Street by Street

LANCASHIRE

Enlarged areas BLACKBURN, BLACKPOOL, BURNLEY, LANCASTER, PRESTON, SOUTHPORT

Plus Formby, Littleborough, Maghull, Orrell, Rainford, Ramsbottom, Rochdale, Settle, Todmorden

CW00870706

3rd edition December 2008
© Automobile Association Developments Limited 2008

Original edition printed May 2001

Enabled by | Ordnance Survey
This product includes map data licensed from Ordnance Survey® with the permission of the Controller of Her Majesty's Stationery Office. © Crown copyright 2008. All rights reserved. Licence number 100021153.

The copyright in all PAF is owned by Royal Mail Group plc.

RoadPilot® DRIVING TECHNOLOGY Information on fixed speed camera locations provided by RoadPilot © 2008 RoadPilot® Driving Technology.

Published by AA Publishing (a trading name of Automobile Association Developments Limited, whose registered office is Fanum House, Basing View, Basingstoke, Hampshire RG21 4EA. Registered number 1878835).

Produced by the Mapping Services Department of The Automobile Association. (A03752)

A CIP Catalogue record for this book is available from the British Library.

Printed by Oriental Press in Dubai

Ref: MX76y

Key to map pages	ii–iii
Key to map symbols	iv–1
Map pages - 1:10,000	2–13
Map pages - 1:17,500	14–263
Map pages - 1:25,000	264–303
Index – towns & villages	304–305
Index – streets	306–348
Index – featured places	348–355
Acknowledgements	355

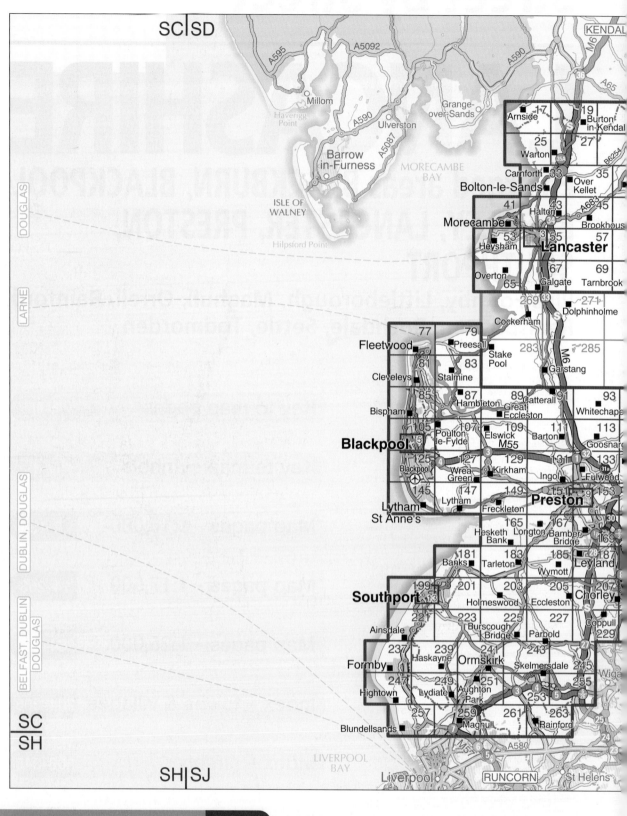

Scale of enlarged map pages 1:10,000   6.3 inches to 1 mile

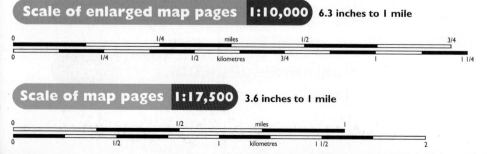

Scale of map pages 1:17,500   3.6 inches to 1 mile

SD|SE

Bedale

YORKSHIRE DALES

NATIONAL

PARK

Ripon

15

Kirkby Lonsdale
23

Burton in Lonsdale
31

Knaresborough

37
39

Hornby

High Bentham

47
49
51
265

Harrogate

Lowgill

Settle

59
61
63

High Salter

267

71
73
75

Long Preston

Tosside

273
275
277
279
281

Skipton

Slaidburn

Forest of Bowland

Bolton-by-Bowland

Gargrave

287
289
291
293
295

Chipping

Waddington

Chatburn

Barnoldswick

Earby

Ilkley

Otley

95
97
99
101
103
297

Hesketh Lane

Clitheroe

Barrowford

Colne

Keighley

Leeds Bradford

115
117
119
121
123

Longridge

Whalley

Sabden

Brierfield

299

135
137
139
141
143

Smargh

Clayton-le-Moors

M65

Burnley

Bradford

Leeds

155
157
159
161
163
301

Blackburn

Accrington

Holme Chapel

Cornholme

Halifax

171
173
175
177
179

Belthorn

Rawtenstall

Bacup

Todmorden

Dewsbury

Wakefield

189
191
193
195
197
303

Anscal

Darwen

Edenfield

M62

Huddersfield

209
211
213
215
217
219

Belmont

Edgworth

Ramsbottom

Littleborough

Holmfirth

233
231
235

Rochdale

Barnsley

Bolton

Oldham

Royston

Leigh

Manchester

Stalybridge

M67

Stocksbridge

SE|SK

CHEADLE

STOCKPORT

SJ|SK

SHEFFIELD

PEAK DISTRICT NATIONAL PARK

Kingston-Upon-Hull

National Grid references are shown on the map frame of each page.
Red figures denote the 100 km square and the blue figures the 1km square.

Example, page 21 : High Biggins 360 478

The reference can also be written using the National Grid two-letter prefix
shown on this page, where 3 and 4 are replaced by SD to give SD6078

2.5 inches to 1 mile   **Scale of map pages 1:25,000**

Junction 9 — Motorway & junction		Underground station	
Services — Motorway service area		Light railway & station	
Primary road single/dual carriageway		Preserved private railway	
Services — Primary road service area		Level crossing (LC)	
A road single/dual carriageway		Tramway	
B road single/dual carriageway		Ferry route	
Other road single/dual carriageway		Airport runway	
Minor/private road, access may be restricted		County, administrative boundary	
One-way street		Mounds	
Pedestrian area		Page continuation 1:25,000 (151)	
Track or footpath		Page continuation 1:17,500 (93)	
Road under construction		Page continuation to enlarged scale 1:10,000 (7)	
Road tunnel		River/canal, lake	
Speed camera site (fixed location) with speed limit in mph (30)		Aqueduct, lock, weir	
Speed camera site (fixed location) with variable speed limit (V)		Peak (with height in metres) — 465 Winter Hill	
Section of road with two or more fixed camera sites; speed limit in mph or variable (40)		Beach	
Average speed (SPECS™) camera system with speed limit in mph (50)		Woodland	
Parking, Park & Ride (P, P+)		Park	
Bus/coach station		Cemetery	
Railway & main railway station		Built-up area	
Railway & minor railway station			

Industrial/business building	Abbey, cathedral or priory
Leisure building	Castle
Retail building	Historic house or building
Other building	Wakehurst Place (NT) National Trust property
City wall	Museum or art gallery
A&E Hospital with 24-hour A&E department	Roman antiquity
PO Post Office	Ancient site, battlefield or monument
Public library	Industrial interest
i Tourist Information Centre	Garden
i Seasonal Tourist Information Centre	Garden Centre Garden Centre Association Member
Petrol station, 24 hour Major suppliers only	Garden Centre Wyevale Garden Centre
Church/chapel	Arboretum
Public toilet, with facilities for the less able	Farm or animal centre
PH Public house AA recommended	Zoological or wildlife collection
Restaurant AA inspected	Bird collection
Madeira Hotel Hotel AA inspected	Nature reserve
Theatre or performing arts centre	Aquarium
Cinema	Visitor or heritage centre
Golf course	Country park
Camping AA inspected	Cave
Caravan site AA inspected	Windmill
Camping & caravan site AA inspected	Distillery, brewery or vineyard
Theme park	Other place of interest

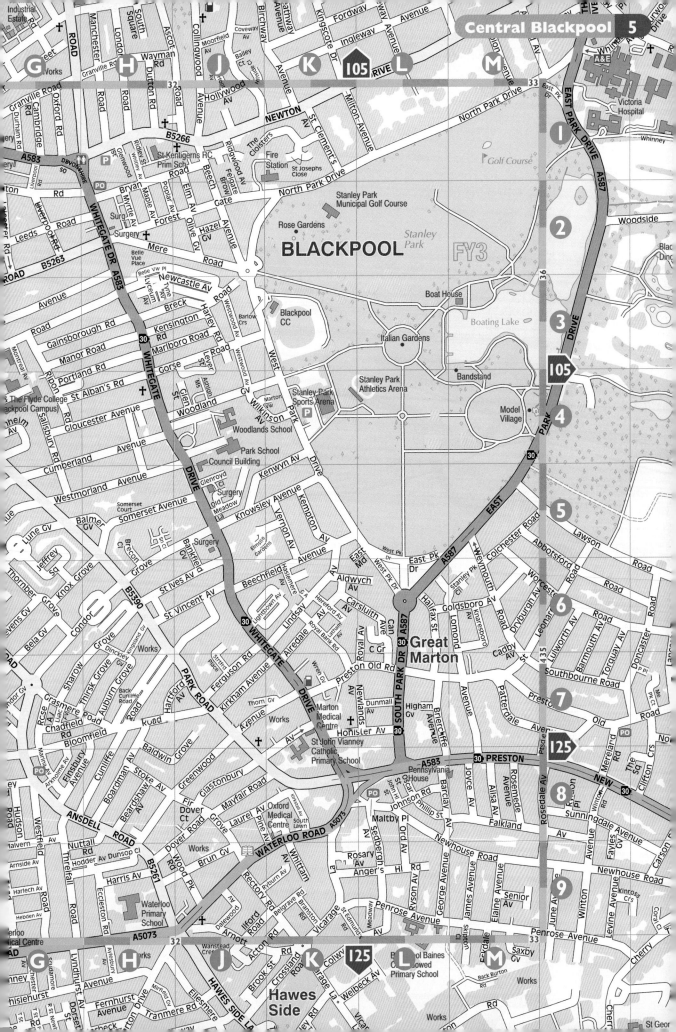

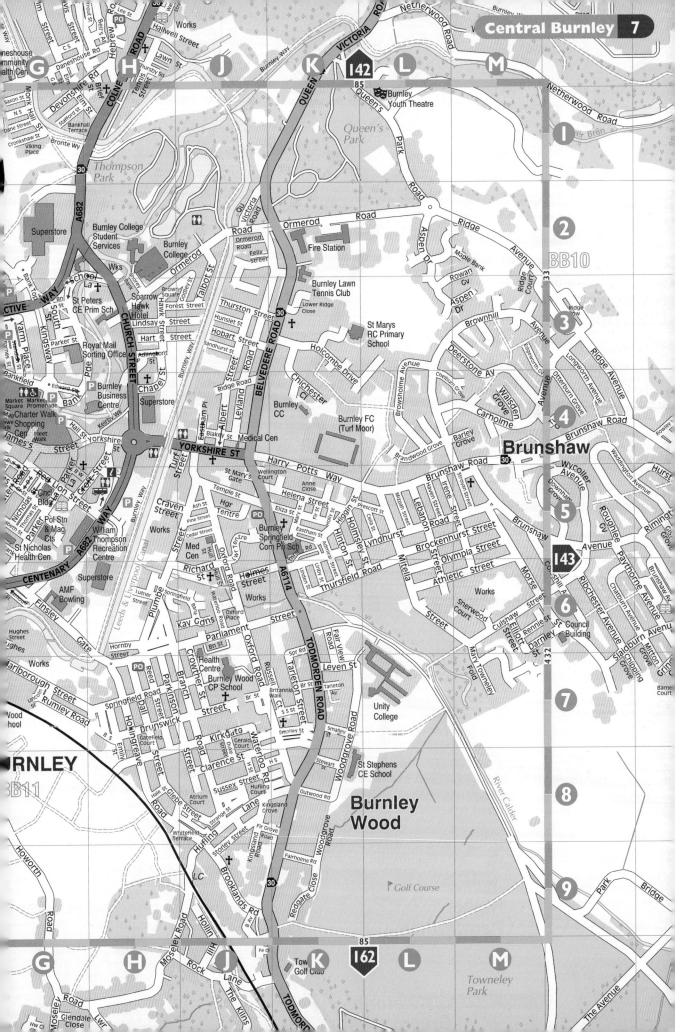

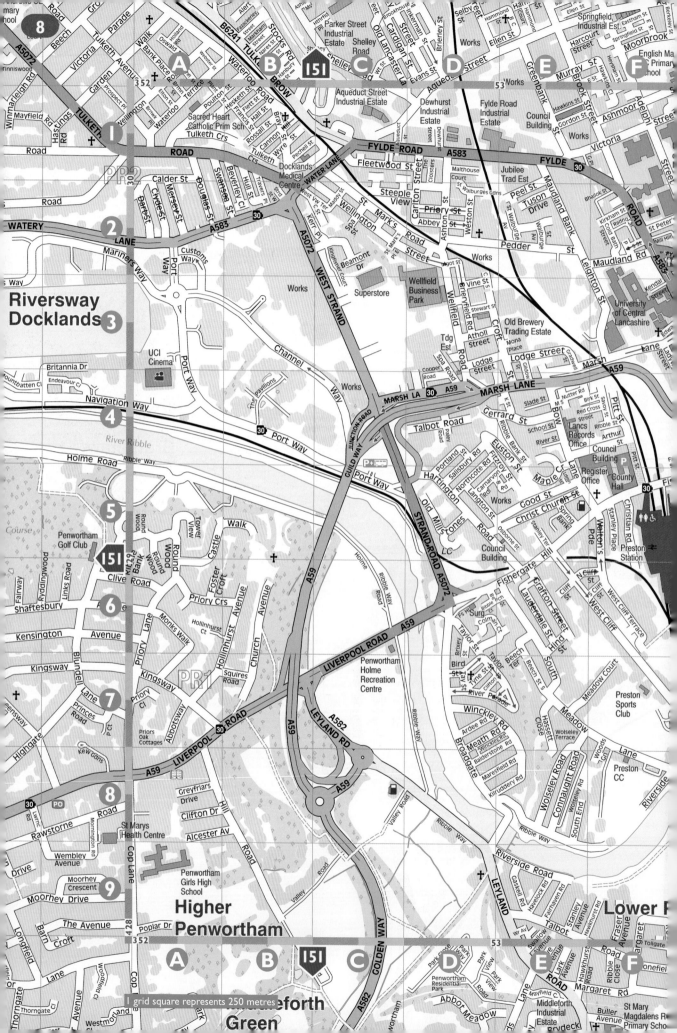

12

SOUTHPORT

1 grid square represents 250 metres

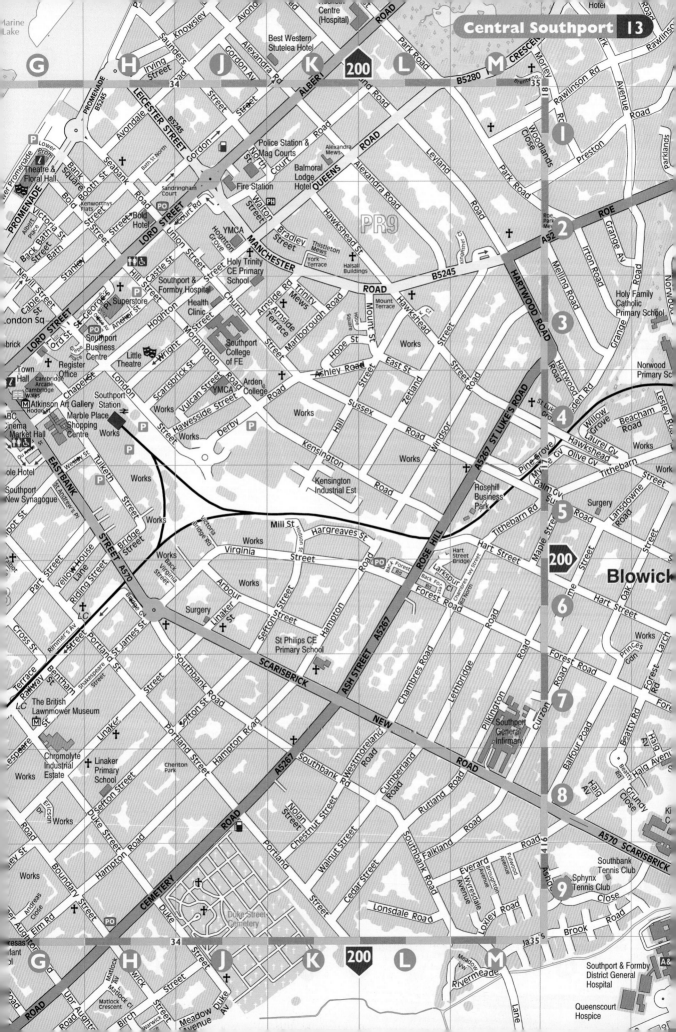

A   B   C   D   E   F

3 65   66   67

83

Barbondale

Barbon Beck

Barbondale Road

Fell Ho

1

2

82

Barbon Low Fell

3

Fell Road

Bullpot Farm

4

Casterton Fell

81

Cow Pot

Gale Garth

Lancaster Hole

5

Hellot Scales Barn

6

80

Ease Gill Kirk

Whittle Hole

Smithy House

Leck Fell

7

8

479

3 65   66   67   Short Drop ve

A   B   C   **23**   D   E   F

High Park   Lost

I grid square represents 500 metres

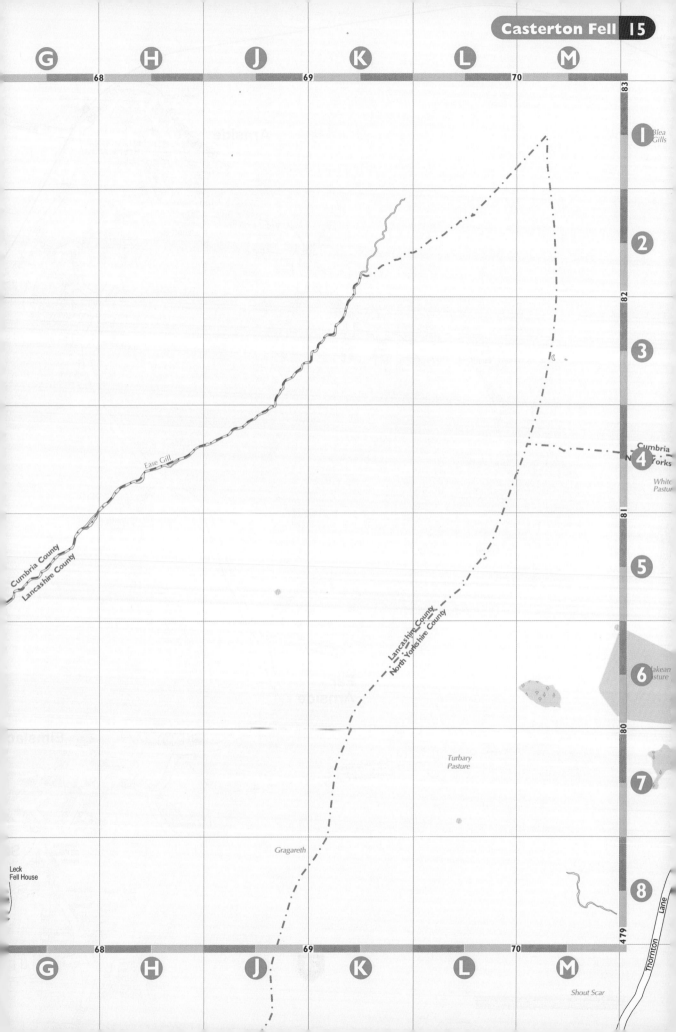

Blea
Gills

Cumbria
N Yorks

White
Pastur

akean
sture

Turbary
Pasture

Gragareth

Leck
Fell House

Lancashire County
North Yorkshire County

Cumbria County
Lancashire County

Ease Gill

Thornton Lane

Shout Scar

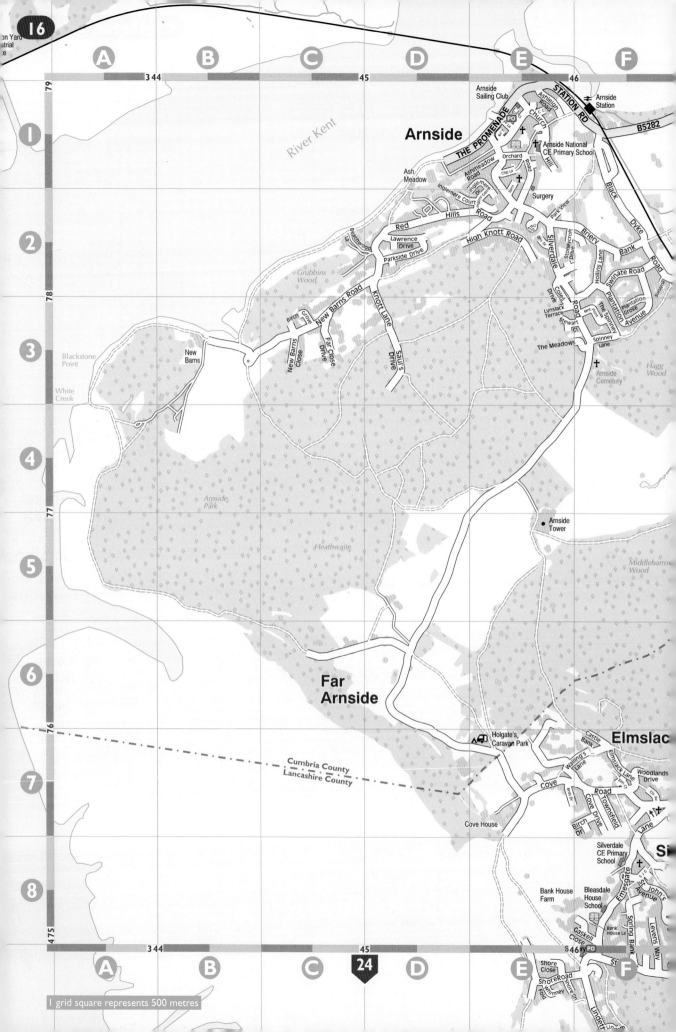

G   H   J   K   L   M

SANDSIDE   47   48   49   79

Carr Bank

Hazelslack

Slack Head

Deepdale Close

Fairy Steps

Limestone Link

Arnside Moss

Highcote Lane   Hillcrest Drive

Leighton Close   Leighton Dr

High Cote

Limestone

Deepdale Farm

Major Woods

Storth Road

Dollywood Lane

Limestone Link

Leighton Beck

Cold Well Lane

Coldwell Farm

Leighton House

Silverdale Moss

Gait Barrows Nature Reserve

Cumbria County
Lancashire County

Brackenthwaite Road

Brackenthwaite

18

Silverdale Moss Road

LC

Thrang End Farm

Eaves Wood

LC

Challan Hall

Hawes Water

Waterslack

Thrang Brow Lane

Yealand Storrs

Silverdale

Brow Foot Farm

Waterslack Road

Ford Lane

Moss Lane

Red Bridge

Red Bridge Lane

Park Road

The Row Road

The Row

Golf Course

Bottoms Farm

Maryland Cl

erdale

Silverdale Green

P   Silverdale Golf Club

Silverdale Station

Storrs Lane

RSPB Leighton
Nature Rese

25

47   48   49

G   H   J   K   L   M

I   2   3   4   5   6   7   8

77   76   475

Park Lane

Yew Tree
Close

Limestone Link

Holme Park Fell (NT)

G H J K L M

53 54 55

Holme
Primary School

Limestone Link

Brookfield
Close

B6384

BURTON ROAD

Holmefield

Ernest Lane

Curwen
Woods

Clawthorpe
Fell

Kelke
Well

Limestone Link

Mills
trial

M6

A6070

New
Mill

Piger's Lane

Clawthorpe

Sandygap
Farm

Slape Lane

A6070

Dalton
Crags

Dalton

20

Vicarage Lane

Hollowgate

Button Close

St James's Drive

Tanpits Lane

Vicarage Close

Glebe

BOON WALKS

Burton Park

Morewood Drive

Burton Morewood
Primary
School

New Lane

Barker
Close

Neddy
Hill

PO

Cocking
Yard

Burton-in-Kendal

Jones's
Yard

Boon
Town

Garden Pl

MAIN STREET

Mowbray Drive

Thornleigh Drive

Home
Farm

Crow
Trees

Dalton Lane

arn Lane

Dalton
Hall

Henridding

A6070

Dalton Old Hall
Farm

Coat
Gree

Dalton
Wood

G H J K L M

53 54 27 55

79

1

2

78

3

4

77

20

5

6

76

7

475

8

20

A   B   C   D   E   F

356   57   58

79

Sealford Lane

I

Limestone Link

Kelker
Well

Kilnerfoot

78

Shortbutts La

Sealford Beck

Gallowber Lane

2

Crag La   Mill Lane

**Hutton
Roof**

PO

Limestone Link

3

Park Wood
National Nature
Reserve

Pegbank Lane

Moor
End

Cumbria County
Lancashire County

*Hutton
Roof
Park*

4

Nanny
Hall

77

19

Johnson
House

5

Mealrigg

Mealrigg Lane

Crag
House

6

New
Park

76

River Keer

West Ha
Park

7

*Docker
Moor*

8

Keer
Side

Docker
Hall

475

356   *Wash Dub
Wood*   57   58

A   B   C   **28**   D   E   F

1 grid square represents 500 metres

r Holme Lane

Docker

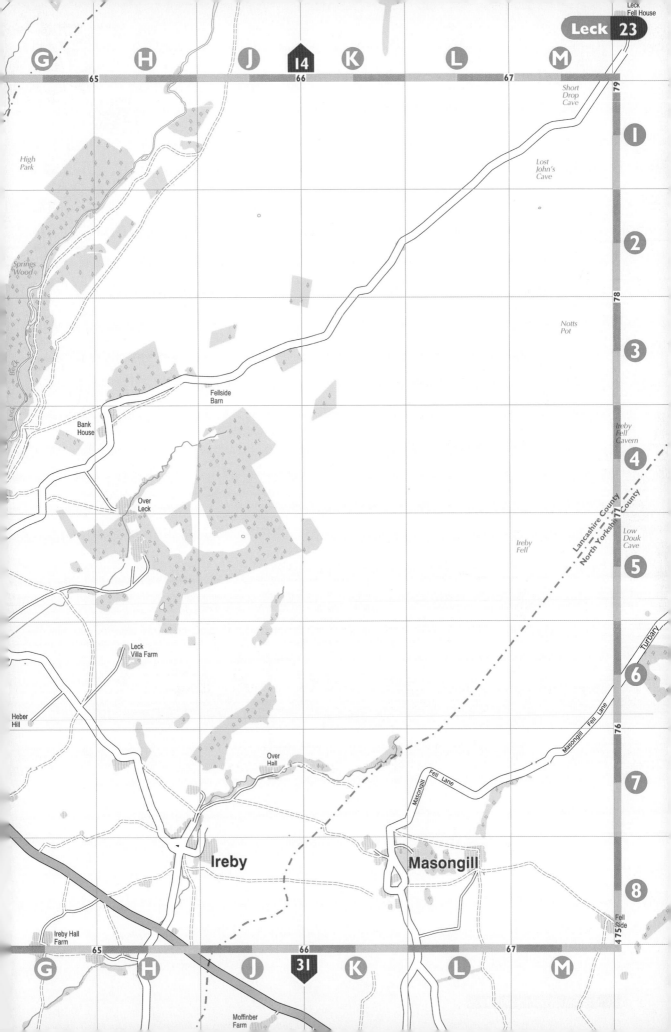

G

H

J

14

K

L

M

65

66

67

79

1

2

78

3

4

5

6

76

7

8

475

65

66

31

67

G

H

J

K

L

M

Leck Fell House

Short Drop Cave

Lost John's Cave

High Park

Springs Wood

Notts Pot

Leck Beck

Fellside Barn

Bank House

Ireby Fell Cavern

Over Leck

Low Douk Cave

Ireby Fell

Lancashire County
North Yorkshire County

Turbary

Leck Villa Farm

Heber Hill

Masongill Fell Lane

Over Hall

Masongill Fell Lane

Ireby

Masongill

Fell Side

Ireby Hall Farm

Moffinber Farm

A   **B**   **C**   **16**   **D**   **E**   **F**

3 44   45

Bank House Farm

Bleasdale House School

Emesgate

St John

Avenue

Bank House Lane

Levens Way

Gaskell

46 Surgery PO

Stankelt

Shore Close

Shore Road

Winney

Shore Gn

1

2

Lindeth Close

Lindeth

Road

Woodwell Lane

Lindeth Tower

3

● Jack Scout (NT)

Ridgeway Park School

4

Jenny Brown's Point

73

5

Warton Sands

6

72

7

471

8

3 44   45   46

A   **B**   **C**   **D**   **E**   **F**

1 grid square represents 500 metres

Bottoms Farm

P Silverdale Station

Silverdale Golf Club

Silverdale Green

The Green

Stankelt Rd

Slackwood Lane

Lane

RSPB Leighton Moss Nature Reserve

Grisedale

Griesdale Wood

Leighton Hall

I

2

74

Heald Brow (NT)

LC

New Road

3

Crag Foot

Crag Road

New Road

Three Brothers

Occupation Road

4

LA5

Warton Crag

26
73

Scar Close

5

New Road

6
Church Avenue
Str
Garr
Main

Town End Fold
72
Farleton Cl
Mill
Hurton Gdns
Sand Lane
Westbourne Road

7 Millh

Cote Stones

River Keer

Grange View
Lane
Hazelmount

8

Galley Hall

471

Warton

Carnforth Station

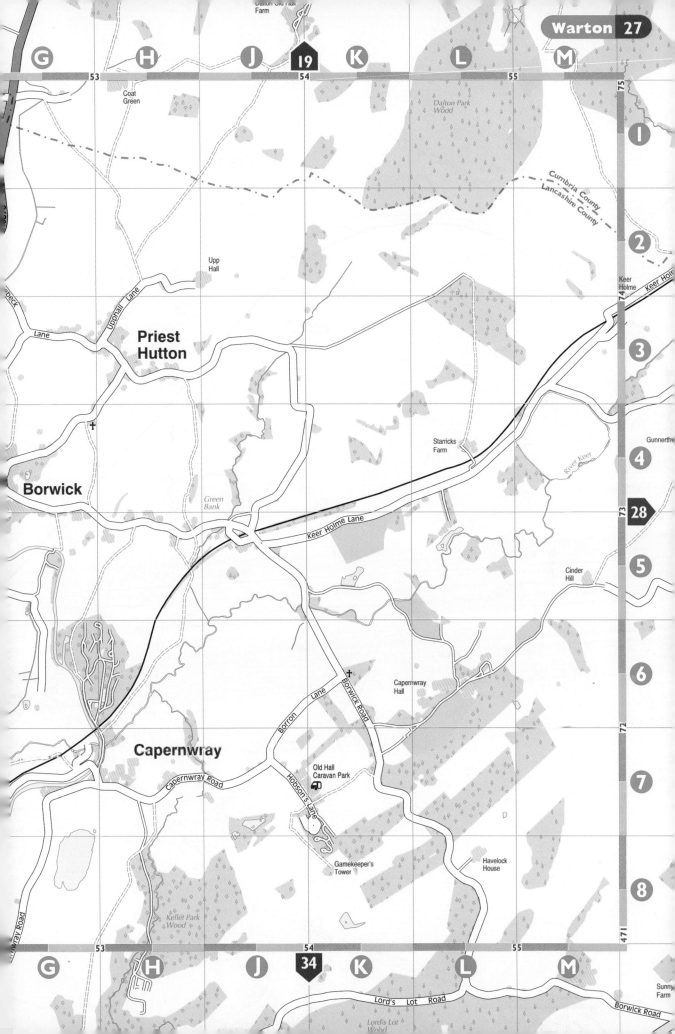

28

A   B   Keer   C   20   Docker   D   E   F
          Side   57   Hall

356

Wash Dub
Wood

75

I

Keer Holme Lane

bria County
hire County

2

Keer
Holme

74

Keer Holme Lane

Docker

Docker Park
Working Farm

3

Brown
Edge

River K

4

Gunnerthwaite

Snab Green
Farm

The High
Farm

27   73

Beck

Cinder
Hill

5

Locka Lane

Craven
View

6

Kitchlow
Farm

Meadow
Wy

PO

Arkh
CE F
Scho

The Herb
Gdns

72

Locka
Farm

7

142

Locka Lane

B6254

Storrs
Hall

8

471

356   B6254   57   Go   35   D   E   F
                        Ha

A   B   C   58

wick Road

Sunny Bank

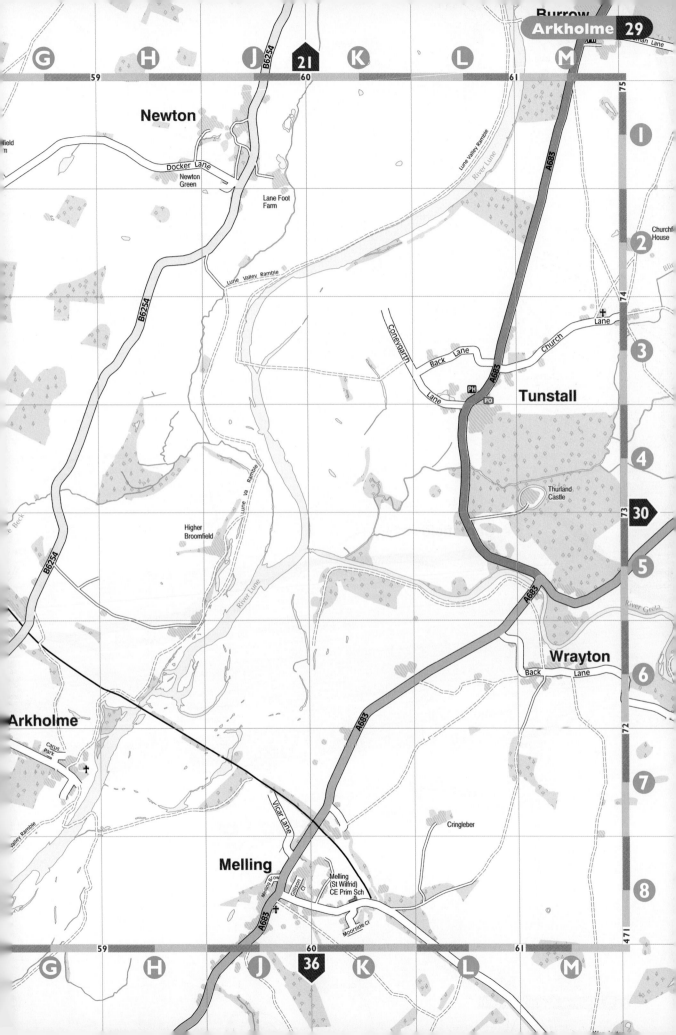

30

Woodman Lane

A   B   C   22   D   E   F

362   63   64

75

1

2

Churchfield
House

74

Blind Cant

Cant

Beck

Collingholme

Laithbutts

Lane

3

4

29

73

Cantsfield

A687

Scaleber

Longber Lane

Lancashire County
North Yorkshire County

5

River Greta

Halfway
House

Longber

Lowfields

Lane

6

72

Bull
Bank

River Greta

7

Back Lane

Spout Lane

Back Lane

Scaleber
Farm

8

471

Gill Farm

Black
Wood

Back Lane

362   63   64

A   B   C   37   D   E   F

Moss
House

Old Hutton

Brow

1 grid square represents 500 metres

G H J **23** K L M

65 66 67 75

I

2

3

Westhouse

4

5

6

7

8

G H J **38** K L M

65 66

Ireby Hall Farm

Moffinber Farm

Anems House

Galegreen

Kirksteads

Stainderber

Whaitber

Westgate Lane

Bank

Smithy Lane

Lower Westhouse

Selber

Low Threaber

High Threaber Farm

Gooda

A65

A687

Lowfields

Lund Fa

Gallaber

74

73

72

471

A687

Blind Lane

Ireby Road

A687

Orchard Thorntons VA Prim Sch

Manor Close

The Croft

Tvine Vw

PO

HIGH STREET

Duke Street

Leeming Lane

Low St

Barnoldswick Lane

Kepp House

Bentham Road

Park Foot

Burton in Lonsdale

Greta Heath

Burton Hill

Brd

River Greta

Bentham Moor Road

River Greta

Bentham Moor Road

Bentham Road

Chalybeate Spring

Bentham Moor

Fourlands Hill

Fourlands House

Dunc om's Lane

Ra

Fell Side

Four Lane Ends

A B C **25** D E F

346 47 48

71
70
69
68
467

1
2
3
4
5
6
7
8

Marsh House Farm

Dertern

Bolton Holmes

Wild Duck Hall

Saint Nicholas La

Merefell Road

Haw

Mill Lane

Sandside Caravan & Camping Park

The shore

Sunnybank

Lowlands Rd

Meadow Dr

Chestnut Av

Shelley

Wordsworth

Byron

Bolton-le-Sands CC

Red Bank Farm

St Michael's Lane

LC

Hillcrest Rd

Monkswell Dr

Monkswell

Clynds Dr

Windermere

St Michael's

Coniston Rd

Rydal Road

ROAD

30

St Michael's La

Red Bank Farm

Pasture Lane

Beech Tree Cl

Church Court

Priest Skear

Bolton Town End

BY-PASS

Clarksfield Road

Main Road

Church Brow

Morecambe Lodge

Pasture Lane

A5105

Garage Ind Est

Town End

Slyne Road

Church Brow Close

ROAD

Lancaster Canal

Broadlands Dr

A B C **42** D E F

346 47 48

Madison Av

Coastal Rd

Baesdale

Whitendale Drive

Greenwood

Pinewood Avenue

Greenacre Rd

Inworth Drive

Bryn Cv

Ash Tree Cv

Fir Tree

Crs

Greenwood Av

A6

ROAD

COASTAL

Morecambe Bay Nature Reserve

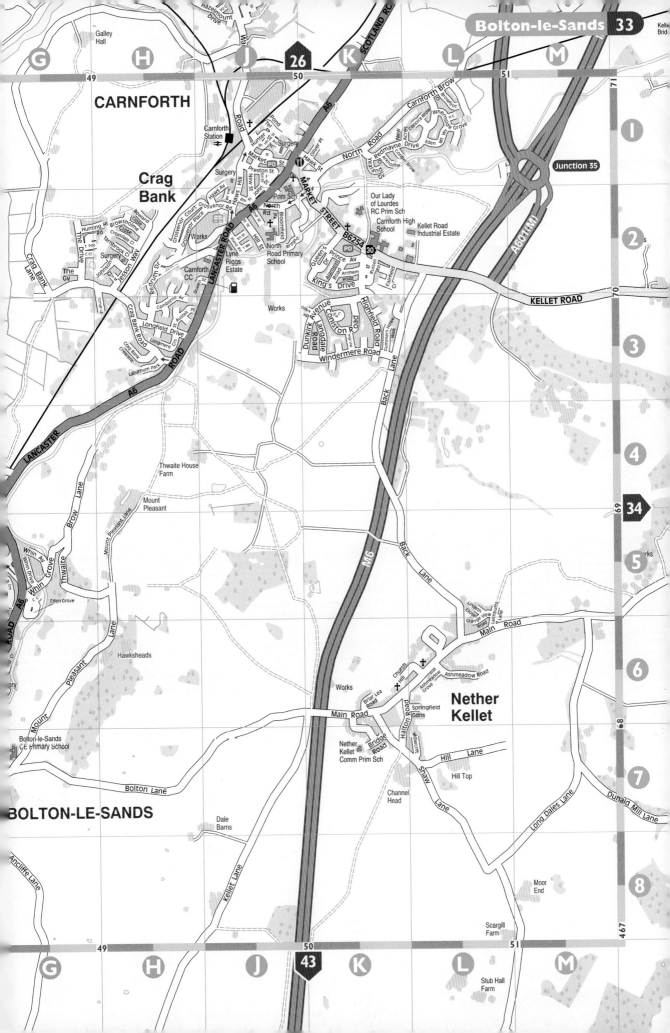

G H J **28** K L M

55 56 57 71

I

House

Road

Sunny Bank
Farm

Borwick Road

B6254

Gowan
Hall

2

70

Fall Kirk

Gress ugh

edwell
sherie

†

3

Fleet

Lea Lane

Eskrigge Lane

Eskrigge

4

Straits
Head

Low House

Lune valley Ramble

River Lune

69

36

Higher
Snab
Farm

Sandbeds Lane

5

Sidegarth

The
Snab

Aughton Road

6

68

Lune Valley Ramble

Camp House

7

Lune Valley Ramble

Aughton

Aughton Brow

8

Meadow View Old Road

Farleton Road

55 56 **45** 57 467

G H J K L M

A683

Farlet

Claughton

Low House

Bank House
Farm

River Lune

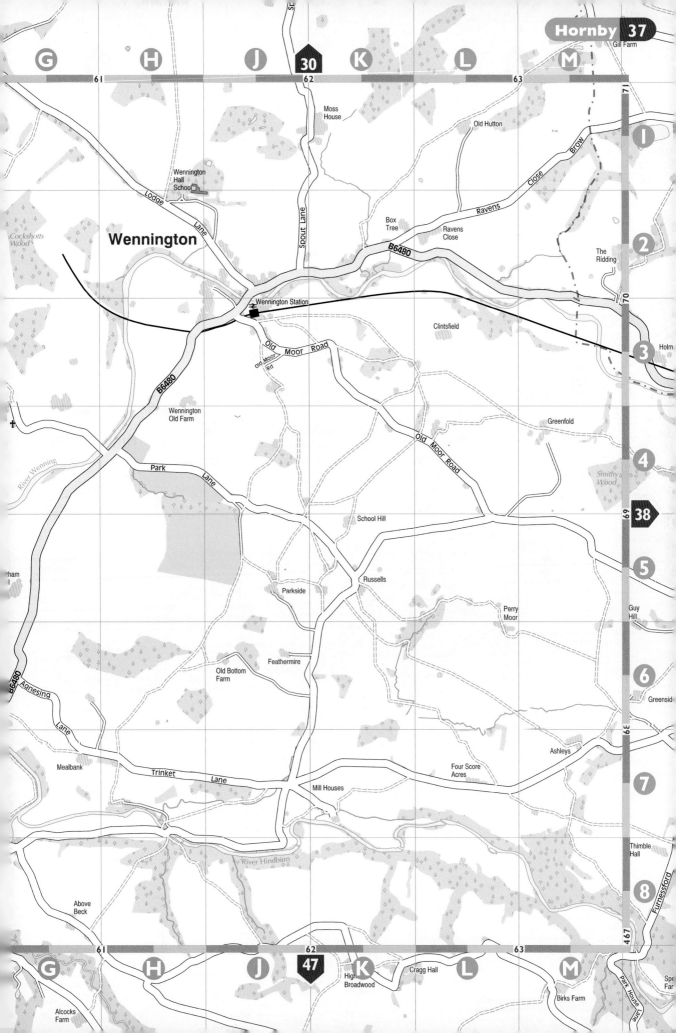

Gill Farm

G H J 30 K L M

61 62 63 71

I

Moss House

Old Hutton

Wennington Hall School

Cockshotts Wood

Lodge Lane

Wennington

Box Tree

Ravens Close

B6480

Ravens Close

Brow

The Ridding

2

70

Spout Lane

Wennington Station

Clintsfield

Holm

3

Old Moor Road

Old Moor Rd

B6480

Wennington Old Farm

Greenfold

Smithy Wood

4

River Wenning

Park Lane

Old Moor Road

School Hill

69

38

Russells

5

Parkside

Perry Moor

Guy Hill

B6480

Agnesing Lane

Featheremire

Old Bottom Farm

Greenside

6

68

Ashleys

Mealbank

Trinket Lane

Four Score Acres

7

Mill Houses

Thimble Hall

River Hindburn

Funessford

8

467

Above Beck

Park House Lane

Alcocks Farm

High Broadwood

Cragg Hall

Birks Farm

Spa Far

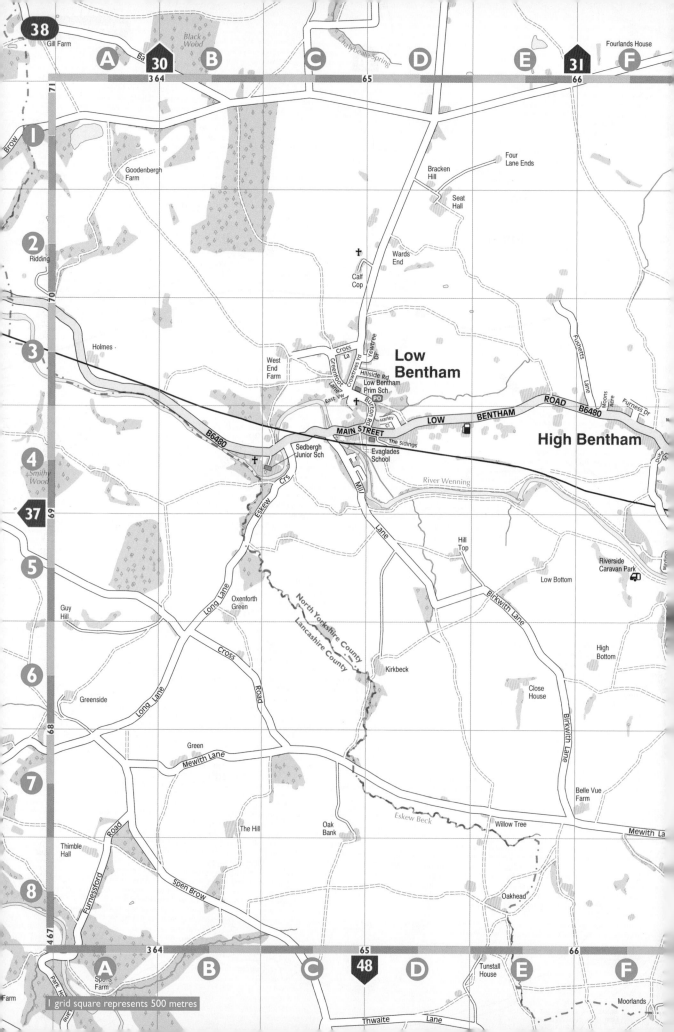

A **30** 364 B C 65 D E **31** 66 F

I Brow 71

Gill Farm

Ba

Black
Wood

Chalybeate Spring

Fourlands House

Four
Lane Ends

Goodenbergh
Farm

Bracken
Hill

Seat
Hall

2 Ridding 70

Wards
End

Calf
Cop

Flushetts Lane

3 Holmes

West
End
Farm

Cross
La

Greenfoot Lane

Crowtrees Rd

Yewtree Dr

Hillside Rd

Low Bentham
Prim Sch

East Vw

PO

**Low
Bentham**

LOW BENTHAM ROAD B6480

Moons
Acre

Furness Dr

B6480

Main Street

Burton Rd

Harley
Cr

The Sidings

High Bentham

Duke St

4 Smithy
Wood

Sedbergh
Junior Sch

Evaglades
School

River Wenning

37 69

Eskew Crs

Mill Lane

Hill
Top

Riverside
Caravan Park

5 Guy
Hill

Long Lane

Oxenforth
Green

North Yorkshire County

Lancashire County

Low Bottom

Birkwith Lane

High
Bottom

6 68

Greenside

Long Lane

Cross Road

Kirkbeck

Close
House

Birkwith Lane

Green

Mewith Lane

7

Belle Vue
Farm

The Hill

Oak
Bank

Eskew Beck

Willow Tree

Mewith La

Thimble
Hall

8 467

Furnessford Road

Spen Brow

Oakhead

A 364 B C 65 **48** D Tunstall
House E 66 F

Spens
Farm

Park Ho
Lane

Thwaite Lane

Moorlands

1 grid square represents 500 metres

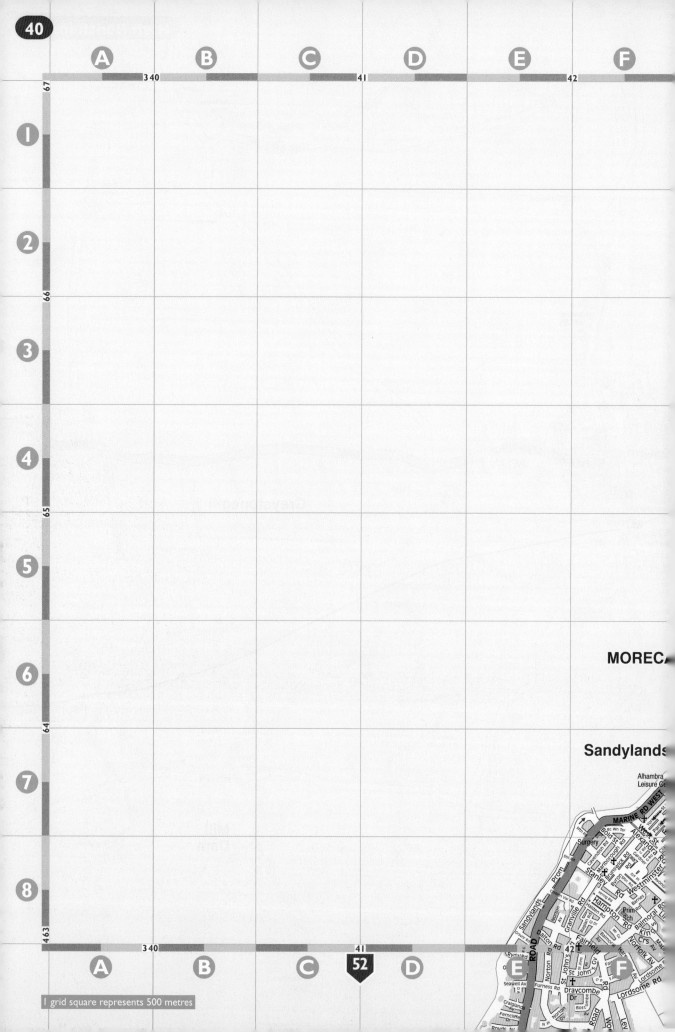

A B C D E F

67

340 41 42

1

2

66

3

4

65

5

6

64

7

MOREC

Sandylands

8

463

340 41

A B C 52 D E F

MARINE RD WEST

Surgery

Sandylands

ROAD

42

Alhambra
Leisure Ce

1 grid square represents 500 metres

G H J K L M

43   44   45   67   99

1
2
3   Scalestones Point
COASTAL ROAD

Morecambe Golf Club

4   42

Morecambe Bay Yacht Club
Hotel Prospect
MARINE ROAD EAST

St Christopher's Wy
Foxholes Rd
Bare Av
Newmarket St

Town Hall
Best Bus Cen
Lifeboat Station
Fire Station
Lord St

Dallam
Royal Av
Rossendale Rd

Colwyn Rd
Mayfield Drive
Bare Lane Station
5   65

Clock Tower
Eric Morecambe Statue

Morecambe High School
St Andrews Grove

Stuart Avenue
Grasmere Dr
Carnvie Av
Lodges Grove
Elms Drive
Ellis Drive

Bare   Fairhope

Poulton le Sands CE Prim Sch
St Marys RC Primary School
Lichfield Av
Wakefield Avenue
Ruskin Drive

Fairlea Av
St Anne's

War Memorial
Midland Hotel
MARINE RD CTRL   A589

Plaza Shop Arcade
Prim Sch
Queen Victoria Hosp
Derwent Avenue
Melrose Av

South Road
Road
Beaufort
Beech Gv
Clifton Dr

6   Torrisholme Primary School

Cinema
Festival Market
Superstore
CENTRAL DR
Morecambe Stn.
EUSTON RD   30
LANCASTER RD

South Gv
Mardale Av
Bowerham
Burlington Av
Anthorn Av
Latham Grove

Greatwood Primary School
Esdale Gv
Azalea Gv
Strickland Drive

Morecambe Super Bowl
Unity Temple

WEST END RD
Corringham Rd
Battismore Rd
Schola Gn
Croft St
Buxton St
Bristol St

LANCASTER RD
Lancaster Rd Prim Sch
Morecambe FC (Christie Park)

BROADWAY
B5321
Lonsdale Rd
Lonsdale Rd
B5321

7   LANC

West End
Morecambe CC
Woodhill Lane
Carleton Street
Hestham
Pennine Vw
Hestham Crs

Hampsfell Drive
Bartholomew Rd
Wingate
Hawkshead Road
Gringley Road
Rochester Av
Winthorpe Av

Christie Av
Branksome Dr
Ennerdale Av
Ullswater Av
Windermere Av
Wyden Av
Warley Av

Cemetery
Homfray Av
Lowther Av
Stanhope Av

Morecambe Road School
MORECAMBE ROAD   A589
Norwood   30

8

West End Primary School
Devonshire Rd   30
Brook Road
Buckingham Rd

Venture Caravan Park
Langridge
Westgate County Prim School
Parkside
Helmside Av
Glentworth Rd W
Westgate   30
Glentworth Road

Westgate
Northgate
White Lund Trading Estate
Whitegate

Hadrian Road
Hadrian Road

Heysham High Sch
Regent Caravan Park
Westgate
Kenilworth Road

White Lund   45

Holder Station and Workshops
Middlegate
A683   463
Trading Estate

G   43   H   J   44   53   K   L   M

OXCLIFFE ROAD

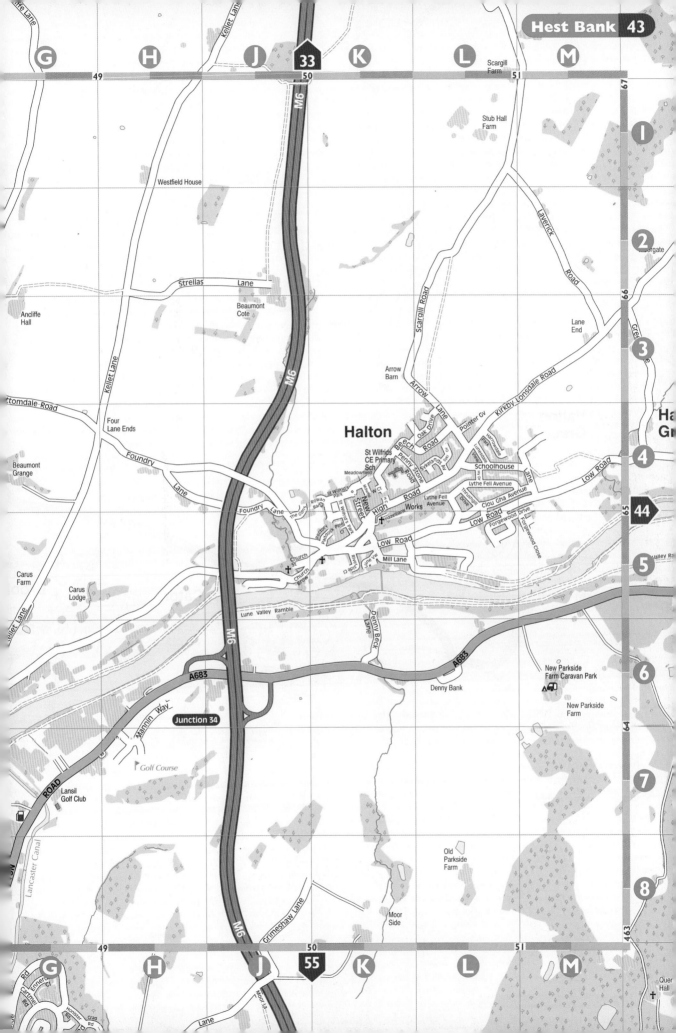

Halton

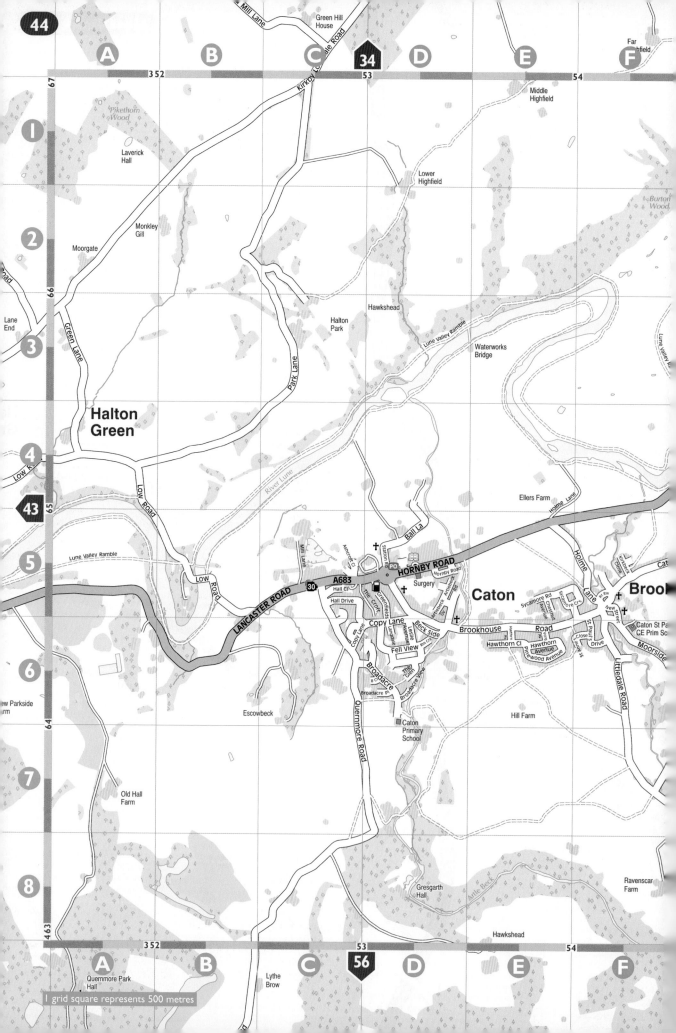

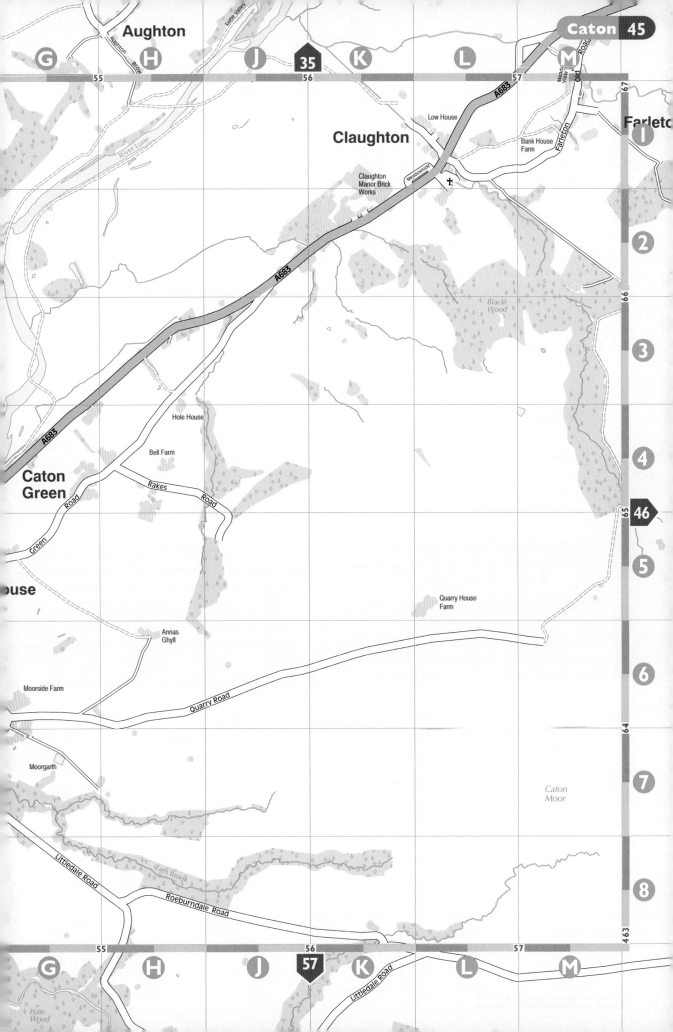

46

A   B   C   36   D   E   F

67   358   59   60

Farleton

Sooby Gill Beck

I

Manor
House

2
66

Scale House
Barn

Cold
Park
Wood

Moor Lane

Hamstone Gill

3

4

Back
Farm

45
65

Barkin
Gate

Thornbush

5

Claughton
Moor

Whit
Moor

6

64

7

Winder
Wood

Lower
Salter
†

8
463

Winder

M
Sa

358   Roeburndale Road   59   60   Ro

A   B   C   58   D   E   F

I grid square represents 500 metres

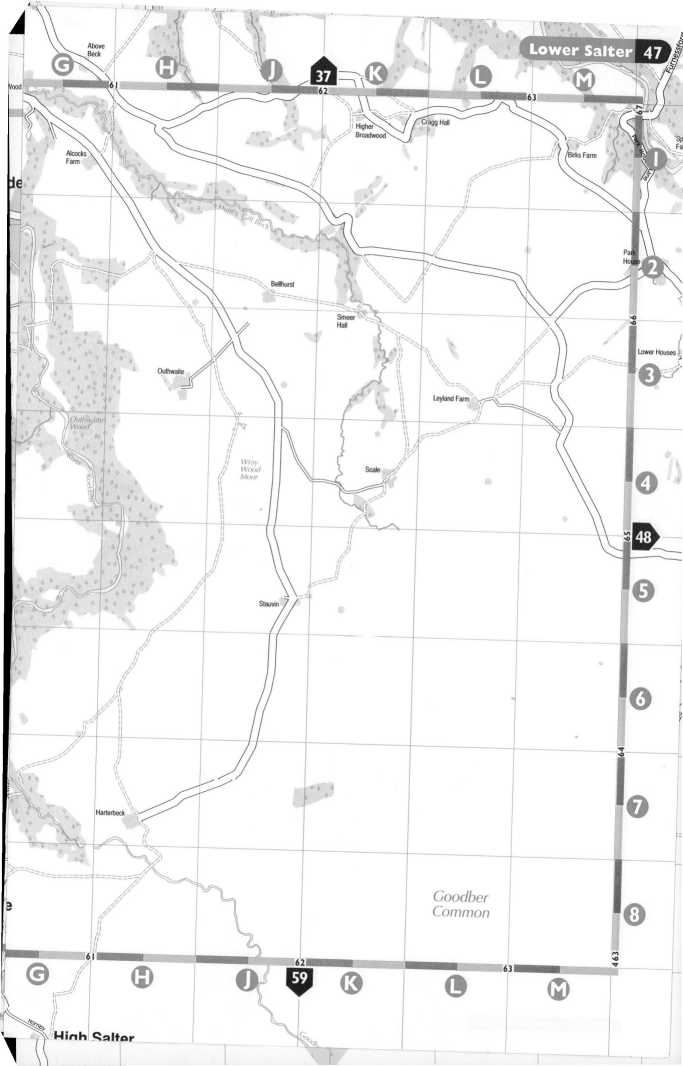

Above Beck

G   H   J   37   K   L   M

61   62   63

Wood

Furnessford

Higher Broadwood

Cragg Hall

Birks Farm

Alcocks Farm

Park House Lane

I

Hunt's Gill Beck

Park House   2

Bellhurst

66

Smeer Hall

Lower Houses   3

Outhwaite

Leyland Farm

Outhwaite Wood

River Roeburn

Wray Wood Moor

Scale   4

65   48

5

Stauvin

6

64

7

Harterbeck

Goodber Common   8

463

Hornby

High Salter

Goodb

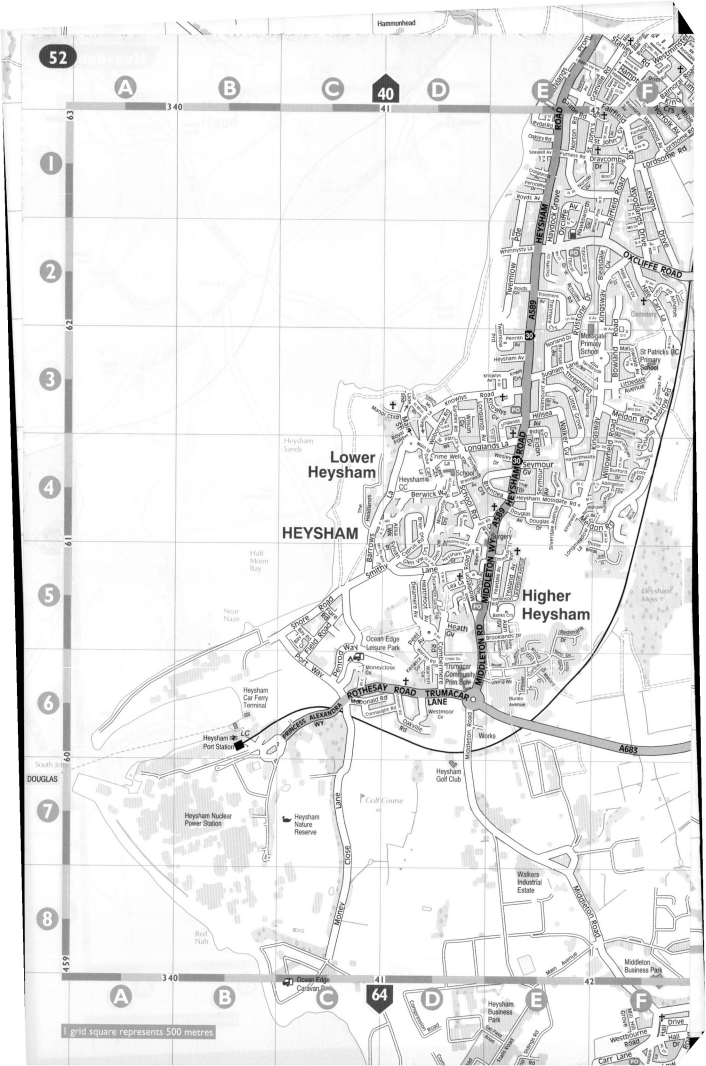

Hammonhead

A B C 40 D E F
41

63 340 42

1

2
62

3

4
61

Lower
Heysham

HEYSHAM

5

Half
Moon
Bay

Near
Naze

6
60

South Jetty
DOUGLAS

7

8
459 340 41 42

A B C 64 D E F

1 grid square represents 500 metres

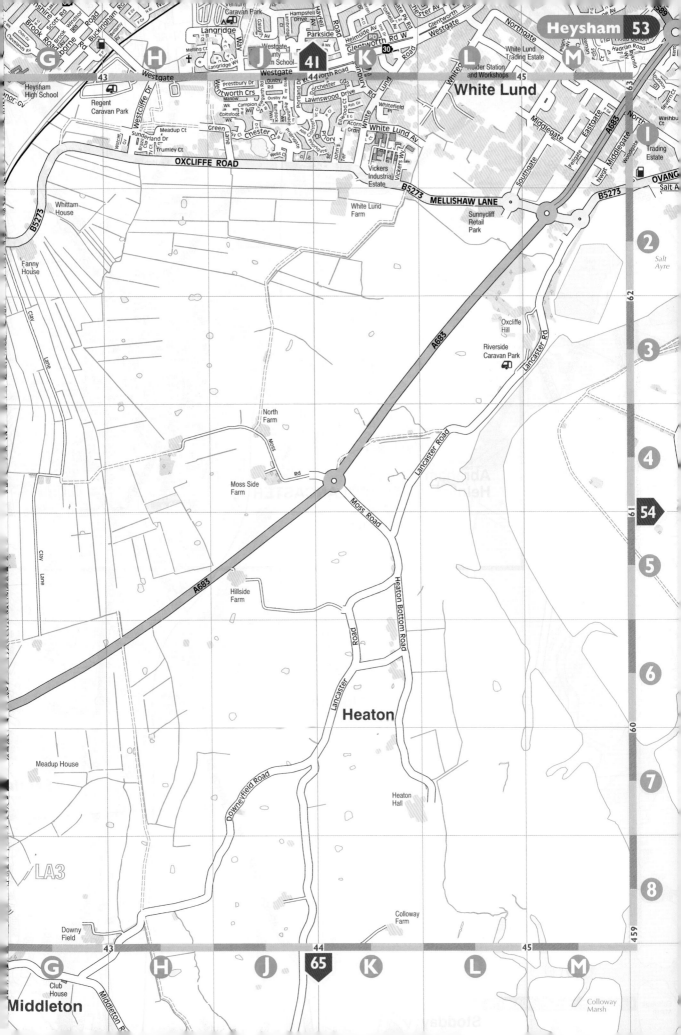

62

A   B   C   **50**   D   E   F

Middlesmoor

3 70   71   72

John Fell

Ing
Close

1

*Fox
Holes*

2

3

Keasden Beck

*Broad
Shaw*

*Claphar
Comma*

*Great
Harlow*

4

*Cold
Stone
Plain*

61

488
▲
Great Harlow

North Yorkshire County
Lancashire County

*Yorkshire Dale
National Park*

5

6

*Catlow
Fell*

*Hasgill
Fell*

7

8

*Cross of Greet
Bridge*

459

3 70   71   72

A   B   C   **74**   D   E   F

River Ho

Catlow

*Low
Laithe*

I grid square represents 500 metres

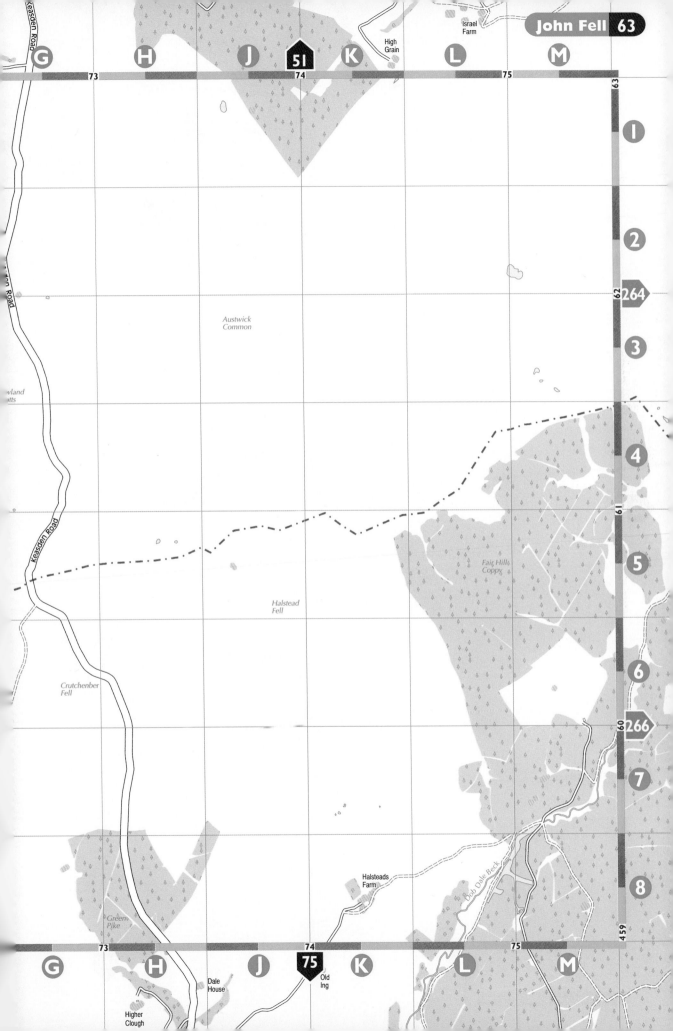

G   H   J   51   K   L   M

73   74   75   63

1

2

62 264

3

61

4

5

6

60 266

7

459

8

G   H   J   75   K   L   M

73   74   75

Israel
Farm

High
Grain

Austwick
Common

Keasden Road

wland
tts

Crutchenber
Fell

Halstead
Fell

Fair Hills
Coppy

Green
Pike

Dale
House

Old
Ing

Higher
Clough

Halsteads
Farm

Halstead
Fell

Bob Dale Beck

A   B   C   D   E   F

340   41   42

59

I

58

2

57

63

4

5

56

6

7

8

455   340   41   42

A   B   C   D   E   **268**   F

Red
Nab

Money

Ocean Edge
Caravan Park

Compression Road

Heysham
Business Park

Gas Field
Road

Stalls Road

Sidings Rd

Workshop
Rd

Main Avenue

Mid
Business Park

Mill Hill
Grove

Hall
Dr

Drive

Westbourne
Road

Hall

Carr Lane

Westmoor
House

Low

PO

Compression road

Holiday
Centre

Melbreak
Caravan
Park

Carr Lane

Brows

Trumley Farm

Potts
Corner

Trailholm

Sunderland
Brows

The

Hall End
Skear

Su
Po

I grid square represents 500 metres

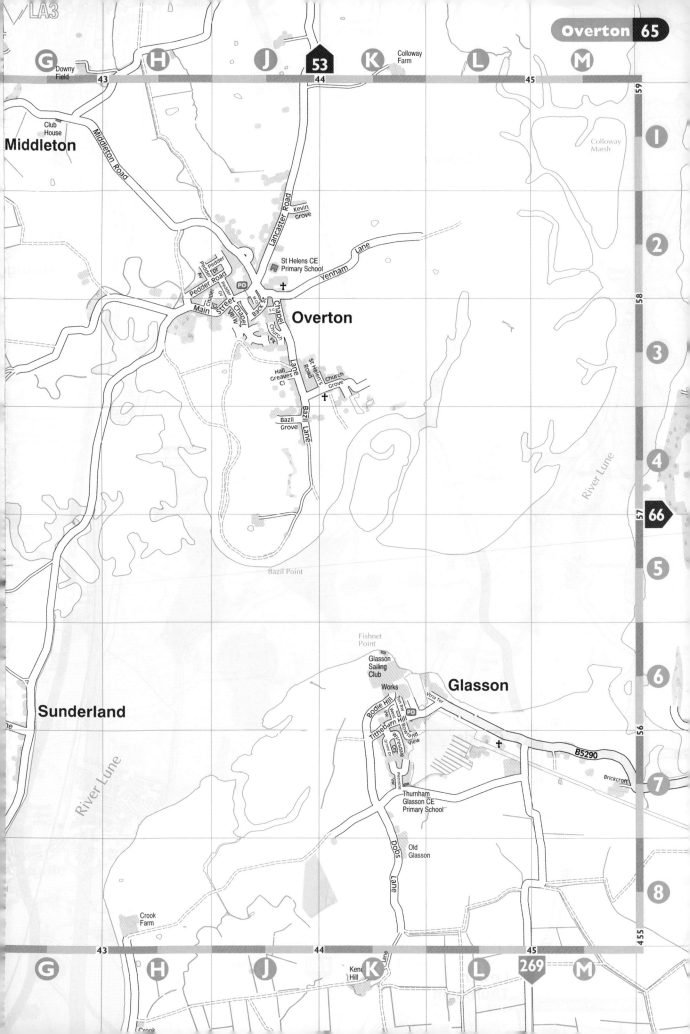

A B C **76** D E **F**

329   30   31

1
2
3
4
5
6
7
8

47
46
45
44
443

Fleetw
Sear C

Princes Way
Chatswor
Lazenby
Alder
Avenue
Burnside
AV
Marine Pde
Marine
Parade
Fairway
Tatham
Court
W Ct
Larkholm
Bowness
Pd
Ben
tham
AV
Burton
Burton
Falmouth
Avenue
Hove
Roundwa
Fairway
Plymouth A
Bristo
AV
Fishermans
WY
W
Rossall
Hospital

Sea Wall
Sea Wall

Promenade
The Bay
Drive
We
Green
thorn
The Car
Corners
North
PREESHL

Promenade
Ocean
Be
Rd
Victor
Coronation
Promenade
Ellerbeck
Rd
Kingswa

CLEVELEYS

A B C **84** D E **F**

329   30   31

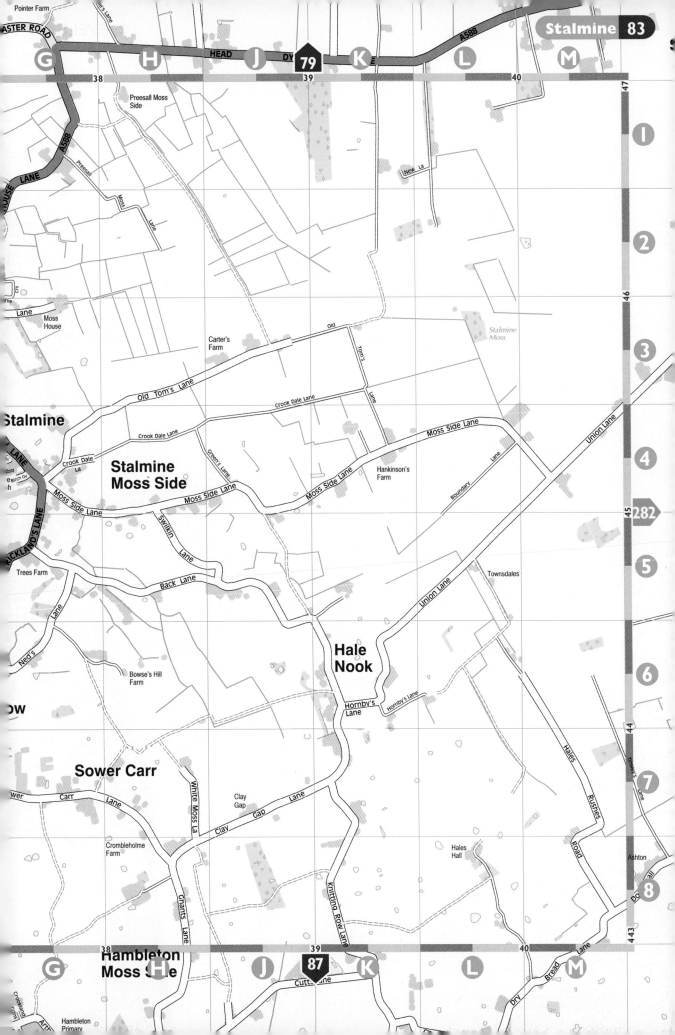

ASTER ROAD

G H HEAD J DY 79 K L M

38 39 40 47

A588

Pointer Farm

Preesall Moss Side

Moss Lane

46

I

2

New La

3

Stalmine Moss

Old Tom's Lane

Carter's Farm

Moss House

The

Lane

Old Tom's Lane

Crook Dale Lane

Moss Side Lane

Stalmine

Crook Dale Lane

Union Lane

4

Green's Lane

Stalmine Moss Side

Crook Dale La

Moss Side Lane

Moss Side Lane

Hankinson's Farm

Boundary Lane

45 282

Moss Side Lane

Swilkin Lane

Lane

Trees Farm

Union Lane

Townsdales

5

RICKLAND'S LANE

Birch Ov

h

Back Lane

Ned's

Lane

Hale Nook

6

ow

Bowse's Hill Farm

Hornby's Lane

Hornby's Lane

44

Tinsley's Lane

7

Sower Carr

White Moss La

Clay Gap Lane

Hales Rushes Road

wer Carr Lane

Clay Gap

Ashton

Do all

8

Crombleholme Farm

Charts Lane

Knitting Row Lane

Hales Hall

443

G H J DY 87 K L M

Hambleton Moss Side

Cutts ne

Hambleton Primary

Crooklan

Art ms

Dry Bread Lane

A   B   C   **80**   D   E   F

329   30   31

43

1

42

2

Little
Bispham

3

41

Norbreck

4

5

Bispham

40

6

7

439

8

329   30   31

A   B   C   **104**   D   E   F

1 grid square represents 500 metres

G   H   J   **83**   K   L   M

38   39   40   43

I

**Hambleton
Moss Side**

Cutts Lane

Chants Lane

Knitting Row Lane

Chapel Lane

Dry Bread Lane

Crookland Farm

Hambleton
Primary
School

Fairmont
Arthur's Lane

Church Lane

Crook Gate Lane

2

42

Sunnybank
Industrial
Estate

...eton

Moss Lane

Mill Lane

Mill Farm

Grange Road

Bournes

Crook
Gate

Chapel Lane

**Out
Rawcliffe**

**Whin Lane
End**

Holme
Nook

Turkey Street

PO

Whin Lane

Leylands

Rawcliffe Road

3

4

Moors Farm

Bodkin Lane

Waterside
Farm

41   **88**

Liscoe
Farm

5

Larbreck

GARS...

Larbreck
Hall

6

40

River Wyre

Bankfield
Farm

Pool Foot Lane

Windy Harbour Road

A586 GARSTANG ROAD

Old Castle

7

Honeypot La

Gosram

B5260

Pool Foot Lane

A585

GARSTANG   NEW   ROAD

Pointer
House

FLEETWOOD ROAD

439

8

**Little
Singleton**

Kirkham i'th'Fields

Road

LODGE

Grange Road

Grange

Fisher's Slack La

B5...

Pitfield
Farm

38   39   **107**   40

G   H   J   K   L   M

Edge

Works

Skitham Ln

Road

A B C D 282 E F

42

Moor
Hi 341

43

Dockinsall

Lane

Bensons

1

Crook Gate Lane

Stone Check
Hall

Out Rawcliffe
CE Primary
School

Crab Tree Lane

ok Gate Lane

2

†

Sandy Lane

Alder

Lane

Belle
Vue

42

Rawcliffe Road

3

Rawcliffe
Hall

Works

Ratten Row

Crabtree
Farm

Crow Lane

Hoskinshire

Lancaster

Road

White
Hall

Rawcliffe Ro

4

Rawcliffe Road

River Wyre

41

Wall Mill Pool

Cartford
Bridge

Cartford C

Cartford Lane

5

Larbreck

Well Lane

Wall Pool
Bridge

Gillow Park

Brow
Close

PH

**Little
Eccleston**

Butt's Lane

GARSTANG

ROAD

Wall
Farm

Meagles Lane

Wall Lane

Blackpool Old Road

Malt Kiln Gv

A586

Great Eccleston
Lane Health Centre

Townside Ca

RAIKES ROAD

Lancaster Av

6

**WEST
END**

HIGH STREET

Back

†

B5293

PO

Barrows Lane East

Wyre
Close

Drive

Chester

York

Ripon
Close

Pennine Way

Lancaster
Close

40

Copp
Lane

South St

St Mary's Road

† St Marys Catholic
Primary School

Pennine
View

7

8

Meagles Lane

Meadow
Farm

Great Eccleston
Copp CE Primary
School

†

Copp

White
Crosses

Copp

439

341

42

43

A B C Langtre 108 D E F

Highbury
Gate

Lane

1 grid square represents 500 metres

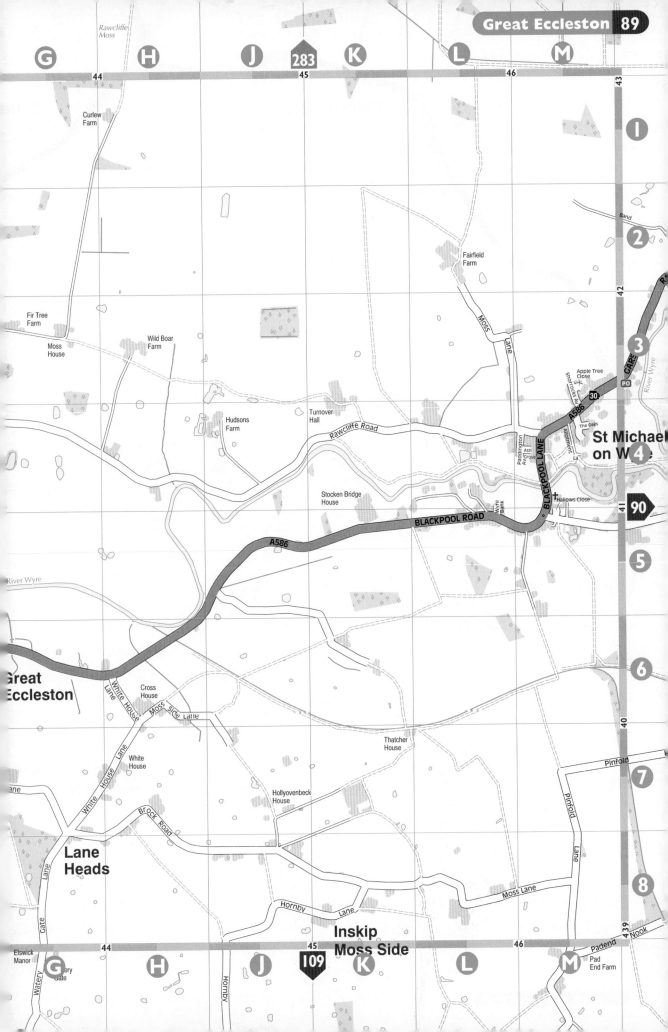

Rawcliffe Moss

G H J 283 K L M

44 45 46 43

I

2

Curlew Farm

Fairfield Farm

Moss Lane

3

Fir Tree Farm

Moss House

Wild Boar Farm

Apple Tree Close

PO

30

River Wyre

CARE

Hudsons Farm

Turnover Hall

Rawcliffe Road

Paddington Av

Ash Grove

The Oaks

St Michael on W 4

A586

BLACKPOOL LANE

Shorrocks Av

Allotment

La

Hallows Close

90

Stocken Bridge House

BLACKPOOL ROAD

Wyre Bank

5

A586

River Wyre

6

Great Eccleston

White House Lane

Cross House

Moss Side Lane

Thatcher House

Pinfold

Pinfold Lane

7

White House

White House Lane

Hollyovenbeck House

Brock Road

Lane Heads

Moss Lane

8

Gate Lane

Elswick Manor

Watery Gate

ery Gate

Hornby Lane

Inskip Moss Side

Padend

439

Nook

Pad End Farm

G H J 109 K L M

44 45 46

Hornby

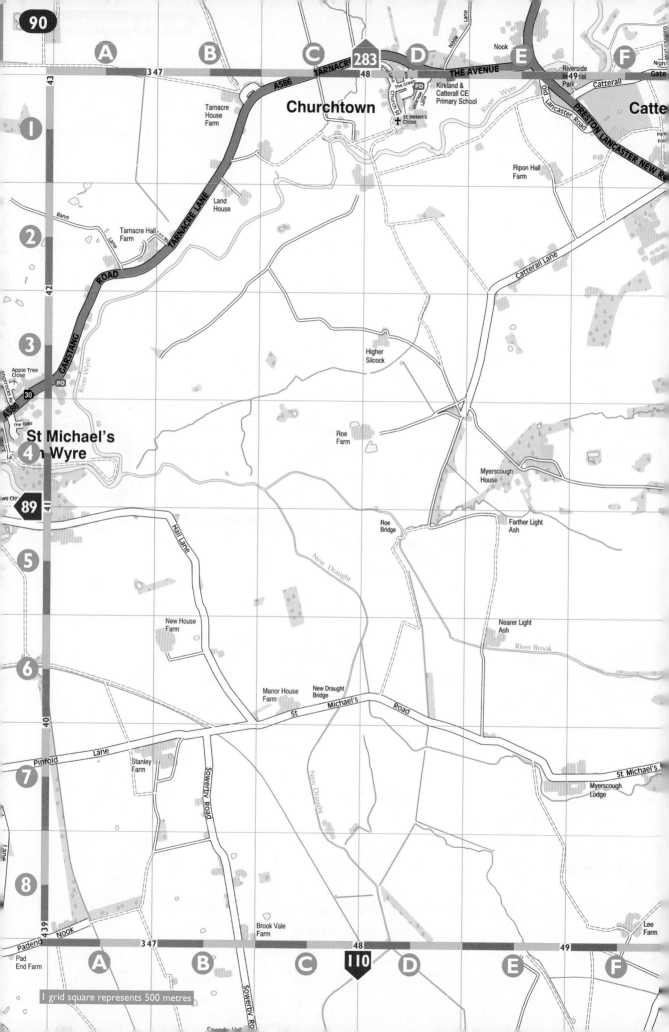

90

A B C **283** D E F

3 47   TARNACRE   48   THE AVENUE   49   Catterall

A586   Nook   Nook   Riverside   Park

Churchtown   River Wyre   Catte

Tarnacre House Farm   The Green   Kirkland & Catterall CE Primary School

St Helen's Close   Ripon Hall Farm

I

Land House

2

Band Lane   Tarnacre Hall Farm   TARNACRE LANE   Catterall Lane

ROAD

GARSTANG

3

River Wyre   Higher Silcock

Apple Tree Close

PO

30

A586   The Oaks   Roe Farm   Myerscough House

St Michael's

4   **n Wyre**

ws Clo

89   41

Hall Lane   Roe Bridge   Farther Light Ash

5

New Draught   Nearer Light Ash

New House Farm   River Brook

6

40

Manor House Farm   New Draught Bridge

St   Michael's   Road

Pinfold   Lane   Stanley Farm   St Michael's

7

Sowerby Road   New Draught   Myerscough Lodge

8

439   Nook   Brook Vale Farm   Lee Farm

Padend

Pad End Farm

A   B   C   **110**   D   E   F

3 47   48   49

I grid square represents 500 metres

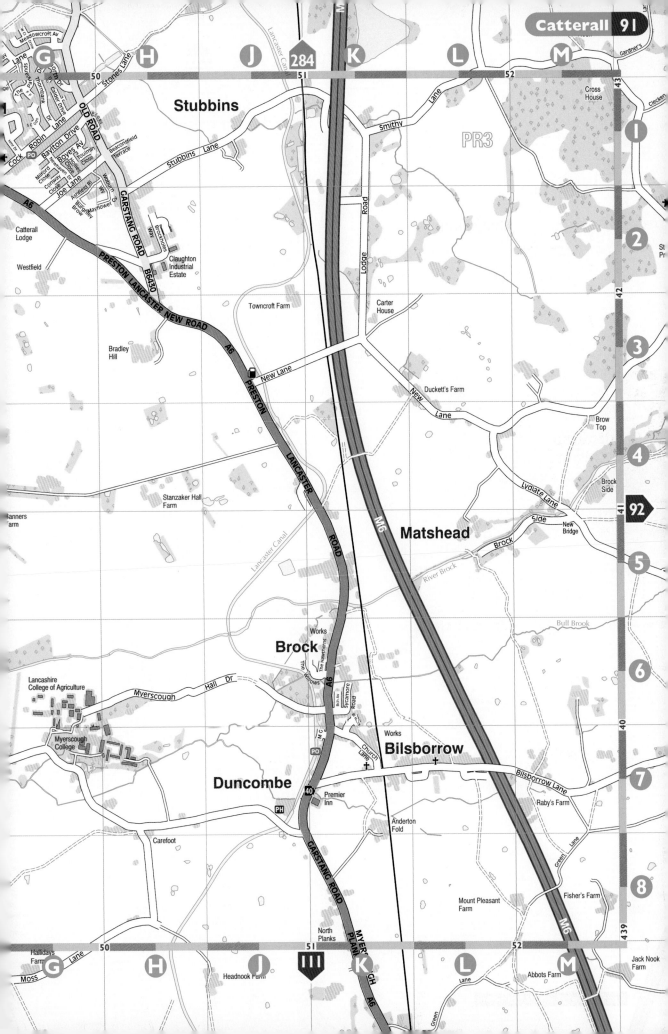

Stubbins

Matshead

Brock

Bilsborrow

Duncombe

PR3

Cross House

Catterall Lodge

Westfield

Bradley Hill

Towncroft Farm

Carter House

Duckett's Farm

Brow Top

Brock Side

New Bridge

Lydiate Lane

River Brock

Bull Brook

Banners Farm

Stanzaker Hall Farm

Lancashire College of Agriculture

Myerscough College

Carefoot

Works

The Hawthorns

The Willows

Works

Church Lane

Premier Inn

Anderton Fold

Raby's Farm

Mount Pleasant Farm

Fisher's Farm

Hallidays Farm

Moss Lane

Headnook Farm

North Planks

Jack Nook Farm

Abbots Farm

St Pr

PRESTON LANCASTER NEW ROAD

CARSTANG ROAD

LANCASTER ROAD

PRESTON

Lancaster Canal

Stubbins Lane

New Lane

New Lane

Lodge Road

Smithy

Brock Side

Bilsborrow Lane

Green Lane

MYERS PLANK

CARSTANG ROAD

Myerscough Hall Dr

Sycamore Road

A6

A6

A6

M6

M6

B6430

OLD ROAD

CARSTANG ROAD

Baylton Drive

Joe Lane

Brockholes Way

Claughton Industrial Estate

Lancaster Canal

284

92

40

PO

PH

PO

G 50 H J 51 K L 52 M 43

1
2
3
4
5
6
7
8

42

41

40

4 39

G 50 H J III K GH L M

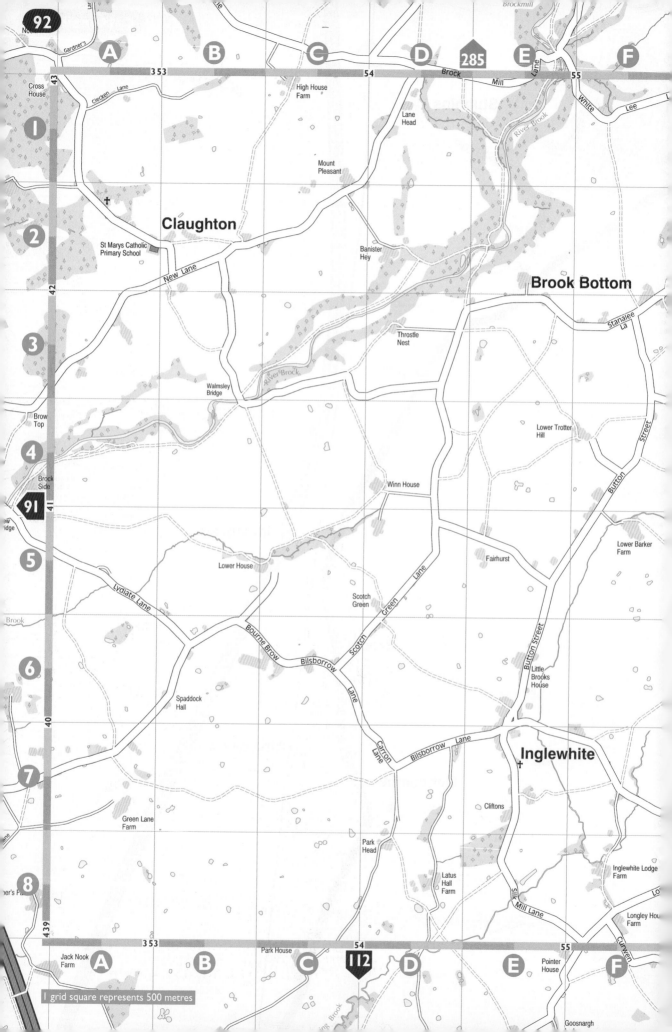

G H J K 286 L M

White
Lee

Fell
Side 56 57 58 43

I

Rigg Lane

Rigg

2

Rigg Lane

Daws

Beacon Fell
Country Park

P

P

Crombleholme
Fold

Wood
Fold

Carwags

Lyndeth

Birch Lane

42

3

Barns
Fold
Reservoirs

Barns Lane

Whitechapel

Church Lane

Oakenhead Cl

Whitechapel
mary School

Fell
Side

Barns Lane
Bottom

4

her
ken
ad

Barns Fold
Farm

41 94

Ashes

Hill House

White
Hill

5

Syke House

Bullsnape

Back Lane

Higher
Barker

Bullsnape
Hall

Horns Lane

6

Plane
Tree

Bullsnape La

Horns Lane

40

Syke House Lane

Fir Trees

7

Isles Field
Farm

Bullsnape La

Inglewhite Road

White Moss
Gate

Palegate Farm

Inglewhite Road

ite Road

Bullsnape Brook

439

8

D
Ba

Lower
Beesley

Higher
Beesley

56 57 58 Inglewhite Road

G H J 113 K Horns
Reservoir L M Oak
Tree

Mill Lane

Ford Lane

Whittingham Brook

St Francis
Catholic

Kidsnape

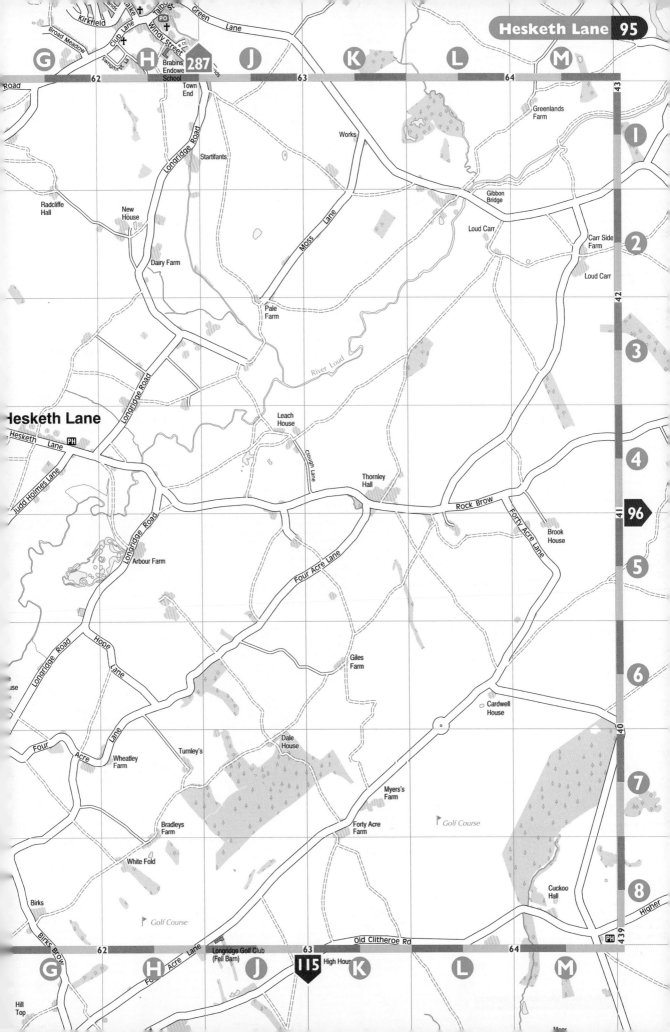

Kirkfield

Broad Meadow

Talbot St

Green Lane

Club Lane

Windy Street

PO

Brabins Endowe School

287

Town End

Road

62

G

H

J

K

L

M

Longridge Road

Startifants

Works

Greenlands Farm

I

Radcliffe Hall

New House

Moss Lane

Gibbon Bridge

Loud Carr

Carr Side Farm

2

Dairy Farm

Loud Carr

Pale Farm

River Loud

3

Hesketh Lane

Leach House

PH

Hesketh Lane

clough Lane

Thornley Hall

4

Judd Holmes Lane

Rock Brow

96

Forty Acre Lane

Brook House

Longridge Road

Arbour Farm

Four Acre Lane

5

Hope Lane

Giles Farm

6

Longridge Road

Cardwell House

40

Lane

Four Acre

Turnley's

Dale House

7

Wheatley Farm

Myers's Farm

Golf Course

Bradleys Farm

Forty Acre Farm

White Fold

Cuckoo Hall

8

Birks

Golf Course

Higher

Birks Brow

62

Fr Acre Lane

Longridge Golf Club (Fell Barn)

63

115

High Hous

Old Clitheroe Rd

64

PH 439

G

H

J

K

L

M

Hill Top

A Doeford B C D 288 E F

365 66 67

I

2 Side

Loud Carr

Yew Tree
Farm

Plantation
Farm

Head o'th
Moor

3 Bradley
Hall

Weed
Acre
Farm

Walker
Fold

Rakefoot

4 Rams
Clough

Longridge Fell

95

Green
Thorn

5

6

Brook
Bottom

Old Clitheroe Road

Lennox Farm

7

Old Clitheroe Road

Intack Crowshaw House

Old Clitheroe Road

8

Higher Road

Huntingdon Hall Road

Low Hill
House

Dutton
Manor

Greengore

A B C 116 D E F

365 66 67

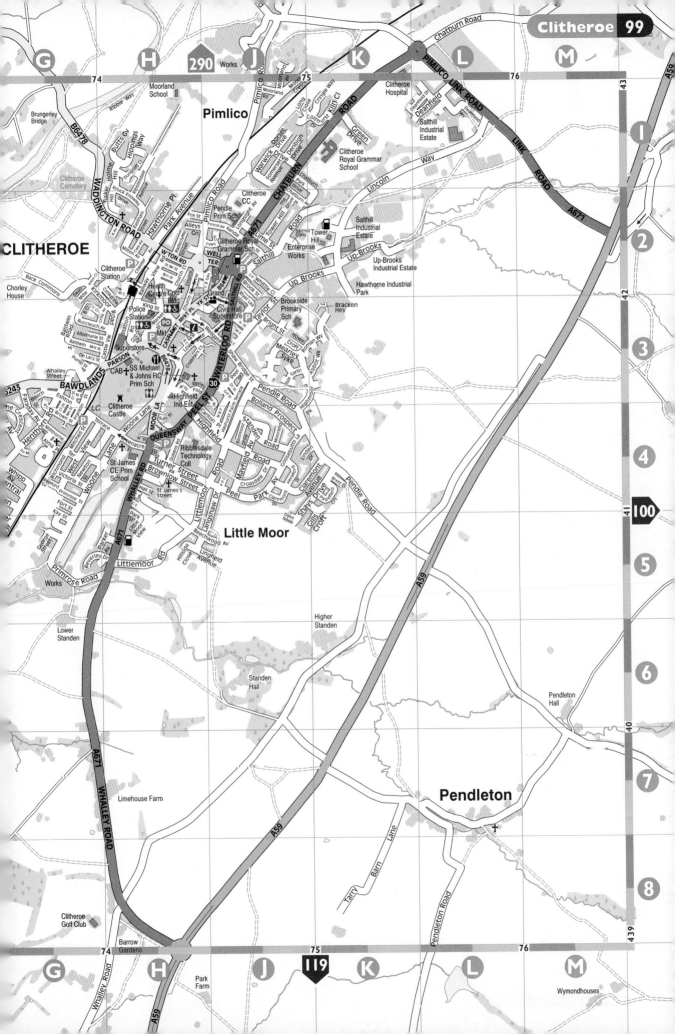

G   H   J   K   292   L   M

80   81   82   43

I

Twiston Moor

2

42

Black Moss

3

Downham Moor

557
▲
Pendle Hill

Windy Harbour Farm

Foot House Gate

4
Blac Moss Rese

Pendle Side

Pendle House

102

41

Ing Head Farm

Over Houses

Pendle Way

Barley Lane

5

Barley Moor

Ing Ends

Boar Clough

+ BARLEY

Under Pendle

Barley Green

The Av

6
Net

Heys La

Ogden Hill

Bridge End

Buttock

40

7

Pendle Way

Spence Moor

Pendle Way

Ogden Resrs

Fell Wood

Cross Lane

Jinny

Newchurch in Pendle

Newchurch in Pendle St Mary CE School

8

BB8

439

Well Head Road

Faughs

Works

Spenbrook Road

Osborne Terrace

80   81   121   82

G   H   J   K   L   M

Well Head Road

Sabden Hall

ddlers

Bull Hole

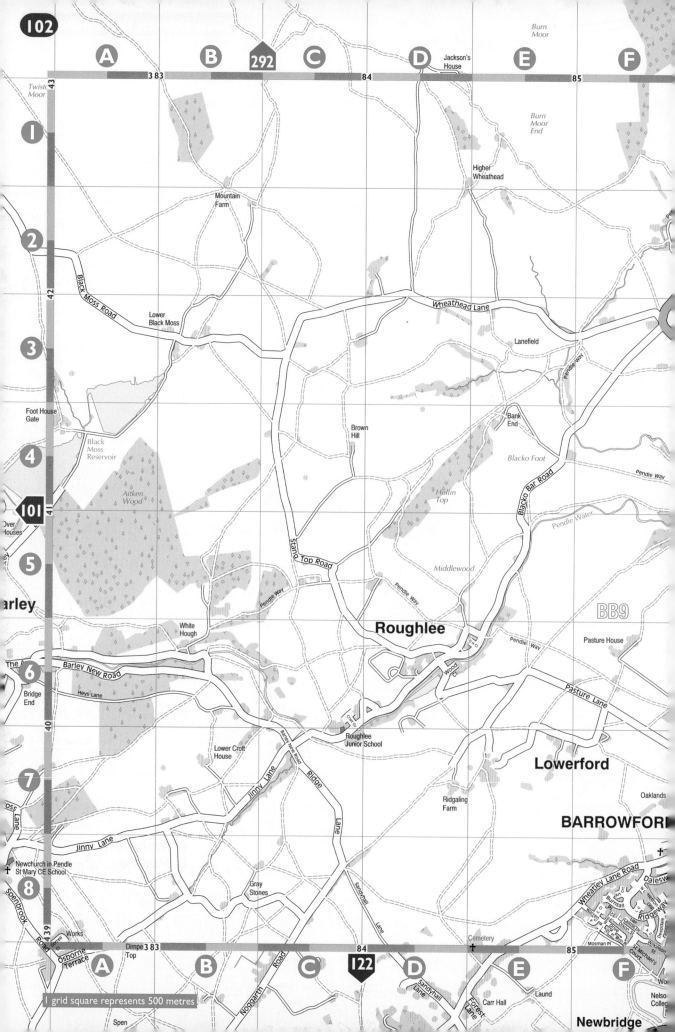

G
H
293
J
K
L
M ley
I

86
87
88
43

Admergill
Pasture

Green
Bank

Sunnybank
Farm

Stone Lane

Standing

WHITEMOOR ROAD

Whitemoor
Reservoir

The Old Sidings
Railway St
Wo

Cocker
Hill

2
51

Reedymoor Lane

Blacko
Hill
Side

Pasture
Head

Holly Bush
Farm

Slipper
Hill
Reservoir

Burwains
Sailing
Club

Foulridge
Lower
Reservoir

3

Brownley
Park

Burnt
House
Farm

Smithy Lane

Back
o' th'
Edge

4

Hollin
Fold

Blacko

Willaston Av

Beverley

Road

Blacko
Primary School

Malkin
Close

GISBURN ROAD

Barnoldswick Road

New House

Red Lane

Alkincoats

Colne Edge

Sacred
RC Primit
School

296

Stone Edge

Pendle Way

GISBURN ROAD A682

Middleton Dr

Stone Edge Road

Peel
Pl
Mfld
Cl

Milton Av

Colne &
Nelson
RUFC

White Gv
Harrison Dr
Rimington
Av

Keats
Cl
Coleridge
Cl

Judge Fields

5

Higherford

The Orchard
Ribblesdale Place

Whittycroft
Av

Blakey
Hall

Akincoats Road

Park Way

Harrison Drive

Birtwis

Slater Av

Milton

Tennyson Rd

NORTH VA

Crow
Trees

Grange
Meadow
Edge

Francis Av

Barrowford
Lock House

Hiers House Lane

Prestfield Av
Milford
Reginald St

Barcroft St
Parker
Selby St

Haverholt

North Va
Moorland

RIGBY

Lord Street
Prim Sch

6

Fold Bank

Park St
East

Nelson
& Colne
College

BARROWFORD ROAD B6247

etherheys

50 A6068

CRWN WY
LORD

OWEN

PO

Colne
Road

ALBERT ROAD

Shaw

7

COLNE ROAD

B6247

VIVARY WAY

Colne Station

Pendle
Leisure
Cen

A56

PRIMET
HILL

Knotts La

7

St Thomas
CE (VA)
Prim Sch

River Av

Barrowford
Cemetery

Pendle
Heritage
Centre

M65

Greenfield
Road

Colne Water

WHITEWALLS DR

A6068

Greenfield
Road

Holker
Business
Cen

Garden Vale
Business Cen

Primet
Business Cen

30

BURNEY ROAD

Primet
Prim Sch

Valley Drive

Dewhurst
Street

8

A682

Clinic

Leeds
Liverpool Canal

Cravendale
Avenue

Bevan
Place

Edward Street

Regent Street

Junction

Superstore

Whitewalls
Industrial
Estate

BURNLEY ROAD

Medical
Centre

Colne Primet
High School

Briercliffe
Avenue

86
87
88
439

G
H
J
123
K
L
M

Holy Saints
RC
Primary School

REEDYFORD ROAD

Swinden
Hall
Road

Rakes
House

Charles Street

A56

Lee Road

Norwood
Road

Oxford Road

Hollins La

Bott House La

John Fisher &
Thomas More High Sch

Pendle
Community
High School

M65

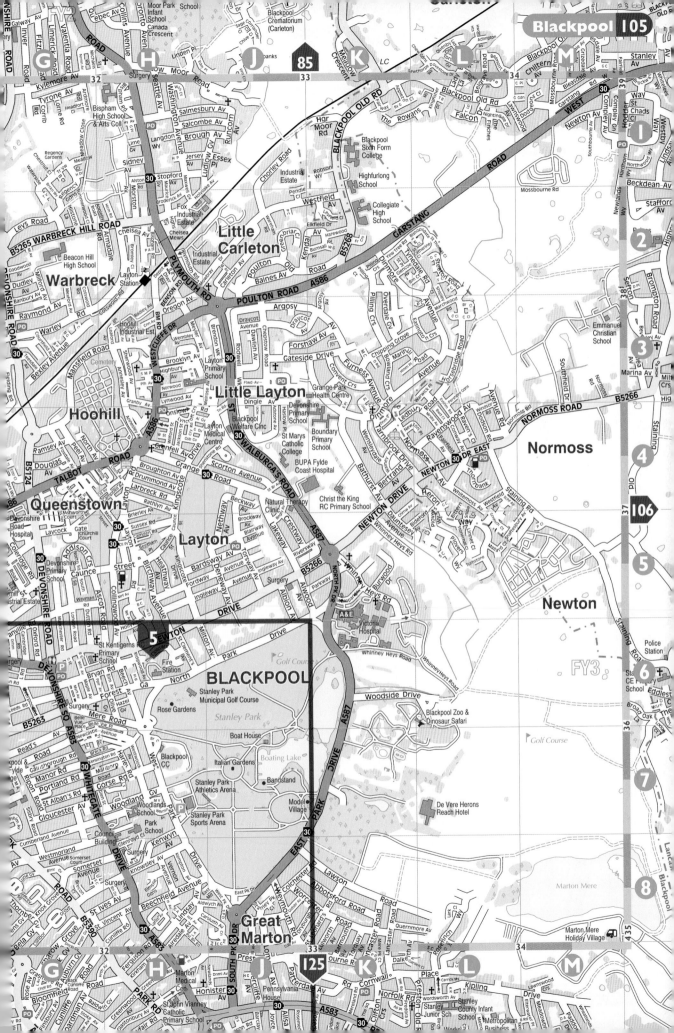

POULTON - LE - FYLDE

Old Field Carr

Puddle House Farm

Hardhorn

Carr Lane

Avenham Hall

STATION

FAIRFIELD ROAD

B5266

Fairfield Rd

LONGHOUSE LANE

HARDHORN ROAD

Smithy Lane

Old Road

Toddestaffe Hall

LC

Staining

Police Station

Staining CE Primary School

Staining Road

Chain Lane

Hawes House

Main Dyke

Lancashire County Blackpool

Mythop Road

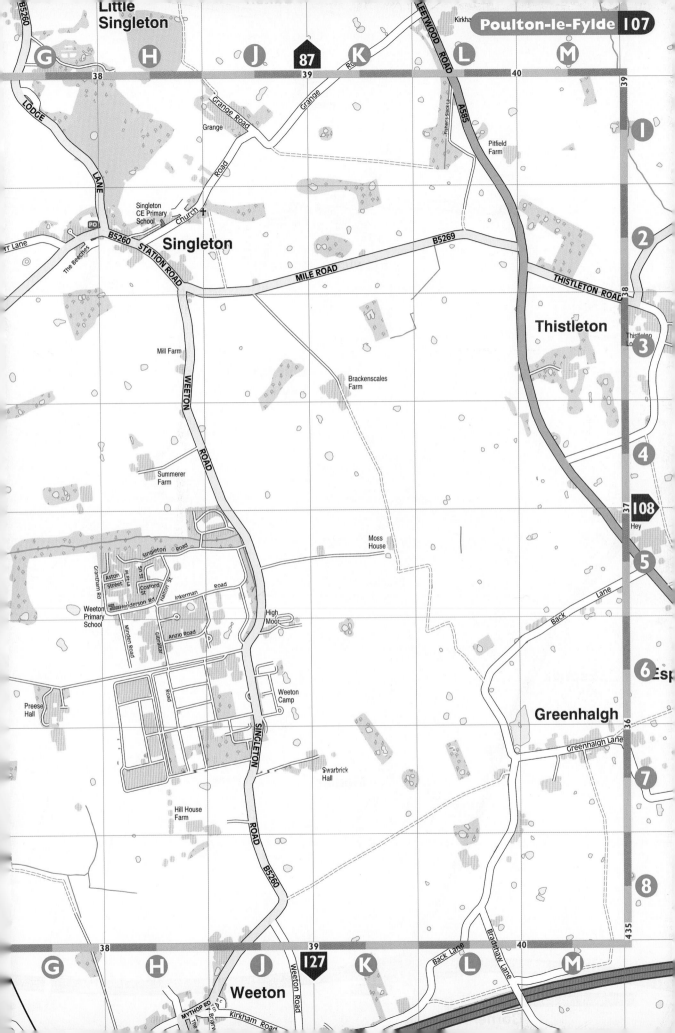

Little Singleton

G   H   J   **87**   K   L   M

38   39   40   39

LODGE LANE

Grange Road

Grange

Grange Rd

FLEETWOOD ROAD

Kirkha

Fisher's Stick La

A585

Pitfield Farm

1

Singleton CE Primary School

Church

PO

B5260   STATION ROAD

The Beeches

rr Lane

Singleton

B5269

THISTLETON ROAD

2

38

Mill Farm

Thistleton

Thistleton Lo

3

MILE ROAD

WEETON

ROAD

Brackenscales Farm

Summerer Farm

4

37   **108**

Hey

Moss House

5

Singleton   Road

Grantham Rd

Aston Street

St St La

Cosford St

Halton St

Inkerman   Road

Henderson Rd

Minden Road

Gibraltar

Weeton Primary School

High Moor

Anzio Road

Road

Back   Lane

6   Esp

Greenhalgh

Preese Hall

Weeton Camp

36

Greenhalgh Lane

7

Swarbrick Hall

Hill House Farm

SINGLETON

ROAD

B5260

8

435

38   39   40

G   H   J   **127**   K   Back Lane   L   Bradshaw Lane   M

Weeton

Weeton Road

MYTHOP RD   Bria   Kirkham Road   The

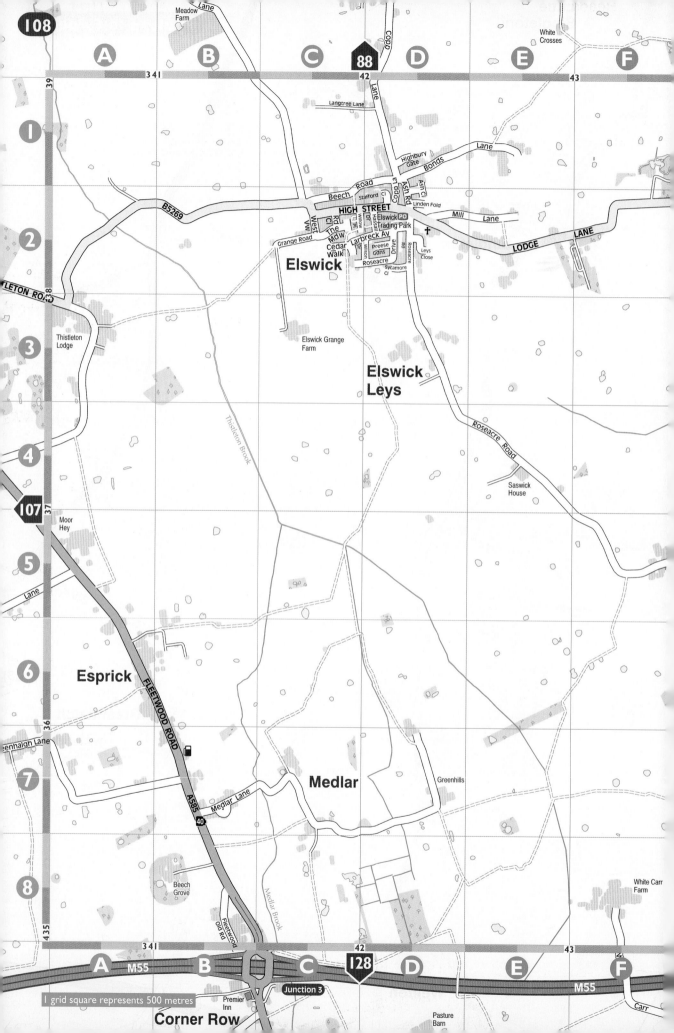

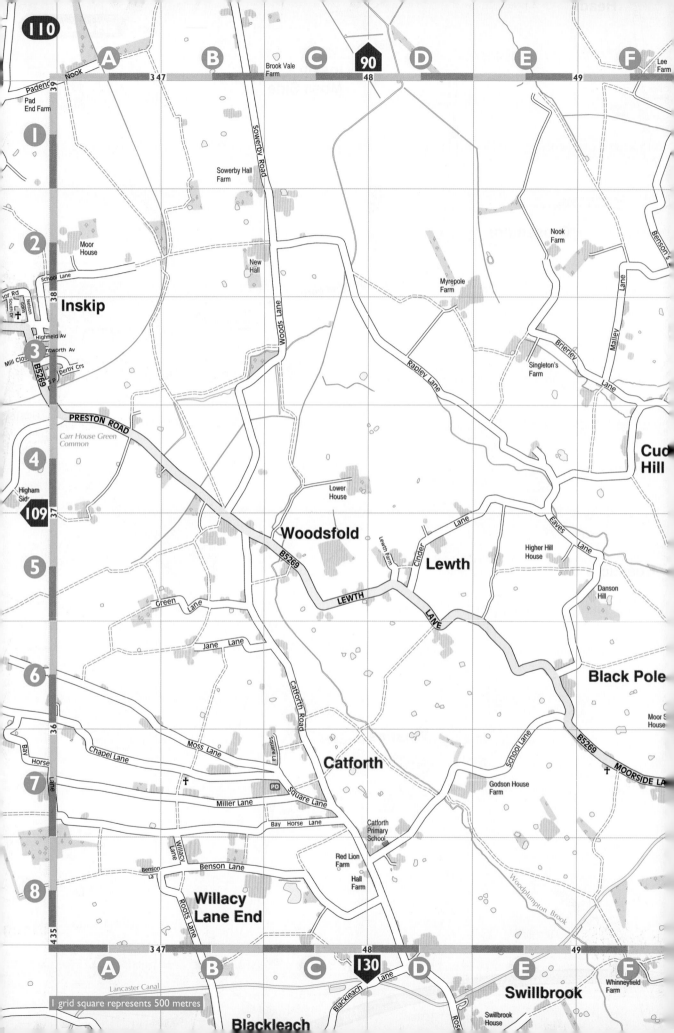

A 347 B Brook Vale Farm C 90 48 D E F 49 Lee Farm

Nook

Padeno
Pad End Farm

1

Sowerby Hall Farm

Sowerby Road

Nook Farm

2
Moor House
New Hall
Myrepole Farm

School Lane
Benson S

Nelson Gdns
nor Rd South Dr
Inskip
Brierley Lane
Malley Lane

Highfield Av
3
ntworth Av
Rapley Lane
Singleton's Farm

Mill Clos
Derby Crs
B5269
S.P.

Woods Lane

PRESTON ROAD

Carr House Green Common
Cuc Hill

4
Lower House

Higham Sid
109 37
Woodsfold
Lewth Farm
Higher Hill House

B5269
Cinder Lane
Lewth
Danson Hill

5
Eaves Lane

Green Lane
LEWTH LANE
Black Pole

6
Jane Lane
Catforth Road
Moor S House

36
Moss Lane
School Lane
B5269 MOORSIDE LA

Chapel Lane
Square La
Catforth
Godson House Farm

Bay Horse Lane
7
PO
Square Lane
Catforth Primary School

Miller Lane

Bay Horse Lane
Red Lion Farm

Willacy Lane
Hall Farm
Woodplumpton Brook

8
Benson La
Benson Lane
Willacy Lane End
Roots Lane

435

A 347 B C 48 130 D E 49 F

Lancaster Canal
Swillbrook
Whinneyfield Farm

1 grid square represents 500 metres
Blackleach Lane
Blackleach
Roos
Swillbrook House

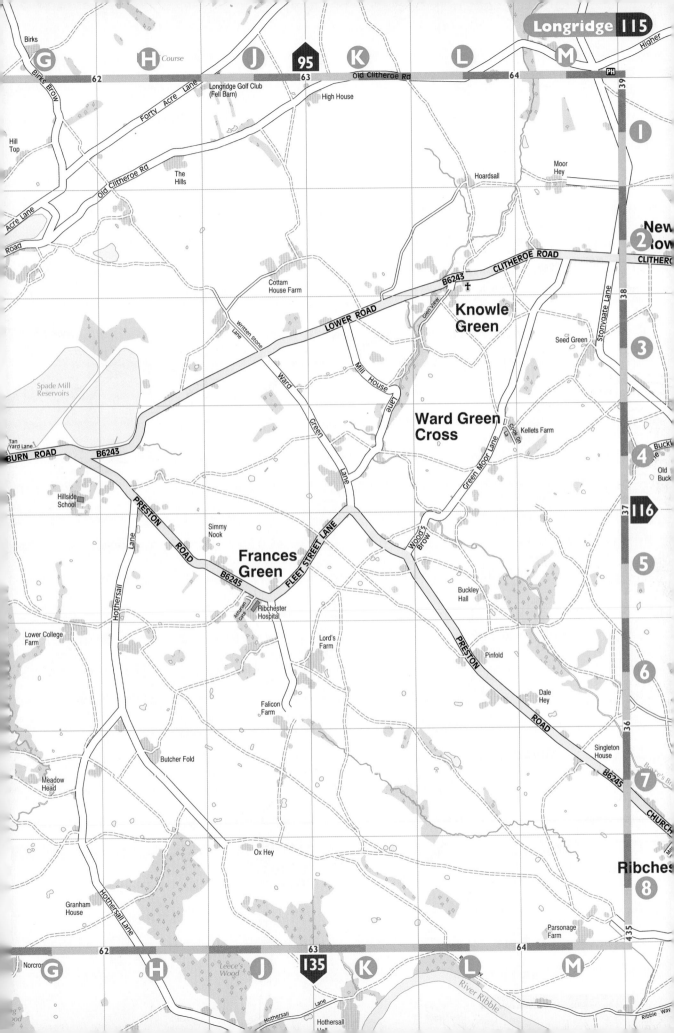

G 62
H Course
J
95
63
K Old Clitheroe Rd
L
M 64
PH 39

Birks

Birks Brow

Longridge Golf Club
(Fell Barn)

High House

1

Moor Hey

Hoardsall

Hill Top

Old Clitheroe Rd

Forty Acre Lane

The Hills

Acre Lane

Road

New Row 2

CLITHEROE

Cottam House Farm

B6243 CLITHEROE ROAD

Glen View

Knowle Green

Seed Green

Storrygate Lane

38

3

Written Stone Lane

LOWER ROAD

Mill House Lane

Ward Green Cross

Kellets Farm

Cook Gn

Spade Mill Reservoirs

Ward Green Lane

Tan Yard Lane

BURN ROAD
B6243

Green Moor Lane

Buckl
Old Buck

37
116

4

Hillside School

PRESTON ROAD

Simmy Nook

FLEET STREET LANE

Wood's Brow

5

Hothersall Lane

Frances Green
B6245

Ribchester Hospital
Ashlands Gaw

Buckley Hall

Lower College Farm

Lord's Farm

Pinfold

PRESTON ROAD

6

Dale Hey

Falicon Farm

36

Butcher Fold

Singleton House
B6245

7

Meadow Head

CHURCH

Granham House

Hothersall Lane

Ox Hey

Ribches 8

Parsonage Farm

435

62
G Norcro

63
H

J Leece's Wood

135

64
K

L

M

River Ribble

Hothersall Lane

Hothersall

B6243

Woodfields

Knowles Brow

Lower Hodder Bridge

G   H   J   97 K   L   M

68   69   70   39

Stonyhurst College

St Marys Hall

River Hodder

Ribble Way

I

Hill Farm

Hall Barn Farm

2

Fox Fields

Hurst Green

St Josephs RC Primary School

WHALLEY   B6243   ROAD

Cross Gills

Jumbles

3

Shire   Lane

ROAD   B6243

The Dene

Avenue Road

Silver St

Smithy Row

Warren Fold   PO

PO

PH   Shireburn Arms Hotel

Ribble Way

Lambing Clough

Ribble Way

River Ribble

4

Brockhall Farm

37   118

Bailey Brook

Bailey Hall

Trough House

Works

Gleneagles Drive

Tuscany   Gv

Provence   Av

St Andrews Rd

The Wynds

5   Broc all Village

Hey Hurst

Ribble Way

Ribble Way

Dinckley Hall

Cherry Cl   Chry Dr   Cherry Dr

Masefield Cl

Damson Close

Bradyll Ct

Pendle Vw   Bradyll

Larkhill

The Avenue Hotel

6

Cravens

Aspinalls

Moorgate La

Dinckley Brook

The Drive

Elm Tree Ct

Highgrove Pk

Brookside

Old Langho

36

Marles Wood

Dinckley

Ribchester Road

Wardfall

Old Langho Road

Hillock Farm

7

Ribchester Road

Lower Fold Farm

Northcote Road

435

8

Dinckley Grange

Chapel Lane

68   69   70

G   H   J   137   K   L   M

Brick House

LONGSIGHT ROAD

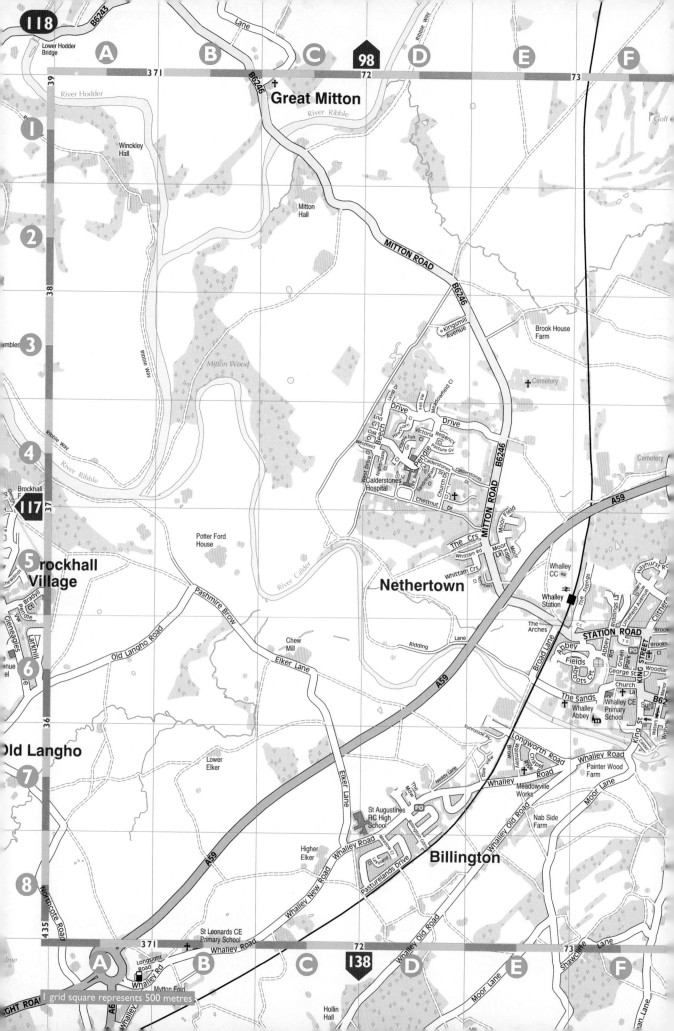

118

Lower Hodder
Bridge

B6243

A 371 **B** B6246 **C** **98** 72 **D** **E** 73 **F**

39 38 37

† Great Mitton

River Hodder

River Ribble

Winckley
Hall

1

Mitton
Hall

2

MITTON ROAD

B6246

3

Mitton Wood

Ribble Way

Kingsmill
Avenue

Brook House
Farm

† Cemetery

Beech Drive

Regency Drive

Victoria

4

River Ribble

Brockhall
F

117

Calderstones
Hospital

Calderstones

Calderstones

B6246

Cemetery

Potter Ford
House

Chestnut
Dr

† Church

Moor Field

Whittam Rd

The Crs

Moor
La

Moor
Edge

Whalley
CC

5

**rockhall
Village**

The Wendy

Bradyll
Pendle

Gleneagles

Larkhill

Pashmire Brow

River Calder

Chew
Mill

Nethertown

Whittam Crs

Whalley
Station

The Arches

CC

STATION ROAD

PO

Green Park

Limefield Avenue

Hayhurst

Clitheroe

6

36

Old Langho Road

Elker Lane

Ridding

Lane

Abbey
Fields

Abbey

Church

King St

B62

Old Langho

Lower
Elker

A59

Sunnyside Av

Whalley
Abbey

Whalley CE
Primary
School

The Sands

Longworth Road

Chapel

Whalley Road

Painter Wood
Farm

Moor Lane

7

435

Northcote Road

A59

Elker Lane

Higher
Elker

St Augustines
RC High
School

PO

Whalley New Road

Pasturelands Drive

Billington

Neddy Lane

Wamsley

Dale Rd

Meadowville
Works

Whalley Old Road

Nab Side
Farm

Moor Lane

8

A A6 Whalley **B** 371 Whalley Road **C** **138** 72 **D** Whalley Old Road **E** 73 Shawcliffe **F**

Longsight
Road

Whalley Rd

Mytton Fold

St Leonards CE
Primary School †

Hollin
Hall

I grid square represents 500 metres

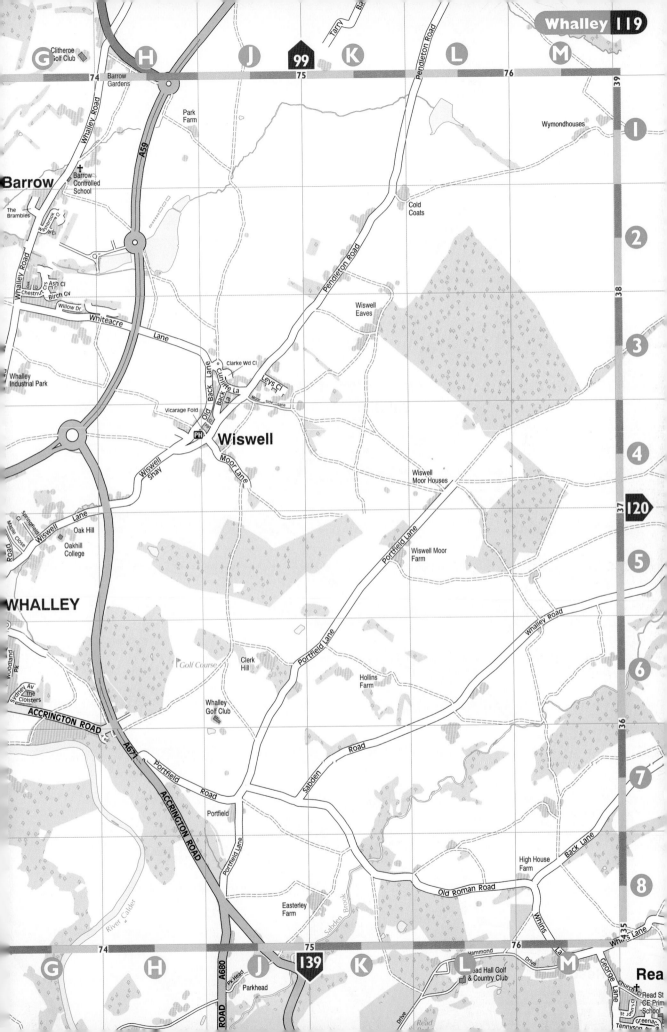

G H J 99 K L M

Clitheroe Golf Club
Barrow Gardens
Park Farm
Wymondhouses

74 75 76

Barrow
The Brambles
Barrow Controlled School
Cold Coats

Whalley Road
A59
Chestnut
Ash Cl
Birch Gv
Willow Dr
Whiteacre Lane

Wiswell Eaves

Whalley Industrial Park
Clarke Wd Cl
Cunliffe La
Back La
Leys Cl
Moor Side Lane
Back Lane
Vicarage Fold
PH **Wiswell**
Pendleton Road

Wiswell Moor Houses

Wiswell Shay
Moor Lane

Wiswell Lane
Oak Hill
Oakhill College
Springfield Cl
Maple Close

Portfield Lane
Wiswell Moor Farm

WHALLEY
120
Whalley Road

Road
Woodland Pk
Sydney Av
The Cloisters
Golf Course
Clerk Hill
Hollins Farm

ACCRINGTON ROAD
A671
Whalley Golf Club
Portfield Lane
Sabden Road

Back Lane

Portfield Road
Portfield
High House Farm

River Calder
A680
Portfield Lane
Easterley Farm
Sabden Brook
Old Roman Road
Whins La
Drive
George Lane
Whins Lane

74 75 139 76

G H J K L M **Rea**

Pk Head
Parkhead
Hammond Drive
ad Hall Golf & Country Club
Read St
St John's CE Prim School
Tennyson Av
Greenac
church

1 2 3 4 5 6 7 8
39 38 37 36 35

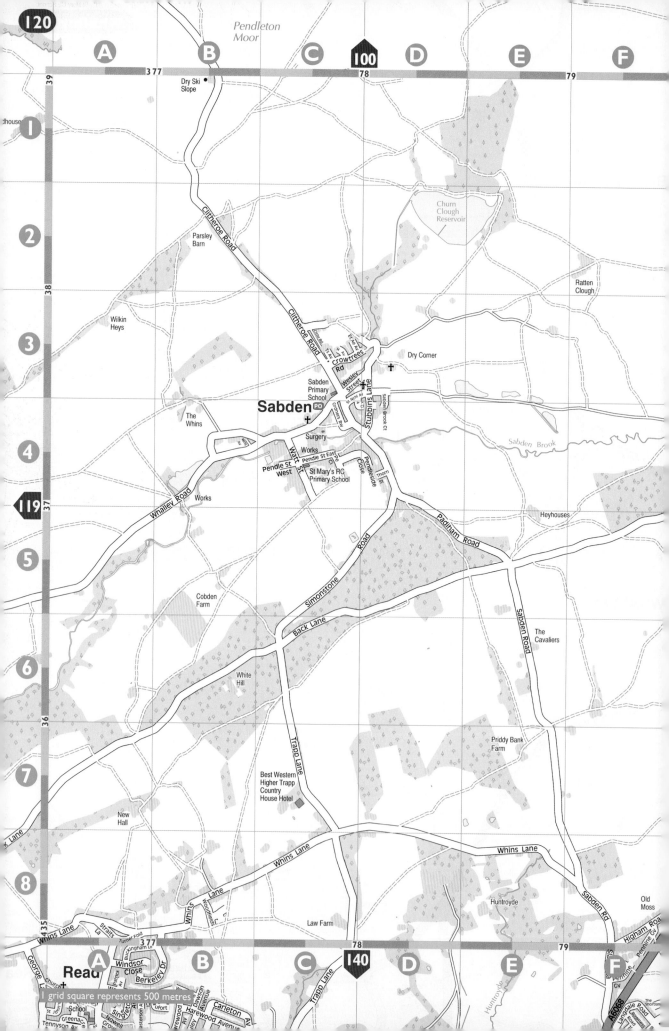

120

A **377** B C **100** D E **79** F

39

Pendleton Moor

1

Dry Ski
Slope •

38

2

Parsley
Barn

Clitheroe Road

Wilkin
Heys

Churn
Clough
Reservoir

Ratten
Clough

3

Crowtrees
Rd

Dry Corner

Sabden
Primary
School

Wesley
Street

Stubbins Lane

Sabden PO

The
Whins

Surgery

Works

Sabden Brook

Sabden Brook Ct

4

Pendle St
West

Watt St

Pendle St East

St Mary's RC
Primary School

Pendleside
Close

Thorn St

37

119

Whalley Road

Works

Heyhouses

5

Padiham Road

Simonstone Road

Sabden Road

The
Cavaliers

Cobden
Farm

White
Hill

Back Lane

36

6

Priddy Bank
Farm

7

Trapp Lane

Best Western
Higher Trapp
Country
House Hotel

New
Hall

Whins Lane

8

Whins Lane

Whins Lane

Sabden Rd

Huntroyde

Old
Moss

435

Whins Lane

377

Windsor
Close

Berkeley Dr

Read

A B C **140** D E F

78

Trapp Lane

Huntroyde

A6068

Higham Road

Pennine Gv

Langdale Road

1 grid square represents 500 metres

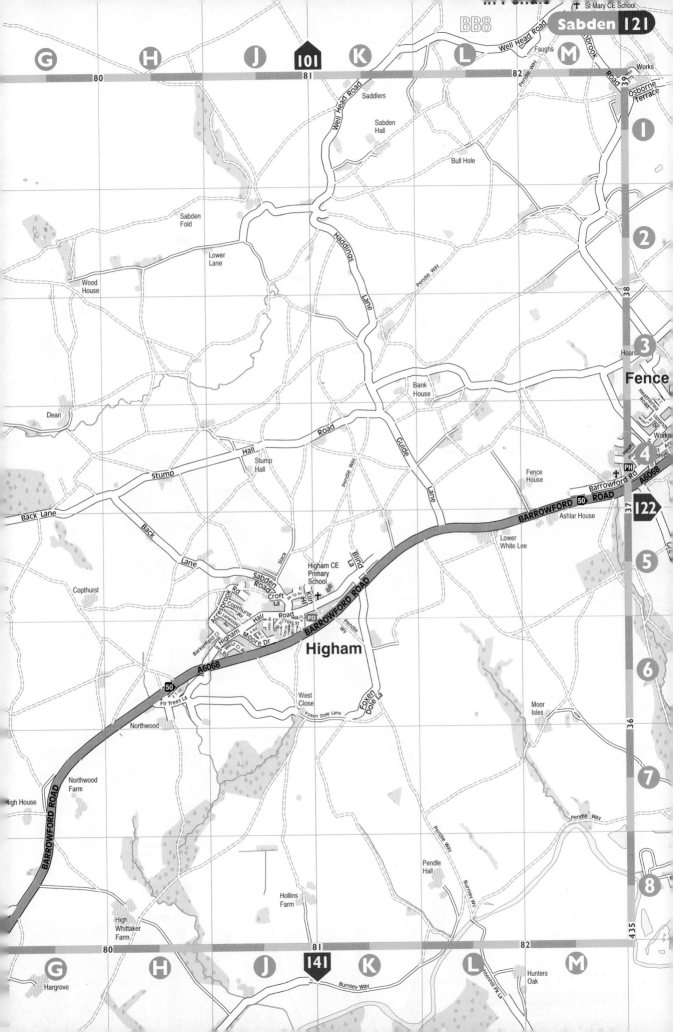

I grid square represents 500 metres

1 grid square represents 500 metres

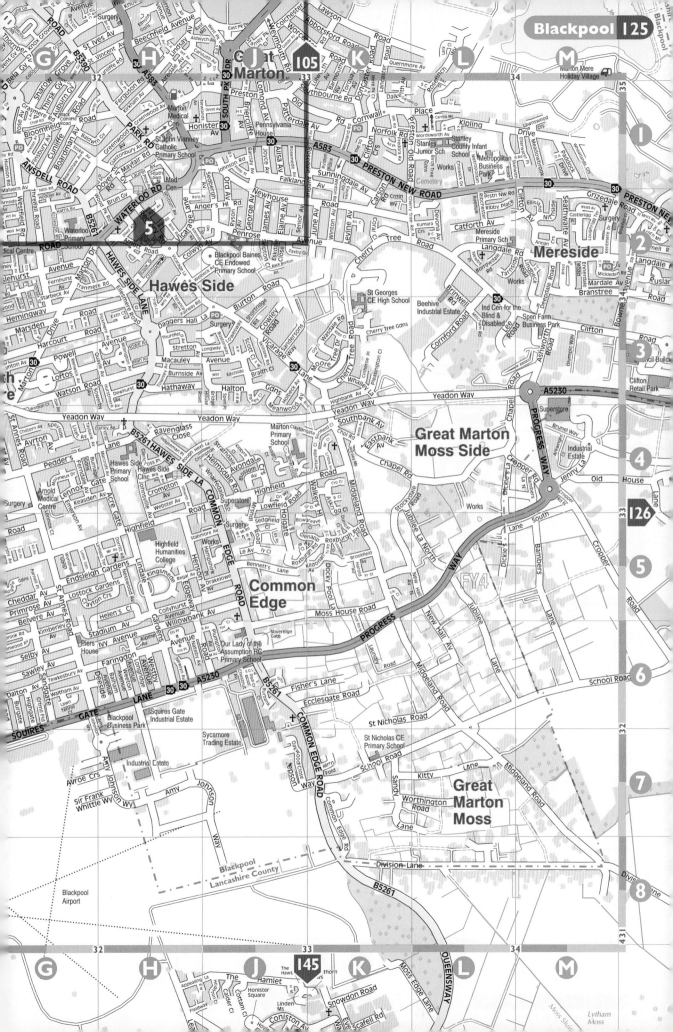

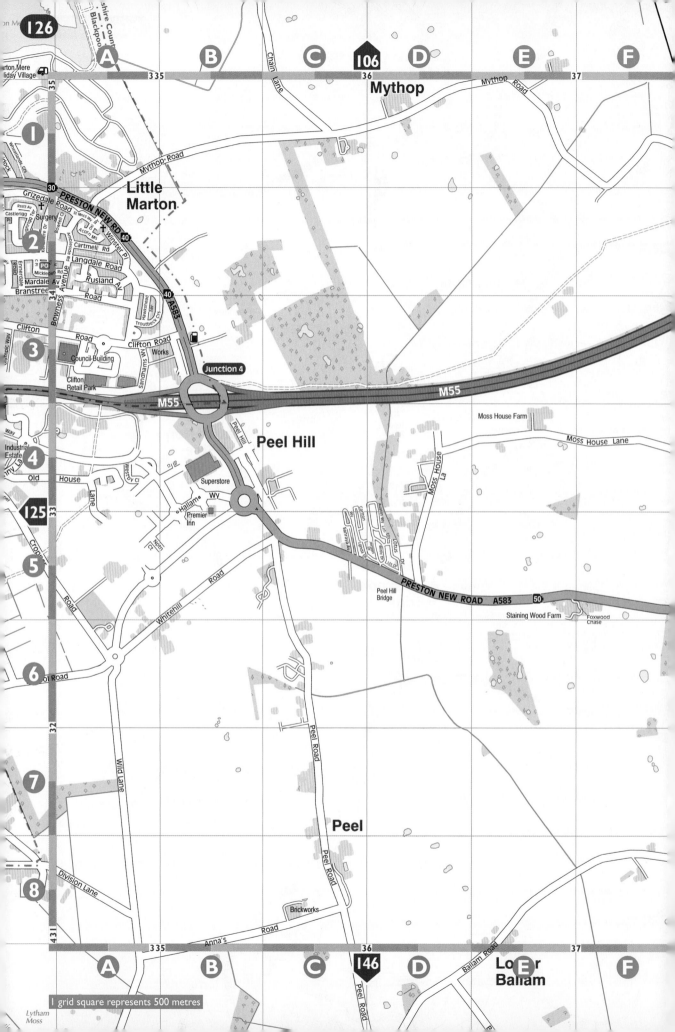

A   B   C   106   D   E   F

335   36   37

Mythop

Mythop Road

I

Little
Marton

30   Mythop Road

Grizedale Road   PRESTON NEW RD

Surgery

Castlerigg   St Mncl Wy

Pl   Winster Pl

2   40

Cartmell   Rd

Acorn Ms

POst   Langdale Road

Mickleden Rd

Mardale Av   Rusland Av

Branstree   Road

34   Bowness Avenue   Hawkshead   A583   40

Troutbeck   Crs

Clifton   Clifton Road

3   Road   Works

Council Building   Sandhams Wy

Clifton   Clifton Road

Clifton
Retail Park   Junction 4

M55   M55   Moss House Farm

Way   Moss House Lane

Industrial
Estate   Peel Hill

4   Peel Hill   Moss House La

Old   House   Superstore

125   33   Hallam   Austin Wy

5   Premier   Carlton   Lotus Dr

Crook   Whitehill Road   Sanraya Av

6   Road   32   Peel Hill   PRESTON NEW ROAD A583   50
Bridge
Staining Wood Farm   Foxwood
Chase

7   Wild Lane   Peel Road

Peel

8   Division Lane

431   Peel Road

Brickworks

Anna's   Road   Ballam Road

335   36   37

A   B   C   146   D   E   Lower   F
Ballam

Peel Road

Lytham
Moss

G H J 107 K L M

Weeton

MYTHOP RD
Briarwood Cl
Kirkham Road
The Cl
Knowsley Crs
Mythop Road
CHURCH ROAD
Weeton Road
Back Lane
Back Lane
Bradshaw Lane

Moss Farm

M55

St Michaels CE
Primary School

Stanley
House
Farm

Weeton Road

B5260

Moss House Lane
Plumpton Lane
The Arbory
Meadow Vw
Corner Bank Cl

Great
Plumpton

WEETON ROAD

128

ON NEW ROAD A583

A583 BLACKPOOL ROAD

Little
Plumpton

Westby Road

BLACKPOOL ROAD

FOX LANE ENDS

Fox La
Ends

Ribby

Ballam Road

B5260

Westby

STATION RD

Vicarage Cl

Wray Crs

B5259 RIBB

Browns

First Av
Elms Dr
The Brooklands
Beverley Cl
RIBBY ROAD
St Nicholas Cl
PH
Manor Rd
Ribby Av
Willow Drive
Beechfield Avenue

Shepherd's
Farm
Mill Lane
McCall Close
PO
Ribby with
Wrea-Endowed
CE Prim Sch
Manor
Moss
Side
Lane
Westbourne Av
Ash Gv
Richmo

The Villa
Country House
Hotel

B5259
SIDE LANE
MOSS
Wrea
Green

Bryning Lane
Bryning
Avenue

G Farm H J 147 K L M

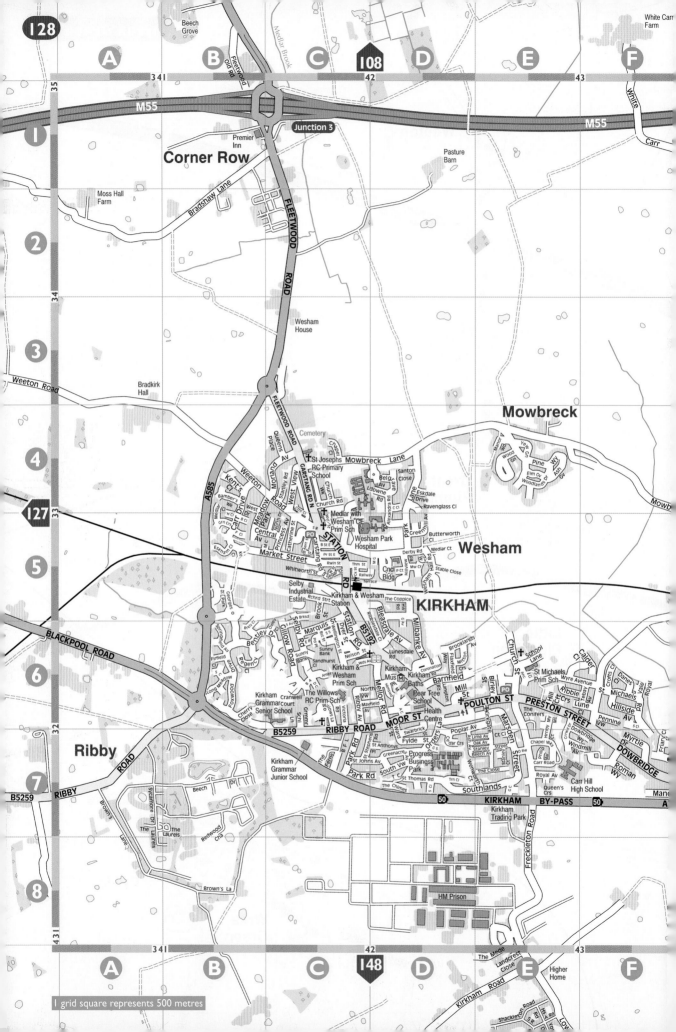

G   H   J   **109**   K   L   M

45

35

I

Moorside

Church Road

44   45   46

Treales CE
Primary School

Blue Moor

M55

Stanley
Lodge

Salwick Road

Kellet's
Bridge

2

Cross Hill
Farm

Stud
Farm

Stanley
Grange

Dagger Road

34

Cross   Lane

**Moor
Side**

Blue Moor

Moss House
Farm

Moss Lane East

3

Moorside

Bolton
Houses

Jacob's Lane

Church Road

4

Moss   Lane   West

Dagger Road

Station   Road

130

33

Treales

Jacob's Lane

Treales
Cottage

5

Kirkham   Road

Sn   La

Works

Treales Road

Moorfield

Treales Road

Carr Lane

Spen   Lane

6

Spen   Brook

Salwick
Station

Station   Road

32

New Hey Lane

Dowbridge

New Hey Lane

Dingle
Farm

7
Works

5192   **BLACKPOOL RD**

50

Moor   Hall   Lane

Oakfield House
School

Church Lane

Clifton Lane

8

431

Highgate
Cl

Vicarage   Lane

G   H   J   **149**   K   L   M

44   45   46

Parrox

Brnying Drive
Hornby Drive

Birch

Cedar

50

Marsh
View

**Newton
with Scales**

Oak Lane

Grange Lane

School

Newton Bluecoat
CE Primary School

Scale Hall Lane

BLACKP

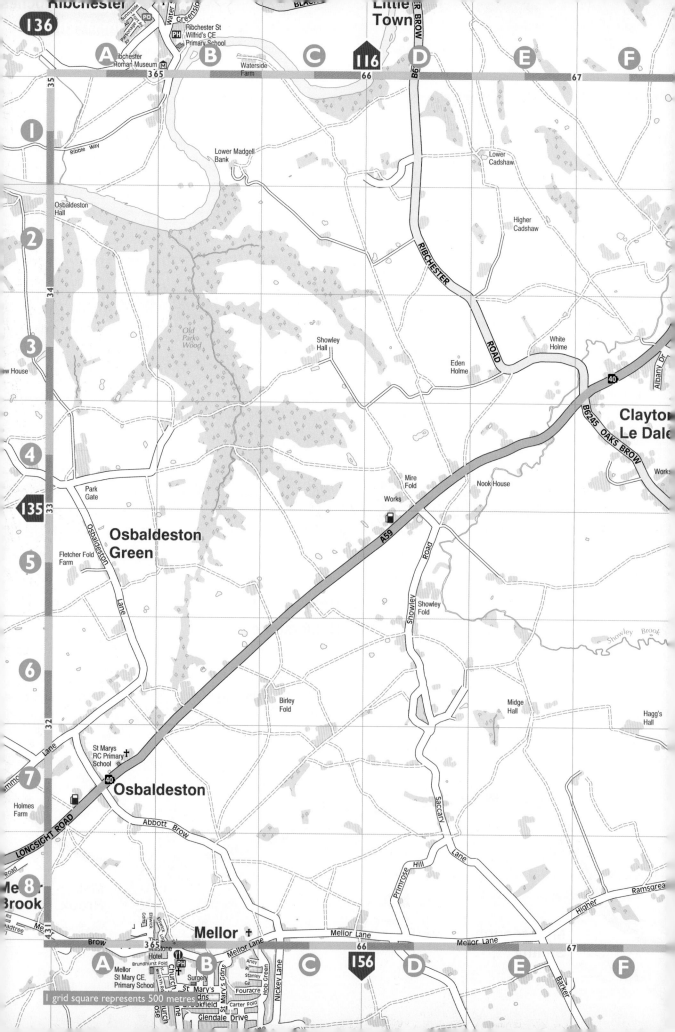

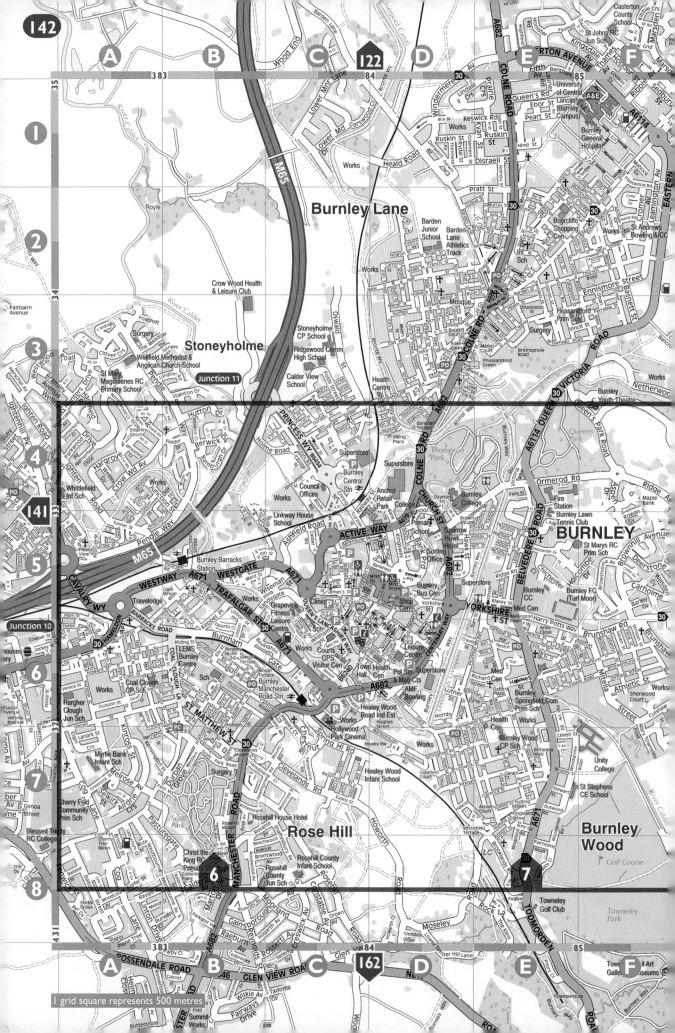

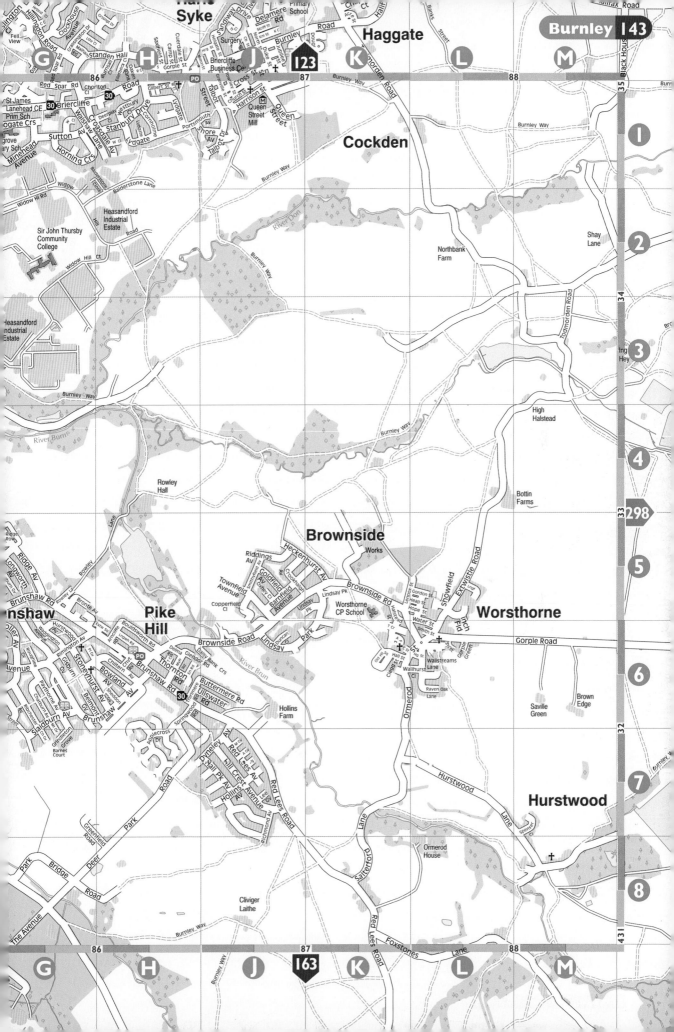

Syke

Haggate

Cockden

Brownside

Worsthorne

Pike Hill

nshaw

Hurstwood

G H J 123 K L M

I
2
3
4
298
5
6
7
8

St James Lanehead CE Prim Sch
Sir John Thursby Community College
Heasandford Industrial Estate
Heasandford Industrial Estate

Briercliffe Business Cen

Queen Street Mill

Northbank Farm

High Halstead

Shay Lane

Ing Hey

Bottin Farms

Rowley Hall

Works

Worsthorne CP School

Gorple Road

Saville Green

Brown Edge

Hollins Farm

Ormerod House

Cliviger Laithe

G H J 163 K L M

86 87 88

86 87 88

35 34 33 32 431

Red Spar Rd
Horning Crs
Widow Hill Rd
Burnley Way
River Don
River Burn
River Brun
Todmorden Road
Extwistle Road
Gorple Road
Brownside Rd
Hurstwood
Red Lees Road
Foxstones
Park Bridge Road
The Avenue
Deer
Greenfield
Brunshaw Rd
Thornton
Springwood

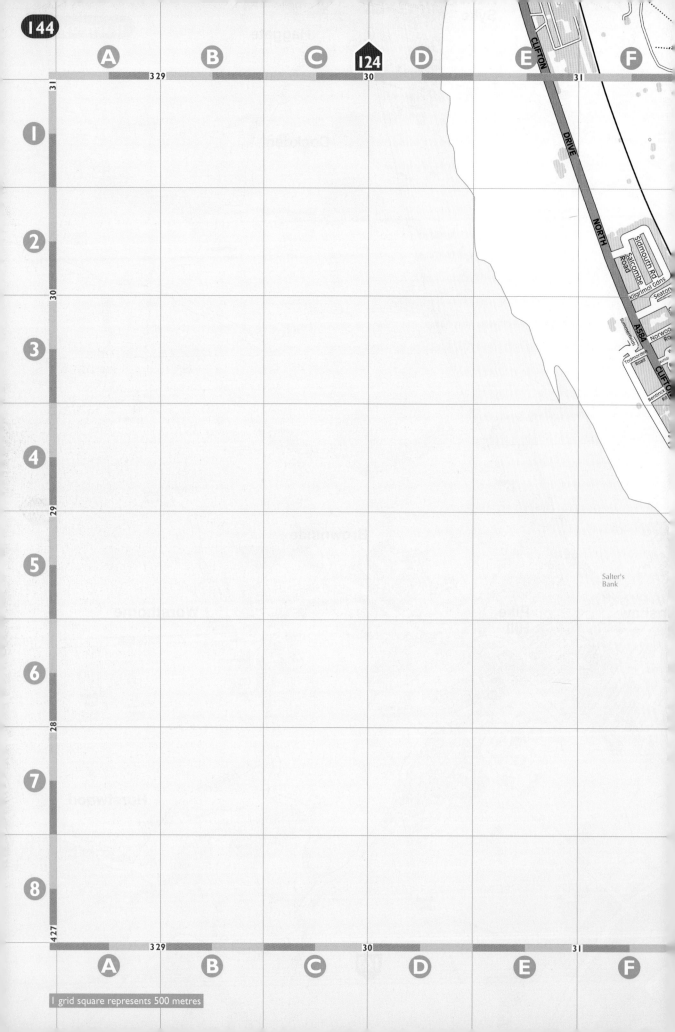

124

A   B   C   D   E   F

31

329   30   31

CLIFTON

DRIVE

NORTH

Sidmouth Rd

Salcombe
Road

Kilgrimol Gdns

Seaton

A584

Summerfields

Norwood
Road

Todmorden
Road

Avenue

CLIFTON

Bentinck Rd

Salter's
Bank

31

30

29

28

427

1

2

3

4

5

6

7

8

329   30   31

A   B   C   D   E   F

I grid square represents 500 metres

G   H   J   127   K   **Wrea Green**   L   M

The Villa Country House Hotel

McCall Close

Side Lane

Westbourne Av

Richmod Av

Bryning Lane

B5259

38

MOSS SIDE LANE

Bryning Avenue

39

40

31

1

North Farm

2

Willowmead Pk

prospect

30

ROAD B5259

LYTHAM

LC

Moss Side

Moss Side Station

New House Farm

Bryning Hall Lane

Bryning Hall La

Bryning

3

Wrea Brook

Bryning Hall Farm

Bryning Lane

Kellam

Cartmell Lane

B5259

Huck Lane

4

Carr Lane

Church

SALTCOTES

Eastham Hall Caravan Site

Eastham Hall

Little Carr Side Farm

29 148

Windy Harbour Farm

Fir Gr

Bece

5

Warto

Lodge Lane

Warton Hall

West End Lane

Woodlands Dr

Meadow

Wicklow Av

Cheviot Av

ROAD

Lidun Park Industrial Estate

Boundary Road

A584

6

errier Bank

Cem

Cotswold Rd

T Birr

W Cramblin C

Bredon Cl

Tewkesbury Dr

Mornington Road

PRESTON ROAD A584

Works

LYTHAM ROAD A584

Works

28

Warto

The Crs

Lane

Bank

7

Saltcotes Road

Lytham Avenue

Bttnet Rd

Graving Dock Rd

Marine Industrial Centre

Marine Business Centre

Back Lane Caravan Park

Tennyson Av

Three Worlds Business Centre

Dock Road

South St

Street

am

Preston Chambers

Lytham Hospital

West

Road

Works

Waterfront Marine Business Park

8

Wrea Brook

38

39

40

427

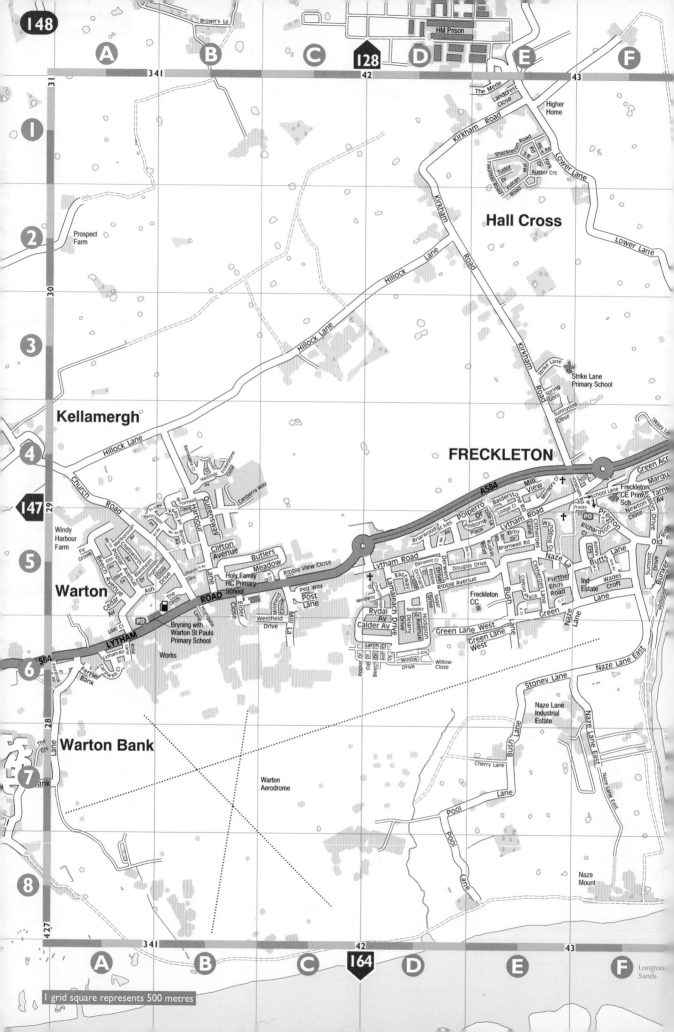

A 341 B C 128 42 D E 43 F

31

I

Brown's La

HM Prison

The Mede
Landcrest
Close
Higher
Home

Shackleton Road
Kirkham Road
Tudor
Dr Vulcan
Road
HS A Rd
York
Auster Crs

Hall Cross

Lower Lane

2
30
Prospect
Farm

Hillock Lane

3
Hillock Lane

Strike Lane
Kirkham Road
Spring
Gdns
Sunnyside
Close
Strike Lane
Primary School

Kellamergh

4
Hillock Lane
Church Road
Ramsgate Cl
Dover
Foxestone
Close
Hastings
Av
Camberra Way

FRECKLETON

A584
Mill
View
School Lane Freckleton
CE Prim
Sch
Green Acre
Marqu
Tarn
Newton
Close
Preston Drive
Old

147
29
Windy
Harbour
Farm
Tn Cam
Cornead
Keats
Av
Tennison
Dr Inglenook
Harbour Road
Queensway
Clifton
Avenue
Polperro
Dr
Briarwood St Ives
Amborne
Place
Balderst
Lodge Cl
Lytham Road
Clitheroes
Memori
Kirby
Dr
Bramwell Rd
Wyndene Gv
Naze La
PO
Richardson
Actiel
Summit
CRS
Butts
Lane
Bunker

5
Warton
Beech Avenue
Poplar Avenue
Chatsworth Av
Blenheim
Dr
Olive
Elm
Ash
Close
Drive
Mahborough
Byron
Av
Church H Av
Church
Gdns
Lane
Butlers
Meadow
Holy Family
RC Primary
School
Ribble View Close
Peg Way
Post
Lane
Derwent
Drive
Ribble
East
Way
Orchard
Orchard
Drive
Douglas Drive
Ribble Avenue
Sagar
Ruskin
Road
Clitheroes Lane
Clifton
Place
C
C
Further
Ends
Road
Green
Ind
Estate
Wades
Croft
Lane

Lilac Cl
PO
The
Orch
Ash
Highgate
Elder
Close
Millfield
Close
Mill
La
Westfield
Drive
Lamaleach Drive
Rydal
Av
Calder Av
Sedgley
Av
Hodgson
Delany
Drive
Freckleton
CC
Green Lane West
Green Lane
West
Bush Lane
Naze
Lane
Green

LYTHAM ROAD
Bryning with
Warton St Pauls
Primary School
Works
Larch Cl
Poplar Dr
Oak Dr
Beech Dr
Ash Dr
Willow
Drive
Willow
Close
Naze Lane East

6
584
Lytham Rd
Ferrier
Bank
Carrwell Cl
Flur
Stoney Lane
Naze Lane
Industrial
Estate

28

Warton Bank
The
Crs
Bank
Cherry Lane
Lane

7
Bank

Warton
Aerodrome
Bush Lane
Pool

Naze Lane East
Naze Lane East

8
427

Pool
Lane
Naze
Mount

Longton
Sands

1 grid square represents 500 metres

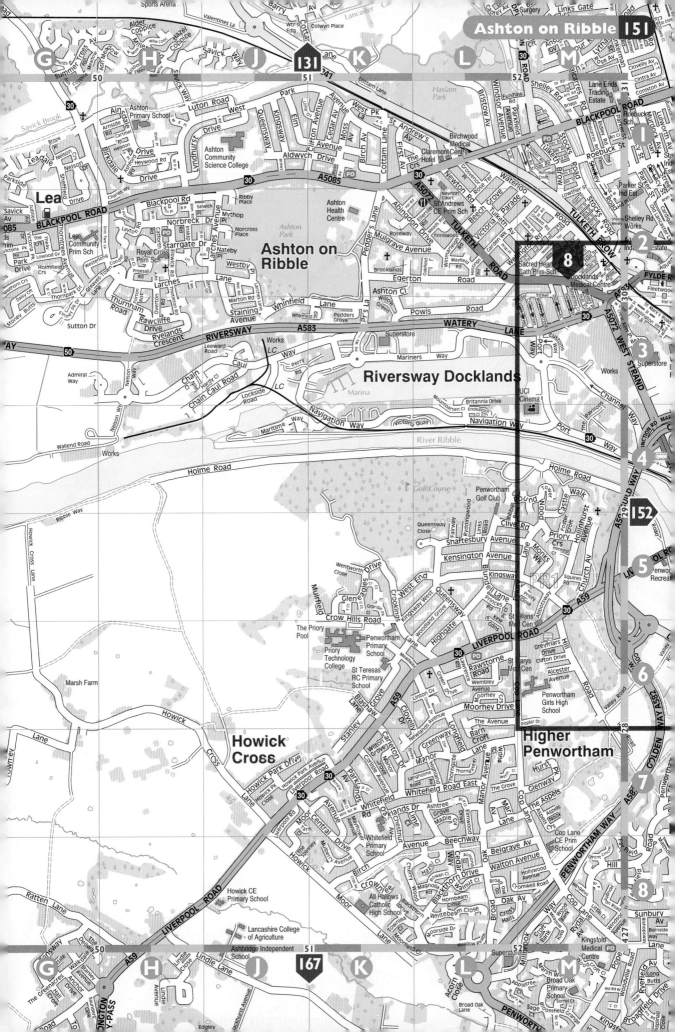

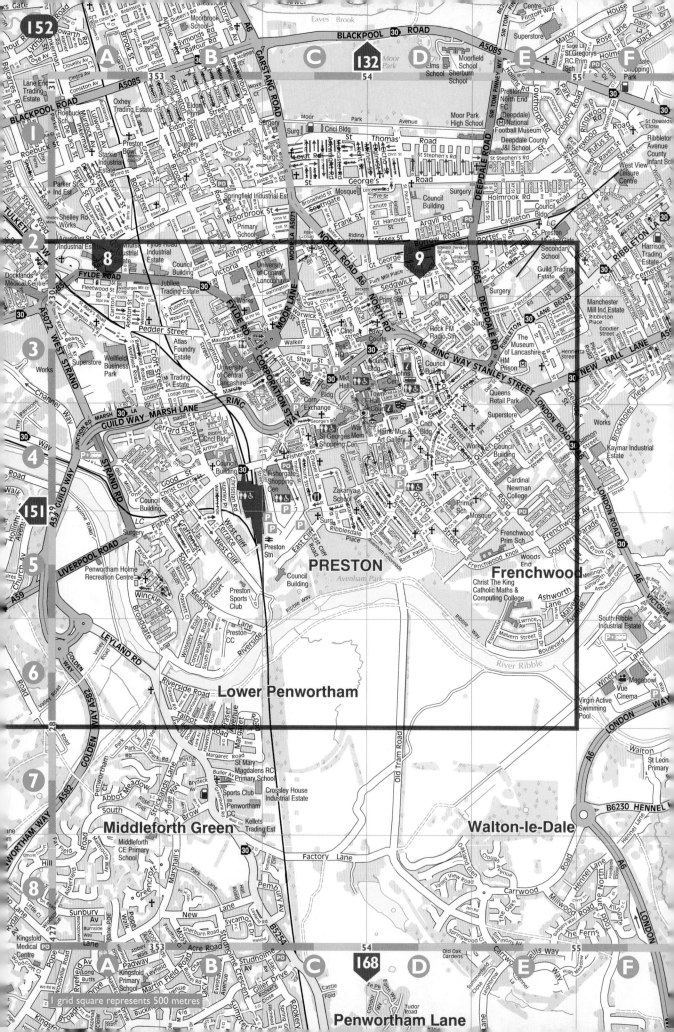

Me 156 Brook

Mellor †

136

A

B

C

D

E

F

1

2

3

4

155

5

6

7

8

A677

A

B

Feniscliffe

C

172

D

E

F

Millstone Hotel
Mellor St Mary CE Primary School
Brundhurst Fold
Church Lane
Church Close
Brookfield
St Mary's Gdns
Glendale Drive
Whitecroft
Mire Ash Brow
Mellor Brow
Mellor Lane
Nickey Lane
Surgery
Arley Rd
Stanley Rd
Hob Green
Carter Fold
Fouracre

Mellor Lane

Lancashire County Blackburn

Whinney Lane

Reaps

A677 PRESTON NEW ROAD

A6119

YEW TREE DRIVE

50

Beardwood

A677 PRESTON NEW ROAD 30

Billinge Scarr

scarr

Carr Lane

scarr La

Westholme School

Heathfield Park

Beardwood School

Beardwood Hospital

Westholme Boys Sch

Westholme Middle School

Westholme Lower School

Meins Road

Meins Road

Meins Croft

Woodgates Rd

BB2

Woodgates

Billinge End Rd

Assheton Road

Lawley Rd

Billinge Av

Billinge Lane

Under Billinge Lane

Witton Weavers Way

Killard Lane

Witton Weavers Way

Witton Country Park

Pleasington Crematorium

Witton Park High School

Witton Park Athletics Track

Witton Weavers Way

OLD ROAD

A674

PRESTON

Tower Road

Hillcrest Rd

Cecilia Rd

Francis Rd

Henry

Lammack

Columbia
Alberta
Calgary Avenue
Ottawa Cl
Quebec
Hudson Cl
Montreal Rd
Vancouver Crescent
Whinney Lane
Cuckoo
Knighton Av
West Leigh Rd
Lammack Prim Sch

Golf Course

Revidge

Blackburn Golf Club

Blackburn Golf Club

NEW BROW

Sacred Heart RC Prim School
Leamington
Dukes
Dukes Brow
West Park
East Lancashire CG
Queen E Gramma School
Adult Education Cen

Al-Asr Primary School
St Silas CE Prim School
Granville

A677

PRESTON NEW

30

BILLINGE

Buncer La

Corse Road

Manor Rd

Taunton

Irene St

Irving Place

Wensley Fold CE Primary School

Livingstone Road

French Rd

Wensley Road

Johnston

Belle Vue St

Rawstorne St

Wensley Business Park

Thompso Street Industrial Estate

Rolleston Road

St Mark's

Pleasington

Hawkshead St
Selborne St

BANK TOP 30

REDLAM

REDLAM BROW

SPRING LANE

Griffin Park Prim Sch

Spring Lane

STANCLIFFE ST

B6447

St Peters RC Primary School

Mill Station

1 grid square represents 500 metres

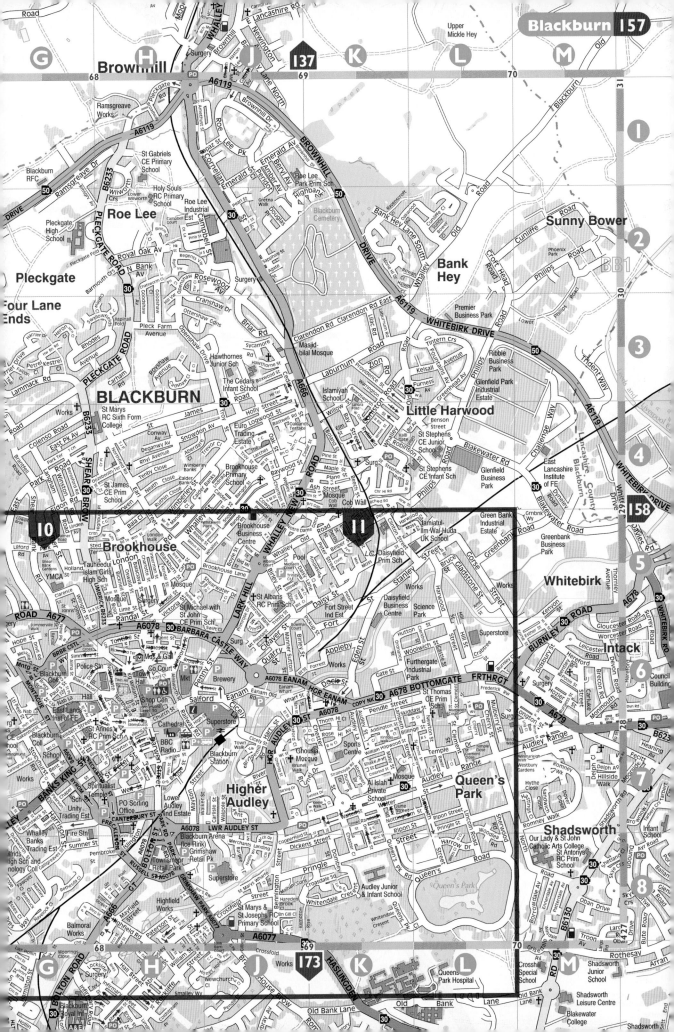

158

A   B   C   **138**   D   E   F ottle

LEE LANE

B6535

RISHTON

HARWOOD ROAD

Dunscar

Lower Cunliffe

Leeds & Liverpool Canal

nny Bower

Rishton
Reservoir

Cut Lane

Sidebeet Lane

BLACKBURN ROAD

A678

M65

M65

Junction 6

157

WHITEBIRK DRIVE

WHITEBIRK ROAD

Davies Rd

A6119

Thornley Avenue

A678

ROAD

Intack
Primary
School

Intack

Council
Building

ACCRINGTON ROAD A679

BANK LANE

KNUZDEN BROOK

B6236

St Ives
Business
Park

**Knuzden
Brook**

B6234 MT ST JAMES

Knuzden St Oswalds
CE Voluntary
Aided Prim Sch

HASLINGDEN OLD ROAD

Haslingden Old Road

Magnoll's Farm

Duckworth Hall

M65

BLACKBURN ROAD A679

M65

Cowhill
Fold

Golf Course

Golf Course

Accrington &
District Golf Club

West End

Devon Avenue

West End
Business
Park

West End
Primary
School

Knuzden
Hall

Stanhill

STANHILL LANE

Hargreaves Road

OSWALDTWISTLE

B6234

White
Ash
School

Moor E
Prim Sc

Industrial
Estate

Works

Works

NEW LANE

B6231

Green
St

Sunnybank
Dr

Willow
Pk

A   B   **174**   C   D   E   F

Rishton
Golf Club

Rishton
Station

Station Close

Churchill
Avenue

Rishton
CC

St Albans
Road

Woodside Av

A678

Works

Cowhill
Lane

Cowhill
Lane

Shadsworth
Junior School

Shadsworth
Leisure Centr

lakewater
college

1 grid square represents 500 metres

ACCRINGTON

G H J 141 K L M

80 81 82 31

1

2

Old Barn

New Barn

Lower Micklehurst

30

3

Burnley Way

4

29 162

5

Burnley Way

New Laithe

Clow Bridge

Springfield View

40

MANCHESTER

Moorland View Childrens Home & School

A682

Works

Wilkinson St

Dunnockshaw

28

6

ROAD

7

Great Clough

Oak Street

L Heber St

Works

Rossendale Way

Limy Water

427

8

Higher Withins

Rossendale Way

Commercial Street

Swinshaw Hall

Rossendale Way

80 81 82

G H 177 K L M

Love Clough

BURNLEY ROAD

silven Clod Rd

L C Rd

Springbank Gardens

meldon Road

Goodshaw Lane

Goodshaw Fold

Goodshaw Chapel

Rossendale Road Industrial Est

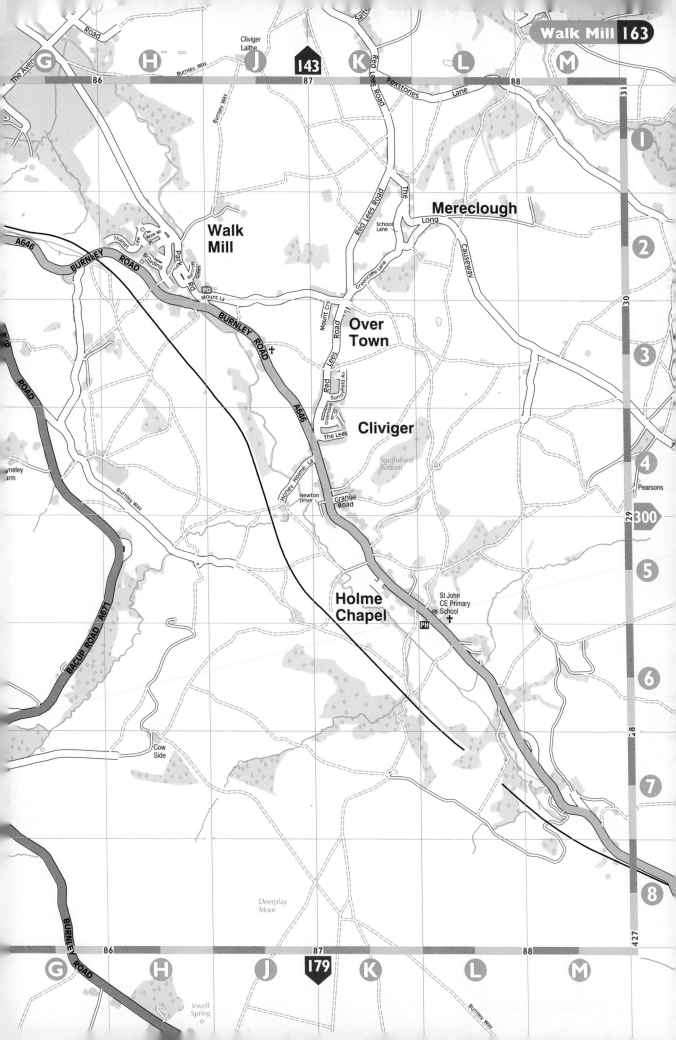

G H J **143** K L M

86 87 88 31

I

2

30

3

4

Pearsons

29 **300**

5

28

6

7

427

8

G H J **179** K L M

86 87 88

Walk Mill

Mereclough

Over Town

Cliviger

Southward Bottom

Holme Chapel

St John CE Primary School

Deerplay Moor

Irwell Spring

A646

BURNLEY ROAD

A646

BACUP ROAD A671

BURNLEY ROAD

Burnley Way

Red Lees Road

Foxstones Lane

Long Causeway

Greencliffe Lane

School Lane

Mount Crs

Mount La

Red Lees Road

Sunnyfield Av

Greendale

Lumb Cl

The Lees

Honey Holme La

Newton Drive

Grange Road

Burnley Way

Cow Side

The Aven

Cliviger Laithe

PO

Lee Cl

Walk Mll Pl

Thanet Cl

Broading

Barcroft Green

Park Rd

PH

Burnley Way

A 341 B C **148** 42 D E 43 F

Longtor
Sands

Mount

Lane

I 27

Meredougs

2 26

3

Hesketh
Out Marsh

Ribble Bank
Farm

4

25

Hesketh
New Marsh

5

Dib Road

6

24

Hundred End Cutter

7

Marsh
Farm

Dib Road

Sh

The Wall

8 423

Ribble View
Farm

Shore Road

A 341 B C 42 **182** D E 43 F

Hutton Sands

Hutton Marsh

Old Grange

Grange

G er Ribble

H

J

149

K

L

M

I

44

45

46

27

Ribble Way

Longton Marsh

2

Grange Lane

Ribble Way

26

3

Marsh Lane

Hall Carr Lane

Guide Road

River Asland or Douglas

4

25

166 Hal

Carr Hey Watercourse

Anchorage Farm

5

Odd House

6

Guide Road

Station Road

24

Hesketh-with-Becconsall All Saints CE Prim Sch

PO Shore Rd

Marsh Road

The Brow

Rose Gdns

Meadow Lane

Marsh Farm

Crk Pk Drive

Schofield

Becsfield

Ribble

Fowpont

7

Langdale Av

Fr Av

Delta

Chapel

Drive

Delta Pk

Avenue

Poppyfields

Thistle

PCt

Station Road

Hesketh Bank

Hazelwood Dr

Cdns

Elderbrook

Ha

The Nurseries

Cropper Gardens

Chandlers Croft

The Green

Th NS

Chapel Rd

Pardoe Cl

Charles Close

Ashbrook Cl

Chapel Road

Silverdale

8

Becconsall Lane

Muc

Newarth Lane

Station Road

Sidney

West Lancashire Light Railway

44

45

183

46

4 23

G

H

J

K

L

M

Becconsall

Cherry Vale

Granville Av

Norwood Av

Meadway

Woodlea Rd

PO

Mill Lane

Moss Lane

Liverpool Old Road

Brookl

New Longton

White Stake

AMS Trading Estate

Thornton Barn

Pleasant View

Midge Hall

Farington **6**

Singleton's Farm

Howick CE Primary School

Lancashire College of Agriculture

Ashbridge Independent School

All Hallows Catholic High School

Hutton Grammar School

Broad Oak Primary School

Kingsfold Medical Centre

Business Park

Nutter's Platt

Moss Side Industrial Estate

Crown Stage & Theatre

New Longton All Saints CE Primary School

Long Moss Meadows

151

168

185

G **H** **J** **K** **L** **M**

1
2
3
4
5
6
7
8

gher Walton

A **B** **C** 154 **D** **E** **F**

THE STRAITS A675

BLACKBURN OLD ROAD

HOGHTON LANE

Hawthorne Avenue

Hoghton Lane

Hall Lane

Manor Close

Quaker PO

Hollins

Blackburn Old Rd

1

Four Lane Ends

Daub Bells

Central Avenue

Gregson Lane

Squires Close

Arrowsmith Drive

Knowsley Close

Brookhouse Close

Brookhouse Drive

Brindle Lodge

Fowler Cl

Conway Court

Lydric Avenue

Rhodesway

Arrowsmith Close

Mintholme Avenue

Friths Avenue

Larch Gate

PO

Gregson Lane

2

Aldersleigh Crs

Alma Row

Alder Drive

Birch Cl

Willow Cl

Hillpark Avenue

Westfield Drive

Hayfield Avenue

Bank Head Lane

Bournesfield

Bourne's Row

Brindle Gregson Lane Primary School

Brindle St Josephs RC Primary School

Back Bourne's Row

Lane

LC

Hatchwood Farm

Cowans Lane

3

Bank Head Lane

Jack Green

Oram Road

Mill House Lane

Hill House Lane

LC

Works Lane

4

M61

Brindle Fold

Dover Lodge School of Equitation

Windmill Lane

Dover Lane

169 169

Junction 9/2

M65

SANDY LANE

5

Brindle Road

Pippin Street

Smithy Lane

Stony Bank

Bateson's Farm

M65

Leigh Farm

6

Brow Lane Brow

Three Nooks

Pippin Street

Smithy Close

Brindle Heights

Marsh Lane

7

Acrefield

Sandall Field

Brook Road

SANDY LANE

Thorpe Green

LANE

Brindle St James CE Primary School

Brindle

Calvert's Farm

High Cop Lane

Hilton's Brow

Marsh Lane

8

M61

OLD RD

B5256

Holt Lane

Top o' th' Lane

Breworth Fold Lane

Water Street

Withnell Fold Industrial Estate

Withnell

Mill Wd Cl

Parke Mews

Withnell Fold Primary School

A **B** **C** 188 **D** **E** **F**

Denham

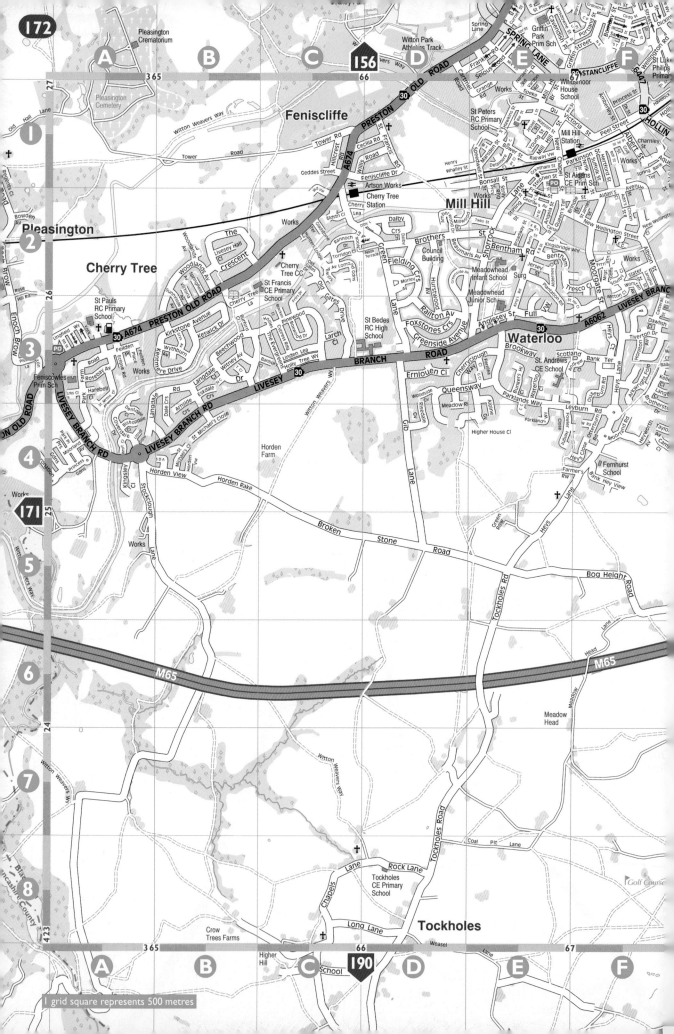

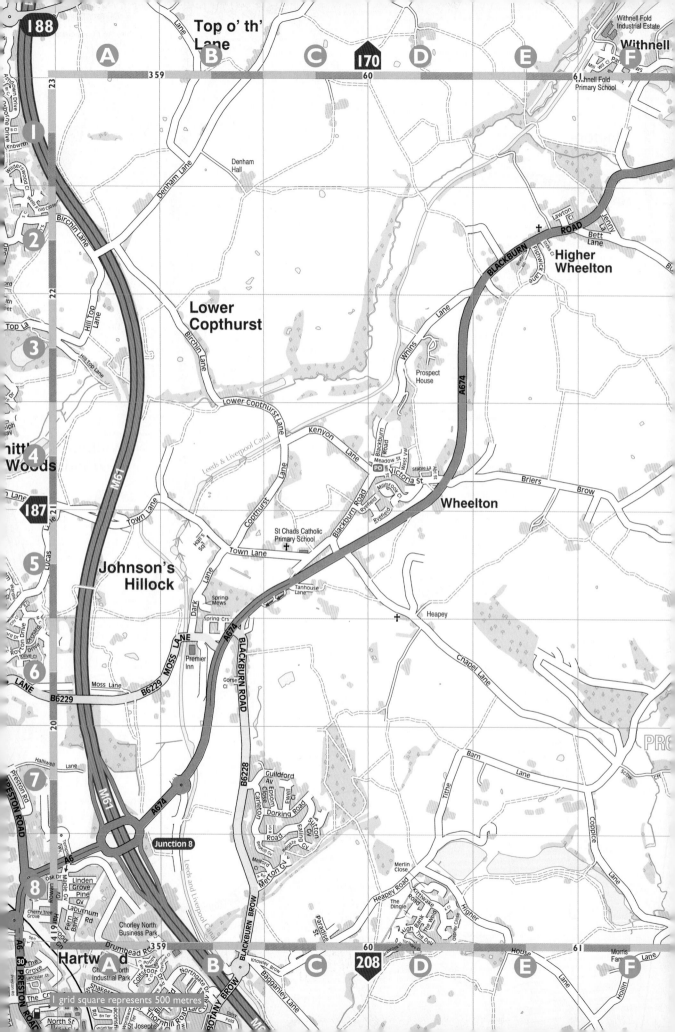

G
H
J
171
K
L
M

62
63
64
23

I

Close House

Abbey Village

Miller Av

Mac Cl

PO

Garrett St

Abbey Village Primary School

A674

30

Oakmere

Avenue

Thirlmere Drive

A675

22

2

Burn Lane

Calder Av

St Josephs RC Primary School

Monks

Ribble Close

Bloomfield Road

Dole Lane

3

Woodsfold

Withnell Fold Old Road

Pleasant View

Fellstone V

PO

Withnell

Mt Pleasant

Lane

Moor

Sandringham Drive

Sandy Lane

Sandringham Drive

Balmoral Dr

Ashmeadow

Works

Surgery

North Av

Norcross Brow

Lane

Lane

Canterbury Cl

Windsor Dr

Road

Withnell Fold Old Rd

Heather Lea Dr

Harrington Rd

Churchill Rd

Derby St

Salisbury Rd

Prospect Ter

Lwr Bank St

Twist

Richmond Cl

Parke Road

Railway

4

School Lane

Chapel St

Urban View

St Johns CE/Methodist Primary School

PO

Brinscall Public Baths

Butterworth Brow

21

190

The Sq

Quarry Rd

Windy Harbour

Brinscall

Larch Dr

Maple Avenue

Bank Lane

Dick Lane

Lodge

Well Lane

Withnell Moor

5

Brinscall Hall

Edge Gate Lane

6

20

Withnell Moor

Trigg Lane

Wheelton Moor

7

8

4 19

62
63
64

W e
Coppice

The Colt

A   B   C   172   D   Tockholes   E   F

Golf Course

Chapels Lane
Rock Lane
Tockholes
CE Primary
School

66   67

Weasel   Lane

Higher
Hill

Old School Lane

Dean   Lane   Witton Weavers Wy

Red Lea
Farm

Brow
Trees Farms

I

Roddlesworth Reservoirs

2

Earnsdale
Reservoir

Trash Lane

22

Roddlesworth
Reservoirs

BOLTON ROAD
Roddlesworth Lane   Roddlesworth

3

Tockholes Road

Ryal Fold

Stepback Brook

Hollinshead
Ter

4

Rake Brook

189   21

New
Barn

5

Watson's
Farm

Mill Lane

BELMONT ROAD

20

Withnell
Moor

6

Witton Weavers Way   Tockholes

7

419

A675

Road

8

Crookfield Road

Witton Weavers Way

A   B   C   210   D   E   F

66   67

1 grid square represents 500 metres

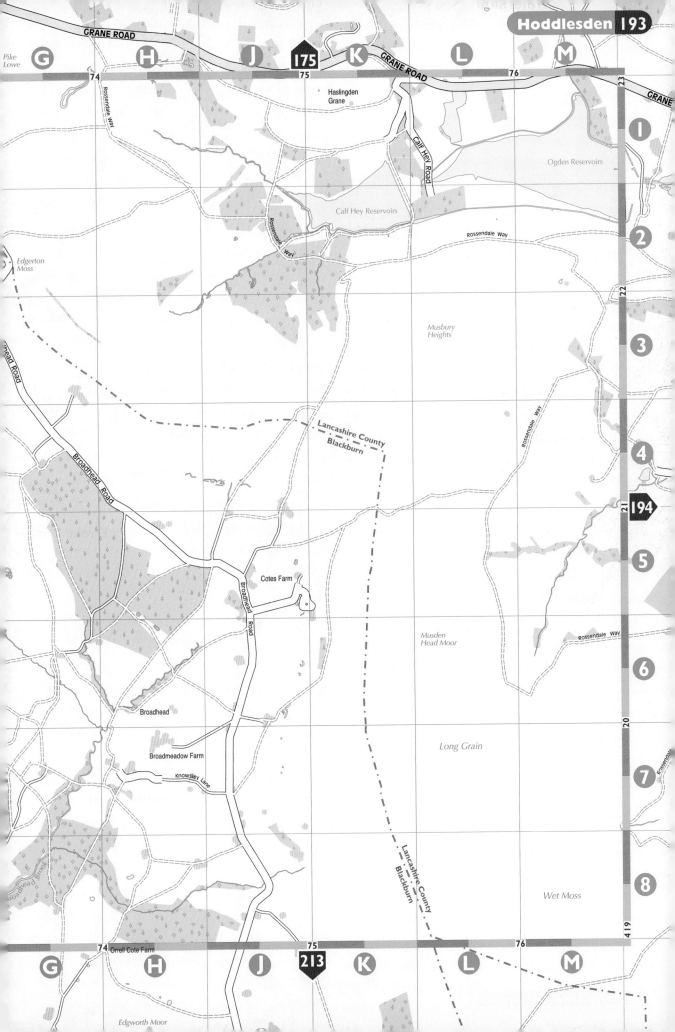

GRANE ROAD

G H J **175** K L M

GRANE ROAD

GRANE

74 75 76 23

Haslingden Grane

1

Calf Hey Road

Ogden Reservoirs

Rossendale Way

2

Calf Hey Reservoirs

22

Rossendale Way

Edgerton Moss

Musbury Heights

3

Rossendale Way

Broadhead Road

Lancashire County
Blackburn

4

21 **194**

5

Cotes Farm

Broadhead Road

Musden Head Moor

Rossendale Way

6

20

Broadhead

Long Grain

Broadmeadow Farm

Knowsley Lane

7

Lancashire County
Blackburn

8

Wet Moss

419

74 Orrell Cote Farm 75 **213** 76

G H J K L M

Edgworth Moor

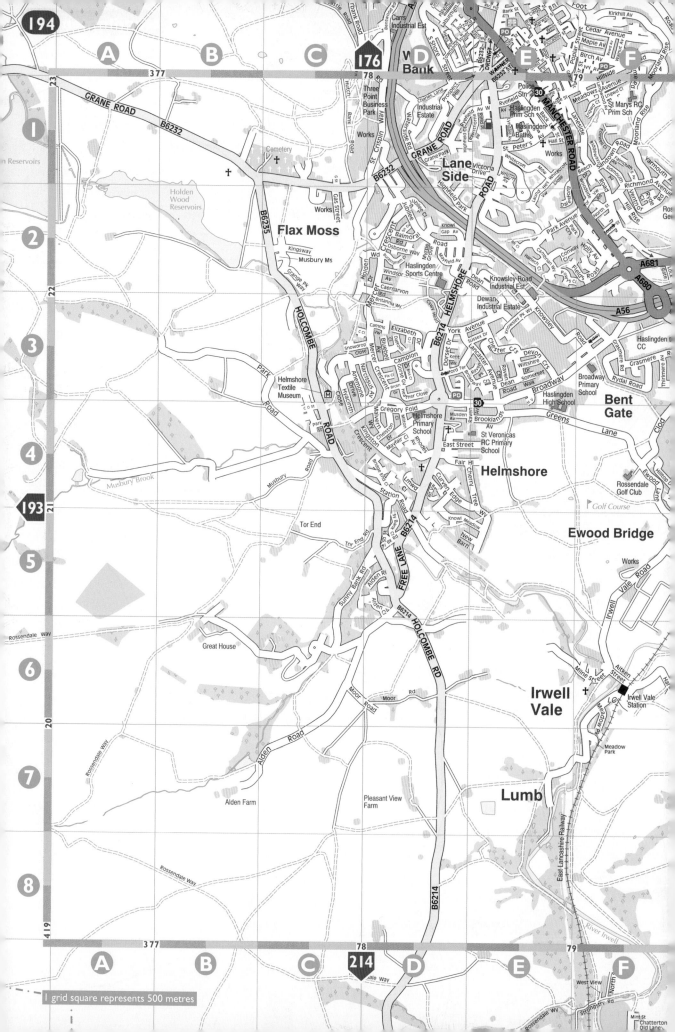

Height End

G H J **177** K L M

Cloughfold

New Hall Hey

Townsend Fold

Balladen

196

Edenfield

G H J **215** K L M

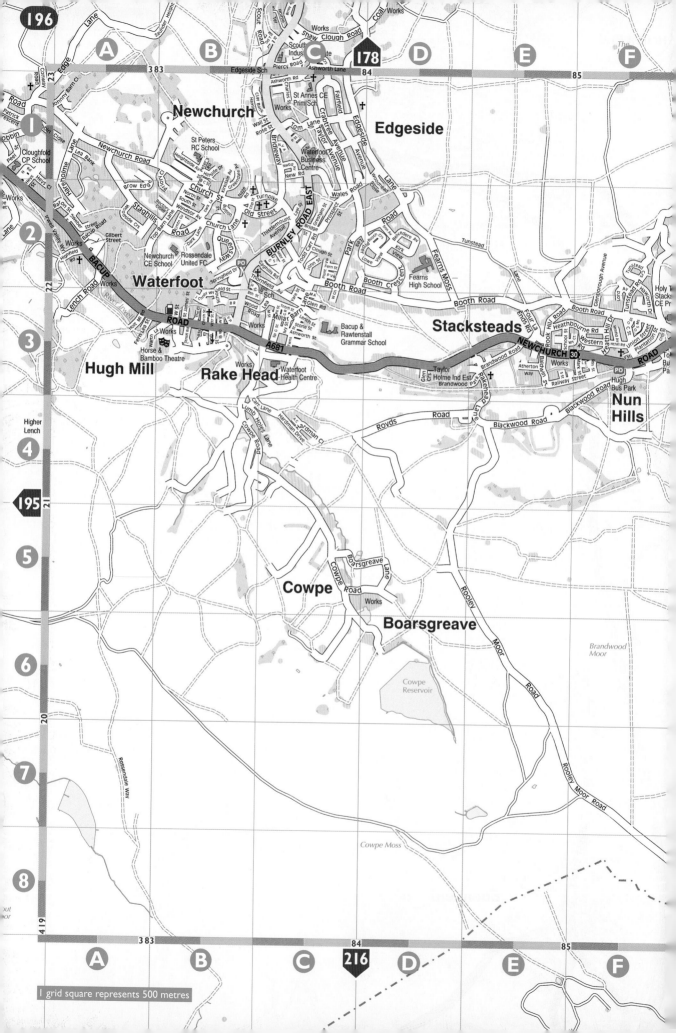

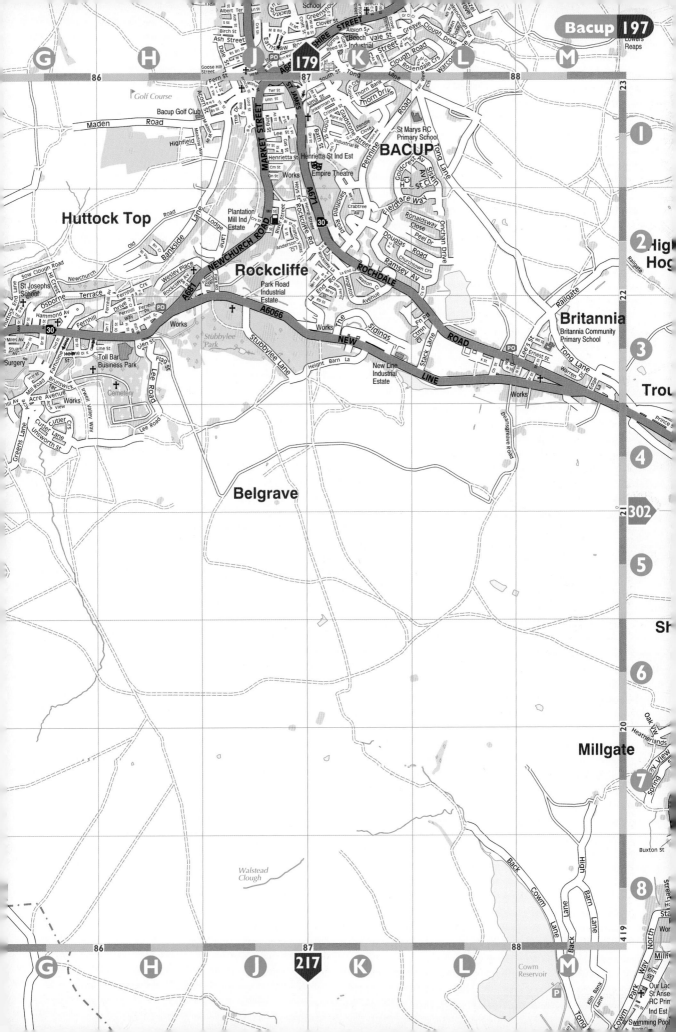

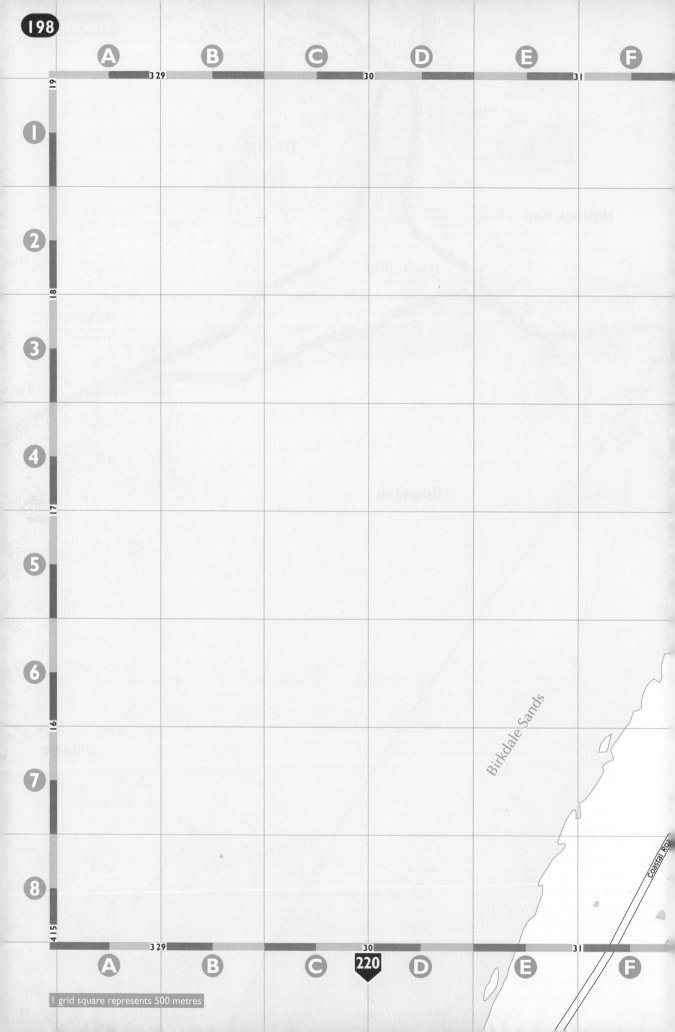

A B C D E F
3 29 30 31
19

1

18

2

3

17

4

5

16

6

7

415

8

Belgrave

Birkdale Sands

Coastal Road

A B C D E F
3 29 30 31

1 grid square represents 500 metres

G H J 181 K L M

Riverside
Holiday Park

1

2

3

202

4

5

6

7

8

Boundary
Dalweb
SOUTHP

Gravel Lane

Bobbiners Lane

Three Pools Waterway

New Lane

New La

Cabin Lane

Dolly's Lane

Dolly's

Moss Lane

Jp La Moss Lane

New Lane

Wyke Wood Lane

Long Meanygate

Winacre Farm

Wyke Hey Farm

The Sluice

Lane

Mere

Common Lane

Sluice Farm

Long Meanygate

Meanygate Farm

Common Lane

Wyke House Farm

Wyke Lane

ke Lane

Perch Pool Lane

The Avenue

Wyke Thorn Farm

Caunce's Road

Mere Hall

Midge Hall Farms

Wyke Wood Lane

Caunce's Road

Shaw's Farm

LC

Wyke Lane

Perch Pool Lane

Wyke Cop Road

Greenings Lane

Greenings

Midge Hall Lane

415

G H J 223 K L M

Wyke Road Farm

Woo

s Lane

Perch Poo

Best

ane

Wholesome Lane

38 39 40 19

38 39 40

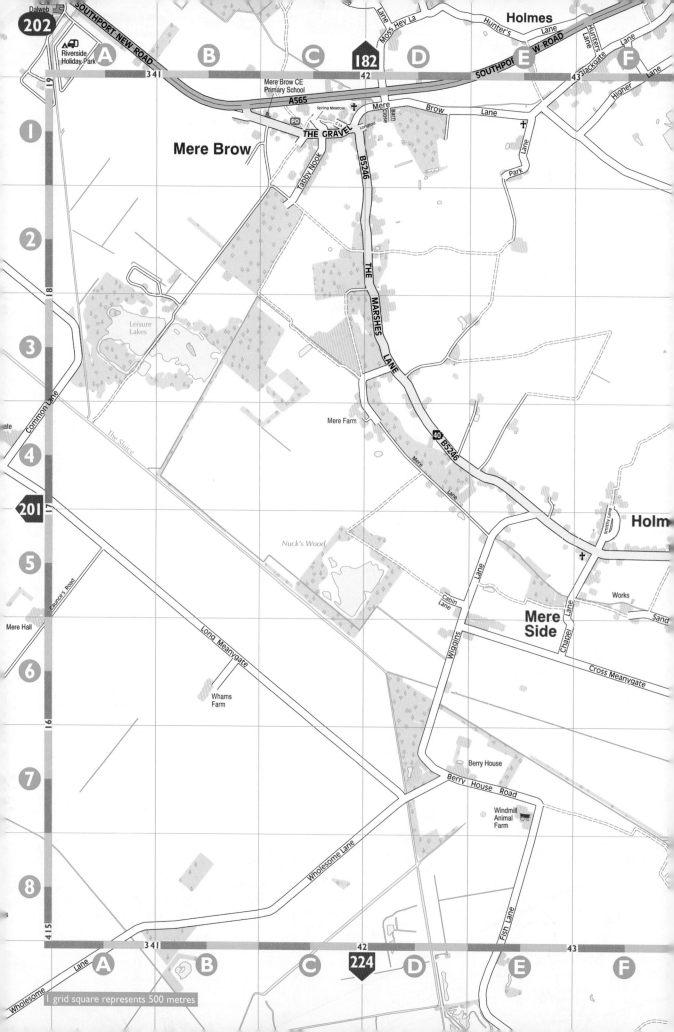

202

Riverside
Holiday Park

SOUTHPORT NEW ROAD

A

B

C

182
42

D

SOUTHPORT NEW ROAD

Holmes

Moss Hey La

Hunter's
Lane

E

Blackgate

Hunter's
Lane

Lane

F

Higher
Lane

341

19

A565

Mere Brow CE
Primary School

Spring Meadow

PO

Mere

Brow

Lane

43

THE GRAVEL

C La

Longford

Mere

Barn
Close

Park
Lane

Lane

Mere Brow

Tabby Nook

B5246

1

18

2

Leisure
Lakes

THE MARSHES LANE

3

Common Lane

The Sluice

Mere Farm

40 B5246

4

Mere

Lane

201

Nuck's Wood

Holm

Smithy Lane

5

Caunce's Road

Cabin
Lane

Works

**Mere
Side**

Sand

Mere Hall

Long Meanygate

Whams
Farm

Wiggins

Lane

Chapel

Lane

Cross Meanygate

6

16

7

Berry House

Berry House Road

Windmill
Animal
Farm

Wholesome Lane

8

415

341

42

43

Wholesome

Lane

A

B

C

224

D

E

F

Fish Lane

1 grid square represents 500 metres

Shaw
Green

EUXTON
Euxton St
Marys RC
Euxton CE
Prim Sch
Firbank
Brookside
Castorton
Church Walk

Euxton Hall
Hospital

RunshawLane
DeanHallLane
DAWBER'S LANE
A581

DAWBER'S LANE
Old Dawber's La
Works
A581
Pincock
Pincock St
Fieldside Av
PincockBrow

River Yarrow

Mill Lane

Bolton
Green

Back Lane

Wood End
Farm
Bradley
Hall

Back Lane

Charnock
Green

SIBBERING BROW
CHARNOCK BROW
PRESTON ROAD

Parr Lane
Sandringham
Rd
Warwick
Windsor
Road

205

pers
enue
PO

Bradley
Lane
Cotswold

Red Lane

Hall Lane
Old Hall
Old

Sagar St
New St

Grove Park
Indus
Esta
THE
GN
30
Shelley Dr
Keats Cl
Langton
LANGTON BROW
B5250

PR7

Whalley Road
Works

WOOD LANE
The Warings

Heskin
Green

PH

Camelot
Theme
Park
Park Hall
Leisure
Centre

Charnock
Richard Golf
Club

Charno
Richard

Brook Lane

A49

B5250

Stocks
Court
Highgrove
Av
Pye Brook
Stocks
La

Park
Hall Hotel
Park Hall Road

Preston
Rd

Welcome
Lodge

Charnock Richard Service Area

Golf Course

Town Lane
353
PO
Withington Lane
The
Meadows
Heskin

B5250

Heskin Pembertons
CE Primary School

228
Lane
54
M6
Lane
55
A49
PRESTON RD
Croston Lane
Chorley La

1 grid square represents 500 metres

G   H   J   **189**   K   L   M
62   63   64

**White
Coppice**

The Goit

I

Round
Loaf

2

18

3

Anglezarke
Moor

4

Moor   Road

17   **210**

Limestone Brook

Lead Mines
Clough

5

Anglezarke
Reservoir

6

River Yarrow

Moor Road

16

Parson's   Bullough   Road

Hodge   Alance
Brow   Bridge

Deanfield   Lane

7

Yarrow
Reservoir

Lane   Ends

Lane

Wilcock's
Farm

Knowsley

Nick Hilton's Lane

Blindhur

Moses
Cocker's

8

Belmont Roa

415

Blindhur 62
Sheepnouse Lane

G   H   J   **231**   K   L   M
62   63   64

Rivington

A   **B**   **C**   190   **D**   **E**   **F**

365   66   67

Crookfield Road

Witton Weavers Way

Witt... vers Way

I   2   3   4   209   5   6   7   8

19   18   16   415

A675

Blackburn Lancashire County

Redmonds Edge

Bromiley

Belmont Reservoir

Sharples Higher End

BELMONT ROAD

Back High Street

Ch Str

ake View W?

South View

Ward's

Turton Belmont Primary School

Ryecroft Lane

HIGH STREET

PO

30

Anshaw Close

Church St

River Yarrow

Rivington Road

Hordern Stoops

Rivington Road

Wards Reservoir

Police Station

Belmont Road

Blackburn Lancashire County

A   **B**   **C**   232   **D**   **E**   **F**

365   66   67

Winter Hill

I grid square represents 500 metres

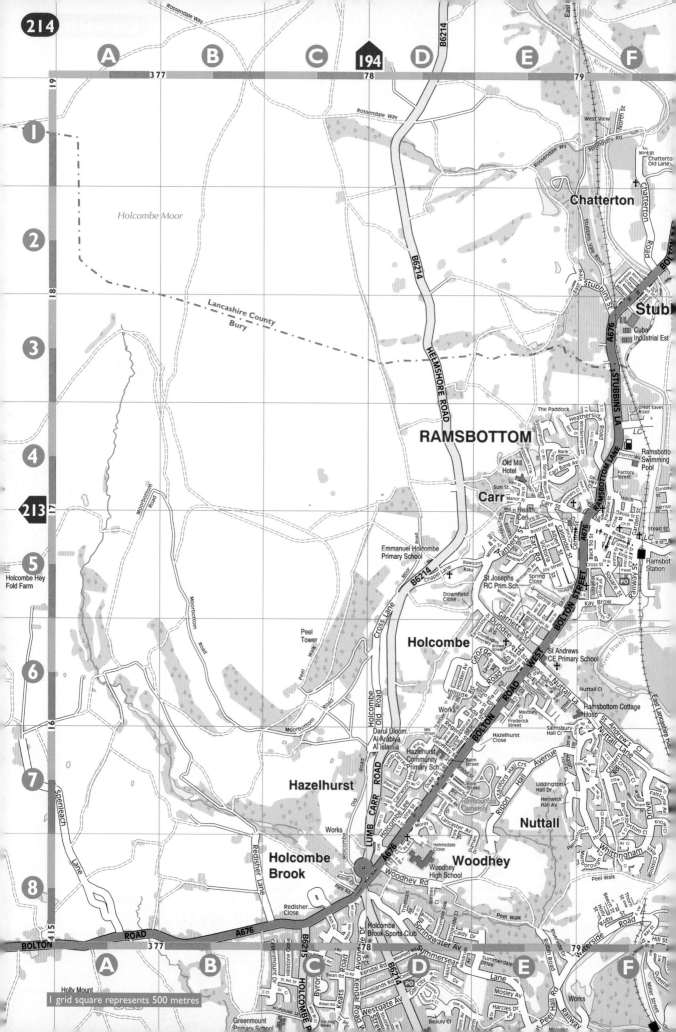

Edenfield

Turn

Shuttleworth

BLO

Twine Valley
Country Park
& Fishery

Rossendale
School

Harden
Moor

Nangreaves

oksbottoms

Junction 1

Junction 1

Stubbins
Primary
School

Summerseat Methodist
Primary School

Turf
Moor

Cheesden

Deeply
Vale

G H J 195 K L M

WOOD LA A56

BOLTON ROAD NORTH
BURY ROAD
WHALLEY ROAD
A56
M66
MANCHESTER RD
MANCHESTER ROAD
A56

Bury Old Rd
ROCHDALE ROAD
A680 ROCHDALE ROAD

Bleakholt Road
Riding Head Lane
Coal Road
Fecit Lane
Fecit Lane

Moor Side Lane
Black Lane
Bamford Road

Whitelow Road
Lancashire County
Bury Old Road
Bury

Croston Close Road
Croston Close Road
Lancashire County

Buckhurst
Rd

Mount
Pisnt

Bass Lane

G H J K L M

216

Rossendale Way

Love
Lane

Leaches Rd

Lower
Rd

Higher
Fold
Lane

Scout
Road

Hollins
Lane

Plunge Road

Dearden
Fold

Dearden
Clough

Michael
Wife Lane

Edenfield
CC

Dean
Close

A B C **196** D E F

84 85

3 83

19

18

17

16

415

1

2

3

4

215

5

6

7

8

Scout
Moor

Turf
Moor

Rossendale way

Lancashire County
Rochdale

Naden Higher
Reservoir

Naden Middle
Reservoir

Knowl
Moor

Roc
Mo

Cheesden

EDENFIELD ROAD

A680

Croston Close

Rochdale
Lancashire County

Ashworth
Moor
Reservoir

Ashworth Road

Knowl Lane

EDENFIELD ROAD

A680

**Red
Lumb**

**Rain
Shore**

Red Lumb St

Over Town Lane

Over Town Lane

Fordœ Lane

Works

A B C D E F

3 83 84 85

EDENFIELD ROAD

A680

Deeply Vale Lane

Windy Hill Farm

Marcroft Gate Farm

Baitings Cl

Fairview

Riviera
Court

Norden Way

1 grid square represents 500 metres

A   B   C   198   D   E   F

3 29   30   31

15

1

2

14

3

13

4

5

Sands

Ainsdale-on-Sea

Ainsdale

Dunes

12

6

7

8

4 11

3 29   30   31

A   B   C   237   D   E   F

Ainsdale Sand Dunes
National S   Reserve

1 grid square represents 500 metres

Willowbank Holiday
Home & Touring Park

Coastal Road

Ainsdale
Hope CE
High School

Chiltern
Road

Chatsworth

Upton
Avenue

Knowle Avenue

Harewood
Road

shore   Rd

shore
Road

stratford Close

Barford
Close

Arden Cl

Grafton
Dr

Chandley
Close

Arlington
Close

Brinklow
Close

Sambourn
Fold

Romwell Dr

Lighthorne
Dr

Pershore

GV Shelton
Cl

Harbury

Quinton Cl

Kingsbury
Cl

Wimcote
Cv

Meriden
Cl

Sevenoaks
Avenue

Westminster
Dr

Wigton

Avenue

Merefield
Special
School

Shoreside
Primary
School

Harrington
Drive

Broadway

Daresbury

Prestbury Av

Barrington
Dr

Daneway

Greyfriars

Chatsworth
Rd

Chartwell Rd

Tavistock Dr

Tudor Rd

Blenheim

Osborne Road

Seaforth

Hatfield

Carlton

Saltringham

Petworth

Chatsworth

Road

Belvedere
Road

Burnley

Delamere Road

Mandeville
Road

Mossdale Av

Chesterfield Rd

Longcliffe Drive

Bridgend Dr

Kenilworth
Road

Hillsview Road

Chesterfield
Cl

Trelley

Greenend

Kendal Way

Woodside
AV

Furness

Thirdmere
Drive

Gleneagles

Newby
Cl

Coastal Road

Pinfold
Lane

Pinfold
Lane

Woodvale

Somerset Dr

Cornwall

Dorset
Avenue

Rose Cl

Ainsdale
Station

PO

Surgery

Ainsdale

Salford

Trevor
Road

Stout
Rd

Stoneleigh
Close

Wentworth
Close

Halifax
Road

The Paddock

Sunbury Drive

Margate
Close

Uldale
Close

Mulfield
Drive

Keswick
Close

Bowness Av

Windermere Crs

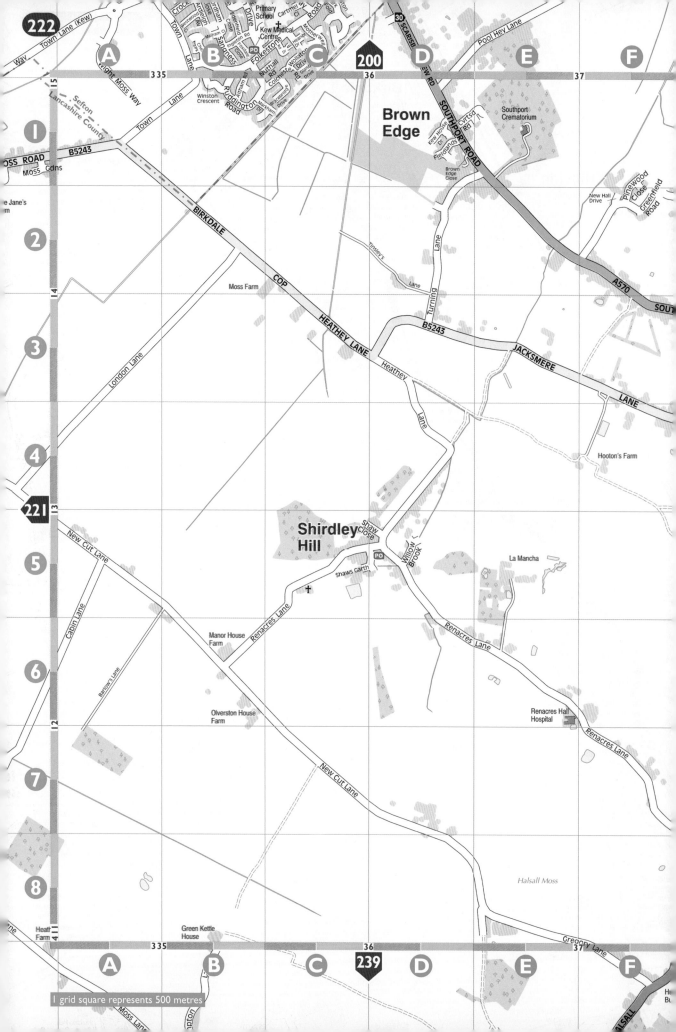

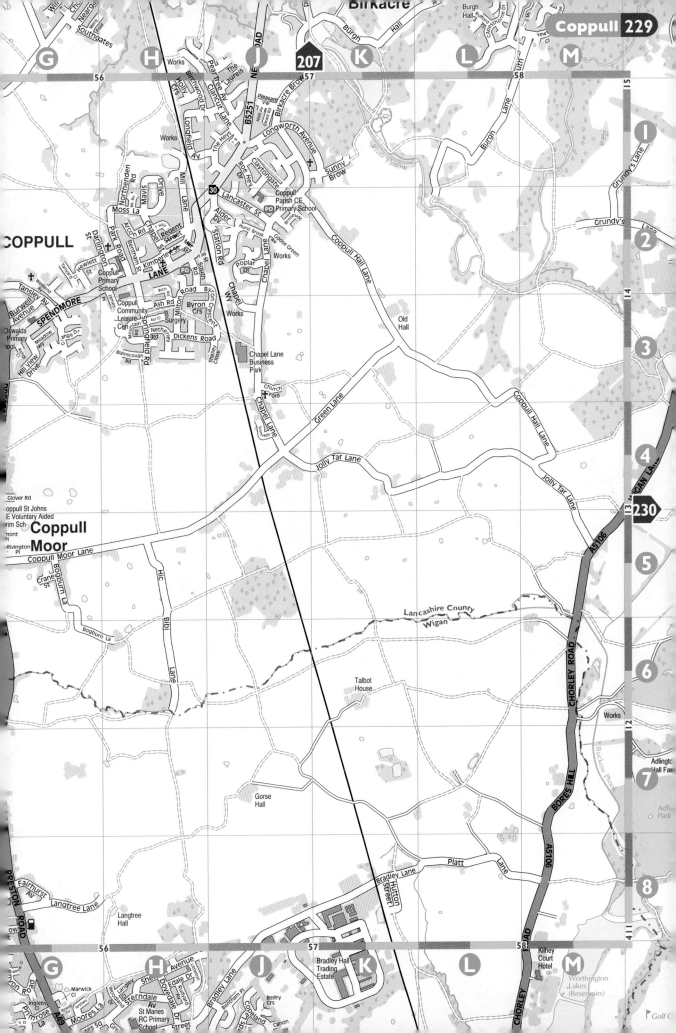

Birkacre

Burgh Hall

G H J K L M

207

57 58 15

1

Grundy's Lane

Grundy's Lane 2

14

River Yarrow

Works

B5251

Pear Tree Av
Birchwood Dr
Clancutt Lane
The Laurels
Longfield Av
Holly Crs

Pleasant VW
Hill VW
Birkacre Brow
Longworth Avenue

Claytongate
Roe Hey Dr
Sunny Brow

COPPULL

Moss La
Mavis Drive
Northenden Rd
Mill Lane
Chapel St
Atcon Rd
Benham St
LANE
Regent Street
Kimberley St

30 Lancaster St
Alder Cv
Station Rd
Hurst Brook
Goose Green
Brookside

Coppull Parish CE Primary School
PO

Coppull Hall Lane

3

Darlington St
Park Road
Coppull Primary School
Hewlett St
PO
Byron Crescent
Poplar Dr
Chapel Lane
Chapel VW
Works

Old Hall

Tansley Av
Burwell Av
SPENDMORE
Meadow Ivy
Hill View Drive
Oswalds Primary School
Coppull Community Leisure Cen
Springfield Rd
Grange Dr
Nether Rd
Ash Rd
Byron Crescent
Surgery
Dickens Road
Shelley Close
Blainscough Rd

Chapel Lane Business Park

Church Fold

Green Lane

Glover Rd
Coppull St Johns CE Voluntary Aided Prim Sch
Rivington Pl

Coppull Moor

Jolly Tar Lane
Jolly Tar Lane

4

Coppull Hall Lane

WIGAN LANE

230

13

A5106

Coppull Moor Lane
Crane St
Bogburn La
HIC
Bibi Lane

5

Lancashire County
Wigan

Bogburn La

6

12

Talbot House

CHORLEY ROAD

Works

Buckow Brook

Adlingto Hall Far

Adli Park

7

Gorse Hall

BORES HILL

A5106

Platt Lane
Bradley Lane
Hutton Street

PRESTON ROAD
Fairhurst Av
Langtree Lane
Langtree Hall

8

11

56 57 58

G H J K L M

A49
Primrose La
Ingleby Cl
Marwick Cl
Sterndale Av
Moores La
Bradley Avenue
Langley
Woodland
Dovedale Dr
Sheldale Dr
St Maries RC Primary School
Copeland St
Benham's
Belfry Crs
Canon

Bradley Hall Trading Estate

Kilhey Court Hotel

CHORLEY ROAD
Worthington Lakes (Reservoirs)

Golf C

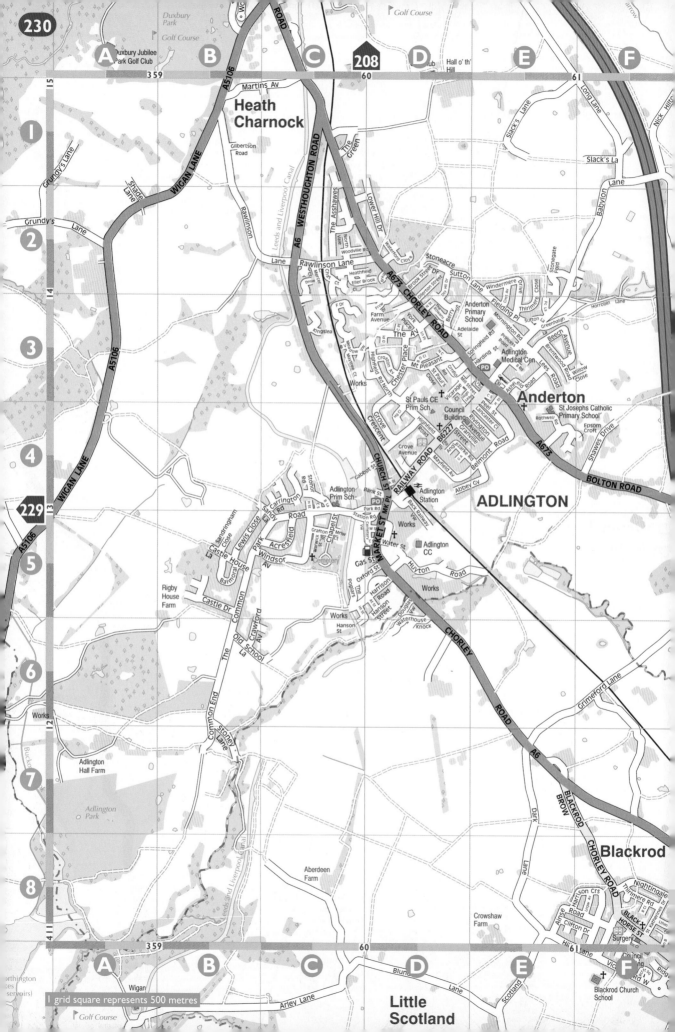

G   H   J   **209**   K   L   M

62   63   64   15

I

2

Moses Cocker's

Belmont Road

Rivington

Sheep House Lane

Hall Lane

Sheephouse Lane

Rivington Lane

Blindhurst

Horrobin Lane

New Road

Rivington Primary School

Rivington Park Independent School

Rivington Country Park

Lever Park

14   3

Belmont Road

Tan Pits Farm

Roscoe Lowe Brow

Rivington Reservoirs

Rivington Lane

4

232

13   5

Headless Cross

Grimeford Village

Grimeford Industrial Estate

Rivington Lane

Rivington Castle

Rivington & Blackrod High School

Royton Road

Old Will's Lane

V   de

Greenland Lane

A673

BOLTON ROAD

Works

Dryfield Lane

Park Avenue

Green Lane

Lever Lane

Heaviley Grove

Whitwell Gdns

Fearnhead Av

Wenlock Close

Malvern

Cotswold Dr

Berwin Cl

Pennine

Snowdon Drive

Pendle

Brownlow Rd

12   6

HORW

M61

Squirrel Lane

SCHOLES BANK

Hope St North

Old Lord's Crs

Ormston Avenue

Ardley Road

Rochaven Avenue

Factory Hill

7

Lancashire County Bolton

Factory Brow

Anderton Lane

Ashness Lane

Travelodge

Bolton West Service Area

LEE LANE

Darley Street

Brady Street

Mary St W

Mary St E

Catherine St E

Dickson St

Lord Street Prim Sch

Albert St Business Park

Singleton Av

Medical Cen

Beaumont Avenue

Ansdell Road

Longworth Road

Treasure House School of Make Up

Horwich Parish CE Primary School

Bridge

King Street

Pembroke St

William St

Offerton St

Dixey St

Leicester Av

Marsh St

Wright St

A673

Mottram Street

Spring Gdn

Winter St

CHURCH STREET

Pearlbrook Industrial Estate

Horwich Leisure Centre

Police Stn

P

Melbourne Rd

Lever Park School

Medway Dr

8

Coniston Road

Whitehall Lane

Lodge Bank

LANE B5238

CROWN

Butterwick Field

James's St

Merefold

Owston

Mallard Ave

Hilton Av

Mason St

Avondale

Coppice

Nuttall St

Berne Av

Greenstone Av

Fernstone Close

St Catherines CE Primary School

Cornerstone

Evanstone Close

Ramscrofton Rd

Stocks

Portland Pl

Cresley Avenue

Brooklands

Fairways

Stephenson St

Victoria Road

CHORLEY NEW ROAD

Horwich Business P

Hartley St

Fairburn Rd

Watts St

Golf C

Thirlmere Avenue

Horwich Golf Club

G   H   J   K   L   M

62   63   64

Blackrod Station

Works

Moss

Fowler Industrial

St Ma

STREET

Vicarage Road

PO

Castle

232

A   B   C   **210**   D   E   F

365   66   67

1

456
▲
Winter Hill

Rivington Moor

2

14

Lancashire County
Bolton

Smithills Moor

3   *Rivington
Pike*

4

Coal Pit Road

Holdens
Farm   Gilligant's
Farm

231   13

5   **Wilderswood**

Old Rake

Burnt Edge Lane

Walke
Fold

6   **Montcliffe**

Brownlow Rd   Marklands Rd   George's Lane   Edge

HORWICH   12   Foxholes Road   Factory Hill   Manor   Makinson Lane

7   Bridge   St   Works   Wallsuches   Matchmoor Lane

Horwich Parish
CE Primary
School   Gingham   **BL6**   **Wallsuches**

HURCH STREET   Ridgmont
Cemetery   B6226   **CHORLEY OLD ROAD**

St George   Melbourne   Medway Dr   Park Lane   PO

8   The Strand   Mayfair   Bottom o' th Moor

ever Park   Kensington Drive   Lambeth
Close   Hgr
Barn   Vicarage Rd   Bottom O' Th Moor   Shepherd's
Drive   B6226   **CHORLEY OLD ROAD**   MONTS

Portland   Lev
Pl   school   **Bottom o' th'
Moor**   Chapel   New
Road

Golf Course   365   66   67

A   B   C   D   E   F

Horwich
Golf Cr

Thirlmere Avenue

St Mary HC
Primary School   Buckingham Avenue   Balmoral Cl   Sandhill   Claypool Rd

I grid square represents 500 metres   RUNSWICK AVENUE

G H J K L M

68 69 70

211

I

2

3

Horrocks Fold 4

5

6

Sharple

7

8

G H J K L M

Folds Pasture

A675

Springs Reservoir

Dingle Reservoir

Hampsons

Golf Course

Deakins Business Park

Dunscar Golf Club

Blackburn Bolton

A675

Scout Road

BELMONT

Horrocks Hill Farm

Scout Road

Coal Pit Road

Cunliffe's Farm

Shoreside

Wilkinson Rd

Colliers Row Road

Longshaw Ford Road

Smithills Dean Road

Athlone Av

Dunoon Dr

Barrow Park Avenue

Walker Fold Road

St Peters Smithills Dean CE Primary School

Smithills Hall Museum

Thornleigh Salesian College

Harts

Barrow Bridge

Bolton Sixth Form College North Campus

BL1

Smithills School

Redcar Road

Limefield Close

Myrton Rd

Abercorn Road

Temple Rd

A58

Thor

Golf Course

First St
Second St
Third St
Fourth St
Bazley Street

Jesmond Road

Smithills Road

Croft Road

Woodburn Dr

Scagfield

Brookdean Cl

Raveden Cl

Loen Cres

Temple Dr

Lumwood

Barrow Bridge Road

Riversleigh Close

Moss Bank Park

Capitol Cl

Moss Lane

Forest Road

Garwick Rd

Kenwood Rd

WAY

BANK

Whalley Avenue

Lightbounds Road

Johnson Fold Community Primary School

Hollin Hey Road

Dunsop Drive

Morston Av

Surgery

A60

Johnson Fold

Bolton Old Links Go Club

68

Romiley Drive

Tattersall Av

Gisyrove Av

Chipping Road

Craven Place

Shackleton

Cargrave Road

Oakenclough Dr

Heaton CC

Harners Lane

Rushey Fold La

St Paul's Cem

BROW

OLD

CHORLEY OLD ROAD

MOSS

69

BANK

70

Doffcocker

Smith IIs Drive

Heaton CC

Church Road Primary School

Back Church Rd

Moorland

Orwell Road

Brentford Avenue

Shepherd Cross

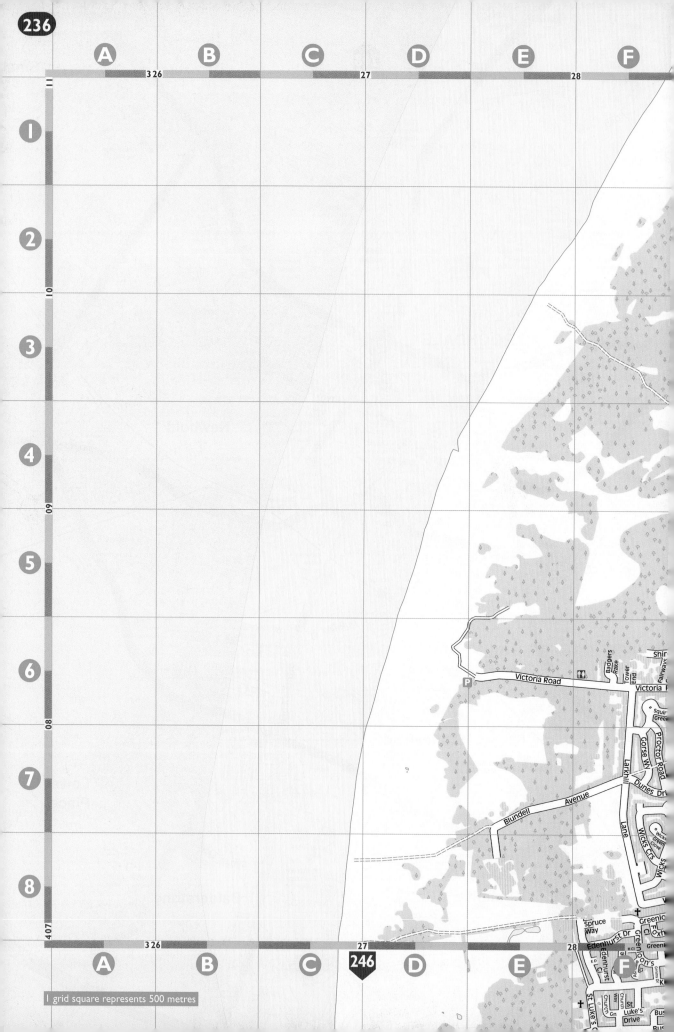

A   B   C   D   E   F

3 26   27   28

1

2

3

4

5

6

7

8

11

10

09

08

407

Victoria Road

Badgers Rake

Tower End

Shir

Fairway

Victoria R

Squir
Gree

Proctor Road

Gorse Wy

Larkhill

Dunes Dri

Blundell   Avenue

Lane

Wicks
Green

Wicks Close

Wicks Cts

Wicks

Spruce
Way

Greenic

Fox

Greenlon's

Green

Edenhurst Dr

Edenhurst
Cl

H C

St
Church

Church
Wk

St Luke's
Drive

St

St Luke's

Bus

+

+

3 26   27   28

I grid square represents 500 metres

238

Ainsdale Clinic
The Brkdle
Kings Meadow
Primary School
Sandbrook
Road

Meadow

Meadow

332

A

B

C

221

33

D

E

34

F

St John Stone
Catholic Primary
School

Rose Crs
Cherry Road
Heather Cl
Lilac Av

I

Woodvale Road

Vale Crescent
Moor Close

Woodvale Road

Plex Moss

Liverpool Old

Moor Lane

Plex Moss Lane

Lancashire County

2

Sefton

Plex Moss Lane

Gettern Farm

Plex Moss Lane

Broad Lane

3

Heathy Lane

Alder Lane

4

North Moss Lane

237

60

Gor

5

Sefton

Lancashire County

Cheshire Lines Path

Downholland Brook

Moss Lane

6

Moss

Lane

Old Moss Le

08

Downholland

Downholland Moss

7

407

Formby's
Farm

8

332

Broad Lane

33

34

A

B

C

248

D

E

F

LORD
SEFTON

Broad
Lane

trons La

County

Middl

1 grid square represents 500 metres

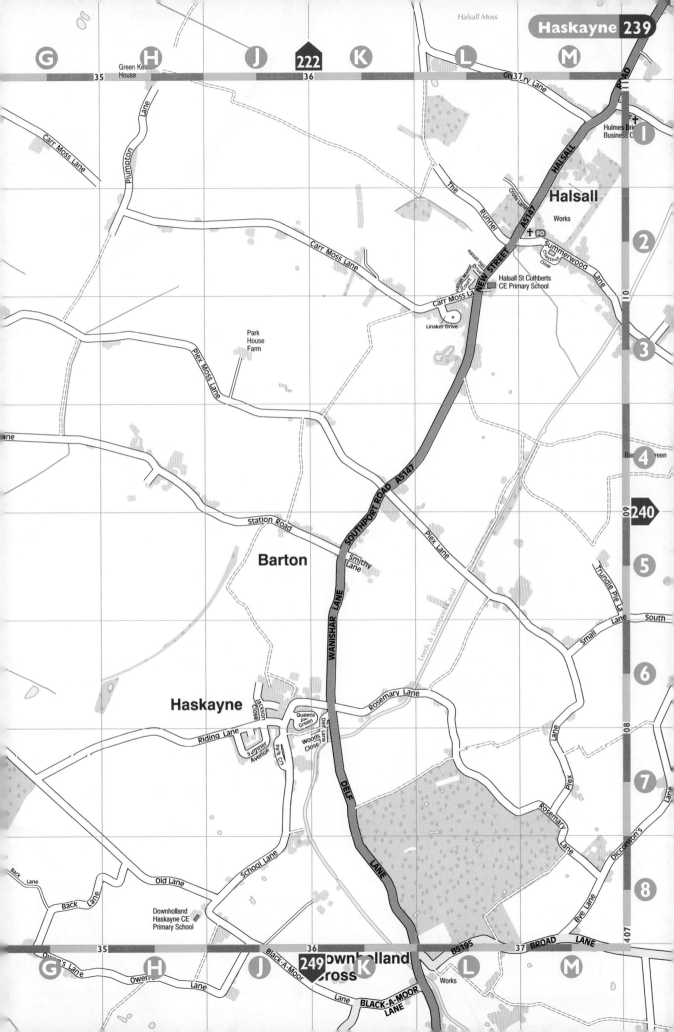

G **H** **J** 222 **K** **L** **M**

35
36
Gr 37 ry Lane
ROAD

Green Ke House

Halsall Moss

Hulmes Bri Business C **1**

Carr Moss Lane

Plumpton Lane

Carr Moss Lane

HALSALL

A5147

Halsall

Cross Lane

Works

The Runnel

PO

Summerwood Lane

Chestnut Close

2

110

Halsall Hall Drive

Halsall Manor Court

NEW STREET

Halsall St Cuthberts CE Primary School

3

Carr Moss La

Park House Farm

Linaker Drive

Plex Moss Lane

Bar reen **4**

Station Road

A5147

SOUTHPORT ROAD

Plex Lane

09 240

Leeds & Liverpool Canal

Trundle Pie La

South

Lane

Small

5

Barton

Smithy Lane

Lane

6

WANISHAR LANE

Lane

08

Rosemary Lane

Plex

7

Haskayne

Jackson Close

Queens Green

Delf Lane

Riding Lane

Sumner Avenue

Park Crs

Woods Close

Rosemary Lane

Dicconson's Lane **8**

DELF LANE

School Lane

407

Back Lane

Old Lane

Downholland Haskayne CE Primary School

Bye Lane

G **H** **J** 249 **K** **L** **M**

35
36
37 BROAD LANE

O en's Lane

wen Lane

BLACK-A-MOOR

ownholland ross

B5195

Works

Lane

BLACK-A-MOOR LANE

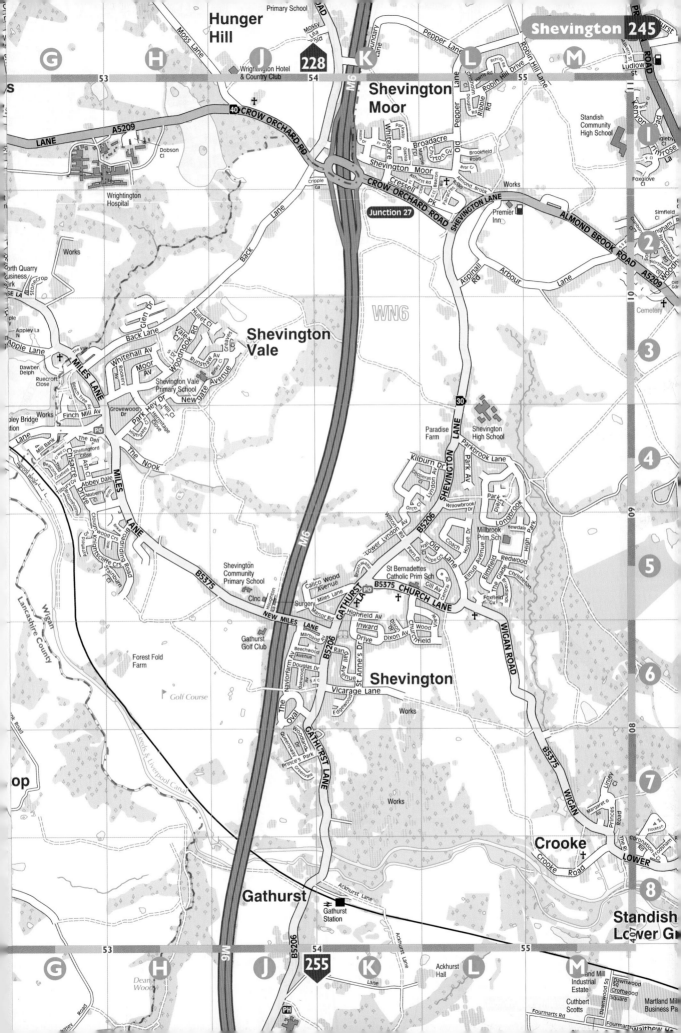

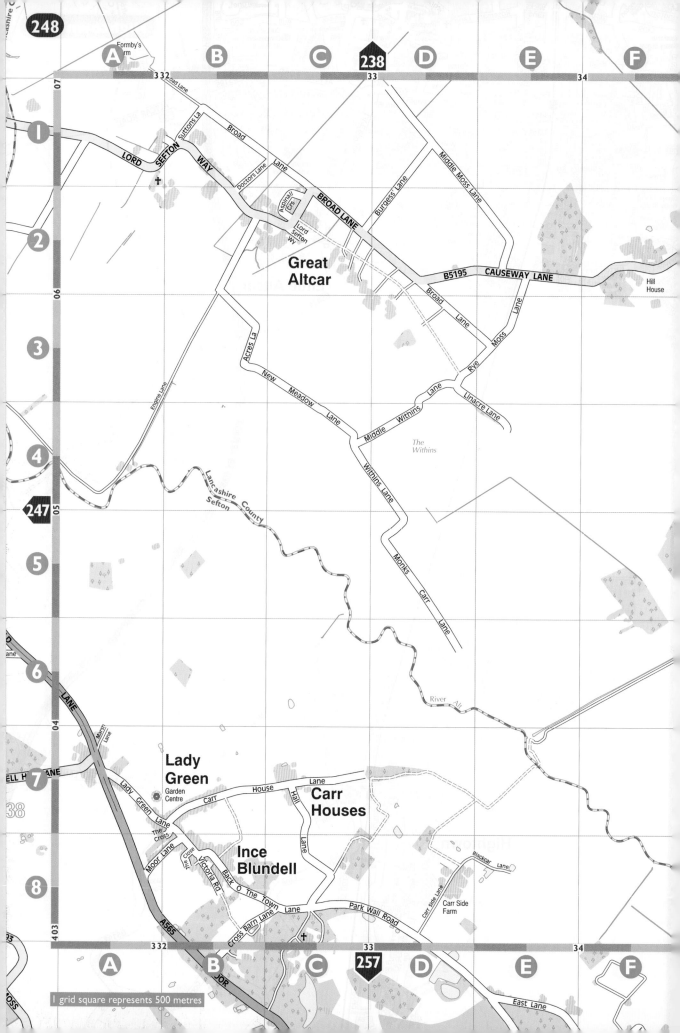

A   B   238   C   D   E   F

332   33   34

1   07

LORD SEFTON WAY

Suttons La   Broad   Doctors Lane   Lane

Aspinall Crs   Lord Sefton Wy

BROAD LANE

Burgess Lane   Middle Moss Lane

2   06

Great
Altcar

Broad   Lane   Moss   Lane   B5195 CAUSEWAY LANE

Hill
House

3   Acres La   Rye   Lane

New   Meadow   Lane   Middle   Withins   Lane   Linacre Lane

Engine Lane

The
Withins

4   05

Lancashire County

Sefton

Withins Lane

5

Monks   Carr   Lane

6   04

LANE

March Lane

River Al

7

Lady
Green

Garden
Centre

House   Lane

Carr   Hall   Lane   Carr
Houses

blackcar   Lane

ELL H   LANE

38

Lady Green Lane

The
Cross

Moor Lane   The Close   Victoria Rd   Ince
Blundell   Back O The Town Lane

Carr Side Lane   Carr Side
Farm

8   03

A565

Cross Barn Lane   Park Wall Road

332   33   34

A   B   257   C   D   E   F

JOR

East Lane

07

3 26

27

28

Spruce Way

Greenlo
Fox
Greenloon's
Greenlo

Edenhurst

Edenhurst Cl

St Luke's Church

I

Kirkdale
Bank

Greenloon's Dr
Ki

St
Luke's
Church
Gn

†

St
Luke's
Drive

Church
Way

Bus

Bus

Lime Tree
Way

2

06

P

Lifeboat   Road

Shorrocks Hill
Country Club

HCl

ED

Trap

Maple
Close

Beechwood

Grove
Grove
Aspen Gv

Cedar
Drive

Ash

Maple
Close

Sycamore

Mayfi

3

Alexandra

Road

Road

Albert

Road

Mitford
Close

Tadlow
Close

Meldreth
Close

Elsworth Cl

Formby Point &
Squirrel Nature
Reserve

St Luke's Church

4

05

5

6

04

7

8

4 03

3 26

27

28

A B C D E F

248

A B C **238** D E F

332 Broad Lane 33 East Lane 34

07

1 LORD SEFTON WAY Suttons La Broad Lane

Doctors Lane

Aspinall Cres

06

2 Broad Lane Burgess Lane Middle Moss Lane

Lord Sefton Wy

Great Altcar Broad Lane B5195 CAUSEWAY LANE Hill House

3 Acres La Moss Lane

Engine Lane New Meadow Lane Rye Lane Linacre Lane

4 Middle Withins Lane

Lancashire County The Withins

05

247 Sefton Withins Lane

5 Monks Carr Lane

6 LANE

04 Marsh Lane River Alt

7 ELL H LANE Lady Green **Carr Houses** Garden Centre Carr House Lane Hall Lane

The Cross Blackcar Lane

Ince Blundell Victoria Rd Moor Lane Carr Side Lane Carr Side Farm

8 Back O The Town Lane

A565 Cross Barn Lane Park Wall Road

403 332 33 34

A B **257** C D E F

JOR East Lane

1 grid square represents 500 metres

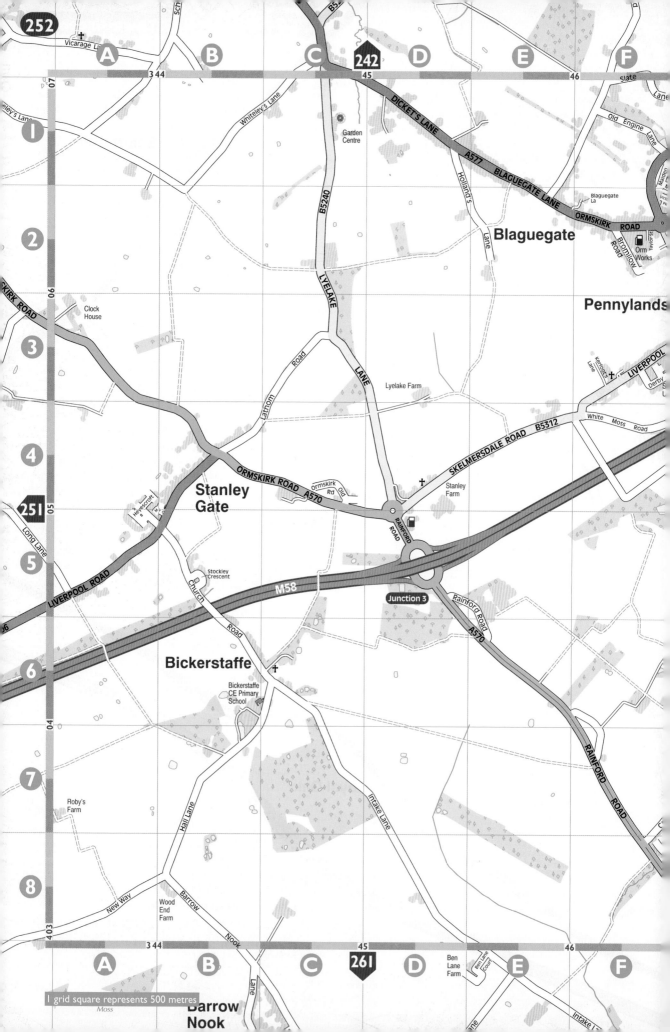

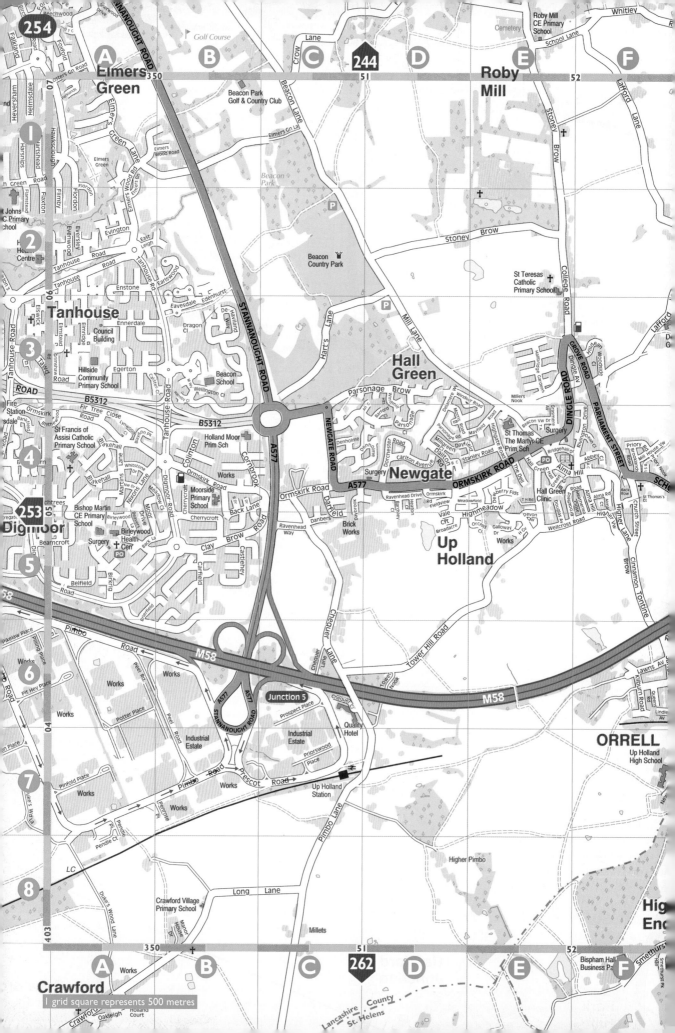

Elmers Green

Roby Mill

Tanhouse

Digmoor

253

Hall Green

Newgate

Up Holland

ORRELL

Up Holland High School

Crawford

Junction 5

244

262

1 grid square represents 500 metres

Higher
End

Crawford Village
Primary School

Long Lane

Dukes Wood Lane

Manor House Dr

G   H   J   K   L   M

50   51   254   52

Works

Crawford

Crawford Road   Oakleigh   Holland Court

Lancashire County
St. Helens

Bispham Hall
Business Park

UPHOLLAND

Smethurst Road   Smethurst Pk

Crank Road

Coppice Rd

Coleridge Cres

Tennyson Dr

I

1

2

Maddocks

Robin's Lane

Pimbo Road

Lane

Brownlow La

Trevel

Brownlow

3

Holiday
Moss

Houghwood
Golf Club

Kings Moss

Golf Course

4

King's Moss La   Fir Tree Cl   Pimbo Rd   Brook La

Crank Road

Houghwood

Red

01

5

Red Cat Lane

Barn

Gores Lane

BACK LANE

Road

6

Moss Lane

RED CAT LANE B5205

GORE'S LANE

Alderley Farm   Alder Lane

Alder Lane

RAINFORD   ROAD

B5205

Rozy Wy

Rainf

1400

HIGHER   LANE B5205

B5207

Highfield Drive

Chapel View

Holt

Holt Avenue

CTS

Delph Meadow Gdns

AS

Crank

CRANK HILL

St. Mary's Avenue

Birchley
St Marys RC
Prim School

7

ROAD

BIRCHLEY

Birchley Avenue

Linden

Avon

Ribble

Trent Road

Lime

Vale

8

Fairfield
Gdns   Fairfield
Hospital

Rainford Hall

G   H   J   K   L   M

50   51   52

NK

BIRCHLEY ROAD

MARTINDAL

Moss Bank Road

Works

03

02

400

399

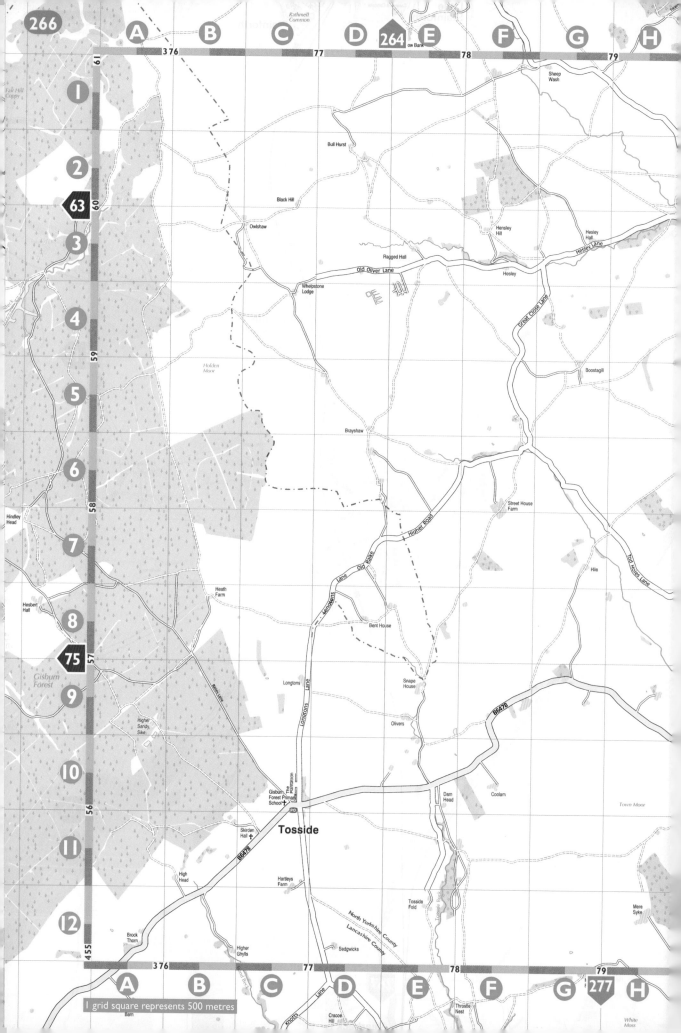

G   H   J   254   K   L   M   Higher End

I

Crawford

Crawford Village Primary School

Long Lane

Duke's Wood Lane

50   51   52   03   UPHOLLAND

Works

Oakleigh   Holland Court

Crawford Road

Lane

Maddocks

Lancashire County
St. Helens

Robin's Lane

Pimbo Road

Brownlow La

Brownlow

Bispham Hall Business Park

Smethurst Road

Crank Road

Coleridge Rd

Tennyson

2

02

3

Holiday Moss

Kings Moss

Kings Moss La

Fir Tree

Brook La

Pimbo Rd

Crank Road

Houghwood Golf Club

Golf Course

Houghwood

01

4

5

Red Cat Lane

Gores Lane

BACK LANE

GORE'S LANE

Red

Barn

Road

B5205   RAINFORD   ROAD

6

Roby

400

Moss Lane

RED CAT LANE B5205

Alderley Farm

Alder Lane

Alder Lane

Delph Meadow Gdns

Holt Ct

Holt Avenue

A57

7

HIGHER   LANE B5205

B5207

Highfield Drive

CRANK HILL

Chapel View

St Mary's Avenue

BIRCHLEY ROAD

Birchley St Marys RC Prim School

Trent Road

Avon Road

Crank

CRANK ROAD

Birchley Avenue

Linden Grove

Lime Vale Road

Ribble Cl

8

3 99

50   51   52

G   H   J   K   L   M

Fairfield Gdns

Fairfield Hospital

Rainford Hall

Works

MARTINDALE

Moss Bank Road

264

A   B   C   D   E   F   G   H

376   77   78   79

67
Waters
Bridge
Gayclops
Fen Beck

Lane

I

Kettlesbeck Brow
Lanshaw
Farm
66

2

Low Dyke
House

Ainswick
Moss

Middlesber

Shepherd Gate

Crow Nest Rd

Lawkland

Rawlinshaw

Brunton
House

Brunton Road

A65

Cave
Hole
Wood

B6480

Slated

3

+   Eldroth Road

Lawkland
Green

Lawkland
Hall Wood

4

65

51

Eldroth

Eldroth Road

Lane End
House

High Paley
Green

Kettles Beck

5

Willow Tree

Blaithwaite

Armistead

A65

6

Lingthu

Barnet
64

Brow Lane

Black Bank

Black Bank Road

Stackhouse Lane

Craven
Ridge

Craven Ridge Lane

Low Paley
Green

7

Ravenshaw

Howith

Butterfield
Gap

Accerhill
Hall

8

63

Rouster

Langrigg

Beck Lane

Cross Lane

Parsons
Close

Parsons Close Lane

Paley Green Lane

9

Storrs Gill Lane

Rome

10

62

63

Wham

Wham Lane

Birchshow
Rocks

11

Gigleswick
Common

Sandford

Sandford Beck

12

461

Rathmell
Common

Low Bank

Sheep
Wash

376   77   78   79

A   B   266   C   D   E   F   G   H

266

1 grid square represents 500 metres

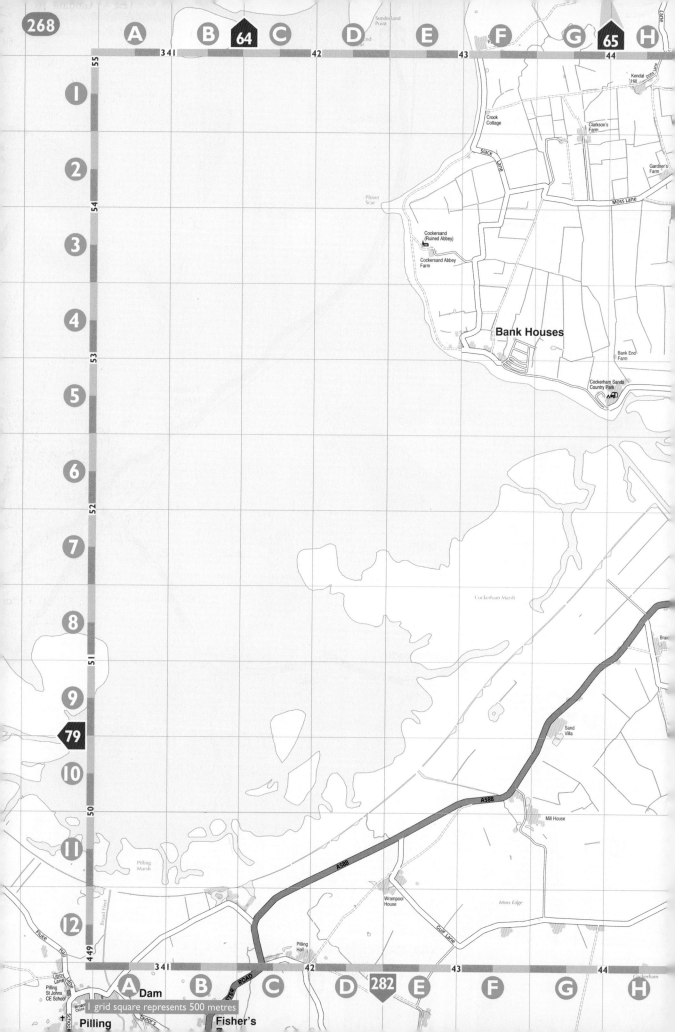

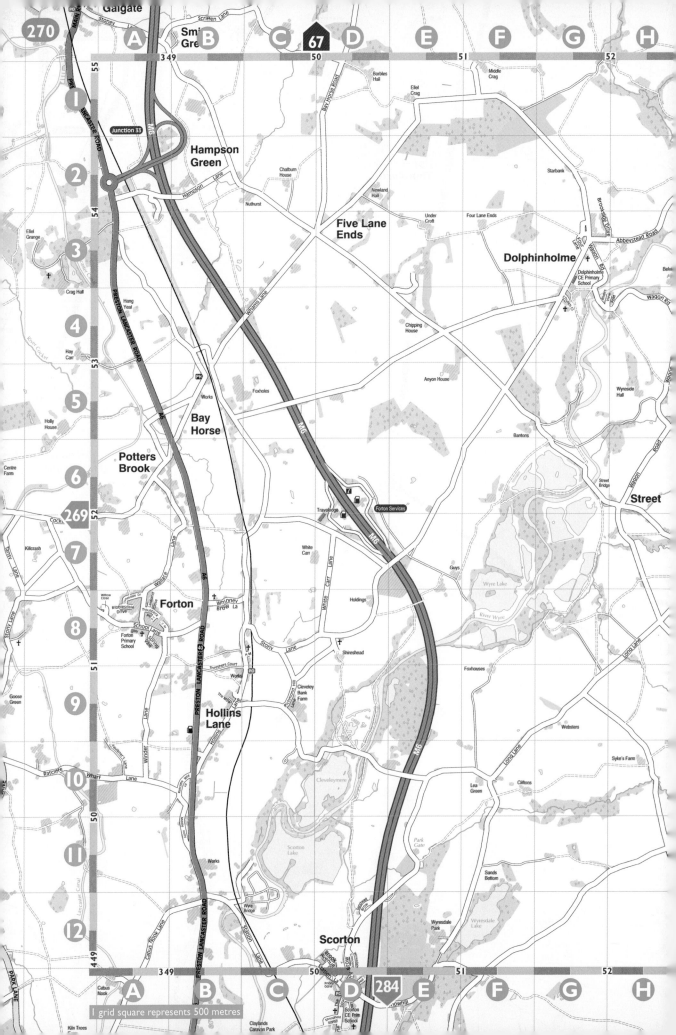

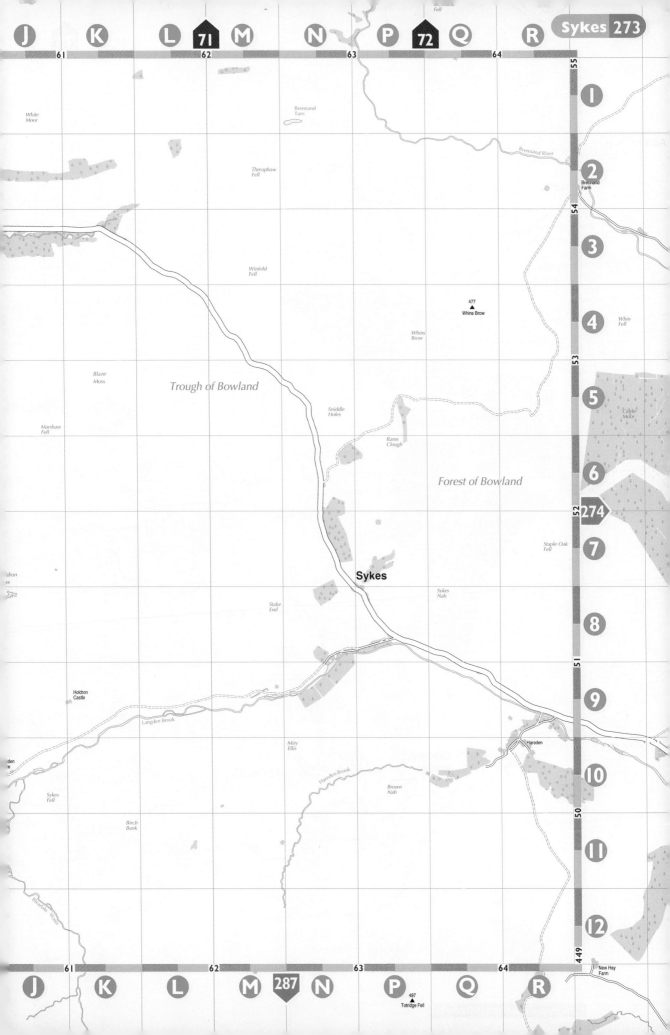

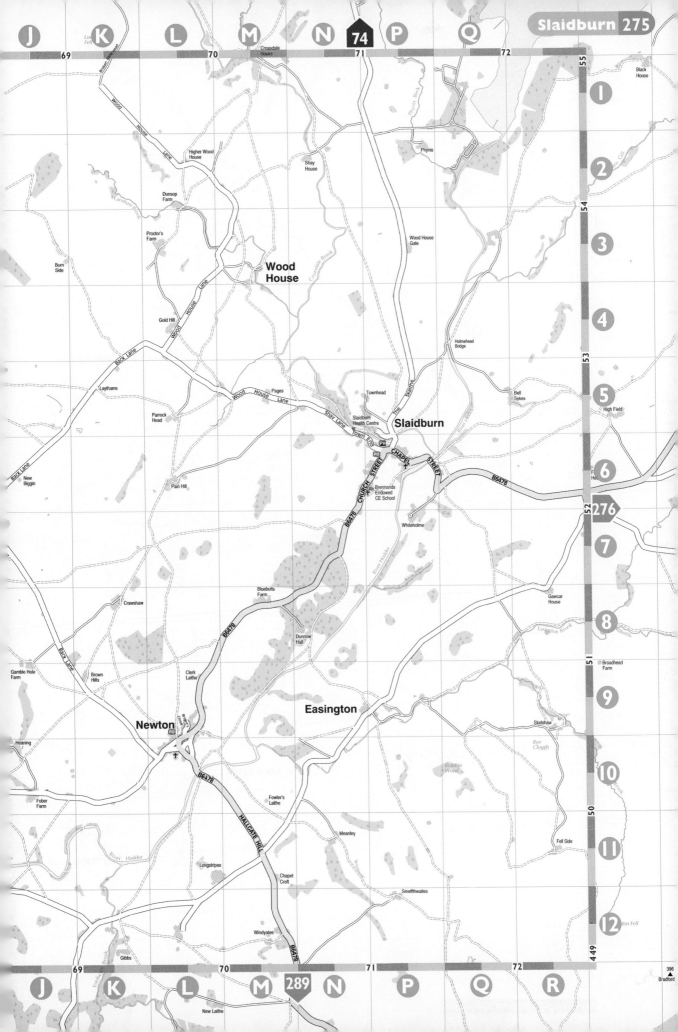

J K L M N **74** P Q

69 70 71 72 55

1
54
2
53
3
4
5 High Field
52 **276**
6
7
8 Broadhead Farm
51
9
50
10
11
12

J K L M **289** N P Q R

69 70 71 72

Croasdale House

Low Fell

Brook Meadow

Wood House Lane

Higher Wood House

Shay House

Phynis

Phynis Beck

Dunsop Farm

Lanshaw Brook

Proctor's Farm

Croasdale Brook

Wood House Gate

Burn Side

Wood House

Holmehead Bridge

Gold Hill

Wood House Lane

Back Lane

Townhead

The Scaithe

Bell Sykes

Laythams

Wood House Lane Pages

Shay Lane

Slaidburn Health Centre

Slaidburn

River Hodder

Parrock Head

Town End

Back Lane

New Biggin

Pain Hill

PO

CHAPEL STREET

CHAPEL STREET

B6478

Brennands Endowed CE School

Whiteholme

CHURCH STREET

B6478

Fell Head

Bluebutts Farm

River Hodder

Gawcar House

Dunnow Hall

Crawshaw

Easington Brook

B6478

Gamble Hole Farm

Brown Hills

Clerk Laithe

Easington

Skelshaw

Heaning

Newton
PO

Brennand's Close

Rye Clough

Brabbin Wood

Fober Farm

B6478

Fowler's Laithe

Fell Side

HALLGATE HILL

Meanley

Longstripes

Chapel Croft

Smelfthwaites

Gibbs

Windyates

B6478

New Laithe

396
▲ Bradford

276

A B C D E F G H

3 73 74 75 76

55

1 Black House

54

2 Rain Gill
Barn Gill
Brook House Green

Dugdale Lane

3 Well House
Stephen Moor Lodge
B6478

Lower Stony Bank

Shays

Far Kno

4 Standridge
Meadow Top
Anna Land End
Fells
Ling Hill

53

B6478

5 Bell Sykes
High Field
Lower Edge
Higher Edge
Threap Green

6 Tinklers Farm
Tinklers Lane
Black Moss
Holden Lane
B6478
Field Head

275

52

7 Dean Slack Head
Dean Slack
Swallow Scars
Champion Farm
Dugdales
Peet Lane
Westmoor

Gawcar House

8 Harrop Hall
Easingto
Broadhead Farm
Cross
Stephensons

51

9 Skelshaw
Harrop Lodge
Wilmans
Barret Hill Brow

Rye Clough

10 Lane Ends
Skelshaw Brook

Smalden Lane

50

11 Bambers
Bay Gate

Fell Brook

Lenning Lane

12 Easington Fell
Harrop Fold
Smalden House
Cottams

449

3 73 396 74 75 76
Bradford Fell

A B C D 290 E F G H
High Heig

Smalden L

Lane

1 grid square represents 500 metres

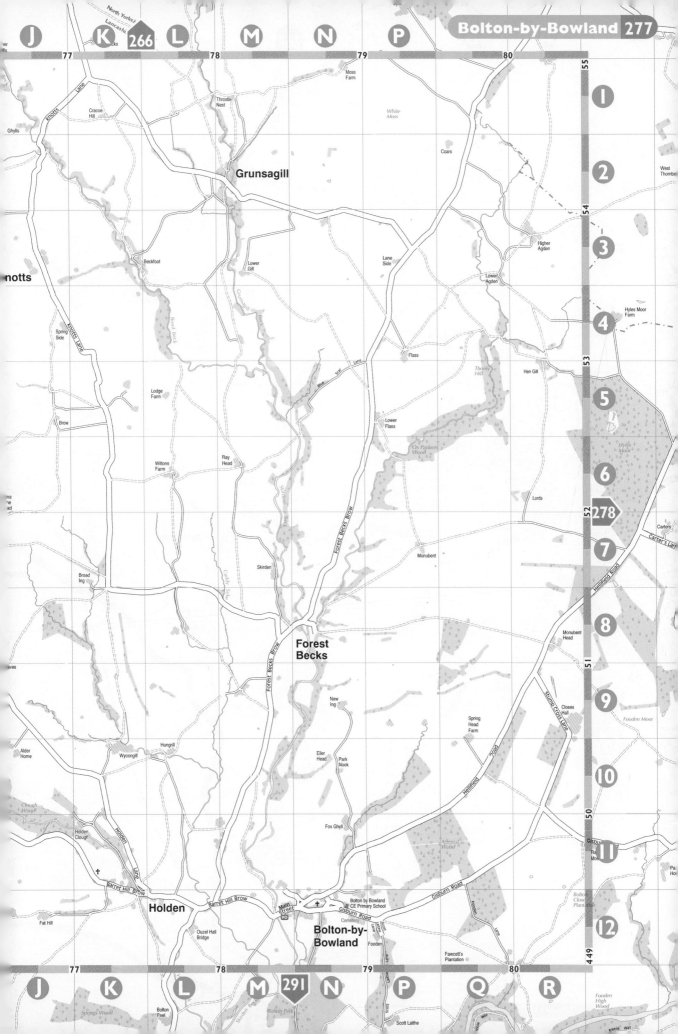

J   K   266   L   M   N   P

77   78   79   80

Bolton-by-Bowland 277

1

2

3

4

5

6

278

7

8

9

10

11

12

Grunsagill

Beckfoot
Lower Gill

Lane Side

Moss Farm

White Moss

Coars

Higher Agden
Lower Agden

Hyles Moor Farm

Flass

Thorny Hill

Hen Gill

Lower Flass

Os Pastures Wood

Hyles Moor

Spring Side
Knotts Lane

Brow

Lodge Farm

Wittons Farm

Ray Head

Skirden

Lords

Monubent

Carters
Carter's Lane

Broad Ing

Forest Becks Brow

Forest
Becks

Monubent Head

New Ing

Closes Hall

Stump Cross Lane

Fooden Moor

Wycongill

Hungrill

Alder Home

Eller Head
Park Nook

Spring Head Farm

Hellifield Road

Holden Clough

Holden Lane

Fox Ghyll

Admiral's Wood

Gisburn Road

Fooden Moss

Bolton Closes Plantation

Holden

Barret Hill Brow

Fat Hill

Ouzel Hall Bridge

Main Street

Bolton by Bowland CE Primary School

Gisburn Road

Cemetery

Bolton-by-Bowland

Fooden

Fawcett's Plantation

J   K   L   M   291   N   P   Q   R

77   78   79   80

Springs Wood

Bolton Peel

Bolton Park

Scott Laithe

Fooden High Wood

Ghylls

Cracoe Hill

Knotts Lane

North Yorks
Lancashire

Throstle Nest

Blue Scar Lane

Crimshall Beck

Bond Beck

Skirden

Cuddy Sykes

Clough Wood

West Thornber

55
54
53
52
51
50
49

J K L M N P Q

85 86 87 88

Halton
Place

Swinden

55

1 Kelber

Millstock
Lane

Mill Lane

2 Winterley
Cobba

54

Swinden Gill Wood

3

Cobers
Laithe

Ash Tree
Farm

4 Litt
Sta

Nappa
Flats

Swinden Moor
Head

53

Nappa

5 Stainton
Hall

A682

Hayber

Greenber Lane

ingthorpe Lane

6 Stainton
House

Slack

North Yorkshire County
Lancashire County

52 **280**

A682

7

olme

Varley
Field

Horton
Pasture

Scar Road

Marton
Scar

8 Gledstone
Hall

Skelda
House

9

Hoober

Lane

Lower
Paradise

Pasture House

Gledstone Road

51

Baxen Lane

Burons
Laithe

A59

10

West Ing Lane

Green Lane

+ **Horton**

Bentha
Plantation

Horton
Green

50

Bale
New
Plantation

Crooks
House

11

Turpit Gate
House

Willcross

Yarlside Lane

B6251

Yarlside

12

Old Park
Laithe

Stock

449

J K L M **293** N P Q R

85 86 87 88

Laithbuts
Laithe

North Yorks
Lancashire

Stock Beck

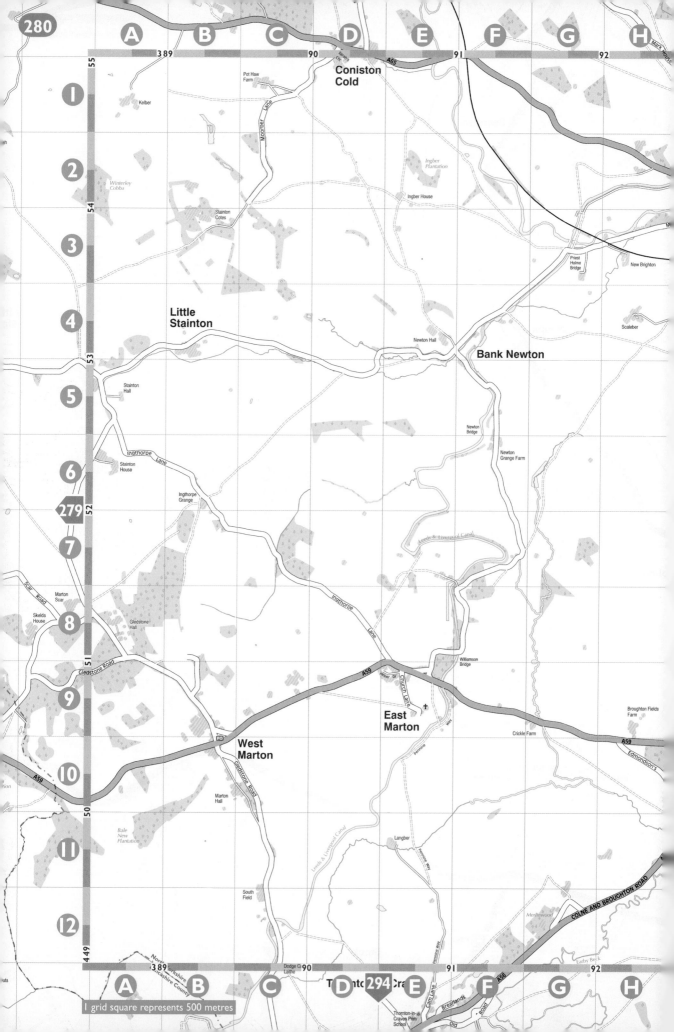

A B C D E F G H

3 89 90 A65 91 92

Mark House

1

Kelber

Pot Haw
Farm

Coniston
Cold

Moorber Lane

2

Winterley
Cobba

Ingber
Plantation

Ingber House

3

Stainton
Cotes

Priest
Holme
Bridge

New Brighton

4

Little
Stainton

Newton Hall

Bank Newton

Scaleber

53

5

Stainton
Hall

Newton
Bridge

Ingthorpe Lane

6

Stainton
House

Newton
Grange Farm

279

52

Ingthorpe
Grange

Leeds & Liverpool Canal

7

Scar Road

Ingthorpe Lane

8

Marton
Scar

Skelda
House

Gledstone
Hall

51

Williamson
Bridge

9

Gledstone Road

A59

East
Marton

Church Lane

Pennine Way

Broughton Fields
Farm

Crickle Farm

A59

Edmondson's

PO

West
Marton

10

A59

50

Marton
Hall

Gledstone Road

Leeds & Liverpool Canal

Langber

Pennine Way

11

Bale
New
Plantation

South
Field

Merlinwood

COLNE AND BROUGHTON ROAD

12

449

North Yorkshire County
Lancashire County

3 89

Dodge Cr
Laithe

90

Thornton 294 Cra

Thornton-in-a
Craven Prim
School

Cam Lane

Breanlands

Old Road

91

A56

92

Earby Beck

A B C D E F G H

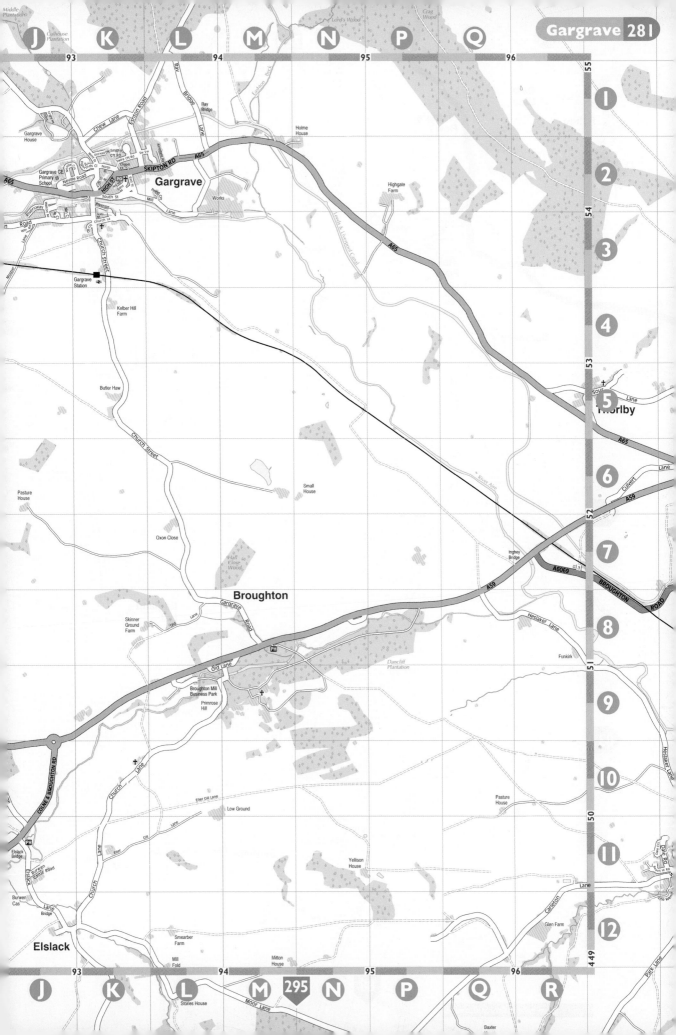

282

268

88

79

83

A B C D E F G H

Pilling
Dam Side
Fisher's Row
Pilling St Johns CE Sch
Libby Lane
School Lane
Surgery
Taylors Lane
Cherry Tree Dr
Taylors Industrial Estate
St John's Avenue
Carr Close
Bluebell
Carr Lane
Lancaster Road
LANCASTER ROAD
A588
Pilling Hall
St Williams Catholic Primary School
Works
Moss House Lane
Bond's Farm
Horse Park Lane
Peahall Lane
Works
Carr Lane Road
Works
Stake Pool
Fold House
Scronkey
DYKE LANE
HEAD
Bradshaw Lane
Pilling Water
Jarvis Carr
Cumming Carr
Pilling Water
Cogie Hill Farm
Isla
Bone Hill Farm
Bone Hill Lane
Black Lane
Kentucky Farm
Pilling Moss
Bradshaw Lane Head
New Union Farm
Rigby Pool
Black Hill Farm
Ivy Farm
Union Lane
Brook Farm
Rawcliffe Moss
Eagland Hill
New Lane
Bradshaw Lane
Birk's Farm
Hornby's
Lousanna
Lancaster Road
Chathill Farm
Ashton Lane
Tinney's Lane
Dockinsall Lane
Skitham
New Eskham
Eskham House
Rigby Pool
Hares Road
Lidney Road
Moor Hall
Bensons
Moss Edge
Works
Skitham Lane
Cuckoo Lane
Lancaster Road
Rawcliffe Moss
Broad Lane
Stone Check
Out Rawcliffe CE Primary
Crook Gate La
Crab Tree Lane
Curlew Farm
Cockerham Moss
Gull Moss
Gulf Lane

49 48 47 46 45 44 44 443

341 42 43 44

I 2 3 4 5 6 7 8 9 10 11 12

1 grid square represents 500 metres

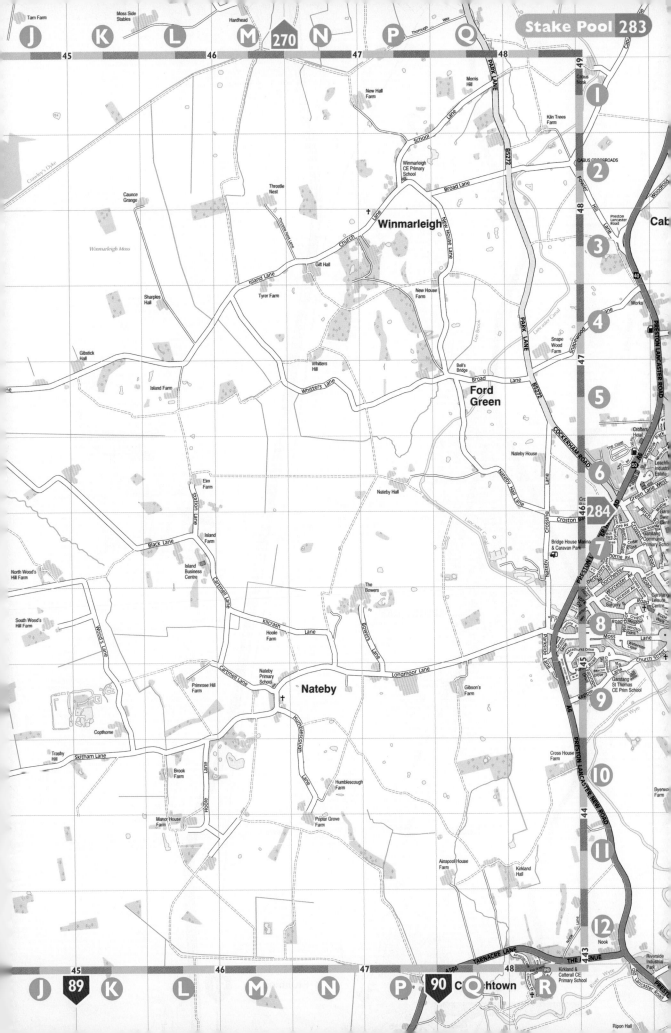

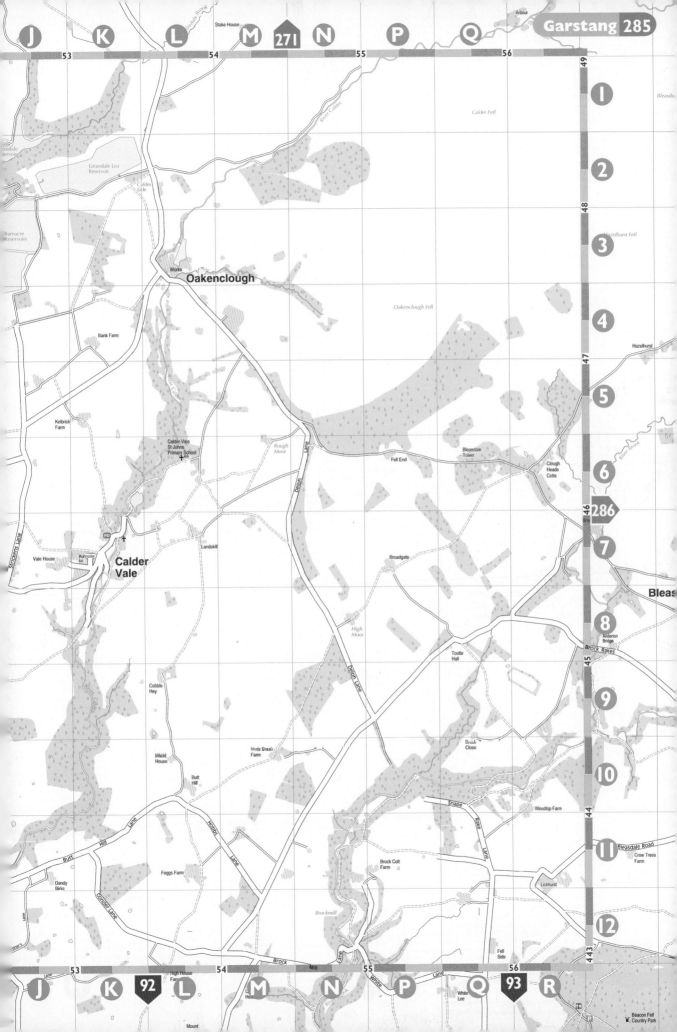

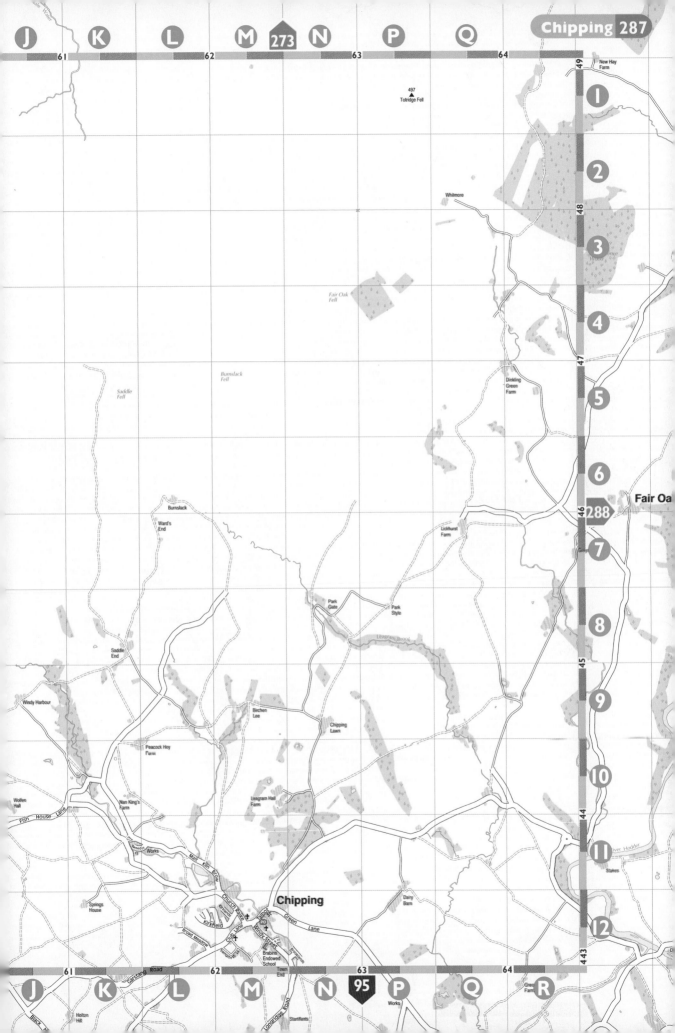

J K L M N P Q

273

61 62 63 64

49

New Hay Farm

1

2

48

Whitmore

3

497
Totridge Fell

4

47

Fair Oak Fell

5

Dinkling Green Farm

Burnslack Fell

6

Saddle Fell

46 288 Fair Oa

7 Greys

Burnslack

Lickhurst Farm

Ward's End

8

Park Gate

Park Style

45

Saddle End

Leagram Brook

9

Windy Harbour

Birchen Lee

10

Chipping Lawn

Peacock Hey Farm

44

Wolfen Hall

Nan King's Farm

Leagram Hall Farm

11 River Hodder

Fish House Lane

Stakes

Breeds Works

Springs House

Malt Kiln Brow

Church Raike

Chipping

Dairy Barn

12

Kirkfield

Windy Street

Green Lane

443

Broad Meadow

Brabins Endowed School

Town End

J K L M N 95 P Q R

61 62 63 64

Holton Hill

Garstang Road

Longridge Road

Startifants

Works

Green Farm

Black F

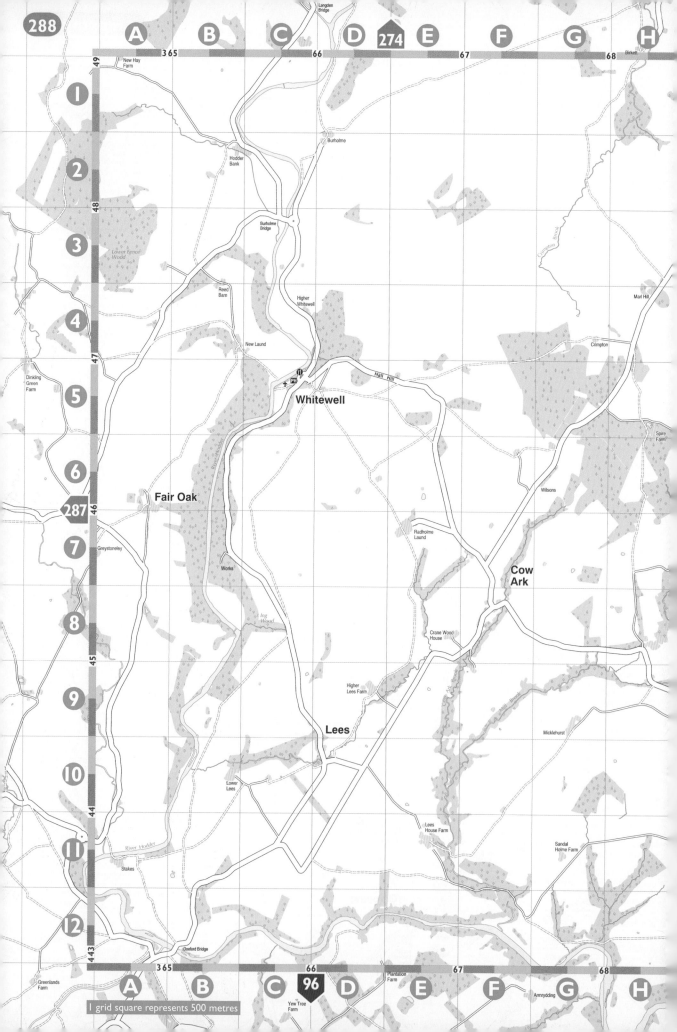

J K L M **275** N P Q

69   70   71   72

I
2
3
4
5
6
7
8
9
10
11
12

▲ 396
Bradford Fell

Slaidburn Road B6478

Underhand

New Laithe

Ing Barn

Ashnott

Gibbs

Crag House

Stone Fold

Newton Fells

Bradford Fell

BB7

Browsholme Moor

Moorcock Inn

New-o-Nook

Elm Clough Wood

Browsholme Road

Hodgson Moor

Daisy Hill

Mill Farm

Mill Lane

290

Buckstall

Leemings

Hare Clough

Flatts

Freeholds Lane

Bookers

Rabbit Lane

Braddup Farm

Cross Lane

Freeholds Lane

Chancery Farm

Kitchens

Talbot Bridge

Cross Lane

Colthurst Hall

Braddup House

Slaidburn Road

B6478

BELLE VUE

West

Wadd

Mason House

Clough Bottom

Page Fold

Lower New House

CLITHEROE

Bashall Eaves

Rugglesmere

Twitter

Fields House

Agden Farm

Cow Hey

Horse Hey

Backridge

J **97** K L M N P **98** Q R

69   70   71   72

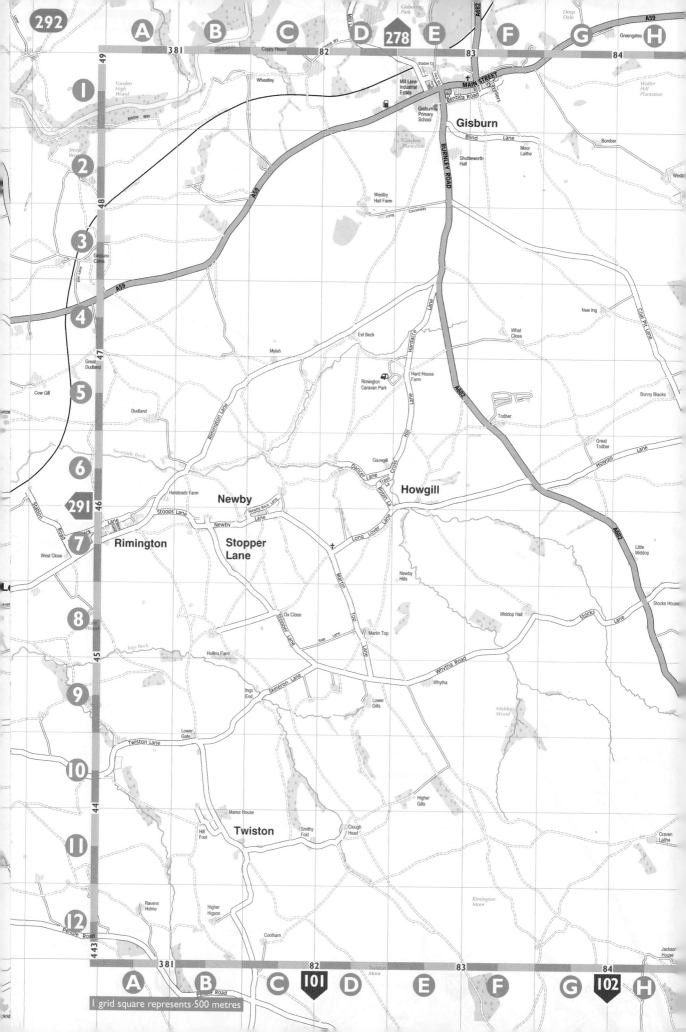

A B C D E F G H

1

Fooden High Wood

Wheatley

Coppy House

Mill Lane Industrial Estate

Stable C

Gisburn Primary School

Park Rd

MAIN STREET

Bentlea Road

Craggiers

Gisburn

Blind Lane

Shuttleworth Hall

Moor Laithe

Bomber

Walter Hill Plantation

Deep Dale

Greengates

A682

A59

2

Steep Wood

Ribble Way

48

Cawber Plantation

Westby Hall Farm

Long Causeway

BURNLEY ROAD

New Ing

Coal Pit Lane

Wedb

3

Gisburn Cotes

Kiln Lane

A59

4

47

Eel Beck

Mylah

Hardacre Lane

What Close

A682

Todber

Bonny Blacks

5

Great Dudland

Cow Gill

Dudland

Rimington Lane

Rimington Caravan Park

Hard House Farm

Great Todber

Howgill Lane

6

Swanside Beck

Hill Lane

Gazegill

Dancer Lane

Trash La

Cross

46

Halsteads Farm

Newby

Howgill

291

Stoops Lane

Newby Back Lane

Newby Lane

Road Ln

Long Lover Lane

Little Middop

7

Station Road

Lane

Rimington

Newby

Stopper Lane

Newby Hills

West Close

Martin Top Lane

8

45

Ings Beck

Ox Close

Stopper Lane

Side Lane

Martin Top

Middop Hall

Stocks Lane

Stocks House

9

Ings End

Skeleron Lane

Lower Gills

Whytha Road

Whytha

Middop Wood

10

44

Twiston Lane

Lower Gate

Higher Gills

11

Hill Foot

Manor House

Twiston

Smithy Fold

Clough Head

Rimington Moor

Craven Laithe

12

Pendle Road

Ravens Holme

Higher Higson

Coolham

443

Twiston Moor

Jackson House

A B C D E F G H

Pendle Road

1 grid square represents 500 metres

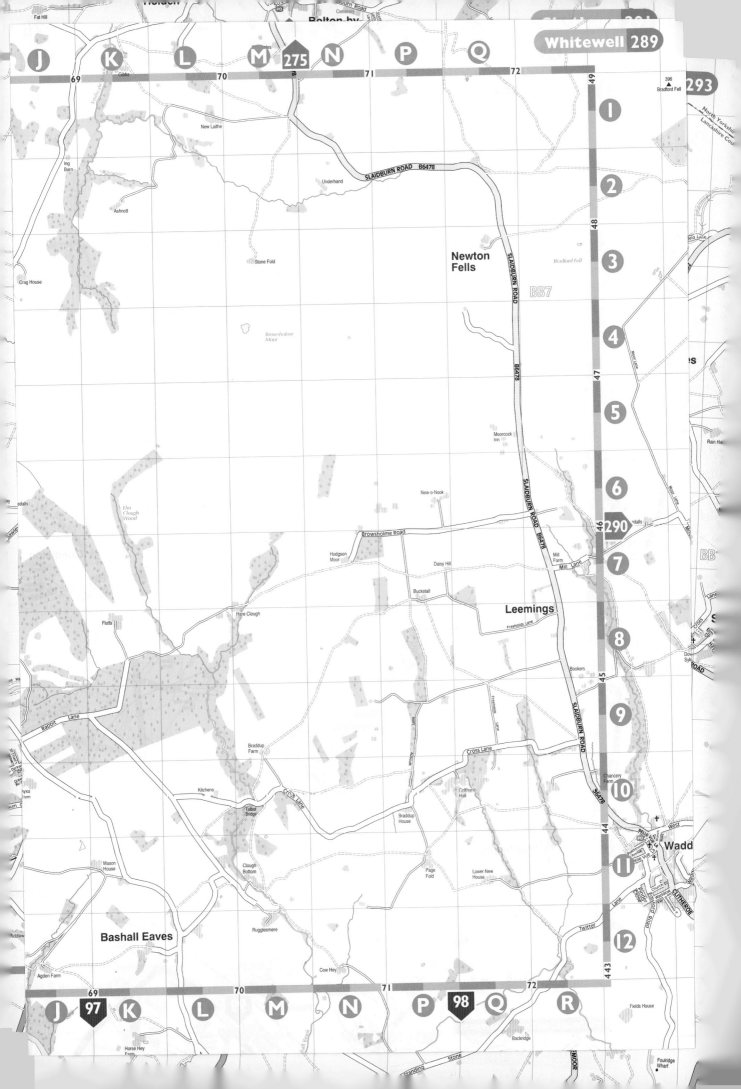

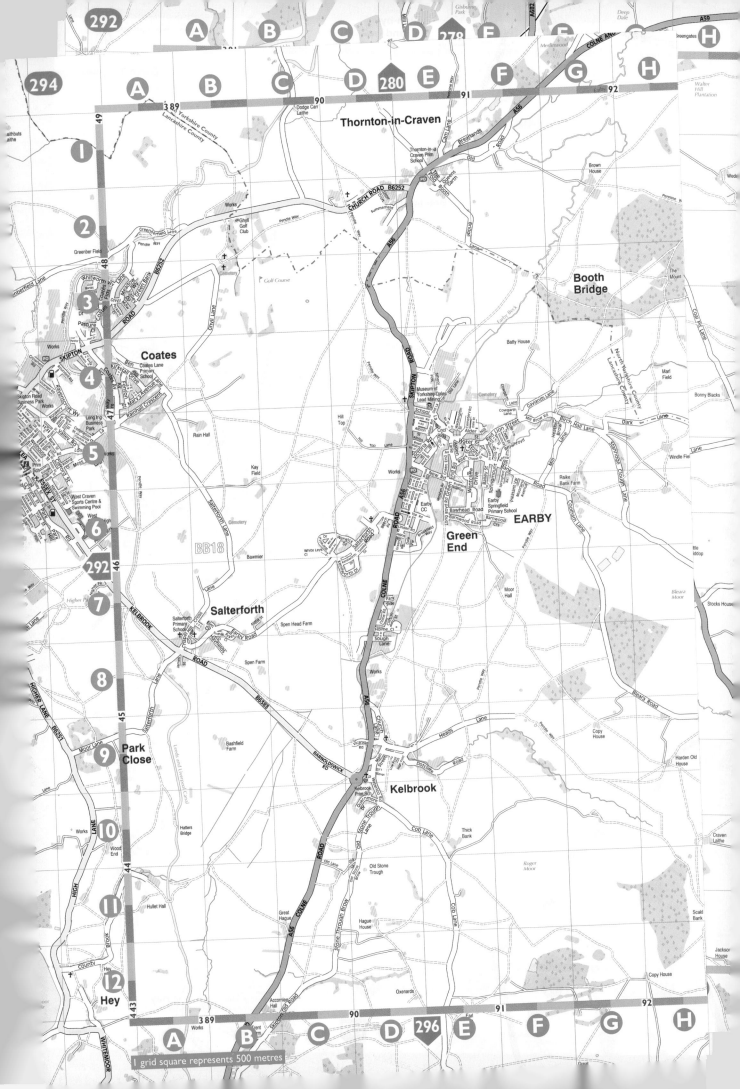

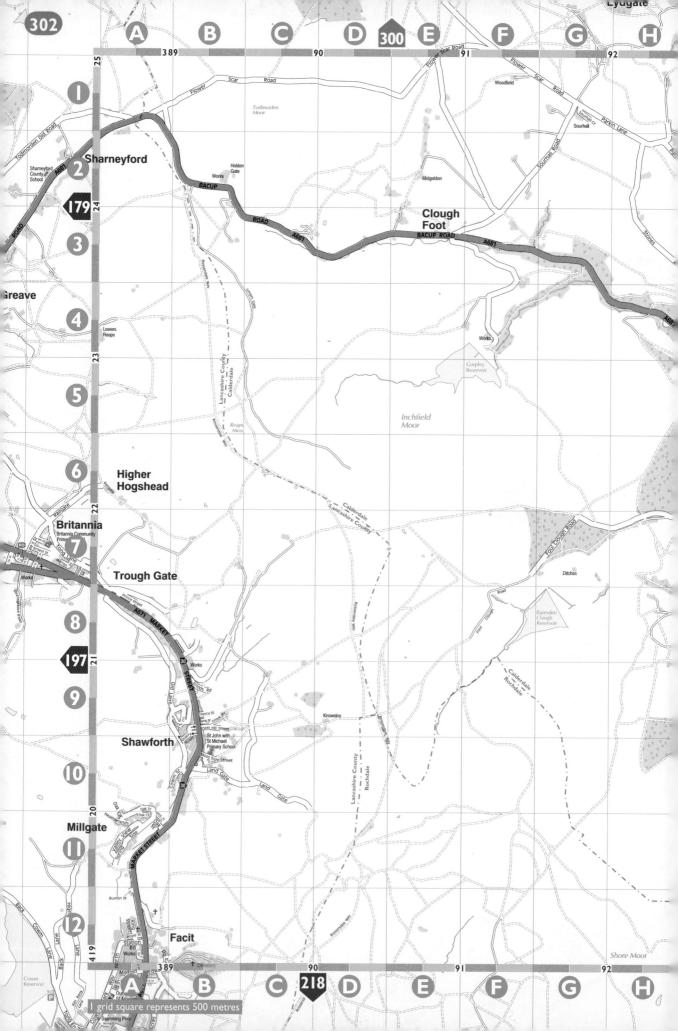

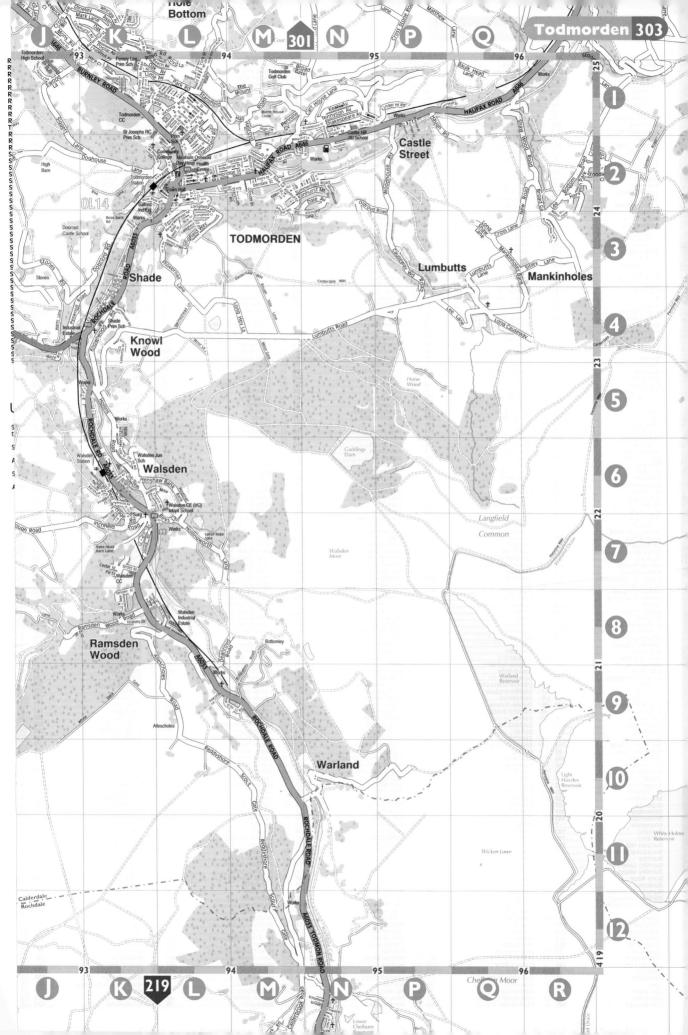

GAR/LONG PR3.........................88 E6
HGHB LA2..............................36 D7
HGHB LA2..............................30 B7
KIRK/FR/WAR PR4.............166 D3
KIRK/FR/WAR PR4.............127 K1
KKBYL LA6............................33 K5
LEYL PR25...........................186 F4
MTHPE LA7............................18 B1
ORM L39..............................250 B4
ORM L39..............................239 B6
PDHM/BLYW BB12.............121 G5
PDHM/BLYW BB12.............119 H3
PLF/KEOS FY6.......................82 D1
RAW/HAS BB4.....................177 J5
RNFD/HAY WA11..................263 J6
SETT BD24...........................267 K3
SETT BD24...........................264 D8
SKEL WN8............................243 G1
WHIT OL12...........................267 R6
Back La East BRSC L40.........227 H2
Back Leach St COL BB8 *.......103 M7
Back Lee St RAW/HAS BB4....194 H1
Back Lines St MCMB LA4.........41 J6
Back Longworth Rd
EDGW/EG BL7......................212 A4
LANC LA1................................3 C4
RAW/HAS BB4......................177 K1
Back Lune St COL BB8 *........296 B6
Back Marine Rd MCMB LA4......41 G7
Back Marine Rd East
MCMB LA4.............................41 L5
Back McDonna St BOL BL1....233 M8
Back Moon Av BPOOL FY1.........4 D8
Back Morecambe St MCMB LA4.41 G5
Back Moss La BRSC L40.........225 J4
Back Mt CHLY/EC PR7............207 A8
Back Nelson St HOR/BR BL6 *.232 A8
Back North Cft LSTA FY8........145 H5
Back Oldham Rd MILN OL16....235 K5
Back O The Town La
HTWN L38.............................248 B8
Back Owen's Rw HOR/BR BL6 *.231 M8
Back Owen St ACC BB5..........159 M4
Back Patience St WHIT OL12...234 F2
Back Pleasant St BPOOL FY1..104 E4
Back Queen St GTH/LHO BB6..138 F7
LANC LA1................................3 G7
MCMB LA4.............................41 J6
Back Railway Vw
CHLY/EC PR7.......................230 D4
Back Raimond St BOL BL1.....233 M8
Back Rawlinson St
HOR/BR BL6 *.......................231 L7
Back Read's Rd BPOOL FY1......4 E3
Back Rhoden Rd ACC BB5......175 G1
Back Ridge St TOD OL14 *.....303 L2
Back Rings Rw RAW/HAS BB4.177 K1
Back Rock Av BOL BL1...........233 M8
Back Roseberry Av North
MCMB LA4.............................41 K6
Back Roseberry Av South
MCMB LA4.............................41 K7
Back Royds St MILN OL16......235 K6
Back Rushton St BCUP OL13 *.197 H3
Back St Anne's Rd West
LSTA FY8..............................145 H5
Back St John St BCUP OL13...179 J8
Back Sandy Bank Rd
EDGW/EG BL7......................213 G6
Back School La SKEL WN8.....254 F4
SKEL WN8............................253 G2
Back Scotland Rd NLSN BB9..123 G3
Back Seed St PRES PR1............9 G3
Back Shannon St BPOOL FY1....4 D5
Back Shannon St
PDHM/BLYW BB12..............140 F3
Back Skull House La
WGNNW/ST WN6.................244 F6
Back Somerville St BOL BL1 *.233 M8
Back Springfield Rd North
LSTA FY8..............................145 H5
Back Square St RAMS BL0.....214 F5
Back Stanley St RAMS BL0.....214 E6
Back Starkie St PRES PR1........9 H4
The Backs GAR/LONG PR3.....114 D5
Back St HEY LA3.....................65 J3
Back Virginia St STHP PR8......13 H6
Back Warbreck Rd BPOOL FY1.104 E4
Back Waterloo Rd
BPOOL FY4...........................124 E2
Back Water St ACC BB5 *......159 M5
Back Wellfield Ter TOD OL14..303 L3
Back Wellington St ACC BB5..159 M6
Back West Crs LSTA FY8 *.....145 H5
Back Willow St
PDHM/BLYW BB12................6 D3
Back Wilmot St BOL BL1 *.....233 M8
Back Winterdyne Ter HEY LA3..40 F7
Back Woodfield Rd BPOOL FY1..4 D8
Back Wood St HOR/BR BL6....231 M8
Back Wright St HOR/BR BL6...231 L7
RAW/HAS BB4......................177 K4
Back York St CLI BB7..............99 H3
Bacon St NLSN BB9...............123 H3
Bacup Old Rd BCUP OL13.....179 J5
Bacup Rd BLY BB11...............163 G6
RAW/HAS BB4......................195 K1
TOD OL14.............................302 B2
Badby Wd NWD/KWIPK L33...260 C7
Baden St BBNW BB2..............172 F2
Badge Brow ACC BB5.............159 H6
Badger Cl MILN OL16.............235 M8
Badger La HBR HX7................301 R7
MILN OL16............................235 M8
Badgers Cft FUL/RIB PR2......153 J2
Badgers Rake FMBY L37........236 F6
Badgers Wk CHLY/EC PR7.....187 L8
Badgers Wk East LSTA FY8...146 F8
Badgers Wy BBR PR5..............152 E8
Badger Wd TOD OL14.............303 M2
Bagganley La CHLY PR6.........208 B2
Bagnall St WHIT OL12.............234 C1
Bagnold Rd PRES PR1............153 G2
Bagot St BPOOL FY1.............124 E2
Bagslate Moor La ROCH OL11.234 C3
Bagslate Moor Rd ROCH OL11.234 C3
Baildon Rd ROCH OL11...........234 E2
Bailey Bank CLI BB7................97 K4
Bailey Cl BBN BB1...................173 J2
Bailey Ct BPOOLE FY3...........105 H5
Bailey La HEY LA3....................52 D3
SKP/WHF BD23....................266 B9
Bailey St BLY BB11....................6 C5
BWCK/EAR BB18..................294 F6
Bailey Wy MCHL L31..............258 F2
Baillie St FUL/RIB PR2...........132 F2

Baillie St MILN OL16 *............235 J4
Baillie St East MILN OL16......235 K3
Bailrigg La LANC LA1...............66 F2
Baines Av BPOOLE FY3...........105 J2
Bainesfield PLF/KEOS FY6....106 A1
Bairstow St BPOOL FY1............4
BWCK/EAR BB18..................293 P6
PRES PR1................................9 H5
Bakers Ct BPOOLE FY4..........125 J4
Baker's La CHTN/BK PR9........180 C8
Bakers Ms KIRK/FR/WAR......183 K5
Baker St BBN BB1.....................11 L5
BCUP OL13...........................197 B6
BLY BB11..............................163 D6
CHLY/EC PR7.......................229 H2
LANC LA1................................42 E8
LEYL PR25...........................186 E1
NLSN BB9.............................123 H2
RAMS BL0............................214 E6
Balaclava St BBN BB1...............10 L1
Bala Cl BBN BB1......................10 L1
Balcarres St CHLY/EC PR7.....186 D2
Balcarres Pl LEYL PR25.........186 D3
Balcarres Rd CHLY/EC PR7...207 L6
FUL/RIB PR2........................131 M8
LEYL PR25...........................186 D3
Balderstone Cl
BRFD/BLYE BB10................143 G1
Balderstone Hall La
BBNW BB2............................134 F5
Balderstone La
BRFD/BLYE BB10................143 H2
Balderstone Rd
KIRK/FR/WAR PR4..............148 E4
PRES PR1................................8 D2
Baldwin Gv BPOOL FY1.............5 H7
Baldwin Hl CLI BB7..................99 G3
Baldwin St CLI BB7..................99 G3
Baldwin St BBNW BB2 *...........10 B7
BBR PR5...............................169 H3
CHLY/EC PR7.......................196 E3
WGNW/BIL/OR WN5............255 L6
The Bales CLV/TH FY5.............86 A4
Balfour Cl CLV/TH FY5.............86 A4
NLSN BB9.............................123 G6
STHP PR8.............................200 B6
WHIT OL12...........................234 F2
Balfour St BBNW BB2................10 A8
GTH/LHO BB6......................139 G6
LEYL PR25...........................186 D3
Balham Av BPOOLS FY4.........125 H6
Ballam Rd FUL/RIB PR2..........151 H2
KIRK/FR/WAR PR4..............127 H7
LSTA FY8..............................146 E7
Ballam St BLY BB11 *..............7 B8
Ballantrae Rd BBN BB1...........158 A8
Ballard Cl LIT OL15................219 L4
Ballater St BLY BB11.................6 A9
Balle St BWN BB2...................191 K3
Ballet Hill Crs GAR/LONG PR3.91 K4
Ball Grove Dr COL BB8...........296 E6
Balliol Cl PDHM/BLYW BB12..141 G5
Ball La FUL/RIB PR2..................44 D5
Ball St BPOOL FY1....................4 D9
MILN OL16............................235 K3
NLSN BB9 *...........................123 G2
PLF/KEOS FY6.......................86 A8
Balmer Gv BPOOL FY1..............5 G5
Balmoral Av BBN BB1.............137 K7
CLI BB7..................................98 F3
CSBY/BLUN LA23................257 H8
HEY LA3.................................40 F8
LEYL PR25...........................186 F3
ROCH OL11..........................234 E3
Balmoral Cl CHTN/BK PR9.....180 E8
NWD/KWIPK L33..................260 B6
Balmoral Crs BBN BB1............158 C2
Balmoral Dr CHLYE PR6.........189 H3
CHTN/BK PR9.......................180 E8
FMBY L37.............................247 H2
Balmoral Pl CLV/TH FY5..........85 M3
Balmoral Rd ACC BB5.............160 A4
BBR PR5...............................153 G8
BPOOLS FY4.........................5 J6
CHLY/EC PR7.......................207 L3
CHLY/EC PR7.......................205 M4
COL BB8................................296 F10
DWN BB3..............................191 K2
EDGW/EG BL7......................212 F7
NLSN BB9.............................122 E5
PDHM/BLYW BB12..............140 F2
RAMS BL0............................215 H4
RAW/HAS BB4......................176 E8
ROCH OL11..........................235 L2
TOD OL14.............................303 L4
Balmoral Ter FTWD FY7...........77 L6
Balm St RAMS BL0.................214 D7
Balniel Cl CHLY/EC PR7..........207 L4
Balshaw Av CHLY/EC PR7......207 G1
Balshaw Crs LEYL PR25.........186 C1
Balshaw La CHLY/EC PR7......207 G2
Balshaw Rd HGHB LA2............49 H6
LEYL PR25...........................186 C2
Balshaw St BBR PR5...............169 H1
Balshaw Ter
KIRK/FR/WAR PR4..............128 E7
Baltic Blds RAW/HAS BB4 *....196 B3
Baltic Rd RAW/HAS BB4.........196 B3
Baltimore Rd LSTA FY8...........145 L5
Bamber Av BISP FY2................84 F7
CHLY/EC PR7.......................187 H4
Bamber Gdns CHTN/BK PR9...200 D3
Bambers La BPOOLS FY4.......125 M5
Bambers La North
BPOOLS FY4.........................125 M4
Bamber St CHLY/EC PR7.......207 L6
Bamber's Wk
KIRK/FR/WAR PR4..............128 B4
Bamburgh Cl BPOOLS FY4.....125 K4
Bamburgh Dr PDHM/BLYW BB12.6 C1
Bamford Cl ROCH OL11..........234 E5
Bamford Crs ACC BB5.............160 A7
Bamford Ms ROCH OL11.........234 B4
Bamford Prec ROCH OL11 *....234 B4
Bamford Rd RAMS BL0...........215 H3
Bamfords Fold
CROS/BRETH PR26..............184 C6
Bamford St BLY BB11 *..............7 J6
LIT OL15...............................219 L4
NLSN BB9.............................123 K3
Bamford Wy ROCH OL11........234 C5
Bampton Dr
KIRK/FR/WAR PR4..............131 G7
Bampton Av BPOOLS FY4.......124 F4
Banastre CHLY/EC PR7..........207 L6
Banastre Rd STHP PR8............12 F8
Banastre St ACC BB5.............159 K2
Banastre St LIT OL15.............219 L5
BISP FY2..............................105 G3
Banbury Cl BBNW BB2...........172 C3
Banbury Dr FUL/RIB PR2........132 B7
Bangor Av HEY LA3..................41 M8
LSTA FY8..............................145 J5
Bargee Cl BBN BB1...................11 G7
Barham St BPOOL FY1..............4 D8

Bancroft Av CLV/TH FY5...........85 L1
Bancroft Fold
BRCK/EAR BB18..................293 P6
Bancroft Rd BRFD/BLYE BB10.142 F3
Bancroft St BBN BB1.................11 H4
Band La GAR/LONG PR3...........90 A7
Banham Av WGNS/IIMK WN3..255 M8
Bank Av WGNW/BIL/OR WN5..255 G6
Bank Barn La WHIT OL12........219 G4
Bank Bottom DWN BB3...........191 K2
Bank Brow SKEL WN8.............244 F6
Bank Cl HGHB LA2...................66 E7
KIRK/FR/WAR PR4..............166 D3
WHIT OL12............................219 K8
Bankcroft Cl
PDHM/BLYW BB12..............141 H3
Bankes Av
WGNW/BIL/OR WN5............255 K5
Bankfield BLY BB11....................7 G4
SKEL WN8............................253 M4
Bankfield Ct CLV/TH FY5...........85 L3
Bankfield Gv CHTN/BK PR9.....200 E1
ROCH OL11..........................234 B3
Bankfield La CHTN/BK PR9.....200 E1
Bank Fold NLSN BB9...............103 H6
Bankhall Ter BRFD/BLYE BB10...7 L1
Bank Head La BBR PR5...........169 M3
Bank Hey La North BBN BB1...137 J8
Bank Hey La South BBN BB1...157 K2
Bank Hey Vw BBNW BB2........172 A4
Bank House La BCUP OL13.....197 J1
CARN LA5...............................16 A1
Bankhouse Rd NLSN BB9.......123 H2
Bank House St NLSN BB9.......103 H7
Bankhouse St
PDHM/BLYW BB12..............6 F3
Bank La BBN BB1....................158 A7
KIRK/FR/WAR PR4..............147 M7
MGHL L31.............................259 M5
NWD/KWIPK L33..................260 A7
WHIT OL12............................218 F4
Bank Meadow HOR/BR BL6....231 M7
Bank Nook CHTN/BK PR9.......180 C8
Bank Pde BBN BB1 *.................7 G4
PRES PR1................................9 J6
Bank Pl FUL/RIB PR2...............151 M2
Bank Rd LANC LA1....................42 E8
SKEL WN8............................245 G6
Banksbarn SKEL WN8.............253 M4
Banks Bridge Cl
BWCK/EAR BB18..................293 R3
Banks Crs LSTA FY8...............52 E5
Banksfield Av FUL/RIB PR2.....131 M8
Banksfield Cl BBR PR5.............169 J4
Banks Hi BWCK/EAR BB18......293 P3
Bankside BBNW BB2.................10 E9
CHLYE PR6...........................187 L2
HTWN L38.............................247 J8
SKEL WN8............................243 L1
TOD OL14.............................303 L1
Bankside Cl BCUP OL13.........197 H2
Bankside La BCUP OL13.........197 H2
Bank Sq CHTN/BK PR9............13 G1
Banks Ri HGHB LA2.................39 G4
FUL/RIB PR2........................131 M8
Banks St BPOOL FY1..............104 E5
BRFD/BLYE BB10................253 L8
Bank St ACC BB5...................197 J1
BCUP OL13...........................197 J1
BWCK/EAR BB18..................293 R5
CHLY/EC PR7.......................230 C4
CHLY/EC PR7.......................207 M3
COL BB8................................296 F10
DWN BB3..............................191 K2
EDGW/EG BL7......................212 F7
NLSN BB9.............................122 E5
PDHM/BLYW BB12..............140 F2
RAMS BL0............................215 H4
RAW/HAS BB4......................176 E8
ROCH OL11..........................235 L2
TOD OL14.............................303 L3
Banks Wy HGHB LA2................39 G4
Bank Top BBNW BB2................10 B7
BLY BB11................................7 G3
Bankwell Cl SETT BD24..........265 M8
Bankwell Rd SETT BD24.........265 M8
Bankwood WGNNW/ST WN6...245 L4
Banner Cl CHLY/EC PR7.........145 J1
Bannerman Rd CHLYE PR6.....208 A1
Bannister Cl BBR PR5.............153 L7
COL BB8................................296 E6
Bannister Ct NLSN BB9 *........123 H4
Bannister Dr LEYL PR25.........186 B2
Bannister Gn CHLY/EC PR7....205 M8
Bannister Hall Crs BBR PR5....153 L7
Bannister Hall Dr BBR PR5......153 L7
Bannister Hall La BBR PR5......153 L7
Bannister La BRSC L40...........227 H5
CROS/BRETH PR26..............168 A7
Bannister's Bit PRES PR1 *.....9 M1
Bannister St CLV/TH FY5.........81 M7
LSTA FY8..............................146 E8
Bannistre Cl LSTA FY8............145 K3
Bannistre Ct
KIRK/FR/WAR PR4..............183 K5
Barathea St ROCH OL11.........234 D8
Barbara Castle Wy BBNW BB2..10 D3
Barberry Gv NTHTN L30...........258 D7
Barbondale Rd KKBYL LA6......14 C1
Barbon Pl LANC LA1.................42 E1
Barbrook Cl WGNNW/ST WN6..245 C4
Barclay Av BLY BB11................141 M7
BPOOLS FY4.........................5 L8
Barclay Rd GAR/LONG PR3.....114 D4
Barclyde St ROCH OL11..........235 H6
Barcroft Gn BRFD/BLYE BB10.163 H2
Barcroft Rd ACC BB5...............158 F7
Barden Cft ACC BB5...............139 J7
Barden La PDHM/BLYW BB12.122 C8
Barden Pl ACC BB5.................133 G7
Barden St ACC BB5.................139 J7
Bardsea Pl FUL/RIB PR2.........131 J8
Bardsley Cl BBNW BB2...........172 C3
Bardsway Av BPOOLE FY3.....105 H5
Bare Av MCMB LA4...................41 H5
Bare La MCMB LA4...................41 M5
Barehill St LIT OL15...............219 L5
Bare La MCMB LA4...................41 M5
Barford Cl SKEL WN8.............254 D4

Barker Brow GAR/LONG PR3...116 D8
Barker Cl KKBYL LA6................19 G5
Barkerfield Cl
PDHM/BLYW BB12..............121 H6
Barkerhouse Rd NLSN BB9.....123 J3
Barker La BBNW BB2..............156 E1
Barker St CLI BB7...................303 L1
BARKE ST LIT OL15...............219 H8
Barkfield Av FMBY L37............237 H7
Barkfield La FMBY L37............237 H7
Barley Bank St DWN BB3........191 J3
Barley Cl BBNW BB2.................10 C4
Barley Cop La LANC LA1...........42 B7
Barleydale Rd NLSN BB9.........103 H6
Barleyfield BBR PR5................169 M8
RAW/HAS BB4......................177 K3
Barley La BBN BB1...................10 C3
NLSN BB9.............................101 K2
Barley New Rd
PDHM/BLYW BB12..............102 A6
Barley St BBN BB1..................140 F4
Barlow Crs BLY BB11................5 J3
Barlow Moor Cl WHIT OL12.....234 B1
Barlow's La ORM L39..............222 A6
Barlow St ACC BB5.................159 K5
MILN OL16............................235 K4
PRES PR1................................9 H5
RAW/HAS BB4......................177 K8
Barmouth Av BPOOLE FY3.....125 K1
Barmouth St BBN BB1.............157 G2
Barmskin La CHLY/EC PR7.....227 L1
Barnacre Cl FUL/RIB PR2........132 D3
Barnacre Rd GAR/LONG PR3...114 D3
Barnard Cl ACC BB5...............158 F7
Barn Cl KIRK/FR/WAR PR4.....202 D1
Barn Cft CROS/BRETH PR26...185 L2
Barncroft Dr HOR/BR BL6......232 C8
Barnes Av RAW/HAS BB4.......195 J1
Barnes La CHLY/EC PR7........227 L1
Barnes Mdw LIT OL15............219 M2
Barnes Dr CLV/TH FY5.............81 L4
ORM L39...............................241 H8
Barnes Sq ACC BB5...............139 J8
Barnes St ACC BB5.................139 J8
BLY BB11................................7 G3
RAW/HAS BB4......................176 E7
TOD OL14.............................303 K6
Barnfield BBR PR5..................168 D3
KIRK/FR/WAR PR4..............184 B1
KIRK/FR/WAR PR4..............128 D6
Barnfield Av BRFD/BLYE BB10.143 J5
Barnfield Cl CLV/TH FY5...........81 J7
Barn Field Cl COL BB8............296 D6
Barnfield Dr SKEL WN8...........254 E4
Barn Field La WHIT OL12........218 D4
Barnfield Mnr BRFD/BLYE BB10.87 G8
Barnfield St ACC BB5..............160 A8
WHIT OL12...........................235 J1
Barnfield Wy ACC BB5............140 B6
Barnflatt Cl BBR PR5...............153 K7
Barn Gill Cl BBNW BB2.............11 M4
Barn Hay Dr
CROS/BRETH PR26..............168 B3
Barn Hey KIRK/FR/WAR PR4...166 D2
Barn Hey Dr
CROS/BRETH PR26..............168 B3
Barn Meadow BBR PR5...........169 L5
Barn Meadow La
GTH/LHO BB6......................138 D6
Barnmeadow La
GTH/LHO BB6......................138 D6
Barnoldswick La KKBYL LA6....31 J5
Barnoldswick Rd
BWCK/EAR BB18..................294 C9
NLSN BB9.............................103 J4
Barnsfold FUL/RIB PR2...........132 A5
Barnside CHLY/EC PR7...........186 F8
Barns La GAR/LONG PR3.........93 M4
Barn Vw CHLYE PR6...............230 C3
Barnwood Crs
BWCK/EAR BB18..................294 F6
Barnwood Rd
BWCK/EAR BB18..................294 E6
Baron Rd BPOOL FY1.................4 D9
Barons Dr DWN BB3...............173 K4
Barons Wy CHLY/EC PR7.......207 G1
DWN BB3..............................173 K5
GTH/LHO BB6......................235 J4
Barracks Rd BLY BB11.............195 A2
Barrel Sykes SETT BD24........265 N6
Barret Hill Brow CLI BB7.........276 G11
Barret St BWCK/EAR BB18.....294 D6
Barrett Av STHP PR8..............221 K1
Barrett Rd STHP PR8..............221 K1
Barrett St BRFD/BLYE BB10....142 D3
Barrington Cr ACC BB5...........159 J4
Barrington Dr STHP PR8..........200 C5
Barrison Dr BRSC L40.............241 H1
Barritt Rd RAW/HAS BB4........195 J1
Barrow Rd BOL BL1.................233 L4
Barrow Bridge Rd BOL BL1.....233 L4
Barrowford Rd COL BB8..........103 K6
NLSN BB9.............................122 F2
PDHM/BLYW BB12..............121 G8
Barrow Nook La ORM L39.......252 B8
Barrows La HEY LA3.................52 E3
Barrow's La GAR/LONG PR3.....88 E6
Barrows La East
GAR/LONG PR3.......................88 E6
Barry Av FUL/RIB PR2.............131 G4
Barry Gv HEY LA3....................52 E5
Barry St PDHM/BLYW BB12....141 G8
Bar St BRFD/BLYE BB10.........143 E3
TOD OL14.............................303 K3
Barton Av BPOOL FY1..............4 C7
PLF/KEOS FY6.......................78 B6
Barton Ct LANC LA1 *..............54 F7
Barton Heys Rd FMBY L37......247 G4
Barton La GAR/LONG PR3.......111 M3
Barton Rd LANC LA1.................54 F7
LSTA FY8..............................145 G3

Bartons Cl CHTN/BK PR9........181 G6
Barton Sq PLF/KEOS FY6.........78 B6
Barton St BBNW BB2.................10 B4
WGNW/BIL/OR WN5............255 K5
Bashall Gv LEYL PR25.............168 C8
Basil Ct MILN OL16.................235 M8
Basil St COL BB8....................296 A7
MILN OL16............................235 L5
PRES PR1..............................152 F1
Basnett St BRFD/BLYE BB10...142 F2
Bassenthwaite Av
NWD/KWIPK L33..................260 A7
Bassenthwaite Rd
BPOOLE FY3.........................125 L1
Bassett Wy WHIT OL12...........235 H1
Bass La BURY BL9..................215 H8
Bastwell Rd BBN BB1.............157 J4
Bateman Gv MCMB LA4...........41 J8
Bateman Rd MCMB LA4...........41 J8
Bates St ACC BB5..................139 H8
Bathgate Wy NWD/KWIPK L33.260 C7
Bath Mill La LANC LA1................3 J7
Bath Mill Sq LANC LA1..............3 J7
Bath Rd LSTA FY8..................146 E8
Bath Springs ORM L39...........241 H6
Bath St ACC BB5....................159 L7
BBNW BB2.............................10 A6
BCUP OL13...........................197 K1
BPOOLS FY4.........................124 E2
CHTN/BK PR9.......................13 G2
COL BB8................................296 B6
DWN BB3..............................191 K2
FUL/RIB PR2 *.......................8 C1
LANC LA1................................3 J6
LSTA FY8..............................146 E8
MCMB LA4.............................41 H6
NLSN BB9.............................123 J3
TOD OL14.............................303 L1
WHIT OL12...........................235 K2
Bath St North CHTN/BK PR9....13 H1
Bathurst Av BPOOLE FY3.......105 K4
Bathurst St BBNW BB2.............10 D3
Batridge Rd EDGW/EG BL7.....212 D4
Battersby St ROCH OL11........234 D5
Battismore Rd MCMB LA4.......41 H6
Battle Wy FMBY L37...............247 L1
The Baum MILN OL16.............235 J4
Bawdlands CLI BB7..................99 G3
Bawhead Rd BWCK/EAR BB18.294 E6
Baxendale St BBR PR5............169 H2
Baxtergate MCMB LA4..............41 J5
Bayard St PDHM/BLYW BB12 *.141 K5
Baycliffe Crs MCMB LA4 *.........41 H6
Bay Cl HEY LA3........................52 C4
Bay Horse La LANC LA1...........55 G8
Bay Horse La
KIRK/FR/WAR PR4..............109 M7
Bay Horse Rd HGHB LA2.........270 D1
Bayley Fold CLI BB7.................99 H3
Bayley St ACC BB5.................139 H8
Bayliss Cl HOR/BR BL6...........232 A7
Baylton Dr GAR/LONG PR3......91 G1
Baynes St DWN BB3...............192 C2
Bay New Dr HEY LA3................52 E3
Bay Rd FUL/RIB PR2................131 J4
HEY LA3.................................52 C5
Bayside FTWD FY7..................77 L7
Bay St BBN BB1......................157 K4
Bayswater BISP FY2................84 F7
The Bay CLV/TH FY5.................85 M8
Baytree Cl BBR PR5................168 F3
CHTN/BK PR9.......................181 G5
Bay Tree Farm FUL/RIB PR2 *..151 G3
Baytree Gv MGHL L31............259 K8
Bay Tree Rd CHLYE PR6..........169 L8
Baytree Wk WHIT OL12..........217 M2
Bay Vw KKBYL LA6..................34 B3
Bay View Ct LANC LA1 *...........2 E6
Bay View Crs HGHB LA2...........42 D3
Baywood St BBN BB1.............157 J4
Bazil Gv HEY LA3.....................65 J4
Bazil La HEY LA3......................65 J4
Bazley Rd LSTA FY8...............146 A8
Bazley St BOL BL1..................233 J8
Beacham Rd STHP PR8..........200 B4
Beach Av CLV/TH FY5..............81 G8
LSTA FY8..............................145 M8
Beachcomber Dr CLV/TH FY5...80 F8
Beach Ct LSTA FY8 *...............146 F8
Beachley Rd FUL/RIB PR2.......131 J4
Beachley Sq PDHM/BLYW BB12..6 C1
Beach Priory Gdns STHP PR8...12 D5
Beach Rd CLV/TH FY5...............80 F8
FTWD FY7..............................77 H7
LSTA FY8..............................145 G4
PLF/KEOS FY6.......................78 E4
Beach St LSTA FY8.................146 F8
MCMB LA4.............................41 M4
Beachwood La CARN LA5.........16 C2
Beacon Av FUL/RIB PR2.........132 A7
Beacon Cl COL BB8.................103 M8
Beacon Crossing SKEL WN8 *.243 M1
Beacon Dr GAR/LONG PR3......113 G5
Beacon Gv FUL/RIB PR2.........132 A7
GAR/LONG PR3.......................284 A9
Beacon La SKEL WN8.............243 K5
Beacon Rd PLF/KEOS FY6.......86 D8
WGNNW/ST WN6.................245 L1
Beaconsfield Av PRES PR1.....153 J2
Beaconsfield St CHTN/BK PR9.200 C5
Beaconsfield St ACC BB5.......160 A6
GTH/LHO BB6......................138 C5
RAW/HAS BB4......................138 D5
TOD OL14.............................303 M2
Beaconsfield Ter CHLYE PR6....91 H1
GAR/LONG PR3.......................91 H1
The Beacons WGNNW/ST WN6.245 G4
Beacon St CHLY/EC PR7.........208 A4
Beacon Vw WGNNW/ST WN6..244 F3
Beacon View Dr SKEL WN8.....254 E4
Beadle Av WHIT OL12.............219 G6
Beaford Cl
WGNW/BIL/OR WN5............255 L6
Beal Crs MILN OL16................235 M2
Beale Cl BBN BB1...................173 L2
Beale Rd NLSN BB9................122 E3
Beamish Av BBNW BB2...........173 G3
Beamont Dr PRES PR1..............8 C2
Bean Av BPOOLS FY4.............125 H3
Beardshaw Av BPOOL FY1........5 H8
Beardsworth St BBN BB1.........157 K3
Beardwood Brow BBNW BB2...156 D3
Beardwood Dr BBNW BB2.......156 D5
Beardwood Fold BBNW BB2....156 D3
Beardwood Meadow
BBNW BB2............................156 D3
Beardwood Pk BBNW BB2.......156 E4
Bearncroft SKEL WN8.............253 M5

Bear St *PDHM/BLYW* BB12 141 H5
Bearswood Cft *CHLYE* PR6 187 L1
Bearwood Wy *CLV/TH* FY5 85 M1
Beatie St *NLSN* BB9 * 122 E5
Beatrice Av *PDHM/BLYW* BB12 141 M4
Beatrice Pl *BBNW* BB2 173 K3
Beatrice St *HOR/BR* BL6 231 L7
ROCH OL11 235 G4
Beattock Cl *NWD/KWIPK* L33 260 A5
Beattock Pl *BISP* FY2 85 J5
Beatty Av *CHLY/EC* PR7 207 L5
Beatty Cl *LSTA* FY8 145 G2
Beatty Rd *STHP* PR8 200 B6
Beauclerk Rd *LSTA* FY8 145 K5
Beaufort *FMBY* L37 247 K1
Beaufort Av *BISP* FY2 84 F6
Beaufort Cl *ORM* L39 250 D2
PDHM/BLYW BB12 140 B1
Beaufort Gv *MCMB* LA4 41 L6
Beaufort Rd *BCUP* OL13 179 K4
MCMB LA4 41 M6
Beaufort St *NLSN* BB9 123 G4
WHIT OL12 235 G2
Beauley Av *PDHM/BLYW* BB12 140 B1
Beaumaris Av *BBNW* BB2 172 D2
Beaumaris Rd *LEYL* PR25 186 F3
Beaumonds Wy *ROCH* OL11 234 C5
Beaumont Av *HOR/BR* BL6 231 M7
Beaumont Cl *LIT* OL15 219 J6
Beaumont Crs *ORM* L39 251 G1
Beaumont Gdns *PLF/KEOS* FY6 85 K6
Beaumont Gv
WGNW/BIL/OR WN5 255 L3
Beaumont Pl *LANC* LA1 42 E7
Beaumont Rd *HOR/BR* BL6 231 L7
Beaumont St *LANC* LA1 42 E7
TOD OL14 303 K1
Beaumont Wy *DWN* BB3 192 A3
Beaver Cl *BBN* BB1 137 J6
Beavers La *SKEL* WN8 254 A5
Beaver Ter *BCUP* OL13 179 K8
Bebles Rd *ORM* L39 240 F8
Becconsall La
KIRK/FR/WAR PR4 165 J8
Beck Ct *FTWD* FY7 81 G2
Beckdean Av *PLF/KEOS* FY6 106 A1
Beckenham Ct
BRFD/BLYE BB10 123 G8
Beckett Ct *PRES* PR1 9 H1
Beck Gv *CLV/TH* FY5 81 H7
Beck Head *KKBYL* LA6 21 L1
Becks Brow *SKP/WHF* BD23 267 J10
Beckside *COL* BB8 296 E8
Beck Side *HGHB* LA2 44 D6
Beck Vw *LANC* LA1 * 54 F8
Beckway Av *BPOOLE* FY3 105 J4
Bective Rd *KKBYL* LA6 21 L1
Bedale Pl *CLV/TH* FY5 85 H2
Beddington St *NLSN* BB9 * 123 G2
Bedford Av *CLV/TH* FY5 81 G7
MGHL L31 259 H5
Bedford Cl *ACC* BB5 158 F7
Bedford Ms *DWN* BB3 173 J7
Bedford Pl *LANC* LA1 54 F7
PDHM/BLYW BB12 141 G4
Bedford Rd *BPOOL* FY1 104 F3
FUL/RIB PR2 132 D7
LSTA FY8 147 G7
STHP PR8 221 K1
Bedfordshire Av
PDHM/BLYW BB12 141 L4
Bedford St *BBNW* BB2 172 F1
DWN BB3 173 J7
NLSN BB9 122 F2
TOD OL14 300 H12
WGNW/BIL/OR WN5 * 255 M6
Bedford Ter *RAW/HAS* BB4 194 D3
Beechacre *RAMS* BL0 215 G6
Beecham St *MCMB* LA4 41 J5
Beech Av *BPOOLE* FY3 5 J1
BWCK/EAR BB18 294 D6
CHLY/EC PR7 186 E8
CHLYE PR6 230 E3
CSBY/BLUN L23 257 K5
DWN BB3 191 L1
GAR/LONG PR3 91 K6
HGHB LA2 66 E7
KIRK/FR/WAR PR4 148 A5
KIRK/FR/WAR PR4 128 D7
LEYL PR25 186 D3
MGHL L31 259 L8
PLF/KEOS FY6 86 A7
SKEL WN8 243 M1
TOD OL14 303 K1
Beech Cl *ACC* BB5 174 F1
BBN BB1 158 E3
BBN BB1 137 H5
BCUP OL13 179 K8
BRSC L40 203 M7
CLI BB7 99 G3
KKBY L32 259 M8
SKEL WN8 253 H2
WHIT OL12 217 M2
Beech Crs *ACC* BB5 159 K2
Beechcroft *CLV/TH* FY5 * 80 F7
Beech Dr *CLI* BB7 118 D4
FMBY L37 237 G7
FUL/RIB PR2 132 A3
GAR/LONG PR3 114 D4
KIRK/FR/WAR PR4 148 D6
KIRK/FR/WAR PR4 128 B7
PLF/KEOS FY6 106 A1
RAW/HAS BB4 194 F1
Beeches Cl *SKP/WHF* BD23 281 J3
Beeches Ct *CLV/TH* FY5 85 M2
The Beeches *CHLYE* PR6 169 M8
KIRK/FR/WAR PR4 183 K4
PLF/KEOS FY6 107 G2
Beechfield *LANC* LA1 2 C6
MGHL L31 259 H2
SKEL WN8 226 F6
Beechfield Av *BPOOLE* FY3 5 J6
KIRK/FR/WAR PR4 127 M8
PLF/KEOS FY6 78 D6
Beechfield Cl *ROCH* OL11 234 B5
Beechfield Ct *LEYL* PR25 186 E3
Beechfield Gdns *STHP* PR8 12 D5
Beechfield Rd *LEYL* PR25 186 D4
Beechfields *CHLY/EC* PR7 205 L5
Beech Gdns *CHLYE* PR6 187 L2
RNFD/HAY WA11 262 B4
Beech Gv *ACC* BB5 159 K7
BRFD/BLYE BB10 122 F7
CHTN/BK PR9 200 B4
CLI BB7 291 J10
CLI BB7 290 C8
DWN BB3 173 G5
FUL/RIB PR2 151 L2
MCMB LA4 41 M6
PLF/KEOS FY6 78 B5
Beech Hill Cl *BBR* PR5 153 H8
Beeching Cl *LANC* LA1 * 54 E5
Beech Meadow *ORM* L39 241 K7
Beech Mt *BBN* BB1 137 J8
Beech Rd *GAR/LONG* PR3 284 A7
HGHB LA2 43 K4
KIRK/FR/WAR PR4 108 C2
LEYL PR25 186 D1
ORM L39 250 D5
Beech St *ACC* BB5 159 M6
BBN BB1 157 K4
BCUP OL13 179 K8
BURY BL9 214 F8
CLI BB7 99 G3
EDGW/EG BL7 213 G6
GTH/LHO BB6 138 F5
LANC LA1 2 D5
NLSN BB9 123 H2
PDHM/BLYW BB12 141 G4
PRES PR1 8 D6
RAW/HAS BB4 177 J8
ROCH OL11 235 G5
Beech St South *PRES* PR1 8 E7
Beech Ter *PRES* PR1 8 E7
Beechthorpe Av *CLI* BB7 290 A11
Beech Tree Av
WGNNW/ST WN6 245 G3
Beech Tree Cl *CARN* LA5 32 F7
NLSN BB9 123 H4
Beechtrees *SKEL* WN8 253 M4
Beechway *FUL/RIB* PR2 * 132 D7
MGHL L31 259 L1
PRES PR1 151 L8
Beechway Av *MGHL* L31 259 K1
Beechwood *SKEL* WN8 243 M8
Beechwood Av *ACC* BB5 160 A8
BBR PR5 152 F7
BLY BB11 6 D9
CLI BB7 99 H5
FUL/RIB PR2 131 M7
LIT OL15 219 K8
RAMS BL0 215 C5
WGNNW/ST WN6 245 J6
Beechwood Ct *CHLY/EC* PR7 * 229 J3
Beechwood Crs
WGNW/BIL/OR WN5 255 H5
Beechwood Cft *CHLYE* PR6 169 K8
Beechwood Dr *BBNW* BB2 172 B3
CLV/TH FY5 85 L3
FMBY L37 246 F2
ORM L39 241 G7
Beechwood Gdns *LANC* LA1 66 F1
Beechwood Gv *BISP* FY2 85 H6
Beechwood Ms *BBNW* BB2 173 K3
Beechwood Rd *BBN* BB1 157 K4
Beecroft La *SKP/WHF* BD23 267 M9
Beeford Dr
WGNW/BIL/OR WN5 255 H6
Bee La *PRES* PR1 168 A2
Beenland St *PRES* PR1 153 G2
Beeston Av *PLF/KEOS* FY6 85 M6
Beeston Dr *NTHTN* L30 258 E6
Beetham Ct *ACC* BB5 139 H8
Beetham Pl *BPOOLE* FY3 105 H5
Beethamway *NWD/KWIPK* L33 260 C8
Begonia St *DWN* BB3 191 L2
Begonia Vw *DWN* BB3 173 K4
Bela Cl *LANC* LA1 * 2 A2
Bela Gv *BPOOL* FY1 4 F7
Beldale Pk *KKBY* L32 259 M7
Belfield *SKEL* WN8 254 A5
Belfield Cl *MILN* OL16 235 M3
Belfield La *MILN* OL16 235 M4
Belfield Mill La *MILN* OL16 235 M3
Belfield Old Rd *MILN* OL16 235 M3
Belfield Rd *ACC* BB5 159 L6
MILN OL16 235 L3
Belford Av *CLV/TH* FY5 81 J7
Belford St *PDHM/BLYW* BB12 6 F1
Belfry Cl *CHLY/EC* PR7 187 G7
Belfry Man *GTH/LHO* BB6 * 117 M5
The Belfry *DWN* BB3 * 191 M3
LSTA FY8 147 G6
Belgarth Rd *ACC* BB5 159 M4
Belgium St *ROCH* OL11 234 B4
Belgrave Av *KIRK/FR/WAR* PR4 128 D4
PRES PR1 151 L8
Belgrave Cl *LSTA* FY8 146 A5
Belgrave Ct *FUL/RIB* PR2 * 132 E4
Belgrave Crs *HOR/BR* BL6 232 A8
Belgrave Pl *PLF/KEOS* FY6 105 L1
Belgrave Rd *BPOOLS* FY4 5 K9
COL BB8 296 A5
DWN BB3 191 J3
LEYL PR25 186 D3
PLF/KEOS FY6 105 L1
STHP PR8 199 J7
Belgrave Sq *DWN* BB3 * 191 K2
Belgrave St *ACC* BB5 176 D3
NLSN BB9 122 D6
PDHM/BLYW BB12 * 6 F1
WHIT OL12 234 F2
Bellair Av *CSBY/BLUN* L23 257 K7
Bellamy Av *MCMB* LA4 41 H8
Belle Field Cl *PRES* PR1 168 D1
Belle Hl *SETT* BD24 265 M6
Belle Isle Av *WHIT* OL12 217 M5
Belle View Pl *BPOOLE* FY3 5 H2
Belle Vue Av *LANC* LA1 54 F5
Belle Vue Dr *LANC* LA1 54 F5
Belle Vue La *CLI* BB7 290 A11
Belle Vue Pl *BLY* BB11 6 D4
BPOOLE FY3 5 H2
Belle Vue St *BBNW* BB2 10 A4
BLY BB11 * 6 D4
Bellfield Rd *MCMB* LA4 41 K6
Bellflower Cl *LEYL* PR25 169 H8
Bellingham Rd *LSTA* FY8 146 E6
Bellis Av *CHTN/BK* PR9 200 B1
Bellis Gv *NWD/KWIPK* L33 * 260 A6
Bellis Wy *BBR* PR5 168 E1
Bell La *ACC* BB5 139 L7
GAR/LONG PR3 284 G11
WGNW/BIL/OR WN5 255 L3
Bell's Ar *BRFD/BLYE* BB10 142 D3
Bell's Br *GAR/LONG* PR3 283 Q5
Bell's Cl *MGHL* L31 249 L7
Bellshill Crs *MILN* OL16 235 M2
Bells La *BBR* PR5 170 B1
Bell's La *MGHL* L31 249 K8
Bell St *MILN* OL16 235 J3
RAW/HAS BB4 176 E8
Belmont Av *BPOOL* FY1 4 E5
FUL/RIB PR2 133 G8
PLF/KEOS FY6 85 L8
WGNW/BIL/OR WN5 255 G8
Belmont Cl *BRSC* L40 225 H8
CHLYE PR6 189 H3
FUL/RIB PR2 153 G1
LANC LA1 42 C8
Belmont Ct *GAR/LONG* PR3 114 E4
Belmont Crs *FUL/RIB* PR2 153 G1
Belmont Dr *CHLYE* PR6 208 B2
Belmont Gv *BRFD/BLYE* BB10 143 G6
Belmont Pl *CHLY/EC* PR7 228 F5
Belmont Rd *CHLYE* PR6 230 E4
CHLYE PR6 190 C6
EDGW/EG BL7 211 G8
FTWD FY7 77 K8
FUL/RIB PR2 151 M1
GTH/LHO BB6 138 E6
HOR/BR BL6 231 M2
LEYL PR25 186 A2
LSTA FY8 145 M6
Belmont St *STHP* PR8 12 E6
Belmont Wy *WHIT* OL12 235 H1
Belper St *BBN* BB1 11 J1
Belsfield Dr *KIRK/FR/WAR* PR4 165 H7
Belthorn Rd *BBN* BB1 174 C5
Belton Av *MILN* OL16 235 M2
Belton Hl *FUL/RIB* PR2 132 A3
Belvedere Av *RAW/HAS* BB4 196 D2
Belvedere Dr *CHLY/EC* PR7 207 L3
FMBY L37 247 J2
Belvedere Pk *ORM* L39 250 F4
Belvedere Rd *BBN* BB1 137 K8
BRFD/BLYE BB10 7 J4
CHLYE PR6 230 E3
CLV/TH FY5 85 M3
LEYL PR25 186 E1
STHP PR8 220 F6
Belverdale Gdns *BPOOLS* FY4 125 J6
Belvere Av *BPOOLS* FY4 125 G6
Belvidere Pk *CSBY/BLUN* L23 257 H8
Belvidere Rd *CSBY/BLUN* L23 257 G8
Belvoir Mdw *MILN* OL16 219 H7
Belvoir St *WHIT* OL12 235 G2
Benbow Cl *LSTA* FY8 145 G2
Bence Rd *PRES* PR1 9 M5
Bence St *COL* BB8 296 B6
Bench Carr *WHIT* OL12 235 H2
Benenden Pl *CLV/TH* FY5 * 85 K1
Bengal St *CHLY/EC* PR7 207 M2
Bengarth Rd *CHTN/BK* PR9 200 C3
Ben La *BWCK/EAR* BB18 294 A4
ORM L39 261 K1
Ben Lane Ct *ORM* L39 261 L1
Bennett Av *BPOOL* FY1 4 F3
Bennett Dr
WGNW/BIL/OR WN5 255 G7
Bennett Rd *CLV/TH* FY5 81 K8
Bennett's La *BPOOLS* FY4 125 J5
Bennett St *NLSN* BB9 123 J1
Bennington St *BBNW* BB2 11 H8
Benson Av *MCMB* LA4 41 L7
Benson La *KIRK/FR/WAR* PR4 110 A8
Benson Rd *BPOOLE* FY3 105 H2
Benson's La *KIRK/FR/WAR* PR4 110 F2
Benson St *BBN* BB1 157 L4
EDGW/EG BL7 213 G6
Bent Gap La *BBNW* BB2 10 A5
Bentham Av *BRFD/BLYE* BB10 122 E8
FTWD FY7 80 F2
Bentham Cl *BBNW* BB2 172 E2
Bentham Moor Rd *KKBYL* LA6 31 J7
Bentham Rd *BBNW* BB2 172 E2
HGHB LA2 31 L8
LANC LA1 66 F1
Bentham St *CHLY/EC* PR7 229 H2
STHP PR8 13 G7
Bentham's Wy *STHP* PR8 221 M1
Bentinck Av *BPOOLS* FY4 124 E6
Bentinck Dr *KKBYL* LA6 21 M2
Bentinck Rd *LSTA* FY8 144 F3
Bentinck St *WHIT* OL12 234 F2
Bent La *COL* BB8 296 E5
LEYL PR25 186 E2
Bentlea Rd *CLI* BB7 292 E1
Bentley Dr *BPOOLS* FY4 126 D5
KIRK/FR/WAR PR4 128 B6
Bentley Gn *CLV/TH* FY5 86 A1
Bentley La *BRSC* L40 227 G4
CHLY/EC PR7 227 L2
Bentley Mnr *FUL/RIB* PR2 * 153 J1
Bentley Ms *WHIT* OL12 * 235 H1
Bentley Park Rd
KIRK/FR/WAR PR4 166 C4
Bentley St *BBN* BB1 157 M6
BCUP OL13 179 K8
DWN BB3 191 L4
NLSN BB9 123 G4
WHIT OL12 235 H1
Bentley Wood Wy *BLY* BB11 141 H7
Bentmeadows *WHIT* OL12 235 H2
Benton Rd *FUL/RIB* PR2 133 G7
Bents *COL* BB8 * 296 E5
Bents Farm Cl *LIT* OL15 * 219 J6
Bent St *ACC* BB5 159 G8
BBNW BB2 10 D5
RAW/HAS BB4 195 G3
Bentwood Rd *RAW/HAS* BB4 176 D8
Beresford Dr *CHTN/BK* PR9 200 C2
Beresford Gdns *CHTN/BK* PR9 200 C1
Beresford Rd *BBN* BB1 157 G4
Beresford St *BLY* BB11 6 A5
BPOOL FY1 104 F4
Bergen St *BLY* BB11 141 L6
Bergerac Crs *CLV/TH* FY5 85 J5
Berkeley Cl *CHLY/EC* PR7 208 A6
NLSN BB9 * 123 H4
Berkeley Crs
PDHM/BLYW BB12 140 F2
Berkeley Dr *BBR* PR5 169 H7
MILN OL16 235 L7
PDHM/BLYW BB12 140 A1
Berkeley Rd *CSBY/BLUN* L23 256 F6
Berkeley St *NLSN* BB9 122 D6
PRES PR1 152 B2
Berkley Cl *KIRK/FR/WAR* PR4 128 B6
Berkley Wk *LIT* OL15 219 J6
Berkshire Av
PDHM/BLYW BB12 141 L4
Berkshire Cl *BBN* BB1 137 J5
Bernard St *WHIT* OL12 218 B8
Berne Av *HOR/BR* BL6 231 K8
Berridge Av
PDHM/BLYW BB12 141 K5
Berriedale Rd *NLSN* BB9 123 K2
Berry Cl *SKEL* WN8 253 J1
Berry Fld *PRES* PR1 151 M8
Berry House Rd *BRSC* L40 202 D7
Berry La *GAR/LONG* PR3 114 D4
Berrys La *CLI* BB7 138 F1
Berry's La *PLF/KEOS* FY6 85 M7
Berry St *BBR* PR5 168 D3
BLY BB11 6 F8
CHLYE PR6 230 D3
NLSN BB9 * 122 E6
PRES PR1 9 K5
SKEL WN8 253 H1
Bertha Rd *MILN* OL16 235 M4
Bertha St *ACC* BB5 160 A5
Bertie St *ROCH* OL11 235 G7
Bertram Av *MCMB* LA4 41 H7
Bertrand Av *BPOOLE* FY3 105 K4
Berwick Av *CLV/TH* FY5 81 J7
STHP PR8 220 F5
Berwick Dr *CSBY/BLUN* L23 256 F6
FUL/RIB PR2 132 A7
PDHM/BLYW BB12 6 C1
Berwick Rd *BPOOLS* FY4 124 F7
LSTA FY8 145 J4
PRES PR1 9 J5
Berwick St *MILN* OL16 235 L5
PRES PR1 * 153 H2
Berwick Wy *HEY* LA3 52 D4
Berwyn Av *MCMB* LA4 41 L6
Berwyn Cl *HOR/BR* BL6 231 M6
Beryl Av *BBN* BB1 157 J1
CLV/TH FY5 85 H2
Besant Cl *BBN* BB1 173 L1
Bescar Brow La *BRSC* L40 223 H4
Bescar La *BRSC* L40 223 K3
Bescot Wy *CLV/TH* FY5 85 J4
Bessie St *BWCK/EAR* BB18 293 Q5
Best St *KIRK/FR/WAR* PR4 128 C6
Beswicke Royds St *MILN* OL16 235 L2
Beswicke St *LIT* OL15 219 M6
WHIT OL12 235 H3
Beswick St *TOD* OL14 303 K8
Bethel Av *BISP* FY2 85 G7
Bethel Gn *LIT* OL15 * 219 M2
Bethel Rd *BBN* BB1 157 K4
Bethel St *BWCK/EAR* BB18 293 Q4
Bethesda Cl *BBNW* BB2 10 D8
Bethesda Rd *BPOOL* FY1 4 D4
Bethesda St *BLY* BB11 6 F4
BWCK/EAR BB18 293 Q6
Betony *MCMB* LA4 42 A4
Betony Cl *WHIT* OL12 218 A8
Bett La *CHLYE* PR6 188 F2
Betula Ms *ROCH* OL11 234 A2
Beulah Av *MCMB* LA4 41 L6
Bevan Pl *NLSN* BB9 123 J1
Beverley Av *PLF/KEOS* FY6 106 A3
Beverley Cl *CHTN/BK* PR9 180 F6
FUL/RIB PR2 8 B1
KIRK/FR/WAR PR4 127 K8
Beverley Dr *CLI* BB7 99 G5
Beverley Gv *BPOOLS* FY4 124 F4
Beverley Pl *MILN* OL16 235 K3
Beverley Rd *NLSN* BB9 103 H3
WGNW/BIL/OR WN5 255 L3
Beverley Rd North *LSTA* FY8 145 K3
Beverley Rd South *LSTA* FY8 145 K3
Beverley St *BBNW* BB2 172 E2
BLY BB11 6 C6
Beverly Cl *CLV/TH* FY5 85 L3
Beverston *ROCH* OL11 * 235 H5
Bevington Cl *BLY* BB11 6 D5
Bewcastle Dr *BRSC* L40 241 L8
Bexhill Rd *FUL/RIB* PR2 131 K8
Bexley Av *BISP* FY2 105 G3
Bexley Pl *LSTA* FY8 146 A6
Bezza La *BBNW* BB2 134 E7
Bhailok St *PRES* PR1 8 E2
Bibby Dr *BPOOLE* FY3 106 B7
Bibby Rd *CHTN/BK* PR9 200 D2
Bickerstaffe St *BPOOL* FY1 4 C5
Bickerton Rd *STHP* PR8 199 J7
Bicknell St *BBN* BB1 10 E2
Bideford Av *BPOOLE* FY3 105 K5
Bideford Rd *ROCH* OL11 234 E8
Bidston St *PRES* PR1 153 H3
Bigdale Dr *NWD/KWIPK* L33 260 D8
Biggins La *KKBYL* LA6 21 J4
Biggins Rd *KKBYL* LA6 21 L2
Bilberry St *MILN* OL16 235 K5
Billinge Av *BBNW* BB2 156 D6
Billinge Cl *BBNW* BB2 156 E6
Billinge End Rd *BBNW* BB2 155 L6
Billinge La *ORM* L39 251 H6
Billinge Rd *WGNS/IIMK* WN3 255 M7
Billinge St *BBN* BB1 11 K5
Billington Av *RAW/HAS* BB4 177 K4
Billington Ct *FUL/RIB* PR2 134 A2
Billington Gdns *CLI* BB7 118 D7
Billington Rd *BLY* BB11 141 K8
Billington St
KIRK/FR/WAR PR4 128 C5
Billington St East
KIRK/FR/WAR PR4 128 C5
Bilsborough Hey *PRES* PR1 168 B2
Bilsborough Meadow
FUL/RIB PR2 131 H8
Bilsborrow La *GAR/LONG* PR3 91 L7
Binbrook Pl *CHLY/EC* PR7 207 K3
Binfold Cft *KKBYL* LA6 21 M2
Bingley Av *BPOOLE* FY3 105 J5
Bingley Cl *CHLYE* PR6 187 M1
Bingley Rd *MILN* OL16 235 M4
Bingley Sq *MILN* OL16 235 M4
Bingley Ter *MILN* OL16 235 M4
Binns Nook Rd *WHIT* OL12 235 K1
Binns St *RAW/HAS* BB4 177 K4
Binyon Ct *LANC* LA1 54 E5
Binyon Rd *LANC* LA1 54 E5
Birbeck Rd *NWD/KWIPK* L33 260 D8
Birch Av *BRSC* L40 225 H7
CHLY/EC PR7 186 F7
CLV/TH FY5 85 H1
FUL/RIB PR2 151 K1
HGHB LA2 66 E7
KIRK/FR/WAR PR4 129 J8
LEYL PR25 160 H10
PRES PR1 151 K8
RAW/HAS BB4 176 F8
TOD OL14 301 K12
WHIT OL12 219 G7
Birchbank Gdns *BBN* BB1 157 K4
Birch Cl *ACC* BB5 160 B1
MGHL L31 259 J2
WHIT OL12 217 M6
Birch Crs *ACC* BB5 159 J8
BBR PR5 170 B2
Birch Dr *CARN* LA5 16 E7
Birchenlee La *COL* BB8 296 A8
Birches Rd *EDGW/EG* BL7 213 G7
The Birches *FMBY* L37 237 H6
Birch Fld *CHLYE* PR6 169 L8
Birchfield *KIRK/FR/WAR* PR4 166 B8
Birchfield Dr *GAR/LONG* PR3 114 D3
ROCH OL11 234 F6
Birchfield Wy *MGHL* L31 249 L6
Birch Gn *FMBY* L37 237 G6
Birch Green Rd *SKEL* WN8 243 L8
Birch Gv *CARN* LA5 16 C3
CLI BB7 119 G3
LANC LA1 2 C5
PLF/KEOS FY6 83 G4
RAMS BL0 214 D8
Birch Hall Av *DWN* BB3 173 H7
Birch Hall La *BWCK/EAR* BB18 294 G5
Birch Hey Cl *WHIT* OL12 218 F7
Birch Hill Crs *WHIT* OL12 219 G7
Birch Hill La *WHIT* OL12 219 G5
Birchin La *CHLYE* PR6 188 A2
Birch La *GAR/LONG* PR3 93 M3
Birchley Av
WGNW/BIL/OR WN5 263 M8
Birchley Rd *RNFD/HAY* WA11 263 L8
Birch Mt *WHIT* OL12 219 H7
Birchover Cl *FUL/RIB* PR2 131 K6
Birch Rd *CHLY/EC* PR7 229 H2
CHLYE PR6 208 A1
GAR/LONG PR3 284 A6
WHIT OL12 218 F5
Birch's Brow *ORM* L39 250 B1
Birch St *ACC* BB5 * 159 L5
BCUP OL13 179 J8
FTWD FY7 77 K7
LSTA FY8 146 F8
SKEL WN8 253 H2
STHP PR8 199 L8
WHIT OL12 218 F5
Birchtree Av *HEY* LA3 52 F2
Birchtree Dr *MGHL* L31 259 K8
Birch Tree Gdns *BPOOLE* FY3 125 L1
Birch Wk *BBN* BB1 11 M5
TOD OL14 * 303 L1
Birch Wy *PLF/KEOS* FY6 85 M7
Birchway Av *BPOOLE* FY3 105 H5
Birchwood *CROS/BRETH* PR26 185 L2
Birchwood Av
KIRK/FR/WAR PR4 166 E2
Birchwood Cl *LSTA* FY8 146 B7
SETT BD24 265 N8
Birchwood Dr *CHLY/EC* PR7 207 H8
FUL/RIB PR2 132 A4
PLF/KEOS FY6 86 F1
Birchwood Wy
NWD/KWIPK L33 260 D6
Bird St *NLSN* BB9 122 E6
PRES PR1 8 D7
Birkacre Brow *CHLY/EC* PR7 229 J1
Birkacre Rd *CHLY/EC* PR7 207 J7
Birkbeck Pl *FTWD* FY7 81 G1
Birkbeck Wy *BRFD/BLYE* BB10 142 D2
Birkdale Av *BISP* FY2 85 H6
FTWD FY7 81 H4
KIRK/FR/WAR PR4 166 C3
LSTA FY8 145 J2
Birkdale Cl *CHLY/EC* PR7 187 G7
CLV/TH FY5 86 A2
KIRK/FR/WAR PR4 166 C3
LANC LA1 42 C8
Birkdale Cop *STHP* PR8 222 B2
Birkdale Dr *FUL/RIB* PR2 151 H1
Birkdale Rd *MILN* OL16 235 M7
Birkenshaw Av
CSBY/BLUN L23 256 E7
Birkett Dr *FUL/RIB* PR2 133 K8
Birkett Pl *FUL/RIB* PR2 133 K8
Birkett Rd *ACC* BB5 159 M4
Birkey La *FMBY* L37 247 J1
Birklands Av *MCMB* LA4 41 K7
Birkrig *SKEL* WN8 254 A5
Birks Brow *GAR/LONG* PR3 95 G8
Birkside Wy *BPOOLS* FY4 125 M2
Birks La *TOD* OL14 303 L7
Birk St *PRES* PR1 8 F4
Birkwith La *HGHB* LA2 38 E6
Birley Bank *PRES* PR1 152 F3
Birley Cl *WGNNW/ST* WN6 245 J3
Birley Pl *BRFD/BLYE* BB10 142 D3
Birley St *BBN* BB1 11 H2
BPOOL FY1 4 C1
KIRK/FR/WAR PR4 128 E6
PRES PR1 9 H3
WHIT OL12 235 K2
Birleywood *SKEL* WN8 254 A5
Birnam Gn *FTWD* FY7 77 H7
Birtwhistle Cl *NLSN* BB9 * 122 E6
Birtwistle Av *COL* BB8 103 M5
Birtwistle Cl *NLSN* BB9 122 E6
Birtwistle Hyde Pk *COL* BB8 * 296 A6
Birtwistle St *ACC* BB5 159 M6
BBR PR5 168 E4
GTH/LHO BB6 138 E6
Bisham Cl *DWN* BB3 191 M3
Bishopdale Cl *BBNW* BB2 172 A4
HEY LA3 42 A8
Bishopdale Ct *SETT* BD24 265 N7
Bishopdale Rd *LANC* LA1 2 C7
Bishopgate *PRES* PR1 9 J3
Bishopsgate *BPOOLE* FY3 105 K2
LANC LA1 54 F7
Bishops Ga *LSTA* FY8 146 A5
Bishopsgate Wk *MILN* OL16 235 M7
Bishopstone Cl *BBNW* BB2 173 K3
Bishop St *ACC* BB5 * 159 M6
BRFD/BLYE BB10 142 E2
MILN OL16 235 L2
Bishopsway *PRES* PR1 152 A8
Bison Pl *CROS/BRETH* PR26 185 M1
Bispham Av
CROS/BRETH PR26 168 B7
Bispham Rd *BISP* FY2 85 G7
BPOOLE FY3 105 H3
CHTN/BK PR9 200 C4
CLV/TH FY5 84 F1
NLSN BB9 123 H5
PLF/KEOS FY6 85 K6
Bispham St *PRES* PR1 * 9 H2
Bittern Cl *BPOOLE* FY3 105 L5
ROCH OL11 234 C4
Bivel St *PDHM/BLYW* BB12 6 B3
Black Abbey St *ACC* BB5 159 M6
Blackacre La *BRSC* L40 241 J2
Black-A-Moor La *ORM* L39 249 J1
Blackamoor Rd *BBN* BB1 173 L4
Black Bank Rd *HGHB* LA2 264 C6
Blackberry Hall Crs *HEY* LA3 52 F3
Blackberry Wy *PRES* PR1 167 L1
Blackbrook Cl *CHLYE* PR6 208 D1
Black Bull La *FUL/RIB* PR2 132 A7
Blackburn Brow *CHLYE* PR6 208 B1
Blackburn Old Rd *BBN* BB1 157 M1
BBR PR5 170 E1
GTH/LHO BB6 138 D5
Blackburn Rd *BBN* BB1 158 B4
BBR PR5 153 L7
CHLYE PR6 188 B6
DWN BB3 211 M3
DWN BB3 173 H7
EDGW/EG BL7 192 D7
GAR/LONG PR3 116 C8
GAR/LONG PR3 114 F4
GTH/LHO BB6 138 F7
PDHM/BLYW BB12 140 D4
RAMS BL0 195 G7
RAW/HAS BB4 195 G5
RAW/HAS BB4 176 E6
Blackburn St *BBN* BB1 10 F1
BLY BB11 6 F3
CHLYE PR6 208 A4
Blackcar La *SFTN* L29 248 D8
Blackchapel Dr *MILN* OL16 235 L8
Black Cft *CHLYE* PR6 169 L8
Black Dyke *TOD* OL14 * 303 Q4
Black Dyke Rd *CARN* LA5 16 F1
Blacker St *BRFD/BLYE* BB10 142 D1
Blackfen Pl *BISP* FY2 105 G3
Blackfield Rd
KIRK/FR/WAR PR4 148 E5

Blackgate La
KIRK/FR/WAR PR4 182 F8
Blackhorse Cl *HOR/BR* BL6 230 F8
Black Horse St *CHLY/EC* PR7 * 207 L5
HOR/BR BL6 230 F8
Black House La
BRFD/BLYE BB10 298 A4
GAR/LONG PR3 94 E1
Blackhurst Av
KIRK/FR/WAR PR4 167 J1
Blackhurst Ct
KIRK/FR/WAR PR4 166 E3
Blackhurst Rd *MGHL* L31 249 M6
Black La *GAR/LONG* PR3 282 H5
RAMS BL0 215 L4
Blacklane Cft *CLI* BB7 99 H2
Blackleach Av *FUL/RIB* PR2 134 A2
Blackleach La
KIRK/FR/WAR PR4 130 C2
Blackledge Cl
WGNW/BIL/OR WN5 255 H6
Blackley Gv *NWD/KWIPK* L33 * 260 D5
Black Moor Rd *BRSC* L40 226 D1
Black Moss La *BRSC* L40 223 G4
ORM L39 251 G1
Black Moss Rd *NLSN* BB9 102 A2
Blacko Bar Rd *NLSN* BB9 102 E5
Blackpits Rd *ROCH* OL11 234 A2
Blackpool La *GAR/LONG* PR3 89 M5
Blackpool Old Rd *BPOOLE* FY3 105 K1
GAR/LONG PR3 88 C6
Blackpool Rd *BISP* FY2 85 G7
FUL/RIB PR2 151 G2
GAR/LONG PR3 114 D4
GAR/LONG PR3 89 L5
KIRK/FR/WAR PR4 127 K5
LSTA FY8 146 A6
PLF/KEOS FY6 85 K7
Blackpool Rd North *LSTA* FY8 145 J1
Blackpool St *ACC* BB5 159 H6
DWN BB3 191 L5
Blackrod Brow *HOR/BR* BL6 230 E7
Blackshaw St *TOD* OL14 303 N2
Blacksmith La *ROCH* OL11 234 E7
Blacksmiths Rw *LSTA* FY8 146 A4
Blacksnape Rd *DWN* BB3 191 M1
Blackstone Av *MILN* OL16 235 M3
Blackstone Rd *CHLYE* PR6 208 B2
Blackthorn Cl *BBN* BB1 157 J4
CLV/TH FY5 81 J6
FUL/RIB PR2 151 G2
KIRK/FR/WAR PR4 149 J1
WHIT OL12 235 H1
Blackthorn Crs *BCUP* OL13 179 J8
Blackthorn Cft *CHLYE* PR6 187 K1
Blackthorn Dr *PRES* PR1 151 K8
Blackthorn Ms *LSTA* FY8 145 M6
WHIT OL12 235 H1
Blackwood Pl *LANC* LA1 55 G6
Blackwood Rd *BCUP* OL13 196 E4
Blades St *LANC* LA1 2 F6
Blaguegate La *SKEL* WN8 252 E1
Blainscough Rd *CHLY/EC* PR7 229 H3
Blairgowrie Gdns *ORM* L39 241 K7
Blair Gv *CHTN/BK* PR9 200 C4
Blair St *WHIT* OL12 235 G2
Blairway Av *BPOOLE* FY3 105 J5
Blake Av *BBR* PR5 168 D4
Blakefield Rd *CSBY/BLUN* L23 257 M5
Blakehall *SKEL* WN8 254 A4
Blakeley Crs *BWCK/EAR* BB18 293 P3
Blake St *ACC* BB5 159 L5
MILN OL16 235 K3
Blakewater Rd *BBN* BB1 157 L4
Blakey Moor *BBNW* BB2 10 D4
Blakey St *BLY* BB11 7 J4
Blakiston St *FTWD* FY7 77 K7
Blanche St *WHIT* OL12 235 K1
Blandford Av *CLV/TH* FY5 84 F2
Blandford Cl *STHP* PR8 12 B7
Blannel St *BLY* BB11 6 C4
Blashaw La *PRES* PR1 151 K6
Blaydike Moss
CROS/BRETH PR26 185 L2
Blaydon Av *CLV/TH* FY5 81 H7
Blaydon Pk *SKEL* WN8 254 A4
Bleachers Dr *LEYL* PR25 186 B2
Blea Cl *PDHM/BLYW* BB12 141 M3
Bleakholt Rd *RAMS* BL0 215 J2
Bleak La *BRSC* L40 226 A6
Bleara Rd *BWCK/EAR* BB18 294 G8
Bleasdale Av *BPOOLE* FY3 106 B6
CLI BB7 98 F4
CLV/TH FY5 85 G2
KIRK/FR/WAR PR4 128 D5
PLF/KEOS FY6 105 M1
Bleasdale Cl *BBR* PR5 169 J3
LEYL PR25 186 E4
ORM L39 251 G4
Bleasdale Gv *HEY* LA3 52 F2
Bleasdale Rd *GAR/LONG* PR3 286 A11
GAR/LONG PR3 113 J5
LSTA FY8 146 F7
PLF/KEOS FY6 78 A6
Bleasdale St East *PRES* PR1 9 M1
Blea Tarn Pl *MCMB* LA4 41 L7
Blea Tarn Rd *HGHB* LA2 67 H1
Blelock St *PRES* PR1 9 K4
Blenheim Av *BPOOL* FY1 5 G4
KIRK/FR/WAR PR4 128 C6
Blenheim Cl *BBN* BB1 157 H2
BBR PR5 168 F3
Blenheim Dr *CLV/TH* FY5 85 M1
KIRK/FR/WAR PR4 148 A5
Blenheim Pl *LSTA* FY8 145 H2
Blenheim Rd *STHP* PR8 220 E5
WGNW/BIL/OR WN5 255 M3
Blenheim St *COL* BB8 296 D6
WHIT OL12 * 234 F2
Blenheim Wy
KIRK/FR/WAR PR4 131 H5
Blesma Ct *BPOOLS* FY4 * 124 F5
Blind La *CLI* BB7 292 E2
KKBYL LA6 31 H5
PDHM/BLYW BB12 121 K5
TOD OL14 303 K1
Blindman's La *ORM* L39 240 F4
Bloomfield Ct *PRES* PR1 152 B1
Bloomfield Gra *PRES* PR1 167 M1
Bloomfield Pk *CARN* LA5 33 J2
Bloomfield Rd *BPOOL* FY1 4 D8
CHLYE PR6 189 K2
Bloom St *RAMS* BL0 214 D7
Blossom Av *ACC* BB5 159 H6
BPOOLS FY4 125 J4
Blossom Ct *BPOOLE* FY3 105 K2
Blossom Pl *MILN* OL16 235 J3
The Blossoms *FUL/RIB* PR2 132 F5
PLF/KEOS FY6 86 C8
Blucher St *COL* BB8 296 B7
Bluebell Av *RAW/HAS* BB4 194 D3
Bluebell Cl *BISP* FY2 105 G1
CHLYE PR6 187 L6
CLV/TH FY5 81 J6
GAR/LONG PR3 79 M6
KIRK/FR/WAR PR4 165 H7
KKBY L32 260 B7
Bluebell Dr *ROCH* OL11 234 E8
Bluebell Gv *BLY* BB11 141 K6
Bluebell La *TOD* OL14 300 F9
Blue Bell Pl *PRES* PR1 9 K3
Bluebell Wy *BBR* PR5 169 K3
FUL/RIB PR2 133 H5
Bluebell Wd *LEYL* PR25 168 C8
Bluecoat Crs
KIRK/FR/WAR PR4 149 K1
Blue Moor *KIRK/FR/WAR* PR4 129 J2
Blue Scar La *CLI* BB7 277 N5
Blue Stone La *BRSC* L40 205 H8
Bluestone La *MGHL* L31 259 H2
Blundell Av *FMBY* L37 236 E7
HTWN L38 247 J8
STHP PR8 221 J1
Blundell Crs *STHP* PR8 221 J1
Blundell Dr *STHP* PR8 221 J1
Blundell Gv *HTWN* L38 247 J8
Blundell La *CHTN/BK* PR9 200 F1
PRES PR1 151 L5
Blundell Rd *FUL/RIB* PR2 132 B8
HTWN L38 256 C1
LSTA FY8 145 J2
Blundellsands Rd East
CSBY/BLUN L23 256 F7
Blundellsands Rd West
CSBY/BLUN L23 256 E8
Blundell St *BPOOL* FY1 4 C6
Blyth Av *LIT* OL15 * 219 J8
Blythe Av *CLV/TH* FY5 81 H6
Blythe La *BRSC* L40 242 B2
Blythe Ms *STHP* PR8 221 J3
Blythewood *SKEL* WN8 253 M4
Blyth Hey *NTHTN* L30 258 A8
Boar Clough *NLSN* BB9 101 H5
Boarded Barn *CHLY/EC* PR7 186 F8
Boardman Av *BPOOL* FY1 5 H8
Boardman St *TOD* OL14 303 L1
Board St *BRFD/BLYE* BB10 142 D2
Boarsgreave La *RAW/HAS* BB4 196 C5
Bobbin Cl *ACC* BB5 * 159 K6
Bobbiners La *CHTN/BK* PR9 181 K8
Bobbin Mill Cl *TOD* OL14 300 E10
Bobby Langton Wy *BRSC* L40 225 H6
Bocholt Wy *RAW/HAS* BB4 195 K1
Bodie Hl *HGHB* LA2 65 K6
Bodkin La *GAR/LONG* PR3 87 J4
Bodmin Av *CHTN/BK* PR9 180 E6
Bodmin St *PRES* PR1 153 G2
Boegrave Av *BBR* PR5 168 D3
Bogburn La *CHLY/EC* PR7 229 G5
Bog Height Rd *DWN* BB3 172 F5
Boland St *BBN* BB1 157 K4
Bold La *ORM* L39 250 E4
Bold St *ACC* BB5 160 A5
BBN BB1 10 D1
BCUP OL13 197 J2
CHTN/BK PR9 13 G2
COL BB8 296 B7
FTWD FY7 77 L6
HEY LA3 40 F7
PRES PR1 152 A1
Bold Venture Wy *ACC* BB5 139 K8
The Boleyn *MGHL* L31 250 B8
Bolland Prospect *CLI* BB7 99 J3
Bolland St *BWCK/EAR* BB18 293 Q4
Bolton Av *ACC* BB5 160 A2
LANC LA1 42 E7
PLF/KEOS FY6 85 M6
Bolton Cl *FMBY* L37 247 K1
Bolton Gv *NLSN* BB9 103 G8
Bolton La *CARN* LA5 33 H7
Bolton Meadow
CROS/BRETH PR26 185 K3
Bolton Rd *BBNW* BB2 173 G3
BBR PR5 171 H4
CHLY/EC PR7 208 B7
CHLYE PR6 171 K6
DWN BB3 191 M8
EDGW/EG BL7 213 G7
HOR/BR BL6 231 H5
ROCH OL11 234 D7
STHP PR8 199 K7
Bolton Rd North *RAMS* BL0 214 F2
Bolton Rd West *RAMS* BL0 214 E7
Bolton's Cop *CHTN/BK* PR9 182 A5
Boltons Ct *PRES* PR1 9 J4
Bolton's Ct *BBN* BB1 * 10 E3
Bolton's Meanygate
KIRK/FR/WAR PR4 182 F4
Bolton St *BPOOL* FY1 4 C8
CHLY/EC PR7 207 M4
COL BB8 103 L7
RAMS BL0 214 E6
RAW/HAS BB4 196 B2
Bombay Rd
WGNW/BIL/OR WN5 255 M3
Bombay St *BBNW* BB2 10 A8
Bonchurch St *BBN* BB1 * 157 M7
Bond Cl *HOR/BR* BL6 231 M8
Bond La *SETT* BD24 265 N7
Bonds La *GAR/LONG* PR3 284 B9
KIRK/FR/WAR PR4 108 D1
Bond's La *CHLY/EC* PR7 230 C4
CHTN/BK PR9 181 K4
Bond St *BRFD/BLYE* BB10 142 D3
COL BB8 296 A6
DWN BB3 173 K8
LANC LA1 3 K6
NLSN BB9 * 123 G4
RAMS BL0 215 H1
TOD OL14 * 303 L2
WHIT OL12 235 K1
Bone Cft *CHLYE* PR6 169 L8
Bone Hill La *GAR/LONG* PR3 282 F5
Bonfire Hill Cl *RAW/HAS* BB4 177 K4
Bonfire Hill Rd *RAW/HAS* BB4 177 K4
Bonney St *CLV/TH* FY5 81 L8
Bonnington Av
CSBY/BLUN L23 256 F6
Bonny St *BPOOL* FY1 4 C4
Bonsall St *BBNW* BB2 172 E1
Boome St *BPOOLS* FY4 124 F5
Boon Town *KKBYL* LA6 19 H6
Boon Wks *KKBYL* LA6 19 H5
Booth Bridge La
SKP/WHF BD23 294 E2
Booth Ct *BRFD/BLYE* BB10 142 D3
Booth Crs *RAW/HAS* BB4 196 C2
Boothley Rd *BPOOL* FY1 104 F5
Boothman Pl *NLSN* BB9 123 H1
Boothman St *BBNW* BB2 * 10 D9
Booth Rd *BCUP* OL13 196 D3
RAW/HAS BB4 196 C2
Boothroyden *BPOOL* FY1 104 E3
Booth's La *ORM* L39 240 C6
Booth St *ACC* BB5 159 M6
BCUP OL13 197 K1
BOL BL1 233 M8
CARN LA5 33 J2
CHTN/BK PR9 13 G2
NLSN BB9 123 G3
RAW/HAS BB4 196 B3
RAW/HAS BB4 176 D7
Bootle St *PRES* PR1 152 F2
Boot St *BWCK/EAR* BB18 294 E5
Boot Wy *BLY* BB11 7 G5
Borage Cl *CLV/TH* FY5 81 K6
Boran Ct *BLY* BB11 141 H7
Bordeaux Crs *BISP* FY2 85 J5
Border Ct *LANC* LA1 2 C4
Bores Hl *WGN* WN1 229 M7
Borough Rd *DWN* BB3 191 J3
Borron La *KKBYL* LA6 27 J7
Borrowdale *FMBY* L37 237 J6
Borrowdale Av *BBN* BB1 157 M8
FTWD FY7 77 H7
Borrowdale Cl
BRFD/BLYE BB10 122 F8
Borrowdale Dr
BRFD/BLYE BB10 122 F7
ROCH OL11 234 E7
Borrowdale Gv *MCMB* LA4 41 L6
Borrowdale Rd *BPOOLS* FY4 125 L2
LANC LA1 3 K5
LEYL PR25 186 E4
WGNW/BIL/OR WN5 * 255 L4
Borwick Av *CARN* LA5 26 B5
Borwick Cl *CARN* LA5 26 B6
Borwick Ct *KKBYL* LA6 26 F4
MCMB LA4 * 41 J8
Borwick Dr *LANC* LA1 2 C1
Borwick La *CARN* LA5 26 C5
Borwick Rd *KKBYL* LA6 27 K6
Bosburn Dr *BBNW* BB2 155 M1
Boscombe Av *HEY* LA3 52 F1
Boscombe Rd *BPOOLS* FY4 124 E5
Bosley Cl *DWN* BB3 192 A3
Bostock St *PRES* PR1 * 9 J4
Boston Av *BISP* FY2 85 G5
Boston Rd *BCUP* OL13 179 J8
LSTA FY8 145 L5
Bostons *GTH/LHO* BB6 138 E6
Boston St *NLSN* BB9 123 J5
Bostonway *BPOOLS* FY4 125 J3
Bosworth Dr *STHP* PR8 220 E7
Bosworth Pl *BPOOLS* FY4 124 E7
Bosworth Sq *ROCH* OL11 * 235 G7
Bosworth St *HOR/BR* BL6 231 L7
ROCH OL11 235 G6
Botanic Rd *CHTN/BK* PR9 200 D2
Botany Brow *CHLYE* PR6 208 B1
Bott House La *COL* BB8 123 K1
Bottomdale Rd *HGHB* LA2 42 E3
Bottomgate *BBN* BB1 11 K4
Bottomley Bank La
RAW/HAS BB4 177 L3
Bottomley Rd *TOD* OL14 303 M9
Bottomley St *NLSN* BB9 123 H3
Bottomley Yd *NLSN* BB9 * 123 H3
Bottom O' Th' Knotts Brow
EDGW/EG BL7 213 J8
Bottom O' Th' Moor
HOR/BR BL6 232 C8
Bottoms La *CARN* LA5 17 G7
Botton Rd *HGHB* LA2 48 C8
Boulder St *RAW/HAS* BB4 177 K4
Bouldsworth Rd
BRFD/BLYE BB10 143 H6
Boulevard *PRES* PR1 9 L8
The Boulevard *LSTA* FY8 145 K7
Boulsworth Cl
BWCK/EAR BB18 * 293 Q8
Boulsworth Crs *NLSN* BB9 123 L2
Boulsworth Dr *COL* BB8 296 F10
Boulsworth Gv *COL* BB8 296 D6
Boulview Ter *COL* BB8 296 D6
Boundary Cl *CHLY/EC* PR7 205 L5
KIRK/FR/WAR PR4 167 J3
Boundary Dr *CSBY/BLUN* L23 256 F5
Boundary Edge *RAMS* BL0 195 H8
Boundary La *BRSC* L40 225 J8
CHTN/BK PR9 182 A6
GAR/LONG PR3 83 L4
KIRK/FR/WAR PR4 182 B4
WGNNW/ST WN6 228 D8
Boundary Meanygate
KIRK/FR/WAR PR4 182 C4
Boundary Rd *ACC* BB5 159 M4
FUL/RIB PR2 132 A8
LANC LA1 3 H9
LSTA FY8 147 H6
Boundary St *BRFD/BLYE* BB10 142 F1
COL BB8 296 A7
LEYL PR25 186 E1
LIT OL15 219 K5
ROCH OL11 235 H6
STHP PR8 13 G9
Boundary Wk *ROCH* OL11 235 J6
Bourble's La *PLF/KEOS* FY6 79 G8
Bourne Brow *GAR/LONG* PR3 92 B6
Bourne May Rd *PLF/KEOS* FY6 78 A6
Bournemouth Rd *BPOOLS* FY4 124 E5
Bourne Rd *CLV/TH* FY5 81 L6
Bournesfield *BBR* PR5 170 B2
Bourne's Rw *BBR* PR5 170 B2
Bourne St *CLV/TH* FY5 81 M7
Bourne Wy *CLV/TH* FY5 81 J7
Bovington Av *CLV/TH* FY5 85 J3
Bow Brook Rd *LEYL* PR25 186 E2
Bowden Av *BBNW* BB2 171 M2
Bowen St *BBNW* BB2 172 E1
Bower Av *WHIT* OL12 219 G7
Bower Cl *BBNW* BB2 172 E1
Bowerham La *LANC* LA1 55 G8
Bowerham Rd *LANC* LA1 3 J9
Bowerham Ter *LANC* LA1 3 J9
Bowers La *GAR/LONG* PR3 283 P8
The Bowers *CHLY/EC* PR7 207 M7
Bower St *BBNW* BB2 172 E1
Bowes Lyon Pl *LSTA* FY8 * 145 M4
Bowfell Av *MCMB* LA4 41 L6
Bowfell Cl *BPOOLS* FY4 126 A2
Bowfield's La *BBNW* BB2 135 J7
Bowgreave Cl *BPOOLS* FY4 125 J5
Bowgreave Dr *GAR/LONG* PR3 284 C11
Bow Hills La *CLI* BB7 278 F7
Bowker Cl *ROCH* OL11 234 B2
Bowker's Green La *ORM* L39 251 H6
Bowland Av *BRFD/BLYE* BB10 143 H6
CHLYE PR6 208 A3
FTWD FY7 81 G3
Bowland Av South *LANC* LA1 66 F3
Bowland Cl *CARN* LA5 33 H2
GAR/LONG PR3 114 E3
Bowland Ct *CLI* BB7 99 H3
Bowland Crs *BPOOLE* FY3 105 K3
Bowland Dr *LANC* LA1 2 C1
LITH L21 257 M7
Bowland Gate La *CLI* BB7 290 D8
Bowland Pl *FUL/RIB* PR2 133 K8
LSTA FY8 145 M5
Bowland Rd *FUL/RIB* PR2 133 K8
GAR/LONG PR3 284 B6
HEY LA3 52 F3
Bowland Vw *GAR/LONG* PR3 284 B6
HGHB LA2 65 K6
NLSN BB9 123 G7
Bowland View Ct
PLF/KEOS FY6 * 83 G5
Bow La *LEYL* PR25 186 F2
PRES PR1 8 E4
Bowlers Cl *FUL/RIB* PR2 132 F6
Bowlers Wk *WHIT* OL12 235 J1
Bowlingfield *FUL/RIB* PR2 131 K5
Bowling Green Cl *DWN* BB3 191 L4
STHP PR8 200 C6
Bowling Green Cots
GTH/LHO BB6 * 117 M5
The Bowling Gn *RAMS* BL0 195 G8
Bowling Green Wy *ROCH* OL11 234 C5
Bowman Ct *BBN* BB1 11 H2
Bowness Av *BPOOLS* FY4 125 M3
CLV/TH FY5 85 L1
FTWD FY7 80 F2
LSTA FY8 145 J2
NLSN BB9 123 H5
STHP PR8 220 F8
WHIT OL12 234 F2
Bowness Cl *BBN* BB1 11 J2
Bowness Rd *LANC* LA1 3 K3
PDHM/BLYW BB12 140 F1
PRES PR1 153 K2
Bowood Ct *BPOOLE* FY3 105 L4
Bowran St *PRES* PR1 9 G3
Bow St *LEYL* PR25 186 E1
ROCH OL11 235 G8
Boxer Pl *CROS/BRETH* PR26 185 M1
Box St *LIT* OL15 219 K6
RAMS BL0 * 215 G5
Boxwood Dr *BBNW* BB2 172 C3
Boxwood St *BBN* BB1 157 J3
Boyer Av *MGHL* L31 259 G4
Boyes Av *GAR/LONG* PR3 91 G1
Boyes Brow *NWD/KWIPK* L33 260 A7
Boyle St *BBN* BB1 11 G2
Boys La *FUL/RIB* PR2 131 M6
Brabazon Pl
WGNW/BIL/OR WN5 255 M3
Brabiner La *FUL/RIB* PR2 113 L8
Bracebridge Dr *STHP* PR8 222 C1
Bracewell Av *PLF/KEOS* FY6 86 D8
Bracewell Cl *NLSN* BB9 * 123 H3
Bracewell La *SKP/WHF* BD23 293 M2
Bracewell Rd *FUL/RIB* PR2 133 H6
Bracewell St *BRFD/BLYE* BB10 142 E2
BWCK/EAR BB18 293 Q4
NLSN BB9 123 J3
Brackenber Cl *SETT* BD24 265 L8
Brackenber La *SETT* BD24 265 L8
Brackenbury Cl *BBR* PR5 168 D4
Brackenbury Rd *FUL/RIB* PR2 132 B8
Brackenbury St *PRES* PR1 152 C1
Bracken Cl *BBNW* BB2 172 C3
CHLYE PR6 208 B3
Bracken Dr *KIRK/FR/WAR* PR4 149 G4
Bracken Gv *RAW/HAS* BB4 194 D3
Bracken Hey *CLI* BB7 99 K3
Bracken Lea Fold *WHIT* OL12 234 E1
Brackenthwaite Rd *CARN* LA5 17 M4
Bracken Wy *BISP* FY2 105 G1
Brackenway *FMBY* L37 237 K5
Bracknel Wy *ORM* L39 250 D2
Braconash Rd *LEYL* PR25 186 B1
Bradda Rd *BBNW* BB2 173 H2
Braddocks Cl *WHIT* OL12 219 G7
Braddon Cl *MCMB* LA4 41 K8
Braddon St *PRES* PR1 153 G2
Brades Av *CLV/TH* FY5 86 A1
Brades La *KIRK/FR/WAR* PR4 149 G4
Brade St *CHTN/BK* PR9 180 F7
Bradfield Av *AIN/FAZ* L10 258 F8
Bradford Gv *HEY* LA3 52 E5
Bradford St *ACC* BB5 160 A5
Bradkirk La *BBR* PR5 169 L3
Bradkirk Pl *BBR* PR5 169 K4
Bradley Fold *NLSN* BB9 * 123 H2
Bradley Gdns
PDHM/BLYW BB12 141 L6
Bradley Hall Rd *NLSN* BB9 123 J2
Bradley La *CHLY/EC* PR7 206 A5
WGN WN1 229 K8
Bradley Rd *NLSN* BB9 123 H2
Bradley Rd East *NLSN* BB9 123 H2
Bradley Smithy Cl *WHIT* OL12 235 H1
Bradley St *CHTN/BK* PR9 13 K2
COL BB8 296 C6
Bradley Vw *NLSN* BB9 * 123 H2
Bradman Rd *NWD/KWIPK* L33 260 F8
Bradshaw Brow *BRSC* L40 227 G2
Bradshaw Cl *BBN* BB1 157 H3
NLSN BB9 123 H4
PLF/KEOS FY6 82 F4
Bradshawgate Dr *CARN* LA5 16 E7
Bradshaw La *BRSC* L40 227 H1
GAR/LONG PR3 282 B5
KIRK/FR/WAR PR4 107 L8
SKEL WN8 243 M2
Bradshaw Rw *ACC* BB5 159 J5
Bradshaw's La *STHP* PR8 221 G5
Bradshaw St *ACC* BB5 * 159 J5
LANC LA1 3 K8
MILN OL16 235 K3
NLSN BB9 123 G4
WGNW/BIL/OR WN5 255 K5
Bradshaw St East *ACC* BB5 * 159 M5
Bradshaw St West *ACC* BB5 * 159 J5
Bradyll Ct *GTH/LHO* BB6 117 M5
Brady St *HOR/BR* BL6 231 K6
Braefield Crs *FUL/RIB* PR2 133 J8
Braemar Av *CHTN/BK* PR9 200 B1
CLV/TH FY5 85 M4
Braemar Wk *BISP* FY2 85 J5
Braeside *BBNW* BB2 10 A1
Braganza Wy *LANC* LA1 2 A6
Braidhaven *WGNNW/ST* WN6 245 H4
Braid's La *GAR/LONG* PR3 284 F8
Braintree Av *PRES* PR1 168 B1
Braith Cl *BPOOLS* FY4 125 J3
Braithwaite *WGNNW/ST* WN6 245 K5
Braithwaite St *BPOOL* FY1 104 E4
Bramble Cl *KIRK/FR/WAR* PR4 128 B5
LIT OL15 219 J6
Bramble Ct *CLV/TH* FY5 85 K1
PRES PR1 168 B1
The Brambles *BBNW* BB2 156 D3
CHLY/EC PR7 229 J1
CLI BB7 119 G2
FUL/RIB PR2 133 G5
Bramble St *BRFD/BLYE* BB10 142 D2
Bramble Wy *BRSC* L40 225 J7
SKEL WN8 243 M2
Bramblewood
CROS/BRETH PR26 204 E1
The Bramblings *PLF/KEOS* FY6 105 L1
Bramcote Cl *NWD/KWIPK* L33 260 D7
Bramcote Rd *NWD/KWIPK* L33 260 C7
Bramcote Wk
NWD/KWIPK L33 260 C7
Bramhall Rd *SKEL* WN8 253 J1
Bramley Av *FTWD* FY7 77 H7
PDHM/BLYW BB12 141 M3
Bramley Cl *ACC* BB5 159 J6
Bramley Gdns *PLF/KEOS* FY6 105 K1
Bramley Rd *ROCH* OL11 234 B3
The Bramleys *MGHL* L31 258 F4
Bramley St *ACC* BB5 159 L5
Brampton Av *CLV/TH* FY5 81 J7
Brampton Cl *KKBY* L32 260 B7
Brampton Dr *MCMB* LA4 42 A6
Brampton St *FUL/RIB* PR2 8 A1
Bramwell Pk *BRSC* L40 223 L7
Bramwell Rd
KIRK/FR/WAR PR4 148 E5
Bramworth Av *RAMS* BL0 214 E5
Branch Rd *ACC* BB5 139 J8
BBNW BB2 155 L1
BLY BB11 7 H7
CLI BB7 290 A11
DWN BB3 173 H4
Branch St *BCUP* OL13 197 G3
NLSN BB9 123 H3
Brancker St *CHLY/EC* PR7 207 K6
Brandiforth St *BBR* PR5 169 H1
Brandon Cl *SKEL* WN8 254 D4
Brandreth Delph *SKEL* WN8 227 G8
Brandreth Dr *SKEL* WN8 243 M1
Brandreth Pk *SKEL* WN8 226 F7
Brandwood *PRES* PR1 151 K7
RAW/HAS BB4 * 196 B2
Brandwood Gv *BRFD/BLYE* BB10 7 L4
Brandwood Pk *BCUP* OL13 196 D3
Brandwood Rd *BCUP* OL13 196 E3
Brandwood St *DWN* BB3 191 L2
Brandy House Brow *BBNW* BB2 11 G9
Branksome Av *CLV/TH* FY5 81 J8
Branksome Dr *MCMB* LA4 41 L7
Branston Rd *BPOOLS* FY4 5 K9
Branstree Rd *BPOOLS* FY4 125 M2
Brant Ct *FTWD* FY7 80 F2
Brantfell Dr
PDHM/BLYW BB12 141 L3
Brantfell Rd *BBN* BB1 157 G4
GTH/LHO BB6 138 F5
Brant Rd *PRES* PR1 153 K2
Brantwood *ACC* BB5 159 H1
Brantwood Av *BBN* BB1 158 B6
MCMB LA4 41 M5
Brantwood Dr *LANC* LA1 54 F8
LEYL PR25 186 E2
Brassey St *PDHM/BLYW* BB12 141 M4
Brathay Pl *FTWD* FY7 81 G1
Braxfield Ct *LSTA* FY8 * 145 G5
Brays Heys *CLV/TH* FY5 * 85 M2
Brays Rd *LSTA* FY8 146 E1
Bray St *FUL/RIB* PR2 8 B1
Brazil Cl *HEY* LA3 53 H1
Bread St *PDHM/BLYW* BB12 * 6 A3
Brearlands *SKP/WHF* BD23 294 E1
Brearley St *BCUP* OL13 197 G3
Breck Cl *PLF/KEOS* FY6 86 B6
Breck Dr *PLF/KEOS* FY6 86 B6
Breck Rd *BPOOLE* FY3 5 H3
CLV/TH FY5 86 B5
PLF/KEOS FY6 86 A7
Breck's Br *HGHB* LA2 269 K8
Breckside Cl *PLF/KEOS* FY6 86 B6
Brecon Av *ACC* BB5 158 F7
Brecon Cl *BPOOL* FY1 5 H5
Brecon Rd *BBN* BB1 157 M6
Bredon Av *CHLY/EC* PR7 207 G2
Bredon Cl *LSTA* FY8 147 G6
Breeze Cl *CLV/TH* FY5 81 K7
COL BB8 296 B2
Breeze Mt *BBR* PR5 168 F4
Breeze Rd *STHP* PR8 221 H1
Brenbar Crs *WHIT* OL12 218 A2
Brenda Crs *CSBY/BLUN* L23 257 K4
Brendale Av *MGHL* L31 258 F3
Brendjean Rd *MCMB* LA4 41 K7
Brendon Wk *BPOOLE* FY3 105 J3
Brennand Cl *BBR* PR5 169 J3
LANC LA1 2 A2
Brennand St *BRFD/BLYE* BB10 142 E2
CLI BB7 99 H2
Brentlea Av *HEY* LA3 52 D4
Brentlea Crs *HEY* LA3 52 D4
Brent St *BRFD/BLYE* BB10 122 F8
Brentwood *FTWD* FY7 81 H1
Brentwood Av *BLY* BB11 6 D9
CLV/TH FY5 85 G2
CSBY/BLUN L23 257 J6
PLF/KEOS FY6 85 M8
Brentwood Cl *HTWN* L38 256 C1
LIT OL15 219 J8
Brentwood Ct *CHTN/BK* PR9 200 A2
Brentwood Rd *CHLYE* PR6 230 E3
NLSN BB9 123 K2
Bretherton Cl
CROS/BRETH PR26 185 M3
Bretherton Rd
CROS/BRETH PR26 184 D7
Bretherton Ter *LEYL* PR25 186 D2
Bretlands Rd *CSBY/BLUN* L23 257 L6
Brettarch Dr *LANC* LA1 54 D6
Brettargh Cl *LANC* LA1 54 D5
Brettargh Dr *LANC* LA1 54 D5
Brett Cl *CLI* BB7 99 K4
Bretton Fold *STHP* PR8 200 C6
Brewery La *FMBY* L37 237 J5
LANC LA1 3 H5
MGHL L31 259 H8
Brewery St *BBNW* BB2 10 C4
GAR/LONG PR3 114 E4
TOD OL14 300 H11
Breworth Fold La *CHLYE* PR6 170 C8
Briar Av *CHLY/EC* PR7 186 F7
Briar Bank Rw *FUL/RIB* PR2 132 C3
Briar Cl *WHIT* OL12 234 D2
Briarcroft *DWN* BB3 173 K5
Briar Cft *KIRK/FR/WAR* PR4 166 D4
Briar Fld *BISP* FY2 85 J5
Briarfield Rd *PLF/KEOS* FY6 85 L5
Briar Gv *FUL/RIB* PR2 131 K7
Briar Hill Cl *BBN* BB1 11 J5
Briar Lea Rd *KKBYL* LA6 33 K6
Briar Ms *CLV/TH* FY5 85 M2
Briar Rd *BBN* BB1 157 J3
CLV/TH FY5 85 L2
STHP PR8 221 G7
Briars Brook *BRSC* L40 225 K8
Briarscroft *CARN* LA5 26 B5
Briars Gn *SKEL* WN8 243 K7
Briars La *BRSC* L40 225 K8
MGHL L31 259 H2
The Briars *CHLY/EC* PR7 205 M5
FUL/RIB PR2 133 G5

STHP PR8 221 J2
Briar St BCUP OL13 197 K2
ROCH OL11 235 G5
Briarwood CSBY/BLUN L23 256 E5
KIRK/FR/WAR PR4 148 D5
Briarwood Cl CLV/TH FY5 85 L4
KIRK/FR/WAR PR4 127 H1
LEYL PR25 186 A3
Briarwood Dr BISP FY2 85 H6
Briary Cft HTWN L38 247 J8
Brickcroft HGHB LA2 65 M7
Brickcroft La
CROS/BRETH PR26 184 D8
Brickfield St MILN OL16 235 L1
Brickhouse Gdns
GAR/LONG PR3 * 287 M12
Brickhouse La PLF/KEOS FY6 82 F7
Brick House La PLF/KEOS FY6 82 E7
Brick Kiln La BRSC L40 203 K8
Brick St BLY BB11 6 F4
Brickwall Gn SFTN L29 258 C4
Brickwall La SFTN L29 258 B5
Bride St TOD OL14 303 L1
Bridge SKP/WHF BD23 281 J12
Bridge Av ORM L39 241 H7
Bridge Bank BBR PR5 152 F5
Bridge Bank Rd LIT OL15 219 J8
Bridge Brow KKBYL LA6 21 M2
Bridge Cl BBR PR5 168 D3
Bridge Cft ACC BB5 139 J7
CARN LA5 32 F7
LITH L21 257 M8
Bridge End BBR PR5 168 F4
Bridge End Cl RAW/HAS BB4 194 D4
Bridge End St TOD OL14 * 300 F10
Bridge Farm Dr MGHL L31 259 J1
Bridgefield St
PDHM/BLYW BB12 140 F7
ROCH OL11 235 G4
Bridgefold Rd ROCH OL11 234 F4
Bridge Gv STHP PR8 13 H6
Bridgehall Dr SKEL WN8 254 E4
Bridge House Rd BPOOLS FY4 125 J3
Bridge La LANC LA1 3 G5
NTHTN L30 258 B8
Bridge Mill Ct CHLYE PR6 208 C5
Bridgemill Rd BBN BB1 11 G5
Bridge Mill Rd NLSN BB9 122 F3
Bridgend Dr STHP PR8 220 E7
Bridgenorth Dr LIT OL15 219 J8
Bridge Rd BBR PR5 168 F3
CLI BB7 291 J10
CSBY/BLUN L23 256 F8
FTWD FY7 77 L7
FUL/RIB PR2 151 M1
KKBYL LA6 33 K7
LANC LA1 54 E6
LSTA FY8 146 A7
MGHL L31 259 G4
Bridgeside CARN LA5 33 J2
LSTA FY8 124 E7
Bridges La SFTN L29 258 C4
Bridge St ACC BB5 159 H5
BBN BB1 158 E1
BBNW BB2 10 F5
BBR PR5 169 H4
BLY BB11 * 7 G4
COL BB8 103 M7
GAR/LONG PR3 284 B9
GTH/LHO BB6 138 F6
HOR/BR BL6 231 M7
NLSN BB9 122 E5
ORM L39 241 H7
PDHM/BLYW BB12 140 E3
RAMS BL0 214 F5
RAW/HAS BB4 196 C2
RAW/HAS BB4 178 D3
STHP PR8 13 H5
TOD OL14 303 L2
WHIT OL12 218 F8
Bridge Ter BBR PR5 152 F5
Bridget St LANC LA1 * 3 H6
Bridgeview Dr
NWD/KWIPK L33 260 C7
Bridgewater Av CLV/TH FY5 85 J4
Bridgewater Cl BLY BB11 141 J7
Bridgeway BBR PR5 168 F3
Bridge Wills La CHTN/BK PR9 180 F6
Bridleway LSTA FY8 146 B4
Bridle Wy NWD/KWIPK L33 260 A5
Bridleway RAW/HAS BB4 196 C1
Brief St BRFD/BLYE BB10 142 D3
Briercliffe Av BPOOLE FY3 5 L7
COL BB8 103 L8
Briercliffe Rd
BRFD/BLYE BB10 142 E3
CHLYE PR6 208 A2
Briercliffe St COL BB8 103 L8
Brier Crs NLSN BB9 123 G5
Brier Dr HEY LA3 52 D4
Brierfield KIRK/FR/WAR PR4 167 J3
SKEL WN8 254 A6
Brier Heights Cl NLSN BB9 123 G6
Brierley Av BPOOLE FY3 105 H5
Brierley Cl NTHTN L30 258 E7
Brierley La KIRK/FR/WAR PR4 110 E3
Brierley Rd BBR PR5 169 K4
Brierley St FUL/RIB PR2 152 A2
Briers Brow CHLYE PR6 188 E4
Briery Bank CARN LA5 16 F2
Briery Cl FUL/RIB PR2 132 F7
Brieryfield Rd PRES PR1 8 D3
Briery Hey BBR PR5 169 M5
Briery St LANC LA1 2 D4
Brigg Fld ACC BB5 139 J7
Briggs Rd FUL/RIB PR2 151 M1
Brighouse Cl ORM L39 241 G5
Brighton Av BPOOLS FY4 124 E3
CLV/TH FY5 85 G1
LSTA FY8 145 J4
Brighton Crs FUL/RIB PR2 131 K8
Brighton Rd BRFD/BLYE BB10 122 F8
STHP PR8 199 K8
Brighton St CHLYE PR6 * 208 B3
TOD OL14 300 F10
Brighton Ter BBNW BB2 156 E5
DWN BB3 191 H1
Bright's Cl CLI BB7 275 L9
Brightstone Cl CHTN/BK PR9 181 L6
Bright St ACC BB5 159 G8
BBN BB1 11 L1
BPOOLS FY4 124 E3
BRFD/BLYE BB10 142 D2
CHTN/BK PR9 200 C4
CLI BB7 99 J3
COL BB8 296 A6
DWN BB3 191 J1
MILN OL16 235 K6
RAW/HAS BB4 177 K8
TOD OL14 303 K4
Bright Ter COL BB8 296 E9
Brigsteer Cl ACC BB5 159 H1
Brimrod La ROCH OL11 235 G6
Brindle Cl BBR PR5 169 L3
GAR/LONG PR3 114 E4
LANC LA1 2 B2
Brindle Ct BBR PR5 169 K1
Brindle Fold BBR PR5 169 M4
Brindle Hts CHLYE PR6 170 C6
Brindle Pl FUL/RIB PR2 134 A2
Brindle Rd BBR PR5 169 J1
CHLYE PR6 170 A5
Brindle St BBNW BB2 172 E2
CHLY/EC PR7 207 M5
PRES PR1 152 F3
Brindley Cl BLY BB11 141 J7
Brindley St
WGNW/BIL/OR WN5 255 M6
Brinklow Cl STHP PR8 220 D6
Brinks Rw HOR/BR BL6 * 232 A6
Brinwell Rd BPOOLS FY4 125 L2
Brisbane Pl CLV/TH FY5 85 J4
Brisbane St ACC BB5 159 K2
Bristol Av BISP FY2 85 H7
FTWD FY7 80 F3
LEYL PR25 168 F7
Bristol Cl BBN BB1 11 J5
Bristol St BLY BB11 6 B8
COL BB8 296 B6
MCMB LA4 41 K7
Bristow Av FUL/RIB PR2 151 L1
Britannia Av BCUP OL13 197 K1
Britannia Dr FUL/RIB PR2 151 L3
Britannia Pl BPOOL FY1 124 E2
Britannia Rd
WGNW/BIL/OR WN5 255 M3
Britannia St GTH/LHO BB6 138 F6
Britannia Wk BLY BB11 7 J7
LSTA FY8 145 M3
Britannia Wy RAW/HAS BB4 194 D3
Briton St MILN OL16 235 K3
Britten Cl BBNW BB2 173 K1
Britten St DWN BB3 191 J1
Britwell Cl BBNW BB2 173 K3
Brixey St PRES PR1 8 D7
Brixham Pl BPOOLS FY4 124 E5
Brixton Rd PRES PR1 9 M5
Broadacre HGHB LA2 44 D6
SKEL WN8 254 D5
WGNNW/ST WN6 245 K1
Broad Acre WHIT OL12 234 B1
Broadacre Cl HGHB LA2 44 D6
Broadacre Pl HGHB LA2 44 C6
Broadacre Vw HGHB LA2 44 D6
Broad Cft KIRK/FR/WAR PR4 166 D2
Broadfield ACC BB5 175 J1
GAR/LONG PR3 131 L1
Broadfield Av BPOOLS FY4 125 H6
PLF/KEOS FY6 86 C8
Broadfield Dr LEYL PR25 186 B2
LIT OL15 219 J8
PRES PR1 168 A1
Broadfield Rd ACC BB5 159 K8
Broadfields CHLY/EC PR7 207 L1
Broadfield Stile MILN OL16 235 H5
Broadfield St ACC BB5 159 J8
MILN OL16 235 H5
Broadfleet Cl GAR/LONG PR3 79 M5
Broadfold Av BBN BB1 157 K4
Broadgate PRES PR1 8 D7
Broad Ga TOD OL14 303 M1
Broadgreen Cl LEYL PR25 186 C2
Broadhalgh Av ROCH OL11 234 D4
Broadhalgh Rd ROCH OL11 234 D5
Broadhead Rd DWN BB3 192 F3
EDGW/EG BL7 213 H4
Broad Hey NTHTN L30 258 A8
Broadhurst La
WGNNW/ST WN6 228 C5
Broadhurst Rd CLV/TH FY5 85 H3
Broadhurst Wy NLSN BB9 122 F7
Broad Ing ROCH OL11 * 234 E2
Broading Cl BRFD/BLYE BB10 163 H2
Broadith La GAR/LONG PR3 113 H1
Broadlands STHP PR8 199 H8
WGNNW/ST WN6 245 L5
Broadlands Dr CARN LA5 32 E8
Broadlands Pl LSTA FY8 146 C7
Broad La CLI BB7 118 E6
FMBY L37 248 C2
GAR/LONG PR3 283 Q5
MILN OL16 235 L8
ORM L39 249 M1
SFTN L29 257 M2
TOD OL14 301 N9
Broadlea Gv WHIT OL12 234 F1
Broadley St RAW/HAS BB4 177 K8
Broadmead SKEL WN8 243 L1
Broad Meadow BBR PR5 168 D3
GAR/LONG PR3 287 L12
Broad Meadow La
CROS/BRETH PR26 184 B8
Broadness Dr NLSN BB9 123 H5
Broad Oak Av GAR/LONG PR3 284 C9
Broad Oak Cl CHLYE PR6 230 D3
Broad Oak Gn PRES PR1 151 L8
Broad Oak La BPOOLE FY3 106 A6
PRES PR1 151 L8
Broad Oak Rd ACC BB5 159 M6
Broadoak Rd MGHL L31 259 H2
ROCH OL11 234 B5
Broadpool La PLF/KEOS FY6 86 F2
Broadriding Rd
WGNNW/ST WN6 245 H5
Broad Sq LEYL PR25 186 D3
Broadstone Cl WHIT OL12 234 D2
Broadstone Cl LANC LA1 55 H4
Broadstone Dr CHLY/EC PR7 187 H4
Broadstone St TOD OL14 303 N1
Broad St LEYL PR25 186 D3
NLSN BB9 123 G3
TOD OL14 303 L1
Broadtree Cl BBNW BB2 135 M8
Broadwater Av FTWD FY7 81 H3
Broadwater Gdns FTWD FY7 * 81 H3
Broadway ACC BB5 159 M5
BBN BB1 157 H1
BPOOLS FY4 124 F4
CLV/TH FY5 81 G5
FUL/RIB PR2 151 J1
HOR/BR BL6 232 A8
LANC LA1 3 H1
LEYL PR25 186 E3
MCMB LA4 41 L6
NLSN BB9 123 G3
RAW/HAS BB4 194 E3
Broadway Cl STHP PR8 220 E6
Broadway Crs RAW/HAS BB4 194 D3
Broadway Pl NLSN BB9 103 G8
Broadway St BBNW BB2 172 E2
Broadwood Av MGHL L31 258 F4
Broadwood Cl PRES PR1 151 L7
Broadwood Dr FUL/RIB PR2 132 B4
Broadwood Wy LSTA FY8 146 B7
Broche Cl ROCH OL11 234 E8
Brock Av FTWD FY7 81 G1
Brockbank Av LANC LA1 54 A3
Brock Cl LANC LA1 42 D8
Brock Clough Rd
RAW/HAS BB4 178 C7
Brockenhurst St
BRFD/BLYE BB10 7 L5
Brockholes Brow PRES PR1 153 J2
Brockholes Crs PLF/KEOS FY6 106 B1
Brockholes Vw PRES PR1 152 F4
Brockholes Wy GAR/LONG PR3 91 H2
Brocklebank Rd CHTN/BK PR9 200 B2
Brocklehurst Av ACC BB5 159 L8
Brocklewood Av
PLF/KEOS FY6 106 A3
Brock Mill La GAR/LONG PR3 285 M12
Brock Rakes GAR/LONG PR3 286 A8
Brock Rd CHLYE PR6 208 A2
GAR/LONG PR3 89 H7
Brock Side GAR/LONG PR3 91 L5
Brock St LANC LA1 3 G6
Brockway MILN OL16 235 M8
PLF/KEOS FY6 106 A1
Brockway Av BPOOLE FY3 105 J5
Brodick Rd BBN BB1 158 A8
Brodie Cl BPOOLS FY4 125 J5
Brogden La BWCK/EAR BB18 293 K6
Brogden St BWCK/EAR BB18 293 Q4
Brogden Vw BWCK/EAR BB18 293 P3
Broken Bank Head CLI BB7 275 K1
Broken Banks COL BB8 296 B7
Broken Stone Rd BBNW BB2 172 C5
Bromfield WHIT OL12 * 235 J3
Bromilow Rd SKEL WN8 252 F2
Bromley Cl BISP FY2 105 H2
Bromley Gn CHLYE PR6 188 C7
Bromley Rd LSTA FY8 145 J5
Bromley St BBNW BB2 10 A3
PRES PR1 * 8 D2
Brompton Av CSBY/BLUN L23 256 F8
NWD/KWIPK L33 260 D6
Brompton Cl LSTA FY8 146 A5
Brompton Rd PLF/KEOS FY6 106 A2
STHP PR8 200 B4
Bromsgrove Av BISP FY2 84 F7
Bromsgrove Rd
BRFD/BLYE BB10 142 E3
Bronte Av BRFD/BLYE BB10 143 G5
Bronte Cl CSBY/BLUN L23 256 E7
WHIT OL12 234 D1
Bronte Wy BRFD/BLYE BB10 298 A7
BRFD/BLYE BB10 7 G1
COL BB8 297 J7
PDHM/BLYW BB12 141 J3
Brooden Dr NLSN BB9 122 F7
Brook Av GAR/LONG PR3 270 D12
HEY LA3 41 G8
MGHL L31 259 H1
Brook Cft FUL/RIB PR2 131 L8
Brookdale CHLYE PR6 230 D2
EDGW/EG BL7 210 F7
KIRK/FR/WAR PR4 167 K5
WHIT OL12 218 B8
Brookdale Av CLV/TH FY5 85 H3
Brookdale Cl LEYL PR25 186 E5
The Brookdale STHP PR8 221 G8
Brookdean Cl BOL BL1 233 M8
Brooke Cl ACC BB5 176 B1
CHTN/BK PR9 200 E4
Brooke's La CLI BB7 118 F6
Brookes St BCUP OL13 197 G3
The Brookes CHLYE PR6 208 B4
Brooke St CHLY/EC PR7 208 A4
Brook Farm Cl ORM L39 241 H7
Brookfield BBNW BB2 156 B1
BRSC L40 226 F1
CROS/BRETH PR26 184 E8
SKEL WN8 243 M1
Brookfield Av BPOOLS FY4 125 K5
CLV/TH FY5 85 M1
CSBY/BLUN L23 257 G8
FUL/RIB PR2 132 F7
Brookfield Cl CARN LA5 33 G6
KKBYL LA6 19 G1
Brookfield Ct GAR/LONG PR3 287 M12
Brookfield Dr FUL/RIB PR2 132 B3
LIT OL15 219 H5
Brookfield La ORM L39 250 D6
Brookfield Pl BBR PR5 169 K5
Brookfield Rd CLV/TH FY5 85 M1
SKEL WN8 254 F5
WGNNW/ST WN6 245 L1
Brookfields
WGNW/BIL/OR WN5 * 255 L6
Brookfield St BBN BB1 10 F1
PRES PR1 152 C2
TOD OL14 300 F10
Brookfield Wy
BWCK/EAR BB18 294 E6
Brookford Cl
PDHM/BLYW BB12 142 A3
Brook Gv CLV/TH FY5 81 H7
HEY LA3 41 G8
Brook Hey KIRK/FR/WAR PR4 166 C3
Brook Hey Cl WHIT OL12 219 G7
Brook Hey Dr NWD/KWIPK L33 260 C7
Brookholme Ct LANC LA1 2 B8
Brookhouse Cl BBN BB1 11 G1
BBR PR5 170 C1
Brookhouse Dr BBR PR5 170 C1
Brookhouse Gdns BBN BB1 * 11 G1
Brookhouse La BBN BB1 11 G1
Brookhouse Rd HGHB LA2 44 D6
ORM L39 241 G5
Brookhouse St FUL/RIB PR2 152 A2
Brookland KKBYL LA6 31 H6
Brookland Cl ACC BB5 139 H7
Brooklands FUL/RIB PR2 151 K2
GAR/LONG PR3 287 N12
HOR/BR BL6 231 M8
ORM L39 241 J5
Brooklands Av BLY BB11 7 J9
FUL/RIB PR2 132 B4
KIRK/FR/WAR PR4 128 D6
RAW/HAS BB4 194 E4
Brooklands Ct LANC LA1 * 54 F7
ROCH OL11 234 F5
Brooklands Dr GAR/LONG PR3 284 B9
HEY LA3 52 D5
MGHL L31 259 G3
WGNW/BIL/OR WN5 255 G6
Brooklands Gv BRSC L40 225 J8
Brooklands Rd BLY BB11 7 J9
LSTA FY8 145 M5
SKEL WN8 254 F4
Brooklands Ter BBN BB1 * 157 K4
The Brooklands
KIRK/FR/WAR PR4 127 K7
Brookland St MILN OL16 * 235 L8
Brook La CHLY/EC PR7 206 E7
CROS/BRETH PR26 168 A5
KIRK/FR/WAR PR4 168 A4
KIRK/FR/WAR PR4 166 B8
MILN OL16 235 L8
ORM L39 241 H7
RNFD/HAY WA11 263 J4
SKP/WHF BD23 278 G1
WGNW/BIL/OR WN5 255 K6
Brooklawns
KIRK/FR/WAR PR4 184 A1
Brooklyn Av BPOOLE FY3 105 H3
MILN OL16 219 G7
Brooklyn Rd BBN BB1 137 H6
Brook Meadow
KIRK/FR/WAR PR4 131 J5
Brook Pk MGHL L31 258 F4
Brook Pl FUL/RIB PR2 151 G1
Brook Rd CSBY/BLUN L23 257 K5
HEY LA3 41 G8
LSTA FY8 146 F7
MGHL L31 259 H3
Brook Rd North FUL/RIB PR2 132 A8
Brooksbottom Cl RAMS BL0 214 F7
Brooks End ROCH OL11 234 B2
Brookside BRSC L40 223 L7
CHLY/EC PR7 229 J2
CHLY/EC PR7 206 F1
CLI BB7 291 N10
CLI BB7 * 290 C8
CLV/TH FY5 81 M8
GTH/LHO BB6 117 M6
KIRK/FR/WAR PR4 128 C5
LANC LA1 54 F7
Brookside Av RNFD/HAY WA11 262 B4
Brookside Cl CLI BB7 118 F6
CROS/BRETH PR26 168 B8
RAMS BL0 214 D8
Brookside Crs CLI BB7 290 C8
Brookside Dr HGHB LA2 270 G2
Brookside La ACC BB5 158 C8
Brookside Rd FUL/RIB PR2 132 A4
STHP PR8 221 M2
Brookside St ACC BB5 158 F8
Brookside Vw ACC BB5 158 E7
Brook's Pl WHIT OL12 * 235 H3
Brooks Rd FMBY L37 247 G1
Brook St ACC BB5 159 H8
BBN BB1 158 E2
BBNW BB2 172 E1
BBR PR5 153 L8
BPOOLS FY4 125 H2
BWCK/EAR BB18 293 Q5
CHLYE PR6 230 D2
CHTN/BK PR9 180 F7
CLI BB7 99 J2
COL BB8 296 A6
FTWD FY7 81 H3
FUL/RIB PR2 132 A8
KIRK/FR/WAR PR4 128 C5
LANC LA1 2 F8
LIT OL15 219 M6
NLSN BB9 123 H3
RAW/HAS BB4 176 E6
WHIT OL12 218 F5
Brooks Wy FMBY L37 247 G1
The Brook LIT OL15 219 M2
Brookview FUL/RIB PR2 132 E6
Brookway BBNW BB2 172 E3
KIRK/FR/WAR PR4 166 C3
LIT OL15 219 K7
Brooky Moor EDGW/EG BL7 * 213 H5
Broom Cl BRSC L40 225 J7
LEYL PR25 169 H8
Broome Cl STHP PR8 199 L8
Broome Rd STHP PR8 199 L8
Broom Fld GAR/LONG PR3 284 C11
Broomfield Mill St PRES PR1 152 C2
Broomfield Pl BBNW BB2 156 E8
Broomfield Rd FTWD FY7 77 J8
Broomfield Sq ROCH OL11 * 235 J6
Broom Hill Coppice
GAR/LONG PR3 284 B6
Broomholme
WGNNW/ST WN6 245 G4
Brotherod Hall Rd WHIT OL12 234 F1
Brothers St BBNW BB2 172 D2
Brotherston Dr BBNW BB2 172 F3
Brotherton Mdw CLI BB7 99 J3
Brougham St PDHM/BLYW BB12 6 E1
Brough Av BISP FY2 105 H1
Broughton Av BPOOLE FY3 105 H4
STHP PR8 13 M9
Broughton Cl BBNW BB2 173 K2
Broughton Gv HEY LA3 41 K8
Broughton St DWN BB3 191 J1
PDHM/BLYW BB12 6 A3
PRES PR1 132 B8
Broughtons Yd ACC BB5 * 159 M5
Broughton Tower Wy
FUL/RIB PR2 132 D3
Broughton Wy PLF/KEOS FY6 85 M5
Brow Cl GAR/LONG PR3 88 D5
Brow Edge RAW/HAS BB4 196 A2
Browfoot Cl CARN LA5 33 L1
Browgate CLI BB7 281 L7
Browgill Pl LANC LA1 2 D2
Browhead Rd
BRFD/BLYE BB10 142 E3
Brow Hey BBR PR5 169 L5
Brow La HGHB LA2 39 M7
Brown Bank Rd LIT OL15 219 J8
Brown Birks Rd ACC BB5 160 B3
Brown Birks St TOD OL14 300 D10
Brownedge Cl BBR PR5 169 G2
Brown Edge Cl STHP PR8 222 D1
Brownedge La BBR PR5 169 H2
Brownedge Rd BBR PR5 168 E3
Brownhill Av
BRFD/BLYE BB10 7 M3
Brownhill Dr BBN BB1 157 J1
Brown Hill La COL BB8 296 C4
HBR HX7 301 P7
Brownhill La
KIRK/FR/WAR PR4 167 G4
Brownhill Rd BBN BB1 137 J8
LEYL PR25 186 C2
Brownhill Vw WHIT OL12 235 H2
Browning Av ACC BB5 158 F6
CLV/TH FY5 81 K8
LSTA FY8 147 G7
Browning Cl COL BB8 296 A5
Browning Crs PRES PR1 * 153 G1
Browning Rd PRES PR1 153 G1
Browning St DWN BB3 192 C2
Brown La BBR PR5 169 J1
Brownley St CHLYE PR6 208 B4
CHLYE PR6 187 L2
Brown Lodge St LIT OL15 219 J8
Brownlow La
WGNW/BIL/OR WN5 263 M2
Brownlow Rd HOR/BR BL6 231 L7
Brownlow St BBN BB1 158 A7
CLI BB7 99 H4
Brownmoor Cl
CSBY/BLUN L23 257 K7
Brownmoor La
CSBY/BLUN L23 257 J8
Brownmoor Pk
CSBY/BLUN L23 257 J8
Brownroyd BWCK/EAR BB18 294 F5
Browns Hey CHLY/EC PR7 207 K1
Brownside Cl MILN OL16 218 F8
Brownside Rd
BRFD/BLYE BB10 143 H6
Brown's La KIRK/FR/WAR PR4 128 A7
NTHTN L30 258 C8
PLF/KEOS FY6 82 B4
Brown Sq BLY BB11 7 H3
Brown St ACC BB5 159 L6
BBN BB1 10 F3
BBR PR5 169 J3
BCUP OL13 179 J7
BLY BB11 6 F3
CHLYE PR6 208 A3
CLI BB7 99 G4
CLV/TH FY5 81 L8
FTWD FY7 77 K8
LIT OL15 219 K6
RAMS BL0 214 E6
Brown St East COL BB8 296 A6
Brown St West COL BB8 * 103 M7
Brows Cl FMBY L37 237 H8
Browsholme LANC LA1 2 A2
Browsholme Av
BRFD/BLYE BB10 7 L4
FUL/RIB PR2 133 J8
Browsholme Cl BPOOLE FY3 105 L3
CARN LA5 33 H2
Browsholme Rd CLI BB7 289 N7
Brows La FMBY L37 237 H8
Brow St ROCH OL11 235 K7
The Brow KIRK/FR/WAR PR4 165 H7
Brow Vw BRFD/BLYE BB10 * 142 E3
Broxholme Wy MGHL L31 259 G4
Broxton Av
WGNW/BIL/OR WN5 255 J4
Broyd Vw LANC LA1 54 E6
Bruce St BBN BB1 11 L2
BLY BB11 6 A5
BWCK/EAR BB18 293 Q4
ROCH OL11 234 F7
Bruna La GAR/LONG PR3 284 D11
Brundhurst Fold BBNW BB2 156 A1
Brunel Dr BBN BB1 11 H5
Brunel St PDHM/BLYW BB12 141 M4
Brunel Wk BBN BB1 11 H5
Brunel Wy BPOOLS FY4 125 M4
Brungerley Av CLI BB7 99 H2
Brungerley Br CLI BB7 99 G1
Brun Gv BPOOL FY1 5 J9
Brunshaw Av BRFD/BLYE BB10 7 M5
Brunshaw Rd BRFD/BLYE BB10 7 L5
Brun St BLY BB11 6 F4
Brunswick Dr COL BB8 103 K8
Brunswick Pl FUL/RIB PR2 8 A1
Brunswick Rd HEY LA3 40 F8
Brunswick St BBNW BB2 10 C6
BLY BB11 7 H7
CHLYE PR6 208 A3
DWN BB3 191 L3
MILN OL16 235 K3
NLSN BB9 123 H4
Brunswick Ter ACC BB5 159 L5
BCUP OL13 197 G3
Brunton Rd HGHB LA2 264 G1
LANC LA1 54 E6
Brush St BLY BB11 141 M6
Brussells Rd DWN BB3 191 M2
Bryan Rd BPOOLE FY3 5 H2
Bryan St BBNW BB2 173 H1
Brydeck Av PRES PR1 152 B7
Bryer's Cft BBN BB1 137 J5
Bryer St LANC LA1 3 H6
Bryn Gv HGHB LA2 42 D1
Bryning Av BISP FY2 84 F7
KIRK/FR/WAR PR4 127 L8
Bryning Fern La
KIRK/FR/WAR PR4 128 C7
Bryning Hall La LSTA FY8 147 J2
Bryning La KIRK/FR/WAR PR4 147 L1
KIRK/FR/WAR PR4 129 J8
Bryn Lea Ter BOL BL1 233 J7
Bryony Cl CLV/TH FY5 81 J6
WGNW/BIL/OR WN5 255 G6
Buccleuch Av CLI BB7 99 G3
Buccleuch Cl CLI BB7 99 G3
Buccleuch St BLY BB11 6 C5
Buchanan St BPOOL FY1 104 F5
CHLYE PR6 208 A4
RAMS BL0 214 E5
Buckden Cl CLV/TH FY5 84 F1
Buckden Ga NLSN BB9 * 102 F8
Buckden Pl HEY LA3 52 E3
Buckden Rd ACC BB5 159 J7
Buckfast Cl NTHTN L30 258 C7
Buckfast Dr FMBY L37 247 L1
Buck Haw Brow SETT BD24 264 H3
Buckholes La CHLYE PR6 188 F2
Buckhurst Rd BURY BL9 215 L8
Buckingham Av PRES PR1 168 A1
Buckingham Cl NTHTN L30 257 M8
RAW/HAS BB4 194 D2
Buckingham Ct
NWD/KWIPK L33 260 C8
Buckingham Dr
PDHM/BLYW BB12 140 A1
Buckingham Gv ACC BB5 159 J4
FMBY L37 247 H1
Buckingham Pl HEY LA3 41 G8
Buckingham Rd HEY LA3 41 G8
LSTA FY8 146 A7
MGHL L31 258 F3
Buckingham St CHLYE PR6 208 A4
MILN OL16 235 K3
Buckingham Wy PLF/KEOS FY6 85 M6
Buckland Dr
WGNW/BIL/OR WN5 255 L2
Bucklands Av FUL/RIB PR2 152 A1
Buckley Brook St WHIT OL12 235 L1
Buckley Crs CLV/TH FY5 84 F4
Buckley Farm La WHIT OL12 218 E8
Buckley Flds WHIT OL12 235 K1
Buckley Hill La NTHTN L30 258 A6
Buckley La WHIT OL12 218 E8
Buckley Rd WHIT OL12 218 E8
Buckley St HEYW OL10 234 A8
MILN OL16 235 K3
Buckley Vw TOD OL14 303 K1
WHIT OL12 218 E8
Buckley Wood Bottom
TOD OL14 303 L2
Bucknell Pl CLV/TH FY5 85 H4
Buckshaw Hall Cl
CHLY/EC PR7 207 L1
Bucks La SETT BD24 265 M7
Buck St BLY BB11 6 B5
CLI BB7 290 G8
COL BB8 296 B6
Buckthorn Pl PLF/KEOS FY6 78 C5
Buckton Cl CHLYE PR6 187 M5

Bude Cl KIRK/FR/WAR PR4 131 J5
Buersil Av MILN OL16 235 L7
Buersil St MILN OL16 235 L8
Buffet Hill La HGHB LA2 39 M6
Buff St DWN BB3 191 J3
Bulcock St BRFD/BLYE BB10 142 E2
Bulk Rd LANC LA1 3 H4
Bulk St LANC LA1 3 H6
Bull Cop FMBY L37 237 K8
Bullens La BRSC L40 223 G4
Buller Av PRES PR1 152 B7
Buller St LANC LA1 42 E8
RAW/HAS BB4 195 K1
Bullfinch St PRES PR1 * 152 E2
Bullough Cl ACC BB5 159 K6
Bull Park La PLF/KEOS FY6 86 F3
Bullsnape La GAR/LONG PR3 93 J7
Bull St BLY BB11 7 G4
Bulmer St FUL/RIB PR2 151 M1
Bulwer St MILN OL16 235 K3
The Bungalows
BWCK/EAR BB18 * 294 E6
Bunkers Hill Cl BBNW BB2 172 E3
Bunker St KIRK/FR/WAR PR4 148 F5
Bunting Pl CLV/TH FY5 85 J2
Bunyan St WHIT OL12 235 J2
Burbank Cl BPOOLS FY4 125 J6
Burbo Bank Rd
CSBY/BLUN L23 256 D7
Burbo Bank Rd North
CSBY/BLUN L23 256 C6
Burbo Bank Rd South
CSBY/BLUN L23 256 E8
Burbo Crs CSBY/BLUN L23 256 E8
Burbo Man CSBY/BLUN L23 * 256 E8
Burchall Fld MILN OL16 235 L4
Burdett Av WHIT OL12 234 C2
Burdett St BLY BB11 6 A5
Burdock Wk HEY LA3 53 J1
Burford Cl BBNW BB2 172 B3
BPOOLE FY3 105 K4
Burford Dr HEY LA3 52 F4
Burgate BPOOLS FY4 125 G6
Burgess Av BPOOLS FY4 125 H4
Burgess Gdns MGHL L31 258 F1
Burgess' La FMBY L37 248 D2
Burgess St BBN BB1 157 M6
Burgh Hall Rd CHLY/EC PR7 207 K8
Burgh La CHLY/EC PR7 207 M7
Burgh La South CHLY/EC PR7 229 L1
Burghley Brow GAR/LONG PR3 91 G2
Burghley Cl CHLYE PR6 187 M1
Burghley Ct LEYL PR25 * 186 E2
Burgh Mdw CHLY/EC PR7 207 M7
Burgh Wood Wy CHLY/EC PR7 207 J5
Burgundy Crs CLV/TH FY5 85 J4
Burholme Br CLI BB7 288 C3
Burholme Cl FUL/RIB PR2 153 K1
Burholme Pl FUL/RIB PR2 153 K1
Burholme Rd FUL/RIB PR2 153 K1
Burleigh Rd PRES PR1 8 D5
Burleigh St PDHM/BLYW BB12 6 E1
Burlington Av FMBY L37 237 L8
MCMB LA4 41 L6
Burlington Gdns LEYL PR25 186 E3
Burlington Gv MCMB LA4 41 L6
Burlington Rd BPOOLS FY4 124 E5
STHP PR8 199 J8
Burlington Rd West
BPOOLS FY4 124 D5
Burlington St BBNW BB2 10 A3
CHLY/EC PR7 208 A4
NLSN BB9 122 F4
ROCH OL11 235 K7
Burnage Gdns BPOOLS FY4 125 G4
Burnedge Cl WHIT OL12 218 A1
Burned House La
PLF/KEOS FY6 82 F2
Burneside Cl MCMB LA4 41 K7
Burnet Cl MILN OL16 235 M7
Burnfell Rd LANC LA1 2 C1
Burn Gv CLV/TH FY5 81 H7
Burnham Cl BLY BB11 6 C5
Burnham Ct HEY LA3 52 F2
Burnham Ga BLY BB11 6 B5
Burnley Cl BBN BB1 11 M3
Burnley La ACC BB5 160 C1
Burnley Rd ACC BB5 139 L8
BBN BB1 157 M6
BCUP OL13 179 J7
BCUP OL13 163 G8
BLY BB11 163 G2
BLY BB11 160 E2
BRFD/BLYE BB10 163 J3
BRFD/BLYE BB10 123 J8
CLI BB7 292 E2
COL BB8 296 E10
COL BB8 123 K1
NLSN BB9 122 E7
PDHM/BLYW BB12 141 H4
RAMS BL0 195 G6
RAW/HAS BB4 177 J5
STHP PR8 220 F6
TOD OL14 303 J1
TOD OL14 300 B9
Burnley Rd East
RAW/HAS BB4 196 C2
Burnley Wy BCUP OL13 179 L1
BLY BB11 162 B4
BLY BB11 140 E8
BLY BB11 6 E4
HBR HX7 298 G10
PDHM/BLYW BB12 140 E7
PDHM/BLYW BB12 6 C2
RAW/HAS BB4 161 H5
TOD OL14 300 A10
Burnsall Av BPOOLE FY3 105 K2
HEY LA3 52 E3
Burnsall Cl BRFD/BLYE BB10 123 H8
Burnsall Pl FUL/RIB PR2 133 H7
NLSN BB9 102 F8
Burnsall Rd ACC BB5 159 J7
Burns Av ACC BB5 158 F6
CLV/TH FY5 85 J1
LSTA FY8 147 G7
Burns Dr ACC BB5 176 B1
Burnside RAMS BL0 215 G1
SKEL WN8 243 L1
Burnside Av BPOOLS FY4 125 H3
FTWD FY7 80 F1
FUL/RIB PR2 133 J8
GAR/LONG PR3 285 K7
Burnside Rd MILN OL16 235 M5
Burnside Wy PRES PR1 152 A8
Burnslack Rd FUL/RIB PR2 133 J8
Burns Pl BPOOLS FY4 125 J3
Burns Rd FTWD FY7 77 K6
Burns St NLSN BB9 123 G2
PDHM/BLYW BB12 140 F7
PDHM/BLYW BB12 6 F1
PRES PR1 153 G1
Burns Wk DWN BB3 191 M2
Burns Wy GTH/LHO BB6 138 E7
Burnt Edge La HBR HX7 301 N7
HOR/BR BL6 232 E6
Burnthorpe Cl ROCH OL11 234 B5
Burnt House Cl TOD OL14 303 M1
Burrell Av COL BB8 296 A5
Burrington Cl FUL/RIB PR2 133 G5
Burrow Heights La HGHB LA2 66 E3
Burrow Rd KKBYL LA6 21 M6
PRES PR1 9 K1
Burrow's La PLF/KEOS FY6 82 C5
Burscough Rd ORM L39 241 J5
Burscough St ORM L39 241 H6
Burton Av LANC LA1 42 B8
Burton Ct FTWD FY7 80 F3
Burton Gdns NLSN BB9 122 E6
Burton Hl KKBYL LA6 31 H6
Burton Pk KKBYL LA6 19 G5
Burton Rd BPOOLS FY4 125 J3
HGHB LA2 38 C3
KKBYL LA6 19 G1
Burton St BBN BB1 158 F2
BLY BB11 7 J6
Burwains Av COL BB8 296 A2
Burwell Av CHLY/EC PR7 229 G3
FMBY L37 247 G2
Burwell Cl WHIT OL12 218 A8
Burwen Castle Rd
SKP/WHF BD23 281 J11
Burwen Cl BLY BB11 142 A8
Burwood Cl PRES PR1 168 C1
Burwood Dr BPOOLE FY3 105 K5
FUL/RIB PR2 153 H1
Bury Fold La DWN BB3 191 K5
Bury La CHLYE PR6 189 J1
Bury New Rd RAMS BL0 215 G5
Bury Old Rd BURY BL9 215 J7
Bury Rd EDGW/EG BL7 213 J8
RAMS BL0 215 G1
RAW/HAS BB4 176 E8
ROCH OL11 234 C5
STHP PR8 199 K8
Bury St ACC BB5 159 G8
DWN BB3 191 K2
Buseph Barrow MCMB LA4 42 A6
Buseph Ct MCMB LA4 42 A7
Buseph Dr MCMB LA4 42 A7
Bushburn Dr GTH/LHO BB6 137 M2
Bushby's La FMBY L37 246 F1
Bushby's Pk FMBY L37 246 F1
Bushell Pl PRES PR1 9 J6
Bushell St PRES PR1 9 G1
Bushey La RNFD/HAY WA11 262 B1
Bush La KIRK/FR/WAR PR4 148 E7
Bush St BRFD/BLYE BB10 142 D3
Bussel Rd PRES PR1 168 B1
Butcher Brow BBR PR5 153 H6
Butchers La ORM L39 250 C6
Bute Av BPOOL FY1 104 E4
Bute Rd BBN BB1 174 A1
Bute St BLY BB11 6 B9
Butler Pl PRES PR1 152 C1
Butler Rd BPOOL FY1 4 C6
Butlers Farm Ct LEYL PR25 186 A4
Butlers Meadow
KIRK/FR/WAR PR4 148 B5
Butler St BBN BB1 158 F2
BPOOL FY1 104 F5
BRFD/BLYE BB10 * 142 D3
PRES PR1 9 G5
RAMS BL0 214 D7
Butterbergh HGHB LA2 39 G3
Buttercross Cl BLY BB11 162 A1
Buttercup Dr ROCH OL11 234 E8
Butterfield Gdns ORM L39 241 G8
Butterfield St LANC LA1 * 3 G5
Butterlands PRES PR1 153 J3
Buttermere Av ACC BB5 159 G6
CHLY/EC PR7 207 K5
COL BB8 296 C5
FTWD FY7 80 F2
MCMB LA4 * 41 L7
Buttermere Cl BBN BB1 11 H2
BBR PR5 169 G1
FMBY L37 237 G8
FUL/RIB PR2 132 F7
MGHL L31 259 G2
NWD/KWIPK L33 260 A7
Buttermere Ct LANC LA1 * 3 L3
Buttermere Crs
RNFD/HAY WA11 262 C1
Buttermere Dr PLF/KEOS FY6 78 C6
RAMS BL0 214 E4
Buttermere Rd
BRFD/BLYE BB10 143 H6
GAR/LONG PR3 114 C6
LANC LA1 3 L3
WGNW/BIL/OR WN5 255 M4
Butterwick Fld HOR/BR BL6 231 J8
Butterworth Brow
CHLY/EC PR7 207 J7
CHLYE PR6 189 J4
Butterworth Cl
KIRK/FR/WAR PR4 128 D5
Butterworth St LIT OL15 219 K6
Butt Hill La GAR/LONG PR3 285 J11
Button St GAR/LONG PR3 92 E6
Butts BWCK/EAR BB18 293 Q5
GTH/LHO BB6 138 E6
The Butts Av MILN OL16 * 235 J4
Butts Cl CLV/TH FY5 81 M7
Butts Gv CLI BB7 99 H1
Butts La HGHB LA2 39 G3
KIRK/FR/WAR PR4 148 F5
STHP PR8 200 C6
TOD OL14 301 P11
Butt's La GAR/LONG PR3 88 E5
Butts Mt GTH/LHO BB6 138 F6
Butts Rd CLV/TH FY5 81 L7
Buxton Av BISP FY2 85 G7
Buxton Crs MILN OL16 235 L7
Buxton St ACC BB5 159 K6
MCMB LA4 41 K7
WHIT OL12 302 A12
Bye La ORM L39 239 M8
Bye Rd RAMS BL0 215 H4
Byerworth La North
GAR/LONG PR3 284 B10
Byerworth La South
GAR/LONG PR3 284 B10
Byfield Av CLV/TH FY5 85 H4
Byland Cl BPOOLS FY4 124 F6
FMBY L37 247 L1
PDHM/BLYW BB12 140 A2
Bymbrig Cl BBR PR5 169 H3
By-Pass Rd CARN LA5 24 E5
The By-Pass CSBY/BLUN L23 257 H7
Byrom St BBNW BB2 10 D6
CHTN/BK PR9 200 C5
TOD OL14 303 L1
Byron Av CARN LA5 32 F6
CLV/TH FY5 81 K8
KIRK/FR/WAR PR4 148 B5
LSTA FY8 147 G7
Byron Cl ACC BB5 176 B1
ACC BB5 158 F7
FMBY L37 237 J7
KIRK/FR/WAR PR4 183 J6
WGNW/BIL/OR WN5 255 J4
Byron Crs CHLY/EC PR7 229 H2
Byron Gv BWCK/EAR BB18 293 P4
Byron Rd COL BB8 296 C6
CSBY/BLUN L23 256 E7
HEY LA3 40 F8
MGHL L31 250 A8
Byron Sq GTH/LHO BB6 * 138 E7
Byron St BPOOLS FY4 124 E2
CHLY/EC PR7 207 M3
FTWD FY7 77 K7
PDHM/BLYW BB12 141 J4
The Byway CSBY/BLUN L23 257 H6

C

Cabin La BRSC L40 202 D5
CHTN/BK PR9 181 H8
MGHL L31 249 J7
ORM L39 222 A6
Cable St CHTN/BK PR9 13 G3
FMBY L37 237 K7
LANC LA1 3 G5
Cabus Cross Roads
GAR/LONG PR3 284 A2
Cabus Nook La GAR/LONG PR3 270 A12
Cadby Av BPOOLE FY3 5 M7
Cadley Av FUL/RIB PR2 131 L8
Cadley Cswy FUL/RIB PR2 131 M7
Cadley Dr FUL/RIB PR2 131 L8
Cadogan Pl PRES PR1 9 J6
Cadogan St NLSN BB9 123 G1
Cadshaw Cl BBN BB1 157 H3
Cadwell Rd MGHL L31 249 L6
Caernarfon Cl CLV/TH FY5 86 A1
Caernarvon Av
PDHM/BLYW BB12 141 K4
Caernarvon Rd RAW/HAS BB4 194 D2
Cage La KIRK/FR/WAR PR4 167 L3
Cairndale Dr LEYL PR25 186 E5
Cairn Dr ROCH OL11 234 B6
Cairn Gv BPOOLS FY4 124 F7
Cairns Cl NLSN BB9 102 F8
Cairnsmore Av PRES PR1 153 J2
Cairo St PDHM/BLYW BB12 6 B3
Caister Cl SKEL WN8 254 A3
Caithness Dr CSBY/BLUN L23 257 J8
Caithness Rd HEYW OL10 234 B6
Calcott St BLY BB11 162 B1
Caldbeck Cl NLSN BB9 123 H5
Caldbeck Rd LANC LA1 3 M3
Calder Av CHLY/EC PR7 207 L6
CHLYE PR6 189 K2
CLI BB7 118 D4
CLV/TH FY5 85 J1
DWN BB3 173 G7
FTWD FY7 81 G1
FUL/RIB PR2 132 C5
GAR/LONG PR3 114 D4
KIRK/FR/WAR PR4 148 C6
LIT OL15 219 K4
ORM L39 241 H7
Calder Bank BBN BB1 157 H4
Calderbank Cl
CROS/BRETH PR26 185 K2
Calder Banks BBN BB1 157 H4
Calderbrook Av BLY BB11 142 B8
Calderbrook Pl BLY BB11 6 C9
Calderbrook Rd LIT OL15 219 L3
Calder Cl CARN LA5 33 G2
KIRK/FR/WAR PR4 128 E6
LSTA FY8 145 J1
NLSN BB9 123 G2
NWD/KWIPK L33 260 C5
Calder Ct ACC BB5 140 B5
Calderdale Wy TOD OL14 302 H2
TOD OL14 301 K11
Calder Dr GAR/LONG PR3 91 G1
MGHL L31 259 J1
Calder Edge TOD OL14 * 301 R12
Calder House La
GAR/LONG PR3 284 C11
Calder Pl GTH/LHO BB6 139 H5
WGNW/BIL/OR WN5 255 M4
Calder Rd BISP FY2 104 F2
RAW/HAS BB4 177 K7
Caldershaw La WHIT OL12 234 D1
Caldershaw Rd WHIT OL12 234 D2
Calderstones Dr CLI BB7 118 D4
Calder St BBN BB1 157 J4
BLY BB11 6 F3
COL BB8 103 M7
FUL/RIB PR2 8 A2
MILN OL16 235 L1
NLSN BB9 123 G2
PDHM/BLYW BB12 140 F3
TOD OL14 303 L2
Calder V CLI BB7 118 F7
NLSN BB9 123 G1
Caldervale Av PLF/KEOS FY6 85 M8
Calder Vale Rd
PDHM/BLYW BB12 6 E3
Calder Wy HEY LA3 54 A1
Caldicott Cl TOD OL14 303 J4
Caldicott Wy PLF/KEOS FY6 85 M5
Caldwell Cl NWD/KWIPK L33 * 260 C7
Caldy Dr RAMS BL0 214 D8
Caleb St NLSN BB9 123 H2
Caledonian Av BPOOLE FY3 105 G4
Calfcote La GAR/LONG PR3 114 E4
Calf Croft Pl LSTA FY8 146 D7
Calf Hall La BWCK/EAR BB18 293 P5
Calf Hey ACC BB5 139 J7
LIT OL15 219 J5
Calf Hey North ROCH OL11 235 K7
Calf Hey Rd RAW/HAS BB4 193 L1
Calf Hey South ROCH OL11 235 K7
Calf Wood La AIRE BD20 295 N6
Calgary Av BBNW BB2 156 E3
Calico Cl ACC BB5 158 F7
Calico Dr GAR/LONG PR3 284 C12
Calico St BBNW BB2 173 G2
Calico Wood Av
WGNNW/ST WN6 245 J5
California Dr TOD OL14 303 K5
Calkeld La LANC LA1 3 G5
Calla Dr GAR/LONG PR3 284 B7
Callander Cl FUL/RIB PR2 132 F4
Callender St RAMS BL0 214 E5
Calliards Rd MILN OL16 219 H7
Callon St PRES PR1 153 H3
Caltha Dr DWN BB3 173 K4
Caltha St RAMS BL0 214 E5
Calva Cl PDHM/BLYW BB12 141 L3
Calverley St PRES PR1 153 G2
Calverley Wy WHIT OL12 218 B7
Calvert Pl BPOOLE FY3 105 K4
Cambell's Ct LSTA FY8 145 H4
Camberley Cl STHP PR8 12 A8
Camberly Dr ROCH OL11 234 C5
Camborne Av CARN LA5 33 H3
Camborne Ct BPOOLE FY3 125 L1
Camborne Pl
KIRK/FR/WAR PR4 148 D5
Cambray Rd BPOOL FY1 104 F3
Cambrian Cl BBN BB1 137 J8
Cambrian Wy RAW/HAS BB4 194 E2
Cambridge Ar STHP PR8 13 G4
Cambridge Av CHTN/BK PR9 200 C1
CSBY/BLUN L23 257 G7
LANC LA1 55 G6
ROCH OL11 234 D5
Cambridge Cl BBN BB1 11 H5
PDHM/BLYW BB12 141 G5
PRES PR1 152 B1
Cambridge Dr BBN BB1 158 B7
CSBY/BLUN L23 256 F6
GAR/LONG PR3 284 A8
PDHM/BLYW BB12 141 G4
Cambridge Gdns
CHTN/BK PR9 200 C1
Cambridge Pl TOD OL14 303 L2
Cambridge Rd BBR PR5 169 J3
BPOOL FY1 5 G1
CHTN/BK PR9 200 B2
CLV/TH FY5 80 F8
CSBY/BLUN L23 256 F6
FMBY L37 247 G2
FTWD FY7 77 H8
HEY LA3 40 F8
LSTA FY8 146 B8
SKEL WN8 253 H2
WGNW/BIL/OR WN5 255 H3
Cambridge St ACC BB5 * 159 M4
BBN BB1 11 H5
BLY BB11 * 6 A5
CHLY/EC PR7 207 M4
COL BB8 * 296 A7
DWN BB3 191 M2
GTH/LHO BB6 139 G6
NLSN BB9 * 122 E6
PRES PR1 152 B1
TOD OL14 303 L2
Cambridge Wk PRES PR1 152 B1
Cambridge Wks STHP PR8 13 G4
Cam Cl BBR PR5 169 J3
Camden Pl PRES PR1 9 H5
Camden Rd BPOOLE FY3 105 H5
Camden St NLSN BB9 123 G4
Camellia Dr LEYL PR25 187 H1
Cameron Av BPOOLE FY3 105 H4
Cameron Cft CHLYE PR6 * 208 A3
Cameron St BRFD/BLYE BB10 142 D2
Camforth Hall La
GAR/LONG PR3 113 J5
Cam La CHLYE PR6 169 K8
SKP/WHF BD23 294 E1
Cammock La SETT BD24 265 N8
Camms Vw RAW/HAS BB4 194 D3
Camomile Cl CHLY/EC PR7 * 187 K8
Campbell Av BPOOLE FY3 105 H4
Campbell Cl BBNW BB2 172 F4
Campbell Ct BBN BB1 157 H2
Campbell Crs NWD/KWIPK L33 260 A5
Campbell St BBN BB1 157 H2
PDHM/BLYW BB12 140 A2
PRES PR1 9 M2
WHIT OL12 * 235 H1
Campion Cl CLV/TH FY5 81 J6
Campion Dr FUL/RIB PR2 150 F2
RAW/HAS BB4 194 D3
The Campions FUL/RIB PR2 150 F2
Campion Wy HEY LA3 53 J1
WHIT OL12 217 M8
Camp St BRFD/BLYE BB10 123 H8
Cam St PRES PR1 152 F1
Camwood BBR PR5 169 L7
Camwood Dr BBR PR5 168 E2
Cam Wood Fold CHLYE PR6 169 K8
Canada Crs BISP FY2 85 H8
Canada St HOR/BR BL6 231 L8
Canal Bank BRSC L40 * 224 E5
Canal Bank Pygons Hl
MGHL L31 249 M4
Canal Cl KKBYL LA6 19 G1
Canal Gdns CARN LA5 33 G5
Canalside BBNW BB2 11 H7
BRSC L40 223 L7
Canal Side NLSN BB9 123 G1
Canal St ACC BB5 159 H5
BBNW BB2 172 E2
BLY BB11 6 E5
CHLY/EC PR7 230 D5
LIT OL15 219 L6
ROCH OL11 235 K6
Canal Wk CHLYE PR6 208 C3
LANC LA1 3 J5
Canberra Cl CLV/TH FY5 85 J4
Canberra Ct BPOOLS FY4 * 125 H7
Canberra La
KIRK/FR/WAR PR4 131 H7
Canberra Rd LEYL PR25 186 E2
WGNW/BIL/OR WN5 255 M2
Canberra Wy
KIRK/FR/WAR PR4 148 B4
ROCH OL11 235 K8
Candlemakers Ct CLI BB7 99 H3
Cann Bridge St BBR PR5 153 K7
Canning Rd CHTN/BK PR9 200 D4
Canning St PDHM/BLYW BB12 6 E1
Cannock Av BPOOLE FY3 105 H3
Cannock Gn MGHL L31 258 E2
Cannon Hl FUL/RIB PR2 8 B1
LANC LA1 * 2 C7
Cannon St ACC BB5 159 L6
NLSN BB9 123 J2
PRES PR1 9 H5
RAMS BL0 214 D7
TOD OL14 303 K4
Canon Flynn Ct MILN OL16 235 M4
Canon St MILN OL16 235 L1
Canterbury Av BPOOLE FY3 5 L6
CSBY/WL L22 257 G8
LANC LA1 55 G5
Canterbury Cl CHLYE PR6 189 H3
FMBY L37 237 J6
GAR/LONG PR3 283 R8
PLF/KEOS FY6 85 M6
ROCH OL11 234 D4
STHP PR8 12 C9
Canterbury Rd PRES PR1 153 G2
Canterbury St BBNW BB2 10 D6
CHLYE PR6 208 B5
Canterbury Wy
GAR/LONG PR3 283 R8
NTHTN L30 258 C7
Cantlow Fold STHP PR8 220 D7
Cantsfield Av FUL/RIB PR2 131 L7
Canute St PRES PR1 152 D2
Capernwray Rd KKBYL LA6 34 C1
Capesthorne Dr CHLY/EC PR7 207 L8
Cape St RAW/HAS BB4 195 K1
Capilano Pk ORM L39 250 F3
Capitol Cl BOL BL1 233 K8
Capitol Wy BBR PR5 152 F6
Caplin Cl NWD/KWIPK L33 260 B5
Capstan Cl LSTA FY8 145 H2
Captains Rw LANC LA1 3 H3
Captain St BCUP OL13 179 K4
HOR/BR BL6 231 L7
Caraway Cl CSBY/BLUN L23 257 L6
Carawood Cl WGNNW/ST WN6 245 G4
Carbis Av FUL/RIB PR2 134 A3
Carcroft Av BISP FY2 85 G7
Cardale KIRK/FR/WAR PR4 167 G1
Cardiff St SKEL WN8 253 G2
Cardigan Av ACC BB5 158 F7
CLI BB7 99 H3
PDHM/BLYW BB12 141 K4
Cardigan Cl CLI BB7 99 G3
Cardigan Pl BPOOLS FY4 124 D6
Cardigan Rd STHP PR8 221 J2
Cardigan St FUL/RIB PR2 152 A2
WHIT OL12 218 B8
Cardigan Wy NTHTN L30 * 258 E7
Cardinal Gdns LSTA FY8 146 A5
Cardinal Pl CLV/TH FY5 81 H8
Cardinal St BRFD/BLYE BB10 142 E2
Cardwell Cl KIRK/FR/WAR PR4 148 A6
Cardwell Pl BBNW BB2 10 E4
Cardwell St PDHM/BLYW BB12 141 G4
Carfax Fold WHIT OL12 234 E1
Carfax Rd NWD/KWIPK L33 260 D7
Carfield SKEL WN8 254 B5
Carham Rd BBN BB1 157 H3
Carholme Av BRFD/BLYE BB10 7 M4
Carisbrooke Av BPOOLS FY4 125 K4
Carisbrooke Cl PLF/KEOS FY6 85 M5
Carisbrooke Dr CHTN/BK PR9 200 C2
Carleton Av BPOOLE FY3 105 J2
FUL/RIB PR2 133 G7
PDHM/BLYW BB12 140 B1
Carleton Dr PRES PR1 151 K7
Carleton Gdns PLF/KEOS FY6 85 L6
Carleton Ga PLF/KEOS FY6 85 M7
Carleton La SKP/WHF BD23 281 R12
Carleton Rd CHLYE PR6 188 B7
COL BB8 103 K8
Carleton St MCMB LA4 41 H7
NLSN BB9 123 H4
Carleton Wy PLF/KEOS FY6 85 L6
Carley St DWN BB3 191 H1
Carlile Wy NWD/KWIPK L33 260 C5
Carlin Ga BISP FY2 104 E1
Carlinghurst Rd BBNW BB2 10 C5
Carlisle Av FTWD FY7 81 G2
PRES PR1 151 K7
Carlisle Gv CLV/TH FY5 85 L1
Carlisle Pl CHLYE PR6 230 D3
Carlisle Rd ACC BB5 * 160 A3
STHP PR8 221 K1
Carlisle St BBN BB1 11 G6
PRES PR1 9 J3
WHIT OL12 218 B8
Carloway Av FUL/RIB PR2 132 F6
Carl's Wy NWD/KWIPK L33 260 D5
Carlton Av CHLYE PR6 187 L1
SKEL WN8 254 D4
Carlton Dr PRES PR1 9 M8
Carlton Gdns BBN BB1 10 E1
Carlton Gv BISP FY2 84 E7
Carlton Pl CLI BB7 99 H4
Carlton Rd BBN BB1 10 D1
BLY BB11 6 D6
LEYL PR25 186 C3
LSTA FY8 145 J4
STHP PR8 220 F5
Carlton St BCUP OL13 179 K8
FUL/RIB PR2 8 D2
NLSN BB9 122 E6
Carlton Ter CSBY/BLUN L23 * 257 G7
Carlton Wy BPOOLS FY4 126 C4
Carluke St BBN BB1 157 M6
Carlyle Av BPOOLS FY4 124 E5
Carlyle Gv MCMB LA4 41 M5
Carmel Cl ORM L39 251 G1
Carnarvon Rd BBNW BB2 156 E6
PRES PR1 8 D5
STHP PR8 221 J2
Carnegie Av CSBY/BLUN L23 257 G8
Carnfield Pl BBR PR5 169 K3
Carnforth Av BISP FY2 85 H6
Carnforth Brow CARN LA5 33 L1
Carnforth Cl BBNW BB2 173 K2
Carnoustie Dr CHLY/EC PR7 187 G7
Carnoustie Cl FUL/RIB PR2 131 L4
STHP PR8 12 C9
Carnoustie Ct PRES PR1 151 K5
Carnoustie Dr RAMS BL0 214 D6
Caroline Cl HEY LA3 52 E3
Caroline St BPOOL FY1 4 D5
PRES PR1 152 F3
Carpenters Wy MILN OL16 235 L7
Carradice Cl NLSN BB9 123 G4
Carr Bank Av RAMS BL0 214 E4
Carr Bank Dr RAMS BL0 214 E4
Carr Bank Rd MTHPE LA7 17 H1
RAMS BL0 214 E4
Carr Barn Brow BBR PR5 169 M5
Carr Brook Cl CHLYE PR6 187 L3
Carr Cl GAR/LONG PR3 79 M6
PLF/KEOS FY6 106 B1
PLF/KEOS FY6 82 F7
Carr Cft LITH L21 257 L8
Carr Dr KIRK/FR/WAR PR4 128 B5
Carr End La PLF/KEOS FY6 82 F4
Carr Fld BBR PR5 169 M7
Carrfield Av CSBY/BLUN L23 257 K8
Carr Fold RAMS BL0 214 E4
Carr Ga CLV/TH FY5 80 F7
Carr Hall Cl NLSN BB9 122 E2
Carr Hall Dr NLSN BB9 122 E2
Carr Hall Gdns NLSN BB9 122 E1
Carr Hall Rd NLSN BB9 122 E1
Carr Hall St RAW/HAS BB4 176 D6
Carr Head La PLF/KEOS FY6 106 B1
Carr Hey CLV/TH FY5 * 85 K1
Carr Holme Gdns
GAR/LONG PR3 284 B5
Carr House La
CROS/BRETH PR26 184 A4
HTWN L38 248 B7
LANC LA1 2 F8
TOD OL14 303 N1
WGNNW/ST WN6 228 C3
Carriage Dr LIT OL15 219 L4
Carrick Ms BPOOLE FY3 125 L1
Carrier's Rw COL BB8 296 H5
Carrington Cl MILN OL16 219 G8
Carrington Gv MCMB LA4 41 M6
Carrington Rd CHLY/EC PR7 230 C4
CHLY/EC PR7 207 L4
Carr La BBNW BB2 156 B5

BRSC L40.....225 L8
CHLY/EC PR7.....207 M6
CROS/BRETH PR26.....204 E4
GAR/LONG PR3.....79 M7
HEY LA3.....64 E3
HGHB LA2.....66 D1
KIRK/FR/WAR PR4.....183 J4
KIRK/FR/WAR PR4.....147 L5
KIRK/FR/WAR PR4.....129 C5
LEYL PR25.....168 D8
MGHL L31.....249 J6
PLF/KEOS FY6.....106 E2
PLF/KEOS FY6.....82 F8
RAW/HAS BB4.....195 K2
STHP PR8.....221 J4
Carr Meadow BBR PR5.....169 M5
Carr Moss La STHP PR8.....221 H7
Carroll Crs ORM L39.....241 J4
Carrol St PRES PR1.....9 J4
Carron La GAR/LONG PR3.....92 D7
Carr Pl BBR PR5.....169 L4
Carr Rd BLY BB11.....6 D9
BWCK/EAR BB18.....293 P4
CHLYE PR6.....187 L1
CLV/TH FY5.....85 G5
COL BB8.....296 B5
DWN BB3.....191 L3
FTWD FY7.....77 K6
HOR/BR BL6.....231 L6
KIRK/FR/WAR PR4.....128 E7
NLSN BB9.....122 F2
PLF/KEOS FY6.....86 F1
RAW/HAS BB4.....195 J2
RAW/HAS BB4.....178 L3
TOD OL14.....300 D11
Carr's Crs FMBY L37.....247 G2
Carr's Crs West FMBY L37.....247 G2
Carr Side La SFTN L29.....248 D8
Carr St BBN BB1.....10 F2
BBR PR5.....169 L3
CHLYE PR6.....208 B2
PRES PR1.....9 L5
RAMS BL0.....214 E4
Carrs Wd COL BB8.....156 C5
Carruthers Cl HEYW OL10.....234 C8
Carrwood Dr KIRK/FR/WAR PR4.....128 E7
Carrwood Gdns HGHB LA2.....66 E7
Carrwood Gn PDHM/BLYW BB12.....140 F3
Carrwood Rd RAMS BL0.....214 D7
Carrwood Pk STHP PR8.....199 L8
Carrwood Rd BBR PR5.....152 E8
Carrwood Wy BBR PR5.....168 E1
Carry La COL BB8.....296 B6
Carshalton Rd BPOOL FY1.....104 E4
Carsluith Av BPOOLS FY4.....5 K2
Carson Rd BPOOLS FY4.....125 K2
Carter Av BLY BB11.....140 F7
RNFD/HAY WA11.....262 D6
Carter Fold BBNW BB2.....156 B1
Carter Pl NLSN BB9.....123 J3
Carter's La CLI BB7.....278 A7
The Carters NTHTN L30.....258 D7
Carter St ACC BB5.....159 L7
BPOOL FY1.....4 E1
PDHM/BLYW BB12.....141 M4
Carterville Cl BPOOLS FY4.....125 K4
Cartford Av GAR/LONG PR3.....88 D5
Cartford Cl GAR/LONG PR3.....88 D5
Cartford La GAR/LONG PR3.....88 D5
Cartford Pk GAR/LONG PR3.....88 D5
Cart Ga PLF/KEOS FY6.....78 E8
Cartmel Cl WHIT OL12.....235 J2
Cartmel Av ACC BB5.....159 K8
FTWD FY7.....80 F2
MGHL L31.....259 H1
Cartmel Cl STHP PR8.....200 C8
FMBY L37.....247 L1
PDHM/BLYW BB12.....141 L3
Cartmel Fold BPOOLS FY4.....125 L6
Cartmel La GAR/LONG PR3.....283 L7
LSTA FY8.....147 G4
Cartmell Rd BPOOLS FY4.....126 A2
LSTA FY8.....145 J7
Cartmel Pl FUL/RIB PR2.....133 J4
MCMB LA4.....41 K7
Cartmel Rd BBNW BB2.....156 D8
LANC LA1.....3 L1
LEYL PR25.....186 A3
Cartwright Ct LANC LA1.....54 D6
Carus Av BBN BB1.....192 B3
Carus Pk KKBYL LA6.....29 G7
Carus St DWN BB3.....192 C2
Carvel Wy BRSC L40.....225 J8
Carvers Brow CROS/BRETH PR26.....204 E2
Carwood La CHLYE PR6.....187 M4
Caryl Rd LSTA FY8.....144 F3
Cascades SKEL WN8.....253 M4
Caspian Wy LANC LA1.....54 D7
Casserley Rd COL BB8.....296 C5
Casson Ga WHIT OL12.....235 H2
Castercliffe Rd NLSN BB9.....123 L3
Casterton CHLY/EC PR7.....206 F1
Casterton Av BRFD/BLYE BB10.....122 E8
Casterway Vw CLI BB7.....99 H2
Castle Av PLF/KEOS FY6.....85 H5
ROCH OL11.....235 H5
Castle Bank CARN LA5.....16 F1
Castlebergh La SETT BD24.....265 P7
Castle Cl COL BB8.....296 C5
Castle Ct COL BB8.....296 C5
Castle Crs HOR/BR BL6.....231 M6
Castle Dr CHLY/EC PR7.....230 B5
FMBY L37.....247 J2
Castle Fold PRES PR1.....168 C1
Castlegate BPOOL FY1.....4 D9
Castlehey SKEL WN8.....254 A5
Castle HI LANC LA1.....2 F5
SETT BD24.....265 P7
Castle Hill Crs ROCH OL11.....235 H5
Castle House La CHLY/EC PR7.....230 N1
Castlekeep Vw CLI BB7.....99 H2
Castle La BPOOLE FY3.....106 A6
BRSC L40.....242 A6
GAR/LONG PR3.....284 C9
TOD OL14.....303 N1
Castle Lane Cl TOD OL14.....303 N1
Castlemere Cl ROCH OL11.....235 L1
Castlemere Ter ROCH OL11.....235 L1
Castle Mt FUL/RIB PR2.....132 C4
Castle Pk LANC LA1.....2 F5
Castle Park Ms LANC LA1.....2 F5
Castlerigg Dr PDHM/BLYW BB12.....141 L3
Castlerigg Pl BPOOLS FY4.....125 M4
Castle Rd COL BB8.....296 B5
BBN BB1.....11 L3
CHLY/EC PR7.....208 A4
CHTN/BK PR9.....13 H3
CLI BB7.....99 H3

NLSN BB9.....123 J3
PDHM/BLYW BB12.....6 E1
PRES PR1.....9 E2
Castleton Dr NTHTN L30.....258 E7
Castleton Rd PRES PR1.....152 E2
Castletown Dr BCUP OL13.....197 L3
Castletown St BCUP OL13.....197 L3
CLI BB7.....99 H3
Castle Wk PRES PR1.....8 A6
STHP PR8.....12 A6
Catches Cl ROCH OL11.....234 E3
Catches La ROCH OL11.....234 E2
Catforth Av BPOOLS FY4.....125 L2
Catforth Rd FUL/RIB PR2.....151 M1
KIRK/FR/WAR PR4.....110 C6
Catharine's La ORM L39.....251 J1
Cathedral Cl BBNW BB2.....10 F5
Cathedral Dr HEY LA3.....53 J1
Catherine Cl KIRK/FR/WAR PR4.....128 C4
Catherine St CHLY/EC PR7.....207 M5
KIRK/FR/WAR PR4.....128 C5
PRES PR1.....9 M2
Catherine St East HOR/BR BL6.....231 L7
Catherine St West HOR/BR BL6.....231 K6
Cathrow Dr KIRK/FR/WAR PR4.....167 L4
Cathrow Wy CLV/TH FY5.....86 A1
Catley Cl CHLYE PR6.....187 M6
Catlow Hall St ACC BB5.....159 H8
Caton Av FTWD FY7.....81 G2
Caton Cl CHTN/BK PR9.....180 C7
GAR/LONG PR3.....114 E3
LEYL PR25.....187 H1
Caton Green Rd HGHB LA2.....44 A2
Caton Gv BPOOLE FY3.....105 J4
Caton Rd LANC LA1.....3 J5
Caton St MILN OL16.....235 J5
Cato St RAMS BL0.....214 D7
Cat Tail La STHP PR8.....223 H2
Catterall Cl BPOOL FY1.....105 G4
Catterall Gates La GAR/LONG PR3.....90 F1
Catterall La GAR/LONG PR3.....90 E2
Catterall St BBNW BB2.....172 F3
Catterick Fold STHP PR8.....200 C8
Cattle St GTH/LHO BB6.....138 F6
Caunce Av CHTN/BK PR9.....181 K5
Caunce's Rd CHTN/BK PR9.....201 M6
Caunce St BPOOL FY1.....4 E1
BPOOLE FY3.....105 G5
Causeway End RAW/HAS BB4.....194 D4
Causeway Head RAW/HAS BB4.....194 D3
Causeway La BRSC L40.....225 L2
FMBY L37.....248 E2
Causeway Side TOD OL14.....303 N9
The Causeway CHLYE PR6.....208 B3
CHTN/BK PR9.....180 F6
CROS/BRETH PR26.....185 J5
Causeway Wood Rd TOD OL14.....303 P9
Causey Foot NLSN BB9.....123 G4
Cavalry Wy BLY BB11.....7 A4
Cavell Cl BBN BB1.....173 L2
Cavendish Ct CARN LA5.....32 F6
Cavendish Crs FUL/RIB PR2.....133 J4
Cavendish Man CLV/TH FY5.....80 F3
Cavendish Pl BBNW BB2.....156 E8
BBR PR5.....153 G8
Cavendish Rd BISP FY2.....84 F7
CSBY/BLUN L23.....256 F8
HEY LA3.....40 F8
LSTA FY8.....144 F3
PRES PR1.....153 H2
ROCH OL11.....235 H8
STHP PR8.....199 J8
Cavendish St ACC BB5.....159 M8
BWCK/EAR BB18.....293 P6
CHLYE PR6.....208 A4
DWN BB3.....173 J8
LANC LA1.....2 C6
Cave St BBNW BB2.....172 E2
Cavour St PDHM/BLYW BB12.....141 L3
The Cawsey PRES PR1.....168 C1
Cawthorne St LANC LA1.....2 C5
Caxton Av BISP FY2.....84 F7
Caxton Rd FUL/RIB PR2.....132 E3
Cayley St MILN OL16.....235 L4
Cecilia Rd BBNW BB2.....172 C1
Cecilia St PRES PR1.....153 G2
Cecil St ACC BB5.....159 M7
BBN BB1.....158 F2
BPOOL FY1.....104 F4
BWCK/EAR BB18.....293 P4
LIT OL15.....219 J6
LSTA FY8.....144 F3
ROCH OL11.....235 H8
Cedar Av BBR PR5.....168 E3
CHLY/EC PR7.....186 F7
CLV/TH FY5.....85 H1
FTWD FY7.....81 H3
FUL/RIB PR2.....151 K1
KIRK/FR/WAR PR4.....148 A5
PLF/KEOS FY6.....106 A3
PLF/KEOS FY6.....78 D6
RAW/HAS BB4.....176 F8
Cedar Cl BBN BB1.....158 E3
FUL/RIB PR2.....134 A2
GAR/LONG PR3.....284 A7
KIRK/FR/WAR PR4.....129 C8
ORM L39.....240 D7
RAMS BL0.....214 D7
Cedar Crs KIRK/FR/WAR PR4.....128 D2
Cedar Dr FMBY L37.....246 F2
Cedar Fld CHLYE PR6.....187 M1
Cedar Gv KIRK/FR/WAR PR4.....166 D2
MGHL L31.....259 G5
SKEL WN8.....253 G5
WGNW/BIL/OR WN5.....255 J5
Cedar Rd CHLYE PR6.....208 A4
FUL/RIB PR2.....153 H1
LANC LA1.....2 P6
Cedars Cl BWCK/EAR BB18.....293 P6
Cedar Sq BPOOL FY1.....4 D6
The Cedars CHLY/EC PR7.....207 L5
CHLY/EC PR7.....205 L5
KIRK/FR/WAR PR4.....167 J3
Cedar St ACC BB5.....160 A5
BBN BB1.....157 P3
BLY BB11.....7 H6
MCMB LA4.....41 H6
STHP PR8.....200 C7
TOD OL14.....303 K9
WHIT OL12.....235 H2
Cedar Wk KIRK/FR/WAR PR4.....108 C3
Cedar Wy PRES PR1.....151 L8
Cedarwood Cl LSTA FY8.....146 B7

Cedarwood Dr LEYL PR25.....186 B3
Cedarwood Pl LANC LA1.....55 L4
Cedric Pl BISP FY2.....84 F7
Celandine Cl CLV/TH FY5.....81 J6
LIT OL15.....219 J5
Celandine Wk WGNS/IIMK WN3.....255 M7
Celia St BRFD/BLYE BB10.....7 A1
Cemetery La BLY BB11.....141 K7
PLF/KEOS FY6.....82 E2
Cemetery Rd BWCK/EAR BB18.....294 F6
DWN BB3.....173 M6
PRES PR1.....152 F2
RAMS BL0.....214 D7
Cemetery Vw CHLY/EC PR7.....230 C5
Centenary Wy BLY BB11.....7 G6
Central Av ACC BB5.....158 F7
BBR PR5.....170 B1
CLI BB7.....99 G4
KIRK/FR/WAR PR4.....128 E7
LANC LA1.....42 E7
LIT OL15.....219 L5
ROCH OL11.....215 G1
STHP PR8.....221 J3
Central Av North CLV/TH FY5.....81 J8
Central Beach LSTA FY8.....146 A6
Central Blds CSBY/BLUN L23.....257 H7
Central Dr BPOOL FY1.....4 D4
LSTA FY8.....145 M4
MCMB LA4.....41 G6
PRES PR1.....151 K7
RNFD/HAY WA11.....262 C4
WGNNW/ST WN6.....245 L5
Central Sq MGHL L31.....259 G1
Central St RAMS BL0.....214 E5
Central Vw BCUP OL13.....197 K1
Centre Dr CHLYE PR6.....169 L7
Centre Rd AIRE BD20.....295 J3
Centre Vale Cl LIT OL15.....219 M4
Centurian Wy CROS/BRETH PR26.....168 D7
Century Gdns WHIT OL12.....235 J3
Ceres La LANC LA1.....2 A6
Chaddock St PRES PR1.....9 H5
Chadfield Rd BPOOL FY1.....5 G5
Chad St COL BB8.....296 C1
Chadwell Rd NWD/KWIPK L33.....260 F1
Chadwick Gdns BBR PR5.....168 D4
Chadwick Hall Rd ROCH OL11.....234 E5
Chadwick St BBNW BB2.....10 B8
BPOOL FY1.....4 A5
ROCH OL11.....235 G4
Chadwick Wy NWD/KWIPK L33.....260 F1
Chaffinch Cl CLV/TH FY5.....81 J6
Chaffinch Ct BPOOLE FY3.....105 L5
Chaigley Cl CLI BB7.....97 K3
Chaigley Rd GAR/LONG PR3.....114 E3
Chain Caul Rd FUL/RIB PR2.....151 J3
Chain Caul Wy FUL/RIB PR2.....151 J3
Chain House La KIRK/FR/WAR PR4.....167 M4
Chain La BPOOLE FY3.....106 C8
Chalfont Fld FUL/RIB PR2.....131 M6
Challenge Wy BBN BB1.....157 M4
WGNW/BIL/OR WN5.....255 M2
Chamber House Dr ROCH OL11.....234 E8
Chamberlain Dr NWD/KWIPK L33.....260 C6
Chambres Rd STHP PR8.....13 M6
Chambres Rd North STHP PR8.....13 M6
Champagne Av CLV/TH FY5.....85 J3
Champness Hall MILN OL16.....235 J4
Chancellors Whf LANC LA1.....3 G8
Chancel Pl DWN BB3.....191 M4
MILN OL16.....235 J4
Chancel Wy DWN BB3.....191 M3
Chancery Rd CHLY/EC PR7.....207 K2
Chandlers Cft KIRK/FR/WAR PR4.....165 H4
Chandlers Ford PLF/KEOS FY6.....86 E6
Chandlers Rest LSTA FY8.....147 G4
Chandler St PRES PR1.....9 J4
Chandley Cl STHP PR8.....220 F6
Change Cl BCUP OL13.....179 L7
Changford Rd NWD/KWIPK L33.....260 D6
Channel Av CSBY/BLUN L23.....256 F8
Channel Wy FUL/RIB PR2.....8 B7
Channing Rd LSTA FY8.....145 M7
Channing Sq MILN OL16.....235 L5
Channing St MILN OL16.....235 L5
Chanters Wy DWN DD3.....173 K6
Chapel Brow GAR/LONG PR3.....114 D4
LEYL PR25.....186 E2
Chapel Cl CLI BB7.....98 E3
HEY LA3.....65 H3
HGHB LA2.....66 H3
KIRK/FR/WAR PR4.....128 C4
Chapel Ct BRFD/BLYE BB10.....123 K8
SKP/WHF BD23.....281 K2
Chapel Fld EDGW/EG BL7.....212 F7
Chapel Fold CLI BB7.....119 J4
COL BB8.....296 A7
Chapel Gdns GAR/LONG PR3.....91 G3
KIRK/FR/WAR PR4.....165 H4
Chapel Gra EDGW/EG BL7.....212 F7
Chapel HI BWCK/EAR BB18.....294 F6
GAR/LONG PR3.....114 D5
LIT OL15.....219 J5
Chapel Hill La RAW/HAS BB4.....177 H5
Chapel House La KKBYL LA6.....22 F8
Chapel House Rd NLSN BB9.....123 G5
Chapelhouse Wk FMBY L37.....237 G6
Chapel La BBR PR5.....171 G1
BRSC L40.....242 B1
BRSC L40.....202 E6
CARN LA5.....16 E1
CHLY/EC PR7.....206 F1
CHLYE PR6.....188 D6
CHTN/BK PR9.....181 H4
CLI BB7.....290 D10
FMBY L37.....237 J8
GAR/LONG PR3.....91 L1
HEY LA3.....65 J3
HGHB LA2.....66 J3
KIRK/FR/WAR PR4.....166 F1
KIRK/FR/WAR PR4.....110 A4
KKBYL LA6.....31 H6
NTHTN L30.....258 D6
SKEL WN8.....244 A2
TOT/BURYW BL8.....214 D7
Chapel Meadow KIRK/FR/WAR PR4.....166 F3

Chapel Mdw KIRK/FR/WAR PR4.....183 K6
Chapel Ms BWCK/EAR BB18.....294 E6
ORM L39.....241 H7
Chapel Park Rd KIRK/FR/WAR PR4.....166 F3
Chapel Ri CLI BB7.....118 F2
Chapel Rd BPOOLS FY4.....125 K4
FUL/RIB PR2.....132 D7
KIRK/FR/WAR PR4.....165 H4
Chapels DWN BB3.....173 K8
Chapel St South TOD OL14.....303 K6
Chapels Brow DWN BB3.....173 K8
Chapelside Cl GAR/LONG PR3.....91 G1
Chapels La DWN BB3.....172 C8
Chapel Sq ACC BB5.....159 H7
Chapel St ACC BB5.....159 H7
BBN BB1.....174 C5
BBN BB1.....158 F2
BBNW BB2.....10 B5
BCUP OL13.....196 F3
BLY BB11.....7 H4
BPOOL FY1.....4 C4
BRFD/BLYE BB10.....143 K6
BWCK/EAR BB18.....294 D5
CHLY/EC PR7.....230 C5
CHLY/EC PR7.....229 H2
CHLY/EC PR7.....207 M3
CHLYE PR6.....189 H3
CLI BB7.....275 P6
COL BB8.....296 A7
DWN BB3.....191 K3
EDGW/EG BL7.....212 A8
EDGW/EG BL7.....210 F6
GAR/LONG PR3.....114 D4
GAR/LONG PR3.....88 C5
HGHB LA2.....66 F8
HOR/BR BL6.....231 M8
LANC LA1.....3 G1
LSTA FY8.....146 D3
MCMB LA4.....41 H6
NLSN BB9.....123 G5
ORM L39.....241 J6
PDHM/BLYW BB12.....121 J6
PLF/KEOS FY6.....86 A7
PRES PR1.....9 G4
RAW/HAS BB4.....196 B2
RAW/HAS BB4.....176 B8
ROCH OL11.....235 K7
SETT BD24.....265 N7
STHP PR8.....13 G4
WGNW/BIL/OR WN5.....255 L5
WHIT OL12.....218 F4
WHIT OL12.....217 M3
Chapel Vw RNFD/HAY WA11.....263 J7
Chapel Vls BCUP OL13.....179 L7
Chapel Wk CARN LA5.....26 B5
KIRK/FR/WAR PR4.....167 G3
PDHM/BLYW BB12.....140 F2
SKP/WHF BD23.....267 R6
Chapel Wks KIRK/FR/WAR PR4.....128 C3
PRES PR1.....9 H4
Chapel Wy CHLY/EC PR7.....229 J2
Chapel Yd BBR PR5.....153 G6
Chapman Cl BWCK/EAR BB18.....293 Q4
Chapman Rd DWN BB3.....192 C2
FUL/RIB PR2.....132 D8
Chapter Rd DWN BB3.....191 M3
Chardonnay Crs CLV/TH FY5.....85 J3
Charlbury Gv HEY LA3.....52 F2
Charles Av STHP PR8.....221 H5
Charlesbye Av ORM L39.....241 K5
Charles Cl LANC LA1.....3 H1
Charles Crs BBR PR5.....153 M8
Charles Gv GAR/LONG PR3.....114 C4
Charles La RAW/HAS BB4.....194 D1
Charles St ACC BB5.....159 H8
ACC BB5.....139 H6
BBN BB1.....10 C9
BPOOL FY1.....4 E1
COL BB8.....296 B6
DWN BB3.....191 J3
GTH/LHO BB6.....138 F7
LANC LA1.....3 H9
LIT OL15.....219 K6
MCMB LA4.....41 G6
NLSN BB9.....123 H1
RAW/HAS BB4.....196 C1
Charles Wy FUL/RIB PR2.....151 K1
Charlesway CHLY/EC PR7.....151 J1
Charles Whittaker St WHIT OL12.....234 C2
Charlesworth Cl MGHL L31.....249 L6
Charlock Cl NTHTN L30.....258 F7
Charlotte Pl PRES PR1.....9 F5
Charlotte St BBN BB1.....10 E5
BLY BB11.....6 F5
EDGW/EG BL7.....212 A7
MILN OL16.....235 J5
PRES PR1.....9 G5
RAMS BL0.....214 E6
Charnley Cl PRES PR1.....167 M1
Charnley Ct BBR PR5.....153 J8
Charnley Fold BBR PR5.....169 J1
Charnley Fold La BBR PR5.....153 J8
Charnley Rd BPOOL FY1.....4 D3
Charnley's La CHTN/BK PR9.....181 H3
Charnley St BBNW BB2.....172 H1
LANC LA1.....2 C5
PRES PR1.....9 G4
Charnock Brow Preston Rd CHLY/EC PR7.....206 F1
Charnock Fold PRES PR1.....152 F1
Charnock Moss BBR PR5.....168 C3
Charnock St CHLYE PR6.....208 A4
KIRK/FR/WAR PR4.....128 D2
LEYL PR25.....186 D2
ORM L39.....241 J6
Charnwood Av BPOOLE FY3.....105 K5
Charnwood Cl BBNW BB2.....156 D3
Charter Brook GTH/LHO BB6.....139 G6
Charterhouse Pl BBNW BB2.....156 E8
Charter La CHLY/EC PR7.....207 L8
Charter St ACC BB5.....159 J6
MILN OL16.....235 K7
Chartford Cl CHLYE PR6.....187 M1
Chartwell Cl CHLYE PR6.....187 M1
Chartwell Ri BBR PR5.....168 F3
Chartwell St STHP PR8.....220 F6
Chase Cl STHP PR8.....12 B7
Chase Heys CHTN/BK PR9.....200 F1
Chaseley Rd WHIT OL12.....235 H1
The Chase BPOOLE FY3.....105 M4
CARN LA5.....25 H1
CLV/TH FY5.....81 K6
LEYL PR25.....186 F1
PDHM/BLYW BB12.....142 A3
Chase Wd KIRK/FR/WAR PR4.....166 F3

CLI BB7.....99 J2
GTH/LHO BB6.....139 H6
RAW/HAS BB4.....195 K7
Chatburn Old Rd CLI BB7.....290 E12
Chatburn Park Dr CLI BB7.....99 J1
NLSN BB9.....122 D5
Chatburn Rd BOL BL1.....233 J8
CLI BB7.....290 G12
FUL/RIB PR2.....133 H7
GAR/LONG PR3.....114 D5
Chatburn St South TOD OL14.....303 H4
Chatham Av LSTA FY8.....145 K4
Chatham Crs COL BB8.....296 B5
Chatham Pl CHLYE PR6.....208 B3
PRES PR1.....152 E1
Chatham St COL BB8.....296 B5
NLSN BB9.....123 G2
Chatsworth Av BISP FY2.....84 F5
FTWD FY7.....80 F1
KIRK/FR/WAR PR4.....148 A5
Chatsworth Cl BBN BB1.....173 L3
CHLY/EC PR7.....207 L3
CLV/TH FY5.....86 A2
NLSN BB9.....122 F2
Chatsworth Ct CHLYE PR6.....230 F3
Chatsworth Rd BBR PR5.....153 G8
HEY LA3.....41 G8
LANC LA1.....54 E7
LEYL PR25.....186 C3
LSTA FY8.....145 G4
STHP PR8.....220 D5
Chatsworth St PRES PR1.....152 F3
WGNW/BIL/OR WN5.....255 M6
WHIT OL12.....218 B8
Chatteris Pl CLV/TH FY5.....84 F2
Chatterton Old La RAMS BL0.....214 B1
Chatterton Rd RAMS BL0.....214 H1
Chaucer Av CLV/TH FY5.....81 J8
Chaucer Cl CHLY/EC PR7.....205 L5
Chaucer Gdns GTH/LHO BB6.....138 F2
Chaucer Pl BISP FY2.....5 J6
Chaucer Rd FTWD FY7.....77 K7
Chaucer St PRES PR1.....153 G1
Cheam Av CLV/TH FY5.....208 A5
Cheapside BPOOL FY1.....4 C1
CHLY/EC PR7.....207 M3
FMBY L37.....247 K1
LANC LA1.....3 H2
PRES PR1.....9 H4
SETT BD24.....265 N7
Cheddar Av BPOOLS FY4.....125 L6
Cheddar Dr FUL/RIB PR2.....133 G5
Chedworth Av HEY LA3.....52 F4
Cheetham Meadow CROS/BRETH PR26.....185 K2
Cheetham St BBNW BB2.....10 A4
MILN OL16.....235 J3
Chelburn Gv BRFD/BLYE BB10.....7 J13
Chelburn Vw LIT OL15.....219 M2
Chelford Av BPOOLS FY4.....105 H3
Chelford Cl PRES PR1.....168 C1
Chellowdene CSBY/BLUN L23.....257 H5
Chelmsford Cl LANC LA1.....55 H6
Chelmsford Gv CHLY/EC PR7.....207 L3
Chelmsford Pl CHLY/EC PR7.....207 L5
Chelmsford Wk CROS/BRETH PR26.....185 K3
Chelsea Av BISP FY2.....105 K3
Chelsea Ms BISP FY2.....105 K2
LANC LA1.....3 H2
Chelsea St ROCH OL11.....235 G6
Chelston Dr RAW/HAS BB4.....194 D4
Cheltenham Av BISP FY2.....159 H4
Cheltenham Crs CLV/TH FY5.....86 A3
LSTA FY8.....147 G6
Cheltenham Rd BBNW BB2.....10 A3
BPOOL FY1.....104 E4
LANC LA1.....54 E6
Cheltenham Wy STHP PR8.....200 C7
Chepstow Cl ROCH OL11.....234 C3
Chepstow Gdns GAR/LONG PR3.....284 C9
Chepstow Rd BPOOLS FY3.....105 J3
Chequer Cl SKEL WN8.....254 C5
Chequer La SKEL WN8.....254 C5
Chequers ACC BB5.....159 J1
Chequers Av LANC LA1.....55 G7
Cheriton Fld FUL/RIB PR2.....131 M4
Cheriton Pk STHP PR8.....199 G7
The Cherries CHLY/EC PR7.....187 G8
Cherry Cl BBN BB1.....11 M4
FUL/RIB PR2.....133 G5
KIRK/FR/WAR PR4.....128 D2
Cherryclough Wy BBNW BB2.....172 D3
Cherry Crs ACC BB5.....175 G1
RAW/HAS BB4.....195 J3
Cherrycroft SKEL WN8.....254 B5
Cherrydale BISP FY2.....85 G5
Cherry Dr GTH/LHO BB6.....117 L5
Cherry Gn ORM L39.....250 F5
Cherry Gv BRSC L40.....225 H5
CHLYE PR6.....189 L1
GAR/LONG PR3.....114 D3
ROCH OL11.....234 D3
Cherry La KIRK/FR/WAR PR4.....148 E7
Cherry Lea BBNW BB2.....172 C4
Cherry Rd STHP PR8.....238 A1
Cherry St SBN BB1.....11 M4
Cherry Tree Cl CARN LA5.....42 G1
GAR/LONG PR3.....282 B2
HEY LA3.....52 D5
PLF/KEOS FY6.....78 D5
Cherry Tree Dr LANC LA1.....54 E7
Cherry Tree Gdns BPOOLS FY4.....125 L5
Cherry Tree Gv CHLYE PR6.....187 M8
Cherry Tree La BBNW BB2.....172 B3
BRSC L40.....223 K7
ORM L39.....250 E2
RAW/HAS BB4.....195 A2
Cherry Tree Rd BLY BB11.....7 H1
Cherry Tree Rd North BPOOLS FY4.....125 K2
Cherry Trees BBR PR5.....152 E8
Cherry Tree Wy RAW/HAS BB4.....194 B1
Cherry V KIRK/FR/WAR PR4.....183 H1
Cherry Wd NWD/KWIPK L33.....260 C6
Cherry Wd PRES PR1.....151 L8
Cherrywood Av CLV/TH FY5.....84 B7
Cherrywood Cl LEYL PR25.....186 B3
Chervil Wk WGNS/IIMK WN3.....255 M7
Cheryl Dr CLV/TH FY5.....81 K8
Chesham Dr KIRK/FR/WAR PR4.....167 J4
Chesham Ldg GAR/LONG PR3.....88 E6
Chesham St GAR/LONG PR3.....177 G8
Cheshire Ct CHLY/EC PR7.....187 J5

314 Che - Clo

RAMS BL0 215 G5
Cheshire House Cl
CROS/BRETH PR26 * 168 C4
Cheshire Lines Pth ORM L39 238 C5
Chesmere Cft PRES PR1 * 151 L6
Chesmere Dr PRES PR1 151 L6
Chesnell Gv NWD/KWIPK L33 260 C6
Chester Av CHLY/EC PR7 208 B7
CHTN/BK PR9 200 C3
CLI BB7 99 H2
CLV/TH FY5 85 G1
PLF/KEOS FY6 85 M8
ROCH OL11 234 D5
Chesterbrook GAR/LONG PR3 116 B7
Chester Cl BBN BB1 11 J7
CSBY/BLUN L23 257 L7
GAR/LONG PR3 284 A8
HEY LA3 53 J1
Chester Crs RAW/HAS BB4 194 E3
Chester Dr RAMS BL0 214 D7
Chesterfield Cl STHP PR8 220 E7
Chesterfield Dr
NWD/KWIPK L33 260 B6
Chesterfield Rd BPOOL FY1 104 E4
CSBY/BLUN L23 257 K6
STHP PR8 220 E7
Chester Pl CHLYE PR6 230 D3
GAR/LONG PR3 88 F6
LANC LA1 54 F6
Chester Rd BPOOLE FY3 * 105 G4
CHTN/BK PR9 200 C3
PRES PR1 152 F2
Chester St ACC BB5 159 K6
BBN BB1 11 J5
Chestnut Av BPOOLS FY4 125 J6
CARN LA5 32 F6
CHLY/EC PR7 186 F7
CHLYE PR6 208 B1
CSBY/BLUN L23 257 J5
HGHB LA2 44 E5
PRES PR1 151 K7
TOD OL14 301 K12
Chestnut Cl BBR PR5 169 H1
BISP FY2 105 G1
KIRK/FR/WAR PR4 128 E7
ORM L39 239 M2
Chestnut Ct LEYL PR25 186 D4
ORM L39 241 J5
Chestnut Crs CLI BB7 119 G2
FUL/RIB PR2 153 H1
KIRK/FR/WAR PR4 166 C3
Chestnut Dr BWCK/EAR BB18 293 P6
CLI BB7 118 D4
FUL/RIB PR2 132 A4
MCMB LA4 42 A4
RAW/HAS BB4 195 J3
Chestnut Gdns CLV/TH FY5 81 L8
Chestnut Gra ORM L39 241 G8
Chestnut Gv ACC BB5 159 K7
ACC BB5 139 K7
DWN BB3 191 K6
LANC LA1 2 C5
Chestnut Ri BLY BB11 6 E6
Chestnut St STHP PR8 13 K9
Chestnut Wk BBN BB1 11 M4
MGHL L31 259 K7
Chestnut Wy FMBY L37 246 F2
LIT OL15 219 H6
Chethams Cl CLV/TH FY5 85 K1
Chetwood Av CSBY/BLUN L23 257 J6
Chevassut Cl NLSN BB9 122 F2
Cheviot Av BRFD/BLYE BB10 143 H6
CLV/TH FY5 81 J7
LSTA FY8 147 H6
Cheviot Cl HOR/BR BL6 231 M6
RAMS BL0 214 F7
Cheviot St PRES PR1 8 B2
Cheviot Wy NWD/KWIPK L33 260 C5
Chevron Cl ROCH OL11 234 E8
Chew Gdns PLF/KEOS FY6 85 L8
Chew La SKP/WHF BD23 281 K1
Cheyne Cl CSBY/BLUN L23 256 D8
Chichester Cl BRFD/BLYE BB10 7 K4
CLV/TH FY5 85 K1
LIT OL15 219 J8
Chichester St MILN OL16 235 K4
Chicken St BBNW BB2 10 B6
Chilham St
WGNW/BIL/OR WN5 255 K5
Chiltern Av BPOOLS FY4 125 G4
BRFD/BLYE BB10 143 H6
CHLY/EC PR7 207 G2
PLF/KEOS FY6 85 M8
Chiltern Cl HOR/BR BL6 231 M6
LSTA FY8 147 G6
RAMS BL0 214 F7
Chiltern Dr KKBY L32 259 M7
WGNS/IIMK WN3 255 M8
Chiltern Meadow LEYL PR25 187 G2
Chiltern Rd RAMS BL0 214 F7
STHP PR8 220 D5
Chilton Cl MGHL L31 259 G2
Chilton Ms MGHL L31 259 G2
The Chimes KIRK/FR/WAR PR4 183 K6
KIRK/FR/WAR PR4 128 D7
China St ACC BB5 159 J5
LANC LA1 3 G6
Chindit Cl FMBY L37 247 G1
Chindits Wy FUL/RIB PR2 132 E7
The Chines FUL/RIB PR2 132 B7
Chingford Bank
BRFD/BLYE BB10 123 G8
Chingle Cl FUL/RIB PR2 133 H5
Chipping Av STHP PR8 220 D6
Chipping Gv BPOOLE FY3 105 K3
BRFD/BLYE BB10 143 G7
Chipping La GAR/LONG PR3 114 D2
Chipping St PDHM/BLYW BB12 141 G2
Chirk Dr CLV/TH FY5 * 86 A1
Chisacre Dr WGNNW/ST WN6 245 G4
Chisholm Cl WGNNW/ST WN6 228 E8
Chislehurst Av BPOOLS FY4 124 F2
Chislehurst Gv
BRFD/BLYE BB10 123 G7
Chislehurst Pl LSTA FY8 146 A5
Chislett Cl BRSC L40 * 225 G7
Chisnall Av WGNNW/ST WN6 228 C6
Chisnall La CHLY/EC PR7 228 C1
Chiswell Gv CLV/TH FY5 86 B3
Chiswell St
WGNW/BIL/OR WN5 255 M6
Chiswick Gv BPOOLE FY3 125 L1
Chive Cl BISP FY2 85 J8
Chorley Cl CHTN/BK PR9 181 H6
Chorley Hall Rd CHLY/EC PR7 207 M1
Chorley New Rd HOR/BR BL6 231 L8
Chorley Old Rd CHLYE PR6 187 M3
HOR/BR BL6 232 B8
Chorley Rd BBR PR5 153 G8
BPOOLE FY3 105 J1
CHLYE PR6 171 G8
HOR/BR BL6 230 F8
SKEL WN8 226 F7
WGN WN1 229 M6
Chorley St CHLYE PR6 230 E3
Chorlton Cl BRFD/BLYE BB10 143 G1
Chorlton St BBN BB1 157 J4
Christ Church Sq ACC BB5 * 159 M6
Christ Church St ACC BB5 * 159 M6
BCUP OL13 179 K8
PRES PR1 8 E5
Christian Rd PRES PR1 8 F5
Christie Av MCMB LA4 41 L7
Christines Crs BRSC L40 225 G7
Christleton WGNNW/ST WN6 245 L5
Christleton Cl
BRFD/BLYE BB10 123 J8
Christopher Acre ROCH OL11 234 B2
Church Aly ACC BB5 * 159 J1
Church Av ACC BB5 176 B1
LANC LA1 54 E7
PRES PR1 153 H3
PRES PR1 8 B7
Church Bank ACC BB5 159 H4
KKBYL LA6 34 B3
Church Bank St DWN BB3 * 191 K2
Church Br ACC BB5 * 159 J5
Church Brow BBR PR5 153 G6
CARN LA5 32 F8
CLI BB7 99 H2
HGHB LA2 43 J5
Church Brow Cl CARN LA5 32 F8
Church Brow Gdns CLI BB7 99 J2
Church Cl BBNW BB2 156 B1
CHTN/BK PR9 200 D3
CLI BB7 99 H2
FMBY L37 237 K8
HGHB LA2 270 G4
KIRK/FR/WAR PR4 148 D5
PDHM/BLYW BB12 139 M1
RAMS BL0 214 E6
Church Close Ct FMBY L37 * 237 K8
Church Ct CARN LA5 32 F8
PRES PR1 152 F1
RAMS BL0 195 G7
Church Cft SKP/WHF BD23 281 K3
Church Dr CLI BB7 118 D4
LSTA FY8 146 C8
WGNW/BIL/OR WN5 255 G6
Churchfield FUL/RIB PR2 132 C5
WGNNW/ST WN6 245 K5
Church Flds BRSC L40 223 J4
ORM L39 241 H6
Churchfields STHP PR8 199 J8
Church Fold CHLY/EC PR7 207 H7
Church Gdns
KIRK/FR/WAR PR4 148 B5
Churchgate CHTN/BK PR9 200 C2
GAR/LONG PR3 113 G5
Churchgate Ms CHTN/BK PR9 200 D2
Church Gn FMBY L37 246 F1
KKBY L32 260 B8
SKEL WN8 253 J2
Church Gv HEY LA3 65 K3
Church Hall ACC BB5 159 J5
Church Hl CARN LA5 16 E1
CHLYE PR6 187 L4
KKBYL LA6 33 K6
TOD OL14 300 H11
Church Hill Av CARN LA5 26 A6
Church Hill Rd BBN BB1 157 K4
ORM L39 241 G5
Churchill Av BBN BB1 158 D3
CHTN/BK PR9 200 C1
Churchill Cl CLV/TH FY5 85 L1
Churchill Ct BPOOLE FY3 105 G5
Churchill Dr FUL/RIB PR2 133 G7
Churchill Rd CHLYE PR6 189 K3
FUL/RIB PR2 132 F7
NLSN BB9 122 E2
Churchill St TOD OL14 300 H11
WHIT OL12 234 F2
Churchill Wy LEYL PR25 186 D1
NLSN BB9 122 E4
Church La ACC BB5 159 K2
BBNW BB2 156 B1
BWCK/EAR BB18 294 D9
CHLY/EC PR7 207 G7
CLI BB7 118 F6
CLI BB7 98 B8
CROS/BRETH PR26 168 B4
GAR/LONG PR3 283 N3
GAR/LONG PR3 132 A2
GAR/LONG PR3 113 G5
GAR/LONG PR3 93 G4
GAR/LONG PR3 91 K7
GTH/LHO BB6 138 F5
KIRK/FR/WAR PR4 129 M8
KKBYL LA6 29 M3
MCMB LA4 41 J5
MGHL L31 249 J3
MILN OL16 * 235 J4
ORM L39 250 D4
PDHM/BLYW BB12 140 F2
PLF/KEOS FY6 87 G2
RAMS BL0 195 G7
RAW/HAS BB4 196 B2
SKP/WHF BD23 281 K3
SKP/WHF BD23 281 K12
SKP/WHF BD23 280 E9
SKP/WHF BD23 267 N9
WGNNW/ST WN6 245 K5
WGNNW/ST WN6 228 A3
Church Mdw COL BB8 296 A6
Church Ms BBR PR5 169 H4
Church Pk HEY LA3 65 J3
KIRK/FR/WAR PR4 130 C8
Church Raike GAR/LONG PR3 287 M12
Church Rd BBR PR5 169 J5
BRSC L40 203 M7
CHTN/BK PR9 181 K5
CLV/TH FY5 85 J1
CSBY/BLUN L23 257 H7
FMBY L37 237 K7
KIRK/FR/WAR PR4 183 K6
KIRK/FR/WAR PR4 148 A4
KIRK/FR/WAR PR4 127 H1
KIRK/FR/WAR PR4 109 J7
LEYL PR25 186 D3
LSTA FY8 145 J4
MGHL L31 259 G4
MILN OL16 235 L5
ORM L39 252 B5
PLF/KEOS FY6 107 H2
RAMS BL0 215 H3
RNFD/HAY WA11 262 C5
SKEL WN8 253 J2
SKP/WHF BD23 294 D2
TOD OL14 300 H11
Church Rw KIRK/FR/WAR PR4 127 L7
PRES PR1 9 J3
Churchside KIRK/FR/WAR PR4 167 J3
Church Srteet
PDHM/BLYW BB12 140 F7
Church Stile MILN OL16 235 J4
Church St ACC BB5 159 J1
ACC BB5 159 G8
BBN BB1 158 D2
BBN BB1 10 F4
BBR PR5 153 L8
BCUP OL13 196 F3
BLY BB11 7 H3
BPOOL FY1 4 C2
BRFD/BLYE BB10 143 J1
BWCK/EAR BB18 293 Q5
CHLY/EC PR7 230 D4
CHLY/EC PR7 * 207 M4
CHTN/BK PR9 13 J3
CLI BB7 275 N6
CLI BB7 99 H3
COL BB8 296 A6
CROS/BRETH PR26 204 E2
DWN BB3 191 K2
EDGW/EG BL7 210 F7
FTWD FY7 77 L7
GAR/LONG PR3 116 A7
GAR/LONG PR3 114 E4
GAR/LONG PR3 90 D1
GTH/LHO BB6 138 F6
HGHB LA2 43 J5
HOR/BR BL6 231 M8
KIRK/FR/WAR PR4 128 E6
KKBYL LA6 21 K6
LANC LA1 2 F5
LEYL PR25 186 E1
LIT OL15 219 L6
MCMB LA4 41 K5
MILN OL16 219 G8
NLSN BB9 122 E6
NLSN BB9 103 G7
ORM L39 241 H6
PDHM/BLYW BB12 140 E3
PLF/KEOS FY6 * 86 A8
PRES PR1 9 J4
RAMS BL0 214 F5
RAW/HAS BB4 176 E8
SETT BD24 265 L6
SKEL WN8 254 F4
SKP/WHF BD23 281 K5
TOD OL14 301 J11
WGNW/BIL/OR WN5 255 G6
WHIT OL12 235 H4
WHIT OL12 217 M3
Church Ter DWN BB3 * 191 K2
Churchtown Crs BCUP OL13 197 K2
Church Vw KIRK/FR/WAR PR4 183 K6
ORM L39 250 D4
WHIT OL12 234 B1
Church Wk BBN BB1 137 J8
CHLY/EC PR7 206 F1
FUL/RIB PR2 133 J6
KIRK/FR/WAR PR4 183 K5
KIRK/FR/WAR PR4 128 C4
TOD OL14 303 K6
Church Wy FMBY L37 246 F1
KKBY L32 260 B8
NLSN BB9 123 G5
Churton Gv WGNNW/ST WN6 245 L1
Chysden Cl CHLYE PR6 187 M6
Cicely La BBN BB1 11 G4
Cicely St BBN BB1 11 G5
Cinamon St WHIT OL12 235 G3
Cinderbarrow La KKBYL LA6 26 F1
Cinder Hill Rd TOD OL14 303 P1
Cinder La KIRK/FR/WAR PR4 202 C1
KIRK/FR/WAR PR4 110 D5
LANC LA1 54 E8
Cinnamon Brow SKEL WN8 254 F5
Cinnamon Ct PRES PR1 167 M1
Cinnamon Hill Dr North
BBR PR5 153 G8
Cinnamon Hill Dr South
BBR PR5 153 G8
Cintra Av FUL/RIB PR2 152 A1
Cintra Ter FUL/RIB PR2 132 A8
Cirrus Dr ORM L39 250 D2
City Heights Cl LANC LA1 3 J6
City Rd WGNW/BIL/OR WN5 255 L4
Clairane Av FUL/RIB PR2 132 B5
Clancut La CHLY/EC PR7 229 J1
Clanfield FUL/RIB PR2 132 B4
Clapgate Rd ROCH OL11 234 B2
Clara Gorton Ct MILN OL16 * 235 L5
Clara St PRES PR1 152 F4
ROCH OL11 235 J6
WHIT OL12 218 A2
Clare Av COL BB8 123 K1
Claremont Av CHLY/EC PR7 207 L4
CLI BB7 99 J4
MGHL L31 258 E3
STHP PR8 12 E9
Claremont Ct BPOOL FY1 104 F4
Claremont Crs MCMB LA4 41 G7
Claremont Dr CLI BB7 99 J4
ORM L39 241 G8
Claremont Gdns STHP PR8 12 E9
Claremont Pl LSTA FY8 145 H3
Claremont Rd ACC BB5 159 L3
BPOOL FY1 104 F4
CHLY/EC PR7 207 L6
CSBY/BLUN L23 257 G7
ROCH OL11 234 F4
Claremont St NLSN BB9 122 D6
PDHM/BLYW BB12 6 A3
Claremont Ter
CSBY/BLUN L23 * 257 G6
NLSN BB9 123 G4
Claremount Av LEYL PR25 186 E3
Clarence Av CLV/TH FY5 81 G8
PLF/KEOS FY6 78 B6
Clarence Pk BBNW BB2 156 E4
Clarence Rd ACC BB5 159 K7
STHP PR8 199 K7
Clarence St BBN BB1 10 D2
BLY BB11 7 J8
BWCK/EAR BB18 293 R6
CHLY/EC PR7 * 208 A4
COL BB8 296 D6
DWN BB3 173 J8
GAR/LONG PR3 114 D4
LANC LA1 3 J8
LEYL PR25 186 E1
MCMB LA4 41 J5
RAW/HAS BB4 177 K4
WHIT OL12 235 G1
Clarendon Gv MGHL L31 249 M6
Clarendon Rd BBN BB1 157 J3
BPOOL FY1 4 D7
LANC LA1 42 E8
LSTA FY8 145 J3
Clarendon Rd East BBN BB1 157 K3
HEY LA3 41 G7
Clarendon Rd North LSTA FY8 145 J3
Clarendon Rd West HEY LA3 40 F8
Clarendon St ACC BB5 160 A5
CHLYE PR6 208 B4
COL BB8 296 E6
MILN OL16 235 L7
PRES PR1 9 K6
Clare Rd BPOOL FY1 4 D9
LANC LA1 2 F1
Clare St BLY BB11 6 C4
Claret St ACC BB5 159 K6
Clarke Holme St
RAW/HAS BB4 * 196 C1
Clarke's La WHIT OL12 235 G3
Clarke St BBN BB1 158 E2
MILN OL16 235 L1
Clarke Wood Cl CLI BB7 119 J3
Clarkfield Cl BRSC L40 225 J8
Clarkfield Dr MCMB LA4 41 L6
Clarksfield Rd CARN LA5 32 F7
Clark St MCMB LA4 41 J5
PLF/KEOS FY6 86 C8
Claughton Av LEYL PR25 187 H2
Claughton Dr LANC LA1 54 F8
Claughton St BRFD/BLYE BB10 142 E2
Claybank PDHM/BLYW BB12 140 F2
Claybridge Cl
WGNW/BIL/OR WN5 255 L2
Clay Brow Rd SKEL WN8 254 B5
Clayburn Cl CHLYE PR6 208 B1
Clayfield Dr ROCH OL11 234 C3
Clay Gap La PLF/KEOS FY6 83 J7
Claylands Dr CARN LA5 32 F7
Clay La HEY LA3 53 G5
ROCH OL11 234 A3
Claymere Av ROCH OL11 234 B3
Clay St BLY BB11 141 M6
LIT OL15 219 J6
Clayton Av LEYL PR25 186 A4
RAW/HAS BB4 195 H3
Clayton Brook Rd BBR PR5 169 L6
Clayton Cl NLSN BB9 123 G2
Clayton Ct GAR/LONG PR3 114 E4
Clayton Crs BPOOLS FY4 125 G5
Clayton Fold
PDHM/BLYW BB12 141 K5
Clayton Gdns BRSC L40 225 H7
Claytongate BPOOLS FY4 125 J4
CHLY/EC PR7 229 J1
Claytongate Dr PRES PR1 168 D1
Clayton Green Rd CHLYE PR6 169 L8
Clayton Gv BBN BB1 137 G5
Claytonhalgh GAR/LONG PR3 116 B8
Clayton Hall Dr ACC BB5 139 J7
Clayton Ms SKEL WN8 253 G2
Clayton Rw GTH/LHO BB6 138 A2
Clayton's Ga PRES PR1 9 G3
Clayton St BBNW BB2 10 E5
BBR PR5 169 H2
BWCK/EAR BB18 293 R5
COL BB8 296 B7
GTH/LHO BB6 138 F6
NLSN BB9 123 G2
SKEL WN8 253 G2
WHIT OL12 235 L1
Clayton Wy ACC BB5 139 K8
BBNW BB2 173 G4
Cleator Av BISP FY2 104 F2
Cleaver St BBN BB1 11 H3
BRFD/BLYE BB10 142 E3
Clecken La GAR/LONG PR3 92 A1
Clegg Av CLV/TH FY5 80 F8
Clegg St BRFD/BLYE BB10 143 K6
BRFD/BLYE BB10 142 D3
KIRK/FR/WAR PR4 * 128 D6
LIT OL15 219 J4
NLSN BB9 122 E6
RAW/HAS BB4 176 E8
SKEL WN8 253 G2
WHIT OL12 217 M1
Clegg St East
BRFD/BLYE BB10 * 142 D3
Cleggswood Av LIT OL15 219 K8
Clematis Cl CHLY/EC PR7 187 K8
Clematis St BBNW BB2 156 E6
Clement Ct MILN OL16 * 235 L5
Clementina Rd
CSBY/BLUN L23 256 E7
Clementina St WHIT OL12 235 J2
Clement Royds St WHIT OL12 * 235 H3
Clements Dr NLSN BB9 122 F7
Clement St ACC BB5 159 M6
DWN BB3 191 K3
Clements Wy NWD/KWIPK L33 260 A6
Clengers Brow CHTN/BK PR9 180 D8
Clent Av MGHL L31 249 M8
Clent Gdns MGHL L31 250 A8
Clent Rd MGHL L31 258 F1
Clerkhill St BBN BB1 11 L3
Clevedon Dr WGNS/IIMK WN3 255 M7
Clevedon Rd BPOOL FY1 104 E4
FUL/RIB PR2 131 K7
Cleveland Av FUL/RIB PR2 132 F7
Cleveland Cl KKBY L32 259 M7
RAMS BL0 214 F8
Cleveland Dr LANC LA1 2 C8
Cleveland Rd LEYL PR25 186 C1
LSTA FY8 146 E8
Clevelands Av CARN LA5 16 F7
HEY LA3 41 G8
Clevelands Gv BLY BB11 6 D7
HEY LA3 41 G8
Clevelands Mt BLY BB11 6 D7
Clevelands Rd BLY BB11 6 D7
Cleveland St CHLY/EC PR7 * 229 H2
CHLY/EC PR7 207 M3
COL BB8 296 C5
Clevelands Wk HEY LA3 41 G8
Cleveleys Av CHTN/BK PR9 180 D7
CLV/TH FY5 81 G8
FUL/RIB PR2 131 M7
LANC LA1 42 B8
MILN OL16 235 L8
Cleveleys Rd ACC BB5 159 K3
BBNW BB2 173 H2
BBR PR5 154 B8
CHTN/BK PR9 180 D8
The Cleves MGHL L31 250 B8
Cleve Wy FMBY L37 247 L1
Clieves Hl ORM L39 240 A4
Clieves Hills La ORM L39 250 A1
Cliff Bank Hamlet
RAW/HAS BB4 196 B1
Cliffe Ct PRES PR1 153 G3
Cliffe Dr CHLYE PR6 187 L3
Cliffe La GTH/LHO BB6 138 E4
Cliffe St NLSN BB9 123 H2
Clifford Av KIRK/FR/WAR PR4 166 D2
MCMB LA4 41 L5
Clifford Rd BPOOL FY1 104 E4
STHP PR8 221 K2
Clifford St BWCK/EAR BB18 293 R5
CHLY/EC PR7 208 A3
COL BB8 296 B6
ROCH OL11 235 J6
Cliff Pl BISP FY2 84 E7
Cliff Rd CHTN/BK PR9 200 A1
Cliff St BBN BB1 158 E1
COL BB8 103 L8
MILN OL16 235 L2
PDHM/BLYW BB12 141 G2
PRES PR1 8 E6
Clifton Av ACC BB5 159 M4
BPOOLS FY4 125 M2
FUL/RIB PR2 151 K1
KIRK/FR/WAR PR4 148 B5
LEYL PR25 186 E3
Clifton Cl CLV/TH FY5 85 M2
Clifton Ct LSTA FY8 146 F8
Clifton Crs BPOOLE FY3 125 K1
PRES PR1 152 F1
Clifton Dr BPOOLS FY4 124 D5
GTH/LHO BB6 138 F5
HOR/BR BL6 230 E8
LSTA FY8 145 M7
MCMB LA4 41 M6
PRES PR1 8 A8
Clifton Dr North LSTA FY8 144 F3
Clifton Dr South LSTA FY8 145 H5
Clifton Flds
KIRK/FR/WAR PR4 * 149 L4
Clifton Gdns LSTA FY8 145 M5
Clifton Ga LSTA FY8 146 E7
Clifton Gn KIRK/FR/WAR PR4 149 M2
Clifton Gv CHLY/EC PR7 207 L4
PRES PR1 132 F8
Clifton La KIRK/FR/WAR PR4 150 A1
Clifton Pl FUL/RIB PR2 * 151 L1
KIRK/FR/WAR PR4 148 E5
Clifton Rd BPOOLS FY4 125 M3
FMBY L37 237 K6
FTWD FY7 77 K8
NLSN BB9 122 F7
PDHM/BLYW BB12 141 M4
STHP PR8 200 C5
Clifton St ACC BB5 159 K7
BBN BB1 158 E2
BPOOL FY1 4 C1
BWCK/EAR BB18 294 D7
COL BB8 296 A6
DWN BB3 173 H7
LSTA FY8 146 E8
PDHM/BLYW BB12 6 D3
PRES PR1 8 D7
ROCH OL11 * 235 K6
Clinkham Rd GTH/LHO BB6 138 D6
Clinning Rd STHP PR8 221 K1
Clinton Av BPOOL FY1 4 F4
Clinton St BBN BB1 11 K1
Clippers Quay BBN BB1 * 11 G6
Clitheroe Cl HEYW OL10 234 A8
Clitheroe Pl BPOOLS FY4 125 K3
Clitheroe Rd CLI BB7 290 A11
CLI BB7 118 F6
GAR/LONG PR3 115 L2
LSTA FY8 145 M5
NLSN BB9 122 C6
Clitheroes La
KIRK/FR/WAR PR4 148 E5
Clitheroe St
PDHM/BLYW BB12 140 F3
PRES PR1 152 F4
Clive Av LSTA FY8 145 H2
Clive Ldg STHP PR8 221 J1
Clive Rd PRES PR1 151 L5
STHP PR8 221 J2
Clive St PDHM/BLYW BB12 142 C3
Clockhouse Av
BRFD/BLYE BB10 123 G8
Clockhouse Ct
BRFD/BLYE BB10 123 G8
Clockhouse Gv
BRFD/BLYE BB10 123 G8
Clod La RAW/HAS BB4 194 F4
Clods Carr La PLF/KEOS FY6 78 C8
Clogger La SKP/WHF BD23 295 K3
Cloister Dr DWN BB3 191 M2
Cloisters HEY LA3 53 J1
The Cloisters BPOOLE FY3 5 J1
CLI BB7 119 G6
CSBY/BLUN L23 257 G8
FMBY L37 * 237 J8
FUL/RIB PR2 8 D1
KIRK/FR/WAR PR4 183 K5
LEYL PR25 186 F1
MILN OL16 235 L2
RAW/HAS BB4 196 B3
Clorain Rd NWD/KWIPK L33 260 D8
The Close ACC BB5 176 D3
ACC BB5 139 J7
CHLYE PR6 188 F1
CHTN/BK PR9 181 K6
CLV/TH FY5 85 G1
CSBY/BLUN L23 257 G8
FUL/RIB PR2 133 H5
GAR/LONG PR3 284 A6
HTWN L38 248 B8
KIRK/FR/WAR PR4 167 K4
KIRK/FR/WAR PR4 128 E7
KIRK/FR/WAR PR4 127 H1
Clou Gha Av HGHB LA2 43 L4
Clougha Av LANC LA1 3 L9
Clough Acre CHLY/EC PR7 207 K1
Clough Av BBR PR5 152 E8
BRSC L40 225 J7
Clough Bank CLI BB7 291 J10
Clough End Rd RAW/HAS BB4 176 E6
Cloughfield PRES PR1 168 A2
Clough Gdns RAW/HAS BB4 176 E6
Clough House La WHIT OL12 218 E5
Clough La GAR/LONG PR3 95 J4
PDHM/BLYW BB12 140 C1
Clough Mi TOD OL14 * 303 K6
Clough Rd BCUP OL13 179 K8
LIT OL15 219 K3
NLSN BB9 123 K3
TOD OL14 303 K6
Clough St BCUP OL13 197 G3
BLY BB11 6 A5
DWN BB3 191 M5
RAW/HAS BB4 196 C2
WHIT OL12 218 F5
Clough Ter LIT OL15 * 219 K4
The Clough CHLYE PR6 169 K8
Cloughwood Crs
WGNNW/ST WN6 245 G4
Clovelly Av BISP FY2 84 F5
FUL/RIB PR2 132 A8
Clovelly Dr PRES PR1 151 K6
SKEL WN8 243 K2
STHP PR8 221 H3
Clovelly St ROCH OL11 234 E8
Clover Av LSTA FY8 145 K2
Clover Ct BISP FY2 85 J5
Clover Crs PDHM/BLYW BB12 142 A3
Clover Dr KIRK/FR/WAR PR4 149 G4
Clover Fld CHLYE PR6 187 L1
Cloverfield PRES PR1 151 L7
Cloverfields BBN BB1 11 J1
Clover Hall Crs MILN OL16 235 M2
Clover Hl BCUP OL13 * 179 K8
Clover Hill Rd NLSN BB9 123 J4
Clover Ms BPOOLE FY3 * 105 H5

Clover Rd CHLY/EC PR7 — 207 K6
Clover St BCUP OL13 — 179 K8
WHIT OL12 — 235 H3
Clover Ter DWN BB3 — 173 K8
Clover Vw MILN OL16 * — 235 M4
Club La GAR/LONG PR3 — 287 M12
Club St BBR PR5 — 169 H4
TOD OL14 — 300 E10
Clucas Gdns ORM L39 — 241 H5
Clyde Ct MILN OL16 — 235 L5
Clydesdale Pl
CROS/BRETH PR26 — 185 M1
Clyde St BBNW BB2 — 156 E8
BPOOL FY1 — 104 E4
FUL/RIB PR2 — 8 A2
Clyffes Farm Cl BRSC L40 — 223 K4
Coach House Cots
RAW/HAS BB4 * — 194 E1
Coach House Ct BRSC L40 — 225 H8
Coach House Dr
WGNNW/ST WN6 — 245 L5
Coach La ROCH OL11 — 234 B6
Coach Ms MCMB LA4 * — 41 G7
Coach Rd ACC BB5 — 159 H6
CARN LA5 — 26 A4
ORM L39 — 261 J2
Coal Clough La BLY BB11 — 6 C8
Coal Clough Rd TOD OL14 — 300 D4
Coal Pit La ACC BB5 — 159 J7
BCUP OL13 — 179 J8
CLI BB7 — 292 H4
COL BB8 — 296 C7
DWN BB3 — 172 G6
ORM L39 — 252 F4
RAW/HAS BB4 — 178 D7
Coal Pit Rd BOL BL1 — 232 C4
Coal Rd RAMS BL0 — 215 K3
Coal St BLY BB11 — 6 F4
Coastal Dr HGHB LA2 — 42 C2
Coastal Ri HGHB LA2 — 42 C1
Coastal Rd MCMB LA4 — 42 A4
STHP PR8 — 220 D5
Coastline Ms CHTN/BK PR9 — 180 D7
Coates Av BWCK/EAR BB18 — 293 R4
Coates Flds BWCK/EAR BB18 — 293 R3
Coates La BWCK/EAR BB18 — 293 R3
Cobb's Brow La BRSC L40 — 243 K6
Cobb's Clough Rd BRSC L40 — 243 J6
Cobbs St ACC BB5 — 175 L4
Cob Castle Rd RAW/HAS BB4 — 176 C8
Cobden Ct BBN BB1 — 10 A4
Cobden Rd CHTN/BK PR9 — 200 C5
Cobden St BCUP OL13 — 197 L3
BRFD/BLYE BB10 — 142 G3
BWCK/EAR BB18 — 293 P4
CHLYE PR6 — 208 B2
DWN BB3 — 191 K3
NLSN BB9 — 123 G4
PDHM/BLYW BB12 — 140 F7
TOD OL14 — 303 L2
Cobham Rd ACC BB5 — 159 M6
Cob La BWCK/EAR BB18 — 294 D10
Cobourg Cl BBNW BB2 — 10 B9
Cob Wall BBN BB1 — 157 M4
Cochran St DWN BB3 * — 191 K3
Cock Br GTH/LHO BB6 — 139 J2
Cocker Br BBR PR5 — 169 K4
Cocker Bar Rd
CROS/BRETH PR26 — 184 F4
Cockerham Rd GAR/LONG PR3 — 283 R5
HGHB LA2 — 269 R7
Cocker House Br HGHB LA2 — 269 R7
Cockerill St RAW/HAS BB4 — 176 E7
Cocker La CROS/BRETH PR26 — 185 M2
Cocker Rd BBR PR5 — 169 K4
Cockersand Av
KIRK/FR/WAR PR4 — 166 C2
Cockersand Dr LANC LA1 — 54 F8
Cocker Sq BPOOL FY1 — 104 E5
Cocker St BPOOL FY1 — 104 E5
Cockhall La WHIT OL12 — 217 M2
Cockhill La COL BB8 — 296 C6
Cocking Yd KKBYL LA6 — 19 L1
Cockle Dick's La CHTN/BK PR9 — 200 B1
Cockridge Cl BBNW BB2 — 172 K4
Cock Robin Cots
CROS/BRETH PR26 — 204 F1
Cock Robin La GAR/LONG PR3 — 91 G1
Codale Av BISP FY2 — 85 G6
Coddington St BBN BB1 — 11 L3
Coe La KIRK/FR/WAR PR4 — 183 K5
Cog La BLY BB11 — 6 A8
Cog St BLY BB11 — 6 A8
Coibern Cl MGHL L31 — 259 H3
Coibran St BRFD/BLYE BB10 — 142 G2
NLSN BB9 — 123 J1
Colburne St BRSC L40 — 225 J4
Colchester Av LANC LA1 — 55 C6
Colchester Rd BPOOLE FY3 — 5 M6
STHP PR8 — 222 A1
Coldale St BPOOLS FY4 * — 124 E5
Cold Bath St PRES PR1 — 8 A1
Colden La HBR HX7 — 301 Q5
Coldstream Pl BBNW BB2 — 173 H1
Coldweather Av NLSN BB9 — 123 J4
Cold Well La MTHPE LA7 — 17 J2
Colebatch Rd FUL/RIB PR2 — 132 A6
Cole Crs ORM L39 — 253 J5
Coleman St NLSN BB9 — 123 J4
FUL/RIB PR2 — 151 M1
Coleridge Av CLV/TH FY5 — 81 J3
WGNNW/ST WN6 — 255 K5
Coleridge Cl COL BB8 — 296 B5
KIRK/FR/WAR PR4 — 131 H7
Coleridge Dr ACC BB5 — 176 B1
Coleridge Pl GTH/LHO BB6 — 138 E1
Coleridge Rd BPOOL FY1 — 105 G5
BBNW BB2 — 10 A7
Colesberg Ct CARN LA5 — 16 E1
Coles Dr CARN LA5 — 16 E2
Colesville Av CLV/TH FY5 — 85 L2
Colinmander Gdns ORM L39 — 240 F8
Colin St BLY BB11 — 6 B6
BWCK/EAR BB18 — 293 Q4
Colinton Av CLV/TH FY5 — 84 F2
College Av NLSN BB9 — 123 J3
CSBY/BLUN L23 — 257 G8
FMBY L37 — 237 J5
College Ct PRES PR1 — 152 B4
College Ga CLV/TH FY5 — 80 C3
College Pth FMBY L37 — 237 G6
College Rd CSBY/BLUN L23 — 256 F7
SKEL WN8 — 254 E2
WHIT OL12 — 235 G4
College Rd North
CSBY/BLUN L23 — 256 F6

College St ACC BB5 — 159 K5
TOD OL14 — 300 F10
Colley St MILN OL16 — 235 K2
Colliers Row Rd BOL BL1 — 233 L6
Colliers St ACC BB5 — 159 H6
Collier St ACC BB5 — 176 B1
Collinge Fold La RAW/HAS BB4 — 177 J7
Collingham Pk LANC LA1 — 66 E2
Colling St RAMS BL0 — 214 E6
Collingwood ACC BB5 — 159 H1
Collingwood Av PDHM/BLYW BB12 — 105 H5
LSTA FY8 — 145 H2
Collingwood Pl CHLY/EC PR7 — 207 K4
Collingwood St COL BB8 — 103 L7
Collins Av BISP FY2 — 85 H8
Collins Dr ACC BB5 — 176 B1
Collin's Hill La GAR/LONG PR3 — 286 H12
Collins Rd BBR PR5 — 169 J2
Collins Rd North BBR PR5 — 169 J1
Collisdene Rd
WGNW/BIL/OR WN5 — 255 G5
Collyhurst Av CHLY/EC PR7 — 207 L3
Collyhurst Av BPOOLS FY4 — 125 H5
Colman Ct PRES PR1 — 9 H4
Colnbrook WGNNW/ST WN6 — 245 L2
Colne And Broughton Rd
SKP/WHF BD23 — 280 G12
Colne La COL BB8 — 296 B7
Colne Rd BRFD/BLYE BB10 — 7 H1
BWCK/EAR BB18 — 293 P6
COL BB8 — 296 D9
HWTH BD22 — 297 R1
NLSN BB9 — 122 E6
Colt House Cl LEYL PR25 — 186 D4
Colthurst Dr CLI BB7 — 99 J7
Coltsfoot Dr CHLYE PR6 — 208 A1
Coltsfoot Wk HEY LA3 — 53 J1
Columban St NTHTN L30 — 258 B6
Columbia Wy BBNW BB2 — 156 C8
Columbine Cl CHLY/EC PR7 * — 187 K8
MGHL L31 — 259 K8
WHIT OL12 — 217 M8
Colville Av BPOOLS FY4 — 124 F6
Colville Rd DWN BB3 — 173 H7
Colville St BRFD/BLYE BB10 — 142 D5
Colwyn Av BPOOLS FY4 — 125 H2
MCMB LA4 — 41 L8
Colwyn Pl FUL/RIB PR2 — 131 K8
Colyton Cl CHLYE PR6 — 208 B3
Colyton Rd CHLYE PR6 — 208 B3
Colyton Rd East CHLYE PR6 — 208 B3
Combermere Gv HEY LA3 — 52 D6
Combermere Rd HEY LA3 — 52 D5
Comer Gdns MGHL L31 — 249 M8
Comet Av CROS/BRETH PR26 — 185 M1
WGNW/BIL/OR WN5 — 255 M3
Comet St BCUP OL13 — 179 J4
Commerce St BCUP OL13 — 197 J1
Commercial Rd CHLY/EC PR7 — 207 M2
DWN BB3 — 173 J6
GTH/LHO BB6 — 139 J2
NLSN BB9 — 123 H3
Commercial St ACC BB5 — 159 G8
BBN BB1 — 158 E1
BCUP OL13 — 197 G3
BPOOL FY1 — 124 E4
BWCK/EAR BB18 — 293 Q5
RAW/HAS BB4 — 161 K8
SETT BD24 — 265 P8
TOD OL14 — 303 M2
Common Bank La
CHLY/EC PR7 — 207 H4
Common Edge Rd
BPOOLS FY4 — 125 J6
Common End CHLY/EC PR7 — 207 H4
Common Garden St LANC LA1 — 3 G6
Commonside CHTN/BK PR9 — 201 L1
Commonside LSTA FY8 — 146 A7
Commons La BBNW BB2 — 135 J5
The Common CHLY/EC PR7 — 207 H4
SKEL WN8 — 226 F8
Commonwealth Cl LSTA FY8 — 145 M3
Como Av BLY BB11 — 141 M7
Company St BBN BB1 * — 158 E2
Compass Cots CHLYE PR6 * — 188 E4
Compley Av PLF/KEOS FY6 — 105 M1
Compley Gn PLF/KEOS FY6 — 105 M1
Compression Rd HEY LA3 — 64 D1
Compston Av RAW/HAS BB4 — 177 K2
Compton Cl PLF/KEOS FY6 — 85 M6
Compton Gn FUL/RIB PR2 — 131 M4
Compton Rd PDHM/BLYW BB12 — 199 L8
Como Av BLY BB11 — 141 M7
Conder Av CLV/TH FY5 — 85 J1
Conder Brow CARN LA5 — 33 K1
Conder Green Rd HGHB LA2 — 66 C6
Conder Pl LANC LA1 — 2 E1
Condor Gv BPOOL FY1 — 5 G7
LSTA FY8 — 145 G3
Condor Wy PRES PR1 — 168 D7
Conduit St NLSN BB9 — 123 G1
Coney Crs CSBY/BLUN L23 — 257 L6
Coneygarth La KKBYL LA6 — 21 L7
Congress St CHLY/EC PR7 — 207 M2
Conifer Cl NWD/KWIPK L33 — 260 B2
Conifer Ct FMBY L37 — 247 J1
The Conifers GAR/LONG PR3 — 111 L3
KIRK/FR/WAR PR4 — 128 C6
MGHL L31 — 249 M8
PLF/KEOS FY6 — 86 F1
KIRK/FR/WAR PR4 — 166 C2
KIRK/FR/WAR PR4 — 128 D5
MCMB LA4 — 41 M6
RAMS BL0 — 214 D7
Coningsby Dr FUL/RIB PR2 — 131 H4
Coniston Av ACC BB5 — 159 J7
BWCK/EAR BB18 — 293 P4
CHLY/EC PR7 — 207 G2
CHLYE PR6 — 230 E3
CLV/TH FY5 — 85 L1
FTWD FY7 — 77 H7
FUL/RIB PR2 — 152 A1
LSTA FY8 — 145 J4
PDHM/BLYW BB12 — 140 F1
WGNW/BIL/OR WN5 — 255 K5
Coniston Cl GAR/LONG PR3 — 114 D6
NWD/KWIPK L33 — 260 A3
RAMS BL0 — 214 D7
Coniston Dr BBR PR5 — 169 H1
DWN BB3 — 191 M1
Coniston Gv COL BB8 — 296 C5
Coniston Rd BBN BB1 — 158 D1
BPOOLS FY4 — 124 F5
CARN LA5 — 32 C4
CHLY/EC PR7 — 207 L5
FMBY L37 — 247 G1
FUL/RIB PR2 — 132 C7
HOR/BR BL6 — 231 G4
LANC LA1 — 3 L3

MCMB LA4 — 41 K6
MGHL L31 — 259 H1
Coniston St PDHM/BLYW BB12 — 141 M5
Coniston Wy BBN BB1 — 158 C2
BCUP OL13 — 179 K7
CROS/BRETH PR26 — 204 E1
RNFD/HAY WA11 — 262 C1
Connaught Av MILN OL16 — 235 L8
Connaught Dr CLV/TH FY5 — 86 A1
Connaught Rd HEY LA3 — 52 C6
LANC LA1 — 55 G6
PRES PR1 — 8 B4
Connell Wy HEYW OL10 * — 234 C8
Consett Av CLV/TH FY5 — 81 H6
Constable Av BBR PR5 — 168 D4
Constable Lee Crs
RAW/HAS BB4 — 177 K7
Constable St PRES PR1 — 9 K2
Constantine Rd MILN OL16 * — 235 K7
Constitution Hl SETT BD24 — 265 P7
Convent Crs BPOOLE FY3 — 105 L4
Convent Gv ROCH OL11 — 235 G6
Convent Yd BOL BL1 * — 292 H6
BPOOLE FY3 — 105 L4
CLI BB7 — 98 F3
CLV/TH FY5 — 85 G1
LEYL PR25 — 186 D1
PRES PR1 — 168 C2
Conway Cl CHLY/EC PR7 — 207 H2
GAR/LONG PR3 — 91 G2
NWD/KWIPK L33 — 260 A5
RAMS BL0 — 214 E5
RAW/HAS BB4 — 194 C1
Conway Crs BWCK/EAR BB18 — 293 N1
Conway Dr ACC BB5 — 158 E7
FUL/RIB PR2 — 131 M5
Conway Gv BRFD/BLYE BB10 — 122 F8
Conway Rd CHLY/EC PR7 — 205 M4
RAW/HAS BB4 — 177 M3
Conway St
WGNW/BIL/OR WN5 — 255 M6
Conyers Av STHP PR8 — 199 J8
Cooke St HOR/BR BL6 — 232 A7
Cook Gdns BBN BB1 — 11 L5
Cook Green La GAR/LONG PR3 — 115 L4
Cook House Rd COL BB8 — 296 B5
Cooks Ct CSBY/BLUN L23 — 256 F5
Cookson Cl KIRK/FR/WAR PR4 — 148 C5
Cookson Rd CLV/TH FY5 — 81 K8
Cook St MILN OL16 — 235 L2
Cook Ter MILN OL16 — 235 L2
Coolham La BWCK/EAR BB18 — 294 C6
Coolidge Av LANC LA1 — 2 C7
The Coombes FUL/RIB PR2 — 132 C6
The Cooperage ACC BB5 — 159 G8
Co-Operation St BCUP OL13 * — 197 K1
RAW/HAS BB4 — 195 L1
Co-operative St BBR PR5 — 169 H5
Co-Operative St
BWCK/EAR BB18 — 293 Q5
RAW/HAS BB4 — 194 C4
Cooperative St TOD OL14 — 303 M4
Cooper Hill Cl BBR PR5 — 153 G6
Cooper Hill Dr BBR PR5 — 153 G6
Cooper Rd PRES PR1 — 8 A1
Coopers Cl ACC BB5 * — 159 G8
Cooper's La CHLY/EC PR7 — 227 L3
Coopers Rw LSTA FY8 — 146 A4
Cooper St BCUP OL13 — 179 J8
BLY BB11 — 7 G1
HOR/BR BL6 — 231 L7
NLSN BB9 — 123 H3
TOD OL14 — 303 P1
WHIT OL12 — 219 H8
Coopers End MILN OL16 — 235 M1
Coopers Wy BPOOL FY1 — 105 G4
Cooper's Wy BPOOL FY1 * — 105 G4
Cooper Ter MILN OL16 * — 235 L2
Coop St BPOOL FY1 * — 4 D4
Coote La KIRK/FR/WAR PR4 — 168 C4
Copeland Pl LSTA FY8 — 146 A7
Copenhagen Sq MILN OL16 — 235 K3
Copenhagen St MILN OL16 — 235 L3
Cop La PRES PR1 — 151 L1
Copperas Ct WGNNW/ST WN6 — 245 L4
Copperas House Ter TOD OL14 — 303 K5
Copper Beech Cl
KIRK/FR/WAR PR4 — 166 C2
Copper Beeches BBNW BB2 * — 156 E6
PRES PR1 — 168 A2
Copperfield Cl
BRFD/BLYE BB10 — 143 J5
Copperfield St BBN BB1 — 11 H1
Copperwood Wy CHLY/EC PR7 — 207 H4
Coppice Av ACC BB5 — 160 A4
Coppice Brow CARN LA5 — 33 L1
Coppice Cl CHLYE PR6 — 208 B7
Coppice Dr WHIT OL12 — 217 M4
Coppice La CHLYE PR6 — 188 F7
Coppice Leys FMBY L37 — 237 H8
The Coppice ACC BB5 — 139 J7
BBN BB1 — 156 D4
BLY BB11 — 6 D8
FUL/RIB PR2 — 131 K7
KIRK/FR/WAR PR4 — 166 C2
KIRK/FR/WAR PR4 — 128 D5
MCMB LA4 — 41 M6
RAMS BL0 — 214 D7
Coppull Hall La CHLY/EC PR7 — 229 G5
Coppull Moor La CHLY/EC PR7 — 229 G5
Coppull Rd CHLY/EC PR7 — 207 M7
MGHL L31 — 249 M7
Copse Cl BBN BB1 — 157 G5
Copse Rd FTWD FY7 — 81 J2
The Copse ACC BB5 — 159 M4
Copster Hill Cl BBN BB1 — 174 A1
Copthurst Av
PDHM/BLYW BB12 — 121 F2
Copthurst La CHLYE PR6 — 188 B5
Copthurst St
PDHM/BLYW BB12 * — 140 F2
Coptrod Head La WHIT OL12 — 218 B7
Copy La HGHB LA2 — 44 D7
NTHTN L30 — 258 C2
Copy Nook BBN BB1 — 11 L5
Copy Wy NTHTN L30 — 258 C2
Coral Cl BPOOLS FY4 — 125 K3
Corbett St BBN BB1 — 157 K3
Corbridge Cl BPOOLS FY4 — 125 K3
Corcas St PLF/KEOS FY6 — 82 C3

Cordwainers Ct CHLY/EC PR7 — 187 H5
Cork Rd LANC LA1 — 55 G5
Corless Rd NLSN BB9 — 103 G8
Cornbrook SKEL WN8 — 254 B4
Cornbrook Cl WHIT OL12 — 218 A3
Corncroft PRES PR1 — 151 M8
Cornel Gv BLY BB11 — 141 M7
Cornelian St BBN BB1 — 157 J3
Cornelian Wy BPOOLS FY4 — 125 K2
Corner Bank Cl
KIRK/FR/WAR PR4 — 127 J4
The Corners CLV/TH FY5 — 80 F7
Cornfield KIRK/FR/WAR PR4 — 131 H5
Cornfield Gv
PDHM/BLYW BB12 — 141 K2
Cornfield St DWN BB3 — 191 K1
TOD OL14 * — 303 N1
Cornflower Cl CHLYE PR6 — 208 A1
KIRK/FR/WAR PR4 — 165 H7
Cornford Rd BPOOLS FY4 — 125 L3
Cornholme BRFD/BLYE BB10 — 143 H1
Corn Mill Cl WHIT OL12 — 218 F1
Cornmill Ct CLI BB7 * — 290 A11
Corn Mill La FTWD FY7 — 77 J7
Cornmill Pl BWCK/EAR BB18 — 293 Q4
Corn Mill Yd ACC BB5 * — 159 J1
Cornthwaite Rd
FUL/RIB PR2 * — 132 B8
Cornwall Av BBN BB1 — 158 B7
BISP FY2 — 104 F1
CLV/TH FY5 — 81 H7
Cornwall Ms CLV/TH FY5 * — 81 J7
Cornwall Pl ACC BB5 * — 159 J4
BPOOLE FY3 — 125 K1
WGNW/BIL/OR WN5 — 255 M5
Cornwall Rd BBN BB1 — 158 B7
Cornwall Wy STHP PR8 — 237 L1
Corona Av MGHL L31 — 249 M6
Coronation Av BBNW BB2 — 171 M4
FMBY L37 — 247 K1
GAR/LONG PR3 — 270 A8
PDHM/BLYW BB12 — 140 F5
Coronation Ct
CROS/BRETH PR26 — 184 E8
Coronation Crs PRES PR1 — 9 M5
Coronation Dr CSBY/BLUN L23 — 257 G8
Coronation La RAW/HAS BB4 — 196 B2
Coronation Pl NLSN BB9 — 103 G8
Coronation Rd CLV/TH FY5 — 84 F7
CSBY/BLUN L23 — 257 G8
KIRK/FR/WAR PR4 — 128 C7
LSTA FY8 — 145 M7
MGHL L31 — 250 A6
NLSN BB9 — 122 F6
Coronation St BPOOL FY1 — 4 E4
BWCK/EAR BB18 — 293 R5
GTH/LHO BB6 — 139 J2
Coronation Wk LANC LA1 — 42 L8
Coronation Wy LANC LA1 — 42 L8
Coronet Ct WGNNW/ST WN6 — 244 F4
Corporation St ACC BB5 — 159 G8
BBNW BB2 — 10 E4
BPOOL FY1 — 4 C2
CHLYE PR6 — 208 A2
CLI BB7 — 99 G3
COL BB8 — 103 K8
PRES PR1 — 9 G3
Corranstone Cl HOR/BR BL6 — 231 L8
Corriander Cl BISP FY2 — 85 L3
Corrib Br BISP FY2 — 105 G1
Corringham Rd MCMB LA4 — 41 H6
Corwen Cl BBN BB1 — 10 E1
Corwen Dr NTHTN L30 — 258 D7
Cosford St KIRK/FR/WAR PR4 — 107 H5
Cosgate Cl
WGNW/BIL/OR WN5 — 255 H4
Costessey Wy
WGNS/IIMK WN3 — 255 M8
Cotaline Cl ROCH OL11 — 234 E8
Cote La LIT OL15 — 219 J4
Cotman Cl BCUP OL13 — 197 L3
Cotswold Av CHLY/EC PR7 — 207 M8
WGNW/BIL/OR WN5 — 255 L6
Cotswold Cl CHLY/EC PR7 — 205 M5
RAMS BL0 — 214 F7
Cotswold Dr HOR/BR BL6 — 231 L6
Cotswold Ms BBN BB1 * — 173 L3
Cotswold Rd BISP FY2 — 105 G4
CHLY/EC PR7 — 207 M5
LSTA FY8 — 147 G3
Cottage Cl ORM L39 — 241 G7
Cottage Flds CHLY/EC PR7 — 207 J1
Cottage Gdns BBR PR5 — 169 L3
Cottage La BBR PR5 — 169 J4
ORM L39 — 241 G7
Cottage Ms ORM L39 — 241 G4
Cottage St PRES PR1 * — 9 H4
Cottam Av FUL/RIB PR2 — 131 J3
Cottam Cl CLI BB7 — 118 F5
LSTA FY8 — 145 J3
Cottam Gn KIRK/FR/WAR PR4 — 131 H1
Cottam La FUL/RIB PR2 — 131 J3
Cottam Pl FUL/RIB PR2 * — 105 M1
Cottam St CHLY/EC PR7 — 207 M5
KIRK/FR/WAR PR4 — 131 H1
Cotterdale Cl NLSN BB9 — 102 F8
Cottesloe Pl NLSN BB9 — 102 F8
Cottesmore Cl WHIT OL12 — 217 M5
Cottom Cft ACC BB5 — 139 J7
Cott St COL BB8 — 103 K8
Cotton Dr ORM L39 — 241 G5
Cotton Fold MILN OL16 — 235 M6
Cotton Hall St DWN BB3 — 191 K1
Cotton Rw BBR PR5 * — 162 F4
Cotton St ACC BB5 — 159 L6
PDHM/BLYW BB12 — 140 F7
Cotton Tree La COL BB8 — 296 F5
Cottys Brow CHTN/BK PR9 — 180 C6
Coudray Rd CHTN/BK PR9 — 200 F7
Coulston Av CLI BB7 — 84 B8
Coulston Rd LANC LA1 — 3 L6
Coulton Rd NLSN BB9 — 122 H4
Counsell Cl CLV/TH FY5 — 85 L1
Countess Cl KIRK/FR/WAR PR4 — 128 C4
Countess Crs BISP FY2 — 84 F7
Countess Rd BBN BB1 — 173 J4
Countess St ACC BB5 — 159 J5
Countesswy PRES PR1 — 9 J2
Countess Wy CHLY/EC PR7 — 207 G2
Country Ms BBNW BB2 — 156 D2
Count St MILN OL16 — 235 K6
County Brook La COL BB8 — 293 R12
County Rd KKBY L32 — 260 D2
ORM L39 — 241 G7
County St LANC LA1 — 2 E1
Coupe Gn BBR PR5 — 154 B7
Coupland St WHIT OL12 — 217 M1

Coupland St WHIT OL12 — 218 A3
Courage Low La
WGNNW/ST WN6 — 228 A7
Course La SKEL WN8 — 243 H2
Courtfield ORM L39 — 241 G4
Courtfield Av BISP FY2 — 105 G3
Court Gn BBR PR5 — 137 H5
Court Ms CHTN/BK PR9 * — 200 D2
The Court FUL/RIB PR2 — 131 M4
PRES PR1 * — 151 M7
The Courtyard BCUP OL13 — 179 K8
CLV/TH FY5 — 85 G2
KIRK/FR/WAR PR4 * — 128 C5
Cousin's La BRSC L40 — 203 K8
Cove Dr CARN LA5 — 16 F7
Coventry St CLV/TH FY5 * — 207 H5
ROCH OL11 — 235 J5
Coverdale Dr BBNW BB2 — 172 A4
Coverdale Rd LANC LA1 — 2 C6
Coverdale Wy
PDHM/BLYW BB12 — 141 K2
Cove Rd CARN LA5 — 16 E1
Covertside Rd STHP PR8 — 222 D1
The Covert CLV/TH FY5 — 81 J7
The Cove FY7 — 80 F7
MCMB LA4 — 41 M4
Coveway Av BPOOLE FY3 — 105 H5
Cowan Brae BBN BB1 — 10 C1
Cow Br SKP/WHF BD23 — 267 G8
Cowell Wy BBNW BB2 — 10 B4
Cowfold St TOD OL14 — 303 L1
Cowgarth La BWCK/EAR BB18 — 294 B5
Cow Gate La SKP/WHF BD23 — 279 L4
Cowgill St BWCK/EAR BB18 — 294 E6
Cowhill La BBN BB1 — 158 C3
Cowhurst Av TOD OL14 — 301 J12
Cow La AIRE BD20 — 295 Q7
BLY BB11 — 6 F4
Cowley Crs PDHM/BLYW BB12 — 141 H4
Cowley Rd BPOOLS FY4 — 125 J3
FUL/RIB PR2 — 133 L8
Cowling Brow CHLYE PR6 — 208 B4
Cowling Hill La HWTH BD22 — 295 R10
Cowling La LEYL PR25 — 186 A2
Cowling Rd CHLYE PR6 — 208 C5
Cowm Park Wy North
WHIT OL12 — 217 M1
Cowm Park Wy South
WHIT OL12 — 217 M3
Cowm St WHIT OL12 — 302 B10
Cowper Av CLI BB7 — 99 J3
Cowper Rd RAW/HAS BB4 — 196 B4
Cowper St BBN BB1 — 157 J4
BLY BB11 — 141 M6
Cowslip Wy CHLYE PR6 — 208 A1
Cowtoot La BCUP OL13 — 179 J8
Cow Well La CHLYE PR6 — 187 L3
Coxfield WGNNW/ST WN6 — 245 G4
Cox Green Cl EDGW/EG BL7 — 212 A8
Cox Green La EDGW/EG BL7 — 212 A7
Coyford Dr CHTN/BK PR9 — 180 D7
Crabtree Av BCUP OL13 — 197 K2
PRES PR1 — 151 K8
RAW/HAS BB4 — 196 C1
Crabtree Cl BRSC L40 — 225 G2
RAW/HAS BB4 — 224 F6
Crab Tree La GAR/LONG PR3 — 88 F2
Crabtree Orch CLV/TH FY5 — 81 L8
Crabtree St BBN BB1 — 11 M3
COL BB8 — 103 M7
NLSN BB9 — 122 E6
RAW/HAS BB4 — 178 C7
Cracoe Gill NLSN BB9 * — 102 F8
Craddock Rd COL BB8 — 296 F6
Crag Bank Crs CARN LA5 — 33 H3
Crag Bank La CARN LA5 — 33 G2
Crag Bank Rd CARN LA5 — 33 H3
Cragdale SETT BD24 — 265 N7
Cragg La HGHB LA2 — 51 K5
Craggs Av HGHB LA2 — 48 F5
Craggs Rw PRES PR1 — 9 G1
Cragg St BPOOL FY1 — 4 C4
COL BB8 — 103 M6
Crag La HGHB LA2 — 20 C3
Crag Rd CARN LA5 — 33 L3
LANC LA1 — 3 L3
Craigflower Ct BBR PR5 — 169 M4
Craiglands Av HEY LA3 — 52 E1
Craiglands Ct LANC LA1 — 54 B6
Craig St HEY LA3 — 40 E8
Crake Av FTWD FY7 — 80 F1
Crake Bank LANC LA1 — 2 A2
Crambe Hts DWN BB3 — 173 H4
Cranberry Cl TOD OL14 — 303 L8
Cranberry Cl DWN BB3 — 192 A5
Cranberry Fold Ct DWN BB3 — 192 A5
Cranberry Ri RAW/HAS BB4 — 177 K2
Cranborne St BBNW BB2 * — 152 H4
Cranbourne Ter BBNW BB2 * — 10 C9
Cranbourne Dr ACC BB5 — 159 K3
CHLYE PR6 — 208 B4
Cranbourne Gv CLV/TH FY5 — 86 A4
Cranbourne Rd ROCH OL11 — 234 B5
Cranbourne St BBR PR5 — 169 H3
CHLYE PR6 — 208 B4
COL BB8 — 296 B5
Cranbrook Av ACC BB5 — 158 F7
BISP FY2 — 85 G6
Cranbrook St BBNW BB2 — 10 C9
Cranesbill PLF/KEOS FY6 * — 78 C5
Cranesbill Cl PLF/KEOS FY6 — 78 C5
Cranes La BRSC L40 — 242 A4
Crane St CHLY/EC PR7 — 229 G5
Cranfield Rd CSBY/BLUN L23 — 257 K6
Cranfield Vw DWN BB3 — 191 M5
Crank Hl RNFD/HAY WA11 — 263 J4
Crankshaw St RAW/HAS BB4 — 177 K8
Cranleigh Av BISP FY2 — 84 F8
Cranmer St BLY BB11 — 6 F2
Cranshaw Dr BBN BB1 — 157 H3
Cranwell Av LANC LA1 — 55 H3
Cranwell Cl BBN BB1 — 11 H5
Cranwell Ct KIRK/FR/WAR PR4 — 128 C5
Craven Bank La SETT BD24 — 264 H5
Craven Cl FUL/RIB PR2 — 132 C4
Cravendale Av NLSN BB9 — 103 H8
Craven Dr BBR PR5 — 169 G4
Craven Gdns ROCH OL11 * — 235 G8
Craven Ridge La SETT BD24 — 264 H8
Craven's Av BBNW BB2 — 173 H5
Cravens Hollow BBNW BB2 — 173 H5
Craven St ACC BB5 — 159 K6
BLY BB11 — 7 H5
BWCK/EAR BB18 — 293 R5
CLI BB7 — 99 H4
COL BB8 — 296 D6
NLSN BB9 — 122 E6
RAW/HAS BB4 — 195 J1
Crawford Av BISP FY2 — 85 G6

CHLY/EC PR7 230 B6
CHLY/EC PR7 207 L4
LEYL PR25 186 D3
MGHL L31 249 L8
PRES PR1 153 J2
Crawford Rd SKEL WN8 263 G1
Crawford St MILN OL16 235 K6
NLSN BB9 123 H2
Crawshaw Dr RAW/HAS BB4 177 K5
Crawshaw Gra RAW/HAS BB4 177 K5
Crawshaw La
BRFD/BLYE BB10 298 A1
Crawshaw St ACC BB5 159 L5
Crediton Av CHTN/BK PR9 180 E6
Crediton Cl BBNW BB2 * 172 F3
Crescent Av FMBY L37 247 H2
Crescent Gn ORM L39 250 E2
Crescent Rd CSBY/BLUN L23 256 E6
PLF/KEOS FY6 86 B7
ROCH OL11 234 E7
STHP PR8 199 J8
Crescent St PRES PR1 152 F2
TOD OL14 303 L2
The Crescent BBNW BB2 172 B2
BBR PR5 168 F3
BPOOLS FY4 124 E4
BRFD/BLYE BB10 143 K6
BRFD/BLYE BB10 122 E7
BWCK/EAR BB18 * 293 Q8
CHLY/EC PR7 207 M1
CHTN/BK PR9 180 F8
CLI BB7 118 D5
CLI BB7 99 G4
COL BB8 296 A5
CSBY/BLUN L23 257 K5
FTWD FY7 81 H3
FUL/RIB PR2 151 G2
HGHB LA2 42 C2
KIRK/FR/WAR PR4 147 M7
KKBYL LA6 18 F1
LSTA FY8 145 H5
MGHL L31 258 F4
PLF/KEOS FY6 85 M7
PLF/KEOS FY6 78 E7
WHIT OL12 * 217 M3
Cressell Pk WGNNW/ST WN6 245 K1
Cressingham Wk LANC LA1 55 G8
Cresswood Av CLV/TH FY5 85 G2
Crestway BPOOLE FY3 105 J5
KIRK/FR/WAR PR4 183 K4
Creswell Av FUL/RIB PR2 131 J8
Creswick Av BLY BB11 162 C1
Creswick Cl BLY BB11 * 6 E9
Crewdson St DWN BB3 191 J1
Crewgarth Rd HEY LA3 53 M2
Cribden End La RAW/HAS BB4 176 F7
Cribden La RAW/HAS BB4 177 G7
Cribden St RAW/HAS BB4 177 J7
Criccieth Cl RAW/HAS BB4 * 194 E2
Criccieth Pl CLV/TH FY5 86 A1
Crichton Pl BPOOLS FY4 124 E6
Cricketers Gn CHLY/EC PR7 205 L4
Cricket Pth FMBY L37 237 J6
STHP PR8 199 J8
Crimble La ROCH OL11 234 B6
Crimbles La HGHB LA2 269 K8
Crimble St WHIT OL12 235 G3
Crimea St BCUP OL13 197 K1
Crime Well La HEY LA3 52 D4
Cringle Wy CLI BB7 99 K1
Cripple Ga WGNNW/ST WN6 245 J1
Cripple Gate La BBR PR5 154 F7
Critchley Cl KIRK/FR/WAR PR4 166 B8
Critchley Wy NWD/KWIPK L33 260 C6
Croasdale LANC LA1 2 A2
Croasdale Av BRFD/BLYE BB10 143 G1
FUL/RIB PR2 133 H6
Croasdale Cl CARN LA5 33 H2
Croasdale Dr CLI BB7 99 J4
CLV/TH FY5 81 J8
SKEL WN8 226 F8
Croasdale Sq BBN BB1 11 J7
Crockleford Av STHP PR8 200 B8
Crocus Cl RAW/HAS BB4 194 C3
Crocus Fld LEYL PR25 186 D4
Croft Acres RAMS BL0 215 G1
Croft Av BRSC L40 225 J8
HGHB LA2 42 D3
WGNW/BIL/OR WN5 255 G6
Croft Bank PRES PR1 151 M8
Croft Cl RAW/HAS BB4 177 K6
Croft Ct CLV/TH FY5 * 81 M7
FTWD FY7 * 81 H1
Crofters Fold HEY LA3 52 F2
HGHB LA2 67 G7
Crofters Gn CHLY/EC PR7 186 F8
PRES PR1 152 B1
Crofters La NWD/KWIPK L33 260 D6
Crofters Meadow
CROS/BRETH PR26 168 B8
Crofters Ms BPOOL FY1 104 F4
Crofters Wk LSTA FY8 146 B4
Croft Fld MGHL L31 259 H2
Croftgate FUL/RIB PR2 132 C6
Croft Head Rd BBN BB1 157 L2
Croft Hey BRSC L40 203 L7
Croft Heys ORM L39 250 E2
Croftland Gdns CARN LA5 32 F5
Croftlands CARN LA5 26 B5
GAR/LONG PR3 282 C3
RAMS BL0 214 D8
WGNW/BIL/OR WN5 255 G7
Croft La PDHM/BLYW BB12 121 J5
Croft Meadow BBR PR5 169 M5
Crofton Av BISP FY2 85 G6
Croft Pk LEYL PR25 * 186 F2
Croft Rd CHLYE PR6 208 B4
Crofts Cl KIRK/FR/WAR PR4 128 F6
Crofts Dr FUL/RIB PR2 134 A2
Croftson Av ORM L39 241 J4
The Crofts KIRK/FR/WAR PR4 166 D2
Croft St ACC BB5 * 159 L5
BCUP OL13 179 J8
BLY BB11 7 G5
BWCK/EAR BB18 294 F5
CLI BB7 99 H4
DWN BB3 * 191 K2
GTH/LHO BB6 138 F7
MCMB LA4 41 K7
PRES PR1 8 D2
WHIT OL12 218 F8
The Croft BBN BB1 157 G4
BBR PR5 * 170 E1
CHLY/EC PR7 205 M4
CLV/TH FY5 85 G1
COL BB8 296 B4
FTWD FY7 81 G1
GAR/LONG PR3 284 A6
GAR/LONG PR3 113 G6
HGHB LA2 44 C5
KKBYL LA6 31 H6
LSTA FY8 145 L2
MGHL L31 249 L6
PLF/KEOS FY6 * 106 A1
WGNW/BIL/OR WN5 255 G7
Croft Wy CLV/TH FY5 85 M3
Croftwood Sq
WGNW/BIL/OR WN5 255 M1
Crombleholme Rd PRES PR1 153 H2
Cromer Av BRFD/BLYE BB10 142 F2
Cromer Gv BRFD/BLYE BB10 142 F2
Cromer Pl BBN BB1 157 H4
Cromer Rd BISP FY2 85 H7
LSTA FY8 145 K2
STHP PR8 221 H1
Cromer St WHIT OL12 235 H2
Cromfield ORM L39 250 F1
Cromford Dr
WGNW/BIL/OR WN5 255 L6
Cromford Wk PRES PR1 * 152 F3
Crompton Av BPOOLS FY4 125 H4
MILN OL16 235 L8
Crompton Pl BBNW BB2 10 A4
Crompton St PRES PR1 152 F2
Cromwell Av PRES PR1 151 M8
Cromwell Cl ORM L39 250 F1
Cromwell Ms GAR/LONG PR3 * 284 C6
Cromwell Rd BPOOL FY1 104 F3
FUL/RIB PR2 133 G8
LANC LA1 2 E8
PRES PR1 151 L8
Cromwell St ACC BB5 159 L3
BBN BB1 11 J6
PDHM/BLYW BB12 6 F1
PRES PR1 9 K1
Cromwell Wy PRES PR1 168 D1
Cronkeyshaw Rd WHIT OL12 235 H2
Cronkeyshaw Vw WHIT OL12 235 H1
Cronkshaw St BRFD/BLYE BB10 7 G1
Cronshaw Dr GTH/LHO BB6 137 M2
Crookall Cl FTWD FY7 81 J1
Crook Dale La PLF/KEOS FY6 83 G4
Crooked La PRES PR1 9 J3
Crooked Shore BCUP OL13 179 J8
Crooke Rd WGNNW/ST WN6 245 M8
Crookfield Rd EDGW/EG BL7 190 D8
Crook Gate La GAR/LONG PR3 87 M2
Crookhalgh Av
BRFD/BLYE BB10 143 J5
Crookhey Gdns HGHB LA2 269 N8
Crookings La PRES PR1 151 K5
Crookland Gdns PLF/KEOS FY6 87 G1
Crooklands Dr GAR/LONG PR3 284 B7
Crookleigh Pl HEY LA3 * 52 E1
Crook St CHLY/EC PR7 230 C4
CHLY/EC PR7 207 L6
MILN OL16 235 K3
PRES PR1 9 M2
Croos St ACC BB5 159 M6
Cropper Gdns
KIRK/FR/WAR PR4 165 G8
Cropper Rd BPOOLS FY4 125 L4
Cropper Rd North
BPOOLS FY4 125 M4
Cropper's La ORM L39 251 K2
Cropton Rd FMBY L37 237 J8
Crosby Cl DWN BB3 191 L5
Crosby Gv BPOOLE FY3 5 L6
Crosby Pl FUL/RIB PR2 131 K7
Crosby Rd BBNW BB2 173 H2
LSTA FY8 145 J2
STHP PR8 199 J8
Crosby St WHIT OL12 235 J1
Crosender Rd CSBY/BLUN L23 256 F8
Crosier Wk KIRK/FR/WAR PR4 131 H6
Crosland Rd North LSTA FY8 145 J2
Crosland Rd South LSTA FY8 145 K3
Crosley Cl ACC BB5 159 L8
Cross Barn Gv DWN BB3 191 L3
Cross Barn La HTWN L38 257 H1
Crossdale Rd CSBY/BLUN L23 256 F8
Crossdale Sq LANC LA1 3 J5
Crosse Hall La CHLYE PR6 208 B4
Crosse Hall St CHLYE PR6 208 C4
Crossens Wy CHTN/BK PR9 180 F5
Cross Fld KIRK/FR/WAR PR4 166 F2
Crossfield Cl WHIT OL12 218 F4
Crossfield Pl ROCH OL11 235 K6
Crossfield Rd SKEL WN8 253 M3
WHIT OL12 218 F5
Crossfield St BBNW BB2 11 G8
Cross Flatts Crs
BWCK/EAR BB18 294 B7
Crossfold BBNW BB2 11 H9
Cross Fold CLI BB7 290 G7
Cross Gates GTH/LHO BB6 138 F6
Cross Green Cl FMBY L37 247 K1
Cross Green Rd FUL/RIB PR2 132 B5
Cross Hagg St COL BB8 * 103 M7
Crosshall Brow BRSC L40 241 M7
Cross Halls PRES PR1 151 L8
Cross Helliwell St COL BB8 * 296 A7
Cross Hey MGHL L31 * 259 H4
Cross Hill La CLI BB7 292 E6
Crosshill Rd BBNW BB2 156 E6
The Crossings BBR PR5 170 E1
Cross Keys Dr CHLYE PR6 187 M4
Crossland Rd BPOOLS FY4 125 H2
Crossland St ACC BB5 159 K6
Cross La BWCK/EAR BB18 294 B7
CLI BB7 289 M10
HGHB LA2 38 C3
KIRK/FR/WAR PR4 129 G2
ORM L39 239 L2
PDHM/BLYW BB12 101 M7
SETT BD24 264 E8
TOD OL14 303 Q3
TOT/BURYW BL8 214 D6
WGNW/BIL/OR WN5 255 G8
Cross Lee TOD OL14 301 J12
Cross Lee Rd TOD OL14 301 J12
Cross Lees WHIT OL12 218 D8
Crossley Fold BLY BB11 6 B8
Crossley New Rd TOD OL14 301 P11
Crossley St TOD OL14 303 L2
Crossmeadow Cl ROCH OL11 234 D3
Cross Meanygate BRSC L40 202 F6
Cross Of Greet Br CLI BB7 62 B8
Cross Pit La RNFD/HAY WA11 262 C5
Cross Rd HGHB LA2 38 B6
Cross School St COL BB8 * 296 A7
Cross Skelton St COL BB8 296 B6
Cross Stone Rd TOD OL14 301 P12
Cross St ACC BB5 159 G7
BPOOL FY1 104 E4
BRFD/BLYE BB10 143 J1
BWCK/EAR BB18 294 D6
CHLY/EC PR7 * 207 M2
CLI BB7 * 99 G3
DWN BB3 191 L4
DWN BB3 173 J4
FTWD FY7 * 77 L6
GAR/LONG PR3 114 C5
GTH/LHO BB6 139 G6
LEYL PR25 186 E1
LSTA FY8 145 G3
MCMB LA4 41 K6
NLSN BB9 122 E6
PDHM/BLYW BB12 121 J6
PRES PR1 9 H5
RAMS BL0 214 F5
RAW/HAS BB4 177 K4
STHP PR8 13 G6
WGNW/BIL/OR WN5 * 255 L5
Cross St North RAW/HAS BB4 176 E7
Cross St West COL BB8 103 L7
The Cross HTWN L38 248 A8
Cross Wy CLV/TH FY5 81 G7
Crossways CLI BB7 290 C8
Croston Av CHLYE PR6 230 D3
Croston Barn Rd
GAR/LONG PR3 283 R7
Croston Dr BRSC L40 203 L5
Croston La CHLY/EC PR7 228 E1
Croston Rd BBR PR5 168 D4
BRSC L40 203 L5
CROS/BRETH PR26 168 B8
GAR/LONG PR3 284 A7
Croston's Brow CHTN/BK PR9 180 C8
Croston St BBN BB1 * 157 M6
Crowder Av CLV/TH FY5 85 L1
Crowell Wy BBR PR5 153 H8
Crow Hills Rd PRES PR1 151 K5
Crowland Cl CHTN/BK PR9 200 D5
Crowland St CHTN/BK PR9 200 D5
Crowland Wy FMBY L37 247 L1
Crow La GAR/LONG PR3 88 B3
RAMS BL0 214 F5
SKEL WN8 244 C8
Crowle St PRES PR1 153 G3
Crown Cl FMBY L37 247 K1
Crowndale EDGW/EG BL7 213 G4
Crowneast St ROCH OL11 234 F4
Crownest Rd BWCK/EAR BB18 293 Q4
Crown Gdns EDGW/EG BL7 213 G5
MILN OL16 235 K6
Crown La FTWD FY7 77 L7
HOR/BR BL6 231 J8
KIRK/FR/WAR PR4 130 D1
Crownlee PRES PR1 151 K8
Crown Ms KIRK/FR/WAR PR4 128 D6
Crown Point Rd BLY BB11 162 D4
Crown St ACC BB5 159 K6
CHLY/EC PR7 207 M3
DWN BB3 191 K3
LEYL PR25 168 E8
MILN OL16 235 K6
PRES PR1 9 H2
Crown Wy COL BB8 103 M6
Crow Orchard Rd
WGNNW/ST WN6 245 J1
Crow Park La CLI BB7 278 G12
Crowshaw Dr WHIT OL12 218 B8
Crowther St ACC BB5 139 H8
BLY BB11 7 J6
MILN OL16 235 K7
Crowthorn Rd EDGW/EG BL7 213 J2
Crow Tree Av BCUP OL13 * 196 E3
Crow Trees Brow CLI BB7 291 J11
Crow Trees Gdns CLI BB7 291 J10
Crowtrees Gv NLSN BB9 102 C6
Crow Trees La EDGW/EG BL7 212 F4
Crowtrees Rd CLI BB7 120 C3
Crowtrees Yd HGHB LA2 38 C3
Crow Wood Av
PDHM/BLYW BB12 6 B1
Crow Wood Ct
PDHM/BLYW BB12 * 6 C1
Crow Wood Rd RAW/HAS BB4 195 G5
Croxteth Cl MGHL L31 250 B8
Croxteth Dr RNFD/HAY WA11 262 C4
Croxton Av MILN OL16 235 M3
Croyde Cl CHTN/BK PR9 180 E6
Croyde Rd LSTA FY8 145 K6
Croydon Rd BPOOLE FY3 105 H4
Croydon St BBNW BB2 10 A3
Crummock Pl BPOOLS FY4 125 M2
Crummock Rd PRES PR1 153 K2
Crumpax Av GAR/LONG PR3 114 D3
Crumpax Cft GAR/LONG PR3 114 D3
Crumpax Meadow
GAR/LONG PR3 114 D3
Crystal Gv LSTA FY8 145 H3
Crystal Ms BPOOL FY1 4 C9
Crystal Rd BPOOL FY1 4 C9
CLV/TH FY5 81 L6
Cuba St NLSN BB9 * 123 G3
Cuckoo Brow BBN BB1 156 F3
Cuckoo La GAR/LONG PR3 282 E12
Cuckstool La
PDHM/BLYW BB12 122 A4
Cudworth Rd LSTA FY8 145 J2
Cuerdale La BBR PR5 153 J6
Cuerdale St BRFD/BLYE BB10 123 H8
Cuerden Av LEYL PR25 186 A4
Cuerden Cl BBR PR5 169 H7
Cuerden Ri BBR PR5 168 F4
Cuerden St CHLYE PR6 208 B4
COL BB8 103 L8
Cuerden Wy BBR PR5 169 G3
Culbeck La CHLY/EC PR7 186 C8
Culcross Av WGNS/IIMK WN3 255 M7
Culshaw St BBN BB1 11 J4
BRFD/BLYE BB10 7 M6
Culshaw Wy BRSC L40 223 J4
Culvert La SKEL WN8 243 K1
SKP/WHF BD23 281 R7
Cumberland Av ACC BB5 139 K8
BPOOL FY1 5 G5
CLV/TH FY5 81 G7
LEYL PR25 186 B4
NTHTN L30 257 M8
PDHM/BLYW BB12 141 K4
Cumberland Cl DWN BB3 191 M5
Cumberland Ga NTHTN L30 258 D7
Cumberland Rd STHP PR8 13 L8
Cumberland St BBN BB1 11 K5
NLSN BB9 * 123 H2
Cumberland View Rd HEY LA3 40 E8
Cumbrian Av BPOOLE FY3 * 105 H4
Cumbrian Wy
PDHM/BLYW BB12 141 L3
Cumeragh La GAR/LONG PR3 113 J6
Cumpstey St BBNW BB2 10 F8
Cunliffe Av RAMS BL0 214 D7
Cunliffe Cl BBN BB1 157 L2
Cunliffe La CLI BB7 119 J3
Cunliffe Rd BBN BB1 157 M2
BPOOL FY1 5 H8
Cunliffe St CHLY/EC PR7 207 M4
PRES PR1 9 K2
RAMS BL0 214 F4
Cunnery Meadow LEYL PR25 187 H2
Cunningham Av CHLY/EC PR7 207 K5
Cunningham Gv
PDHM/BLYW BB12 141 L5
Cunscough La MGHL L31 260 A1
Curate St CHLYE PR6 208 B2
GTH/LHO BB6 138 F6
Curlew Cl ACC BB5 159 G8
BBN BB1 157 H2
CLV/TH FY5 81 J7
LEYL PR25 185 M4
ROCH OL11 234 C4
Curlew Gdns BLY BB11 141 L6
Curlew Gv HEY LA3 52 E6
Curlew La BRSC L40 225 H2
Curran Wy NWD/KWIPK L33 260 A5
Curteis St HOR/BR BL6 231 L7
Curtis Dr FTWD FY7 77 G8
Curtis St RAW/HAS BB4 177 K8
Curven Edge RAW/HAS BB4 194 D4
Curve St BCUP OL13 197 J2
Curwen La GAR/LONG PR3 92 F8
Curwen St PRES PR1 152 F2
Curzon Pl BBNW BB2 * 10 A7
Curzon Rd LSTA FY8 145 K4
PLF/KEOS FY6 86 B8
STHP PR8 13 M7
Curzon St BLY BB11 6 F3
CLI BB7 99 G4
Custom House La FTWD FY7 77 L6
Customs Wy FUL/RIB PR2 8 A2
Cutgate Rd WHIT OL12 234 E2
Cuthbert Mayne Ct MILN OL16 235 H5
Cutland Wy LIT OL15 219 K7
Cut La BBN BB1 158 C2
BRSC L40 240 C3
WHIT OL12 234 C2
Cutler Cl BBNW BB2 10 B4
Cutler Crs BCUP OL13 197 G4
Cutler La BCUP OL13 197 G4
GAR/LONG PR3 94 F3
Cutt Cl CROS/BRETH PR26 185 J5
Cutts La GAR/LONG PR3 87 J1
Cygnet Cl ORM L39 250 F1
Cypress Av CLV/TH FY5 85 H1
Cypress Cl FUL/RIB PR2 133 K7
LEYL PR25 187 H1
MGHL L31 259 K8
Cypress Gv BBR PR5 168 E3
BPOOLE FY3 * 105 G4
Cypress Rdg BBNW BB2 172 C3
Cypress Rd STHP PR8 200 B5
Cyprus Av LSTA FY8 145 L7
Cyprus Rd HEY LA3 52 D5
Cyprus St DWN BB3 191 L5

D

Dacre Rd ROCH OL11 235 J7
Daffodil Cl RAW/HAS BB4 194 D3
WHIT OL12 218 B8
Dagger Rd KIRK/FR/WAR PR4 129 M4
Daggers Hall La BPOOLS FY4 125 H3
Daggers La PLF/KEOS FY6 78 E8
Dahlia Cl DWN BB3 173 K4
WHIT OL12 218 A8
Dailton Rd SKEL WN8 254 D4
Dairy Farm Rd
RNFD/HAY WA11 262 A4
Daisy Bank BCUP OL13 * 179 J8
Daisy Bank Cl LEYL PR25 186 A2
Daisy Bank Crs
BRFD/BLYE BB10 143 H6
Daisy Bank St TOD OL14 300 E10
Daisy Cft FUL/RIB PR2 151 G3
Daisyfields
KIRK/FR/WAR PR4 * 131 J4
Daisyfield St DWN BB3 173 H6
Daisy Fold CHLYE PR6 208 B1
Daisy Hl RAW/HAS BB4 177 K8
Daisy Hill Ct ACC BB5 160 B1
Daisy Hill Dr CHLYE PR6 230 D3
Daisy Hill Fold CHLY/EC PR7 207 G2
Daisy La BBN BB1 11 H1
BRSC L40 225 L7
PRES PR1 132 F8
Daisy Meadow BBR PR5 169 L6
Daisy Mt MGHL L31 259 H3
Daisy St BBN BB1 11 J2
COL BB8 296 A7
LANC LA1 42 E8
WHIT OL12 235 H3
Daisy Wy STHP PR8 221 L1
Dalby Cl CLV/TH FY5 85 J4
PRES PR1 133 G8
Dalby Crs BBNW BB2 172 D2
Dalby Lea BBNW BB2 172 C2
Dale Acre Dr NTHTN L30 257 M8
Dale Av CHLY/EC PR7 207 G2
HGHB LA2 42 D3
KIRK/FR/WAR PR4 166 B4
TOD OL14 303 N2
Dale Cl MGHL L31 258 F1
PDHM/BLYW BB12 6 B3
SKEL WN8 243 L1
Dale Crs BBNW BB2 172 B4
Dale Dyke Wk PLF/KEOS FY6 85 L8
Dalegarth Cl BPOOLS FY4 125 M2
Dalehead Rd LEYL PR25 186 E5
Dale La NWD/KWIPK L33 260 D7
Dalesford RAW/HAS BB4 194 E2
Dalesford Cl CLV/TH FY5 85 M3
Daleside TOD OL14 303 K3
Daleside Rd NWD/KWIPK L33 260 C8
The Dales BWCK/EAR BB18 * 293 Q8
GTH/LHO BB6 137 K3
Dale St ACC BB5 159 K6
BBNW BB2 * 10 C6
BCUP OL13 179 J8
BPOOL FY1 4 C5
BWCK/EAR BB18 294 E5
COL BB8 103 M6
LANC LA1 3 J8
MILN OL16 235 M4
NLSN BB9 122 D6
PDHM/BLYW BB12 * 6 B3
PRES PR1 9 L3
RAMS BL0 214 F3
RAW/HAS BB4 176 E8
TOD OL14 303 L2
Dale Street Ms BPOOL FY1 4 C5
Dalesview Crs HEY LA3 52 E4
Dalesway NLSN BB9 102 F8
Dale Vw BBNW BB2 173 H5
BWCK/EAR BB18 294 D6
CHLY/EC PR7 207 M7
CLI BB7 118 E7
Dalewood Av BPOOLS FY4 5 J9
Dalglish Dr BBNW BB2 173 G4
Dalkeith Av BPOOLE FY3 125 K1
Dalkeith Rd NLSN BB9 * 122 F3
Dallam Av MCMB LA4 41 K5
Dallam Dell CLV/TH FY5 81 L7
Dallas Ct MCMB LA4 42 A7
Dallas Rd LANC LA1 2 F8
MCMB LA4 42 A7
Dallas St PRES PR1 132 B8
Dall St BLY BB11 7 H7
Dalmeny Ter ROCH OL11 235 J7
Dalmore Rd FUL/RIB PR2 131 K8
Dalton Av BPOOLS FY4 125 G6
Dalton Cl BBN BB1 11 K4
RAMS BL0 214 D7
WGNW/BIL/OR WN5 255 L4
Dalton La KKBYL LA6 19 J6
Dalton Rd HEY LA3 40 E8
LANC LA1 3 K5
Dalton Sq LANC LA1 3 H6
Dalton St BLY BB11 6 A9
LSTA FY8 145 G3
NLSN BB9 123 H2
Dame Fold PDHM/BLYW BB12 121 J5
Damfield La MGHL L31 258 F2
Dam Head Rd
BWCK/EAR BB18 293 Q5
Dampier St TOD OL14 303 K6
Dam Side COL BB8 296 A7
Damside St LANC LA1 3 G4
Damson Cl GTH/LHO BB6 117 M5
Dam Wood La BRSC L40 223 M6
Danbers SKEL WN8 254 C5
Dancer La CLI BB7 292 D6
Dandy's Meanygate
KIRK/FR/WAR PR4 182 E4
Dane Ms PLF/KEOS FY6 106 B3
Danesbury Pl BPOOL FY1 4 F1
Danes Cl KIRK/FR/WAR PR4 128 F6
Danes Dr BBR PR5 169 G2
Daneshouse Rd
BRFD/BLYE BB10 142 D3
Dane St PDHM/BLYW BB12 7 G1
ROCH OL11 235 H4
Danesway BBR PR5 169 G2
CHLY/EC PR7 230 C2
PRES PR1 151 K7
Daneswood Av WHIT OL12 217 M4
Daneswood Cl WHIT OL12 217 L3
Daneswood Meadow
WHIT OL12 217 L3
Daneway STHP PR8 220 E5
Danewerke St PRES PR1 * 9 K2
Daniel Fold WHIT OL12 234 E1
Daniel Fold La GAR/LONG PR3 90 F1
Daniell St BBN BB1 158 D1
Daniels La SKEL WN8 253 M4
Daniel St ACC BB5 139 H8
WHIT OL12 218 A2
Danson Gdns BISP FY2 105 G3
Danvers St BBN BB1 158 E1
Darbishire Rd FTWD FY7 77 J6
Daresbury Av STHP PR8 220 D6
Darfield SKEL WN8 254 C4
Darkinson La
KIRK/FR/WAR PR4 150 C1
Dark La BRSC L40 241 L5
BRSC L40 205 H8
BWCK/EAR BB18 294 G5
CHLYE PR6 188 B5
HOR/BR BL6 230 E7
MGHL L31 259 G2
RAW/HAS BB4 196 B2
Darkwood Crs CLI BB7 291 J10
Dark Wood La BBR PR5 154 E5
Darley Av BPOOLS FY4 125 G4
Darley Rd ROCH OL11 235 J7
Darley St HOR/BR BL6 231 L6
Darlington Rd ROCH OL11 235 J8
Darlington St CHLY/EC PR7 229 G2
Darmond Rd NWD/KWIPK L33 260 D8
Darnbrook Rd
BWCK/EAR BB18 293 P5
Darnley St BRFD/BLYE BB10 7 M6
Dartford Cl BBN BB1 11 H5
Dartmouth Cl
KIRK/FR/WAR PR4 128 C6
Dartmouth Dr NTHTN L30 257 M7
Dart St FUL/RIB PR2 8 A2
Darwen Cl GAR/LONG PR3 114 E4
Darwen St BBNW BB2 10 E4
BBR PR5 153 L7
PDHM/BLYW BB12 * 140 F3
PRES PR1 * 152 F4
Darwen Vw BBR PR5 153 H6
Darwin St BRFD/BLYE BB10 142 D1
Datchett Ter ROCH OL11 235 J7
Daub Hall La BBR PR5 170 B1
Daub La BRSC L40 226 D3
Dauntesey Av BPOOLE FY3 105 K5
Davenham Rd DWN BB3 173 H8
FMBY L37 237 J7
Davenport Av BISP FY2 84 F6
Davenport Gv
NWD/KWIPK L33 260 B7
Daventry Av BISP FY2 84 E7
Daventry Rd ROCH OL11 235 J8
Davey La HBR HX7 301 Q8
David Lewis Cl MILN OL16 235 M5
Davidson St LANC LA1 3 K6
David St BCUP OL13 197 G3
NLSN BB9 103 G7
WHIT OL12 235 J2
David St North WHIT OL12 * 235 J2
Davies Rd BBN BB1 158 A5
Davis St GAR/LONG PR3 114 D3
Davy Field Brow BBN BB1 173 L5
Davy Field Rd BBN BB1 173 K5
Davyhulme St WHIT OL12 235 K2
Dawber Delph
WGNNW/ST WN6 245 G3
Dawber's La CHLY/EC PR7 206 B1
Dawlish Av BPOOLE FY3 105 J3
Dawlish Cl BBNW BB2 172 F3
Dawlish Dr CHTN/BK PR9 180 D6
Dawlish Pl FUL/RIB PR2 131 K8
Dawnay Rd FUL/RIB PR2 133 H8
Dawnwood Sq
WGNW/BIL/OR WN5 255 M1
Dawson Av CHTN/BK PR9 180 F6
PDHM/BLYW BB12 140 B1
Dawson Gdns MGHL L31 258 F1
Dawson La CHLY/EC PR7 187 H4
Dawson Pl BBR PR5 169 K4
Dawson Rd LSTA FY8 145 J2
ORM L39 241 J4
Dawson Sq BLY BB11 * 7 H2
Dawson Wk PRES PR1 9 H1
Daybrook SKEL WN8 254 C5
Dayfield SKEL WN8 254 D4
Day St NLSN BB9 123 H4
Dayton Pl BPOOLS FY4 124 F5
Deacon St MILN OL16 235 L2
Deal Pl LSTA FY8 145 J2
Dean Brow GAR/LONG PR3 116 C3
Dean Cl RAMS BL0 195 G8
SKEL WN8 254 F4
Dean Ct FTWD FY7 81 G3
Deancourt ROCH OL11 235 H7
Dean Crs WGNW/BIL/OR WN5 255 L3
Deancroft Av HEY LA3 52 F1
Deanfield CLI BB7 99 L1
Deanfield Dr CLI BB7 99 L1

Deanfield Wy *CLI* BB7........................99 L1
Dean Fold *RAW/HAS* BB4..............178 D3
Deanhall La *CHLY/EC* PR7...........206 A1
Dean Head *LIT* OL15 *.................303 M12
Deanhead La *HOR/BR* BL6.............239 J7
Dean La *BBR* PR5............................134 C8
CLI BB7...138 F1
DWN BB3...190 E4
GTH/LHO BB6.................................138 E4
RAW/HAS BB4................................178 D3
Dean Meadow *CLI* BB7....................99 G4
Dean Rd *RAW/HAS* BB4.................194 D2
Deanroyd Rd *TOD* OL14.................303 D11
Deans Ct *BBR* PR5..........................237 J6
Deansgate *BPOOL* FY1.........................4 C3
MCMB LA4...41 L6
Deansgate La *FMBY* L37..............237 L6
Deansgate La North
FMBY L37..237 K5
Deansgreave Rd *BCUP* OL13........197 L4
Deans La *BRSC* L40.......................226 B7
SKEL WN8..243 J1
Dean St *BBR* PR5............................169 H2
BLY BB11...6 C4
BPOOLS FY4.....................................124 F5
COL BB8..296 E9
DWN BB3...173 J7
MILN OL16..235 L2
PDHM/BLYW BB12..........................141 G2
Dean Wood Av
WGNW/BIL/OR WN5....................255 M5
Dearden Clough *RAMS* BL0..........215 H1
Dearden Fold *RAMS* BL0..............215 H1
Dearden Nook *RAW/HAS* BB4.....195 K2
Dearden St *LIT* OL15......................219 J7
Dearnley Cl *LIT* OL15....................219 J7
Deborah Av *FUL/RIB* PR2..............132 C4
Debra Cl *MGHL* L31.......................259 L2
Dee Cl *NWD/KWIPK* L33...............260 C5
PLF/KEOS FY6....................................85 L6
Deepdale Av *MILN* OL16................235 M5
Deepdale Cl *MTHPE* LA7.................17 M1
Deepdale Cl *NLSN* BB9..................102 F8
Deepdale Dr *BRFD/BLYE* BB10....122 F7
Deepdale Gn *NLSN* BB9.................102 F8
Deepdale Houses *PRES* PR1 *...........9 L1
Deepdale La
KIRK/FR/WAR PR4........................130 A8
Deepdale Mill St *PRES* PR1 *............9 L1
Deepdale Pk *PRES* PR1 *................133 G1
Deepdale Rd *BPOOLS* FY4............125 M3
FTWD FY7...77 K8
PRES PR1...9 L2
Deepdale St *PRES* PR1......................9 L2
Deeplish Rd *ROCH* OL11................235 J6
Deeplish St *ROCH* OL11.................235 J6
Deerbarn St *NTHTN* L30................258 E4
Deerbolt Cl *KKBY* L32...................259 M8
Deerbolt La *KKBY* L32...................259 M8
Deerbolt Wy *KKBY* L32..................259 M8
Deer Chace *PDHM/BLYW* BB12....122 H4
Deerfold *CHLY/EC* PR7...................207 L1
Deerhurst Rd *CLV/TH* FY5...............85 L4
Dee Rd *LANC* LA1................................2 D2
Deer Pk *ACC* BB5...........................160 D3
Deer Park La *HGHB* LA2...................36 H5
Deer Park Rd
BRFD/BLYE BB10..........................143 C8
Deerplay Cl *BRFD/BLYE* BB10......143 H1
Deerplay Cl *BCUP* OL13................179 K3
Deerplay Rd *BCUP* OL13................179 K3
Deerstone Av *BRFD/BLYE* BB10.......7 L3
Deerstone Rd *NLSN* BB9................123 G5
Deeside *BPOOLS* FY4.....................125 G4
Dee St *LSTA* FY8.............................145 H5
Deganwy Av *BBN* BB1....................157 H4
Deighton Cl *LEYL* PR25.................186 D3
Deighton Rd *CHLY/EC* PR7............207 L5
Dekker Rd *NWD/KWIPK* L33.........260 C5
De Lacy St *CLI* BB7...........................99 G3
FUL/RIB PR2....................................152 A1
Delamere Av *HEY* LA3......................52 D5
Delamere Cl *ACC* BB5....................159 L2
BBNW BB2...A3
Delamere Pl *BRFD/BLYE* BB10........7 A3
Delamere Rd *BRFD/BLYE* BB10....122 J8
MILN OL16..235 M7
SKEL WN8..253 J1
STHP PR8..220 E6
Delamere St *SKEL* WN8.................254 D4
Delany Dr *KIRK/FR/WAR* PR4.......148 D5
Delaware Crs *KKBY* L32................259 M8
Delaware Rd *BPOOLE* FY3.............105 K2
Delaware St *PRES* PR1...................152 F2
TOD OL14...300 D9
Delf La *ORM* L39.............................239 K6
Delius Cl *BBNW* BB2......................173 K2
Dellar St *WHIT* OL12......................234 F2
Dellfield La *MGHL* L31..................259 H2
Dell Gdns *WHIT* OL12....................234 E1
Dell La *PDHM/BLYW* BB12.............140 F7
Dell Meadow *WHIT* OL12...............217 M6
Dell Rd *WHIT* OL12........................217 L7
Dell Side Wy *WHIT* OL12...............234 F1
The Dell *BBNW* BB2.......................173 G5
CHLY PR6..188 D8
FUL/RIB PR2.....................................132 H4
KIRK/FR/WAR PR4........................127 L8
SKEL WN8..254 D4
WGNW/ST WN6...............................245 G4
The Dellway
KIRK/FR/WAR PR4........................151 H6
Delma Rd *BRFD/BLYE* BB10.........143 H6
Delph Ap *BBN* BB1.........................157 M7
Delph Av *EDGW/EG* BL7................212 A8
Delph Cl *BBN* BB1...........................157 M7
Delph Common Rd *ORM* L39.........250 C2
Delph Ct *GTH/LHO* BB6.................138 F6
Delph Dr *BRSC* L40........................225 J7
Delphene Av *BISP* FY2.....................85 G5
CLV/TH FY5..85 G4
Delphinium Wy *DWN* BB3.............173 K4
Delph La *BBN* BB1 *.......................157 M8
CHLY/EC PR7....................................207 G6
FMBY L37..236 F8
GAR/LONG PR3...............................284 F2
ORM L39..250 D2
Delph Meadow Gdns
WGNW/BIL/OR WN5....................263 M7
Delph Mt *GTH/LHO* BB6................138 G5
Delph Park Av *ORM* L39................250 D4
Delph Rd *CSBY/BLUN* L23............257 G3
GTH/LHO BB6..................................138 E6
Delphside Cl
WGNW/BIL/OR WN5....................255 G6
Delphside Rd
WGNW/BIL/OR WN5....................254 F6
Delph St *DWN* BB3.........................173 J6
The Delph *SKEL* WN8....................226 F8
Delph Top *ORM* L39.......................241 K9
Delph Wy *CHLYE* PR6...................187 M4

Delta Park Av
KIRK/FR/WAR PR4........................165 H7
Delta Park Dr
KIRK/FR/WAR PR4........................165 H7
Delves La *BRFD/BLYE* BB10.........123 M4
Demming Cl *FUL/RIB* PR2.............150 F3
Dempsey Av *CHTN/BK* PR9..........180 C8
Denaby Av *CLV/TH* FY5....................85 H2
Denbigh Cl *LEYL* PR25...................186 E2
Denbigh Dr *CLI* BB7..........................99 J1
Denbigh Wy *PRES* PR1........................9 K5
Denby Cl *BBR* PR5..........................152 F8
Denebank *BISP* FY2..........................85 G6
Dene Bank Rd *ACC* BB5.................159 H8
The Dene *BBNW* BB2.....................156 D3
CLI BB7..117 H3
Deneway Av *BPOOLE* FY3..............105 J3
Denford Av *LEYL* PR25..................186 E3
Denham Wy *FTWD* FY7....................81 J1
Denham Wood Cl
CHLY/EC PR7....................................207 J5
Denholme *SKEL* WN8.....................254 C4
Denholme Gv *BISP* FY2....................85 H6
Denholme Rd *ROCH* OL11..............235 J7
Denhurst Rd *LIT* OL15....................219 K8
Denis St *LANC* LA1...............................3 J1
Denmark Av *CHTN/BK* PR9...........200 D1
MILN OL16..235 K3
Denmark St *LANC* LA1.......................2 B7
Dennett Cl *MGHL* L31....................259 G4
Dennis Gv *MCMB* LA4 *...................41 L7
Denny Av *LANC* LA1...........................2 E7
Denny Beck La *HGHB* LA2...............43 K5
Denstone Av *BISP* FY2.....................85 G7
Dent Dl *ACC* BB5............................160 A6
Dentdale Cl *BBNW* BB2.................172 A4
Denton Gv
WGNW/BIL/OR WN5....................255 J5
Denton St *BWCK/EAR* BB18..........293 P4
WHIT OL12.......................................235 J2
Dent Rw *BLY* BB11.............................6 E6
Dent St *COL* BB8.............................103 L8
Denver Rd *ROCH* OL11...................235 J7
Denville Av *CLV/TH* FY5...................85 J3
PRES PR1..9 L2
Denville St *BBNW* BB2.....................10 C3
Depot Rd *BPOOLE* FY3...................105 H2
NWD/KWIPK L33...........................260 C3
Derbe Rd *LSTA* FY8........................145 J2
Derby Cl *DWN* BB3.........................191 L6
Derby Crs *KIRK/FR/WAR* PR4.......110 A3
Derby Dr *RNFD/HAY* WA11..........262 D6
Derby Hall Rd *ORM* L39................241 K6
Derby Hill Crs *ORM* L39................241 K6
Derby Pl *CHLYE* PR6......................230 D7
Derby Rd *BPOOL* FY1.....................104 E4
CHTN/BK PR9..................................200 C2
CLV/TH FY5..85 J5
FMBY L37..237 H7
FUL/RIB PR2.....................................132 B7
GAR/LONG PR3...............................284 A8
GAR/LONG PR3...............................114 D4
KIRK/FR/WAR PR4........................128 D5
LANC LA1...3 H4
LSTA FY8...145 M7
PLF/KEOS FY6....................................86 A7
SKEL WN8..243 F3
Derbyshire Av *GAR/LONG* PR3 *..284 C11
Derby Sq *PRES* PR1........................152 F3
Derby St *ACC* BB5...........................159 M5
BBN BB1..158 F2
BBN BB1...11 J1
BLY BB11...6 C5
CHLYE PR6..189 K3
CLI BB7..99 J3
COL BB8..296 A6
LEYL PR25...186 E1
NLSN BB9..123 H2
ORM L39..241 J6
PRES PR1..9 K3
RAMS BL0...215 G5
ROCH OL11.......................................235 K6
Derby Ter *RAW/HAS* BB4..............195 K1
Derdale St *TOD* OL14.....................303 M4
Derek Rd *CHLYE* PR6.....................187 M2
Derham St *BBNW* BB2......................10 F8
Derry Rd *FUL/RIB* PR2...................133 H8
Der St *TOD* OL14............................303 M4
Dertern La *CARN* LA5......................32 F4
Derwent Av *BRFD/BLYE* BB10......142 D1
CHTN/BK PR9...................................200 C2
FMBY L37..247 G1
FTWD FY7..81 G1
MCMB LA4...41 H4
PDHM/BLYW BB12..........................140 F7
Derwent Cl *BBN* BB1......................158 C2
COL BB8..296 B7
DWN BB3..191 M3
KIRK/FR/WAR PR4........................148 D5
MGHL L31...259 J1
NWD/KWIPK L33...........................260 A7
PLF/KEOS FY6.....................................78 D7
RAW/HAS BB4................................176 D1
Derwent Crs *CLI* BB7.......................98 F3
Derwent Dr *GAR/LONG* PR3.........114 C3
KIRK/FR/WAR PR4........................148 D5
Derwent Pl *CLV/TH* FY5.................106 A2
WGNW/BIL/OR WN5....................255 M4
Derwent Rd *CHLY/EC* PR7.............207 L3
LANC LA1...3 J4
LSTA FY8...145 K1
WGNW/BIL/OR WN5....................255 J3
Derwent St *DWN* BB3....................191 M3
WHIT OL12.......................................217 L7
Derwentwater Pl *PRES* PR1 *.......152 F1
Desmond Dr *CSBY/BLUN* L23.......257 J9
Deva Cl *NWD/KWIPK* L33..............260 A7
De Villiers Av *CSBY/BLUN* L23.....257 J11
De Vitre St *LANC* LA1..........................3 J2
Devona Av *BPOOLS* FY4................125 L2
Devon Av *ACC* BB5.........................158 C4
FTWD FY7..81 G1
SKEL WN8..254 E5
Devon Cl *BBR* PR5..........................153 J6
CSBY/BLUN L23..............................256 D7
WGNW/BIL/OR WN5....................255 M5
Devon Crs *RAW/HAS* BB4..............194 B4
Devon Farm Wy *FMBY* L37............248 D3
Devon Gv *PDHM/BLYW* BB12.......141 M3
Devon Pl *ACC* BB5 *.........................54 C4
Devonport Cl *BBR* PR5...................153 J6
Devonport Rd *BBNW* BB2...............10 B4

Devonport Rd *BBNW* BB2...............10 B4
Devonport Rd *CHLYE* PR6.............208 D7
Devon Rd *BBN* BB1........................157 M6
Devonshire Av *CLV/TH* FY5............85 L2
Devonshire Cl
NWD/KWIPK L33...........................260 B7
Devonshire Ct *CHLY/EC* PR7 *.....207 M3
Devonshire Dr *ACC* BB5.................139 J8
GAR/LONG PR3...............................284 A7
Devonshire Ms *CLV/TH* FY5...........85 J3
Devonshire Pl *PRES* PR1................153 H2
Devonshire Rd *BBN* BB1................158 D2
BISP FY2...85 G7
BPOOLE FY3.....................................105 G5
CHLY/EC PR7...................................207 M4
CHTN/BK PR9..................................200 D4
FUL/RIB PR2 *.................................132 D7
HEY LA3...41 G8
LSTA FY8...145 G4
Devonshire Sq *BPOOL* FY1................5 C1
Devonshire St *ACC* BB5.................159 L4
LANC LA1...5 G2
Devon St *BPOOLS* FY4...................125 G2
DWN BB3...191 L5
ROCH OL11.......................................235 J5
Dewberry Flds *SKEL* WN8.............254 E4
Dew Forest *GAR/LONG* PR3...........284 C11
Dewhirst Rd *WHIT* OL12................218 C8
Dewhirst Wy *WHIT* OL12...............218 C7
Dewhurst Av *BPOOLS* FY4.............191 M5
Dewhurst Cl *DWN* BB3...................191 M5
Dewhurst Rd *EDGW/EG* BL7.........212 A8
Dewhurst Rd *GTH/LHO* BB6.........137 J2
Dewhurst Rw *BBR* PR5...................169 G4
COL BB8..296 A8
DWN BB3..191 L5
Dew Meadow Cl *WHIT* OL12.........260 D7
Deycroft Av *NWD/KWIPK* L33......260 D7
Deyes End *MGHL* L31.....................259 H2
Deyes La *MGHL* L31.......................259 J3
Diamond Jubilee La *BRSC* L40......203 M7
Dianne Rd *CLV/TH* FY5....................85 M1
Dibb La *CSBY/BLUN* L23................256 F4
Dibbs Pocket
CHLY PR6..149 G4
Dib Rd *KIRK/FR/WAR* PR4............164 D1
Dicconson's La *LSTA* FY8..............239 M8
Dicconson Ter *LSTA* FY8...............146 E3
Dicconson Wy *ORM* L39 *.............241 K7
Dicken Gn *ROCH* OL11...................235 J7
Dicken Green La *ROCH* OL11.........235 J7
Dickens Av *BWCK/EAR* BB18........293 P4
Dickens Rd *CHLY/EC* PR7.............229 H3
Dickens St *BBN* BB1..........................11 H7
Dicket's La *SKEL* WN8...................252 D1
Dickie's La *BPOOLS* FY4................125 L6
Dickie's La South *BPOOLS* FY4.....125 L5
Dickinson Cl *FMBY* L37..................10 B7
FMBY L37..247 J1
Dickinson Rd *FMBY* L37................247 J1
Dick La *CHLYE* PR6........................189 H7
Dick's La *BRSC* L40........................242 C7
Dickson Av *PRES* PR1....................153 G1
Dickson Hey
KIRK/FR/WAR PR4........................167 J3
Dickson Rd *BPOOL* FY1.................104 E5
PDHM/BLYW BB12..........................141 M5
PRES PR1 *..9 J3
Dickson St West *HOR/BR* BL6........231 K7
Didsbury St *BBN* BB1.....................157 M6
Digby Rd *ROCH* OL11....................235 J7
Diggle Sq *PRES* PR1......................152 F3
Diggles La *ROCH* OL11..................234 D5
Digham Av *BISP* FY2.........................85 G5
Digmoor Dr *SKEL* WN8..................253 M4
Digmoor Rd *SKEL* WN8..................253 M4
Dill Hall La *ACC* BB5.......................159 K5
Dilworth Ct *GAR/LONG* PR3.........114 A6
Dilworth La *GAR/LONG* PR3..........114 A6
Dimple Pk *EDGW/EG* BL7..............212 A8
Dimple Rd *EDGW/EG* BL7.............211 M7
Dimples La *GAR/LONG* PR3..........284 C9
Dinckley Gv *BPOOL* FY1....................5 H6
Dinckley Sq *BPOOL* FY1.....................5 H6
Dineley Av *TOD* OL14.....................301 J12
Dinely St *ACC* BB5.........................159 J5
Dingle Av *BPOOLS* FY3..................105 K4
SKEL WN8..254 E3
Dingle Cl *ORM* L39........................250 F2
Dingle Rd *SKEL* WN8.....................254 E4
The Dingle *CHLYE* PR6..................188 D8
FUL/RIB PR2.....................................132 A4
Dinmore Av *BPOOLE* FY3..............105 K4
Dinmore Pl *BPOOLE* FY3...............105 K4
Dinorwic Rd *STHP* PR8..................199 H8
Dirty Leech *WHIT* OL12.................218 C5
Disley St *ROCH* OL11.....................235 G7
Disraeli St *BRFD/BLYE* BB10 *......112 J1
Ditchfield *FMBY* L37......................247 K1
Ditton Mead Cl *WHIT* OL12..........235 L1
Division La *BPOOLS* FY4................125 K6
Division St *WHIT* OL12...................235 H1
Dixey St *HOR/BR* BL6....................231 K8
Dixon Av *WGNNW/ST* WN6..........245 K6
Dixon Closes *ROCH* OL11..............234 B4
Dixon Dr *WGNNW/ST* WN6...........245 K6
Dixon Rd *GAR/LONG* PR3..............114 A4
Dixon's Farm Ms
KIRK/FR/WAR PR4........................150 A2
Dixons Cl *FUL/RIB* PR2..................133 M1
Dixon St *BBNW* BB2.........................10 A9
HOR/BR BL6.....................................231 J8
NLSN BB9..102 H3
ROCH OL11.......................................235 K6
Doals Ga *BCUP* OL13.....................179 K3
Dobbin Cl *RAW/HAS* BB4...............195 H4
Dobbin Dr *RAW/HAS* BB4..............195 H4
Dobbin La *RAW/HAS* BB4...............195 M1
Dob Brow *CHLY/EC* PR7................207 J7
Dobbs St *FUL/RIB* PR2...................237 K7
Dobbrow Rd *TOD* OL14..................303 N5
Dobs La *HGHB* LA2.........................268 H1
Dobson Av *LSTA* FY8......................145 H5
Dobson St *WGNNW/ST* WN6.........245 M1
Dobson St *DWN* BB3......................191 J1
Dock Av *FTWD* FY7..........................81 K7
Docker La *KKBY* LA6.........................29 H1
Dockinsall La *GAR/LONG* PR3.......282 A12
Dockray St *COL* BB8.......................296 B6
Dock La *LSTA* FY8...........................147 K7
Dock St *BBN* BB1...............................11 J5
FTWD FY7..77 M3
Docky Pool La *BPOOLS* FY4..........125 K5
Doctors La *FMBY* L37.....................248 B2
Doctor's La *CHLY/EC* PR7..............205 K5
KIRK/FR/WAR PR4........................183 J4
Doctors Rw *GAR/LONG* PR3..........114 D7
Dodd's La *MGHL* L31......................259 J4

Dodd Wy *BBR* PR5..........................169 K5
Dodgeons Cl *PLF/KEOS* FY6..........105 M1
Dodgson La *BWCK/EAR* BB18.......295 P5
Dodgson Pl *PRES* PR1....................152 F2
Dodgson Rd *PRES* PR1...................152 F2
Dodney Dr *FUL/RIB* PR2...............150 F2
Dodson Rd *FUL/RIB* PR2...............105 J4
Dodworth Av *STHP* PR8.................200 B6
Doeford Br *GAR/LONG* PR3...........288 B12
Doeholme Rake *HGHB* LA2...........271 J2
Doe Meadow *SKEL* WN8................243 H5
Doghouse La *TOD* OL14.................303 N2
Dog Pits La *BCUP* OL13.................179 J5
Dole La *CHLY/EC* PR7....................189 M2
CHLYE PR6..189 M2
Doles La *CROS/BRETH* PR26.........184 D3
Dolly's La *CHTN/BK* PR9...............201 G3
Dollywood La *MTHPE* LA7................17 J2
Dombey St *BBN* BB1.........................11 J6
Domingo Dr *NWD/KWIPK* L33......260 B5
Dominica Av *DWN* BB3..................173 J5
Dominion Rd *BBNW* BB2...............156 F5
Doncaster Rd *BPOOLS* FY4...........125 K1
Donnington Rd *LSTA* FY8..............145 J4
Donnington Rd *LSTA* FY8..............145 J4
PLF/KEOS FY6....................................85 M1
Donshort Ms *NLSN* BB9 *..............122 J7
Don St *LSTA* FY8............................145 H4
Doodstone Av *BBR* PR5..................168 G2
Doodstone Cl *BBR* PR5..................168 G2
Doodstone Nook *BBR* PR5.............168 G2
Dooley Dr *NTHTN* L30...................258 H4
Dora Cl *BLY* BB11.............................7 J8
Dora St *ROCH* OL11........................214 D7
Dorchester Av *ACC* BB5.................158 F7
Dorchester Cl *BBN* BB1....................11 L1
CLV/TH FY5...85 M3
Dorchester Dr
NWD/KWIPK L33...........................260 D6
Dorchester Gdns *HEY* LA3...............53 K1
Dorchester Rd *BPOOL* FY1............104 E3
GAR/LONG PR3...............................284 A4
SKEL WN8..254 D4
Doric Gn *WGNW/BIL/OR* WN5......255 J6
Doris Henderson Wy *LANC* LA1........3 K4
Doris St *BLY* BB11..............................7 J8
Dorking Rd *CHLYE* PR6..................188 C5
Dorman Rd *FUL/RIB* PR2...............133 H4
Dorothy Av *LEYL* PR25...................186 E5
Dorothy St *PRES* PR1..........................9 J8
RAMS BL0...214 C3
Dorrington Rd *LANC* LA1.................54 E6
Dorritt St *BPOOLS* FY4..................125 H5
Dorritt St *BBN* BB1...........................11 J7
Dorset Av *CLV/TH* FY5.....................81 G7
DWN BB3...173 J8
PDHM/BLYW BB12..........................141 G4
STHP PR8..237 M1
Dorset Cl *WGNW/BIL/OR* WN5.....255 M7
Dorset Dr *BBN* BB1........................158 A7
CLI BB7..99 J1
RAW/HAS BB4................................194 D2
LSTA FY8...145 J4
Dorset Rd *BPOOLS* FY4.................125 G5
FUL/RIB PR2.....................................132 B5
MGHL L31...258 F1
ROCH OL11.......................................235 D6
Dotcliffe Rd *BWCK/EAR* BB18......294 D9
Double Rw *PDHM/BLYW* BB12......140 E3
Doughty St *COL* BB8.......................296 A4
Douglas Av *BPOOLE* FY3................105 H4
HEY LA3...52 E4
HOR/BR BL6.....................................231 H1
KIRK/FR/WAR PR4........................183 J2
PLF/KEOS FY6....................................82 F7
SKEL WN8..254 D4
Douglas Cl *BBNW* BB2...................173 G4
BBR PR5..169 J3
BRSC L40...203 M8
HOR/BR BL6.....................................231 H4
Douglas Ct *FUL/RIB* PR2...............132 A4
Douglas Dr *HEY* LA3........................52 E4
KIRK/FR/WAR PR4........................148 D5
MGHL L31...259 J1
ORM L39..241 G4
Douglas Gv *DWN* BB3.....................173 G4
Douglas Pl *BBN* BB1......................157 M7
FTWD FY7..77 G8
Douglas Rd *BCUP* OL13.................197 G5
BRFD/BLYE BB10..........................123 K8
CHTN/BK PR9..................................180 F7
FUL/RIB PR2.....................................132 A4
WGNNW/ST WN6...........................245 L1
Douglas Rd North
FUL/RIB PR2.....................................132 A8
Douglas St *COL* DD0 *....................296 A5
FUL/RIB PR2...8 A1
LSTA FY8...145 J4
RAMS BL0...214 B5
Douglas Vw *HOR/BR* BL6...............230 F7
Douglas Wy *NWD/KWIPK* L33......260 H5
The Doultons *BBR* PR5...................152 E8
Dove Cl *PRES* PR1.............................85 J8
Dovecote *CHLYE* PR6......................169 K8
Dovecote Av *BPOOLE* FY3.............125 M1
Dovedale Cl *BRFD/BLYE* BB10......122 F7
CHTN/BK PR9..................................180 D6
LEYL PR25...186 D5
PDHM/BLYW BB12..........................141 M3
Dovedale Dr
PDHM/BLYW BB12..........................141 M3
WHIT OL12.......................................219 G8
Dovedale Gdns *GAR/LONG* PR3....114 A5
Dovedale Rd *DWN* BB3...................191 J1
Dove La *DWN* BB3..........................191 J1
Dover Cl *BBN* BB1..........................157 M7
KIRK/FR/WAR PR4........................148 B4
Dover Ct *BPOOL* FY1........................5 J8
Dover Gdns *PLF/KEOS* FY6.............85 J8
Dover La *CHLYE* PR6......................170 F4
Dover Rd *BPOOL* FY1........................5 H9
LSTA FY8...145 J4
MGHL L31...258 F1
Dover St *ACC* BB5...........................159 K4
DWN BB3...173 J4
MILN OL16..235 L1
NLSN BB9..123 G1
TOD OL14...303 N2
Dovestone Cl *PLF/KEOS* FY6..........85 L1
Dove St *LSTA* FY8...........................145 G4

Dovetree Cl *BBR* PR5 *...................152 E8
KIRK/FR/WAR PR4........................128 F7
Dowbridge Wy
KIRK/FR/WAR PR4........................128 E6
Dowhills Dr *CSBY/BLUN* L23........256 E6
Dowhills Pk *CSBY/BLUN* L23........256 E6
Dowhills Rd *CSBY/BLUN* L23........256 E6
Dowling St *ROCH* OL11.................235 J5
Downes Gv *MCMB* LA4.....................41 L7
Downesfield Rd *HEY* LA3.................53 J7
Downfield Cl *RAMS* BL0.................214 D5
Downham Av *GTH/LHO* BB6.........139 H5
RAW/HAS BB4................................177 K7
Downham Cots *HEY* LA3 *...............66 F7
Downham Dr *ACC* BB5...................159 K8
Downham Gv
BRFD/BLYE BB10..........................143 G6
Downham Pl *BPOOLS* FY4.............124 E7
Downham Rd *CLI* BB7....................291 J10
LEYL PR25...185 M3
Downham St *BBNW* BB2................156 F7
Downholland Moss La
FMBY L37..237 M7
Downing Ct *GAR/LONG* PR3..........111 M8
Downing St *PRES* PR1....................153 H3
Downley Cl *FUL/RIB* PR2...............234 D1
Downside Cl *NTHTN* L30................258 H5
The Downs *PLF/KEOS* FY6...............86 A7
WGNS/IIMK WN3.............................255 M5
Dowry St *ACC* BB5.........................159 M5
Dragon Cl *SKEL* WN8.....................254 E4
Drake Cl *LSTA* FY8..........................145 H2
ORM L39..250 F1
Drakelowe Av *BPOOLS* FY4...........125 J3
Drake Rd *LIT* OL15.........................219 M2
Drakes Cft *FUL/RIB* PR2................132 D7
Drakes Hollow *BBR* PR5................153 G7
Drake St *ROCH* OL11.....................235 J5
Drammen Av *BLY* BB11...................141 L6
Drapers Av *CHLY/EC* PR7..............205 M5
Draycombe Dr *HEY* LA3...................52 E1
Draycot Av *BPOOLE* FY3.................105 J3
Drayton Rd *HEY* LA3.........................52 F4
Drewitt Crs *CHTN/BK* PR9.............180 F7
Drew St *BLY* BB11...........................141 L6
Drewton Av *HEY* LA3........................52 E1
Drinkhouse La
CROS/BRETH PR26........................204 D2
Drinkhouse Rd
CROS/BRETH PR26........................204 E2
Driscoll St *PRES* PR1..........................9 L2
Driver St *RAW/HAS* BB4................177 K4
The Drive *BBR* PR5.........................153 J6
BCUP OL13.......................................197 J1
CARN LA5..32 H6
CHLYE PR6..171 H8
FUL/RIB PR2.....................................132 D7
GTH/LHO BB6..................................117 M6
HEY LA3...52 E4
HGHB LA2...42 C2
KIRK/FR/WAR PR4........................166 D3
Driving Ga *RAW/HAS* BB4.............177 K2
Dronsfield Rd *FTWD* FY7.................77 J6
Drovers Wy *LSTA* FY8....................146 A4
Druids Cl *EDGW/EG* BL7...............212 A8
Drumacre La East
KIRK/FR/WAR PR4........................166 D5
Drumacre La West
KIRK/FR/WAR PR4........................166 D5
Drumhead Rd *CHLYE* PR6..............208 A1
Drummersdale La *BRSC* L40..........223 L2
Drummond Av *BPOOLS* FY4..........105 H4
Drummond Rd
CSBY/BLUN L23..............................257 G3
Dry Bread La *GAR/LONG* PR3..........87 L1
Dryburgh Av *BPOOLE* FY3................5 M8
Dryden Gv *GTH/LHO* BB6.............138 E7
Dryden Rd *FTWD* FY7.......................77 K7
Dryden St *ACC* BB5.........................139 J8
PDHM/BLYW BB12..........................141 G4
Dryfield La *HOR/BR* BL6................231 K6
Duchess Dr *BISP* FY2........................84 F8
Duchess St *DWN* BB3.....................173 J4
Duchy Av *FUL/RIB* PR2..................132 E7
Ducie Pl *PRES* PR1.........................153 J2
Duckett St *BLY* BB11..........................6 F1
Duckshaw Rd *DWN* BB3.................191 J5
GAR/LONG PR3..................................79 K4
HGHB LA2..43 J6
Duckworth Cl *GAR/LONG* PR3.......91 G1
Duckworth Dr *GAR/LONG* PR3......284 C12
Duckworth Hall Brow
ACC BB5..174 D1
Duckworth Hill La *ACC* BB5..........174 F1
Duckworth La *ACC* BB5..................174 F1
KIRK/FR/WAR PR4........................183 H3
RAW/HAS BB4................................195 H3
Duckworth St *ACC* BB5..................159 H5
BBNW BB2...10 C7
DWN BB3...191 J1
NLSN BB9..123 G1
Duddle La *BBR* PR5........................169 G1
Duddle Av *DWN* BB3......................173 G8
FTWD FY7..81 M2
MGHL L31...259 J1
Duddon Cl *HEY* LA3.........................42 H8
Dudley Av *ACC* BB5........................158 F7
BISP FY2...105 G2
Dudley Cl *KIRK/FR/WAR* PR4.......166 D2
Dudley St *COL* BB8........................296 C6
MCMB LA4...41 K7
NLSN BB9..122 F8
Duerden St *NLSN* BB9....................123 G3
Duffins Cl *WHIT* OL12...................218 A8
Dugdale Ct *BPOOLS* FY4................125 J6
Dugdale La *SKP/WHF* BD23..........276 E11
Dugdale Rd *PDHM/BLYW* BB12....141 G4
Dugdales Cl *BPOOLS* FY4..............126 B4
Dugdale St *BLY* BB11..........................7 H4
Dugie Pl *RAMS* BL0........................214 E4
Duke Av *STHP* PR8.........................199 M7
Duke of Sussex St
BBNW BB2...172 E3
Dukes Brow *BBNW* BB2....................10 B2
Dukes Ct *BBN* BB1.........................156 E5
Dukes Cut *TOD* OL14.....................301 K8
Duke St *DWN* BB3..........................192 B2
Dukes Meadow *FUL/RIB* PR4........131 K6
Duke St *ACC* BB5............................158 F2
BBNW BB2...169 H4
BBR PR5..169 J4
BLY BB11...7 H1
BPOOL FY1..4 D9
BRFD/BLYE BB10..........................207 M5
COL BB8..296 A7
FMBY L37..247 H1
GTH/LHO BB6..................................138 D4
HEY LA3...52 D4

HGHB LA2 .... 38 F4
KKBYL LA6 .... 31 H6
KKBYL LA6 .... 18 L8
LANC LA1 .... 2 H4
LIT OL15 .... 219 K6
PRES PR1 .... 9 L4
RAMS BL0 .... 214 D7
RAW/HAS BB4 .... 196 B3
SETT BD24 .... 265 N8
STHP PR8 .... 12 E5
WHIT OL12 .... 235 M4
Dukes Wy FMBY L37 ... 247 J4
Duke's Wood La SKEL WN8 . 253 M7
Dumbarton Cl BPOOLS FY4 . 125 K5
Dumbarton Rd LANC LA1 .. 3 J7
Dumb Tom's La HGHB LA2 . 31 L8
Dumfries Cl BISP FY2 ... 85 J6
Dumfries Hollow HEYW OL10 . 234 C8
Dumfries Wy NWD/KWIPK L33 . 260 A5
Dunald Mill La KKBYL LA6 . 33 M7
Dunbar Cl BPOOLS FY4 .. 125 K5
Dunbar Crs STHP PR8 ... 221 J5
Dunbar Dr FUL/RIB PR2 . 132 A7
HEY LA3 .... 52 D4
Dunbar Rd FUL/RIB PR2 . 131 J8
STHP PR8 .... 221 H2
Duncan Av BBR PR5 ...... 84 F5
Duncan Cl BRFD/BLYE BB10 . 143 J6
LSTA FY8 .... 145 G1
Duncan Pl FTWD FY7 ..... 77 H7
Duncan St HOR/BR BL6 .. 231 M8
PDHM/BLYW BB12 .... 141 K6
Duncroft Cl CLI BB7 ..... 99 H1
Dundas St COL BB8 ..... 103 M7
Dundee Dr BBN BB1 ...... 11 J5
Dundee La RAMS BL0 .... 214 E5
Dundee Rd TOD OL14 ... 300 C10
Dundee St LANC LA1 ...... 3 K7
Dunderdale Av NLSN BB9 . 122 F4
Dunderdale St GAR/LONG PR3 . 114 C4
Dundonald St PRES PR1 .. 153 L8
Dundonnell Rd NLSN BB9 . 123 K2
Dunelt Rd BPOOL FY1 ..... 5 G8
Dunes Av BPOOLS FY4 ... 124 E6
Dunes Dr FMBY L37 ..... 236 F7
Dungeon La SKEL WN8 ... 243 M4
Dunham Dr CHLYE PR6 ... 187 M5
Dunkeld St LANC LA1 ...... 3 K7
Dunkenhalgh Wy ACC BB5 . 159 L4
Dunkenshaw Crs LANC LA1 . 67 G1
Dunkirk Av CARN LA5 .... 33 J5
FUL/RIB PR2 .... 131 M7
Dunkirk La CROS/BRETH PR26 . 185 K2
Dunkirk Ri WHIT OL12 * . 235 H4
Dunkirk Rd STHP PR8 ... 221 J5
Dunlin Av HEY LA3 ...... 52 L6
ROCH OL11 .... 234 C4
Dunlin Cl CLV/TH FY5 .... 81 J5
ROCH OL11 .... 235 H8
STHP PR8 .... 237 M1
Dunlop Av ROCH OL11 ... 235 H8
Dunlop Dr MGHL L31 .... 259 L2
Dunmail Av BPOOLE FY3 ... 5 L7
Dunmore St PRES PR1 ..... 9 M2
Dunnings Bridge Rd
   NTHTN L30 .... 258 E7
Dunnock La KIRK/FR/WAR PR4 . 131 H7
Dunny Shop Av ACC BB5 . 159 K7
Dunoon Cl FUL/RIB PR2 . 131 J7
Dunoon Dr BBN BB1 ..... 158 A8
BOL BL1 .... 233 M6
Dunoon St BLY BB11 .... 6 A6
Dunrobin Dr CHLY/EC PR7 . 207 G2
Dunscar Dr CHLYE PR6 .. 208 B2
Dunscombe Ter
   GAR/LONG PR3 * 91 K7
Dunsop Cl BBR PR5 * 169 J4
BPOOL FY1 .... 5 H9
Dunsop Dr BOL BL1 ..... 233 J8
Dunsop Rd FUL/RIB PR2 . 133 G7
Dunsop St BBN BB1 ...... 11 G1
Dunstable WHIT OL12 * .. 235 J3
Dunster Av ACC BB5 .... 158 F6
ROCH OL11 .... 235 H6
Dunster Gv CLI BB7 ...... 98 F5
Dunster Rd STHP PR8 ... 221 H3
Dunvegan Cl BPOOLS FY4 . 125 K5
Durban Gv BLY BB11 .... 6 C6
Durham Av CLV/TH FY5 .. 81 H8
LANC LA1 .... 54 F7
LSTA FY8 .... 145 H4
PDHM/BLYW BB12 .... 141 L4
Durham Cl BBN BB1 ...... 11 H6
HEY LA3 .... 52 J1
Durham Dr ACC BB5 .... 159 J8
BBN BB1 .... 137 J5
CHLY/EC PR7 .... 187 H5
RAMS BL0 .... 214 D8
Durham Gv GAR/LONG PR3 . 284 A8
Durham Rd BBN BB1 ..... 137 J4
BPOOL FY1 .... 5 G1
DWN BB3 .... 191 H1
Durham St ACC BB5 .... 160 A4
ROCH OL11 .... 235 K6
SKEL WN8 .... 253 G1
Durley Rd BPOOL FY1 ...... 4 F8
Durnford Cl WHIT OL12 .. 234 A1
Durnlaw Cl LIT OL15 ... 219 M6
Durn St LIT OL15 ...... 219 M5
D'Urton La GAR/LONG PR3 . 132 G2
Dutch Barn Cl CHLY/EC PR7 . 187 L8
Duttonfield Cl
   CROS/BRETH PR26 .... 168 B8
Dutton Cl BPOOLE FY3 .. 105 G5
Dutton St ACC BB5 ..... 159 M5
Duttons Wy BBN BB1 .... 174 A1
Duxbury Cl MGHL L31 ... 250 D8
RNFD/HAY WA11 .... 262 C4
Duxbury Hall Rd CHLY/EC PR7 . 208 A7
Duxbury St BWCK/EAR BB18 . 294 F5
DWN BB3 .... 191 L5
Dye House La LANC LA1 * ... 3 J5
MILN OL16 .... 218 F8
Dyers Ct LIT OL15 ..... 219 K5
Dyers La ORM L39 ...... 241 H7
Dyer St KIRK/FR/WAR PR4 . 128 C6
Dyke Nook CLI BB7 ...... 99 J5
Dykes La CARN LA5 ...... 26 C1
Dymock Rd PRES PR1 * .. 153 G2
Dymock Rd North PRES PR1 * . 153 G2
Dyneley Av BRFD/BLYE BB10 . 143 J7
Dyneley Rd BBN BB1 .... 157 M4
Dyson St BBNW BB2 * ... 173 G1

E

Eachill Gdns BBN BB1 ... 158 E3
Eachill Rd BBN BB1 .... 158 E2
Eafield Rd LIT OL15 ... 219 H8
MILN OL16 .... 235 M2

Eager La MGHL L31 ..... 249 L3
Eagle Brow CLV/TH FY5 .. 81 L6
Eagle Crs RNFD/HAY WA11 . 262 D5
The Eagles PLF/KEOS FY6 . 86 B6
Eagle St ACC BB5 ...... 174 F1
   BBN BB1 .... 157 M7
   NLSN BB9 .... 123 J2
   TOD OL14 .... 303 L2
Eagleton Wy PRES PR1 .. 168 D1
Eagley Rd BRFD/BLYE BB10 . 122 F7
Ealand Cha HOR/BR BL6 . 231 J8
Ealees Rd LIT OL15 .... 219 M6
Ealing Gv CHLYE PR6 ... 188 C7
Eamont Av CHTN/BK PR9 . 180 E6
Eamont Pl FTWD FY7 ..... 81 G1
Eanam BBN BB1 .... 11 G4
Eanam Old Rd BBN BB1 .. 11 G4
Eanam Whf BBN BB1 ..... 11 H4
Earby Rd BWCK/EAR BB18 . 294 F1
Eardley Rd HEY LA3 ..... 52 D3
Earlesdon Av BWCK/EAR BB18 . 294 C6
Earlham St BWCK/EAR BB18 . 294 F5
Earl Av BPOOLS FY4 ... 105 H3
Earl Rd RAMS BL0 ..... 214 F5
Earl's Cl CSBY/BLUN L23 . 257 J8
Earls Dr DWN BB3 ..... 192 B2
Earl St ACC BB5 .... 159 J1
   BBN BB1 .... 157 H4
   BRFD/BLYE BB10 ...... 142 D3
   BWCK/EAR BB18 .... 293 R5
   COL BB8 .... 296 A7
   GTH/LHO BB6 .... 138 E6
   LANC LA1 .... 3 G3
   NLSN BB9 .... 123 J2
   PRES PR1 .... 9 H3
   RAMS BL0 .... 215 G5
Earlsway BPOOLE FY3 ... 106 A6
Earls Wy CHLY/EC PR7 .. 207 L5
Earlswood SKEL WN8 .... 254 B6
Earnsdale Av DWN BB3 .. 191 G1
Earnsdale Cl DWN BB3 .. 191 H1
Earnsdale Rd DWN BB3 .. 173 H8
Earnshaw Av WHIT OL12 . 218 B8
Earnshaw Dr LEYL PR25 . 186 A2
Earnshaw Rd BCUP OL13 . 179 J8
Earnshaw Rw BCUP OL13 . 179 J8
Easby Cl FMBY L37 ..... 247 K1
Easdale Av MCMB LA4 ... 41 M6
Easedale Cl CARN LA5 ... 42 E1
   PDHM/BLYW BB12 ..... 141 L3
Easedale Wk NWD/KWIPK L33 . 260 B6
Easington LANC LA1 ...... 2 A2
Easington Crs BPOOLS FY3 . 105 K3
East Av BWCK/EAR BB18 . 293 Q5
East Bank NLSN BB9 .... 103 J3
Eastbank Av RAW/HAS BB4 * . 194 F1
East Bank Av RAW/HAS BB4 . 194 F1
Eastbank Rd STHP PR8 .. 145 H6
Eastbank St STHP PR8 ... 13 G4
East Beach LSTA FY8 .... 146 F8
East Boothroyden
   BPOOL FY1 * 104 E3
Eastbourne Cl FUL/RIB PR2 . 131 J6
Eastbourne Rd BPOOLS FY4 . 124 E5
   STHP PR8 .... 199 K8
Eastbourne St ROCH OL11 . 235 H6
East Cecil St LSTA FY8 . 146 D8
East Cliff PRES PR1 ..... 9 G5
East Cliffe LSTA FY8 ... 146 F8
East Cliff Rd PRES PR1 .. 9 G6
Eastcott Cl BBNW BB2 .. 173 K3
East Ct CLV/TH FY5 ..... 81 K6
East Crs ACC BB5 ...... 159 L3
East Croft NWD/KWIPK L33 . 260 C6
East Dene SKEL WN8 .... 243 L1
East End St COL BB8 ... 103 M7
Eastern Av BRFD/BLYE BB10 . 142 F2
Eastfield Dr CLI BB7 ... 290 E9
   KIRK/FR/WAR PR4 .... 166 D2
Eastgate ACC BB5 ...... 159 M5
   FUL/RIB PR2 .... 132 A6
   GAR/LONG PR3 .... 116 B7
   HEY LA3 .... 53 M4
   WHIT OL12 .... 217 M4
East Gate Cl LSTA FY8 . 124 F7
East Gate St MILN OL16 . 235 J3
Eastham Pl BLY BB11 ..... 7 L5
Eastham St BRFD/BLYE BB10 . 7 L1
   CLI BB7 .... 99 H2
   LANC LA1 .... 3 J8
   PRES PR1 .... 152 B2
East Holme LSTA FY8 ... 147 G7
East Lancashire Rd BBN BB1 . 137 J8
Eastlands CROS/BRETH PR26 . 185 M4
   HEY LA3 .... 52 F4
East Leigh SKEL WN8 ... 254 A2
East Lodge Pl
   BRFD/BLYE BB10 * 163 H2
East Md BPOOLE FY3 ..... 5 K6
   ORM L39 .... 250 E2
East Meade MGHL L31 .. 258 F1
Eastmoor Dr CLI BB7 .... 99 K5
East Mt WGNW/BIL/OR WN5 . 255 J5
Easton Cl FUL/RIB PR2 . 133 G5
East Pde BWCK/EAR BB18 . 293 Q5
   RAW/HAS BB4 .... 177 K8
East Park Av BBN BB1 .. 157 G4
   DWN BB3 .... 191 K3
East Park Dr BPOOLE FY3 . 5 K6
East Park Rd BBN BB1 .. 10 F3
Eastpines Dr CLV/TH FY5 . 85 J4
East Rd CLV/TH FY5 .... 82 A7
   FUL/RIB PR2 .... 132 D7
   LANC LA1 .... 3 J6
Eastside BPOOLS FY4 ... 125 J3
East Sq KIRK/FR/WAR PR4 . 166 D2
East St BBNW BB2 ...... 10 A7
   BBR PR5 .... 169 H4
   CHTN/BK PR9 .... 13 L3
   HEY LA3 .... 40 F7
   LEYL PR25 .... 186 C2
   LIT OL15 .... 219 M6
   MILN OL16 .... 235 L3
   NLSN BB9 .... 122 F6
   PDHM/BLYW BB12 ..... 140 F7
   PRES PR1 .... 9 K2
   RAMS BL0 .... 195 G7
   RAW/HAS BB4 .... 194 D4
   RAW/HAS BB4 .... 177 J8
   SKP/WHF BD23 .... 281 K5
   WHIT OL12 .... 218 A1
East Ter CHLY/EC PR7 .. 187 G2
East Topping St BPOOL FY1 . 4 D1
East Vw BBR PR5 .... 152 F5
   BCUP OL13 .... 197 J1
   BURY BL9 .... 214 F8
   COL BB8 .... 296 F8
   HGHB LA2 .... 38 G5
   KIRK/FR/WAR PR4 * ... 148 F5

PDHM/BLYW BB12 .... 140 A1
PRES PR1 .... 9 H1
RAMS BL0 .... 214 E2
East View Ct LANC LA1 * . 42 C8
East Wy CHLYE PR6 ..... 208 A3
Eastway MILN OL16 .... 131 M3
   KIRK/FR/WAR PR4 .... 148 D5
   MGHL L31 .... 259 G1
Eastwood Av BPOOLE FY3 . 105 H3
   FTWD FY7 .... 77 J8
Eastwood Crs RAW/HAS BB4 . 195 M1
Eastwood La TOD OL14 .. 301 R10
Eastwood Rd LEYL PR25 . 186 C2
   TOD OL14 .... 301 K8
Eastwood St BBN BB1 ... 11 K1
   BWCK/EAR BB18 .... 293 H4
   LIT OL15 .... 219 L6
   RAW/HAS BB4 .... 195 M1
Eaton Av BPOOL FY1 ..... 4 F9
Eaton Cl LSTA FY8 ..... 145 J5
Eaton Pl KIRK/FR/WAR PR4 . 128 C6
Eaton St NLSN BB9 ..... 123 J6
Eaves Av BLY BB11 ..... 162 A1
Eaves Cl ACC BB5 ..... 160 C2
Eavesdale SKEL WN8 .... 254 B3
Eaves Green La
   GAR/LONG PR3 .... 113 J3
Eavesham Cl PRES PR1 .. 168 D2
Eaves La CHLYE PR6 .... 208 B3
   FUL/RIB PR2 .... 132 B8
Eaves Rd LSTA FY8 ..... 145 K2
Eaves St BPOOL FY1 .... 104 E4
Eaveswood Cl FUL/RIB PR2 . 169 H2
Ebony St BBN BB1 ...... 157 K4
Ecclesgate St BPOOLS FY4 . 125 J4
Eccleshill Gdns DWN BB3 . 173 M7
Eccleshill Rd DWN BB3 .. 173 J5
Eccleshill St
   PDHM/BLYW BB12 ..... 140 F3
Eccles La BRSC L40 .... 226 E5
Eccles Rd FMBY L37 .... 247 G2
   WGNW/BIL/OR WN5 .... 255 L3
Eccles St ACC BB5 ..... 159 L4
   BBNW BB2 .... 10 E8
   PRES PR1 * 152 F2
   RAMS BL0 .... 214 E5
Eccleston Rd BPOOL FY1 .. 5 H9
Eckersley Cl BBNW BB2 .. 173 G3
Eckroyd Cl NLSN BB9 ... 123 G5
Eclipse Cl MILN OL16 .. 235 M4
Eclipse Rd BBNW BB2 .. 172 A3
Ecroyd Rd FUL/RIB PR2 * . 151 H1
Ecroyd St LEYL PR25 ... 186 D2
   NLSN BB9 .... 122 E3
Edale Av RAW/HAS BB4 .. 194 F1
Edale Cl PRES PR1 ..... 152 C2
Eddington Rd LSTA FY8 . 145 L7
Eddie Cl LEYL PR25 .... 186 D4
Eddleston Cl BPOOLE FY3 . 106 A6
Edelston Rd BPOOL FY1 .. 5 H9
Eden Av CHTN/BK PR9 .. 180 C8
   FTWD FY7 .... 81 G1
   LSTA FY8 .... 146 B3
   MCMB LA4 .... 42 A6
   RAMS BL0 .... 215 G1
   RNFD/HAY WA11 .... 262 B4
Eden Cl NLSN BB9 ...... 103 G7
   NWD/KWIPK L33 ...... 260 G7
Eden Ct RAMS BL0 ..... 215 G1
Eden Dr North CSBY/BLUN L23 . 257 K8
Eden Dr South
   CSBY/BLUN L23 ...... 257 K8
Edenfield KIRK/FR/WAR PR4 . 166 B7
Edenfield Cl PLF/KEOS FY6 . 106 C1
Edenfield Cl STHP PR8 .. 200 B8
Edenfield Rd ROCH OL11 . 234 D7
   WHIT OL12 .... 216 C8
Edenfield St ROCH OL11 . 234 F1
Eden Gdns GAR/LONG PR3 . 114 A3
Eden Gv CARN LA5 ...... 33 J1
Edenhurst SKEL WN8 .... 254 B3
Edenhurst Cl FMBY L37 . 246 F1
Edenhurst Dr FMBY L37 . 246 F1
Eden Mount Wy CARN LA5 . 33 L1
Eden Pk BBNW BB2 .... 156 D3
Edensor Ter DWN BB3 .. 191 J1
Edgar St ACC BB5 ...... 159 L5
   MILN OL16 .... 235 M1
   NLSN BB9 * 123 J2
   RAMS BL0 .... 214 E6
Edgar St West RAMS BL0 . 214 E6
Edgecott Cl HEY LA3 .... 52 F4
Edge End GTH/LHO BB6 . 138 E6
Edge End La NLSN BB9 . 123 G6
Edge End Nth GTH/LHO BB6 . 138 E5
   NLSN BB9 .... 123 G5
Edge End Rd GTH/LHO BB6 . 138 E6
Edgefield CHLY/EC PR7 . 207 L1
Edge Gate La CHLYE PR6 . 189 G7
Edge Hall Rd
   WGNW/BIL/OR WN5 .... 255 H6
Edgehill Cl FUL/RIB PR2 . 132 B1
Edgehill Crs LEYL PR25 . 186 B1
Edgehill Dr FUL/RIB PR2 . 132 B1
Edge La BCUP OL13 .... 197 M3
   BWCK/EAR BB18 .... 293 M6
   CSBY/BLUN L23 .... 257 K5
   EDGW/EG BL7 .... 212 D3
   HOR/BR BL6 .... 232 F4
   RAW/HAS BB4 .... 196 A1
   SKP/WHF BD23 .... 267 G2
Edgeley Ct PDHM/BLYW BB12 . 6 B1
Edgemoor Dr CSBY/BLUN L23 . 257 K6
   ROCH OL11 .... 234 B7
Edgeside GTH/LHO BB6 .. 138 E6
Edgeside La RAW/HAS BB4 . 196 C1
Edgeware Rd BPOOLS FY4 . 125 H5
Edgeworth Gv BRFD/BLYE BB10 * . 7 M3
Edgeworth V EDGW/EG BL7 . 213 H5
Edge Yate La RAW/HAS BB4 . 177 L2
Edgley Ct KIRK/FR/WAR PR4 . 167 H1

Edgley Dr ORM L39 .... 241 K6
Edinburgh Cl LEYL PR25 . 186 F2
Edinburgh Dr ACC BB5 . 159 J8
Edinburgh Rd FMBY L37 . 247 G5
Edinburgh Wy ROCH OL11 . 235 G7
Edington St BLY BB11 ... 6 F1
Edisford Rd CLI BB7 .... 83 G3
Edison St DWN BB3 .... 191 J2
Edith St BBN BB1 .... 11 K6
   BWCK/EAR BB18 .... 293 Q4
   NLSN BB9 .... 123 J3
Edleston St ACC BB5 ... 159 J6
Edlingham ROCH OL11 * . 235 H5
Edmondson St
   BWCK/EAR BB18 .... 293 Q4
Edmonton Dr BBNW BB2 . 156 C4
Edmonton Pl BISP FY2 .. 85 H8
Edmund Gennings Ct CLI BB7 . 291 J10
Edmunds Fold LIT OL15 . 219 J5
Edmundson St ACC BB5 . 159 H4
   BBNW BB2 .... 10 B4
   BBR PR5 .... 173 G4
   BRFD/BLYE BB10 ...... 142 E2
   DWN BB3 .... 191 J2
   PRES PR1 .... 9 J3
   TOD OL14 .... 303 K7
   WHIT OL12 .... 235 G3
Edward Av LIT OL15 .... 219 J8
Edward Cl KIRK/FR/WAR PR4 . 183 K6
Edward Ct ACC BB5 .... 159 H5
Edward Jenner Av NTHTN L30 . 258 C8
Edward Sq PRES PR1 ... 9 K1
Edward St ACC BB5 .... 176 B2
   ACC BB5 .... 159 H5
   BBN BB1 .... 158 E2
   BBR PR5 .... 152 F5
   BCUP OL13 .... 179 K8
   BLY BB11 .... 7 G5
   BPOOL FY1 .... 4 D1
   BWCK/EAR BB18 .... 294 E5
   CARN LA5 .... 33 J1
   CHLY/EC PR7 .... 208 A4
   CLV/TH FY5 .... 81 J7
   DWN BB3 .... 191 H1
   GTH/LHO BB6 .... 138 F6
   HOR/BR BL6 .... 231 K8
   LANC LA1 .... 3 J6
   LEYL PR25 .... 186 D3
   LSTA FY8 .... 145 J4
   MCMB LA4 .... 41 H6
   MILN OL16 .... 235 K3
   NLSN BB9 .... 123 J1
   PRES PR1 .... 8 F3
   RAW/HAS BB4 .... 176 B8
   WHIT OL12 .... 219 G1
   WHIT OL12 .... 218 A1
Edward Vii Quay
   FUL/RIB PR2 * 151 L3
Edwell Av BPOOLS FY4 .. 125 L3
Edwinstowe Rd LSTA FY8 . 145 M5
Egan St PRES PR1 .... 9 J1
Egbert St PRES PR1 ..... 152 D2
Egerton SKEL WN8 ..... 254 A3
Egerton Ct FUL/RIB PR2 * . 151 L2
Egerton Gv CHLY/EC PR7 . 207 L5
Egerton Rd BPOOL FY1 .. 104 E4
   EDGW/EG BL7 .... 211 H7
   FUL/RIB PR2 .... 151 K2
   LEYL PR25 .... 186 C1
Egremont Av CLV/TH FY5 . 81 J6
Eider Cl CLV/TH FY5 .... 81 J6
Eidsforth La GAR/LONG PR3 . 284 F6
Eidsforth Rd MCMB LA4 . 41 J5
Eight Acre Av CLI BB7 . 120 C3
Eight Acre La CARN LA5 . 18 D7
   FMBY L37 .... 237 L5
   GAR/LONG PR3 .... 79 H5
Eildon Dr PLF/KEOS FY6 . 106 C1
Elaine Av BPOOLS FY4 .. 5 M9
Elbow La ROCH OL11 ... 235 K5
Elbow St BBR PR5 ...... 187 K8
Elcho St PRES PR1 ..... 9 L4
Elderberry Cl CLV/TH FY5 . 81 D1
Elderbrook Ct
   KIRK/FR/WAR PR4 .... 165 H7
Elder Cl CHLYE PR6 .... 187 M1
   FUL/RIB PR2 .... 151 K2
   KIRK/FR/WAR PR4 .... 148 G5
Elder St MILN OL16 .... 235 L6
   NLSN BB9 .... 123 J1
Elderwood Av CLV/TH FY5 . 85 L2
Eldon Gv HEY LA3 ...... 52 K5
Eldons Cft STHP PR8 ... 221 G6
Eldon St CHLYE PR6 .... 208 A4
   PRES PR1 .... 152 D1
   TOD OL14 .... 303 M2
Eldon V NTHTN L30 ..... 258 B7
Eldroth Rd HGHB LA2 ... 51 L2
Eldwick St BRFD/BLYE BB10 . 142 F4
Eleanor St BBN BB1 .... 11 H4
   NLSN BB9 .... 123 H2
Electricity St ACC BB5 . 159 L4
Elgar Cl BBNW BB2 ..... 173 K2
Elgin Crs BLY BB11 ...... 6 A7
Elgin Pl BPOOLE FY3 ... 105 K4
Elgin St LANC LA1 ...... 3 K5
   PRES PR1 .... 152 D1
Elijah St PRES PR1 ..... 153 G3
Elim Gdns BBNW BB2 ... 172 C8
Elim St LIT OL15 ...... 219 M4
Elizabeth Av STHP PR8 . 221 H6
Elizabeth Cl BPOOLS FY4 . 106 A6
Elizabeth Dr RAW/HAS BB4 . 194 D3
Elizabeth Sq PRES PR1 . 9 K1
Elizabeth St ACC BB5 .. 159 J4
   BBN BB1 .... 11 H4
   BLY BB11 .... 7 G5
   BPOOL FY1 .... 77 L6
   FTWD FY7 .... 77 L6
   GTH/LHO BB6 .... 138 C7
   NLSN BB9 .... 123 H2
   RAMS BL0 .... 195 M4
   RAW/HAS BB4 .... 177 J8
   WHIT OL12 .... 235 J2
   WHIT OL12 .... 218 A1

WHIT OL12 .... 234 D1
Ellenshaw St DWN BB3 . 191 L2
Ellen St BBR PR5 ...... 169 H2
   BOL BL1 .... 233 M8
   DWN BB3 .... 191 K4
   NLSN BB9 .... 123 G3
   PRES PR1 .... 152 A2
Ellerbeck Av FUL/RIB PR2 . 130 C2
Ellerbeck Rd BWCK/EAR BB18 . 143 H1
Ellerbeck Rd ACC BB5 . 159 L4
   CLV/TH FY5 .... 84 F1
Eller Brook Cl CHLYE PR6 . 230 C2
Ellerbrook Dr BRSC L40 . 225 J8
Ellerbrook Wy ORM L39 . 241 L2
Ellerslie Av CLV/TH FY5 . 86 A2
Ellerslie Rd FUL/RIB PR2 . 151 L2
Ellesmere Av CLV/TH FY5 . 86 A2
   COL BB8 .... 296 C6
Ellesmere Gv MCMB LA4 . 41 H8
Ellesmere Rd BPOOLS FY4 . 125 L8
   DWN BB3 .... 173 H8
   MCMB LA4 .... 41 G7
Ellesmere St ROCH OL11 . 235 J6
Elletson St PLF/KEOS FY6 . 86 A7
Elliot St BOL BL1 ...... 233 M8
Elliott Av DWN BB3 .... 191 L5
Elliott Cl PRES PR1 .... 152 B1
Elliott St BRFD/BLYE BB10 . 7 M6
   PRES PR1 .... 152 B1
   WHIT OL12 .... 235 K3
Elliott Wk PRES PR1 ... 152 B1
Ellis Dr MCMB LA4 ..... 41 M5
Ellisland BPOOLS FY4 .. 125 M2
Ellison Fold ACC BB5 .. 139 H8
Ellison Fold La DWN BB3 . 191 M2
Ellison St ACC BB5 .... 159 L5
   BBN BB1 .... 191 K1
Ellis St BLY BB11 .... 6 C5
   BWCK/EAR BB18 .... 293 Q5
Ellwood Av LANC LA1 ... 42 F7
Ellwood Ct HEY LA3 .... 53 L1
Ellwood Gv HEY LA3 .... 53 L1
Elm Av BPOOLE FY3 ..... 5 J3
   CSBY/BLUN L23 ...... 257 J6
   FUL/RIB PR2 .... 151 J1
   HGHB LA2 .... 66 E7
   KIRK/FR/WAR PR4 .... 148 A5
   PLF/KEOS FY6 .... 86 A8
   TOD OL14 .... 301 L2
Elmbank Av CLV/TH FY5 . 85 L2
Elm Brow GAR/LONG PR3 . 94 F7
Elm Cl BBN BB1 .... 158 E3
   BWCK/EAR BB18 .... 293 P6
   RAW/HAS BB4 .... 176 B8
Elm Ct PLF/KEOS FY6 * . 86 A8
Elmcroft La HTWN L38 .. 247 K8
Elmdale Cl FMBY L37 ... 247 L5
Elm Dr BBR PR5 .... 169 J2
   FMBY L37 .... 247 L5
Elmers Gn SKEL WN8 ... 254 A1
Elmer's Green La SKEL WN8 . 254 A1
Elmers Wood Rd SKEL WN8 . 254 A1
Elmfield WGNNW/ST WN6 . 245 L7
Elmfield Dr BBR PR5 ... 169 M5
Elmfield St ACC BB5 ... 159 J4
Elm Gdns RNFD/HAY WA11 . 262 C5
Elm Gv CHLYE PR6 ..... 208 B2
   DWN BB3 .... 173 L8
   FUL/RIB PR2 .... 153 H1
   KIRK/FR/WAR PR4 .... 148 E4
   LEYL PR25 .... 169 G8
   MCMB LA4 .... 41 M4
   ROCH OL11 .... 235 H6
   SKEL WN8 .... 253 H2
   WHIT OL12 .... 218 F6
Elmhurst Rd LSTA FY8 .. 145 L4
Elmore Wd LIT OL15 ... 219 H5
Elm Park Dr STHP PR8 . 221 H6
Elmpark Ga WHIT OL12 . 217 L8
Elmpark Gv WHIT OL12 . 217 L8
Elmpark V WHIT OL12 .. 217 L8
Elmpark Vw WHIT OL12 . 217 L8
Elmpark Wy WHIT OL12 . 217 L8
Elm Pl ORM L39 .... 241 H7
Elmridge SKEL WN8 .... 254 A3
Elmridge Crs BISP FY2 . 85 J8
Elm Rd BRSC L40 ...... 225 H8
   KKBY L32 .... 260 A8
   STHP PR8 .... 13 G9
Elms Av CLV/TH FY5 .... 85 L2
   LSTA FY8 .... 146 A2
Elmsdale Cl LANC LA1 ... 2 C2
Elms Dr KIRK/FR/WAR PR4 . 127 L7
   MCMB LA4 .... 41 M5
Elmsfield Av ROCH OL11 . 234 B3
Elmsfield Pk ORM L39 .. 250 D5
Elmsfield Rd CSBY/BLUN L23 . 257 L5
Elmside Cl CLV/TH FY5 . 86 A1
Elmslack La CARN LA5 .. 16 F7
Elmslack La CARN LA5 .. 16 F7
Elmsley St PRES PR1 ... 152 B8
Elmslie Gdns BPOOLE FY3 . 5 J5
Elms Rd MCMB LA4 ..... 41 M4
   MGHL L31 .... 258 F5
Elmstead SKEL WN8 .... 254 A3
The Elms CHLYE PR6 .... 187 M1
   LIT OL15 .... 219 H5
   MGHL L31 .... 250 A8
Elm St BBN BB1 .... 157 K4
   BCUP OL13 .... 179 K8
   BRFD/BLYE BB10 ...... 7 K8
   COL BB8 .... 296 C6
   FTWD FY7 .... 77 L6
   GTH/LHO BB6 .... 138 C7
   NLSN BB9 .... 123 H2
   RAMS BL0 .... 195 M4
   RAW/HAS BB4 .... 177 J8
   WHIT OL12 .... 235 J2
   WHIT OL12 .... 218 A1
Elmswood Cl LSTA FY8 .. 146 C1
Elm Tree Gv GTH/LHO BB6 . 117 M6
Elmwood CHLY/EC PR7 .. 207 L2
   GAR/LONG PR3 .... 114 D3
   SKEL WN8 .... 243 M4
Elmwood Av CSBY/BLUN L23 . 257 J7
   LEYL PR25 .... 186 B2
   PLF/KEOS FY6 .... 86 A7
Elmwood Cl ACC BB5 ... 160 A5
Elmwood Ct
   KIRK/FR/WAR PR4 .... 127 L1
Elmwood Dr CLV/TH FY5 . 85 L2
Elmwood St BLY BB11 .... 6 B5
Elnup Av WGNNW/ST WN6 . 245 L5
Elsby Av CLV/TH FY5 ... 85 M3
Elsie La CLV/TH FY5 .... 85 L2
Elsie St RAMS BL0 ..... 214 D7
Elsinore Cl FTWD FY7 .. 77 J6
Elslack Br SKP/WHF BD23 . 281 J11
Elslack La SKP/WHF BD23 . 281 J11
Elson Rd FMBY L37 ..... 247 G5

...ston Av *BPOOLE* FY3 * 105 K3
...ston Gn *FUL/RIB* PR2 ......134 B2
...ston La *FUL/RIB* PR2 ......134 D5
...swick *SKEL* WN8 ......253 M3
...swick Gdns *BBN* BB2 ......136 A4
...swick Ldg *BBNW* BB2 ......136 H6
...swick Pl *LSTA* FY8 ......145 L3
...swick Rd *CHTN/BK* PR9 ......180 C7
...*FUL/RIB* PR2 ......151 H2
...LEYL PR25 ......186 A4
...swick St *DWN* BB3 ......191 L1
...cerwater *FMBY* L37 ......246 F3
...cerwater *BPOOLE* FY3 *......125 M1
...LANC LA1 ......3 L3
...ton Av *CSBY/BLUN* L23 ......256 F7
...NTHTN L30 ......258 B8
...ton Rd *BBN* BB1 ......174 C5
...ton St *FUL/RIB* PR2 ......8 A1
...vaston *PLF/KEOS* FY6 ......85 M6

...bankment Cl
...*WGNW/BIL/OR* WN5 ......255 L5
...vington Rd *HTWN* L38 ......256 D1
...wood Cl *NWD/KWIPK* L33 ......260 B5
...y Cl *BBN* BB1 ......137 J5
...DWN BB3 ......191 K4
...y Ms *CHTN/BK* PR9 ......200 D1

...bankment Rd
...EDGW/EG BL7 ......212 F6
...merald Av *BBN* BB1 ......157 H3
...merald St *NTHTN* L30 ......258 B8
...merald St *BBN* BB1 ......157 J2
...merson Av *BPOOLS* FY4 ......125 C4
...merson Cl *HTWN* L38 ......247 K7
...merson Rd *PRES* PR1 ......153 C1
...merson St *LANC* LA1 ......54 F1
...mesgate La *CARN* LA5 ......16 F4
...mily St *BBN* BB1 ......11 J1
...BBR PR5 ......168 D3
...BLY BB11 ......7 H7
...mlsett Rd *BBR* PR5 ......153 J8
...manuel Rd *CHTN/BK* PR9 ......200 C1
...manuel St *PRES* PR1 ......152 A1
...ma St *ACC* BB5 ......159 J5
...WHIT OL12 ......235 H3
...maus Rd *HEY* LA3 ......52 E1
...merdale Cl *ACC* BB5 ......159 G6
...mmett St *HOR/BR* BL6 ......231 L8
...PRES PR1 ......9 H1
...mott Ct *COL* BB8 ......296 C4
...mott La *COL* BB8 ......296 G4
...msix *BRSC* L40 ......223 L5
...nnie La *CROS/BRETH* PR26 ...185 M5
...mpire St *GTH/LHO* BB6 ......139 G5
...mpire Pl *BPOOLE* FY3 * 105 C4
...mpress St *GTH/LHO* BB6 ......139 G5
...mpress Cl *MGHL* L31 ......258 E2
...mpress Dr *BISP* FY2 ......104 E2
...mpress St *ACC* BB5 ......159 J5
...COL BB8 ......296 B6
...mpress Wy *CHLY/EC* PR7 ......207 H1
...dbutt La *CSBY/BLUN* L23 ....257 H8
...dcliffe Rd *MCMB* LA4 ......41 L6
...deavour St *FUL/RIB* PR2 ......151 L4
...derley Cl *CLV/TH* FY5 ......85 H2
...ding Rake *WHIT* OL12 ......217 M7

...dsleigh Gdns
...BPOOLS FY4 ......125 C5
...dsleigh La *LANC* LA1 ......42 B4
...d St *COL* BB8 ......103 L7
...field Av *CSBY/BLUN* L23 ......257 H7
...field Cl *CHLY/EC* PR7 ......205 M2
...ROCH OL11 ......234 E7
...field Rd *ACC* BB5 ......160 A4
...BPOOL FY1 ......104 F4
...field Vw *WGNW/BIL/OR* WN5...255 L6
...gine La *FMBY* L37 ......248 A4
...gland Av *BBNW* BB2 ......173 G3
...BISP FY2 ......84 F7
...glish Martyrs' Pl *PRES* PR1 ...152 C1
...nerdale *SKEL* WN8 ......254 A1
...nerdale Av *BBN* BB1 ......157 M8
...FTWD FY7 ......80 D5
...MCMB LA4 ......41 L7
...MGHL L31 ......259 H1
...nerdale Cl *CLI* BB7 ......98 F4
...FMBY L37 ......237 C8
...GAR/LONG PR3 ......270 A8
...LANC LA1 ......3 L1
...LEYL PR25 ......186 A4
...NWD/KWIPK L33 ......260 B5
...PLF/KEOS FY6 ......78 C5
...nerdale Dr *BBR* PR5 ......153 H6
...ORM L39 ......250 E1
...nerdale Rd *BPOOLS* FY4 ......125 G4
...BRFD/BLYE BB10 ......143 H6
...CHLY/EC PR7 ......207 K6
...CLI BB7 ......98 A3
...FMBY L37 ......237 C8
...GAR/LONG PR3 ......114 C6
...ROCH OL11 ......234 E7

...nilsmore Rd
...CSBY/BLUN L23 ......256 F6
...nismore St
...BRFD/BLYE BB10 ......142 F2
...noch Brow *BBNW* BB2 ......171 M2
...nstone *SKEL* WN8 ......254 A1
...terprise Dr
...CROS/BRETH PR26 ......168 C7
...terprise Wy *COL* BB8 ......103 J8
...FTWD FY7 ......81 K5
...twisle Rd *ACC* BB5 ......159 L2
...twistle Hall La
...EDGW/EG BL7 ......212 C4
...twistle Rd *MILN* OL16 ......235 K4
...twistle St *DWN* BB3 ......191 K2
...hraim St *PRES* PR1 ......152 A1
...ping Av *ACC* BB5 ......159 L2
...ping Cl *BISP* FY2 ......85 H6
...ping Pl *CHLYE* PR6 ......208 A3
...som Cl *CHLYE* PR6 ......188 B5
...ROCH OL11 ......234 B5
...som Cft *CHLYE* PR6 ......230 F4
...som Rd *NWD/KWIPK* L33 ....260 C5
...som Gv *NWD/KWIPK* L33 ....260 C5
...som Wy *ACC* BB5 ......160 A6
...worth St *DWN* BB3 ......191 K3
...uity St *DWN* BB3 ......191 K3
...dington St *BPOOL* FY1 ......4 E5
...cson Dr *STHP* PR8 ......13 G8
...c St *LIT* OL15 ......219 K5
...mine *CLI* BB7 ......84 F6
...nest St *ACC* BB5 ......173 J4
...BCUP OL13 ......197 M5
...TOD OL14 ......300 F10
...nest Ter *WHIT* OL12 ......235 H3
...niquen Cl *BBNW* BB2 ......172 D3
...son Fold *TOD* OL14 ......303 M2
...ingden Vw *HBR* HX7 ......301 Q7
...rskine Rd *CHLYE* PR6 ......208 B2
...r St *BLY* BB11 * 6 E5

Escott Gdns
BRFD/BLYE BB10 * 142 D3
Eshe Rd *CSBY/BLUN* L23 ......256 F7
Eshe Rd North
CSBY/BLUN L23 ......256 F7
Esher Pond *FUL/RIB* PR2 ......131 M5
Esher Rd *SKP/WHF* BD23 ......281 K1
Eshton Ter *CLI* BB7 ......99 G3
Esk Av *FTWD* FY7 ......81 G1
Eskbank *SKEL* WN8 ......253 M3
Eskbrook *SKEL* WN8 ......253 M2
Eskdale *SKEL* WN8 ......253 M2
Eskdale Av *FTWD* FY7 ......81 G2
ORM L39 ......250 F1
ROCH OL11 ......234 E7
Eskdale Cl *BPOOLS* FY4 ......125 C3
BRFD/BLYE BB10 ......122 E7
FMBY L37 ......247 C3
FUL/RIB PR2 ......132 C3
Eskdale Dr *FMBY* L37 ......247 C3
KIRK/FR/WAR PR4 ......128 D4
MGHL L31 ......259 H1
Eskdale Gv *PLF/KEOS* FY6 ......78 C5
LEYL PR25 ......186 E4
Eskdale Pl *MCMB* LA4 ......41 L7
Eskdale Rd *GAR/LONG* PR3 ....114 C5
Eskham Cl
KIRK/FR/WAR PR4 ......128 B5
Eskrigge Cl *LANC* LA1 * 42 D7
Eskrigge La *HGHB* LA2 ......35 M4
Esp La *BWCK/EAR* BB18 ......293 N6
Esplen *CSBY/BLUN* L23 ......257 H8
Essex Av *PDHM/BLYW* BB12 ...141 L4
Essex Cl *BBNW* BB2 ......10 C8
Essex Pl *BISP* FY2 ......105 J1
Essex Rd *BBN* BB1 ......158 D2
MCMB LA4 ......42 A4
STHP PR8 ......221 K3
Essex St *ACC* BB5 ......160 A5
BWCK/EAR BB18 ......293 Q5
COL BB8 ......296 B7
DWN BB3 ......191 L2
NLSN BB9 ......123 H5
ROCH OL11 ......235 J4
Essington Av *MCMB* LA4 ......41 H7
Est Bank Rd *RAMS* BL0 ......214 D4
Esther St *BBN* BB1 ......157 M6
Esthwaite Gdns *LANC* LA1 * 3 L4
Ethel Ct *MILN* OL16 * 235 L5
Ethel St *BWCK/EAR* BB18 ......293 K5
WHIT OL12 ......218 A1
Ethersall Rd *NLSN* BB9 ......123 H5
Eton Av *ACC* BB5 ......159 M4
Eton Cl *PDHM/BLYW* BB12 ....141 M5
ROCH OL11 ......234 E5
Eton Pk *FUL/RIB* PR2 ......132 F6
Eton Wy
WGNW/BIL/OR WN5 ......255 L5
Ettington Dr *STHP* PR8 ......220 D6
Ettrick Av *FTWD* FY7 ......77 J9
Ettrick Cl *NWD/KWIPK* L33 ....260 A5
Europa Wy *LANC* LA1 ......3 J4
Euston Gv *MCMB* LA4 ......41 H6
Euston Rd *MCMB* LA4 ......41 H6
Euston St *PRES* PR1 ......8 D4
Euxton Cl *BPOOLS* FY4 ......125 H5
Euxton Hall Gdns
CHLY/EC PR7 ......206 F1
Euxton La *CHLY/EC* PR7 ......187 C7
PRES PR1 ......152 A2
Evans St *BLY* BB11 ......6 F8
Evanstone Cl *HOR/BR* BL6 ......231 K8
Eva St *WHIT* OL12 ......235 J1
Evelyn Av *DWN* BB3 ......173 H6
Evelyn St *BRFD/BLYE* BB10 ....142 D2
Evenwood *SKEL* WN8 ......254 A1
Evenwood Ct *SKEL* WN8 * 253 M2
Everard Av *BRSC* L40 ......223 J4
Everard Rd *STHP* PR8 ......13 M9
Everdon Wd *NWD/KWIPK* L33 ..260 D5
Everest Cl *LSTA* FY8 ......145 K2
Everest Dr *BISP* FY2 ......84 F5
Everest Rd *CSBY/BLUN* L23 ....257 G7
LSTA FY8 ......145 K1
Evergreen Av *LEYL* PR25 ......186 D1
Evergreen Cl *CHLY/EC* PR7 ....207 L6
The Evergreens *BBNW* BB2 ...172 C3
FMBY L37 ......237 G7
KIRK/FR/WAR PR4 ......131 M5
Eversham Cl *CHTN/BK* PR9 ....181 K6
Eversham Rd
PDHM/BLYW BB12 ......141 J7
Eversleigh Av *CLV/TH* FY5 ......81 J8
Eversleigh St *PRES* PR1 ......152 B2
Eversley *SKEL* WN8 ......254 A2
Everton Rd *BPOOLS* FY4 * 125 K3
STHP PR8 ......199 K7
Everton St *DWN* BB3 * 191 J2
Every St *BLY* BB11 ......6 D5
NLSN BB9 ......122 F4
RAMS BL0 ......215 G5
TOD OL14 ......303 M2
Evesham Av *PRES* PR1 ......168 B4
Evesham Cl *CLV/TH* FY5 ......85 H4
HEY LA3 ......52 F5
KIRK/FR/WAR PR4 ......166 D2
Evesham Rd *BPOOLE* FY3 ......145 G3
LSTA FY8 ......145 G3
Evington *SKEL* WN8 ......243 M8
Ewell Cl *CHLYE* PR6 ......188 C3
Ewood *BBNW* BB2 ......173 G3
Ewood La *RAW/HAS* BB4 ......194 H4
TOD OL14 ......303 J1
Exbury *WHIT* OL12 * 235 H3
Excelsior Ter *LIT* OL15 ......219 J4
Exchange St *ACC* BB5 ......159 J6
BBN BB1 ......11 G3
BPOOL FY1 ......104 E4
COL BB8 ......296 A7
DWN BB3 ......191 L1
RAMS BL0 ......195 H4
Exe St *PRES* PR1 ......152 B1
Exeter Av *LANC* LA1 ......42 A5
Exeter Dr *CLV/TH* FY5 ......85 G1
Exeter Rd *MILN* OL16 ......235 J6
Exeter Pl *FUL/RIB* PR2 ......131 H1
Exeter St *BBN* BB1 ......10 D1
BPOOLS FY4 ......124 F5
ROCH OL11 ......235 J4
Exmoor Cl *CHTN/BK* PR9 ......180 C5
Exmouth Pl *MILN* OL16 ......235 K6
Exmouth Sq *MILN* OL16 * 235 K7
Exmouth St *BLY* BB11 ......7 G4

MILN OL16 ......235 K8
Exton St *NLSN* BB9 ......122 D6
Extwistle Rd
BRFD/BLYE BB10 ......143 L5
Extwistle Sq
BRFD/BLYE BB10 ......143 G6
Extwistle St
BRFD/BLYE BB10 * 142 D3
Eyes La *CROS/BRETH* PR26 ....184 D3

F

Factory Brow *GAR/LONG* PR3 ...284 D1
HOR/BR BL6 ......231 G8
Factory Hl *HOR/BR* BL6 ......232 A7
LANC LA1 ......3 J4
Factory La *CHLYE* PR6 ......230 E3
PDHM/BLYW BB12 ......140 F2
PRES PR1 ......152 C8
Factory St *RAMS* BL0 ......214 F4
Faircres *WGNNW/ST* WN6 ......245 L2
Fairbairn Av
PDHM/BLYW BB12 ......141 M3
Fairbank Gv *MCMB* LA4 ......41 H6
Fairbank Wk *RAW/HAS* BB4 ...177 K2
Fairburn *SKEL* WN8 ......243 J6
Fairclough Rd *ACC* BB5 ......159 K8
CLV/TH FY5 ......81 K7
Fairfax Av *BISP* FY2 ......85 H5
Fairfax Cl *GAR/LONG* PR3 ......284 C9
Fairfax Pl *BBR* PR5 ......169 G1
Fairfax Rd *FUL/RIB* PR2 ......133 J7
Fairfield Av *BPOOLE* FY3 ......105 L4
GAR/LONG PR3 ......284 A9
RAW/HAS BB4 ......196 C5
Fairfield Cl *CARN* LA5 ......33 K4
CLI BB7 ......98 A3
LANC LA1 ......2 E6
ORM L39 ......241 H4
Fairfield Ct *FTWD* FY7 ......81 J1
Fairfield Dr *BRFD/BLYE* BB10 ..122 B8
CLI BB7 ......98 A3
FUL/RIB PR2 ......151 L1
ORM L39 ......241 H4
Fairfield Gv *HEY* LA3 ......52 F1
Fairfield Rd *BPOOL* FY1 ......104 D7
FUL/RIB PR2 ......132 D7
HEY LA3 ......52 F2
LANC LA1 ......2 E1
LEYL PR25 ......186 C3
NLSN BB9 ......123 L3
PLF/KEOS FY6 ......106 C4
STHP PR8 ......220 F5
Fairfields Dr *DWN* BB3 ......173 J5
Fairfield St *ACC* BB5 ......159 J7
BBR PR5 ......168 E4
WGNW/BIL/OR WN5 ......255 M6
Fairgarth Dr *KKBYL* LA6 ......21 L1
Fairham Av *PRES* PR1 * 168 A1
Fairhaven *NWD/KWIPK* L33 ....260 B6
SKEL WN8 ......243 L6
Fairhaven Av *FTWD* FY7 ......81 G4
Fairhaven Cl *CLV/TH* FY5 ......86 A3
Fairhaven La *LSTA* FY8 ......145 H6
Fairhaven Rd *BBNW* BB2 ......173 J2
CHTN/BK PR9 ......180 E7
LEYL PR25 ......186 A2
LSTA FY8 ......145 H6
PRES PR1 ......8 E7
Fairhaven Wy *MCMB* LA4 ......41 H7
Fairheath Rd *HGHB* LA2 ......48 C3
Fair Hl *RAW/HAS* BB4 ......194 D4
Fairholme Rd *BLY* BB11 * 7 H7
CSBY/BLUN L23 ......257 H7
Fairholmes Cl *CLV/TH* FY5 ......81 L8
Fairholmes Wy *CLV/TH* FY5 ......81 L8
Fairhope Av *LANC* LA1 ......42 D3
MCMB LA4 ......42 A1
Fair Hope Ct *BBNW* BB2 ......10 A2
Fairhurst Av *WGNNW/ST* WN6 ..229 G8
Fairhurst's Dr *BPOOL* FY1 ......104 D4
Fairhurst St *BPOOL* FY1 ......104 D4
Fairlawne Wd *NWD/KWIPK* L33 .260 B6
Fairlea Av *MCMB* LA4 ......42 A4
Fairlie *SKEL* WN8 ......243 M8
Fairmont Dr *PLF/KEOS* FY6 ......87 G1
Fairoak Cl *FUL/RIB* PR2 ......133 J8
Fairsnape Av *GAR/LONG* PR3 ..114 C6
Fairsnape Rd *LSTA* FY8 ......147 H3
Fairstead *SKEL* WN8 ......243 M8
Fairview *RAW/HAS* BB4 ......177 M5
Fairview Av *LSTA* FY8 ......145 K4
Fairview Cl *KIRK/FR/WAR* PR4 ..166 D2
Fair View Crs *BCUP* OL13 ......197 L1
Fairview Dr *CHLYE* PR6 ......230 C3
Fair View Rd *BLY* BB11 ......7 K6
Fairway *CHLY/EC* PR7 ......207 L1
CHTN/BK PR9 ......199 M1
FTWD FY7 ......80 D7
PLF/KEOS FY6 ......105 K4
Fair Wy *PLF/KEOS* FY6 ......82 F7
Fairway *PRES* PR1 ......151 L5
WHIT OL12 ......217 M4
Fairway Gdns *PLF/KEOS* FY6 ......78 A6
Fairway Rd *BPOOLS* FY4 ......125 H5
Fairways *CSBY/BLUN* L23 ......257 H7
FMBY L37 ......236 F2
Fairways Av *GAR/LONG* PR3 ...111 M8
Fairways Ct *BBN* BB1 ......137 J6
Fairways Dr *FMBY* L37 ......236 F2
The Fairways *SKEL* WN8 ......244 A8
Fairwinds Av
KIRK/FR/WAR PR4 ......165 J7
Falcon Av *DWN* BB3 ......173 H4
Falcon Cl *BBN* BB1 ......157 G3
SETT BD24 ......265 N6
WHIT OL12 ......234 A1
Falcon Dr *PLF/KEOS* FY6 ......105 L1
Falcon Gdns *SETT* BD24 ......265 N9
Falcon Ms *PLF/KEOS* FY6 ......78 C5
Falcon St *PRES* PR1 ......152 B1
Falinge Fold *WHIT* OL12 ......235 G2
Falinge Ms *WHIT* OL12 ......235 H3
Falinge Rd *WHIT* OL12 ......235 G2
Falkirk Av *BISP* FY2 ......85 J4
Falkirk Gv *WGNW/BIL/OR* WN5 .255 N8
Falkland *SKEL* WN8 ......243 M8
Falkland Av *BPOOLS* FY4 ......5 M8
ROCH OL11 ......234 F3
Falkland Rd *STHP* PR8 ......13 L1
Fallbarn Crs *RAW/HAS* BB4 ...195 K2

Fall Barn Rd *RAW/HAS* BB4 ....195 L1
Fallbarn Rd *RAW/HAS* BB4 ....195 L1
Fall Kirk *HGHB* LA2 ......35 K2
Fallowfield *NWD/KWIPK* L33 ....260 B6
Fallowfield Cl
KIRK/FR/WAR PR4 ......128 B5
Fallowfield Dr
PDHM/BLYW BB12 ......142 A3
WHIT OL12 ......218 G5
Fallowfield La *LSTA* FY8 ......145 M5
Falmouth Av *ROCH* OL11 ......80 A7
RAW/HAS BB4 ......194 F1
Falmouth Rd *BPOOL* FY1 ......4 F8
Falmouth St *ROCH* OL11 ......235 K6
Falstone Av *RAMS* BL0 ......214 F4
Faraday Av *CLI* BB7 ......99 G3
Faraday Dr *FUL/RIB* PR2 ......132 A4
Faraday Rd *MILN* OL16 ......234 E2
Faraday St *PDHM/BLYW* BB12 .141 M4
Far Close Dr *CARN* LA5 ......16 C3
Far Cft *BBR* PR5 ......168 D2
Fareham Cl *CHTN/BK* PR9 ......181 K6
FUL/RIB PR2 ......132 D6
Fareham Dr *CHTN/BK* PR9 ......181 K6
Far Fld *PRES* PR1 ......151 M8
Farholme La *BCUP* OL13 ......197 G3
Faringdon *ROCH* OL11 * 235 H5
Faringdon Av *BPOOLS* FY4 ....125 G2
Farington Ga *LEYL* PR25 ......186 E1
Farington Rd
CROS/BRETH PR26 ......168 C5
Farlands Ri *MILN* OL16 ......235 M3
Far La *PRES* PR1 ......167 M1
Farleton Cl *CARN* LA5 ......25 J7
Farleton Ct *LANC* LA1 ......42 E7
Farleton Old Rd *HGHB* LA2 ......45 M1
Farley La *SKEL* WN8 ......244 B8
Farm Av *BCUP* OL13 ......179 J7
CHLYE PR6 ......230 D3
Farm Cl *CHTN/BK* PR9 ......200 D3
CLV/TH FY5 ......85 L1
Farmdale Dr *MGHL* L31 ......259 H2
Farmdale Rd *LANC* LA1 ......3 J6
Farmend *KIRK/FR/WAR* PR4 ...166 E3
Farmer's Rw *BBN* BB1 ......172 A3
Farm House La *BBN* BB1 ......157 M7
CHLYE PR6 ......187 M5
Farm Meadow Rd
WGNW/BIL/OR WN5 ......255 H6
Far Moor La *LANC* LA1 ......55 H3
Far Moss La *CSBY/BLUN* L23 ...256 E5
Farm Wk *LIT* OL15 ......219 J6
MILN OL16 ......235 M2
Farnboro St *TOD* OL14 ......303 K6
Farnborough Av *STHP* PR8 ......221 J3
Farnell Pl *BPOOLS* FY4 ......125 G5
Farnham Wy *PLF/KEOS* FY6 ......85 M1
Farnlea Dr *MCMB* LA4 ......41 M6
Farnley Cl *WHIT* OL12 ......234 C1
Far Nook *CHLYE* PR6 ......187 L4
Farnworth Gv
NWD/KWIPK L33 ......260 B6
Farnworth Rd *CLV/TH* FY5 ......85 M2
Faroes Cl *BBNW* BB2 ......173 J2
Farrell Cl *MGHL* L31 ......259 L7
Farrell St *WGNW/BIL/OR* WN5 ..255 M6
Farrer Av *LANC* LA1 ......66 F4
Farriers La *ROCH* OL11 ......235 J3
Farriers Cl *PLF/KEOS* FY6 ......86 E1
Farrier Wy *WGNNW/ST* WN6 ...244 F4
Farringdon Crs *PRES* PR1 ......153 J2
Farringdon Pl *PRES* PR1 ......153 J2
Farringdon Rd *BBNW* BB2 ......172 F2
BLY BB11 ......141 M8
Farrington Ct *BLY* BB11 ......141 M8
Farrington Ct *BLY* ORM L39 ....241 H5
Farrington Pl *BLY* BB11 ......141 M8
Farrington Pl *BCUP* OL13 ......197 L3
BLY BB11 ......141 M8
Farrington St *CHLY/EC* PR7 ......207 M3
Fatherside Dr *NTHTN* L30 ......257 M8
Faulkner Cl *STHP* PR8 ......220 F2
Faulkner Gdns *MILN* OL16 ......235 M4
Faulkner's La *GAR/LONG* PR3 ...270 A10
Favordale Rd *COL* BB8 ......296 D5
Fawcett *SKEL* WN8 ......243 L8
Fawcett Cl *BBNW* BB2 ......10 A1
Fawcett Rd *MGHL* L31 ......250 F5
Fayles Gv *BPOOLS* FY4 ......125 K5
Fazackerley St *FUL/RIB* PR2 ....151 M2
Feardown Av *CHLY/EC* PR7 ....207 H1
Fearnhead Av *HOR/BR* BL6 ....231 M3
Fearns Moss *BCUP* OL13 ......196 D2
Featherstall Brook Vw
LIT OL15 ......219 J6
Featherstall Rd *LIT* OL15 ......219 J6
February Cl *WHIT* OL12 ......235 J1
Fecit La *RAMS* BL0 ......215 L3
Fecitt Brow *BBN* BB1 ......158 A3
Fecitt Rd *BBNW* BB2 ......156 E5
Federation St
BWCK/EAR BB18 ......293 P4
Feilden Pl *CHLYE* PR6 ......230 C3
Feildens Farm La *BBNW* BB2 ...135 L3
Feilden St *BBN* BB1 ......10 B5
Felgate Brow *BPOOLE* FY3 * 5 J2
Fell Brow *GAR/LONG* PR3 ......114 C5
Fell Cl *BBR* PR5 ......169 J4
Fellery St *CHLY/EC* PR7 ......207 M3
Fellgate *KEY* LA3 ......53 M1
Fell Rd *KKBYL* LA6 ......14 D3
MCMB LA4 ......42 A1
Fellside Gdns *LIT* OL15 ......219 J4
Fellside Vw *HEY* LA3 ......52 F1
Fellstone V *CHLYE* PR6 ......189 K2
Fell Vw *BRFD/BLYE* BB10 ......123 G8
CHLYE PR6 ......208 B5
Fellview *CHTN/BK* PR9 ......181 G5
Fell Vw *CLI* BB7 ......290 C8
CLI BB7 ......118 C4
FUL/RIB PR2 ......133 M1
GAR/LONG PR3 ......284 D7
HGHB LA2 ......44 D6
MILN OL16 ......235 M2
Fell View Gv *GAR/LONG* PR3 ...284 B7
Fell Vw Pl *PLF/KEOS* FY6 ......85 G4
Fellway Cl *BBR* PR5 ......168 F5
Felsted *SKEL* WN8 ......253 M2
Felstead St *PRES* PR1 ......153 C5
Feltons *SKEL* WN8 ......253 M2
Fenber Av *BPOOLS* FY4 ......124 D4
Fengrove Av *RAW/HAS* BB4 ...196 D3
Fenham Carr La *LANC* LA1 ......55 H4
Feniscliffe Dr *BBNW* BB2 ......172 C1
Fennel Cl *BISP* FY2 ......85 J3
Fenney Ct *SKEL* WN8 ......253 M2
Fensway *KIRK/FR/WAR* PR4 ....167 G1

Fenton Av *BWCK/EAR* BB18 ....294 A4
Fenton Ms *ROCH* OL11 * 235 H6
Fenton Rd *BPOOL* FY1 ......104 F5
FUL/RIB PR2 ......132 F7
Fenton St *BLY* BB11 ......141 M8
WHIT OL12 ......235 H4
Ferguson Gdns *WHIT* OL12 ....218 C3
Ferguson St *BPOOL* FY1 * 5 J7
Ferguson St *BBNW* BB2 ......173 G4
Fermor Rd *KIRK/FR/WAR* PR4 ...183 H2
PRES PR1 ......153 H2
Fern Av *ACC* BB5 ......159 J8
LANC LA1 ......54 F1
NLSN BB9 ......123 H4
Fern Bank *CHLYE* PR6 ......188 A8
Fern Bank Av *BWCK/EAR* BB18 .293 P4
Fernbank Dr *NTHTN* L30 ......258 C7
Ferncliffe Dr *HEY* LA3 ......52 E1
Fern Cl *BBR* PR5 ......168 E5
KKBY L32 ......260 B7
SKEL WN8 ......253 H2
WGNNW/ST WN6 ......245 K5
Ferndale Av *BPOOLS* FY4 ......125 G4
Ferndale Cl *CLV/TH* FY5 ......85 G1
LEYL PR25 ......186 B4
Ferndale St *BRFD/BLYE* BB10 ..142 F3
Fern Dene *WHIT* OL12 ......234 C1
Ferney Lee Rd *TOD* OL14 ......303 K1
Fern Gore Av *ACC* BB5 ......159 K8
Fern Gv *BPOOL* FY1 ......4 F5
Fern Hey *CSBY/BLUN* L23 ......257 K6
Fernhill Av *BCUP* OL13 ......197 H3
Fernhill Cl *BCUP* OL13 ......197 H3
Fernhill Crs *BCUP* OL13 ......197 H3
Fernhill Dr *BCUP* OL13 ......197 H3
Fernhill Gv *BCUP* OL13 ......197 H3
Fern Hill La *WHIT* OL12 ......217 K7
Fernhill Pk *BCUP* OL13 ......197 H3
Fernhill Wy *BCUP* OL13 ......197 H3
Fernlea Av *ACC* BB5 ......159 K8
BWCK/EAR BB18 ......293 P4
Fernlea Cl *BBNW* BB2 ......172 E3
WHIT OL12 ......234 E1
Fern La *ACC* BB5 ......139 H7
Fern Lea *RAW/HAS* BB4 ......196 A3
Fernleigh *CROS/BRETH* PR26 ...185 K3
Fernleigh Cl *BISP* FY2 ......85 G6
Fern Meadow *CHLYE* PR6 ......187 M1
Fern St *BBR* PR5 ......6 B8
Fernside Wy *WHIT* OL12 ......234 D2
The Ferns *BBR* PR5 ......152 E8
BCUP OL13 ......197 K2
FUL/RIB PR2 ......151 M1
KIRK/FR/WAR PR4 ......128 C7
Fernstone Cl *HOR/BR* BL6 ......231 K8
Fern St *BCUP* OL13 ......197 J1
COL BB8 ......296 C5
RAMS BL0 ......215 G4
RAW/HAS BB4 ......196 C2
ROCH OL11 ......235 J5
WHIT OL12 ......218 F5
Fern Ter *RAW/HAS* BB4 * 176 D8
Fern Valley Cha *TOD* OL14 ......303 J1
Fernwood Av *CLV/TH* FY5 ......85 L1
Fernwood Cl *LSTA* FY8 ......146 B7
Fernyhalgh Ct *FUL/RIB* PR2 * ...133 G5
Fernyhalgh Gdns *FUL/RIB* PR2 .133 G5
Fernyhalgh La *FUL/RIB* PR2 ....133 G5
Fernyhalgh Pl *FUL/RIB* PR2 ....133 G5
Ferny Knoll Rd
RNFD/HAY WA11 ......253 J7
Ferrand Ldg *LIT* OL15 ......219 M4
Ferrand Rd *LIT* OL15 ......219 L5
Ferrier Bank
KIRK/FR/WAR PR4 ......148 A6
Ferry Side La *CHTN/BK* PR9 ....180 F6
Festival Rd *RNFD/HAY* WA11 ...262 D6
Fiddlers Fold Ct
KIRK/FR/WAR PR4 ......130 C7
Fiddler's La *CHLYE* PR6 ......286 F11
Fidler La *CROS/BRETH* PR26 ...168 C5
Field Cl *BRSC* L40 ......225 J8
Fieldcroft *ROCH* OL11 ......234 E4
Fielden Sq *TOD* OL14 ......303 L3
Fielden St *CHLYE* PR6 ......208 B3
LEYL PR25 ......186 A2
TOD OL14 ......303 P1
Fieldfare Cl *CLV/TH* FY5 ......81 K6
PRES PR1 ......152 B8
Fieldfare Ct *CHLY/EC* PR7 ......207 J4
Fieldfare Wy *BCUP* OL13 ......197 K2
Fieldhead Av *ROCH* OL11 ......234 D2
Fieldhouse Av *CLV/TH* FY5 ......86 A1
Fieldhouse Rd *WHIT* OL12 ......235 J1
Fielding Crs *BBNW* BB2 ......172 D2
Fielding La *ACC* BB5 ......159 H8
GTH/LHO BB6 ......138 E6
Fielding Rd *BPOOL* FY1 ......132 A8
MGHL L31 ......249 L7
The Fieldings *FUL/RIB* PR2 ......132 A8
Fieldings Cl *BBN* BB1 ......158 F2
Fieldlands *STHP* PR8 ......222 D1
Field Maple Dr *FUL/RIB* PR2 ...133 J7
Fields End *GTH/LHO* BB6 ......137 M3
Fieldsend *HEY* LA3 ......52 F5
Fieldside Av *CHLY/EC* PR7 ......206 F3
Fieldside Cl *BBR* PR5 ......152 E8
Fields Rd *RAW/HAS* BB4 ......194 E2
The Fields *CHLY/EC* PR7 ......205 L4
Field St *BBNW* BB2 ......172 E1
BPOOL FY1 ......4 B5
ROCH OL11 ......235 K7
Fieldview *SKEL* WN8 ......254 D4
Field Wk *ORM* L39 ......241 L6
Fieldway *LSTA* FY8 ......145 H4
MGHL L31 ......259 H4
Fife Cl *CHLYE* PR6 ......208 B5
Fife St *ACC* BB5 ......159 K7
NLSN BB9 ......123 J1
Fifth Av *BPOOLS* FY4 ......124 D4
BRFD/BLYE BB10 ......142 F3
Fifth St *BOL* BL1 ......233 J7
Filberts Cl *FUL/RIB* PR2 ......131 M7
The Filberts *FUL/RIB* PR2 ......131 M8
File St *CHLY/EC* PR7 ......207 M4
Filey Pl *BPOOL* FY1 ......104 E5
Filey Rd *LSTA* FY8 ......145 K2

Filey St MILN OL16 .... 235 M1
Filton Gv HEY LA3 .... 41 M8
Finance St LIT OL15 .... 219 H6
Finch Av RNFD/HAY WA11 .... 262 C6
Finch Cl BBN BB1 .... 10 F2
Finches Cots PRES PR1 * 152 B7
The Finches PLF/KEOS FY6 .... 105 L1
Finch La KIRK/FR/WAR PR4 .... 131 H1
WGNNW/ST WN6 .... 244 E2
Finchley Rd BPOOL FY1 .... 104 E3
Finch Mill La WGNNW/ST WN6 .... 245 G4
Finch St DWN BB3 * 191 J1
Findon SKEL WN8 .... 253 L2
Fine Jane's Wy CHTN/BK PR9 .... 200 E3
Finney Park Dr FUL/RIB PR2 .... 151 J2
Finnington La BBNW BB2 .... 171 K5
Finsbury Av BPOOL FY1 .... 5 J1
LSTA FY8 .... 145 L7
Finsbury Pl BBNW BB2 .... 173 L7
Finsbury St ROCH OL11 .... 235 G6
Finsley Ga BLY BB11 .... 7 G4
Finsley St BRFD/BLYE BB10 * 123 H8
Firbank BBR PR5 .... 169 G2
CHLY/EC PR7 .... 206 F1
Firbank Av KIRK/FR/WAR PR4 .... 183 K4
Firbank Rd LANC LA1 .... 3 K4
Firbeck SKEL WN8 .... 253 M2
Fir Cl FTWD FY7 .... 80 F1
Fircroft WGNNW/ST WN6 .... 245 K1
Firfield Cl KIRK/FR/WAR PR4 .... 128 B6
Fir Gv BPOOL FY1 .... 5 J3
KIRK/FR/WAR PR4 .... 148 A3
Fir Grove Rd BLY BB11 .... 7 J8
Firs Crs FMBY L37 .... 237 G6
Firshill Cl CLV/TH FY5 .... 85 L3
Firs La ORM L39 .... 240 C7
Firs Link FMBY L37 .... 237 G7
First Av ACC BB5 .... 159 K7
BPOOL FY4 .... 124 C4
CLI BB7 .... 290 C8
CSBY/BLUN L23 * 257 G7
FUL/RIB PR2 .... 151 J1
KIRK/FR/WAR PR4 .... 149 M2
KIRK/FR/WAR PR4 .... 127 L3
PLF/KEOS FY6 .... 86 B8
First St BOL BL1 .... 82 C7
Fir St BBN BB1 .... 157 J4
BRFD/BLYE BB10 * 7 K5
NLSN BB9 .... 123 J3
RAMS BL0 .... 215 G4
RAW/HAS BB4 .... 176 F8
STHP PR8 .... 200 C5
TOD OL14 .... 303 P1
First St BOL BL1 .... 233 J7
Firswood Cl LSTA FY8 .... 146 B2
Firswood Rd SKEL WN8 .... 242 F7
Fir Tree Av FUL/RIB PR2 .... 131 L7
Fir Tree Cl CARN LA5 .... 32 E8
Firtree Cl CHLY/EC PR7 .... 207 M8
Fir Tree Cl KIRK/FR/WAR PR4 .... 166 B8
RNFD/HAY WA11 .... 263 J4
SKEL WN8 .... 254 A4
Fir Tree La ORM L39 .... 250 D1
Fir Tree Pl CLV/TH FY5 .... 85 J3
Fir Trees Av BBR PR5 .... 168 C2
FUL/RIB PR2 .... 133 J7
Fir Trees Cl NLSN BB9 .... 123 K4
Fir Trees Crs BBR PR5 .... 168 D2
Firtrees Dr BBNW BB2 .... 172 C3
Fir Trees Gv
PDHM/BLYW FY3 .... 121 H6
Fir Trees La PDHM/BLYW BB12..121 H6
Fir Trees Pl FUL/RIB PR2 .... 133 J7
Fir Trees Rd BBR PR5 .... 168 D2
Firwood SKEL WN8 .... 244 A8
Firwood La BBR PR5 .... 154 G6
Fisher Dr CHTN/BK PR9 .... 200 C4
WGNNW/BIL/OR WN5 .... 255 H6
Fisherfield WHIT OL12 .... 234 C2
Fishergate PRES PR1 .... 8 F5
Fishergate Ct PRES PR1 * 8 F5
Fishergate HI PRES PR1 .... 8 D6
Fishermans Cl FMBY L37 .... 237 H6
Fishermans Wy FTWD FY7 .... 80 F3
Fisherman's La BPOOL FY4 .... 125 J6
Fisher's Slack La
PLF/KEOS FY6 * 107 L1
Fisher St BPOOL FY1 .... 104 F5
Fish House La GAR/LONG PR3....287 J11
Fish La BRSC L40 .... 202 E8
Fishmoor Dr BBNW BB2 .... 173 J3
Fish Rake La RAW/HAS BB4 .... 195 G5
Fish St PRES PR1 .... 9 H1
Fishwick La CHLYE PR6 .... 188 C4
Fishwick Pde PRES PR1 .... 153 G3
Fishwick Rd PRES PR1 .... 152 F3
Fishwick St MILN OL16 .... 235 K5
Fishwick Vw PRES PR1 .... 153 G3
Fitchfield PRES PR1 * 168 C1
Fitzgerald St PRES PR1 .... 152 F2
Fitzroy Rd BISP FY2 .... 85 G8
Fitzroy St PRES PR1 .... 8 C4
Five Acres CROS/BRETH PR26..168 B7
Five Ashes La HGHB LA2 .... 66 E4
Flag La CHLYE PR6 .... 208 C6
CROS/BRETH PR26 .... 184 D6
Flag St BCUP OL13 .... 197 H3
Flakefleet Av FTWD FY7 .... 81 H2
Flamingo Wy PLF/KEOS FY6 .... 78 D6
Flamstead SKEL WN8 .... 253 M2
Flannel St WHIT OL12 * 235 K3
Flare Rd HEY LA3 .... 52 C5
Flash La BRSC L40 .... 203 L7
Flatfield Wy MGHL L31 .... 259 H2
Flat La CARN LA5 .... 18 B8
SKP/WHF BD23 .... 267 K9
Flatman's La ORM L39 .... 249 H2
Flax Cl RAW/HAS BB4 .... 194 D3
Flaxfield Rd FMBY L37 .... 237 K8
Flaxfields BRSC L40 .... 225 J8
Flaxfield Wy
KIRK/FR/WAR PR4 .... 128 D6
Flax La BRSC L40 .... 242 C1
Flax St RAMS BL0 .... 214 D7
Flaxton SKEL WN8 .... 253 M2
Fleck Rd ACC BB5 .... 159 M5
Fleece St MILN OL16 .... 235 L5
Fleetgreen LANC LA1 .... 42 D8
Fleet La HGHB LA2 .... 67 G2
Fleet St BPOOL FY1 .... 4 E3
CHLY/EC PR7 .... 207 M4
GAR/LONG PR3 .... 114 D4
HOR/BR BL6 .... 232 A4
LSTA FY8 .... 145 G4
NLSN BB9 .... 123 H1
PRES PR1 .... 9 G4
WGNNW/ST WN6 .... 245 K1
Fleet Street La GAR/LONG PR3..115 J5

Fleet Wk BLY BB11 * 7 G4
Fleetwood Cl BBNW BB2 * 173 J2
CHTN/BK PR9 .... 180 C8
Fleetwood Crs CHTN/BK PR9....181 K5
Fleetwood Rd CHTN/BK PR9....181 K5
Fleetwood Gdns
NWD/KWIPK L33 .... 260 C6
Fleetwood Old Rd
KIRK/FR/WAR PR4 .... 108 B8
Fleetwood Rd
BRFD/BLYE BB10 .... 142 F1
BRFD/BLYE BB10 .... 199 M2
CLV/TH FY5 .... 85 G5
FTWD FY7 .... 81 H5
KIRK/FR/WAR PR4 .... 108 A6
PDHM/BLYW BB12 .... 141 G3
PLF/KEOS FY6 .... 87 L3
Fleetwood Rd North
CLV/TH FY5 .... 85 K1
Fleetwood Rd South
CLV/TH FY5 .... 85 K3
Fleetwood's La NTHTN L30 .... 258 A7
Fleetwood St FUL/RIB PR2 .... 8 L7
LEYL PR25 .... 186 E1
Fleming Cl WHIT OL12 .... 219 G6
Fleming Sq BBNW BB2 .... 10 E5
Flensburg Wy
CROS/BRETH PR26 .... 168 A8
Fletcher Rd KIRK/FR/WAR PR4..183 K4
Fletcher Rd BBN BB1 * 158 D2
PRES PR1 .... 9 L2
Fletcher's Dr BRSC L40 .... 225 H7
Fletcher's Rd LIT OL15 .... 219 H8
Fletcher St LIT OL15 .... 219 H8
NLSN BB9 .... 123 J4
ROCH OL11 .... 235 K6
Fletton Cl WHIT OL12 .... 235 H1
Fletton Ms WHIT OL12 .... 234 F1
Flett St FUL/RIB PR2 .... 8 B1
Flimby SKEL WN8 .... 254 A2
Flimby Cl BBNW BB2 .... 173 J3
Flintoff Wy PRES PR1 .... 132 E8
Flintron Brow HGHB LA2 .... 69 M7
Flip Rd RAW/HAS BB4 .... 176 C8
Floodgates Rd HTWN L38 .... 247 J6
Flordon SKEL WN8 .... 254 A2
Florence Av BLY BB11 .... 141 M7
KIRK/FR/WAR PR4 .... 148 A4
Florence Nightingale Cl
NTHTN L30 .... 258 C7
Florence Pl BBN BB1 .... 11 J1
Florence Steet MILN OL16 .... 235 L5
Florence St ACC BB5 .... 159 H5
BBN BB1 .... 11 J1
BLY BB11 .... 141 M6
BPOOL FY1 .... 125 K5
MILN OL16 .... 235 L5
Flowerfield KIRK/FR/WAR PR4..131 H5
Flower Flds GAR/LONG PR3 .... 91 G1
Flower Scar Rd BCUP OL13 .... 302 B1
Floyd Rd FUL/RIB PR2 * 133 H4
Floyer St PRES PR1 .... 9 M4
Fluke Hall La GAR/LONG PR3 .... 79 J3
Flyde Av LANC LA1 * 67 G4
Fold Gdns WHIT OL12 .... 217 L8
Fold La HBR HX7 .... 301 P5
Folds HOR/BR BL6 .... 230 F8
Foldside KIRK/FR/WAR PR4 .... 148 F4
Folds St PDHM/BLYW BB12 * 6 F1
Fold St HEY OL10 .... 234 B8
The Fold SKP/WHF BD23 .... 294 E1
Folkestone Rd CLV/TH FY5 .... 81 J7
KIRK/FR/WAR PR4 .... 148 B4
Folkestone Rd LSTA FY8 .... 145 J3
STHP PR8 .... 200 B8
Folly La BWCK/EAR BB18 .... 293 N9
LANC LA1 .... 42 C7
Folly Wk WHIT OL12 .... 235 J2
Folly Wood Dr CHLY/EC PR7 .... 207 K5
Fooden La CLI BB7 .... 277 Q12
Footeran La CARN LA5 .... 18 B8
Foot Mill Crs WHIT OL12 .... 235 G1
Foot Wood Crs WHIT OL12 .... 235 G1
Ford Av NWD/KWIPK L33 .... 260 E5
Ford Gdns ROCH OL11 .... 234 E5
Fordham Cl STHP PR8 .... 200 B8
Ford La CARN LA5 .... 17 H6
GAR/LONG PR3 .... 113 J1
LITH L21 .... 257 L8
Fordoe La WHIT OL12 .... 216 F7
Fordside Av ACC BB5 .... 139 H7
Fordstone Av PLF/KEOS FY6 .... 78 D7
Ford St BRFD/BLYE BB10 .... 142 E2
LANC LA1 .... 2 D4
NLSN BB9 .... 103 H7
Ford Vw LITH L21 .... 257 L8
Fordway Av BPOOL FY3 .... 105 H5
Forefield La CSBY/BLUN L23....257 J7
Foregate FUL/RIB PR2 .... 132 B7
Foreside NLSN BB9 .... 103 H6
Forest Bank Rd RAW/HAS BB4..177 K4
Forest Becks Brow CLI BB7 .... 277 M9
Forest Cl BBR PR5 .... 152 F8
Forest Dr LSTA FY8 .... 146 B7
SKEL WN8 .... 243 M8
WGNNW/ST WN6 .... 245 K1
Forester Dr PDHM/BLYW BB12..122 A3
Forest Ga BPOOL FY3 .... 53 M1
HEY LA3 .... 53 M1
Forest Gv GAR/LONG PR3 .... 113 L3
Forest Holme Cl
RAW/HAS BB4 .... 178 D4
Forest La NLSN BB9 .... 122 F1
Forest Pk LANC LA1 .... 2 C7
Fore St DWN BB3 .... 191 J4
Forest Rd BOL BL1 .... 233 J8
STHP PR8 .... 13 L6
Forest St BLY BB11 .... 7 H3
NLSN BB9 .... 123 G2
RAW/HAS BB4 .... 178 D4
Forest Vw WHIT OL12 .... 235 G1
Forest Wy FUL/RIB PR2 .... 132 G6
Forestway LEYL PR25 .... 186 C3
Forfar Gv BLY BB11 .... 142 A8
Forfar St BLY BB11 .... 142 A8
Forge La BRSC L40 .... 242 F7
Forge La GAR/LONG PR3 .... 284 D7
Forge St BCUP OL13 .... 197 J3
Forgewood Cl HGHB LA2 .... 43 M5
Forgewood Dr HGHB LA2 .... 43 L5
Formby Av FTWD FY7 .... 81 G4
Formby By-Pass FMBY L37 .... 247 H1
Formby Cl BBNW BB2 .... 173 J3
Formby Crs KIRK/FR/WAR PR4..166 C4
Formby Flds FMBY L37 .... 237 K1
Formby Rd FMBY L37 .... 237 J7
Formby Rd LSTA FY8 .... 145 H1
Formby St FMBY L37 .... 247 J2
Forrester Cl LEYL PR25 .... 186 D1
Forrestside BBNW BB2 .... 173 G4
Forrest St BBN BB1 .... 11 J3

Forshaw Av BPOOLE FY3 .... 105 J3
LSTA FY8 .... 145 G3
Forshaw Rd PRES PR1 .... 81 H1
Forsythia Dr CHLYE PR6 .... 169 L7
Forsyth St WHIT OL12 .... 234 B1
Fort Av GAR/LONG PR3 .... 116 A8
Forton Lodge Flats
CSBY/BLUN L23 * 256 F7
Forton Rd FUL/RIB PR2 .... 151 H3
Fort's Blds BWCK/EAR BB18....294 D9
Fort St ACC BB5 .... 139 J8
BBN BB1 .... 11 J3
CLI BB7 .... 99 G4
PDHM/BLYW BB12 .... 140 A1
Forty Acre La GAR/LONG PR3 .... 114 F2
Foscote Rd NWD/KWIPK L33....260 D7
Foss Ct HEY LA3 .... 41 M8
Fossdale Moss
CROS/BRETH PR26 .... 185 M2
Fosse Cl BBNW BB2 .... 173 K3
Foster Cft PRES PR1 * 8 A6
Foster Rd BWCK/EAR BB18....293 P4
Fosters Cl CHTN/BK PR9 .... 200 E3
Fosters Green Rd SKEL WN8....253 M1
Foster St ACC BB5 .... 159 M4
CLI BB7 .... 208 B2
Fothergill St COL BB8 .... 103 M6
Foul Clough Rd TOD OL14 .... 302 F8
Fouldrey Av PLF/KEOS FY6 .... 86 B6
Foulds Cl COL BB8 .... 103 M7
Foulds St CHTN/BK PR9 .... 200 D7
STHP PR8 .... 200 D7
Foundary Gdns CARN LA5 .... 26 A8
Foundry La HGHB LA2 .... 43 J5
Foundry St BBNW BB2 .... 10 B6
BCUP OL13 .... 197 J1
BLY BB11 .... 6 F3
CHLY/EC PR7 * 207 M3
RAW/HAS BB4 .... 195 J2
Fountain Cl PDHM/BLYW BB12..141 G3
Fountain Ct CSBY/BLUN L23....256 D6
Fountain Pl ACC BB5 .... 159 L6
Fountains Av BBN BB1 .... 157 L3
PDHM/BLYW BB12 .... 140 A2
Fountains Sq NLSN BB9 .... 103 G8
Fountains St ACC BB5 .... 159 K6
BWCK/EAR BB18 .... 293 P5
COL BB8 .... 296 A7
DWN BB3 * 191 K3
NLSN BB9 .... 123 H2
TOD OL14 .... 303 P1
Fountains Wy ACC BB5 .... 158 G6
PDHM/BLYW BB12 .... 140 A2
Fouracre BBNW BB2 .... 156 D1
Four Acre Dr LITH L21 .... 257 L8
Four Acre La GAR/LONG PR3 .... 95 G7
Fouracres MGHL L31 .... 258 E4
Fourfields BBR PR5 .... 169 H2
Four Lane Ends LANC LA1 .... 270 C5
Four Lane Ends BBR PR5 .... 170 A1
Four Lane Ends Rd BCUP OL13..196 C5
Fourmarts Rd
WGNNW/BIL/OR WN5 .... 255 M1
Four Oaks Rd BBR PR5 .... 169 L4
Four Stalls End LIT OL15 .... 219 K7
Fourth Av BPOOLS FY4 .... 124 F4
Fourth St BOL BL1 .... 233 J7
Fowler Av CROS/BRETH PR26..168 E5
Fowler Cl BBR PR5 .... 170 E1
Fowler Height Cl BBNW BB2....172 E4
Fowler Hill La GAR/LONG PR3..284 A2
Fowler La CROS/BRETH PR26..168 C5
Fowler St FUL/RIB PR2 .... 132 A4
CHLY/EC PR7 .... 207 L1
Foxcroft PDHM/BLYW BB12....142 A3
Foxcroft St LIT OL15 .... 219 J6
Foxdale Av BPOOLE FY3 .... 105 J4
Foxdale Cl BCUP OL13 .... 197 G2
EDGW/EG BL7 .... 213 H6
STHP PR8 .... 200 B8
Foxdale Gv PRES PR1 .... 133 G8
Foxen Dole La
PDHM/BLYW BB12 .... 121 J6
Foxes Ter GAR/LONG PR3 * 89 M4
Foxfield Cl ACC BB5 .... 159 G7
Foxfield Dr
WGNNW/ST WN6 .... 245 L5
Foxfields PLF/KEOS FY6 .... 82 F3
Foxfold SKEL WN8 .... 244 A8
Foxglove Cl BLY BB11 .... 142 E8
KIRK/FR/WAR PR4 .... 165 H7
Foxglove Ct WHIT OL12 .... 218 A4
Foxglove Dr CHLYE PR6 .... 187 L6
Fox Gv HEY LA3 .... 40 F8
Foxhall Rd BPOOL FY1 .... 4 C6
Foxhall Sq BPOOL FY1 .... 4 C6
Foxhill Bank Brow
ACC BB5 .... 159 G6
Foxhill Cl FMBY L37 .... 236 F8
Foxhill Dr RAW/HAS BB4 .... 178 A4
Foxhole Rd CHLY/EC PR7 .... 207 H2
Foxholes Cl WHIT OL12 .... 235 K2
Foxholes La WHIT OL12 .... 235 L1
Foxholes Rd HOR/BR BL6 .... 232 A7
MCMB LA4 .... 41 L5
WHIT OL12 .... 235 K1
Foxhouse La MGHL L31 .... 259 H3
Foxhouse St BBNW BB2 .... 10 A3
Fox La BBR PR5 .... 154 B8
LEYL PR25 .... 186 A3
Fox Lane Ends
KIRK/FR/WAR PR4 .... 127 K6
Foxstones Crs BBNW BB2 .... 172 D3
Foxstones La
BRFD/BLYE BB10 .... 143 K8
Fox St ACC BB5 .... 159 L5
CLI BB7 .... 99 H3
MILN OL16 .... 235 L3
PDHM/BLYW BB12 .... 141 J5
PRES PR1 .... 9 J3
Foxwell Cl RAW/HAS BB4 .... 194 F1
Foxwood Cha ACC BB5 .... 160 B3
KIRK/FR/WAR PR4 .... 126 F5
Foxwood Cl
WGNNW/BIL/OR WN5 .... 255 M3
Foxwood Dr
KIRK/FR/WAR PR4 .... 128 B6
The Foxwood CHLY/EC PR7 .... 228 B2
Frailey Cl STHP PR8 .... 220 F2
Frances St DWN BB3 .... 191 J1
NLSN BB9 .... 103 M5
Francis Av NLSN BB9 .... 103 J1
Francis St ACC BB5 * 139 J8
BBNW BB2 .... 10 D5
Fylde School Cots
BPOOLE FY3 * 105 M3
Fylde St KIRK/FR/WAR PR4....128 D7
PRES PR1 .... 8 F2

Franklands
Franklands Dr FUL/RIB PR2 .... 133 J6
Franklands Fold
NTHTN L30 * 258 C7
Franklin Gv NWD/KWIPK L33....260 D6
Franklin Rd BBNW BB2 .... 156 E8
Franklin St CLI BB7 .... 99 G3
DWN BB3 .... 191 K1
LANC LA1 .... 54 E8
PDHM/BLYW BB12 * 141 M5
Frank St ACC BB5 .... 159 K7
BWCK/EAR BB18 .... 293 Q5
PRES PR1 .... 152 C2
Fraser Av PRES PR1 .... 152 C7
Fraser St ACC BB5 .... 159 K7
BRFD/BLYE BB10 .... 142 E2
MILN OL16 .... 235 L7
Frazer Gv BPOOLS FY4 .... 124 E2
Freckleton Dr
NWD/KWIPK L33 .... 260 D6
Freckleton Rd CHTN/BK PR9....180 C7
KIRK/FR/WAR PR4 .... 128 E3
Freckleton St BBNW BB2 .... 10 D5
BPOOL FY1 .... 4 F8
LSTA FY8 .... 146 F8
Frederick Banting Cl
NTHTN L30 .... 258 C7
Frederick Rw BBN BB1 * 11 M4
Frederick St ACC BB5 .... 159 H7
BBNW BB2 * 10 E8
BPOOLS FY4 .... 125 K1
BWCK/EAR BB18 .... 293 P4
CHLYE PR6 .... 208 A3
DWN BB3 .... 191 K1
LIT OL15 .... 219 K5
RAMS BL0 .... 214 E6
Fredora Av BPOOLS FY3 .... 125 K1
Freeholds La CLI BB7 .... 289 Q9
Freeholds Rd WHIT OL12 .... 302 B3
Freehold St ROCH OL11 .... 235 H6
Free La RAW/HAS BB4 .... 194 D5
Freemans La CHLY/EC PR7 .... 207 H8
Freemantle Av PLF/KEOS FY6..104 A6
Freeport Village FTWD FY7 * 77 L8
Free Trade St BLY BB11 * 6 F4
Freetrade St ROCH OL11 .... 235 H6
French Cl BBNW BB2 .... 156 C7
French Rd BBNW BB2 .... 156 C7
Frenchwood Av FUL/RIB PR2 .... 9 M6
PRES PR1 * 9 M6
Frenchwood Knoll PRES PR1 .... 9 M7
Frenchwood St PRES PR1 .... 9 M6
Freshfield Av ACC BB5 .... 139 H8
FMBY L37 .... 237 H8
Freshfields FUL/RIB PR2 .... 131 G8
Friargate PRES PR1 .... 8 F3
Friar's Moss Rd HGHB LA2 .... 56 A3
Friar's Pas LANC LA1 * 3 H6
The Friars FUL/RIB PR2 .... 132 B7
Friars St LANC LA1 .... 3 H5
Friars Wk FMBY L37 .... 247 L1
Friary Cl KIRK/FR/WAR PR4 .... 128 F7
Friday St CHLYE PR6 .... 208 A3
Fieldhurst Rd TOD OL14 .... 300 F10
Frieston WHIT OL12 * 235 J3
Frinton Gv BISP FY2 .... 85 H5
Frobisher Dr LSTA FY8 .... 145 H2
Frobisher Rd LIT OL15 .... 219 M2
Frog La BRSC L40 .... 203 M8
Frome St PRES PR1 .... 153 G2
Froom St CHLYE PR6 .... 208 B3
Fry St NLSN BB9 .... 123 H1
Fulford Av FUL/RIB PR2 .... 150 F2
Fulham St BBNW BB2 .... 173 G4
Fullers Ter BCUP OL13 .... 197 J2
Full Pot La ROCH OL11 .... 234 B3
Full Vw BBNW BB2 .... 172 E3
Fulmar Gdns ROCH OL11 .... 234 C4
The Fulmars
PLF/KEOS FY6 * 105 L1
Fulshaw Rd FUL/RIB PR2 .... 151 L1
Fulwood Av BPOOLS FY3 .... 105 J3
KIRK/FR/WAR PR4 .... 183 J2
STHP PR8 .... 13 M9
Fulwood Dr MCMB LA4 .... 42 A6
Fulwood Hall La
FUL/RIB PR2 * 132 E7
Fulwood Hts
FUL/RIB PR2 .... 132 F6
Fulwood Rw FUL/RIB PR2 .... 133 H6
Fummerber La
HGHB LA2 .... 51 L2
Funchal Av FMBY L37 .... 247 G2
Furbank La ROCH OL11 .... 234 A3
Furbarn Rd ROCH OL11 .... 234 A3
Furlong Crs BPOOLS FY3 .... 105 K2
Furlong La PLF/KEOS FY6 .... 86 A6
Furness Av BBN BB1 .... 157 L3
BPOOLS FY3 .... 105 K3
FMBY L37 .... 237 J8
FTWD FY7 .... 81 G2
LIT OL15 .... 219 K5
ORM L39 .... 241 H7
Furness Cl CHLY/EC PR7 .... 208 A6
STHP PR8 .... 220 E8
Furness Dr HGHB LA2 .... 38 F3
PLF/KEOS FY6 .... 86 C8
Furness St BRFD/BLYE BB10....142 E2
LANC LA1 .... 2 D4
Furnival Dr BRSC L40 .... 225 G7
Further Ends Rd
KIRK/FR/WAR PR4 .... 148 E5
Further Fld BBR PR5 .... 169 K3
ROCH OL11 .... 234 F4
Furthergate BBN BB1 .... 11 L4
Further Heights Rd
WHIT OL12 .... 235 H1
Further La BBNW BB2 .... 155 M2
BBR PR5 .... 155 H4
Further Pits ROCH OL11 .... 234 F4
Furzegate MILN OL16 .... 235 M8
Fushetts La HGHB LA2 .... 38 E3
Fusiliers Cl CHLY/EC PR7 .... 187 J4
Fylde Av CROS/BRETH PR26..168 B7
Fylde Rd CHTN/BK PR9 .... 180 C7
FUL/RIB PR2 .... 8 C1
LSTA FY8 .... 146 A4
PLF/KEOS FY6 .... 86 B7
PRES PR1 .... 8 E1

BPOOL FY1 .... 104 E5
BRFD/BLYE BB10 .... 142 D3
COL BB8 .... 103 L8
FUL/RIB PR2 .... 8 L7

Fylde View Cl PLF/KEOS FY6......106 A1

G

Gabbot St CHLY/EC PR7 230
Gables Pl MCMB LA4 * 41
The Gables KIRK/FR/WAR PR4..131
MGHL L31 259
Gabriel Cl SKEL WN8 244
Gadfield St DWN BB3 191
Gadsby St BPOOL FY1 4
Gage St LANC LA1 3
Gaghills Rd RAW/HAS BB4 196
Gainsborough Av BBNW BB2 10
BBR PR5 168
BLY BB11 142
MCMB LA4 41
MGHL L31 258
Gainsborough Dr ROCH OL11....235
Gainsborough Rd BPOOL FY1 5
STHP PR8 199
Gaisgill Av MCMB LA4 41
Galbraith Wy ROCH OL11 234
Gale Cl LIT OL15 219
Gales La BRSC L40 204
Gales Ter ROCH OL11 235
Gale St WHIT OL12 218
Galligreaves St BBNW BB2 10
Galligreaves Wy BBNW BB2 10
Gall La TOD OL14 300
Galloway Crs BISP FY2 85
Galloway Dr SKEL WN8 254
Galloway Rd FTWD FY7 77
Gallowber La KKBYL LA6 20
Gallows La GAR/LONG PR3 116
Galston Cl NWD/KWIPK L33....260
Galway Av BISP FY2 85
Gamble Rd CLV/TH FY5 81
Gambleside Cl RAW/HAS BB4..177
Game St GTH/LHO BB6 138
Gamull La PDHM/BLYW BB12 133
Gandy La WHIT OL12 217
Gannow La PDHM/BLYW BB12..141
Gantley Av
WGNNW/BIL/OR WN5 255
Gantley Crs
WGNNW/BIL/OR WN5 255
Gantley Rd
WGNNW/BIL/OR WN5 255
Ganton Cl STHP PR8 200
Ganton Ct PRES PR1 151
Garbett St ACC BB5 159
Garden Av KIRK/FR/WAR PR4 127
Garden Cl BPOOLS FY3 125
PLF/KEOS FY6 86
Gardeners Ms BPOOL FY1 104
Gardeners Rw CLI BB7 120
Gardeners Vw
NWD/KWIPK L33 260
Gardenia Cl CHLYE PR6 169
Garden La MILN OL16 235
Garden Pl KKBYL LA6 19
Gardens Gv MCMB LA4 41
The Gardens EDGW/EG BL7 213
HGHB LA2 43
Garden St ACC BB5 159
BBNW BB2 10
BWCK/EAR BB18 * 293
CHLYE PR6 189
COL BB8 296
GTH/LHO BB6 138
KIRK/FR/WAR PR4 127
LSTA FY8 145
NLSN BB9 123
PDHM/BLYW BB12 140
PRES PR1 9
RAMS BL0 214
TOD OL14 303
Garden Ter AIRE BD20 295
BPOOLS FY4 124
CHLY/EC PR7 207
Garden Wk FUL/RIB PR2 151
Gardiners Pl SKEL WN8 253
Gardner Av CARN LA5 26
FMBY L37 237
HEY LA3 40
LANC LA1 3
Gardner's La GAR/LONG PR3 285
Gardner St PRES PR1 9
Garfield Av LANC LA1 2
Garfield Cl ROCH OL11 234
Garfield Pl MCMB LA4 42
Garfield St ACC BB5 159
FTWD FY7 77
TOD OL14 300
Garfield Ter CHLYE PR6 208
Garforth Crs BBR PR5 169
Gargrave Av BLL 233
Gargrave House Gdns
SKP/WHF BD23 281
Gargrave Rd SKP/WHF BD23 281
Garland Gv FTWD FY7 * 77
Garlicks Cots LSTA FY8 * 146
Garner Av BBNW BB2 173
Garnet Brow La HGHB LA2 51
Garnet St LANC LA1 3
Garnett Gdns ORM L39 241
Garnett Pl SKEL WN8 253
Garnett Rd CLI BB7 98
Garnett St DWN BB3 191
NLSN BB9 123
RAMS BL0 214
Garrick Gv BPOOLE FY3 105
Garrick Pde STHP PR8 12
Garrick St NLSN BB9 123
Garrison Rd FUL/RIB PR2 132
Garsdale Av BRFD/BLYE BB10..122
Garsdale Cl BBR PR5 153
Garsdale Rd FUL/RIB PR2 132
Garsden Av BBN BB1 174
Gars End HGHB LA2 36
Garstang New Rd
PLF/KEOS FY6 87
Garstang Rd CHTN/BK PR9 180
FUL/RIB PR2 132
GAR/LONG PR3 88
HGHB LA2 269
PLF/KEOS FY6 87
PRES PR1 132
Garstang Rd East
PLF/KEOS FY6 86
Garstang Rd North
KIRK/FR/WAR PR4 128
Garstang Rd South
KIRK/FR/WAR PR4 128
Garstang Rd West
BPOOLS FY3 105
PLF/KEOS FY6 105
Garstang St DWN BB3 191
The Gars HGHB LA2 36

Garstone Cft FUL/RIB PR2........131 M5
Garswood Av RNFD/HAY WA11..262 D4
Garswood Rd MGHL L31.........250 B8
  PDHM/BLYW BB12............142 C1
Garton Av BPOOLS FY4.........124 F5
Garwick Rd BOL BL1...........233 E8
Gas Field Rd HEY LA3...........64 E1
Gas House La HGHB LA2..........39 L4
Gaskell Cl CARN LA5.............16 E8
  LIT OL15 *...................219 K5
Gaskell Crs CLV/TH FY5.........85 K1
Gaskell Rd PRES PR1.............8 E2
Gaskell St CHLYE PR6..........208 B3
  BLY BB11.......................6 F4
  CHLY/EC PR7..................230 C5
  GAR/LONG PR3...............114 D3
  RAW/HAS BB4.................194 C2
  ROCH OL11....................235 H4
Gas St BCUP OL13.............197 J1
Gatefield St PRES PR25.........186 E1
Gate Ter LEYL PR25..............7 H7
Gate House Br HGHB LA2........68 A6
Gategarth Av FUL/RIB PR2....132 C4
Gateside Dr BPOOLE FY3......105 J3
Gate St BBN BB1................11 L4
  ROCH OL11....................235 J6
Gateway Cl CLV/TH FY5.........86 A4
Gathurst Hall
  WGNNW/ST WN6.............245 J8
Gathurst La WGNNW/ST WN6.245 J8
Gathurst Rd FUL/RIB PR2.....151 M1
  WGNW/BIL/OR WN5.........255 H2
Gatley Dr MCHL L31............259 H3
Gaulter's La PLF/KEOS FY6.....78 F7
Gauxholme Fold TOD OL14....303 J14
Gaw's Hill La ORM L39.........240 D8
Gaw's Hill Vw ORM L39........240 E8
Gawthorpe Edge
  PDHM/BLYW BB12..........141 J4
Gawthorpe Rd
  PDHM/BLYW BB12.............6 B1
Gawthorpe St
  PDHM/BLYW BB12..........140 F2
Gawthorpe Vw *
  PDHM/BLYW BB12..........121 J6
Gaydon Av CLV/TH FY5.........85 K4
Gaylands La BWCK/EAR BB18..294 F3
Gaythorne Av PRES PR1........153 J2
Geddes St BBNW BB2...........172 C1
Geldof Dr BPOOL FY1..........104 F3
General St BPOOL FY1.........104 E5
Geneva Rd FUL/RIB PR2.......132 F7
Geneva Ter ROCH OL11........234 F3
Genoa St BLY BB11.............141 M7
Geoffrey St CHLYE PR6........208 A2
  PRES PR1....................152 F2
  RAMS BL0....................214 D7
George Av BPOOLS FY4..........5 J8
  GTH/LHO BB6.................138 E7
George Dr STHP PR8...........221 H6
George Fox Av LANC LA1.......67 G4
George La PDHM/BLYW BB12..139 M1
George Moore Ct
  CSBY/BLUN L23 *............257 M5
George Rd RAMS BL0...........214 E4
George's La CHTN/BK PR9......181 J4
  HOR/BR BL6.................232 A4
George's Rd PRES PR1............9 L5
George's Rw RAW/HAS BB4....196 C3
George's Ter
  WGNW/BIL/OR WN5.........255 G6
George St ACC BB5............159 H8
  ACC BB5 *...................159 J8
  BBN BB1....................158 E2
  BBNW BB2....................10 E1
  BLY BB11.......................6 E5
  BPOOL FY1.....................4 E1
  BWCK/EAR BB18...........294 E5
  CHLY/EC PR7................207 M4
  CLI BB7.....................118 F6
  CLI BB7.......................99 G5
  DWN BB3....................191 K4
  GAR/LONG PR3..............114 D3
  GTH/LHO BB6................138 G6
  HOR/BR BL6.................231 M8
  LANC LA1......................3 G7
  LEYL PR25...................186 E1
  LIT OL15 *..................219 L6
  LSTA FY8....................146 E1
  MCMB LA4.....................41 M6
  MILN OL16...................235 K3
  NLSN BB9....................123 C2
  PRES PR1......................9 L5
  RAW/HAS BB4 *.............176 B4
  TOD OL14....................303 L1
  WHIT OL12...................217 M3
George St West BBNW BB2......10 E1
Georgia Av NWD/KWIPK L33..260 A5
Georgian Pl FMBY L37.........247 H2
Gerald Ct BLY BB11..............7 J7
German La CHLY/EC PR7.......207 C3
Gerrard Pl SKEL WN8...........253 J4
Gerrard's Ter PLF/KEOS FY6...85 M7
Gerrard St LANC LA1 *...........2 C1
  PRES PR1......................8 D4
Gertrude St NLSN BB9.........123 D1
Ghants La PLF/KEOS FY6........83 H1
Ghyll La BWCK/EAR BB18......294 C1
Ghyll Mdw BWCK/EAR BB18...294 A1
Gibbon Rd GAR/LONG PR3......95 C3
Gib Field Rd COL BB8.........103 K8
Gib Hey La RAW/HAS BB4.....177 L2
Gib Hill La RAW/HAS BB4.....177 M1
Gib Hill Rd NLSN BB9.........123 K1
Gib La BBNW BB2.............172 G4
  BBR PR5.....................154 F8
Gibraltar Rd
  KIRK/FR/WAR PR4..........107 H6
Gibraltar St BBNW BB2........156 C6
Gibson La NWD/KWIPK L33...260 A5
Gibson St MILN OL16..........235 M3
  NLSN BB9 *..................123 C1
  TOD OL14....................303 M2
Giddygate La MGHL L31........259 H4
Gidlow Av CHLYE PR6..........230 D4
Gifford Wy DWN BB3...........191 L1
Gilbert Pl BRSC L40...........224 C4
Gilbertson Rd CHLY/EC PR7...230 B1
Gilbert St BRFD/BLYE BB10...143 H1
  CHLY/EC PR7 *..............207 M5
  RAMS BL0....................214 A1
  RAW/HAS BB4................196 A2
Gildabrook Rd BPOOLS FY4...125 G6
Gilderdale Ct LSTA FY8.......146 F2
Gildow St PRES PR1..............8 E3
Giles St CLI BB7................99 H4
  NLSN BB9....................123 C1
Gilhouse Av FUL/RIB PR2.....150 F1
Gill Av WGNNW/ST WN6.......245 L5
Gillcroft CHLY/EC PR7.........205 L1
Giller Cl PRES PR1............168 B1
Giller Dr PRES PR1............168 B1
Giller Fold PRES PR1..........168 C1

Gillett St PRES PR1............152 F2
Gillians La BWCK/EAR BB18....293 P6
Gillibrand Cl PRES PR1........167 G3
Gillibrand Link Rd
  CHLY/EC PR7................207 J5
Gillibrands Rd SKEL WN8......253 K4
Gillibrand St BBR PR5.........153 G6
  CHLY/EC PR7................207 M4
  DWN BB3....................173 J1
Gillibrand Wks CHLY/EC PR7..207 M5
Gillies St ACC BB5............159 M5
  BBNW BB2....................11 G8
Gillison Cl KKBYL LA6..........29 J8
Gillisons Bungalows LANC LA1 *..3 G7
Gill La KIRK/FR/WAR PR4......166 D6
Gill Nook KIRK/FR/WAR PR4...166 D6
Gillow Av LANC LA1.............66 H4
Gillow Ct LANC LA1.............54 E8
Gillow Pk GAR/LONG PR3.......88 C5
Gillow Rd KIRK/FR/WAR PR4..128 C8
Gills St COL BB8..............103 H3
Gilpin Av MGHL L31...........259 H1
Gilpin Cl LANC LA1 *............2 A1
Gilsecroft Av NWD/KWIPK L33.260 D8
Gilstead Av HEY LA3............52 F3
Gin Bow CHLY/EC PR7.........207 M4
Gin Croft La RAMS BL0........195 H8
Gingham Brow HOR/BR BL6...232 A7
Gipsy La ROCH OL11...........234 F8
Girvan Gv BLY BB11...........145 M5
Gisburn Av LSTA FY8..........145 H4
Gisburn Gv BPOOLE FY3.......105 H4
  BRFD/BLYE BB10...........143 G6
Gisburn Old Rd CLI BB7.......293 M8
Gisburn Pl BBNW BB2..........10 A5
Gisburn Rd BWCK/EAR BB18..293 P4
  CLI BB7....................277 N12
  FUL/RIB PR2................133 H7
  NLSN BB9....................103 G8
  ROCH OL11..................235 K6
Gisburn St BBNW BB2..........10 A5
  BWCK/EAR BB18............293 P4
Gladden Pl SKEL WN8.........253 H8
The Glades LSTA FY8..........146 F2
The Glade MCMB LA4...........41 M6
  WGNNW/ST WN6.............245 J8
Gladeway CLV/TH FY5..........86 A4
Gladstone Cl BBNW BB2......172 C2
Gladstone Crs BCUP OL13....197 K1
  ROCH OL11..................235 K8
Gladstone Rd CHTN/BK PR9..200 C5
Gladstone St BBN BB1.........197 K1
  BCUP OL13...................197 K1
  BPOOL FY1..................124 F2
  GTH/LHO BB6................138 F6
  PDHM/BLYW BB12..........300 E10
Gladstone Ter BBNW BB2.....172 C2
  LANC LA1 *....................3 G7
Gladstone Wy CLV/TH FY5.....85 K2
Glaisdale Dr STHP PR8........200 C8
Glamis Dr CHLY/EC PR7.......207 L3
  CHTN/BK PR9................180 E8
Glamis Rd LEYL PR25.........186 F5
Glamorgan Gv
  PDHM/BLYW BB12..........141 J4
Glasson Cl BBNW BB2.........173 J2
Glastonbury WHIT OL12 *.....235 H3
Glastonbury Rd FUL/RIB PR2..5 J8
Glasven Rd NWD/KWIPK L33..260 D8
Glebe Cl ACC BB5.............159 L6
  FUL/RIB PR2................132 C7
  KKBYL LA6....................30 H5
  MGHL L31...................258 E2
Glebe End SFTN L29...........258 M4
Glebelands KIRK/FR/WAR PR4.183 K6
Glebe La CHTN/BK PR9........181 J4
Glebe Ms KIRK/FR/WAR PR4..150 A1
Glebe Rd SKEL WN8...........253 K3
Glebe St BLY BB11...............7 H8
  GTH/LHO BB6................138 G6
The Glebe CROS/BRETH PR26.185 L3
Gledhill St TOD OL14.........303 L1
Gledstone Rd SKP/WHF BD23..279 R9
Gledstone Vw
  BWCK/EAR BB18............293 P4
Glenapp Av BPOOLS FY4.......125 J3
Glenarden Av CLV/TH FY5......85 H3
Glen Av TOD OL14.............301 J12
Glenavon Dr WHIT OL12.......218 A4
Glenborough Av BCUP OL13..196 F3
Glenbrook Cl BBNW BB2......172 B5
Glenburn Rd SKEL WN8........243 H7
Glencarron Cl DWN BB3.......192 C3
Glencoe Av BPOOLE FY3......105 K2
  DWN BB3....................192 B4
Glencoe Rd FUL/RIB PR2.....235 G6
Glenden Foot WHIT OL12......235 G1
Glen Dr WCNNW/ST WN6......245 H3
Gleneagles Av DWN BB3......192 B2
Gleneagles Ct NWD/KWIPK L33.260 A5
Gleneagles Ct
  KIRK/FR/WAR PR4..........128 C6
  GTH/LHO BB6................117 M6
  LANC LA1.....................41 J5
  MCMB LA4....................41 M6
  PRES PR1....................151 K2
  STHP PR8....................220 E5
Gleneagles Wy RAMS BL0.....214 A6
Glen Eldon Rd LSTA FY8......145 H4
Glenfield Av CLV/TH FY5.......85 H5
Glenfield Pk NLSN BB9 *.......123 J2
Glenfield Rd NLSN BB9.........123 J2
Glen Gdns WHIT OL12.........218 C8
Glen Garth BWCK/EAR BB18..294 E4
Glengreave Av BBN BB1.......137 H8
Glen Gv FUL/RIB PR2..........133 K8
Glenholme Gdns
  KIRK/FR/WAR PR4 ....105 L1
Glenholme Rd MGHL L31 *....258 H4
Glenluce Crs BBN BB1.........158 A8
Glenluce Dr PRES PR1.........153 J2

Glenmarsh Wy FMBY L37......237 L8
Glenmere Crs CLV/TH FY5......84 H4
Glenmore CHLYE PR6..........187 K1
Glenmore Av CLV/TH FY5.......85 L1
Glenmore Rd ACC BB5.........176 B1
  ROCH OL11..................234 B6
Glen Park Dr
  KIRK/FR/WAR PR4..........165 G7
Glen Rd RAW/HAS BB4........196 C3
Glenrose Ter FUL/RIB PR2......12 F8
Glenroy Av COL BB8...........296 A5
Glen Royd WHIT OL12.........234 F2
Glenshiels Av DWN BB3.......192 B3
Glenside WGNNW/ST WN6....244 E1
Glen Sq BLY BB11.............162 C1
Glen St BCUP OL13............197 H3
  BLY BB11......................6 D3
  BPOOLE FY3.................105 J5
  COL BB8....................296 A5
  RAMS BL0...................214 E4
The Glen BBNW BB2...........173 H6
  FUL/RIB PR2................153 J2
  HGHB LA2....................44 D7
  PLF/KEOS FY6................78 D7
  TOD OL14...................301 J12
Glentworth Cl MGHL L31......259 C3
Glentworth Rd East MCMB LA4.41 L8
Glentworth Rd
  West MCMB LA4.............41 K8
Glen View Av HEY LA3..........52 D5
Glen View Cl FUL/RIB PR2....133 K8
Glenview Crs HEY LA3.........52 D5
Glen View La HEY LA3..........52 D5
Glen View Rd BLY BB11.......162 B1
Glen Wy NLSN BB9............122 D4
Glenway NWD/KWIPK L33.....260 C5
  PRES PR1...................151 M7
Glenwood St BPOOLE FY3.......5 J5
Global Wy DWN BB3...........173 K6
Globe La EDGW/EG BL7.......212 A8
Glossop Ct BISP FY2...........84 F5
Gloucester Av ACC BB5.......159 K4
  BPOOL FY1....................5 G4
  CLV/TH FY5..................81 G7
  LANC LA1.....................54 F7
  LEYL PR25..................168 F8
  WHIT OL12..................219 G7
Gloucester Dr HEY LA3.........40 F8
Gloucester Rd BBN BB1......157 M6
  CHLY/EC PR7................207 M6
  LSTA FY8...................146 A7
  STHP PR8....................12 D7
Glover Cl CROS/BRETH PR26.185 J5
Glover St BRFD/BLYE BB10...143 K4
  CHLY/EC PR7................229 G4
Glover's Brow KKBY L32......259 M7
Glover's Ct PRES PR1............9 J4
Glover's La NTHTN L30........258 B7
Glover St HOR/BR BL6.........231 L7
  PRES PR1.....................9 J4
Glynn St ACC BB5.............159 J4
Godiva St BRFD/BLYE BB10..142 D2
Godley St BLY BB11.............7 J5
Godwin Av BPOOLE FY3.........5 K6
Goe La KIRK/FR/WAR PR4.....148 K4
Goffa Mill SKP/WHF BD23....281 K3
Goitside NLSN BB9............123 H3
Goit St BBNW BB2............172 F1
  RAW/HAS BB4................196 C2
Golbourne St PRES PR1..........9 L1
Goldacre La GTH/LHO BB6....138 D4
Goldbourne Cl FTWD FY7......81 G1
Goldburn Cl FUL/RIB PR2....131 G1
Goldcrest Av BPOOL FY1......131 L3
Goldcrest Dr BBR PR5.........169 K1
Golden Hl LEYL PR25.........186 E1
Golden Hill La LEYL PR25....186 C1
Golden Wy PRES PR1.........152 A7
Goldfield Av BRFD/BLYE BB10.143 J5
Goldfinch Cl WHIT OL12.......235 H3
Goldfinch Dr GAR/LONG PR3.284 B12
Goldfinch St PRES PR1........152 E1
Goldhey St BBN BB1 *.........157 K4
Goldsboro Av BPOOLE FY3......5 J5
Goldstone Dr CLV/TH FY5.......5 H4
Golf Rd FMBY L37.............237 G6
Golf Vw FUL/RIB PR2.........131 K5
Golgotha Rd LANC LA1.........54 F7
Golgotha Village LANC LA1 *..54 F7
Gonder La GAR/LONG PR3....285 K12
Goodall Cl BWCK/EAR BB18..294 E5
Goodenber Crs HGHB LA2......39 G4
Goodenber Rd HGHB LA2......39 G4
Goodier St PRES PR1..........152 F1
Goodrich ROCH OL11 *........235 H5
Goodshaw Av BBN BB1........157 H2
  RAW/HAS BB4................177 K2
Goodshaw Av North
  RAW/HAS BB4................177 H1
Goodshaw Cl BBN BB1 *......157 H2
Goodshaw Fold Cl
  RAW/HAS BB4................177 K1
Goodshaw Fold Rd
  RAW/HAS BB4................177 J1
Goodshaw La ACC BB5........176 F2
Good Shepherd Cl MILN OL16.235 L5
Good St PRES PR1..............8 E5
Goodwood Av BISP FY2........132 C4
Goodwood Cl LANC LA1.........55 L5
Goodwood Rd LANC LA1.........55 L5
Goosebutts La CLI BB7..........99 J4
Goose Foot Cl BBR PR5.......154 E5
Goosefoot La KIRK/FR/WAR PR4.229 J2
Goose Green Av CHLY/EC PR7.229 J2
Goose Green La COL BB8......296 A5
Goose Hill St BCUP OL13.....179 J8
Goose House La DWN BB3....173 K4
Gooselands SETT BD24........267 A3
Goose La WHIT OL12..........235 J3
Gooseleach La
  PDHM/BLYW BB12..........140 D3
Goosnargh La GAR/LONG PR3.112 C4
Gordale Cl BPOOLS FY4.......125 K3
  BWCK/EAR BB18............293 P4
Gordon Av ACC BB5...........159 L4
  CHTN/BK PR9................199 M2
  CLV/TH FY5...................85 J1
  MGHL L31...................249 M8
Gordon Ct LANC LA1..........219 L5
Gordon Rd FTWD FY7..........77 J8
  LSTA FY8...................145 M2
  NLSN BB9 *..................123 M3
Gordonstoun Crs
  WGNW/BIL/OR WN5.........255 K2
Gordonstoun Pl BBNW BB2....10 A7

CLV/TH FY5...................85 K1
Gordon St ACC BB5...........159 H6
  BCUP OL13.................179 J7
  BPOOLS FY4 *................4 C5
  CHLYE PR6...................208 A4
  COL BB8....................296 B6
  DWN BB3....................173 K6
  PDHM/BLYW BB12.............6 E1
  PRES PR1.....................8 E1
  ROCH OL11..................235 K6
Gore Dr ORM L39.............241 H8
Gores La FMBY L37...........237 H6
  RNFD/HAY WA11............263 J5
Gore's La WGNW/BIL/OR WN5.255 J5
Goring St CHLY/EC PR7.......208 A4
Gorple Gn BRFD/BLYE BB10..143 L6
Gorple Rd BRFD/BLYE BB10..143 M6
Gorple Rd BRFD/BLYE BB10..123 H8
Gorrell Cl PDHM/BLYW BB12.122 A1
Gorrells Wy ROCH OL11.......235 G8
Gorrels Cl ROCH OL11........235 K6
Gorse Av CLV/TH FY5...........81 H8
Gorse Cl CHLYE PR6..........188 B6
  KIRK/FR/WAR PR4..........183 K5
Gorsefield FMBY L37..........237 K5
Gorse Gv FUL/RIB PR2........133 H8
  KIRK/FR/WAR PR4..........166 D3
Gorse La KIRK/FR/WAR PR4..183 J5
Gorse Rd BBNW BB2..........156 E6
  CHTN/BK PR9................181 M4
  HTWN L38...................247 M8
  NTHTN L30..................258 M8
  ORM L39....................238 F4
Gorsey Hill SKEL WN8.........253 K4
Gorsey Bank LIT OL15........219 M4
Gorst La BRSC L40............224 C5
Gorsuch La BRSC L40.........223 G7
Gorton St BPOOL FY1.........104 F5
  CHTN/BK PR9................200 C3
Gosforth Rd BISP FY2.........200 C3
Gough La BBR PR5............169 G6
Goulding Av LEYL PR25.......186 C1
Goulding St CHLY/EC PR7....208 A3
Gowans La CHLYE PR6........170 D3
Gower Ct CROS/BRETH PR26.186 A1
Gower Gdns BRSC L40........225 J4
Gower Gv KIRK/FR/WAR PR4.148 A6
Gowers St MILN OL16.........235 L3
Goyt St LANC LA1...............55 J4
Grab La LANC LA1..............55 H4
Graburn Rd FMBY L37........237 J7
Gracamy Av
  KIRK/FR/WAR PR4 *........148 A6
Grace St HOR/BR BL6.........231 L7
  RAW/HAS BB4................235 K1
Graduate La HGHB LA2.........66 H5
Gradwell St PRES PR1...........8 E5
Grafton Av ACC BB5..........160 B8
  BRFD/BLYE BB10...........122 A4
  DWN BB3....................191 J1
  MILN OL16..................235 L5
Grafton Ct CHLY/EC PR7......13 J1
Grafton Dr STHP PR8.........220 B1
Grafton Gdns ACC BB5........160 B7
Grafton Pl HEY LA3............40 C9
Grafton Rd FUL/RIB PR2......133 J7
  HEY LA3......................40 F9
Grafton St BBNW BB2..........10 C9
  BPOOL FY1.................104 C2
  CHLY/EC PR7................230 D4
  CLI BB7......................99 G5
  MILN OL16..................235 L5
  NLSN BB9...................123 J2
Grafton Vls BCUP OL13......197 G3
Graham Av BBR PR5..........168 F3
Graham Rd GAR/LONG PR3...284 A9
  WGNNW/ST WN6............244 F9
Graham St LANC LA1...........54 C1
  MCMB LA4 *..................41 M6
  PDHM/BLYW BB12..........141 J4
  PRES PR1...................152 F2
Grammar School La
  KIRK/FR/WAR PR4..........128 C7
Grampian Wy LSTA FY8.......147 G6
Granams Cft NTHTN L30......258 M4
Granborne Cha KKBY L32.....259 J8
Granby Av BPOOLE FY3.......105 H3
Granby Cl CHTN/BK PR9......180 C8
Granby St PDHM/BLYW BB12....6 C1
Grandage La HWTH BD22.....295 P9
Grandidge St ROCH OL11.....235 H6
Grand Manor Dr LEYL PR25..186 A4
Grane Pk RAW/HAS BB4......194 D1
Grane Rd BBN BB1............175 M8
Grane St RAW/HAS BB4.......176 B4
Grange Av BN CHTN/BK PR9..85 L1
  CLV/TH FY5 *................85 L1
  FUL/RIB PR2................133 G4
  GTH/LHO BB6................138 G5
  PLF/KEOS FY6................78 C5
  RAW/HAS BB4................177 K2
  WGNW/BIL/OR WN5.........255 M4
Grange Crs RAW/HAS BB4....195 K1
  CHLY/EC PR7................229 G3
Grange Dr BBR PR5...........169 A7
  CHLY/EC PR7................229 G3
  CHLY/EC PR7................186 F7
Grangefield KIRK/FR/WAR PR4.166 C4
Grange Gdns PLF/KEOS FY6.106 A1
Grange La LANC LA1...........55 M6
  FMBY L37...................237 H7
  KIRK/FR/WAR PR4..........166 A2
  KIRK/FR/WAR PR4..........149 J2
  PLF/KEOS FY6................78 C5
Grange Pk RAW/HAS BB4.....159 H8
Grange Park Cl PRES PR1....151 K2
Grange Park Wy
  RAW/HAS BB4................194 D2
Grange Pl FUL/RIB PR2.......133 G4
Grange Rd BBNW BB2........105 L4
  BPOOLS FY3..................4 F4
  BRFD/BLYE BB10...........143 G4
  DWN BB3....................200 B4
  FTWD FY7.....................77 G8
  FUL/RIB PR2................133 M8

HTWN L38...................247 H5
  KIRK/FR/WAR PR4..........108 C2
  LEYL PR25..................186 A2
  LSTA FY8...................145 H4
  PLF/KEOS FY6................87 G2
  RAW/HAS BB4................195 L1
  WHIT OL12..................218 A4
Grange Ter ACC BB5..........139 H8
  BLY BB11.....................6 F1
  BWCK/EAR BB18............294 A5
  MCMB LA4....................41 M4
Grange Ter RAW/HAS BB4 *..137 K8
The Grange BBNW BB2.......137 J2
  CHTN/BK PR9................180 F8
  KIRK/FR/WAR PR4..........131 K8
  LSTA FY8....................145 H4
Grange Vw CARN LA5..........32 E8
  CARN LA5....................26 A7
Grange View Rd KKBYL LA6...33 J3
The Granings
  KIRK/FR/WAR PR4..........131 G5
Grant Cl LANC LA1.............54 C8
Grant Dr KIRK/FR/WAR PR4..166 D6
Grantham Cl STHP PR8.......221 H2
Grantham Rd BPOOL FY1 *..104 F4
  KIRK/FR/WAR PR4..........107 C5
  NWD/KWIPK L33............260 B6
  STHP PR8...................221 H2
Grantham St BBNW BB2......172 E1
Grantham Wy NTHTN L30....258 H8
Granton Cl FMBY L37........237 H8
Grants La RAMS BL0.........214 F5
Grant St ACC BB5............159 K5
  BLY BB11.....................6 D1
Granville Av KIRK/FR/WAR PR4.183 H1
  MGHL L31....................258 F1
Granville Cl ORM L39.........250 E1
Granville Gdns ACC BB5......160 A7
Granville Pk ORM L39.........250 E1
Granville Pk West ORM L39..250 E1
Granville Rd ACC BB5.........159 M8
  BBNW BB2...................156 E6
  BPOOL FY1....................5 G1
  CHLYE PR6..................208 B2
  DWN BB3....................191 J3
  GTH/LHO BB6................139 G4
  HEY LA3......................40 E8
  LANC LA1.....................42 C4
  NLSN BB9...................122 F5
  STHP PR8...................199 C3
Granville St BRFD/BLYE BB10.142 D3
  CHLYE PR6..................230 D4
  COL BB8....................296 B6
  TOD OL14 *.................303 K6
Grape La CROS/BRETH PR26.204 F2
Grasmere Av BBN BB1........156 F2
  CLV/TH FY5...................85 L1
  FTWD FY7.....................77 H7
  LEYL PR25..................186 D1
  PDHM/BLYW BB12..........140 F1
  SKEL WN8...................254 E3
  WGNW/BIL/OR WN5.........255 J3
Grasmere Cl ACC BB5.........160 A3
  BBN BB1....................158 D2
  BBR PR5....................169 G1
  CHLY/EC PR7................207 G2
  FUL/RIB PR2................132 F7
  NWD/KWIPK L33............260 A7
Grasmere Dr HGHB LA2........39 G4
Grasmere Gdns
  CSBY/BLUN L23 *...........257 J8
Grasmere Gv CHLYE PR6.....187 L4
  GAR/LONG PR3..............114 C5
Grasmere Rd BPOOL FY1.......4 F5
  FMBY L37...................237 G5
  LANC LA1.....................3 K5
  LSTA FY8...................145 H2
  MCMB LA4....................41 L5
  MGHL L31...................259 G4
  PLF/KEOS FY6................78 C5
  RAW/HAS BB4................194 F3
  WGNW/BIL/OR WN5.........255 M4
Grasmere St BRFD/BLYE BB10.142 D1
Grasmere Ter BCUP OL13....179 J8
  CHLY/EC PR7................207 L6
Grasscroft FTWD FY7...........81 G1
Grassington Dr
  BRFD/BLYE BB10...........123 G8
Grassington Pl CLV/TH FY5...85 G3
Grassington Rd LSTA FY8....145 L4
Gratton Pl SKEL WN8.........253 K3
Gravel La CHTN/BK PR9......181 J4
The Gravel KIRK/FR/WAR PR4.202 C3
Grave-Yard La ORM L39......251 K6
Graving Dock Rd LSTA FY8...147 G7
Gravners Fld CLV/TH FY5......86 A1
Grayrigg Dr MCMB LA4........41 J7
Graysons Rd RNFD/HAY WA11.262 J3
Grays Pl HEY LA3..............52 F1
Great Avenham St PRES PR1 *..9 Jb
Great Bent Cl WHIT OL12.....219 G7
Great Bolton St BBNW BB2 *..10 A6
Great Close La SETT BD24....266 C1
Great Croft Cl
  BWCK/EAR BB18............293 P4
Great Eaves Rd RAMS BL0...214 E4
Great Flatt WHIT OL12........234 E2
Great Gates Ct ROCH OL11..235 K7
Great George St COL BB8.....296 A4
  MILN OL16..................235 J4
Great Gill KIRK/FR/WAR PR4.166 D1
Great Greens La BBR PR5....169 G1
Great Hanging Br
  CROS/BRETH PR26..........204 A3
Great Hanover St PRES PR1..152 A2
Great Hey KIRK/FR/WAR PR4.184 A1
  NTHTN L30..................258 A6
Great House Rd WHIT OL12..301 J11
Great Howarth WHIT OL12...218 A7
Great Lee WHIT OL12..........3 H6
Great John St LANC LA1........2 E4
Great Lee Wk WHIT OL12....235 G1
Great Meadow NTHTN L30...258 B3
  CHLY/EC PR7................207 K1
Great Park Dr LEYL PR25....186 D1
Great Shaw St PRES PR1.......9 G3
Great Townley St PRES PR1..153 G2
Great Tunstead
  KIRK/FR/WAR PR4..........166 A2
Greave Av ROCH OL11........234 E5
Greave Cl RAW/HAS BB4.....177 K5
Greave Clough Cl BCUP OL13.179 L8
Greave Clough Dr BCUP OL13.179 L8
Greave Rd BCUP OL13........179 L8
Greaves Av CHTN/BK PR9....181 K6
  WGNNW/ST WN6............245 J3
Greaves Hall Av CHTN/BK PR9.181 K6
Greave Meadow PRES PR1...168 G4

Greaves Rd LANC LA1 ...... 3 H9
Greaves St GTH/LHO BB6 ...... 138 F1
  PRES PR1 * 9 K4
  RAW/HAS BB4 ...... 194 C1
Greaves-Town La FUL/RIB PR2.. 151 G2
Grebe Cl BPOOLE FY3 ...... 105 L4
  WGNS/IIMK WN3 ...... 255 L7
Grebe Whf LANC LA1 ...... 3 L4
Greenacre GAR/LONG PR3 ...... 113 C5
Greenacre Cl RAMS BL0 ...... 215 H4
Greenacre Ct LANC LA1 ...... 55 G8
Greenacre Pk HGHB LA2 ...... 42 D1
Greenacre Rd HGHB LA2 ...... 42 D1
Greenacres EDGW/EG BL7 ...... 213 H5
  FUL/RIB PR2 ...... 131 L2
Green Acres
  KIRK/FR/WAR PR4 ...... 148 F4
Greenacres Av
  KIRK/FR/WAR PR4 ...... 128 D7
Greenacres Dr CHLY/EC PR7 .. 187 G7
  GAR/LONG PR3 ...... 284 C9
The Greenacres
  KIRK/FR/WAR PR4 ...... 167 G1
Greenacre St CLI BB7 ...... 99 H4
Green Av BPOOLS FY4 ...... 124 F5
Green Bank BCUP OL13 ...... 197 G3
  BWCK/EAR BB18 ...... 294 A3
  PLF/KEOS FY6 ...... 86 B8
Greenbank Av MGHL L31 .... 249 M8
  PRES PR1 ...... 152 A1
  WGNW/BIL/OR WN5 ...... 255 G8
Greenbank Dr LIT OL15 ...... 219 L4
  PDHM/BLYW BB12 ...... 122 B3
  STHP PR8 ...... 221 H1
Greenbank Pk RAW/HAS BB4... 195 L1
Greenbank Pl PRES PR1 ...... 8 E1
  PRES PR1 ...... 152 A1
  WHIT OL12 ...... 235 J1
Greenbanks BISP FY2 ...... 85 L8
Greenbank St PRES PR1 ...... 152 A1
  RAW/HAS BB4 ...... 195 L1
Greenbank Ter DWN BB3 ...... 173 L6
Greenbank Wy BBN BB1 ...... 157 M5
Greenberfield La
  BWCK/EAR BB18 ...... 293 Q3
Greenbooth Rd WHIT OL12 .... 217 D8
Greenbriar Cl BPOOLE FY3 .... 105 J2
Green Bridge Cl ROCH OL11 *.. 235 J7
Greenbrook Cl
  PDHM/BLYW BB12 ...... 141 J5
Greenbrook Rd
  PDHM/BLYW BB12 ...... 141 J5
Greencliffe La
  BRFD/BLYE BB10 ...... 163 K2
Green Cl BLY BB11 ...... 162 B1
Green Close Pk BBNW BB2 .... 172 H1
Green Cft CSBY/BLUN L23 .... 257 L6
Greencroft PRES PR1 ...... 152 A4
Greencroft Wy MILN OL16 .... 219 G8
Greendale Av RAW/HAS BB4 .. 196 B3
Greendale Cl BRFD/BLYE BB10.. 163 L4
  FTWD FY7 ...... 80 F1
Greendale Dr CARN LA5 ...... 26 A8
Greendale Ms FUL/RIB PR2 .. 151 H1
Green Dick's La GAR/LONG PR3.. 79 H6
Green Dr BBR PR5 ...... 168 F2
  CLI BB7 ...... 99 K1
  CLV/TH FY5 ...... 80 F7
  FUL/RIB PR2 ...... 132 B4
  GAR/LONG PR3 ...... 111 L3
  LSTA FY8 ...... 146 D6
  PLF/KEOS FY6 ...... 106 B3
  PRES PR1 ...... 151 L6
Green End BBR PR5 ...... 155 H4
Green End Av BWCK/EAR BB18. 294 E5
Green End Cl BCUP OL13 *.... 179 K8
Green End Rd
  BWCK/EAR BB18 ...... 294 E6
Greenfield Av CLI BB7 ...... 291 J10
  CLI BB7 * 98 F3
  SKEL WN8 ...... 243 L1
Greenfield Cl FTWD FY7 .... 81 J1
Greenfield Ct LANC LA1 * .. 3 J7
  BBR PR5 ...... 168 D3
Greenfield La ROCH OL11 .... 235 K7
Greenfield Rd
  BRFD/BLYE BB10 ...... 143 G7
  CHLYE PR6 ...... 230 D3
  CHLYE PR6 ...... 208 B3
  CLV/TH FY5 ...... 85 H3
  COL BB8 ...... 103 K7
  FTWD FY7 ...... 81 J1
  STHP PR8 ...... 222 F2
Greenfields BBNW BB2 ...... 173 G4
  HGHB LA2 ...... 44 D5
Greenfields Crs
  KIRK/FR/WAR PR4 ...... 128 B5
Greenfield St DWN BB3 ...... 191 M5
  LANC LA1 ...... 3 J6
  RAW/HAS BB4 ...... 176 E8
  ROCH OL11 ...... 235 K7
Greenfield Ter TOD OL14 .... 300 D10
Greenfield Vw DWN BB3 ...... 173 K4
Greenfield Wy FUL/RIB PR2 .. 131 L6
Greenfinch Ct BPOOLE FY3 .. 105 L5
Greenfold Cots
  RAW/HAS BB4 * 177 L2
Greenfold Dr RAW/HAS BB4 .. 177 K1
Greenfoot La HGHB LA2 ...... 38 C3
Greenford Cl
  WGNW/BIL/OR WN5 ...... 255 G5
Greenford Rd STHP PR8 .... 220 F7
Green Ga FUL/RIB PR2 ...... 131 M8
  KIRK/FR/WAR PR4 ...... 166 F2
Greengate Cl
  PDHM/BLYW BB12 ...... 6 A2
  WHIT OL12 ...... 219 G7
Greengate La CARN LA5 .... 33 H3
Green Gate La SKP/WHF BD23.. 267 R5
Greengrove Bank MILN OL16.. 218 F4
Greenhalgh La CHLYE PR6 .... 230 L3
  KIRK/FR/WAR PR4 ...... 107 M7
Greenhalgh Cl GAR/LONG PR3. 284 C5
Greenham Av NWD/KWIPK L33.260 C5
Greenhead Av BBN BB1 .... 157 L3
Greenhead La
  PDHM/BLYW BB12 ...... 122 A6
Green Head La SETT BD24 .... 286 F7
Green Hey KIRK/FR/WAR PR4.. 184 A1
  LSTA FY8 ...... 147 G2
Greenhey WGNW/BIL/OR WN5.. 255 K4
Greenhey Pl SKEL WN8 ...... 253 J3
Greenheys Dr MGHL L31 .... 259 J1
Greenhill GTH/LHO BB6 ...... 138 D5
Greenhill Av KIRK/FR/WAR PR4. 128 D5
  WHIT OL12 ...... 235 G3

Green Hill La HGHB LA2 ...... 34 B7
Green Hill Rd BCUP OL13 .... 197 D2
Greenholme Av MCMB LA4 .. 41 J8
Green Howarth Vw ACC BB5 .. 159 M8
Greenhurst La CHTN/BK PR9.. 201 M8
Greenland La CHLY/EC PR6 .. 231 G6
Greenland St HOR/BR HX7.... 301 L6
Greenings La CHTN/BK PR9.... 201 M8
Green La BBNW BB2 ...... 172 D2
  BBR PR5 ...... 154 C5
  BRSC L40 ...... 225 J7
  BRSC L40 ...... 229 K4
  CHLY/EC PR7 ...... 181 M7
  CLI BB7 ...... 290 F7
  CROS/BRETH PR26 ...... 184 F4
  CSBY/BLUN L23 ...... 257 L5
  FMBY L37 ...... 237 J5
  GAR/LONG PR3 ...... 287 M12
  GAR/LONG PR3 ...... 283 R8
  GAR/LONG PR3 ...... 114 E3
  GAR/LONG PR3 ...... 111 L1
  HEY LA3 ...... 53 J1
  HGHB LA2 ...... 44 A3
  HOR/BR BL6 ...... 231 L6
  KIRK/FR/WAR PR4 ...... 182 F7
  KIRK/FR/WAR PR4 ...... 167 M2
  KIRK/FR/WAR PR4 ...... 148 E5
  KIRK/FR/WAR PR4 ...... 110 A5
  LANC LA1 ...... 67 C5
  LANC LA1 ...... 3 J5
  MGHL L31 ...... 258 D1
  ORM L39 ...... 241 H5
  PDHM/BLYW BB12 ...... 140 F3
  RNFD/HAY WA11 ...... 262 D6
  SKEL WN8 ...... 243 J5
  SKP/WHF BD23 ...... 279 K10
  WGNW/BIL/OR WN5 ...... 255 G8
  WHIT OL12 ...... 235 H3
Green Lane Av ORM L39 * 241 H5
Green La East GAR/LONG PR3.. 284 B6
Green La West GAR/LONG PR3.. 284 A5
  KIRK/FR/WAR PR4 ...... 148 D6
Greenlea Cl
  WGNW/BIL/OR WN5 ...... 255 G6
Greenlea Dr MCMB LA4 ...... 41 J8
Greenlees St WHIT OL12 .... 235 J3
Green Link MGHL L31 ...... 258 E1
Greenloon's Dr FMBY L37 .... 236 F8
Greenloon's Wk FMBY L37 .. 246 F1
Greenmead
  KIRK/FR/WAR PR4 ...... 131 H6
Green Meadow COL BB8 ...... 296 E9
  WHIT OL12 ...... 219 G7
Green Meadow La
  PLF/KEOS FY6 ...... 86 E3
Green Moor La GAR/LONG PR3. 115 L4
Greenmount Av CLV/TH FY5.. 81 K8
  KIRK/FR/WAR PR4 ...... 128 D5
Greenmount Dr
  TOT/BURYW BL8 ...... 214 C8
Green Nook La GAR/LONG PR3. 114 C5
Green Oak Pl CLV/TH FY5 .... 85 J3
Greenock Cl BLY BB11 ...... 6 A8
Greenock St BLY BB11 ...... 6 A8
Green Pk CLI BB7 ...... 118 F6
Green Park Dr MGHL L31 .... 258 C2
Green Pl BBR PR5 ...... 169 K5
Green Ridge Cl NLSN BB9 .... 123 G6
Green Rd COL BB8 ...... 103 M7
Green Rw DWN BB3 ...... 172 E5
Greenroyde ROCH OL11 *.... 235 H6
Greens Arms Rd EDGW/EG BL7. 212 B4
Greenset Cl LANC LA1 ...... 42 D7
Greenshank Cl ROCH OL11 *.. 234 C4
Greenside CHLY/EC PR7 ...... 186 F8
  GAR/LONG PR3 ...... 116 B8
  KIRK/FR/WAR PR4 ...... 131 G7
Greenside Av BBNW BB2 .... 172 G2
  FUL/RIB PR2 ...... 150 F2
Greenside Cl NWD/KWIPK L33. 260 D5
  TOT/BURYW BL8 ...... 213 L8
Greenside Gdns
  CROS/BRETH PR26 ...... 185 L4
Greens La BCUP OL13 ...... 197 G3
  RAW/HAS BB4 ...... 194 E4
Greens La MGHL L31 ...... 249 M8
Green's La CARN LA5 ...... 25 D3
Greenslate Ct
  WGNW/BIL/OR WN5 ...... 255 C8
Greenslate Rd
  WGNW/BIL/OR WN5 ...... 255 H8
Greensnook La BCUP OL13 .. 179 K8
Greensnook Ter BCUP OL13 .. 179 K8
The Greens WHIT OL12 ...... 217 M2
Greenstone Av HOR/BR BL6... 231 K8
Green St ACC BB5 ...... 159 F1
  BRFD/BLYE BB10 ...... 142 E2
  BWCK/EAR BB18 ...... 293 Q5
  CHLY/EC PR7 ...... 207 K6
  CHLYE PR6 ...... 230 E3
  DWN BB3 ...... 191 K2
  GTH/LHO BB6 ...... 138 F6
  LANC LA1 ...... 3 J6
  LSTA FY8 ...... 146 D8
  MCMB LA4 ...... 41 H7
  PDHM/BLYW BB12 ...... 140 F4
  RAMS BL0 ...... 195 H8
  RAW/HAS BB4 ...... 177 L8
Green St East DWN BB3 .... 191 K2
Greensward Cl
  WGNW/BIL/OR WN5 ...... 245 L2
Greensway GAR/LONG PR3 .. 111 M8
The Green CARN LA5 ...... 32 F6
  CARN LA5 ...... 25 C1
  CHLY/EC PR7 ...... 205 M6
  CHLYE PR6 ...... 230 C1
  COL BB8 ...... 296 C5
  DWN BB3 * 191 K2
  FUL/RIB PR2 ...... 153 J2
  GAR/LONG PR3 ...... 90 D1
  KIRK/FR/WAR PR4 ...... 165 L8
  KIRK/FR/WAR PR4 ...... 127 L8
  KIRK/FR/WAR PR4 ...... 127 J1
  ROCH OL11 ...... 234 F8
  SKEL WN8 ...... 243 L1
  WGNW/BIL/OR WN5 ...... 255 L4
Greenthorn Crs FUL/RIB PR2. 153 K1
Greenthorne Cl EDGW/EG BL7. 213 H4
Greenvale ROCH OL11 ...... 234 A3
Greenview Dr ROCH OL11.... 234 C3
Greenville Dr HEY LA3 ...... 258 F2
Green Wk BWCK/EAR BB18.... 294 D6
  STHP PR8 ...... 221 G6
Green Wy BPOOLS FY4 ...... 125 L4
Greenway CHLY/EC PR6 ...... 205 L8
  CSBY/BLUN L23 ...... 257 K6
  FUL/RIB PR2 ...... 132 A4
  GAR/LONG PR3 ...... 284 C12
  HOR/BR BL6 ...... 232 C8

  PRES PR1 ...... 151 L7
Greenway Av SKEL WN8 ...... 253 L4
Greenway Cl SKEL WN8 ...... 253 H1
Greenways KIRK/FR/WAR PR4.. 183 J2
  KKBYL LA6 ...... 34 B3
  LSTA FY8 ...... 145 L5
Greenway St DWN BB3 ...... 173 J8
Greenwood La ORM L39 ...... 222 E8
Greenwich Cl ROCH OL11 .... 234 C5
Greenwich Dr LSTA FY8 ...... 146 A4
Greenwood BBR PR5 ...... 169 L7
Greenwood Av BPOOL FY1 .. 42 A1
  CARN LA5 ...... 25 D3
Greenwood Cl LSTA FY8 ...... 146 B7
  ORM L39 ...... 250 D7
Greenwood Crs CARN LA5 .. 42 E1
Greenwood Dr CARN LA5 ...... 42 E1
Greenwood St BBR PR5 ...... 169 H2
  LIT OL15 ...... 219 L6
  MILN OL16 ...... 235 J4
The Greenwood BBNW BB2 .. 173 G5
Greetby HI ORM L39 ...... 241 K6
Greetby Pl SKEL WN8 ...... 253 K3
Gregareth La LANC LA1 ...... 2 F7
Gregory Av BISP FY2 ...... 84 F6
Gregory Fold RAW/HAS BB4.... 194 D4
Gregory La ORM L39 ...... 222 E8
Gregory Meadow
  GAR/LONG PR3 ...... 284 A8
Gregory Pl LSTA FY8 ...... 146 D8
Gregory's Ct LANC LA1 ...... 54 F7
Gregson Cl BPOOLS FY4 ...... 125 J4
Gregson Dr FTWD FY7 ...... 81 J1
Gregson La BBNW BB2 * 10 D4
  BBR PR5 ...... 169 M1
Gregson Rd LANC LA1 ...... 3 K7
Gregson's Av FMBY L37 ...... 237 H6
Gregson St DWN BB3 ...... 191 K3
Gregson Wy FUL/RIB PR2 .. 132 E6
Grenada Cl DWN BB3 ...... 173 J5
Grenfell Av BPOOLE FY3 .... 105 H4
Grenville Av BBR PR5 ...... 169 G1
  FUL/RIB PR2 ...... 145 H2
Gresham Rd CLV/TH FY5 .... 85 G2
Gresham St RAW/HAS BB4.... 196 C2
Gresley Av HOR/BR BL6 ...... 231 M8
Gresley Ct LANC LA1 ...... 54 E5
Gresley Pl BISP FY2 ...... 105 H1
Gressingham Dr LANC LA1.... 54 F7
Greta Heath KKBYL LA6 ...... 31 H6
Greta Pl FTWD FY7 ...... 81 J1
  LANC LA1 ...... 3 K6
Gretdale Av LSTA FY8 ...... 145 H3
Gretna Crs CLV/TH FY5 ...... 85 G3
Gretna Rd BBN BB1 ...... 157 J2
Gretna Wk BBN BB1 ...... 157 J2
Greyfriars Av FUL/RIB PR2 .. 132 A6
Greyfriars Crs FUL/RIB PR2 .. 132 A6
Greyfriars Rd STHP PR8 .... 220 F8
Grey Heights Vw CHLYE PR6.. 208 B3
Greyhound Bridge Rd LANC LA1. 3 F6
Greystock Av FUL/RIB PR2 .. 132 B5
Greystock Cl BBR PR5 ...... 169 L3
Greystoke Av BBNW BB2 .... 172 B3
Greystoke Pl BPOOLS FY4 .. 124 E6
Greystone Av ORM L39 ...... 251 G1
Greystonegill La HGHB LA2 .. 39 M5
Grey Stone La TOD OL14 .... 301 Q10
Greystones CROS/BRETH PR26..185 L2
Greystones Dr
  PDHM/BLYW BB12 ...... 122 A3
Grey St BRFD/BLYE BB10 .... 142 D3
  NLSN BB9 ...... 123 C1
Greythwaite Ct LANC LA1 .... 2 C9
Griffin Cl ACC BB5 ...... 160 C2
  BLY BB11 ...... 141 L6
Griffin St BBNW BB2 ...... 156 E8
Griffiths Dr CHTN/BK PR9.... 200 C3
Grimeford La HOR/BR BL6.... 230 F6
Grimshaw La LANC LA1 ...... 55 J1
Grimes St WHIT OL12 ...... 234 C2
Grime St CHLY/EC PR7 ...... 208 A5
  NLSN BB9 ...... 191 J1
  RAMS BL0 ...... 214 D2
Grimrod Pl SKEL WN8 ...... 253 K4
Grindlestone Ct
  GAR/LONG PR3 ...... 113 H5
Grindlestone Hirst COL BB8 .. 103 M8
Grindleton Brow CLI BB7 .... 290 G8
Grindleton Cl BPOOLE FY3.... 105 L3
Grindleton Gv
  BRFD/BLYE BB10 ...... 143 C7
Grindleton Rd BBNW BB2 .. 10 A5
  CLI BB7 ...... 290 E9
Gringley Rd MCMB LA4 ...... 41 K8
Grinstead Dr STHP PR8 .... 221 J2
Grisedale Av GAR/LONG PR3 .. 284 A8
  LANC LA1 ...... 55 K4
  PLF/KEOS FY6 ...... 85 M8
Grisedale Br HGHB LA2 ...... 69 L8
Grisedale Cl ACC BB5 ...... 159 H1
  CLV/TH FY5 ...... 81 M4
Grisedale Crs FUL/RIB PR2 .. 153 K1
Grisedale Dr FUL/RIB PR2 .. 153 K1
  HEY LA3 ...... 52 F3
Grisedale Rd BPOOLS FY4.... 125 M4
  LANC LA1 ...... 55 K1
Grisedale Dr
  PDHM/BLYW BB12 ...... 141 L3
Grosvenor Cl NTHTN L30.... 258 C8
  STHP PR8 ...... 199 H8
Grosvenor Ct CARN LA5 .... 33 H1
Grosvenor Gdns STHP PR8.. 199 J8
  KIRK/FR/WAR PR4 ...... 33 H1
Grosvenor Pl CLV/TH FY5 .... 85 H4
Grosvenor Rd CARN LA5 .... 33 G1
  CHLY/EC PR7 ...... 207 K5
  HEY LA3 ...... 52 F2
  MGHL L31 ...... 258 F5
  STHP PR8 ...... 199 H7
Grosvenor St BPOOL FY1 .... 4 C6
  COL BB8 ...... 296 C6
  LSTA FY8 ...... 146 F8

  PDHM/BLYW BB12 ...... 6 E2
  PRES PR1 ...... 9 M4
Grouse St WHIT OL12 ...... 235 J2
Grove Av CHLYE PR6 ...... 230 D4
  KIRK/FR/WAR PR4 ...... 166 C3
Grove Ct ACC BB5 ...... 158 F8
Grove Crs CHLYE PR6 ...... 230 D4
Grove La PDHM/BLYW BB12 .. 141 H2
Grove Pk CHTN/BK PR9 ...... 200 C2
  ORM L39 ...... 241 J4
Grove Park Gdns SETT BD24 .. 265 K8
Grove Rd BBR PR5 ...... 152 F5
  SKEL WN8 ...... 254 E3
Grove St ACC BB5 ...... 158 F8
  BBNW BB2 ...... 10 E8
  BBR PR5 ...... 169 J3
  BCUP OL13 ...... 179 K8
  BLY BB11 * 6 E7
  BWCK/EAR BB18 ...... 294 A3
  LEYL PR25 ...... 186 A3
  LSTA FY8 ...... 145 L4
  MCMB LA4 ...... 41 G7
  NLSN BB9 ...... 103 H3
  ROCH OL11 ...... 235 H6
  STHP PR8 ...... 12 C1
Grove Ter STHP PR8 ...... 12 B8
The Grove ACC BB5 ...... 159 H6
  CARN LA5 ...... 33 G2
  CHLY/EC PR7 ...... 207 M1
  CLI BB7 ...... 118 F6
  CLI BB7 ...... 99 J2
  CLV/TH FY5 ...... 81 H8
  LANC LA1 ...... 3 J1
  ORM L39 ...... 250 F4
  PDHM/BLYW BB12 * .. 141 L5
  PRES PR1 ...... 151 J7
  WGNNW/ST WN6 ...... 244 F1
Grovewood STHP PR8 ...... 12 B8
Grovewood Dr
  WGNNW/ST WN6 ...... 245 H4
Grundy Cl WHIT OL12 ...... 200 B6
Grundy Ms BPOOLS FY4 .... 124 F4
Grundy's La CHLY/EC PR7 .... 229 M2
Guardian La WHIT OL12 .... 219 G6
Gubberford La GAR/LONG PR3. 284 A4
Guernsey Av CHLY/EC PR7 .. 187 C5
Guide La KIRK/FR/WAR PR4.. 121 K4
Guide Rd KIRK/FR/WAR PR4.. 164 C1
Guide Sq BBR PR5 ...... 173 L3
Guildford Av BISP FY2 ...... 84 F5
  CHLYE PR6 ...... 188 C7
Guildford Rd PRES PR1 ...... 9 K7
  STHP PR8 ...... 12 A1
Guildford St MILN OL16 .... 235 K4
Guildhall St PRES PR1 ...... 9 G6
Guild Rw PRES PR1 ...... 9 G5
Guild Wy FUL/RIB PR2 ...... 8 C5
Guilford St NLSN BB9 ...... 103 H3
Guinea Hall Cl CHTN/BK PR9.. 181 K6
Guinea Hall La CHTN/BK PR9. 181 K6
Gulf La GAR/LONG PR3 ...... 268 E12
  HGHB LA2 ...... 269 K10
Gummers Howe Wk CARN LA5. 33 K3
Gurney St BBNW BB2 ...... 156 E8
Gutter La RAMS BL0 ...... 214 E4
Guysyke COL BB8 ...... 103 M7
Gynn Av BPOOL FY1 ...... 104 E3
Gypsy La ROCH OL11 ...... 234 F8

H

Habergham Dr
  PDHM/BLYW BB12 ...... 141 J3
Habergham St
  PDHM/BLYW BB12 ...... 140 F2
Hackensall Rd PLF/KEOS FY6.. 78 B7
Hacking Cl GTH/LHO BB6 .... 137 M2
Hacking Dr GAR/LONG PR3.... 114 C6
Hacking St DWN BB3 ...... 191 J2
  NLSN BB9 ...... 123 J1
Hacklands Av FUL/RIB PR2.... 150 E2
Haddings La
  PDHM/BLYW BB12 ...... 121 K2
Haddon Pl FUL/RIB PR2 ...... 132 A3
Haddon Rd BISP FY2 ...... 84 F6
Haddon St ROCH OL11 ...... 235 H6
Hadlee Ter LANC LA1 ...... 2 C4
Hadleigh Rd PLF/KEOS FY6.. 85 M5
Hadrian's Av HEY LA3 ...... 41 M8
Hadstock Av FMBY L37 ...... 247 G2
Hagg St COL BB8 ...... 103 M7
Haig Av FUL/RIB PR2 * 152 A1
Haig La GAR/LONG PR3 ...... 88 F3
  KIRK/FR/WAR PR4 ...... 183 K4
  LANC LA1 ...... 2 E2
  LEYL PR25 ...... 186 C2
  STHP PR8 ...... 200 B6
Haighton Green La
  FUL/RIB PR2 ...... 133 H1
Haig Rd BPOOL FY1 ...... 4 C9
Hail St RAMS BL0 * 214 D2
Hala Crs LANC LA1 ...... 54 F8
Hala Gv LANC LA1 ...... 54 F8
Hala Hi LANC LA1 ...... 55 G8
Hala Rd LANC LA1 ...... 54 F8
Hala Sq LANC LA1 ...... 54 F8
Halcyon Cl WHIT OL12 ...... 234 L1
Haldane Rd DWN BB3 ...... 173 H7
Haldane St BRFD/BLYE BB10 *. 142 E1
Halden Rd HEY LA3 ...... 40 F8
Hale Carr Gv HEY LA3 ...... 52 F2
Hale Carr La HEY LA3 ...... 52 F2
Hales Rushes Rd
  GAR/LONG PR3 ...... 83 M8
Hale St BLY BB11 ...... 7 H8
Half Acre BBR PR5 ...... 168 D3
Half Acre Dr ROCH OL11 .... 234 E5
Half Acre La ROCH OL11 .... 234 E5
Half Acre Ms ROCH OL11 .... 234 E5
Half Acre Rd ROCH OL11 .... 234 E5
Halford Pl CLV/TH FY5 ...... 85 H4
Halfpenny La CHLY/EC PR7 .. 205 L8
Halifax Crs CSBY/BLUN L23 .. 257 L5
  NLSN BB9 ...... 122 F1
  STHP PR8 ...... 199 H7
Halifax St BPOOLE FY3 ...... 5 F8

Haliwell St LIT OL15 ...... 219 H5
Hallam Crs NLSN BB9 ...... 123 J1
Hallam La HEY LA3 64
Hallam Rd NLSN BB9 ...... 123 L1
Hallam St ACC BB5 ...... 159 L4
Hallam Wy BPOOLS FY4 .... 126 B3
Hallbridge Gdns WGNW/BIL/OR WN8. 254 F2
Hall Av BPOOLS FY4 ...... 126 F5
Hall Brow ORM L39 ...... 241 H8
Hall Carr La KIRK/FR/WAR PR4.. 166 A4
Hall Carr Rd RAW/HAS BB4 .. 195 J3
Hall Cl HGHB LA2 44
  RAW/HAS BB4 177
  WGNNW/ST WN6 245
Hall Cft KIRK/FR/WAR PR4 .. 167 C2
Hallcroft SKEL WN8 253
Hall Dr HEY LA3 64
  HGHB LA2 44
  MCMB LA4 41
Halley Rd DWN BB3 ...... 173 H5
Hallfield Rd GTH/LHO BB6.... 138
Hall Fold WHIT OL12 217
Hall Gdns WHIT OL12 234
Hall Ga CHLY/EC PR7 207
Hallgate HI CLI BB7 ...... 275 M4
Hall Gate La BRSC L40 205
Hall Gn SKEL WN8 254
Hall Green Cl SKEL WN8 254
Hall Green La BRSC L40 205
Hall Gv HEY LA3 64
Hall HI CLI BB7 288
Halling Pl TOD OL14 303
Halliwell Cl CHLY/EC PR7 *.. 207
Halliwell Hts BBR PR5 153
Halliwell La CHLYE PR6 187
Halliwell Pl CHLY/EC PR7 .. 207
Halliwell St ACC BB5 176
  CHLY/EC PR7 207
  WHIT OL12 235
Hall La BRSC L40 ...... 242 C2
  GAR/LONG PR3 88
  HOR/BR BL6 231
  HTWN L38 248
  KIRK/FR/WAR PR4 166
  LEYL PR25 186
  MGHL L31 259
  MGHL L31 249
  NWD/KWIPK L33 260
  ORM L39 252
  WGNNW/ST WN6 244
  WGNW/BIL/OR WN5 255
Hallmoor Cl ORM L39 251
Hallows Cl GAR/LONG PR3.... 89
Hallows Farm Av WHIT OL12. 235
Hall Pk LANC LA1 54
Hall Park Av BRFD/BLYE BB10.. 143
Hall Park Dr CLV/TH FY5 146
Hall Rd BRSC L40 223
  COL BB8 296
  FUL/RIB PR2 132
  PRES PR1 152
Hall Rd East CSBY/BLUN L23 .. 256
Hall Rd West CSBY/BLUN L23.. 256
Hallroyd Crs TOD OL14 303
Hallroyd Pl TOD OL14 303
Hallroyd Rd TOD OL14 303
Hallsall Dr MCMB LA4 42
Hall's Sq CHLYE PR6 188
Hall St BBNW BB2 10
  BCUP OL13 179
  BLY BB11 7
  BRFD/BLYE BB10 143
  CHTN/BK PR9 13
  CLI BB7 99
  COL BB8 296
  FUL/RIB PR2 7
  MCMB LA4 41
  RAW/HAS BB4 194
  WHIT OL12 217
Halltine Cl CSBY/BLUN L23 .. 256
Hallwell St BRFD/BLYE BB10.. 142
Hallwood Cl BRFD/BLYE BB10.. 122
Hallwood Cl CHLY/EC PR7 .. 207
Halmote Av
  PDHM/BLYW BB12 121
Halsall Blds CHTN/BK PR9 .. 13
Halsall Cl CSBY/BLUN L23 .. 257
Halsall Hall Dr ORM L39 239
Halsall La FMBY L37 237
  ORM L39 240
Halsall Manor Ct ORM L39 .. 239
Halsall Rd ORM L39 239
  STHP PR8 221
Halsbury St PRES PR1 9
Halstead Cl NLSN BB9 103
Halstead La NLSN BB9 103
Halstead Rd FUL/RIB PR2 .. 133
Halston St BLY BB11 6
Halton Av CLV/TH FY5 81
  LEYL PR25 187
Halton Cha BRSC L40 242
Halton Ct MCMB LA4 41
Halton Gdns BPOOLS FY4 .. 125
Halton Pl CLV/TH FY5 133
  GAR/LONG PR3 114
Halton Rd KKBYL LA6 33
  LANC LA1 3
  MGHL L31 250
Halton St KIRK/FR/WAR PR4.. 166
Halton Wd KKBY L32 259
Hambledon Dr PRES PR1 168
Hambledon St
  PDHM/BLYW BB12 141
Hambledon Vw
  PDHM/BLYW BB12 140
Hambleton Cl
  KIRK/FR/WAR PR4 166
Hameldon Ap BLY BB11 6
Hameldon Av ACC BB5 176
Hameldon Cl BLY BB11 140
Hameldon Rd BLY BB11 160
  RAW/HAS BB4 177
Hameldon Vw GTH/LHO BB6.. 139
Hamer Av BBN BB1 158
  RAW/HAS BB4 177
Hamer Hall Crs WHIT OL12... 235
Hamer La MILN OL16 235
Hamer Rd FUL/RIB PR2 133
Hamer St DWN BB3 191
Hamerswood Dr
  GAR/LONG PR3 91
Hamilton Cl LSTA FY8 147
Hamilton Ct LANC LA1 3
Hamilton Gv FUL/RIB PR2.... 133
Hamilton Rd CHLY/EC PR7 .. 187
  COL BB8 123
  FUL/RIB PR2 8
  MCMB LA4 42

NLSN BB9 ....122 F2
Hamilton St BBNW BB2.........10 B8
Hamlet Cl BBNW BB2 *...........10 B7
Hamlet Gv KIRK/FR/WAR PR4 ...109 J7
Hamlet Rd FTWD FY7 ....77 H7
The Hamlet CHLY/EC PR7 *....230 C2
LSTA FY8 ....145 J1
Hammerton Gn BCUP OL13 ....179 K8
Hammerton Hall La LANC LA1...42 C7
Hammerton Pl BPOOLE FY3.....105 K3
Hammerton St BCUP OL13 ....179 J7
BLY BB11 ....6 G1
Hammond Av BCUP OL13 ....197 G3
Hammond Ct PRES PR1...........152 D4
Hammond Dr
 PDHM/BLYW BB12 ....139 K2
Hammond Rd
 NWD/KWIPK L33 ....260 F8
Hammond's Rw PRES PR1 ....9 J4
Hammond St NLSN BB9 ....123 J4
 PRES PR1.............................152 B2
Hampden Av DWN BB3...........191 L4
Hampden Rd LEYL PR25 ....186 D1
Hampden St BLY BB11..............7 J8
 LSTA FY8 ....235 J5
Hampsfell Dr MCMB LA4..........41 J8
Hampshire Av NTHTN L30 ......257 M8
Hampshire Cl BBN BB1...........137 K4
Hampshire Pl BPOOLS FY4 .....125 J3
Hampshire Rd BBN BB1..........158 D2
 BBR PR5 ....153 G8
Hampson Av LEYL PR25 ....187 G2
Hampson Gv PLF/KEOS FY6 .....78 D7
Hampson La HGHB LA2..........270 B2
Hampson St HOR/BR BL6........231 L7
Hampstead Cl LSTA FY8 ....146 B5
Hampstead Ms BPOOLS FY1 *...104 F4
Hampstead Rd FUL/RIB PR2....153 G1
Hampton Cl CHLY/EC PR7 ......207 L5
Hampton Ct LSTA FY8.............145 M3
Hampton Pl CLV/TH FY5............81 H8
Hampton Rd BPOOLS FY4.......124 C3
 FMBY L37 ....40 F8
 HEY LA3................................52 E3
 STHP PR8............................13 H9
The Hamptons PLF/KEOS FY6...78 C5
Hampton St FUL/RIB PR2.......151 M1
Hanbury Rd FUL/RIB PR2 *.....151 M2
Hancock St BBNW BB2............10 B7
The Handbridge FUL/RIB PR2..152 B6
Hand La BRSC L40..................205 J6
Handley Rd BPOOL FY1 ....104 F5
Handley St WHIT OL12 ....235 G3
Handshaw Dr PRES PR1.........168 D1
Hands La ROCH OL11 ....234 D4
Handsworth Cl BPOOL FY1 ....104 F4
Handsworth Rd BPOOL FY1....104 F4
Hanging Green La HGHB LA2 *....5
Hangington Clough Br
 HGHB LA2 ....272 D2
Hanley Cl PLF/KEOS FY6 ....82 F1
Hannah Ct CHLY/EC PR7.........187 H5
Hannah St ACC BB5...............159 L6
 BCUP OL13 ....179 K8
 DWN BB3 ....191 K2
Hanover Crs BISP FY2 ....84 F1
Hanover St B COL BB8 ....296 F5
 LIT OL15 ....219 K6
 MCMB LA4..............................41 J8
 PRES PR1...............................9 H1
Hansby Cl SKEL WN8..............254 B3
Hanson St BBN BB1 *............158 D7
 CHLY PR7 ....230 C1
 GTH/LHO BB6.......................138 F7
Hanstock Cl
 WGNW/BIL/OR WN5............255 G6
Hants La ORM L39..................241 H5
Happy Mount Ct MCMB LA4...42 A4
Happy Mount Dr MCMB LA4...41 M4
Hapton Rd PDHM/BLYW BB12 ..140 F8
Hapton St CLV/TH FY5...............81 G7
 PDHM/BLYW BB12 ....140 K1
Hapton Wy RAW/HAS BB4.....177 K1
Harbour Av KIRK/FR/WAR PR4..148 B5
Harbour Cl FTWD FY7...............81 J1
Harbour La CHLYE PR6...........189 G4
 EDGW/EG BL7.......................213 C4
 KIRK/FR/WAR PR4................148 B4
Harbour Wy FTWD FY7.............77 G2
Harbury Av STHP PR8............220 D7
Harcourt Rd ACC BB5.............160 A8
 BBNW BB2.............................10 A2
 BPOOLS FY4 ....125 G3
 LANC LA1...............................42 D8
Harcourt St BCUP OL13 ....179 K8
 BLY BB11 *..............................6 A5
 PRES PR1...........................152 B2
Hardacre La CHLYE PR6.........187 G4
 CLI BB7 ....292 E4
Hardacre St ORM L39.............241 J5
Hardhorn Rd PLF/KEOS FY6...106 C4
Hardhorn Wy PLF/KEOS FY6...106 K1
Harding Rd BRSC L40..............205 U7
Harding St BCUP OL13...........230 K3
Hard Knott Ri CARN LA5...........33 K3
Hardlands Av MCMB LA4.........42 A7
Hard La WHIT OL12 ....218 A1
Hardman Av RAW/HAS BB4 ...195 K4
Hardman Cl BBN BB1..............158 D1
 RAW/HAS BB4.....................196 C4
Hardman Dr RAW/HAS BB4...196 C3
Hardman St BBNW BB2..........10 B8
 BPOOL FY1..........................104 F1
Hardman Wy DWN BB3...........191 K4
Hardsough La RAMS BL0........194 F3
Hardwicke St PRES PR1 *..........9 J2
 ROCH OL11 ....235 K1
Hardy Av NLSN BB9 ....122 G3
Hardy Cl FUL/RIB PR2............151 J3
 ROCH OL11 ....235 K3
Hardy Ct NLSN BB9 *.............123 J4
Hardy Dr CHLY/EC PR7 ....207 L4
Hardy St BBN BB1..................157 J2
 NLSN BB9............................122 F3
Harebell Cl BBNW BB2 *.........247 J2
 WHIT OL12 ....218 A4
Hare Clough Cl BBNW BB2 *.....11 H8
Hare Ct TOD OL14 ....301 K12
Hareholme La RAW/HAS BB4..196 A2
Hare Hill Rd LIT OL15 ....219 K6
Harehill St TOD OL14 ....303 K1
Hareholme La RAW/HAS BB4..196 A2
Hares La STHP PR8 ....223 J4
Harestone CHLY/EC PR7.......207 L4
Hare St ROCH OL11 ....235 J6
Harefield Av ROCH OL11 ......235 D2
Harefield Ri
 PDHM/BLYW BB12 ....142 A3

Harewood CHLY/EC PR7........207 L1
Harewood Av BPOOLE FY3.....105 K2
 HEY LA3.................................52 F1
 LANC LA1.............................54 F8
 PDHM/BLYW BB12 ....140 B3
 ROCH OL11 ....234 A1
 STHP PR8 ....220 F5
Harewood Cl PLF/KEOS FY6 ...85 M6
Harewood Rd PRES PR1........152 C6
Hargate Av ROCH OL11........234 D1
Hargate Rd CLV/TH FY5...........85 M1
Hargher St BLY BB11 *..............6 F2
Hargreaves Av LEYL PR25 .....186 A5
Hargreaves Ct CLI BB7............98 F4
Hargreaves Dr
 FUL/RIB PR2 ....131 J7
 RAW/HAS BB4 ....178 C5
Hargreaves Fold La
 RAW/HAS BB4 ....178 C4
Hargreaves La BBNW BB2.....123 J8
Hargreaves Rd ACC BB5.......158 C2
Hargreaves St ACC BB5........159 M6
 BLY BB11................................6 A1
 BRFD/BLYE BB10 ....123 J8
 CLV/TH FY5.............................81 L8
 COL BB8 ....103 J1
 NLSN BB9............................122 F3
 RAW/HAS BB4 ....178 A4
 RAW/HAS BB4 ....178 C5
 ROCH OL11 ....234 F7
 STHP PR8 ....13 K5
Hargrove Av
 PDHM/BLYW BB12 ....140 F2
 PDHM/BLYW BB12 ....6 A2
Harington Cl FMBY L37..........237 E2
Harington Rd FMBY L37.........237 F2
Harington Rd FMBY L37.........236 F7
Harland St FUL/RIB PR2........131 A8
Harland Wy WHIT OL12..........234 D1
Harlech Av BPOOL FY1..............5 L6
Harlech Cl RAW/HAS BB4......194 A3
Harlech Dr ACC BB5..............158 F7
 LEYL PR25 ....186 E2
Harlech Gv CLV/TH FY5...........86 A1
Harleston Rd NWD/KWIPK L33..260 D3
Harley Cl HGHB LA2 ....38 C7
Harley St BPOOLS FY4............125 J3
 TOD OL14 ....303 L1
Harley Wd TOD OL14 ....300 H11
Harling Bank KKBYL LA6..........21 L1
Harling Rd PRES PR1.............153 G2
Harling St PDHM/BLYW BB12 ..141 L5
 BPOOLS FY4 ....125 K5
Harold Av BLY BB11................141 M7
Harold Lees Rd HEYW OL10 ...234 A6
Harold St BLY BB11 ....6 C8
 COL BB8 ....103 M7
 MILN OL16 ....235 M1
Harold Ter BBN BB1...............168 D5
Harpers La PDHM/BLYW BB12 ..122 A3
Harper's La CHLYE PR6...........208 A2
Harper St BWCK/EAR BB18....293 P5
 ROCH OL11 ....235 M6
Harp's Cft NTHTN L30............257 M8
Harridge Av WHIT OL12..........217 M8
Harridge La ORM L39..............240 C3
Harridge St WHIT OL12...........217 M8
The Harridge WHIT OL12.......217 M8
Harrier Ct LANC LA1.................2 A1
Harrier Dr BBN BB1................157 G3
Harriet St BLY BB11..................6 D6
Harriett St MILN OL16............235 K4
Harrington Av BPOOL FY1........5 L7
Harrington Rd CHLY/EC PR7 ...207 L3
 CSBY/BLUN L23....................257 C7
 HEY LA3.................................40 F3
Harrington St ACC BB5..........159 K2
Harris Av BPOOL FY1 ....5 L7
Harris Ct CLI BB7 *..................99 H3
Harrison Av CLV/TH FY5...........85 L1
Harrison Cl WHIT OL12..........234 A1
Harrison Crs HEY LA3...............52 E2
 HOR/BR BL6........................230 F6
Harrison Dr COL BB8.............103 M5
 RNFD/HAY WA11................262 C4
Harrison La KIRK/FR/WAR PR4..167 L1
Harrison Rd CHLY/EC PR7 .....230 D5
 CHLY/EC PR7.......................207 M5
Harrison St BBNW BB2..........10 C8
 BCUP OL13 ....197 G3
 BPOOL FY1 ....4 F7
 BRFD/BLYE BB10 ....143 J4
 BWCK/EAR BB18 ....231 L7
 HOR/BR BL6........................231 G7
 RAMS BL0 ....215 M6
 TOD OL14 ....300 E10
Harris Rd WGNNW/ST WN6...245 L1
Harris St FTWD FY7..................77 K7
 PRES PR1...............................9 J1
Harrock Cl BRSC L40..............227 J3
 WGNNW/ST WN6................227 K7
Harrock Rd LEYL PR25............187 G2
Harrocks St NTHTN L30..........258 C6
Harrock Vw CHLY/EC PR7 *....227 M2
Harrod St STHP PR8..............199 J3
Harrogate Crs
 PDHM/BLYW BB12 ....143 G1
Harrogate Rd LSTA FY8.........145 M4
Harrogate Wy CHTN/BK PR9...180 D3
Harrop Pl FUL/RIB PR2...........133 H7
Harrops Cft NTHTN L30 ....258 B6
Harrow Av ACC BB5...............159 M4
 FTWD FY7.............................77 J7
 ROCH OL11 ....234 D5
Harrow Cl NTHTN L30............258 C8
 PDHM/BLYW BB12 ....141 H5
 WGNW/BIL/OR WN5............255 J3
Harrowdale Pk HGHB LA2......43 L4
Harrow Dr BBN BB1.................11 L4
Harrow Gv MCMB LA4............42 A7
Harrow Pl BPOOLS FY4..........124 A6
 LSTA FY8 ....146 A6
Harrowside BPOOLS FY4........124 D5
Harrowside West BPOOLS FY4..124 D6
Harrow Stiles La BCUP OL13 ..179 L6
Harrow St LANC LA1...............159 H7
Harry Potts Wy
 BRFD/BLYE BB10 ....7 J4
Harry St NLSN BB9................103 J8
 ROCH OL11 ....234 E8
Harsnips SKEL WN8...............253 M1
Harswell Cl
 WGNW/BIL/OR WN5............255 H6
Hartdale Rd CSBY/BLUN L23..257 K5
Hartford Av BPOOL FY3 *........85 J1
Hartington Rd CHLYE PR6......189 J3
 DWN BB3 *...........................173 H7
 PRES PR1...............................8 D5

Hartington St BBN BB1 *.......158 D2
 LANC LA1................................3 H1
 NLSN BB9............................122 E6
Hartland Av TOT/BURYW BL8 ..180 K5
Hartlands Cl BRFD/BLYE BB10 ..123 G8
Hartlebury Rd BBN BB1 *.......235 H5
Hartlet St GTH/LHO BB6 ......139 G6
Hartley Av ACC BB5..............159 K8
Hartley Crs STHP PR8............221 J1
Hartley Gn SKP/WHF BD23....267 K6
Hartley Gv
 WGNW/BIL/OR WN5............255 L4
Hartley La ROCH OL11...........235 H7
Hartley Rd STHP PR8.............221 J1
Hartleys Ter COL BB8.............296 F2
Hartleys St ACC BB5..............159 H7
 BBN BB1 *............................10 E2
 BLY BB11..............................141 M6
 BWCK/EAR BB18..................294 D6
 COL BB8 ....296 F5
 GTH/LHO BB6.....................139 G5
 LIT OL15 ....219 K6
 NLSN BB9............................123 H4
 WGNW/BIL/OR WN5............255 L5
 WHIT OL12 ....218 A5
Hartmann St ACC BB5............159 K5
Hartshead SKEL WN8.............253 M1
Hart's La SKEL WN8...............254 C3
Hart St BBN BB1 ....11 H5
 BLY BB11 *...........................7 H3
 STHP PR8............................13 M5
Hart Street Br STHP PR8........13 M5
Hartwood Gn CHLY/EC PR6 ...197 M8
Hartwood Rd CHTN/BK PR9 ...13 M2
Harvard St ROCH OL11...........235 K7
Harvelin Pk TOD OL14...........303 M1
Harvester Dr CHLYE PR6........187 M5
Harvesters Fold
 KIRK/FR/WAR PR4 ....109 J7
Harvester Wy NTHTN L30......258 D7
Harvey St COL BB8................159 G7
 NLSN BB9............................123 H7
 WHIT OL12 ....235 L2
Harvington Dr STHP PR8........220 D6
Harwich Rd LSTA FY8.............145 J2
Harwin Cl WHIT OL12............218 A8
Harwood Av LSTA FY8............145 H3
Harwood Av PLF/KEOS FY6.....82 F4
Harwood Ga GTH/LHO BB6....139 H5
Harwood New Rd
 GTH/LHO BB6......................139 H5
 BBN BB1 ....138 A7
Harwood's La DWN BB3.........192 A2
Harwood St BBN BB1..............11 L2
 DWN BB3 ....191 H1
 RAMS BL0 ....215 H1
 WHIT OL12 ....219 J6
Hasburry Dr CLV/TH FY5..........85 M1
Haslam Cl BRFD/BLYE BB10...142 D3
Haslam Dr ORM L39...............241 G4
Haslam St WHIT OL12............235 G3
Haslemere Av BPOOLS FY4......5 G6
Haslingden New Rd BBN BB1...174 A3
Haslingden Old Rd BBN BB1...158 B6
 RAW/HAS BB4 ....195 H1
Haslingden Rd ACC BB5.........174 A5
 BBN BB1...............................11 J9
 RAW/HAS BB4 ....195 G2
Haslow Pl BPOOLE FY3...........105 J4
Hassall Dr KIRK/FR/WAR PR4...108 D2
Hassett Cl PRES PR1...............8 E7
Hastings Av BISP FY2...............85 H6
Hastings Cl
 KIRK/FR/WAR PR4 ....148 B4
Hastings Pl LSTA FY8.............146 D8
Hastings Rd CLV/TH FY5..........85 M2
 FUL/RIB PR2 ....151 L2
 KIRK/FR/WAR PR4................148 C3
 LANC LA1.............................54 E6
 LEYL PR25 ....186 E1
 STHP PR8............................221 H2
Hatfield Av FTWD FY7..............81 H1
 MCMB LA4............................42 A7
Hatfield Gdns FTWD FY7..........81 H1
Hatfield Ms FTWD FY7 *...........81 J1
Hatfield Rd ACC BB5..............160 A3
 FUL/RIB PR2 ....133 H8
Hatfield Wk FTWD FY7 *..........81 H1
Hathaway BPOOLS FY4..........125 J3
Hathaway Cl MGHL L31.........258 E4
Hathaway Fold
 PDHM/BLYW BB12 ....141 G4
Hathaway Rd FTWD FY7...........77 H4
Hatlex Dr HGHB LA2...............42 D1
Hatlex HI HGHB LA2...............42 D1
Hatlex La HGHB LA2 ....42 D1
Hatters Br BWCK/EAR BB18 ...294 A10
Hattersley St BLY BB11 *...........6 D3
Hatton St CHLY/EC PR7..........230 C5
Haugh Av PDHM/BLYW BB12 ..140 B2
Haugh Rd TOD OL14 ....303 M1
Haunders La
 KIRK/FR/WAR PR4 ....183 L2
 BBR PR5 *............................169 H1
 BRFD/BLYE BB10 ....142 F7
Haydon Av STHP PR8 ....168 D4
Hayes Dr MGHL L31...............259 J1
Hayfell Av MCMB LA4..............41 J8
Hayfell Crs MCMB LA4.............42 C2
Hayfell Gv HGHB LA2 ....42 D2
Hayfield Av BBR PR5...............170 B2
Hayfield Av BBR PR5...............170 H1
 BISP FY2 ....105 H1
Hayfield Cl BBR PR5...............170 H1
Hayfield Rd ORM L39.............241 H4
Hayfields BWCK/EAR BB18 ....294 D5
Hayhurst Cl CLI BB7 *............118 C5
Hayhurst Farm Ter CLI BB7....99 H5
Hayhurst Rd CLI BB7..............118 C5
Hayling Pl FUL/RIB PR2..........131 J7
Haylot Dr HGHB LA2...............43 L4
Haylot Sq LANC LA1.................3 H1
Haymaker Ri WHIT OL12........218 A5
Haymans Gn MGHL L31.........259 J2
Haynes St WHIT OL12............235 H9
Hays La GTH/LHO BB6............139 H4
Haysworth St PRES PR1.........152 C1
Haywards Ms CAR/LONG PR3..159 G2
Haywood Av ACC BB5............159 L5
 FUL/RIB PR2 ....132 D7
Haywood Rd ACC BB5............159 J4
Hazel Av ACC BB5..................160 A7
 BBNW BB2.............................11 C8
 DWN BB3 ....173 J7
 FTWD FY7..............................81 J3

Haweswater Rd ACC BB5.......160 A2
Hawfinch Cl BCUP OL13.........197 K1
Hawick Cl NWD/KWIPK L33....260 K1
Hawkhurst Av HEY LA3............52 E1
Hawkhurst Rd PRES PR1...........8 E1
Hawking Pl BISP FY2...............85 H3
Hawkins Cl PRES PR1.............152 E1
Hawkins St BBNW BB2.............8 E1
Hawkley Wy LIT OL15 ....219 M2
Hawksbury Dr PRES PR1........168 A1
Hawksclough SKEL WN8.........253 M1
Hawks Gv RAW/HAS BB4........195 K2
Hawkshaw Av DWN BB3.........173 H8
Hawkshaw Bank Rd BBN BB1..157 G3
Hawkshaw Cl
 TOT/BURYW BL8..................213 L8
Hawkshaw La
 TOT/BURYW BL8..................213 L7
Hawkshead PRES PR1............152 B8
Hawkshead Av CHLY/EC PR7 ..207 G2
Hawkshead Cl MGHL L31........259 H1
Hawkshead Dr MCMB LA4.......41 K8
Hawkshead Rd FUL/RIB PR2...133 H6
 PLF/KEOS FY6 ....78 C5
Hawkshead St BBNW BB2......156 F7
 CHTN/BK PR9........................13 K2
Hawkstone Cl ACC BB5..........160 C2
Hawk St BLY BB11 ....7 H5
 CARN LA5...............................33 K1
Hawkswood CHLY/EC PR7 .....205 L5
Hawksworth Cl FMBY L37......237 E5
Hawksworth Dr FMBY L37......237 K5
Hawksworth Gv HEY LA3..........52 E3
Hawkwood St ACC BB5..........159 L3
Hawthorn Av ACC BB5...........225 J7
 DWN BB3 ....191 M1
 FTWD FY7..............................81 H3
 HGHB LA2..............................44 E6
 RAMS BL0 ....215 H1
 WGNW/BIL/OR WN5............255 J5
Hawthorn Bank ACC BB5 *.....139 K8
Hawthorn Cl CLI BB7..............118 D4
 CROS/BRETH PR26 *............186 A1
 GTH/LHO BB6......................138 A3
 HGHB LA2..............................44 E6
 KIRK/FR/WAR PR4................167 K4
 KIRK/FR/WAR PR4................128 D5
Hawthorn Crs FUL/RIB PR2....151 G2
 SKEL WN8............................253 H2
Hawthorn Dr BBN BB1............158 E3
 BBR PR5...............................153 M8
 BRFD/BLYE BB10 ....123 G8
 GAR/LONG PR3....................284 A7
 KIRK/FR/WAR PR4................129 J3
Hawthorne Crs FMBY L37......247 E2
Hawthorne Dr
 BWCK/EAR BB18..................293 R4
Hawthorne Gv CHTN/BK PR9..200 C4
 NLSN BB9 *...........................103 C8
 PLF/KEOS FY6 ....85 K6
Hawthorne Mdw
 RAW/HAS BB4 ....177 K2
Hawthorne Pl CLI BB7.............99 H4
Hawthorne Rd BLY BB11...........6 A3
 CLV/TH FY5.............................85 L3
Hawthorne St BBN BB1..........157 H3
Hawthorn Pl TOD OL14 *........303 M1
Hawthorn Rd BPOOL FY1.......104 F4
 CARN LA5...............................32 F5
 FUL/RIB PR2 ....153 H1
 MCMB LA4............................42 A7
 ROCH OL11 ....234 B3
The Hawthorns BBN BB1 *.....205 H4
 CHLY/EC PR7.......................205 L4
 FUL/RIB PR2 ....132 C5
 GAR/LONG PR3....................284 A7
 GAR/LONG PR3......................91 K7
 KIRK/FR/WAR PR4................131 H1
 LANC LA1.............................66 F1
 LSTA FY8 ....145 J3
The Haw Thorns SKEL WN8....243 H7
Hawthorn Wk LIT OL15 ....219 K6
Hawton Rd BLY BB11..............157 H3
 HOR/BR BL6........................231 G7
Haydock Av LEYL PR25...........186 D3
Haydock Gv HEY LA3...............52 E2
Haydock Park Rd AIN/FAZ L10..259 H3
Haydock Rd LANC LA1.............55 G3
Haydocks
 KIRK/FR/WAR PR4 ....131 G6
Haydock St BBN BB1..............157 H2
 BBR PR5 *............................169 H1
 BRFD/BLYE BB10 ....142 F7
Haydon Av STHP PR8 ....168 D4
Hayes Dr MGHL L31...............259 J1

KKBY L32 ....259 M8
Hazel Bank BBNW BB2 *.........10 A1
 HEY LA3.................................52 E4
Hazelbank HGHB LA2 ....43 K5
Hazelbank Gdns FMBY L37 *..237 H6
Hazel Cl BBNW BB2................169 J2
 BBR PR5...............................169 J3
 BLY BB11 *.............................78 C5
 PRES PR1.............................151 L8
Hazel Coppice FUL/RIB PR2 ...131 H6
Hazeldene Rd FTWD FY7..........81 H1
Hazel Gv ACC BB5..................159 K1
 BBN BB1...............................158 D6
 BBR PR5...............................169 J2
 BCUP OL13 ....179 L8
 BPOOLE FY3..........................5 J2
 CHLYE PR6............................187 M8
 CLI BB7 ....98 F4
 CSBY/BLUN L23....................257 J8
 FUL/RIB PR2 ....133 K7
 GAR/LONG PR3....................114 E3
 KIRK/FR/WAR PR4................183 J3
 LANC LA1...............................2 C5
 RAW/HAS BB4 ....177 J3
 STHP PR8............................220 D5
Hazelhurst St ACC BB5 *........214 D2
Hazelhurst Dr GAR/LONG PR3..288 R8
Hazelhurst Rd FUL/RIB PR2....153 K1
Hazel La SKEL WN8................243 G7
Hazelmere Rd FUL/RIB PR2....151 G2
Hazel Ms MGHL L31 *.............259 L8
Hazelmount Av CARN LA5.......26 A8
Hazelmount Crs CARN LA5......26 A8
Hazelrigg La HGHB LA2 ....42 A1
The Hazels BBN BB1...............137 H5
 CHLY/EC PR7.......................229 H2
Hazel St ACC BB5..................176 D3
 RAMS BL0 ....214 D7
Hazelwood CARN LA5.............16 J7
Hazelwood Av BRSC L40........225 H7
Hazelwood Cl BBN BB1...........157 K2
 LEYL PR25 ....186 E2
Hazelwood Dr
 KIRK/FR/WAR PR4 ....165 G7
 MCMB LA4............................42 A5
Hazelwood Gdns LANC LA1...66 F1
Hazelwood Rd NLSN BB9.......123 K3
Hazelwood St TOD OL14........303 C3
Hazelhurst Cl FMBY L37.........246 F1
Hazlewood Cl CLV/TH FY5.......85 K1
Headbolt La NWD/KWIPK L33..260 K7
 ORM L39..............................221 G7
Head Dyke La GAR/LONG PR3...79 J8
Headen Av
 WGNW/BIL/OR WN5............255 L6
Headfort Cl BISP FY2..............105 L2
Headingley Cl ACC BB5..........160 C2
Headingly St WHIT OL12........234 C5
Headlands St WHIT OL12.......235 H2
The Headlands HEY LA3..........52 C4
Headley Rd LEYL PR25...........186 B2
Headroomgate Back Rd
 LSTA FY8 ....145 J3
Headroomgate Rd LSTA FY8...145 J3
Heads La BWCK/EAR BB18.....294 E6
Heald Cl BCUP OL13...............219 K3
 WHIT OL12 ....217 M8
Heald Cft GAR/LONG PR3......284 C9
Heald Dr WHIT OL12..............217 M8
Heald House Rd LEYL PR25....186 F3
Heald La BCUP OL13..............179 K4
 LIT OL15 ....219 K8
Heald Rd BRFD/BLYE BB10....142 D1
Heald St CHLYE PR6..............208 A3
Healdwood Cl
 PDHM/BLYW BB12 ....122 C8
Healdwood Dr
 PDHM/BLYW BB12 ....122 C8
Healey Av HEYW OL10 *.........234 B8
 WHIT OL12 ....218 A1
Healey Ct BLY BB11..................6 E6
Healey Gv WHIT OL12............217 M6
Healey La WHIT OL12.............218 B7
Healey Mt BLY BB11.................6 E7
Healey Rw BLY BB11................6 E7
Healey St BPOOLE FY3...........105 G5
Healey Wood Rd BLY BB11 *....6 H1
Healing St ROCH OL11 *........235 K6
Heaning Av ACC BB5..............160 A3
 BBN BB1...............................158 A4
Heanor Dr STHP PR8.............200 C8
Heapey Fold La CHLYE PR6 ...208 A4
Heapey Rd CHLYE PR6...........188 D4
Heap St WHIT OL12...............234 A1
Heap St BRFD/BLYE BB10......142 E2
 RAW/HAS BB4 ....177 K3
Heapworth Av RAMS BL0........214 E5
Heartwood Cl BBNW BB2......156 D3
Heathbourne Rd BCUP OL13...196 E3
Heather Bank BLY BB11..........141 M7
 RAW/HAS BB4 ....195 J2
 TOD OL14 ....303 L6
Heather Brow
 BWCK/EAR BB18..................294 G5
Heather Cl BRSC L40..............225 H7
 CHLYE PR6............................208 B3
 FMBY L37 ....237 L6
 HOR/BR BL6........................231 G7
 NLSN BB9............................123 G8
 RAW/HAS BB4 ....194 D3
 STHP PR8............................238 A1
Heatherfield EDGW/EG BL7....213 D5
Heatherfield Cl FUL/RIB PR2 ..151 M2
Heather Gv FUL/RIB PR2........133 J8
Heatherlands WHIT OL12.......302 A11
Heatherlea Cl SKEL WN8........254 C4
Heather Lea Dr CHLYE PR6.....189 J3
Heatherlea Rd
 PDHM/BLYW BB12 ....122 A3
Heatherleigh
 CROS/BRETH PR26...............186 A1
Heatherleigh Gdns BBNW BB2..173 E3
Heathers Cft NTHTN L30........258 B8
Heatherside RAMS BL0..........214 E4
The Heathers BBR PR5...........169 C6
 PLF/KEOS FY6 ....85 L6
Heather St CSBY/BLUN L23....257 J5
Heatherway FMBY L37............237 K5
Heathey La STHP PR8.............222 C3
Heathfield CHLYE PR6............230 C2
Heathfield Av FMBY L37.........237 K5
Heathfield Dr PRES PR1.........133 H7
 NWD/KWIPK L33...................260 K1
Heathfield Pk BBNW BB2.......156 C5
Heathfield Rd BCUP OL13.......196 F3
 FTWD FY7..............................81 H1

MGHL L31 ....259 J4
STHP PR8 ....221 H6
Heathfoot Av HEY LA3 ....52 D5
Heathfoot Dr HEY LA3 ....52 D5
Heathgate PDHM/BLYW BB12 ..122 A3
SKEL WN8 ....253 M1
Heath Gv HEY LA3 ....52 E3
Heath Hill Dr BCUP OL13 ......196 H5
Heath Rd WHIT OL12 ....218 F4
Heathrow Pl CHLY/EC PR7 .....207 K4
Heath St BRFD/BLYE BB10 ......142 E3
ROCH OL11 ....235 G5
Heath Vw LITH L21 ....257 L8
Heathway FUL/RIB PR2 ....132 D2
Heathway Av BPOOLE FY3 ......105 H5
Heathy La ORM L39 ....238 D3
Heatley Cl BBNW BB2 ....10 C7
Heatley St PRES PR1 ....8 F4
Heaton Bottom Rd HEY LA3 .....53 K5
Heaton Cl BBR PR5 ....153 G7
BRSC L40 ....225 G7
CLV/TH FY5 ....85 M3
HEY LA3 ....41 M8
PLF/KEOS FY6 ....85 M6
SKEL WN8 ....254 D4
Heaton Mount Av
FUL/RIB PR2 ....132 C4
Heaton Pl PRES PR1 ....153 H7
Heaton Rd LANC LA1 ....54 E6
LSTA FY8 ....145 K4
Heaviley Gv HOR/BR BL6 ....231 K6
Hebden Av BPOOL FY1 ....5 C9
Heber Dr SKP/WHF BD23 ....280 D9
Heber Pl LIT OL15 ....219 L6
Heber St BLY BB11 ....161 L7
Hebrew Rd BRFD/BLYE BB10 ..142 D3
Hebrew Sq BRFD/BLYE BB10 * 142 D3
Heckenhurst Av
BRFD/BLYE BB10 ....143 J5
Hector Av MILN OL16 ....235 H1
Hector Rd DWN BB3 ....173 H6
Hedgecroft CSBY/BLUN L23 ...257 M5
Hedge Rw WHIT OL12 *............127 L8
Hedge Rows WHIT OL12 ....217 M1
Hedgerows Rd
CROS/BRETH PR26 ....185 K3
The Hedgerow BBNW BB2 ......156 D3
Hedgeview BRSC L40 ....223 L7
Heeley Rd LSTA FY8 ....145 G3
Height Barn La BCUP OL13 .....197 K3
Height Cft NLSN BB9 ....123 H6
Height La GAR/LONG PR3 ....94 B4
Heights Av WHIT OL12 ....235 H1
Heights Cl WHIT OL12 ....235 H1
Heightside Av RAW/HAS BB4 ..196 D3
Height Side La RAW/HAS BB4 ..177 L4
Heights La WHIT OL12 ....235 H2
Heights Rd NLSN BB9 ....123 G5
Helena St BRFD/BLYE BB10 ....7 K5
Helen Bank Dr
RNFD/HAY WA11 ....262 C3
Helen's Cl BPOOLS FY4 ....125 H5
Helks Brow HGHB LA2 ....48 B7
Hellifield FUL/RIB PR2 ....132 B4
Hellifield Rd CLI BB7 ....277 Q10
Helm Cl BLY BB11 ....162 A1
Helmn Wy NLSN BB9 ....123 K3
Helmsdale SKEL WN8 ....253 M1
Helmsdale Cl RAMS BLO 214 D8
Helmsdale Rd BPOOLS FY4 .....125 J4
NLSN BB9 ....123 K2
Helmshore Rd RAW/HAS BB4 ..194 D3
TOT/BURYW BL8 ....214 D3
Helmside Av MCMB LA4 ....41 K8
Helmsley Gn LEYL PR25 ....186 E1
Helston Cl NLSN BB9 ....103 G7
CHTN/BK PR9 ....180 E6
Helton Cl NLSN BB9 ....103 G7
Helvellyn Dr
PDHM/BLYW BB12 ....141 M3
Helvellyn Rd
WGNW/BIL/OR WN5 ....255 L4
Hemingway BPOOLS FY4 ....125 G3
Hempshaw Av RAW/HAS BB4 ..177 K1
Hemp St BCUP OL13 ....197 J2
Henderson Dr
RNFD/HAY WA11 ....262 D3
Henderson Rd FTWD FY7 ....81 J1
KIRK/FR/WAR PR4 ....107 H5
PRES PR1 ....132 B8
WHIT OL12 ....235 L1
Henderville St LIT OL15 ....219 K5
Hendon Pl FUL/RIB PR2 ....151 H1
Hendon Rd NLSN BB9 ....123 J3
Hendriff Pl WHIT OL12 *..........235 J2
Hendry La BBNW BB2 ....173 G3
Henley Av CLV/TH FY5 ....85 G1
Henley Ct BISP FY2 * 105 J3
Henley Dr CHTN/BK PR9 ....200 B2
Henley Ms HEY LA3 * 40 F7
Henley St WHIT OL12 ....235 H2
Henley Ter ROCH OL11 ....235 H5
Hennel La BBR PR5 ....168 E1
Henrietta St BBNW BB2 * 10 B4
BCUP OL13 ....197 J2
PRES PR1 ....9 M2
Henry Hickman La NTHTN L30 ..258 C7
Henry St ACC BB5 ....159 J5
BBN BB1 ....158 E2
BPOOL FY1 ....4 D7
COL BB8 ....123 M7
LANC LA1 ....3 G7
LIT OL15 ....219 J8
LSTA FY8 ....146 D8
MILN OL16 ....235 K3
NLSN BB9 * 123 G2
RAMS BLO 215 G4
RAW/HAS BB4 ....195 J1
WHIT OL12 ....218 F4
Henry Whalley St BBNW BB2 ..172 D1
Henshaw Bank TOD OL14 ....303 H6
Henshaw Woods TOD OL14......303 K6
Henson Av BPOOLS FY4 ....125 H5
Henthorne St BPOOL FY1 ....104 C7
Henthorn Rd CLI BB7 ....98 E7
Henwick Hall Av RAMS BLO 214 A7
Herbert St BBNW BB2 * 10 C9
BCUP OL13 ....197 G3
BLY BB11 ....6 D6
HOR/BR BL6 ....231 K7
LEYL PR25 ....186 D1
PDHM/BLYW BB12 ....141 G4
PRES PR1 ....9 J1
The Herb Gdns KKBYL LA6 ....28 F6
Hereford Av BPOOLE FY3 ....5 K6
GAR/LONG PR3 ....284 A7
PDHM/BLYW BB12 ....141 G4
Hereford Cl ACC BB5 ....159 L4
Hereford Dr CLI BB7 ....99 J4

Hereford Gv CHLY/EC PR7 ....187 H5
KIRK/FR/WAR PR4 ....131 G2
SKEL WN8 ....254 E5
Hereford Rd BBN BB1 ....157 M6
CHTN/BK PR9 ....200 C4
COL BB8 ....123 K1
Hereford St NLSN BB9 ....122 F3
ROCH OL11 ....235 K6
Herevale Hall Dr RAMS BLO 214 E7
Heriot Cl CLV/TH FY5 ....85 J2
Heritage Wy CLV/TH FY5 ....85 J3
KIRK/FR/WAR PR4 ....183 K6
Herkomer Av BLY BB11 ....162 B1
Herlebeck Ri LANC LA1 ....3 L1
Hermitage Cl WGNNW/ST WN6..245 G4
Hermitage St BBN BB1 ....158 F2
The Hermitage CLV/TH FY5 ....85 J1
Hermitage Wy LSTA FY8 ....146 A4
Hermon Rd CLV/TH FY5 ....81 H7
Hermon St PRES PR1 ....152 F7
Hern Av BBR PR5 ....168 D3
CLV/TH FY5 ....81 J6
Heron Cl BBN BB1 ....157 G3
CLV/TH FY5 ....81 J6
Heron Ct BLY BB11 ....141 M6
Heron Dr MCMB LA4 ....41 M8
Heron Gv RNFD/HAY WA11 ......262 E6
Heron Wy ACC BB5 ....159 H8
BPOOLE FY3 ....105 L4
KIRK/FR/WAR PR4 ....148 E1
Herring Arm Rd FTWD FY7 ....81 K1
Herschel Av
PDHM/BLYW BB12 ....141 M3
Herschell St BBNW BB2 ....172 C2
PRES PR1 ....9 K6
Hertford St BBNW BB2 ....172 F1
Hesketh Av BISP FY2 ....84 E7
Hesketh Cl FUL/RIB PR2 ....153 H2
Hesketh Ct GTH/LHO BB6 ....139 G5
CHTN/BK PR9 ....200 B1
MGHL L31 ....259 J1
WGNNW/ST WN6 ....245 K1
Hesketh Dr BRSC L40 ....203 K8
CHTN/BK PR9 ....200 B1
FUL/RIB PR2 ....153 H2
GAR/LONG PR3 ....114 C3
HEY LA3 ....52 D3
LSTA FY8 ....145 K2
MILN OL16 ....235 H4
Hesketh Gn BRSC L40 ....203 L7
Hesketh La GAR/LONG PR3 ....95 G4
KIRK/FR/WAR PR4 ....183 J2
Hesketh Pl FTWD FY7 ....77 L6
Hesketh Rd BBNW BB2 ....225 G7
CHTN/BK PR9 ....180 A4
FUL/RIB PR2 ....153 H2
GAR/LONG PR3 ....114 C3
HEY LA3 ....52 D3
LSTA FY8 ....145 K2
MILN OL16 ....235 H4
Hesketh St FUL/RIB PR2 ....8 B1
GTH/LHO BB6 ....138 F6
Heskin Av MGHL L31 ....250 A7
Heskin La ORM L39 ....241 G3
Heslaker La SKP/WHF BD23 .....281 R8
Hesley La SETT BD24 ....266 G3
Hesse St DWN BB3 * 191 K3
Hest Bank La HGHB LA2 ....42 D4
Hest Bank Rd MCMB LA4 ....41 M5
Hester Cl HTWN L38 ....247 J7
Hestham Av MCMB LA4 ....41 J7
Hestham Crs MCMB LA4 ....41 J7
Hestham Dr MCMB LA4 ....41 J7
Hestham Pde MCMB LA4 ....41 J7
Hetherington Pl BISP FY2 ....105 H1
Hetton Lea NLSN BB9 ....102 F8
Heversham Av FUL/RIB PR2 ......132 B3
Heversham Cl LANC LA1 ....55 G8
MCMB LA4 ....41 K8
Hewart St PDHM/BLYW BB12 ...141 K4
Hewitt Cl KIRK/FR/WAR PR4 .....167 H2
Hewitt La AIRE BD20 ....295 Q5
Hewitt St LEYL PR25 ....186 E1
Hewlett St CHLY/EC PR7 ....229 G2
Hexham Av CLV/TH FY5 ....81 H7
Hexham Cl ACC BB5 ....160 B8
Hexham Rd MCMB LA4 ....42 A8
Hey Bottom La WHIT OL12 ....218 C5
Heybrook St MILN OL16 ....235 L3
Heycrofts Vw RAMS BLO 195 G8
Heydon Cl FMBY L37 ....247 G2
Hey End KIRK/FR/WAR PR4 ....167 J3
Heyes Av RNFD/HAY WA11 ....262 D5
Heyescroft Orm L39 ....252 A5
Heyes Gv RNFD/HAY WA11 ....262 D1
Heyes Rd WGNW/BIL/OR WN5 ..262 E6
Heyes St WGNNW/ST WN6 ....244 F4
The Heyes CHLY PR6 ....187 L1
Heyfold Gdns DWN BB3 ....173 J8
Hey Head Av RAW/HAS BB4 * ...196 D2
Hey Head La LIT OL15 ....219 K3
TOD OL14 ....301 N12
Heyhead St NLSN BB9 ....122 F6
Heyhouses La LSTA FY8 ....145 L3
Heyhurst Rd BBNW BB2 ....10 C4
Heymoor Av GTH/LHO BB6 ......139 G5
Heys ACC BB5 ....159 H8
Heys Cl BBNW BB2 ....172 E4
BBNW BB2 ....195 M1
Heys Ct ACC BB5 ....159 M1
BBNW BB2 ....172 F3
Heysham Av HEY LA3 ....52 E4
Heysham Crs BBNW BB2 ....173 J2
Heysham Hall Dr HEY LA3 ....52 D5
Heysham Hall Gv HEY LA3 ....52 D4
Heysham Mossgate Rd
HEY LA3 ....52 E4
Heysham Pk HEY LA3 ....52 D4
Heysham Rd CHTN/BK PR9 ....200 C4
HEY LA3 ....52 D4
WGNW/BIL/OR WN5 ....255 L4
Heysham St PRES PR1 ....152 B2
Heys Hunt Av LEYL PR25 ....186 D1
Heys La ACC BB5 ....159 H8
BBNW BB2 ....172 E4
DWN BB3 ....172 E5
GTH/LHO BB6 ....139 G6
LEYL PR25 ....186 C1
WGNNW/ST WN6 ....245 K5
Heys St MILN OL16 ....235 K3
Hey St NLSN BB9 ....123 H2
The Heys CHLY/EC PR7 ....229 J7
Heyworth Av BBNW BB2 ....172 F4
Hibbert Ter LANC LA1 ....54 E8
Hibson Av WHIT OL12 ....234 B1
Hibson Cl WHIT OL12 ....218 F3

Hibson Rd NLSN BB9 ....123 G5
Hic Bibi La CHLY/EC PR7 ....229 H3
Hickson Av MGHL L31 ....249 M8
Hick's Ter BBN BB1 ....158 F2
Hidings Court La MCMB LA4 ....41 L7
Hiers House La COL BB8 ....103 J3
Higgin's La BRSC L40 ....224 F7
Higgin St BRFD/BLYE BB10 ....7 J1
COL BB8 ....103 H6
Higham Gv BPOOLE FY3 ....5 L7
Higham Hall Rd
PDHM/BLYW BB12 ....121 J6
Higham Rd PDHM/BLYW BB12 ..120 F8
Higham Side Rd
KIRK/FR/WAR PR4 ....109 L5
Highbank BBN BB1 ....157 J2
Highbank Av BPOOLS FY4 ....125 K3
High Bank CHLYE PR6 ....188 D8
High Bank Cescent DWN BB3 ...191 K4
High Banks MGHL L31 ....249 M8
High Barn Cl ROCH OL11 ....235 H6
High Barn La WHIT OL12 ....197 M8
Highbury Av BPOOLE FY3 ....105 H3
FTWD FY7 ....77 J8
Highbury Ga
KIRK/FR/WAR PR4 ....108 D3
Highbury Pl BBN BB1 ....10 E1
Highbury Rd LSTA FY8 ....145 G3
Highbury Rd East LSTA FY8 .....145 G3
High Cl PDHM/BLYW BB12 ......141 H5
High Cop CHLYE PR6 ....170 C7
Highcote La MTHPE LA7 ....17 L1
High Ct MCMB LA4 ....42 H6
High Crag Ct CARN LA5 ....26 B5
Highcroft HGHB LA2 ....39 G4
Highcroft Av BISP FY2 ....85 H6
High Croft La TOD OL14 ....303 H1
Highcroft Wy WHIT OL12 ....218 C7
Highcross Av PLF/KEOS FY6 .....106 A3
Highcross Hl PLF/KEOS FY6 .....106 A3
Highcross Rd PLF/KEOS FY6 .....106 A3
Highdale HEY LA3 * 52 E4
Higher Antley St ACC BB5 ....159 K6
Higher Ashenhurst TOD OL14 ...301 K12
Higher Audley St BBN BB1 ....11 H5
LIT OL15 ....219 K8
Higher Bank Rd FUL/RIB PR2 ...132 C8
Higher Bank St CHLYE PR6 ....189 K2
Higher Barn HOR/BR BL6 ....232 C8
Higher Barn St BBN BB1 ....11 J4
Higher Booths La
RAW/HAS BB4 ....177 K2
Higher Calderbrook Rd
LIT OL15 ....219 M2
Higher Cswy NLSN BB9 ....103 G8
Higher Cleggswood Av
LIT OL15 ....219 K8
Higher Commons La
BBNW BB2 ....135 M7
Higher Cft PRES PR1 ....167 M1
Higher Croft Cots DWN BB3 * ...173 J3
Higher Croft Rd DWN BB3 ....173 J3
Higher Cross Rw BCUP OL13 * ..179 J8
Higher Eanam BBN BB1 ....11 J4
Higher End Pk NTHTN L30 ....258 A6
Higher Feniscowles La
BBNW BB2 ....171 L3
Higher Fld GTH/LHO BB6 ....137 M3
Higher Firs Dr ACC BB5 ....139 K8
Higher Fold La RAMS BLO 215 H4
Higher Furlong
KIRK/FR/WAR PR4 ....166 C5
Highergate Cl ACC BB5 ....160 C1
Higher Gate Rd ACC BB5 ....160 C2
Higher Gn PLF/KEOS FY6 ....86 A3
Higher Greenfield
FUL/RIB PR2 ....131 L6
Higher Heys ACC BB5 ....159 H8
Higher House Fld BBNW BB2 ....172 E4
Higher House La CHLYE PR6 .....188 D3
Higherlands Cl SKP/WHF BD23 ..281 K2
Higher La BWCK/EAR BB18 ......293 Q8
GAR/LONG PR3 ....284 C8
KIRK/FR/WAR PR4 ....202 F1
RAW/HAS BB4 ....176 E7
RNFD/HAY WA11 ....262 D5
SKEL WN8 ....254 F4
SKEL WN8 ....243 L2
Higher Lawrence St
DWN BB3 ....191 J1
Higher London Ter DWN BB3* ..191 L1
Higher Meadow LEYL PR25 ....187 H2
Higher Mill St RAW/HAS BB4 ....177 K8
Higher Moor Rd BPOOLE FY3 ...105 K1
Higher Park Rd
BWCK/EAR BB18 ....293 R7
Higher Peel St ACC BB5 ....159 G8
Higher Perry St DWN BB3 ....191 L1
Higher Ramsgreave Rd
BBN BB1 ....136 F8
Higher Reedley Rd NLSN BB9 ...122 F7
Higher Rd GAR/LONG PR3 ....114 E3
SKP/WHF BD23 ....266 E7
Higher Saxifield
BRFD/BLYE BB10 ....123 H8
Higher Shore Rd LIT OL15 ....219 H8
Higher South St DWN BB3* 191 L2
Higher Syke CHTN/BK PR9 ....200 C4
Higher Tentre BLY BB11 ....7 J5
Higher Vw SKEL WN8 ....254 F5
Higher Walton Rd BBR PR5 ......153 H7
Higher Wheat La MILN OL16 .....235 M3
Higher Witton Rd BBNW BB2 ....156 E7
Highfield BCUP OL13 ....197 H1
CHLYE PR6 ....189 J3
GTH/LHO BB6 ....138 E6
NWD/KWIPK L33 ....254 F5
Highfield Av BBR PR5 ....168 F2
BRFD/BLYE BB10 ....123 H8
COL BB8 ....296 B2
FUL/RIB PR2 ....132 C2
KIRK/FR/WAR PR4 ....109 M3
LEYL PR25 ....168 F8
WGNNW/ST WN6 ....245 K5
Highfield Cl ACC BB5 ....159 J8
CHLYE PR6 ....230 D4
KIRK/FR/WAR PR4 ....183 K6
RAW/HAS BB4 ....194 D1
Highfield Crs MCMB LA4 ....41 D1
NLSN BB9 ....103 G3
Highfield Dr FUL/RIB PR2 ....132 B3
GAR/LONG PR3 ....114 E2
HGHB LA2 ....42 D2
PRES PR1 ....167 H4
RNFD/HAY WA11 ....263 H1
Highfield Gdns BBNW BB2 ....10 E9
Highfield Gv BBR PR5 ....168 F2
CSBY/BLUN L23 ....257 J6

Highfield La BRSC L40 ....223 M4
DWN BB3 ....191 L3
Highfield Ms DWN BB3 ....191 L3
Highfield Pk MGHL L31 ....259 G6
RAW/HAS BB4 ....194 D1
Highfield Rd BBN BB1 ....158 D2
BBNW BB2 ....124 F5
BPOOLS FY4 ....124 F5
BWCK/EAR BB18 ....294 E5
CARN LA5 ....33 G4
CHTN/BK PR9 ....180 E8
COL BB8 ....230 D4
CROS/BRETH PR26 ....204 F1
DWN BB3 ....191 L2
ORM L39 ....241 H5
RAMS BLO 195 G8
RAW/HAS BB4 ....196 A2
ROCH OL11 ....234 B2
Highfield Rd North
CHLY/EC PR7 ....207 M1
CHLYE PR6 ....230 D3
Highfield Rd South
CHLY/EC PR7 ....207 M2
Highfield St DWN BB3 ....191 L2
High Fold BWCK/EAR BB18 ....294 D9
Highgale Gdns BBR PR5 ....168 C4
Highgate BPOOLS FY4 ....125 G6
High Ga FTWD FY7 ....77 G8
Highgate GAR/LONG PR3 ....113 G5
NLSN BB9 ....123 G4
PRES PR1 ....151 L6
Highgate Av FUL/RIB PR2 ....132 C2
Highgate Cl FUL/RIB PR2 ....132 C2
KIRK/FR/WAR PR4 ....129 J8
Highgate Crs WGNNW/ST WN6 ..245 J4
Highgate La
KIRK/FR/WAR PR4 ....148 B5
High Gate La FUL/KEOS FY6 ......82 D7
Highgate La WHIT OL12 ....217 M5
Highgate Pl LSTA FY8 ....146 A5
Highgate Rd MGHL L31 ....250 A8
SKEL WN8 ....254 E4
High Gn LEYL PR25 ....186 C2
Highgrove Cl MCMB LA4 ....41 H7
Highgrove Ct
CROS/BRETH PR26 ....185 J3
Highgrove Rd LANC LA1 ....54 D7
High Hill Grove SETT BD24 ......265 N8
High Hill La SETT BD24 ....265 P8
High Knott Rd CARN LA5 ....16 C7
Highland Av PRES PR1 ....151 L7
Highland Brow HGHB LA2 ....66 F5
Highland Dr RAW/HAS BB4 ....187 H5
Highlands LIT OL15 ....219 K8
Highlands Rd ROCH OL11 ....234 A6
High La BRSC L40 ....241 K3
BWCK/EAR BB18 ....293 R11
ORM L39 ....251 M3
High Lea CHLYE PR6 ....230 D3
High Level Rd ROCH OL11 ....235 K6
High Meadow BBR PR5 ....168 E1
Highmeadow SKEL WN8 ....254 D5
Highmoor NLSN BB9 ....123 J5
High Moor La
WGNNW/ST WN6 ....227 K7
Highmoor Pk CLI BB7 ....99 J4
High Moss ORM L39 ....241 H8
High Pk BWCK/EAR BB18 ....245 M5
Higher Pk Pl CHTN/BK PR9 ....200 D3
Higher Pk Rd CHTN/BK PR9 ......200 D3
High Peak Rd WHIT OL12 ....217 M5
Highrigg Dr GAR/LONG PR3 .....132 C2
High Rd HGHB LA2 ....48 C2
HGHB LA2 ....43 K5
Highsands Av BRSC L40 ....203 H5
Highsted Gv NWD/KWIPK L33 ...260 B6
High St ACC BB5 ....159 J8
BBN BB1 ....158 E2
BBN BB1 ....158 E2
BPOOL FY1 ....104 E5
BRSC L40 ....226 E2
CHLY/EC PR7 ....207 M3
CLI BB7 ....98 E5
COL BB8 ....296 A7
CSBY/BLUN L23 ....257 J6
MILN OL16 ....235 L3
NLSN BB9 ....122 C5
PDHM/BLYW BB12 ....140 F4
PRES PR1 ....9 J1
RAW/HAS BB4 ....177 K4
Hillsview Rd STHP PR8 ....220 F7
Hill Top KIRK/FR/WAR PR4 ....167 K5
NLSN BB9 ....103 G7
Hill Top Cl CARN LA5 ....18 A7
RAW/HAS BB4 ....149 G4
Hilltop Dr RAW/HAS BB4 ....194 A4
Hill Top La BWCK/EAR BB18 .....294 D5
CHLYE PR6 ....187 M3
Hilltop Wk ORM L39 ....240 F8
Hill Vw BBN BB1 ....157 H3
RAW/HAS BB4 ....195 J2
Hill View Dr CHLY/EC PR7 ....229 J7
Hill View Rd GAR/LONG PR3 .....284 B6
Hillview Rd KIRK/FR/WAR PR4 ..128 D5
Hill Wk LEYL PR25 ....186 D1
Hillylaid Rd CLV/TH FY5 ....85 M1
Hilmar St BBN BB1 ....157 J4
Hilstone La BISP FY2 ....105 G2
Hilton Av BPOOL FY1 ....124 E2
HOR/BR BL6 ....231 K8
LSTA FY8 ....145 K4
Hilton Dr DWN BB3 ....191 L3
Hilton's Brow CHLYE PR6 ....170 F7
Hilton St DWN BB3 ....191 K3
Hinchley Gn MGHL L31 ....258 F7
Hindburn Av NLSN BB9 ....259 J1
Hindburn Cl CARN LA5 ....33 L1
Hindburn Pl LANC LA1 * 2 E7
Hinde St LANC LA1 ....3 J4
Hindle Fold La GTH/LHO BB6 ...138 F5
Hindle St ACC BB5 ....159 K5
BCUP OL13 ....197 G3
DWN BB3 ....191 J4
Hindley Beech MGHL L31 ....258 F1
Hindley Cl FUL/RIB PR2 ....132 C4
Hindley Ct NLSN BB9 ....122 F2
Hindley St CHLY/EC PR7 ....207 L5
Hind's Head Av
WGNNW/ST WN6 ....228 C5
Hind St BRFD/BLYE BB10 ....142 E1
PRES PR1 ....8 E1
Hinton WHIT OL12 * 235 H3
Hinton Cl ROCH OL11 ....234 B5
Hinton St BRFD/BLYE BB10 ....7 J1
Hippings Wy CLI BB7 ....99 H1
Hirst St BLY BB11 * 7 L1
PDHM/BLYW BB12 ....141 G4
TOD OL14 * 300 E10
Hoarstones Av
PDHM/BLYW BB12 ....122 A4
Hobart St BBN BB1 ....157 L3
Hobart St NWD/KWIPK L33 ......260 B5
Hobart Pl CLV/TH FY5 ....85 J3
Hobart St BLY BB11 ....7 J4
Hobbs La GAR/LONG PR3 ....285 L11

Hill Cft KIRK/FR/WAR PR4 ....128 E6
Hilldean SKEL WN8 ....254 F7
Hill End La HWTH BD22 ....297 P1
RAW/HAS BB4 ....195 M2
Hill Field Cft GAR/LONG PR3 ....284 D6
Hill House Fold La
WGNNW/ST WN6 ....227 M6
Hill House La CHLYE PR6 ....170 D3
Hill Houses DWN BB3 ....191 K3
Hillingdon Rd
BRFD/BLYE BB10 ....123 G8
Hillingdon Rd North
BRFD/BLYE BB10 ....122 F7
Hillkirk Dr WHIT OL12 ....217 M8
Hill La COL BB8 ....296 E5
HOR/BR BL6 ....230 E8
KKBYL LA6 ....33 L7
Hillmount Av HEY LA3 ....52 E3
Hillock Cl BRSC L40 ....223 K4
Hillock La BRSC L40 ....223 K4
KIRK/FR/WAR PR4 ....148 A3
SKEL WN8 ....243 M5
Hill Rd South PRES PR1 ....151 M8
Hillsborough Av NLSN BB9 ....123 G6
Hills Ct LANC LA1 ....3 L3
Hillsea Av HEY LA3 ....52 E3
Hillside BLY BB11 ....142 A8
KIRK/FR/WAR PR4 ....183 K5
Hill Side LANC LA1 ....2 F5
Hillside Av BBN BB1 ....122 F7
BRFD/BLYE BB10 ....122 F7
CROS/BRETH PR26 ....168 C4
FUL/RIB PR2 ....231 M7
HOR/BR BL6 ....231 M7
KIRK/FR/WAR PR4 ....128 F7
ORM L39 ....251 M3
PLF/KEOS FY6 ....78 E7
SKEL WN8 ....227 G6
Hillside Cl BLY BB11 ....142 A8
BPOOLS FY4 ....105 H5
CHLY/EC PR7 ....206 F2
CLI BB7 ....99 H5
CLV/TH FY5 ....86 A3
GTH/LHO BB6 ....138 F5
NLSN BB9 ....122 F6
Hillside Crs BCUP OL13 ....179 J4
CHLYE PR6 ....187 M3
Hillside Dr CLI BB7 ....290 D9
PLF/KEOS FY6 ....82 F4
RAW/HAS BB4 ....196 B1
Hillside Gdns DWN BB3 ....191 K3
Hillside Rd HGHB LA2 ....191 K3
PRES PR1 ....152 F5
RAMS BLO 214 D6
RAW/HAS BB4 ....194 F1
STHP PR8 ....221 H2
Hillside Vw NLSN BB9 ....122 F6
Hillside Wk BBN BB1 ....157 M7
Hillside Wy WHIT OL12 ....217 M2
The Hills FUL/RIB PR2 ....133 L4
Hillstone Av WHIT OL12 ....217 M7
Hill St ACC BB5 ....159 L4
BBN BB1 ....11 L2
BPOOLS FY4 ....124 E5
BURY BL9 ....214 F8
BWCK/EAR BB18 ....293 Q5
CARN LA5 ....33 J2
CHTN/BK PR9 ....180 D3
COL BB8 ....296 A7
CSBY/BLUN L23 ....257 J6
MILN OL16 ....235 L3
NLSN BB9 ....122 C5
PDHM/BLYW BB12 ....140 F4
PRES PR1 ....9 J1
RAW/HAS BB4 ....177 K4

Hobcross La BRSC L40 242 D2
Hob Gn BBNW BB2 156 C1
Hob La EDGW/EG BL7 212 F4
Hobson's La KKBYL LA6 27 J7
Hobson St RAW/HAS BB4 177 J7
Hockley Pl BPOOLE FY3 105 J4
Hodder Av BPOOL FY1 5 G9
CHLY/EC PR7 207 L6
FTWD FY7 81 G1
HEY LA3 42 A8
LIT OL15 219 J5
MGHL L31 259 J1
Hodder Bridge Cots CLI BB7 * 97 L4
Hodder Brook FUL/RIB PR2 133 K8
Hodder Cl BBR PR5 169 J3
Hodder Dr CLI BB7 290 C8
Hodder Gv CLI BB7 98 F4
DWN BB3 173 H7
Hodder Pl BBN BB1 11 G1
LANC LA1 55 G6
LSTA FY8 145 L4
Hodder St ACC BB5 160 A5
BBN BB1 10 F1
BRFD/BLYE BB10 122 F8
GAR/LONG PR3 114 E4
Hodder Wy PLF/KEOS FY6 106 A1
Hoddlesden Rd DWN BB3 192 B2
Hodge Brow HOR/BR BL6 209 J7
Hodge La BWCK/EAR BB18 293 Q7
Hodge St STHP PR8 13 G4
Hodgson Av
KIRK/FR/WAR PR4 148 D5
Hodgson Pl PLF/KEOS FY6 106 A1
Hodgson Rd BPOOL FY1 104 E2
Hodgson St ACC BB5 159 H7
DWN BB3 191 L2
Hodson St BBR PR5 169 H2
STHP PR8 13 K5
Hogarth Av BLY BB11 142 B8
Hogarth Crs
KIRK/FR/WAR PR4 * 109 J7
Hoggs Hill La FMBY L37 247 H3
Hogg's La CHLY/EC PR7 208 B6
Hoghton Av BCUP OL13 197 K2
Hoghton Cl LANC LA1 2 C9
LSTA FY8 145 J1
Hoghton Gv CHTN/BK PR9 13 J2
Hoghton La BBR PR5 154 A8
Hoghton Rd GAR/LONG PR3 114 E4
LEYL PR25 186 A2
Hoghton St BBR PR5 168 D3
CHTN/BK PR9 13 H3
Hoghton Vw PRES PR1 152 F4
Holbeck Av BPOOLS FY4 125 J3
MCMB LA4 42 A7
WHIT OL12 218 A7
Holbeck St BRFD/BLYE BB10 142 D3
Holborn Dr ORM L39 240 F8
Holborn Gdns ROCH OL11 235 G6
Holborn Hl ORM L39 240 F8
Holborn Sq ROCH OL11 235 G6
Holborn St ROCH OL11 235 G6
Holcombe Dr BRFD/BLYE BB10 7 K3
Holcombe Gv CHLYE PR6 208 B2
Holcombe Lee RAMS BL0 214 D8
Holcombe Old Rd
TOT/BURYW BL8 214 C8
Holcombe Rd BISP FY2 105 H2
RAW/HAS BB4 194 D6
Holcroft Pl LSTA FY8 146 C7
Holden Av RAMS BL0 214 D6
Holden Cl NLSN BB9 122 F2
Holden Fold DWN BB3 173 L8
Holden La CLI BB7 276 G6
Holden Rd NLSN BB9 122 D6
Holden St ACC BB5 * 159 L6
BBN BB1 174 C5
BBNW BB2 10 A5
BLY BB11 6 F4
CHLY/EC PR7 230 C4
CLI BB7 99 J3
WHIT OL12 * 235 K1
Holden Wy LANC LA1 * 54 E6
Holden Wood Dr
RAW/HAS BB4 194 C2
Holderness St TOD OL14 303 M2
Hole Bottom Rd TOD OL14 303 L1
Hole House La CLI BB7 75 J6
Hole House St BBN BB1 157 M6
Holgate BPOOLS FY4 125 J4
CSBY/BLUN L23 257 L4
Holgate Dr
WGNW/BIL/OR WN5 255 H6
Holgate Pk CSBY/BLUN L23 257 L4
Holgate St BRFD/BLYE BB10 123 J8
GTH/LHO BB6 138 F6
Holker Cl BBR PR5 154 B8
LANC LA1 2 C9
Holker La CROS/BRETH PR26 185 K7
Holker St COL BB8 103 L7
DWN BB3 191 L3
Holland Av BBR PR5 169 H1
RAW/HAS BB4 177 J7
Holland Ct SKEL WN8 263 G1
Holland House Ct BBR PR5 153 H8
Holland House Rd BBR PR5 153 H8
Holland Moss SKEL WN8 253 K6
Holland Pl NLSN BB9 123 H1
Holland Ri WHIT OL12 * 235 H3
Holland Rd FUL/RIB PR2 151 M2
Holland's La SKEL WN8 252 D1
Holland St ACC BB5 159 J5
BBN BB1 10 D2
MILN OL16 219 G7
PDHM/BLYW BB12 * 140 E3
WHIT OL12 235 H3
Hollies Cl BBNW BB2 172 C3
GAR/LONG PR3 91 G1
Hollies Rd BBN BB1 137 K4
Hollin Bridge St BBNW BB2 10 B9
Hollin Fold NLSN BB9 103 G3
Hollinghurst Rd
NWD/KWIPK L33 260 C6
Hollingreave Rd BLY BB11 7 H7
Hollings KIRK/FR/WAR PR4 167 J4
Hollington St COL BB8 296 E6
Hollingworth La TOD OL14 303 L7
Hollingworth Rd LIT OL15 219 L7
Hollinhead Crs FUL/RIB PR2 131 L7
Hollinhey Cl NTHTN L30 258 D6
Hollin Hey Rd BOL BL1 233 H8
Hollin Hl BLY BB11 7 J9
Hollinhurst Av PRES PR1 8 A7
Hollinhurst Brow HGHB LA2 48 D7
Hollinhurst Ct PRES PR1 8 A6
Hollin La CHLYE PR6 208 F1
RAW/HAS BB4 177 K7
ROCH OL11 234 B5
Hollin Mill St NLSN BB9 122 E5
Hollins Av BRFD/BLYE BB10 143 J7
Hollins Cl ACC BB5 159 M7
BBR PR5 154 F8
Hollins Gv FUL/RIB PR2 131 L8
Hollins Grove St DWN BB3 173 J8
Hollinshead St CHLY/EC PR7 207 M3
Hollinshead Ter DWN BB3 190 E4
Hollins La ACC BB5 159 M7
CARN LA5 25 G2
CARN LA5 16 F2
CROS/BRETH PR26 185 M7
GAR/LONG PR3 270 B10
RAMS BL0 215 H2
Hollins Meadow TOD OL14 303 K6
Hollins Pl TOD OL14 303 K6
Hollins Rd BWCK/EAR BB18 293 P5
DWN BB3 173 H7
NLSN BB9 123 K1
PRES PR1 132 E8
TOD OL14 303 K5
Hollins St TOD OL14 303 K7
The Hollins TOD OL14 303 L1
Hollin St BBNW BB2 10 B9
Hollin Wy RAW/HAS BB4 177 K6
Hollinwood Dr RAW/HAS BB4 177 K6
Hollowbrook Wy WHIT OL12 235 G1
Hollowfield ROCH OL11 234 A2
Hollowford La BRSC L40 225 M8
Hollowforth La
KIRK/FR/WAR PR4 111 H7
Hollow Gill Brow SETT BD24 267 K5
Hollowhead Av BBN BB1 137 J6
Hollowhead La BBN BB1 137 J6
Hollowrane KKBYL LA6 19 H5
Hollowspell WHIT OL12 218 F8
Holly Av RAW/HAS BB4 194 F2
Holly Bank ACC BB5 159 M7
CARN LA5 26 A6
Hollybank Cl FUL/RIB PR2 131 J6
Hollybrook Rd STHP PR8 12 E7
Holly Cl BRSC L40 242 B7
CHLYE PR6 187 L1
CLV/TH FY5 81 M8
SKEL WN8 253 H2
Holly Crs CHLY/EC PR7 207 H8
RNFD/HAY WA11 262 D6
Holly Fold La ORM L39 253 H8
Holly Gv GAR/LONG PR3 114 D3
KIRK/FR/WAR PR4 183 K4
Holly La BRSC L40 203 M8
ORM L39 253 G7
ORM L39 240 E7
Holly Ms LSTA FY8 145 J1
Holly Pl BBR PR5 169 L5
Holly Rd BPOOL FY1 104 F2
CLV/TH FY5 81 L8
Holly St ACC BB5 159 G7
BBN BB1 157 J4
BRFD/BLYE BB10 7 K5
BURY BL9 214 F8
NLSN BB9 123 J3
WHIT OL12 218 F5
Holly Ter BBN BB1 157 J3
Holly Tree Cl DWN BB3 191 K6
RAW/HAS BB4 177 J6
Holly Tree Wy BBNW BB2 172 C3
Holly Wk LANC LA1 * 2 C5
Hollywood Av BPOOLE FY3 5 J1
PRES PR1 151 M8
Hollywood Gv FTWD FY7 77 J7
Holman St PRES PR1 152 F2
Holmbrook Cl BBNW BB2 173 J3
Holmby St BRFD/BLYE BB10 142 E1
Holmdale Av CHTN/BK PR9 180 F7
Holme Av FTWD FY7 81 G3
Holme Bank RAW/HAS BB4 195 J2
Holme Cl BWCK/EAR BB18 294 D7
Holme Crs COL BB8 296 E8
Holme End PDHM/BLYW BB12 122 C7
Holmefield KKBYL LA6 19 G2
Holmefield Av CLV/TH FY5 85 H1
Holmefield Cl CLV/TH FY5 85 H1
Holmefield Gv MGHL L31 258 F2
Holmefield Rd LSTA FY8 145 J4
PLF/KEOS FY6 78 B6
Holmehead SETT BD24 265 N4
Holmehead Br CLI BB7 275 Q4
Holme Hl CLI BB7 99 H1
Holme House Rd TOD OL14 300 F10
Holme La HGHB LA2 44 E5
RAW/HAS BB4 195 G3
Holme Lea ACC BB5 139 J7
Holme Pk HGHB LA2 39 G5
Holme Rd ACC BB5 139 H7
BBR PR5 169 G3
FUL/RIB PR2 151 H4
PDHM/BLYW BB12 6 D1
PRES PR1 8 C5
Holmes Cots BOL BL1 * 233 M8
Holmes Ct PRES PR1 132 B8
Holmes Dr BCUP OL13 179 J7
Holmes House Av
WGNS/IIMK WN3 255 M8
Holme Slack La PRES PR1 132 F8
Holmes La BCUP OL13 179 J8
Holmes Meadow
CROS/BRETH PR26 185 L2
Holmes Rd CLV/TH FY5 81 K8
WHIT OL12 235 G4
Holmes St BLY BB11 7 J6
PDHM/BLYW BB12 141 G3
RAW/HAS BB4 177 L8
WHIT OL12 235 G3
Holmes Ter RAW/HAS BB4 177 J6
The Holmes RAW/HAS BB4 177 J6
Holmestrand Av BLY BB11 141 K7
Holme St ACC BB5 159 L5
BCUP OL13 197 G3
COL BB8 296 E6
DWN BB3 191 K3
NLSN BB9 123 G1
Holmeswood
KIRK/FR/WAR PR4 128 D6
Holmeswood Crs G
AR/LONG PR3 111 L4
Holmeswood Pk
RAW/HAS BB4 195 H3
Holmeswood Rd BRSC L40 203 G5
Holmfield Crs FUL/RIB PR2 151 G2
Holmfield Pk FMBY L37 237 G7
Holmfield Rd BISP FY2 104 E2
FUL/RIB PR2 132 D7
Holmrook Rd PRES PR1 152 E2
Holmsley St BRFD/BLYE BB10 7 K5
Holmwood Cl FMBY L37 237 G8
Holmwood Dr FMBY L37 237 G7
Holmwood Gdns FMBY L37 237 G7
Holroyd St MILN OL16 235 K4
Holsands Cl FUL/RIB PR2 133 H5
Holstein Av WHIT OL12 218 A7
Holstein St PRES PR1 9 K2
Holt Av CHLY/EC PR7 229 J1
Holt Brow LEYL PR25 186 D5
Holt Coppice ORM L39 250 D4
Holt La CHLYE PR6 170 A8
Holt Mill Rd RAW/HAS BB4 196 A3
Holts La PLF/KEOS FY6 86 C8
Holt Sq NLSN BB9 103 H6
Holts Ter WHIT OL12 235 H1
Holt St BBN BB1 158 F1
RAMS BL0 215 G5
RAW/HAS BB4 196 B2
WGNW/BIL/OR WN5 255 G6
WHIT OL12 217 M2
Holt St West RAMS BL0 214 E6
Holyoake Av BISP FY2 105 H2
Holyoake St
PDHM/BLYW BB12 141 K5
TOD OL14 300 D10
Holyrood CSBY/BLUN L23 256 D7
Homecare Av CLI BB7 120 C3
Home Farm Cl HGHB LA2 36 F7
Home Fld GAR/LONG PR3 284 B7
Homer Av KIRK/FR/WAR PR4 183 J4
Homer St BLY BB11 141 M6
Homestead BBR PR5 169 L7
Homestead Av NTHTN L30 258 E8
Homestead Cl LEYL PR25 186 A2
Homestead Dr FTWD FY7 81 H2
Homestead Gdns WHIT OL12 219 G6
The Homestead LSTA FY8 * 146 D8
Homestead Wy FTWD FY7 81 H2
Homewood Av MCMB LA4 42 A5
Homfray Av HEY LA3 41 M8
Homfray Gv HEY LA3 41 M8
Honey Hole BBNW BB2 11 G9
Honey Hole Cl TOD OL14 303 L3
Honey Hole Rd TOD OL14 303 L3
Honey Holme La
BRFD/BLYE BB10 163 J4
Honey Moor Dr CLV/TH FY5 81 K7
Honeypot La PLF/KEOS FY6 87 G7
Honeysuckle Cl CHLYE PR6 187 L6
Honeysuckle Ct ACC BB5 160 B2
Honeysuckle Gv
KIRK/FR/WAR PR4 165 H7
Honeysuckle Pl BISP FY2 85 J5
Honeysuckle Wy WHIT OL12 218 A8
Honeywood Cl RAMS BL0 214 D8
Honister Av BPOOLE FY3 5 K7
Honister Rd BRFD/BLYE BB10 122 E8
LANC LA1 3 M2
WGNW/BIL/OR WN5 255 L5
Honister Sq LSTA FY8 145 J1
Honister Wy ROCH OL11 234 E7
Honiton Av BBNW BB2 172 F3
Honiton Wy KIRK/FR/WAR PR4 131 J5
Hood House St BLY BB11 6 D8
Hood St ACC BB5 159 M4
Hoole La CHTN/BK PR9 181 K5
GAR/LONG PR3 283 L10
Hools La GAR/LONG PR3 79 K6
Hope Cl CLV/TH FY5 81 L7
Hope Crs WGNNW/ST WN6 245 L5
Hope Island SKEL WN8 253 J3
Hope La GAR/LONG PR3 95 G6
Hope Sq CHTN/BK PR9 13 K3
Hope St ACC BB5 159 L6
BBNW BB2 10 C3
BCUP OL13 179 J7
BRFD/BLYE BB10 143 K5
CHLY/EC PR7 207 M2
CHLYE PR6 230 E4
CHTN/BK PR9 13 K3
DWN BB3 191 J2
GTH/LHO BB6 138 F7
HOR/BR BL6 231 L7
LANC LA1 3 J8
LSTA FY8 145 K4
MCMB LA4 41 K7
NLSN BB9 122 E6
PDHM/BLYW BB12 * 141 G3
PRES PR1 9 G3
RAMS BL0 214 E6
RAW/HAS BB4 195 M2
RAW/HAS BB4 194 E1
WHIT OL12 235 J3
Hope St North HOR/BR BL6 231 L6
Hope Ter BBNW BB2 10 A2
Hopkinson St COL BB8 * 296 E8
Hopton Rd BPOOL FY1 4 C7
Hopwood Av HOR/BR BL6 231 M7
Hopwood Crs
RNFD/HAY WA11 262 D6
Hopwood St ACC BB5 159 K7
BBR PR5 169 H3
BLY BB11 * 6 D4
PRES PR1 9 K2
Horace St PDHM/BLYW BB12 * 6 B3
Horden Rake BBNW BB2 172 B4
Horden Vw BBNW BB2 172 A4
Hordley St PDHM/BLYW BB12 141 K5
Hornbeam Cl PRES PR1 151 L8
Hornby Av FTWD FY7 81 G3
FUL/RIB PR2 133 H7
Hornby Bank HGHB LA2 36 C4
Hornby Cha MGHL L31 259 G4
Hornby Ct BBNW BB2 10 A6
KIRK/FR/WAR PR4 128 E7
LANC LA1 42 D7
Hornby Cft CROS/BRETH PR26 185 L4
Hornby Dr KIRK/FR/WAR PR4 129 J8
LANC LA1 54 F7
Hornby Hall Cl HGHB LA2 36 B5
Hornby La KIRK/FR/WAR PR4 89 J8
Hornby Rd BPOOL FY1 4 F3
CHLYE PR6 208 B5
CHTN/BK PR9 180 D7
GAR/LONG PR3 114 E3
HGHB LA2 46 F8
HGHB LA2 44 D5
HGHB LA2 36 F7
LSTA FY8 145 H6
Hornby's La GAR/LONG PR3 83 K6
Hornby St ACC BB5 159 H8
BLY BB11 7 H6
CSBY/BLUN L23 * 257 H7
Hornby Ter MCMB LA4 41 K5
Hornchurch Dr CHLY/EC PR7 207 K3
Horncliffe Cl RAW/HAS BB4 195 H3
Horncliffe Rd BPOOLS FY4 124 E5
Horncliffe Vw RAW/HAS BB4 194 E3
Horne St ACC BB5 159 M4
Horning Crs BRFD/BLYE BB10 143 G1
Hornsea Cl CLV/TH FY5 86 A1
FUL/RIB PR2 131 K7
Hornsey Av LSTA FY8 124 E7
Horns La GAR/LONG PR3 113 J2
Horridge Fold EDGW/EG BL7 212 B8
Horrobin La CHLYE PR6 230 F3
Horrocksford Wy LANC LA1 2 D9
Horrocks Rd EDGW/EG BL7 213 G4
Horsebridge Rd BPOOLE FY3 105 L3
Horsefield Av WHIT OL12 217 M5
Horse Market KKBYL LA6 21 M1
Horse Park La GAR/LONG PR3 282 D2
Horsfall Av LSTA FY8 146 D8
Horsfall Cl ACC BB5 159 L4
Horsfall St TOD OL14 303 P1
Horsfall Vls TOD OL14 * 303 P1
Horsfield Cl COL BB8 296 C6
Horton Av BRFD/BLYE BB10 122 E8
Horton Cl NWD/KWIPK L33 260 B5
Hoscar Moss Rd BRSC L40 225 M8
Hospital Br SKP/WHF BD23 267 R7
Hosta Cl NWD/KWIPK L33 260 A6
Hosticle La KKBYL LA6 21 J5
Hothersall La GAR/LONG PR3 115 G8
Houghclough La
GAR/LONG PR3 94 B1
Hough La LEYL PR25 186 D2
Houghton Av BPOOLS FY4 125 G3
Houghton Cl MILN OL16 235 M5
PRES PR1 152 A8
Houghton Ct HGHB LA2 43 K4
Houghton La WGNNW/ST WN6 245 J5
Houghton Rd PRES PR1 151 M8
Houghton's La SKEL WN8 253 M2
Houghtons Rd SKEL WN8 243 K8
Houghton St CHLYE PR6 208 A3
Houldsworth Rd FUL/RIB PR2 132 B8
Houseman Pl BPOOLS FY4 125 H4
Hove Av FTWD FY7 80 F3
Hove Rd LSTA FY8 145 J5
Hovingham St MILN OL16 235 L3
Howard Cl ACC BB5 159 J6
LSTA FY8 145 H2
MGHL L31 259 J2
Howard Dr KIRK/FR/WAR PR4 183 J4
Howard Florey Av NTHTN L30 258 C7
Howard Ms CARN LA5 33 H2
Howard Pl MILN OL16 235 J3
Howard Rd CHLY/EC PR7 207 L6
Howards La
WGNW/BIL/OR WN5 255 J4
Howard St BBN BB1 158 D2
BLY BB11 6 A6
BPOOL FY1 104 F5
NLSN BB9 * 122 F3
WGNW/BIL/OR WN5 255 M6
WHIT OL12 235 J3
Howard Wy LIT OL15 219 M2
Howarth Av ACC BB5 159 J4
Howarth Cl BLY BB11 142 D8
Howarth Crs PLF/KEOS FY6 86 B8
Howarth Cross St MILN OL16 235 L1
Howarth Farm Wy WHIT OL12 218 F8
Howarth Fold EDGW/EG BL7 * 212 A8
Howarth Rd FUL/RIB PR2 131 M8
Howarth Sq MILN OL16 235 K3
Howarth St LIT OL15 219 L5
RAW/HAS BB4 178 C3
Howden Hts PLF/KEOS FY6 85 L8
Howe Av BPOOLS FY4 125 H3
Howe Cft CLI BB7 99 J3
Howe Gv CHLY/EC PR7 207 K4
Howells Cl MGHL L31 259 G1
Howe Wk BLY BB11 7 G4
Howgill Av LANC LA1 42 E7
Howgill Cl NLSN BB9 123 J5
Howgill La CLI BB7 292 G6
The Howgills FUL/RIB PR2 132 D4
Howgill Wy LSTA FY8 147 G6
Howick Cross La FUL/RIB PR2 151 G5
Howick Moor La PRES PR1 151 J8
Howick Park Av PRES PR1 151 J7
Howick Park Cl PRES PR1 151 J7
Howick Park Dr PRES PR1 151 J7
Howorth Rd BLY BB11 7 G9
Howsin St BRFD/BLYE BB10 142 D2
Howson La SETT BD24 265 P4
Hoylake Cl FUL/RIB PR2 131 L5
Hoyle Av LSTA FY8 145 J1
Hoyles La KIRK/FR/WAR PR4 130 F6
Hoyle St ACC BB5 176 D3
BCUP OL13 197 H3
WHIT OL12 302 A12
Hozier St BBN BB1 157 M6
Hubert Pl LANC LA1 2 D5
Hubie St PDHM/BLYW BB12 6 E1
Huck La LSTA FY8 147 H4
Hud Hey Rd RAW/HAS BB4 176 D5
Hud Rake RAW/HAS BB4 176 E6
Hudson Cl BBNW BB2 156 E3
Hudson Ct BBR PR5 169 M3
Hudson Rd BPOOL FY1 5 G8
MGHL L31 259 G4
Hudson St ACC BB5 159 M7
BLY BB11 6 B5
NLSN BB9 * 122 E6
PRES PR1 9 K5
TOD OL14 300 F10
Hudsons Wk ROCH OL11 234 E4
Hufling Ct BLY BB11 7 J8
Hufling La BLY BB11 7 J9
Hugh Barn La
KIRK/FR/WAR PR4 167 H4
Hughes Av HOR/BR BL6 231 K7
Hughes Gv BISP FY2 105 H2
Hughes St BLY BB11 7 G6
Hugh La CROS/BRETH PR26 168 A8
Hugh Rake RAW/HAS BB4 177 J5
Hugh St MILN OL16 235 K3
Hughtrede St MILN OL16 * 235 L8
Hullet Cl WGNNW/ST WN6 245 H3
Hull Rd BPOOL FY1 4 D3
Hull St BLY BB11 7 J5
FUL/RIB PR2 8 B1
Hulme St STHP PR8 12 F4
Hulton Dr NLSN BB9 123 H5
Humber Av BPOOLE FY3 * 105 H3
Humber Pl
WGNW/BIL/OR WN5 255 M4
Humber St GAR/LONG PR3 114 D4
Humblescough La
GAR/LONG PR3 283 N9
Hume St MILN OL16 235 K6
Humphreys Hey
CSBY/BLUN L23 257 L6
Humphrey St NLSN BB9 122 E5
Hundred End La CHTN/BK PR9 182 C1
Hungerford Rd LSTA FY8 145 J6
Hunniball Ct FUL/RIB PR2 151 M1
Hunslet St BLY BB11 7 J3
NLSN BB9 123 J4
Hunstanton Cl CHLY/EC PR7 187 G6
Hunter Av KIRK/FR/WAR PR4 183 K5
Hunter Rd KIRK/FR/WAR PR4 148 E1
Hunters Cl ORM L39 260 D1
Hunters Fold
KIRK/FR/WAR PR4 166 D6
Hunters Ga LANC LA1 54 D6
Hunters Gn RAMS BL0 214 C8
Hunters La TOD OL14 303 J1
Hunter's La KIRK/FR/WAR PR4 182 E8
MILN OL16 235 J3
Hunters Ldg BBNW BB2 172 C2
BBR PR5 153 G8
Hunters Rd LEYL PR25 187 G2
Hunter St CARN LA5 33 J1
Huntingdon Ct
CHTN/BK PR9 * 200 D1
Huntingdon Gv MGHL L31 249 M7
Huntingdon Hall Rd
GAR/LONG PR3 116 C2
Huntingdon Rd CLV/TH FY5 84 F2
Hunting Hill Rd CARN LA5 33 G2
Huntington Dr DWN BB3 191 K4
Huntley Av BPOOLE FY3 105 H4
Huntley Cl MCMB LA4 41 M6
Huntley La BBR PR5 155 G1
Hunt Rd MGHL L31 259 G2
Huntroyde Av
PDHM/BLYW BB12 140 E3
Huntroyde Cl PDHM/BLYW BB12 6 B1
Hunts Fld CHLYE PR6 187 M1
Huntsman Cha
KIRK/FR/WAR PR4 * 129 J5
Hunt St PRES PR1 * 8 D4
Hurlston Av SKEL WN8 * 253 M3
Hurlston Dr ORM L39 241 H4
Hurlston La BRSC L40 240 E2
Hurn Gv CHLY/EC PR7 207 K4
Hurst Brook CHLY/EC PR7 229 J2
Hurst Crs RAW/HAS BB4 177 L8
Hurstdene Cl PLF/KEOS FY6 86 C8
Hurstead Gn WHIT OL12 * 219 G7
Hurstead St ACC BB5 176 B2
Hurst Gn BRSC L40 226 F1
Hurst La RAW/HAS BB4 177 L8
Hurstleigh Dr HEY LA3 52 F4
Hurstleigh Hts CLV/TH FY5 86 B1
Hurstmere Av BPOOLS FY4 125 H3
Hurst Pk PRES PR1 151 M7
Hurst Rd MGHL L31 259 H4
Hurst's La ORM L39 260 D1
Hurst St ROCH OL11 235 K6
Hurstway FUL/RIB PR2 132 A4
Hurstway Cl FUL/RIB PR2 132 A4
Hurstwood Av BBNW BB2 172 D2
BRFD/BLYE BB10 143 G6
Hurstwood Dr BISP FY2 105 G1
Hurstwood Gdns NLSN BB9 123 G7
Hurstwood La
BRFD/BLYE BB10 143 L7
Hurtley St BRFD/BLYE BB10 142 D3
Hutch Bank Rd RAW/HAS BB4 176 C8
Hutchinson Ct DWN BB3 191 J2
Hutchinson Rd ROCH OL11 234 A2
Hutchinson St BBNW BB2 * 10 F8
ROCH OL11 234 E5
Hut La CHLYE PR6 208 E7
Huttock End La BCUP OL13 197 G3
Hutton Cl KKBYL LA6 19 H5
Hutton Ct SKEL WN8 253 G2
Hutton Crs MCMB LA4 41 H7
Hutton Dr PDHM/BLYW BB12 6 C1
Hutton Gdns CARN LA5 25 M7
Hutton Gv MCMB LA4 41 H7
Hutton Hall Av
KIRK/FR/WAR PR4 167 H1
Hutton Rd SKEL WN8 253 G2
Hutton St BBN BB1 11 K3
WGN WN1 229 K8
Hutton Wy LANC LA1 2 D4
ORM L39 241 H6
Huyton Rd CHLY/EC PR7 230 D5
Hyacinth Cl RAW/HAS BB4 194 C3
Hyatt Crs WGNNW/ST WN6 228 F8
Hydeaway Ct MCMB LA4 41 J7
Hyde Rd BPOOL FY1 4 D7
MCMB LA4 42 A7
Hyde's Brow RNFD/HAY WA11 262 D3
Hydon Brook Wk ROCH OL11 234 F7
Hyndburn Br GTH/LHO BB6 139 J6
Hyndburn Dr DWN BB3 173 G7
Hyndburn Rd ACC BB5 159 J5
GTH/LHO BB6 139 H6
Hyndburn St ACC BB5 159 J5
Hyning Rd CARN LA5 26 B3
The Hynings GTH/LHO BB6 138 E5
Hythe Cl BBN BB1 157 M7
STHP PR8 200 B8

I

Ibbison Ct BPOOL FY1 4 E5
Ibbotroyd Av TOD OL14 301 K12
Ibsley WHIT OL12 * 235 H3
Icconhurst Cl ACC BB5 176 A1
Ice St BBN BB1 157 H4
Iddesleigh Rd PRES PR1 * 153 H2
Iddon Ct BPOOL FY1 104 F5
Idlewood Pl CLV/TH FY5 85 J3
Idstone Cl BBNW BB2 173 K3
Ightenhill Park La
PDHM/BLYW BB12 141 M3
Ightenhill Park Ms
PDHM/BLYW BB12 141 M4
Ightenhill St
PDHM/BLYW BB12 140 F2
Ighten Rd PDHM/BLYW BB12 6 A2
Ilford Av CSBY/BLUN L23 257 G6
Ilford Rd BPOOLS FY4 5 J9
Ilkley Av CHTN/BK PR9 180 F5
LSTA FY8 145 M5
Ilkley Gv CLV/TH FY5 85 G3
The Illawalla CLV/TH FY5 86 B5
Illingworth Rd PRES PR1 153 H2
Illston Ms NLSN BB9 * 122 E6
Ilminster ROCH OL11 * 235 H5
Ilway BBR PR5 153 G8
Imperial Yd BPOOL FY1 * 104 E4
Ince Av CSBY/BLUN L23 256 F6
Ince Crs FMBY L37 237 G8
Ince La CHLY/EC PR7 205 M6
SFTN L29 257 J2
Ince Rd CSBY/BLUN L23 257 K4
Inch Fld BRFD/BLYE BB10 143 L5
Inchfield SKEL WN8 253 L1
Inchfield Cl ROCH OL11 234 B2
Inchfield Rd TOD OL14 303 K7
India St ACC BB5 159 J5
DWN BB3 191 L3
Industrial Pl BCUP OL13 197 J1
Industrial St BCUP OL13 197 K1
RAMS BL0 214 F2
TOD OL14 303 L2
Industry Rd WHIT OL12 235 J2
Industry St DWN BB3 191 L1
LIT OL15 219 L6
ROCH OL11 234 B2
TOD OL14 303 K6
WHIT OL12 218 A1
Infant St ACC BB5 159 M5
Infirmary Cl BBNW BB2 * 10 D9
Infirmary Rd BBNW BB2 10 D9
Infirmary St BBNW BB2 10 D9
Ing Dene Av COL BB8 103 L7
Ing Dene Cl COL BB8 103 L7
Ingfield Est SETT BD24 265 N9
Ingfield La SETT BD24 265 N8
Inghams La LIT OL15 219 L6
Ingham St NLSN BB9 103 G8

Inghey Br SKP/WHF BD23 281 Q7
Ingleborough Dr
BWCK/EAR BB18 293 P5
Ingleborough Rd LANC LA1 42 B8
Ingleborough Vw CARN LA5 33 K3
HGHB LA2 * 39 G3
Ingleborough Wy LEYL PR25 186 F1
Ingleby Cl CLV/TH FY5 81 J6
Ingle Cl CHLYE PR6 208 A2
Inglefield ROCH OL11 234 B2
Ingle Gn CSBY/BLUN L23 256 D6
Ingle Head FUL/RIB PR2 132 A5
Inglehurst Rd BLY BB11 141 L6
Inglemere Ct CARN LA5 16 D1
Inglemere Dr CARN LA5 16 E2
Inglemere Gdns CARN LA5 16 E2
Ingle Nook BRFD/BLYE BB10 143 J7
Inglenook Cl CLV/TH FY5 85 J2
Inglesby Cnr BRSC L40 223 L7
Ingleton Av BISP FY2 85 J7
Ingleton Cl ACC BB5 160 A6
Ingleton Dr LANC LA1 54 F7
Ingleton Rd FUL/RIB PR2 133 H7
STHP PR8 200 B8
Ingleway CLV/TH FY5 81 H8
Ingleway Av BPOOLE FY3 105 H5
Inglewhite SKEL WN8 253 K1
Inglewhite Fold
PDHM/BLYW BB12 141 G4
Inglewhite Rd
GAR/LONG PR3 114 D3
Inglewood Cl FTWD FY7 80 F2
KIRK/FR/WAR PR4 148 A5
Inglewood Gv BISP FY2 85 H6
Inglis St LIT OL15 219 L5
Ingoe Cl HEYW OL10 234 C8
Ingol Gv PLF/KEOS FY6 86 F1
Ingol La PLF/KEOS FY6 87 G1
Ingot St PRES PR1 8 D2
Ingram SKEL WN8 253 L2
Ings Av BWCK/EAR BB18 293 Q4
WHIT OL12 234 E1
Ings La WHIT OL12 234 E1
Ingthorpe Av BISP FY2 85 G6
Ingthorpe La
SKP/WHF BD23 280 A6
Inkerman Rd
KIRK/FR/WAR PR4 107 H5
Inkerman St BBN BB1 10 F1
BCUP OL13 197 K1
FUL/RIB PR2 131 M8
PDHM/BLYW BB12 * 140 F3
WHIT OL12 * 235 J2
Ink St MILN OL16 235 J4
Inner Prom LSTA FY8 145 M8
Inskip SKEL WN8 253 K1
Inskip Pl LSTA FY8 145 K3
Inskip Rd CHTN/BK PR9 180 D7
FUL/RIB PR2 151 H2
KIRK/FR/WAR PR4 109 K7
LEYL PR25 186 A1
Inskip St PDHM/BLYW BB12 140 F3
Institute St PDHM/BLYW BB12 141 G3
Intack La BBNW BB2 155 L1
Intack Rd KIRK/FR/WAR PR4 166 E3
Intake Crs COL BB8 296 C5
Intake La ORM L39 252 D7
ORM L39 249 H3
Inverness Rd DWN BB3 191 J3
Inver Rd BISP FY2 85 G8
Inward Dr WGNNW/ST WN6 245 K6
Ipswich Pl CLV/TH FY5 84 F1
Ipswich Rd FUL/RIB PR2 153 G1
Ipswich St ROCH OL11 235 J6
Ireby Rd KKBYL LA6 31 H5
Irene Pl BBNW BB2 156 E6
Irene St BRFD/BLYE BB10 7 L5
Iris Park Wk MGHL L31 259 K8
Iris St RAMS BL0 214 E5
Irongate BBR PR5 168 F3
Ironside Cl FUL/RIB PR2 132 E7
Iron St BBNW BB2 10 D8
Irton Rd CHTN/BK PR9 200 B3
Irvin Av CHTN/BK PR9 180 F6
Irvine St NLSN BB9 * 123 J1
Irving Cl BISP FY2 85 J6
Irving Pl BBNW BB2 156 E6
Irving St CHTN/BK PR9 199 L2
Irvin St PRES PR1 9 M1
Irwell SKEL WN8 243 K8
Irwell Pl WGNW/BIL/OR WN5 255 M5
Irwell Rd WGNW/BIL/OR WN5 255 J4
Irwell St BCUP OL13 197 J1
GAR/LONG PR3 114 E3
PDHM/BLYW BB12 141 K5
RAMS BL0 214 F5
Irwell Ter BCUP OL13 179 J8
Irwell Vale Rd RAW/HAS BB4 194 F5
Irwell Valley Wy BCUP OL13 197 G3
BCUP OL13 179 K2
RAMS BL0 214 F7
RAW/HAS BB4 195 G4
Isabella St GAR/LONG PR3 114 D3
WHIT OL12 235 J1
Isa St RAMS BL0 214 D7
Isherwood Fold EDGW/EG BL7 213 G4
Isherwood St BBNW BB2 173 G2
PRES PR1 152 F2
ROCH OL11 235 K6
Island La GAR/LONG PR3 282 H5
Islay Cl BPOOLS FY4 125 J5
Islay Rd LSTA FY8 146 A5
Isle of Man BBN BB1 137 H7
Isle of Man St RAW/HAS BB4 178 C4
Isleworth Dr CHLY/EC PR7 207 L4
Islington BBNW BB2 10 E7
CSBY/BLUN L23 257 G7
Islington Cl BRFD/BLYE BB10 123 G8
Ivanhoe Rd CSBY/BLUN L23 256 F8
Ivan St BRFD/BLYE BB10 142 E1
Iveagh Ct MILN OL16 * 235 L5
Ivegate COL BB8 296 A6
Ivinson Rd DWN BB3 173 L8
Ivor St ROCH OL11 234 E8
Ivory Dr NWD/KWIPK L33 260 B6
Ivory St PDHM/BLYW BB12 141 M5
Ivy Av BPOOLS FY4 125 H6
RAW/HAS BB4 176 F8
Ivy Bank FUL/RIB PR2 133 G5
Ivybridge SKEL WN8 253 L1
Ivy Cl BRSC L40 225 K8
LEYL PR25 187 H1
Ivy Cots WHIT OL12 * 234 F2
Ivydale SKEL WN8 253 L1
Ivy Dene Cl SETT BD24 265 N8
Ivy Gdns CLV/TH FY5 81 K7
Ivy House Gdns
SKP/WHF BD23 281 K2
Ivy Pl TOD OL14 300 C10
Ivy St BBNW BB2 10 D9
BRFD/BLYE BB10 142 E2
RAW/HAS BB4 196 C3
STHP PR8 13 M6
Ivy Ter DWN BB3 191 L5

J

Jack Anderton Br
GAR/LONG PR3 286 A8
Jack Br HBR HX7 301 R6
Jack La SKP/WHF BD23 267 L8
Jacks Key Dr DWN BB3 191 M6
Jacksmere La BRSC L40 222 E3
Jackson Cl LANC LA1 2 B8
ORM L39 239 J6
Jackson Heights Rd BBN BB1 174 E7
Jackson Rd CHLY/EC PR7 * 207 K6
LEYL PR25 186 A2
Jackson's Banks Rd
BBNW BB2 135 G6
Jackson's Common La
BRSC L40 240 D2
Jackson's La BRSC L40 227 H4
Jackson St ACC BB5 * 159 H6
BBR PR5 * 169 J3
BPOOLE FY3 105 H4
BRFD/BLYE BB10 * 142 D3
CHLY/EC PR7 208 A5
MILN OL16 235 L5
WHIT OL12 218 F5
Jackson Ter CARN LA5 26 A7
Jack Taylor Ct WHIT OL12 * 235 L2
Jack Walker Wy BBNW BB2 173 G4
Jacob Bright Ms WHIT OL12 235 J1
Jacob's La KIRK/FR/WAR PR4 129 J3
Jacob St ACC BB5 159 M6
Jacson St PRES PR1 9 J4
Jade Cl NWD/KWIPK L33 260 C8
Jagoe Rd BWCK/EAR BB18 294 D6
James Av BPOOLS FY4 5 M9
GTH/LHO BB6 138 E6
James Butterworth Ct
MILN OL16 * 235 L5
James Butterworth St
MILN OL16 235 L4
James Hill St LIT OL15 219 L6
Jameson Rd FTWD FY7 81 K2
Jameson St BPOOL FY1 4 F5
James Pl CHLY/EC PR7 229 H2
James St ACC BB5 159 G7
BBN BB1 174 C5
BBN BB1 * 158 F2
BBN BB1 10 F3
BBR PR5 169 H2
BCUP OL13 * 196 D4
BRFD/BLYE BB10 142 D2
BWCK/EAR BB18 293 Q6
COL BB8 * 296 B6
DWN BB3 191 J2
EDGW/EG BL7 212 A8
GTH/LHO BB6 138 E6
HOR/BR BL6 231 J8
LIT OL15 219 J6
MCMB LA4 41 K6
PRES PR1 9 M5
RAW/HAS BB4 195 K1
WHIT OL12 235 K3
WHIT OL12 218 A1
James St West DWN BB3 191 K2
Jamieson Av CSBY/BLUN L23 257 K7
Jane La CROS/BRETH PR26 167 K8
KIRK/FR/WAR PR4 110 B6
Jane's Brook Rd STHP PR8 200 A7
Janes Meadow
KIRK/FR/WAR PR4 183 K6
Jane St WHIT OL12 302 B9
WHIT OL12 235 H3
Janice Dr FUL/RIB PR2 132 A4
Janine Cl MCMB LA4 41 H7
Jannat Cl ACC BB5 * 159 L6
Jarrett Rd NWD/KWIPK L33 260 D7
Jarvis St WHIT OL12 235 J2
Jasmine Rd BBR PR5 152 D8
Jasper St BBN BB1 157 J2
Jedburgh Dr NWD/KWIPK L33 260 A5
Jefferson Cl LANC LA1 2 C7
Jefferson Wy WHIT OL12 218 C8
Jeffrey Av GAR/LONG PR3 114 E4
Jeffrey Hill Cl FUL/RIB PR2 133 M4
Jeffrey Sq BPOOL FY1 5 G6
Jellicoe Cl LSTA FY8 145 H1
Jem Ga CLV/TH FY5 85 G3
Jemmett St PRES PR1 132 B8
Jenny La BPOOLS FY4 125 M4
CHLYE PR6 188 F2
Jenny Nook HEY LA3 52 F4
Jensen Cl LANC LA1 54 D5
Jensen Dr BPOOLS FY4 126 D5
Jepheys Pl WHIT OL12 235 J2
Jepheys St WHIT OL12 235 J2
Jepp Hl BWCK/EAR BB18 293 Q5
Jepps Av GAR/LONG PR3 111 L3
Jepps La GAR/LONG PR3 111 L3
Jepson St DWN BB3 191 K3
Jepson Wy BPOOLS FY4 125 J7
Jermyn St WHIT OL12 235 K3
Jerrold St LIT OL15 219 L6
Jersey Av BISP FY2 105 H1
Jersey St BBNW BB2 172 E2
Jervis Cl LSTA FY8 145 G2
Jesmond Av BPOOLS FY4 124 E4
Jesmond Gv MCMB LA4 41 L8
Jesmond Rd BOL BL1 233 L7
Jessel St BBNW BB2 172 E1
Jesson Wy CARN LA5 33 H2
Jevington Wy HEY LA3 52 F4
Jingling La KKBYL LA6 21 M1
Jinny La PDHM/BLYW BB12 102 A8
Jobling St COL BB8 * 103 J8
Jockey St BLY BB11 141 M6
Joe Connolly Wy
RAW/HAS BB4 196 B3
Joe La GAR/LONG PR3 91 G2
John Ashworth St WHIT OL12 235 L2
John Eastwood Homes
TOD OL14 * 303 K6
John Hill St BPOOLS FY4 5 L8
John Hunter Wy NTHTN L30 258 C8
Johnny Barn Cl RAW/HAS BB4 195 M1
John O'Gaunt St
PDHM/BLYW BB12 140 F2
John Roberts Cl ROCH OL11 235 H6
Johnson Cl CARN LA5 33 H2
LANC LA1 2 B7
Johnson New Rd DWN BB3 174 B8
Johnson Rd BPOOLS FY4 5 L8
DWN BB3 173 M7
Johnson's Meanygate
KIRK/FR/WAR PR4 182 F2
Johnson St
WGNW/BIL/OR WN5 255 L5
Johnspool FUL/RIB PR2 131 M5
Johnston WHIT OL12 * 235 H3
Johnston Av LIT OL15 * 219 J8
Johnston Cl BBNW BB2 10 B4
Johnston St BBNW BB2 10 B4
John St ACC BB5 159 G8
ACC BB5 139 J8
BBR PR5 169 H2
BPOOL FY1 4 D8
BWCK/EAR BB18 294 E6
CARN LA5 33 J2
CHLY/EC PR7 * 229 H2
CLV/TH FY5 81 L7
COL BB8 103 M7
DWN BB3 191 J1
HEYW OL10 234 A8
HGHB LA2 66 F8
LEYL PR25 186 D2
LIT OL15 219 K6
MILN OL16 218 F8
NLSN BB9 122 E5
NLSN BB9 103 H7
RAW/HAS BB4 196 C2
WHIT OL12 217 M2
Johnsville Av BPOOLS FY4 125 H4
John William St PRES PR1 * 152 F3
Joiners Aly GTH/LHO BB6 * 138 F6
Joiner's Rw BBNW BB2 10 F7
Jolly Tar La CHLY/EC PR7 229 K4
Jonathan Cl RAW/HAS BB4 194 D3
Jones St HOR/BR BL6 231 L7
MILN OL16 235 K5
Jones's Yd KKBYL LA6 19 G6
Joseph Lister Cl NTHTN L30 258 C8
Joseph St DWN BB3 191 K2
LIT OL15 219 L5
NLSN BB9 123 G1
WHIT OL12 235 G1
Joshua St TOD OL14 303 L1
Jowkin La ROCH OL11 234 A4
Joyce Av BPOOLS FY4 5 M8
Joy St RAMS BL0 214 E5
WHIT OL12 235 J1
Jubilee Av FUL/RIB PR2 151 G2
ORM L39 241 J5
PLF/KEOS FY6 78 D7
WGNW/BIL/OR WN5 255 G7
Jubilee Cl DWN BB3 191 M2
RAW/HAS BB4 194 D2
Jubilee Dr CLV/TH FY5 80 F8
SKEL WN8 253 H3
Jubilee La BPOOLS FY4 125 L5
Jubilee La North BPOOLS FY4 125 K4
Jubilee Pl CHLYE PR6 208 A2
Jubilee Rd ACC BB5 159 J4
BBR PR5 168 D4
CSBY/BLUN L23 256 F8
FMBY L37 247 G2
KIRK/FR/WAR PR4 166 C7
RAW/HAS BB4 194 D2
Jubilee St ACC BB5 159 H7
BBN BB1 10 F5
BRFD/BLYE BB10 123 J8
DWN BB3 191 K2
PDHM/BLYW BB12 * 140 A1
Jubilee Ter
KIRK/FR/WAR PR4 * 149 M2
KIRK/FR/WAR PR4 148 F4
Jubilee Wy CROS/BRETH PR26 184 E8
LSTA FY8 145 M3
Judd Holmes La GAR/LONG PR3 95 G5
Judeland CHLY/EC PR7 207 K1
Judge Flds COL BB8 296 A5
Judith St WHIT OL12 217 M8
Julia St HOR/BR BL6 231 L7
WHIT OL12 235 H3
July St BBN BB1 11 L6
Jumps La TOD OL14 300 H10
Junction Aly MILN OL16 235 J4
Junction La BRSC L40 225 H7
Junction Rd FUL/RIB PR2 8 C4
RNFD/HAY WA11 262 B3
Junction St COL BB8 103 J8
DWN BB3 191 L4
NLSN BB9 122 E5
PDHM/BLYW BB12 6 B2
June Av BPOOLS FY4 125 K2
June St BBN BB1 11 K6
June's Wk KIRK/FR/WAR PR4 166 C6
Juniper Cl PLF/KEOS FY6 78 D6
Juniper Cft CHLYE PR6 187 K2
Juniper Gdns CSBY/BLUN L23 257 L5
Juniper St BBN BB1 157 K4
Juno St NLSN BB9 123 J1
Jutland Av ROCH OL11 234 F3
Jutland St PRES PR1 9 K2

K

Kaigh Av CSBY/BLUN L23 257 G6
Kairnryan Cl BISP FY2 85 J6
Kale Gv NWD/KWIPK L33 260 D6
Kane St FUL/RIB PR2 151 M2
Karan Wy MGHL L31 259 K8
Kateholm BCUP OL13 179 K4
Kate St RAMS BL0 * 214 E5
Kathan Cl MILN OL16 235 L4
Kathleen St WHIT OL12 235 G3
Kay Brow RAMS BL0 214 F5
Kay Gdns BLY BB11 7 H6
Kayley La CLI BB7 291 K10
Kay St ACC BB5 159 G7
BPOOL FY1 4 D4
BURY BL9 214 F8
CLI BB7 99 G4
DWN BB3 191 L2
EDGW/EG BL7 212 F7
PDHM/BLYW BB12 141 G2
PRES PR1 * 8 E4
RAW/HAS BB4 195 K1
ROCH OL11 235 H6
Kayswell Rd MCMB LA4 42 A6
Kearsley Av KIRK/FR/WAR PR4 183 K5
Keasden Av BPOOLS FY4 125 G4
Keasden Rd CLI BB7 63 G5
HGHB LA2 63 G2
Keats Av CARN LA5 32 F6
KIRK/FR/WAR PR4 148 B5
TOD OL14 303 N1
WHIT OL12 234 D2
Keats Cl ACC BB5 176 B1
CHLY/EC PR7 206 A6
CLV/TH FY5 85 K1
COL BB8 296 A5
Keats Fold PDHM/BLYW BB12 141 J4
Keats Ter STHP PR8 200 C5
Keats Wy KIRK/FR/WAR PR4 131 G7
Keble Dr AIN/FAZ L10 258 F8
Keele Cl CLV/TH FY5 85 K1
Keele Wk BBN BB1 11 H6
Keelham La TOD OL14 301 N9
Keepers Dr WHIT OL12 234 B1
Keepers Ga LSTA FY8 146 A4
Keeper's Hey CLV/TH FY5 81 K7
Keeper's La GAR/LONG PR3 284 E5
Keepers Wood Wy
CHLY/EC PR7 207 K5
Keer Bank LANC LA1 2 A1
Keer Holme La KKBYL LA6 27 K5
Keighley Av COL BB8 296 A5
Keighley Rd COL BB8 296 C6
HWTH BD22 297 Q1
Keirby Wk BLY BB11 7 H4
Keith Gv CLV/TH FY5 85 G2
Keith St PDHM/BLYW BB12 141 M5
Kelbrook Dr BLY BB11 6 C9
Kelbrook Rd BWCK/EAR BB18 294 A7
Kelkbeck Cl MGHL L31 259 J1
Kellet Acre BBR PR5 168 D4
Kellet Av LEYL PR25 187 G2
Kellet Ct LANC LA1 2 E6
Kellet La BBR PR5 169 L5
CARN LA5 33 J8
HGHB LA2 43 G6
KKBYL LA6 34 A1
Kellet Lane Br KKBYL LA6 26 E8
Kellet Rd KKBYL LA6 33 M3
Kellett St CHLY/EC PR7 * 207 M3
MILN OL16 235 L3
Kelley Cl BBNW BB2 172 F3
Kelmarsh Cl BPOOLE FY3 125 L1
Kelsall Av BBN BB1 157 L3
Kelsall St MILN OL16 * 235 J3
Kelsey St LANC LA1 2 E6
Kelso Av CLV/TH FY5 85 G2
Kelso Cl NWD/KWIPK L33 260 A5
Kelsons Av CLV/TH FY5 85 M1
Kelswick Dr NLSN BB9 123 H5
Kelverdale Rd CLV/TH FY5 85 J3
Kelvin Rd CLV/TH FY5 85 G5
Kelvin St DWN BB3 191 J2
Kem Mill La CHLYE PR6 187 L3
Kemp Av ROCH OL11 235 G6
Kemp Ct BBN BB1 137 J8
Kemple Vw CLI BB7 98 F5
Kemp St FTWD FY7 77 L6
Kempton Av BPOOLE FY3 5 K5
Kempton Park Fold STHP PR8 200 C8
Kempton Ri BBN BB1 11 H8
Kempton Rd LANC LA1 55 G7
Kenbury Cl NWD/KWIPK L33 260 D7
Kenbury Rd NWD/KWIPK L33 260 D7
Kendal Av BPOOLE FY3 105 J2
CLV/TH FY5 81 G7
NLSN BB9 103 G7
WHIT OL12 234 B1
Kendal Cl RNFD/HAY WA11 262 C1
Kendal Dr MCMB LA4 42 A7
MGHL L31 259 G1
RNFD/HAY WA11 262 C2
Kendall Cl BBNW BB2 173 G3
Kendalmans SETT BD24 265 M7
Kendal Rd KKBYL LA6 21 K1
LSTA FY8 145 G2
NWD/KWIPK L33 260 A7
Kendal Rw BBN BB1 174 C5
Kendal St BBN BB1 10 F2
CLI BB7 99 J2
NLSN BB9 123 G2
PRES PR1 8 F2
Kendal Wy STHP PR8 220 E8
Kenilworth ROCH OL11 * 235 H5
Kenilworth Av FTWD FY7 77 H8
Kenilworth Cl
PDHM/BLYW BB12 141 H3
Kenilworth Dr
BWCK/EAR BB18 294 D7
CLI BB7 98 F5
Kenilworth Gdns BPOOLS FY4 124 E4
Kenilworth Pl LANC LA1 54 F6
Kenilworth Rd CSBY/BLUN L23 256 F8
HEY LA3 53 J1
LSTA FY8 145 J5
STHP PR8 220 F7
Kenion Rd ROCH OL11 234 D5
Kenion St MILN OL16 235 J4
Kenlis Rd GAR/LONG PR3 284 E11
Kenmore Cots LITH L21 * 257 M8
Kenmure Pl PRES PR1 152 C1
Kennedy Cl LANC LA1 2 C8
Kennelwood Av
NWD/KWIPK L33 260 C8
Kennessee Cl MGHL L31 259 H3
Kennet Dr FUL/RIB PR2 132 C3
Kenneth Cl NTHTN L30 258 B8
Kennett Dr LEYL PR25 186 E1
Kennington Rd FUL/RIB PR2 132 D7
Kensington Av PRES PR1 151 L5
Kensington Dr HOR/BR BL6 231 M8
Kensington Gdns BBR PR5 168 F2
Kensington Pl BLY BB11 6 B7
Kensington Rd BPOOLE FY3 5 H3
CHLY/EC PR7 207 L4
CHTN/BK PR9 13 K4
CLV/TH FY5 80 F8
FMBY L37 247 H2
LANC LA1 54 E6
LSTA FY8 146 A7
MCMB LA4 * 41 J6
Kensington St NLSN BB9 122 F4
ROCH OL11 235 H7
Kent Av BBR PR5 * 153 G8
CLV/TH FY5 81 H7
FMBY L37 247 K2
Kent Ct NLSN BB9 103 G7
Kent Dr BBN BB1 158 B7
LEYL PR25 187 G1
Kentmere Av BBR PR5 169 G1
LEYL PR25 168 D8
WHIT OL12 218 E8
Kentmere Cl
PDHM/BLYW BB12 141 L3
Kentmere Dr BBNW BB2 172 B3
BPOOLS FY4 125 M2
KIRK/FR/WAR PR4 166 E3
Kentmere Gv MCMB LA4 41 L7
Kentmere Rd LANC LA1 3 K4
Kenton Cl FMBY L37 237 J5
Kent Rd BPOOL FY1 4 E5
FMBY L37 247 K2
STHP PR8 12 F9
Kent's Cl KIRK/FR/WAR PR4 128 B4
Kent St BBN BB1 11 G6
FTWD FY7 77 L6
LANC LA1 3 H1
PDHM/BLYW BB12 6 E1
PRES PR1 152 C1
ROCH OL11 235 J5
Kent Wk RAW/HAS BB4 194 D3
Kent Wy HEY LA3 42 A8
Kenway RNFD/HAY WA11 262 D5
Kenwood Av MCMB LA4 41 H7
Kenwood Rd BOL BL1 233 L8
Kenworthys Flats
CHTN/BK PR9 13 G2
Kenworthy St BBN BB1 11 H1
MILN OL16 235 M4
Kenworthy Ter MILN OL16 235 M4
Kenwyn Av BPOOLE FY3 5 J5
Kenyon Cl NWD/KWIPK L33 260 C5
Kenyon Fold ROCH OL11 234 B6
Kenyon La CHLYE PR6 188 C4
Kenyon Rd MCMB LA4 42 A6
NLSN BB9 122 D4
Kenyons La FMBY L37 237 K8
MGHL L31 250 A7
Kenyon St ACC BB5 159 L5
BBN BB1 157 M5
BCUP OL13 197 L3
RAMS BL0 214 F4
RAW/HAS BB4 177 K8
Keppel Pl BLY BB11 6 C5
Keppers Wood Wy
GAR/LONG PR3 284 B12
Kepple La GAR/LONG PR3 283 R9
Kerenhappuch St RAMS BL0 214 E6
Kerfoot's La SKEL WN8 252 F3
Kerr Cl NWD/KWIPK L33 260 B5
Kerr Pl PRES PR1 8 B2
Kershaw Av CSBY/BLUN L23 257 J8
Kershaw Cl RAW/HAS BB4 177 K4
Kershaw Rd TOD OL14 303 K6
Kershaw St ACC BB5 159 H5
BCUP OL13 * 197 J1
CHLYE PR6 208 B3
WGNW/BIL/OR WN5 255 L5
WHIT OL12 * 235 J3
Kerslake Wy HTWN L38 247 J7
Kerslea Av PLF/KEOS FY6 106 A3
Kerton Rw STHP PR8 * 199 J7
Keston Gv BPOOLS FY4 124 F6
Kestor La GAR/LONG PR3 114 D4
Kestral Pk SKEL WN8 243 M7
Kestrel Cl BBN BB1 157 G3
CHLYE PR6 188 D8
CLV/TH FY5 81 J6
Kestrel Ct CHTN/BK PR9 13 L3
Kestrel Dr DWN BB3 173 G8
Kestrel Ms SKEL WN8 243 M7
Keswick Cl ACC BB5 160 A2
MGHL L31 259 H1
STHP PR8 220 F8
TOD OL14 301 J12
Keswick Ct LANC LA1 3 L3
Keswick Dr BBNW BB2 172 B3
Keswick Gv HEY LA3 52 D6
PLF/KEOS FY6 78 C6
Keswick Rd BPOOL FY1 4 F5
BRFD/BLYE BB10 142 D1
LANC LA1 3 K4
LSTA FY8 145 H3
Keswick Wk LANC LA1 3 L3
Keswick Wy RNFD/HAY WA11 262 C1
Kettering Rd STHP PR8 220 E6
Kettlesbeck Brow HGHB LA2 51 K6
Kevin Av PLF/KEOS FY6 86 C6
Kevin Gv HEY LA3 65 J2
Kew Gdns LEYL PR25 168 E8
PRES PR1 151 L5
Kew Gv CLV/TH FY5 85 G2
Kew House Dr STHP PR8 222 D1
Kew Rd FMBY L37 247 G2
ROCH OL11 235 J8
STHP PR8 199 K8
Keynsham Gv
PDHM/BLYW BB12 6 B1
Key Syke La TOD OL14 303 M2
Key Vw DWN BB3 191 M6
Khyber St COL BB8 103 M7
Kibble Crs BRFD/BLYE BB10 122 F8
Kibble Gv NLSN BB9 123 G7
Kibboth Crew RAMS BL0 214 E4
Kibbrooke Av BPOOLS FY4 124 E7
Kidder St BBNW BB2 173 G3
Kiddlington Cl BBR PR5 168 F3
Kiddrow La PDHM/BLYW BB12 141 K4
Kidsgrove FUL/RIB PR2 131 J6
Kielder Ct LSTA FY8 146 F7
Kielder Dr PDHM/BLYW BB12 6 C1
Kiers Ct HOR/BR BL6 232 B7
Kilbane St FTWD FY7 81 J2
Kilburn Dr WGNNW/ST WN6 245 K4
Kilburn Rd
WGNW/BIL/OR WN5 254 F6
Kilcrash La GAR/LONG PR3 283 M8
Kildale Cl MGHL L31 258 F1
Kildare Av CLV/TH FY5 81 K7
Kildare Rd BISP FY2 85 G8
Kildonan Av BPOOLS FY4 125 J5
Kilgrimol Gdns LSTA FY8 144 F3
Kilkerran Cl CHLYE PR6 208 A3
Killer St RAMS BL0 * 214 F5
Killiard La BBNW BB2 156 B7
Killingbeck Cl BRSC L40 225 G7
Killington St BRFD/BLYE BB10 142 F1
Kilmory Pl BISP FY2 85 J6
Kilmuir Cl FUL/RIB PR2 * 132 F6
Kilnbank Av MCMB LA4 41 H6
Kiln Bank La WHIT OL12 217 M1
Kiln Cl CLI BB7 99 K1
Kiln Cft CHLYE PR6 169 K8
Kilnerdeyne Ter MILN OL16 * 235 H5
Kilngate BBR PR5 152 F8
Kiln Hl PDHM/BLYW BB12 121 J5
Kilnhouse La LSTA FY8 145 J2
Kiln House Wy ACC BB5 159 K8
Kilnhurst La TOD OL14 303 N3
Kilnhurst Mt TOD OL14 303 M2
Kilnhurst Rd TOD OL14 303 M2
Kiln La CLI BB7 291 R3
CLI BB7 278 E7
PLF/KEOS FY6 86 E1
SKEL WN8 253 H1
The Kilns BLY BB11 142 E8
Kiln St NLSN BB9 123 G3
RAMS BL0 214 E6
Kiln Wk WHIT OL12 235 H1
Kilnyard Rd CSBY/BLUN L23 257 G7
Kilruddery Rd PRES PR1 8 D8
Kilsby Cl BBR PR5 153 H8
Kilshaw St
WGNW/BIL/OR WN5 255 M6
Kilworth Height FUL/RIB PR2 131 M6
Kilworth St ROCH OL11 235 G6
Kimberley Av BPOOLS FY4 125 G6
CSBY/BLUN L23 * 257 G8
Kimberley Cl BRFD/BLYE BB10 123 J8
Kimberley Dr CSBY/BLUN L23 257 G8
Kimberley Rd FUL/RIB PR2 151 M1
Kimberley St BCUP OL13 * 196 D4
BRFD/BLYE BB10 123 J8
CHLY/EC PR7 229 H2
Kimberly Cl KIRK/FR/WAR PR4 148 E5
Kime St PDHM/BLYW BB12 141 M5
Kincraig Pl BISP FY2 85 J5
Kincraig Rd BISP FY2 85 J7
Kinders Fold LIT OL15 219 J4
King Edward Av BISP FY2 104 E2
LSTA FY8 145 K7
King Edward St ACC BB5 158 F8

Kingfisher Bank BLY BB11 141 L7
Kingfisher Cl BBN BB1 157 H3
NWD/KWIPK L33 260 B5
Kingfisher Ct CHTN/BK PR9 13 M2
PRES PR1 8 C2
Kingfisher Dr PLF/KEOS FY6 105 L1
Kingfisher Ms PLF/KEOS FY6 105 L1
Kingfisher Pk SKEL WN8 243 M7
Kingfisher St PRES PR1 152 E1
Kingfisher Wy FTWD FY7 77 H8
King George Av BISP FY2 104 E2
King La CLI BB7 99 H3
Kingsacre GAR/LONG PR3 283 R12
Kings Ar LANC LA1 3 G6
Kings Arms Cl LANC LA1 * 3 G6
Kings Av RAW/HAS BB4 195 K2
Kingsbridge Cl PRES PR1 168 B2
King's Bridge Cl BBNW BB2 172 E2
King's Bridge St BBNW BB2 172 E2
Kingsbridge Whf BBNW BB2 172 E2
Kingsbury Cl STHP PR8 220 D7
Kingsbury Ct SKEL WN8 243 M7
King's Cswy NLSN BB9 123 G6
Kings Cl BPOOLE FY3 106 B6
CARN LA5 16 E2
CHLY/EC PR7 187 J5
FMBY L37 247 H1
King's Cl PLF/KEOS FY6 86 B8
Kingscote Dr BPOOLE FY3 105 H4
Kings Ct LEYL PR25 186 D2
Kings Crs LEYL PR25 186 D2
King's Crs HEY LA3 40 F8
King's Cft BBR PR5 153 G6
Kingsdale Av BRFD/BLYE BB10 122 E8
FUL/RIB PR2 133 G6
HEY LA3 52 E2
Kingsdale Cl BBR PR5 153 J6
LEYL PR25 186 E5
Kingsdale Rd LANC LA1 2 C7
Kings Dr DWN BB3 192 B2
FUL/RIB PR2 132 A6
PDHM/BLYW BB12 141 G5
King's Dr CARN LA5 33 K2
Kingsfield Rd MGHL L31 258 F4
Kingsfold Dr PRES PR1 167 M1
Kings Gv WHIT OL12 218 F7
Kingshaven Dr PRES PR1 168 B2
Kings Hey Dr CHTN/BK PR9 200 C2
King's Hwy ACC BB5 176 E3
RAW/HAS BB4 176 E5
Kingshotte Gdns NLSN BB9 102 F8
Kingsland Gv BLY BB11 7 J8
BPOOL FY1 5 H7
Kingsland Rd BLY BB11 7 J9
ROCH OL11 234 E8
Kingslea CHLY/EC PR7 230 C3
Kingsley Av PDHM/BLYW BB12 141 H4
Kingsley Cl ACC BB5 159 J4
BBNW BB2 172 A4
CLV/TH FY5 81 K8
MGHL L31 249 M6
Kingsley Dr CHLY/EC PR7 207 K6
Kingsley Rd BPOOLE FY3 125 L1
COL BB8 296 G5
KIRK/FR/WAR PR4 131 H5
Kingsley St NLSN BB9 123 J1
Kingsmead BBN BB1 158 A7
CHLY/EC PR7 207 M6
Kings Meadow STHP PR8 221 G8
Kingsmede BPOOLS FY4 125 H5
Kingsmere Av LSTA FY8 145 J2
Kingsmill Av CLI BB7 118 D3
Kings Mill La SETT BD24 265 M7
King's Moss La
RNFD/HAY WA11 263 H4
Kingsmuir Av FUL/RIB PR2 * 133 G7
Kingsmuir Cl HEY LA3 52 D4
Kings Rd CLV/TH FY5 84 F1
CSBY/BLUN L23 257 G7
FMBY L37 247 H1
King's Rd ACC BB5 159 L3
BBNW BB2 172 E3
LSTA FY8 145 H6
MILN OL16 235 L6
Kingston Av ACC BB5 159 K7
BPOOLS FY4 124 F6
Kingston Cl PLF/KEOS FY6 78 C5
Kingston Crs CHTN/BK PR9 180 F6
RAW/HAS BB4 194 C4
Kingston Dr LSTA FY8 146 A5
Kingston Pl DWN BB3 173 H4
King St ACC BB5 159 L5
BBNW BB2 10 D5
BBR PR5 168 E4
BCUP OL13 197 J1
BPOOL FY1 4 E1
BRFD/BLYE BB10 123 J8
CARN LA5 33 J2
CHLY/EC PR7 208 A5
CLI BB7 118 F6
CLI BB7 99 H3
COL BB8 296 B6
FTWD FY7 77 K7
GAR/LONG PR3 114 F4
GTH/LHO BB6 138 F6
HOR/BR BL6 231 K7
LANC LA1 3 G6
LEYL PR25 186 D2
MCMB LA4 41 J6
MILN OL16 235 J4
NLSN BB9 122 D6
PDHM/BLYW BB12 140 F3
RAMS BL0 214 F5
RAW/HAS BB4 196 B3
RAW/HAS BB4 176 E7
STHP PR8 12 F5
TOD OL14 303 N1
WHIT OL12 302 A12
King St East ROCH OL11 235 H6
King St South ROCH OL11 235 H6
King's Wk CLV/TH FY5 81 G6
Kingsway ACC BB5 159 K3
BBR PR5 169 H3
BLY BB11 7 G3
BPOOLS FY4 124 F4
CHLY/EC PR7 207 H1
CLV/TH FY5 84 F1
DWN BB3 173 K4
FUL/RIB PR2 151 J1
GTH/LHO BB6 139 J5
HEY LA3 52 E4
LANC LA1 3 J3
LEYL PR25 186 B4
LSTA FY8 145 M7
MILN OL16 235 M5
PRES PR1 8 A7
RAW/HAS BB4 194 C2
STHP PR8 12 E4
Kingsway Av GAR/LONG PR3 111 M8
Kingsway Ct HEY LA3 52 F2
Kingsway West PRES PR1 151 K6
Kingswood CHLY/EC PR7 207 L6
Kingswood Cl LSTA FY8 146 B7
Kingswood Ct
NWD/KWIPK L33 260 C7
Kingswood Dr CSBY/BLUN L23 257 G8
Kingswood Pk STHP PR8 12 C6
Kingswood Rd LEYL PR25 186 D1
Kingswood St PRES PR1 8 E4
King William St BBN BB1 10 E4
Kinlet Rd WGNS/IIMK WN3 255 M7
Kinloch Wy ORM L39 241 G6
Kinnerton Pl CLV/TH FY5 85 J3
Kinnical La MTHPE LA7 18 C1
Kinross Cl BBN BB1 11 K5
Kinross Crs BPOOLS FY4 125 K2
Kinross St BLY BB11 6 B6
Kinross Wk BBN BB1 11 K5
Kintbury Rd LSTA FY8 145 J7
Kintour Rd LSTA FY8 146 B5
Kintyre Cl BPOOLS FY4 125 J4
Kintyre Wy HEY LA3 52 C4
Kipling Dr BPOOLE FY3 125 L1
Kipling Pl GTH/LHO BB6 138 E7
Kirby Dr KIRK/FR/WAR PR4 148 E5
Kirby Rd BBNW BB2 173 G2
BPOOL FY1 4 C7
NLSN BB9 122 E3
Kirk Av CLI BB7 98 F3
Kirkbeck Cl HGHB LA2 44 F5
Kirkby Av CLV/TH FY5 81 H7
LEYL PR25 187 H2
Kirkby Lonsdale Rd
KKBYL LA6 34 F5
Kirkby Lonsdale Rd HGHB LA2 43 L4
KKBYL LA6 34 C3
Kirkby Rw KKBY L32 259 M8
Kirkdale Av LSTA FY8 145 J4
RAW/HAS BB4 196 B2
Kirkdale Cl DWN BB3 191 M5
Kirkdale Gdns SKEL WN8 * 254 C4
Kirkdale Rd GTH/LHO BB6 137 M3
Kirkdene Av COL BB8 296 A2
Kirkes Rd LANC LA1 3 K7
Kirkfell Dr PDHM/BLYW BB12 141 M3
Kirkfield GAR/LONG PR3 287 L12
Kirkgate BLY BB11 7 J7
KIRK/FR/WAR PR4 128 E6
SETT BD24 265 N7
Kirkgate La KKBYL LA6 26 F4
Kirkham Av BPOOL FY1 5 J7
Kirkham By-Pass
KIRK/FR/WAR PR4 128 E7
Kirkham Cl LEYL PR25 186 A2
Kirkham Rd CHTN/BK PR9 180 D7
KIRK/FR/WAR PR4 129 G5
KIRK/FR/WAR PR4 127 J1
Kirkham St PRES PR1 8 F2
Kirk Head KIRK/FR/WAR PR4 184 B1
Kirkhill Av RAW/HAS BB4 176 F8
Kirk Hill Rd RAW/HAS BB4 176 F8
Kirklake Bank FMBY L37 246 F1
Kirklake Rd FMBY L37 246 F1
Kirklands GAR/LONG PR3 287 M12
HGHB LA2 42 D2
Kirklands Rd KKBYL LA6 34 B3
Kirklees Rd STHP PR8 221 J2
Kirkmoor Cl CLI BB7 99 G2
Kirkmoor Rd CLI BB7 99 G2
Kirk Rd ACC BB5 159 H4
Kirkside Vw BLY BB11 140 F7
Kirkstall WHIT OL12 * 235 H3
Kirkstall Av BPOOL FY1 5 K8
LIT OL15 219 K5
PDHM/BLYW BB12 140 A2
Kirkstall Cl CHLY/EC PR7 208 A6
Kirkstall Dr BWCK/EAR BB18 293 R4
CHLY/EC PR7 208 A6
FMBY L37 247 L1
Kirkstall Rd CHLY/EC PR7 208 A6
STHP PR8 221 J1
Kirkstead Wk MGHL L31 259 L8
Kirkstone WGNW/BIL/OR WN5 255 M4
Kirkstone Av BBNW BB2 172 B3
FTWD FY7 81 G2
Kirkstone Dr CLV/TH FY5 84 F5
MCMB LA4 41 L6
Kirkstone Rd LSTA FY8 145 G2
Kirk Vw RAW/HAS BB4 196 D2
Kirton Crs LSTA FY8 145 M5
Kirton Pl CLV/TH FY5 85 H2
Kit Brow La HGHB LA2 67 H6
Kitchen St MILN OL16 235 K3
Kitson Wood Rd TOD OL14 300 H11
Kitter St WHIT OL12 218 E8
Kitt Green Rd
WGNW/BIL/OR WN5 255 M3
Kittiwake Cl CLV/TH FY5 85 J2
Kittiwake Rd CHLYE PR6 188 D8
Kittlingborne Brow BBR PR5 153 K8
Kittygill La KKBYL LA6 21 K2
Kitty La BPOOLS FY4 125 L7
Knacks La WHIT OL12 217 K6
Knaresboro Av BPOOLE FY3 5 M6
Knaresborough Cl
PLF/KEOS FY6 85 M6
Knebworth Cl CHLYE PR6 187 M1
Knighton Av BBNW BB2 156 F3
Knightsbrdige Cl
KIRK/FR/WAR PR4 128 B5
Knightsbridge Av BPOOLS FY4 125 G5
COL BB8 103 L6
Knightsbridge Cl LSTA FY8 146 A5
Knightsbridge Wk
NWD/KWIPK L33 260 A5
Knightscliffe Crs
WGNNW/ST WN6 245 G5
Knights Cl CLV/TH FY5 85 J2
Knitting Row La GAR/LONG PR3 83 K8
Knob Hall Gdns CHTN/BK PR9 180 C8
Knob Hall La CHTN/BK PR9 180 C8
Knoll La KIRK/FR/WAR PR4 166 C7
Knoll St ROCH OL11 234 E8
The Knoll HGHB LA2 42 D3
Knot Acre KIRK/FR/WAR PR4 167 K3
Knot La BBR PR5 153 H6
SKP/WHF BD23 278 H9
Knott Hill St WHIT OL12 302 B9
Knott La CARN LA5 16 D2
Knotts Brow EDGW/EG BL7 213 J7
Knotts Dr COL BB8 103 M8
Knotts La COL BB8 103 M7
PDHM/BLYW BB12 141 J5
SKP/WHF BD23 277 J4
Knotts Mt COL BB8 103 M8
Knotts Rd TOD OL14 300 G11
Knott St DWN BB3 191 K2
Knotwood Ct ACC BB5 159 H6
Knowe Hill Crs LANC LA1 55 G8
Knowl Cl RAMS BL0 214 F7
Knowle Av BISP FY2 104 F2
CLV/TH FY5 85 H2
STHP PR8 220 F5
Knowle La DWN BB3 173 K8
Knowles Brow CLI BB7 97 L8
Knowlesly Rd DWN BB3 191 L5
Knowles Rd LSTA FY8 145 H4
Knowles St BBN BB1 158 E2
CHLY/EC PR7 207 M5
PRES PR1 153 G3
The Knowle BISP FY2 104 F1
CSBY/BLUN L23 256 E8
Knowley Brow CHLYE PR6 208 B1
Knowl Gap Av RAW/HAS BB4 194 D2
Knowl Hill Dr WHIT OL12 234 B1
Knowl La WHIT OL12 216 E6
Knowl Meadow RAW/HAS BB4 194 D5
Knowlmere St ACC BB5 159 L5
Knowl Syke St WHIT OL12 218 F4
Knowlwood Rd TOD OL14 303 K4
Knowlys Av HEY LA3 52 D3
Knowlys Crs HEY LA3 52 E3
Knowlys Dr HEY LA3 52 E3
Knowlys Gv HEY LA3 52 D3
Knowlys Rd HEY LA3 52 D3
Knowsley Av BPOOLE FY3 5 J5
LEYL PR25 168 F7
TOD OL14 * 303 K6
Knowsley Cl BBR PR5 170 B1
LANC LA1 2 C9
Knowsley Crs CLV/TH FY5 85 M1
KIRK/FR/WAR PR4 127 H2
WHIT OL12 302 B9
Knowsley Dr BBR PR5 170 C1
Knowsley Ga FTWD FY7 77 G7
Knowsley La CHLYE PR6 209 G7
EDGW/EG BL7 193 H7
Knowsley Ms ORM L39 241 J6
Knowsley Park Wy
RAW/HAS BB4 194 E3
Knowsley Rd BBN BB1 137 J6
CHTN/BK PR9 199 L2
LEYL PR25 186 F3
ORM L39 241 J7
RAW/HAS BB4 194 E3
Knowsley Rd West BBN BB1 137 H5
Knowsley St COL BB8 * 296 A7
PRES PR1 9 K5
WHIT OL12 235 H3
Knowsley Vw
RNFD/HAY WA11 262 B3
Knox Gv BPOOL FY1 5 G6
Knuck Knowles Dr CLI BB7 99 H1
Knutsford Rd BPOOLE FY3 125 L1
Knutsford Wk MGHL L31 250 A7
Knuzden Brook BBN BB1 158 A7
Korea Rd FUL/RIB PR2 132 E6
Kumara Crs BPOOLS FY4 125 L2
Kyan St BRFD/BLYE BB10 142 E1
Kylbarrow La CARN LA5 26 C1
Kylemore Av BISP FY2 105 G1
Kyston Cl BPOOL FY1 105 G4

L

Laburnum Av BBR PR5 168 E3
LSTA FY8 146 E6
Laburnum Cl BLY BB11 6 B8
PRES PR1 132 F8
Laburnum Cots
GAR/LONG PR3 * 282 B2
Laburnum Crs KKBY L32 260 A8
Laburnum Dr ACC BB5 159 J8
FUL/RIB PR2 132 A3
SKEL WN8 253 G2
Laburnum Gv BRSC L40 225 J5
LANC LA1 2 C5
MGHL L31 259 J2
STHP PR8 200 C4
Laburnum Pk CARN LA5 33 H3
Laburnum Rd BBN BB1 157 K3
CHLYE PR6 188 A8
LANC LA1 3 H1
Laburnum St BPOOLE FY3 105 G4
RAW/HAS BB4 176 D8
Laburnum Ter ROCH OL11 235 H7
Laburnum Wy LIT OL15 219 J6
Lachman Rd COL BB8 296 E8
Lacy Av PRES PR1 168 B1
TOD OL14 303 K6
Ladbrooke Gv BLY BB11 162 B1
Lade End HEY LA3 52 D3
Ladies Rw
KIRK/FR/WAR PR4 * 109 J7
Ladies Wk LANC LA1 3 J2
Lady Acre BBR PR5 169 K3
Lady Alice's Dr BRSC L40 242 B3
Ladybank Av FUL/RIB PR2 132 F4
Lady Bower La PLF/KEOS FY6 85 L8
Ladybower La
PLF/KEOS FY6 85 L8
Lady Cl DWN BB3 173 K5
Lady Crosse Dr CHLYE PR6 187 M5
Lady Green Cl HTWN L38 * 248 B8
Lady Green La HTWN L38 248 A7
Lady Hartley Ct COL BB8 296 G5
Lady Hey Crs FUL/RIB PR2 150 F2
Ladyman St PRES PR1 8 E5
Lady Pl BBR PR5 153 H7
Ladysmith Rd FUL/RIB PR2 151 M1
Lady St PRES PR1 9 H2
Lady's Wk BRSC L40 241 L6
Lady Well Dr FUL/RIB PR2 132 F4
Ladywell St PRES PR1 8 F3
Lafford La SKEL WN8 244 F8
Lagonda Dr BPOOLS FY4 126 C5
Laidley's Wk FTWD FY7 77 H6
Laithbutts La KKBYL LA6 33 L6
Laithe St BLY BB11 6 F7
COL BB8 103 M7
Lake Av MCMB LA4 41 G7
Lake Bank LIT OL15 219 K8
Lakeber Av HGHB LA2 39 G4
Lakeber Cl HGHB LA2 39 G4
Lakeber Dr HGHB LA2 39 G3
Lake Gv MCMB LA4 41 G7
Lakeland Cl CLI BB7 118 D8
GAR/LONG PR3 270 A8
Lakeland Dr CLI BB7 118 D3
Lakeland Gdns CHLY/EC PR7 207 K6
Lakeland Wy
PDHM/BLYW BB12 141 L3
Lake Rd HEY LA3 41 G8
LSTA FY8 145 M8
Lake Rd North LSTA FY8 145 M7
Lakes Dr WGNW/BIL/OR WN5 255 H5
Lakeside PLF/KEOS FY6 78 E6
Lakeside Av
WGNW/BIL/OR WN5 255 H8
Lakeside Ct RNFD/HAY WA11 262 D5
STHP PR8 * 13 G2
Lakeside Gdns
RNFD/HAY WA11 262 D5
Lake Vw EDGW/EG BL7 210 F6
Lake View Rd COL BB8 296 A4
Lakeway BPOOLE FY3 105 J5
Lakewood Av CLV/TH FY5 85 G2
Lamaleach Dr
KIRK/FR/WAR PR4 148 D5
Lamberhead Rd
WGNW/BIL/OR WN5 255 L5
Lambert Cl FUL/RIB PR2 133 H8
Lambert Rd FUL/RIB PR2 133 H8
LANC LA1 42 D8
Lambert St COL BB8 296 F9
Lambeth Cl BBN BB1 11 K5
HOR/BR BL6 232 A8
Lambeth St BBN BB1 11 K4
Lambeth Ter ROCH OL11 235 G6
Lambing Clough La CLI BB7 117 H3
Lambourne SKEL WN8 243 L7
Lambridge Cl MCMB LA4 41 J8
Lambshear La MGHL L31 249 M7
Lambs Hill Cl CLV/TH FY5 86 A2
Lamb's La GAR/LONG PR3 79 K7
Lambs Rd CLV/TH FY5 86 A2
Lambton Gates RAW/HAS BB4 195 M1
Lambton St
WGNW/BIL/OR WN5 255 L6
Lamlash Rd BBN BB1 158 A7
Lammack Rd BBN BB1 157 G3
Lanark Av BISP FY2 84 F5
Lanark St BLY BB11 6 A7
Lancambe Ct LANC LA1 2 A2
Lancashire Dr CHLY/EC PR7 187 J5
Lancashire St MCMB LA4 40 F7
Lancaster Av ACC BB5 159 K4
CLV/TH FY5 85 M1
CSBY/BLUN L23 257 G8
GAR/LONG PR3 88 F6
LEYL PR25 187 H2
LSTA FY8 145 J7
RAMS BL0 214 D7
RAW/HAS BB4 194 D3
Lancaster Cl CHLYE PR6 230 E4
GAR/LONG PR3 88 F6
MGHL L31 259 J2
PLF/KEOS FY6 78 C6
STHP PR8 199 H7
Lancaster Ct CHLY/EC PR7 207 M1
Lancaster Crs SKEL WN8 253 H2
Lancaster Dr ACC BB5 139 J8
CHLYE PR6 189 H3
CHTN/BK PR9 181 H6
CLI BB7 98 F3
PDHM/BLYW BB12 141 G5
Lancaster Ga CHTN/BK PR9 181 J6
FTWD FY7 77 G8
LANC LA1 * 3 H6
Lancastergate LEYL PR25 186 C3
Lancaster Ga NLSN BB9 122 F4
Lancaster La LEYL PR25 187 G2
SKEL WN8 226 F8
Lancaster Pl BBNW BB2 156 E6
CHLYE PR6 230 D3
Lancaster Rd BPOOLE FY3 125 K1
CARN LA5 33 G4
FMBY L37 247 H2
GAR/LONG PR3 284 B5
GAR/LONG PR3 282 B7
GAR/LONG PR3 88 D4
HEY LA3 65 J2
HGHB LA2 269 M5
HGHB LA2 44 B6
HGHB LA2 36 B6
MCMB LA4 41 K6
PLF/KEOS FY6 78 C6
PRES PR1 9 H2
STHP PR8 199 H7
WGNW/BIL/OR WN5 255 M2
Lancaster St ACC BB5 158 F8
BBNW BB2 10 A6
CHLY/EC PR7 229 J2
COL BB8 296 A6
Lanchester Ct
CROS/BRETH PR26 186 A5
Lancia Crs BPOOLS FY4 126 D5
Lancing Pl BBNW BB2 10 A7
Landcrest Cl
KIRK/FR/WAR PR4 148 E1
Land End MGHL L31 259 M2
Land Ga WHIT OL12 302 B10
Landing La CLI BB7 276 E12
Land La CHTN/BK PR9 180 F7
KIRK/FR/WAR PR4 167 G5
Landseer Av BISP FY2 84 F7
Landseer Cl BLY BB11 6 C9
Landseer St PRES PR1 152 F2
Landsmoor Dr
KIRK/FR/WAR PR4 166 D2
Lane Bottom BWCK/EAR BB18 293 P8
Lanedale KIRK/FR/WAR PR4 166 D2
Lane End La BCUP OL13 197 K2
Lane End Rd BCUP OL13 197 K3
Lanefield Dr CLV/TH FY5 81 G7
Lane Foot Brow HGHB LA2 48 F4
Lane Head HGHB LA2 36 F7
Lane Head La BCUP OL13 179 J8
Lane House COL BB8 296 F10
Lane House Cl BBNW BB2 * 172 E3
Lane House Rd HWTH BD22 295 Q11
Laneshaw Cl DWN BB3 173 H7
Laneside ACC BB5 140 A5
Laneside Av ACC BB5 159 L3
PDHM/BLYW BB12 121 J5
Laneside Cl CLI BB7 118 D4
LIT OL15 219 K5
Laneside Rd RAW/HAS BB4 194 E1
Laneside St TOD OL14 303 K3
The Lane HEY LA3 64 F6
PLF/KEOS FY6 85 K8
Lane Top COL BB8 296 F7
Langber End La KKBYL LA6 39 M1
Langcliffe Rd FUL/RIB PR2 133 H7
SETT BD24 265 N6
Langdale HGHB LA2 44 D6
Langdale Av CLI BB7 98 F4
CROS/BRETH PR26 184 E8
FMBY L37 237 G8
KIRK/FR/WAR PR4 165 G7
RAW/HAS BB4 195 H1
Langdale Cl ACC BB5 160 A2
BBNW BB2 172 B3
BBR PR5 169 G2
CLV/TH FY5 85 L1
FMBY L37 247 G1
KIRK/FR/WAR PR4 148 D5
Langdale Crs FUL/RIB PR2 133 H8
WGNW/BIL/OR WN5 255 L3
Langdale Dr BRSC L40 225 H7
MGHL L31 259 H1
Langdale Gdns STHP PR8 221 J2
Langdale Gv CHLYE PR6 187 L4
Langdale Pl BPOOLS FY4 125 M2
LANC LA1 * 3 K2
Langdale Ri COL BB8 296 C5
Langdale Rd BBNW BB2 172 A4
BPOOLS FY4 125 L2
CARN LA5 33 K3
FUL/RIB PR2 133 H8
GAR/LONG PR3 114 C5
LANC LA1 3 K2
LEYL PR25 186 E5
LSTA FY8 145 G3
MCMB LA4 41 K6
PDHM/BLYW BB12 140 F1
WGNW/BIL/OR WN5 255 L4
Langden Br CLI BB7 274 D12
Langden Brook Ms HEY LA3 54 A1
Langden Brook Sq BBN BB1 11 J7
Langden Crs BBR PR5 169 J4
Langden Dr FUL/RIB PR2 133 K8
Langden Fold FUL/RIB PR2 134 A2
Langdon Wy BISP FY2 105 H1
Langfield BRFD/BLYE BB10 143 L5
Langfield Av BPOOLS FY4 124 F6
Langfield Cl FUL/RIB PR2 132 C3
Langford St ACC BB5 176 B2
Langham Av ACC BB5 159 L3
Langham Rd BBN BB1 157 G4
Langham St
PDHM/BLYW BB12 141 L5
Langholm Cl LEYL PR25 186 A3
Langholme Cl NLSN BB9 122 F2
Langholme Rd PRES PR1 151 K7
Langholme St NLSN BB9 123 H5
Langho St BBNW BB2 172 F2
Langley Cl HTWN L38 256 C1
Langley La GAR/LONG PR3 112 C3
Langley Pl BRSC L40 224 E7
Langley Rd BRSC L40 224 E7
LANC LA1 3 K8
Langport Cl FUL/RIB PR2 132 C3
Langridge Wy MCMB LA4 41 H8
Langroyd Rd COL BB8 296 B6
Langshaw Dr CLI BB7 99 H5
Langshaw La HGHB LA2 67 J6
Langstone Cl HOR/BR BL6 231 L8
Lang St ACC BB5 159 K5
BPOOL FY1 104 F5
Langthwaite Rd HGHB LA2 55 K6
Langton Brow CHLY/EC PR7 206 A6
GAR/LONG PR3 114 E4
Langton Cl BBNW BB2 172 F3
CHLY/EC PR7 206 A6
CROS/BRETH PR26 185 M3
LANC LA1 42 F7
Langton Rd KIRK/FR/WAR PR4 128 D6
NWD/KWIPK L33 260 C6
Langton St PRES PR1 8 D5
Langton Ter ROCH OL11 235 H7
Langtree SKEL WN8 243 L8
Langtree La KIRK/FR/WAR PR4 108 C1
WGNNW/ST WN6 229 G8
Langwood FTWD FY7 81 H1
Langwood Av RAW/HAS BB4 194 F1
Langwood Cl RAW/HAS BB4 194 F1
Langwood Ct RAW/HAS BB4 194 F1
Langwood La
RNFD/HAY WA11 262 F2
Langwyth Rd
BRFD/BLYE BB10 143 H6
Lansborough Cl
CROS/BRETH PR26 185 L3
Lansbury Pl NLSN BB9 123 J1
Lansbury St
WGNW/BIL/OR WN5 255 K5
Lansdowne Cl BLY BB11 6 D7
RAMS BL0 214 E6
Lansdowne Gv MCMB LA4 41 M4
Lansdowne Pl BPOOL FY1 104 E5
Lansdowne Rd
KIRK/FR/WAR PR4 128 C4
LSTA FY8 146 A6
MCMB LA4 41 M4
STHP PR8 200 B5
Lansdowne St BBNW BB2 156 E8
ROCH OL11 234 F4
Lansdown Hl FUL/RIB PR2 131 M4
Lansil Wk LANC LA1 42 F8
Lansil Wy LANC LA1 42 F8
The Lanterns PLF/KEOS FY6 86 A7
Lapford Crs NWD/KWIPK L33 260 D7
Lappet Gv KIRK/FR/WAR PR4 131 H6
Lapwing Cl ROCH OL11 234 B4
Lapwing Rw LSTA FY8 146 B4
The Lapwings PLF/KEOS FY6 105 L1
Larbreck Av KIRK/FR/WAR PR4 108 C2
Larbreck Rd BPOOLE FY3 105 H4
Larch Av ACC BB5 159 J8
CHLYE PR6 208 B1
Larch Cl BBNW BB2 172 C3
KIRK/FR/WAR PR4 148 D6
PLF/KEOS FY6 78 D6
RAW/HAS BB4 195 J3
SKEL WN8 253 H2
Larch Dr CHLYE PR6 189 J4
KIRK/FR/WAR PR4 * 148 D6
Larches Av FUL/RIB PR2 151 J2
Larches La FUL/RIB PR2 151 H2
The Larches BBN BB1 157 J4
Larchfield Rd CSBY/BLUN L23 257 K0
Larch Ga BBR PR5 170 B1
Larchgate FUL/RIB PR2 132 F4
Larch Gv BBR PR5 169 J2
GAR/LONG PR3 284 B7
LANC LA1 2 C5
Larch St NLSN BB9 123 J3
PDHM/BLYW BB12 * 141 M4
STHP PR8 200 B6
Larch Wy FMBY L37 237 G7
Larchway GAR/LONG PR3 114 E3
Larchwood FUL/RIB PR2 151 H2
LANC LA1 55 G7
PRES PR1 * 151 L7
Larchwood Av MGHL L31 258 F4
Larchwood Cl LSTA FY8 146 C7
Larchwood Crs LEYL PR25 186 B2
Largs Rd BBN BB1 157 M8
Lark Av PRES PR1 152 B7
Lark Cl BPOOLE FY3 105 L8
Lark Ct FTWD FY7 81 G2
Larkfield CHLY/EC PR7 205 L5
Larkfield La CHTN/BK PR9 180 D8
Lark Hl BBN BB1 11 G2
BBR PR5 153 L8
Larkhill GTH/LHO BB6 117 M6
Lark Hl RAW/HAS BB4 177 K8
Larkhill SKEL WN8 243 L7
Larkhill Av BRFD/BLYE BB10 122 F6
Larkhill Gv HTWN L38 247 J8
Larkhill La FMBY L37 236 F7
Larkhill Pl WHIT OL12 235 H2
Larkhill Rd PRES PR1 9 L5
Larkhill St BPOOL FY1 * 104 F5
PRES PR1 9 M5
Larkholme Av FTWD FY7 81 H2
Larkholme La FTWD FY7 81 H2
Larkholme Pde FTWD FY7 80 F2
Larkspur Cl BBNW BB2 172 A3
STHP PR8 13 L6
Lark St COL BB8 296 B5
DWN BB3 191 L6

PDHM/BLYW BB12 ....141 M4
Latham Av BPOOLE FY3 ....5 K6
  ORM L39 ....241 K6
Latham Crs KIRK/FR/WAR PR4...183 J5
Latham La
  WGNW/BIL/OR WN5 ....255 K3
Latham Rd HOR/BR BL6....230 A7
Latham St BRFD/BLYE BB10...142 E2
  PRES PR1 ....9 J6
Lathom Av MCMB LA4........41 L1
  SKEL WN8 ....243 J8
Lathom Cl BRSC L40........225 H7
Lathom Dr MGHL L31 ......250 B8
  RNFD/HAY WA11.......262 C4
Lathom La MCMB LA4........41 M4
Lathom Rd CHTN/BK PR9...199 M2
  ORM L39 ....252 C6
Lathom Wy GAR/LONG PR3...284 C9
Latimer Cl
  WGNW/BIL/OR WN5 ....255 J4
Latimer Dr KIRK/FR/WAR PR4..167 J2
Latin St MILN OL16 *......235 H5
Lauder Cl NWD/KWIPK L33...260 C5
Lauderdale Av CLV/TH FY5...85 G2
Lauderdale Rd FUL/RIB PR2...133 J2
Lauderdale St PRES PR1....8 A8
Laund Ga PDHM/BLYW BB12...122 A3
Laund Gv ACC BB5 ....160 A8
Laund Hey Vw RAW/HAS BB4...194 A8
Laund La CHLYE PR6........171 H6
  RAW/HAS BB4 ....176 F8
Laund Rd ACC BB5 ....176 A1
Laundry Rd BPOOLS FY4...125 K6
Laundry Rd North
  BPOOLS FY4 ....125 K5
Laund St RAW/HAS BB4....177 J3
The Laund
  CROS/BRETH PR26.....185 K2
Laurel Av BPOOL FY1 ....5 J3
  BRSC L40 ....225 H5
  CHLY/EC PR7 ....186 E6
  DWN BB3 ....191 L1
  FTWD FY7 ....81 J3
  LSTA FY8 ....146 E6
Laurel Bank LANC LA1 .....2 C7
Laurel Bank Av FUL/RIB PR2..131 M8
Laurel Ct MILN OL16 *......235 L5
Laurel Dr CLV/TH FY5......85 L3
  SKEL WN8 ....253 H1
Laurel Gv STHP PR8 ....200 B4
The Laurels CHLY/EC PR7...207 J8
  KIRK/FR/WAR PR4....128 E2
Laurel St BCUP OL13......179 J8
  BLY BB11 ....9 K4
  PRES PR1 ....9 K4
Laureston Av HEY LA3.......52 E5
Laurie Pl WHIT OL12 *.....235 J4
Laurier Av BPOOLS FY4....124 F5
Laurier Rd BRFD/BLYE BB10...122 E8
Lauriston Cl BPOOLS FY4...125 K5
Lavender Cl FUL/RIB PR2...132 F5
Lavender Gv CLV/TH FY5...207 M6
Lavender Hl RAW/HAS BB4...195 J4
Lavender Wy PLF/KEOS FY6...78 C7
Laverick Rd HGHB LA2......43 M2
Laverton Rd LSTA FY8 .....145 J6
Lawflat WHIT OL12 ....218 F6
Lawley Rd BBNW BB2 ......156 D6
The Lawns CHTN/BK PR9....200 C1
Lawn St BRFD/BLYE BB10...142 D3
Lawnswood Av LANC LA1....54 F7
Lawnswood Av
  PLF/KEOS FY6 ....105 L1
Lawnswood Crs BPOOLE FY3...125 M1
Lawnswood Dr HEY LA3......53 J1
Lawn Tennis Ct BPOOLS FY4...125 G6
Lawnwood Av CHLY/EC PR7...207 K6
Lawrence Av BBR PR5 ......169 G1
  BLY BB11 ....141 M6
  LSTA FY8 ....145 K4
  PDHM/BLYW BB12 ....140 B2
Lawrence Cl WHIT OL12 ...234 D2
Lawrence Dr CARN LA5.....16 D2
Lawrence La CHLY/EC PR7...205 M4
  PRES PR1 ....151 L6
Lawrence Rw FTWD FY7 .....77 K7
Lawrence St BBNW BB2.....10 A4
  BPOOLS FY4 * 124 E2
  FUL/RIB PR2 ....132 A8
  PDHM/BLYW BB12 ....141 G2
  RAW/HAS BB4 ....178 C7
Lawrie Av RAMS BL0........214 C6
Lawsings Brow HGHB LA2...51 J1
Lawson Cl LANC LA1 ....54 E8
Lawson Gdns HGHB LA2....42 D3
Lawson Pl HGHB LA2.......42 D3
Lawson Rd BPOOLE FY3....105 K8
  LSTA FY8 ....145 K1
Lawsons Ct CLV/TH FY5....85 M2
Lawsons Rd CLV/TH FY5....85 M1
Lawson St CHLYE PR6......208 B3
  CHTN/BK PR9 ....200 D4
  PRES PR1 ....9 H2
  RAW/HAS BB4 ....177 K3
Law St RAW/HAS BB4......196 C2
  ROCH OL11 ....234 F6
  TOD OL14 ....300 E10
Lawton Cl CHLYE PR6.......188 E2
Lawton St WHIT OL12 .....235 K2
Laxey Gv PRES PR1........133 G8
Laxey Rd BBNW BB2 ......173 H2
Laycock Ga BPOOLE FY3....105 G5
Laycock St MILN OL16......109 H5
Layton Rd BPOOLE FY3....105 H5
  FUL/RIB PR2 ....151 H2
Lazenby Av FTWD FY7......80 F1
Lea Bank RAW/HAS BB4....196 A1
Leach Cl MILN OL16........235 M1
Leach Crs LSTA FY8.......145 J1
Leaches Rd RAMS BL0......215 G3
Leachfield Rd HGHB LA2...66 E7
Leach La LANC LA1.........145 H1
Leach Pl BBR PR5.........169 L5
Leach St BBNW BB2 ....10 E1
  MILN OL16 ....235 L5
Leach Vls KIRK/FR/WAR PR4 *...109 J2
Lea Crs ORM L39...........241 H4
Leadale FUL/RIB PR2......151 G1
Leadale Rd LEYL PR25.....186 A2
Leader St WGNW/BIL/OR WN5...255 M5
Lea Dr BBNW BB2..........173 H5
Leaford Av BPOOLE FY3....105 H3
Leafy Cl LEYL PR25.......186 E4
Leagram Crs FUL/RIB PR2...133 J8
Lea Gate St MILN OL16....235 K6
Leah St LIT OL15 *........219 L6
Lea La HEY LA3...........52 D5

HGHB LA2 ....35 K4
KIRK/FR/WAR PR4 ......150 C1
Leamington Av
  BRFD/BLYE BB10 ......142 F2
Leamington Rd BBNW BB2...156 B5
  BPOOL FY1 ....4 F7
  LSTA FY8 ....145 J3
  MCMB LA4 ....41 K8
  STHP PR8 ....220 F8
Leamington St NLSN BB9...123 H4
  WHIT OL12 ....235 H3
Leamington Gdns PLF/KEOS FY6...106 A1
Leapers Vw KKBYL LA6.....34 B3
Lea Rd CHLYE PR6.........187 M6
  KIRK/FR/WAR PR4 ....130 F8
Leaside Cl WHIT OL12 ....235 G1
Leatherbarrows La MGHL L31...259 K4
Leathercote GAR/LONG PR3...284 B9
Leathwood MGHL L31 *.....259 H3
Leaverholme Cl
  BRFD/BLYE BB10 .....163 K4
Leaver St PDHM/BLYW BB12...141 M3
Leavesley Rd BPOOL FY1...104 F3
Leaway WHIT OL12.........218 F5
Lea Way CLV/TH FY5.......86 A4
Lebanon St BRFD/BLYE BB10...7 J1
Leckhampton Rd FUL/RIB PR2...104 E3
Leckonby St GAR/LONG PR3...88 F5
Leckwith Rd NTHTN L30...258 E8
Ledburn SKEL WN8........243 H8
Ledbury Rd BPOOLE FY3...105 K4
Ledson Gv ORM L39........250 F4
Ledsons Vw MGHL L31.....259 K8
Lee Bottom Rd TOD OL14...303 F22
Lee Br HGHB LA2..........69 L8
Lee Brook Cl RAW/HAS BB4...177 K7
Lee Brook La RAW/HAS BB4...177 J7
Leeds Cl BBN BB1.........11 L6
  NLSN BB9 ....123 J2
Leeds Rd BPOOL FY1.......5 G2
  NLSN BB9 ....123 J1
Lee Green St BRFD/BLYE BB10...142 E3
Lee Gv BRFD/BLYE BB10...143 J7
Leehouse Dr PLF/KEOS FY6...106 A3
Leek St PRES PR1.........113 H3
Lee La BBN BB1...........138 F8
  BRSC L40 ....226 F4
  EDGW/EG BL7 ....212 F1
  HOR/BR BL6 ....231 K7
  TOD OL14 ....303 J1
Leeming La KKBYL LA6.....31 H6
Lee Rd BCUP OL13........197 H3
  BPOOLS FY4 ....125 G1
  NLSN BB9 ....123 J1
Lees Cl DWN BB3 *........173 H7
  HEY LA3 ....52 D4
Lees La SKEL WN8........243 M3
Leeson Av CHLY/EC PR7....207 G7
Lees Rd BRFD/BLYE BB10...230 E3
Lee's St BCUP OL13.......197 M3
The Lees BRFD/BLYE BB10...163 K4
Lee St ACC BB5...........159 M8
  BCUP OL13 ....197 J1
  BRFD/BLYE BB10 .....142 D1
  GAR/LONG PR3 ....114 C4
  LIT OL15 ....219 J1
  NLSN BB9 ....103 L8
Leeswood SKEL WN8.......243 M8
Leet Rd PDHM/BLYW BB12...121 J6
Leeward Cl DWN BB3.......173 J5
Leeward Rd FUL/RIB PR2...151 J1
Legh La KIRK/FR/WAR PR4...182 F7
Leicester Av CLV/TH FY5...81 G8
  GAR/LONG PR3 ....284 A8
  HOR/BR BL6 ....231 K8
Leicester Ga CLV/TH FY5...81 H8
Leicester Rd BBN BB1.....157 M6
  BPOOL FY1 ....5 G2
  PRES PR1 ....152 C2
  ROCH OL11 ....235 K6
Leighbrow BBR PR5.......168 E1
Leigh House Ctyd BBR PR5 *...152 F3
Leigh Pk BLY BB11........140 F8
Leigh Rw CHLY/EC PR7....207 M4
Leighton Av FTWD FY7....247 K2
  MGHL L31 ....259 G1
Leighton Cl MTHPE LA7...17 J1
Leighton Dr LANC LA1....2 C8
  MTHPE LA7 ....17 L1
Leighton St PRES PR1.....8 E2
Leinster St LANC LA1.....54 F6
Leith Av CLV/TH FY5.....85 G1
Lemonious St WGNW/BIL/OR WN5...159 M7
Lenches Fold COL BB8....296 A8
Lenches Rd COL BB8......296 A8
Lench Rd RAW/HAS BB4...196 A5
Lench St RAW/HAS BB4....196 C5
Lendel Cl FMBY L37......237 H8
Lennon St CHLY/EC PR7...207 M4
Lennox Ct BPOOLS FY4...125 C4
Lennox Ga BPOOLS FY4...125 C4
Lennox Rd TOD OL14......300 D10
Lennox St BRFD/BLYE BB10...143 K5
  PRES PR1 ....9 J5
Lenton Av FMBY L37......237 G7
Lentworth Av BISP FY2...85 G6
Lentworth Dr LANC LA1...54 F7
Leo Case Ct PRES PR1....153 G3
Leonard Cheshire Dr
  NTHTN L30 ....258 C8
Leonard St BWCK/EAR BB18...293 Q5
  NLSN BB9 ....123 H4
Leopold Gv BPOOL FY1....4 D2
Leopold Rd BBNW BB2.....156 E5
Leopold St COL BB8......103 L7
  ROCH OL11 ....235 G4
  WGNW/BIL/OR WN5....255 M4
Leopold Wy BBNW BB2....173 K3
Lesley Rd STHP PR8......200 B4
Leslie Av CLV/TH FY5.....85 M1
  HGHB LA2 ....42 D6
Letchworth Av ROCH OL11...235 K6
Letchworth Dr CHLY/EC PR7...207 L5
Letchworth Wks CHLY/EC PR7...207 L5
Lethbridge Rd STHP PR8...13 L8
Letitia St HOR/BR BL6....231 K8
Levant St PDHM/BLYW BB12...140 F2
Leven Av FTWD FY7........77 G8
Leven Gv DWN BB3.........173 J4
Levens Cl BBNW BB2......173 J5
  CHTN/BK PR9 ....181 K6
  LANC LA1 ....2 B5
Levens Dr HEY LA3........52 E1
  LEYL PR25 ....187 G1
Levens Pl WGNW/BIL/OR WN5...255 M4
Levens St BBN BB1.......11 K7
Levens Wy CARN LA5......16 F8
Levensgarth Av FUL/RIB PR2...132 C3

Lever Cl BBNW BB2........156 C3
Lever Rd CHLY/EC PR7....186 F1
Lever Park Av HOR/BR BL6...231 K6
Lever St BPOOLE FY3......5 J2
  HEYW OL10 ....234 A8
  RAMS BL0 ....214 F5
  RAW/HAS BB4 ....195 L1
Levine Av BPOOLS FY4....125 K2
Lewis Cl CHLY/EC PR7....230 K5
Lewis St GTH/LHO BB6....139 G6
Lewis Wk NWD/KWIPK L33...260 B5
Lewtas St BPOOL FY1.....104 E3
Lewth Farm
  KIRK/FR/WAR PR4 ....110 D5
Lewth La KIRK/FR/WAR PR4...110 D5
Lexington Wy
  NWD/KWIPK L33 .....260 A5
Lex St PRES PR1.........152 F3
Lexton Dr CHTN/BK PR9...180 F4
Leybourne Av STHP PR8...221 J4
Leyburn Av BISP FY2.....84 F1
Leyburn Cl ACC BB5......160 E6
  FUL/RIB PR2 ....133 H6
Leyburn Rd BBNW BB2....172 E4
Leycester Dr LANC LA1...42 E8
Ley Cl LANC LA1.........2 B7
Leyfield Av PRES PR1....168 A1
Leyfield Cl BPOOLE FY3...105 K2
Leyfield Rd LEYL PR25...186 C2
Leyland Cl CLV/TH FY5....85 L1
Leyland St CHTN/BK PR9...181 H6
  COL BB8 ....296 B8
Leyland La CROS/BRETH PR26...185 M8
Leyland Rd LEYL PR25.....186 A4
  LEYL PR25 ....186 A4
Leyland St ACC BB5......159 J6
Leyland Wy LEYL PR25....186 F2
  ORM L39 ....241 J6
Leys Cl CLI BB7..........119 J3
Leys Rd BISP FY2........105 G2
Leyster St MCMB LA4.....41 K6
Ley St ACC BB5..........176 B1
Leyton Av LEYL PR25.....186 A4
Leyton St WHIT OL12.....235 J1
Libby La GAR/LONG PR3...79 M5
Library Av LANC LA1.....66 F4
Library Rd CHLYE PR6....169 L7
Library St ACC BB5......159 H5
  CHLY/EC PR7 ....207 M4
  PRES PR1 ....9 G7
Lichen Cl CHLY/EC PR7...207 G7
Lichfield Av CSBY/WL L22...257 C8
  MCMB LA4 ....41 L8
Lichfield Rd BPOOL FY1...104 F3
  CHLY/EC PR7 ....207 M5
  FUL/RIB PR2 ....151 J8
Lichfield St
  WGNW/BIL/OR WN5 ...255 M6
Lichfield Ter MILN OL16...235 M7
Liddell Av MGHL L31.....259 H7
Liddesdale Rd BBNW BB2...123 L1
Liddington Hall Dr RAMS BL0...214 E7
Lidgate Cl NWD/KWIPK L33...260 B6
Lidget Av FUL/RIB PR2...150 F2
Liege Rd LEYL PR25......186 D3
Lifeboat Rd FMBY L37....246 D2
Lightbounds Rd BOL BL1...233 J8
Lightbown Av BPOOLS FY3...5 J8
Lightbown St DWN BB3...173 K8
Lightburne Av LIT OL15...219 H7
Lighthurne Av LSTA FY8...145 J6
Lightfoot Cl FUL/RIB PR2...132 A3
Lightfoot Green La
  KIRK/FR/WAR PR4 ....131 L3
Lightfoot La FUL/RIB PR2...132 A3
  KIRK/FR/WAR PR4 ....131 J4
Lighthorne Dr STHP PR8...220 D7
Lighthouse La FMBY L37...247 K2
Lighthurst Av CHLY/EC PR7...207 M6
Lighthurst La CHLY/EC PR7...207 M6
Lightwood Av BPOOLS FY4...124 F3
  LSTA FY8 ....146 E6
Lilac Av BPOOL FY1......5 G2
  LSTA FY8 ....146 E6
  PRES PR1 ....168 C5
  STHP PR8 ....238 A1
Lilac Cl RAW/HAS BB4....148 A6
Lilac Gv CHLYE PR6......189 L1
  CLI BB7 ....98 F4
  DWN BB3 ....173 H5
  PLF/KEOS FY6 ....78 B6
  PRES PR1 ....132 F8
  SKEL WN8 ....253 H7
Lilac Rd BBN BB1........157 K3
The Lilacs CLV/TH FY5...81 K8
Lilac St COL BB8........296 C5
Lilac Ter BCUP OL13.....197 G3
Lilburn Cl RAMS BL0.....214 F7
Liley St MILN OL16......235 K4
Lilford Cl KIRK/FR/WAR PR4...183 K6
Lilford Rd BBN BB1......10 C1
Lily Gv LANC LA1........54 F6
  PRES PR1 ....132 E2
Lily St BCUP OL13.......197 J1
  BPOOL FY1 ....4 F1
  DWN BB3 ....191 L2
  NLSN BB9 ....123 J5
  TOD OL14 ....300 H11
Lima Rd LSTA FY8........145 K5
Limbrick BBN BB1........10 E2
Limbrick Rd CHLYE PR6...208 A3
Lime Av ACC BB5.........175 G1
  HGHB LA2 ....66 F7
  KIRK/FR/WAR PR4 ....128 D2
  TOD OL14 ....303 K1
Limebrest Av CLV/TH FY5...86 A3
Lime Cha FUL/RIB PR2....131 M3
Limechase Cl BPOOLS FY4...125 K5
Lime Cl PRES PR1........151 K7
Limefield BBNW BB2......10 A3
Limefield Av CLI BB7....118 F6
Limefield Dr SKEL WN8...254 A8
Limefield St ACC BB5....160 A6
Limefield St BOL BL1....233 K7
Lime Gv BISP FY2........105 H1
  CHLY/EC PR7 ....207 K4
  CLV/TH FY5 ....85 J4
  FUL/RIB PR2 ....151 J1
  GAR/LONG PR3 ....114 C2
  LANC LA1 ....2 D7
  LIT OL15 ....219 J6
  LSTA FY8 ....145 G3
  PLF/KEOS FY6 ....106 B1

RAMS BL0 ....215 G4
RNFD/HAY WA11.........262 C5
SKEL WN8 ....253 H2
Limekiln La SKP/WHF BD23...279 J2
Limerick Rd BISP FY2....85 G8
Lime Rd ACC BB5.........159 L4
  RAW/HAS BB4 ....176 B8
  WHIT OL12 ....218 C6
Limers Ct TOD OL14......302 C6
  WHIT OL12 ....218 C6
Limes Av CHLY/EC PR7....186 F7
  DWN BB3 ....191 J3
  HEY LA3 ....40 F8
Limestone Link CARN LA5...17 C2
  MTHPE LA7 ....17 J1
Lime St BBN BB1.........10 E2
  CLI BB7 ....99 J2
  COL BB8 ....296 B5
  GTH/LHO BB6 ....138 F5
  NLSN BB9 ....122 F3
  ROCH OL11 ....234 F7
  STHP PR8 ....200 B5
  TOD OL14 ....303 K1
Lime Tree Gv RAW/HAS BB4...177 K7
Lime Tree Wy FMBY L37...246 F1
Lime Vale Rd
  WGNW/BIL/OR WN5 ...263 M8
Limewood Cl ACC BB5....160 A5
  RAW/HAS BB4 ....194 D4
Limey La BLY BB11.......162 B5
Limont Rd STHP PR8......221 G6
Linacre La FMBY L37.....248 D3
Linadale Av CLV/TH FY5...85 L1
Linadale Cl CARN LA5....16 E1
Linadale Crs BRFD/BLYE BB10...142 D1
Linadale Gdns BPOOLS FY4...125 H5
Linadale Rd GAR/LONG PR3...114 C6
Lindbeck Rd BPOOLS FY4...125 M2
Lindbergh Av LANC LA1...54 E7
Lindel Rd FTWD FY7......81 H1
Linden Av BBN BB1.......10 D1
  CLV/TH FY5 ....81 J8
  CSBY/BLUN L23 .....256 F7
  RAMS BL0 ....215 G5
  TOD OL14 ....303 K1
  WGNW/BIL/OR WN5 ...255 H5
Linden Cl BBR PR5.......168 E2
  CLV/TH FY5 ....85 J1
  KIRK/FR/WAR PR4 ....150 A2
  NLSN BB9 ....123 J2
  RAMS BL0 ....215 G1
Linden Dr BBR PR5.......168 E2
Linden Fold KIRK/FR/WAR PR4...130 J8
Linden Gn CLV/TH FY5....81 J8
Linden Gv BPOOLE FY3....188 G4
  FUL/RIB PR2 ....133 H8
  GAR/LONG PR3 ....284 B7
  WGNW/BIL/OR WN5 ...255 H5
Linden Lea BBNW BB2....172 C3
  RAW/HAS BB4 ....195 J3
Linden Ms LSTA FY8......145 J1
Linden Pl BISP FY2......85 H8
Linden Rd BWCK/EAR BB18...294 D6
  COL BB8 ....296 A6
Lindens SKEL WN8........243 L7
The Lindens MGHL L31...258 F4
Linden St BRFD/BLYE BB10...143 J8
  WGNW/BIL/OR WN5 ...255 M6
Linderbreck La PLF/KEOS FY6...106 B3
Lindeth Cl CARN LA5.....24 F1
  KKBYL LA6 ....33 L5
Lindfield Gdns LANC LA1...42 E8
Lindeth Rd CARN LA5....24 F1
Lindholme SKEL WN8.....243 M8
Lindisfarne Av BBNW BB2...173 J2
Lindisfarne Cl PDHM/BLYW BB12...6 C1
Lindle Av KIRK/FR/WAR PR4...167 H1
Lindle Cl KIRK/FR/WAR PR4...167 H1
Lindle Crs KIRK/FR/WAR PR4...167 H1
Lindley Av
  WGNW/BIL/OR WN5 ...254 F9
Lindley Cft CLV/TH FY5...86 B1
Lindley Dr SKEL WN8....226 F8
Lindley St BBNW BB2....172 E1
  BBR PR5 ....168 E3
Lindon Park Rd RAW/HAS BB4...194 F4
Lindow Cl LANC LA1......3 G7
Lindow Sq LANC LA1.....3 G7
Lindow St LANC LA1.....3 G7
Lindred Rd NLSN BB9....122 D4
Lindsay Av BPOOLE FY3...5 K6
  LEYL PR25 ....186 D2
  LSTA FY8 ....145 J5
  PLF/KEOS FY6 ....106 A1
Lindsay Ct HEY LA3.....53 K1
Lindsay Dr CHLY/EC PR7...207 K4
Lindsay Pk BRFD/BLYE BB10...143 J3
Lindsay St BLY BB11.....7 H3
  CLV/TH FY5 ....85 H5
  FUL/RIB PR2 ....151 J2
  GAR/LONG PR3 ....114 A7
  LANC LA1 ....2 C6
  LIT OL15 ....219 J6
  LSTA FY8 ....145 G3
  PLF/KEOS FY6 ....106 B1

Lingfield Cl LANC LA1....55 G8
Lingfield Rd FTWD FY7...81 H2
Lingfield Wy BBNW BB2...172 A3
Lingham La HGHB LA2.....39 L5
Lingmoor Dr
  PDHM/BLYW BB12 ....141 G3
Lingmoor Rd LANC LA1...3 L1
Lingwell Cl CHLYE PR6...187 M6
Link Av CSBY/BLUN L23...257 H6
Link Dr HGHB LA2........39 G3
Links Av CHTN/BK PR9...200 B1
Links Fld FUL/RIB PR2...131 M8
Links Ga CLV/TH FY5.....86 A4
  FUL/RIB PR2 ....131 M8
  LSTA FY8 ....145 K5
Linkside Av NLSN BB9....123 L3
Links La BBNW BB2......171 M3
Links Rd BPOOL FY1.....104 F2
  FUL/RIB PR2 ....145 H6
  PLF/KEOS FY6 ....78 A6
  PRES PR1 ....151 L5
The Links CLV/TH FY5...80 F8
Links Vw LSTA FY8......145 M6
  ROCH OL11 ....234 D3
Linley Av WGNW/ST WN6...245 M7
Linnell Dr ROCH OL11...234 B3
Linnet Cl BPOOLE FY3...105 L5
Linnet Hl ROCH OL11....234 B5
Linnet La LSTA FY8......146 B4
Linnet St PRES PR1.....152 E1
Linnet Wy NWD/KWIPK L33...260 B4
Linslade Cl NWD/KWIPK L33...260 C7
Linslade Crs NWD/KWIPK L33...260 C7
Linton Av HEY LA3......52 B3
Linton Dr BLY BB11.....142 A8
Linton Gdns NLSN BB9...102 F3
Linton Gv PRES PR1.....152 E1
Linton St FUL/RIB PR2...132 A8
Linville Av CSBY/BLUN L23...256 F7
Lion Ct ACC BB5.........159 H5
Lionel St PDHM/BLYW BB12...141 M5
Lions Dr BBN BB1........174 A3
Lion St ACC BB5........159 H4
Liptrott Rd CHLY/EC PR7...207 K6
Lisbon Dr BLY BB11......6 D5
  DWN BB3 ....191 M2
Lisbon Drive BLY BB11...6 D4
Lisbon St ROCH OL11....234 E3
Liskeard Cl MILN OL16...235 K3
Lisle St PRES PR1.......133 K3
Lismore Av BPOOLS FY4...125 C4
Lister Ct SKP/WHF BD23...294 D2
Lister Gv HEY LA3......52 E3
Lister St ACC BB5.......159 L3
  BBNW BB2 ....10 E8
Lister Well Rd BWCK/EAR BB18...293 P10
Little Acre CLV/TH FY5...86 A3
  KIRK/FR/WAR PR4 ....166 D3
  MGHL L31 ....259 H3
Little Banks Cl BBR PR5 *...169 L5
Little Barn Hey NTHTN L30...258 A7
Little Carr La CHLY/EC PR7...208 A6
Little Cl CROS/BRETH PR26...168 B4
  PRES PR1 ....151 M8
Little Crosby Rd
  CSBY/BLUN L23 .....257 H4
Littledale Av HEY LA3...52 F3
Littledale Rd HGHB LA2...55 L5
Littledale St WHIT OL12...235 G3
Little Fell La HGHB LA2...234 F7
Little Flatt WHIT OL12...234 F7
Little Hey La FMBY L37...237 L7
Littleholme St TOD OL14...303 K4
Little Howarth Wy
  WHIT OL12 * 218 F7
Little La CHTN/BK PR9...200 D4
  GAR/LONG PR3 ....111 K3
Littlemoor Rd CLI BB7...99 H5
Little Moor Vw CLI BB7...99 H5
Little Peel St BBNW BB2...10 C4
Little Poulton La PLF/KEOS FY6...106 C1
Little Queen St COL BB8...103 M7
Little St ACC BB5........159 K5
Little Toms La
  BRFD/BLYE BB10 .....123 G8
Little Tongues La PLF/KEOS FY6...78 E7
Little Twining
  KIRK/FR/WAR PR4 ....166 D4
Little Wood Cl CHLY/EC PR7...207 H4
Littondale Gdn BBNW BB2 *...172 A4
Littondale Gdns BBNW BB2...172 A4
Liverpool New Rd
  KIRK/FR/WAR PR4 ...166 C7
Liverpool Old Rd FMBY L37...203 K1
  KIRK/FR/WAR PR4 ...166 C7
  KIRK/FR/WAR PR4 ...183 K7
  MGHL L31 ....250 A7
  ORM L39 ....251 J7
  ORM L39 ....240 F8
  PDHM/BLYW BB12 ....141 K5
  PRES PR1 ....8 A8
  SKEL WN8 ....252 F1
  STHP PR8 ....237 M1
Liverpool Rd North BRSC L40...183 M5
  MGHL L31 ....258 F4
Liverpool Rd South BRSC L40...241 H1
  MGHL L31 ....258 F4
Livesey Branch Rd BBNW BB2...172 B4
Livesey Hall Cl BBNW BB2...172 B2
Livesey St BBN BB1......158 D1
  LSTA FY8 ....146 D8
  PDHM/BLYW BB12 ....9 M5
  PRES PR1 ....9 M5
Livet Av BPOOLS FY4....125 G4
Livingstone Rd ACC BB5...159 L3
Livingstone St NLSN BB9...122 E6
Livsey St MILN OL16....235 K4
Lloyd Cl LANC LA1......123 H3
Lloyd's Av MCMB LA4....41 H7
Lloyd St DWN BB3.......173 J8
  ROCH OL11 ....235 G7
  TOD OL14 ....303 L1
  WHIT OL12 ....217 M2
Lobden Crs WHIT OL12...218 A4
Lobley Cl WHIT OL12....235 L1
Lochinch Cl BPOOLS FY4...125 C5
Loch St WGNW/BIL/OR WN5...255 L5
Locka La KKBYL LA6......42 A5
  LANC LA1 ....42 D7
Lock Br Cl BBR PR5......74 D2
Lockerbie Av CLV/TH FY5...85 G3
Lockfield Dr BWCK/EAR BB18...293 R3
Lock Ga RAW/HAS BB4....194 F2

Lockhart Rd PRES PR1 152 C1
Lockhart St MILN OL16 235 L6
Lockhurst Av CLV/TH FY5 85 J3
Lock La KIRK/FR/WAR PR4 203 L1
Locks Barn SETT BD24 265 N4
Lockside BBNW BB2 10 D9
Lockside Rd FUL/RIB PR2 151 J3
Lock St ACC BB5 * 159 H7
TOD OL14 303 K4
Lockwood Av PLF/KEOS FY6 86 A7
Lockyer Av PDHM/BLYW BB12 141 L5
Lodge Bank CHLYE PR6 189 J4
HOR/BR BL6 231 J8
Lodge Bank Rd LIT OL15 219 J8
Lodge Cl BBR PR5 169 J2
CLV/TH FY5 84 F4
KIRK/FR/WAR PR4 148 E5
KKBYL LA6 18 F1
Lodge Ct BPOOLE FY3 106 A6
Lodge La BCUP OL13 197 J2
CROS/BRETH PR26 168 B5
HGHB LA2 37 H2
KIRK/FR/WAR PR4 150 A2
KIRK/FR/WAR PR4 108 E2
LSTA FY8 147 J6
ORM L39 261 M2
PLF/KEOS FY6 107 G1
Lodge Mill La RAMS BL0 215 K2
Lodge Pk GAR/LONG PR3 91 G1
Lodge Rd GAR/LONG PR3 91 K2
SETT BD24 265 N10
WGNW/BIL/OR WN5 255 H7
Lodges Gv MCMB LA4 41 M5
Lodgeside ACC BB5 139 J8
Lodge St ACC BB5 159 M5
LANC LA1 3 H5
LIT OL15 219 L5
PRES PR1 8 D3
RAMS BL0 214 F5
WHIT OL12 218 F5
Lodge Ter ACC BB5 159 H6
The Lodge GTH/LHO BB6 138 E6
Lodge Vw CROS/BRETH PR26 168 B4
GAR/LONG PR3 * 114 D5
RAMS BL0 215 K3
The Lodgings FUL/RIB PR2 132 F5
Lodore Rd BPOOLS FY4 124 F5
Loen Crs BOL BL1 233 M8
Loftos Av BPOOLS FY4 125 G3
Logwood St BBN BB1 157 J4
Loisine Cl ROCH OL11 234 D8
Lois Pl BBNW BB2 * 10 B3
Lomas La RAW/HAS BB4 195 J4
Lomax Cl GTH/LHO BB6 139 G5
Lomax St GTH/LHO BB6 138 F6
WHIT OL12 235 J2
Lombard St WHIT OL12 235 G3
Lomeshaye Rd NLSN BB9 122 F3
Lomeshaye Wy NLSN BB9 122 F3
Lomond Av BPOOLE FY3 5 M6
LSTA FY8 145 L6
Lomond Cl CHLY/EC PR7 187 G7
Lomond Gdns BBNW BB2 172 C2
Lomond Ter MILN OL16 235 M7
Londonderry Rd HEY LA3 52 D6
London La STHP PR8 222 A3
London Rd BBN BB1 10 E1
BPOOLE FY3 105 G5
PRES PR1 9 M4
London Sq STHP PR8 13 G3
London St FTWD FY7 77 K6
STHP PR8 13 H4
London Ter DWN BB3 191 L1
London Wk BBN BB1 10 E1
London Wy BBR PR5 152 F8
Long Acre BBR PR5 169 M6
Longacre CHTN/BK PR9 180 C8
Long Acre Cl CARN LA5 * 33 H3
Long Acre Pl LSTA FY8 146 D7
Long Acres Dr WHIT OL12 218 A2
Longacres La WHIT OL12 218 A1
Long Bank La SKP/WHF BD23 278 D2
Long Barn Brow BBR PR5 171 H1
Longber La KKBYL LA6 30 E4
Longbrook WGNNW/ST WN6 245 L5
Longbrook Av BBR PR5 169 H1
Long Butts PRES PR1 168 A1
Long Cswy CLI BB7 292 D3
HBR HX7 301 P7
TOD OL14 303 Q4
The Long Cswy
BRFD/BLYE BB10 163 K1
HBR HX7 301 L8
TOD OL14 300 C5
Longcliffe Dr STHP PR8 220 E7
Long Cl CLI BB7 99 J1
CROS/BRETH PR26 185 K3
Long Copse CHLY/EC PR7 207 J2
Long Cft GAR/LONG PR3 111 L3
KIRK/FR/WAR PR4 166 D2
Long Croft Meadow
CHLY/EC PR7 207 L1
Longdale Av SETT BD24 265 N8
Longdale La SFTN L29 258 A4
Long Dales La KKBYL LA6 245 M7
Longfield FMBY L37 237 L6
FUL/RIB PR2 132 C3
PRES PR1 151 L6
Longfield Av CHLY/EC PR7 229 H1
CSBY/BLUN L23 257 H5
PLF/KEOS FY6 86 A7
Longfield Cl TOD OL14 303 L5
Longfield Ct BWCK/EAR BB18 293 Q6
Longfield Dr CARN LA5 33 H3
Longfield Gv TOD OL14 303 L3
Longfield Mnr CHLY/EC PR7 207 K6
Longfield Pl PLF/KEOS FY6 86 A7
Longfield Rd ROCH OL11 234 F3
TOD OL14 303 L2
Longfield Wy TOD OL14 303 L3
Longfold KIRK/FR/WAR PR4 202 C1
MGHL L31 259 H2
Longford Av BISP FY2 85 H6
Longford Rd STHP PR8 221 K1
Long Gn BWCK/EAR BB18 294 F5
Longhey SKEL WN8 243 M7
Long Hey La DWN BB3 192 C2
TOD OL14 303 M4
Long Heys La SKEL WN8 244 B7
Long Heys Or Back La
SKEL WN8 244 E5
Long Hl ROCH OL11 235 G7
Longhirst Cl BOL BL1 233 L8
Longholme Rd RAW/HAS BB4 195 K1
Longhouse La PLF/KEOS FY6 106 A3
Long Ing La BWCK/EAR BB18 293 R5
Longlands Av HEY LA3 52 D3
Longlands Crs HEY LA3 52 E3
Longlands La HEY LA3 52 D4
Longlands Rd LANC LA1 42 D8
Long La BBNW BB2 171 K1
CHLYE PR6 208 D7
CHTN/BK PR9 181 L5
COL BB8 296 G3
DWN BB3 172 C8
GAR/LONG PR3 284 H6
GAR/LONG PR3 270 F10
HGHB LA2 272 A1
HGHB LA2 67 L3
HGHB LA2 38 A6
ORM L39 240 F8
SFTN L29 257 K3
SKEL WN8 254 B8
Long Level KKBYL LA6 22 C3
Longley Cl FUL/RIB PR2 132 C3
Longley La GAR/LONG PR3 112 C5
Long Lover La CLI BB7 292 D7
Long Marsh La LANC LA1 2 D4
Long Meadow BBNW BB2 155 L1
CHLY/EC PR7 207 K6
COL BB8 * 296 D6
KIRK/FR/WAR PR4 166 C7
KIRK/FR/WAR PR4 128 B6
Longmeadow La CLV/TH FY5 81 M8
HEY LA3 52 E5
Long Meanygate
CHTN/BK PR9 201 J3
Longmeanygate
CROS/BRETH PR26 185 K1
Longmere Crs CARN LA5 33 H3
Longmire Wy MCMB LA4 41 H6
Longmoor La GAR/LONG PR3 283 P9
Long Moss CROS/BRETH PR26 185 K3
Long Moss La
KIRK/FR/WAR PR4 167 H5
Long Moss Mdw
KIRK/FR/WAR PR4 167 J5
Longridge Av BPOOLS FY4 125 H6
Longridge Heath NLSN BB9 123 G7
Longridge Rd CLI BB7 116 F3
FUL/RIB PR2 133 J7
GAR/LONG PR3 114 D1
Longridge Road Elm Brow
GAR/LONG PR3 94 F7
Long Royd Rd
BWCK/EAR BB18 294 E6
Longsands La FUL/RIB PR2 132 F6
Longshaw Cl BRSC L40 203 K6
Longshaw Ford Rd BOL BL1 233 J6
Longshaw La BBNW BB2 173 G1
Long Shaw La TOD OL14 303 Q3
Longshaw St BBNW BB2 173 G2
Longsight Av ACC BB5 160 C3
CLI BB7 99 J2
Longsight Rd BBN BB1 137 H2
BBNW BB2 135 M8
GTH/LHO BB6 137 M1
Longton Av CLV/TH FY5 85 L1
Longton By-Pass
KIRK/FR/WAR PR4 166 D7
Longton Cl BBN BB1 11 M4
Longton Dr FMBY L37 237 K5
HEY LA3 41 M7
Longton Rd BPOOL FY1 4 F2
PDHM/BLYW BB12 142 A3
Longtons La SKP/WHF BD23 266 C9
Longton St CHLYE PR6 208 B3
Longway BPOOLS FY4 125 J3
Long Wham La
KIRK/FR/WAR PR4 185 G2
Longworth Av
BRFD/BLYE BB10 143 G5
CHLY/EC PR7 229 J1
HOR/BR BL6 230 F8
Longworth Rd CLI BB7 118 E7
EDGW/EG BL7 211 M8
HOR/BR BL6 231 M7
Longworth Rd North
EDGW/EG BL7 211 H6
Longworth St BBR PR5 169 H1
CHLY/EC PR7 207 L5
PRES PR1 152 F2
Lonmore Cl CHTN/BK PR9 181 K6
Lonsdale Av FTWD FY7 77 H8
MCMB LA4 41 M7
MILN OL16 235 L6
ORM L39 241 J4
Lonsdale Cha BBR PR5 * 168 D3
Lonsdale Cl LEYL PR25 186 D5
Lonsdale Crs FTWD FY7 77 H8
Lonsdale Dr
CROS/BRETH PR26 184 E8
Lonsdale Gdns NLSN BB9 103 G8
Lonsdale Gv MCMB LA4 41 M7
Lonsdale Ms BBR PR5 * 168 D3
Lonsdale Pl LANC LA1 54 F5
Lonsdale Ri KKBYL LA6 21 M1
Lonsdale Rd BPOOL FY1 4 D7
FMBY L37 237 H8
MCMB LA4 41 M7
PRES PR1 152 F2
STHP PR8 13 L9
Lonsdale St ACC BB5 159 J5
NLSN BB9 123 J2
PDHM/BLYW BB12 * 141 M4
Lonsdale Wk
WGNW/BIL/OR WN5 255 L5
Lord Av BCUP OL13 196 F3
Lord's Av BBR PR5 168 E4
Lord's Cl SETT BD24 265 M7
Lord's Close Rd HGHB LA2 49 H6
Lord's Crs DWN BB3 173 K5
Lords Cft CHLYE PR6 187 K1
Lord Sefton Wy FMBY L37 248 A1
Lords Fold RNFD/HAY WA11 262 B4
Lordsgate Dr BRSC L40 225 H8
Lordsgate La BRSC L40 241 L1
Lord's La GAR/LONG PR3 114 E1
PRES PR1 168 B2
Lord's Lot Rd KKBYL LA6 34 E2
Lordsome Rd HEY LA3 52 F1
Lord Sq BBN BB1 10 E4
MILN OL16 * 235 J4
Lord St ACC BB5 159 H7
BBN BB1 158 E2
BBNW BB2 10 E4
BCUP OL13 197 J1
BPOOL FY1 104 E5
BRSC L40 225 H6
CHLY/EC PR7 205 M6
CHLYE PR6 208 A4
CHLYE PR6 187 M2
CHTN/BK PR9 13 H2
COL BB8 103 M6
DWN BB3 191 K1
FTWD FY7 77 K7
GTH/LHO BB6 138 F7
HOR/BR BL6 231 L7
LANC LA1 3 G4
LSTA FY8 145 G4
MCMB LA4 41 J5
NLSN BB9 122 D6
PRES PR1 9 J3
RAW/HAS BB4 195 K1
STHP PR8 12 E5
TOD OL14 303 K6
Lord Street Ml BBN BB1 10 E4
Lord St West BBNW BB2 10 E4
STHP PR8 12 E6
Lord's Wk PRES PR1 9 K3
Lorne Rd BISP FY2 105 G1
Lorne St CHLY/EC PR7 207 M4
DWN BB3 191 J1
LSTA FY8 146 F7
WHIT OL12 218 E8
Lorraine Av FUL/RIB PR2 132 B8
Lorton Cl FUL/RIB PR2 132 C5
PDHM/BLYW BB12 141 L3
Lostock Ct BBR PR5 * 168 E4
Lostock Gdns BPOOLS FY4 125 G5
Lostock La BBR PR5 168 F4
Lostock Meadow CHLYE PR6 187 K2
Lostock Rd CROS/BRETH PR26 184 F8
Lostock Sq BBR PR5 168 E4
Lostock Vw BBR PR5 168 D4
Lothersdale Cl
BRFD/BLYE BB10 123 G8
Lothian Av FTWD FY7 77 G8
Lothian Pl BISP FY2 85 H6
Lottice La BBN BB1 174 C2
Lotus Dr BPOOLS FY4 126 D5
Loughlin Dr NWD/KWIPK L33 260 C6
Loughrigg Cl
PDHM/BLYW BB12 141 L3
Loughrigg Ter BPOOLS FY4 125 M2
Louis Braille Cl NTHTN L30 258 C7
Louise Cl WHIT OL12 218 F8
Louise Gdns WHIT OL12 218 E8
Louise St BPOOL FY1 4 D5
WHIT OL12 218 E8
Louis Pasteur Av NTHTN L30 258 C7
Louis Pollard Crs
GTH/LHO BB6 139 G5
Louis St RAMS BL0 195 G6
Louis William St BBN BB1 174 A3
Loupsfell Dr MCMB LA4 41 K7
Louvaine Av BOL BL1 233 J7
Lourdes Av BBR PR5 168 D2
Louvain St BWCK/EAR BB18 293 P4
Lovat Rd PRES PR1 152 C1
Loveclough Pk RAW/HAS BB4 161 J8
Love Clough Rd RAW/HAS BB4 177 J1
Love La RAMS BL0 215 H2
Lovely Hall La BBN BB1 137 G4
Low Bank PDHM/BLYW BB12 141 H5
Low Bentham Rd HGHB LA2 38 D4
Lowcroft GAR/LONG PR3 111 L8
HGHB LA2 39 G4
SKEL WN8 243 M8
Lowcross Rd PLF/KEOS FY6 106 B1
Lower Abbotsgate KKBYL LA6 21 L1
Lower Alt Rd HTWN L38 247 J7
Lower Antley St ACC BB5 159 J6
Lower Ashworth Cl BBNW BB2 10 B5
Lower Audley St BBN BB1 10 F6
Lower Back La HBR HX7 301 Q7
Lower Bank Rd FUL/RIB PR2 132 C8
Lower Bank St CHLYE PR6 189 K3
Lower Barnes St ACC BB5 139 H7
Lower Barn St DWN BB3 191 M4
Lower Beechwood ROCH OL11 235 G6
Lower Burgh Rd CHLY/EC PR7 207 K7
Lower Burgh Wy CHLY/EC PR7 207 K7
Lower Chapel La CLI BB7 290 G7
Lower Clough Fold NLSN BB9 122 F1
Lower Clough St NLSN BB9 122 F1
Lower Clowes Rd
RAW/HAS BB4 195 H3
Lower Cockcroft BBNW BB2 10 E4
Lower Copthurst CHLYE PR6 * 188 B3
Lower Copthurst La
CHLYE PR6 188 B4
Lower Cribden Av
RAW/HAS BB4 195 H1
Lower Croft St
BWCK/EAR BB18 294 E5
Lower Cross St DWN BB3 191 K2
Lower East Av
BWCK/EAR BB18 293 Q4
Lower Eccleshill Rd DWN BB3 173 K6
Lower Falinge WHIT OL12 235 J3
Lower Ferney Lee TOD OL14 303 K1
Lower Fld CROS/BRETH PR26 168 C5
Lowerfield GTH/LHO BB6 137 L3
Lowerfields
PDHM/BLYW BB12 141 J5
Lowerfold GTH/LHO BB6 138 F5
Lowerfold Cl WHIT OL12 217 M7
Lowerfold Crs WHIT OL12 217 M7
Lowerfold Dr WHIT OL12 217 M7
Lowerfold Rd GTH/LHO BB6 138 F5
Lowerfold Wy WHIT OL12 217 M7
Lowergate CLI BB7 99 H3
Lower Gate Rd ACC BB5 160 C1
Lower George St TOD OL14 303 L2
Lower Gn PLF/KEOS FY6 86 B8
WHIT OL12 234 F2
Lower Greenfield FUL/RIB PR2 131 L6
Lower Greenfoot SETT BD24 266 N0
Lower Hazel Cl BBNW BB2 10 B5
Lower Hey CSBY/BLUN L23 257 L6
KIRK/FR/WAR PR4 166 D2
Lower Hill Dr CHLYE PR6 230 D2
Lower Hodder Br CLI BB7 97 M8
Lower Hollin Bank St
BBNW BB2 10 C9
Lowerhouse Crs
PDHM/BLYW BB12 141 K5
Lower House Gn
RAW/HAS BB4 178 C3
Lowerhouse La
PDHM/BLYW BB12 141 J5
Lower House La WHIT OL12 218 E4
Lower House Rd LEYL PR25 186 A3
Lower Jowkin La ROCH OL11 234 A4
Lower Laith Av TOD OL14 303 M2
Lower Laithe Dr NLSN BB9 102 F8
Lower La GAR/LONG PR3 114 E4
HBR HX7 301 P8
KIRK/FR/WAR PR4 148 E1
MILN OL16 235 M8
RAW/HAS BB4 176 E7
Lower Lune St FTWD FY7 77 L6
Lower Lyndon Av
WGNNW/ST WN6 245 K5
Lower Manor La
PDHM/BLYW BB12 142 C1
Lower Mead Dr
PDHM/BLYW BB12 142 C1
Lower Meadow EDGW/EG BL7 213 G5
Lower North Av
BWCK/EAR BB18 293 Q5
Lower Park St
BWCK/EAR BB18 293 R6
Lower Parrock Rd NLSN BB9 122 F2
Lower Philips Rd BBN BB1 157 M2
Lower Prom STHP PR8 12 E3
Lower Ridge Cl BRFD/BLYE BB10 7 K3
Lower Rd GAR/LONG PR3 115 K3
RAMS BL0 215 G3
Lower Rosegrove La
PDHM/BLYW BB12 141 J6
Lower School St COL BB8 296 A7
Lower Sheriff St WHIT OL12 235 H3
Lower Sherriff St WHIT OL12 235 H3
Lower St MILN OL16 235 K7
Lower Tenterfield ROCH OL11 234 A1
Lower Tentre BLY BB11 7 J6
Lower Timber Hill La BLY BB11 142 D8
Lower Tweedale St
ROCH OL11 235 J5
Lower Wk CLV/TH FY5 84 F4
Lower West Av
BWCK/EAR BB18 293 Q4
Lower Wheat End MILN OL16 235 L3
Lower Wilworth BBN BB1 157 H2
Lowesby Cl BBR PR5 153 H8
Lowes Gn FMBY L37 237 L8
Lowe's La SKEL WN8 243 H3
Loweswater Cl ACC BB5 160 C3
Loweswater Crs
PDHM/BLYW BB12 141 L3
Loweswater Dr MCMB LA4 41 L7
Loweswater Wy
NWD/KWIPK L33 260 A7
Lowesway BPOOLS FY4 125 J3
CLV/TH FY5 81 L8
Lowe Vw RAW/HAS BB4 196 C2
Lowfield Cl KIRK/FR/WAR PR4 149 J1
Lowfield Rd BPOOLS FY4 125 J4
Low Fold BWCK/EAR BB18 294 D9
Lowgill La HGHB LA2 48 D5
Low Gn LEYL PR25 186 C2
Low Hl WHIT OL12 218 F8
Lowick Cl BBR PR5 154 B7
Lowick Dr PLF/KEOS FY6 106 A2
Lowlands Rd CARN LA5 32 F5
MCMB LA4 41 K6
Lowland Wy BISP FY2 85 J5
Low La KKBYL LA6 22 F5
MCMB LA4 42 A6
SKP/WHF BD23 267 M9
Low Moor La BWCK/EAR BB18 293 Q6
Low Moor Rd BISP FY2 85 H8
Lowood Gv FUL/RIB PR2 151 G2
Lowood Pl BBNW BB2 156 D5
Lowrey Ter BPOOL FY1 4 D8
Low Rd HEY LA3 64 F1
HGHB LA2 43 K5
Lowry Cl BBR PR5 168 D4
NWD/KWIPK L33 260 B5
Lowry Hill La BRSC L40 242 E1
Low's Pl WHIT OL12 235 K1
Low St KKBYL LA6 31 H6
Lowther Av BISP FY2 104 E1
HEY LA3 41 M8
MGHL L31 259 H1
Lowther Crs
CROS/BRETH PR26 186 A1
Lowther Dr CROS/BRETH PR26 186 A1
Lowther La COL BB8 296 A2
Lowther Pl BBN BB1 157 K3
Lowther Rd FTWD FY7 77 J7
LANC LA1 3 M3
ROCH OL11 235 H7
Lowther St FUL/RIB PR2 151 M2
NLSN BB9 122 F3
Lowther Ter LSTA FY8 146 D8
Lowthian St PRES PR1 9 H3
Lowthorpe Crs PRES PR1 152 E1
Lowthorpe Rd PRES PR1 152 E1
Lowthwaite Dr NLSN BB9 123 H5
Lowton Rd LSTA FY8 145 K3
Lowwood HTWN L38 247 J5
Loxham Gdns BPOOLS FY4 125 G5
Loxley Gdns
PDHM/BLYW BB12 141 J5
Loxley Gn FUL/RIB PR2 132 F5
Loxley Pl CLV/TH FY5 85 H4
Loxley Pl East CLV/TH FY5 85 H4
Loxley Rd STHP PR8 13 M9
Lubbock St PDHM/BLYW BB12 141 M5
Lucas Av CHLY/EC PR7 207 G4
Lucas La CHLYE PR6 187 M5
Lucerne Rd FUL/RIB PR2 132 F7
Lucknow St ROCH OL11 235 J6
Lucy St LANC LA1 3 G6
MCMB LA4 41 J5
NLSN BB9 103 G8
Ludlow SKEL WN8 243 M7
Ludlow Dr ORM L39 241 G4
Ludlow Gv BISP FY2 105 J1
Ludlow St WGNNW/ST WN6 228 F8
Luke St BCUP OL13 196 F3
Lulworth SKEL WN8 243 M7
Lulworth Av BPOOLE FY3 125 K1
FUL/RIB PR2 152 A1
Lulworth Pl BBR PR5 169 G1
Lulworth Rd FUL/RIB PR2 * 132 D7
STHP PR8 12 C8
Lumb Carr Av RAMS BL0 214 D7
Lumb Carr Rd RAMS BL0 214 D8
Lumb Holes La RAW/HAS BB4 196 B6
Lumb La HWTH BD22 297 R2
RAW/HAS BB4 178 C7
Lumb Scar BCUP OL13 197 J1
Lumbutts La TOD OL14 303 Q3
Lumbutts Rd TOD OL14 303 N4
Lumwood BOL BL1 233 L8
Lunar Dr NTHTN L30 258 C6
Lund Cl BRSC L40 242 B7
Lunds La KIRK/FR/WAR PR4 184 A2
Lund St BBNW BB2 10 A5
PRES PR1 9 H2
Lune Av MGHL L31 259 H1
Lune Cl KIRK/FR/WAR PR4 128 E6
KKBYL LA6 21 M1
Lunedale Av BPOOL FY1 4 F9
Lune Dr HEY LA3 42 A8
LEYL PR25 187 H1
Lunefield Dr KKBYL LA6 21 M2
Lune Gv BPOOL FY1 4 E7
Lune Rd FTWD FY7 77 J7
LANC LA1 2 D4
Lunesdale Cl LSTA FY8 145 M4
Lunesdale Ct HGHB LA2 36 B7
LANC LA1 42 C8
Lunesdale Dr GAR/LONG PR3 270 A8
Lunesdale Rd
KIRK/FR/WAR PR4 128 D6
Lunesdale Vw HGHB LA2 43 L4
Lune St COL BB8 296 B7
CSBY/BLUN L23 257 H7
GAR/LONG PR3 88 C3
LANC LA1 3 G3
PDHM/BLYW BB12 141 G3
PRES PR1 9 G4
Lune Ter LANC LA1 3 G4
Lune Valley Ramble HGHB LA2 35 H3
KKBYL LA6 29 L1
LANC LA1 3 H4
Lune Vw HGHB LA2 43 K5
PLF/KEOS FY6 78 B6
Lunt Rd SFTN L29 257 M1
Lupin Cl ACC BB5 159 K4
CHLYE PR6 187 L6
Lupin Rd ACC BB5 159 L4
Lupton Dr CSBY/BLUN L23 257 K7
NLSN BB9 103 G7
Lupton Pl LANC LA1 42 C8
Lupton St CHLY/EC PR7 207 M5
Lutner St BLY BB11 7 H6
Luton Rd CLV/TH FY5 85 G2
FUL/RIB PR2 151 H1
Lutwidge Av PRES PR1 152 F2
Lyceum Av BPOOLE FY3 5 H3
Lyceum Pas MILN OL16 * 235 J4
Lychfield Dr BBR PR5 169 H4
Lychgate PRES PR1 9 K3
Lyddesdale Av CLV/TH FY5 85 G2
Lydd Gv CHLY/EC PR7 207 K4
Lydford ROCH OL11 * 235 H5
Lydgate BRFD/BLYE BB10 143 H1
CHLY/EC PR7 207 K6
Lydia St ACC BB5 159 L7
Lydiate La CHLY/EC PR7 205 L2
CSBY/BLUN L23 257 L5
GAR/LONG PR3 91 M4
LEYL PR25 168 F7
Lydiate Pk CSBY/BLUN L23 257 L5
Lydiate Station Rd MGHL L31 249 H6
Lydric Av BBR PR5 170 B1
Lyefield Wk MILN OL16 235 L5
Lyelake La BRSC L40 252 C2
Lyme Gv PLF/KEOS FY6 78 B6
Lymington Gv NTHTN L30 258 C8
Lymm Av LANC LA1 42 B8
Lynbridge Cl
WGNW/BIL/OR WN5 255 H6
Lyncroft Crs BPOOLE FY3 105 H4
Lyndale SKEL WN8 243 L7
Lyndale Av BBN BB1 137 K4
BBR PR5 168 F2
RAW/HAS BB4 194 E1
Lyndale Cl BBN BB1 * 137 K4
LEYL PR25 186 E5
RAW/HAS BB4 177 K4
Lyndale Dr LIT OL15 219 K5
Lyndale Gv BBR PR5 168 F1
Lyndale Rd BLY BB11 140 F8
Lynden Av MCMB LA4 41 M7
Lyndeth Cl FUL/RIB PR2 133 H5
Lyndhurst SKEL WN8 243 L7
Lyndhurst Av BBN BB1 158 B6
Lyndhurst Dr FUL/RIB PR2 151 H1
Lyndhurst Gv GTH/LHO BB6 139 H5
Lyndhurst Rd BBNW BB2 173 H1
BRFD/BLYE BB10 7 L5
CSBY/BLUN L23 257 K7
DWN BB3 173 H8
STHP PR8 221 K1
Lyndon Av GTH/LHO BB6 139 H5
WGNNW/ST WN6 245 L4
Lyndon Ct GTH/LHO BB6 139 H5
Lynfield Rd GTH/LHO BB6 139 H5
Lynn Gv BPOOL FY1 104 E4
Lynn Pl FUL/RIB PR2 * 153 G1
Lynnwood Dr ROCH OL11 234 E3
Lynroyle Wy ROCH OL11 235 G8
Lynslack Ter CARN LA5 16 E3
Lynthorpe Rd BBNW BB2 173 H1
NLSN BB9 123 K2
Lynton Av BPOOLS FY4 125 G3
LEYL PR25 186 F3
ROCH OL11 234 E8
Lynton Ct FTWD FY7 80 F3
Lynton Dr STHP PR8 221 H2
Lynton Rd ACC BB5 159 J7
STHP PR8 221 H3
Lynwood Av ACC BB5 139 J7
BPOOLE FY3 105 H3
DWN BB3 173 H8
FUL/RIB PR2 133 M2
ORM L39 240 F8
Lynwood Cl ACC BB5 139 J7
CLI BB7 118 D4
COL BB8 296 A4
DWN BB3 173 H8
SKEL WN8 254 A4
Lynwood Dr PLF/KEOS FY6 82 F4
Lynwood End ORM L39 * 240 F8
Lynwood Rd ACC BB5 160 B1
BBNW BB2 156 E5
Lyons La CHLY/EC PR7 208 A4
Lyons La South CHLY/EC PR7 208 A4
Lyons Rd STHP PR8 12 F8
Lythall Av LSTA FY8 147 G7
Lytham Cl LANC LA1 55 H4
Lytham Ct CHLY/EC PR7 187 G7
KKBY L32 259 M7
Lytham Rd BBNW BB2 173 J3
BPOOLS FY4 124 E3
BRFD/BLYE BB10 142 F1
CHTN/BK PR9 180 D7
FUL/RIB PR2 131 M8
KIRK/FR/WAR PR4 148 A6
LSTA FY8 147 G2
Lytham St CHLYE PR6 208 B4
WHIT OL12 218 B8
Lythcoe Av FUL/RIB PR2 131 M7
Lythe Fell Av HGHB LA2 43 L4
Lythe Fell Rd HGHB LA2 49 J8
Lythe La HGHB LA2 49 G8
Lyth Rd LANC LA1 3 M3
Lytles Cl FMBY L37 247 K1
Lytton St PDHM/BLYW BB12 141 J4

M

Mabel St COL BB8 296 C6
WHIT OL12 235 G1
Maberry Cl WGNNW/ST WN6 245 G4
Macaulay St BLY BB11 141 M6
Macauley Av BPOOLS FY4 125 H3
Macbeth Rd FTWD FY7 77 H7
Macdonald St
WGNW/BIL/OR WN5 255 L5
Mackay Cft CHLYE PR6 208 A3
Mackenzie Cl CHLYE PR6 208 A3
Maclaren Cl BPOOLE FY3 106 A6
Macleod St NLSN BB9 123 G3
Maclure Rd ROCH OL11 235 J5
Maddy St PRES PR1 8 C2
Madeley Gdns WHIT OL12 235 G2
Maden Rd BCUP OL13 197 G1
Maden's Sq LIT OL15 219 L6
Maden St ACC BB5 159 H5
Maden Wy BCUP OL13 197 J1
Madingley Ct CHTN/BK PR9 * 200 C1
Madison Av BISP FY2 84 E6
CARN LA5 42 D1
Maesbrook Cl CHTN/BK PR9 181 L6
Mafeking Rd FUL/RIB PR2 151 M1

Magdalen Av *CLV/TH* FY5 .... 85 G2
Magdalene Sq *NTHTN* L30 * 258 C7
Maggots Nook Rd
  RNFD/HAY WA11 .... 262 D2
Maghull La *MGHL* L31 .... 259 D2
Magnolia Cl *FUL/RIB* PR2 ...... 132 F5
Magnolia Dr *LEYL* PR25 .... 187 H1
Magnolia Rd *PRES* PR1 .... 151 L8
Magpie Cl *BLY* BB11 .... 141 M6
Maida V *CLV/TH* FY5 .... 85 G3
Maiden Cl *SKEL* WN8 .... 252 F1
Maiden St *RAW/HAS* BB4 .... 176 B5
Maiden Wy *LANC* LA1 .... 52 E8
Main Cl *HEY* LA3 .... 65 J2
Main Dr *PLF/KEOS* FY6 .... 86 B8
Main Rd *HGHB* LA2 .... 66 F8
  HGHB LA2 .... 42 A2
  KKBYL LA6 .... 33 K6
Mainsfield Si *SETT* BD24 ...... 265 M6
Mainsfield Ri *SETT* BD24 ...... 265 M6
Mains La *BRSC* L40 .... 226 C5
  PLF/KEOS FY6 .... 86 D6
Main Sprit Weind *PRES* PR1 .... 9 J4
The Mains *SETT* BD24 .... 265 M6
Main Sq *CHLY/EC* PR7 .... 187 H5
Main St *BWCK/EAR* FY18 .... 294 D9
  CARN LA5 .... 25 M6
  CLI BB7 .... 292 E1
  CLI BB7 .... 290 G2
  CLI BB7 .... 277 M12
  HEY LA3 .... 65 H3
  HEY LA3 .... 52 D3
  HGHB LA2 .... 269 N7
  HGHB LA2 .... 38 C4
  HGHB LA2 .... 36 B5
  KKBYL LA6 .... 21 K6
  KKBYL LA6 .... 19 G3
  LANC LA1 .... 3 H2
  SETT BD24 .... 267 K3
  SKP/WHF BD23 .... 267 K6
Mainway *LANC* LA1 .... 3 H2
Mainway V *BBR* PR5 .... 169 H3
Mairscough La *ORM* L39 .... 249 K3
Maitland Av *CLV/TH* FY5 .... 85 G2
Maitland Cl *PRES* PR1 .... 152 F3
  WHIT OL12 .... 218 F8
Maitland Pl *RAW/HAS* BB4 ...... 195 K2
Maitland St *BCUP* OL13 .... 197 J1
  PRES PR1 .... 153 J8
  TOD OL14 .... 303 K4
Major St *ACC* BB5 .... 159 L7
  RAMS BL0 .... 214 E5
  RAW/HAS BB4 * 177 K4
  WCNW/BIL/OR WN5 .... 255 H9
Makinson La *HOR/BR* BL6 .... 232 C7
Malcolm Pl *FTWD* FY7 .... 77 H7
Malcolm St *PRES* PR1 .... 153 G8
  ROCH OL11 .... 235 G8
Malden St *LEYL* PR25 .... 186 D2
Maldern Av *PLF/KEOS* FY6 ...... 85 M6
Maldon Pl *FUL/RIB* PR2 * 153 G1
Maldon St *ROCH* OL11 .... 235 J6
Malham Av *ACC* BB5 .... 159 J7
  BPOOLS FY4 .... 125 G3
  STHP PR8 .... 200 B8
Malham Cl *LANC* LA1 .... 42 C8
Malham Pl *FUL/RIB* PR2 .... 133 H7
Malham Rd *BRFD/BLYE* BB10 ..... 123 G8
Malham View Cl
  BWCK/EAR BB18 .... 293 P6
Malham Wend *NLSN* BB9 .... 102 F8
Malkin Cl *NLSN* BB9 .... 103 H3
Malkin La *CLI* BB7 .... 98 C6
Mallard Av *PLF/KEOS* FY6 ...... 78 E7
Mallard Cl *CLV/TH* FY5 .... 81 K7
  HEY LA3 .... 53 J3
  LEYL PR25 .... 185 M3
  ORM L39 .... 250 F1
Mallard Ct *BPOOLE* FY3 .... 105 L5
  LANC LA1 .... 42 C8
Mallard Dr *HOR/BR* BL6 .... 231 K8
The Mallards *CHTN/BK* PR9 ..... 180 D8
Mallards Wk *BBR* PR5 .... 169 K6
Mallee Av *CHTN/BK* PR9 .... 180 D8
Mallee Crs *CHTN/BK* PR9 .... 180 D8
Malley La *KIRK/FR/WAR* PR4 .... 110 F3
Mallom Av *MGHL* L31 .... 249 L7
Mallory Av *MGHL* L31 .... 249 L7
Mallow Cft *MILN* OL16 .... 235 M7
Mallow Dl *FUL/RIB* PR2 .... 131 L6
Mallowdale Av *HEY* LA3 .... 52 F8
Mallowdale Rd *LANC* LA1 .... 2 C1
Mallow Wk *HEY* LA3 .... 53 J1
The Mall *BLY* BB11 .... 6 F4
  FUL/RIB PR2 .... 153 H1
  LSTA FY8 .... 145 M4
Maltby Pl *BPOOLS* FY4 .... 5 L8
Malthouse Ct *FUL/RIB* PR2 ..... 8 D1
Malthouse Wy *PRES* PR1 .... 152 A8
The Maltings *CLV/TH* FY5 ...... 81 K7
  KIRK/FR/WAR PR4 .... 166 C3
Malt Kiln Brow *GAR/LONG* PR3 .. 287 L11
Malt Kiln Gv *GAR/LONG* PR3 .... 88 D6
Maltkiln La *BRSC* L40 .... 226 C5
  ORM L39 .... 251 H3
The Maltings *KKBYL* LA6 .... 21 K6
Malton Dr *BBR* PR5 .... 168 C4
Malt St *ACC* BB5 .... 159 L4
Malvern Av *ACC* BB5 .... 159 H8
  BBNW BB2 .... 173 G2
  BPOOL FY1 .... 5 L8
  LANC LA1 .... 54 F5
  PDHM/BLYW BB12 .... 141 L8
  PLF/KEOS FY6 .... 82 F4
  PRES PR1 .... 9 M8
Malvern Cl *PRES* PR1 .... 168 F5
  HOR/BR BL6 .... 231 M6
  KKBY L32 .... 259 M7
  WGNS/IIMK WN3 .... 255 M8
Malvern Rd *LSTA* FY8 .... 146 A6
  NLSN BB9 .... 123 J2
  PRES PR1 .... 9 M7
Malvern St *PRES* PR1 .... 9 M8
  WGNNW/ST WN6 .... 228 F4
Malvern St East *ROCH* OL11 .... 234 F4
Malvern St West *ROCH* OL11 .... 234 F4
Malvern Wy *RAW/HAS* BB4 .... 194 D4
Manby Cl *BBR* PR5 .... 154 C8
Manchester Rd *ACC* BB5 .... 159 M6
  BLY BB11 .... 6 D7
  BPOOLS FY4 .... 105 G5
  BURY BL9 .... 215 H6
  BWCK/EAR BB18 .... 293 Q7
  CHTN/BK PR9 .... 13 J2
  NLSN BB9 .... 123 K2
  PDHM/BLYW BB12 .... 140 F7
  PRES PR1 .... 9 K4
  RAMS BL0 .... 215 H5
  RAW/HAS BB4 .... 194 D4
  ROCH OL11 .... 234 F8

Mandella Ct *BBN* BB1 .... 10 F1
Mandeville Rd *STHP* PR8 .... 220 E6
Manfield Cl *SKEL* WN8 .... 243 K7
Manion Av *MGHL* L31 .... 249 L6
Manion Cl *MGHL* L31 .... 249 L6
Manitoba Cl *BBNW* BB2 .... 156 F3
Mankinholes Bank *TOD* OL14 .... 303 Q3
Manley Rd *PRES* PR1 .... 151 H7
Manner Sutton St *BBN* BB1 ..... 11 H3
Manning Rd *PRES* PR1 .... 153 H2
  STHP PR8 .... 200 B5
Mannin Wy *LANC* LA1 .... 43 H7
Manor Av *BRSC* L40 .... 242 A1
  CSBY/BLUN L23 .... 257 D8
  FUL/RIB PR2 .... 132 E7
  GAR/LONG PR3 .... 116 A8
  HGHB LA2 .... 42 D3
  PRES PR1 .... 151 L7
Manor Brook *ACC* BB5 .... 159 M5
Manor Cl *BBR* PR5 .... 154 C8
  HGHB LA2 .... 42 D3
  KKBYL LA6 .... 31 H6
  TOD OL14 .... 303 R3
Manor Ct *FUL/RIB* PR2 .... 131 K4
Manor Ctyd *HEY* LA3 .... 52 C3
Manor Crs *BRSC* L40 .... 242 A1
  HGHB LA2 .... 42 D3
Manorcroft *KIRK/FR/WAR* PR4 ... 166 C3
Manor Dr *BRSC* L40 .... 242 A1
  CLV/TH FY5 .... 81 G8
  CSBY/BLUN L23 .... 257 D8
  HGHB LA2 .... 42 D3
  KIRK/FR/WAR PR4 .... 128 N7
  NTHTN L30 .... 258 E8
Manor Farm *KKBYL* LA6 .... 21 K4
Manor Fids *CLI* BB7 .... 118 F6
Manor Gdns *BRSC* L40 .... 242 A1
Manor Gv *HEY* LA3 .... 53 G1
  PRES PR1 .... 151 L7
  SKEL WN8 .... 253 J2
  WGNW/BIL/OR WN5 .... 255 L3
Manor House Cl
  CROS/BRETH PR26 .... 185 L3
  MGHL L31 .... 258 F2
Manor House Crs *PRES* PR1 ..... 132 E8
Manor House Dr *SKEL* WN8 ...... 254 B8
Manor House La *PRES* PR1 ...... 132 E8
Manor La *HGHB* LA2 .... 42 D3
  PRES PR1 .... 151 L7
Manor Ldg *FMBY* L37 .... 237 H7
Manor Mill Cl *MILN* OL16 ...... 219 G4
Manor Pk *PRES* PR1 .... 132 F8
Manor Pl *ACC* BB5 .... 159 J4
Manor Rd *BBNW* BB2 .... 156 E4
  BPOOL FY1 .... 5 G3
  BRSC L40 .... 242 A1
  CHLY PR6 .... 169 L8
  CHTN/BK PR9 .... 200 D1
  CLI BB7 .... 118 F6
  COL BB8 .... 296 B6
  CSBY/BLUN L23 .... 257 D8
  DWN BB3 .... 191 J3
  FTWD FY7 .... 77 H6
  HGHB LA2 .... 42 E3
  HOR/BR BL6 .... 232 A7
  KIRK/FR/WAR PR4 .... 127 L7
  KIRK/FR/WAR PR4 .... 109 M3
  PDHM/BLYW BB12 .... 141 L4
  WGNNW/ST WN6 .... 245 J5
Manor St *ACC* BB5 .... 160 A4
  BCUP OL13 .... 197 J2
  NLSN BB9 .... 123 J3
  RAMS BL0 .... 214 E4
Manor Wy *KIRK/FR/WAR* PR4 ..... 127 L8
  KIRK/FR/WAR PR4 .... 128 E4
Manor Wd *FTWD* FY7 .... 77 H7
Manse Av *WGNNW/ST* WN6 .... 228 C5
Mansergh St
  BRFD/BLYE BB10 * 142 F1
Mansfield Crs *NLSN* BB9 .... 122 F8
Mansfield Dr *BBR* PR5 .... 154 B8
Mansfield Gra *ROCH* OL11 ...... 234 F6
Mansfield Gv *NLSN* BB9 .... 122 F5
Mansfield Rd *BPOOLE* FY3 ...... 105 G3
  ROCH OL11 .... 234 B4
Mansion St South *ACC* BB5 * ... 160 A5
Manston Gv *CHLY/EC* PR7 .... 207 K4
Manx Jane's La *CHTN/BK* PR9 ... 180 D7
Manxman Rd *BBNW* BB2 .... 173 H2
Maple Av *BPOOLE* FY3 .... 5 H2
  BRSC L40 .... 225 H7
  CHLY PR6 .... 189 J4
  CLV/TH FY5 .... 85 M3
  FTWD FY7 * 81 J3
  HEY LA3 .... 40 F8
  RAW/HAS BB4 .... 176 F8
Maple Bank *BRFD/BLYE* BB10 * .. 142 M2
Maplebank *FUL/RIB* PR2 .... 150 F2
Maple Cl *BBN* BB1 .... 137 H5
  CLI BB7 .... 119 G5
  FMBY L37 .... 246 F2
  KIRK/FR/WAR PR4 .... 128 J1
Maple Ct *LEYL* PR25 .... 169 G8
Maple Crs *BBN* BB1 .... 158 E5
  PRES PR1 .... 8 E5
Maple Dr *ACC* BB5 .... 159 J8
  PLF/KEOS FY6 .... 106 A1
Maple Gv *CHLY* PR6 .... 188 A8
  FUL/RIB PR2 .... 133 G7
  KIRK/FR/WAR PR4 .... 148 A5
  LANC LA1 .... 2 C1
  PRES PR1 .... 151 L7
  RAMS BL0 .... 215 G6
Maple Rd *GAR/LONG* PR3 .... 284 B6
The Maples *CROS/BRETH* PR26 ... 185 D3
Maple St *BBN* BB1 .... 158 A4
  BBN BB1 .... 157 K4
  ROCH OL11 .... 235 G6
  STHP PR8 .... 200 E4
  TOD OL14 .... 303 K8
Maplewood *SKEL* WN8 .... 243 K7
Maplewood Av *PLF/KEOS* FY6 .... 78 D6
Maplewood Cl *LEYL* PR25 .... 186 B3
Maplewood Dr *CLV/TH* FY5 ...... 84 F3
Maplewood Gdns *LANC* LA1 ...... 66 F1
Marabou Dr *DWN* BB3 .... 173 H2
Marathon Pl
  CROS/BRETH PR26 .... 167 M8
Marble Av *CLV/TH* FY5 .... 85 J4
Marble St *ACC* BB5 .... 159 M4
Marchbank Rd *SKEL* WN8 .... 253 K5
Marchbanks Cl
  PDHM/BLYW BB12 .... 6 F7
Marchwood Rd *BPOOLS* FY4 ...... 105 L3
Marcliffe Dr *ROCH* OL11 .... 234 E6
Marcroft Av *BPOOLS* FY4 .... 125 H4
Marcroft Pl *ROCH* OL11 .... 235 K7
Mardale Av *BPOOLS* FY4 .... 125 M2
  MCMB LA4 .... 41 L6

Mardale Cl *STHP* PR8 .... 220 E7
Mardale Crs *LEYL* PR25 .... 186 E4
Mardale Rd *GAR/LONG* PR3 ...... 114 C6
  LANC LA1 .... 3 K3
  PRES PR1 .... 153 K2
Mardyke *WHIT* OL12 * 235 M3
Maresfield Rd *PRES* PR1 .... 8 C1
Margaret Av *LANC* LA1 .... 54 E7
  WGNNW/ST WN6 .... 245 M7
Margaret Rd *CSBY/BLUN* L23 .... 256 D7
  PRES PR1 .... 152 B7
Margaret St *BBN* BB1 .... 158 A7
  BRFD/BLYE BB10 * 142 F8
  PRES PR1 .... 9 H4
  RAW/HAS BB4 .... 177 J7
Margate Av *BPOOLS* FY4 .... 125 H5
Margate Rd *FUL/RIB* PR2 .... 131 K2
  PRES PR1 .... 145 J3
Margroy Cl *WHIT* OL12 .... 235 K1
The Mariari Cl *NTHTN* L30 ..... 258 C7
Marians Dr *ORM* L39 .... 241 H3
The Marian Sq *NTHTN* L30 ...... 258 B7
The Marian Wy *NTHTN* L30 ...... 258 B8
Maria Sq *EDGW/EG* BL7 .... 210 F7
Maria St *BBN* BB1 .... 191 L5
Maricourt Av *BBN* BB1 .... 158 A6
Marie Curie Av *NTHTN* L30 ..... 258 C7
Marigold St *ROCH* OL11 .... 235 J6
Marilyn Av *BBR* PR5 .... 168 A3
Marina Av *BPOOL* FY1 .... 5 G7
  BPOOLE FY3 .... 106 A3
Marina Cl *BBR* PR5 .... 168 A3
Marina Dr *BBR* PR5 .... 168 A3
  FUL/RIB PR2 .... 132 B5
Marina Gv *BBR* PR5 .... 168 D2
Marina Ms *FTWD* FY7 .... 77 L8
Marina Rd *FMBY* L37 .... 247 J2
Marine Av *BLY* BB11 .... 141 M7
Marine Crs *CHLY/EC* PR7 .... 187 J5
Marine Dr *CHTN/BK* PR9 .... 199 L1
  CHTN/BK PR9 .... 180 B5
  HGHB LA2 .... 42 A5
  LSTA FY8 .... 145 M8
  STHP PR8 .... 12 A6
Marine Gate Man
  CHTN/BK PR9 * 13 H1
Marine Pde *FTWD* FY7 .... 80 F1
  STHP PR8 .... 12 E1
Marine Road Central
  MCMB LA4 .... 41 H6
Marine Rd East *MCMB* LA4 ...... 41 K5
Marine Rd West *HEY* LA3 .... 40 F7
Mariners Cl *FTWD* FY7 .... 81 K7
Mariners Wy *FUL/RIB* PR2 ...... 151 K5
Marino Cl *CLV/TH* FY5 .... 86 A3
Maritime Ct *FTWD* FY7 .... 81 J1
Maritime Wy *FUL/RIB* PR2 ...... 151 L4
Mark Cl *PRES* PR1 .... 168 J3
Market Bids *LSTA* FY8 * 145 J5
Market Pl *CHLY/EC* PR7 .... 230 D5
  CLI BB7 .... 99 H3
  COL BB8 .... 296 B6
  GAR/LONG PR3 .... 284 B8
  GAR/LONG PR3 .... 114 C4
  PRES PR1 .... 9 H4
  RAMS BL0 .... 214 F4
  SETT BD24 .... 265 N7
Market Prom *BLY* BB11 .... 7 G4
Market Sq *BLY* BB11 .... 7 G4
  KKBYL LA6 .... 21 M1
  LSTA FY8 .... 146 B1
  NLSN BB9 .... 123 G3
Market St *ACC* BB5 .... 159 L6
  BCUP OL13 .... 197 J1
  BPOOL FY1 .... 4 E4
  CARN LA5 .... 33 J1
  CHLY PR6 .... 230 D5
  CHLY/EC PR7 .... 207 M3
  COL BB8 .... 296 B6
  DWN BB3 .... 191 K2
  KIRK/FR/WAR PR4 .... 128 C6
  KKBYL LA6 .... 21 M1
  LANC LA1 .... 3 H4
  MCMB LA4 .... 41 H6
  PLF/KEOS FY6 .... 86 F1
  PRES PR1 .... 9 H3
  RAMS BL0 .... 195 G7
  RAW/HAS BB4 .... 196 C5
  STHP PR8 .... 12 E4
  WHIT OL12 .... 217 M5
Market Street La *BBNW* BB2 .... 10 E3
Market St West *PRES* PR1 ...... 9 G3
Market Wy *BBN* BB1 .... 10 E1
  ORM L39 .... 241 H6
Markham Dr *STHP* PR8 .... 222 B1
Markham Rd *BBNW* BB2 .... 156 E8
Markham St *FUL/RIB* PR2 .... 151 M2
Marklands Rd *HOR/BR* BL6 ...... 232 B6
Markland St *PRES* PR1 .... 8 E4
  RAMS BL0 * 214 F5
Mark La *TOD* OL14 .... 301 J12
Mark Rd *HTWN* L38 .... 247 J7
Markross St *RAW/HAS* BB4 ...... 195 J4
Mark's Av *CROS/BRETH* PR26 .... 166 F8
Mark St *BCUP* OL13 .... 196 F5
  BRFD/BLYE BB10 .... 142 E2
  WHIT OL12 .... 235 L2
Marland Av *BPOOLE* FY3 .... 125 K7
Marland Cl *ROCH* OL11 .... 234 E7
Marland Cl *ROCH* OL11 .... 234 E6
Marland Fold *ROCH* OL11 .... 234 E7
Marland Gn *ROCH* OL11 .... 234 E7
Marland Old Rd *ROCH* OL11 ..... 234 E7
Marl Av *PRES* PR1 .... 151 L7
Marlboro Rd *BPOOLS* FY4 .... 5 H3
Marlborough Av *CLV/TH* FY5 .... 80 F6
  KIRK/FR/WAR PR4 .... 148 A5
  MGHL L31 .... 250 A8
Marlborough Cl *RAMS* BL0 ...... 214 F8
Marlborough Dr *BBR* PR5 .... 152 F2
  FUL/RIB PR2 .... 132 A3
Marlborough Rd *ACC* BB5 .... 159 J5
  CHTN/BK PR9 .... 13 K3
  CSBY/BLUN L23 .... 257 C6
  HEY LA3 .... 40 F8
  LSTA FY8 .... 145 H2
Marlborough St *BLY* BB11 ...... 7 H3
  CHLY PR6 .... 208 B2
  WHIT OL12 .... 234 F7
Marl Cop *CROS/BRETH* PR26 ..... 184 D5
Marl Cft *PRES* PR1 .... 168 A1
Marled Hey *EDGW/EG* BL7 .... 213 G6
Marles Ct *BRFD/BLYE* BB10 ..... 142 A3
Marlfield *KIRK/FR/WAR* PR4 .... 166 C7
Marl Gv *WGNW/BIL/OR* WN5 ...... 255 L5
Marl Hill Crs *FUL/RIB* PR2 .... 153 K1
Marl Hill La *AIRE* BD20 .... 295 A8
Marlhill Rd *BPOOLE* FY3 .... 105 K3

Marlin St *NLSN* BB9 .... 123 J1
Marlow Ct *CHLY/EC* PR7 .... 230 C5
Marlowe Av *ACC* BB5 .... 176 B1
Marl Pits *RAW/HAS* BB4 .... 177 L8
Marl Pl *ACC* BB5 * 160 A2
Marl Rd *NTHTN* L30 .... 258 D8
  NWD/KWIPK L33 .... 260 F8
Marlton Rd *BBNW* BB2 .... 173 G2
Marlton Wy *LANC* LA1 .... 54 F5
Marne Crs *ROCH* OL11 .... 234 F4
Marple Cl *DWN* BB3 .... 173 J4
Marquis Cl *KIRK/FR/WAR* PR4 ... 128 C6
Marquis Dr *KIRK/FR/WAR* PR4 ... 128 C6
Marron Cl *LEYL* PR25 .... 186 B2
Marsden Cl *BRFD/BLYE* BB10 .... 122 F8
Marsden Dr *NLSN* BB9 .... 123 G5
Marsden Gv *NLSN* BB9 .... 122 F6
Marsden Hall Rd North
  NLSN BB9 .... 123 K2
Marsden Hall Rd South
  NLSN BB9 .... 123 K3
Marsden Height Cl *NLSN* BB9 ... 123 H6
Marsden Mi *NLSN* BB9 * 123 G5
Marsden Pl *NLSN* BB9 .... 123 K3
Marsden Rd *BPOOLS* FY4 .... 125 G3
  BRFD/BLYE BB10 .... 122 F8
  CHTN/BK PR9 .... 200 B4
Marsden St *ACC* BB5 .... 159 L7
  BBNW BB2 .... 172 E4
  KIRK/FR/WAR PR4 .... 128 C6
Marsett Cl *WHIT* OL12 .... 234 C2
Marsett Pl *FUL/RIB* PR2 .... 133 H6
Marshall Av *ACC* BB5 .... 160 A3
Marshall Gv *FUL/RIB* PR2 ...... 131 K7
Marshallsay *FMBY* L37 .... 247 L5
Marshall's Brow *PRES* PR1 ..... 152 B8
Marshall's Cl *MGHL* L31 .... 249 M7
Marshall St *MILN* OL16 .... 235 L4
Marsham Cl *GAR/LONG* PR3 * 284 C9
Marsham Gv *DWN* BB5 .... 191 M2
Marshaw Pl *GAR/LONG* PR3 ...... 283 R9
Marshaw Rd *LANC* LA1 .... 2 D2
Marsh Brows *FMBY* L37 .... 247 H4
Marsh Cl *HGHB* LA2 .... 269 L7
Marsh Crs *MCMB* LA4 .... 42 A8
Marshdale Rd *BPOOLS* FY4 ...... 125 G4
Marsh Dr *KIRK/FR/WAR* PR4 ..... 149 G4
The Marshes La
  KIRK/FR/WAR PR4 .... 202 D2
Marshfield Rd *SETT* BD24 ...... 265 N7
Marsh Ga *DWN* BB3 .... 191 M2
Marsh House La *DWN* BB3 .... 191 M2
Marsh La *CHLYE* PR6 .... 170 A4
  HBR HX7 .... 301 K8
  HGHB LA2 .... 269 L7
  HTWN L38 .... 248 A7
  KIRK/FR/WAR PR4 .... 165 L2
  PLF/KEOS FY6 .... 86 F2
  PRES PR1 .... 8 C4
Marsh Moss La *BRSC* L40 .... 224 F4
Marsh Prom *BLY* BB11 .... 7 H4
Marsh Rd *CHTN/BK* PR9 .... 181 K1
  CLV/TH FY5 .... 85 K1
  KIRK/FR/WAR PR4 .... 165 J2
Marshside Rd *CHTN/BK* PR9 ..... 180 B6
Marsh St *BBN* BB1 .... 10 F1
  HOR/BR BL6 .... 231 K7
  LANC LA1 .... 3 H4
Marsh Ter *DWN* BB3 .... 191 K1
Marsh Vw *KIRK/FR/WAR* PR4 ..... 149 J1
Marsh Wy *PRES* PR1 .... 167 M4
Mars St *EDGW/EG* BL7 .... 213 H5
Marston Cl *FUL/RIB* PR2 .... 131 M4
Marston Crs *HTWN* L38 .... 256 D1
Marston Moor *FUL/RIB* PR2 ..... 131 M4
Martha's Ter *MILN* OL16 .... 218 F8
Martholme Av *ACC* BB5 .... 139 K8
Martholme La *GTH/LHO* BB6 ..... 139 J3
Martin Av *LSTA* FY8 .... 145 H4
Martin Croft Rd *RAW/HAS* BB4 .. 176 B6
Martindale Cl *BBN* BB1 * 173 M1
Martin Dr *DWN* BB3 .... 191 M1
Martine Cl *MGHL* L31 .... 259 J4
Martinfield Rd *PRES* PR1 ...... 168 A1
Martinfields *BRFD/BLYE* BB10 .. 122 F8
Martinique Dr *DWN* BB3 .... 173 J5
Martin La *BRSC* L40 .... 224 B3
  WHIT OL12 .... 234 D1
Martins Av *CHLY/EC* PR7 .... 230 B1
Martins Fld *WHIT* OL12 .... 234 C1
Martins La *SKEL* WN8 .... 254 A4
Martin St *BRFD/BLYE* BB10 ..... 142 A4
  EDGW/EG BL7 .... 213 G4
Martin Top La *CLI* BB7 .... 292 D5
Martland Av *AIN/FAZ* L10 ...... 259 H8
  WGNNW/ST WN6 .... 245 J8
Mart La *BRSC* L40 .... 225 H4
Martlet Av *ROCH* OL11 .... 234 E4
Marton Dr *BLY* BB11 .... 142 B8
  BPOOLS FY4 .... 125 G3
  MCMB LA4 * 41 K7
Marton Fold *BPOOLS* FY4 .... 125 K7
Marton Pl *MCMB* LA4 * 42 A6
Marton Rd *FUL/RIB* PR2 .... 151 L7
  SKP/WHF BD23 .... 280 H3
Marton St *LANC* LA1 .... 3 G7
Marton Vw *BPOOLE* FY3 .... 5 J4
Mary Av *STHP* PR8 .... 221 H5
Marybank Cl *FUL/RIB* PR2 ...... 132 F5
Mary Ct *BBN* BB1 * 158 A1
Maryland *BPOOLS* FY4 .... 126 D5
Maryland Cl *CARN* LA5 .... 17 G3
Mary St *BBN* BB1 .... 158 E2
  BBN BB1 .... 11 K5
  BRFD/BLYE BB10 .... 7 K5
  CARN LA5 .... 26 A2
  COL BB8 .... 103 M7
  LANC LA1 .... 3 H4
  RAMS BL0 .... 214 E6
Mary St East *HOR/BR* BL6 ...... 231 L7
Mary St West *GAR/LONG* PR3 .... 114 D3
  HOR/BR BL6 .... 231 L7
Mary Towneley Fold
  BRFD/BLYE BB10 .... 7 M6
Masefield Av *CLV/TH* FY5 ...... 85 H3
  PDHM/BLYW BB12 .... 141 L7
  WGNNW/BIL/OR WN5 .... 255 H1
Masefield Rd *GTH/LHO* BB6 ..... 138 D7
  GTH/LHO BB6 .... 138 D7
Masefield Pl *BBR* PR5 .... 169 G1
Masefield Rd *CSBY/BLUN* L23 ... 257 M5
Mason Cl *KIRK/FR/WAR* PR4 ..... 148 D1
Masonfield Crs *LANC* LA1 ...... 55 H4

Masongill Fell La *KKBYL* LA6 .. 23 L7
Mason Hill Vw *FUL/RIB* PR2 .... 132 D7
Mason House Crs
  FUL/RIB PR2 .... 131 K6
Mason's St *ACC* BB5 .... 296 A6
Mason St *ACC* BB5 .... 159 A6
  CHLYE PR6 .... 208 B2
  HOR/BR BL6 .... 231 K8
  MILN OL16 .... 235 L4
Masons Wy *BWCK/EAR* BB18 ...... 293 Q4
Masonwood *FUL/RIB* PR2 .... 132 D5
Massam Cl *FUL/RIB* PR2 .... 132 D5
Massam's La *FMBY* L37 .... 237 H5
Massey Cft *WHIT* OL12 .... 217 M4
Massey La *NLSN* BB9 .... 122 C6
Massey St *BLY* BB11 * 7 H4
  NLSN BB9 .... 122 D7
Masterson Av
  PDHM/BLYW BB12 .... 140 A1
Matcham Ct *BPOOL* FY1 .... 5 A2
Matchmoor La *HOR/BR* BL6 ...... 232 C7
Mather Av *ACC* BB5 .... 159 L3
Mather St *BPOOLE* FY3 .... 105 H4
Mathias Ct *MCMB* LA4 * 41 J5
Matlock Ct *HOR/BR* BL6 .... 232 B7
Matlock Gv *BRFD/BLYE* BB10 .... 142 F1
Matlock Pl *FUL/RIB* PR2 .... 131 K6
Matlock St *STHP* PR8 .... 199 L8
Matterdale Rd *LEYL* PR25 ...... 186 E4
Matthew Cl *COL* BB8 .... 296 B4
Matthew La *TOD* OL14 .... 301 P12
Matthew Moss La *ROCH* OL11 .... 234 E7
Matthews Ct *BPOOLS* FY4 .... 125 G4
Matthew St *BBNW* BB2 .... 172 E1
Matthias Ct *MCMB* LA4 * 41 J5
Matthias St *MCMB* LA4 * 41 J5
Mattock Crs *MCMB* LA4 .... 42 A6
Maudland Bank *PRES* PR1 .... 8 E1
  PRES PR1 .... 8 F2
Maudsley Dr *ACC* BB5 .... 159 M5
Maud St *CHLY/EC* PR7 .... 207 L5
  NLSN BB9 .... 123 G1
  WHIT OL12 .... 235 K1
Maunders Ct *CSBY/BLUN* L23 .... 257 C6
Maureen Av *BBR* PR5 .... 168 E3
Maureen St *WHIT* OL12 .... 235 K1
Maurice Gv *BISP* FY2 .... 105 H1
Maurice Dr *CHLY/EC* PR7 .... 229 H1
Mavis Rd *BBNW* BB2 .... 156 D6
Mawdsley Cl *FMBY* L37 .... 237 L8
Mawdsley Ter *ORM* L39 .... 241 J3
Maxwell Gv *BISP* FY2 .... 105 H1
Maybank Cl *CHTN/BK* PR9 .... 200 D4
May Bell Av *CLV/TH* FY5 .... 81 J8
Maybury Av
  PDHM/BLYW BB12 .... 141 L4
Maybury Cl *RAMS* BL0 .... 214 E6
Maycroft Av *PLF/KEOS* FY6 ..... 85 M6
Mayfair *HOR/BR* BL6 .... 232 A8
Mayfair Av *CSBY/BLUN* L23 ..... 257 H6
Mayfair Cl *HTWN* L38 .... 256 C1
  LSTA FY8 .... 146 A5
  RAW/HAS BB4 .... 194 D4
Mayfair Crs *BBN* BB1 .... 137 J6
Mayfair Dr *CLV/TH* FY5 .... 85 M3
Mayfair Gdns *FUL/RIB* PR2 ..... 132 F6
  ROCH OL11 .... 235 G6
Mayfayre Av *MGHL* L31 .... 249 L6
Mayfield Av *ACC* BB5 .... 159 J7
  BBR PR5 .... 168 F3
  BPOOLS FY4 .... 124 F5
  CHLYE PR6 .... 230 D4
  CLI BB7 .... 99 J4
  CLV/TH FY5 .... 81 K7
  FMBY L37 .... 246 F2
  FUL/RIB PR2 .... 131 K6
  KIRK/FR/WAR PR4 .... 128 C6
  KKBYL LA6 .... 18 F7
  LANC LA1 .... 42 D8
  RAW/HAS BB4 .... 194 D2
Mayfield Cl *PRES* PR1 .... 152 B7
Mayfield Ct *MCMB* LA4 .... 41 J5
Mayfield Dr *MCMB* LA4 .... 41 M5
Mayfield Fold *BLY* BB11 .... 142 E8
Mayfield Rd *BBN* BB1 .... 137 H8
  CHLYE PR6 .... 208 A2
  HGHB LA2 .... 38 F5
  LEYL PR25 .... 186 D4
  LSTA FY8 .... 145 L3
  SKEL WN8 .... 254 D4
  WGNW/BIL/OR WN5 .... 255 L3
Mayfield St *BBNW* BB2 .... 10 B8
  NLSN BB9 .... 123 L2
Mayfield Ter *MILN* OL16 .... 235 L2
  MILN OL16 .... 235 L2
Mayflower Av *PRES* PR1 .... 151 L7
Mayflower Gv *GAR/LONG* PR3 .... 91 G2
Mayflower Cl *CHLY/EC* PR7 ..... 187 J4
Mayflower St *BBNW* BB2 .... 172 E1
Maylands Pl *NLSN* BB9 .... 102 F8
Maynard St *FUL/RIB* PR2 .... 152 A1
Mayor Dr *KIRK/FR/WAR* PR4 ..... 183 K5
Mayor Av *BPOOL* FY1 .... 4 E7
Maypark *BBR* PR5 .... 169 K6
Maypole St *NTHTN* L30 .... 258 K6
Mayson St *BBNW* BB2 .... 10 B5
May St *BBN* BB1 .... 11 K6
  EDGW/EG BL7 .... 213 H5
  NLSN BB9 .... 123 G1
Maytree Ct *CHLYE* PR6 .... 230 C3
Maytree Wk *SKEL* WN8 .... 243 L7
Mayville Rd *NLSN* BB9 .... 122 E5
McCall Cl *KIRK/FR/WAR* PR4 .... 127 K8
McDonald Rd *HEY* LA3 .... 52 D4
McDonna St *BOL* BL1 .... 233 M8
McKenzie St *BBR* PR5 .... 169 J3
McNaught St *MILN* OL16 .... 235 L5
Mead Av *LEYL* PR25 .... 186 E5
Meadow Av *FTWD* FY7 .... 81 J4
  PLF/KEOS FY6 .... 78 D5
  STHP PR8 .... 199 M7
Meadoway *ACC* BB5 .... 159 J4
  KIRK/FR/WAR PR4 .... 183 K6
Meadow Bank
  BRFD/BLYE BB10 .... 122 F6
Meadow Bank Rd *NLSN* BB9 ...... 122 F4
Meadowbarn Cl
  KIRK/FR/WAR PR4 .... 131 H6
Meadow Bottom Rd
  TOD OL14 .... 303 L1
Meadowbridge Cl *BRSC* L40 ..... 242 B7

Meadowbrook BPOOLE FY3 125 M1
BRSC L40 242 A1
Meadow Brow CHTN/BK PR9 181 G6
Meadow Cl ACC BB5 160 C2
BISP FY2 105 G1
BRFD/BLYE BB10 122 E7
BRSC L40 242 B7
CLI BB7 118 D8
COL BB8 296 A2
KIRK/FR/WAR PR4 150 A2
KIRK/FR/WAR PR4 127 L8
SKEL WN8 254 A4
Meadow Clough SKEL WN8 243 L7
Meadow Ct PRES PR1 8 E7
Meadow Court Rd MCMB LA4 41 K7
Meadow Crs
KIRK/FR/WAR PR4 128 C5
PLF/KEOS FY6 85 K8
Meadowcroft CHLY/EC PR7 186 E8
Meadow Cft CLI BB7 290 D10
Meadowcroft DWN BB3 173 K5
FMBY L37 247 J1
KKBYL LA6 33 L7
LSTA FY8 145 K2
SKEL WN8 243 L7
Meadowcroft Av CLV/TH FY5 85 H1
GAR/LONG PR3 284 C12
PLF/KEOS FY6 86 F2
Meadowcroft Cl
RAW/HAS BB4 177 K6
Meadowcroft Gv HEY LA3 52 F2
Meadowcroft La ROCH OL11 234 C5
Meadowcroft Rd LEYL PR25 186 A4
Meadow Dr CARN LA5 32 F6
KIRK/FR/WAR PR4 147 M6
ORM L39 250 F1
Meadow Edge NLSN BB9 103 J6
Meadowfield FUL/RIB PR2 132 C4
HGHB LA2 43 K4
MILN OL16 235 L8
Meadow Fld PRES PR1 168 B1
Meadowfield SKEL WN8 254 D4
Meadowfield Cl CLI BB7 118 D4
Meadow Head Av WHIT OL12 218 A5
Meadow Head La DWN BB3 172 F6
KIRK/FR/WAR PR4 166 C4
Meadowland Cl
CROS/BRETH PR26 168 B8
Meadowlands CHLY/EC PR7 207 G7
Meadow La BBR PR5 169 L7
BRSC L40 225 M8
CROS/BRETH PR26 204 A2
KIRK/FR/WAR PR4 165 H7
LSTA FY8 147 G7
MGHL L31 259 H2
PLF/KEOS FY6 78 C7
STHP PR8 220 F8
Meadow Pk BPOOLE FY3 106 A6
GAR/LONG PR3 284 A6
HGHB LA2 66 E7
KIRK/FR/WAR PR4 183 L5
KIRK/FR/WAR PR4 128 B5
RAMS BL0 194 F6
Meadow Reach PRES PR1 167 L1
Meadow Ri BBNW BB2 172 D4
SETT BD24 265 M6
Meadows Av BCUP OL13 179 J7
CLV/TH FY5 81 J8
RAW/HAS BB4 194 E1
Meadows Cl CARN LA5 18 B7
Meadows Dr RAW/HAS BB4 177 K2
Meadowside CLI BB7 290 H7
CROS/BRETH PR26 204 D1
HGHB LA2 45 K1
KIRK/FR/WAR PR4 166 D6
LANC LA1 3 H8
Meadowside Av ACC BB5 139 H8
Meadowside Dr BBR PR5 170 B2
NWD/KWIPK L33 260 C5
The Meadows ACC BB5 159 J8
BBR PR5 * 169 J1
CARN LA5 18 B7
CARN LA5 16 E3
CHLY/EC PR7 228 A1
CLI BB7 118 D7
CLV/TH FY5 85 J1
COL BB8 296 A5
CROS/BRETH PR26 185 L3
GAR/LONG PR3 270 B9
KIRK/FR/WAR PR4 108 C2
MGHL L31 259 G2
PDHM/BLYW BB12 142 A3
STHP PR8 * 221 G7
WHIT OL12 217 M2
Meadow St ACC BB5 159 M5
BLY BB11 * 6 F4
BWCK/EAR BB18 293 P3
CHLYE PR6 188 D4
DWN BB3 191 L4
GTH/LHO BB6 138 F7
LANC LA1 2 D5
LEYL PR25 186 D2
PDHM/BLYW BB12 140 F2
PRES PR1 9 K2
Meadow Ter DWN BB3 173 H6
Meadow V BBNW BB2 173 H5
CROS/BRETH PR26 185 K3
Meadowvale Dr
WGNW/BIL/OR WN5 255 M5
Meadow Vw CHLYE PR6 230 C3
CLI BB7 98 F3
HGHB LA2 45 M1
KIRK/FR/WAR PR4 127 J4
LITH L21 257 L8
STHP PR8 200 A7
WHIT OL12 234 D2
Meadow Wk LIT OL15 * 219 J6
Meadow Wy BCUP OL13 197 H1
BWCK/EAR BB18 294 A3
CHLY/EC PR7 229 G3
EDGW/EG BL7 213 G5
GAR/LONG PR3 284 B5
KKBYL LA6 28 F6
Meads Rd FUL/RIB PR2 151 L2
Meadup Ct HEY LA3 53 H1
Meadway BPOOLS FY4 5 L9
CHLYE PR6 169 L8
KIRK/FR/WAR PR4 183 J1
MGHL L31 258 E4
PDHM/BLYW BB12 140 D4
PRES PR1 151 K6
RAMS BL0 214 F2
ROCH OL11 234 E7
SKEL WN8 243 K7
Meadway Cl HOR/BR BL6 232 A8
Meagles La GAR/LONG PR3 88 B8
Mealhouse La CHLY/EC PR7 207 M3
Mealrigg La KKBYL LA6 20 C6
Meanwood Av BPOOLS FY4 125 J4
Meanwood Fold ROCH OL11 234 F3
Meanygate BBR PR5 169 H3
Mearley Brook Fold CLI BB7 99 J4
Mearley Rd FUL/RIB PR2 133 H7
Mearley St CLI BB7 99 H4
Mearley Syke CLI BB7 99 J3
Meath Rd PRES PR1 8 D8
The Mede KIRK/FR/WAR PR4 148 E1
Medina Cl ACC BB5 159 L6
Medlar Cl KIRK/FR/WAR PR4 128 B5
Medlar Ct KIRK/FR/WAR PR4 128 D5
Medlar Ga KIRK/FR/WAR PR4 128 D5
Medlar La KIRK/FR/WAR PR4 108 B7
Medley St WHIT OL12 235 J2
Medlock Av FTWD FY7 76 F8
Medway FUL/RIB PR2 132 C5
Medway Av FTWD FY7 81 G3
Medway Cl BBR PR5 168 E2
Medway Dr HOR/BR BL6 232 A8
Meeting House La LANC LA1 2 F6
Meins Cft BBNW BB2 156 D6
Meins Rd BBNW BB2 156 B5
Melba Rd FUL/RIB PR2 133 H8
Melbert Av FUL/RIB PR2 131 L8
Melbourne Av CLV/TH FY5 85 J4
FTWD FY7 81 G3
Melbourne Cl HOR/BR BL6 231 M8
Melbourne Gv HOR/BR BL6 231 M8
Melbourne Rd LANC LA1 3 J6
TOD OL14 303 K6
Melbourne St ACC BB5 159 K2
DWN BB3 * 191 L5
PDHM/BLYW BB12 141 G4
PRES PR1 9 H2
RAW/HAS BB4 196 C2
Melbreck SKEL WN8 243 K7
Meldon Gra HEY LA3 52 F3
Meldon Rd HEY LA3 52 E4
Meldreth Cl FMBY L37 246 F2
Melford Cl CHLYE PR6 188 B8
Melford Dr
WGNW/BIL/OR WN5 255 G8
Melia Cl RAW/HAS BB4 195 J1
Melita St DWN BB3 191 L3
Melling Brow KKBYL LA6 29 J8
Melling Cl CHLYE PR6 * 230 D2
Melling Ct MCMB LA4 41 H8
Melling Dr KKBY L32 260 B8
Melling La MGHL L31 259 H4
Melling Ms GAR/LONG PR3 * 284 C6
Melling Rd CHTN/BK PR9 200 B3
HGHB LA2 36 B4
Mellings PRES PR1 152 F5
Mellings Fold PRES PR1 * 152 F5
Melling's La LSTA FY8 145 K2
Melling St PRES PR1 9 H2
Mellings Wd LSTA FY8 145 K2
Melling Wy KKBY L32 260 B8
Mellishaw La HEY LA3 53 L2
Mellor Brow BBNW BB2 135 M8
Mellor Cl BBNW BB2 156 C3
BLY BB11 142 A8
Mellor Ct GAR/LONG PR3 114 E4
Mellor La BBNW BB2 156 B1
Mellor Pl PRES PR1 * 9 M5
Mellor Rd KIRK/FR/WAR PR4 128 D6
LEYL PR25 186 A1
Mellors Cl STHP PR8 200 C6
Mellor St ROCH OL11 235 G4
Mellwood Av BPOOLE FY3 105 J2
Melrose WHIT OL12 * 235 H3
Melrose Av ACC BB5 159 J8
BLY BB11 6 A7
BPOOLE FY3 105 J3
CHTN/BK PR9 180 E6
CSBY/BLUN L23 257 H8
FUL/RIB PR2 132 F6
LIT OL15 219 K4
MCMB LA4 41 K6
Melrose Gdns
CROS/BRETH PR26 204 F1
Melrose Rd NWD/KWIPK L33 260 A5
Melrose St DWN BB3 191 J1
LANC LA1 3 K7
ROCH OL11 235 G4
Melrose Wy CHLY/EC PR7 208 A5
Melton Gv LSTA FY8 146 B8
Melton Pl CLV/TH FY5 84 F3
LEYL PR25 186 E1
Melville Dr BBNW BB2 10 C3
Melville Gdns DWN BB3 191 K3
Melville Rd BISP FY2 84 F7
HEY LA3 * 52 D6
Melville St BRFD/BLYE BB10 142 F2
DWN BB3 191 K3
Memorial Gdns GAR/LONG PR3 91 K7
Memory Cl KIRK/FR/WAR PR4 148 E4
Menai Dr FUL/RIB PR2 132 A4
Mendip Av WGNS/IIMK WN3 255 M8
Mendip Cl HOR/BR BL6 231 M6
LSTA FY8 147 G6
Mendip Rd LEYL PR25 187 G2
Menivale Cl CHTN/BK PR9 180 D5
Meols Cl FMBY L37 247 H1
Meols Cop Rd STHP PR8 200 C6
Meolsgate Av
KIRK/FR/WAR PR4 183 K4
Mercer Ct CHLY/EC PR7 230 C2
Mercer Crs RAW/HAS BB4 194 D3
Mercer Dr GTH/LHO BB6 139 H5
Mercer La ROCH OL11 234 B3
Mercer Rd BBR PR5 168 D2
Mercer's La ORM L39 251 L7
Mercer St GTH/LHO BB6 139 G6
PDHM/BLYW BB12 141 J4
PRES PR1 152 F3
Mercers Wy BBN BB1 174 A2
Merchants House BBN BB1 * 11 H6
Merchants Landing BBN BB1 11 G7
Merchants Quay BBN BB1 11 H7
Merclesden Av NLSN BB9 123 L2
Mercury Ri ACC BB5 140 B5
Mercury Wy SKEL WN8 254 B3
Mere Av BRSC L40 225 H5
FTWD FY7 81 G2
Merebank Cl ROCH OL11 234 B3
Merebrook Gv
NWD/KWIPK L33 260 C6
Mere Brow La
KIRK/FR/WAR PR4 202 D1
Mere Cl GAR/LONG PR3 111 M8
SKEL WN8 253 J1
Mere Ct BLY BB11 141 L7
Meredith St NLSN BB9 123 H4
Merefell Rd CARN LA5 32 F5
Merefield CHLY/EC PR7 207 K2
Merefield Av ROCH OL11 235 H6
Merefield St ROCH OL11 235 H6
Merefield Ter ROCH OL11 * 235 H6
Mere Fold CHLY/EC PR7 207 G8
Merefold HOR/BR BL6 231 J8
Mereland Cl
WGNW/BIL/OR WN5 255 H5
Mereland Rd BPOOLE FY3 125 K1
Mere La BRSC L40 203 G8
CHTN/BK PR9 181 K8
ROCH OL11 235 J6
Mere Park Ct BPOOLE FY3 105 K8
Merepark Dr CHTN/BK PR9 180 E7
Mere Rd BPOOLE FY3 5 H2
FMBY L37 247 G1
Mereside Cl KIRK/FR/WAR PR4 166 C4
Mere St ROCH OL11 235 J5
Meres Wy STHP PR8 221 L1
Merewood SKEL WN8 243 K7
Meribel Cl CSBY/BLUN L23 257 K6
Meriden Cl STHP PR8 220 E6
Merinall Cl MILN OL16 235 M4
Merlecrest Dr
KIRK/FR/WAR PR4 183 K3
Merlewood RAMS BL0 195 H8
Merlewood Av CHTN/BK PR9 180 E8
Merlin Cl CHLYE PR6 188 D8
Merlin Dr ACC BB5 159 G8
Merlin Gv LEYL PR25 185 M3
PDHM/BLYW BB12 141 H5
Merlin Rd BBNW BB2 156 E5
Merlyn Rd CLV/TH FY5 85 H2
Merrick Av PRES PR1 153 J3
Merrilocks Rd CSBY/BLUN L23 256 D6
Merrilox Av MGHL L31 259 G1
Merrybents St TOD OL14 303 N2
Merryburn Cl FUL/RIB PR2 132 D7
Merryman Hall WHIT OL12 * 235 L1
Merry Trees La
KIRK/FR/WAR PR4 131 H6
Merscar La BRSC L40 224 A5
Mersey Av DWN BB3 173 G7
FMBY L37 237 H5
MGHL L31 259 J1
Mersey Rd BPOOLS FY4 124 E3
CSBY/BLUN L23 256 F8
FTWD FY7 77 H7
WGNW/BIL/OR WN5 255 J4
Mersey St BCUP OL13 197 K2
FUL/RIB PR2 8 A2
GAR/LONG PR3 114 D4
PDHM/BLYW BB12 141 K5
Merton Av FUL/RIB PR2 132 C5
Merton Ct FUL/RIB PR2 132 C5
Merton Gv CHLYE PR6 188 B8
CSBY/BLUN L23 256 F8
Merton Rd WGNS/IIMK WN3 255 L7
Merton St NLSN BB9 * 123 G2
PDHM/BLYW BB12 6 E1
Messenger St NLSN BB9 123 J4
Meta St BBNW BB2 173 H1
Metcalf Cl NWD/KWIPK L33 260 A5
Metcalf Dr ACC BB5 140 A5
Metcalfe Cl BBNW BB2 173 G3
Metcalfe St PDHM/BLYW BB12 141 L6
Mete St PRES PR1 153 G3
Methuen Av BBR PR5 154 B8
FUL/RIB PR2 132 B5
Methuen Cl BBR PR5 154 C8
Methuen Dr BBR PR5 154 C8
Metropolitan Dr BPOOLE FY3 125 L1
Mettle Cote BCUP OL13 197 K2
Mewith La HGHB LA2 38 B7
The Mews MCMB LA4 41 M6
PDHM/BLYW BB12 * 140 F3
STHP PR8 12 F7
Mexford Av BISP FY2 105 G2
Meyler Av BPOOLE FY3 105 H5
Miall St ROCH OL11 235 J5
Michael Pl MCMB LA4 41 L6
Michaels Cl FMBY L37 237 H8
Michaelson Av MCMB LA4 41 M7
Michael Wife La RAMS BL0 215 H1
Mickering La ORM L39 250 F5
Mickleden Av FUL/RIB PR2 132 C4
Mickleden Rd BPOOLS FY4 125 M2
Micklegate CLV/TH FY5 84 F4
Micklehurst Crs BLY BB11 162 A1
Mickleton Dr STHP PR8 220 D6
Middlecot Cl
WGNW/BIL/OR WN5 255 H6
Middle Craven Rd SETT BD24 265 N7
Middlefield CROS/BRETH PR26 185 K3
Middle Fld ROCH OL11 234 B2
Middleforth Gn PRES PR1 152 B7
Middlegate HEY LA3 53 M1
Middlegate Gn RAW/HAS BB4 177 K2
Middle Hey KIRK/FR/WAR PR4 184 B1
Middle Hl WHIT OL12 218 C7
Middle Holly GAR/LONG PR3 270 B10
Middle Meanygate
KIRK/FR/WAR PR4 182 F4
Middle Moss La FMBY L37 248 D1
Middlesex Av
PDHM/BLYW BB12 141 K4
Middle St BPOOL FY1 4 D5
COL BB8 103 M7
LANC LA1 3 G6
WHIT OL12 217 M2
Middleton Av FTWD FY7 81 G2
Middleton Dr NLSN BB9 103 H5
Middleton Rd HEY LA3 52 D5
Middleton Wy HEY LA3 52 D4
Middle Turn EDGW/EG BL7 213 G4
Middle Withins La FMBY L37 248 C4
Middlewood SKEL WN8 243 K7
Middlewood Cl CHLY/EC PR7 205 M5
ORM L39 250 F4
Middlewood Dr ORM L39 250 F4
Middle Wood La LIT OL15 219 H5
Middlewood Rd ORM L39 250 F4
Midfield GTH/LHO BB6 137 M3
Midge Hall Dr ROCH OL11 234 D5
Midge Hall La CHTN/BK PR9 223 M1
KIRK/FR/WAR PR4 167 J7
Midgeland Rd BPOOLS FY4 125 K4
Midgeland Ter BPOOLS FY4 * 125 M6
Midgery La GAR/LONG PR3 132 D3
Midgley St COL BB8 296 B7
Midhurst Dr STHP PR8 220 E7
Midhurst St ROCH OL11 235 J6
Midland St ACC BB5 159 M6
NLSN BB9 123 H2
Midlothian Dr CSBY/BLUN L23 256 F8
Midsummer St BBNW BB2 10 B3
Milbanke Av
KIRK/FR/WAR PR4 128 D5
Milbeck Cl GAR/LONG PR3 114 C6
Milbourne St BPOOL FY1 4 E1
Milbrook Cl BLY BB11 141 L6
Milbrook Crs KKBY L32 260 B8
Milbrook Dr KKBY L32 260 B8
Milburn Av CLV/TH FY5 81 J6
Mildred Cl CLV/TH FY5 81 K8
Mile End Cl COL BB8 296 A2
Mile End Rw BBNW BB2 156 E5
Mile Rd PLF/KEOS FY6 107 J2
Miles Av BCUP OL13 197 G3
Miles La WGNNW/ST WN6 245 G3
Miles St PRES PR1 153 C1
Mile Stone Meadow
CHLY/EC PR7 187 G7
Milestone Pl HGHB LA2 * 44 D6
Miles Wk PRES PR1 152 B1
Miletas Pl LSTA FY8 145 M8
Milford Av BISP FY2 105 G2
Milford Cl FMBY L37 246 F2
GAR/LONG PR3 91 G1
Milford Crs LIT OL15 219 L5
Milford St COL BB8 103 M6
WHIT OL12 235 J2
Milford Ter CLV/TH FY5 * 81 L8
Milking La DWN BB3 173 K5
Milking Stile La LANC LA1 2 C6
Milkstone Pl ROCH OL11 * 235 J5
Milkstone Rd ROCH OL11 235 J5
Milk St RAMS BL0 214 E6
ROCH OL11 235 J5
Millar Barn La RAW/HAS BB4 196 C3
Millar's Pace CHTN/BK PR9 180 E5
Millbank FUL/RIB PR2 131 M8
Mill Bank WGNNW/ST WN6 245 G4
Millbank Brow BRSC L40 225 J8
Millbank La MGHL L31 250 C8
Millbeck Cl KKBY L32 260 B7
Mill Br SKP/WHF BD23 267 R7
Millbrook PDHM/BLYW BB12 122 B3
Millbrook Bank ROCH OL11 * 234 A2
Millbrook Cl ACC BB5 159 G8
CHLYE PR6 188 D4
SKEL WN8 253 H1
Millbrook Ct CLI BB7 290 D10
COL BB8 296 E6
Millbrook St DWN BB3 173 J4
Millbrook Wy PRES PR1 167 M1
Mill Brow HGHB LA2 48 C7
KKBYL LA6 21 M1
Mill Brow Rd BWCK/EAR BB18 294 F5
Mill Cl CSBY/BLUN L23 257 H5
KIRK/FR/WAR PR4 109 M3
SETT BD24 265 N7
Millcombe Wy BBR PR5 153 H8
Mill Ct GAR/LONG PR3 114 E3
NTHTN L30 258 A6
Millcroft CSBY/BLUN L23 257 K6
FUL/RIB PR2 131 M7
Millcroft Av
WGNW/BIL/OR WN5 255 G6
Mill Dam Cl BRSC L40 241 M1
Mill Dam La BRSC L40 241 M1
Milldyke Cl BPOOLS FY4 125 J5
Mill Entrance ACC BB5 159 J1
Miller Ar PRES PR1 9 J4
Miller Av CHLYE PR6 189 L1
CSBY/BLUN L23 257 G6
Miller Cl ACC BB5 158 F6
Miller Ct LANC LA1 54 D6
Miller Fld FUL/RIB PR2 131 H8
Miller Fold Av ACC BB5 159 L8
Miller La KIRK/FR/WAR PR4 131 H6
KIRK/FR/WAR PR4 110 B7
Miller Rd PRES PR1 153 G2
Millers Brook Cl HEYW OL10 * 234 A8
Millers Cl LSTA FY8 146 A4
Millers Ct ORM L39 241 J6
Millerscroft KKBY L32 259 M8
Millersdale Cl CLV/TH FY5 86 B4
Millersgate KIRK/FR/WAR PR4 131 H7
Millers Nook SKEL WN8 254 E3
Miller St BPOOL FY1 4 C9
Millett St RAMS BL0 215 G4
Mill Fld ACC BB5 139 J7
SKEL WN8 243 M2
Millfield Cl KIRK/FR/WAR PR4 148 C5
Millfield Gv MILN OL16 235 L5
Millfield Rd BPOOLS FY4 125 J5
CHLY/EC PR7 207 L2
Millfold WHIT OL12 218 A1
Mill Fold Gdns LIT OL15 219 K7
Mill Ga FUL/RIB PR2 132 A8
MILN OL16 235 L1
Millgate Rd RAW/HAS BB4 177 K8
Mill Gn COL BB8 296 A7
Millgreen Cl SKEL WN8 254 D4
Millham St BBN BB1 10 F1
Mill Hvn FUL/RIB PR2 132 A8
Mill Hey Av PLF/KEOS FY6 106 B2
Mill Hey La BRSC L40 203 M8
Mill Hl ACC BB5 159 G7
PRES PR1 8 F2
Mill Hill Bridge St BBNW BB2 172 E1
Mill Hill Gv HEY LA3 64 F1
Mill Hill La BLY BB11 160 D1
SETT BD24 265 L5
Mill Hill St BBNW BB2 172 E1
Millholme Dr HGHB LA2 39 G5
Mill House Cl WHIT OL12 219 G7
Mill House La CHLYE PR6 170 B3
GAR/LONG PR3 115 K3
Mill House Ms LANC LA1 * 3 J6
Millhouse St RAMS BL0 215 H3
Mill House Vw SKEL WN8 254 F4
Millington Av BPOOLS FY4 125 H3
Millionaire Rw BRSC L40 223 L7
Mill La BBNW BB2 10 E5
BBR PR5 153 G6
BPOOLE FY3 106 A6
BRSC L40 225 H6
BWCK/EAR BB18 294 F5
CARN LA5 32 F5
CARN LA5 25 M7
CHLY/EC PR7 228 D1
CHLY/EC PR7 206 D2
CHLYE PR6 190 C5
CHLYE PR6 187 M2
CHTN/BK PR9 200 D2
CLI BB7 289 R7
CLI BB7 278 D12
CROS/BRETH PR26 168 B8
FTWD FY7 77 L7
FUL/RIB PR2 131 M7
GAR/LONG PR3 113 G5
GAR/LONG PR3 94 F4
GTH/LHO BB6 139 J5
HGHB LA2 43 K5
HGHB LA2 46 H2
HOR/BR BL6 232 A7
KIRK/FR/WAR PR4 183 J1
KIRK/FR/WAR PR4 127 K8
KIRK/FR/WAR PR4 108 D2
KKBY L32 259 M7
KKBYL LA6 20 C3
LEYL PR25 186 A3
ORM L39 250 C2
PLF/KEOS FY6 87 H5
PLF/KEOS FY6 82 F4
RNFD/HAY WA11 262 F7
SKEL WN8 254 D3
SKEL WN8 253 J1
SKEL WN8 243 M2
SKP/WHF BD23 281 L2
SKP/WHF BD23 279 L2
SKP/WHF BD23 267 Q8
WGNNW/ST WN6 244 F4
Mill Leat Cl SKEL WN8 243 M1
Mill Nook WHIT OL12 218 C8
Millom Av BISP FY2 85 G7
Millom Cl FTWD FY7 80 F3
MILN OL16 235 M2
Mill Rd STHP PR8 221 G6
WGNW/BIL/OR WN5 255 G6
Mill Rw RAW/HAS BB4 177 J6
Mills St WHIT OL12 218 A2
Millstone Ct LANC LA1 * 42 D8
Mill St ACC BB5 176 B2
ACC BB5 159 J1
ACC BB5 159 G8
BCUP OL13 179 J8
BWCK/EAR BB18 293 P5
CHLY/EC PR7 229 H2
CHLYE PR6 230 D3
CHLYE PR6 188 D4
CLI BB7 290 D10
GTH/LHO BB6 138 F6
KIRK/FR/WAR PR4 128 D6
LANC LA1 3 J5
LEYL PR25 186 A3
NLSN BB9 103 G7
ORM L39 241 J7
PDHM/BLYW BB12 140 F3
PLF/KEOS FY6 78 E8
PRES PR1 * 8 D3
RAMS BL0 214 D7
RAW/HAS BB4 176 E7
STHP PR8 13 K5
Millthorne Av CLI BB7 99 G4
Mill Vw KIRK/FR/WAR PR4 148 E4
Mill View Ct ORM L39 252 A5
Mill View La HOR/BR BL6 232 B7
Millwood Cl BBNW BB2 172 D2
Mill Wood Cl CHLYE PR6 170 F8
Millwood Gld CHLY/EC PR7 207 L2
Millwood La TOD OL14 303 M2
Millwood Rd BBR PR5 152 E8
Milman Cl ORM L39 241 G8
Milner Rd DWN BB3 173 H7
LSTA FY8 146 A7
Milner St BRFD/BLYE BB10 142 D3
PRES PR1 152 C1
WHIT OL12 217 M2
Milne St RAMS BL0 194 F6
Milngate Cl MILN OL16 235 M8
Milnholme BOL BL1 233 L8
Milnrow Rd MILN OL16 235 L4
Milnshaw Gdns ACC BB5 159 K4
Milnshaw La ACC BB5 159 L5
Milnthorpe Av CLV/TH FY5 81 G6
Milnthorpe Rd KKBYL LA6 18 F1
Milton Av BPOOLE FY3 5 K1
CLI BB7 99 H2
CLV/TH FY5 81 K8
Milton Cl BBR PR5 169 G1
DWN BB3 191 M2
GTH/LHO BB6 138 E7
RAW/HAS BB4 194 D4
Milton Crs PLF/KEOS FY6 106 A3
Milton Dr ORM L39 241 K7
Milton Gv BWCK/EAR BB18 293 P4
Milton Pl BISP FY2 85 J5
Milton Rd CHLY/EC PR7 229 H3
COL BB8 296 A6
Milton St ACC BB5 159 G7
ACC BB5 139 J8
BBN BB1 11 J3
BRFD/BLYE BB10 123 H8
CHTN/BK PR9 200 D4
FTWD FY7 77 K6
MILN OL16 235 J3
NLSN BB9 123 G2
PDHM/BLYW BB12 141 G4
RAMS BL0 214 E5
Milton Ter CHLYE PR6 208 A1
Milton Wy MGHL L31 258 E2
Mimosa Cl CHLY/EC PR7 187 K8
Mimosa Rd FUL/RIB PR2 153 H1
Mincing La BBNW BB2 10 E5
Minden Rd KIRK/FR/WAR PR4 107 H6
Minehead Av BRFD/BLYE BB10 143 G1
Minerva Rd LANC LA1 2 A6
Mine St HEYW OL10 234 A7
Minnie St WHIT OL12 * 218 A1
Minnie Ter BBNW BB2 10 A1
Minorca Cl ROCH OL11 234 B3
Minor St RAW/HAS BB4 177 K4
Minster Crs DWN BB3 191 M3
Minster Pk KIRK/FR/WAR PR4 131 H6
Minstrel Wk PLF/KEOS FY6 86 A7
Mint Av NLSN BB9 103 G7
Mintholme Av BBR PR5 170 B1
Mint St RAMS BL0 214 F1
Mire Ash Brow BBNW BB2 156 A2
Mire Close La HWTH BD22 295 R9
Mire Rdg COL BB8 296 D8
Mirfield Gv BPOOLS FY4 125 G2
Miry La SKEL WN8 244 A1
Mitcham Rd BPOOLS FY4 125 L3
Mitchelgate KKBYL LA6 21 L1
Mitchell Hey WHIT OL12 235 H4
Mitchell La SETT BD24 265 P8
Mitchell St CLI BB7 99 G4
COL BB8 296 A6
MILN OL16 218 F8
PDHM/BLYW BB12 141 M5
TOD OL14 300 H12
WHIT OL12 235 G3
Mitella St BRFD/BLYE BB10 7 L5
Mitre St BLY BB11 6 C4
Mitton Av NLSN BB9 103 J5
RAW/HAS BB4 177 K7
Mitton Cl BBNW BB2 172 F3
Mitton Cots NLSN BB9 * 103 J5
Mitton Crs KIRK/FR/WAR PR4 128 D6
Mitton Dr FUL/RIB PR2 133 K8
Mitton Gv BRFD/BLYE BB10 143 G6
Mitton La AIRE BD20 295 L6
Mitton Rd CLI BB7 118 D2
Mitton St BBN BB1 157 J4
Mizpah St BRFD/BLYE BB10 7 L5
Mizzy Rd WHIT OL12 235 H2
Moira Crs FUL/RIB PR2 133 H7
Moleside Cl ACC BB5 160 A5
Molesworth St MILN OL16 235 K4
Mollington Rd BBNW BB2 156 E4
Molly Wood La BLY BB11 141 J6
Molyneux Ct PRES PR1 9 K3
Molyneux Dr BPOOLS FY4 125 G4
Molyneux Pl LSTA FY8 146 D7
Molyneux Rd MGHL L31 259 J4
ORM L39 250 F4
Molyneux St WHIT OL12 235 G3
Molyneux Wy AIN/FAZ L10 258 F8
Mona Pl PRES PR1 8 E3
Monarch Crs LSTA FY8 145 L3
Monarch St ACC BB5 159 H7
Mona Rd BBNW BB2 173 H2
Moneyclose Gv HEY LA3 52 C6
Money Close La HEY LA3 52 C8
Monk Hall St BRFD/BLYE BB10 142 D3
Monkroyd Av BWCK/EAR BB18 293 P5
Monks Carr La HTWN L38 248 D5

Monks Cl FMBY L37 247 K2
Monks Dr CHLYE PR6 189 K2
FMBY L37 247 K2
GAR/LONG PR3 114 D5
Monks Hill Cots CHLYE PR6 * 188 F5
Monk's La PLF/KEOS FY6 82 D2
Monk St ACC BB5 159 K5
CLI BB7 99 G4
Monks Wk PRES PR1 8 A6
Monkswell Av CARN LA5 32 F6
Monkswell Dr CARN LA5 32 F6
Monkswood Av MCMB LA4 41 M6
Monmouth Rd BBN BB1 157 M6
Monmouth St COL BB8 296 D6
PDHM/BLYW BB12 6 A3
ROCH OL11 235 J5
Monomer Rd CLV/TH FY5 81 M7
Monroe Dr FTWD FY7 77 G8
Mons Av ROCH OL11 234 F3
Mons Rd TOD OL14 301 J12
Montague Cl BBNW BB2 10 C5
BPOOLE FY3 105 K3
Montague Rd BLY BB11 6 D6
Montague St BBNW BB2 10 C4
BPOOLS FY4 124 E3
CLI BB7 99 G3
COL BB8 296 B5
NLSN BB9 122 E6
Montagu Rd FMBY L37 237 H6
Montcliffe Rd CHLYE PR6 208 B2
Monteagle Dr HGHB LA2 36 B5
Monteagle Sq HGHB LA2 36 C5
Montford Rd NLSN BB9 122 C6
Montgomery ROCH OL11 * 235 H5
Montgomery Av CHTN/BK PR9 200 D5
Montgomery Gv
PDHM/BLYW BB12 141 M4
Montgomery St BBR PR5 169 J3
ROCH OL11 234 F7
Monthall Ri LANC LA1 3 K3
Montjoly St PRES PR1 * 152 F4
Monton Rd DWN BB3 173 H7
Montpelier Av BISP FY2 84 F6
Montreal Av BPOOL FY1 5 G3
Montreal Rd BBNW BB2 156 F3
Montreal St TOD OL14 303 K6
Montrose Av BPOOL FY1 4 E5
WGNW/BIL/OR WN5 255 M4
Montrose Cl CHLYE PR6 208 B5
Montrose Crs HEY LA3 52 D4
Montrose Dr CHTN/BK PR9 200 C2
Montrose St BBNW BB2 10 A7
BLY BB11 6 E8
NLSN BB9 122 E6
Montserrat Brow BOL BL1 232 F8
Moody La BRSC L40 227 H2
Moon Av BPOOL FY1 4 D8
Moon Bay Whf HEY LA3 52 C4
Moons Acre HGHB LA2 38 F3
Moon St BBR PR5 169 H3
Moor Av PRES PR1 151 J7
WGNNW/ST WN6 245 H3
Moorber La SKP/WHF BD23 280 C2
Moorbottom Rd
TOT/BURYW BL8 214 C7
Moorbridge Cl NTHTN L30 258 D7
Moorbrook St PRES PR1 152 B2
Moor Cl CSBY/BLUN L23 257 J6
DWN BB3 192 A3
LANC LA1 3 J6
STHP PR8 237 M1
Moor Close La KKBYL LA6 34 B2
Moorcock Rd HBR HX7 301 M6
Moor Coppice CSBY/BLUN L23 257 J6
Moorcroft DWN BB3 173 K5
GAR/LONG PR3 131 L1
RAMS BL0 215 G1
ROCH OL11 235 J8
Moorcroft Crs FUL/RIB PR2 133 G8
Moor Dr CSBY/BLUN L23 257 H6
SKEL WN8 254 A4
Moor Edge CLI BB7 118 E5
Moore Dr PDHM/BLYW BB12 121 J6
Moorend CLI BB7 99 J4
Moorend Cots GTH/LHO BB6 * 117 K7
Moore St BPOOLS FY4 124 E2
COL BB8 * 103 M6
MILN OL16 235 J4
NLSN BB9 123 J4
PDHM/BLYW BB12 141 J4
PRES PR1 152 F4
Moore Tree Dr BPOOLS FY4 125 K3
Moor Fld CLI BB7 118 E5
Moorfield EDGW/EG BL7 213 G5
Moor Fld KIRK/FR/WAR PR4 167 J4
Moorfield NWD/KWIPK L33 260 C6
Moorfield Av ACC BB5 160 C3
BBN BB1 137 H8
BPOOLE FY3 105 H5
LIT OL15 219 K4
PLF/KEOS FY6 85 L6
Moorfield Cl ACC BB5 139 L8
FUL/RIB PR2 132 B3
PRES PR1 151 K8
Moorfield Dr ACC BB5 139 L8
FUL/RIB PR2 133 H8
LSTA FY8 146 D7
Moorfield La BRSC L40 223 L8
Moorfield Pl WHIT OL12 * 235 H2
Moorfield Rd CSBY/BLUN L23 257 K6
LEYL PR25 185 M3
Moorfields BISP FY2 85 J7
CHLYE PR6 208 B2
Moorfields Av FUL/RIB PR2 132 B3
Moorfield Wy ACC BB5 139 L8
Moorfoot Wy NWD/KWIPK L33 260 A5
Moorgate ACC BB5 175 L2
BPOOLS FY4 125 J5
FUL/RIB PR2 132 C6
Moor Ga LANC LA1 3 J6
Moorgate ORM L39 241 H7
Moor Ga TOD OL14 303 M4
Moorgate Av CSBY/BLUN L23 257 H8
ROCH OL11 234 D4
Moorgate Gdns BBNW BB2 172 F2
Moorgate La GTH/LHO BB6 117 K6
LIT OL15 219 H4
Moorgate Rd BWCK/EAR BB18 293 P6
Moorgate St BBNW BB2 172 F2
Moor Hall La
KIRK/FR/WAR PR4 129 J7
Moor Hall St PRES PR1 152 B1
Moorhead Gdns
KIRK/FR/WAR PR4 148 B4
Moorhead St COL BB8 103 M6
Moorhen Pl CLV/TH FY5 85 J2
Moorhey Crs BBR PR5 169 K3
PRES PR1 151 L6
Moorhey Dr PRES PR1 151 L6
Moorhey Rd MGHL L31 259 G5
Moor Hl ROCH OL11 234 B2
Moorhouse Av ACC BB5 159 K7
Moorhouse Cl ACC BB5 159 K7
Moorhouses HTWN L38 247 J8
Moorhouse St ACC BB5 159 K7
BLY BB11 141 M6
BPOOL FY1 104 E4
Moor House Vw HBR HX7 301 Q7
Moorings Cl BBNW BB2 10 D9
The Moorings CHLYE PR6 208 B3
MGHL L31 249 L7
PDHM/BLYW BB12 6 C2
Moorland Av BBNW BB2 172 A4
BWCK/EAR BB18 294 F6
CLI BB7 99 J1
CSBY/BLUN L23 257 H6
DWN BB3 191 G1
FUL/RIB PR2 133 G6
PLF/KEOS FY6 86 B7
ROCH OL11 234 C2
WHIT OL12 217 M5
Moorland Cl NLSN BB9 103 H5
Moorland Ct PLF/KEOS FY6 * 86 B7
Moorland Crs CLI BB7 99 J1
FUL/RIB PR2 133 G6
WHIT OL12 217 M4
Moorland Dr HOR/BR BL6 232 C8
NLSN BB9 123 G7
Moorland Gdns PLF/KEOS FY6 86 B7
Moorland Ga CHLYE PR6 208 C5
Moorland Ri RAW/HAS BB4 176 F8
Moorland Rd BBNW BB2 172 F4
BLY BB11 142 B8
CLI BB7 99 J1
GTH/LHO BB6 137 M2
LSTA FY8 145 K4
MGHL L31 258 F5
PLF/KEOS FY6 86 B7
Moorlands Gv HEY LA3 40 F8
Moorlands Rd CSBY/BLUN L23 257 L5
Moorlands Ter BCUP OL13 197 K2
The Moorlands BCUP OL13 179 K3
Moorland St WHIT OL12 235 H2
Moorland Ter WHIT OL12 234 D2
Moorland Vw DWN BB3 * 173 K8
NLSN BB9 123 H5
Moor La BWCK/EAR BB18 293 R9
CLI BB7 138 C2
CLI BB7 99 H4
CSBY/BLUN L23 257 H6
DWN BB3 173 K8
HGHB LA2 46 D1
HTWN L38 248 A8
KIRK/FR/WAR PR4 167 G2
LANC LA1 3 J6
PDHM/BLYW BB12 140 F2
PRES PR1 9 G1
RAW/HAS BB4 176 B5
SKP/WHF BD23 295 M1
SKP/WHF BD23 267 R5
STHP PR8 237 M1
TOD OL14 303 L4
Moor Park Av BISP FY2 85 H8
PRES PR1 152 C1
Moor Park Ct PRES PR1 * 152 C1
Moor Platt Cl HOR/BR BL6 232 C8
Moor Rd CHLY/EC PR7 207 K6
CHLYE PR6 209 H6
CROS/BRETH PR26 184 F8
LIT OL15 219 M2
RAW/HAS BB4 194 C6
WGNW/BIL/OR WN5 255 H5
Moorside KIRK/FR/WAR PR4 129 G3
ROCH OL11 235 J8
Moorside Av BBN BB1 158 A7
FUL/RIB PR2 133 J8
HOR/BR BL6 231 M7
NLSN BB9 123 G7
Moorside Cl CSBY/BLUN L23 257 J7
KKBYL LA6 29 K8
Moorside Crs BCUP OL13 179 K7
Moorside Dr ACC BB5 159 K1
PRES PR1 151 L8
Moorside Fold
KIRK/FR/WAR PR4 166 E5
Moor Side La CLI BB7 119 J3
Moorside La
KIRK/FR/WAR PR4 110 F7
Moor Side La RAMS BL0 215 K4
Moorside Rd CSBY/BLUN L23 257 J7
EDGW/EG BL7 213 G2
HGHB LA2 44 F6
Moorside Wk
WGNW/BIL/OR WN5 255 L3
Moor St ACC BB5 139 J8
KIRK/FR/WAR PR4 128 D6
LANC LA1 * 3 H6
Moorsview RAMS BL0 214 E5
Moorthorpe Cl DWN BB3 191 K5
Moor Vw BCUP OL13 179 K7
Moorview Cl BRFD/BLYE BB10 143 H1
Moor View Cl WHIT OL12 234 C2
Moorview Ct BPOOLS FY4 * 125 J4
Moorway PLF/KEOS FY6 86 C7
Moor Wy TOT/BURYW BL8 213 L8
Moray Cl RAMS BL0 214 D7
Morecambe Rd BBNW BB2 173 J2
LANC LA1 2 D3
Morecambe St East MCMB LA4 41 J5
Morecambe St
West MCMB LA4 * 41 J6
Moresby Av BPOOLE FY3 105 L4
Moret Cl CSBY/BLUN L23 257 K6
Moreton Dr BPOOLE FY3 106 A6
PLF/KEOS FY6 106 A1
Moreton Gn HEY LA3 52 E4
Moreton St ACC BB5 159 L5
Morewood Dr KKBYL LA6 19 H5
Morgan Ms NTHTN L30 258 A8
Morgan St LIT OL15 219 L6
Morland Av BBR PR5 168 D4
KIRK/FR/WAR PR4 128 C4
Morley Av BBNW BB2 172 D2
Morley Cl LANC LA1 42 D8
Morley Cft
CROS/BRETH PR26 168 B8
Morley Rd BPOOLS FY4 125 H3
CHTN/BK PR9 200 B3
LANC LA1 42 D8
Morley St MILN OL16 235 L2
PDHM/BLYW BB12 140 F3
Morningside CSBY/BLUN L23 257 J8
LANC LA1 2 F8
Morningside Cl MILN OL16 * 235 L5
Mornington Rd CHLYE PR6 230 E3
CHTN/BK PR9 13 J3
LSTA FY8 147 H7
PRES PR1 152 J2
PRES PR1 * 151 L6
ROCH OL11 235 K8
Morris Cl LEYL PR25 186 D3
Morris Ct FUL/RIB PR2 * 153 G1
Morris Crs FUL/RIB PR2 153 G1
Morris La ORM L39 223 G8
Morrison St CHLYE PR6 208 A1
Morris Rd CHLYE PR6 * 208 B2
FUL/RIB PR2 153 G1
SKEL WN8 254 D4
Morse St BRFD/BLYE BB10 7 M6
Morston Av BISP FY2 105 H1
Mortimer Gv HEY LA3 52 F3
Morton St BBN BB1 10 E3
Mort St HOR/BR BL6 231 L7
Morven Gv STHP PR8 200 B4
Mosber La SKP/WHF BD23 281 J3
Moscow Mill St ACC BB5 159 H6
Mosedale Dr
PDHM/BLYW BB12 141 L3
Moseley Av BWCK/EAR BB18 294 C6
Moseley Rd BLY BB11 142 D8
Mosley St BBNW BB2 10 E9
BWCK/EAR BB18 293 Q5
LEYL PR25 186 D2
NLSN BB9 123 G3
PRES PR1 152 F3
STHP PR8 13 G9
Mosman Pl NLSN BB9 102 F8
Moss Acre Rd PRES PR1 152 B8
Moss Av FUL/RIB PR2 151 K1
MILN OL16 235 M5
WGNW/BIL/OR WN5 255 G8
Mossbank BBN BB1 * 11 J2
Moss Bank CHLY/EC PR7 229 H2
ORM L39 251 G1
Moss Bank Pk BOL BL1 * 233 J8
Moss Bank Pl BPOOLS FY4 125 J3
Mossborough Hall La
RNFD/HAY WA11 261 M8
Mossbourne Rd PLF/KEOS FY6 105 M2
Moss Bridge La BRSC L40 242 F1
Moss Bridge Pk BBR PR5 168 E3
Moss Bridge Rd MILN OL16 235 L5
Mossbrook Dr
KIRK/FR/WAR PR4 131 H6
Moss Brow RNFD/HAY WA11 262 B4
Moss Cl CHLYE PR6 208 B3
RAW/HAS BB4 194 D3
Mossdale BBN BB1 11 J1
Mossdale Rd NWD/KWIPK L33 260 C6
Moss Delph La ORM L39 250 E1
Moss Dr HOR/BR BL6 232 C8
Moss Edge La LSTA FY8 145 K1
Moss End La HWTH BD22 297 P1
Moss End Wy
NWD/KWIPK L33 261 G8
Mossfield Cl BBR PR5 168 E3
Mossfield Rd CHLYE PR6 208 B3
Moss Fold Rd DWN BB3 173 H6
Moss Gdns STHP PR8 221 M1
Moss Ga BBN BB1 11 K1
Mossgate Pk HEY LA3 52 E6
Mossgiel Av STHP PR8 220 E6
Moss Hall La HBR HX7 301 P7
LSTA FY8 146 B3
Moss Hall Rd ACC BB5 159 L3
Moss Hey La
KIRK/FR/WAR PR4 182 D8
Mosshill Cl MGHL L31 249 M8
Moss House La GAR/LONG PR3 282 C3
KIRK/FR/WAR PR4 184 C1
KIRK/FR/WAR PR4 126 D4
PLF/KEOS FY6 82 F2
Moss House Rd BPOOLS FY4 125 K5
KIRK/FR/WAR PR4 131 L1
Mosslands LEYL PR25 186 A2
Moss La BBN BB1 158 C7
BBR PR5 168 E3
BOL BL1 233 K8
BRSC L40 225 J5
CARN LA5 18 D4
CARN LA5 17 J7
CHLY/EC PR7 229 H2
CHLYE PR6 187 M6
CHTN/BK PR9 200 E3
CHTN/BK PR9 181 M5
CROS/BRETH PR26 204 D3
CROS/BRETH PR26 184 E4
GAR/LONG PR3 284 A8
GAR/LONG PR3 111 G1
GAR/LONG PR3 95 J2
GAR/LONG PR3 89 L3
HGHB LA2 268 H2
HTWN L38 247 L6
KIRK/FR/WAR PR4 182 B4
KIRK/FR/WAR PR4 167 H4
KIRK/FR/WAR PR4 110 B7
KIRK/FR/WAR PR4 89 L8
KKBYL LA6 18 D2
LEYL PR25 186 F1
MCMB LA4 41 H7
MGHL L31 250 A6
MILN OL16 235 K5
NWD/KWIPK L33 260 C3
ORM L39 261 J1
ORM L39 238 D6
PLF/KEOS FY6 87 G2
PRES PR1 168 B2
RNFD/HAY WA11 263 H6
SKEL WN8 253 J5
WGNNW/ST WN6 228 B8
WHIT OL12 217 L4
Moss La East
KIRK/FR/WAR PR4 129 K3
Moss Lane Vw SKEL WN8 253 J5
Moss La West
KIRK/FR/WAR PR4 129 H4
Moss Lea KIRK/FR/WAR PR4 183 K3
Mosslea Dr GAR/LONG PR3 111 L3
Moss Mill St MILN OL16 235 L6
Moss Nook BRSC L40 225 H5
ORM L39 * 250 F1
Moss Nook La MGHL L31 259 L3
RNFD/HAY WA11 262 B5
Mossom La CLV/TH FY5 84 F4
Moss Pl LANC LA1 42 F7
Moss Rd HEY LA3 53 J4
STHP PR8 221 M1
WGNW/BIL/OR WN5 255 G8
Moss Side BWCK/EAR BB18 293 R5
FMBY L37 237 L7
Moss Side La GAR/LONG PR3 89 H6
KIRK/FR/WAR PR4 182 C8
LSTA FY8 147 J1
MILN OL16 235 M6
PLF/KEOS FY6 83 G4
Moss Side St WHIT OL12 302 B10
Moss Side Wy
CROS/BRETH PR26 185 L4
Moss St BBN BB1 11 K2
BBR PR5 168 E3
CLI BB7 99 G3
GTH/LHO BB6 138 F7
MILN OL16 235 L5
PRES PR1 * 8 F2
WGNW/BIL/OR WN5 * 255 L5
Moss Ter MILN OL16 235 K5
WGNW/BIL/OR WN5 255 L6
Moss Wy MGHL L31 259 J2
Moss Wy BPOOLS FY4 * 125 J4
Mossway KIRK/FR/WAR PR4 167 J5
Mossy Lea Fold
WGNNW/ST WN6 228 C8
Mossy Lea Rd
WGNNW/ST WN6 228 B5
Mostyn Av BWCK/EAR BB18 294 E6
Mostyn St DWN BB3 173 H7
Motherwell Crs STHP PR8 200 C8
Mottram Cl CHLYE PR6 187 M5
Mottram St HOR/BR BL6 231 L7
Moulden Brow BBNW BB2 171 L4
Moulding Cl BBNW BB2 156 E7
Mounsey Rd BBR PR5 169 J3
Mountain Ash WHIT OL12 217 L8
Mountain Ash Cl WHIT OL12 217 L8
Mountain La ACC BB5 159 M7
Mountain Rd CHLY/EC PR7 229 H3
Mount Av LANC LA1 42 E8
LIT OL15 219 K4
MCMB LA4 41 M4
RAW/HAS BB4 196 C3
WHIT OL12 219 H7
Mountbatten Cl FUL/RIB PR2 151 L3
Mountbatten Rd
CHLY/EC PR7 207 K5
Mount Cl KKBY L32 259 M7
Mount Crs BRFD/BLYE BB10 163 K3
KKBY L32 259 M7
WGNW/BIL/OR WN5 255 J5
Mount Gdns MCMB LA4 41 M4
Mount House Cl FMBY L37 237 L6
Mount House Rd FMBY L37 237 L6
Mount La BRFD/BLYE BB10 163 H3
TOD OL14 300 F8
Mount Pleasant BBN BB1 11 G3
BURY BL9 215 J8
CARN LA5 16 F3
CHLYE PR6 230 D3
CHLYE PR6 189 K3
CHLYE PR6 187 M3
HGHB LA2 39 G4
LIT OL15 * 219 M3
PRES PR1 * 9 G3
RAW/HAS BB4 195 H1
Mount Pleasant La CARN LA5 33 G7
Mount Pleasant St ACC BB5 * 159 H7
BLY BB11 * 6 F5
TOD OL14 300 D10
Mount Pleasant Ter
HGHB LA2 * 39 G4
Mount Pleasant Vw TOD OL14 303 K2
Mount Rd BLY BB11 6 E7
FTWD FY7 77 K6
KKBY L32 259 L7
Mount St James BBN BB1 158 B7
Mountside Cl WHIT OL12 235 J1
Mount St ACC BB5 159 K1
BPOOL FY1 104 E5
CHTN/BK PR9 13 L3
FTWD FY7 77 K7
GTH/LHO BB6 138 F5
NLSN BB9 122 E6
PRES PR1 9 G5
RAMS BL0 214 E4
RAW/HAS BB4 195 H1
WHIT OL12 * 235 H3
Mount Ter CHTN/BK PR9 13 L3
RAW/HAS BB4 195 K1
The Mount BBNW BB2 10 B2
SKEL WN8 * 253 L1
TOD OL14 303 M1
Mount Trinity BBN BB1 11 G3
Mount Vw COL BB8 * 103 M1
Mountwood SKEL WN8 243 K7
Mount Zion Ct TOD OL14 300 E10
Mowbray Av BBNW BB2 173 J1
Mowbray Dr BPOOLE FY3 105 H2
KKBYL LA6 19 G6
Mowbray Rd FTWD FY7 77 H7
Mowbray St ROCH OL11 234 E8
Mowbreck Ct
KIRK/FR/WAR PR4 128 D5
Mowbreck La
KIRK/FR/WAR PR4 128 C4
Mowbrick La HGHB LA2 42 C2
Muirfield PRES PR1 151 K5
Muirfield Cl CHLY/EC PR7 187 G7
FUL/RIB PR2 131 L5
Muirfield Dr STHP PR8 220 F7
Mulberry Av PRES PR1 151 K8
Mulberry Cl
KIRK/FR/WAR PR4 149 M2
NWD/KWIPK L33 260 C5
ROCH OL11 235 H6
Mulberry Ms BISP FY2 85 J4
KIRK/FR/WAR PR4 128 E6
Mulberry St BBN BB1 11 L4
Mulberry Wk BBN BB1 11 M5
Mulgrave Av FUL/RIB PR2 151 K2
Mullion Cl CHTN/BK PR9 180 E6
Muncaster Dr
RNFD/HAY WA11 262 D4
Muncaster Rd PRES PR1 152 C1
Munro Av
WGNW/BIL/OR WN5 255 H5
Munro Crs FUL/RIB PR2 133 H8
Munster Av BISP FY2 85 G8
Murchison Gv CLV/TH FY5 85 H3
Murdock Av FUL/RIB PR2 152 A1
Murdock St BBNW BB2 * 156 E7
Muriel St MILN OL16 235 L6
Murray Av
CROS/BRETH PR26 168 B6
Murrayfield ROCH OL11 234 B5
Murray St BRFD/BLYE BB10 142 E2
LEYL PR25 186 E2
PRES PR1 152 B2
Musabbir Sq MILN OL16 * 235 K3
Musbury Crs RAW/HAS BB4 195 J2
Musbury Ms RAW/HAS BB4 194 C2
Musbury Rd RAW/HAS BB4 194 C4
Musden Av RAW/HAS BB4 194 D4
Museum St BBN BB1 10 E3
Musker Dr NTHTN L30 257 M8
Musker St CSBY/BLUN L23 257 J8
Mutual St HEYW OL10 234 B8
Myerscough Av BPOOLS FY4 125 J6
LSTA FY8 145 G3
Myerscough Hall Dr
GAR/LONG PR3 91 H6
Myerscough Planks
GAR/LONG PR3 91 K8
Myerscough Smithy Rd
BBNW BB2 135 G8
Myers Rd East
CSBY/BLUN L23 257 H8
Myers Rd West
CSBY/BLUN L23 257 G8
Myers St BRFD/BLYE BB10 142 D3
BWCK/EAR BB18 293 Q6
Myndon St LANC LA1 42 E8
Myra Av MCMB LA4 41 K7
Myra Rd LSTA FY8 145 L7
Myrescough Smithy Rd
BBNW BB2 135 L8
Myrtle Av BLY BB11 * 6 A7
BPOOLE FY3 5 H2
CLV/TH FY5 81 J6
PLF/KEOS FY6 86 B6
Myrtle Bank Rd BBNW BB2 * 172 F3
BCUP OL13 179 J8
Myrtle Dr KIRK/FR/WAR PR4 128 F7
Myrtle Gv BRFD/BLYE BB10 143 J7
HEY LA3 40 F8
RAW/HAS BB4 194 D2
STHP PR8 13 M5
Mythop Av LSTA FY8 146 F7
Mythop Cl LSTA FY8 146 E7
Mythop Pl FUL/RIB PR2 151 J2
Mythop Rd BPOOLS FY4 126 A1
KIRK/FR/WAR PR4 127 H1
LSTA FY8 146 F7
Mytton Rd BOL BL1 233 L8
Mytton St PDHM/BLYW BB12 141 G3
Mytton Vw CLI BB7 98 F4

N

Naarian Ct BBN BB1 157 J4
Nabbs Fold TOT/BURYW BL8 214 C8
Nab La ACC BB5 158 E7
BBNW BB2 10 C4
Nab Rd CHLYE PR6 208 B2
Nab's Head La BBR PR5 155 H3
Naburn Dr
WGNW/BIL/OR WN5 255 H6
Nab Wood Dr CHLY/EC PR7 207 K5
Nairn Av SKEL WN8 243 L6
Nairn Cl BPOOLS FY4 125 K4
Nairne St BLY BB11 6 B5
Nancy St DWN BB3 191 K2
Nansen Rd BBNW BB2 172 E1
FTWD FY7 77 J8
Nantwich Av WHIT OL12 218 C8
Napier Av BPOOLS FY4 124 E5
KIRK/FR/WAR PR4 183 J3
Napier Cl LSTA FY8 145 G2
Napier St ACC BB5 159 M6
NLSN BB9 123 H4
Napier Ter STHP PR8 12 F8
Naples Av BLY BB11 * 6 A7
Naples Rd DWN BB3 191 M2
Naptha La KIRK/FR/WAR PR4 167 M5
Narcissus Av RAW/HAS BB4 194 C3
Nares Rd BBNW BB2 156 E8
Nares St FUL/RIB PR2 151 M2
Narrow Croft Rd ORM L39 250 E2
Narrow La CROS/BRETH PR26 185 J1
ORM L39 250 E2
Narrow Moss La BRSC L40 241 G1
Narvik Av BLY BB11 141 L7
Nasmyth St HOR/BR BL6 231 M8
Nateby Av BPOOLS FY4 125 H6
Nateby Cl GAR/LONG PR3 114 C3
LSTA FY8 145 L4
Nateby Ct GAR/LONG PR3 283 R8
Nateby Crossing La
GAR/LONG PR3 283 R7
Nateby Hall La GAR/LONG PR3 283 Q6
Nateby Pl FUL/RIB PR2 151 J2
Nathan Gv NWD/KWIPK L33 260 C7
Nave Cl DWN BB3 191 M2
Navena Av FTWD FY7 81 G1
Navigation Cl NTHTN L30 258 D7
Navigation Wy BBN BB1 11 G7
FTWD FY7 77 K8
FUL/RIB PR2 151 K4
Naylorfarm Av
WGNNW/ST WN6 245 J6
Naylor's Ter EDGW/EG BL7 210 F6
Nazeby Av CSBY/BLUN L23 257 J8
Naze La KIRK/FR/WAR PR4 148 E5
Naze La East
KIRK/FR/WAR PR4 148 F6
Naze Rd RAW/HAS BB4 196 B2
TOD OL14 303 J4
Naze View Av RAW/HAS BB4 196 C1
Neales Fold CHTN/BK PR9 181 G6
Neapsands Cl FUL/RIB PR2 133 G6
Neargates CHLY/EC PR7 207 G8
Near Meadow CHLYE PR6 169 M8
Neath Cl BBN BB1 157 H4
BBR PR5 153 H8
Neddy Hl KKBYL LA6 19 G5
Neddy La CLI BB7 118 D7
Nedens Gv MGHL L31 249 M8
Nedens La MGHL L31 249 M8
Ned's La GAR/LONG PR3 79 K6
PLF/KEOS FY6 83 G6
Needham Av MCMB LA4 41 H8
Needham Ri MCMB LA4 41 H8
Needham Wy SKEL WN8 243 L6
Nell Carrs RAMS BL0 215 H4
Nell La LEYL PR25 169 G7
Nell's La ORM L39 250 C6
Nelson Av LEYL PR25 186 E2
Nelson Ct STHP PR8 199 J7
Nelson Crs FUL/RIB PR2 151 G1
Nelson Dr FUL/RIB PR2 151 G1
Nelson Gdns
KIRK/FR/WAR PR4 109 M3
Nelson Rd BPOOL FY1 4 C8
BRFD/BLYE BB10 123 J7
CHLY/EC PR7 207 M4
FTWD FY7 77 J8
Nelson Sq BLY BB11 6 F5
Nelson St ACC BB5 159 M6
BBR PR5 169 H3
BCUP OL13 197 M3
CLI BB7 98 E3
DWN BB3 191 J1
GTH/LHO BB6 * 139 G5
HOR/BR BL6 232 A8
KIRK/FR/WAR PR4 128 C6
LANC LA1 3 H6
LIT OL15 219 L6
LSTA FY8 147 G8
MCMB LA4 * 41 H6
MILN OL16 235 J4
STHP PR8 12 F5
Nelson Ter PRES PR1 * 8 D3
Nelson Wy FUL/RIB PR2 151 H3
Nene Cl LEYL PR25 186 E4
Neps La CLI BB7 278 F8
Neptune Ct BPOOLS FY4 126 A5
Neptune St BLY BB11 6 E4
Nesswood Av BPOOLS FY4 125 H5
Neston Rd MILN OL16 235 M7
Neston St PRES PR1 153 H3
Nether Beck KKBYL LA6 26 D8
Netherby St BLY BB11 6 B7
Nethercroft ROCH OL11 234 B3
Netherfield Cl PDHM/BLYW BB12 6 A2
Netherfield Rd NLSN BB9 123 G3

Netherheys Cl COL BB8 103 L6
Nether Kellet Rd KKBYL LA6 34 B2
Netherlands Rd MCMB LA4 41 K7
Netherley Rd CHLY/EC PR7 229 H3
Netherton Gra NTHTN L30 258 E8
Netherton Gn NTHTN L30 258 C6
Netherton La NTHTN L30 258 B6
Nethertown Cl CLI BB7 118 E5
Netherwood Gdns
GTH/LHO BB6 117 L6
Netherwood Rd
BRFD/BLYE BB10 142 F3
Netherwood St
BRFD/BLYE BB10 * 143 H1
Nethway Av BPOOLE FY3 105 J5
Netley Av WHIT OL12 218 C8
Neverstitch Cl SKEL WN8 * 253 J1
Neverstitch Rd SKEL WN8 253 G1
Nevett St PRES PR1 153 G3
Neville Av CLV/TH FY5 85 H3
Neville Crs SKP/WHF BD23 281 J2
Neville Dr CLV/TH FY5 85 L3
Neville Rd SKP/WHF BD23 281 J2
Neville St GAR/LONG PR3 114 D4
Nevill St CHTN/BK PR9 13 G2
Nevy Fold Av HOR/BR BL6 232 C8
New Acres CARN LA5 33 K1
SKEL WN8 243 J2
Newall St LIT OL15 219 L5
TOD OL14 303 K7
Newark Cl NTHTN L30 258 E6
Newark Pl FUL/RIB PR2 132 A3
Newark Rd WHIT OL12 218 C8
Newark Sq WHIT OL12 218 C8
Newark St ACC BB5 159 J6
Newarth La KIRK/FR/WAR PR4 165 H8
New Bank Rd BBNW BB2 156 E5
New Barn RAW/HAS BB4 194 D5
New Barn Ct BBNW BB2 11 G9
New Barn La RAW/HAS BB4 195 J3
ROCH OL11 235 G6
New Barns Cl CARN LA5 16 C3
New Barns Rd CARN LA5 16 C3
New Barn St MILN OL16 235 K5
New Bath St COL BB8 296 B6
Newbigging Av RAW/HAS BB4 196 C1
Newbold Hall Dr MILN OL16 235 M4
Newbold Moss MILN OL16 235 L4
Newbold St MILN OL16 235 M4
New Bonny St BPOOL FY1 4 C3
Newborough Av
CSBY/BLUN L23 257 K7
New Br GAR/LONG PR3 91 M5
New Broad La MILN OL16 235 M8
New Brook Houses
PRES PR1 * 152 F3
New Brown St NLSN BB9 * 123 G2
New Brunswick St
HOR/BR BL6 231 L8
New Buildings Pl MILN OL16 * 235 J3
Newburn Cl SKEL WN8 243 L6
Newbury Av BPOOLS FY4 125 G2
New Bury Cl ACC BB5 158 F8
Newbury Cl FUL/RIB PR2 131 M3
Newbury Dr SKEL WN8 243 L6
Newbury Gn FUL/RIB PR2 131 M3
Newbury Rd LSTA FY8 145 J7
SKEL WN8 243 L6
Newby Av FTWD FY7 81 G2
PLF/KEOS FY6 106 A2
Newby Back La CLI BB7 292 C7
Newby Cl BLY BB11 162 A1
STHP PR8 220 E8
Newby Dr LANC LA1 42 E8
LEYL PR25 187 G1
SKEL WN8 243 L6
Newby La CLI BB7 292 B7
Newby Pl BPOOLS FY4 125 L2
FUL/RIB PR2 133 G7
Newby Sq
WGNW/BIL/OR WN5 * 255 L6
Newcastle Av BPOOLE FY3 5 H3
CLV/TH FY5 81 H7
Newcastle St BBNW BB2 10 A8
New Cswy FMBY L37 247 L3
New Chapel St BBNW BB2 172 E1
New Church Cl ACC BB5 * 139 J8
Newchurch Old Rd BCUP OL13 197 G2
Newchurch Rd BCUP OL13 196 E3
RAW/HAS BB4 177 L8
New Cock Yd PRES PR1 9 H5
New Colliers Rw BOL BL1 * 233 H6
New Court Dr EDGW/EG BL7 212 A8
New Court Wy ORM L39 241 J6
Newcroft CARN LA5 26 B5
New Cut Cl STHP PR8 221 K3
New Cut La STHP PR8 221 K3
New Draught Br
GAR/LONG PR3 90 C6
Newfield Cl CSBY/BLUN L23 257 M5
New Field Cl MILN OL16 235 L3
Newfield Dr BBNW BB2 173 K3
NLSN BB9 123 H3
Newfield Rd BBR PR5 169 K4
New Fold WGNW/BIL/OR WN5 254 F7
New Foul La CHTN/BK PR9 200 C7
New Garden Flds
RAW/HAS BB4 178 C4
New Garden St BBNW BB2 10 E8
Newgate FUL/RIB PR2 132 B7
HEY LA3 53 M1
MILN OL16 235 J4
Newgate Av WGNNW/ST WN6 245 H3
Newgate La KIRK/FR/WAR PR4 167 M3
Newgate Rd SKEL WN8 254 C4
New Ground Ct
BRFD/BLYE BB10 122 F8
New Hall Av BPOOLS FY4 125 L5
New Hall Av North
BPOOLS FY4 125 L5
New Hall Dr STHP PR8 222 F2
New Hall Hey Rd
RAW/HAS BB4 195 J2
New Hall La PRES PR1 9 M3
New Hall St BRFD/BLYE BB10 142 C2
Newhaven Dr GAR/LONG PR3 91 G1
New Hey La KIRK/FR/WAR PR4 129 G7
Newhouse Cl WHIT OL12 218 F5
Newhouse Crs ROCH OL11 234 B3
New House La GAR/LONG PR3 283 Q3
Newhouse Rd ACC BB5 159 M3
BPOOLS FY4 5 L8
New House St COL BB8 296 B6
Newington Av BBN BB1 157 J8
Newlands CHLY/EC PR7 205 M5
Newlands Av BPOOLE FY3 5 K7
BRSC L40 225 J7
CLI BB7 98 F4
LANC LA1 55 G6
PRES PR1 151 K7
WHIT OL12 218 C8
Newlands Cl BBNW BB2 172 B3
WHIT OL12 218 C8
Newlands Rd LANC LA1 55 G7
LSTA FY8 145 M6
MCMB LA4 41 K7
Newlands Wy PLF/KEOS FY6 105 M2
New La ACC BB5 174 F1
BRSC L40 224 E5
CHLY/EC PR7 205 K1
CHTN/BK PR9 181 G7
CLI BB7 98 B5
CLV/TH FY5 85 L4
GAR/LONG PR3 282 H8
GAR/LONG PR3 91 J3
GAR/LONG PR3 83 K1
KIRK/FR/WAR PR4 183 G5
KKBYL LA6 19 G6
ORM L39 251 H1
PRES PR1 152 B8
New Lane Pace CHTN/BK PR9 181 L3
New Line BCUP OL13 197 K3
New Links Av FUL/RIB PR2 131 K5
Newlyn Av BPOOLS FY4 125 H6
MGHL L31 259 H2
Newlyn Dr SKEL WN8 254 A4
Newlyn Pl FUL/RIB PR2 131 J6
Newman Gv CLV/TH FY5 81 H6
Newman Rd BPOOL FY1 105 G3
Newman St BRFD/BLYE BB10 142 D2
MILN OL16 218 F8
Newmarket Av LANC LA1 55 G7
New Market St CHLY/EC PR7 207 M3
CLI BB7 99 H3
COL BB8 296 A6
Newmarket St MCMB LA4 41 L5
New Meadow La FMBY L37 248 B3
New Miles La WGNNW/ST WN6 245 J6
New Mill St BBN BB1 11 G1
CHLY/EC PR7 205 M5
LIT OL15 219 K6
New Moss La CHLYE PR6 187 M6
New Oxford St COL BB8 296 B5
New Park St BBNW BB2 10 D3
New Pastures BBR PR5 168 F3
Newport St NLSN BB9 123 H2
New Preston Mi PRES PR1 * 9 M3
New Quay Rd LANC LA1 2 B4
New Rd BBR PR5 168 E2
BLY BB11 162 D1
BRSC L40 203 L7
BWCK/EAR BB18 294 E5
CARN LA5 25 J3
CHLY/EC PR7 207 J8
CHLYE PR6 231 G3
CROS/BRETH PR26 204 E4
FMBY L37 237 K6
HBR HX7 301 P5
KKBYL LA6 21 L1
LANC LA1 3 G5
LIT OL15 219 H7
LSTA FY8 124 E7
PLF/KEOS FY6 82 D7
RAW/HAS BB4 196 C1
SETT BD24 265 N7
TOD OL14 303 R3
TOD OL14 300 F6
WHIT OL12 217 L3
New Rough Hey FUL/RIB PR2 131 L5
New Rw COL BB8 296 F7
New Row Cots
GAR/LONG PR3 * 116 A2
New Scotland Rd NLSN BB9 123 H2
Newsham Hall La
KIRK/FR/WAR PR4 111 H8
Newsham Pl LANC LA1 54 F6
Newsham Rd LANC LA1 54 F6
Newsham St FUL/RIB PR2 * 8 C1
New Shaw La HBR HX7 301 Q6
News La RNFD/HAY WA11 262 D2
Newsome St LEYL PR25 186 D2
New South Prom BPOOLS FY4 124 D5
New Springs BOL BL1 * 233 L8
Newstead WHIT OL12 * 235 H3
Newstead Av CSBY/BLUN L23 256 E8
New St BRSC L40 226 F1
CARN LA5 33 J1
CHLY/EC PR7 205 M5
CHLYE PR6 189 J3
COL BB8 103 L8
HGHB LA2 44 F8
HGHB LA2 43 K4
LANC LA1 3 G6
LIT OL15 219 J7
MCMB LA4 41 H6
NLSN BB9 123 J2
ORM L39 239 L2
PDHM/BLYW BB12 * 140 E3
RAW/HAS BB4 176 E8
SETT BD24 265 P4
WGNW/BIL/OR WN5 255 L6
WHIT OL12 235 H1
New Taylor Fold
BRFD/BLYE BB10 * 123 J8
Newton Av PLF/KEOS FY6 105 M1
PRES PR1 133 J3
Newton Br SKP/WHF BD23 280 F5
Newton Cl CROS/BRETH PR26 185 L3
KIRK/FR/WAR PR4 148 F5
Newton Ct FUL/RIB PR2 151 L2
Newton Dr ACC BB5 160 A8
BPOOLE FY3 5 K1
BRFD/BLYE BB10 163 J4
SKEL WN8 243 L6
Newton Dr East BPOOLE FY3 105 L4
Newton Gv CLV/TH FY5 85 L4
TOD OL14 301 J12
Newton Pl BPOOLE FY3 105 K4
Newton Rd FUL/RIB PR2 151 L1
LSTA FY8 145 K4
Newton St ACC BB5 * 158 E6
BBN BB1 11 L4
CHTN/BK PR9 200 D4
CLI BB7 99 G4
DWN BB3 191 L1
MILN OL16 235 K6
PDHM/BLYW BB12 141 M4
PRES PR1 9 L2
Newtown BWCK/EAR BB18 293 Q5
Newtown St COL BB8 296 B7
New Wy ORM L39 260 E1
WHIT OL12 217 M2
New Wellington Cl BBNW BB2 172 F2
New Wellington St BBNW BB2 172 F2
Nib La PRES PR1 168 B3
Nicholas Rd CSBY/BLUN L23 256 E7
Nicholas St BLY BB11 7 G5
COL BB8 103 M7
DWN BB3 191 J2
Nicholl St BRFD/BLYE BB10 142 D3
Nicholson Crs MCMB LA4 41 L6
Nicholson St ROCH OL11 235 J6
Nichol St CHLY/EC PR7 * 207 M2
Nickey La BBNW BB2 156 C1
Nick Hilton's Brow CHLYE PR6 230 F1
Nick Hilton's La CHLYE PR6 209 G8
Nicksons La PLF/KEOS FY6 78 E7
Nickson's Weind
GAR/LONG PR3 284 B8
Nicola Cl BCUP OL13 179 K4
Nigher Moss Av MILN OL16 235 M5
Nightfield La BBNW BB2 135 J5
Nightingale Cl BBN BB1 173 L2
CLI BB7 118 D4
KKBY L32 259 L8
Nightingale Crs BLY BB11 * 141 M6
Nightingale Dr PLF/KEOS FY6 105 L1
Nightingale Rd HOR/BR BL6 230 F8
Nightingale St CHLYE PR6 230 D3
Nightingale Wy
CHLY/EC PR7 * 207 M4
GAR/LONG PR3 284 B12
Nile Cl FUL/RIB PR2 151 H3
Nile St LANC LA1 3 H5
MILN OL16 235 K3
NLSN BB9 * 123 G2
PRES PR1 9 K4
Nimes St PRES PR1 153 G3
Nine Elms FUL/RIB PR2 131 M5
Nineteen Acre La CARN LA5 18 C7
Nipe La RNFD/HAY WA11 253 J7
Nithside BPOOLS FY4 125 M2
Niton Cl RAW/HAS BB4 * 194 F2
Nixon La CROS/BRETH PR26 185 J3
Nixons Ct CROS/BRETH PR26 185 J3
Nixons La SKEL WN8 254 A4
Nixon's La STHP PR8 221 H4
Nixon St ROCH OL11 234 E8
Noble Meadow WHIT OL12 * 219 G7
Noble St BBN BB1 158 E2
DWN BB3 191 K3
GTH/LHO BB6 138 F7
Noblett Ct FTWD FY7 81 J1
Noblett St BBN BB1 11 G3
Noel Ga ORM L39 250 E2
Noel Rd LANC LA1 42 D8
Noel Sq FUL/RIB PR2 * 153 H2
Noggarth Rd
PDHM/BLYW BB12 122 A3
Nolan St STHP PR8 13 K8
Nook Crs FUL/RIB PR2 133 M2
Nook Cft BWCK/EAR BB18 294 F5
Nook Farm Av WHIT OL12 218 C8
Nookfield CROS/BRETH PR26 185 K2
Nook Fld GAR/LONG PR3 113 G5
Nookfield Cl LSTA FY8 146 D7
Nook Gld FUL/RIB PR2 133 M2
Nooklands FUL/RIB PR2 132 B7
Nook La ACC BB5 174 E1
BBNW BB2 172 C2
BBR PR5 169 G5
BRSC L40 205 H6
GAR/LONG PR3 283 R12
Nook Ter BBNW BB2 172 D2
The Nook BPOOLE FY3 106 A6
CARN LA5 32 F7
WGNNW/ST WN6 245 H4
Noon Sun St WHIT OL12 235 J2
Noor St PRES PR1 9 K1
Nora St NLSN BB9 103 G8
Norbreck Cl BBNW BB2 173 J3
Norbreck Dr FUL/RIB PR2 151 H2
Norbreck Rd CLV/TH FY5 84 F5
Norburn Crs FMBY L37 247 J1
Norbury Cl CHTN/BK PR9 180 F6
Norbury St MILN OL16 * 235 L7
Norcliffe Rd BISP FY2 84 F6
Norcross Brow CHLYE PR6 189 K3
Norcross La CLV/TH FY5 85 K4
Norcross Pl FUL/RIB PR2 151 J2
Nordale Pk WHIT OL12 234 A1
Norden Rd ROCH OL11 234 A6
Norfolk Av BISP FY2 84 E8
CLV/TH FY5 81 H8
HEY LA3 40 F8
PDHM/BLYW BB12 141 G5
Norfolk Cl ACC BB5 139 J8
LEYL PR25 186 B4
LIT OL15 219 M3
Norfolk Gv ACC BB5 159 K4
STHP PR8 221 J2
Norfolk Rd BBR PR5 153 G7
BPOOLE FY3 125 K1
LSTA FY8 146 E6
MGHL L31 258 F4
PRES PR1 152 D2
STHP PR8 221 J2
Norfolk St ACC BB5 159 M4
BBN BB1 158 D2
BBNW BB2 172 F1
COL BB8 296 B6
DWN BB3 191 L2
LANC LA1 3 H1
NLSN BB9 123 G2
ROCH OL11 235 H5
Norford Wy ROCH OL11 234 B4
Norham Cl PDHM/BLYW BB12 6 D1
Norkeed Rd CLV/TH FY5 84 F4
Norland Dr HEY LA3 52 E3
Norley Hall Av
WGNW/BIL/OR WN5 255 M5
Norley Rd WGNW/BIL/OR WN5 255 L4
Normanby St
WGNW/BIL/OR WN5 255 L5
Norman Cl CLV/TH FY5 85 J2
Normandie Av BISP FY2 85 G8
Normandy Rd
KIRK/FR/WAR PR4 111 L8
Normanhurst ORM L39 241 K7
Norman Rd ACC BB5 158 F6
CSBY/BLUN L23 257 G8
ROCH OL11 235 G5
Norman St BBNW BB2 10 A7
BRFD/BLYE BB10 7 G1
Normoss Av BPOOLE FY3 105 K4
Normoss Rd BPOOLE FY3 105 L4
Norreys St MILN OL16 235 K3
Norris House Dr ORM L39 250 F3
Norris St CHLY/EC PR7 207 M5
DWN BB3 191 L2
PRES PR1 152 A1
Norris Wy FMBY L37 237 L8
North Albion St FTWD FY7 77 K7
Northall KIRK/FR/WAR PR4 184 B1
Northam Cl CHTN/BK PR9 180 D6
North Av BWCK/EAR BB18 293 Q5
HGHB LA2 66 F5
North Bank Av BBN BB1 157 H2
Northbrook Rd LEYL PR25 186 B1
North Church St FTWD FY7 77 L6
Northcliffe GTH/LHO BB6 138 E5
North Cliff St PRES PR1 8 E6
North Clifton St LSTA FY8 146 E8
Northcote Rd GTH/LHO BB6 117 M8
PRES PR1 8 D5
Northcote St DWN BB3 191 L5
LEYL PR25 186 D2
North Ct CLV/TH FY5 81 G6
Northdene SKEL WN8 243 L1
Northdene Dr ROCH OL11 234 C5
North Dr CLV/TH FY5 85 G5
KIRK/FR/WAR PR4 128 C5
KIRK/FR/WAR PR4 109 M2
LANC LA1 67 G3
WGNNW/ST WN6 244 F1
North Dunes HTWN L38 247 J7
North East Av CHLYE PR6 189 K3
Northeast Dr LANC LA1 67 G3
Northenden Rd CHLY/EC PR7 229 H2
North End La HTWN L38 247 K6
Northern Av
KIRK/FR/WAR PR4 184 A1
Northern Perimeter Rd
NTHTN L30 258 B6
The Northern Rd
CSBY/BLUN L23 257 H7
Northfield SKEL WN8 243 L7
Northfield Av BPOOL FY1 104 E3
Northfield Cl NWD/KWIPK L33 260 D7
Northfield Rd ACC BB5 176 D3
BBN BB1 157 H4
Northfields Av SETT BD24 265 N6
Northfields Crs SETT BD24 265 N6
Northfleet Av FTWD FY7 81 H1
Northgate BBNW BB2 10 E3
BISP FY2 84 F7
GAR/LONG PR3 113 G5
HEY LA3 41 L8
LEYL PR25 186 E1
WHIT OL12 217 M4
Northgate Dr CHLYE PR6 208 B1
North Gv BBR PR5 168 F3
North Highfield FUL/RIB PR2 133 H5
North Houses La LSTA FY8 146 A4
Northlands CROS/BRETH PR26 185 M4
FUL/RIB PR2 132 B5
North La WHIT OL12 235 J3
Northleach Av PRES PR1 168 C1
North Leach Dr STHP PR8 220 D6
North Meade MGHL L31 258 E1
North Meadowside
KIRK/FR/WAR PR4 166 D6
North Moor La ORM L39 240 C3
North Moss La FMBY L37 238 A4
North Mount Rd KKBY L32 259 L7
North Pde BWCK/EAR BB18 293 Q4
North Park Av NLSN BB9 122 F2
North Park Dr BPOOLE FY3 5 K2
North Park Rd KKBY L32 259 M7
North Perimeter Rd
NWD/KWIPK L33 261 G7
North Prom LSTA FY8 144 F4
North Ribble St BBR PR5 152 F5
North Rd BBN BB1 11 M6
CARN LA5 33 J2
CHTN/BK PR9 180 E7
CROS/BRETH PR26 184 B5
KKBYL LA6 18 F1
LANC LA1 3 G5
PRES PR1 9 H1
RAW/HAS BB4 195 M1
Northside CHLY/EC PR7 186 F8
North Sq BPOOLE FY3 105 G5
CLV/TH FY5 80 F6
North St BRFD/BLYE BB10 142 D2
BWCK/EAR BB18 293 Q6
CHLY/EC PR7 207 M1
CHTN/BK PR9 13 J1
CLI BB7 99 J2
COL BB8 296 A5
FTWD FY7 77 L6
MCMB LA4 41 J6
MILN OL16 235 K3
NLSN BB9 123 G2
PDHM/BLYW BB12 140 F6
PRES PR1 9 G2
RAMS BL0 214 F1
RAW/HAS BB4 194 F2
RAW/HAS BB4 178 D3
SKP/WHF BD23 281 K2
WHIT OL12 217 M2
North Syke Av FUL/RIB PR2 150 E2
Northumberland Av BISP FY2 104 E2
CLV/TH FY5 81 H7
Northumberland Cl DWN BB3 191 M5
Northumberland St
CHLY/EC PR7 208 A4
MCMB LA4 41 H6
Northumberland Wy
NTHTN L30 257 M8
North Union Vw BBR PR5 168 C3
North V CHLYE PR6 230 C2
North Valley Rd COL BB8 103 M6
North Vw KIRK/FR/WAR PR4 128 C6
North View Cl GAR/LONG PR3 88 F6
North Warton St LSTA FY8 146 F8
Northway FTWD FY7 81 G2
FUL/RIB PR2 132 A5
GAR/LONG PR3 111 M8
MGHL L31 258 F4
ORM L39 250 C5
SKEL WN8 253 L1
North West Dr LANC LA1 66 F3
Northwich Cl CSBY/BLUN L23 257 L5
Northwold Cl WGNS/IIMK WN3 255 M8
Northwood Cl LSTA FY8 146 B7
PDHM/BLYW BB12 6 B1
Northwood Wy PLF/KEOS FY6 106 A1
Norton Av HEY LA3 40 E8
Norton Dr HEY LA3 52 F1
Norton Gv HEY LA3 52 E1
MGHL L31 258 F5
Norton Pl HEY LA3 52 E1
Norton Rd GAR/LONG PR3 284 B5
HEY LA3 52 E1
WHIT OL12 218 C8
Norton St PDHM/BLYW BB12 140 F7
Norton V CLV/TH FY5 86 A1
Norwich Av ROCH OL11 234 D4
Norwich Pl BISP FY2 85 G6
PRES PR1 9 K5
Norwich St ROCH OL11 235 K6
Norwood Av BBNW BB2 173 H1
BPOOLE FY3 105 H3
CHTN/BK PR9 200 B3
KIRK/FR/WAR PR4 183 J1
NLSN BB9 123 J1
Norwood Cl CHLYE PR6 230 D3
Norwood Crs CHTN/BK PR9 200 B3
Norwood Dr MCMB LA4 42 A7
Norwood Gv RNFD/HAY WA11 262 D5
Norwood Rd LSTA FY8 144 F3
STHP PR8 200 C4
Notre Dame Gdns BBN BB1 11 H1
Nottingham Rd PRES PR1 152 D2
Nottingham St BBN BB1 11 K6
Novak Pl MCMB LA4 42 A7
Nova Scotia Whf BBNW BB2 * 10 D9
Nowell Gv PDHM/BLYW BB12 140 A1
Nowell St GTH/LHO BB6 * 138 F6
Noyna Av COL BB8 296 B2
Noyna Rd COL BB8 296 B2
Noyna Vw COL BB8 296 B4
Nun's St LANC LA1 3 J5
The Nurseries FMBY L37 247 K1
KIRK/FR/WAR PR4 165 H8
Nursery Av ORM L39 241 K5
Nursery Cl CHLY/EC PR7 207 H7
LEYL PR25 186 C3
Nursery Dr FMBY L37 247 J1
KIRK/FR/WAR PR4 183 J2
Nursery Gdns MILN OL16 * 235 M3
Nursery La KIRK/FR/WAR PR4 167 H3
Nursery Rd MGHL L31 249 M7
Nutfield St TOD OL14 303 L1
Nutgill La HGHB LA2 39 M4
Nuthall Rd STHP PR8 200 B8
Nuttall Av GTH/LHO BB6 138 F7
HOR/BR BL6 231 K8
Nuttall Cl RAMS BL0 214 F6
Nuttall Hall Rd RAMS BL0 215 G7
Nuttall La RAMS BL0 214 E6
Nuttall Rd BPOOL FY1 5 G9
RAMS BL0 215 G7
Nuttall St ACC BB5 159 M7
BBNW BB2 173 G2
BCUP OL13 179 L8
BLY BB11 * 7 K8
MILN OL16 235 K4
Nutter Crs PDHM/BLYW BB12 121 J6
Nutter Rd ACC BB5 159 M4
CLV/TH FY5 85 G1
PRES PR1 8 E4

O

Oak Av ACC BB5 176 D3
BPOOLS FY4 125 G3
CHLY/EC PR7 187 G8
CLV/TH FY5 85 M3
GAR/LONG PR3 114 D4
HGHB LA2 66 E7
KIRK/FR/WAR PR4 128 D7
MCMB LA4 42 A5
ORM L39 241 G7
PRES PR1 151 L8
TOD OL14 301 K12
Oakbank Dr ACC BB5 159 H6
Oakcliffe Rd WHIT OL12 218 F7
Oak Cl BBN BB1 158 E3
CLI BB7 118 D4
WHIT OL12 302 A11
Oak Crs SKEL WN8 253 G2
Oak Cft CHLYE PR6 187 L1
Oakdene Av ACC BB5 160 B2
Oak Dr BRSC L40 225 J8
CHLYE PR6 187 M8
HGHB LA2 43 L4
KIRK/FR/WAR PR4 148 D6
Oaken Bank BRFD/BLYE BB10 123 H8
Oaken Cl BCUP OL13 179 L8
Oakenclough Rd BCUP OL13 179 L8
Oakeneaves Av BLY BB11 162 A1
Oakengate FUL/RIB PR2 132 F4
Oakenhead Cl GAR/LONG PR3 93 G4
Oakenhead St PRES PR1 * 153 H2
Oakenhead Wood Old Rd
RAW/HAS BB4 177 H8
Oakenhurst Rd BBNW BB2 10 C5
Oakenrod Hl ROCH OL11 234 F4
Oakenshaw Av WHIT OL12 217 M5
Oakenshaw Cft ACC BB5 139 H8
Oakenshaw Vw WHIT OL12 217 M5
Oakfield FUL/RIB PR2 151 L2
FUL/RIB PR2 132 C4
Oakfield Av ACC BB5 139 H8
Oakfield Crs ACC BB5 159 H7
Oakfield Dr CROS/BRETH PR26 185 L3
FMBY L37 237 G7
Oakfield Rd BBNW BB2 173 G4
HTWN L38 256 C1
Oakfields ORM L39 241 K6
Oakfield Ter ROCH OL11 234 F3
Oakford Cl CHTN/BK PR9 181 L6
Oakgate Cl KIRK/FR/WAR PR4 183 J6
Oak Gn ORM L39 241 J6
Oakgrove BPOOLS FY4 125 G5
Oak Gv DWN BB3 191 L1
GAR/LONG PR3 * 284 B8
KIRK/FR/WAR PR4 167 K5
Oakham Ct CHTN/BK PR9 * 13 K2
PRES PR1 9 K5
Oak Hl LIT OL15 219 J6
Oak Hill Cl ACC BB5 159 M7
Oakhill Cl MGHL L31 259 G1
Oakhill Cottage La MGHL L31 250 A7
Oakhill Dr MGHL L31 249 M7
Oakhill Rd MGHL L31 259 G1
Oakhurst Av ACC BB5 160 B2
Oakland Av CLV/TH FY5 85 G5
Oakland Gln BBR PR5 152 D8
Oaklands Av CSBY/BLUN L23 257 H6
KIRK/FR/WAR PR4 183 K4
NLSN BB9 103 G8
Oaklands Ct LANC LA1 54 B6
Oaklands Dr PRES PR1 151 K7
RAW/HAS BB4 195 H1
Oaklands Gv FUL/RIB PR2 151 J2
Oaklands Rd RAMS BL0 215 G1
Oaklands Ter BBN BB1 157 J4
Oakland St BBR PR5 169 H2
NLSN BB9 123 H3
Oak La ACC BB5 160 A6
KIRK/FR/WAR PR4 149 J1
Oaklea WGNNW/ST WN6 245 K1
Oakleaf Cl GAR/LONG PR3 112 F5
Oakleaf Wy BPOOLS FY4 126 A2
Oaklee Gv NWD/KWIPK L33 260 D7
Oakleigh SKEL WN8 263 G1
Oakley Rd HEY LA3 52 E1
RAW/HAS BB4 195 J1
Oakley St RAW/HAS BB4 195 H1
Oakmere CHLYE PR6 169 M8
Oakmere Av CHLYE PR6 189 G1
Oakmere Cl BBNW BB2 173 G5
Oakmoor Av BISP FY2 85 H7
Oak Mt TOD OL14 303 L1
Oak Rdg CLI BB7 290 C8
Oakridge Cl FUL/RIB PR2 132 C4
Oak Rd GAR/LONG PR3 284 A7
Oaks Brow BBN BB1 136 F4
Oakshaw Dr WHIT OL12 234 D2
Oakshott Pl BBR PR5 169 L4
The Oaks BBR PR5 152 E8
CHLY/EC PR7 207 L7
GAR/LONG PR3 89 M4
PLF/KEOS FY6 86 A6
Oak St ACC BB5 159 J2
BBN BB1 157 J4
BLY BB11 161 L7
COL BB8 296 C5
FTWD FY7 77 K7
GTH/LHO BB6 138 F5

LIT OL15 219 M6
MILN OL16 235 J4
NLSN BB9 122 G6
PDHM/BLYW BB12 141 M4
PRES PR1 9 K5
RAMS BL0 * 214 E6
STHP PR8 200 B5
TOD OL14 303 K3
WHIT OL12 302 A10
Oak Ter COL BB8 * 296 H5
Oaktree Av FUL/RIB PR2 131 K7
LEYL PR25 169 G7
Oaktree CI FUL/RIB PR2 131 K7
Oak Tree Ct SKEL WN8 244 A8
Oak Vw LEYL PR25 186 B1
WHIT OL12 302 A10
Oakville Rd HEY LA3 52 D6
Oakway GAR/LONG PR3 * 114 D3
Oakwood SKEL WN8 * 244 A8
Oakwood Av BBN BB1 157 K2
BBR PR5 152 F7
LSTA FY8 146 B7
STHP PR8 221 G5
WGNNW/ST WN6 245 J6
Oakwood CI BPOOLS FY4 125 J7
BRFD/BLYE BB10 123 G8
CLV/TH FY5 86 A1
Oakwood Dr FUL/RIB PR2 132 A3
STHP PR8 221 H6
Oakwood Gdns LANC LA1 66 F1
Oakwood Gv LANC LA5 42 C6
Oakwood Rd ACC BB5 160 C4
CHLY/EC PR7 229 J1
Oakwood Vw CHLY/EC PR7 * 207 L7
Oakworth Av FUL/RIB PR2 133 J6
Oakworth CI NWD/KWIPK L33 260 G5
Oasis CI BRSC L40 203 L8
Oat St PDHM/BLYW BB12 140 F4
Oban Ct FUL/RIB PR2 134 A2
Oban Crs FUL/RIB PR2 133 G8
Oban Dr BBN BB1 157 M8
Oban PI BISP FY2 * 85 H5
Oban Rd BRFD/BLYE BB10 142 F5
Oberlin St ROCH OL11 235 G6
Observatory Rd BBNW BB2 173 K1
Occupation La PLF/KEOS FY6 87 J7
Occupation Rd CARN LA5 25 L4
Ocean Bvd BPOOLS FY4 * 124 D4
Ocean Wy CLV/TH FY5 80 F8
O'Connor Dr NWD/KWIPK L33 260 H5
Oddfellows Ter RAW/HAS BB4 178 H4
Odell Wy BBN BB1 153 H8
Off Botanic Av BBR BL6 231 K8
Offerton St HOR/BR BL6 231 K8
Old Acre HTWN L38 247 J4
Old Back La CLI BB7 119 J4
Old Bank La BBN BB1 11 M9
BBNW BB2 173 J1
Old Bank St BBNW BB2 10 E5
Old Bent La WHIT OL12 218 D4
Old Boundary Wy ORM L39 241 J5
Old Bridge Wy CLV/TH FY5 86 A2
Old Bridge Wy PLF/KEOS FY6 208 A2
Old Brow La MILN OL16 218 H8
Old Buckley La GAR/LONG PR3 116 A4
Oldbury PI CLV/TH FY5 * 85 J7
Old Carr Mill St RAW/HAS BB4 176 A6
Old Chapel Ct CHLYE PR6 * 230 D4
Old Clay Dr WHIT OL12 219 G7
Old Clitheroe Rd
GAR/LONG PR3 115 L2
Old Cock Yd PRES PR1 9 J4
Old Colliers Rw BOL BL1 * 233 H6
Old Cft FUL/RIB PR2 132 A3
Old Dawber's La CHLY/EC PR7 206 E2
Old Delph Rd ROCH OL11 234 D7
Olde Back La BLY BB11 141 M8
Old Engine La SKEL WN8 252 F1
Olde Stonehearth Ct
CHLYE PR6 208 G7
Old Farm Rd CSBY/BLUN L23 257 J7
Old Farmside RAW/HAS BB4 173 G4
Oldfield KIRK/FR/WAR PR4 166 C4
PRES PR1 168 A1
Oldfield Av BISP FY2 84 F1
DWN BB3 173 H8
Oldfield Carr La PLF/KEOS FY6 106 B2
Oldfield CI FUL/RIB PR2 106 B2
Oldfield Crs PLF/KEOS FY6 86 B2
Oldfield Rd BBR PR5 169 K4
Old Fold WGNW/BIL/OR WN5 255 H6
Old Forge CI LSTA FY8 146 A4
Old Gates Dr BBNW BB2 172 C2
Old Ground St RAMS BL0 * 214 F5
Old Hall CI BBR PR5 169 H3
MCMB LA4 42 A7
MGHL L31 259 C4
NLSN BB9 102 D6
Old Hall Dr SKP/WHF BD23 281 K7
Old Hall Dr ACC BB5 160 C2
BBR PR5 169 H3
Old Hall Gdns RNFD/HAY WA11 262 D5
CHLY/EC PR7 206 E2
Old Hall Rd MGHL L31 259 C4
Old Hall Sq BRFD/BLYE BB10 143 K6
Old Hall St BRFD/BLYE BB10 142 D3
Oldham Rd MILN OL16 235 J4
Oldham St BLY BB11 * 6 D7
MCMB LA4 * 41 J5
Old Hey Cft PRES PR1 168 A1
Old House La BPOOLS FY4 124 M4
Old Kiln BCUP OL13 197 G3
Old Lancaster La FUL/RIB PR2 152 C2
Old Lancaster Rd
GAR/LONG PR3 90 E1
Old La BRSC L40 227 G3
BWCK/EAR BB18 293 Q10
FMBY L37 237 J5
MGHL L31 250 B7
ORM L39 239 H8
RNFD/HAY WA11 262 C4
SKP/WHF BD23 281 L8
WGNNW/ST WN6 245 L5
WHIT OL12 302 B9
Old Langho Rd GTH/LHO BB6 117 L8
Old Laund St
PDHM/BLYW BB12 122 B3
Old Links CI CHTN/BK PR9 200 H5
Old Lord's Crs HOR/BR BL6 231 L1
Old Lostock La BBR PR5 169 J5
Old Mains La PLF/KEOS FY6 86 D5
Old Meadow La BPOOLS FY3 5 L8
Old Meadows Rd BCUP OL13 179 J6
Old Mill Ct KIRK/FR/WAR PR4 166 C3
Old Mill Dr COL BB8 296 H5
Old Mill HI ORM L39 241 H6
Old Mill La BRSC L40 227 H4
FMBY L37 237 J5
Old Millstones PRES PR1 * 8 B1
Old Mill St BBN BB1 11 L1
Oldmill St WHIT OL12 217 M8
Old Moor Rd HGHB LA2 37 J3

Old Moss La ORM L39 238 F6
Old Nab Rd GTH/LHO BB6 138 D3
Old Oak Gdns BBR BB8 168 D1
Old Oliver La LEYL PR25 * 169 G7
Old Orch FUL/RIB PR2 132 A7
Old Parsonage La
PDHM/BLYW BB12 140 E3
Old Penny Gdns MCMB LA4 41 M7
Old Pepper La
WGNNW/ST WN6 245 L1
Old Prescot CI MGHL L31 259 M1
Old Racecourse Rd MGHL L31 258 D6
Old Raike SKP/WHF BD23 266 D7
Old Rake HOR/BR BL6 232 A5
Old Rectory Gn ORM L39 250 D4
SFTN L29 258 B4
Old Riggs Yd KKBYL LA6 * 19 H6
Old Rd MILN OL16 219 H7
SKP/WHF BD23 294 E1
Old Roman Rd
PDHM/BLYW BB12 119 L8
Old Rw KIRK/FR/WAR PR4 128 E3
Oldroyd Rd TOD OL14 303 N2
The Old Sawmill SETT BD24 267 J3
Old School La
CROS/BRETH PR26 185 K3
SETT BD24 265 P8
Old School Dr
KIRK/FR/WAR PR4 166 D3
Old School La BBR PR5 168 F5
CHLY/EC PR7 230 B6
CHLY/EC PR7 187 G8
DWN BB3 190 C1
Old School Ms BCUP OL13 196 F3
RAW/HAS BB4 176 H8
Old Shaw La HBR HX7 301 Q7
The Old Sidings COL BB8 296 A2
Old Station CI FUL/RIB PR2 134 A2
Old Station Ct CLI BB7 99 H3
Old Stone Brow
BWCK/EAR BB18 294 D11
Old Stone Trough La
BWCK/EAR BB18 294 D10
Old St RAW/HAS BB4 196 B2
Old Tom's La PLF/KEOS FY6 83 H5
Old Town CI SKEL WN8 253 G3
Old Town La FMBY L37 237 H7
Old Town Wy SKEL WN8 253 G3
Old Tram Rd BBR PR5 152 D7
PRES PR1 9
The Old Tramway BBR PR5 169 L5
Old Vicarage PRES PR1 9 J4
Old Vicarage Rd HOR/BR BL6 232 C8
Old Will's La HOR/BR BL6 231 L5
Olive Ct CHLYE PR6 187 M6
Olive Gv BPOOLE FY3 5 J2
KIRK/FR/WAR PR4 188 A5
SKEL WN8 253 H2
STHP PR8 200 B4
Olive La DWN BB3 191 L1
Oliver CI LIT OL15 219 J6
Olive Rd LANC LA1 * 3 K1
Oliver PI CARN LA5 33 K1
Oliver's PI FUL/RIB PR2 132 D3
Olive St BCUP OL13 196 F3
Olive St BCUP OL13 197 H3
Ollerton Fold CHLYE PR6 * 171 G7
Ollerton La CHLYE PR6 171 H1
Ollerton Rd LSTA FY8 146 A6
Ollerton St CHLYE PR6 230 D3
Ollerton Ter CHLYE PR6 171 H8
Ollery Gn NTHN L30 258 C2
Olney ROCH OL11 * 235 H5
Olympia St BRFD/BLYE BB10 7 L6
Olympic Wy BPOOLS FY4 125 M3
Onchan Dr BCUP OL13 197 L2
Onchan Rd BBNW BB2 173 H2
One Ash CI WHIT OL12 235 J1
Onslow Crs STHP PR8 221 K1
Onslow Rd BPOOLE FY3 105 H4
Onslow St ROCH OL11 234 F7
Ontario CI BBN BB2 156 D3
Oozebooth Ter BBN BB1 157 H4
Oozehead La BBNW BB2 156 E6
Opal CI CLV/TH FY5 85 J4
Opal St BBN BB1 157 H1
Openshaw Dr BBN BB1 157 H6
Oporto CI BLY BB11 * 6 D5
Orama Mi WHIT OL12 * 217 M3
Oram Rd CHLYE PR6 170 C3
Orange St ACC BB5 159 L4
Orchan Rd TOD OL14 301 J12
Orchard Av BPOOLS FY4 124 F5
CARN LA5 32 F5
KIRK/FR/WAR PR4 167 K4
PLF/KEOS FY6 106 B2
Orchard Br BLY BB11 * 6 F4
Orchard CI BBNW BB2 156 E6
CHLY/EC PR7 187 G7
CLV/TH FY5 81 G7
FUL/RIB PR2 131 K6
HGHB LA2 42 E3
KIRK/FR/WAR PR4 165 J8
KIRK/FR/WAR PR4 127 L4
WGNNW/ST WN6 245 K4
WGNW/BIL/OR WN5 255 H6
Orchard Cft BBR PR5 168 D3
Orchard DI CSBY/BLUN L23 257 J7
Orchard Dr ACC BB5 159 J7
CHLYE PR6 187 M6
FTWD FY7 81 H2
Orchard Hey NTHN L30 258 B3
Orchard La KIRK/FR/WAR PR4 166 C3
LANC LA1 * 2 D7
STHP PR8 221 G2
Orchard Mill Dr
CROS/BRETH PR26 204 E1
Orchard Pk DWN BB3 191 J1
Orchard Rd CARN LA5 16 C1
LSTA FY8 145 H5
The Orchards PLF/KEOS FY6 85 L6
WGNNW/ST WN6 255 H6
Orchard St GTH/LHO BB6 138 D7
HEYW OL10 234 B8
LEYL PR25 186 C2
PRES PR1 9 H4
The Orchard
CROS/BRETH PR26 184 F8
GAR/LONG PR3 88 D2
HGHB LA2 36 F7
KIRK/FR/WAR PR4 148 B5
KIRK/FR/WAR PR4 166 C3
ORM L39 241 M4
Orchard Vw ORM L39 251 G2
Orchard Yd KKBYL LA6 * 18 F1
Orchid CI SKEL WN8 254 C5
Ord Av BPOOLS FY4 5 J4

Orders La KIRK/FR/WAR PR4 128 D7
Ordnance St BBN BB1 11 L1
Ord Rd FUL/RIB PR2 151 M1
Oregon Av BPOOLE FY3 105 H3
Oriel CI STHP PR8 199 J7
Oriel Dr AIN/FAZ L10 259 G8
Oriel St ROCH OL11 235 J6
Oriole CI BBN BB1 10 F2
Orion Blds CLV/TH FY5 * 85 G1
Orkney CI BBN BB1 157 M8
Orkney CI BPOOLE FY1 4 F8
Ormerod Bld BLY BB11 7 H1
Ormerod St ACC BB5 176 E4
ACC BB5 159 K7
BLY BB11 7 G5
BRFD/BLYE BB10 143 K6
CLV/TH FY5 81 L8
COL BB8 296 B6
NLSN BB9 123 J8
RAW/HAS BB4 195 K1
Orme St BCUP OL13 4 F5
Ormond Av BPOOLE FY1 104 C3
BRSC L40 242 A7
Ormonde Av MGHL L31 258 A5
Ormonde Dr MGHL L31 258 F3
Ormont Av CLV/TH FY5 85 H1
Ormskirk Old Rd ORM L39 252 C4
Ormskirk Rd ORM L39 251 M2
PRES PR1 9 J3
RNFD/HAY WA11 262 B3
SKEL WN8 252 F2
LANC LA1 42 D8
MCMB LA4 41 M4
NLSN BB9 122 F6
PRES PR1 9 K5
Orms Wy FMBY L37 237 H8
Ornston Av HOR/BR BL6 231 L6
Orpen Av BLY BB11 142 C8
Orpington St
WGNW/BIL/OR WN5 255 M5
Orrell CI LEYL PR25 186 A2
Orrell Gdns
WGNW/BIL/OR WN5 255 J5
Orrell Hall CI
WGNW/BIL/OR WN5 255 L4
Orrell Hill La HTWN L38 247 M7
Orrell La BRSC L40 225 G6
Orrell Ms BRSC L40 * 225 H6
Orrest Rd PRES PR1 153 K2
Orrest St PRES PR1 152 A1
Orxhill R CLV/TH FY5 85 H1
Oxhouse Rd
WGNW/BIL/OR WN5 254 F7
Ox St LANC LA1 54 E8
Orwell CI FMBY L37 247 G2
Osbaldeston La BBNW BB2 136 A5
Osbert Cft KIRK/FR/WAR PR4 166 C3
Osbert Rd CSBY/BLUN L23 256 E7
Osborne CI CLV/TH FY5 85 H1
Osborne Crs HEY LA3 41 G8
Osborne Dr CHLYE PR6 187 M1
Osborne Gv CLV/TH FY5 81 G6
MCMB LA4 41 H8
Osborne PI TOD OL14 303 M2
Osborne Rd BBNW BB2 156 E5
BBR PR5 169 G6
CLV/TH FY5 81 G6
FMBY L37 247 H2
HEY LA3 41 G8
LSTA FY8 145 J4
STHP PR8 220 E5
Osborne St PRES PR1 8 E5
ROCH OL11 235 H6
Osborne Ter BCUP OL13 197 G3
DWN BB3 191 H1
PDHM/BLYW BB12 122 A1
RAW/HAS BB4 178 B7
Osborne Wy RAW/HAS BB4 194 D2
Osbourne Rd BPOOLE FY4 124 E3
Oscar St BPOOLS FY4 5 M6
Oslo Rd BLY BB11 141 L6
Osprey CI BBN BB1 157 G3
CHLYE PR6 188 D8
The Ospreys WGNS/IIMK WN3 255 M8
Oswald Av FUL/RIB PR2 151 M2
LSTA FY8 147 G2
Oswald St ACC BB5 158 F8
BBN BB1 11 G3
BBN BB1 10 E1
MILN OL16 235 K3
Otley Rd LSTA FY8 145 L4
Ottawa CI BBNW BB2 156 D3
Otterburn CI BPOOLE FY3 105 L2
Otterburn Gv
BRFD/BLYE BB10 143 G5
Otterburn Rd BBNW BB2 172 F4
Otters CI FUL/RIB PR2 153 J1
Otterwood Sq
WGNW/BIL/OR WN5 255 M1
Ottery CI CHTN/BK PR9 180 D6
Otway St PRES PR1 152 B1
Oulder HI ROCH OL11 234 D4
Oulder Hill Dr ROCH OL11 234 E4
Oulder Mt ROCH OL11 234 E4
Oldfield CI MILN OL16 * 235 L5
Oulton CI MGHL L31 249 L6
Oundle Dr AIN/FAZ L10 258 F8
Ousby Av HEY LA3 53 J1
Ousby Rd HEY LA3 53 J1
Ouseburn Rd BBNW BB2 172 F3
Outer Prom FTWD FY7 77 G6
Outgate Rd KIRK/FR/WAR PR4 131 C2
Out La CROS/BRETH PR26 204 E1
Outlet La MGHL L31 260 B2
ORM L39 260 C1
Out Moss La MCMB LA4 41 J7
Outram La BBN BB1 157 H2
Outram Wy BBR PR5 169 H5
Outwood Rd BLY BB11 7 K8
The Oval WGNNW/ST WN6 245 M8
Ovangle Rd HEY LA3 54 A1
Overdale Gv BPOOLS FY3 105 K2
Overdell Dr WHIT OL12 217 M8
Overfield Wy WHIT OL12 235 J1
Overshores Rd EDGW/EG BL7 212 D4
Overton Rd FUL/RIB PR2 151 H5
Over Town La WHIT OL12 235 J6
Overt St ROCH OL11 235 J6
Ovington Dr STHP PR8 200 B8
The Ov BLY BB11 141 M8
Owen Av ORM L39 241 J5
Owen Ct ACC BB5 139 J5
Owen Rd LANC LA1 3 G1
Owen's La ORM L39 249 J5
Owen St CHLYE PR6 * 208 B4
Owen St ACC BB5 159 L4
PDHM/BLYW BB12 141 K6
PRES PR1 9 K2
Owlet Hall Rd DWN BB3 191 H1
Owsten Ct HOR/BR BL6 231 H1
Owtram St PRES PR1 152 F5
Oxcliffe Av HEY LA3 52 E2
Oxcliffe Gv HEY LA3 52 E2
Oxcliffe Rd HEY LA3 52 E2
Oxendale Rd CLV/TH FY5 86 A1
Oxenholme Av CLV/TH FY5 81 M7

Oxenhurst Rd BPOOLE FY3 105 K3
Oxford Av ACC BB5 139 K8
ROCH OL11 234 D5
Oxford CI BBN BB1 11 M1
PDHM/BLYW BB12 141 G3
Oxford Ct STHP PR8 199 J7
Oxford Dr BBN BB1 158 A3
KIRK/FR/WAR PR4 128 C7
Oxford Gdns STHP PR8 12 A8
Oxford Ms BBN BB1 158 A3
Oxford PI BLY BB11 7 J6
LANC LA1 42 D8
MILN OL16 235 K6
Oxford Rd BBN BB5 169 J3
BLY BB11 7 J5
BPOOL FY1 5 G1
CLV/TH FY5 80 F8
FTWD FY7 77 H8
FUL/RIB PR2 132 A2
LANC LA1 145 H4
NLSN BB9 123 H4
SKEL WN8 253 H2
STHP PR8 12 A8
WGNW/BIL/OR WN5 255 M4
Oxford St ACC BB5 * 159 L5
CARN LA5 33 J2
CHLY/EC PR7 230 C5
CHLY/EC PR7 207 M4
COL BB8 296 B6
DWN BB3 173 J7
LANC LA1 42 D8
MCMB LA4 41 J6
NLSN BB9 123 H4
SKEL WN8 253 H2
PRES PR1 152 C1
RAMS BL0 215 G5
WCNNW/ST WN6 245 L4
Oxford Wy FTWD FY7 77 H8
WHIT OL12 235 H1
Ox Hey Av FUL/RIB PR2 * 150 F2
Oxhey CI BRFD/BLYE BB10 143 J5
Ox Hey CI RAMS BL0 214 F4
Oxheys St PRES PR1 152 A1
Oxhill R CLV/TH FY5 85 H1
Oxhouse Rd
WGNW/BIL/OR WN5 254 F7
Ox St LANC LA1 54 E8
Oystercatcher Ga LSTA FY8 146 B4
Oystons Mi PRES PR1 * 8 B2

P

Paa La CLI BB7 278 F6
Packer St MILN OL16 235 J4
Packet La CARN LA5 32 F7
Pad Cote La HWTH BD22 297 R3
Paddington Av GAR/LONG PR3 89 M4
Paddock Av
CROS/BRETH PR26 185 K3
Paddock CI CSBY/BLUN L23 256 E5
Paddock Dr BPOOLE FY3 125 M1
Paddock Rd SKEL WN8 253 M6
Paddock St ACC BB5 * 159 H7
The Paddock ACC BB5 159 J7
BBNW BB2 156 D3
BRSC L40 203 M7
CLI BB7 291 C6
CLV/TH FY5 85 L3
FMBY L37 237 H6
FUL/RIB PR2 132 D5
ORM L39 240 F8
PLF/KEOS FY6 85 M6
RAMS BL0 214 G4
Padend Nook
KIRK/FR/WAR PR4 109 M1
Padgate PI BLY BB11 141 M1
Padiham Rd CLI BB7 120 D5
PDHM/BLYW BB12 6 A3
Padstow Ct CHTN/BK PR9 180 D6
Padway PRES PR1 168 A1
Page Ct FMBY L37 237 J8
Pagefield Cr LANC LA1 * 3 J4
Pages Ct BBR PR5 168 E4
Paignton Rd BBN BB1 157 H4
Painley CI LSTA FY8 146 B4
Paisley St BLY BB11 6 B6
Palace Gdns
PDHM/BLYW BB12 141 L4
Palace Rd STHP PR8 12 A8
Palace St PDHM/BLYW BB12 * 141 M4
Palatine Av LANC LA1 54 F7
Palatine CI BPOOLE FY3 105 M5
Palatine Rd BBNW BB2 10 A5
BPOOL FY1 5 H7
CLV/TH FY5 81 G7
ROCH OL11 234 D3
STHP PR8 12 C7
Palatine Sq BLY BB11 6 E4
Palatine St MILN OL16 235 M4
RAMS BL0 214 F5
Paley Green La SETT BD24 264 H7
Paley Rd PRES PR1 8 A2
Palfrey CI PLF/KEOS FY6 106 B2
Pall Mi CHLY/EC PR7 207 M5
HOR/BR BL6 231 K4
Palmaston CI LANC LA1 54 D5
Palma St TOD OL14 300 E10
Palm CI SKEL WN8 253 H4
Palm Dr PLF/KEOS FY6 85 L5
Palmer Av BPOOLS FY6 4 F1
Palmer Gv MCMB LA4 41 H8
Palmer St BBN BB1 10 C1
Palmerston CI RAMS BL0 214 E8
Palmerston St
PDHM/BLYW BB12 141 G4
Palmer St BBN BB1 157 J4
Palm Gv STHP PR8 13 M5
Palm St BBN BB1 157 J4
BLY BB11 6 A5
Panorama Vw
BWCK/EAR BB18 293 Q8
Pansy St North ACC BB5 159 L4
Pansy St South ACC BB5 * 159 L4
The Parade CARN LA5 33 C2
Paradise La CHLYE PR6 187 L3
CROS/BRETH PR26 185 L2
FMBY L37 237 K6
Paradise St ACC BB5 159 L4
BBNW BB2 10 D5
BLY BB11 7 H5
CHLYE PR6 188 C8
NLSN BB9 123 J8
RAMS BL0 214 F5
RAW/HAS BB4 196 C3
Paragon Wy LANC LA1 2 B6
Parbold CI BPOOLE FY3 105 L2
BRSC L40 225 H8

Parbold HI SKEL WN8 244 A1
Pardoe CI KIRK/FR/WAR PR4 165 H8
Pargate Cha ROCH OL11 234 D5
Paris BBN BB1 137 H7
Paris Av WCNS/IIMK WN3 255 M8
Parish Gdns LEYL PR25 169 H7
Parish St PDHM/BLYW BB12 140 F2
Park Av BBN BB1 10 C1
BLY BB11 6 D8
BWCK/EAR BB18 293 Q6
CHLY/EC PR7 207 L5
CHTN/BK PR9 200 B2
CLI BB7 99 H2
CSBY/BLUN L23 257 H6
FMBY L37 247 G8
FTWD FY7 77 J8
GTH/LHO BB6 139 G5
KIRK/FR/WAR PR4 184 H3
KIRK/FR/WAR PR4 167 H2
LANC LA1 3 L1
LSTA FY8 146 B8
MGHL L31 250 A8
NLSN BB9 122 F2
ORM L39 241 H6
PRES PR1 152 C1
RAMS BL0 215 G5
RAW/HAS BB4 176 B3
WCNNW/ST WN6 245 L4
Parkbourn MGHL L31 259 K1
Parkbourn Dr MGHL L31 259 K1
Parkbourn North MGHL L31 259 K1
Parkbourn Sq MGHL L31 259 K1
Park Bridge Rd
BRFD/BLYE BB10 143 G8
Parkbrook La
WGNNW/ST WN6 245 L4
Park CI FMBY L37 247 H3
FUL/RIB PR2 133 L3
KKBY L32 259 L8
PRES PR1 152 A7
SKEL WN8 226 F8
Park Cots BOL BL1 * 233 M8
Park Ct LANC LA1 54 E8
Park Crs ACC BB5 159 K7
BBNW BB2 200 A2
CHTN/BK PR9 200 A2
MCMB LA4 41 M4
ORM L39 239 J7
PLF/KEOS FY6 82 F3
RAW/HAS BB4 194 E2
Parkdale Gdns BBNW BB2 173 G5
Park Dr CSBY/BLUN L23 256 D7
FUL/RIB PR2 151 G2
NLSN BB9 122 F6
Parke Ms CHLYE PR6 170 F3
Parker CI CLI BB7 99 G5
Parker Crs ORM L39 241 J4
Parker La BLY BB11 7 G5
KIRK/FR/WAR PR4 167 H4
Parker Rd CHLYE PR6 189 H3
Parkers Fold GAR/LONG PR3 * 90 F7
Parker St ACC BB5 176 A1
BBN BB1 158 E1
BLY BB11 7 G1
BPOOL FY1 4 F1
BRFD/BLYE BB10 * 123 J8
BWCK/EAR BB18 293 P4
CHLY/EC PR7 207 M2
COL BB8 103 M6
FUL/RIB PR2 151 M1
LANC LA1 3 K4
NLSN BB9 * 123 J7
Parkers Wood CI CHLY/EC PR7 207 L3
Parkes Wy BBNW BB2 172 F4
Park Farm CI
KIRK/FR/WAR PR4 166 C3
Park Farm Rd BBNW BB2 172 A3
Parkfield WGNNW/ST WN6 245 L4
Parkfield Av FUL/RIB PR2 151 L1
Parkfield CI FUL/RIB PR2 150 F2
ORM L39 240 F8
Parkfield Crs FUL/RIB PR2 150 F2
Parkfield Dr LANC LA1 54 F5
Parkgate GAR/LONG PR3 113 G5
Parkgate Dr LANC LA1 55 H4
LEYL PR25 169 H7
Park Gate Rd BBN BB1 157 G2
Park Hall Rd CHLY/EC PR7 206 C4
Park Head CLI BB7 139 J1
Parkhead La GAR/LONG PR3 284 C5
Park Hey Dr WGNNW/ST WN6 245 H4
Park HI BWCK/EAR BB18 293 Q8
Park Hill Ct GAR/LONG PR3 284 B8
Park Hill La GAR/LONG PR3 284 C8
Park House La HGHB LA2 47 M1
Parkhurst CI BBN BB1 173 H3
Parkin La TOD OL14 302 C11
Parkinson La GAR/LONG PR3 94 D3
Parkinson St BBNW BB2 172 E1
BLY BB11 7 H7
COL BB8 296 A2
RAW/HAS BB4 176 B3
Parkinson Wy BPOOLS FY4 124 F2
Parkland CI CLV/TH FY5 84 C3
Parkland Gv HEY LA3 52 F1
Parklands CHTN/BK PR9 200 B3
RNFD/HAY WA11 262 C4
SKEL WN8 254 A1
Parklands Av PRES PR1 151 K7
Parklands CI PRES PR1 151 K7
Parklands Dr FUL/RIB PR2 132 B3
Parklands Gv BBNW BB2 172 E3
The Parklands GAR/LONG PR3 91 J3
Parklands Wy BBNW BB2 172 E3
Parkland Vw BLY BB11 142 B8
Park La ACC BB5 159 K8
GAR/LONG PR3 283 Q1
GTH/LHO BB6 139 G5
HGHB LA2 44 C3
HGHB LA2 32 H4
HOR/BR BL6 232 A4
HWTH BD22 297 Q1
KIRK/FR/WAR PR4 202 E1
KIRK/FR/WAR PR4 128 D5
MGHL L31 250 B8
MILN OL16 235 J3
NLSN BB9 122 F6
PLF/KEOS FY6 78 D7
PRES PR1 151 K7
SKP/WHF BD23 295 R2
Park Lane CI MGHL L31 259 L1
Park La West NTHN L30 258 C4
Park Lee Rd BBNW BB2 173 H2
Park Link ORM L39 250 E2
Park Ms CLI BB7 292 C1
Park Mill PI PRES PR1 9 J1
Park Rd BBNW BB2 172 A4

BCUP OL13 ....197 J2
BPOOL FY1 ....4 F4
BRFD/BLYE BB10 ....163 H2
BWCK/EAR BB18 ....293 Q6
CARN LA5 ....17 G7
CHLY/EC PR7 ....230 B5
CHLY/EC PR7 ....229 F1
CHLY/EC PR7 ....207 M1
CHTN/BK PR9 ....13 M1
CLI BB7 ....292 E1
CLV/TH FY5 ....85 L3
DWN BB3 ....191 L5
FMBY L37 ....247 J2
FUL/RIB PR2 ....132 D7
GTH/LHO BB6 ....139 G5
KIRK/FR/WAR PR4 ....128 C7
KKBY L32 ....259 L8
LANC LA1 ....3 A4
LEYL PR25 ....186 D4
LSTA FY8 ....145 H5
ORM L39 ....241 H4
PDHM/BLYW BB12 ....140 F4
PLF/KEOS FY6 ....86 B7
PRES PR1 ....152 A7
RAMS BL0 ....214 C8
RAW/HAS BB4 ....196 C2
RAW/HAS BB4 ....194 B3
TOD OL14 ....303 L1
WHIT OL12 ....235 L2
Park Rd West CHTN/BK PR9 ....199 M2
Park Side BWCK/EAR BB18 ....294 D7
Parkside
  MCMB LA4 ....41 J8
  PRES PR1 ....132 E8
Parkside Av CHLY/EC PR7 ....207 M4
Parkside Crs
  WGNW/BIL/OR WN5 ....255 J5
Parkside Dr CARN LA5 ....16 D2
  CHLYE PR6 ....187 L5
Parkside Dr South CHLYE PR6 ....187 L5
Parkside La GAR/LONG PR3 ....283 C5
Parkside Rd LSTA FY8 ....145 K4
  NLSN BB9 ....123 L3
  TOD OL14 ....300 D10
Park Sq LANC LA1 ....3 A4
Park St East NLSN BB9 ....103 H4
Parkstone Av PLF/KEOS FY6 ....85 K6
Parkstone Rd GAR/LONG PR3 ....111 J8
Park St ACC BB5 ....159 M5
  BWCK/EAR BB18 ....293 Q6
  CHLY/EC PR7 ....207 J8
  CHLY/EC PR7 ....205 M5
  CLI BB7 ....99 H4
  GTH/LHO BB6 ....139 C6
  LSTA FY8 ....146 D2
  MCMB LA4 ....41 J5
  MILN OL16 ....235 J5
  NLSN BB9 ....103 C2
  RAW/HAS BB4 ....194 C4
Park St East NLSN BB9 ....103 H4
Parksway PLF/KEOS FY6 ....78 A6
Park Ter BBN BB1 ....157 G4
  HEYW OL10 ....234 H4
Parkthorn Rd FUL/RIB PR2 ....150 F1
Park Vw CARN LA5 ....26 A8
  CARN LA5 ....16 E2
  LIT OL15 ....219 L5
  PDHM/BLYW BB12 ....140 F3
  PRES PR1 ....152 A7
  RAW/HAS BB4 ....196 C2
  WGNW/BIL/OR WN5 ....255 J5
Park View FUL/RIB PR2 * 151 L1
Park View St NLSN BB9 ....122 C4
Park View Ct BPOOLS FY4 ....124 F5
Park View Rd LSTA FY8 ....146 E2
Park Wall Rd HTWN L38 ....248 C8
  SFTN L29 ....257 K2
Parkway BPOOLE FY3 ....105 K5
Park Wy COL BB8 ....103 M5
  FMBY L37 ....247 J2
Parkway NTHTN L30 ....258 C6
Park Wy PRES PR1 ....152 A7
Parkway ROCH OL11 ....234 E2
  WGNNW/ST WN6 ....245 K1
Park Wy West KKBY L32 ....259 L8
Parkwood Av
  PDHM/BLYW BB12 ....6 A2
Park Wood Rd RAW/HAS BB4 ....195 H1
Parliament St BLY BB11 ....7 J6
  DWN BB3 ....191 K2
  HEY LA3 ....40 F7
  LANC LA1 ....3 H4
  SKEL WN8 ....254 F3
Parlick Av GAR/LONG PR3 * 114 C2
Parlick Rd FUL/RIB PR2 ....153 K1
  GAR/LONG PR3 ....283 R9
Parramatta St RAW/HAS BB4 ....195 K1
Parr Cottage Cl CHLY/EC PR7 ....205 M4
Parr La CHLY/EC PR7 ....205 L4
Parrock Cl PRES PR1 ....152 E1
Parrock Rd NLSN BB9 ....122 E1
Parrock St BWCK/EAR BB18 * 293 P8
  NLSN BB9 ....123 H3
  RAW/HAS BB4 ....177 K4
Parrox Fold PLF/KEOS FY6 ....79 F8
Parrox La KIRK/FR/WAR PR4 ....94 F2
Parr's La ORM L39 ....251 G3
Parrys Wy PLF/KEOS FY6 ....86 A7
Parsley Cl BISP FY2 ....96 C4
Parsonage Av GAR/LONG PR3 ....116 A8
Parsonage Brow WGN8 LA4 ....254 C3
Parsonage Dr NLSN BB9 ....122 F6
Parsonage Gdns
  KIRK/FR/WAR PR4 ....183 K6
Parsonage La GAR/LONG PR3 ....94 F2
Parsonage Rd BBN BB1 ....137 J8
  SKEL WN8 ....254 D4
Parsonage St ACC BB5 ....159 H6
  COL BB8 ....103 M4
Parson La CLI BB7 ....99 H3
Parson's Brow CHLY/EC PR7 ....207 M4
  RNFD/HAY WA11 ....262 B5
Parson's Bullough Rd
  CHLYE PR6 ....209 H7
Parsons Cl LANC LA1 ....54 E7
Parsons Close La SETT BD24 ....1 J7
Partridge Av CLV/TH FY5 ....81 J7
Partridge Cl ROCH OL11 ....234 C4
Partridge Dr ACC BB5 ....176 B2
Partridge Hl
  PDHM/BLYW BB12 ....141 G2
Partridge Hill St
  PDHM/BLYW BB12 * 141 G3
Partridge CSBY/BLUN L23... ....256 A7
  KKBY L32 ....259 L8
Part St STHP PR8 ....12 F7
Pashmire Brow CLI BB7 ....118 B5
Passmonds Crs ROCH OL11 ....234 E3
Passmonds Wy ROCH OL11 ....234 E3
The Pass MILN OL16 ....235 K4
Past La CLI BB7 ....276 F10

Pasture Cl BLY BB11 ....6 B9
  BWCK/EAR BB18 ....293 R3
Pasture Dr COL BB8 ....296 A2
  GAR/LONG PR3 ....284 C9
Pasture Fld PLF/KEOS FY6 ....85 L5
Pasture Field Cl
  CROS/BRETH PR26 ....185 M3
Pasturegate BLY BB11 ....6 B8
Pasturegate Av BLY BB11 ....6 B8
Pasture Gv CLI BB7 ....118 D4
Pasturelands Dr CLI BB7 ....118 D8
Pasture La CARN LA5 ....32 D8
  NLSN BB9 ....102 E6
  RNFD/HAY WA11 ....262 D7
The Pastures BBNW BB2 ....156 D3
  CHTN/BK PR9 ....181 G6
  FUL/RIB PR2 ....134 A2
Paterson St BBNW BB2 ....10 E8
Pathfinders Dr LANC LA1 ....54 D7
Patience St WHIT OL12 ....234 F2
Patmos St RAMS BL0 ....215 G5
Paton St WHIT OL12 ....218 A8
Patrick Av PDHM/BLYW BB12 ....140 A1
Patrick Crs RAW/HAS BB4 ....195 M1
Patten's Cl NTHTN L30 ....258 A4
Patten St BBN BB1 ....157 M6
  PRES PR1 ....9 G2
Patterdale Av BBN BB1 ....157 M8
  BPOOLE FY3 ....5 M7
  FTWD FY7 ....81 G3
Patterdale Cl BRFD/BLYE BB10...122 F7
  ROCH OL11 ....234 F3
  STHP PR8 ....220 E8
Patterdale Crs MGHL L31 ....259 H1
Patterdale Rd LANC LA1 ....3 K7
Pattison St BRFD/BLYE BB10 ....142 E1
Paul's La CHTN/BK PR9 ....180 C8
Paulhan St BRFD/BLYE BB10 ....142 E1
Pavey Cl BPOOLS FY4 ....125 J3
Pavilion Cl WHIT OL12 ....235 J1
The Pavilions FUL/RIB PR2 ....8 B4
Pavilion Vw
  CROS/BRETH PR26 ....204 D1
Paxton Pl SKEL WN8 ....253 M7
Paxton St ACC BB5 ....159 L5
Paynter Cl ACC BB5 ....159 K1
  CLI BB7 ....119 G2
Paythorne Av
  BRFD/BLYE BB10 ....143 G6
Paythorne Br CLI BB7 ....278 F8
Paythorne Cl BPOOLE FY3... ....105 L2
Peabody St DWN BB3 ....191 K1
Peace Cl CLV/TH FY5 ....81 K7
Peace St BLY BB11 ....6 A5
Peach Gv MGHL L31 ....259 L7
Peachtree Ct FUL/RIB PR2 ....133 G5
Peacock Crs LIT OL15 ....42 D4
Peacock Hall Rd LEYL PR25 ....186 A4
Peacock Hill Cl FUL/RIB PR2 ....133 L4
Peacock La HGHB LA2 ....42 D1
  TOD OL14 ....303 L9
Peahall La GAR/LONG PR3 ....282 D5
Pearfield CLI BB7 ....186 D1
Pearl Av BISP FY2 ....105 J2
Pearl St ACC BB5 ....159 J6
  BBN BB1 ....157 J2
  ROCH OL11 ....234 F3
Pear Tree Av CHLY/EC PR7 ....207 J8
Pear Tree Cl HEY LA3 ....169 H1
Pear Tree Crs BBR PR5 ....169 G1
Pear Tree Cft
  KIRK/FR/WAR PR4 ....166 D3
Pear Tree La CHLY/EC PR7 ....187 H3
Pear Tree Rd CHLYE PR6 ....169 L8
Peartree Rd
  CROS/BRETH PR26 ....184 E8
Pear Tree St BBR PR5 ....169 H1
Peart St BRFD/BLYE BB10 ....142 E1
Pechell St FUL/RIB PR2 ....8 B5
Pedder Av HEY LA3 ....65 H2
  HEY LA3 ....65 J2
  PLF/KEOS FY6 ....86 D2
Pedder Rd HEY LA3 ....65 J2
Pedder Gv FUL/RIB PR2 ....151 K3
Pedder's La BPOOLS FY4... ....125 G4
  FUL/RIB PR2 ....151 K2
Pedder St FUL/RIB PR2 ....8 A6
  MCMB LA4 ....41 J8
Pedders Wy FUL/RIB PR2 ....151 L1
Pedler Brow La WHIT OL12 ....219 H5
Peebles Cl NWD/KWIPK L33... ....260 A5
Peebles Gv BLY BB11 ....6 B9
Peel Av BPOOLE FY3 ....105 G4
  HEY LA3 ....52 D5
  LANC LA1 ....3 G1
Peel Bank Rd ACC BB5 ....158 C3
Peel Brow RAMS BL0 ....215 G5
Peel Cl BBNW BB2 ....173 H4
Peel Cottage Rd TOD OL14 ....303 N6
Peel Cott St TOD OL14 ....303 M7
Peel Gdns COL BB8 ....103 M6
Peel Hall St PRES PR1 ....9 L1
Peel Hll Br BPOOLS FY4 ....126 D5
Peel Mt BBN BB1 ....158 D7
  RAMS BL0 ....214 D7
Peel Mount BBN BB1 ....158 D7
Peel Park Av ACC BB5 ....160 A5
  CLI BB7 ....99 J3
Peel Park Cl CLI BB7 ....99 J4
  CLI BB7 ....99 H3
Peel Pl NLSN BB9 ....103 H5
Peel Rd COL BB8 ....103 L5
  FTWD FY7 ....77 J8
  LSTA FY8 ....146 C1
  SKEL WN8 ....254 A6
Peel St ACC BB5 ....159 G6
  BBNW BB2 ....10 A9
  CHLY/EC PR7 ....207 M4
  CHLYE PR6 ....99 H4
  CLI BB7 ....99 H3
  FUL/RIB PR2 ....8 B1
  LIT OL15 ....219 L6
  PDHM/BLYW BB12 ....141 J4
  RAW/HAS BB4 ....196 B3
  STHP PR8 ....200 D5
  WHIT OL12 ....235 M2
Peel Wk RAMS BL0 ....214 E7
  TOT/BURYW BL8 ....214 C6
Peers Clough Rd
  RAW/HAS BB4 ....195 G7
Peet Av ORM L39 ....241 G7
Peet's La CHTN/BK PR9 ....180 D2
Pegasus St ROCH OL11... ....234 F1
Pegbank La KKBY LA6... ....20 D3
Peg's La CLI BB7 ....146 F3

Peg Wy KIRK/FR/WAR PR4 ....148 C5
Pelham Av BPOOLE FY3 ....105 H1
Pelham St BBN BB1 ....11 J1
Pellon St TOD OL14 ....303 J4
Pemberton Dr MCMB LA4 ....41 M6
Pemberton Pl MCMB LA4 ....42 A6
Pemberton St BBN BB1 ....157 K7
Pembroke Av BISP FY2 ....84 E8
  MCMB LA4 ....41 J8
Pembroke Cl HOR/BR BL6 ....231 J7
Pembroke St WHIT OL12 *... ....235 K7
Pembroke Pl CHLY/EC PR7 ....207 L5
  LEYL PR25 ....186 D3
  PRES PR1 * 9 K4
Pembroke Rd LSTA FY8 ....146 A1
Pembroke St ACC BB5 ....159 M5
  BBNW BB2 ....10 A8
  BRFD/BLYE BB10 ....142 E2
  LIT OL15 ....219 L5
Pembury Av PRES PR1 ....152 B6
Penda Dr NWD/KWIPK L33... ....260 B5
Pendennis ROCH OL11 * 235 H5
Pendle Av ACC BB5 ....159 J7
  BCUP OL13 ....179 K7
  CLI BB7 ....291 K10
  LANC LA1 ....67 G4
Pendlebury Cl
  KIRK/FR/WAR PR4 ....166 E3
Pendle Cl BCUP OL13 ....197 K1
  BPOOLE FY3 ....105 J2
Pendle Ct GAR/LONG PR3 ....114 D5
  KIRK/FR/WAR PR4 ....128 D5
  SKEL WN8 ....254 A8
Pendle Dr BBNW BB2 ....173 J1
  CLI BB7 ....118 D4
  HOR/BR BL6 ....231 M6
  LITH L21 ....257 M7
  ORM L39 ....241 K5
Pendle Flds
  PDHM/BLYW BB12 ....122 A4
Pendle Hill Cl FUL/RIB PR2 ....133 M4
Pendlehurst St FUL/RIB PR2 ....6 D1
Pendlemist Vw COL BB8 ....103 M8
Pendle Pl LSTA FY8 ....146 F7
  SKEL WN8 ....254 A7
Pendle Rd CLI BB7 ....291 N10
  CLI BB7 ....99 J3
  GTH/LHO BB6 ....139 H5
  LANC LA1 ....42 C9
  LEYL PR25 ....187 G2
  NLSN BB9 ....122 A4
Pendle St ACC BB5 ....159 K7
  BBN BB1 ....11 K4
  NLSN BB9 ....103 G5
  PDHM/BLYW BB12 ....141 G3
Pendle St East CLI BB7 ....120 C4
Pendle St West CLI BB7 ....120 C4
Pendleton Av ACC BB5 ....159 J7
  RAW/HAS BB4 ....177 K7
Pendleton Rd CLI BB7 ....119 G2
Pendle Vw ACC BB5 * 160 C1
  CLI BB7 ....290 C8
  GTH/LHO BB6 ....117 M5
Pendle Wy COL BB8 ....295 J12
  PDHM/BLYW BB12 ....121 K6
  PDHM/BLYW BB12 ....6 B2
  SKP/WHF BD23 ....294 C2
Penfold MGHL L31 ....259 H2
Pengarth Rd HOR/BR BL6 ....231 M6
Penguin St PRES PR1 ....152 E2
Penhale Cl HEY LA3 ....52 D5
Penhale Ct HEY LA3 ....52 D5
Penhale Gdns HEY LA3 * 52 D5
Penhill Cl BISP FY2 ....105 G3
Penistone Av MILN OL16 ....235 K5
Penistone St PDHM/BLYW BB12...6 D1
Penketh Pl SKEL WN8 ....253 M6
Pennine Av CHLY/EC PR7 ....207 G2
  WGNS/IIMK WN3 ....255 M8
Pennine Bridleway WHIT OL12..218 A5
Pennine Cl BPOOLE FY1 ....4 E5
  HOR/BR BL6 ....231 M6
Pennine Crs NLSN BB9 ....122 F6
Pennine Dr WHIT OL12 ....218 A5
Pennine Gdns GAR/LONG PR3...283 R8
Pennine Pl PDHM/BLYW BB12..140 F2
  TOD OL14 ....303 M1
Pennine Pl SKEL WN8 ....253 L5
Pennine Rd BCUP OL13 ....197 K1
  CHLYE PR6 ....208 B2
  HOR/BR BL6 ....231 M6
The Pennines FUL/RIB PR2 ....132 C4
Pennine Vw GAR/LONG PR3 ....88 G6
  GAR/LONG PR3 ....88 G2
  KKBY L32 ....259 M8
  NLSN BB9 ....122 F6
  PLF/KEOS FY6 ....83 G3
  SKP/WHF BD23 ....294 C2
Pennington Av ORM L39 ....241 H6
Penn St HOR/BR BL6 ....231 M8
  MILN OL16 ....235 J4
Pennyfarthing La CLV/TH FY5..85 K1
Penny Gn SETT BD24 ....265 M8
Penny House La ACC BB5 ....159 M4
Pennystone Rd BISP FY2 ....84 D7
Penny Stone Rd HGHB LA2 ....43 K4
Penny St BBN BB1 ....10 F5
  LANC LA1 ....3 G6
  PRES PR1 ....9 G4
Penrhos St FTWD FY7 ....81 K7
Penrhyn Rd LANC LA1 ....2 C8
Penrith Av CLV/TH FY5 ....81 K7
  HEY LA3 ....52 D5
  STHP PR8 ....220 E8
Penrith Crs COL BB8 ....123 L1
  MGHL L31 ....259 H1
Penrith Rd COL BB8 * 103 M8
Penrith St ROCH OL11 ....235 H6
Penrod Wy HEY LA3 ....52 C5
Penrose Av BPOOLS FY4 ....5 J1
Penrose Pl SKEL WN8 ....254 B7
Penshaw Av CLV/TH FY5 ....81 L7
Penswick Av CLV/TH FY5 ....85 H2
Pentland Av NWD/KWIPK L33..260 A5
Pentland Rd LANC LA1 ....54 C8
Penwortham Hall Gdns
  PRES PR1 ....152 B8
Penwortham Wy PRES PR1 ....167 J2
Pen-Y-Ghent Wy
  BWCK/EAR BB18 ....293 P5
Penzance St BBNW BB2 * 172 C1
Peplow Rd HEY LA3 ....52 D5
Pepper La WGNNW/ST WN6...228 E8
Perch Pool La CHTN/BK PR9 ....201 J7
Percival St ACC BB5 ....159 J5
  BBN BB1 ....11 H1

DWN BB3 ....173 J8
Percy Rd LANC LA1 ....3 H9
Percy St ACC BB5 ....158 E6
  BBN BB1 ....157 J1
  BPOOL FY2 ....104 B7
  CHLY/EC PR7 ....208 A4
  COL BB8 ....296 B5
  FTWD FY7 ....77 J7
  MILN OL16 ....235 J4
  NLSN BB9 ....123 G4
  PRES PR1 ....9 K3
  RAMS BL0 ....214 E6
  WHIT OL12 ....302 B6
Peregrine Dr DWN BB3 ....173 G8
Peregrine Pl LEYL PR25 ....186 A1
Peridot Cl BBN BB1 ....157 J1
Perimeter Rd NWD/KWIPK L33..261 H8
Peronne Crs BBN BB1 ....158 A6
Perpignam Wy LANC LA1 * 3 H7
Perry Cl ROCH OL11 ....235 G6
Perry Rd FUL/RIB PR2 ....151 J3
Perry St DWN BB3 ....191 K1
Pershore Gdns BPOOLE FY3....105 G5
Pershore Gv STHP PR8 ....220 D7
Pershore Rd LSTA FY8 ....145 J4
Persia St ACC BB5 ....159 J5
Perth Cl CLV/TH FY5 ....85 J4
  NWD/KWIPK L33 ....260 A5
Perthshire Gv CHLY/EC PR7 ....187 J3
Perth St ACC BB5 ....159 K6
  BBNW BB2 ....10 A8
  BLY BB11 ....6 A5
  LANC LA1 ....3 J2
Peter Birtwistle Cl COL BB8 ....296 B6
Peterborough Dr NTHTN L30..258 B7
Peterfield Rd PRES PR1 * 168 F3
Peter Martin St HOR/BR BL6..231 J7
Peters Av BRSC L40 ....225 H7
Petersbottom La HGHB LA2 ....49 H4
Peters Bldgs BPOOLE FY3 * 105 G5
Peters Rw BBN BB1 * 158 F2
Peter St ACC BB5 ....159 K6
  BBN BB1 ....11 J1
  BPOOL FY1 ....4 D4
  CHLY/EC PR7 ....207 M3
  COL BB8 ....296 B5
  LANC LA1 * 3 H7
  LEYL PR25 ....187 G2
  NLSN BB9 * 103 G5
  RAW/HAS BB4 ....195 K1
  WGNW/BIL/OR WN5 ....255 K5
Petre Crs BBN BB1 ....158 E3
Petrel Cl BBN BB1 ....157 M4
  ROCH OL11 ....234 C4
Petre Rd ACC BB5 ....159 G2
Petrie St WHIT OL12 * 235 J2
Petts Crs LIT OL15 ....219 K5
Petunia Cl CLV/TH FY5 ....85 H2
Petworth Rd STHP PR8 ....220 E5
Pexwood Rd TOD OL14 ....303 J4
Pharos Pl FTWD FY7 ....77 L6
Pharos St FTWD FY7 ....77 L6
Pheasant Gn
  BRFD/BLYE BB10 ....142 E3
Pheasantford St
  BRFD/BLYE BB10 ....142 E3
Pheasant Wood Dr
  CLV/TH FY5 ....81 J6
Philip Av KIRK/FR/WAR PR4 ....128 C7
Philip Dr STHP PR8 ....221 H5
Philips Rd BBN BB1 ....157 L4
Philip St BWCK/EAR BB18 ....293 Q5
  DWN BB3 ....191 L2
  MILN OL16 ....235 J6
Phillips Cl CSBY/BLUN L23 ....257 L5
Phillip's Cl FMBY L37 ....247 J1
Phillips La COL BB8 ....103 L7
Phillips St BBN BB1 * 11 J1
Phillip St BPOOLS FY4 ....5 J8
Phoenix Cl TOD OL14 ....303 N2
Phoenix Pk BBN BB1 ....157 M4
Phoenix St LANC LA1 ....3 H4
  LIT OL15 ....219 L5
  TOD OL14 ....303 N1
  WHIT OL12 ....234 F2
Phyllis St BCUP OL13 ....197 L6
Physics Av LANC LA1 ....67 G3
Piccadilly Cl LANC LA1 ....54 C7
Piccadilly Rd BLY BB11 ....6 C5
Piccadilly Sq BLY BB11 ....6 C5
Pickard Cl BWCK/EAR BB18 ....294 A3
Pickard St LANC LA1 ....54 C7
Pickering Fold BBN BB1 ....173 L4
The Pickerings BBR PR5 * 168 F3
Pickering St NLSN BB9 * 122 A4
Picket Cl TOD OL14 ....300 G11
Pickle Cl BRSC L40 ....225 H7
Pickles St PDHM/BLYW BB12 ....6 B2
Pickmere Av BPOOLS FY4 ....125 J3
Pickmere Cl CLV/TH FY5 ....81 K7
Pickthall Ter CLV/TH FY5 ....303 N2
Pickthorn Cl LANC LA1 ....42 C7
Pickup Fold Rd DWN BB3 ....191 M4
Pickup Rd BBN BB1 ....158 D3
Pickup St ACC BB5 ....159 J6
  BBN BB1 ....11 H2
  BCUP OL13 * 179 K8
  MILN OL16 ....235 K4
  PRES PR1 ....9 H2
Picton Cl BBNW BB2 * 172 C1
Pierce St LANC LA1 ....2 C8
  PDHM/BLYW BB12 ....140 E2
Piercefield Rd FMBY L37 ....237 J7
Piercy St RAW/HAS BB4 ....178 C8
Pier La CARN LA5 ....16 F1
Pierston Av BISP FY2 ....104 F2
Pigot St WGNW/BIL/OR WN5..255 L5
Pike Ct BPOOL FY1 ....80 F4
Pikelaw Pl SKEL WN8 ....253 M6
Pikestone Cl CHLYE PR6 ....208 F4
Pike St ROCH OL11 ....235 J6
Pilgrim St NLSN BB9 ....123 J1
Pilgrims Wy PRES PR1 ....152 A7
Pilkington Dr ACC BB5 ....139 J7
Pilkington Rd STHP PR8 ....220 D6
Pilkington St BBNW BB2 ....10 A9
  RAMS BL0 ....214 D6
  RNFD/HAY WA11 ....262 C5
Pilling Av ACC BB5 ....176 A1
Pilling Barn La RAW/HAS BB4..178 E3
Pilling Cl CHLY/EC PR7 ....207 M6
  CHTN/BK PR9 ....180 C5
Pilling Ct BPOOLE FY3 ....105 K2

Pilling Crs BPOOLE FY3 ....105 K2
Pilling La CHLY/EC PR7 ....207 M6
  MGHL L31 ....249 K6
  PLF/KEOS FY6 ....78 D2
Pilling Pl SKEL WN8 ....253 M6
Pilling Wy RAW/HAS BB4 ....196 E5
  WHIT OL12 ....235 G3
Pilmuir Rd BBNW BB2 ....173 H3
Pilot St ACC BB5 ....159 L4
Pilsley St WGNW/BIL/OR WN5..255 K2
Pimbley Gv East MGHL L31 ....258 F5
Pimbley Gv West MGHL L31..258 F5
Pimbo La SKEL WN8 ....254 C8
Pimbo Rd RNFD/HAY WA11 ....263 H3
  SKEL WN8 ....253 M6
Pimlico Link Rd CLI BB7 ....99 L1
Pimlico Rd CLI BB7 ....99 K2
Pinch Clough Rd
  RAW/HAS BB4 ....178 C5
Pincock Brow CHLY/EC PR7 ....206 F3
Pincock St CHLY/EC PR7 ....206 F3
Pinder Cl CLI BB7 ....290 A11
Pinders La KKBY LA6 ....18 F1
Pinder St NLSN BB9 ....123 J1
Pine Av BPOOL FY1 ....5 J8
  KIRK/FR/WAR PR4 ....166 A2
  ORM L39 ....241 J4
Pine Cl CLI BB7 ....158 E3
  FUL/RIB PR2 ....133 J7
  HGHB LA2 ....43 H5
  KKBY L32 ....259 M8
  SKEL WN8 ....253 J2
  SKEL WN8 ....243 K2
Pine Crs ACC BB5 ....175 J1
Pine Crest ORM L39 ....250 E1
Pine Dl RNFD/HAY WA11 ....241 G3
Pine Dr ORM L39 ....241 H3
Pine Gv CHLY/EC PR6 ....188 A8
  CHTN/BK PR9 ....13 M5
  GAR/LONG PR3 ....284 B6
  ORM L39 ....241 J4
Pinehurst Av CSBY/WL L22 ....256 F5
Pine Rd TOD OL14 ....301 J12
Pines Cl BBR PR5 ....169 M7
The Pines CROS/BRETH PR26..185 J3
Pine St BBN BB1 ....157 K4
  BLY BB11 ....7 J5
  DWN BB3 ....191 L3
  LANC LA1 ....2 F4
  LIT OL15 ....219 L5
  MCMB LA4 * 41 K7
  MILN OL16 ....235 L4
  NLSN BB9 ....123 J3
Pinetree Cl NTHTN L30 ....258 C8
Pine Wks FUL/RIB PR2 ....150 F2
Pineway CLV/TH FY5 ....85 H7
Pine Wy KIRK/FR/WAR PR4 ....128 C7
Pinewood BBNW BB2 ....172 C3
  SKEL WN8 ....244 A8
Pinewood Av BISP FY2 ....85 H7
  CARN LA5 ....42 E1
  FMBY L37 ....247 G2
  GAR/LONG PR3 ....111 M8
  HGHB LA2 ....44 E6
  MCMB LA4 ....41 J8
  PLF/KEOS FY6 ....78 D6
Pinewood Cl FMBY L37 ....247 G1
  HGHB LA2 ....66 D1
  STHP PR8 ....222 F2
Pinewood Crs LEYL PR25 ....186 B3
  WGNW/BIL/OR WN5 ....255 H5
Pinewood Dr ACC BB5 ....160 A4
  NLSN BB9 ....123 K4
Pinewood Gdns
  NWD/KWIPK L33 ....260 B6
Pinfold KIRK/FR/WAR PR4 ....166 D3
  NLSN BB9 ....123 H6
Pinfold Cl FUL/RIB PR2 ....133 H6
  NTHTN L30 ....258 A6
Pinfold Ct LANC LA1 * 3 H1
Pinfold Cft SKP/WHF BD23 ....281 L2
Pinfold La BRSC L40 ....223 J8
  GAR/LONG PR3 ....114 D7
  GAR/LONG PR3 ....89 M7
  KIRK/FR/WAR PR4 ....109 M2
  LANC LA1 ....3 G1
  STHP PR8 ....220 C6
Pinfold Pl KIRK/FR/WAR PR4..128 C7
  NLSN BB9 ....123 C6
  SKEL WN8 ....254 A7
Pinfold St PRES PR1 ....153 G3
Pingle Cft CHLYE PR6 ....187 K1
Pingwood La NWD/KWIPK L33..260 B6
Pink Pl BBNW BB2 ....156 E8
Pink St PDHM/BLYW BB12 ....141 M5
Pinner La RAW/HAS BB4 ....177 J4
Pinners Cl RAMS BL0 ....214 E6
Pintail Cl CROS/BRETH PR26..185 J2
  WHIT OL12 ....235 H5
Pioneer Cl HOR/BR BL6 ....231 M7
Pioneer St HOR/BR BL6 ....231 M7
  LIT OL15 ....219 L6
  ROCH OL11 ....234 F1
  TOD OL14 ....303 K8
Piper Lea RAW/HAS BB4 ....196 C2
Pipers Cl ROCH OL11 ....234 A3
Piper's La KKBY LA6 ....19 J2
Pippin St BRSC L40 ....241 K1
  CHLYE PR6 ....170 B7
Pit Hey Pl SKEL WN8 ....253 M6
Pit La KKBYL LA6 ....17 G8
Pits Farm Av ROCH OL11 ....234 F3
Pitshouse La WHIT OL12 ....234 B1
Pittman Ct FUL/RIB PR2 ....132 E3
Pittman Wy FUL/RIB PR2 ....132 E3
Pittsdale Av BPOOLS FY4 ....125 K1
Pitts House La CHTN/BK PR9..200 C5
Pitt St CHTN/BK PR9 ....200 C5
  LANC LA1 ....3 H5
  PDHM/BLYW BB12 * 141 G3
  PRES PR1 ....9 G3
  TOD OL14 ....303 N2
  WHIT OL12 ....235 J3
Pitville Av BPOOLS FY4 ....173 J8
Pitville St BLY BB11 ....162 A1
Plainmoor Dr CLV/TH FY5 ....85 J4
Plain Pl BBNW BB2 ....157 K4
Plane St BBN BB1 ....157 K4
  BCUP OL13 ....179 J7
  TOD OL14 ....300 H12
Plane Tree Cl BLY BB11 ....162 A1
Plantain Wk HEY LA3 ....53 G1
Plantation Av CARN LA5 ....16 F2
  PLF/KEOS FY6 ....78 F3
Plantation Gv CARN LA5 ....16 F2
Plantation La HGHB LA2 ....271 N1
Plantation Rd ACC BB5 ....160 A5
  BBNW BB2 ....172 E2
  BRSC L40 ....224 E7

EDGW/EG BL7 ... 213 J4
Plantation Sq ACC BB5 ... 160 A5
Plantation St ACC BB5 ... 159 M6
  BCUP OL13 ... 196 F3
  BRFD/BLYE BB10 * ... 7 H1
  NLSN BB9 ... 123 H2
  RAW/HAS BB4 ... 195 L1
The Plantation SKP/WHF BD23... 266 C10
The Planters NTHTN L30 ... 258 D7
Plant St ACC BB5 ... 159 G8
Platt Cl ACC BB5 ... 159 G8
Platten Gv MCMB LA4 ... 41 H6
Platting La ROCH OL11 ... 235 K7
Platt La WGN WN1 ... 229 L8
Platts La LEY L40 ... 242 A1
Platt St BPOOL FY1 ... 104 F5
Pleasant Gv CLV/TH FY5 ... 85 L1
Pleasant Pl BLY BB11 * ... 6 F5
Pleasant St BPOOL FY1 ... 104 E4
  LSTA FY8 ... 146 E8
Pleasant Vw BPOOLS FY4 * ... 125 K7
  BWCK/EAR BB18 ... 294 F6
  CHLY/EC PR7 ... 229 J1
  CHLYE PR6 ... 189 K2
  DWN BB3 ... 192 C2
  RAW/HAS BB4 ... 196 C2
Pleasington Av
  GAR/LONG PR3 ... 284 C9
Pleasington Cl BBNW BB2 ... 156 E7
  BPOOLS FY4 ... 125 K3
Pleasington Gv
  BRFD/BLYE BB10 ... 143 G6
Pleasington La BBNW BB2 ... 171 M3
Pleasington St BBNW BB2 ... 156 E7
Pleck Farm Av BBN BB1 ... 157 H3
Pleckgate Fold BBN BB1 ... 157 G2
Pleckgate Rd BBN BB1 ... 157 G3
Pleck Pl PLF/KEOS FY6 ... 85 L5
Plevna Rd PRES PR1 ... 152 F3
Plex La ORM L39 ... 239 L5
Plex Moss La STHP PR8 ... 238 F2
The Ploughlands FUL/RIB PR2 ... 151 H2
Plough La BRSC L40 ... 242 D8
Ploughmans Ct FUL/RIB PR2 ... 134 A2
Plover Cl CLV/TH FY5 ... 81 J6
  ROCH OL11 ... 234 B4
Plover Dr HEY LA3 ... 52 H4
Plover St PDHM/BLYW BB12 ... 6 A3
  PRES PR1 ... 152 E1
Plovers Wy BPOOLE FY3 ... 105 L5
Plover Vw PDHM/BLYW BB12 ... 6 A3
Plox Brow KIRK/FR/WAR PR4 ... 183 K5
Plumbe St BLY BB11 ... 7 H6
Plumpton Av BPOOLS FY4 ... 125 J6
Plumpton Rd
  KIRK/FR/WAR PR4 ... 131 H1
Plumpton La
  KIRK/FR/WAR PR4 ... 127 H4
  ORM L39 ... 239 H1
Plumpton Rd FUL/RIB PR2 ... 151 M1
Plumtree Cl FUL/RIB PR2 ... 132 F5
Plunge Rd RAMS BL0 ... 195 H8
Plungington Rd PRES PR1 ... 152 B1
Plymouth Av FTWD FY7 ... 80 F4
Plymouth Gv CHLYE PR6 ... 208 B3
Plymouth Rd BISP FY2 ... 105 J2
Poachers Trail LSTA FY8 ... 146 B4
Poachers Wy CLV/TH FY5 ... 81 K7
Pochard Cl CLV/TH FY5 ... 85 J2
Pocklington St ACC BB5 ... 176 A9
Poets' Rd PDHM/BLYW BB12 ... 141 J4
Pointer Ct LANC LA1 ... 3 H9
Pointer Gv HCHB LA2 ... 43 L4
Poke St WGNW/BIL/OR WN5 ... 255 J6
Poland St ACC BB5 ... 159 J6
Polefield FUL/RIB PR2 ... 132 B4
Pole La DWN BB3 ... 191 M4
Pole St PRES PR1 ... 9 K5
Police Cots BBN BB1 * ... 173 L4
Police St DWN BB3 ... 191 K2
Pollard Gv LIT OL15 ... 219 H6
Pollard Pl LANC LA1 ... 42 F7
Pollard St ACC BB5 ... 159 M4
  BLY BB11 ... 6 A5
  PRES PR1 ... 8 F2
  TOD OL14 ... 300 H12
Pollux Ga LSTA FY8 ... 145 M7
Polperro Dr KIRK/FR/WAR PR4 .. 148 C5
Pomfret St BBNW BB2 ... 10 B4
  BLY BB11 ... 6 C4
Pomona St ROCH OL11 ... 235 J6
Pompian Brow
  CROS/BRETH PR26 ... 184 B5
Pond Cl KIRK/FR/WAR PR4 ... 183 H4
Pond Gdns PLF/KEOS FY6 ... 85 L5
Pond St CARN LA5 * ... 33 J1
Pond Ter CARN LA5 ... 33 J1
Pont St NLSN BB9 ... 123 C4
Pool Cl FTWD FY7 ... 80 F2
Poole Rd FUL/RIB PR2 ... 132 D7
Poole St BBN BB1 ... 157 M6
Pool Foot La
  KIRK/FR/WAR PR4 ... 107 H5
  PLF/KEOS FY6 ... 87 G7
Pool Hey La STHP PR8 ... 200 E8
Poolhill Cl CLV/TH FY5 ... 85 H4
Pool House La FUL/RIB PR2 ... 131 J6
Pool La KIRK/FR/WAR PR4 ... 148 D7
Poolside KIRK/FR/WAR PR4 ... 148 F5
Poolside Wk CHTN/BK PR9 ... 180 F7
Pool St CHTN/BK PR9 ... 180 F7
Pope La FUL/RIB PR2 ... 153 J1
  KIRK/FR/WAR PR4 ... 167 L2
Pope Wk PRES PR1 ... 152 B1
Poplar Av BBR PR5 ... 169 J2
  BPOOLE FY3 ... 5 H1
  CHLY/EC PR7 ... 186 F7
  CSBY/BLUN L23 ... 257 J6
  GTH/LHO BB6 ... 139 G5
  KIRK/FR/WAR PR4 ... 148 E3
  KIRK/FR/WAR PR4 ... 148 C6
  KIRK/FR/WAR PR4 ... 128 D1
  PLF/KEOS FY6 ... 106 D1
  TOD OL14 ... 301 K12
Poplar Cl ACC BB5 ... 159 J8
  BBN BB1 ... 158 A4
  BBR PR5 ... 169 J2
Poplar Dr CHLY/EC PR7 ... 229 J1
  CHLY/EC PR7 ... 230 C5
Poplar St CHLY/EC PR7 ... 229 J1
  NLSN BB9 ... 123 J2
  RAW/HAS BB4 ... 176 B1
  STHP PR8 ... 200 B5
Poppy Av CHLYE PR6 ... 208 A1

Poppyfield KIRK/FR/WAR PR4 . 131 J5
Poppyfields KIRK/FR/WAR PR4. 165 H2
Poppyfield Vw ROCH OL11 ... 234 B3
Poppy La ORM L39 ... 251 J2
Porritt Av LANC LA1 ... 2 D6
Porritt Cl ROCH OL11 ... 234 B5
Porritt Wy RAMS BL0 ... 214 F4
Portal Gv PDHM/BLYW BB12 ... 141 L5
Portal Pl PRES PR1 ... 9 J6
Porters Rw PLF/KEOS FY6 * ... 82 F4
Porter St ACC BB5 ... 159 J5
Porter St East
  KIRK/FR/WAR PR4 ... 128 C5
Porters Wood Ct
  WGNW/BIL/OR WN5 ... 255 L4
Portfield La CLI BB7 ... 119 J8
Portfield Rd CLI BB7 ... 119 H7
Portland Dr HEY LA3 ... 53 J1
Portland Rd BPOOL FY1 ... 5 G4
  GTH/LHO BB6 ... 137 M3
Portland St ACC BB5 ... 159 K5
  BBNW BB2 ... 10 A3
  CHLY/EC PR7 ... 208 A7
  COL BB8 ... 296 C6
  DWN BB3 ... 191 L5
  LANC LA1 ... 3 G3
  NLSN BB9 ... 123 G3
  PRES PR1 ... 8 D5
  STHP PR8 ... 12 C1
Portman St PRES PR1 ... 9 M1
Portree Cl FUL/RIB PR2 ... 132 F6
Portree Crs BISP FY2 ... 158 A8
Portree Rd BISP FY2 ... 85 H5
Port Royal Av LANC LA1 ... 2 A7
Portsmouth Av
  BRFD/BLYE BB10 ... 143 H1
Portsmouth Cl CLV/TH FY5 ... 81 J7
Portsmouth Dr CHLYE PR6 ... 208 A3
Portway BISP FY2 ... 85 H5
Port Wy FUL/RIB PR2 ... 8 A2
Poston Av LANC LA1 ... 52 C6
Postern Gate Rd HCHB LA2 ... 55 M3
Post Horse La HCHB LA2 ... 36 B6
Post La KIRK/FR/WAR PR4 ... 148 C5
Post Office Av CHTN/BK PR9 ... 13 H1
Pot House La ACC BB5 ... 175 H2
  DWN BB3 ... 173 M8
Potter La BBR PR5 ... 154 A4
Potter Pl SKEL WN8 ... 254 C4
Poulton Av ACC BB5 ... 159 K3
Poulton Crs BBR PR5 ... 154 A4
Poulton Dr PLF/KEOS FY6 ... 86 C8
Poulton Gdns PLF/KEOS FY6 ... 86 C8
Poulton Old Rd BPOOLE FY3 ... 105 J2
Poulton Rd BPOOLE FY3 ... 105 J3
  CHTN/BK PR9 ... 200 C4
  FTWD FY7 ... 77 H8
  MCMB LA4 ... 41 J6
  PLF/KEOS FY6 ... 85 M7
Poulton Sq MCMB LA4 ... 41 J6
Poulton St FTWD FY7 ... 77 K7
  FUL/RIB PR2 ... 8 A1
  KIRK/FR/WAR PR4 ... 128 D6
Poverty La MGHL L31 ... 259 J4
Powder House La HCHB LA2 ... 42 F6
Powderworks La MGHL L31 ... 250 F8
Powell Av BPOOLS FY4 ... 125 G3
Powell St BLY BB11 ... 6 D7
  BWCK/EAR BB18 ... 293 G4
  DWN BB3 ... 191 K1
Powis Dr KIRK/FR/WAR PR4 ... 183 K3
Powis Rd FUL/RIB PR2 ... 151 K3
Powys Cl RAW/HAS BB4 ... 194 E2
Poynter St PRES PR1 ... 152 F2
Prairie Crs BRFD/BLYE BB10 ... 122 E8
Pratt St BRFD/BLYE BB10 ... 142 D2
The Precincts CSBY/BLUN L23 .. 257 H7
Preesall Cl CHTN/BK PR9 ... 180 C7
  FUL/RIB PR2 ... 151 H2
  LANC LA1 ... 145 L4
Preesall Moss La PLF/KEOS FY6 .. 83 G1
Preesall Rd FUL/RIB PR2 ... 151 H2
Preese Gdns
  KIRK/FR/WAR PR4 ... 108 D2
Prefect Pl WGNW/BIL/OR WN5 .. 255 M3
Premier Wy PLF/KEOS FY6 ... 86 C8
Prenton Gdns CLV/TH FY5 ... 85 J4
Prescot Gn ORM L39 ... 241 G6
Prescot Pl BPOOLE FY3 ... 125 K1
  CLV/TH FY5 ... 85 M1
Prescot Rd KKBY L32 ... 260 E8
  ORM L39 ... 251 G7
Prescott Av BRSC L40 ... 203 K4
Prescott Br BRSC L40 ... 225 M3
Prescott La
  WGNW/BIL/OR WN5 ... 255 L3
Prescott Rd SKEL WN8 ... 254 D7
Prescott St BRFD/BLYE BB10 * .. 7 K5
  MILN OL16 ... 235 M1
Preseland La CSBY/BLUN L23 .. 257 H6
Press Rd LSTA FY8 * ... 145 G3
Prestbury Av BPOOLS FY4 * ... 124 F6
Prestbury Dr HEY LA3 ... 53 J1
Preston Lancaster New Rd
  GAR/LONG PR3 ... 90 E1
Preston Lancaster Old Rd
  GAR/LONG PR3 ... 91 G1
Preston Lancaster Rd
  GAR/LONG PR3 ... 284 B4
  GAR/LONG PR3 ... 91 J3
  HCHB LA2 ... 66 F5
Preston New Rd BBNW BB2... 10 D3
  BBR PR5 ... 153 L2
  BPOOLS FY4 ... 5 M8
  CHTN/BK PR9 ... 180 B7
  FUL/RIB PR2 ... 153 L2
  KIRK/FR/WAR PR4 ... 149 G4
  KIRK/FR/WAR PR4 ... 126 F5
Preston Nook CHLY/EC PR7 .. 205 M6
Preston Old Rd BBNW BB2... 171 M4
  BPOOLE FY3 ... 5 K7
  KIRK/FR/WAR PR4 ... 149 M2
  KIRK/FR/WAR PR4 ... 148 F5
  PORTWAY BISP FY2 * ... 148 F5
Preston Rd BBR PR5 ... 169 L6
  CHLY/EC PR7 ... 228 E1
  CHLYE PR6 ... 187 L5
  CHTN/BK PR9 ... 200 B3
  FUL/RIB PR2 ... 133 M2
  KIRK/FR/WAR PR4 ... 109 K2
  LEYL PR25 ... 186 F1
  LSTA FY8 ... 145 L1
  WGNNW/ST WN6 ... 229 G4
Preston St CARN LA5 ... 33 J1
  CHLY/EC PR7 ... 207 H1
  CHLYE PR6 ... 187 K8
  FTWD FY7 ... 77 L7
  KIRK/FR/WAR PR4 ... 148 F5
  WHIT OL12 ... 234 F7
Prestwich St BLY BB11 ... 6 B7

Prestwick Dr CSBY/BLUN L23 .. 256 F5
Pretoria St WHIT OL12 * ... 234 F2
Price La LANC LA1 ... 42 A1
Price St BPOOLS FY4 ... 124 A2
Prickshaw La WHIT OL12 ... 217 H1
Priestfield CLV/TH FY5 ... 85 J2
Priestland Av COL BB8 ... 103 L6
Priest Holme Br
  SKP/WHF BD23 ... 280 G3
Priesthouse Cl FMBY L37 ... 237 K8
Priesthouse La FMBY L37 ... 237 K8
Primary Av NTHTN L30 ... 258 E7
Primet Br COL BB8 ... 103 M7
Primet Hts COL BB8 ... 103 L8
Primet Hl COL BB8 ... 103 M7
Primet St COL BB8 ... 103 M7
Primrose Av BPOOLS FY4 ... 125 G5
Primrose Bank BBN BB1 ... 11 G2
  BISP FY2 ... 85 H8
Primrose Cl BBNW BB2 ... 172 E1
  CHTN/BK PR9 ... 180 D5
  FMBY L37 ... 237 L6
  KIRK/FR/WAR PR4 ... 165 H7
Primrose Ct LANC LA1 * ... 3 K8
  MCMB LA4 ... 41 J4
Primrose Dr BBN BB1 ... 11 G3
Primrose Gv PRES PR1 ... 132 F8
Primrose Hl BBNW BB2 ... 136 D8
  PRES PR1 ... 9 G5
Primrose Hill Rd CHLY/EC PR7 .. 186 E7
Primrose La PRES PR1 ... 132 F8
Primrose Rd CLI BB7 ... 99 G5
  PRES PR1 ... 132 F8
Primrose St ACC BB5 ... 159 K7
  BRFD/BLYE BB10 * ... 142 F2
  CHLYE PR6 ... 208 A3
  CLI BB7 ... 99 G4
  DWN BB3 ... 191 L3
  LANC LA1 ... 3 J8
  MCMB LA4 * ... 41 J4
  NLSN BB9 ... 122 F6
  WHIT OL12 ... 235 G3
Primrose Ter BBNW BB2 ... 172 E1
  BPOOLS FY4 * ... 125 K7
Primrose Wy PLF/KEOS FY6 ... 85 L5
Primula Dr DWN BB3 ... 173 K4
Prince Av CARN LA5 ... 33 J4
Prince Charles La STHP PR8 ... 12 D8
Prince Lee Mdw DWN BB3 ... 191 M4
Princes Ct PRES PR1 ... 151 L2
Princes Crs MCMB LA4 ... 41 M4
Princes Dr FUL/RIB PR2 ... 132 A5
Princes Gdn STHP PR8 ... 200 B6
Prince's Pk WGNNW/ST WN6 .. 245 J7
Princes Rd LSTA FY8 ... 146 A7
  PRES PR1 ... 151 L5
Princess Alexandra Wy
  HEY LA3 ... 52 C6
Princess Av CLI BB7 ... 99 J2
  KIRK/FR/WAR PR4 ... 128 C5
  LANC LA1 ... 54 E6
  PLF/KEOS FY6 ... 86 A8
  WHIT OL12 ... 218 F7
Princess Ct BPOOL FY1 * ... 4 D5
Princess Gdns BBNW BB2 ... 171 M4
Princess Rd CHLYE PR6 ... 230 E3
  CLV/TH FY5 ... 84 F1
  WGNNW/ST WN6 ... 245 M7
Princess St ACC BB5 ... 159 H5
  BBNW BB2 ... 10 A9
  BBR PR5 ... 168 E4
  BCUP OL13 ... 179 J8
  BPOOL FY1 ... 4 C1
  CHLY/EC PR7 ... 208 A5
  CLI BB7 ... 118 F6
  COL BB8 ... 103 M6
  GTH/LHO BB6 ... 139 G6
  LEYL PR25 ... 186 E2
  NLSN BB9 ... 123 G4
  PDHM/BLYW BB12 ... 141 G5
  PRES PR1 ... 9 L1
  WHIT OL12 ... 235 J2
  STHP PR8 ... 12 B1
Princes St BBN BB1 ... 158 E2
  STHP PR8 ... 12 B1
Prince's St BBNW BB2 ... 10 D5
Princess Wy CHLY/EC PR7 ... 207 C1
  PDHM/BLYW BB12 ... 6 E1
Prince St BCUP OL13 ... 302 A8
  BLY BB11 ... 6 C6
  DWN BB3 ... 191 J2
  MILN OL16 ... 235 L6
  RAMS BL0 ... 214 F5
Princes Wy CLV/TH FY5 ... 84 F2
  FTWD FY7 ... 80 F1
Princeway BPOOLS FY4 ... 124 F4
Pringle Bank CARN LA5 ... 26 A5
Pringle St BBN BB1 ... 11 H7
Pringle Wd CARN LA5 ... 26 A6
Prinny Hill Rd RAW/HAS BB4 .. 176 D8
Printers Fold
  PDHM/BLYW BB12 ... 141 H4
Priorsgate HEY LA3 ... 53 J1
Priors Oak Cots PRES PR1 * ... 8 A7
Priors Wk CLI BB7 ... 291 F1
Priorswood Pl SKEL WN8 ... 254 C7
Priory Cl BRSC L40 ... 225 G6
  FMBY L37 ... 247 L5
  HEY LA3 ... 53 L1
  KIRK/FR/WAR PR4 ... 183 K5
  LEYL PR25 ... 186 F1
  RAW/HAS BB4 ... 196 A5
  WGNW/BIL/OR WN5 ... 255 L5
Priory Ct BBNW BB2 ... 171 M1
  BLY BB11 ... 162 E1
  BPOOL FY1 ... 4 F2
Priory Dr DWN BB3 ... 191 M3
Priory Ga BPOOLS FY4 ... 124 F6
Priory Gra DWN BB3 ... 191 M3
  STHP PR8 ... 12 B1
Priory Gv ORM L39 ... 241 G7
Priory La HCHB LA2 ... 36 B5
  PRES PR1 ... 9 M3
Priory Ms STHP PR8 ... 12 A7
Priory Nook SKEL WN8 ... 254 F4
Priory Rd SKEL WN8 ... 254 F4
Priory St FUL/RIB PR2 ... 8 A1
  NLSN BB9 ... 123 J2
Priory Wk LANC LA1 ... 3 J1
Priory Wy BWCK/EAR BB18 .. 293 H5
Pritchard St BBNW BB2 ... 173 H1
Procter Moss Rd HCHB LA2... 67 J2
Procter St BBNW BB2 ... 11 G8
Proctor Cl NLSN BB9 ... 123 H4
Proctor Fold BBNW BB2 * ... 136 A4
Proctor Rd FMBY L37 ... 236 F7

Progress Av BBN BB1 * ... 157 K4
Progress Ct FY3 ... 105 L3
Progress Rd NLSN BB9 ... 103 J8
  DWN BB3 ... 191 L2
Progress St CHLYE PR6 ... 208 B3
  DWN BB3 ... 191 L2
Progress Wy BPOOLS FY4 ... 125 K6
Promenade BPOOL FY1 ... 104 B3
  BPOOLS FY4 ... 124 D4
  STHP PR8 ... 11 L8
  STHP PR8 ... 12 F3
Promenade North CLV/TH FY5 ... 80 F8
Promenade Rd FTWD FY7 ... 77 K6
Promenade South CLV/TH FY5 .. 84 F1
The Promenade CARN LA5 ... 16 D1
Prospect Av BBR PR5 ... 168 E3
  DWN BB3 ... 191 H1
  HGHB LA2 ... 42 D2
Prospect Dr HGHB LA2 ... 42 D2
Prospect Gdns DWN BB3 ... 191 H1
Prospect Gv MCMB LA4 ... 41 K7
Prospect Hl RAW/HAS BB4 ... 194 D1
Prospect Pl FUL/RIB PR2 ... 151 L2
  HEYW OL10 ... 234 A8
  PRES PR1 ... 152 B7
  SKEL WN8 ... 254 C6
Prospect Rd RAW/HAS BB4 ... 177 J8
Prospect St GTH/LHO BB6 ... 138 F6
  HOR/BR BL6 ... 231 K8
  LANC LA1 ... 3 J8
  LIT OL15 ... 219 L6
  LSTA FY8 ... 146 D8
  NLSN BB9 ... 103 G7
  ORM L39 ... 241 H7
  PDHM/BLYW BB12 ... 140 F3
  PRES PR1 ... 9 L4
  RAMS BL0 ... 214 E6
  RAW/HAS BB4 ... 195 K1
  TOD OL14 ... 303 L2
Prospect Ter CHLYE PR6 ... 189 K5
  NLSN BB9 ... 103 G7
Prospect Wy NTHTN L30 ... 258 E8
Provence Av GTH/LHO BB6 ... 117 M5
Providence St BBN BB1 ... 157 K3
  TOD OL14 ... 303 K6
Prudy Hl PLF/KEOS FY6 ... 86 A7
Prunella Dr DWN BB3 ... 173 K4
Pudding La TOD OL14 ... 300 F9
Pudding Pie Nook La
  GAR/LONG PR3 ... 112 C7
Puddle House La
  PLF/KEOS FY6 ... 106 C3
Pudsey Rd TOD OL14 ... 300 E10
Pullman St ROCH OL11 ... 235 J6
Pump House La
  CROS/BRETH PR26 ... 185 J3
Pump St BBNW BB2 ... 10 B5
  BLY BB11 ... 6 C4
  CLI BB7 ... 99 G3
  PRES PR1 ... 9 J2
Punnell's La MGHL L31 ... 249 J6
Punstock Rd DWN BB3 ... 191 J2
Pye Busk CLI BB7 ... 39 H4
Pye Busk Cl HGHB LA2 ... 39 H4
Pyes Bridge La MTHPE LA7 ... 18 C1
Pygon's Hill La MGHL L31 ... 250 A4

Q

Quail Holme Rd PLF/KEOS FY6 .. 78 A6
Quaker Brook La BBR PR5 ... 154 D8
Quakerfields DWN BB3 ... 191 J8
Quaker La DWN BB3 ... 191 H1
Quakers Vw FUL/RIB PR2 ... 133 G2
Quarlton Dr TOT/BURYW BL8... 213 L8
Quarrybank CLV/TH FY5 ... 85 J3
Quarry Bank GAR/LONG PR3 ... 284 B9
  NWD/KWIPK L33 ... 260 C8
Quarry Bank St
  PDHM/BLYW BB12 ... 141 M4
Quarry Cl NWD/KWIPK L33 ... 260 C8
Quarry Dl NWD/KWIPK L33 ... 260 C8
Quarry Dr ORM L39 ... 250 C7
Quarry Farm Cl CLI BB7 ... 291 J10
Quarry Hey NWD/KWIPK L33... 260 C8
Quarry Hey NWD/KWIPK L33... 260 C8
Quarry Mt ORM L39 ... 241 K5
Quarry Mount Ms LANC LA1 * .. 3 J1
Quarry Rd CHLYE PR6 ... 208 B5
  CHLYE PR6 ... 189 J4
  CSBY/BLUN L23 ... 257 K5
  HGHB LA2 ... 45 H7
  LANC LA1 ... 3 L6
Quarry St ACC BB5 ... 159 M6
  BBN BB1 ... 11 H3
  BCUP OL13 ... 197 K5
  PDHM/BLYW BB12 ... 141 G2
  RAMS BL0 ... 215 G5
  WHIT OL12 ... 302 B10
  WHIT OL12 ... 235 H2
Quayle Av BPOOLS FY4 ... 125 G3
Quayside FTWD FY7 ... 77 L8
The Quayside FTWD FY7 * ... 77 M8
Quebec Av BISP FY2 ... 85 G6
Quebec Rd BBNW BB2 ... 156 E3
  TOD OL14 ... 303 K6
Queen Anne St STHP PR8 ... 13 G4
Queen Elizabeth Ct
  MCMB LA4 * ... 41 H6
Queen Elizabeth Crs ACC BB5... 160 A6
Queen Mary Av LSTA FY8 ... 145 K6
Queens Av FMBY L37 ... 237 H6
  WHIT OL12 ... 218 F7
Queensberry Rd BLY BB11 ... 6 E4
Queensborough Rd ACC BB5 .. 159 L4
Queensbury Rd CLV/TH FY5 ... 84 F2
Queen's Cl PLF/KEOS FY6 ... 86 B8
Queenscourt Av PRES PR1 ... 168 B1
Queen's Crs KIRK/FR/WAR PR4 .. 128 E1
Queens Cft FMBY L37 ... 247 G1
Queensdale Cl BBR PR5 ... 153 H7
Queens Dr BPOOLE FY3 ... 106 A6
  CARN LA5 ... 16 E2
  FUL/RIB PR2 ... 132 A5
  GAR/LONG PR3 ... 114 C4
  MCMB LA4 ... 41 M5
  ROCH OL11 ... 235 H8
Queen's Dr ACC BB5 ... 159 J8
  CARN LA5 ... 33 J4
Queens Garth SKP/WHF BD23... 294 E2
Queensgate CHLY/EC PR7 ... 207 L4
  NLSN BB9 ... 122 F4
Queens Gn ORM L39 ... 239 J6
Queen's Gv CHLY/EC PR7 ... 207 M3
Queen's Lancashire Wy
  BLY BB11 ... 6 E4
Queens Pl KIRK/FR/WAR PR4... 128 E1
Queen's Prom BISP FY2 ... 104 E1
Queen Sq LANC LA1 ... 3 G7
Queens Rd ACC BB5 ... 159 M4

  BBN BB1 ... 11 L7
  BBR PR5 ... 153 H7
  BRFD/BLYE BB10 ... 7 H1
  CHLY/EC PR7 ... 207 L3
  DWN BB3 ... 191 L6
  FMBY L37 ... 247 G1
  FUL/RIB PR2 ... 132 B2
  LIT OL15 ... 219 L6
  LSTA FY8 ... 145 J6
Queens Rd West ACC BB5 ... 159 K4
Queen's Sq PLF/KEOS FY6 ... 86 A8
Queen's Ter BBNW BB2 ... 172 E2
  BCUP OL13 ... 197 H3
  FTWD FY7 ... 77 L6
Queen St ACC BB5 ... 159 H7
  ACC BB5 ... 139 J8
  BBR PR5 ... 168 E4
  BCUP OL13 ... 197 J1
  BLY BB11 ... 6 C1
  BPOOL FY1 ... 4 C1
  BRFD/BLYE BB10 ... 123 H8
  CARN LA5 ... 33 H2
  CLI BB7 ... 98 F3
  COL BB8 ... 103 M6
  DWN BB3 ... 191 J1
  FTWD FY7 ... 77 K7
  GTH/LHO BB6 ... 138 F6
  HOR/BR BL6 ... 231 K8
  LANC LA1 ... 3 L6
  LIT OL15 ... 219 L6
  LSTA FY8 ... 146 D8
  NLSN BB9 ... 103 G7
  ORM L39 ... 241 H7
  PDHM/BLYW BB12 ... 140 F3
  PRES PR1 ... 9 L4
  RAMS BL0 ... 214 E6
  RAW/HAS BB4 ... 195 K1
  TOD OL14 ... 303 L2
  WGNW/BIL/OR WN5 ... 255 L5
  WHIT OL12 ... 235 L3
Queensway CI PRES PR1 ... 151 L5
  BBNW BB2 ... 172 D3
  BBR PR5 ... 169 G2
  BPOOLS FY4 ... 124 F4
  CHLY/EC PR7 ... 207 H1
  CHLYE PR6 ... 189 J3
  CLI BB7 ... 99 H4
  KIRK/FR/WAR PR4 ... 148 J1
  LEYL PR25 ... 186 A6
  LSTA FY8 ... 145 L6
Queens Wy PLF/KEOS FY6 ... 86 A7
Queensway PRES PR1 ... 151 L5
  RAW/HAS BB4 ... 196 B2
  RNFD/HAY WA11 ... 262 A6
  ROCH OL11 ... 235 G8
  WGNNW/ST WN6 ... 245 J7

R

Rabbit La BRSC L40 ... 224 C8
  CLI BB7 ... 289 J3
Raby Sq MCMB LA4 * ... 41 J5
Raby St MCMB LA4 * ... 41 J5
  RAW/HAS BB4 ... 195 K1
Radburn Brow CHLYE PR6 ... 169 K4
Radburn Cl CHLYE PR6 ... 169 K4
  CSBY/BLUN L23 ... 257 J2
Radcliffe Rd FTWD FY7 ... 77 K8
Radcliffe Rd FTWD FY7 ... 77 K8
Radfield Rd DWN BB3 ... 191 J3
Radford Gdns DWN BB3 ... 191 K4
Radford St DWN BB3 ... 191 K3
Radley Av BPOOLE FY3 ... 105 J1
Radley Dr AIR/FAZ L10 ... 258 F8
Radnor Av CLV/TH FY5 ... 85 J2
Radnor Cl ACC BB5 ... 158 F7
Radnor Dr CHTN/BK PR9 ... 180 C8
Radnor St ACC BB5 ... 159 L4
  PRES PR1 ... 8 F2
Radway Cl CLV/TH FY5 ... 85 J4
Radworth Crs BPOOLS FY4 ... 125 L2
Raeburn Av BLY BB11 ... 142 B8
Raedale Av BRFD/BLYE BB10 .. 122 F4
Raglan Cl BLY BB11 ... 6 C6
  HEY LA3 ... 40 F7
Raglan St COL BB8 * ... 296 A7
  FUL/RIB PR2 ... 152 A1
  NLSN BB9 ... 123 G2
  TOD OL14 ... 303 L1
Raikes Hl BPOOL FY1 ... 4 F1
Raikes Hill Dr HGHB LA2 ... 42 C3
Raikes Ms BPOOL FY1 ... 4 F2
Raikes Pde BPOOL FY1 ... 4 F1
Raikes Rd CLV/TH FY5 ... 86 B3
  GAR/LONG PR3 ... 88 B5
  PRES PR1 ... 152 F2
Rail Cl RNFD/HAY WA11 ... 262 C1
Railgate BCUP OL13 ... 197 M3
Railton Av BBNW BB2 ... 172 D3
Railway Ap ORM L39 ... 241 H6
Railway Crossing La LANC LA1.. 54 B6
Railway Gv GBN BB21 ... 157 K4
Railway Pth ORM L39 ... 241 H7
Railway Rd BBN BB1 ... 10 F4
  CHLY/EC PR7 ... 230 D4
  CHLYE PR6 ... 208 A2
  CHLYE PR6 ... 187 K8
  DWN BB3 ... 191 J1
  RAW/HAS BB4 ... 176 E2
  SKEL WN8 ... 253 G3
Railway St BCUP OL13 ... 196 E3
  BLY BB11 ... 6 F3

BWCK/EAR BB18 ...... 293 Q5
CHLY/EC PR7 ...... 208 A4
COL BB8 ...... 296 A2
LANC LA1 ...... 3 H9
LEYL PR25 ...... 186 E1
MILN OL16 ...... 235 K5
NLSN BB9 ...... 122 D6
RAMS BL0 ...... 214 F5
STHP PR8 ...... 13 G7
TOD OL14 ...... 303 L1
Railway Ter GTH/LHO BB6 ...... 138 F7
KIRK/FR/WAR PR4 ...... 128 C5
NLSN BB9 ...... 122 N6
STHP PR8 ...... 12 F7
Railway Vw ACC BB5 ...... 159 M5
BBNW BB2 ...... 172 E1
Railway View Av CLI BB7 * 99 L7
Railway View Rd CLI BB7 * 99 L5
Raimond St BOL BL1 ...... 233 M8
Rainbow Dr MGHL L31 ...... 259 L7
Raines Rd SETT BD24 ...... 265 L9
Rainford By-Pass
RNFD/HAY WA11 ...... 262 A4
Rainford Rd ORM L39 ...... 252 D5
WGNW/BIL/OR WN5 ...... 263 L6
Rainhall Crs BWCK/EAR BB18 ...... 294 A6
Rainhall Rd BWCK/EAR BB18 ...... 293 Q5
Rake ROCH OL11 ...... 234 A4
Rake Foot RAW/HAS BB4 ...... 176 B8
Rake Head Barn La TOD OL14 ...... 303 K7
Rakehead La BCUP OL13 ...... 196 B5
Rakehouse Brow HGHB LA2 ...... 69 K7
Rake La KIRK/FR/WAR PR4 ...... 148 A5
Rakes Br BBN BB3 ...... 173 K4
Rakes House Rd NLSN BB9 ...... 123 H1
Rakes La SKP/WHF BD23 ...... 279 L9
Rakes Rd HGHB LA2 ...... 45 H4
Rake Ter LIT OL15 ...... 219 M5
Rake Top Av
PDHM/BLYW BB12 ...... 121 J5
Rakewood Rd LIT OL15 ...... 219 L8
Raleigh Av BPOOLS FY4 ...... 124 C6
Raleigh Cl LSTA FY8 ...... 145 G2
Raleigh Gdns LIT OL15 ...... 219 M2
Raleigh Rd FUL/RIB PR2 ...... 132 B5
Raleigh St PDHM/BLYW BB12 ...... 141 G3
Ralph St ACC BB5 ...... 159 M5
WHIT OL12 ...... 235 K2
Ralph's Wife's La
CHTN/BK PR9 ...... 181 J5
Ramlen Cl CSBY/BLUN L23 ...... 256 C8
Ramleh Pk CSBY/BLUN L23 ...... 256 D8
The Ramparts LANC LA1 ...... 3 H1
Ramper Ga CLV/TH FY5 ...... 85 G1
Ramsay Ct PLF/KEOS FY6 ...... 78 D3
Ramsay Pl MILN OL16 ...... 235 K3
Ramsay St MILN OL16 ...... 235 K3
Ramsay Ter MILN OL16 ...... 235 K3
Rambottom La RAMS BL0 ...... 214 F4
Ramsbottom Rd HOR/BR BL6 ...... 231 G2
Ramsbottom St ACC BB5 ...... 159 L4
RAW/HAS BB4 ...... 196 A5
Rams Clough La ACC BB5 ...... 175 K3
Ramsden La TOD OL14 ...... 302 H8
Ramsden Rd WHIT OL12 ...... 218 F5
Ramsden St CARN LA5 ...... 33 J1
TOD OL14 ...... 303 H8
Ramsden Wood Rd TOD OL14 ...... 303 J8
Ramsey Av BCUP OL13 ...... 197 K2
BPOOLE FY3 ...... 105 G4
PRES PR1 ...... 132 B2
Ramsey Cl LSTA FY8 ...... 145 G2
Ramsey Gv BRFD/BLYE BB10 ...... 142 F3
Ramsey Rd BBNW BB2 ...... 173 G2
Ramsgate Cl
KIRK/FR/WAR PR4 ...... 148 C5
Ramsgate Rd LSTA FY8 ...... 145 J3
Ramsgreave Av BBN BB1 ...... 157 G1
Ramsgreave Dr BBN BB1 ...... 156 F2
Ramsgreave Rd BBN BB1 ...... 137 H8
Ramshill Av PLF/KEOS FY6 ...... 85 J1
Ranaldsway LEYL PR25 ...... 185 M3
Randall Av WGNNW/ST WN6 ...... 245 K6
Randall Dr NTHTN L30 ...... 257 M8
Randall St BRFD/BLYE BB10 ...... 142 E3
Randal St BBN BB1 ...... 10 E2
Randle Av RNFD/HAY WA11 ...... 262 B3
Randle Brook Ct
RNFD/HAY WA11 ...... 262 B3
Randolph St BBN BB1 ...... 11 K6
Ranelagh Dr STHP PR8 ...... 221 J4
Ranger St ACC BB5 ...... 159 K6
Rangeway Av BPOOLS FY4 ...... 124 F4
Ranglet Rd BBR PR5 ...... 169 L2
Rangletts Av CHLY/EC PR7 ...... 207 M5
Ranglit Av FUL/RIB PR2 ...... 150 F2
Rankin Dr DWN BB3 ...... 192 B3
Ranlea Av MCMB LA4 ...... 42 A7
Ranleigh Dr SKEL WN8 ...... 243 K2
Rannoch Dr BBNW BB2 ...... 172 E1
Rantreefold Rd HGHB LA2 ...... 48 D3
Rapley La KIRK/FR/WAR PR4 ...... 110 F3
Ratcliffe Fold RAW/HAS BB4 ...... 176 D4
Ratcliffe St DWN BB3 ...... 191 M4
RAW/HAS BB4 ...... 176 D8
Ratcliffe Wharf La
GAR/LONG PR3 ...... 260 R10
Rathbone Rd RNFD/HAY WA11 L38 ...... 247 J7
Rathbone St MILN OL16 ...... 235 M4
Rathlyn Av BPOOLE FY3 ...... 105 H4
Rathmell Av BPOOLS FY3 * 105 L2
Rathmore Crs CHTN/BK PR9 ...... 180 E6
Ratten La KIRK/FR/WAR PR4 ...... 150 F5
Raveden Cl BOL BL1 ...... 233 M8
Raven Av RAW/HAS BB4 ...... 194 A5
Raven Cft RAW/HAS BB4 ...... 194 A5
Ravendale Cl WHIT OL12 ...... 234 D1
Ravenglass Av MGHL L31 ...... 259 G1
Ravenglass Cl BBNW BB2 ...... 173 K2
BPOOLS FY4 ...... 125 H4
KIRK/FR/WAR PR4 ...... 128 D4
Ravenhead Dr SKEL WN8 ...... 254 D1
Ravenhill Dr CHLY/EC PR7 ...... 207 M2
Raven Meols La FMBY L37 ...... 247 H1
Raven Oak La
BRFD/BLYE BB10 ...... 143 L6
Raven Pk RAW/HAS BB4 ...... 194 E3
Raven Rd BBNW BB2 * 156 N6
Ravens Cl LANC LA1 ...... 42 D8
Ravens's Cl BPOOLE FY3 ...... 105 H4
Ravens Close Brow HGHB LA2 ...... 37 L3
Ravenscroft Av ORM L39 ...... 241 J1
Ravenscroft Cl BBN BB1 ...... 157 K2
Ravenscroft Wy
BWCK/EAR BB18 ...... 293 R4
The Ravens FMBY L37 ...... 247 H1
Raven St NLSN BB9 ...... 123 J2
PRES PR1 ...... 152 F1
ROCH OL11 ...... 234 D7

Ravenswing Av BBNW BB2 ...... 156 E4
Ravenswood FUL/RIB PR2 ...... 153 H1
Ravenswood Av BPOOLE FY5 ...... 105 L4
Ravenwood Av BPOOLS FY4 ...... 125 G6
Rawcliffe Dr FUL/RIB PR2 ...... 151 L5
Rawcliffe Rd CHLY/EC PR7 ...... 207 M4
GAR/LONG PR3 ...... 87 N3
Rawcliffe St BLY BB11 * 7 H3
Rawcliffe St BPOOLS FY4 ...... 124 E3
Rawlinson Ct CHTN/BK PR9 * 13 M1
Rawlinson La CHTN/BK PR9 ...... 200 B2
Rawlinson La CHLY/EC PR9 ...... 230 B2
Rawlinson Rd DWN BB3 * 200 B2
Rawlinson St DWN BB3 * 191 L5
KIRK/FR/WAR PR4 ...... 128 C5
Raws Ct BLY BB11 * 7 G3
Rawson Av ACC BB5 ...... 159 K7
Rawsons Rake
TOT/BURYW BL8 ...... 214 D5
Rawson St BRFD/BLYE BB10 ...... 142 E2
Rawsthorne Av RAMS BL0 ...... 215 G1
Rawstorne Cl
KIRK/FR/WAR PR4 ...... 167 J1
Rawstorne Rd KIRK/FR/WAR PR4 ...... 167 H2
Rawstorne Rd PRES PR1 ...... 151 L6
Rawstron St BBNW BB2 ...... 10 A5
Rawthey Rd LANC LA1 ...... 2 C8
Raybourne Av PLF/KEOS FY6 ...... 85 M8
Ray Br SKP/WHF BD23 ...... 281 L1
Ray Bridge La SKP/WHF BD23 ...... 281 L1
Raygill Av BLY BB11 ...... 142 A8
Raygill La AIRE BD20 ...... 295 M7
Raygill Pl LANC LA1 ...... 2 D2
Ray La GAR/LONG PR3 ...... 284 E11
Raymond Av BISP FY2 * 105 G3
Raynor St BBNW BB2 ...... 10 A3
Rays Dr LANC LA1 ...... 54 E8
Read Hall Ct
PDHM/BLYW BB12 * 139 L1
Reading Cl BBN BB1 * 11 J6
Read's Av BPOOL FY1 * 4 E4
Read St ACC BB5 ...... 159 K2
Reaney Wy BPOOLS FY4 ...... 125 H4
Reapers Wy NTHTN L30 ...... 258 D7
Rectory Cl CHLY/EC PR7 ...... 207 M3
CROS/BRETH PR26 ...... 204 E1
DWN BB3 ...... 191 M3
RAW/HAS BB4 ...... 196 A2
Rectory Gdns HGHB LA2 ...... 269 M6
KIRK/FR/WAR PR4 ...... 183 K6
Rectory Paddock HGHB LA2 ...... 43 K5
Rectory Rd BPOOLS FY4 ...... 5 J9
CHTN/BK PR9 ...... 200 D3
PDHM/BLYW BB12 ...... 6 B1
Red Bank Rd BISP FY2 ...... 84 E7
Red Br KIRK/FR/WAR PR4 ...... 203 M1
Red Bridge La CARN LA5 ...... 17 H7
Red Brook St ROCH OL11 ...... 235 G4
Redbrow Wy NWD/KWIPK L33 ...... 260 B7
Redcar Av CLV/TH FY5 ...... 81 M6
FUL/RIB PR2 ...... 131 J7
Redcar Cl STHP PR8 ...... 200 C8
BPOOL FY1 ...... 104 E3
LANC LA1 ...... 55 G8
Redcar St WHIT OL12 ...... 235 H4
Red Cat La BRSC L40 ...... 225 H5
Redcliffe Gdns ORM L39 ...... 241 G6
Red Cross St PRES PR1 ...... 8 E4
Redcross St North
WHIT OL12 ...... 235 J3
Red Delph La RNFD/HAY WA11 ...... 262 A4
Reddyshore Scout Ga
TOD OL14 ...... 303 L10
Redearth Rd DWN BB3 ...... 191 K3
Redearth St DWN BB3 ...... 191 K3
Rede Av FTWD FY7 ...... 80 H1
Redeswood Av CLV/TH FY5 ...... 85 G3
Redfearn Wd WHIT OL12 ...... 234 E1
Redfern Wy ROCH OL11 ...... 234 A2
Red Fold ORM L39 ...... 250 F1
Redgate FMBY L37 ...... 247 K1
ORM L39 ...... 241 G6
Redgate Av CSBY/BLUN L23 ...... 257 K7
Redgate Cl BLY BB11 * 7 K9
Redgate Dr FMBY L37 ...... 247 L1
Redhill Av KIRK/FR/WAR PR4 ...... 166 F2
Redhill Dr STHP PR8 ...... 200 C8
Redhills Dr STHP PR8 ...... 200 C8
Red Hills Rd CARN LA5 ...... 16 D2
Red House La CHLY/EC PR7 ...... 205 L5
Redisher Cl RAMS BL0 ...... 214 C8
Redisher Cft RAMS BL0 ...... 214 C8
Redisher La TOT/BURYW BL8 ...... 214 B8
Rediam BBNW BB2 ...... 156 E4
Redland Cl LIT OL15 ...... 219 L5
Red La CHLY/EC PR7 ...... 206 B5
COL BB8 ...... 103 L4
WHIT OL12 ...... 235 L1
Red Lees Av BRFD/BLYE BB10 ...... 143 J8
Red Lees Rd BRFD/BLYE BB10 ...... 143 J7
Red Lion Cl MGHL L31 ...... 258 F2
Red Lion St BLY BB11 ...... 7 G5
BWCK/EAR BB18 ...... 294 F5
Red Lomes NTHTN L30 ...... 258 A6
Red Lumb St WHIT OL12 ...... 216 D7
Redman Rd BRFD/BLYE BB10 ...... 122 D6
Red Marsh Dr CLV/TH FY5 ...... 81 M7
Redmayne Dr CARN LA5 ...... 33 K1
Redmoor Crs NWD/KWIPK L33 ...... 260 B7
Redness St NLSN BB9 ...... 123 H1
Red Rake BBN BB1 ...... 156 F4
Redruth St PDHM/BLYW BB12 ...... 141 A3
Red Sands CARN LA5 * ...... 33 H
Redsands Dr FUL/RIB PR2 ...... 133 G6
Red Scar St COL BB8 ...... 103 M7
Redshank Dr HEY LA3 ...... 52 E5
Red Shell La ACC BB5 ...... 174 A5
Red Spar Rd BRFD/BLYE BB10 ...... 142 F1
Redstart Pl CLV/TH FY5 ...... 85 J2
Redvers Rd BRFD/BLYE BB10 ...... 173 H6
Redvers St BRFD/BLYE BB10 ...... 142 F2
Redvers Ter BPOOL FY1 ...... 104 E3
Redwald Cl NWD/KWIPK L33 ...... 260 C6
Redway CLV/TH FY5 ...... 81 J7
GTH/LHO BB6 ...... 138 G5
Redwing Dr CHLY/EC PR7 ...... 207 K4

Redwood WGNNW/ST WN6 ...... 245 L5
Redwood Av LEYL PR25 ...... 186 B3
MGHL L31 ...... 249 M8
WGNW/BIL/OR WN5 ...... 255 K5
Redwood Cha
KIRK/FR/WAR PR4 ...... 128 B8
Redwood Cl BPOOLS FY4 ...... 124 F7
WHIT OL12 ...... 217 G8
Redwood Dr CHLY/EC PR7 ...... 208 A5
GAR/LONG PR3 ...... 114 D9
MCMB LA4 ...... 41 M6
ORM L39 ...... 241 G7
RAW/HAS BB4 ...... 195 J3
Redwood Gdns CLV/TH FY5 ...... 86 B4
Redwood Hts LANC LA1 ...... 55 H4
Reebys La HGHB LA2 ...... 50 E1
Reedfield St BBR PR5 ...... 169 M7
Reedham Cl BBR PR5 ...... 169 J4
Reedley Dr BRFD/BLYE BB10 ...... 122 E8
Reedley Gv BRFD/BLYE BB10 ...... 122 E8
Reedmace Wk HEY LA3 ...... 53 J1
Reeds Brow RNFD/HAY WA11 ...... 262 E3
Reeds Cl RAW/HAS BB4 ...... 177 K5
Reedshaw La HWTH BD22 ...... 297 Q2
Reedsholme Cl RAW/HAS BB4 ...... 177 K5
Reeds La RAW/HAS BB4 ...... 177 K5
The Reeds LANC LA1 * 2 E4
ORM L39 ...... 241 G5
Reed St BCUP OL13 ...... 179 K8
BLY BB11 ...... 7 G8
Reedy Acre Pl LSTA FY8 ...... 146 C7
Reedyford Rd NLSN BB9 ...... 123 H1
Reedymoor La COL BB8 ...... 103 M2
Rees Pk BRSC L40 ...... 225 J8
Reeval Cl BWCK/EAR BB18 ...... 294 F5
Reeveswood CHLY/EC PR7 ...... 205 L5
Refuge Blds BBN BB1 * 10 F3
Regal Av BPOOLS FY4 ...... 125 H5
Regal Fold WHIT OL12 ...... 218 E7
Regal Ter LANC LA1 * 42 E8
Regency Av BBR PR5 ...... 169 G3
Regency Cl CLI BB7 ...... 118 D4
KIRK/FR/WAR PR4 ...... 148 D5
ROCH OL11 ...... 234 C4
Regency Ct LANC LA1 * 3 G7
Regency Gdns BISP FY2 ...... 105 G3
CHLY/EC PR7 ...... 208 A5
STHP PR8 ...... 199 H7
Regent Av COL BB8 ...... 296 B5
LSTA FY8 ...... 146 A5
NTHTN L30 ...... 258 A6
Regent Cl PDHM/BLYW BB12 ...... 140 F8
STHP PR8 ...... 199 J7
Regent Ct FUL/RIB PR2 ...... 132 C2
Regent Barnes FUL/RIB PR2 ...... 132 A2
Regent Gv FUL/RIB PR2 ...... 132 B2
Regent Ms STHP PR8 ...... 199 J7
Regent Pk FUL/RIB PR2 ...... 132 B5
Regent Park Av
KIRK/FR/WAR PR4 41
Regent Park Gv MCMB LA4 ...... 41 M7
Regent Pl NLSN BB9 ...... 123 H1
Regent Rd ACC BB5 ...... 159 J4
BBR PR5 ...... 153 G2
BPOOL FY1 ...... 4 E2
CHLY/EC PR7 ...... 207 A4
CSBY/BLUN L23 ...... 257 G7
HEY LA3 ...... 40 F7
LEYL PR25 ...... 186 C2
STHP PR8 ...... 199 H7
Regent Rd East BPOOL FY1 ...... 4 E2
Regents Cl BBNW BB2 ...... 171 H4
Regents Fld FMBY L37 * 237 G6
Regents Ter PLF/KEOS FY6 ...... 86 B3
Regent St BBN BB1 ...... 157 H2
BCUP OL13 ...... 197 K3
CHLY/EC PR7 ...... 229 H7
CLI BB7 ...... 290 A11
COL BB8 ...... 103 J8
GAR/LONG PR3 ...... 114 C4
LANC LA1 ...... 2 E4
LIT OL15 ...... 219 L5
NLSN BB9 ...... 122 E6
PRES PR1 ...... 9 H6
RAMS BL0 ...... 214 D6
RAW/HAS BB4 ...... 176 D8
TOD OL14 ...... 303 D8
WHIT OL12 ...... 235 J2
Regents Vw BBN BB1 ...... 157 H2
Regentsway BBR PR5 ...... 169 H3
Regents Wy CHLY/EC PR7 ...... 207 M5
Regiment Dr CHLY/EC PR7 ...... 187 J5
Reginald St COL BB8 ...... 103 J8
Reigate CHLYE PR6 ...... 188 D7
Reiver Rd CROS/BRETH PR26 ...... 167 H4
Renacres La ORM L39 ...... 222 B6
Rendel St PDHM/BLYW BB12 ...... 141 M4
Rendsburg Wy LANC LA1 * 3 M1
Renfrey Cl ORM L39 ...... 241 J1
Rennie Cl GAR/LONG PR3 ...... 284 C9
Rennie St LANC LA1 ...... 54 C1
Rennie St BRFD/BLYE BB10 ...... 142 F3
Renshaw Dr BBR PR5 ...... 169 H1
Renshaw St BRFD/BLYE BB10 ...... 142 E2
Renwick Av BPOOLS FY4 ...... 125 G3
Repton Av BPOOLE FY3 ...... 104 E2
MCMB LA4 ...... 42 A7
Reservoir Rd CLV/TH FY5 ...... 81 M7
Reservoir St BLY BB11 * 6 F7
DWN BB3 ...... 191 L3
MILN OL16 ...... 235 M8
Reta Dr CLV/TH FY5 ...... 81 K8
Retford Rd MILN OL16 ...... 235 M7
Revidge Rd BBN BB1 ...... 156 D2
BBNW BB2 ...... 156 D5
Revoe St BPOOL FY1 ...... 4 E4
Rewe Cl BBNW BB2 * 171 G3
Reynolds St BLY BB11 ...... 142 B8
LANC LA1 ...... 2 F3
Rhoda St NLSN BB9 ...... 123 J2
Rhodden Rd CROS/BRETH PR26 ...... 185 M2
Rhodes Av ACC BB5 ...... 159 H5
Rhodes Dr BBN BB1 ...... 157 G3
RAW/HAS BB4 ...... 194 D4
Rhodes Crs WHIT OL12 ...... 235 J3
Rhodes St WHIT OL12 ...... 218 G3
Rhodesway BBR PR5 ...... 170 B1
Rhuddlan Cl RAW/HAS BB4 ...... 194 D4
Rhuddlan Gdns CLV/TH FY5 ...... 86 A1
Rhyddings St ACC BB5 ...... 159 H1
Rhyl Av BBN BB1 ...... 157 H4
Rhyl St FTWD FY7 ...... 77 L6
Ribbesford Rd
WGNS/IIMK WN3 ...... 255 M7
Ribble Av BRFD/BLYE BB10 ...... 142 F1
CHTN/BK PR9 ...... 180 F5

CLI BB7 ...... 118 D4
DWN BB3 ...... 173 H7
KIRK/FR/WAR PR4 ...... 148 D5
LIT OL15 ...... 219 J5
MGHL L31 ...... 259 H1
Ribble Bank St PRES PR1 ...... 151 L5
SETT BD24 ...... 265 P3
Ribble Bank St PRES PR1 * 8 D1
Ribble Cl CHLYE PR6 ...... 189 K2
KIRK/FR/WAR PR4 ...... 148 D5
PRES PR1 ...... 152 B7
Ribble Ct FUL/RIB PR2 * 8 A1
Ribble Crs BBR PR5 * 128 E6
KIRK/FR/WAR PR4 ...... 128 E6
WGNW/BIL/OR WN5 ...... 263 M8
Ribble Dr CLI BB7 ...... 290 C8
KIRK/FR/WAR PR4 ...... 128 C5
WGNW/BIL/OR WN5 ...... 255 M4
Ribble Rd BPOOL FY1 ...... 4 E4
FTWD FY7 ...... 77 J7
LEYL PR25 ...... 186 A3
WGNNW/ST WN6 ...... 245 L1
Ribblesdale Av ACC BB5 ...... 159 L3
BBN BB1 ...... 137 K4
CLI BB7 ...... 99 J8
Ribblesdale Cl BPOOLS FY4 ...... 125 H3
KIRK/FR/WAR PR4 ...... 128 C5
Ribblesdale Ct MCMB LA4 * 41 J6
Ribblesdale Dr FUL/RIB PR2 ...... 133 G3
BBNW BB2 ...... 10 A1
CHLY/EC PR7 ...... 207 L4
NLSN BB9 ...... 103 H6
PRES PR1 ...... 9 H6
Ribblesdale Rd GAR/LONG PR3 ...... 116 D9
Ribblesdale St
BRFD/BLYE BB10 ...... 142 E3
CROS/BRETH PR26 ...... 185 G8
MGHL L31 ...... 259 G2
Ribble St BBN BB1 ...... 10 D1
BCUP OL13 ...... 197 K3
LSTA FY8 ...... 145 G5
ROCH OL11 8
Ribbleton Av FUL/RIB PR2 ...... 133 G3
Ribbleton Dr ACC BB5 ...... 159 L3
Ribbleton Gv BPOOLE FY3 ...... 118 D4
Ribbleton Hall Crs FUL/RIB PR2 ...... 133 J8
Ribbleton Hall Dr FUL/RIB PR2 ...... 133 J8
Ribbleton La PRES PR1 ...... 9 J2
Ribbleton Pl PRES PR1 ...... 9 M2
Ribble Vw Cl KIRK/FR/WAR PR4 ...... 153 C5
CLI BB7 ...... 278 F5
FUL/RIB PR2 ...... 8 A6
GTH/LHO BB6 ...... 117 M4
KIRK/FR/WAR PR4 ...... 165 L2
PRES PR1 8
SKP/WHF BD23 ...... 278 H2
Ribby Av FUL/RIB PR2 ...... 127 M7
Ribby Pl BPOOLS FY4 ...... 125 G2
FUL/RIB PR2 ...... 151 J2
Ribby Rd KIRK/FR/WAR PR4 ...... 127 L4
Ribchester Av BPOOLS FY4 ...... 125 H3
Ribchester Br GAR/LONG PR3 ...... 116 D9
Ribchester Rd BBN BB1 ...... 137 H8
GAR/LONG PR3 ...... 117 J2
LSTA FY8 ...... 147 H3
Ribchester Wy NLSN BB9 ...... 122 F7
Rice Gv BPOOL FY1 ...... 105 G4
Richard Rd CSBY/BLUN L23 ...... 256 D5
Richardson Cl KIRK/FR/WAR PR4 ...... 148 C5
Richardson St BPOOL FY1 ...... 4 C5
Richards Rd WGNNW/ST WN6 ...... 228 C4
Richard St BBNW BB2 ...... 10 A5
BLY BB11 7
NLSN BB9 ...... 122 E6
RAMS BL0 ...... 215 H4
ROCH OL11 ...... 235 J5
Richards Wk LANC LA1 * 2 F7
Richard's Wy LSTA FY8 ...... 145 G2
Richmond Av BRFD/BLYE BB10 ...... 143 J8
BRSC L40 ...... 225 H4
BWCK/EAR BB18 ...... 293 R5
CLV/TH FY5 ...... 85 H1
KIRK/FR/WAR PR4 ...... 127 L4
LANC LA1 ...... 42 F7
MCMB LA4 ...... 41 J6
RAW/HAS BB4 ...... 194 F1
Richmond Cl CHLY/EC PR7 ...... 207 M5
CROS/BRETH PR26 ...... 185 L2
Richmond Crs BBN BB1 ...... 157 H2
Richmond Gv MGHL L31 ...... 259 G2
Richmond Hl BBN BB1 * 10 B4
WGNW/BIL/OR WN5 ...... 255 M5
Richmond Hill La GAR/LONG PR3 ...... 270 C9
Richmond Hill St ACC BB5 ...... 159 K6
Richmond Ms BRSC L40 ...... 225 H4
Richmond Pk BBN BB1 ...... 191 K1
Richmond Rd ACC BB5 ...... 159 K6
BPOOL FY1 ...... 104 C4
BWCK/EAR BB18 ...... 293 R5
CHLY/EC PR7 ...... 205 M4
CHLYE PR6 ...... 208 B4
CSBY/BLUN L23 ...... 257 H6
LSTA FY8 ...... 145 G5
STHP PR8 ...... 221 J4
Richmond St ACC BB5 ...... 159 K6
BLY BB11 6
HOR/BR BL6 231
PRES PR1 8
TOD OL14 ...... 303 M2
Richmond Ter BBN BB1 ...... 10 B4
DWN BB3 ...... 191 K1
Rickard Rd NLSN BB9 ...... 123 H1
Ridding La CLV/TH FY5 ...... 118 D4
Riddings Av BRFD/BLYE BB10 ...... 143 J8
Riddings La HGHB LA2 48
Ridehalgh La BRFD/BLYE BB10 298
HBR HX7 298
Ridehalgh St COL BB8 ...... 103 J8
Ridge Av BRFD/BLYE BB10 143
Ridge Bank TOD OL14 303

Ridge Cl CHTN/BK PR9 ...... 180 F6
Ridge Ct BRFD/BLYE BB10 ...... 7 M3
GAR/LONG PR3 ...... 114 F3
Ridgeford Gdns FUL/RIB PR2 ...... 132 A6
Ridge La LANC LA1 ...... 52 E3
Ridge La LANC LA1 ...... 3 J4
Ridgemont PDHM/BLYW BB12 ...... 102 C7
Ridgemont FUL/RIB PR2 ...... 131 M5
Ridgemont HOR/BR BL6 ...... 232 D4
Ridge Rd BLY BB11 ...... 7 J4
CHLYE PR6 ...... 208 B4
TOD OL14 ...... 303 L2
Ridge Rw BRFD/BLYE BB10 ...... 143 G5
Ridge Sq LANC LA1 ...... 3 J4
Ridge St LANC LA1 ...... 3 J4
Ridgeway GTH/LHO BB6 ...... 138 C5
NLSN BB9 ...... 102 F8
Ridgeway Dr CLV/TH FY5 ...... 86 A3
MGHL L31 ...... 250 A8
Ridgeways RAW/HAS BB4 ...... 194 F1
The Ridgeway FTWD FY7 ...... 77 G8
LANC LA1 ...... 123 G4
Ridgmont Dr HOR/BR BL6 ...... 232 C8
Riding Barn St ACC BB5 ...... 159 J5
Riding Cl BWCK/EAR BB18 ...... 293 R5
Riding Head La RAMS BL0 ...... 215 J3
Riding La ORM L39 ...... 239 H7
The Ridings CHLYE PR6 ...... 187 K5
CHTN/BK PR9 ...... 180 D8
GAR/LONG PR3 ...... 142 A3
Riding St BLY BB11 ...... 6 C5
CHLYE PR6 ...... 230 D4
PRES PR1 ...... 152 C2
STHP PR8 ...... 13 G8
Ridley La BRSC L40 ...... 227 J1
CROS/BRETH PR26 ...... 185 G8
MGHL L31 ...... 259 G2
Ridley Rd FUL/RIB PR2 ...... 151 M1
Ridley St BPOOLS FY3 ...... 5 H1
Riefield BOL BL1 ...... 233 L8
Riesling Dr NWD/KWIPK L33 ...... 260 B6
Rifle St RAW/HAS BB4 ...... 194 E1
Rigby Ct KIRK/FR/WAR PR4 ...... 148 D6
Rigby Rd BPOOL FY1 ...... 4 D6
MGHL L31 ...... 249 L8
Rigbys Houses CHLY/EC PR7 * 230 D5
Rigby St COL BB8 ...... 103 M6
NLSN BB9 ...... 123 G3
PRES PR1 ...... 152 F2
Rigby Wk CHLY/EC PR7 * 207 M3
Rigg La GAR/LONG PR3 ...... 93 L3
HGHB LA2 ...... 56 B7
Rigg St NLSN BB9 ...... 123 H3
Rildene Wk ROCH OL11 ...... 234 A3
Riley Av LSTA FY8 ...... 145 J6
Riley Cl LEYL PR25 ...... 186 D3
Riley Green Switch Rd
BBR PR5 ...... 171 G4
Rileys Cft SKP/WHF BD23 ...... 267 R6
Riley St ACC BB5 ...... 159 L5
BCUP OL13 ...... 179 J6
BLY BB11 * 7 J8
BWCK/EAR BB18 ...... 294 E5
NLSN BB9 ...... 122 E6
Rimington Av ACC BB5 ...... 159 K8
BRFD/BLYE BB10 ...... 143 G6
COL BB8 ...... 103 M5
Rimington Cl BBNW BB2 ...... 11 C9
Rimington Pl LSTA FY8 ...... 145 L5
NLSN BB9 ...... 123 L2
Rimmer Gv PRES PR1 ...... 223 G2
Rimmer's Av FMBY L37 ...... 237 H5
STHP PR8 ...... 13 G4
Rimrose Valley Rd
CSBY/BLUN L23 ...... 257 K8
Ring Dyke Wy LSTA FY8 ...... 146 D7
Ring Lows La WHIT OL12 ...... 218 D7
Ring O'Bells La BRSC L40 ...... 242 E1
Rings Nook RAW/HAS BB4 * 177 K1
Ringstone Crs NLSN BB9 ...... 123 L3
Ringstones La HGHB LA2 ...... 48 A7
Ringtail Cl BRSC L40 ...... 224 D7
Ringtail Pl BRSC L40 ...... 224 D7
Ringtail Rd BRSC L40 ...... 224 D7
Rington Av PLF/KEOS FY6 ...... 85 L2
Ringway CHLY/EC PR7 ...... 207 K4
STHP PR8 ...... 81 H7
Ring Wy PRES PR1 ...... 9 G4
Ringwood Cl ACC BB5 ...... 159 L2
LSTA FY8 ...... 146 B8
Ringwood Rd PRES PR1 ...... 152 F1
Ripley Cl MGHL L31 ...... 259 H2
Ripley Ct LANC LA1 * 54 E5
Ripley Dr LSTA FY8 ...... 145 L5
WGNS/IIMK WN3 ...... 255 M7
Ripon Av LANC LA1 * 42 E7
Ripon Cl CLV/TH FY5 ...... 81 H6
GAR/LONG PR3 ...... 88 F6
STHP PR8 ...... 200 C8
Ripon Hall Av RAMS BL0 ...... 214 E7
Ripon Rd HEY LA3 ...... 52 D5
BPOOL FY1 ...... 5 G4
LSTA FY8 ...... 146 A6
Ripon St BBN BB1 ...... 11 K6
NLSN BB9 ...... 123 G4
PRES PR1 ...... 152 B1
Ripon Ter PRES PR1 ...... 153 G2
Risedale Dr GAR/LONG PR3 ...... 114 G4
Risedale Gv BBNW BB2 ...... 172 D3
Rise La TOD OL14 ...... 303 K2
The Rise CARN LA5 ...... 33 G5
WGNNW/ST WN6 ...... 245 M4
Rishton Rd ACC BB5 ...... 159 H8
BBN BB1 ...... 137 M6
Rishton St BPOOL FY1 ...... 4 D4
Rising Bridge Rd
RAW/HAS BB4 ...... 176 D4
Ritherham St CLV/TH FY5 ...... 81 J7
River Cl FMBY L37 ...... 247 L2
River Dr PDHM/BLYW BB12 ...... 168 F3
River Hts BBR PR5 ...... 168 G3
River Lea Gdns CLI BB7 ...... 99 J3
Rivermead Ct GAR/LONG PR3 ...... 284 D6
Rivermeade STHP PR8 ...... 200 A7
River Pde PRES PR1 ...... 8 D7
River Rd CLV/TH FY5 ...... 86 B1
Riversdale SETT BD24 ...... 265 M7
Riversdale Cl NWD/KWIPK L33 ...... 260 B7
Riversedge Rd LEYL PR25 ...... 185 M3
The Rivers Edge WHIT OL12 ...... 217 M3
Riversgate FTWD FY7 ...... 77 J7
Riverside CARN LA5 * 26 A8
HTWN L38 ...... 247 J7
PRES PR1 ...... 8 F8

SKP/WHF BD23 281 K2
Riverside Av
 CROS/BRETH PR26 168 B7
Riverside Cl
 CROS/BRETH PR26 204 D1
 CROS/BRETH PR26 168 B7
 HGHB LA2 43 K5
Riverside Cots CHLYE PR6 * 188 B3
Riverside Crs
 CROS/BRETH PR26 204 D1
Riverside Dr BURY BL9 214 E8
 MILN OL16 235 L7
 PLF/KEOS FY6 86 E1
Riverside Vw ACC BB5 139 H7
Riversleigh Av RNFD/HAY FY1 104 F2
 LSTA FY8 146 B8
Riverslea Cl BOL BL1 233 J8
Rivers St WGNW/BIL/OR WN5 255 H5
Riverstone Br LIT OL15 219 K6
River St BBN BB1 11 G5
 BCUP OL13 197 J2
 COL BB8 296 A7
 DWN BB3 191 J1
 HEYW OL10 234 A7
 LANC LA1 2 E3
 PRES PR1 8 D9
 RAMS BL0 214 F5
 TOD OL14 303 M2
Rivers View Fold HGHB LA2 270 G4
Riversway BPOOLE FY3 105 J5
 FUL/RIB PR2 150 F7
 PLF/KEOS FY6 86 E1
 SKP/WHF BD23 281 J3
Riversway Dr BBN BB1 173 J5
River Vw KIRK/FR/WAR PR4 183 K3
River Wy NLSN BB9 103 G7
Riverway Cl BBR PR5 168 F3
Rivington Av BISP FY2 84 F6
 CHLYE PR6 230 D4
Rivington Cl
 KIRK/FR/WAR PR4 183 J3
 PLF/KEOS FY6 86 A8
 STHP PR8 199 K8
Rivington Dr BRSC L40 225 H8
 SKEL WN8 254 F4
Rivington La CHLYE PR6 231 G4
Rivington Pl CHLY/EC PR7 229 G5
Rivington Rd CHLYE PR6 208 D2
 HOR/BR BL6 210 C7
Rivington St BBN BB1 11 L4
 WHIT OL12 235 J2
Rixton Gv CLV/TH FY5 81 L7
Roach Pl MILN OL16 235 K3
Roach Rd BBR PR5 154 D4
Roach V MILN OL16 235 M1
Road La WHIT OL12 218 A7
Roberts Cl CHLY/EC PR7 207 M4
Roberts St CHLY/EC PR7 186 B3
 NLSN BB9 177 K8
 RAW/HAS BB4 * 177 K8
Robert St ACC BB5 159 G8
 BBNW BB2 10 F8
 BWCK/EAR BB18 293 Q5
 COL BB8 296 B6
 DWN BB3 191 J2
 GTH/LHO BB6 * 139 G6
 LANC LA1 3 H6
 RAMS BL0 214 F2
 RAW/HAS BB4 * 196 C1
Robin Bank Rd DWN BB3 191 K1
Robin Cl CHLY/EC PR7 207 G8
Robin Crs HEY LA3 52 E5
Robin Hey CROS/BRETH PR26 185 L2
Robin Hill Dr WGNNW/ST WN6 245 L1
Robin Hill Dr WGNNW/ST WN6 228 C8
Robin Hood La
 WGNNW/ST WN6 227 L8
Robin House La
 BRFD/BLYE BB10 123 H8
Robin La CLI BB7 292 D6
 HGHB LA2 39 G2
 SKEL WN8 226 F6
Robin Rd BURY BL9 214 E8
Robins Cl PLF/KEOS FY6 85 K7
Robins La BISP FY2 85 J6
Robin's La RNFD/HAY WA11 263 J3
Robinson Fold
 BWCK/EAR BB18 293 H4
Robinson La NLSN BB9 122 D1
Robinson St BBN BB1 157 K4
 BRFD/BLYE BB10 142 D2
 CLI BB7 291 K10
 COL BB8 296 A2
 FUL/RIB PR2 132 A8
 HOR/BR BL6 231 L7
 MILN OL16 235 K4
Robin St PRES PR1 153 G2
Robraine KKBYL LA6 21 M2
Robson St NLSN BB9 122 E5
Robson Wy BPOOLE FY3 105 K1
Roby Mi SKEL WN8 244 E8
Rochburry Cl MILN OL16 234 C5
Rochdale Rd BCUP OL13 197 G2
 RAMS BL0 215 K2
 TOD OL14 303 M6
Rochdale Rd East HEYW OL10 234 C8
 MCMB LA4 41 L6
Rochester Av CLV/TH FY5 81 J7
Rochester Cl BCUP OL13 179 G4
Rochester Dr BRFD/BLYE BB10 122 H4
Rochford Av CLV/TH FY5 85 H2
Roch Mills Crs ROCH OL11 234 F6
Roch Mills Gdns ROCH OL11 234 F6
Roch St MILN OL16 235 L2
Roch Valley Wy ROCH OL11 234 F5
Rock Bridge Fold
 RAW/HAS BB4 178 B6
Rock Brow GAR/LONG PR3 95 L4
Rockburgh Crs
 KIRK/FR/WAR PR4 166 D6
Rockcliffe Av BCUP OL13 197 H2
Rockcliffe Dr BCUP OL13 197 H2
Rockcliffe Rd BCUP OL13 197 J2
Rockfield Rd ACC BB5 160 A5
Rockfield St BBNW BB2 10 E9
Rock Hall Rd RAW/HAS BB4 176 E7
Rockhaven Av HOR/BR BL6 231 M7
Rockingham Ct
 NWD/KWIPK L33 * 260 C7
Rockingham Rd BISP FY2 85 J6
Rock La BLY BB11 142 A8
 DWN BB3 172 D8
 MGHL L31 258 D6
Rockliffe La BCUP OL13 197 K2
Rockliffe St BBNW BB2 173 H1
 RAW/HAS BB4 177 K8
Rock St ACC BB5 176 B1
 CLI BB7 99 H3
 CLV/TH FY5 81 L7
 HOR/BR BL6 231 L4
 RAMS BL0 215 H4
 RAW/HAS BB4 176 E8

Rock Ter CARN LA5 16 E1
 CLI BB7 * 138 D1
 RAW/HAS BB4 * 177 K4
Rock Vw MGHL L31 259 K7
Rockville Rd CHLYE PR6 * 187 M3
Rockwood Cl BRFD/BLYE BB10 123 H8
Roddlesworth La CHLYE PR6 190 B2
Rodhill La CLI BB7 290 G2
Rodney Av CLV/TH FY5 145 L2
Rodney St BBNW BB2 10 B8
 PRES PR1 8 B5
Rodwell Wk BPOOLE FY3 105 J3
Roe Br GAR/LONG PR3 90 D5
Roebuck Cl BBNW BB2 10 C8
Roebuck St RAW/HAS BB4 151 M1
Roeburndale Crs HEY LA3 52 F3
Roeburndale Rd HGHB LA2 45 H8
Roeburn Dr HEY LA3 54 A1
Roeburn Pl LANC LA1 2 E2
Roedean Av MCMB LA4 42 A7
Roedean St MGHL L31 259 G4
Roefield Ter WHIT OL12 234 F3
Roe Greave Rd ACC BB5 175 G4
Roehampton Cl CLV/TH FY5 85 K1
Roehampton Dr
 CSBY/BLUN L23 256 F5
Roe Hey Dr CHLY/EC PR7 229 F5
Roe La CHLY/BK PR9 200 B3
Roe Lee Pk BBN BB1 157 L1
Roe St WHIT OL12 234 F2
Rogerley Cl LSTA FY8 146 D7
Rogersfield BRFD/BLYE BB10 137 L3
Roleton Cl NTHTN L30 258 E7
Rolleston Rd BBNW BB2 156 E7
Roman Crs HGHB LA2 44 D6
Roman Pl LANC LA1 2 C5
Roman Rd BBN BB1 173 J1
 DWN BB3 192 C7
 PRES PR1 9 M5
Roman Wy CLI BB7 99 J3
 CLV/TH FY5 85 J2
 FUL/RIB PR2 133 M5
 KIRK/FR/WAR PR4 128 F7
Rome Av BLY BB11 141 M7
Romford Rd PRES PR1 152 F7
Romford St
 PDHM/BLYW BB12 141 M4
Romiley Dr SKEL WN8 253 J1
Romney Av BLY BB11 142 B8
 BPOOLS FY4 124 F2
 FTWD FY7 77 H8
 NLSN BB9 103 C8
Romney St NLSN BB9 123 G4
Romney Wk BBN BB1 157 M7
Romsey WHIT OL12 * 235 H3
Romsey Av FMBY L37 247 L1
Rona Av BPOOLS FY4 125 J5
Ronald Ross Av NTHTN L30 258 C6
Ronald St BBN BB1 157 M6
 PDHM/BLYW BB12 141 K6
Ronaldsway CSBY/BLUN L23 257 K5
 PRES PR1 151 J8
Ronaldsway Cl BCUP OL13 197 K2
Ronbury Cl NLSN BB9 * 122 F2
Roney St BBNW BB2 10 B3
Ronwood Cl
 KIRK/FR/WAR PR4 108 C2
The Roods CARN LA5 26 B5
Rookery Av WGNNW/ST WN6 245 H3
Rookery Cl CHLY/EC PR7 207 K5
 PRES PR1 168 B1
Rookery Dr PRES PR1 168 C1
 RNFD/HAY WA11 262 D6
Rookery La RNFD/HAY WA11 262 D6
Rookery Nook Vls
 BCUP OL13 * 179 J7
Rookery Rd BWCK/EAR BB18 293 R5
Rook Hill Rd BCUP OL13 196 E3
 BWCK/EAR BB18 295 Q7
 COL BB8 296 A6
 NLSN BB9 123 G2
 PRES PR1 152 E1
 RAMS BL0 214 F5
Rookswood Dr ROCH OL11 234 E8
Rookwood Cl CHLY/EC PR7 205 L5
Rookwood Av CHLY/EC PR7 207 M1
 CLV/TH FY5 85 G3
Rooley Moor Rd
 RAW/HAS BB4 196 D5
 WHIT OL12 234 F1
 WHIT OL12 196 E2
Rooley St WHIT OL12 234 F2
Rooley Vw BCUP OL13 197 H2
Roomfield St TOD OL14 303 H2
Roosevelt Av LANC LA1 2 C8
Root Hill Cots CLI BB7 * 274 C11
Rope St KIRK/FR/WAR PR4 130 B1
Ropefield Wy WHIT OL12 218 B8
Rope St WHIT OL12 131 M1
Rope Wk GAR/LONG PR3 284 B8
Rosary Av BPOOLS FY4 5 K9
Roscoe Av CLV/TH FY5 86 A1
Roseacre BPOOLS FY4 124 F6
Roseacre Dr
 KIRK/FR/WAR PR4 108 C2
Rose Acre La CARN LA5 26 C1
Roseacre Pl FUL/RIB PR2 151 L2
 LSTA FY8 145 L3
Roseacre Rd
 KIRK/FR/WAR PR4 109 H6
Rose Av BLY BB11 6 D8
 FUL/RIB PR2 131 M8
 LIT OL15 219 J8
 ROCH OL11 234 A1
Rosebank CLV/TH FY5 85 L1
 BBR PR5 150 F2
 RAMS BL0 215 G2
Rose Bank RAW/HAS BB4 177 K8
Rose Bank Rd TOD OL14 303 K2
Rose Bank St BCUP OL13 179 G8
Rosebay Av BBNW BB2 172 A3
Rosebay Cl FMBY L37 237 M5
Roseberry Av
 KIRK/FR/WAR PR4 131 H6
Roseberry Cl RAMS BL0 214 F2
Roseberry St TOD OL14 300 E10
 LANC LA1 54 A7
 LSTA FY8 145 L2
 MCMB LA4 41 M6
Roseberry St BRFD/BLYE BB10 142 D1
 CHTN/BK PR9 200 D5
Rosebowl Vw BRSC L40 223 L7
Rose Cl LEYL PR25 187 H1
Rose Ct FTWD FY7 * 81 J7
Rose Crs SKEL WN8 253 L4

STHP PR8 237 M1
Rosecroft Cl ORM L39 241 H5
Rosedale Av BPOOLS FY4 125 K1
 CSBY/BLUN L23 257 H7
 HEY LA3 52 F3
Rosedene Cl
 KIRK/FR/WAR PR4 131 H6
Rose Dr RNFD/HAY WA11 262 D6
Rosefield Ct MILN OL16 235 M4
Rosefinch Wy BPOOLE FY3 125 L1
Rose Fold CLV/TH FY5 81 K7
 PRES PR1 152 A7
Rose Gdns KIRK/FR/WAR PR4 165 H1
Rose Gv HGHB LA2 66 E7
Rosegrove La
 PDHM/BLYW BB12 141 L6
Rose Hi CHLY/EC PR7 186 F7
 STHP PR8 13 L5
Rose Hill Av BBN BB1 11 J5
Rosehill Av BLY BB11 6 D9
 NLSN BB9 * 123 J3
Rose Hill Av
 WGNW/BIL/OR WN5 255 M5
Rosehill Dr ORM L39 250 F1
Rose Hill Rd BBNW BB2 171 M2
Rosehill Rd BBNW BB2 6 D8
 COL BB8 123 K1
Rose Hill St BCUP OL13 197 G5
 DWN BB3 191 L3
 RAW/HAS BB4 177 L3
Roseland Av NLSN BB9 122 F5
Roseland Cl FUL/RIB PR2 249 C3
Rose La PRES PR1 132 F8
Rose Lea FUL/RIB PR2 133 L1
Roselea Dr CHTN/BK PR9 180 F7
Roselyn Av BPOOLS FY4 124 F6
Rosemary Av BPOOLS FY4 124 F6
 CLV/TH FY5 81 J9
Rosemary Cl PRES PR1 167 M1
Rosemary Dr LIT OL15 219 J5
Rosemary La FMBY L37 237 H5
 KIRK/FR/WAR PR4 130 D1
 LANC LA1 3 H1
 ORM L39 239 K6
Rosemeade Av BBR PR5 168 A5
Rosemede Av BPOOLS FY4 5 M8
Rosemoor Dr CSBY/BLUN L23 257 K7
Rosemount BCUP OL13 179 K1
Rosemount Av BLY BB11 6 D6
 PLF/KEOS FY6 78 D6
Rosendale Cl BCUP OL13 179 K1
Rosendale Crs BCUP OL13 179 K1
Rose Pth FMBY L37 247 K1
Rose Pl ORM L39 251 G1
 RNFD/HAY WA11 262 D6
Rose St ACC BB5 159 G1
 BBNW BB2 10 F8
 BBN BB1 197 J1
 DWN BB3 191 J2
 LEYL PR25 168 E8
 MCMB LA4 41 J5
 PRES PR1 9 A7
 RAW/HAS BB4 196 B1
 TOD OL14 303 L2
Rose Ter FUL/RIB PR2 133 L2
Rose Vale St RAW/HAS BB4 195 L1
Roseway BPOOLS FY4 124 F6
 FUL/RIB PR2 151 K2
 LSTA FY8 145 L2
 NLSN BB9 122 D4
 PLF/KEOS FY6 85 M8
Rosewood KIRK/FR/WAR PR4 131 K5
 ROCH OL11 234 B2
Rosewood Av BBN BB1 157 H2
 BBR PR5 153 M8
 BLY BB11 6 D9
 RAW/HAS BB4 176 F8
Rosewood Cl CHLY/EC PR7 208 A5
 CLV/TH FY5 86 A2
 LSTA FY8 146 B7
Rosewood Ct BBR PR5 153 L8
Rosewood Dr BBR PR5 153 L8
Roshaw FUL/RIB PR2 133 M2
Rosklyn Rd CHLYE PR6 208 B4
Rosley St COL BB8 296 E6
Rossall Av AIN/FAZ L10 259 J7
Rossall Cl BBR PR5 154 B7
 FTWD FY7 81 G3
 PDHM/BLYW BB12 141 G5
Rossall Ct CLV/TH FY5 * 80 F6
 FTWD FY7 77 H8
Rossall Dr FUL/RIB PR2 131 M7
Rossall Gdns CLV/TH FY5 81 G5
Rossall Ga FUL/RIB PR2 132 A8
Rossall Grange La FTWD FY7 77 G8
Rossall La FTWD FY7 81 G4
Rossall Rd BPOOLE FY3 105 G4
 CHLYE PR6 208 B2
 CLV/TH FY5 81 G7
 KIRK/FR/WAR PR4 131 M7
 LANC LA1 54 F1
 LSTA FY8 146 A7
 WHIT OL12 235 K1
Rossall St FUL/RIB PR2 8 B1
Rossall Ter BBNW BB2 173 H2
Rossendale Av BLY BB11 162 A1
 LANC LA1 67 G3
 MCMB LA4 41 K5
Rossendale Av North
 CLV/TH FY5 85 L1
Rossendale Av South
 CLV/TH FY5 85 L2
Rossendale Rd BLY BB11 141 L1
 LSTA FY8 145 K4
Rossendale Vw TOD OL14 303 R3
 BBN BB1 193 H1
 RAW/HAS BB4 193 M6
 WHIT OL12 217 J3
Rosset Ct NLSN BB9 123 G2
Rossetti Av BLY BB11 162 B1
Rossett Rd CSBY/BLUN L23 256 F8
Rossington Av BISP FY2 85 J7
Rosslyn Av MGHL L31 258 E3
 PLF/KEOS FY6 78 D5
Rosslyn Crs PLF/KEOS FY6 78 D5
Rosslyn Crs East PLF/KEOS FY6 78 D5
Rossmere Av ROCH OL11 234 F5
Rossmoyne Rd LANC LA1 54 F3
Ross St DWN BB3 191 K5
 PRES PR1 9 J2
Rostle Top Rd
 BWCK/EAR BB18 294 D6
Rostrevor Cl
 CROS/BRETH PR26 185 L2
Rostron Crs FMBY L37 247 H2
Rostron Rd RAMS BL0 214 H5
Rothay Av FTWD FY7 81 G1
Rothbury Pl LSTA FY8 146 F7
Rotherwick Av CHLY/EC PR7 207 L4

Rothesay Cresent HEY LA3 52 C6
Rothesay Rd CSBY/BLUN L23 257 H6
Rothesay Rd BBN BB1 173 M1
 HEY LA3 52 C6
 NLSN BB9 122 F5
Rothesay Ter STHP PR8 220 D7
Rothley Av STHP PR8 220 C7
Rothwell Av ACC BB5 159 M7
Rothwell Cl ORM L39 241 G6
Rothwell Crs FUL/RIB PR2 133 J7
Rothwell Dr FTWD FY7 77 G8
 ORM L39 250 E1
Rothwell Rd CHLYE PR6 230 E4
Rothwells Cl CSBY/BLUN L23 257 L5
Rothwell St RAMS BL0 214 G5
 WHIT OL12 235 K2
Rotten Rw HGHB LA2 44 F5
STHP PR8 12 B7
Rough Hey Pl FUL/RIB PR2 133 L4
Rough Hey Rd FUL/RIB PR2 133 L4
Rough Heys La BPOOLS FY4 125 H4
Rough Hey Wk MILN OL16 235 L5
Rough Lea Rd CLV/TH FY5 86 A1
Rough Lee Rd ACC BB5 159 M7
Roughlee St NLSN BB9 123 G1
Rough Side La TOD OL14 303 M3
Roughwood Dr
 NWD/KWIPK L33 260 C8
Round Acre BBR PR5 155 H4
Round Barn EDGW/EG BL7 * 192 E3
Roundell St BWCK/EAR BB18 293 R4
Roundel St BRFD/BLYE BB10 * 142 E1
Roundhay BPOOLS FY4 125 J3
Roundhill La RAW/HAS BB4 176 C5
Round Hill Pl
 BRFD/BLYE BB10 * 163 H2
Roundhill Rd ACC BB5 176 B4
Roundhill Vw ACC BB5 176 D3
The Round Meade MGHL L31 258 C1
Round Meadow
 CROS/BRETH PR26 185 M2
Roundway FTWD FY7 80 F7
Roundway Down
 FUL/RIB PR2 131 M4
The Roundway HTWN L38 247 M8
Round Wd PRES PR1 8 A5
Roundwood Av
 BRFD/BLYE BB10 122 D7
Rouse St ROCH OL11 234 F7
Rowan Av ACC BB5 175 G1
 FUL/RIB PR2 133 K7
Rowan Bank HGHB LA2 43 K4
Rowan Cl BBN BB1 157 K2
 BRSC L40 225 J5
 GAR/LONG PR3 284 C9
 KIRK/FR/WAR PR4 150 A1
 PRES PR1 151 L8
Rowan Cft CHLYE PR6 187 K2
Rowan Dr KKBY L32 260 A8
Rowangate FUL/RIB PR2 132 F4
Rowan Gv BRFD/BLYE BB10 7 L3
 CHLYE PR6 187 M8
Rowan La SKEL WN8 243 L7
The Rowans CHLYE PR6 230 D3
 ORM L39 250 D4
 PLF/KEOS FY6 105 K1
Rowan Tree Cl ACC BB5 * 160 A4
Rowberrow Cl FUL/RIB PR2 133 G5
Rowen Pk BBNW BB2 156 D3
Rowland Av CLV/TH FY5 85 J1
Rowland Ct MILN OL16 * 235 L5
Rowland Ct CLV/TH FY5 85 J1
Rowland La CLV/TH FY5 85 J1
Rowland St ACC BB5 159 K6
 MILN OL16 235 L5
Rowley La BRFD/BLYE BB10 143 G5
Rowley Rd FTWD FY7 77 J8
Roworth Cl BBR PR5 153 L8
Rowsley St LSTA FY8 145 G4
The Row CARN LA5 17 H7
Rowton Heath FUL/RIB PR2 131 M4
Roxburgh Rd BPOOLS FY4 125 J5
Royal Av BPOOLE FY3 5 G6
 FUL/RIB PR2 132 B5
 KIRK/FR/WAR PR4 128 C2
 LEYL PR25 186 B4
Royal Bank Rd BPOOLE FY3 5 K6
Royal Cl FMBY L37 247 K2
Royal Crs FMBY L37 247 K1
Royal Dr FUL/RIB PR2 132 A8
Royal Fold HEY LA3 52 D6
Royal Oak Av BBN BB1 157 H2
Royal Oak Meadow HGHB LA2 36 F3
Royal Pk STHP PR8 199 H4
Royal Pl LSTA FY8 145 M1
Royal Rd MCMB LA4 41 K5
Royal St MILN OL16 235 M1
Royal Ter STHP PR8 12 F4
Royal Troon Ct
 KIRK/FR/WAR PR4 * 128 D7
Royalty Av KIRK/FR/WAR PR4 167 K3
Royalty Gdns
 KIRK/FR/WAR PR4 167 K3
Royalty La KIRK/FR/WAR PR4 167 K3
Royd La LEYL 301 L12
Royds Av ACC BB5 159 M7
 HEY LA3 52 E2
Royds Pl MILN OL16 235 M4
Royds St ACC BB5 159 M7
 LIT OL15 219 J6
 LSTA FY8 145 G4
 MILN OL16 235 L4
Royds St West MILN OL16 235 L4
Royd St TOD OL14 303 K1
Royle Av PLF/KEOS FY6 78 D6
Royle Rd CHLY/EC PR7 187 M6
 PDHM/BLYW BB12 140 F2
 ROCH OL11 235 G8
Royles Ct CLV/TH FY5 85 L1
Royton Rd HOR/BR BL6 231 M7
Royshaw Av BBN BB1 157 H3
Royshaw Cl BBN BB1 157 H3
Royston Rd PLF/KEOS FY6 86 C6
Royton Dr CHLYE PR6 187 M6
Ruby St BBN BB1 * 157 J3
 BURY BL9 214 E6
Ruddington Rd STHP PR8 222 B1
Rudman St WHIT OL12 234 F1
Rudyard Dr DWN BB3 191 M3
Rudyard Pl BPOOLS FY3 * 5 M4
Ruecroft Cl WGNNW/ST WN6 245 G3
Ruff La ORM L39 241 K7

Rufford Av MGHL L31 250 B8
 ROCH OL11 235 G7
Rufford Cl CHLY/EC PR7 207 L8
Rufford Dr CHTN/BK PR9 181 J6
Rufford Park La BRSC L40 203 K6
 CHTN/BK PR9 180 E5
 LSTA FY8 145 L4
 RNFD/HAY WA11 262 C3
Rufus St PRES PR1 152 F1
Rugby Av ACC BB5 159 M4
Rugby Dr WGNW/BIL/OR WN5 255 K4
Rugby Rd WHIT OL12 235 K2
Rugby St BPOOLS FY4 125 K1
Rumley Rd BLY BB11 7 G7
Rumleys Fold BLY BB11 162 A1
Runcorn Av BISP FY2 105 J1
Rundle Rd FUL/RIB PR2 132 B5
Runnells La CSBY/BLUN L23 257 M6
Runnell Vls BPOOLS FY4 * 125 K4
The Runnel ORM L39 239 L1
Runshaw Av WGNNW/ST WN6 245 H3
Runshaw Hall La CHLY/EC PR7 186 F7
Runshaw La CHLY/EC PR7 206 A1
Rupert St CARN LA5 24 A8
 NLSN BB9 122 F4
Rushbed Dr RAW/HAS BB4 177 K5
Rushes Farm Cl ACC BB5 158 F8
Rushey Cl RAW/HAS BB4 177 K5
Rushlake Gdns ROCH OL11 234 B3
Rushley Dr HGHB LA2 42 C2
Rushley Mt HGHB LA2 42 C2
Rushley Wy HGHB LA2 42 C2
Rushton Cl NLSN BB9 123 L1
Rushton St BCUP OL13 197 H3
 GTH/LHO BB6 138 E7
 NLSN BB9 103 G8
Rushworth St East
 BRFD/BLYE BB10 * 142 E2
Rushworth St West
 BRFD/BLYE BB10 * 142 E2
Rushy Fld ACC BB5 139 J8
Rushy Hey BBR PR5 168 D3
Rushy Hill Vw WHIT OL12 * 234 E2
Ruskin Av ACC BB5 158 F6
 BPOOL FY1 4 F2
 CLV/TH FY5 81 K8
 COL BB8 296 A6
 LEYL PR25 186 D1
 PDHM/BLYW BB12 141 G4
Ruskin Cl KIRK/FR/WAR PR4 183 J5
Ruskin Dr KKBYL LA6 21 J4
 MCMB LA4 41 L5
Ruskin Gv BLY BB11 140 F7
 CARN LA5 32 F6
 LANC LA1 * 42 E8
Ruskin St BRFD/BLYE BB10 142 D7
 PRES PR1 9 M6
Russell Av CHTN/BK PR9 200 D4
 CLV/TH FY5 85 G3
 LEYL PR25 186 F3
 PRES PR1 153 K3
Russell Ct LSTA FY8 145 H7
Russell Dr MCMB LA4 42 B7
Russell Pl GTH/LHO BB6 138 E6
Russell Rd CARN LA5 33 K2
 CHTN/BK PR9 200 D4
Russell Sq CHLYE PR6 208 A2
Russell Sq West CHLYE PR6 208 A2
Russell St ACC BB5 159 M6
 BBNW BB2 10 E7
 LANC LA1 3 G6
 NLSN BB9 123 G2
 TOD OL14 303 M2
Russell Ter PDHM/BLYW BB12 141 G4
Russel St BCUP OL13 179 J7
Russia St ACC BB5 159 J5
Rutherford Pl BPOOLS FY4 125 K1
Rutherford Rd MGHL L31 259 H4
Ruthin Cl BBN BB1 157 H4
Ruthin Dr CLV/TH FY5 86 A1
Ruth St WHIT OL12 218 A2
Rutland ROCH OL11 235 H5
Rutland Av BBN BB1 158 B7
 BBR PR5 * 153 C8
 CLV/TH FY5 81 H8
 FTWD FY7 77 H8
 KIRK/FR/WAR PR4 148 F4
 LANC LA1 54 F1
 PDHM/BLYW BB12 141 K5
 PLF/KEOS FY6 85 M8
Rutland Cl ACC BB5 * 139 J8
 GAR/LONG PR3 284 A7
Rutland Ct LSTA FY8 * 146 A6
Rutland Crs ORM L39 241 G4
Rutland Rd LSTA FY8 146 A6
Rutland St ACC BB5 159 M6
 BBNW BB2 156 E8
 COL BB8 296 C6
 HEYW OL10 234 C8
 NLSN BB9 123 H2
 PRES PR1 152 F1
Ryan St LEYL PR25 186 B2
Ryburn Av BBNW BB2 156 D4
 BPOOLS FY4 5 J9
Ryburn Dr ORM L39 241 G4
Rycliffe St PDHM/BLYW BB12 140 F2
Rydal Av BBR PR5 169 G2
 BPOOL FY1 5 K8
 CLV/TH FY5 81 L2
 DWN BB3 191 K3
 FMBY L37 247 K1
 FTWD FY7 77 H7
 KIRK/FR/WAR PR4 148 F5
 PLF/KEOS FY6 85 M8
 PRES PR1 151 M8
 WGNW/BIL/OR WN5 255 J4
Rydal Cl ACC BB5 160 A7
 BRFD/BLYE BB10 122 F7
 FUL/RIB PR2 132 F7
 HOR/BR BL6 230 F7
 PDHM/BLYW BB12 140 F2
Rydal Gv HEY LA3 52 E2
 PLF/KEOS FY6 78 D5
Rydal Mt BBN BB1 174 C5
Rydal Pl CHLY/EC PR7 207 L4
 CLV/TH FY5 86 A1
 COL BB8 296 A6
Rydal Rd BBN BB1 157 K4
 CARN LA5 32 E7
 HEY LA3 52 E1
 LANC LA1 54 F1
 LSTA FY8 145 H3

PLF/KEOS FY6 .... 86 F1
PRES PR1 .... 153 G1
RAW/HAS BB4 .... 194 F3
Rydal St BRFD/BLYE BB10 .... 142 F1
Ryddingwood PRES PR1 .... 151 L5
Ryde Cl RAW/HAS BB4 .... 194 D1
Ryden Av CLV/TH FY5 .... 81 G8
LEYL PR25 .... 186 F1
Ryden Rd BBN BB1 .... 137 C5
Ryder Cl ORM L39 .... 250 F1
Ryder Crs ORM L39 .... 250 F2
STHP PR8 .... 221 H3
Ryding Cl CROS/BRETH PR26 .... 168 D3
The Rydinge FMBY L37 .... 237 H5
Rydings La CHTN/BK PR9 .... 182 A4
Rydings La WHIT OL12 .... 218 D5
Rydings Rd WHIT OL12 .... 218 E6
The Rydings GTH/LHO BB6 .... 137 K3
Rye Cft LITH L21 .... 257 L8
Ryecroft Av PLF/KEOS FY6 .... 86 F2
Ryecroft La EDGW/EG BL7 .... 210 F4
Ryefield CHLYE PR6 .... 188 C5
Ryefield Av PRES PR1 .... 168 A1
RAW/HAS BB4 .... 194 E1
Ryefield Av West
RAW/HAS BB4 .... 194 D1
Ryefield La LITH L21 .... 257 L8
Ryefield Pl RAW/HAS BB4 .... 194 E1
Ryefields ROCH OL11 .... 234 D5
Rye Gdns BBN BB2 .... 173 G5
Ryeground La FMBY L37 .... 237 K6
Ryeheys Rd LSTA FY8 .... 145 G3
Ryeland Cl MILN OL16 .... 235 L7
Ryelands Crs FUL/RIB PR2 .... 151 K1
Ryelands Rd LANC LA1 .... 2 D1
Rye Moss La FMBY L37 .... 248 D3
Rye St HEYW OL10 .... 234 B4
PRES PR1 .... 152 D2
Ryknild Wy HEY LA3 .... 42 A8
Ryland Av PLF/KEOS FY6 .... 85 M8
Rylands Rd CHLY/EC PR7 .... 207 L4
Rylands St BRFD/BLYE BB10 .... 142 E2
Ryldon Pl BPOOLS FY4 .... 125 K1
Rylstone Dr BWCK/EAR BB18 .... 293 P5
HEY LA3 .... 52 E3
Rymers Gn FMBY L37 .... 237 H7
Ryscar Wy BISP FY2 .... 85 J5
Ryson Av BPOOLS FY4 .... 5 L9

S

Sabden Brook Ct CLI BB7 .... 120 D3
Sabden Pl LSTA FY8 .... 145 M4
Sabden Rd CLI BB7 .... 120 J7
PDHM/BLYW BB12 .... 120 D5
Saccary La BBN BB1 .... 136 D7
Sackville St BLY BB11 .... 6 E4
BPOOLS FY4 .... 124 F4
BWCK/EAR BB18 .... 293 P6
CHLYE PR6 .... 208 B4
NLSN BB9 .... 122 D6
TOD OL14 .... 303 M2
Saddleback Crs
WGNW/BIL/OR WN5 .... 255 L4
Saddleback Rd
WGNW/BIL/OR WN5 .... 255 L4
Saddler Nook La KKBYL LA6 .... 21 H4
Sadlers Rw LSTA FY8 .... 146 A4
Sadler St ACC BB5 .... 159 H6
Saer Cl FTWD FY7 .... 77 C8
Saffron Cl NLSN BB9 .... 122 F2
Saffron Ms CSBY/BLUN L23 .... 257 L5
Sagar Dr KIRK/FR/WAR PR4 .... 148 D5
Sagar Fold COL BB8 .... 296 C6
ORM L39 .... 251 G3
Sagar Holme Ter
RAW/HAS BB4 .... 178 B6
Sagar La TOD OL14 .... 300 H8
Sagar St CHLY/EC PR7 .... 205 M5
NLSN BB9 .... 123 H3
Sage Cl BISP FY2 .... 85 J3
Sage Ct PRES PR1 .... 167 M1
Sage La PRES PR1 .... 132 E8
Sahara Fold BBN BB1 .... 157 K4
St Aidan's Av BBNW BB2 .... 172 F2
DWN BB3 .... 191 L3
St Aidan's Cl BBNW BB2 .... 172 F2
ROCH OL11 .... 235 C6
St Aidans Pk BBN BB1 .... 169 H1
St Aidan's Wy NTHTN L30 .... 258 A8
St Albans Cl BBN BB1 .... 11 M2
DWN BB3 .... 173 H7
LSTA FY8 .... 145 H4
St Alban's St MILN OL16 .... 235 H5
St Albans Ter CLV/TH FY5 .... 235 H5
St Ambrose Ter NTHTN L30 .... 258 B7
St Ambrose Ter LEYL PR25 .... 186 F1
St Andrew's Av CLV/TH FY5 .... 85 G1
FUL/RIB PR2 .... 151 K1
St Andrews Cl CHLY/EC PR7 .... 187 D7
LANC LA1 .... 55 H3
LIT OL15 .... 219 H7
St Andrew's Cl ACC BB5 .... 159 G7
LEYL PR25 .... 186 D3
RAMS BL0 .... 214 F7
St Andrew's Dr
CSBY/BLUN L23 .... 256 C5
St Andrews Gv MCMB LA4 .... 41 L5
St Andrew's La NTHTN L30 .... 257 M8
St Andrews Pl STHP PR8 .... 13 G1
St Andrews Rd GTH/LHO BB6 .... 117 M5
St Andrew's Rd
CSBY/BLUN L23 .... 256 E4
PRES PR1 .... 152 D4
St Andrew's Rd North
LSTA FY8 .... 145 G3
St Andrew's Rd South
LSTA FY8 .... 145 H5
St Andrew's Vw BBN BB1 .... 10 A4
BRFD/BLYE BB10 .... 142 E2
St Andrew's Vw
NWD/KWIPK L33 .... 260 B6
St Anne's Av LEYL PR25 .... 186 H5
St Annes Cl MCMB LA4 .... 42 A5
St Anne's Cl ACC BB5 .... 159 H6
BBNW BB2 .... 172 F2
St Annes Ct BPOOLS FY4 .... 124 F2
HCHB LA2 .... 44 F2
St Anne's Crs RAW/HAS BB4 .... 178 C8
St Anne's Dr
PDHM/BLYW BB12 .... 122 A4
WGNW/ST WN6 .... 245 K6
St Anne's Pth FMBY L37 .... 237 J5

St Anne's Pl LANC LA1 * 3 H5
St Annes Rd BPOOLS FY4 .... 124 F3
CHLYE PR6 .... 208 B4
CHTN/BK PR9 .... 180 C2
GAR/LONG PR3 .... 88 F6
HOR/BR BL6 .... 231 M7
St Anne's Rd LEYL PR25 * 237 J5
LEYL PR25 .... 186 F1
ORM L39 .... 241 G7
St Anne's Rd East LSTA FY8 .... 145 H4
St Anne's Rd West LSTA FY8 .... 145 G5
St Anne's St
PDHM/BLYW BB12 .... 140 F4
PRES PR1 .... 152 D1
St Anne's Wy
PDHM/BLYW BB12 .... 122 A4
St Ann's Rd MILN OL16 .... 235 M3
St Ann's Sq CLI BB7 .... 98 E3
St Ann's St BBNW BB2 .... 10 F8
St Anthony's Cl FUL/RIB PR2 * 131 M7
St Anthony's Crs FUL/RIB PR2 .... 131 M7
St Anthony's Gv NTHTN L30 .... 258 A8
St Anthonys Pl
KIRK/FR/WAR PR4 .... 128 D7
St Anthony's Pl BPOOL FY1 * 104 F1
St Anthony's Rd
CSBY/BLUN L23 .... 256 E7
PRES PR1 * 152 D1
St Augustine's Wy NTHTN L30 .... 258 A7
St Austell Pl CARN LA5 .... 33 H3
St Austin's Pl PRES PR1 * 9 K5
St Austin's Rd PRES PR1 .... 9 K5
St Barnabas' Pl PRES PR1 * 9 K1
St Barnabas's Dr LIT OL15 .... 219 K5
St Barnabas St BBNW BB2 .... 10 A1
DWN BB3 .... 191 L5
St Bede's Av BPOOLS FY4 .... 124 E2
St Bedes Cl DWN BB3 * 173 H6
St Bedes Pk DWN BB3 .... 173 J2
St Bee's Cl BBNW BB2 .... 173 J2
St Benet's Av BBR PR5 .... 169 G2
St Benet's Wy NTHTN L30 .... 258 B8
St Bernard's Av BPOOLE FY3 .... 105 J4
St Bernard's Cl NTHTN L30 .... 258 A8
St Bernard's Dr NTHTN L30 .... 258 A8
St Bernard's Rd PLF/KEOS FY6 .... 78 B6
St Brides Cl HOR/BR BL6... .... 231 K7
St Bridget's Gv NTHTN L30 * 258 A8
St Catherine Cl BPOOLE FY3 .... 105 L2
St Catherines Dr LEYL PR25 .... 186 F1
St Catherines Ct LANC LA1 * 3 H4
St Catherine's Dr FUL/RIB PR2 .... 131 M7
St Catherines Wy BBR PR5 .... 168 F4
St Cecilia St GTH/LHO BB6 .... 139 G6
St Celia's Wy MCMB LA4 .... 41 M5
St Chads Av BPOOLS FY4 .... 291 J10
St Chads Cl PLF/KEOS FY6 .... 106 A1
St Chads Ct MILN OL16 .... 235 J4
St Chads St MILN OL16 .... 235 J4
St Chad's Dr LANC LA1 .... 42 D8
St Chad's Rd BPOOL FY1 * 4 B4
PRES PR1 .... 152 F2
St Charles' Rd BBN BB1 * 158 D2
St Christines Av LEYL PR25 .... 168 F7
St Christopher Ct
WGNW/ST WN6 * 245 M7
St Christopher's Rd
PRES PR1 .... 152 D1
St Christopher's Wy MCMB LA4 .... 41 L5
St Clair Cl CHTN/BK PR9 .... 200 D2
St Clair St TOT/BURYW BL8 * 214 C8
St Clares Av FUL/RIB PR2 .... 132 C5
St Clement Cl BBN BB1 .... 11 L1
St Clements Av LEYL PR25 .... 168 F4
St Clement's Av BPOOLE FY3 .... 5 L4
St Clement St BBN BB1 .... 11 L4
St Crispin Wy RAW/HAS BB4 .... 194 D1
St Cuthberts Cl DWN BB3 * 173 H6
St Cuthbert's Cl FUL/RIB PR2 .... 132 A4
LSTA FY8 .... 146 D8
St Cuthbert's Rd BBR PR5 .... 168 D2
CHTN/BK PR9 .... 200 C1
PRES PR1 * 152 D1
St Cuthbert St
BRFD/BLYE BB10 .... 142 E1
St Damian's Rd NTHTN L30 .... 258 B8
St David's Av BBNW BB2 .... 172 A4
CLV/TH FY5 .... 85 G1
St David's Gv LSTA FY8 .... 145 G3
St David's Rd LEYL PR25 .... 186 F1
PRES PR1 .... 152 D1
St David's Rd North LSTA FY8 .... 145 H5
St David's Rd South LSTA FY8 .... 145 H5
St David's Wd ACC BB5 .... 160 A4
St Edmund Hall Cl RAMS BL0 .... 214 F7
St Edmund's Rd BPOOLS FY4 .... 105 K9
St Edmund's St GTH/LHO BB6 * 139 G6
St Francis Cl FUL/RIB PR2 .... 132 D4
St Francis' Rd BBNW BB2 .... 172 D1
St Gabriel's Av BBN BB1 .... 137 J3
St George Cl BPOOL FY1 * 105 G5
St George Av BBNW BB2 .... 172 E2
CLV/TH FY5 .... 85 H4
LSTA FY8 * 145 H4
St Georges Cl COL BB8 * 103 M8
St George La CLV/TH FY5 * 85 G1
St Georges Pk
KIRK/FR/WAR PR4 .... 128 B5
St George's Pl CHTN/BK PR9 * 13 G5
St George's Quay LANC LA1 .... 2 D2
St George's Rd BPOOLS FY4 .... 124 F6
FMBY L37 .... 237 H7
HTWN L38 .... 247 J6
LSTA FY8 .... 145 G6
PRES PR1 .... 152 C1
ROCH OL11 .... 234 C1
St George's Sq LSTA FY8 .... 145 G4
St George's St CHLY/EC PR7 .... 207 M4
St Georges Ter DWN BB3 * 191 L5
RAW/HAS BB4 * 196 D5
St Gerrard's Rd BBR PR5 .... 168 D2
St Giles St PDHM/BLYW BB12 .... 140 F2
St Gregory Rd PRES PR1 .... 152 E1
St Gregory's Pl CHLY/EC PR7 .... 207 M6
St Helens Ct NLSN BB9 .... 123 J8
St Helens Rd GAR/LONG PR3 .... 90 C6
St Helens Rd ORM L39 .... 241 D7
St Helen's Rd CHLYE PR6 .... 187 M2
HEY LA3 .... 65 J3
St Helen's Well
KIRK/FR/WAR PR4 .... 183 K6
St Helier Cl BBNW BB2 .... 172 A4
St Helier's Pl BPOOL FY1 * 4 E8
St Heliers Rd BPOOL FY1 .... 4 E8
St Hilda's Cl CHLY/EC PR7 .... 207 M7
St Hilda's Rd LSTA FY8 .... 145 H5
St Hubert's Pl GTH/LHO BB6 * 138 D7
St Hubert's St GTH/LHO BB6 .... 139 G5

St Ignatius' Sq PRES PR1 .... 9 J1
St Ives Av RAW/HAS BB4 * 5 H6
KIRK/FR/WAR PR4 .... 148 D5
St Ives Crs FUL/RIB PR2 .... 131 K7
St Ives Rd BBN BB1 .... 158 A7
St James Cl ACC BB5 .... 159 H4
BBR PR5 .... 168 A3
BRSC L40 .... 241 M8
RAW/HAS BB4 * 176 B8
St James Pl ACC BB5 .... 159 H4
St James's Cl DWN BB3 * 191 K1
LANC LA1 .... 2 F6
St James's Crs DWN BB3 * 191 K1
St James's Ct ACC BB5 .... 159 C4
BBN BB1 .... 157 A1
BPOOLS FY4 * 124 F5
St James's Gdns
CROS/BRETH PR26 .... 185 K3
St James La BLY BB11 * 7 G4
St James's Pl BBN BB1 .... 157 H4
CHLYE PR6 .... 208 B4
St James's Sq
BWCK/EAR BB18 * 293 Q5
St James's Rd PRES PR1 .... 152 C1
St James's Rw BLY BB11 .... 6 F4
St James's St BLY BB11 .... 6 F4
CLI BB7 .... 99 H4
St James St BCUP OL13 .... 197 J1
NLSN BB9 .... 122 E6
STHP PR8 .... 13 H7
St James' St ACC BB5 .... 159 L6
BBNW BB2 .... 172 F2
RAW/HAS BB4 .... 196 B3
St Jerome's Wy NTHTN L30 .... 258 B7
St John Av FTWD FY7 .... 81 G1
St Johns BBN BB1 .... 10 D2
St John's Av CLV/TH FY5 .... 85 G1
GAR/LONG PR3 .... 79 M6
St Johns Cl KIRK/FR/WAR PR4 .... 128 C7
St Johns Cl ACC BB5 .... 159 L6
PDHM/BLYW BB12 .... 139 M1
RAW/HAS BB4 .... 177 J4
St Johns Ct GAR/LONG PR3 .... 132 C2
MILN OL16 .... 235 L5
STHP PR8 * 221 G7
St John's Dr MILN OL16 .... 235 L5
St Johns Gn LEYL PR25 .... 186 B2
St John's Gv CARN LA5 .... 16 F8
HEY LA3 .... 52 E1
St Johns Ms LANC LA1 * 3 G4
St John's Pl NLSN BB9 .... 123 K3
PRES PR1 .... 9 G3
St John's Rd BBR PR5 .... 155 G6
HEY LA3 .... 52 E1
PDHM/BLYW BB12 .... 140 F5
PRES PR1 .... 9 F5
St John's St DWN BB3 .... 191 L3
GTH/LHO BB6 .... 138 F7
LSTA FY8 .... 146 F8
RAW/HAS BB4 .... 196 C3
St John St BCUP OL13 .... 179 J8
HOR/BR BL6 .... 231 L7
WGNW/BIL/OR WN5 .... 255 L5
St Josephs Cl BPOOLE FY3 .... 5 K1
St Joseph's Dr MILN OL16 .... 235 L7
St Joseph's Pl CHLYE PR6 .... 208 A2
St Joseph's Ter PRES PR1 * 152 F2
St Judes Av LEYL PR25 .... 168 F7
St Jude's Av BBNW BB2 .... 172 E2
St Katherines Dr HOR/BR BL6... .... 230 F8
St Kevin's Dr KKBY L32 .... 260 B7
St Kitts Cl DWN BB3 .... 173 H5
St Lawrence Av BBNW BB2 .... 156 C3
St Lawrence's
GAR/LONG PR3 .... 111 L3
St Lawrence St GTH/LHO BB6 .... 138 D7
St Leonard Cl LANC LA1 * 3 J4
St Leonard's Cl NTHTN L30 .... 258 A7
St Leonard's Ga LANC LA1 .... 3 H5
St Leonard's Rd East LSTA FY8 * 145 M7
St Leonard's Rd West
LSTA FY8 .... 145 G3
St Louis Av PDHM/BLYW BB12 .... 140 F2
St Lucia Cl DWN BB3 .... 173 H5
St Luke's Church Rd FMBY L37 .... 246 F3
St Lukes Cl LANC LA1 * 3 E6
St Luke's Dr FMBY L37 * 246 F1
WGNW/BIL/OR WN5 .... 255 M4
NTHTN L30 .... 258 A7
St Luke's Pl PRES PR1 * 9 H3
St Luke's Rd BPOOLS FY4 * 124 F5
CSBY/BLUN L23 .... 257 G7
St Luke St ROCH OL11 .... 235 G6
St Margarets Cl FUL/RIB PR2 .... 131 K7
St Margarets Ct BBN BB1 * 11 L4
St Margaret's Gdns BLY BB11 .... 140 F7
St Margaret's Rd CARN LA5 .... 32 F5
LEYL PR25 .... 186 F1
MCMB LA4 .... 41 L5
St Margarets Wy BBN BB1 .... 11 M4
St Mark's Gv NTHTN L30 .... 257 M7
St Mark's Pl BBNW BB2 * 156 F7
BPOOLE FY3 .... 105 H3
St Mark's Pl West PRES PR1 * 8 C2
St Mark's Rd BBNW BB2 .... 8 C2
PRES PR1 .... 8 C2
St Marlow Av LEYL PR25 * 168 F7
St Martins Cl PLF/KEOS FY6 .... 85 M7
St Martin's Cl CLV/TH FY5 .... 85 J1
St Martin's Dr BBNW BB2 .... 172 A4
St Martin's Rd BPOOLS FY4 .... 124 F5
LANC LA1 .... 3 K9
PRES PR1 * 152 D1
St Mary Cl BPOOLS FY4 .... 105 J2
St Mary's Av BBR PR5 .... 169 K2
BWCK/EAR BB18 .... 294 D4
WGNW/BIL/OR WN5 .... 263 M7
St Marys Cl BBN BB1 .... 11 G5
GAR/LONG PR3 * 114 D2
PRES PR1 .... 9 J1
St Mary's Cl BBR PR5 .... 169 K2
MILN OL16 .... 235 L7
St Marys Ct BBNW BB2 * 136 A8
St Mary's Ct ACC BB5 * 159 J1
St Mary's Ct SKEL WN8 .... 254 F4

St Mary's Dr GTH/LHO BB6 .... 137 M3
St Mary's Gdns BBNW BB2 .... 156 F7
STHP PR8 .... 221 J4
St Mary's Ga BRFD/BLYE BB10 * 7 J5
CHLY/EC PR7 .... 186 F6
MILN OL16 .... 235 H4
St Mary's Pde LANC LA1 * 2 F6
St Mary's Pl BBR PR5 .... 195 H2
GAR/LONG PR3 .... 88 D3
HEY LA3 .... 52 D3
St Mary's St CLI BB7 .... 99 H2
NLSN BB9 .... 122 F3
PRES PR1 .... 9 L2
St Mary's St North PRES PR1 .... 9 L2
St Mary's Ter RAW/HAS BB4 .... 195 K1
St Mary's Wy RAW/HAS BB4 .... 195 K1
St Marys Wharfe BBN BB1 .... 11 G2
BBNW BB2 .... 11 G8
St Matthew's Cl
WGNS/IIMK WN3 .... 255 M7
St Matthew St BLY BB11 .... 6 D6
St Michael Rd ORM L39 .... 250 C4
St Michael's Cl FUL/RIB PR2 .... 132 A8
St Michaels Cl BBNW BB2 .... 172 B4
CARN LA5 .... 32 F6
CHLY/EC PR7 .... 207 L2
CHTN/BK PR9 .... 180 C8
St Michaels Ct BBN BB1 .... 11 H1
NLSN BB9 .... 122 F1
St Michael's Crs CARN LA5 .... 32 F6
St Michael's Gv MCMB LA4 .... 41 K7
NTHTN L30 .... 257 M8
St Michael's La CARN LA5 .... 32 E6
St Michael's Pk ORM L39 .... 250 D4
St Michaels Pl CARN LA5 .... 32 F7
St Michaels Rd BISP FY2 .... 85 Q3
KIRK/FR/WAR PR4 .... 128 F6
St Michael's Rd
CHLY/EC PR7 .... 256 C6
GAR/LONG PR3 .... 90 C6
LEYL PR25 * 168 F8
PRES PR1 * 152 D1
St Michael's St BBN BB1 .... 157 J4
St Mildred's Wy HEY LA3 .... 52 E1
St Monica's Av NTHTN L30 .... 258 A8
St Monica's Wy BPOOLS FY4 .... 126 A2
St Nicholas' Av CLI BB7 .... 120 C4
St Nicholas Crs CARN LA5 .... 33 G5
St Nicholas Gv
KIRK/FR/WAR PR4 .... 127 L6
St Nicholas La CARN LA5 .... 32 F5
St Nicholas Rd ACC BB5 * 159 J4
BPOOLS FY4 .... 125 K6
St Ogg's Rd MCMB LA4 .... 41 K8
St Oswald's Ct PRES PR1 .... 152 F1
St Oswald's St BBN BB1 .... 158 B7
St Oswald's Cl NTHTN L30 .... 258 C7
St Oswald's Wy NTHTN L30 .... 258 C7
St Oswald St LANC LA1 .... 3 J9
St Patrick's Cl
NWD/KWIPK L33 * 260 A6
St Patrick's Dr NTHTN L30 .... 258 A7
St Patricks Rd North LSTA FY8 .... 145 H3
St Patrick's Rd South
LSTA FY8 .... 145 J4
St Patrick's Wk HEY LA3 .... 52 D4
St Paul's Av BBNW BB2 .... 156 C3
LSTA FY8 .... 145 L7
PRES PR1 .... 9 H1
St Pauls Cl CROS/BRETH PR26 .... 168 C4
NWD/KWIPK L33 .... 260 A6
St Paul's Cl CHLYE PR6 .... 230 D3
CLI BB7 .... 98 F5
St Paul's Ct BLY BB11 * 6 F5
St Paul's Dr HCHB LA2 .... 44 F1
LANC LA1 .... 54 E6
St Paul's Pas STHP PR8 * 12 F6
St Paul's Rd BBN BB1 * 11 J1
BPOOL FY1 .... 104 D3
LANC LA1 .... 54 E6
NLSN BB9 .... 123 G5
PRES PR1 .... 9 K2
St Paul's Sq PRES PR1 * 9 K2
St Paul's St ACC BB5 .... 159 H7
BBNW BB2 .... 10 C4
CLI BB7 .... 98 F5
RAMS BL0 .... 214 F7
STHP PR8 .... 12 E6
St Paul's Ter CLI BB7 * 98 F5
St Peter's Av FMBY L37 .... 237 G7
RAW/HAS BB4 .... 196 B1
St Peters Cl NWD/KWIPK L33 .... 260 A6
St Peter's Cl BBN BB1 .... 137 G5
DWN BB3 .... 191 L3
FMBY L37 .... 237 H7
St Peter's Pl FTWD FY7 .... 77 H1
St Peter's Rd LANC LA1 * 3 H5
RAW/HAS BB4 .... 196 B1
STHP PR8 .... 199 H8
St Peter's Sq PRES PR1 * 8 F2
St Peter St BBN BB1 .... 10 D5
BBNW BB2 .... 10 D5
St Philip's Rd BBNW BB2 .... 156 F7
St Philip's St BBNW BB2 .... 156 F7
NLSN BB9 .... 123 H2
St Philip St BRFD/BLYE BB10 .... 142 D1
St Robert Cl SKP/WHF BD23 .... 281 K7
St Robert St SKP/WHF BD23 .... 281 K7
St Saviour's St BBR PR5 .... 169 G4
St Silas's St BBNW BB2 .... 156 F7
St Stephen's Av LEYL PR25 .... 168 F7
St Stephen's Cv NTHTN L30 .... 258 A8
St Stephens Rd
KIRK/FR/WAR PR4 .... 128 D7
St Stephen's Rd BBN BB1 .... 157 K4
HTWN L38 .... 247 J7
PRES PR1 * 8 F2
WGNW/ST WN6 * 245 M7
St Stephen's Wy COL BB8 .... 296 C6
St Teresa's Dr CLV/TH FY5 .... 85 G2
St Teresa's Dr FUL/RIB PR2 .... 131 M7
St Thomas Cl BPOOLE FY3 .... 105 L2
St Thomas' Pl PRES PR1 * 9 G1
St Thomas Rd
KIRK/FR/WAR PR4 .... 128 D7
PRES PR1 * 152 C1
St Thomas's Ct SKEL WN8 .... 254 F4
St Thomas's Dr NTHTN L30 .... 258 A8

St Thomas's Rd CHLY/EC PR7 .... 207 M3
RAW/HAS BB4 .... 177 K4
St Thomas St BBN BB1 .... 11 L1
St Vincent Av BPOOL FY1 .... 5 H6
St Vincents Cl DWN BB3 .... 173 H5
St Vincents Rd FUL/RIB PR2 .... 132 B6
St Vincent's Wy STHP PR8 .... 12 D9
St Walburga's Rd BISP FY2 .... 105 J2
St Walburga Av FUL/RIB PR2 .... 132 B8
St Walburges Gdns FUL/RIB PR2 * 8 A1
St Wilfred's Dr WHIT OL12 .... 218 A7
St Wilfrid's Pk HGHB LA2 .... 43 K4
St Wilfrid's Ter GAR/LONG PR3 .... 114 C3
St Wilfrid St PRES PR1 .... 9 G4
St William Rd CSBY/BLUN L23 .... 257 G5
Salcombe Av BISP FY2 .... 105 H1
Salcombe Dr CHTN/BK PR9 .... 180 C6
Salcombe Rd LSTA FY8 .... 144 F2
Salem Ms HEY LA3 * 52 D3
Salerno St BLY BB11 .... 141 M6
Salesbury Av BPOOL FY1 .... 137 J7
Sale St LIT OL15 .... 219 L5
Salford BBN BB1 .... 10 F4
Salford Rd HGHB LA2 .... 66 F7
STHP PR8 .... 220 F6
Salford Wy TOD OL14 .... 303 K3
Salik Gdns ROCH OL11 .... 235 G6
Salisbury Av FUL/RIB PR2 .... 134 A2
PLF/KEOS FY6 .... 78 A6
Salisbury Cl HEY LA3 .... 53 J1
Salisbury Rd BPOOL FY1 .... 5 G4
CHLYE PR6 .... 189 J3
DWN BB3 .... 173 H8
LANC LA1 .... 8 D5
PRES PR1 .... 8 D5
Salisbury Rd CHLY/EC PR7 .... 208 A4
CHTN/BK PR9 .... 200 D5
GTH/LHO BB6 .... 139 G5
PRES PR1 .... 153 G2
Salkeld St ROCH OL11 .... 235 J6
Sallowfields
WGNW/BIL/OR WN5 .... 255 J6
Sally Barn Cots
RAW/HAS BB4 .... 195 H3
Sally's La CHTN/BK PR9 .... 200 D1
Salmesbury Av BISP FY2 .... 105 H1
Salmon St PRES PR1 .... 152 F4
Saimsbury Hall Cl RAMS BL0 .... 214 F7
Salop Av BISP FY2 .... 84 F7
Saltash Rd CLV/TH FY5 .... 81 C8
Salt Ayre La LANC LA1 .... 2 C3
Saltburn St
PDHM/BLYW BB12 .... 141 L5
Saltcotes Pl LSTA FY8 .... 147 G6
Saltcotes Rd LSTA FY8 .... 147 G6
Salter Fell Rd LANC LA1 .... 2 C1
Salterforth La BRFD/BLYE BB10 .... 143 K8
Salterforth La
BWCK/EAR BB18 .... 294 D8
Salterforth Rd
BWCK/EAR BB18 .... 294 D8
Salter Rake Ga TOD OL14 .... 303 L7
Salter St PRES PR1 .... 152 C2
Salthill Gdns CLI BB7 * 99 J2
Salthill Rd CLI BB7 .... 99 J2
Salthouse Av BPOOL FY1 * 4 E6
Salt Marsh La PLF/KEOS FY6 .... 86 C2
Salt Pie La KKBYL LA6 .... 21 M1
Salt Pit La BRSC L40 .... 227 J1
Saltpit La MGHL L31 .... 259 H2
Saltram Rd WGNS/IIMK WN3 .... 255 M7
Salts Dr LIT OL15 .... 219 K5
Salus St BRFD/BLYE BB10 .... 142 F2
Salvia Wy NWD/KWIPK L33 .... 260 A6
Salwick Av BISP FY2 .... 85 G6
Salwick Cl CHTN/BK PR9 .... 180 C6
Salwick Pl FUL/RIB PR2 .... 151 K2
LSTA FY8 .... 145 K3
Salwick Rd KIRK/FR/WAR PR4 .... 150 C5
Sambourn Fold STHP PR8 .... 220 D6
Samson St MILN OL16 .... 235 M5
Samuel St PRES PR1 .... 153 G3
The Sanctuary BPOOLS FY4 .... 124 F6
Sandbank Gdns WHIT OL12 .... 217 M5
Sandbeds La HGHB LA2 .... 35 M5
Sand Beds La RAMS BL0 .... 195 J7
Sandbrook Gdns
WGNW/BIL/OR WN5 .... 255 G6
Sandbrook Pk ROCH OL11 .... 235 H7
Sandbrook Rd STHP PR8 .... 220 F6
WGNW/BIL/OR WN5 .... 254 F6
Sandbrook Wy ROCH OL11 .... 235 H7
Sanderling Cl CLV/TH FY5 .... 85 J2
LSTA FY8 .... 146 B4
Sanderling Rd
NWD/KWIPK L33 .... 260 D8
Sanders Gv MCMB LA4 .... 41 M4
Sanderson La CHLY/EC PR7 .... 227 K3
Sandersons Wy BPOOLS FY4 .... 125 J3
Sandfield CLV/TH FY5 * 81 C8
Sandfield Pl ORM L39 .... 251 G1
Sandfield Rd BCUP OL13 .... 197 K2
MILN OL16 .... 235 L6
Sandfield St LEYL PR25 .... 186 E2
Sandford Dr MGHL L31 .... 259 G1
Sandgate CHLY/EC PR7 .... 208 A6
LSTA FY8 .... 144 F4
Sandham St CHLYE PR6 .... 208 A3
Sandhams Wy BPOOLS FY4 .... 126 A3
Sandheys Dr CHTN/BK PR9 .... 200 C3
Sandhills HTWN L38 .... 247 J8
Sandhills Av BPOOLS FY4 .... 124 F6
Sandhills Cl BWCK/EAR BB18 .... 294 B7
Sandhill St DWN BB3 .... 191 H6
Sandhole La ROCH OL11 .... 234 B6
Sandholme Cl SETT BD24 .... 265 M8
Sandholme La GAR/LONG PR3 .... 284 F10
Sandhurst Av BISP FY2 .... 84 F7
LSTA FY8 .... 145 H4
Sandhurst Cl FMBY L37 .... 246 F2
Sandhurst Dr KIRK/FR/WAR PR4 .... 128 C6
Sandhurst Wy MGHL L31 .... 249 L6
Sandicroft Pl PLF/KEOS FY6 .... 86 F2
Sandicroft Rd BPOOL FY1 .... 104 F2
Sandilands Gv HTWN L38 .... 247 J8
Sandiways Dr BRFD/BLYE BB10 .... 123 J8
Sandiways Cl CLV/TH FY5 .... 85 M3
Sandlewood Gv
NWD/KWIPK L33 .... 260 C2
Sandon Gv RNFD/HAY WA11 .... 262 D9
Sandon Pl BPOOLS FY4 .... 124 F7
Sandon Rd STHP PR8 .... 221 D2
DWN BB3 .... 191 L5
Sandon Ter BBN BB1 * 10 B2
Sandown Cl KIRK/FR/WAR PR4 .... 128 B6
Sandown Park Rd
AIN/FAZ L10 .... 259 H8

Sandown Rd *CLV/TH* FY5 .... 85 L2
  LANC LA1 .... 55 C8
  RAW/HAS BB4 .... 194 F1
Sandpiper Cl *BBN* BB1 .... 11 G2
  BPOOLE 105 L5
  ROCH 234 C4
Sandpiper Rd
  WGNS/IIMK WN3 .... 255 L7
Sandpiper Sq *BLY* BB11 .... 141 L6
Sandridge Av *CHLY/EC* PR7 .... 207 L4
Sandridge Pl *BPOOLS* FY4 .... 124 E7
Sandringham Av *CLV/TH* FY5 .... 85 L2
  LEYL PR25 .... 186 F2
Sandringham Cl *BBN* BB1 .... 157 H2
  CHLY/EC PR7 .... 230 B5
  CLI BB7 .... 118 D4
  KIRK/FR/WAR PR4 .... 183 K5
  NWD/KWIPK L33 .... 260 B6
Sandringham Ct *CHTN/BK* PR9 .... 13 H2
  LSTA FY8 .... 146 A2
Sandringham Dr *CHLYE* PR6 .... 189 H3
Sandringham Gv
  RAW/HAS BB4 .... 194 D2
Sandringham Park Dr
  KIRK/FR/WAR PR4 .... 167 J3
Sandringham Rd *BBR* PR5 .... 153 G8
  CHLY/EC PR7 .... 207 L3
  CHLY/EC PR7 .... 205 M4
  DWN BB3 .... 173 H7
  FMBY L37 .... 247 H1
  LSTA FY8 .... 145 K6
  MCMB LA4 .... 41 L5
  MGHL L31 * 258 F3
  STHP PR8 .... 220 F6
Sandringham Wy
  KIRK/FR/WAR PR4 .... 131 H5
Sandsdale Av *FUL/RIB* PR2 .... 132 F6
Sandside Dr *MCMB* LA4 .... 41 M8
Sandside Rd *CARN* LA5 .... 17 C1
Sands Rd *BBN* BB1 .... 158 E1
The Sands *CLI* BB7 .... 118 E6
Sands Wy *BPOOL* FY1 .... 4 D6
Sandwash Cl *RNFD/HAY* WA11 .... 262 C2
Sandwell Av *CLV/TH* FY5 .... 85 M1
Sandwell Brow
  GAR/LONG PR3 .... 270 D12
Sandwich Cl *BBN* BB1 .... 157 M7
Sandwick Cl *FUL/RIB* PR2 .... 132 A7
Sandybeds Cl *ACC* BB5 .... 176 A1
Sandybrook Cl *FUL/RIB* PR2 .... 133 H6
Sandy Cl *CLV/TH* FY5 .... 80 F3
  SKEL WN8 .... 243 K1
Sandycroft *FUL/RIB* PR2 .... 153 J1
Sandyfields *KIRK/FR/WAR* PR4 .... 131 H6
Sandyforth Av *CLV/TH* FY5 .... 81 L1
Sandyforth La *HWTH* BD22 .... 297 N1
  KIRK/FR/WAR PR4 .... 131 K4
Sandygate *BLY* BB11 .... 6 D4
Sandygate La *GAR/LONG* PR3 .... 131 L1
Sandyhall La
  PDHM/BLYW BB12 .... 102 C8
Sandylands Prom *HEY* LA3 .... 40 E8
Sandy La *ACC* BB5 .... 159 M6
  BBNW 171 M1
  BPOOLS FY4 .... 125 K7
  BRSC L40 .... 242 A4
  BRSC L40 .... 202 F5
  CHLY/EC PR7 .... 230 C4
  CHLYE PR6 .... 169 M8
  DWN BB3 .... 173 H5
  FTWD FY7 .... 81 G4
  GAR/LONG PR3 .... 88 C2
  HTWN L38 .... 247 K8
  KIRK/FR/WAR PR4 .... 131 L4
  LEYL PR25 .... 186 D3
  MGHL L31 .... 259 K6
  MGHL L31 .... 249 M6
  NLSN BB9 .... 123 G1
  ORM L39 .... 250 E5
  PLF/KEOS FY6 .... 86 F2
  PLF/KEOS FY6 .... 78 E7
  ROCH OL11 .... 234 F4
  SKEL WN8 .... 253 G2
  SKEL WN8 .... 243 J2
  WGNW/BIL/OR WN5 .... 255 G7
Sandy Pl *LEYL* PR25 .... 186 D3
Sandy Wy *BRSC* L40 .... 203 G7
Sanfield Cl *ORM* L39 .... 241 G5
Sangara Dr *DWN* BB3 .... 173 J4
Sangness Dr *STHP* PR8 .... 200 B8
Sankey Rd *MGHL* L31 .... 259 G4
Sanraya Av *BPOOLS* FY4 .... 126 C5
Sansbury Crs *NLSN* BB9 .... 123 K2
Santon Cl *KIRK/FR/WAR* PR4 .... 128 C3
Sanvino Av *STHP* PR8 .... 221 G6
Sanworth St *TOD* OL14 .... 303 M2
Sapphire Dr *NWD/KWIPK* L33 .... 260 B6
Sapphire St *BBN* BB1 .... 157 J2
Sarah Butterworth Ct
  MILN OL16 .... 235 L4
Sarah La *CROS/BRETH* PR26 .... 184 C6
Sarah's Cft *NTHTN* L30 .... 258 B8
Sarahs Fold *PLF/KEOS* FY6 .... 82 F4
Sarah St *BCUP* OL13 .... 197 M3
  DWN BB3 .... 191 L4
  RAMS BL0 .... 195 H8
  ROCH OL11 .... 235 J5
Sark Gdns *BBNW* BB2 .... 173 J2
Sarmatian Fold
  GAR/LONG PR3 .... 116 A8
Sarscow La *CROS/BRETH* PR26 .... 205 H2
Satinwood Crs *MGHL* L31 .... 259 K8
Saul's Dr *CARN* LA5 .... 16 D3
Saul St *PRES* PR1 .... 9 H3
Saunder Bank *BLY* BB11 .... 6 F5
Saunder Height La
  RAW/HAS BB4 .... 178 A8
Saunders La *RAW/HAS* BB4 .... 177 K4
Saunders'
  KIRK/FR/WAR PR4 .... 167 G1
Saunders Ms *CHLY/EC* PR7 .... 207 M8
Saunders Rd *BBNW* BB2 .... 10 A4
Saunders St *CHTN/BK* PR9 .... 199 L2
Savick Av *FUL/RIB* PR2 .... 151 G2
Savick Cl *BBR* PR5 .... 169 J3
Savick Rd *FUL/RIB* PR2 .... 132 A7
Savick Wy *FUL/RIB* PR2 .... 131 H8
Saville Av *PLF/KEOS* FY6 .... 85 L5
Saville Rd *BPOOL* FY1 .... 4 A5
  MGHL L31 .... 249 M8
Saville St *CHLY/EC* PR7 .... 207 M6
Savon Hook *FMBY* L37 .... 247 G4
Savoy Av *HEY* LA3 .... 41 M6
Savoy St *ACC* BB5 .... 159 J6
  PRES PR1 .... 8 F4
  ROCH OL11 .... 234 F1
Sawdon Av *STHP* PR8 .... 200 B7
Sawley Av *ACC* BB5 .... 160 A4
  BPOOLS FY4 .... 125 G6
  LIT OL15 .... 219 K4

  WHIT OL12 * 235 J3
  PDHM/BLYW BB12 .... 140 A2
Sawley Cl *DWN* BB3 .... 191 M3
Sawley Crs *FUL/RIB* PR2 .... 133 J8
Sawley Dr *GTH/LHO* BB6 .... 139 H6
Sawley Rd *CLI* BB7 .... 291 J7
Sawmill Wy *LIT* OL15 .... 219 K7
Sawrey Ct *ACC* BB5 .... 139 H8
Sawthorpe Wk *PLF/KEOS* FY6 .... 85 K8
Sawyer St *WHIT* OL12 .... 235 J2
Saxby Gv *BPOOLS* FY4 .... 125 J2
Saxifield St *BRFD/BLYE* BB10 .... 124 E8
Saxon Cl *ACC* BB5 .... 158 F6
  CLV/TH FY5 .... 85 L3
Saxon Hey *FUL/RIB* PR2 .... 131 M8
Saxon St *CSBY/BLUN* L23 .... 257 G6
  STHP PR8 .... 12 D8
  TOD OL14 .... 303 K6
Saxthorpe Wk *CLV/TH* FY5 .... 260 B5
Saxwood Cl *WHIT* OL12 .... 234 C2
Scafell Av *MCMB* LA4 .... 41 L6
Scafell Cl *PDHM/BLYW* BB12 .... 141 M3
Scafell Dr *WGNW/BIL/OR* WN5 .... 255 G1
Scafell Rd *LANC* LA1 .... 3 K1
  LSTA FY8 .... 145 K1
Scaffold La *HTWN* L38 .... 247 M5
Scaitcliffe St *ACC* BB5 .... 159 L6
Scale Farm Rd *LANC* LA1 .... 2 A2
Scale Hall La
  KIRK/FR/WAR PR4 .... 149 K1
  LANC LA1 .... 2 C1
Scant Rw *NOR/BR* BL6 * 232 F8
Scape La *CSBY/BLUN* L23 .... 257 H6
Scarborough Rd *BBNW* BB2 .... 173 K2
  LSTA FY8 .... 145 K2
Scarfield Dr *ROCH* OL11 .... 234 B2
Scargill Rd *HGHB* LA2 .... 43 L3
Scarisbrick Av *SKEL* WN8 .... 243 M1
  STHP PR8 .... 12 F3
Scarisbrick Cl *MGHL* L31 .... 250 B8
Scarisbrick New Rd *STHP* PR8 .... 13 J7
Scarisbrick St
  RNFD/HAY WA11 .... 262 C4
  ORM L39 .... 241 H5
Scarlet St *CHLYE* PR6 .... 208 B4
Scarlett Dr *KIRK/FR/WAR* PR4 .... 167 H2
Scarlett St *BLY* BB11 .... 6 C6
Scarr Dr *WHIT* OL12 .... 235 J1
Scarr La *BBNW* BB2 .... 156 C4
Scar Rd *SKP/WHF* BD23 .... 279 K7
Scarsdale Av *BPOOLS* FY4 .... 124 F6
Scar St *BBNW* BB2 .... 156 E8
Scarth Hill La *ORM* L39 .... 251 H1
Scarth La *PDHM/BLYW* BB12 .... 140 E7
Scarth Pk *SKEL* WN8 .... 253 M4
Scawfell Rd *CHLY/EC* PR7 .... 207 L6
Sceptre Wy *BBR* PR5 .... 169 L5
Schleswig St *PRES* PR1 .... 9 K2
Schleswig Wy *LEYL* PR25 .... 185 M4
Schofield Av *BPOOLS* FY4 .... 105 L4
Schofield Cl *RAW/HAS* BB4 .... 195 J1
Schofield Rd *RAW/HAS* BB4 .... 195 J1
Schofield St *DWN* BB3 .... 191 J1
  LIT OL15 .... 219 M5
  RAW/HAS BB4 .... 196 B3
  RAW/HAS BB4 .... 194 D5
  ROCH OL11 .... 235 K7
Schola Green La *MCMB* LA4 .... 41 J6
Scholars Gn *FUL/RIB* PR2 .... 150 F2
Scholefield La *NLSN* BB9 .... 123 H6
Scholefield La *NLSN* BB9 .... 123 H6
Scholes Bank *HOR/BR* BL6 .... 231 K6
Scholes St *DWN* BB3 .... 191 J2
Scholfield St *TOD* OL14 .... 303 L1
School Av *FMBY* L37 .... 237 J8
School Cl *ORM* L39 * 250 F2
  STHP PR8 .... 221 L1
School Ct *RAMS* BL0 .... 215 G2
School Fld *BBR* PR5 .... 169 L6
School Flds *BWCK/EAR* BB18 .... 294 E4
Schoolfold *KIRK/FR/WAR* PR4 .... 165 C7
School HI *SETT* BD24 .... 265 P7
Schoolhouse Fold *BLY* BB11 .... 140 F8
School House La *BBR* PR5 .... 169 L4
School House Gv *BRSC* L40 .... 225 G6
School House La *ACC* BB5 .... 175 L1
Schoolhouse La *HGHB* LA2 .... 43 L4
School Houses *SKEL* WN8 * 253 L3
School Land La *HBR* HX7 .... 301 L5
School La *BBN* BB1 .... 174 A3
  BLY BB11 .... 7 G3
  BRFD/BLYE BB10 .... 163 K2
  BRSC L40 .... 242 B8
  BWCK/EAR BB18 .... 294 E5
  CHLY/EC PR7 .... 187 G8
  CHLYE PR6 .... 189 H3
  CLI BB7 .... 75 H5
  COL BB8 .... 296 H5
  EDGW/EG BL7 .... 213 H5
  FMBY L37 .... 237 J8
  GAR/LONG PR3 .... 283 P2
  GAR/LONG PR3 .... 88 C1
  GAR/LONG PR3 .... 79 M5
  HGHB LA2 .... 264 A5
  HGHB LA2 .... 36 F8
  KIRK/FR/WAR PR4 .... 166 D4
  KIRK/FR/WAR PR4 .... 148 C4
  KIRK/FR/WAR PR4 .... 109 M2
  LEYL PR25 .... 186 C1
  LSTA FY8 .... 146 C5
  MGHL L31 .... 259 K2
  MILN OL16 .... 235 J2
  ORM L39 .... 239 J8
  PDHM/BLYW BB12 .... 140 B2
  PLF/KEOS FY6 .... 78 E8
  SKEL WN8 .... 254 L4
  SKEL WN8 .... 253 G2
  SKEL WN8 .... 244 E8
  SKP/WHF BD23 .... 267 R6
  TOD OL14 .... 303 L2
School Rd *BPOOLS* FY4 .... 125 K7
  CLV/TH FY5 .... 85 M3
  HEY LA3 .... 52 D1
  HTWN L38 .... 247 J7
School St *ACC* BB5 .... 159 L6
  BBN BB1 .... 158 E2
  BBR PR5 .... 153 L8
  BCUP OL13 .... 196 E3
  BWCK/EAR BB18 * 294 D8
  DWN BB3 .... 191 K2
  GTH/LHO BB6 .... 138 D7
  HOR/BR BL6 .... 231 M8
  KIRK/FR/WAR PR4 .... 166 C1
  LEYL PR25 .... 186 E1
  LIT OL15 .... 219 L4
  NLSN BB9 .... 122 F3
  PRES PR1 .... 8 E1
  RAMS BL0 .... 214 E6
  RAW/HAS BB4 .... 177 L7

School Wy
  WGNW/BIL/OR WN5 .... 255 M5
Schwartzman Dr
  CHTN/BK PR9 .... 181 K5
Scorton Av *BPOOLS* FY3 .... 105 J4
Scorton Hall Pk
  GAR/LONG PR3 .... 284 D1
Scotch Green La
  GAR/LONG PR3 .... 92 C6
Scotforth Ct *LANC* LA1 * 54 F7
Scotforth Rd *HGHB* LA2 .... 66 F3
  PRES PR1 .... 152 F7
Scotland Bank Ter *BBNW* BB2 .... 172 E3
Scotland Rd *CARN* LA5 .... 26 D3
  NLSN BB9 .... 123 G1
Scotswood Av *BPOOLS* FY4 .... 125 G6
Scott Av *ACC* BB5 .... 176 B1
  MCMB LA4 .... 41 J8
  PDHM/BLYW BB12 .... 140 B2
Scott Cl *ACC* BB5 .... 159 G6
  BPOOLS FY4 .... 125 J3
  MGHL L31 .... 259 G2
Scott Dr *ORM* L39 .... 241 J4
Scott Gv *MCMB* LA4 .... 41 H7
Scott Laithe La *CLI* BB7 .... 291 P1
Scott Ms *BPOOLS* FY4 .... 125 J3
Scott Park Rd *BLY* BB11 .... 6 C1
Scott Rd *HEY* LA3 .... 41 G8
Scott St *ACC* BB5 .... 139 L4
  CHTN/BK PR9 .... 200 D4
  NLSN BB9 .... 123 G4
  PDHM/BLYW BB12 .... 141 J4
  TOD OL14 .... 303 K7
Scott's Wd *FUL/RIB* PR2 .... 131 M5
Scout Rd *RAMS* BL0 .... 215 K1
  RAW/HAS BB4 .... 178 B8
Scowcroft Dr *MCMB* LA4 .... 41 M6
Scow Croft La *CHLY/EC* PR7 .... 188 F7
Scrapers La *TOD* OL14 .... 301 L11
Scriffen La *HGHB* LA2 .... 67 M8
Scudamore Crs *BPOOLS* FY4 .... 125 G2
The Scythes *NTHTN* L30 .... 258 C7
Seabank Rd *CHTN/BK* PR9 .... 13 H1
  FTWD FY7 .... 77 K6
Seaborn Gv *MCMB* LA4 .... 41 L5
Seaborn Rd *MCMB* LA4 .... 41 L5
Seabourne Av *BPOOLS* FY4 .... 124 E4
Seabrook Dr *CLV/TH* FY5 .... 85 H3
Seacole Cl *BBN* BB1 .... 173 L2
Seacrest Av *BPOOL* FY1 .... 104 F3
Seacroft Crs *CHTN/BK* PR9 .... 180 E6
Seafield *FMBY* L37 .... 247 K4
Seafield Av *CSBY/BLUN* L23 .... 257 L6
Seafield Rd *BPOOL* FY1 .... 104 E3
  LSTA FY8 .... 146 C8
  STHP PR8 .... 220 F6
Seafore Cl *MGHL* L31 .... 249 L7
Sealand Av *FMBY* L37 .... 247 G1
Sealand Cl *FMBY* L37 .... 247 G1
Seascale Cl *BBNW* BB2 .... 173 J2
Seasiders Wy *BPOOL* FY1 .... 4 D4
Seaside Wy *BPOOL* FY1 .... 4 D4
Seathwaite Av *BPOOLS* FY4 .... 125 M2
  HEY LA3 .... 52 F1
Seathwaite Cl *CSBY/BLUN* L23 .... 256 B8
Seathwaite Crs
  NWD/KWIPK L33 .... 260 A7
Seathwaite Wy *ACC* BB5 .... 160 B3
Seatoller Pl
  WGNW/BIL/OR WN5 .... 255 L4
Seaton Av *CLV/TH* FY5 .... 81 H7
Seaton Crs *LSTA* FY8 .... 144 F3
Seaton Pl *SKEL* WN8 .... 243 H8
Seaton Wy *CHTN/BK* PR9 .... 180 D6
Seattle Av *BISP* FY2 .... 85 H8
Sea Vw *KIRK/FR/WAR* PR4 .... 166 C6
Sea View Dr *HGHB* LA2 * 42 C3
Sea View Dr *HGHB* LA2 .... 42 C3
Seaview Wy *FTWD* FY7 .... 77 L7
Sea Wall *FTWD* FY7 .... 80 F3
Seawell Av *HEY* LA3 .... 52 E1
Seawell Gdns *HEY* LA3 .... 52 E1
Second Av *ACC* BB5 .... 159 K8
  BPOOLS FY4 .... 124 F4
  CSBY/BLUN L23 * 257 G7
  PLF/KEOS FY6 .... 82 F2
Second St *BOL* BL1 .... 233 J7
Sedbergh Av *AIN/FAZ* L10 .... 258 F1
  BPOOLS FY4 .... 5 L8
Sedbergh Cl *ACC* BB5 .... 160 A6
Sedberg St *FUL/RIB* PR2 .... 132 A8
Sedburgh St *BRFD/BLYE* BB10 .... 142 F1
Seddon St *SKEL* WN8 .... 243 H8
Sedge Ct *HEY* LA3 .... 53 J1
Sedgefield La *BPOOLS* FY4 .... 125 J5
Sedgefield Dr *BOL* BL1 .... 233 L8
Sedgeley Ms
  KIRK/FR/WAR PR4 .... 148 D5
Sedgley Av *KIRK/FR/WAR* PR4 .... 148 D5
  MILN OL16 .... 235 L7
Sedgwick St *PRES* PR1 .... 9 J1
Sedum Gdns *ACC* BB5 .... 160 B1
Sedum Gv *NWD/KWIPK* L33 .... 260 A6
Sedwell Cl *LSTA* FY8 .... 146 C7
Seeall Av *CLI* BB7 .... 98 F3
Seedhill Ter *NLSN* BB9 * 123 G2
Seedlee Rd *BBR* PR5 .... 169 K5
Sefton Av *BLY* BB11 * 6 D5
  PLF/KEOS FY6 .... 106 A2
  WGNW/BIL/OR WN5 .... 255 G6
Sefton Cl *ACC* BB5 .... 139 K8
  DWN BB3 .... 191 M5
  KKBY L32 .... 259 M8
  WGNW/BIL/OR WN5 .... 255 G6
Sefton Coastal Footpath
  CSBY/BLUN L23 .... 256 C5
Sefton Dr *CSBY/BLUN* L23 .... 257 K4
  KKBY L32 .... 259 M8
  LANC LA1 .... 2 C1
  MGHL L31 .... 258 D3
Sefton Gdns *ORM* L39 .... 251 G4
Sefton La *MGHL* L31 .... 259 G8
Sefton Mill Ct *SFTN* L29 .... 258 C4
Sefton Mill La *SFTN* L29 .... 258 C4
Sefton Moss La *NTHTN* L30 .... 258 A8
Sefton Rd *BBR* PR5 .... 153 G8
  FMBY L37 .... 247 H1
  HEY LA3 .... 40 F7
  LSTA FY8 .... 145 J4
Sefton St *COL* BB8 .... 296 C6
  NLSN BB9 .... 122 E6
  ROCH OL11 .... 235 H6
  STHP PR8 .... 12 B6
Sefton Ter *BLY* BB11 .... 6 D5
Sefton Vw *CSBY/BLUN* L23 * 257 J7
Segar's La *ORM* L39 .... 221 L7
Segar St *STHP* PR8 .... 221 L7

Segar St *GTH/LHO* BB6 * 138 F6
  KIRK/FR/WAR PR4 .... 128 C5
Selborne St *BBNW* BB2 .... 156 F7
  PRES PR1 .... 9 K7
Selbourne Rd *BPOOL* FY1 .... 104 F5
Selbourne Ter
  BWCK/EAR BB18 .... 294 F5
Selby Av *BPOOLS* FY4 .... 125 G6
  CLV/TH FY5 .... 81 H6
  LANC LA1 .... 42 F7
Selby Cl *ACC* BB5 .... 160 B8
Selby Dr *FMBY* L37 .... 247 L1
  WGNS/IIMK WN3 .... 255 M7
Selby Pl *SKEL* WN8 .... 243 G8
Selby Rd *KIRK/FR/WAR* PR4 .... 128 C5
Selby St *COL* BB8 .... 103 M6
  FUL/RIB PR2 .... 152 A2
  MILN OL16 .... 235 L3
  NLSN BB9 .... 123 H4
Seldon St *COL* BB8 * 296 A7
  NLSN BB9 .... 123 H2
Selkirk Cl *WHIT* OL12 .... 218 A8
Selkirk Dr *BBR* PR5 .... 169 G1
Selkirk St *BLY* BB11 .... 6 G3
Sellers St *PRES* PR1 .... 152 F2
Selous Rd *BBNW* BB2 .... 156 E8
Selside Dr *MCMB* LA4 .... 41 J8
Selworthy Rd *STHP* PR8 .... 199 G8
Senior Av *BPOOLS* FY4 .... 5 M9
Seniors Dr *CLV/TH* FY5 .... 81 J8
Sephton Dr *ORM* L39 .... 241 J4
Sephton St *BBR* PR5 .... 168 D3
Serenade Rd *NWD/KWIPK* L33 .... 260 C5
Sergeant St *BBR* PR5 .... 169 J3
Serpentine Rd *BLY* BB11 .... 6 E7
The Serpentine South
  CSBY/BLUN L23 .... 256 D7
The Serpentine
  CSBY/BLUN L23 .... 256 D7
  LSTA FY8 .... 146 D8
  ORM L39 .... 251 G3
Sett End Rd North *BBN* BB1 .... 174 A1
Sett End Rd West *BBN* BB1 .... 173 M2
Settle Cl *CLI* BB7 .... 278 D4
Settle HI *LSTA* FY8 .... 145 M4
Settle Ter *BRFD/BLYE* BB10 .... 142 F1
Seven Acres Rd *CSBY/BLUN* L23 .... 257 L6
Seven Acres La *WHIT* OL12 .... 234 B1
Seven Acres Rd *WHIT* OL12 .... 234 B1
Sevenoaks *CHLY/EC* PR7 .... 207 M7
Sevenoaks Av *STHP* PR8 .... 220 F7
Sevenoaks Dr *CLV/TH* FY5 .... 85 J3
Seven Sands
  KIRK/FR/WAR PR4 .... 166 C2
Seven Stars Rd *LEYL* PR25 .... 186 A4
Seventh Av *BPOOLS* FY4 .... 124 F4
Seven Trees Av *BBN* BB1 * 157 K3
Severn Av *FTWD* FY7 .... 81 G3
Severn Ct *HEY* LA3 .... 54 A1
Severn Dr *BBR* PR5 .... 169 G1
  WGNW/BIL/OR WN5 .... 255 M5
Severn HI *FUL/RIB* PR2 .... 131 M3
Severn Rd *BPOOLS* FY4 .... 124 E4
  NWD/KWIPK L33 .... 260 C5
Severn St *GAR/LONG* PR3 .... 114 D4
Seymour Av *HEY* LA3 .... 52 E4
Seymour Ct *PRES* PR1 .... 152 A1
Seymour Dr *MGHL* L31 .... 250 B8
Seymour Gv *HEY* LA3 .... 52 E4
  MILN OL16 .... 235 L2
Seymour Rd *BPOOL* FY1 .... 4 B2
  FUL/RIB PR2 .... 131 M8
  LSTA FY8 .... 146 A6
Seymour St *CHLYE* PR6 .... 208 A3
  FTWD FY7 .... 77 J7
  LANC LA1 * 3 J5
Shacklady Rd *NWD/KWIPK* L33 .... 260 D7
Shackleton Rd
  KIRK/FR/WAR PR4 .... 148 E1
Shackleton St
  BRFD/BLYE BB10 .... 142 E3
  TOD OL14 .... 300 F10
Shaddock Av *WHIT* OL12 .... 234 C2
Shade La *CHLY/EC* PR7 .... 230 A1
Shade St *TOD* OL14 .... 303 K4
Shadsworth Rd *BBN* BB1 .... 157 M7
Shadwell St East *HEYW* OL10 .... 234 A8
Shadwell St West *HEYW* OL10 .... 234 A8
Shady La *BBR* PR5 .... 169 H7
  HGHB LA2 .... 42 D3
  LEYL PR25 .... 169 K8
Shaftesbury Av *BISP* FY2 .... 104 F1
  BLY BB11 .... 6 E9
  BPOOLE FY3 .... 174 L5
  CLV/TH FY5 .... 80 F5
  DWN BB3 .... 191 H8
  GTH/LHO BB6 .... 139 H5
  KIRK/FR/WAR PR4 .... 151 L5
  PRES PR1 .... 151 L2
  STHP PR8 .... 221 K4
Shaftesbury Cl *LSTA* FY8 .... 146 A4
Shaftesbury Gv *STHP* PR8 .... 221 K4
Shaftesbury Pl *CHLY/EC* PR7 .... 207 J7
  LANC LA1 .... 54 E7
Shaftesbury Av
  CSBY/BLUN L23 .... 257 G7
  STHP PR8 .... 221 K4
Shaftsbury Av
  NWD/KWIPK L33 .... 260 A6
Shaftsbury Rd
  WGNW/BIL/OR WN5 .... 255 K3
Shakeshaft St *BBN* BB1 .... 11 K5
Shakespeare Av *GTH/LHO* BB6 * 138 D7
  TOD OL14 .... 303 N1
Shakespeare Cl *LIT* OL15 .... 219 K4
Shakespeare Rd *FTWD* FY7 .... 77 H7
  LANC LA1 .... 42 H7
  PRES PR1 .... 153 G2
Shakespeare St
  PDHM/BLYW BB12 .... 141 G4
  STHP PR8 .... 13 G4
Shakespeare Ter *CHLYE* PR6 .... 208 A3
Shakespeare Wy *BBNW* BB2 .... 10 B7
Shalbourn Rd *LSTA* FY8 .... 145 K7
Shale St *PDHM/BLYW* BB12 .... 141 G5
Shalgrove Fld *FUL/RIB* PR2 .... 131 M4
Shannon St *BPOOL* FY1 .... 4 E6
Shap Cl *ACC* BB5 .... 160 B8
  NLSN BB9 .... 103 H3
Shap Ct *FTWD* FY7 .... 81 G2
Shap Gv *WGNW/BIL/OR* WN5 .... 255 K4
Shap Gv *BRFD/BLYE* BB10 .... 122 D8
Shard La *PLF/KEOS* FY6 .... 86 E5
Shard Rd *PLF/KEOS* FY6 .... 86 E5
Sharman Rd *LSTA* FY8 .... 145 J3
Sharoe Green La *FUL/RIB* PR2 .... 132 B4
Sharoe Green Pk *FUL/RIB* PR2 .... 132 C4
Sharoe Mount Av *FUL/RIB* PR2 .... 132 C4
Sharow Gv *BPOOL* FY1 .... 5 G1
Sharpe's Av *LANC* LA1 * 54 F7

Sharphaw Vw *SKP/WHF* BD23 .... 281 K2
Sharples Crs *CSBY/BLUN* L23 .... 257 J8
Sharples Gn *EDGW/EG* BL7 .... 213 G5
Sharples St *ACC* BB5 .... 159 J6
  BBNW BB2 .... 10 B1
Sharp St *BRFD/BLYE* BB10 .... 142 E1
  NLSN BB9 .... 103 H8
Sharratts Pth *CHLY/EC* PR7 .... 207 J7
Shawbridge Ct *CLI* BB7 .... 99 J3
Shaw Bridge St *CLI* BB7 .... 99 J3
Shaw Brook Cl *BBN* BB1 .... 158 D3
Shawbrook Cl *BLY* BB11 .... 140 F7
  CHLY/EC PR7 .... 186 F6
Shaw Brook Rd *LEYL* PR25 .... 186 B5
Shaw Brow *CHLYE* PR6 .... 187 L4
  GTH/LHO BB6 .... 138 D3
Shaw Cl *BBNW* BB2 .... 10 B4
Shawclough Cl *WHIT* OL12 .... 218 A8
Shawclough Dr *WHIT* OL12 .... 217 M8
Shawclough Rd *WHIT* OL12 * 235 G1
Shaw Clough Rd
  RAW/HAS BB4 .... 178 C8
Shawclough Rd *WHIT* OL12 .... 217 M8
Shaw Clough St
  RAW/HAS BB4 .... 178 C8
Shawclough Wy *WHIT* OL12 .... 217 M8
Shaw Crs *FMBY* L37 .... 237 L2
Shawes Dr *CHLYE* PR6 .... 230 F4
Shawfield *RAW/HAS* BB4 .... 195 J2
Shawfield La *WHIT* OL12 .... 234 C1
Shaw HI *CHLYE* PR6 .... 187 L5
Shaw Hill Cl *CHLYE* PR6 .... 187 L5
Shaw Hill St *CHLY/EC* PR7 .... 207 M4
Shaw La *KKBYL LA6 .... 33 L7
  TOD OL14 .... 300 E8
Shaw Rd *BPOOL* FY1 .... 124 E2
  HOR/BR BL6 .... 231 L6
Shaw's Av *STHP* PR8 .... 221 K2
Shaws Garth *ORM* L39 .... 222 C5
Shaw's La *GAR/LONG* PR3 .... 79 A3
Shaw's Rd *STHP* PR8 .... 221 K2
Shaw St *BBNW* BB2 .... 10 B8
  COL BB8 .... 103 M7
  LANC LA1 .... 3 J5
  PRES PR1 .... 9 G4
  RAW/HAS BB4 .... 176 B3
  WHIT OL12 .... 235 L1
Shaw Wood Rd *TOD* OL14 .... 303 G1
Shay La *CLI* BB7 .... 275 N5
  GAR/LONG PR3 .... 114 C6
Shays Dr *CLI* BB7 .... 99 J3
The Shay *CLV/TH* FY5 .... 85 J4
Shear Bank Cl *BBN* BB1 .... 10 C1
Shear Bank Gdns *BBN* BB1 .... 10 C1
Shear Bank Rd *BBN* BB1 .... 10 C1
Shear Brow *BBN* BB1 .... 10 B1
Shearing Av *WHIT* OL12 .... 234 C1
Shearwater Dr *BBN* BB1 .... 11 G2
Sheddon Gv *BRFD/BLYE* BB10 .... 143 H4
Shed St *ACC* BB5 .... 159 G8
  COL BB8 .... 103 M7
  WHIT OL12 .... 218 A2
Sheep Gap *WHIT* OL12 .... 234 E2
Sheep Gn *RAW/HAS* BB4 .... 176 B8
Sheep Hey *RAMS* BL0 * 215 G2
Sheep Hill Brow *CHLYE* PR6 .... 187 K1
Sheep Hill La *CHLYE* PR6 .... 187 J1
Sheephill La *KIRK/FR/WAR* PR4 .... 167 J4
Sheephouse La *HOR/BR* BL6 .... 231 K1
Sheep House La *HOR/BR* BL6 .... 231 J1
Sheernest La *WALSEY LA6 .... 18 F2
Sheffield Dr *FUL/RIB* PR2 .... 151 G1
Sheldon Ct *PRES* PR1 * 152 C2
Shelfield La *BRFD/BLYE* BB10 .... 296 B12
  ROCH OL11 .... 234 C2
Shelfield Rd *NLSN* BB9 .... 123 L2
Shelley Cl *BISP* FY2 .... 85 J8
  CARN LA5 .... 32 F6
  CHLY/EC PR7 .... 229 J3
Shelley Dr *ACC* BB5 .... 176 B1
  CHLY/EC PR7 .... 206 A6
  ORM L39 .... 241 G5
  WGNW/BIL/OR WN5 .... 255 K5
Shelley Gdns *GTH/LHO* BB6 * 138 C7
Shelley Gv *CLV/TH* FY5 .... 85 G3
  DWN BB3 .... 191 M2
  STHP PR8 .... 200 C4
Shelley Ms *FUL/RIB* PR2 .... 151 K2
Shelley Rd *FUL/RIB* PR2 .... 151 M1
Shelifield La *CHTN/BK* PR9 .... 180 C3
Shellingford Cl
  WGNNW/ST WN6 .... 245 G4
Shelly Road Mi *FUL/RIB* PR2 * 151 M2
Shelton Dr *STHP* PR8 .... 220 D7
Shenley Wy *CHTN/BK* PR9 * 181 G6
Shenstone Rd *BPOOLE* FY3 .... 105 H4
Shepherd Ga *HGHB* LA2 .... 264 D2
Shepherd St *LSTA* FY8 .... 145 K4
Shepherd Rd North *LSTA* FY8 .... 145 K3
Shepherd's Av *GAR/LONG* PR3 .... 284 C11
Shepherds Cl *HOR/BR* BL6 .... 230 F8
Shepherd's Dr *HOR/BR* BL6 .... 232 D4
Shepherds Gn *RAW/HAS* BB4 .... 178 D3
Shepherd's La *ORM* L39 .... 240 A4
Shepherd St *BCUP* OL13 .... 179 J8
  DWN BB3 .... 191 K4
  LSTA FY8 .... 146 E8
  PRES PR1 .... 9 K4
  ROCH OL11 .... 234 A2
  WHIT OL12 .... 235 J3
Shepherds Wy *CHLYE* PR6 .... 208 A3
Sheppard St *BPOOL* FY1 .... 4 D2
Sheraton Cl
  WGNW/BIL/OR WN5 .... 255 L2
Sheraton Pk *FUL/RIB* PR2 .... 131 K5
Sherborne Rd
  WGNW/BIL/OR WN5 .... 255 K3
Sherbourne Cl *PLF/KEOS* FY6 .... 85 M6
Sherbourne Crs *PRES* PR1 .... 132 E3
Sherbourne Rd *ACC* BB5 .... 160 B8
  BPOOL FY1 .... 104 E3
  PLF/KEOS FY6 .... 86 F1
Sherbourne St *CHLYE* PR6 .... 208 A4
Sherburne Av
  KIRK/FR/WAR PR4 .... 128 C6
Sherburn Rd *PRES* PR1 .... 152 B8
Sherdley Rd *BBR* PR5 .... 168 E4
Sheridan Rd *COL* BB8 .... 296 C5
Sheridan St *NLSN* BB9 .... 123 G2
Sheriff St *WHIT* OL12 .... 235 H2
Sheringham Av *CLV/TH* FY5 .... 85 G5
Sheringham Wy *PLF/KEOS* FY6 .... 86 B8
Sherrat St *SKEL* WN8 .... 253 G2
Sherringham Rd *STHP* PR8 .... 221 H5
Sherwood Av *BPOOLS* FY3 .... 105 H3
  CSBY/BLUN L23 .... 257 G6
  ORM L39 .... 251 G3
Sherwood Ct *BPOOLE* FY3 * 105 H3
  BRFD/BLYE BB10 .... 7 M6
Sherwood Dr *SKEL* WN8 .... 244 M7

Sherwood Pl *CHLYE* PR6 208 A3
CLV/TH FY5 85 J2
Sherwood Rd *BBN* BB1 11 M6
CSBY/BLUN L23 256 F6
LSTA FY8 145 M5
Sherwood Wy *ACC* BB5 159 K2
FUL/RIB PR2 132 D5
Shetland Cl *BBN* BB1 157 M8
BBN BB1 137 J5
Shetland Rd *BPOOL* FY1 4 F8
Shevington Cswy
CROS/BRETH PR26 204 D1
Shevington La
WGNNW/ST WN6 245 L4
Shevington Moor
WGNNW/ST WN6 245 K1
Shevington's La
NWD/KWIPK L33 260 B6
Shilton St *RAMS* BL0 214 E6
Shipley Cl *BPOOLE* FY3 105 L2
Shipley Rd *LSTA* FY8 145 L4
Shipper Bottom La *RAMS* BL0 215 G6
Shirburn *ROCH* OL11 * 235 H5
Shirdley Crs *STHP* PR8 220 F8
Shire Bank Crs *FUL/RIB* PR2 132 B5
Shireburn Av *CLI* BB7 98 F4
Shireburn Rd *FMBY* L37 236 F6
Shire La *CLI* BB7 117 G3
Shireshead Crs *LANC* LA1 66 F1
The Shires *BBNW* BB2 173 G5
Shirewell Rd
WGNW/BIL/OR WN5 255 H6
Shirley Crs *BISP* FY2 85 C5
Shirley Hts *PLF/KEOS* FY6 86 A7
Shirley La *KIRK/FR/WAR* PR4 166 D2
Shoebroad La *TOD* OL14 303 L3
Shop La *ACC* BB5 160 A7
BBR PR5 153 L7
MGHL L31 258 F2
Shore Av *BRFD/BLYE* BB10 143 H1
Shore Cl *CARN* LA5 24 E1
Shore Fold *LIT* OL15 219 J5
Shore Gn *CARN* LA5 24 E1
CLV/TH FY5 81 J8
TOD OL14 300 F9
Shore Hl *LIT* OL15 219 M5
Shore Lea *LIT* OL15 219 J5
Shore Mt *LIT* OL15 219 J5
Shore New Rd *TOD* OL14 300 E9
Shore Rd *CARN* LA5 24 E1
CLV/TH FY5 84 F3
HEY LA3 52 C5
KIRK/FR/WAR PR4 164 D8
LIT OL15 219 J4
STHP PR8 220 C5
The Shore *CARN* LA5 32 D6
Shorey Bank *BLY* BB11 7 H2
Shorrock La *BBNW* BB2 172 E2
Shorrocks Av *GAR/LONG* PR3 89 M3
Shorrock St *DWN* BB3 191 K3
Shortbutts La *KKBYL* LA6 20 D2
Short Clough Cl *RAW/HAS* BB4 177 K5
Short Clough La
RAW/HAS BB4 177 K5
Shorten Brook Dr *ACC* BB5 140 B5
Shorten Brook Wy *ACC* BB5 140 B5
Shortlands Dr *HEY* LA3 52 D4
The Shortlands
PDHM/BLYW BB12 140 F1
Short La *GAR/LONG* PR3 112 C6
Shortridge Rd *BPOOLS* FY4 125 J3
Short St *BCUP* OL13 196 E3
COL BB8 296 A7
WGNW/BIL/OR WN5 255 L5
Shottwood Fold *LIT* OL15 219 M3
Showfield *BRFD/BLYE* BB10 143 L5
Showley Brook Cl *BBN* BB1 137 J7
Showley Ct *BBN* BB1 137 H5
Showley Rd *BBN* BB1 136 D6
Shrewsbury Av *CSBY/WL* L22 257 G8
Shrewsbury Cl
KIRK/FR/WAR PR4 128 F6
Shrewsbury Dr *CLV/TH* FY5 85 K1
LANC LA1 55 G6
Shropshire Cl *NTHTN* L30 258 D7
Shropshire Dr *BBN* BB1 137 J5
Shuttle Cl *ACC* BB5 159 K5
Shuttleworth Md
PDHM/BLYW BB12 * 140 A2
Shuttleworth Rd *PRES* PR1 152 C1
Shuttleworth St *BBN* BB1 158 E1
BRFD/BLYE BB10 * 142 E1
BWCK/EAR BB18 * 294 E5
Shuttling Fields La *BBR* PR5 169 L1
Sibbering Brow Preston Rd
CHLY/EC PR7 206 F4
Sibsey St *LANC* LA1 2 E7
Siddows Av *CLI* BB7 98 F4
Sidebeet La *BBN* BB1 158 B3
Sidegarth La *HGHB* LA2 34 F5
Sidegate La *AIRE* BD20 295 P8
Side La *CLI* BB7 292 D8
Sidgreaves La
KIRK/FR/WAR PR4 130 E6
Siding La *RNFD/HAY* WA11 262 A2
Siding Rd *FTWD* FY7 77 K8
Sidings Rd *HEY* LA3 64 E1
The Sidings *BCUP* OL13 197 K3
CLI BB7 118 F5
COL BB8 103 M7
DWN BB3 191 L4
HGHB LA2 38 D4
SETT BD24 265 N8
Siding St *BCUP* OL13 196 F3
Sidmouth Av *RAW/HAS* BB4 194 F1
Sidmouth Rd *LSTA* FY8 144 F2
Sidney Av *BISP* FY2 105 H1
KIRK/FR/WAR PR4 183 H1
Sidney Rd *CHTN/BK* PR9 200 C3
Sidney Ter *LANC* LA1 * 3 J5
Siebers Bank *WHIT* OL12 * 235 G1
Siggett La *TOD* OL14 303 J1
Silbury Cl *BBNW* BB2 173 K3
Silk Mill La *GAR/LONG* PR3 92 E8
Silk St *ROCH* OL11 235 G7
Silloth Cl *BBNW* BB2 173 H2
Silly La *HGHB* LA2 49 G7
Silsden Cl *BPOOLE* FY3 105 L2
Silver Birch Wy *MGHL* L31 249 L6
Silverdale *BISP* FY2 85 H5
KIRK/FR/WAR PR4 165 J8
Silverdale Av *FTWD* FY7 80 F2
HEY LA3 52 E5
Silverdale Cl *ACC* BB5 159 H1
BBNW BB2 173 J3
BBR PR5 154 B7
BRFD/BLYE BB10 122 E8
LEYL PR25 186 E5
Silverdale Dr *FUL/RIB* PR2 133 G6
Silverdale Moss Rd *CARN* LA5 17 G4
Silverdale Rd *CARN* LA5 16 E2
CHLYE PR6 208 B4
LSTA FY8 145 M4
WGNW/BIL/OR WN5 255 L3
Silversmiths Rw *LSTA* FY8 146 A4
Silverstone Gv *MGHL* L31 249 L6
Silver St *CLI* BB7 117 H2
KIRK/FR/WAR PR4 150 A2
PRES PR1 9 K6
RAMS BL0 214 F5
TOD OL14 303 K8
WHIT OL12 * 235 G3
Silverthorne Dr
CHTN/BK PR9 200 C2
Silverwell St *HOR/BR* BL6 231 L7
Silverwood Av *BPOOLS* FY4 124 F3
Silverwood Cl *LSTA* FY8 146 B7
Silvester Rd *CHLY/EC* PR7 207 M5
Silvia Wy *FTWD* FY7 77 H7
Simeon St *TOD* OL14 303 K7
Simmonds Wy *NLSN* BB9 122 E4
Simmons Av *BBR* PR5 152 E8
Simmons' St *BBNW* BB2 10 D3
Simmons Wy *ACC* BB5 139 K8
Simon's Cft *NTHTN* L30 257 M8
Simonstone La
PDHM/BLYW BB12 140 B3
Simonstone Rd *CLI* BB7 120 C5
Simonswood La *ORM* L39 251 J8
Simpson Cl *BWCK/EAR* BB18 294 A4
Simpson Hill Cl *HEYW* OL10 234 C8
Simpson St *ACC* BB5 159 G8
BPOOLS FY4 124 E3
PDHM/BLYW BB12 140 F7
PRES PR1 * 9 G3
Sinclair St *ROCH* OL11 235 G8
Sineacre La *ORM* L39 261 H2
Singleton Av *HOR/BR* BL6 231 M6
LSTA FY8 145 L4
PDHM/BLYW BB12 140 A1
Singleton Cl *FUL/RIB* PR2 132 C4
Singleton Rd
KIRK/FR/WAR PR4 107 H5
Singleton Rw *PRES* PR1 9 G2
Singleton St *BPOOL* FY1 4 C5
Singleton Wy *FUL/RIB* PR2 132 C4
Sion Cl *FUL/RIB* PR2 133 J7
Sir Frank Whittle Wy
BPOOLS FY4 125 G7
Sir Simon's Ar *LANC* LA1 * 3 G6
Sir Tom Finney Wy *PRES* PR1 152 E1
Sir William Hartley Ct *COL* BB8 296 F5
Siskin Av *BCUP* OL13 197 L1
Sisley La *TOD* OL14 303 R3
Six Acre La *KIRK/FR/WAR* PR4 166 F5
Sixfields *CLV/TH* FY5 85 J4
Sixth Av *BPOOLS* FY4 124 F4
Sizehouse St *PRES* PR1 9 H2
Sizergh Ct *LANC* LA1 2 C9
Sizergh Rd *MCMB* LA4 41 M6
Sizer St *PRES* PR1 152 C2
Size St *WHIT* OL12 218 A2
The Skaithe *CLI* BB7 275 P5
Skeffington Rd *PRES* PR1 152 E1
Skeleron La *CLI* BB7 292 C9
Skelmersdale Rd *ORM* L39 252 D4
Skelshaw Cl *BBN* BB1 11 J8
Skelton St *COL* BB8 296 B6
Skelwith Rd *BPOOLE* FY3 125 L1
Skerton *LANC* LA1 3 G1
Skiddaw Cl *PDHM/BLYW* BB12 141 M2
Skiddaw Pl
WGNW/BIL/OR WN5 255 M5
Skiddaw Rd *LANC* LA1 3 K2
Skiddaw St *BBN* BB1 11 K4
Skip La *KIRK/FR/WAR* PR4 166 E1
Skippool Av *PLF/KEOS* FY6 86 B6
Skippool Br *PLF/KEOS* FY6 86 C5
Skippool Rd *CLV/TH* FY5 86 B4
Skipton Av *CHTN/BK* PR9 180 F5
PLF/KEOS FY6 85 M6
Skipton Cl *BBR* PR5 169 H1
BPOOLS FY4 5 M9
Skipton Crs *FUL/RIB* PR2 133 H6
Skipton Old Rd *COL* BB8 296 B1
Skipton Rd *BWCK/EAR* BB18 293 Q5
COL BB8 296 B5
LSTA FY8 145 L5
SKP/WHF BD23 281 K2
Skipton St *MCMB* LA4 * 41 H6
Skitham La *GAR/LONG* PR3 282 D12
Skull House La
WGNNW/ST WN6 244 F3
Skull House Ms
WGNNW/ST WN6 244 F2
Skye Crs *BBN* BB1 157 M8
Slack *PDHM/BLYW* BB12 121 J5
Slackey La *CHTN/BK* PR9 180 F7
Slack Ga *WHIT* OL12 218 B3
Slack La *HGHB* LA2 268 F2
Slack's La *CHLYE* PR6 230 E1
Slack St *MILN* OL16 235 J4
Slackwood La *CARN* LA5 25 H1
Slade La *PDHM/BLYW* BB12 140 F1
Sladen St *WHIT* OL12 235 J2
Slade St *PRES* PR1 8 E4
Slaidburn Av *BRFD/BLYE* BB10 143 G7
RAW/HAS BB4 177 K7
Slaidburn Crs *CHTN/BK* PR9 180 D6
Slaidburn Dr *ACC* BB5 159 J7
LANC LA1 54 F8
Slaidburn Pl *FUL/RIB* PR2 153 K1
Slaidburn Rd *CLI* BB7 289 N2
FUL/RIB PR2 153 J1
HGHB LA2 49 H3
Slant La *TOD* OL14 303 N1
Slape La *KKBYL* LA6 19 J4
Slate La *SKEL* WN8 252 F1
Slater Av *COL* BB8 296 A5
HOR/BR BL6 231 M7
Slater La *CROS/BRETH* PR26 185 L3
Slater Rd *CLV/TH* FY5 84 F1
Slater St *BBNW* BB2 172 F2
Slawson Wy *HEYW* OL10 234 C8
Sledbrook St
WGNW/BIL/OR WN5 * 255 M6
Slinger Rd *CLV/TH* FY5 80 F8
Sliven Clod Rd *RAW/HAS* BB4 177 H1
Sluice La *BRSC* L40 203 L8
Slyne Rd *MCMB* LA4 42 A7
Smalden La *CLI* BB7 276 F11
Smalley Cft *PRES* PR1 152 C8
Smalley St *BLY* BB11 7 K7
Smalley Thorn Brow
GTH/LHO BB6 138 C6
Smalley Wy *BBNW* BB2 10 F9
The Smallholdings *MGHL* L31 * 250 D8
Small La *BRSC* L40 224 B3
ORM L39 240 C8
Small La North *ORM* L39 240 A1
Small La South *ORM* L39 239 M6
Smallshaw La *BLY* BB11 141 L6
Smallshaw Rd *WHIT* OL12 217 K7
Smallwood Hey Rd
GAR/LONG PR3 79 L6
Smelt Mill Cots *CLI* BB7 * 273 Q9
Smethurst La
WGNW/BIL/OR WN5 255 M6
Smethurst Park Hall
WGNW/BIL/OR WN5 263 M1
Smethurst Rd
WGNW/BIL/OR WN5 263 M1
Smethurst St
WGNW/BIL/OR WN5 255 M6
Smirthwaite St *BLY* BB11 6 A6
Smith Av *KIRK/FR/WAR* PR4 183 J2
WGNW/BIL/OR WN5 255 L3
Smith Cl *FUL/RIB* PR2 133 M2
Smith Cft *CROS/BRETH* PR26 185 K3
Smithills Cl *CHLYE* PR6 208 B2
Smithills Croft Rd *BOL* BL1 233 K8
Smithills Dean Rd *BOL* BL1 233 K6
Smithills Hall Cl *RAMS* BL0 214 E7
Smith Rd *CLV/TH* FY5 85 G1
Smith's La *KIRK/FR/WAR* PR4 203 K2
Smith St *BBR* PR5 169 J3
BRFD/BLYE BB10 143 L6
BWCK/EAR BB18 293 P6
CHLY/EC PR7 208 A5
CHLYE PR6 187 M3
COL BB8 103 M7
KIRK/FR/WAR PR4 128 C6
LIT OL15 219 L6
MILN OL16 235 J4
NLSN BB9 123 H3
PDHM/BLYW BB12 6 D3
RAMS BL0 214 E6
SKEL WN8 253 G2
Smithybridge Rd *MILN* OL16 219 H7
Smithy Bridge St *ACC* BB5 159 G8
Smithy Brow *SKEL* WN8 243 K2
WGNNW/ST WN6 227 M3
Smithy Brow Ct *RAW/HAS* BB4 176 E7
Smithy Cl *CHLYE* PR6 170 C6
FMBY L37 237 L7
GAR/LONG PR3 284 B7
PLF/KEOS FY6 82 E4
Smithy Croft Rd
SKP/WHF BD23 281 K2
Smithyfield Av
BRFD/BLYE BB10 143 J5
Smithy Fold
KIRK/FR/WAR PR4 * 127 L7
WHIT OL12 234 E2
Smithy Glen Dr
WGNW/BIL/OR WN5 255 H7
Smithy Gn *FMBY* L37 237 K7
Smithy La *BPOOLE* FY3 106 A5
BRSC L40 226 E1
BRSC L40 223 M7
BRSC L40 202 F5
CHLYE PR6 170 B5
COL BB8 103 L3
GAR/LONG PR3 91 K1
HBR HX7 301 R6
HEY LA3 52 C5
KIRK/FR/WAR PR4 184 B1
KKBYL LA6 31 M3
LSTA FY8 145 M5
ORM L39 250 C5
ORM L39 239 K5
PLF/KEOS FY6 82 F4
Smithy Ms *BPOOL* FY1 104 F4
Smithy Rw *CLI* BB7 117 H2
Smithy St *BBR* PR5 169 H3
RAMS BL0 * 214 F5
The Smithy *CLI* BB7 * 118 F6
Snaefell Rd *BBNW* BB2 173 H2
Snape Gn *STHP* PR8 223 G3
Snape La *CARN* LA5 26 C2
Snape Rake La *GAR/LONG* PR3 285 Q10
Snape St *DWN* BB3 173 J8
Snapewood La *GAR/LONG* PR3 283 R4
Snell Gv *COL* BB8 296 C5
Sniddle Hill La *DWN* BB3 191 H3
Snipe Av *ROCH* OL11 234 C4
Snipe Cl *BPOOLE* FY3 105 L5
CLV/TH FY5 81 J6
Snipewood *CHLY/EC* PR7 205 L5
Snoballey *BRSC* L40 223 L7
Snodworth Rd *GTH/LHO* BB6 138 A4
Snowden St
PDHM/BLYW BB12 141 L5
Snowdon Av *BBN* BB1 157 H4
Snowdon Cl *BPOOL* FY1 5 H5
Snowdon Dr *HOR/BR* BL6 231 M6
Snowdon Rd *LSTA* FY8 145 K1
Snowdrop Cl *LEYL* PR25 187 H1
RAW/HAS BB4 194 C3
Snow Hl *PRES* PR1 9 H2
Snowhill La *GAR/LONG* PR3 284 E1
Snowshill Crs *CLV/TH* FY5 85 J4
Snowshill Dr *WGNS/IIMK* WN3 255 M7
Snow St *BBN* BB1 11 G1
Sod Hall La *KIRK/FR/WAR* PR4 167 K5
Sollam's Cl *BBR* PR5 169 J1
Sollom La *KIRK/FR/WAR* PR4 203 L1
Solway Av *BBNW* BB2 172 C2
Solway Cl *BISP* FY2 84 F5
PRES PR1 152 D8
Somerby Rd *MCMB* LA4 41 K7
Somerford Cl *PDHM/BLYW* BB12 6 A1
Somerset Av *BBN* BB1 137 J5
BPOOL FY1 5 H5
CHLY/EC PR7 207 M2
CLI BB7 99 J1
DWN BB3 173 J8
LANC LA1 54 F5
Somerset Cl *ACC* BB5 159 J8
Somerset Ct *BPOOL* FY1 5 H5
Somerset Dr *STHP* PR8 237 M1
Somerset Gv *ACC* BB5 159 J4
ROCH OL11 234 D3
Somerset Pk *FUL/RIB* PR2 131 L4
Somerset Pl *NLSN* BB9 123 K2
Somerset Rd *BBN* BB1 158 C2
LEYL PR25 186 E1
PRES PR1 152 D2
WGNW/BIL/OR WN5 255 M5
Somerset St *BLY* BB11 * 7 H8
Somerset Wk *RAW/HAS* BB4 194 E3
Somerville Sq *BOL* BL1 233 M8
Somerville St *BOL* BL1 233 M8
Sorany Cl *CSBY/BLUN* L23 257 L5
Sorrel Cl *CLV/TH* FY5 81 J6
PLF/KEOS FY6 78 D5
Sorrel Ct *PRES* PR1 167 M1
Sorrel Dr *LIT* OL15 219 J5
Soudan St *BRFD/BLYE* BB10 * 142 E1
Soughbridge Mi
BWCK/EAR BB18 * 294 D8
Sough La *BBN* BB1 174 C2
BWCK/EAR BB18 294 D8
Sough Rd *DWN* BB3 191 L3
Soulby Cl *BBNW* BB2 172 F2
Sourhall Ct *TOD* OL14 302 G1
Sourhall Rd *TOD* OL14 302 G2
South Av *BWCK/EAR* BB18 293 Q4
CHLY/EC PR7 208 A5
CLV/TH FY5 80 F7
HGHB LA2 66 F5
KIRK/FR/WAR PR4 167 J3
MCMB LA4 41 G4
Southbank Av *BPOOLS* FY4 125 K4
Southbank Rd *STHP* PR8 13 H7
Southbourne Av
PLF/KEOS FY6 105 M1
Southbrook Rd *LEYL* PR25 186 B2
Southcliffe *GTH/LHO* BB6 138 E5
Southcliffe Av
PDHM/BLYW BB12 141 M4
South Cliff St *PRES* PR1 8 F6
South Clifton St *LSTA* FY8 146 E8
Southdene *SKEL* WN8 243 L2
Southdown Cl *ROCH* OL11 234 F7
Southdown Dr *CLV/TH* FY5 86 A3
Southdowns Rd *CHLY/EC* PR7 208 A6
South Dr *FUL/RIB* PR2 132 B3
KIRK/FR/WAR PR4 109 M3
LANC LA1 67 G5
PDHM/BLYW BB12 141 G3
South East Dr *LANC* LA1 67 G4
South End *PRES* PR1 8 E8
Southern Av
PDHM/BLYW BB12 141 M4
PRES PR1 9 M6
Southern Cl *GAR/LONG* PR3 114 D5
Southern Pde *PRES* PR1 9 M6
Southern Rd *STHP* PR8 12 E6
Southern's La
RNFD/HAY WA11 262 D5
Southey Cl *FUL/RIB* PR2 132 C4
Southey Gv *MGHL* L31 259 G5
Southey St *BLY* BB11 6 C4
Southfield *KIRK/FR/WAR* PR4 166 B8
Southfield Dr *BPOOLE* FY3 105 M3
CLI BB7 290 E9
KIRK/FR/WAR PR4 167 J4
Southfield La
BRFD/BLYE BB10 123 M5
COL BB8 296 A10
Southfield Sq *NLSN* BB9 * 123 J3
Southfield St *NLSN* BB9 123 J3
Southfleet Av *FTWD* FY7 81 H2
Southfleet Pl *FTWD* FY7 81 H2
Southfold Pl *LSTA* FY8 146 D7
Southgate *FTWD* FY7 81 G3
FUL/RIB PR2 132 A6
HEY LA3 53 L1
WHIT OL12 217 L4
Southgates *CHLY/EC* PR7 207 G8
South Gv *FUL/RIB* PR2 132 B3
GAR/LONG PR3 111 L3
MCMB LA4 41 K6
South Hey *LSTA* FY8 145 M5
South Holme *LSTA* FY8 146 E7
South Holme Ter
RAW/HAS BB4 178 C8
South King St *BPOOL* FY1 4 E2
Southlands *KIRK/FR/WAR* PR4 128 D7
Southlands Av *BBR* PR5 168 E2
Southlands Dr
CROS/BRETH PR26 185 M3
South Lawn *BPOOLS* FY4 5 K8
South Meade *MGHL* L31 258 E2
South Meadow La *PRES* PR1 8 E7
South Meadow St *PRES* PR1 * 9 L3
South Moss Rd *LSTA* FY8 145 M4
South Pde *CLV/TH* FY5 85 H2
MILN OL16 235 J4
South Pk *LSTA* FY8 146 C7
South Park Dr *BPOOLE* FY3 5 L7
South Park Rd *KKBY* L32 259 M8
Southport New Rd
CHTN/BK PR9 181 L7
KIRK/FR/WAR PR4 182 E8
Southport Old Rd *FMBY* L37 237 L4
Southport Rd *BRSC* L40 240 D1
CROS/BRETH PR26 205 K1
CSBY/BLUN L23 257 K4
FMBY L37 237 K6
MGHL L31 249 K6
ORM L39 241 H5
ORM L39 239 K5
STHP PR8 222 D1
Southport Ter *CHLYE* PR6 208 B4
South Prom *LSTA* FY8 145 H6
South Ribble St *BBR* PR5 152 F5
South Rd *CHLY/EC* PR7 229 H2
CLV/TH FY5 86 A1
CROS/BRETH PR26 184 B6
LANC LA1 3 H8
MCMB LA4 41 K6
South Shore St *ACC* BB5 159 H6
RAW/HAS BB4 176 D8
South Sq *BPOOLE* FY3 105 G5
CLV/TH FY5 80 F6
South Strd *FTWD* FY7 81 G4
South St *ACC* BB5 159 M6
BCUP OL13 197 K1
BLY BB11 7 G3
DWN BB3 191 K3
GAR/LONG PR3 88 E6
LSTA FY8 147 G7
MILN OL16 235 K3
RAMS BL0 215 G5
RAW/HAS BB4 194 F2
SKP/WHF BD23 281 K2
South Ter *ORM* L39 241 H7
South Terrace Ct *MILN* OL16 235 K6
South Valley Dr *COL* BB8 103 M8
South Vw *BBR* PR5 * 168 D4
EDGW/EG BL7 210 F6
KIRK/FR/WAR PR4 128 D7
NLSN BB9 123 G4
PDHM/BLYW BB12 * 120 B8
ROCH OL11 234 B5
South View Rd *MILN* OL16 219 H8
South View St *TOD* OL14 300 F10
South View Ter *LEYL* PR25 186 D3
MILN OL16 219 H7
South Warton St *LSTA* FY8 146 F8
Southway *FTWD* FY7 81 G2
SKEL WN8 253 L3
South Westby St *LSTA* FY8 146 E8
South West Dr *LANC* LA1 66 F4
Southwood Av *FTWD* FY7 77 H8
Southwood Cl *LSTA* FY8 146 B7
Southwood Dr *ACC* BB5 160 B8
Southworth Av *BPOOLS* FY4 125 H4
Southworth St *BBNW* BB2 173 G1
Southworth Wy *CLV/TH* FY5 81 H6
Sovereign Ga *BPOOLS* FY4 125 J6
Sowarth Fld *SETT* BD24 265 M7
Sow Clough Rd *BCUP* OL13 197 G2
Sowerby Av *BPOOLS* FY4 125 G3
Sowerby Rd *GAR/LONG* PR3 110 B1
Sowerby St
PDHM/BLYW BB12 140 F3
Sower Carr La *PLF/KEOS* FY6 83 G7
Spa Fold *BRSC* L40 242 D7
Spa Garth *CLI* BB7 99 J3
Spa La *BRSC* L40 242 E7
Spalding Av *GAR/LONG* PR3 284 C9
Spark La *BRSC* L40 203 L5
Spa Rd *PRES* PR1 8 D3
Sparrowhawk Dr
PLF/KEOS FY6 78 E7
Sparrow Hl *MILN* OL16 235 H4
SKEL WN8 244 D1
Sparth Av *ACC* BB5 139 J8
Sparth Bottoms Rd
ROCH OL11 235 G5
Sparthfield Av *ROCH* OL11 235 H6
Sparth Rd *ACC* BB5 139 J8
Spa St *PDHM/BLYW* BB12 141 G3
PDHM/BLYW BB12 6 C2
PRES PR1 8 C2
Speakmana Dr
WGNNW/ST WN6 244 F5
Speedie Cl *BBNW* BB2 173 G3
Speedwell Cl *CLV/TH* FY5 81 J6
Speedwell St *BBNW* BB2 172 E1
Speke St *BBNW* BB2 172 E1
Spenbrook Rd
PDHM/BLYW BB12 101 M8
Spen Brow *HGHB* LA2 38 B8
Spencer Ct *BPOOL* FY1 104 F4
Spencer Gv *GTH/LHO* BB6 138 E6
Spencer La *ROCH* OL11 234 B6
Spencer Pl *CHTN/BK* PR9 * 13 K4
Spencers Dr
KIRK/FR/WAR PR4 183 K3
Spencers La *ORM* L39 221 M8
SKEL WN8 253 L5
Spencer's La *MGHL* L31 259 J8
WGNW/BIL/OR WN5 255 G4
Spencer St *ACC* BB5 160 A5
BRFD/BLYE BB10 142 D2
RAMS BL0 214 E6
RAW/HAS BB4 177 K4
Spendmore La *CHLY/EC* PR7 229 G3
Spen Fold *LIT* OL15 219 K7
Spen La *KIRK/FR/WAR* PR4 129 H5
Spenleach La *TOT/BURYW* BL8 213 M7
Spen Pl *BPOOLS* FY4 125 J3
Spenser Cl *BRFD/BLYE* BB10 143 M7
Spenser St *PDHM/BLYW* BB12 141 G4
Spenwood Rd *LIT* OL15 219 J6
Spey Cl *LEYL* PR25 186 B3
Speyside *BPOOLS* FY4 125 G4
Spindle Berry Ct *ACC* BB5 159 L7
Spinners Ct *CHLY/EC* PR7 187 H5
LANC LA1 3 G7
Spinners Gdns *WHIT* OL12 218 F7
Spinners Gn *WHIT* OL12 235 J1
Spinners Sq *BBR* PR5 * 169 H4
Spinney Brow *FUL/RIB* PR2 133 G7
Spinney Cl *CHLYE* PR6 187 L5
KIRK/FR/WAR PR4 167 J3
ORM L39 241 G8
Spinney Crs *CSBY/BLUN* L23 256 E5
Spinney Cft *GAR/LONG* PR3 114 D4
Spinney La *CARN* LA5 16 F3
The Spinney *BBNW* BB2 156 D3
CARN LA5 16 F3
CHLYE PR6 207 M1
CLV/TH FY5 85 J4
FMBY L37 237 K6
KIRK/FR/WAR PR4 183 K4
LANC LA1 55 G6
PDHM/BLYW BB12 142 A3
PLF/KEOS FY6 86 B7
PRES PR1 151 J8
RNFD/HAY WA11 262 C4
WHIT OL12 218 A8
Spinning Av *BBN* BB1 174 A3
The Spinnings *BURY* BL9 * 214 F8
Spire Cl *DWN* BB3 191 M3
Spires Gv *KIRK/FR/WAR* PR4 131 H6
Spodden Fold *WHIT* OL12 217 M3
Spodden St *WHIT* OL12 235 G3
Spod Rd *WHIT* OL12 234 F2
Spokeshave Wy *MILN* OL16 235 M1
Spotland Rd *WHIT* OL12 235 G3
Spotland Tops *WHIT* OL12 234 D2
Spouthouse La *ACC* BB5 160 C2
Spout La *HGHB* LA2 37 J2
Spread Eagle St *ACC* BB5 158 E6
Spring Av *GTH/LHO* BB6 138 F5
Spring Bank *CARN* LA5 16 F8
GAR/LONG PR3 284 B9
PRES PR1 8 E5
Springbank Av *CLV/TH* FY5 85 M1
Springbank Gdns
RAW/HAS BB4 177 J1
Spring Bank La *ROCH* OL11 234 B3
Spring Bank Ter *BBNW* BB2 172 F1
Springbrook Av *CLV/TH* FY5 85 H3
Spring Cl *NWD/KWIPK* L33 * 260 D6
RAMS BL0 214 E5
STHP PR8 12 E8
Spring Crs *CHLYE* PR6 188 B6
Springcroft *LEYL* PR25 168 F8
Springdale Rd *GTH/LHO* BB6 137 M3
Springfield *CARN* LA5 16 E2
HGHB LA2 39 H4
NLSN BB9 103 G3
Spring Fld *RNFD/HAY* WA11 262 B1
Springfield Av *ACC* BB5 159 J7
BBNW BB2 172 B2
BCUP OL13 179 K8
BWCK/EAR BB18 294 F6
KIRK/FR/WAR PR4 128 B6
LIT OL15 219 K4
Springfield Bank *BLY* BB11 7 H6
Springfield Cl *BRSC* L40 242 A1
CLI BB7 119 G4
FMBY L37 246 F1
Springfield Crs *HGHB* LA2 39 H4
Springfield Dr *CLV/TH* FY5 81 L7
RAW/HAS BB4 196 B2
Springfield Gdns
GAR/LONG PR3 284 D1
KKBYL LA6 33 L6
Springfield La *MILN* OL16 219 G8
Springfield Rd *BLY* BB11 7 H7
BPOOL FY1 104 E5
CHLY/EC PR7 229 H3
CHLY/EC PR7 * 207 M3
CHLYE PR6 230 D3
GTH/LHO BB6 138 E7
LEYL PR25 186 A4
LSTA FY8 145 H5
NLSN BB9 123 G5
ORM L39 250 C6
RAW/HAS BB4 177 L8
Springfield Rd North
CHLY/EC PR7 * 229 H2
Springfield St *ACC* BB5 159 G8
BBNW BB2 156 E8
DWN BB3 191 K3
HEY LA3 41 G7
LANC LA1 3 H8
PRES PR1 152 B2

Springfield Ter BBNW BB2 172 C2
Springfield Vw BLY BB11 161 M6
Spring Gdns ACC BB5 159 M6
BCUP OL13 179 K8
CLI BB7 * 290 B11
DWN BB3 191 K3
HOR/BR BL6 231 L7
KIRK/FR/WAR PR4 148 E3
LEYL PR25 186 C3
LSTA FY8 145 J2
MGHL L31 259 H3
PRES PR1 168 C1
Spring Gardens Rd COL BB8 296 A7
Spring Gardens St
RAW/HAS BB4 196 C3
Spring Gardens Ter
PDHM/BLYW BB12 140 F2
Spring Garden St LANC LA1 3 G6
Spring Gv COL BB8 296 F5
Spring Hall ACC BB5 139 J6
Spring Hl BBN BB1 10 E4
KIRK/FR/WAR PR4 149 G4
Springhill Av BCUP OL13 196 F4
Spring Hill Rd ACC BB5 159 J7
BLY BB11 6 E6
Springhill Vls BCUP OL13 197 G3
Spring La BBNW BB2 156 E8
BBR PR5 154 F3
COL BB8 296 A6
RAW/HAS BB4 176 E7
Spring Meadow
KIRK/FR/WAR PR4 202 C1
LEYL PR25 187 H1
Spring Mdw ACC BB5 139 K8
DWN BB3 191 M4
Spring Ms CHLYE PR6 188 B5
Spring Mill Wk MILN OL16 235 M1
Springmount BWCK/EAR BB18 294 F6
Springmount Dr SKEL WN8 226 F6
Spring Pl WHIT OL12 302 A12
Spring Rd WGNW/BIL/OR WN5 255 J3
Spring Rw COL BB8 * 296 F5
Springsands Cl FUL/RIB PR2 * 133 H6
Spring Side WHIT OL12 302 A11
Springs Rd CHLYE PR6 208 A1
GAR/LONG PR3 114 E3
The Springs ROCH OL11 234 B4
Spring St ACC BB5 159 H7
BBN BB1 158 E1
BCUP OL13 * 197 J2
LEYL PR25 186 E2
NLSN BB9 122 F4
RAMS BL0 214 E5
RAW/HAS BB4 177 K3
TOD OL14 300 F10
Springthorpe St DWN BB3 191 L5
Spring Thyme Fold LIT OL15 219 K6
Springvale ACC BB5 159 J7
Spring V GAR/LONG PR3 270 A8
Spring Vale Garden Vil
DWN BB3 191 M5
Springvale Mi RAW/HAS BB4 * 194 D1
Spring Vale Rd DWN BB3 191 L4
Spring Vale Ter LIT OL15 219 L6
Spring Vw BBNW BB2 10 B3
Spring Vls TOD OL14 300 E10
Springwater Av RAMS BL0 214 D8
Springwood Cl BBR PR5 152 D8
Springwood Cots
CHLY/EC PR7 * 208 B6
Springwood Dr BRSC L40 203 K5
CHLY/EC PR7 208 B6
Springwood Rd
BRFD/BLYE BB10 143 H6
Spring Wood St RAMS BL0 214 E4
Spring Yd COL BB8 296 A6
Sprodley Dr WGNNW/ST WN6 244 E1
Spruce Av LANC LA1 54 E7
Spruce Cl FUL/RIB PR2 132 F4
Spruce St RAMS BL0 214 D7
Spruce Wy FMBY L37 236 F8
Sprucewood Cl ACC BB5 160 A5
Spurrier's La MGHL L31 260 A3
Spurrier St CROS/BRETH PR26 168 D7
The Spur CSBY/BLUN L23 257 G8
Spymers Cft FMBY L37 237 K5
Square House La
CHTN/BK PR9 181 M5
Square La BRSC L40 225 H8
KIRK/FR/WAR PR4 110 C7
Square Rd TOD OL14 303 K7
Square St RAMS BL0 214 F5
The Square BPOOLE FY3 125 K1
BRSC L40 223 L7
CHLYE PR6 189 J4
GAR/LONG PR3 284 D1
GAR/LONG PR3 113 J6
LEYL PR25 186 E1
Squire Rd NLSN BB9 123 J3
Squires Cl BBR PR5 170 B1
Squires Gate La BPOOLS FY4 124 D7
Squire's Gate Rd FUL/RIB PR2 131 M8
Squires Rd PRES PR1 8 B7
Squires Wd FUL/RIB PR2 133 G5
Squirrel Fold FUL/RIB PR2 153 J1
Squirrel Gn FMBY L37 236 F6
Squirrel La HOR/BR BL6 231 K7
Squirrels Cha
KIRK/FR/WAR PR4 150 A2
Squirrel's Cha BBR PR5 168 D4
Squirrels Cl ACC BB5 160 B3
Stable Cl CLI BB7 292 E1
KIRK/FR/WAR PR4 128 D5
Stable La CHLYE PR6 188 D4
Stables Cl RAW/HAS BB4 177 K5
The Stables CLV/TH FY5 81 L8
CSBY/BLUN L23 * 257 K6
WHIT OL12 217 M2
Stable Yd ACC BB5 * 159 J5
GAR/LONG PR3 282 B2
Stack Cft CHLYE PR6 187 K1
Stackhills Rd TOD OL14 303 M2
Stackhouse La SETT BD24 265 M5
SETT BD24 264 D7
Stack La BCUP OL13 197 L3
Stadium Av BPOOLS FY4 125 G6
Staffa Crs BBN BB1 158 A7
Stafford Av PLF/KEOS FY6 106 A2
Stafford Cl KIRK/FR/WAR PR4 108 C2
Stafford Moreton Wy
MGHL L31 * 258 F2
Stafford Rd PRES PR1 152 D2
STHP PR8 221 K2
Stafford St BRFD/BLYE BB10 7 G1
DWN BB3 173 J7
NLSN BB9 123 K3
SKEL WN8 253 G1
Staghills Rd RAW/HAS BB4 196 A2
Stainburn Cl WGNNW/ST WN6 245 G5
Stainforth Av BISP FY2 85 H6
Stainforth La SETT BD24 265 N3
Stainforth Rd SETT BD24 265 P4
Staining Av FUL/RIB PR2 151 J3
Staining Old Rd PLF/KEOS FY6 106 A4
Staining Ri BPOOLE FY3 106 A6
Staining Rd BPOOLE FY3 105 L4
Staining Rd West BPOOLE FY3 106 A6
Stainton Dr PDHM/BLYW BB12 142 B3
Stainton Gv MCMB LA4 * 41 M7
Stainton St CARN LA5 26 A8
Stakepool Dr GAR/LONG PR3 282 B2
Stakes Hall Pl BBNW BB2 172 F1
Staley Av CSBY/BLUN L23 257 J8
Stalls Rd HEY LA3 64 E1
Stamford Av BPOOLS FY4 125 G4
Stamford Ct LSTA FY8 * 145 G3
Stamford Dr CHLYE PR6 187 M6
Stamford Pl CLI BB7 99 J2
Stamford Rd STHP PR8 199 L8
Stamford St MILN OL16 235 L5
Stanah Gdns CLV/TH FY5 86 B1
Stanah Rd CLV/TH FY5 86 A2
Stanalee La GAR/LONG PR3 92 F3
Stanbury Dr BRFD/BLYE BB10 143 H1
Stancliffe St BBNW BB2 10 A8
Standen Hall Cl
BRFD/BLYE BB10 * 123 H8
Standen Hall Dr
BRFD/BLYE BB10 123 G8
Standen Rd CLI BB7 99 J4
Standhouse La ORM L39 250 F1
Standing Stone La COL BB8 103 K1
Standish Dr RNFD/HAY WA11 262 D4
Standish St BLY BB11 7 G3
CHLY/EC PR7 207 M4
Standroyd Dr COL BB8 296 D6
Standroyd Rd COL BB8 296 D6
Standside Pk SKEL WN8 253 G3
Stanedge Cl RAMS BL0 214 F7
Stanford Gdns BBNW BB2 173 K2
Stanford Hall Crs RAMS BL0 214 E7
Stangate MGHL L31 258 E1
Stang Top Rd NLSN BB9 102 C5
Stanhill La ACC BB5 158 E7
Stanhill St ACC BB5 158 F8
Stanhope Av HEY LA3 41 M8
Stanhope Ct HEY LA3 * 42 A8
Stanhope Rd BPOOL FY1 104 F3
Stanhope St DWN BB3 191 K1
PDHM/BLYW BB12 * 6 F2
PRES PR1 152 A1
ROCH OL11 235 J6
Stanifield Cl LEYL PR25 168 E8
Stanifield La LEYL PR25 186 E1
Stankelt Rd CARN LA5 24 F1
Stanlawe Rd FMBY L37 237 H5
Stanley Av CLV/TH FY5 85 G1
KIRK/FR/WAR PR4 167 G1
LEYL PR25 168 F7
PLF/KEOS FY6 86 A8
PRES PR1 8 E9
RNFD/HAY WA11 262 B4
STHP PR8 221 J1
Stanley Cl GAR/LONG PR3 114 E4
Stanley Ct ACC BB5 160 A4
BRSC L40 225 H6
KIRK/FR/WAR PR4 128 E7
Stanley Cft KIRK/FR/WAR PR4 111 L8
Stanley Dr DWN BB3 191 L5
HGHB LA2 36 B5
Stanleyfield Cl PRES PR1 9 K1
Stanleyfield Rd PRES PR1 9 K1
Stanley Fold BBR PR5 168 C3
Stanley Ga BBNW BB2 156 B1
FTWD FY7 77 G8
Stanley Gv PRES PR1 151 K7
Stanley Mt BCUP OL13 179 J8
Stanley Park Cl BPOOLE FY3 5 M6
Stanley Pl CHLY/EC PR7 207 M3
LANC LA1 2 D5
PRES PR1 8 F5
WHIT OL12 235 H3
Stanley Range BBNW BB2 172 E1
Stanley Rd BPOOL FY1 4 E3
FMBY L37 237 H5
FTWD FY7 77 J8
HEY LA3 40 E8
KIRK/FR/WAR PR4 128 C4
LEYL PR25 168 F7
LSTA FY8 146 A8
MGHL L31 258 F5
SKEL WN8 254 D4
Stanley St ACC BB5 159 G8
BBN BB1 11 K2
BLY BB11 6 F6
CARN LA5 33 J2
CHTN/BK PR9 13 G3
COL BB8 296 A6
GAR/LONG PR3 * 114 D3
KIRK/FR/WAR PR4 128 D7
LEYL PR25 186 E2
MCMB LA4 41 J5
NLSN BB9 123 G3
ORM L39 241 J6
PRES PR1 9 L3
RAMS BL0 214 E6
WHIT OL12 235 H2
Stanley Ter PRES PR1 8 E5
Stanley Wy SKEL WN8 243 H8
Stanmere Ct TOT/BURYW BL8 213 L8
Stanmore Av BPOOLS FY4 125 H5
Stanmore Dr LANC LA1 54 D6
Stannanought Rd SKEL WN8 254 B6
Stanneybrook Cl MILN OL16 235 L3
Stanning Cl LEYL PR25 186 B3
Stannyfield Cl CSBY/BLUN L23 257 L5
Stanny Field Dr
CSBY/BLUN L23 257 L5
Stanridge Clough La
BWCK/EAR BB18 294 G5
Stansfeld St BBNW BB2 10 B7
Stansfield Av MGHL L31 259 J2
Stansfield Brow AIRE BD20 295 R7
Stansfield Dr ROCH OL11 234 B2
Stansfield Hall LIT OL15 219 M2
Stansfield Hall Rd TOD OL14 303 L1
Stansfield Rd RAW/HAS BB4 196 B3
TOD OL14 303 L2
Stansfield St BLY BB11 141 L6
BPOOL FY1 4 E9
DWN BB3 191 K3
NLSN BB9 123 H2
TOD OL14 303 L1
Stansford Ct PRES PR1 152 A7
Stansted Rd CHLY/EC PR7 207 K4
Stansy Av HEY LA3 52 F2
Stanthorpe Wk
BRFD/BLYE BB10 142 D2
Stanton Cl NTHTN L30 258 A6
Stanworth Brow CHLYE PR6 171 K7
Stanworth Rd NLSN BB9 123 G3
Stanworth St
BRFD/BLYE BB10 143 L6
Stapleton Rd FMBY L37 247 G3
Star Bank BCUP OL13 * 197 G4
Starbeck Av BPOOLS FY4 125 G3
Starfield Cl LSTA FY8 146 D7
Starkey St HEYW OL10 234 A8
Starkie St BBN BB1 11 G4
BLY BB11 6 C5
DWN BB3 191 L3
LEYL PR25 186 E2
PRES PR1 9 H5
Star La HOR/BR BL6 231 J8
Starr Ga BPOOLS FY4 124 E7
Starrgate Dr FUL/RIB PR2 151 H2
Starring La LIT OL15 219 H6
Starring Rd LIT OL15 219 H6
Starring Wy LIT OL15 219 J6
Star St ACC BB5 159 J6
DWN BB3 191 L2
Startifants La GAR/LONG PR3 286 G11
Startley Nook
KIRK/FR/WAR PR4 167 L5
States Rd LSTA FY8 145 L5
Statham Rd BRSC L40 242 F7
Statham Wy ORM L39 241 H7
Station Ap BRSC L40 225 H6
ORM L39 * 241 J6
TOD OL14 303 L2
Station Av
WGNW/BIL/OR WN5 255 G6
Station Cl BBN BB1 158 D3
BBN BB1 137 J7
HGHB LA2 36 C6
Station Ct RAW/HAS BB4 * 195 J2
Stationers Entry MILN OL16 235 J4
Station La GAR/LONG PR3 283 L6
GAR/LONG PR3 270 D12
GAR/LONG PR3 111 J5
KKBYL LA6 18 F5
Station Ms KKBY L32 * 259 M8
Station Pde TOD OL14 300 C10
Station Rd ACC BB5 160 B1
BBN BB1 158 D2
BBR PR5 170 E1
BBR PR5 169 H3
BPOOLS FY4 124 E3
BRSC L40 204 A7
CARN LA5 16 E1
CHLY/EC PR7 230 C5
CHLY/EC PR7 229 J2
CHTN/BK PR9 181 J6
CLI BB7 291 R6
CLI BB7 118 F6
CLI BB7 99 H3
CLV/TH FY5 85 M2
COL BB8 296 A2
CROS/BRETH PR26 184 E8
CROS/BRETH PR26 167 J8
EDGW/EG BL7 212 F7
FTWD FY7 77 K7
GTH/LHO BB6 139 G6
HGHB LA2 44 D5
HGHB LA2 42 C2
HGHB LA2 39 G4
HGHB LA2 36 C6
KIRK/FR/WAR PR4 167 J3
KIRK/FR/WAR PR4 165 H7
KIRK/FR/WAR PR4 129 M5
KIRK/FR/WAR PR4 127 L7
KKBYL LA6 18 F3
LANC LA1 2 E5
LIT OL15 219 L6
LSTA FY8 146 E8
MCMB LA4 41 J6
MGHL L31 259 H3
MGHL L31 249 K5
ORM L39 241 J5
ORM L39 239 J5
PDHM/BLYW BB12 140 F3
PLF/KEOS FY6 107 H2
PLF/KEOS FY6 86 B7
RAW/HAS BB4 194 D4
ROCH OL11 235 J5
SETT BD24 265 M8
SKEL WN8 243 M1
SKP/WHF BD23 267 R7
STHP PR8 220 F6
TOD OL14 300 F10
WHIT OL12 217 L6
Station Sq LSTA FY8 146 D8
Station Ter BPOOLS FY4 124 E3
Station to Station Wk
LIT OL15 219 L8
Station Wy GAR/LONG PR3 284 B7
HGHB LA2 36 B6
Staups La HBR HX7 301 Q9
Staveley Av BRSC L40 225 H7
Staveley Gv FTWD FY7 81 G1
Staveley Pl FUL/RIB PR2 151 H1
Staveley Rd SKEL WN8 243 H8
STHP PR8 221 G7
Stavordale WHIT OL12 * 235 H3
Staynall La PLF/KEOS FY6 82 E7
Stead St RAMS BL0 214 F5
Sted Ter BBN BB1 10 D1
Steeley La CHLYE PR6 208 A4
Steeple Vw FUL/RIB PR2 8 C2
NWD/KWIPK L33 260 B6
Steer St BRFD/BLYE BB10 142 E2
Steeton Rd BPOOLE FY3 105 L2
Stefano Rd PRES PR1 152 F3
Steiner's La ACC BB5 159 H5
Steiner St ACC BB5 159 K5
Stephenage Pk PRES PR1 168 D1
Stephendale Av BBR PR5 169 L3
Stephens Gv HEY LA3 65 J3
Stephenson Dr
PDHM/BLYW BB12 141 M3
Stephenson St CHLYE PR6 208 B4
Stephenson Wy FMBY L37 237 L8
Stephen St BBNW BB2 172 E1
LSTA FY8 145 H4
Steps Meadow WHIT OL12 218 F7
Stevenson Av LEYL PR25 168 F8
Stevenson Sq WHIT OL12 218 E8
Stevenson St East ACC BB5 159 J6
Stevenson St West ACC BB5 159 J7
Steward Av LANC LA1 55 G6
Stewart Cl CARN LA5 16 E3
Stewart St BBNW BB2 173 G3
BLY BB11 7 K8
PRES PR1 8 D3
Stile Hey CSBY/BLUN L23 257 L6
Stilemoor Ri TOD OL14 301 K12
Stile Rd TOD OL14 301 K12
Stiles Av KIRK/FR/WAR PR4 166 F2
Stiles Rd NWD/KWIPK L33 260 C5
The Stiles ORM L39 241 H6
Stirling Av CSBY/BLUN L23 257 H8
Stirling Cl CHLYE PR6 * 208 B4
CLI BB7 98 F5
LEYL PR25 186 F2
Stirling Ct BRFD/BLYE BB10 123 L7
Stirling Dr BBN BB1 11 H6
Stirling Rd BPOOLE FY3 105 G5
LANC LA1 3 J7
Stirling St BBNW BB2 172 E2
Stiups La MILN OL16 235 L7
Stockbridge Dr
PDHM/BLYW BB12 141 H3
Stockbridge Rd
PDHM/BLYW BB12 141 G3
Stock Cl WHIT OL12 235 H1
Stockclough La BBNW BB2 172 A4
Stockdale Crs BBR PR5 169 J4
Stockdove Wy CLV/TH FY5 81 G8
Stockdove Wd CLV/TH FY5 81 H8
Stockholm St BLY BB11 141 L6
Stockley Crs ORM L39 252 B5
Stockley Dr WGNNW/ST WN6 245 H3
Stocks Cl CHLYE PR6 188 E2
Stocks Cots HOR/BR BL6 * 232 A7
Stocks Ct CHLY/EC PR7 206 B8
PLF/KEOS FY6 86 A8
Stocksgate WHIT OL12 234 E1
Stocks La CHLY/EC PR7 206 B8
CLI BB7 292 G8
PLF/KEOS FY6 85 K7
Stocks Park Dr HOR/BR BL6 231 M8
Stocks Rd FUL/RIB PR2 151 M1
Stocks St PRES PR1 8 F2
Stockton Crs NWD/KWIPK L33 260 A5
Stockton St LIT OL15 219 K6
Stockwood Cl BBNW BB2 156 D3
Stockydale Rd BPOOLS FY4 125 K4
Stoke Av BPOOL FY1 5 H8
Stokes Hall Av LEYL PR25 186 D3
Stoke St MILN OL16 235 L5
Stoneacre Dr CHLYE PR6 230 D2
Stonebarn Dr MGHL L31 249 M8
Stonebridge Cl BBR PR5 168 F3
Stone Bridge La ACC BB5 159 G8
Stonebridge Ter
GAR/LONG PR3 * 114 D4
Stonechat Cl BCUP OL13 197 L2
BPOOLE FY3 105 L5
Stone Cl RAMS BL0 214 D7
Stone Cft PRES PR1 168 A1
Stonecroft Rd LEYL PR25 186 A4
Stonecrop WGNNW/ST WN6 245 G2
Stonecross Cl ACC BB5 159 H6
Stone Cross Gdns
GAR/LONG PR3 91 G1
Stone Edge Rd NLSN BB9 103 H5
Stonefield KIRK/FR/WAR PR4 166 C3
PRES PR1 152 B7
Stonefold Av
KIRK/FR/WAR PR4 166 F2
Stonegate Fold CHLYE PR6 230 E2
Stonehall La SKEL WN8 244 D6
Stone Head La HWTH BD22 295 N11
Stonehill Crs WHIT OL12 217 K8
Stone Hill Dr BBN BB1 157 K2
Stonehill Dr WHIT OL12 217 K8
Stone Hill La WHIT OL12 234 D1
Stonehill Rd WHIT OL12 217 K8
Stoneholme Rd RAW/HAS BB4 177 K3
Stone House Fold BLY BB11 * 163 H5
Stonehouse Gn CHLYE PR6 169 L8
Stoneleigh Cl STHP PR8 220 F7
Stonely Dr TOD OL14 303 K8
Stone Pits RAMS BL0 195 H8
Stone Row Head LANC LA1 55 H3
Stones Bank Rd EDGW/EG BL7 211 J6
Stones La GAR/LONG PR3 91 H1
TOD OL14 302 H3
Stones Rd TOD OL14 303 J3
Stones Ter TOD OL14 * 303 K5
Stone St RAW/HAS BB4 196 C3
Stone Through Brow
BWCK/EAR BB18 294 C12
Stoneway Rd CLV/TH FY5 85 H2
Stonewell LANC LA1 * 3 H5
Stoney Brow SKEL WN8 254 D2
Stoney Butts FUL/RIB PR2 151 G3
Stoneycroft Av HOR/BR BL6 232 A7
Stoneycroft Cl HOR/BR BL6 232 A6
Stoney Croft Dr CARN LA5 26 B5
Stoneycroft Dr CARN LA5 16 E2
Stoneygate CLV/TH FY5 85 J2
PRES PR1 9 J4
Stoneygate La
WGNNW/ST WN6 244 E1
Stoney Holt LEYL PR25 187 H2
Stoneyhurst Av AIN/FAZ L10 258 F8
BRFD/BLYE BB10 143 G6
CLV/TH FY5 86 A3
Stoneyhurst Height NLSN BB9 123 G7
Stoney La BBR PR5 168 F5
CHLY/EC PR7 230 B7
COL BB8 296 B2
HGHB LA2 67 G8
KIRK/FR/WAR PR4 148 E6
PLF/KEOS FY6 86 F1
Stoneyroyd WHIT OL12 * 218 A1
Stoney Royd La TOD OL14 301 J11
Stoney St BLY BB11 7 J9
Stonie Heyes Av WHIT OL12 235 L1
Stonor Rd CHLY/EC PR7 230 C4
Stony Bank CHLYE PR6 170 D6
Stony Bank Rd
BWCK/EAR BB18 294 E5
Stonybutts BBN BB1 10 E4
Stonycroft Av BPOOLS FY4 124 F6
Stony Croft Pl BPOOLS FY4 * 124 F6
Stonyfield NTHTN L30 258 B6
Stonygate La GAR/LONG PR3 115 M3
Stony Hill Av BPOOLS FY4 124 E5
Stonyhurst CHLY/EC PR7 207 M7
Stonyhurst Cl BBNW BB2 * 10 C6
PDHM/BLYW BB12 141 G5
Stonyhurst Rd BBNW BB2 10 C5
Stony La GAR/LONG PR3 269 Q8
SKEL WN8 226 F7
Stoodley Cl TOD OL14 303 R2
Stoodley Gra TOD OL14 * 303 R2
Stoodley La TOD OL14 301 R12
Stoopes Hl BWCK/EAR BB18 294 F5
Stoops Fold BBNW BB2 136 B8
Stoops La CLI BB7 292 A7
Stoop St BLY BB11 141 M6
Stopes Brow DWN BB3 173 K4
Stopford Av BISP FY2 105 H1
LIT OL15 219 H7
Stopgate La NWD/KWIPK L33 260 D5
Stopper La CLI BB7 292 C8
Stopping Hey BBN BB1 * 137 L6
Store St DWN BB3 173 K4
HOR/BR BL6 231 M7
ROCH OL11 234 B2
Storey Av LANC LA1 2 D6
Storey Home LANC LA1 * 54 D6
Stork Cl CLV/TH FY5 85 J2
Stork St DWN BB3 192 A3
Storrs La CARN LA5 17 J8
Storth Gill La SETT BD24 264 G9
Storth Rd MTHPE LA7 17 H2
Storwood Cl
WGNW/BIL/OR WN5 255 H6
Stott St MILN OL16 219 G7
NLSN BB9 123 G3
WHIT OL12 235 J2
Stour Ldg FUL/RIB PR2 131 M5
Stourton Rd STHP PR8 220 F7
Stourton St BBN BB1 158 D1
Stout St BBNW BB2 * 10 C6
Straight Up La CHTN/BK PR9 200 F3
Strait La HGHB LA2 271 R2
Straits ACC BB5 159 H7
Straits La PDHM/BLYW BB12 120 A8
The Straits BBR PR5 170 D1
Strand Farm Ct HGHB LA2 36 B6
Strand Rd PRES PR1 8 D5
Strand St West FUL/RIB PR2 8 B2
The Strand BPOOL FY1 4 C1
FTWD FY7 80 F3
HOR/BR BL6 232 A8
Strange St BLY BB11 7 J8
Strang Stee CLI BB7 99 H3
Strang St RAMS BL0 214 F5
Stranraer Rd
WGNW/BIL/OR WN5 255 M2
Stransdale Cl GAR/LONG PR3 283 R8
Stratfield Pl LEYL PR25 186 E2
Stratford Av ROCH OL11 235 H6
Stratford Cl LANC LA1 42 D8
STHP PR8 220 D5
Stratford Dr FUL/RIB PR2 132 A7
Stratford Pl BPOOL FY1 5 J7
Stratford Rd CHLYE PR6 208 A3
LSTA FY8 145 L5
Strathclyde Rd BBN BB1 11 J5
Strathdale BPOOLS FY4 125 J4
Strathmore Cl RAMS BL0 214 F8
Strathmore Dr
CSBY/BLUN L23 257 H8
Strathmore Gv CHLY/EC PR7 207 L4
Strathmore Rd FUL/RIB PR2 132 B7
Strathyre Cl BISP FY2 85 J6
Stratton Ct NLSN BB9 123 H5
Strawberry Bank BBNW BB2 10 D3
Strawberry Flds CHLY/EC PR7 187 L8
Street COL BB8 103 M7
Street Br HGHB LA2 270 G6
Strellas La CARN LA5 43 H2
Stretford Cl NWD/KWIPK L33 260 B6
Stretton Av BPOOLS FY4 125 H3
Stretton Dr CHTN/BK PR9 200 C3
Strickens La GAR/LONG PR3 284 G9
Strickland Dr MCMB LA4 41 M6
Stricklands La PRES PR1 152 A7
Strickland's La PLF/KEOS FY6 83 G5
Strike La KIRK/FR/WAR PR4 148 E3
Strines St TOD OL14 303 K8
The Strine BRSC L40 203 K2
Strongstry Rd RAMS BL0 214 F1
Stronsay Pl BISP FY2 85 J5
Stroyan St BRFD/BLYE BB10 7 M5
Strutt St PRES PR1 152 E2
Stryands KIRK/FR/WAR PR4 166 F2
Stuart Av BCUP OL13 197 G3
MCMB LA4 41 L5
Stuart Cl FUL/RIB PR2 133 H8
Stuart Pl BPOOLE FY3 105 K2
Stuart Rd CLV/TH FY5 85 M1
FUL/RIB PR2 133 H8
MGHL L31 259 L8
Stuart St ACC BB5 159 L4
BWCK/EAR BB18 293 R5
MILN OL16 235 K5
Stubbins La CLI BB7 120 D4
GAR/LONG PR3 91 H1
RAMS BL0 214 F3
Stubbins St RAMS BL0 214 F2
Stubbins Vale Rd RAMS BL0 214 F2
Stubbylee La BCUP OL13 197 J3
Stub La BRSC L40 241 K1
Stubley Gdns LIT OL15 219 K6
Stubley Holme TOD OL14 300 D10
Stubley La LIT OL15 219 J7
TOD OL14 300 D10
Stubley Mill Rd LIT OL15 219 H7
Studfold CHLY/EC PR7 207 L1
Studholme Av PRES PR1 168 B1
Studholme Cl PRES PR1 168 B1
Studholme Crs PRES PR1 152 B8
Stump Cross La CLI BB7 277 R9
Stump Hall Rd
PDHM/BLYW BB12 121 H4
Stump La CHLYE PR6 208 A3
Stunstead Rd COL BB8 296 F8
Sturgess Cl ORM L39 241 J4
Sturminster Cl PRES PR1 168 B1
Styan St FTWD FY7 77 K7
Stydd La GAR/LONG PR3 116 B7
Sudden St ROCH OL11 234 F7
Sudell Av MGHL L31 259 J1
Sudell Cl DWN BB3 191 M2
Sudell Cross BBNW BB2 * 10 E3
Sudell La MGHL L31 250 A5
Sudell Rd DWN BB3 191 K2
Sudellside St DWN BB3 191 L1
Sudley Rd ROCH OL11 234 F6
Sudlow St MILN OL16 235 L1
Suffolk Av PDHM/BLYW BB12 141 K5
Suffolk Rd BPOOLE FY3 125 K1
PRES PR1 152 D2
STHP PR8 221 K3
Suffolk St BBNW BB2 172 F1
ROCH OL11 235 J5
Sugar Stubbs La CHTN/BK PR9 181 M7
Sugham La HEY LA3 52 E3
Sulby Cl STHP PR8 199 J8
Sulby Dr FUL/RIB PR2 133 J6
LANC LA1 3 H9
Sulby Gv FUL/RIB PR2 133 J6
MCMB LA4 41 M5
Sulby Rd BBNW BB2 173 H2
Sullivan Dr BBNW BB2 173 K2
Sullom Side La GAR/LONG PR3 284 H10
Sullom Vw GAR/LONG PR3 284 B9
Sultan St ACC BB5 159 M5
Sulyard St LANC LA1 3 H6
Summer Castle MILN OL16 * 235 J4
Summerfield LEYL PR25 168 C8
SKP/WHF BD23 294 D2
Summerfield Cl BBR PR5 168 D1
Summerfield Dr HGHB LA2 42 D4
Summerfield Rd TOD OL14 303 M2
Summerfields CHLY/EC PR7 229 J4
LSTA FY8 144 F3
Summerhill Dr MGHL L31 259 J4
Summersgill Rd LANC LA1 2 C2
Summer St HOR/BR BL6 231 L7
MILN OL16 235 K4
NLSN BB9 122 F4
SKEL WN8 243 J7
Summer Trees Av
FUL/RIB PR2 131 G8
Summerville BPOOLS FY4 124 F5
Summerville Av BPOOLE FY3 106 A6
Summerville Wk BBNW BB2 10 C3
Summerwood Cl BISP FY2 105 G1

Summerwood La ORM L39 239 M2
Summit Dr KIRK/FR/WAR PR4 148 F5
The Summit BWCK/EAR BB18 * 293 Q8
Sumner Av ORM L39 239 J7
Sumner Gv NWD/KWIPK L33 260 C6
Sumner Rd FMBY L37 237 J8
Sumners Barn FUL/RIB PR2 133 H5
Sumner's La
CROS/BRETH PR26 204 D4
Sumner St BBNW BB2 10 D7
LEYL PR25 186 D2
Sumpter Cft PRES PR1 168 B1
Sunbank Cl WHIT OL12 235 G1
Sunbury Av PRES PR1 152 A8
Sunbury Dr STHP PR8 220 E7
Suncliffe Rd NLSN BB9 123 G7
Sunderland Av CLV/TH FY5 81 H7
PLF/KEOS FY6 87 G1
Sunderland Dr HEY LA3 53 H1
Sunderland St
PDHM/BLYW BB12 141 L6
Sunfield Cl BPOOLS FY4 125 K4
Sunindale Av RAW/HAS BB4 196 D2
Sunningdale GAR/LONG PR3 111 L8
Sunningdale Av BPOOLS FY4 125 K1
FTWD FY7 81 G4
HGHB LA2 42 C2
Sunningdale Cl
KIRK/FR/WAR PR4 128 D7
Sunningdale Ct LSTA FY8 145 K5
Sunningdale Crs HGHB LA2 42 C3
Sunningdale Dr CLV/TH FY5 86 A3
CSBY/BLUN L23 256 F5
Sunningdale Gdns
BRFD/BLYE BB10 123 G8
FMBY L37 237 H8
Sunningdale Pl
KIRK/FR/WAR PR4 109 M3
Sunny Bank BCUP OL13 * 179 M6
KIRK/FR/WAR PR4 128 C6
Sunny Bank Av BISP FY2 84 F7
KIRK/FR/WAR PR4 149 K1
Sunny Bank Cl RAW/HAS BB4 194 D5
Sunnybank Dr ACC BB5 174 F1
Sunnybank Gdns BBNW BB2 173 H2
Sunny Bank Rd BBNW BB2 173 G2
Sunnybank Rd CARN LA5 32 F6
Sunny Bank Rd RAW/HAS BB4 194 C5
Sunnybank St DWN BB3 * 191 K2
RAW/HAS BB4 176 D8
Sunny Bank Ter TOD OL14 300 E10
Sunny Bower Cl BBN BB1 157 L2
Sunny Brow CHLY/EC PR7 229 K1
Sunny Dr WGNW/BIL/OR WN5 255 J5
Sunnyfield Av
BRFD/BLYE BB10 163 K3
MCMB LA4 41 M5
Sunnyfield La DWN BB3 192 C3
Sunnyfields ORM L39 241 K6
Sunnyhill FUL/RIB PR2 132 F6
Sunny Hl LANC LA1 * 2 D7
Sunnyhill Cl DWN BB3 191 G1
Sunnyhurst Av BPOOLS FY4 125 G5
Sunnyhurst Cl DWN BB3 191 G1
Sunnyhurst La DWN BB3 191 G1
Sunnyhurst Rd BBNW BB2 10 C5
Sunny Lea St RAW/HAS BB4 177 J6
Sunnymede Dr MGHL L31 250 A8
Sunnymede V RAMS BL0 214 D8
Sunnymere Dr DWN BB3 191 H1
Sunny Rd CHTN/BK PR9 200 D1
Sunnyside ORM L39 250 F4
STHP PR8 199 J8
TOD OL14 303 K2
Sunnyside Av BBN BB1 137 K4
BBNW BB2 172 B2
CLI BB7 118 E6
GAR/LONG PR3 116 A8
KIRK/FR/WAR PR4 148 A5
Sunnyside Cl
KIRK/FR/WAR PR4 148 E4
LANC LA1 2 D7
RAW/HAS BB4 177 K5
Sunnyside La LANC LA1 2 D7
Sunnyside Rd CSBY/BLUN L23 256 F8
Sunset Cl NWD/KWIPK L33 260 D6
Sun St ACC BB5 159 H7
CLI BB7 99 H4
COL BB8 296 B6
LANC LA1 3 G5
NLSN BB9 122 F3
RAMS BL0 214 E4
Sun Ter TOD OL14 300 E10
Sun Vale Av TOD OL14 303 L8
Super St ACC BB5 139 H7
Surgeon's Ct PRES PR1 9 G4
Surma Cl MILN OL16 235 L6
Surrey Av DWN BB3 173 J8
PDHM/BLYW BB12 141 L4
Surrey Rd BBN BB1 158 A5
NLSN BB9 123 G1
Surrey St ACC BB5 160 A5
PRES PR1 152 F3
TOD OL14 * 303 L1
Suruyne CARN LA5 16 F2
Sussex Cl ACC BB5 159 J4
Sussex Dr BBN BB1 11 J6
GAR/LONG PR3 284 A7
RAW/HAS BB4 194 D3
Sussex Rd BBN BB1 158 C3
BPOOLE FY3 105 H5
CHTN/BK PR9 13 K4
MGHL L31 259 G4
STHP PR8 200 B5
Sussex St BLY BB11 7 J8
BWCK/EAR BB18 293 Q5
NLSN BB9 123 H2
PRES PR1 152 D2
ROCH OL11 * 235 J5
Sutch La BRSC L40 225 L7
Sutcliffe St BCUP OL13 197 M3
BLY BB11 6 F4
BRFD/BLYE BB10 123 J8
CHLY/EC PR7 208 A4
LIT OL15 219 L5
Sutherland Cl BBN BB1 137 K4
Sutherland Rd BPOOL FY1 104 F4
Sutherland St COL BB8 103 M7
Sutherland Vw BPOOL FY1 104 F4
Sutton Av BRFD/BLYE BB10 143 G1
KIRK/FR/WAR PR4 183 K3
Sutton Crs ACC BB5 160 C2
Sutton Dr FUL/RIB PR2 151 G3
Sutton Gv CHLYE PR6 188 C7
Sutton La CHLYE PR6 230 D2
KIRK/FR/WAR PR4 183 J6
Sutton Pl BPOOL FY1 4 F4
Sutton Rd FMBY L37 247 H2
Suttons La FMBY L37 248 B1
Sutton St BBNW BB2 172 A3
KIRK/FR/WAR PR4 107 H5
Swainbank St BLY BB11 * 7 J6
Swaine St NLSN BB9 122 F3
Swainson St BPOOL FY1 * 104 F5
LSTA FY8 146 C8
Swainstead Rake SETT BD24 266 H12
Swain St WHIT OL12 * 235 H2
Swalegate MGHL L31 258 F1
Swallow Av PRES PR1 152 B7
Swallow Bank Dr ROCH OL11 * 234 E8
Swallow Cl BPOOLE FY3 125 L1
CLV/TH FY5 81 K7
NWD/KWIPK L33 260 B4
Swallow Ct CHLYE PR6 187 M2
Swallow Dr BBN BB1 10 F2
ROCH OL11 234 C4
Swallow Fld
KIRK/FR/WAR PR4 166 B8
Swallowfields BBN BB1 157 G3
KIRK/FR/WAR PR4 131 H6
Swallowfold FUL/RIB PR2 134 A2
Swallow Pk BLY BB11 141 M6
Swallow Whf LANC LA1 3 J4
Swanage Av BPOOLS FY4 124 E5
Swanage Rd BRFD/BLYE BB10 142 F2
Swan Ctyd CLI BB7 * 99 H3
Swan Delph ORM L39 250 F1
Swan Dr CLV/TH FY5 85 J2
Swan Farm Cl DWN BB3 173 J4
Swan Hey MGHL L31 * 259 H4
Swan La ORM L39 250 B5
Swan Meadow CLI BB7 99 G2
Swanpool La ORM L39 250 F1
Swansea St FUL/RIB PR2 8 A1
Swansey La CHLYE PR6 187 L2
Swan St BBNW BB2 10 F8
DWN BB3 191 L5
PRES PR1 9 M2
Swan Wk MGHL L31 259 H4
Swan Yd LANC LA1 3 J7
Swarbrick Av FUL/RIB PR2 134 A2
Swarbrick Cl BPOOL FY1 105 G4
Swarbrick Ct GAR/LONG PR3 114 E4
Swarbrick St
KIRK/FR/WAR PR4 128 D7
Sweet Briar Cl WHIT OL12 235 H1
Sweet Briar La WHIT OL12 235 H1
Swift Cl BBN BB1 11 G3
BPOOLE FY3 125 L1
Swift Gdns HEY LA3 52 E6
Swift Rd ROCH OL11 234 C4
Swift's Cl NTHTN L30 258 A7
Swift's Fold SKEL WN8 253 G3
Swift's La NTHTN L30 258 A7
Swilkin La PLF/KEOS FY6 83 H5
Swill Brook La PRES PR1 152 F5
Swinate Rd CARN LA5 16 F2
Swinburne Cl ACC BB5 176 B1
Swinden Hall Rd NLSN BB9 123 H1
Swinden La COL BB8 123 K1
Swinderby Dr MGHL L31 259 L8
Swindon Av BPOOLS FY4 125 G3
Swindon St BLY BB11 6 B6
Swineshead La TOD OL14 303 L4
Swineshead Rd TOD OL14 303 K4
Swinglehurst Cots
GAR/LONG PR3 * 287 M12
Swinglehurst La
GAR/LONG PR3 287 M12
Swinless St BRFD/BLYE BB10 142 E2
Swinshaw Cl RAW/HAS BB4 177 K1
Swinside KIRK/FR/WAR PR4 131 G7
Swire Croft Rd SKP/WHF BD23 281 K2
Swiss St ACC BB5 159 J5
Swithemby St HOR/BR BL6 231 K7
Sword Meanygate
KIRK/FR/WAR PR4 182 E5
Swords Cross Cl CHLY/EC PR7 207 K6
Sybil St LIT OL15 219 K5
Sycamore Av BPOOLS FY4 * 125 J6
CHLY/EC PR7 187 G8
CSBY/BLUN L23 257 J5
GAR/LONG PR3 284 A7
PDHM/BLYW BB12 141 K4
TOD OL14 301 K12
Sycamore Cl BBN BB1 158 E3
BBN BB1 * 157 J3
BRSC L40 226 F1
FUL/RIB PR2 132 F5
KIRK/FR/WAR PR4 108 D2
LIT OL15 219 J6
PDHM/BLYW BB12 141 M5
Sycamore Ct CHLY/EC PR7 207 L6
Sycamore Crs ACC BB5 139 J7
HGHB LA2 44 E5
Sycamore Dr
KIRK/FR/WAR PR4 128 A7
PRES PR1 152 B8
SKEL WN8 253 H1
Sycamore Gdns COL BB8 103 M5
HEY LA3 52 D5
Sycamore Gv ACC BB5 160 B8
DWN BB3 191 L1
FMBY L37 246 F2
LANC LA1 2 C5
Sycamore Ri COL BB8 296 A2
Sycamore Rd BBN BB1 157 J3
CHLYE PR6 208 A1
FUL/RIB PR2 153 H1
GAR/LONG PR3 91 K6
HGHB LA2 44 E5
Sycamore Wy
BWCK/EAR BB18 293 P6
Syd Brook La BRSC L40 205 H5
Sydney Av CLI BB7 119 G6
Sydney Gdns LIT OL15 219 M2
Sydney St ACC BB5 159 K2
DWN BB3 191 L4
LSTA FY8 145 J5
PDHM/BLYW BB12 6 F3
Sykefield NLSN BB9 122 D6
Syke Hl PRES PR1 9 K5
Syke House La GAR/LONG PR3 93 H7
Sykelands Av HGHB LA2 43 L4
Sykelands Gv HGHB LA2 43 L4
Syke La WHIT OL12 218 C7
Syke Rd WHIT OL12 218 C7
Sykes Cl BWCK/EAR BB18 294 B7
Sykes Ct MILN OL16 * 235 L5
Syke Side Dr ACC BB5 140 B5
Sykes St MILN OL16 235 L5
Syke St PRES PR1 9 J5
Sylvancroft FUL/RIB PR2 131 K6
Sylvan Dr BLY BB11 141 K7
Sylvan Gv BBR PR5 169 K1
Sylvan Pl HEY LA3 52 D4
Sylvester St LANC LA1 2 E7
Symonds Rd FUL/RIB PR2 132 B8

T

Tabby Nook KIRK/FR/WAR PR4 202 C2
Tabby's Nook SKEL WN8 243 K2
Tabley La KIRK/FR/WAR PR4 131 H3
Tabor St PDHM/BLYW BB12 141 M4
Tadema Gv BLY BB11 162 C1
Tadlow Cl FMBY L37 246 F2
Tag Cft FUL/RIB PR2 131 J6
Tag Farm Ct FUL/RIB PR2 131 J6
Tag La FUL/RIB PR2 131 K7
KIRK/FR/WAR PR4 131 J4
Tag Wood Vw RAMS BL0 214 D7
Tailor's La MGHL L31 259 H3
Talaton Cl CHTN/BK PR9 180 D6
Talbot Av ACC BB5 159 J1
Talbot Br CLI BB7 289 M10
Talbot Cl RAW/HAS BB4 195 H3
Talbot Dr BRFD/BLYE BB10 143 J1
CHLY/EC PR7 207 H1
STHP PR8 13 G5
Talbot Gv ROCH OL11 234 C4
Talbot Rd ACC BB5 159 K3
BPOOL FY1 4 C1
BPOOLE FY3 105 G4
LEYL PR25 186 B1
LSTA FY8 146 F6
PRES PR1 8 D4
Talbot Rw CHLY/EC PR7 * 207 G2
Talbot Sq BPOOL FY1 4 C1
Talbot St BBN BB1 158 F2
BLY BB11 7 J3
BRFD/BLYE BB10 143 J1
CHLYE PR6 * 208 B2
COL BB8 296 A5
FUL/RIB PR2 132 A7
GAR/LONG PR3 287 M12
ROCH OL11 235 J5
STHP PR8 12 F6
Talbot Ter LSTA FY8 146 E8
Tall Trees LANC LA1 42 F7
Tamar Cl LEYL PR25 186 E4
Tamar St PRES PR1 153 H3
The Tamneys SKEL WN8 253 J2
Tanfield Nook SKEL WN8 243 M1
Tanfields SKEL WN8 253 J2
Tanglewood FUL/RIB PR2 132 E6
Tan Hill Dr LANC LA1 42 E8
Tan House Cl SKEL WN8 226 F8
Tanhouse La CHLYE PR6 188 C5
Tan House La SKEL WN8 243 M1
Tanhouse Rd CSBY/BLUN L23 257 L6
SKEL WN8 253 M3
Tanners Cft RAMS BL0 214 E5
Tannersmith La BRSC L40 205 J6
Tanners St RAMS BL0 214 E5
Tanner St BLY BB11 * 6 F4
Tanners Wy LSTA FY8 146 A4
Tanpits La KKBYL LA6 19 G5
Tanpits Rd ACC BB5 159 H5
Tansley Av CHLY/EC PR7 229 G2
Tansy La GAR/LONG PR3 269 Q7
Tanterton Hall Rd
FUL/RIB PR2 131 J5
Tanyard Cl CHLY/EC PR7 229 G2
Tan Yard La GAR/LONG PR3 114 F3
Taper St RAMS BL0 214 E5
Tapestry St BBNW BB2 173 G2
Tarbert Crs BBN BB1 158 A7
Tarbet St LANC LA1 3 K7
Tarleswood SKEL WN8 253 J2
Tarleton Av BLY BB11 7 K7
Tarleton Rd CHTN/BK PR9 200 D3
Tarleton St BLY BB11 7 K7
Tarlscough La BRSC L40 224 F2
Tarlswood SKEL WN8 253 J2
Tarnacre Hall Farm Ms
GAR/LONG PR3 90 A2
Tarnacre La GAR/LONG PR3 90 B2
Tarnacre Vw GAR/LONG PR3 284 B9
Tarn Av ACC BB5 139 J7
Tarnbeck Dr BRSC L40 204 F8
Tarnbrick Av
KIRK/FR/WAR PR4 148 F4
Tarn Brook Cl ACC BB5 160 C2
Tarnbrook Cl CARN LA5 42 E1
CARN LA5 33 H2
Tarnbrook Cots
GAR/LONG PR3 * 282 B2
Tarnbrook Ct MCMB LA4 * 41 J6
Tarnbrook Dr BPOOLE FY3 105 K4
Tarnbrook Rd HEY LA3 52 E3
LANC LA1 2 C2
Tarn Brow ORM L39 240 F8
Tarn Cl PRES PR1 151 J7
Tarn Ct FTWD FY7 81 G2
Tarn Hows Cl CHLY/EC PR7 * 207 L6
Tarn La KKBYL LA6 19 G7
Tarn Rd CLV/TH FY5 86 A4
FMBY L37 237 G8
Tarnside BPOOLS FY4 125 L2
Tarnside Cl MILN OL16 218 F8
Tarnside Rd
WGNW/BIL/OR WN5 255 H5
Tarnsyke Rd LANC LA1 2 D2
Tarnway Av CLV/TH FY5 86 A3
Tarradale KIRK/FR/WAR PR4 166 C2
Tarragon Dr BISP FY2 85 J7
Tarry Barn La CLI BB7 99 K8
Tarvin Cl BRFD/BLYE BB10 123 J8
CHTN/BK PR9 181 G6
Tasker St ACC BB5 159 M5
Tatham Ct FTWD FY7 80 F2
Tattersall St ACC BB5 159 G7
BBNW BB2 * 10 E6
RAW/HAS BB4 176 E5
Tatton St COL BB8 103 L8
Taunton Rd BBNW BB2 156 E6
Taunton St BPOOLS FY4 125 G2
PRES PR1 153 G2
Tavistock Dr STHP PR8 220 E5
Tavistock Rd ROCH OL11 235 J8
Tavistock St NLSN BB9 123 J3
Tawd Rd SKEL WN8 253 M3
Taybank Av BPOOLS FY4 125 G4
Taylor Av BBNW BB2 172 F4
ORM L39 241 K6
RAW/HAS BB4 196 C1
ROCH OL11 234 C3
Taylor Cl BBNW BB2 10 B7
Taylor Ct RAW/HAS BB4 176 D8
Taylor Gv MCMB LA4 42 A5
Taylors Cl PLF/KEOS FY6 85 M6
Taylor's La GAR/LONG PR3 282 A1
Taylor's Meanygate
KIRK/FR/WAR PR4 182 C3
Taylors Pl WHIT OL12 * 235 J2
Taylor St BBNW BB2 10 C8
BRFD/BLYE BB10 143 D3
BWCK/EAR BB18 293 P5
CHLY/EC PR7 207 L6
CLI BB7 99 J3
DWN BB3 191 K3
HOR/BR BL6 231 L8
NLSN BB9 122 E5
PRES PR1 8 D6
RAW/HAS BB4 177 K8
SKEL WN8 252 F2
WHIT OL12 235 J2
WHIT OL12 218 A3
Taylor St West ACC BB5 * 159 L5
Taymouth Rd BPOOLS FY4 125 K5
Tay St BLY BB11 6 B5
PRES PR1 8 D7
Taywood Cl PLF/KEOS FY6 86 C7
Taywood Rd CLV/TH FY5 81 K8
Tbirdy Brow CLI BB7 97 K5
Teal Cl BBN BB1 157 G3
CLV/TH FY5 81 K7
LEYL PR25 186 A4
ORM L39 250 F1
WGNS/IIMK WN3 255 L7
Teal Ct BPOOLE FY3 105 L5
ROCH OL11 234 C4
Teal La LSTA FY8 146 A4
Tears La SKEL WN8 243 J2
Teasel Wk HEY LA3 53 J1
Tebay Av CLV/TH FY5 81 G7
KIRK/FR/WAR PR4 128 F6
Tebay Cl MGHL L31 259 J1
Tebay Ct LANC LA1 42 D7
Tedder Av CHTN/BK PR9 200 D4
PDHM/BLYW BB12 141 L5
Teenadore Av BPOOLS FY4 125 H4
Tees Ct FTWD FY7 81 G1
Teesdale Av BISP FY2 105 G3
Tees St MILN OL16 * 235 L5
PRES PR1 152 F1
Teil Gn FUL/RIB PR2 133 H5
Telford St PDHM/BLYW BB12 141 M4
Tell St WHIT OL12 235 G4
Temperance St CHLYE PR6 208 B3
Temple Cl BBN BB1 11 M5
Temple Ct PRES PR1 9 H4
Temple Dr BBN BB1 11 L5
BOL BL1 233 M8
Temple Flds CHLYE PR6 * 188 D8
Temple La LIT OL15 219 M2
Temple Rd BOL BL1 233 M8
Temple St BLY BB11 7 J5
BPOOL FY1 4 C2
COL BB8 296 B5
NLSN BB9 123 J3
Templeton Cl DWN BB3 191 K1
Temple Wy CHLYE PR6 188 A8
Tems St SETT BD24 265 M7
Tenby Cl BBN BB1 157 H4
Tenby Gv WHIT OL12 234 F2
Tenby Rd PRES PR1 9 K6
Tenby St WHIT OL12 234 F2
Tennis St BRFD/BLYE BB10 7 H1
Tennyson Av ACC BB5 158 F7
CHLY/EC PR7 207 M5
CLV/TH FY5 81 K8
KIRK/FR/WAR PR4 148 A5
LSTA FY8 147 G7
PDHM/BLYW BB12 141 H4
PDHM/BLYW BB12 139 M1
TOD OL14 303 N1
Tennyson Cl CARN LA5 32 F6
Tennyson Dr BISP FY2 85 J5
ORM L39 241 G5
Tennyson Gdns
KIRK/FR/WAR PR4 148 A5
Tennyson Mill Ct PRES PR1 153 G2
Tennyson Pl BBR PR5 169 G1
GTH/LHO BB6 138 E7
Tennyson Rd BPOOLE FY3 105 J4
COL BB8 103 M6
FTWD FY7 77 K7
PRES PR1 153 G2
Tennyson St BLY BB11 6 C5
BRFD/BLYE BB10 * 123 J8
PDHM/BLYW BB12 140 F7
ROCH OL11 235 K6
Ten Rw HGHB LA2 65 K6
Tensing Av BISP FY2 85 G6
Tensing Rd MGHL L31 259 G2
Tentercroft WHIT OL12 * 235 H4
Tenterfield St PRES PR1 9 H3
RAW/HAS BB4 196 C3
Tenterhill La ROCH OL11 234 A1
Terance Rd BPOOLS FY4 125 H2
Tern Cl NWD/KWIPK L33 260 B4
ROCH OL11 234 C4
Tern Gv HEY LA3 52 E5
Terrace St PRES PR1 152 F2
Terry St NLSN BB9 123 K1
Tetbury Cl BBNW BB2 172 B3
Teven St BBR PR5 169 H2
Teversham SKEL WN8 253 J1
Teviot Av FTWD FY7 77 G8
Tewkesbury SKEL WN8 * 253 H1
Tewkesbury Av BPOOLS FY4 125 H2
Tewkesbury Cl ACC BB5 160 A8
Tewkesbury Dr LSTA FY8 147 G6
Tewksbury St BBNW BB2 172 E2
Thames Av BRFD/BLYE BB10 122 F8
Thames Dr
WGNW/BIL/OR WN5 255 J4
Thames Rd BPOOLS FY4 124 E4
Thames St KIRK/FR/WAR PR4 149 J1
MILN OL16 235 L5
Thanet SKEL WN8 253 J1
Thanet Lee Cl
BRFD/BLYE BB10 163 H2
Thealby Cl SKEL WN8 253 H1
Theatre St PRES PR1 9 G5
Thelma St RAMS BL0 214 E5
Thermdale Cl GAR/LONG PR3 * 284 A8
Thetford WHIT OL12 * 235 H3
Thetis Rd LANC LA1 2 A5
Thickrash Brow HGHB LA2 39 G6
Thickwood Moss La
RNFD/HAY WA11 262 C6
Thimble Cl WHIT OL12 219 G7
The Thimbles WHIT OL12 219 G7
Third Av BPOOLS FY4 124 F4
CSBY/BLUN L23 * 257 G7
PLF/KEOS FY6 82 F3
Third St BOL BL1 233 J7
Thirlmere Av
BRFD/BLYE BB10 142 D1
COL BB8 296 C5
FMBY L37 247 K1
FTWD FY7 80 F3
PDHM/BLYW BB12 140 F1
PLF/KEOS FY6 85 L7
RAW/HAS BB4 194 F3
SKEL WN8 254 E4
Thirlmere Cl ACC BB5 160 A2
BBN BB1 * 11 H2
CHLYE PR6 230 E3
KIRK/FR/WAR PR4 166 E3
MGHL L31 259 H1
PLF/KEOS FY6 78 C5
Thirlmere Ct LANC LA1 * 3 L3
Thirlmere Dr CHLYE PR6 189 G1
DWN BB3 191 M1
GAR/LONG PR3 114 C6
MCMB LA4 41 J7
STHP PR8 220 E8
Thirlmere Gv MCMB LA4 41 J7
Thirlmere Ms HTWN L38 * 247 K7
Thirlmere Rd BPOOLS FY4 124 F3
BRFD/BLYE BB10 143 H6
CHLY/EC PR7 207 K5
HOR/BR BL6 230 F8
HTWN L38 247 K7
LANC LA1 3 L2
PRES PR1 153 J2
ROCH OL11 234 E7
WGNW/BIL/OR WN5 255 L4
Thirlmere Wk NWD/KWIPK L33 260 A7
Thirsk SKEL WN8 253 H1
Thirsk Av LSTA FY8 145 L4
Thirsk Gv BPOOL FY1 5 H7
Thirsk Rd LANC LA1 55 G7
Thistle Break HEY LA3 52 E4
Thistle Cl CHLYE PR6 208 B3
CLV/TH FY5 81 J6
KIRK/FR/WAR PR4 165 H7
Thistlecroft FUL/RIB PR2 131 K6
Thistlemount Av
RAW/HAS BB4 196 C2
Thistle St BCUP OL13 197 J1
Thistleton Ms CHTN/BK PR9 13 K2
Thistleton Rd FUL/RIB PR2 151 H2
KIRK/FR/WAR PR4 107 M2
Thomas Gv MCMB LA4 41 J6
Thomas Henshaw Ct
ROCH OL11 234 F7
Thomas St ACC BB5 * 159 G8
BBNW BB2 10 C6
BLY BB11 7 G5
COL BB8 103 M7
MILN OL16 235 K3
NLSN BB9 123 H4
PRES PR1 9 M5
TOD OL14 300 F10
Thompson Av ORM L39 241 K6
Thompson St DWN BB3 191 L4
HOR/BR BL6 231 K8
KIRK/FR/WAR PR4 128 C5
PDHM/BLYW BB12 140 F3
PRES PR1 153 G1
Thonock Rd MCMB LA4 41 L8
Thorburn Dr WHIT OL12 217 L4
Thorburn Rd
WGNW/BIL/OR WN5 255 M5
Thorn Bank BCUP OL13 197 K1
Thornbank BPOOLE FY3 105 L4
Thornbank Dr GAR/LONG PR3 284 C12
Thornbeck Av HTWN L38 247 J8
Thornber Ct BRFD/BLYE BB10 142 F2
Thornber Gv BPOOL FY1 5 G6
Thornber St BBNW BB2 10 B9
Thornbridge Av BRSC L40 225 H8
Thornbury ROCH OL11 * 235 H5
SKEL WN8 253 J1
Thornbush Wy MILN OL16 235 M3
Thorncliffe Dr DWN BB3 192 A3
Thorn Crs BCUP OL13 197 K1
Thorncross CLV/TH FY5 85 J3
Thorn Dr BCUP OL13 197 K1
Thorne St NLSN BB9 123 K1
Thorney Bank St BLY BB11 * 6 E6
Thorneycroft Cl PLF/KEOS FY6 85 L6
Thorneyholme Rd ACC BB5 159 M4
Thorneylea WHIT OL12 218 A2
Thornfield CROS/BRETH PR26 184 B6
KIRK/FR/WAR PR4 166 B8
Thornfield Av FUL/RIB PR2 133 J8
GAR/LONG PR3 114 D3
RAW/HAS BB4 196 B2
Thornfield Rd CSBY/BLUN L23 257 K5
Thorn Gdns BCUP OL13 * 197 K1
Thorngate PRES PR1 151 L7
Thorngate Cl PRES PR1 151 L7
Thorn Gv BPOOL FY1 5 J7
COL BB8 296 C5
Thornhill ORM L39 250 E2
Thornhill Av BBN BB1 158 D3
PLF/KEOS FY6 78 D6
Thorn Hill Cl BBN BB1 11 J4
Thornhill Cl BPOOLS FY4 125 J6
Thornhill Rd CHLYE PR6 208 A1
LEYL PR25 185 M3
Thorn La GAR/LONG PR3 134 D1
Thornlea Dr WHIT OL12 234 E1
Thornleigh Cl CLV/TH FY5 85 K1
Thornleigh Dr KKBYL LA6 19 H6
Thornley Av BBN BB1 157 M5
Thornley Pl FUL/RIB PR2 133 K8
Thornley Rd FUL/RIB PR2 133 K8
Thornpark Dr FUL/RIB PR2 151 G3
Thorns Av HGHB LA2 42 C2
The Thorns MGHL L31 258 E1
Thorn St BCUP OL13 197 K1
BRFD/BLYE BB10 142 D3
BURY BL9 214 F8
CLI BB7 120 D4
GTH/LHO BB6 138 F5
PRES PR1 152 F1
RAW/HAS BB4 177 J6
Thornthwaite Rd
KIRK/FR/WAR PR4 131 G7
Thornton Av FUL/RIB PR2 131 L7
LSTA FY8 145 L3
MCMB LA4 41 K5
Thornton Cl ACC BB5 159 K3
BBNW BB2 173 J3
BRSC L40 203 M8
Thornton Crs BRFD/BLYE BB10 143 H6
MCMB LA4 41 K6
Thornton Dr BBR PR5 154 B8
CROS/BRETH PR26 168 B7
Thornton Ga CLV/TH FY5 80 F7
Thornton Gv MCMB LA4 41 K6
Thornton La MCMB LA4 41 K5
Thornton Ms CLV/TH FY5 * 86 B4
Thornton Rd BRFD/BLYE BB10 143 H6
CHTN/BK PR9 200 C4
MCMB LA4 41 K6
Thornton St ROCH OL11 * 235 J6
Thorntree Pl WHIT OL12 235 G3
Thorntrees Av FUL/RIB PR2 151 G2
GAR/LONG PR3 111 L6
Thornway Av CLV/TH FY5 86 A3
Thornwood SKEL WN8 253 J1
Thornwood Cl BBN BB1 157 H2
LSTA FY8 146 B7
Thornylea BBNW BB2 173 G4
Thoroughgood Cl BRSC L40 242 A1
Thorough Wy GAR/LONG PR3 269 P12
Thorpe SKEL WN8 253 J1
Thorpe Av MCMB LA4 42 A7
Thorpe Cl PRES PR1 152 C2
Thorpe St RAMS BL0 * 214 E6
Thorvald Gdns MCMB LA4 42 A7
Thrang Brow La CARN LA5 17 M6
Threagill La CARN LA5 26 C6
Threefields FUL/RIB PR2 131 K6
Three Nooks BBR PR5 169 M6

Three Oaks Cl BRSC L40 242 E1
Three Pools CHTN/BK PR9 180 F8
Three Tuns La FMBY L37 237 J8
Threlfall CHLY/EC PR7 207 J1
Threlfall Rd BPOOL FY1 5 G9
Threlfalls La CHTN/BK PR9 200 C1
Threlfall St FUL/RIB PR2 151 M2
Threshers Ct GAR/LONG PR3 270 B9
The Threshers NTHTN L30 * 258 E7
Threshfield Av HEY LA3 52 E3
Thropps La KIRK/FR/WAR PR4 166 F5
Throstle Cl PDHM/BLYW BB12 6 F1
Throstle Gv HGHB LA2 42 D4
Throstle Nest La
GAR/LONG PR3 283 M3
Throstle St BBNW BB2 10 B6
NLSN BB9 123 H2
Throstle Wk HGHB LA2 42 E3
Throstle Wy CLV/TH FY5 85 J2
Throup Pl NLSN BB9 123 H1
Thrum Fold WHIT OL12 218 A7
Thrum Hall La WHIT OL12 218 B8
Thrushgill Dr HGHB LA2 43 L4
Thrush St WHIT OL12 234 F2
Thurcroft Dr SKEL WN8 253 H1
Thurland Ct MCMB LA4 41 H8
Thurnham Rd FUL/RIB PR2 151 H3
Thurnham St LANC LA1 3 H7
Thursby Av BPOOLS FY4 125 G5
Thursby Cl STHP PR8 220 E8
Thursby Pl NLSN BB9 * 123 J1
Thursby Rd BRFD/BLYE BB10 142 F2
NLSN BB9 123 J1
Thursby Sq BRFD/BLYE BB10 142 D3
Thursden Av
BRFD/BLYE BB10 * 123 J8
Thursden Pl NLSN BB9 123 L2
Thursfield Av BPOOLS FY4 125 H3
Thursfield Rd BRFD/BLYE BB10 7 K6
Thursgill Av MCMB LA4 41 K8
Thurston SKEL WN8 253 H1
Thurston Rd LEYL PR25 186 D2
Thurston St BLY BB11 7 J3
Thwaite Brow La CARN LA5 33 G5
Thwaite La HGHB LA2 48 C1
Thwaites Av BBNW BB2 156 B1
Thwaites Cl BBN BB1 174 A1
Thwaites Rd ACC BB5 158 F7
Thwaites St ACC BB5 158 F8
Thyme Cl BISP FY2 85 J8
Tiber Av BLY BB11 141 M7
Tiber St PRES PR1 9 L5
Tibicar Dr East HEY LA3 52 E2
Tibicar Dr West HEY LA3 52 E2
Tib St RAMS BL0 * 214 E6
Tideswell Av
WGNW/BIL/OR WN5 255 K2
Tiflis St WHIT OL12 235 H3
Tilbury Gv WGNNW/ST WN6 245 G4
Tilcroft SKEL WN8 253 H1
Timber St ACC BB5 159 M6
BCUP OL13 197 J2
NLSN BB9 * 122 E5
Timbrills Av CLI BB7 120 C3
Timms Cl FMBY L37 237 J6
Timms La FMBY L37 237 J6
Tincklers La CHLY/EC PR7 205 J5
Tinedale Vw
PDHM/BLYW BB12 141 G2
Tinkerfield FUL/RIB PR2 132 B4
Tinker's La HGHB LA2 271 J5
Tinklers La CLI BB7 276 D6
Tinniswood FUL/RIB PR2 151 L2
Tinsley Av STHP PR8 200 B8
Tinsley's La GAR/LONG PR3 282 A11
STHP PR8 222 C2
Tintagel SKEL WN8 253 G1
Tintagell Cl BBNW BB2 171 M4
Tintern Av CHLY/EC PR7 208 A6
LIT OL15 219 K4
WHIT OL12 235 H1
Tintern Cl ACC BB5 160 B8
PDHM/BLYW BB12 140 A2
Tintern Crs BBN BB1 157 L3
Tintern Dr FMBY L37 247 L1
Tippet Cl BBNW BB2 173 K2
Titan Wy CROS/BRETH PR26 185 L2
Tithe Barn Cl WHIT OL12 * 219 G7
Tithebarn Ga PLF/KEOS FY6 86 A7
Tithebarn Hl HGHB LA2 65 K7
Tithe Barn La CHLYE PR6 188 D7
GAR/LONG PR3 284 D2
LEYL PR25 186 C6
Tithebarn La MGHL L31 259 K6
Tithebarn Pl PLF/KEOS FY6 86 A7
Tithebarn Rd CSBY/BLUN L23 257 J6
STHP PR8 13 M5
Tithebarn St PLF/KEOS FY6 85 M7
PRES PR1 9 J3
SKEL WN8 * 254 E4
Tiverton Av SKEL WN8 253 H1
Tiverton Cl FUL/RIB PR2 132 C3
Tiverton Dr BBNW BB2 172 F3
BRFD/BLYE BB10 123 J8
Toad Carr TOD OL14 * 303 K1
Toad La WHIT OL12 235 H3
Tockholes Rd CHLYE PR6 190 E7
DWN BB3 190 D3
Todd Carr Rd RAW/HAS BB4 196 C2
Todd Hall Rd RAW/HAS BB4 176 C7
Todd La North BBR PR5 168 F2
Todd La South BBR PR5 168 F3
Todd's La CHTN/BK PR9 181 K5
Todd St MILN OL16 235 K4
Tod Holes La SKP/WHF BD23 266 H7
Todmanhaw La
SKP/WHF BD23 267 Q10
Todmorden Old Rd BCUP OL13 179 K7
Todmorden Rd BCUP OL13 179 K8
BLY BB11 7 K6
BRFD/BLYE BB10 143 M3
LIT OL15 219 M5
LSTA FY8 144 F3
Toll Bar Crs LANC LA1 54 E8
Tollgate PRES PR1 152 B7
Tollgate Crs BRSC L40 224 F8
Tollgate Rd BRSC L40 241 L1
Tollgate Wy MILN OL16 235 M3
Tolsey Dr KIRK/FR/WAR PR4 167 G1
Tom Benson Wy FUL/RIB PR2 131 J4
Tom La HWTH BD22 295 M10
RAW/HAS BB4 196 C1
Tomlinson Rd FUL/RIB PR2 151 M1
HEY LA3 52 E5
LEYL PR25 186 C1
Tomlinson St HOR/BR BL6 231 L8
ROCH OL11 234 F7
Tonacliffe Rd WHIT OL12 217 M6
Tonacliffe Ter WHIT OL12 217 M4
Tonacliffe Wy WHIT OL12 217 M5
Tonbridge Dr AIN/FAZ L10 259 G8
Tongbarn SKEL WN8 253 H1
Tong End WHIT OL12 217 M1
Tonge St MILN OL16 * 235 K5
Tong La BCUP OL13 179 K8
WHIT OL12 217 M2
Tongues La PLF/KEOS FY6 78 F6
Tontine Rd SKEL WN8 254 F5
Tontine St BBN BB1 10 E3
Toogood La WGNNW/ST WN6 228 A4
Tootell St CHLY/EC PR7 207 L5
Tootle La BRSC L40 203 J8
Tootle Rd GAR/LONG PR3 114 E3
Top O' Th' Cft BBNW BB2 * 173 G3
Top Acre KIRK/FR/WAR PR4 166 F2
Top Acre Rd SKEL WN8 253 M4
Topaz St BBN BB1 157 J1
Topaz Wy CHLYE PR6 208 B5
Top Barn La RAW/HAS BB4 196 A2
Topiary Gdns GAR/LONG PR3 284 C11
Top O'Th' Close Rd TOD OL14 303 L9
Top O' Th' Hill Rd TOD OL14 303 K6
The Toppings GAR/LONG PR3 284 B9
Topping St BPOOL FY1 4 D1
Top St TOD OL14 303 J8
Torcross Cl CHTN/BK PR9 180 D6
Tor End Rd RAW/HAS BB4 194 C5
Tormore Cl CHLYE PR6 188 D8
Toronto Av BISP FY2 85 H8
FTWD FY7 81 G1
Toronto Rd BBNW BB2 156 F3
Torquay Av BPOOLE FY3 125 K1
BRFD/BLYE BB10 142 F1
Torra Barn Cl EDGW/EG BL7 212 B8
Torridon Cl BBNW BB2 172 C2
Torrisholme Rd LANC LA1 2 F1
Torrisholme Sq MCMB LA4 * 42 A7
Torside Gv PLF/KEOS FY6 85 L8
Torsway Av BPOOLE FY3 105 J5
Torver Cl PDHM/BLYW BB12 141 L3
Tor Vw RAW/HAS BB4 195 K2
Tor View Rd RAW/HAS BB4 194 F2
Totnes Cl PLF/KEOS FY6 85 M6
Totnes Dr CHTN/BK PR9 180 D6
Tottenham Rd DWN BB3 173 J5
Tottleworth Rd BBN BB1 158 F1
Toulmin Cl GAR/LONG PR3 91 G1
Tourer Ter BRSC L40 223 L7
Towbreck Gdns PLF/KEOS FY6 106 B3
Tower Av LANC LA1 67 G4
RAMS BL0 214 D6
Tower Blds CHTN/BK PR9 * 13 J1
HOR/BR BL6 * 232 D8
Tower Cswy TOD OL14 300 E11
Tower Cl CLV/TH FY5 81 K7
Tower Ct EDGW/EG BL7 212 F7
LANC LA1 3 H8
Tower End FMBY L37 236 F6
Tower Gn FUL/RIB PR2 132 C4
Tower Hl CLI BB7 99 J2
ORM L39 241 K6
Tower Hill Rd SKEL WN8 254 D6
Tower La FUL/RIB PR2 132 C4
Tower Nook SKEL WN8 254 D6
Tower Rd BBNW BB2 172 B1
DWN BB3 191 L3
Towers Av MGHL L31 258 F1
Tower St ACC BB5 158 E6
BCUP OL13 197 J1
BPOOL FY1 4 D2
EDGW/EG BL7 212 F7
TOD OL14 300 D10
Tower Vw BISP FY2 105 G1
DWN BB3 191 M2
PRES PR1 8 A5
Town Brow LEYL PR25 187 J1
Towneley Av ACC BB5 160 C1
Towneley Rd GAR/LONG PR3 114 D4
Towneley Rd West
GAR/LONG PR3 114 D4
Towneleyside BLY BB11 162 E1
Towneley St BRFD/BLYE BB10 142 E1
Town End CARN LA5 32 F8
CLI BB7 275 N5
CLV/TH FY5 * 85 K1
Town End Cl ORM L39 241 G7
Town End Fold CARN LA5 25 M6
Townfield Av BRFD/BLYE BB10 143 J5
Townfield Cl
KIRK/FR/WAR PR4 166 C4
Townfield La HGHB LA2 42 C4
Towngate CHLY/EC PR7 205 L3
COL BB8 296 A2
LEYL PR25 186 C4
Town Green La ORM L39 250 F3
Town Hall St BBNW BB2 10 E4
GTH/LHO BB6 138 F6
Townhead SETT BD24 265 N7
Town Head Av SETT BD24 265 P7
Townhead Cft SETT BD24 265 P6
Townhead Wy SETT BD24 265 N6
Town Hill Bank
PDHM/BLYW BB12 141 G2
Town House Rd LIT OL15 219 L5
NLSN BB9 123 L3
Town La CHLY/EC PR7 227 M2
CHLYE PR6 187 M4
KIRK/FR/WAR PR4 184 A1
STHP PR8 222 A1
Town Lane (Kew) STHP PR8 199 M8
Townlea Cl PRES PR1 151 K8
Townley Av BPOOLS FY4 125 H3
Townley Cl LANC LA1 2 C8
Townley La PRES PR1 151 G7
Townley St BRFD/BLYE BB10 123 J8
CHLYE PR6 208 A4
COL BB8 296 B6
MCMB LA4 41 J5
NLSN BB9 122 E6
Town Mdw MILN OL16 235 H4
Town Mill Brow WHIT OL12 * 235 H4
Town Rd CROS/BRETH PR26 204 E1
Townsend St RAW/HAS BB4 196 C3
RAW/HAS BB4 176 D8
Townsfield CARN LA5 16 F7
Townside Ga GAR/LONG PR3 88 E6
Townsley St NLSN BB9 123 H5
Townsway BBR PR5 168 F3
Town Vw BBN BB1 11 G5
Town Wk BBN BB1 11 G5
Towpath Wk CARN LA5 33 J2
Tow Top La AIRE BD20 295 R6
Toxhead Cl HOR/BR BL6 231 K8
Tracks La WGNW/BIL/OR WN5 255 G8
Trafalgar Cl FUL/RIB PR2 132 A8
Trafalgar Rd BPOOL FY1 4 C7
LANC LA1 54 F6
STHP PR8 199 H8
Trafalgar St BLY BB11 6 D4
CHLY/EC PR7 207 M2
LSTA FY8 145 J4
MILN OL16 235 K3
Trafford St PRES PR1 * 152 B1
ROCH OL11 235 H6
Tram La KKBYL LA6 21 L1
Tramway La BBR PR5 169 L5
Tranmere Av HEY LA3 52 E2
Tranmere Ct SKP/WHF BD23 267 R6
Tranmere Crs HEY LA3 52 E2
Tranmere Rd BPOOLS FY4 125 G2
Tranmoor KIRK/FR/WAR PR4 166 C5
Trans Pennine Trail
NTHTN L30 258 E8
Trap Hl FMBY L37 246 F1
Trapp La PDHM/BLYW BB12 140 C1
Trash La CLI BB7 292 D6
DWN BB3 190 E1
Travellers Ct CLI BB7 292 F1
Travers Pl FUL/RIB PR2 8 B1
Travis St BRFD/BLYE BB10 142 D3
Trawden Cl ACC BB5 159 M7
Trawden Crs FUL/RIB PR2 133 H7
Trawden Rd COL BB8 296 E7
Traylen Wy WHIT OL12 234 D2
Treales Rd KIRK/FR/WAR PR4 129 J5
Trecastle Rd NWD/KWIPK L33 260 D7
Treen Cl CHTN/BK PR9 180 E5
Treesdale Cl STHP PR8 199 J7
Treetops Av RAMS BL0 214 D8
Treetop Vls CHTN/BK PR9 * 180 C7
Trefoil Cl CLV/TH FY5 81 K6
Trefoil Wy LIT OL15 219 J5
Tremellen St ACC BB5 159 K5
Trengrove St WHIT OL12 * 234 F2
Trent Av MGHL L31 259 J1
Trent Cl BRSC L40 225 J6
HEY LA3 54 A1
Trent Rd BPOOLS FY4 124 E4
NLSN BB9 123 K3
WGNW/BIL/OR WN5 263 M7
WGNW/BIL/OR WN5 255 M4
Trent St GAR/LONG PR3 114 C4
LSTA FY8 147 G8
MILN OL16 235 L5
Tresco Cl BBNW BB2 172 E2
Tretower Wy CLV/TH FY5 86 A1
Treviot Cl NWD/KWIPK L33 260 A5
Trevor Cl BBN BB1 157 J4
Trevor Dr CSBY/BLUN L23 257 J8
Trevor Rd BRSC L40 225 G7
STHP PR8 220 F7
Trevor St ROCH OL11 234 E8
The Triangle ACC BB5 160 B3
FUL/RIB PR2 132 B7
Tricklebanks GAR/LONG PR3 * 90 D1
Trident Wy BBN BB1 157 M3
Trigg La CHLYE PR6 189 G6
Trillium Wy DWN BB3 173 K4
Trinity Cl KIRK/FR/WAR PR4 148 F4
NLSN BB9 122 F6
PDHM/BLYW BB12 141 G5
Trinity Ct BBN BB1 11 H2
Trinity Dr KKBYL LA6 18 F1
Trinity Fold PRES PR1 * 9 H2
Trinity Gdns CLV/TH FY5 81 K8
STHP PR8 12 F6
Trinity Ms CHTN/BK PR9 13 K3
Trinity Pl PRES PR1 * 9 H3
Trinity Rd CHLY/EC PR7 * 207 L4
Trinity St ACC BB5 159 G8
BBN BB1 11 H3
BCUP OL13 196 F3
Trinity Wks KIRK/FR/WAR PR4 183 K6
Trinket La HGHB LA2 37 H7
Tristan Av KIRK/FR/WAR PR4 166 D6
Troon Av BBN BB1 157 M8
CLV/TH FY5 86 A3
Troon Cl CHLY/EC PR7 187 G7
Troon Ct PRES PR1 151 K5
Troughton Crs BPOOLS FY4 125 H3
Trout Beck ACC BB5 139 J7
Troutbeck Av FTWD FY7 81 G1
GAR/LONG PR3 270 A8
MGHL L31 259 H1
Troutbeck Cl
PDHM/BLYW BB12 141 L3
Troutbeck Crs BPOOLS FY4 126 A3
Troutbeck Dr RAMS BL0 214 F4
Troutbeck Pl FUL/RIB PR2 133 H6
Troutbeck Ri
WGNW/BIL/OR WN5 255 L5
Troutbeck Rd CHLY/EC PR7 207 L6
LANC LA1 3 K4
LSTA FY8 145 G2
Troutbeck Wy ROCH OL11 234 E7
Trout St BRFD/BLYE BB10 142 D3
PRES PR1 * 152 F4
Trower St PRES PR1 9 M6
Troy St BBN BB1 157 J4
Trumacar La HEY LA3 52 D6
Truman Av LANC LA1 2 B8
Trumley Ct HEY LA3 53 H1
Trundle Pie La ORM L39 239 M5
Trunnah Gdns CLV/TH FY5 81 L8
Trunnah Rd CLV/TH FY5 81 L8
Truro Av CHTN/BK PR9 180 E6
NTHTN L30 258 C7
Truro Pl PRES PR1 153 G2
Truro St BPOOLS FY4 125 G2
Truscott Rd BRSC L40 225 G7
Tucker Hl CLI BB7 99 H2
Tudor Av FUL/RIB PR2 150 F1
PRES PR1 153 J3
Tudor Cl CLV/TH FY5 85 J2
DWN BB3 191 K1
GTH/LHO BB6 137 M2
PLF/KEOS FY6 85 K7
RNFD/HAY WA11 262 B3
Tudor Ct WHIT OL12 * 235 L2
Tudor Cft BBR PR5 168 F4
Tudor Dr KIRK/FR/WAR PR4 148 E1
Tudor Ga LSTA FY8 145 L3
Tudor Gv MCMB LA4 41 M5
Tudor Pl BPOOLS FY4 124 E5
Tudor Rd CSBY/BLUN L23 257 G8
LSTA FY8 145 G3
PRES PR1 168 D1
STHP PR8 220 E5
Tudor Vw NWD/KWIPK L33 260 B6
Tuer St LEYL PR25 186 C1
Tulip Gv WHIT OL12 218 B8
Tulketh Av FUL/RIB PR2 151 L2
Tulketh Brow FUL/RIB PR2 151 M1
Tulketh Crs FUL/RIB PR2 8 A1
Tulketh Rd FUL/RIB PR2 151 L2
Tulketh St STHP PR8 13 H4
Tunbridge Pl PRES PR1 153 G2
Tunbrook Av FUL/RIB PR2 134 B2
Tunley Holme BBR PR5 169 L6
Tunley La WGNNW/ST WN6 228 B6
Tunley Moss WGNNW/ST WN6 228 B7
Tunnel St PDHM/BLYW BB12 6 B3
Tunstall Dr ACC BB5 159 L2
Tunstall St MCMB LA4 41 H6
Tunstead Av
PDHM/BLYW BB12 140 B3
Tunstead Crs BCUP OL13 196 F2
Tunstead La RAW/HAS BB4 196 D2
Tunstead Rd BCUP OL13 196 F3
Tunstill St BRFD/BLYE BB10 142 E2
The Turbary FUL/RIB PR2 131 M8
Turf Hill Rd MILN OL16 235 L7
Turf House Cl LIT OL15 219 J4
Turflands CROS/BRETH PR26 204 E2
Turf St BLY BB11 7 H5
Turf Ter LIT OL15 219 K5
Turkey St ACC BB5 160 A4
GAR/LONG PR3 87 K3
Turks Head Yd PRES PR1 9 J4
Turnacre FMBY L37 237 L5
Turnberry SKEL WN8 253 G1
Turnberry Av CLV/TH FY5 86 A3
Turnberry Cl
KIRK/FR/WAR PR4 128 D7
MCMB LA4 41 K6
Turnberry Wy CHTN/BK PR9 181 G6
Turnbridge Rd MGHL L31 249 M8
Turnbury Cl CHLY/EC PR7 187 G7
Turncroft Rd DWN BB3 191 L3
Turner Av BBR PR5 168 D5
Turner Fold PDHM/BLYW BB12 140 A1
Turner Gv NWD/KWIPK L33 260 B5
Turner Rd NLSN BB9 122 E3
Turner's Pl WHIT OL12 218 B8
Turner St BWCK/EAR BB18 293 R5
CLI BB7 99 H4
PRES PR1 9 K1
WHIT OL12 235 H2
Turners Yd
WGNW/BIL/OR WN5 * 255 H5
Turness Av PDHM/BLYW BB12 140 A2
Turnfield FUL/RIB PR2 131 J5
Turnfield Cl MILN OL16 219 G8
Turnhill Rd MILN OL16 235 L8
Turning La STHP PR8 222 D3
Turn La DWN BB3 191 H2
Turnpike RAW/HAS BB4 196 B2
Turnpike Fold HGHB LA2 42 E6
Turnpike Rd ORM L39 250 D1
The Turnpike FUL/RIB PR2 132 A5
Turn Rd RAMS BL0 215 H3
Turnstone BPOOLE FY3 105 L5
Turpin Green La LEYL PR25 186 E2
Turton Dr CHLYE PR6 208 B2
Turton Gv BRFD/BLYE BB10 143 G5
Turton Hollow Rd
RAW/HAS BB4 177 K3
Tuscan Av BLY BB11 141 M6
Tuscany Gv GTH/LHO BB6 117 M5
Tuson Cft KIRK/FR/WAR PR4 166 C3
Tuson Dr FUL/RIB PR2 8 E2
Tuxbury Dr CLV/TH FY5 86 A3
Tuxford Rd LSTA FY8 145 M5
Tweedale St ROCH OL11 235 H6
Tweed St BBNW BB2 173 G3
HGHB LA2 39 G4
LSTA FY8 145 H5
NLSN BB9 123 K3
Tweedys Ct GAR/LONG PR3 287 K11
Twemlow Pde HEY LA3 52 E2
Twenty Acre La
KIRK/FR/WAR PR4 184 E2
Twickenham Pl LSTA FY8 146 A5
Twig La MGHL L31 259 G2
Twinegate WHIT OL12 218 B8
Twine Wk KKBYL LA6 31 H6
Twistfield Cl STHP PR8 12 D7
Twist Moor La CHLYE PR6 189 K3
Twiston La CLI BB7 291 N10
Twitter La CLI BB7 98 B2
Two Acre La PRES PR1 * 167 M2
Two Gates Dr DWN BB3 * 191 L1
Twyford Cl MGHL L31 * 259 H2
Tyldesley Rd BPOOL FY1 4 C6
Tyne Av BPOOLE FY3 5 H3
Tyne Cl CLV/TH FY5 81 H6
Tynedale Rd BPOOLE FY3 105 K2
Tyne St BBR PR5 169 J2
PRES PR1 8 D7
Tynwald Rd BBNW BB2 173 H2
Tyrer Rd ORM L39 241 J4
Tyrer's Av MGHL L31 249 M6
Tyrers Cl FMBY L37 247 J1
Tyrone Av BISP FY2 105 G1
Tyrone Dr ROCH OL11 234 C6
Tyseley Gv BWCK/EAR BB18 294 D6
Tythebarn St DWN BB3 191 L2

U

Udale Pl LANC LA1 2 E1
Uggle La LANC LA1 54 E8
Uldale Cl NLSN BB9 123 H5
STHP PR8 220 E8
Ullesthorpe WHIT OL12 * 235 H3
Ulleswater Rd LANC LA1 3 K6
Ullswater Av ACC BB5 160 A2
CLV/TH FY5 85 L1
FTWD FY7 81 G3
MCMB LA4 41 L7
WGNW/BIL/OR WN5 255 J4
WHIT OL12 234 F2
Ullswater Cl BBN BB1 158 D2
BBN BB1 11 H2
NWD/KWIPK L33 260 A7
PLF/KEOS FY6 86 F1
Ullswater Crs CARN LA5 33 K3
Ullswater Rd BPOOLS FY4 124 F3
BRFD/BLYE BB10 143 H6
CHLY/EC PR7 207 L5
FUL/RIB PR2 132 F7
Ullswater Wy RAW/HAS BB4 177 K2
Ulnes Walton La
CROS/BRETH PR26 185 J7
Ulpha Cl PDHM/BLYW BB12 141 L3
Ulster Av ROCH OL11 235 H6
Ulster Rd LANC LA1 54 F6
Ulster St BLY BB11 6 B6
Ulverston Cl BBNW BB2 173 K2
MGHL L31 259 H1
Ulverston Crs LSTA FY8 145 M4
Ulverston Dr BBN BB1 158 D2
Underbank Cl BCUP OL13 179 J8
Underbank Rd ACC BB5 176 D4
CLV/TH FY5 86 B2
RAW/HAS BB4 176 C8
Underbank Wy RAW/HAS BB4 176 C8
Under Billinge La BBNW BB2 156 B7
Underley St BRFD/BLYE BB10 122 F8
Under Wd FUL/RIB PR2 131 M8
Underwood WHIT OL12 * 235 H4
Unicon Pk RAW/HAS BB4 176 C8
Union La GAR/LONG PR3 83 L5
Union Pas KIRK/FR/WAR PR4 * 128 D6
Union Rd ACC BB5 159 G7
RAW/HAS BB4 195 G1
WHIT OL12 219 H7
Union St ACC BB5 159 L5
BBNW BB2 10 E8
BCUP OL13 196 F3
CHLY/EC PR7 207 M3
CHLYE PR6 187 M3
CHTN/BK PR9 13 H2
CLI BB7 98 F3
COL BB8 296 B6
DWN BB3 191 K2
MCMB LA4 41 H6
MILN OL16 235 J3
NLSN BB9 122 E6
PRES PR1 9 G3
RAMS BL0 214 F5
RAW/HAS BB4 177 K8
WHIT OL12 217 M3
Union St South TOD OL14 303 L2
Unit Rd STHP PR8 221 G6
Unity St BBNW BB2 10 F8
BWCK/EAR BB18 * 294 D9
TOD OL14 303 K7
Unity Wy RAW/HAS BB4 177 J8
Unsworth Av PLF/KEOS FY6 78 D7
Unsworth St BCUP OL13 197 G4
Up Brooks CLI BB7 99 J2
Upholland Rd
WGNW/BIL/OR WN5 255 G8
Uplands Cha FUL/RIB PR2 131 L5
Uplands Dr PDHM/BLYW BB12 122 A4
Upper Aughton Rd STHP PR8 12 F8
Upper Cliffe (Bersham Drive)
GTH/LHO BB6 138 F5
Upper George St WHIT OL12 * 235 J2
Upper Hayes Cl MILN OL16 235 M3
Upper Hill Wy
BWCK/EAR BB18 293 Q8
Upper La TOD OL14 301 M10
Upper Lune St FTWD FY7 77 L6
Upper Passmonds Gv
ROCH OL11 234 E3
Upper Raglan St TOD OL14 * 303 L1
Upper Westby St LSTA FY8 146 D8
Upphall La KKBYL LA6 27 H3
Uppingham SKEL WN8 253 G2
Uppingham Dr RAMS BL0 214 E4
Upton ROCH OL11 235 H5
Upton Av STHP PR8 220 E5
Upton Barn MGHL L31 258 F1
Upwood Cl BISP FY2 85 H6
Urban Vw CHLYE PR6 189 J3
Ushers Meadow LANC LA1 2 F8
Usk Av CLV/TH FY5 86 A1
Uttley St ROCH OL11 234 F7

V

Vale Av HOR/BR BL6 231 K8
Vale Cl WGNNW/ST WN6 245 H3
Vale Coppice HOR/BR BL6 231 K8
RAMS BL0 214 F8
Vale Cots LIT OL15 219 K6
Vale Ct ACC BB5 160 C2
Vale Crs STHP PR8 237 M1
Vale Cft SKEL WN8 254 D5
Vale House Cl CLI BB7 * 118 F6
Vale La BRSC L40 243 H6
Valentia Rd BISP FY2 85 G8
Valentines La FUL/RIB PR2 131 J8
Valentines Meadow
KIRK/FR/WAR PR4 131 H7
Vale Rd CSBY/BLUN L23 257 G7
LANC LA1 42 D8
Vale Royal KIRK/FR/WAR PR4 128 F6
Vale St BBNW BB2 10 F9
BCUP OL13 179 K8
DWN BB3 191 J2
EDGW/EG BL7 213 G7
NLSN BB9 123 J3
RAW/HAS BB4 176 D7
The Vale FUL/RIB PR2 132 C6
WGNNW/ST WN6 245 G3
Valeway Av CLV/TH FY5 85 G3
Valley Cl CSBY/BLUN L23 257 L7
NLSN BB9 123 K3
Valley Dr BWCK/EAR BB18 294 A3
PDHM/BLYW BB12 141 G3
Valley Gdns BLY BB11 141 J7
Valley Mill Ct COL BB8 296 H5
Valley Rd BBN BB1 137 J6
BBR PR5 155 J8
BWCK/EAR BB18 293 R5
GAR/LONG PR3 114 F4
PRES PR1 8 B9
Valley St BLY BB11 141 L7
Valley Vw CHLYE PR6 208 B4
FUL/RIB PR2 132 D7
WHIT OL12 302 A11
Valley View Rd BBR PR5 152 D8
Valli Ga BBN BB1 157 K4
Valligates BBN BB1 157 K4
Vanbrugh Gv
WGNW/BIL/OR WN5 255 L2
Vance Rd BPOOL FY1 4 D3
Vancouver Crs BBNW BB2 156 F3
Vandyck Av BLY BB11 162 B1
Vandyke St WHIT OL12 234 C2
Vardon Rd BBNW BB2 172 E1
Varley St COL BB8 296 B5
DWN BB3 * 191 K2
PRES PR1 152 D1
Varlian Cl BRSC L40 241 M8
Vaughan Cl FMBY L37 237 G7
Vaughan Rd STHP PR8 199 K7
Vaughan St NLSN BB9 123 J4
Vauxhall St BBNW BB2 * 156 E8
Vavasour Ct MILN OL16 * 235 L5
Vaynor WHIT OL12 * 235 H3
Veevers St BLY BB11 6 F4
NLSN BB9 122 D5
PDHM/BLYW BB12 141 G3
Velvet St BBNW BB2 * 173 G3
Venables Av COL BB8 296 C5
Venice Av BLY BB11 141 M7
Venice St BLY BB11 6 A6
Ventnor Pl FUL/RIB PR2 131 K7
Ventnor Rd BPOOLS FY4 124 E5
CHLY/EC PR7 207 L5
RAW/HAS BB4 194 F2
Ventnor St ROCH OL11 235 J6
Venture Ct ACC BB5 140 A6
Venture Rd FTWD FY7 81 K5
Venture St BCUP OL13 179 K8
Verax St BCUP OL13 197 J2
Verbena Cl DWN BB3 173 K4
Verbena Dr PLF/KEOS FY6 78 C5
Verdant Wy MILN OL16 235 M8
Verdun Crs ROCH OL11 234 F3
Vermont Av CSBY/BLUN L23 257 G7
Vermont Cl NWD/KWIPK L33 260 A4
Vermont Gv CLV/TH FY5 85 H3
Vermont Rd CSBY/BLUN L23 257 G7
Vernon Av BPOOLE FY3 5 K5
Vernon Crs HGHB LA2 66 F8
Vernon Rd CHTN/BK PR9 200 D3

COL BB8 296 G5
LSTA FY8 145 H2
Vernon St BBNW BB2 10 E5
DWN BB3 191 L2
NLSN BB9 123 H4
PRES PR1 152 C2
TOD OL14 303 K4
Verona Av BLY BB11 141 M6
Veronica St DWN BB3 173 H7
Verulam Rd CHTN/BK PR9 180 E8
Vesta St RAMS BL0 214 E5
Vevey St LEYL PR25 186 D3
Viaduct Rd BBR PR5 171 J1
Vicarage Av CLV/TH FY5 85 G1
HGHB LA2 44 E6
PDHM/BLYW BB12 140 E3
Vicarage Cl BRSC L40 241 L8
CHLY/EC PR7 187 G8
CHLYE PR6 230 D3
FMBY L37 237 G7
FUL/RIB PR2 132 C7
HEY LA3 53 K1
KIRK/FR/WAR PR4 127 L7
KKBYL LA6 19 H5
LSTA FY8 145 J4
Vicarage Dr DWN BB3 191 M3
MILN OL16 218 F8
Vicarage Fold CLI BB7 119 H4
Vicarage Gdns BRSC L40 225 G6
Vicarage La ACC BB5 176 B2
BBN BB1 137 J5
BBR PR5 154 B2
BPOOLS FY4 5 K9
BRSC L40 242 A8
CHTN/BK PR9 181 J4
FUL/RIB PR2 132 C7
GAR/LONG PR3 90 D1
KIRK/FR/WAR PR4 129 K8
KKBYL LA6 21 M1
KKBYL LA6 19 H5
RAW/HAS BB4 195 J1
WGNNW/ST WN6 245 K6
Vicarage Rd BWCK/EAR BB18 293 Q4
FMBY L37 237 G7
PLF/KEOS FY6 86 A8
WGNW/BIL/OR WN5 255 G7
Vicarage St CHLYE PR6 208 A2
Vicarage Wk ORM L39 241 H6
Vicar La KKBYL LA6 29 J7
Vicar's Dr MILN OL16 235 J4
Vicarsfields Rd LEYL PR25 186 D4
Vicar's Ga MILN OL16 235 H4
Vicar St BBN BB1 * 11 G4
GTH/LHO BB6 * 138 F7
Vickers Wy HEY LA3 53 K1
Victor Av MCMB LA4 41 M6
Victoria Av ACC BB5 176 A1
BBNW BB2 172 B2
CLI BB7 291 K10
CSBY/BLUN L23 256 F7
LANC LA1 54 E6
NLSN BB9 122 E5
Victoria Bank DWN BB3 * 191 K1
Victoria Bridge Rd STHP PR8 13 J5
Victoria Cl CLI BB7 118 D4
Victoria Ct BBN BB1 10 E4
CLI BB7 291 J10
CROS/BRETH PR26 184 E8
GAR/LONG PR3 131 M1
STHP PR8 12 D9
Victoria Dr RAW/HAS BB4 194 E1
Victoria Gdns NLSN BB9 122 F1
Victoria Ldg
PDHM/BLYW BB12 140 A1
Victoria Ms MCMB LA4 41 K5
Victoria Pde FUL/RIB PR2 151 L2
MCMB LA4 41 K5
RAW/HAS BB4 196 B3
Victoria Pk SKEL WN8 252 F2
Victoria Park Av FUL/RIB PR2 151 G2
LEYL PR25 185 M4
Victoria Park Dr FUL/RIB PR2 151 G2
Victoria Pl LANC LA1 3 G7
Victoria Quay FUL/RIB PR2 151 K4
Victoria Rd BBNW BB2 171 M1
BBR PR5 152 F5
BWCK/EAR BB18 293 R5
FMBY L37 236 E6
FUL/RIB PR2 132 C8
HOR/BR BL6 231 M8
HTWN L38 248 B8
KIRK/FR/WAR PR4 128 C6
LSTA FY8 145 J6
ORM L39 240 F8
PDHM/BLYW BB12 141 G3
PLF/KEOS FY6 86 B7
TOD OL14 303 L1
Victoria Rd East CLV/TH FY5 85 K2
Victoria Rd West CLV/TH FY5 84 F1
CSBY/BLUN L23 257 G7
Victoria St ACC BB5 159 G8
BBN BB1 158 E2
BBN BB1 10 F2
BBR PR5 168 E3
BCUP OL13 197 G3
BLY BB11 6 F4
BPOOL FY1 4 C2
BRSC L40 225 H6
BWCK/EAR BB18 294 E5
CHLY/EC PR7 208 A4
CHLYE PR6 188 D4
CHTN/BK PR9 13 G2
CLI BB7 99 G4
DWN BB3 191 K2
FTWD FY7 77 L6
GAR/LONG PR3 114 D4
GTH/LHO BB6 139 G6
LIT OL15 219 L6
LSTA FY8 146 F8
MCMB LA4 41 H6
NLSN BB9 122 F3
PRES PR1 8 F1
RAMS BL0 214 E5
RAW/HAS BB4 195 M2
RAW/HAS BB4 176 D8
RNFD/HAY WA11 262 C4
SETT BD24 265 P7
TOD OL14 300 F10
WHIT OL12 235 J2
WHIT OL12 * 217 M3
Victoria Ter CHLYE PR6 208 A2
HGHB LA2 65 K6
Victoria Wy FMBY L37 237 G6
RAW/HAS BB4 195 M1
STHP PR8 12 D4
Victor St ACC BB5 139 J8
Victory Av CHTN/BK PR9 200 D4
Victory Cl NLSN BB9 123 H3
Victory Rd BPOOL FY1 104 F5
Victrex Rd CLV/TH FY5 82 A7
Viewfield Ms BBNW BB2 * 156 E6
View Rd DWN BB3 173 H6
Vihiers Cl CLI BB7 118 F5
Viking Cl STHP PR8 199 K7
Viking Pl BRFD/BLYE BB10 7 G1
Viking St ROCH OL11 234 F3
Viking Wy HEY LA3 52 E6
Village Cl SKEL WN8 253 G3
Village Ct PLF/KEOS FY6 * 86 A8
Village Cft CHLY/EC PR7 186 F8
Village Dr FUL/RIB PR2 153 J1
Village Green La FUL/RIB PR2 151 J5
Village Wks PLF/KEOS FY6 * 86 A8
Village Wy BISP FY2 85 G6
HTWN L38 247 J7
SKEL WN8 253 G3
Villas Ct LANC LA1 2 F8
Villas Rd MGHL L31 259 L1
The Villas KIRK/FR/WAR PR4 131 H6
Villa Wy GAR/LONG PR3 284 B9
Villiers Ct PRES PR1 152 B1
Villiers St PDHM/BLYW BB12 141 G4
PRES PR1 152 B1
Vincent Ct BBNW BB2 173 G3
Vincent Rd NLSN BB9 123 J3
Vincent St BBNW BB2 173 G3
COL BB8 296 C6
LANC LA1 3 K8
LIT OL15 219 K5
MILN OL16 * 235 K6
Vincit St BRFD/BLYE BB10 142 E3
Vine Ct MILN OL16 235 L5
Vine Pl ROCH OL11 235 J6
The Vinery KIRK/FR/WAR PR4 167 J3
Vine St ACC BB5 158 F8
CHLY/EC PR7 207 M2
LANC LA1 54 E5
PRES PR1 8 D3
RAMS BL0 214 D7
Vineyard Cl WHIT OL12 218 F4
Violet St BRFD/BLYE BB10 142 D2
Virginia Av MGHL L31 249 M8
Virginia Gv MGHL L31 250 A8
Virginia St ROCH OL11 * 235 H7
STHP PR8 13 J5
Virginia Wy
WGNW/BIL/OR WN5 255 M3
Virgin's La CSBY/BLUN L23 257 J4
Viscount Av DWN BB3 173 K5
Viscount Dr LANC LA1 54 D8
Vivary Wy COL BB8 103 L7
Vivian Dr STHP PR8 221 K1
Vivian St ROCH OL11 235 H6
Vogan Av CSBY/BLUN L23 257 K8
Vulcan Rd KIRK/FR/WAR PR4 148 E2
Vulcan St BLY BB11 6 F4
CHTN/BK PR9 13 J4
NLSN BB9 123 J2
TOD OL14 303 K6

W

Wackersall Rd COL BB8 103 L8
Wadacre La MGHL L31 259 K7
Waddington Av
BRFD/BLYE BB10 143 G6
Waddington Rd ACC BB5 160 A4
CLI BB7 99 G1
FUL/RIB PR2 153 K1
LSTA FY8 145 M5
Waddington St
BWCK/EAR BB18 294 E5
PDHM/BLYW BB12 141 G3
Waddow Gn CLI BB7 98 F3
Waddow Gv CLI BB7 290 B11
Waddow Vw CLI BB7 290 A11
Wade Brook Rd
CROS/BRETH PR26 185 J5
Wades Cft KIRK/FR/WAR PR4 148 F5
Wade St PDHM/BLYW BB12 141 G2
Wadham Rd PRES PR1 9 L6
Wagon Rd GAR/LONG PR3 270 H6
HGHB LA2 270 G3
Wagstaff Cl BBNW BB2 172 F3
Waidshouse Cl NLSN BB9 123 H5
Waidshouse Rd NLSN BB9 123 H5
Waingap Crs WHIT OL12 218 A3
Waingap Ri WHIT OL12 218 C7
Waingap Vw WHIT OL12 218 A4
Waingate FUL/RIB PR2 133 M2
Waingate Cl RAW/HAS BB4 177 L8
Waingate La RAW/HAS BB4 177 L8
Waithlands Rd MILN OL16 235 L5
Waitholme La CARN LA5 18 D5
Wakefield Av MCMB LA4 41 L6
Wakefield Dr LANC LA1 54 F7
Wakefield Rd BISP FY2 85 H7
NTHTN L30 258 E8
Walden Rd BBN BB1 137 J7
Waldon St PRES PR1 153 G2
Walesby Pl LSTA FY8 146 A6
Wales Rd RAW/HAS BB4 196 C2
Walgarth Dr CHLY/EC PR7 207 K4
Walkdale KIRK/FR/WAR PR4 167 G1
Walkden St WHIT OL12 * 235 J2
Walker Av ACC BB5 159 K7
Walker Cl FMBY L37 247 J1
Walker Fold Rd BOL BL1 233 G6
Walker Gv HEY LA3 52 E3
Walker La FUL/RIB PR2 131 K4
Walker Pl PRES PR1 9 L4
Walker Rd BBN BB1 173 M4
Walkers Hl BPOOLS FY4 125 K4
Walker St BBN BB1 11 G6
BPOOL FY1 104 E5
CLI BB7 99 J3
MILN OL16 235 K4
PRES PR1 9 H2
Walker Wy CLV/TH FY5 81 L7
Walk Mill Cl WHIT OL12 219 G7
Walk Mill Pl BRFD/BLYE BB10 163 H2
The Walk KIRK/FR/WAR PR4 164 F7
MILN OL16 235 J4
STHP PR8 12 E6
Wallace Hartley Ms COL BB8 * 296 A6
Wallace La GAR/LONG PR3 270 A7
Wallbank Dr WHIT OL12 217 L4
Wallcroft St SKEL WN8 253 H3
The Walled Gdn CHLYE PR6 187 L5
Wallend Rd FUL/RIB PR2 151 G4
Waller Av BISP FY2 84 F6
Waller Hl COL BB8 296 A2
Waller St TOD OL14 303 L2
Wallets Wood Ct CHLY/EC PR7 207 K6
Walletts Rd CHLY/EC PR7 207 L5
Wallhurst Cl BRFD/BLYE BB10 143 K6
Walling's La CARN LA5 16 E7
Wall La GAR/LONG PR3 88 B6
Wall Pool Br GAR/LONG PR3 88 B5
Wallstreams La
BRFD/BLYE BB10 143 L6
Wall St BPOOL FY1 104 F4
RAW/HAS BB4 196 B1
Wallsuches HOR/BR BL6 232 C7
Wallwork Cl ROCH OL11 234 B2
Walmer Ct STHP PR8 199 J8
Walmer Gn KIRK/FR/WAR PR4 166 C6
Walmer Rd LSTA FY8 145 J3
STHP PR8 199 K8
Walmesley Dr
RNFD/HAY WA11 262 D6
Walmsgate BWCK/EAR BB18 293 Q6
Walmsley Av BBN BB1 158 D3
LIT OL15 219 J8
Walmsley Br GAR/LONG PR3 92 B3
Walmsley Brow CLI BB7 118 E7
Walmsley Cl ACC BB5 159 H5
GAR/LONG PR3 284 B8
Walmsley Ct ACC BB5 159 J2
Walmsley St BBN BB1 158 E2
DWN BB3 191 L1
FTWD FY7 77 K7
Walney Gdns BBNW BB2 173 J2
Walney Pl BPOOLE FY3 105 K4
Walnut Av RAW/HAS BB4 176 F8
Walnut Cl PRES PR1 151 L8
Walnut Gv MGHL L31 259 K8
Walnut St BBN BB1 157 J4
BCUP OL13 179 K8
STHP PR8 13 K9
Walpole Av BPOOLS FY4 124 E6
Walpole St BBN BB1 11 G6
BRFD/BLYE BB10 142 E2
MILN OL16 235 K4
Walro Ms CHTN/BK PR9 180 D8
Walsden Gv BRFD/BLYE BB10 7 M4
Walshaw La BRFD/BLYE BB10 143 G1
Walsh St BBNW BB2 10 E9
HOR/BR BL6 231 L7
Walter Av LSTA FY8 145 K1
Walter St ACC BB5 160 B1
ACC BB5 159 G8
BBN BB1 11 J6
DWN BB3 * 191 L6
NLSN BB9 122 E6
Waltham Av BPOOLS FY4 125 G6
Waltham Cl ACC BB5 160 B8
Waltham Ct HGHB LA2 43 K4
Walthew House La
WGNW/BIL/OR WN5 255 L2
Waltho Av MGHL L31 259 H2
Walton Av MCMB LA4 41 M6
PRES PR1 151 L8
SKP/WHF BD23 281 J2
Walton Cl BCUP OL13 197 K2
Walton Crs BBNW BB2 173 K2
Walton Fold TOD OL14 303 N1
Walton Gn BBR PR5 152 F7
Walton Gv MCMB LA4 42 A6
Walton La NLSN BB9 123 J1
Walton Rd SKP/WHF BD23 281 J3
Walton's Pde PRES PR1 8 F5
Walton St ACC BB5 159 K2
CHLY/EC PR7 230 D5
CHTN/BK PR9 13 J2
COL BB8 296 A7
NLSN BB9 123 H2
Walton Summit Rd BBR PR5 169 K5
Walton Vw PRES PR1 153 G3
Walverden Av BPOOLS FY4 125 G3
Walverden Crs NLSN BB9 123 J3
Walverden Rd
BRFD/BLYE BB10 123 K6
NLSN BB9 123 G6
Wandales La KKBYL LA6 22 C1
Wanes Blades Rd BRSC L40 226 B7
Wanishar La ORM L39 239 K6
Wansbeck Av FTWD FY7 81 G1
Wansfell Rd CLI BB7 98 F4
Wanstead St PRES PR1 153 H3
Warbreck Dr BISP FY2 104 E2
Warbreck Hill Rd BPOOL FY1 104 E3
Warbury St PRES PR1 153 H2
Warcock La BCUP OL13 179 L8
Ward Av ACC BB5 158 F8
CLV/TH FY5 81 G8
FMBY L37 247 G1
Warde St NLSN BB9 123 H3
Ward Green La GAR/LONG PR3 115 J3
Wardle Ct CHLYE PR6 187 M5
Wardle Dr CLV/TH FY5 81 J8
Wardle Edge WHIT OL12 218 E8
Wardle Fold WHIT OL12 218 F4
Wardle Gdns WHIT OL12 218 F4
Wardle Rd WHIT OL12 218 F6
Wardle St BCUP OL13 * 197 G3
LIT OL15 219 K5
Wardley's La PLF/KEOS FY6 82 D7
Wardley St
WGNW/BIL/OR WN5 255 L6
Wardlow Av
WGNW/BIL/OR WN5 255 K3
Ward Rd CSBY/BLUN L23 256 D5
Ward's End PRES PR1 9 J4
Ward St BBR PR5 168 E4
BLY BB11 6 D4
BPOOL FY1 4 D9
CHLYE PR6 208 B4
EDGW/EG BL7 210 F6
GTH/LHO BB6 138 F6
KIRK/FR/WAR PR4 128 D6
Wareham Cl ACC BB5 159 L2
Wareham Rd BPOOLE FY3 105 J2
Wareham St BBN BB1 157 K4
Warehouse La COL BB8 296 A1
Wareings Yd ROCH OL11 235 K7
Waring Dr CLV/TH FY5 81 K8
The Warings CHLY/EC PR7 206 A7
NLSN BB9 123 H5
Warley Av HEY LA3 41 M8
Warley Dr HEY LA3 41 M7
Warley Rd BPOOL FY1 104 E3
Warley St LIT OL15 219 L5
Warley Wise La COL BB8 295 K12
Warmden Av ACC BB5 160 B8
Warmden Gdns BBN BB1 157 K4
Warner Rd PRES PR1 153 G2
Warner St ACC BB5 159 M6
RAW/HAS BB4 176 E8
War Office Rd ROCH OL11 234 B5
Warpers Moss Cl BRSC L40 225 J6
Warper's Moss La BRSC L40 225 J5
Warren Av North FTWD FY7 77 J7
Warren Av South FTWD FY7 77 J7
Warren Cl HGHB LA2 42 D3
Warren Ct STHP PR8 12 B7
Warren Dr BCUP OL13 197 M3
CLV/TH FY5 85 G3
HGHB LA2 42 D3
NLSN BB9 102 F8
Warren Fold CLI BB7 117 J2
Warren Gn FMBY L37 237 G7
Warren Gv CLV/TH FY5 85 H3
HEY LA3 52 D6
Warrenhouse Rd
NWD/KWIPK L33 260 D7
Warrenhurst Rd FTWD FY7 77 J8
Warren Rd CHTN/BK PR9 200 D3
CSBY/BLUN L23 256 D6
HEY LA3 52 D5
Warrenside Cl BBN BB1 137 K7
Warren St FTWD FY7 77 L6
The Warren BBNW BB2 156 D4
FUL/RIB PR2 133 G5
Warrington St BBN BB1 157 K3
Warth La RAW/HAS BB4 196 A3
Warton Av HEY LA3 52 D5
Warton Pl CHLY/EC PR7 207 K3
Warton Rd CARN LA5 26 A8
Warton St LSTA FY8 146 F8
PRES PR1 * 8 E7
Wartonwood Vw CARN LA5 33 J2
Warwick Av ACC BB5 159 K4
CLV/TH FY5 81 H7
CSBY/BLUN L23 257 G8
LANC LA1 54 F6
MCMB LA4 42 A5
Warwick Cl ACC BB5 159 J4
FUL/RIB PR2 132 B7
STHP PR8 199 L8
Warwick Dr BWCK/EAR BB18 294 C6
CLI BB7 99 J1
NLSN BB9 123 G6
PDHM/BLYW BB12 141 G4
Warwick Pl BPOOLE FY3 105 L3
Warwick Rd BBR PR5 153 G7
BPOOLE FY3 105 G5
CHLY/EC PR7 205 M4
LEYL PR25 186 B4
LSTA FY8 145 J5
Warwick St ACC BB5 159 J4
CHLY/EC PR7 230 C5
GAR/LONG PR3 114 D3
NLSN BB9 123 H4
PRES PR1 9 G2
RAW/HAS BB4 176 E8
STHP PR8 199 L7
WHIT OL12 235 L1
Wasdale Av BBN BB1 157 M8
MGHL L31 259 J1
Wasdale Cl LEYL PR25 186 E5
PDHM/BLYW BB12 140 F2
Wasdale Gv GAR/LONG PR3 114 C6
Wasdale Rd BPOOLS FY4 125 K3
Washbrook Cl CLI BB7 119 G2
Washbrook Wy ORM L39 241 H7
Washburn Ct HEY LA3 54 A1
Washington Av BISP FY2 105 H1
Washington Cl LANC LA1 2 C7
Washington Ct BISP FY2 105 H1
Washington Dr CARN LA5 26 B5
NWD/KWIPK L33 260 A5
Washington La CHLY/EC PR7 207 H1
Washington St ACC BB5 159 M5
Wasp Av ROCH OL11 235 K8
Wasp Mill Dr WHIT OL12 218 F5
Waste La HGHB LA2 271 L6
Wastwater Dr MCMB LA4 41 M7
Watchyard La FMBY L37 237 K8
Waterbarn La BCUP OL13 * 196 E3
Waterbarn St
BRFD/BLYE BB10 142 E2
Watercroft ROCH OL11 234 A2
Waterdale BISP FY2 85 H6
Waterfield Av DWN BB3 191 L5
Waterfoot Av BPOOLE FY3 105 H5
STHP PR8 220 E8
Waterford Cl CHLYE PR6 230 D2
FUL/RIB PR2 132 F6
Waterford St NLSN BB9 123 J2
Waterfront BBN BB1 * 11 H7
Water Head FUL/RIB PR2 131 L8
Waterhead Crs CLV/TH FY5 84 F5
Waterhouse Cl WHIT OL12 218 F6
Waterhouse Knock
HOR/BR BL6 230 D6
Waterhouse St WHIT OL12 235 J3
Watering Pool La BBR PR5 168 E2
Water La CHTN/BK PR9 181 G6
FUL/RIB PR2 8 B2
RAMS BL0 215 G1
Waterleat Gld PLF/KEOS FY6 106 B3
Waterloo Cl BBNW BB2 172 E3
Waterloo Rd BLY BB11 7 J6
BPOOLS FY4 124 F2
BWCK/EAR BB18 294 D9
CLI BB7 99 J3
FUL/RIB PR2 151 L1
STHP PR8 221 H1
Waterloo St ACC BB5 159 K2
CHLY/EC PR7 207 M2
Waterloo Ter FUL/RIB PR2 8 A1
Watermans Cl HOR/BR BL6 231 M7
Waterman Vw MILN OL16 * 235 M3
Water Mdw BBNW BB2 173 G4
Watermede
WGNW/BIL/OR WN5 255 H8
Waters Br HGHB LA2 51 L1
Waters Edge BBN BB1 11 G7
CLI BB7 118 F7
Water's Edge FUL/RIB PR2 131 J8
Waters Edge Gn
GAR/LONG PR3 284 B9
Waterside BISP FY2 105 G1
LANC LA1 3 G4
NTHTN L30 258 B6
Waterside Cl GAR/LONG PR3 284 A8
Waterside La MILN OL16 235 L3
Waterside Ms
PDHM/BLYW BB12 140 F3
Waterside Rd COL BB8 296 A7
RAW/HAS BB4 194 D1
Waterslack Rd CARN LA5 17 H5
Waters Reach LSTA FY8 * 146 A8
Water St ACC BB5 159 M5
ACC BB5 139 J6
BBR PR5 169 H1
BRFD/BLYE BB10 143 L6
BWCK/EAR BB18 294 E5
CHLY/EC PR7 230 D5
CHLY/EC PR7 207 M3
CHLYE PR6 170 C6
CSBY/BLUN L23 257 L5
GAR/LONG PR3 116 B8
GTH/LHO BB6 138 F6
LANC LA1 3 G4
MILN OL16 235 K4
NLSN BB9 123 H3
PDHM/BLYW BB12 140 F7
RAW/HAS BB4 177 K4
TOD OL14 303 L2
WHIT OL12 217 L3
Waterway Av NTHTN L30 258 E8
Waterworks Rd ORM L39 241 K5
Watery Gate La
GAR/LONG PR3 109 G1
Watery La DWN BB3 191 L5
FUL/RIB PR2 151 L3
GAR/LONG PR3 284 D6
LANC LA1 42 C8
PRES PR1 153 G3
SETT BD24 265 K9
Watford St BBN BB1 10 E3
Watkin La BBR PR5 168 E4
Watkin Rd CHLYE PR6 187 L3
Watkins Cl NLSN BB9 122 F7
Watling Cl BBNW BB2 173 K3
HEY LA3 41 M8
Watling Ga GTH/LHO BB6 * 117 M5
Watling St LIT OL15 219 J6
Watling Street Rd
FUL/RIB PR2 132 B8
Watson Ct BPOOLS FY4 125 G4
Watson Gdns WHIT OL12 218 A8
Watson Rd BPOOLS FY4 125 G3
Watson St ACC BB5 159 H7
BBNW BB2 172 E1
Watton Beck Cl MGHL L31 259 J1
Watts Cl NWD/KWIPK L33 260 D7
Watts St WHIT OL12 235 K3
Watt St CLI BB7 120 C4
PDHM/BLYW BB12 141 M4
Watty La TOD OL14 303 J4
Wavell Av CHTN/BK PR9 200 E4
Wavell Cl ACC BB5 176 C1
CHTN/BK PR9 200 E4
Wavell St PDHM/BLYW BB12 141 M5
Waverledge Rd GTH/LHO BB6 138 E7
Waverledge St GTH/LHO BB6 138 F7
Waverley SKEL WN8 253 G2
WHIT OL12 * 235 H3
Waverley Av BPOOL FY1 104 F3
FTWD FY7 77 G8
Waverley Cl NLSN BB9 123 G7
PDHM/BLYW BB12 140 A2
Waverley Dr
KIRK/FR/WAR PR4 183 J5
KIRK/FR/WAR PR4 167 J4
Waverley Gdns FUL/RIB PR2 153 H1
Waverley Pl BBNW BB2 156 E6
Waverley Rd ACC BB5 160 B8
BBN BB1 158 B7
BBN BB1 137 H7
CSBY/BLUN L23 256 F8
PRES PR1 153 G2
Waverley St BLY BB11 6 C4
STHP PR8 12 F3
Waxy La KIRK/FR/WAR PR4 148 F4
Wayfarers Av STHP PR8 * 13 G3
The Way Ga CLV/TH FY5 81 G6
Wayman Rd BPOOLE FY3 105 G5
Wayoh Cft EDGW/EG BL7 213 G5
Wayside PLF/KEOS FY6 78 A6
The Way HEY LA3 42 A8
The Weald KIRK/FR/WAR PR4 131 G6
Weasel La DWN BB3 190 D1
Weatherhill Crs NLSN BB9 123 H6
Weaver Av BRSC L40 225 J6
NWD/KWIPK L33 260 C5
Weaver's Brow CHLYE PR6 208 C5
Weavers La MGHL L31 259 J5
Weavers Ms DWN BB3 191 J2
Weber St RAW/HAS BB4 196 A2
Webster Av BPOOLS FY4 125 H4
Webster Gdns
KIRK/FR/WAR PR4 166 D7
Webster Gv MCMB LA4 42 B5
Webster St FUL/RIB PR2 151 M2
Wedgewood Rd ACC BB5 160 C2
Weedon St MILN OL16 235 L3
Weeton Av BPOOLS FY4 125 H6
CLV/TH FY5 81 G8
Weeton Pl FUL/RIB PR2 151 H2
Weeton Rd KIRK/FR/WAR PR4 127 J4
PLF/KEOS FY6 107 H3
Weets Vw BWCK/EAR BB18 293 R4
The Weind GAR/LONG PR3 88 E6
Weirden Cl PRES PR1 167 M2
Weir La BCUP OL13 179 K4
Weir St BBNW BB2 10 E6
TOD OL14 303 K4
Welbeck Av BBN BB1 157 L3
BPOOLS FY4 125 H2
FTWD FY7 77 J7
LIT OL15 219 K5
Welbeck Rd MILN OL16 235 L7
STHP PR8 199 J7
Welbeck Ter STHP PR8 199 J7
Welbourne SKEL WN8 253 G2
Welburn St ROCH OL11 235 J6
Welbury Cl BWCK/EAR BB18 294 E5
Weld Av CHLY/EC PR7 207 M6
Weldbank La CHLY/EC PR7 207 M6
Weldbank St CHLY/EC PR7 207 M6
Weld Blundell Av MGHL L31 249 L7
Weldburn Wk CLV/TH FY5 86 A1
Weld Dr FMBY L37 237 G7
Weldon Dr ORM L39 241 J7
Weldon St BLY BB11 * 6 C5
Weld Pde STHP PR8 12 D9
Weld Rd CSBY/BLUN L23 256 F8
STHP PR8 12 B7
Welland Cl BISP FY2 85 H7
Wellbank Vw WHIT OL12 234 C1
Wellbeck Cl BBR PR5 169 H2
Wellbrow Dr GAR/LONG PR3 114 E3
Wellbrow Ter WHIT OL12 235 G2
Wellcross Rd SKEL WN8 254 E5
Wellesley St
PDHM/BLYW BB12 141 J5
Well Fld ACC BB5 159 K1
Wellfield KIRK/FR/WAR PR4 166 C2
RNFD/HAY WA11 262 D7
Wellfield Av LEYL PR25 186 C2
Wellfield Dr
PDHM/BLYW BB12 141 M3
Wellfield La BRSC L40 251 M1
Wellfield Pl ROCH OL11 235 K6
Wellfield Rd BBNW BB2 10 A2
BBR PR5 168 D4
PRES PR1 8 D3
Wellfield St ROCH OL11 235 K6
Wellfield Ter TOD OL14 303 L3
Wellgate CLI BB7 99 J3
Well Head Rd
PDHM/BLYW BB12 121 K1
Wellhouse Rd
BWCK/EAR BB18 293 Q5
Wellhouse St BWCK/EAR BB18 293 Q5
Wellington Av LEYL PR25 186 E3
Wellington Cl AIN/FAZ L10 258 F8
SKEL WN8 254 B3
Wellington Ct BRFD/BLYE BB10 7 J3
KKBYL LA6 21 L1
Wellington Ms EDGW/EG BL7 213 G7
Wellington Pl BBR PR5 169 G1
MILN OL16 235 K3
Wellington Rd BBNW BB2 10 B8
BPOOL FY1 4 C8
EDGW/EG BL7 213 G7
FUL/RIB PR2 151 L2
LANC LA1 54 F6
TOD OL14 303 L2

Wil - Wor 347

Wilfield St BLY BB11 * 6 C4
Wilford St BPOOLE FY3 105 H4
Wilfred St ACC BB5 159 M7
Wilkie Av BLY BB11 162 B1
Wilkinson Av BPOOLE FY3 5 J4
Wilkinson Mt
BWCK/EAR BB18 * 294 E5
Wilkinson St BBR PR5 168 E3
BLY BB11 161 L7
NLSN BB9 102 F8
PDHM/BLYW BB12 121 J6
RAW/HAS BB4 176 E7
Wilkinson Wy PLF/KEOS FY6 78 C6
Wilkin Sq CLI BB7 99 H3
Willacy La KIRK/FR/WAR PR4 110 B8
Willacy Pde HEY LA3 52 F2
Willard Av WGNW/BIL/OR WN5 255 G8
Willaston Av NLSN BB9 103 H3
Willbutts La ROCH OL11 234 F3
Willedstan Av CSBY/BLUN L23 257 H8
William Harvey Cl NTHTN L30 258 C8
William Henry St PRES PR1 152 F3
ROCH OL11 235 K7
William Herbert St BBN BB1 11 G1
William Hopwood St BBN BB1 11 K5
Williams Av MCMB LA4 42 B5
Williams Dr BBNW BB2 173 K2
Williams La FUL/RIB PR2 132 F4
Williamson Br SKP/WHF BD23 280 F8
Williamson Rd LANC LA1 3 J6
Williams Pl NLSN BB9 123 J3
Williams Rd BRFD/BLYE BB10 142 E2
William St ACC BB5 159 K2
BBNW BB2 10 F9
BBR PR5 * 168 D3
BCUP OL13 197 M3
BPOOLE FY3 105 H4
BWCK/EAR BB18 294 E6
COL BB8 296 B7
DWN BB3 * 191 K2
HOR/BR BL6 231 K8
LIT OL15 219 K6
MILN OL16 219 G7
NLSN BB9 122 E5
RAMS BL0 214 F2
ROCH OL11 235 J5
WHIT OL12 217 M2
William Young Cl PRES PR1 * 152 F1
Willis Rd BBNW BB2 172 C1
Willis St BLY BB11 6 D6
Willoughby Av CLV/TH FY5 85 G1
Willoughby St BBN BB1 10 E2
Willow Av KKBY L32 259 M8
RAW/HAS BB4 177 K7
Willow Bank DWN BB3 191 K5
GAR/LONG PR3 * 91 K6
TOD OL14 303 L1
Willowbank Av BPOOLS FY4 125 H6
Willowbank Ct PLF/KEOS FY6 * 85 L6
Willow Bank La DWN BB3 191 J2
Willow Brook ORM L39 222 D5
Willowbrook Dr
WGNNW/ST WN6 245 L4
Willow Cl BBR PR5 170 B2
BBR PR5 168 D3
CHLYE PR6 230 E3
CLV/TH FY5 86 A2
GAR/LONG PR3 270 A8
KIRK/FR/WAR PR4 148 D6
NLSN BB9 122 E2
PLF/KEOS FY6 78 D5
PRES PR1 151 K7
Willow Coppice FUL/RIB PR2 131 H8
Willow Crs BRSC L40 225 J5
FUL/RIB PR2 153 G1
KIRK/FR/WAR PR4 * 148 D6
LEYL PR25 169 G8
Willowcroft Dr PLF/KEOS FY6 86 E2
Willow-Dale CLV/TH FY5 86 A2
Willowdene CLV/TH FY5 85 H2
Willow Dr CHLY/EC PR7 207 G8
CLI BB7 119 G3
GAR/LONG PR3 284 B6
KIRK/FR/WAR PR4 148 D6
KIRK/FR/WAR PR4 127 M7
PLF/KEOS FY6 106 A3
SKEL WN8 253 H2
Willow End BRSC L40 225 J7
Willow Fld CHLYE PR6 169 M8
Willow Field Cha BBR PR5 * 170 E1
Willowfield Rd HEY LA3 52 F4
Willow Gn BRSC L40 203 K8
FUL/RIB PR2 151 K3
ORM L39 241 J6
Willow Gv BPOOLE FY3 105 K2
CLI BB7 290 C8
FMBY L37 237 J7
GAR/LONG PR3 112 F5
MCMB LA4 42 A5
PLF/KEOS FY6 86 E1
STHP PR8 200 B4
Willow Grove Pk
PLF/KEOS FY6 * 78 D6
Willowhey CHTN/BK PR9 180 C8
Willow Hey KIRK/FR/WAR PR4 183 J4
MGHL L31 259 H4
SKEL WN8 253 J2
Willow La LANC LA1 2 B7
Willowmead Pk LSTA FY8 147 J1
Willowmead Wy WHIT OL12 234 D1
Willow Mt BBN BB1 137 J8
Willow Pk ACC BB5 174 F1
Willow Pl KIRK/FR/WAR PR4 108 C2
Willow Ri LIT OL15 219 J8
Willow Rd CHLYE PR6 208 B1
CROS/BRETH PR26 185 J5
Willow Rocks
BWCK/EAR BB18 * 293 Q8
Willows Av CLV/TH FY5 85 H2
LSTA FY8 146 B8
Willows La ACC BB5 159 K8
KIRK/FR/WAR PR4 128 C6
Willows Park La
GAR/LONG PR3 114 E3
The Willows BBNW BB2 135 M8
BRSC L40 226 F1
CHLY/EC PR7 207 L7
GAR/LONG PR3 91 J6
STHP PR8 * 13 J9
Willow St ACC BB5 139 H8
BBN BB1 157 K4
DWN BB3 191 J2
FTWD FY7 77 K7
GTH/LHO BB6 138 F7
PDHM/BLYW BB12 6 D3
RAW/HAS BB4 196 B3
Willow Ter BPOOLE FY3 * 105 M5
Willow Tree Av GAR/LONG PR3 112 A8
RAW/HAS BB4 195 H1
Willow Tree Crs LEYL PR25 186 A2
Willow Trees Dr BBN BB1 156 F3
Willow Wk SKEL WN8 243 L7
Willow Wy CSBY/BLUN L23 257 H6
KIRK/FR/WAR PR4 167 J4
Wills Av MGHL L31 258 F1
Willsford Av MGHL L31 259 L8
Willshaw Rd BISP FY2 104 E2
Willy La HGHB LA2 269 N5
Wilmar Rd LEYL PR25 186 F1
Wilmcote Gv STHP PR8 220 E7
Wilmore Cl COL BB8 103 M6
Wilmot Rd FUL/RIB PR2 133 H8
Wilmot St BOL BL1 233 M8
Wilpshire Banks BBN BB1 137 J7
Wilpshire Rd BBN BB1 137 M6
Wilsham Rd
WGNW/BIL/OR WN5 255 H6
Wilson Cl KIRK/FR/WAR PR4 183 K4
TOD OL14 301 J12
Wilson Dr KIRK/FR/WAR PR4 108 D2
Wilson Gv HEY LA3 52 D3
Wilson Sq CLV/TH FY5 84 F4
Wilson St BBNW BB2 10 C9
COL BB8 296 A2
HOR/BR BL6 231 K7
WHIT OL12 235 J3
Wilton Cl BBNW BB2 156 C3
LANC LA1 * 42 F7
Wilton Gv PRES PR1 151 K7
Wilton Pde BPOOL FY1 104 E4
Wilton Pl LEYL PR25 * 186 E2
Wilton Rd WGNNW/ST WN6 245 K5
Wilton St BRFD/BLYE BB10 142 E2
NLSN BB9 122 E6
Wilton Ter WHIT OL12 235 H3
Wiltshire Av
PDHM/BLYW BB12 141 L4
Wiltshire Dr RAW/HAS BB4 194 E3
Wiltshire Ms
KIRK/FR/WAR PR4 131 G6
Wiltshire Pl
WGNW/BIL/OR WN5 255 M5
Wilvere Dr CLV/TH FY5 84 F3
Wilworth Crs BBN BB1 157 H2
Wimberley Banks BBN BB1 157 H4
Wimberley Gdns BBN BB1 10 E1
Wimberley Pl BBN BB1 * 10 E1
Wimberley St BBN BB1 10 E1
Wimbledon Av CLV/TH FY5 85 G5
Wimbledon Dr ROCH OL11 235 G6
Wimborne Rd
WGNW/BIL/OR WN5 255 K3
Wimbourne Pl BPOOLS FY4 124 D5
Wimbrick Cl ORM L39 241 G7
Wimbrick Crs ORM L39 241 G8
Winchcombe Rd CLV/TH FY5 85 H4
Winchester Av ACC BB5 * 159 M4
AIN/FAZ L10 259 G8
BPOOLS FY4 125 G2
CHLY/EC PR7 208 B8
LANC LA1 55 G6
MCMB LA4 41 L5
Winchester Cl HEY LA3 * 53 J1
ROCH OL11 234 C4
WGNW/BIL/OR WN5 255 J4
Winchester Dr PLF/KEOS FY6 85 K5
Winchester Rd
PDHM/BLYW BB12 141 G5
Winckley Rd ACC BB5 159 J1
PRES PR1 8 D7
Winckley Sq PRES PR1 9 H5
Winckley St PRES PR1 9 G6
Winder Garth KKBYL LA6 34 C2
Winder La GAR/LONG PR3 270 A10
Windermere Av ACC BB5 160 A2
BRFD/BLYE BB10 142 D1
CLI BB7 98 F4
COL BB8 296 C5
FTWD FY7 81 G3
LEYL PR25 168 D8
MCMB LA4 41 L7
Windermere Cl BBN BB1 11 H2
Windermere Crs STHP PR8 220 F8
Windermere Dr BBN BB1 158 D2
CHLYE PR6 230 E2
DWN BB3 173 M8
MGHL L31 259 H1
NWD/KWIPK L33 260 A7
RAMS BL0 214 F4
RNFD/HAY WA11 262 C1
Windermere Rd BCUP OL13 179 K8
BPOOLS FY4 124 E3
CARN LA5 32 E6
CHLYE PR6 * 208 B4
FUL/RIB PR2 132 F7
HTWN L38 247 K7
LANC LA1 3 L6
PDHM/BLYW BB12 140 F2
PRES PR1 153 J2
WGNW/BIL/OR WN5 255 J3
Windermere Sq LSTA FY8 145 J1
Windfield Cl NWD/KWIPK L33 260 D5
Windflower Dr LEYL PR25 187 H1
Windgate KIRK/FR/WAR PR4 183 K6
Windgate Fold
KIRK/FR/WAR PR4 183 K6
Windham Pl LANC LA1 42 B8
Windham St MILN OL16 218 F8
Windholme LANC LA1 2 A7
Windle Ash MGHL L31 258 F1
Windle Av CSBY/BLUN L23 257 K7
Windle Cl BPOOLS FY4 124 F7
Windmill Av CSBY/BLUN L23 257 J6
KIRK/FR/WAR PR4 128 E7
ORM L39 241 J6
Windmill Cl BPOOLE FY3 106 B6
NWD/KWIPK L33 * 260 B6
Windmill Ct LANC LA1 54 F8
MILN OL16 * 235 L5
Windmill Hts SKEL WN8 254 D3
Windmill La CHLYE PR6 170 E4
Windmill Pl BPOOLS FY4 125 J5
Windmill St LANC LA1 2 D5
MILN OL16 235 L5
Windmill Vw
KIRK/FR/WAR PR4 128 D5
Windrows SKEL WN8 253 J2
The Windrush WHIT OL12 217 M7
Windsor Av ACC BB5 159 K3
BPOOLS FY4 124 E3
CHLY/EC PR7 230 B5
CLI BB7 98 F4
CLV/TH FY5 85 L1
FUL/RIB PR2 131 L8
GAR/LONG PR3 114 C4
KIRK/FR/WAR PR4 167 K2
LANC LA1 55 G6
MCMB LA4 41 G8
PRES PR1 151 M8
RAW/HAS BB4 196 B2
RAW/HAS BB4 194 D2
Windsor Cl BBN BB1 11 L7
BRSC L40 225 H8
CHLY/EC PR7 207 L4
LEYL PR25 186 A4
NTHTN L30 258 C6
PDHM/BLYW BB12 140 A1
Windsor Ct PLF/KEOS FY6 86 B8
STHP PR8 12 B9
Windsor Dr CHLYE PR6 189 H3
FUL/RIB PR2 132 A5
Windsor Gdns GAR/LONG PR3 284 A8
Windsor Gv MCMB LA4 41 H7
Windsor Park Rd AIN/FAZ L10 259 H8
Windsor Pl BWCK/EAR BB18 294 A4
Windsor Rd BBN BB1 158 B6
BBNW BB2 156 E5
BBR PR5 153 G8
BPOOLE FY3 105 L4
CHLY/EC PR7 207 L4
CHLY/EC PR7 205 M4
CHTN/BK PR9 13 L4
DWN BB3 173 J8
FMBY L37 247 H2
GAR/LONG PR3 284 A8
GTH/LHO BB6 139 G6
HEY LA3 41 G8
LSTA FY8 145 K6
MGHL L31 258 F3
SKEL WN8 254 D3
TOD OL14 303 K1
Windsor St ACC BB5 * 159 M5
COL BB8 296 B6
NLSN BB9 123 J4
PDHM/BLYW BB12 141 M5
ROCH OL11 235 K6
Windsor Ter FTWD FY7 77 L6
MILN OL16 235 M4
Windy Bank COL BB8 296 B6
Windy Harbour La TOD OL14 301 L10
Windy Harbour Rd
PLF/KEOS FY6 87 K7
STHP PR8 221 H4
Windyhill LANC LA1 3 G6
Windy Strret GAR/LONG PR3 287 M12
Winery La BBR PR5 152 F6
Wineva Gdns CSBY/BLUN L23 257 J8
Winewall La COL BB8 296 F6
Winewall Rd COL BB8 296 E6
Wingate Av CLV/TH FY5 85 G4
MCMB LA4 41 K7
Wingate Pl CLV/TH FY5 85 G3
Wingate Rd NWD/KWIPK L33 260 C7
Wingates PRES PR1 151 M8
Wingate-Saul Rd LANC LA1 2 E6
Wingate St ROCH OL11 234 A2
Wingfield Cl SFTN L29 258 A3
Wingrove Rd FTWD FY7 81 J1
Winifred La ORM L39 250 E2
Winifred St BPOOL FY1 4 C3
RAMS BL0 214 E6
WHIT OL12 234 E2
Winmarleigh Rd FUL/RIB PR2 151 L2
LANC LA1 66 F1
Winmarleigh St BBN BB1 157 M6
Winmarleigh Wk BBN BB1 157 M7
Winmerleigh St BBN BB1 157 M7
Winmoss Dr NWD/KWIPK L33 260 C6
Winnipeg Cl BBNW BB2 156 E3
Winnipeg Ct BISP FY2 85 H8
Winnipeg Pl BISP FY2 85 G8
Winscar Wk PLF/KEOS FY6 85 L8
Winsford Crs CLV/TH FY5 84 F3
Winsford Dr ROCH OL11 234 C6
Winslow Av PLF/KEOS FY6 85 L6
Winslow Cl PRES PR1 168 B1
Winsor Av LEYL PR25 186 E3
Winstanley Gv BPOOL FY1 4 E1
Winstanley Rd SKEL WN8 253 J3
WGNW/BIL/OR WN5 255 J8
Winster Cl BBR PR5 154 B7
Winster Ct ACC BB5 * 159 H1
Winster Pk LANC LA1 2 A1
Winster Pl BPOOLS FY4 126 A2
The Winsters SKEL WN8 253 J2
Winster Wk LANC LA1 2 A2
Winston Av CLV/TH FY5 85 J1
LSTA FY8 145 L5
ROCH OL11 234 B5
Winston Crs STHP PR8 222 B1
Winston Rd BBN BB1 157 G4
Winterburn Rd BBNW BB2 172 F4
Winterbutlee Gv TOD OL14 303 K6
Winterbutlee Rd TOD OL14 303 K6
Winter Gap La AIRE BD20 295 M7
Winter Hey La HOR/BR BL6 231 L8
Winter Hill Cl FUL/RIB PR2 133 M4
Winter Hill Vw EDGW/EG BL7 212 A8
Winterley Dr ACC BB5 160 B2
Winterton Rd DWN BB3 191 K1
Winthorpe Av MCMB LA4 41 L7
Winton Av BPOOLS FY4 125 K2
FUL/RIB PR2 132 C5
Winton Rd BPOOLS FY4 125 K1
Winton St LIT OL15 219 L6
Winward Cl DWN BB3 173 J5
Wiseman St BLY BB11 6 D4
Wisteria Dr DWN BB3 173 L4
Wiswell Cl BRFD/BLYE BB10 143 H1
RAW/HAS BB4 177 K7
Wiswell La CLI BB7 119 G5
Wiswell Shay CLI BB7 119 H4
Witham Cl NTHTN L30 258 D7
Witham Rd SKEL WN8 253 G2
Withens Rd MGHL L31 250 A8
Witherslack Cl MCMB LA4 41 J8
Withers St BBN BB1 11 H5
Within Gv ACC BB5 160 A2
Withington La CHLY/EC PR7 228 B1
Within Lea BBR PR5 169 H3
Withins Fld HTWN L38 247 J8
Withins La FMBY L37 248 C4
Withnell Fold Old Rd
CHLYE PR6 189 H2
Withnell Gv CHLYE PR6 208 B2
Withnell Rd BPOOLS FY4 124 E3
Withy Grove Cl BBR PR5 169 J2
Withy Grove Crs BBR PR5 169 J2
Withy Grove Rd BBR PR5 169 J2
Withy Pde FUL/RIB PR2 132 B7
Withy Trees Av BBR PR5 169 J2
Withy Trees Cl BBR PR5 169 J2
Witley Rd MILN OL16 235 L4
Witney Av BBNW BB2 172 B3
Wittlewood Dr ACC BB5 159 K2
Witton Av FTWD FY7 81 H2
Witton Gv FTWD FY7 81 H2
Witton Pde BBNW BB2 10 A7
Witton St PRES PR1 9 M3
Witton Wy RNFD/HAY WA11 262 D4
Witton Weavers Wy BBR PR5 155 J8
CHLYE PR6 190 D7
EDGW/EG BL7 212 E7
Woborrow Rd HEY LA3 52 D4
Woburn Cl ACC BB5 160 B8
Woburn Gn LEYL PR25 186 E2
Woburn Rd BPOOL FY1 104 F4
Woburn Wy GAR/LONG PR3 91 H1
The Wold CHLYE PR6 188 D8
Wolfenden Gn RAW/HAS BB4 196 C3
Wollaton Dr STHP PR8 200 C8
Wolseley Cl LEYL PR25 186 D3
Wolseley Pl PRES PR1 * 9 J5
Wolseley Rd PRES PR1 8 E8
Wolseley St BBNW BB2 173 G2
LANC LA1 3 J5
Wolseley Ter PRES PR1 8 E7
Wolsey Cl CLV/TH FY5 81 H8
Wolsley Rd BPOOL FY1 124 E2
FTWD FY7 77 J7
Wolverton SKEL WN8 253 J3
Wolverton Av BISP FY2 104 E1
Wolvesey ROCH OL11 * 235 H5
Woodacre Rd FUL/RIB PR2 153 K1
Woodale Laithe NLSN BB9 102 F8
Wood Bank PRES PR1 151 M8
Woodbank Av DWN BB3 * 191 H1
Wood Bank Rd LIT OL15 219 K8
Woodberry Cl
NWD/KWIPK L33 260 C5
Woodbine Gdns
PDHM/BLYW BB12 141 L4
Woodbine Rd BBNW BB2 156 E5
PDHM/BLYW BB12 141 M5
Woodbine St MILN OL16 235 K6
Woodbine St East MILN OL16 235 L6
Woodbine Ter TOD OL14 300 E10
Woodbridge Gdns WHIT OL12 234 F1
Woodburn Cl BBNW BB2 156 D3
Woodburn Dr BOL BL1 233 L8
Woodbury Av BBNW BB2 173 G2
PDHM/BLYW BB12 122 A4
Wood Cl NLSN BB9 102 D6
Wood Clough Platts NLSN BB9 122 D6
Woodcock Cl CLV/TH FY5 81 K6
ROCH OL11 234 C4
Woodcock Fold CHLY/EC PR7 205 M4
Woodcock Hill Rd BBNW BB2 155 L7
Woodcote Cl NWD/KWIPK L33 260 D7
Woodcourt Av BLY BB11 142 A8
Woodcrest BBN BB1 137 J6
Woodcroft SKEL WN8 253 J3
WGNNW/ST WN6 245 H5
Woodcroft Av RAW/HAS BB4 177 J6
Woodcroft Cl PRES PR1 167 M1
Woodcroft St RAW/HAS BB4 177 J6
Wood End PDHM/BLYW BB12 122 C8
PRES PR1 167 M1
Woodend Av CSBY/BLUN L23 257 H5
MGHL L31 258 F4
Woodend La WHIT OL12 219 G5
Wood End Rd CHLYE PR6 169 K8
Woodfall CHLY/EC PR7 207 L1
Woodfield BBR PR5 169 M5
Woodfield Av ACC BB5 160 A8
BPOOL FY1 4 C8
WHIT OL12 * 235 H1
Woodfield Cl PRES PR1 151 L7
Woodfield Rd BPOOL FY1 4 C8
CHLY/EC PR7 207 M2
CLV/TH FY5 86 A2
ORM L39 240 F8
Woodfields PDHM/BLYW BB12 120 B8
Woodfield Vw CLI BB7 118 F7
Woodfold Cl BBNW BB2 135 L8
Woodfold La GAR/LONG PR3 284 B2
Woodfold Pl BBNW BB2 156 E6
Woodford Copse
CHLY/EC PR7 207 J4
Woodford St
WGNW/BIL/OR WN5 255 L5
Woodgate HEY LA3 53 M1
Woodgate Av ROCH OL11 234 D5
Woodgate Pk HEY LA3 * 54 A1
Woodgates Rd BBNW BB2 156 B6
Wood Gn KIRK/FR/WAR PR4 128 E4
LEYL PR25 186 B1
Wood Green Dr CLV/TH FY5 85 J3
Woodgrove Rd BLY BB11 7 K8
Woodhall Crs BBR PR5 154 B7
Woodhall Gdns PLF/KEOS FY6 86 F1
Woodhart La CHLY/EC PR7 205 M6
Woodhead Cl RAMS BL0 214 F7
RAW/HAS BB4 196 D1
Woodhead Rd
PDHM/BLYW BB12 140 A1
Wood Hey Gv WHIT OL12 218 C7
Woodhey Rd RAMS BL0 214 D8
Woodhill Av MCMB LA4 41 H8
Woodhill Cl MCMB LA4 41 H8
Woodhill La MCMB LA4 41 H7
Woodhouse Gv TOD OL14 303 N2
Wood House La CLI BB7 275 K1
Woodhouse La WHIT OL12 217 G8
Woodhouse Rd CLV/TH FY5 86 B3
TOD OL14 303 P2
Woodland Av BCUP OL13 179 J6
BRSC L40 223 J4
CLV/TH FY5 85 L1
Woodland Cl
KIRK/FR/WAR PR4 127 L8
PLF/KEOS FY6 87 G1
Woodland Crs PLF/KEOS FY6 78 D5
Woodland Dr ACC BB5 139 J6
PLF/KEOS FY6 106 B2
Woodland Gv BPOOLE FY3 5 J4
PRES PR1 151 L6
Woodland Pk CLI BB7 118 F6
Woodland Pl DWN BB3 173 J5
Woodland Rd HEYW OL10 234 B8
MGHL L31 259 K7
WHIT OL12 234 F1
Woodlands Av BBNW BB2 172 B2
BBR PR5 169 K1
FUL/RIB PR2 153 H1
KIRK/FR/WAR PR4 128 C6
PRES PR1 152 A8
ROCH OL11 234 D4
TOD OL14 303 L1
Woodlands Cl CHTN/BK PR9 13 M1
FMBY L37 247 G1
KIRK/FR/WAR PR4 129 J8
ORM L39 241 K7
Woodlands Crs GAR/LONG PR3 111 L5
Woodlands Dr CARN LA5 16 F7
CLI BB7 290 C8
CLI BB7 118 F6
FUL/RIB PR2 132 B3
HEY LA3 52 F1
KIRK/FR/WAR PR4 147 M6
KIRK/FR/WAR PR4 128 E4
LEYL PR25 186 C3
WGNNW/ST WN6 245 J7
Woodlands Gv DWN BB3 191 G1
FUL/RIB PR2 134 B2
HEY LA3 52 F1
PDHM/BLYW BB12 140 E3
Woodlands Meadow
CHLY/EC PR7 207 M8
Woodlands Rd FMBY L37 247 G1
LANC LA1 42 F7
LSTA FY8 146 A7
NLSN BB9 123 J3
RAMS BL0 215 G1
The Woodlands BRSC L40 225 K8
FUL/RIB PR2 151 H2
GTH/LHO BB6 117 M5
STHP PR8 220 F6
Woodland St WHIT OL12 235 K1
Woodlands Vw KKBYL LA6 34 B3
LSTA FY8 146 A6
MILN OL16 235 M3
Woodlands Wy GAR/LONG PR3 111 L5
KIRK/FR/WAR PR4 166 C3
Woodland Ter BCUP OL13 179 J6
Woodland Vw BCUP OL13 179 J7
CHLYE PR6 * 189 J4
CSBY/BLUN L23 257 K4
Wood La BRSC L40 226 B6
BRSC L40 205 G6
CHLY/EC PR7 228 B2
FMBY L37 248 F2
RAMS BL0 215 G1
SKEL WN8 244 A1
Wood Lark Dr CHLY/EC PR7 207 J6
Wood Lea TOD OL14 300 H11
Woodlea Cha DWN BB3 191 M8
Woodlea Cl CHTN/BK PR9 181 G6
Woodlea Gdns NLSN BB9 123 G6
Woodlea Rd BBN BB1 11 M6
LEYL PR25 186 C3
Wood Lea Rd RAW/HAS BB4 196 B3
Woodlee Rd
KIRK/FR/WAR PR4 183 J1
Woodleigh Cl MGHL L31 249 L6
Woodley Av ACC BB5 159 M7
CLV/TH FY5 86 A2
Woodley Park Rd SKEL WN8 243 L7
Woodley Rd MGHL L31 258 F5
Woodmancote CHLY/EC PR7 207 L1
Woodman La KKBYL LA6 22 A8
Woodmoss La STHP PR8 223 H1
Woodnook Rd
WGNNW/ST WN6 245 H3
Wood Park Rd BPOOL FY1 5 H9
Woodpecker Hl BLY BB11 * 141 M6
Woodplumpton La
GAR/LONG PR3 111 L8
Woodplumpton Rd BLY BB11 162 C1
KIRK/FR/WAR PR4 131 H1
Woodridge Av CLV/TH FY5 84 F3
Woodrow SKEL WN8 253 H3
Woodrow Dr SKEL WN8 243 J2
Woodruff Cl CLV/TH FY5 81 J6
Woodrush MCMB LA4 42 A5
Woods Brow BBNW BB2 135 G6
Wood's Brow GAR/LONG PR3 115 K5
Woods Cl ORM L39 239 J7
Woods End PRES PR1 9 L6
Woodsend Cl BBNW BB2 173 K3
Woods Gn PRES PR1 8 F8
Woodside CHLY/EC PR7 208 B7
CHLY/EC PR7 186 F8
LEYL PR25 168 F7
RAW/HAS BB4 194 F1
Woodside Av BBN BB1 158 C3
CHLYE PR6 187 L2
FUL/RIB PR2 132 B7
KIRK/FR/WAR PR4 167 J4
STHP PR8 220 E8
Woodside Cl SKEL WN8 254 F3
Woodside Crs RAW/HAS BB4 196 A2
Woodside Dr BPOOLE FY3 105 K6
RAMS BL0 214 D6
Woodside Gv BBNW BB2 172 D3
Woodside Rd ACC BB5 160 B3
PDHM/BLYW BB12 140 B1
Woodside Wy
NWD/KWIPK L33 260 C6
Woods La GAR/LONG PR3 110 C3
Wood's La GAR/LONG PR3 283 K8
The Woods ROCH OL11 234 F7
Woodstock Av CLV/TH FY5 85 M3
Woodstock Cl BBR PR5 168 F3
Woodstock Crs BBNW BB2 * 172 B3
Woodstock Dr STHP PR8 221 J3
Woodstock Gdns BPOOLS FY4 124 E4
Woodstock St WHIT OL12 234 F2
Wood St ACC BB5 159 H6
BPOOL FY1 4 D1
BRFD/BLYE BB10 142 D3
COL BB8 296 B7
DWN BB3 191 J2
FTWD FY7 81 H3
GTH/LHO BB6 139 H6
HOR/BR BL6 231 M8
LANC LA1 3 G5
LIT OL15 219 L6
LSTA FY8 145 H5
MILN OL16 235 K5
NLSN BB9 122 E6
PDHM/BLYW BB12 140 F7
PLF/KEOS FY6 106 C1
RAMS BL0 214 E6
Wood Street Livesey Fold
DWN BB3 191 J1
Woodtop Av ROCH OL11 234 C6
Woodvale CROS/BRETH PR26 185 K3
Woodvale Ct CHTN/BK PR9 181 K6
Woodvale Rd CHLYE PR6 * 169 L7
STHP PR8 237 M1
Wood Vw BBNW BB2 172 C2
WGNNW/ST WN6 245 K6
Wood View La PLF/KEOS FY6 82 F4
Woodville Av CSBY/BLUN L23 257 G8
Woodville Rd BBN BB1 157 K4
CHLY/EC PR7 * 207 M3
CHLYE PR6 230 C2
NLSN BB9 122 E5
PRES PR1 168 A1
Woodville Rd West PRES PR1 167 M1
Woodville St LANC LA1 3 J5
LEYL PR25 168 E8
Woodville Ter DWN BB3 191 L5
LSTA FY8 146 C8
Woodward Rd
NWD/KWIPK L33 260 F7
Woodway FUL/RIB PR2 131 M7
Woodwell La CARN LA5 24 F2
Wookey Cl FUL/RIB PR2 133 G5
Wooley La ACC BB5 176 B1
Woolman Rd BPOOL FY1 4 F4
Woolwich St BBN BB1 11 K3
Woone La CLI BB7 99 G4
Worcester Av ACC BB5 159 K4
GAR/LONG PR3 284 A8
LANC LA1 55 G6
LEYL PR25 186 E3
Worcester Pl CHLY/EC PR7 208 B8
Worcester Rd BBN BB1 157 M6
BPOOLE FY3 5 M6
Worcester St ROCH OL11 235 H7
Worden Cl LEYL PR25 186 C4
Worden La LEYL PR25 186 D4
Worden Rd FUL/RIB PR2 132 A8
Wordsworth Av BPOOLE FY3 125 L1

CARN LA5 .... 32 F6
CLV/TH FY5 .... 85 J1
KIRK/FR/WAR PR4 .... 148 B5
LSTA FY8 .... 147 G7
PDHM/BLYW BB12 .... 141 H4
Wordsworth Cl ACC BB5 .... 158 F7
ORM L39 .... 241 C5
Wordsworth Dr GTH/LHO BB6 .... 138 E6
Wordsworth Pl BPOOLS FY4 .... 124 F4
Wordsworth Rd ACC BB5 .... 159 K7
Wordsworth St
BRFD/BLYE BB10 * 123 J8
PDHM/BLYW BB12 .... 140 F7
Wordsworth Ter CHLYE PR6 .... 208 A1
Wordsworth Wy ROCH OL11 .... 234 B5
Workshop Rd HEY LA3 .... 64 E1
Worrall St WHIT OL12 .... 235 G1
Worsley Av BPOOLS FY4 .... 124 F4
Worsley Cl PLF/KEOS FY6 .... 78 A6
WGNW/BIL/OR WN5 * 255 M6
Worsley Gn
WGNW/BIL/OR WN5 .... 255 L6
Worsley Pl MILN OL16 .... 235 L4
Worsley Rd LSTA FY8 .... 145 M6
Worsley St ACC BB5 .... 176 D4
MILN OL16 .... 235 L4
WGNW/BIL/OR WN5 .... 255 L6
Worsten Av BBNW BB2 .... 172 F2
Worston Cl ACC BB5 .... 159 J7
RAW/HAS BB4 .... 159 J7
Worston La GTH/LHO BB6 .... 139 H5
Worston Pl BBNW BB2 .... 156 E6
Worthalls Rd
PDHM/BLYW BB12 .... 140 A2
Worthing Cl STHP PR8 .... 199 J8
Worthing Rd FUL/RIB PR2 .... 131 K7
Worthington Rd BPOOLS FY4 .... 125 K7
Worthy St CHLYE PR6 .... 208 B4
Wove Ct PRES PR1 .... 152 B1
Wraith St DWN BB3 .... 191 K3
Wray Ct LANC LA1 .... 42 D7
Wray Crs CROS/BRETH PR26 .... 185 J3
KIRK/FR/WAR PR4 .... 127 K7
Wray Gv CLV/TH FY5 .... 85 G3
Wray Pl MILN OL16 .... 235 M5
Wrawood Ct FTWD FY7 .... 80 F2
Wren Av PRES PR1 .... 8 E9
Wrenbury Cl
WGNW/BIL/OR WN5 .... 255 L6
Wrenbury Dr MILN OL16 .... 235 M7
Wren Cl CLV/TH FY5 .... 86 A3
PLF/KEOS FY6 .... 85 K7
WGNW/BIL/OR WN5 .... 255 L2
Wren Gn MILN OL16 .... 235 L5
Wren Gv BPOOLE FY5 .... 5 K7
Wrennalls La CHLY/EC PR7 .... 205 L1
Wren St NLSN BB9 .... 123 J3
PDHM/BLYW BB12 .... 141 M5
PRES PR1 .... 152 E2

Wrights Fold LEYL PR25 .... 186 F3
Wrights Ter STHP PR8 .... 199 L8
Wright St BCUP OL13 .... 179 J7
CHLYE PR6 .... 208 B3
CHTN/BK PR9 .... 13 H3
HOR/BR BL6 .... 231 L7
KIRK/FR/WAR PR4 .... 128 C5
Wrigley Pl LIT OL15 * 219 J8
Wrigleys Cl FMBY L37 .... 237 J6
Wrigleys La FMBY L37 .... 237 J6
Written Stone La
GAR/LONG PR3 .... 115 J3
Wroxham Cl BRFD/BLYE BB10 * 143 G1
Wroxton Cl CLV/TH FY5 .... 85 J2
Wuerdle Cl MILN OL16 .... 219 H8
Wuerdle Farm Wy MILN OL16 .... 219 H7
Wuerdle Pl MILN OL16 .... 219 H7
Wuerdle St MILN OL16 .... 219 H7
Wycherley Rd WHIT OL12 .... 234 E1
Wychnor FUL/RIB PR2 .... 131 L4
Wycollar Cl ACC BB5 .... 159 M7
Wycollar Dr BBNW BB2 .... 156 D5
Wycollar Rd BBNW BB2 .... 156 D5
Wycoller Av BRFD/BLYE BB10 .... 143 K6
Wycoller Vw COL BB8 .... 296 H5
Wycombe Av BPOOLS FY4 .... 124 E5
Wyfordby Av BBNW BB2 .... 156 C4
Wyke Cop Rd CHTN/BK PR9 .... 201 L8
Wykeham Cv WHIT OL12 .... 234 E2
Wykeham Rd LSTA FY8 .... 146 E2
Wyke La CHTN/BK PR9 .... 201 L7
Wyke Wood La CHTN/BK PR9 .... 201 L7
Wylva Av CSBY/BLUN L23 .... 257 K8
Wymundsley CHLY/EC PR7 .... 207 J2
Wyndene Cl GAR/LONG PR3 .... 114 F3
Wyndene Gv
KIRK/FR/WAR PR4 .... 148 E5
Wyndham Gdns BPOOLS FY4 .... 125 G5
Wyndham Pl MCMB LA4 .... 42 A5
Wynfield BBR PR5 .... 169 J1
Wyngarth Cl LANC LA1 * 3 C1
Wynnstay Av MGHL L31 .... 250 A8
Wynnwood Av BPOOL FY1 .... 104 F2
Wynotham St
BRFD/BLYE BB10 .... 142 L1
Wyre Av KIRK/FR/WAR PR4 .... 128 E6
Wyre Bank GAR/LONG PR3 .... 89 L5
Wyre Br GAR/LONG PR3 .... 270 C12
Wyre Cl GAR/LONG PR3 .... 88 F6
LANC LA1 .... 54 A3
Wyre Ct FTWD FY7 * 77 H8
Wyre Crs DWN BB3 .... 173 G7
Wyredale Rd LSTA FY8 .... 144 F3
Wyrefields PLF/KEOS FY6 .... 86 D8
Wyre Gv BPOOL FY1 .... 4 D7
Wyre La GAR/LONG PR3 .... 284 B6
Wyre Rd CLV/TH FY5 .... 86 D5
Wyresdale Av ACC BB5 .... 159 K3

BISP FY2 .... 85 G7
HEY LA3 .... 52 F3
PLF/KEOS FY6 .... 85 M8
STHP PR8 .... 13 M9
Wyresdale Ct LANC LA1 .... 3 L7
Wyresdale Crs FUL/RIB PR2 .... 133 G7
GAR/LONG PR3 .... 270 D12
HGHB LA2 .... 65 K7
Wyresdale Dr LEYL PR25 .... 186 F3
Wyresdale Gdns LANC LA1 .... 3 L8
Wyresdale Pk PLF/KEOS FY6 * 86 E1
Wyresdale Rd HGHB LA2 .... 56 A8
LANC LA1 .... 3 L7
PLF/KEOS FY6 .... 86 A6
Wyreside Cl GAR/LONG PR3 .... 284 B7
Wyreside Dr PLF/KEOS FY6 .... 86 E1
Wyre St FTWD FY7 .... 77 J8
FUL/RIB PR2 .... 8 B1
KIRK/FR/WAR PR4 .... 128 C5
PDHM/BLYW BB12 .... 141 G3
Wytham St PDHM/BLYW BB12 .... 141 G4
Wythburn Av BBNW BB2 .... 172 E8
Wythburn Cl
PDHM/BLYW BB12 .... 141 L3
Wythorpe Cft MCMB LA4 .... 41 J7
Wyvern Wy PLF/KEOS FY6 .... 85 L6

Y

Yare St RAW/HAS BB4 .... 196 C3
Yarlside La SKP/WHF BD23 .... 279 L12
Yarmouth Av RAW/HAS BB4 .... 194 F1
Yarm Pl BLY BB11 .... 7 F3
Yarraville St RAW/HAS BB4 .... 195 K1
Yarrow Av MGHL L31 .... 259 J1
Yarrow Cl CLV/TH FY5 * 189 K2
CROS/BRETH PR26 .... 204 E1
ROCH OL11 .... 235 J6
Yarrow Ga CHLY/EC PR7 .... 208 B5
Yarrow Gv HOR/BR BL6 .... 231 L7
Yarrow Pl LEYL PR25 .... 186 A3
Yarrow Rd CHLYE PR6 .... 208 B5
LEYL PR25 .... 186 A3
Yarrow Wk HEY LA3 * 53 J1
Yarwell WHIT OL12 * 235 H3
Yarwood Cl HEYW OL10 .... 234 B8
Yates Fold BBNW BB2 .... 11 G9
Yates St BPOOL FY1 .... 104 E5
CHLY/EC PR7 .... 207 L6
Yeadon SKEL WN8 .... 253 L2
Yeadon Gv CHLY/EC PR7 .... 207 K4
Yeadon Wy BPOOLS FY4 .... 124 F3
Yea Fold LIT OL15 .... 219 H8
Yealand Av HEY LA3 .... 52 E5
SETT BD24 .... 265 M6
Yealand Cl ROCH OL11 .... 234 E5
Yealand Dr LANC LA1 .... 54 F7

Yealand Gv CARN LA5 .... 33 K1
Yealand Rd CARN LA5 .... 26 B2
Yellow House La STHP PR8 .... 13 G6
Yenham La HEY LA3 .... 65 K2
Yerburgh Rd BBNW BB2 .... 156 B1
Yewbarrow Cl
PDHM/BLYW BB12 .... 141 M2
Yew Ct FTWD FY7 .... 77 J8
Yewdale SKEL WN8 .... 253 K2
WGNNW/ST WN6 .... 245 L5
Yewdale Av HEY LA3 .... 52 E7
Yew Dale Gdns ROCH OL11 .... 234 E7
Yewlands Av BBR PR5 .... 169 J2
CHLY/EC PR7 .... 206 C8
FUL/RIB PR2 .... 132 B5
Yewlands Crs FUL/RIB PR2 .... 132 B5
Yewlands Dr BRFD/BLYE BB10 .... 122 E8
FUL/RIB PR2 .... 132 B5
GAR/LONG PR3 .... 284 B6
LEYL PR25 .... 186 C2
Yew St BBN BB1 * 157 K4
Yew Tree Av CHLY/EC PR7 .... 186 F1
FUL/RIB PR2 .... 133 M1
Yewtree Av FUL/RIB PR2 .... 133 K6
Yew Tree Cl BBN BB1 * 137 H5
Yewtree Cl CHLY/EC PR7 .... 207 M8
Yew Tree Ct GAR/LONG PR3 .... 284 A7
KIRK/FR/WAR PR4 .... 129 J2
Yew Tree Dr ACC BB5 .... 159 J8
BBNW BB2 .... 156 C3
Yewtree Dr HGHB LA2 .... 38 D3
Yew Tree Gdns PLF/KEOS FY6 .... 82 F3
Yew Tree Gn MGHL L31 .... 259 L7
Yewtree Gv BBR PR5 .... 168 D4
Yew Tree Gv RAW/HAS BB4 .... 195 J3
Yew Tree Rd BPOOLE FY3 .... 105 K2
ORM L39 .... 241 J5
Yew Tree Ter WHIT OL12 * 302 B9
Yew Tree Vls CHLY/EC PR7 * 206 B8
York Av CLV/TH FY5 .... 85 G1
CSBY/BLUN L23 .... 257 G7
FTWD FY7 .... 77 H8
FUL/RIB PR2 .... 132 B7
RAW/HAS BB4 .... 194 D3
ROCH OL11 .... 234 D5
STHP PR8 .... 12 E7
York Cl ACC BB5 .... 139 J8
FMBY L37 .... 237 J5
LEYL PR25 .... 186 B2
NTHTN L30 .... 258 C6
York Crs BBN BB1 .... 137 J5
York Dr GAR/LONG PR3 .... 88 F6
KIRK/FR/WAR PR4 .... 148 E1
RAMS BL0 .... 214 D8
Yorke St BLY BB11 .... 6 F5
York Flds BWCK/EAR BB18 .... 293 Q6
York Gdns STHP PR8 .... 12 E8

York Gv GAR/LONG PR3 .... 283 R8
York La GTH/LHO BB6 .... 138 A3
York Pl ACC BB5 .... 159 L4
CHLYE PR6 .... 230 D3
MCMB LA4 .... 41 G6
TOD OL14 .... 303 L2
York Rd BBN BB1 .... 137 M6
BISP FY2 .... 84 E7
CSBY/BLUN L23 .... 257 H7
FMBY L37 .... 237 J8
GTH/LHO BB6 .... 138 A4
LANC LA1 .... 54 F6
LSTA FY8 .... 145 J6
MGHL L31 .... 259 G5
STHP PR8 .... 12 D9
Yorkshire Dr CHLY/EC PR7 .... 187 J5
Yorkshire St ACC BB5 .... 159 M7
BCUP OL13 .... 179 J8
BLY BB11 .... 7 H4
BPOOL FY1 .... 4 C5
MILN OL16 .... 235 J3
NLSN BB9 .... 123 J3
WHIT OL12 .... 235 K3
Yorkshire St West HEY LA3 .... 40 F7
BBN BB1 * 158 D2
BBNW BB2 .... 10 F8
BCUP OL13 .... 179 J6
BPOOL FY1 .... 4 C5
BWCK/EAR BB18 .... 293 Q6
CHLY/EC PR7 .... 208 A4
CLI BB7 .... 99 H3
COL BB8 .... 296 B6
GTH/LHO BB6 .... 139 G6
MILN OL16 .... 235 L5
NLSN BB9 .... 123 J3
RAW/HAS BB4 .... 177 K4
TOD OL14 .... 303 L1
York Ter BBNW BB2 .... 172 A3
CHTN/BK PR9 .... 13 K2
Young Av LEYL PR25 .... 186 F2
Young St BBNW BB2 .... 172 E1
RAMS BL0 .... 214 E5
Yoxall Dr NWD/KWIPK L33 .... 260 A5

Z

Zama St RAMS BL0 * 214 D7
Zebudah St BBNW BB2 .... 172 F1
Zedburgh WHIT OL12 * 235 H3
Zetland St CHTN/BK PR9 .... 13 L4
PRES PR1 .... 9 M5
Zion Rd BBN BB1 .... 157 K3
Zion St BCUP OL13 .... 179 K8
COL BB8 .... 296 A2
Zion Ter WHIT OL12 .... 234 D7

Index - featured places

Abbey Farm Caravan Park
BRSC L40 .... 241 M3
Abbey Gisburn Park
Private Hospital
CLI BB7 .... 278 E11
Abbey Lakes Sports Centre
WGNW/BIL/OR WN5 .... 255 G4
Abbey Lane Industrial Estate
BRSC L40 .... 241 M2
Abbey Road Clinic
BPOOLS FY4 .... 124 F5
Abbey Village Primary School
CHLYE PR6 .... 189 M2
ABC Cinema
STHP PR8 .... 13 G4
Abraham Guest High School
WGNW/BIL/OR WN5 .... 255 K5
Abraham Ormerod
Day Hospital
TOD OL14 .... 303 L2
Accrington Business Centre
ACC BB5 .... 159 L5
Accrington Cemetery
ACC BB5 .... 160 A3
Accrington Crematorium
ACC BB5 .... 160 A3
Accrington Cricket Club
ACC BB5 .... 159 M3
Accrington & District
Golf Club
ACC BB5 .... 158 E5
Accrington Huncoat
Primary School
ACC BB5 .... 160 B1
Accrington &
Rossendale College
ACC BB5 .... 159 L6
RAW/HAS BB4 .... 195 J1
Accrington Stanley FC
ACC BB5 .... 159 L3
Accrington Victoria Hospital
ACC BB5 .... 159 L4
Ackhurst Business Centre
CHLY/EC PR7 .... 207 J3
Ackhurst Park
Industrial Estate
CHLY/EC PR7 .... 207 H3
Adlington CC
CHLY/EC PR7 .... 230 D5
Adlington Cemetery
CHLY/EC PR7 .... 230 C5
Adlington Medical Centre
CHLYE PR6 .... 230 E3
Adlington Primary School
CHLY/EC PR7 .... 230 C4
Admiral Shopping Centre
NLSN BB9 .... 123 G3
The Adult College
LANC LA1 .... 3 H7
Adult Education Centre
BBNW BB2 .... 10 B3
Ainscough Business Park
WGNNW/ST WN6 .... 228 B5
Ainsdale CE Primary School
STHP PR8 .... 221 G7
Ainsdale Clinic
STHP PR8 .... 221 G8
Ainsdale Hope
CE High School
STHP PR8 .... 220 F5
Ainsdale Sand Dunes
National Nature Reserve
STHP PR8 .... 237 H1
AK Business Park
CHTN/BK PR9 .... 200 D5

Al-Asr Primary School
BBNW BB2 .... 156 E5
Albany Science College
CHLY/EC PR7 .... 208 B2
Albert Street Business Park
HOR/BR BL6 .... 231 L6
Albion Road Industrial Estate
ROCH OL11 .... 235 G5
Alder Grange Community &
Technology School
RAW/HAS BB4 .... 177 K7
Alhambra Leisure Centre
HEY LA3 .... 40 F7
Alice Ingham
RC Primary School
MILN OL16 .... 235 M1
Al Islah Private School
BBN BB1 .... 11 J6
All Hallows Catholic
High School
PRES PR1 .... 151 K8
Alliance Business Park
ACC BB5 .... 159 K6
All Saints CE Primary School
ACC BB5 .... 159 H1
CHLY/EC PR7 .... 207 L6
WHIT OL12 .... 235 K2
All Saints RC High School
Language College
RAW/HAS BB4 .... 195 G2
All Seasons Leisure Centre
CHLY/EC PR7 .... 208 A2
All Souls CE
Primary School
HEYW OL10 .... 234 C8
Alma Industrial Estate
WHIT OL12 .... 235 J2
Alston Lane
RC Primary School
GAR/LONG PR3 .... 134 C1
Altham Business Park
ACC BB5 .... 140 C5
Altham CE Primary School
ACC BB5 .... 140 A5
Altham Industrial Estate
ACC BB5 .... 140 B5
AMF Bowling
BLY BB11 .... 7 G3
BPOOL FY1 .... 4 E6
AMS Trading Estate
KIRK/FR/WAR PR4 .... 167 G4
Anchor Retail Park
BLY BB11 .... 6 F3
Anchorsholme
Primary School
CLV/TH FY5 .... 85 H3
Anderton Primary School
CHLYE PR6 .... 230 D3
Ansdell Primary School
LSTA FY8 .... 145 M6
Apollo Cinema
MCMB LA4 .... 41 G6
Apollo Five Cinema
BBN BB1 .... 10 E3
Applegate School
COL BB8 .... 296 A7
Appley Bridge All Saints
CE Primary School
WGNNW/ST WN6 .... 244 F2
Aqueduct Street
Industrial Estate
FUL/RIB PR2 .... 8 C1
Archbishop Huttons
Primary School
CARN LA5 .... 26 A6

Arden College
CHTN/BK PR9 .... 13 J4
The Arena
BPOOLS FY4 .... 124 E4
Argyle Lawn Tennis Club
CHTN/BK PR9 .... 200 B1
Arkholme CE Primary School
KKBYL LA6 .... 28 F6
Arndale Shopping Centre
ACC BB5 .... 159 M5
MCMB LA4 .... 41 H6
Arnold Junior School
BPOOLS FY4 .... 124 F4
Arnold Medical Centre
BPOOLS FY4 .... 125 G4
Arnold School
BPOOLS FY4 .... 124 E4
Arnside Cemetery
CARN LA5 .... 16 F3
Arnside National
CE Primary School
CARN LA5 .... 16 E1
Arnside Sailing Club
CARN LA5 .... 16 E1
Arnside Tower
CARN LA5 .... 16 E5
Ashbridge Independent
School
KIRK/FR/WAR PR4 .... 167 J1
Ashfield Valley
Primary School
ROCH OL11 .... 235 H7
Ashleigh Primary School
DWN BB3 .... 191 K5
Ashton Community
Science College
FUL/RIB PR2 .... 151 J1
Ashton Health Centre
FUL/RIB PR2 .... 151 K2
Ashton & Lea Golf Club
KIRK/FR/WAR PR4 .... 150 F1
Ashton Primary School
FUL/RIB PR2 .... 151 H1
Ashurst Health Centre
SKEL WN8 .... 243 L7
Ashworth Hospital
MGHL L31 .... 259 K1
Asmall Primary School
ORM L39 .... 241 G4
Astley Hall Museum &
Art Gallery
CHLY/EC PR7 .... 207 K2
Astley Park School
CHLY/EC PR7 .... 207 L3
Astra Business Centre
FUL/RIB PR2 .... 133 M5
Astra Industrial Centre
ROCH OL11 .... 234 F8
Atherton House School
CSBY/BLUN L23 .... 257 G7
Atkinson Art Gallery
STHP PR8 .... 13 G4
Audley Infant School
BBN BB1 .... 11 K8
Audley Junior School
BBN BB1 .... 11 K7
Audley Sports &
Neighbourhood Centre
BBN BB1 .... 11 J5
Aughton Christ Church
Primary School
ORM L39 .... 240 F7
Aughton St Michaels
CE Primary School
ORM L39 .... 250 E2

Aughton Town Green
Primary School
ORM L39 .... 250 F3
The Avenue Hotel
GTH/LHO BB6 .... 117 M6
Avondale Primary School
DWN BB3 .... 173 H8
Back Lane Caravan Park
KIRK/FR/WAR PR4 .... 147 M7
Bacup Cemetery
BCUP OL13 .... 197 H3
Bacup FC
BCUP OL13 .... 179 J7
Bacup Golf Club
BCUP OL13 .... 197 H1
Bacup Leisure Hall
BCUP OL13 .... 179 J8
Bacup & Rawtenstall
Grammar School
RAW/HAS BB4 .... 196 C3
Baillie Street Health Centre
MILN OL16 .... 235 J3
Baines Endowed
Primary School
CLV/TH FY5 .... 85 M2
Baines School
PLF/KEOS FY6 .... 106 A2
Balderstone
CE Primary School
BBNW BB2 .... 135 K6
Balderstone
Technology College
ROCH OL11 .... 235 K8
Balladen Community School
RAW/HAS BB4 .... 195 J3
Balmoral Lodge Hotel
CHTN/BK PR9 .... 13 K1
Balshaw Lane Primary School
CHLY/EC PR7 .... 207 H2
Balshaws CE High School
LEYL PR25 .... 186 E4
Bamber Bridge Clinic
BBR PR5 .... 169 J1
Bamber Bridge FC
BBR PR5 .... 169 G3
Bamber Bridge (Withy Park)
Leisure Centre
BBR PR5 .... 169 J2
Bamford Primary School
ROCH OL11 .... 234 B5
Bancroft Mill
BWCK/EAR BB18 .... 293 P6
Banks Health Centre
CHTN/BK PR9 .... 181 J5
Banks Methodist
Primary School
CHTN/BK PR9 .... 181 L5
Bank View Industrial Estate
PLF/KEOS FY6 .... 86 F2
Barden Junior School
BRFD/BLYE BB10 .... 142 D2
Barden Lane Athletics Track
BRFD/BLYE BB10 .... 142 D2
Barnaby's Sands Burrow
Marshes Nature Reserve
FTWD FY7 .... 81 L4
Barnfield Business Centre
NLSN BB9 .... 123 J5
Barnoldswick
CE Primary School
BWCK/EAR BB18 .... 293 Q6
Barnoldswick Civic Centre
BWCK/EAR BB18 .... 293 Q5
Barrow Controlled School
CLI BB7 .... 119 G1

Barrowford Cemetery
NLSN BB9 .... 103 G7
Barrowford Clinic
NLSN BB9 .... 103 G8
Barton Grange Hotel
GAR/LONG PR3 .... 111 L4
Barton St Lawrence
CE Primary School
GAR/LONG PR3 .... 111 L3
Bates Swimming Pool
PLF/KEOS FY6 .... 86 F1
Baxenden & District Golf Club
(Top o' th' Meadows)
ACC BB5 .... 160 C8
Baxenden St John's
CE Primary School
ACC BB5 .... 176 B2
BBC Radio Lancashire
BBNW BB2 .... 10 F5
Beacon Country Park
SKEL WN8 .... 254 C2
Beacon Fell Country Park
GAR/LONG PR3 .... 93 J1
Beacon Hill High School
BISP FY2 .... 105 G2
Beacon Park Golf &
Country Club
SKEL WN8 .... 254 B1
Beacon School
SKEL WN8 .... 254 B3
Beardwood Hospital
BBNW BB2 .... 156 D5
Beardwood School
BBNW BB2 .... 156 D5
Beaumont College of
Further Education
HGHB LA2 .... 42 D7
Bedford Hotel
LSTA FY8 .... 145 H5
Beech House School
ROCH OL11 .... 235 H6
Beech Industrial Estate
BCUP OL13 .... 179 K8
Beech Tree School
BBR PR5 .... 169 K7
Beehive Industrial Estate
BPOOLS FY4 .... 125 L3
Belair Industrial Estate
CSBY/BLUN L23 .... 257 J8
Belfield Community
Primary School
MILN OL16 .... 235 M3
Belgrave Madison Hotel
BISP FY2 .... 84 E6
Belmont School
RAW/HAS BB4 .... 195 H1
Belthorn Primary School
BBN BB1 .... 174 C5
Belvedere & Caldervale
Sports Club
BRFD/BLYE BB10 .... 122 E8
Benjamin Hargreaves
CE Primary School
ACC BB5 .... 160 A6
The Bennett
House School
CHLYE PR6 .... 208 B2
Bentham Golf Club
HGHB LA2 .... 39 G3
Bentham Industrial Estate
HGHB LA2 .... 39 G4
Berry Lane Medical Centre
GAR/LONG PR3 .... 114 D4
Best Business Centre
MCMB LA4 .... 41 J5

Best Western Garstang
　Country Hotel & Golf Club
　GAR/LONG PR3 .... 284 B11
Best Western Higher Trapp
　Country House Hotel
　PDHM/BLYW BB12 .... 120 C7
Best Western Leyland Hotel
　LEYL PR25 .... 186 F2
Best Western
　Royal Clifton Hotel
　STHP PR8 .... 12 H1
Best Western Stutelea Hotel
　CHTN/BK PR9 .... 199 M2
Bickerstaffe
　CE Primary School
　ORM L39 .... 252 B6
Big Blue Hotel
　BPOOLS FY4 .... 124 E5
Bigdale Medical Centre
　NWD/KWIPK L33 .... 260 D8
The Birches
　PLF/KEOS FY6 .... 86 B6
Birchwood Medical Centre
　FUL/RIB PR2 .... 151 L1
Birkdale Cemetery
　STHP PR8 .... 221 H4
Birkdale High School
　STHP PR8 .... 221 H4
Birkdale Primary School
　STHP PR8 .... 199 L8
Birkdale RC Cemetery
　STHP PR8 .... 221 H5
Birkdale Trading Estate
　STHP PR8 .... 221 J1
Birleywood Health Centre
　SKEL WN8 .... 254 A5
Bishop David Sheppard
　CE Primary School
　CHTN/BK PR9 .... 200 E4
Bishop Martin
　CE Primary School
　SKEL WN8 .... 254 A4
Bishop Rawsterne
　CE Language College
　CROS/BRETH PR26 .... 204 F1
Bispham Endowed
　CE Primary School
　BISP FY2 .... 85 G7
Bispham Hall Business Park
　WGNW/BIL/OR WN5 .... 263 M1
Bispham High School &
　Arts College
　BISP FY2 .... 105 G1
Blackburn Arena (Ice Rink)
　BBNW BB2 .... 10 F7
Blackburn Cathedral
　BBN BB1 .... 10 F4
Blackburn Cemetery
　BBN BB1 .... 157 K2
Blackburn College
　BBNW BB2 .... 10 D4
Blackburn Golf Club
　BBNW BB2 .... 156 E4
Blackburn Museum &
　Art Gallery
　BBN BB1 .... 10 E3
Blackburn Ragged School
　BBNW BB2 .... 10 C5
Blackburn RFC
　BBN BB1 .... 157 G1
Blackburn Rovers FC
　(Ewood Park)
　BBNW BB2 .... 173 G3
Blackburn Royal Infirmary
　BBNW BB2 .... 173 G1
Blackburn Shopping Centre
　BBN BB1 .... 10 E4
Black Moss School
　SKEL WN8 .... 253 L1
Blacko Primary School
　NLSN BB9 .... 103 H4
Blackpool Airport
　BPOOLS FY4 .... 125 G8
Blackpool Airport Terminal
　BPOOLS FY4 .... 124 F7
Blackpool Baines CE
　Endowed Primary School
　BPOOLS FY4 .... 125 J2
Blackpool Beach Patrol
　Headquarters
　BPOOL FY1 .... 104 E4
Blackpool Borough
　Indoor Bowls Club
　BPOOL FY1 .... 104 F5
Blackpool Business Park
　BPOOLS FY4 .... 125 H6
Blackpool Crematorium
　(Carleton)
　BISP FY2 .... 85 J8
Blackpool Cricket Club
　BPOOLE FY3 .... 5 K3
Blackpool FC
　(Bloomfield Road)
　BPOOL FY1 .... 4 E7
Blackpool & Fleetwood
　Tramway
　BISP FY2 .... 104 F7
Blackpool Lido
　BPOOLS FY4 .... 124 E2
Model Village
　BPOOLE FY3 .... 5 M4
Blackpool North Shore
　Golf Club
　BISP FY2 .... 104 F1
Blackpool Pleasure Beach
　BPOOLS FY4 .... 124 E4
Blackpool Rugby Club
　CLV/TH FY5 .... 85 G4
Blackpool Sixth Form College
　BPOOLE FY3 .... 105 K1
Blackpool & The Fylde College
　CLV/TH FY5 .... 85 H5
　LSTA FY8 .... 145 M6
Blackpool & The Fylde College
　(Central Blackpool Campus)
　BPOOL FY1 .... 4 F4
Blackpool & The Fylde College
　(Fleetwood Nautical Campus)
　FTWD FY7 .... 81 H4
Blackpool Tower
　BPOOL FY1 .... 4 B2
Blackpool Town Hall &
　Municipal Buildings
　BPOOL FY1 .... 4 C1
Blackpool Welfare Clinic
　BPOOL FY1 .... 105 J4
Blackpool Zoo &
　Dinosaur Safari
　BPOOLE FY3 .... 105 L6
Blakewater College
　BBN BB1 .... 173 M1
Bleasdale CE Primary School
　GAR/LONG PR3 .... 286 B8

Bleasdale House School
　CARN LA5 .... 16 F8
Blessed Trinity RC College
　BLY BB11 .... 141 M7
Bloomfield Medical Centre
　BPOOL FY1 .... 4 F7
Blowick Business Park
　CHTN/BK PR9 .... 200 D5
Bold Hotel
　CHTN/BK PR9 .... 13 H2
Bolton by Bowland
　CE Primary School
　CLI BB7 .... 277 N12
Bolton-le-Sands CC
　CARN LA5 .... 32 F6
Bolton-le-Sands
　CE Primary School
　CARN LA5 .... 33 G7
Bolton Old Links Golf Club
　BOL BL1 .... 233 G8
Bolton Sixth Form College
　North Campus
　BOL BL1 .... 233 L7
Bootle High School
　BOL BL1 .... 258 D7
Botanic Gardens Museum
　CHTN/BK PR9 .... 200 E1
Boundary Primary School
　BPOOLE FY3 .... 105 K4
Bowerham Community
　Primary School
　LANC LA1 .... 3 J9
Bowland College
　LANC LA1 .... 67 G4
Bowland County
　High School
　CLI BB7 .... 291 J6
Brabins Endowed School
　GAR/LONG PR3 .... 287 M12
Bradley Primary School
　NLSN BB9 .... 123 H1
The Breck Primary School
　PLF/KEOS FY6 .... 86 C6
Brennands Endowed
　CE School
　CLI BB7 .... 275 P6
Bretherton Endowed
　CE Primary School
　CROS/BRETH PR26 .... 184 C5
Briar Dene Hotel
　CLV/TH FY5 .... 85 G2
Brickworks
　ACC BB5 .... 160 B1
Bridge House Marina &
　Caravan Park
　GAR/LONG PR3 .... 283 R7
Briercliffe Business Centre
　BRFD/BLYE BB10 .... 123 J8
Briercliffe County
　Primary School
　BRFD/BLYE BB10 .... 123 J8
Briercliffe Shopping Centre
　BRFD/BLYE BB10 .... 142 E2
Brierfield Health Centre
　NLSN BB9 .... 122 E5
Brimrod Primary School
　ROCH OL11 .... 235 G6
Brindle Gregson Lane
　Primary School
　BBR PR5 .... 170 B2
Brindle St James
　CE Primary School
　CHLYE PR6 .... 170 C6
Brindle St Josephs
　RC Primary School
　BBR PR5 .... 170 B2
Brinscall Public Baths
　CHLYE PR6 .... 189 J4
Britannia Community
　Primary School
　BCUP OL13 .... 197 M3
The British Lawnmower
　Museum
　STHP PR8 .... 13 G7
Broadfield Primary School
　MILN OL16 .... 235 J4
Broadfield School
　ACC BB5 .... 175 J1
Broad Oak Industrial Estate
　ACC BB5 .... 159 M6
Broad Oak Primary School
　PRES PR1 .... 167 M1
Broadoaks Centre
　LEYL PR25 .... 186 D2
Broadway Primary School
　RAW/HAS BB4 .... 194 F3
Brockholes Wood
　Primary School
　PRES PR1 .... 153 K2
Brookfield Community
　Primary School
　SKEL WN8 .... 253 G1
Brookfield Primary School
　FUL/RIB PR2 .... 133 H6
Brookfield School
　PLF/KEOS FY6 .... 86 C6
Brookhouse Business Centre
　BBN BB1 .... 11 G1
Brookhouse Primary School
　BBN BB1 .... 157 J4
Brook Lodge Primary School
　RNFD/HAY WA11 .... 262 C3
Brookside Business Park
　RAW/HAS BB4 .... 177 J5
Brookside Primary School
　CLI BB7 .... 99 J3
Broughton Business &
　Enterprise College
　GAR/LONG PR3 .... 131 M1
Broughton CE Primary School
　GAR/LONG PR3 .... 132 A2
Broughton Mill Business Park
　SKP/WHF BD23 .... 281 L9
Broughton Park
　Private Hospital
　GAR/LONG PR3 .... 132 B2
Brownedge St Marys
　RC High School
　BBR PR5 .... 169 J2
Brownhill Special School
　WHIT OL12 .... 235 H2
Bryning with Warton
　St Pauls Primary School
　KIRK/FR/WAR PR4 .... 148 B6
Buckley Road
　Industrial Estate
　WHIT OL12 .... 235 L1
Buckshaw Primary School
　CHLY/EC PR7 .... 207 K1
BUPA Fylde Coast Hospital
　BPOOLE FY3 .... 105 J4
Burn Hall Industrial Estate
　FTWD FY7 .... 81 K5

Burnley Business Centre
　BLY BB11 .... 7 H4
Burnley Cemetery
　BLY BB11 .... 141 K7
Burnley College
　BLY BB11 .... 7 H2
Burnley College
　Student Services
　BLY BB11 .... 7 H2
Burnley Crematorium
　BLY BB11 .... 141 K7
Burnley Cricket Club
　BRFD/BLYE BB10 .... 7 K4
Burnley FC (Turf Moor)
　BRFD/BLYE BB10 .... 7 K4
Burnley General Hospital
　BRFD/BLYE BB10 .... 142 F1
Burnley Golf Club
　BLY BB11 .... 162 C1
Burnley Lawn Tennis Club
　BRFD/BLYE BB10 .... 7 K3
Burnley Road Medical Centre
　COL BB8 .... 103 L8
Burnley Springfield
　Community Primary School
　BLY BB11 .... 7 J5
Burnley Wood CP School
　BLY BB11 .... 7 J7
Burnley Wood Health Centre
　BLY BB11 .... 7 J7
Burnley Youth Theatre
　BRFD/BLYE BB10 .... 7 L1
Burscough Bridge
　Methodist Primary School
　BRSC L40 .... 225 G6
Burscough CC
　BRSC L40 .... 225 J7
Burscough Health Centre
　BRSC L40 .... 225 H6
Burscough Industrial Estate
　BRSC L40 .... 224 E6
Burscough Primary School
　BRSC L40 .... 225 G6
Burscough Priory
　Science College
　BRSC L40 .... 225 G6
Burscough Sports Centre
　BRSC L40 .... 225 H6
Burton Morewood
　Primary School
　KKBYL LA6 .... 19 H5
Burwains Sailing Club
　COL BB8 .... 103 M3
Caldershaw Primary School
　WHIT OL12 .... 234 C2
Calderstones Hospital
　CLI BB7 .... 118 D4
Calder Vale St Johns
　Primary School
　GAR/LONG PR3 .... 285 L6
Calder View School
　PDHM/BLYW BB12 .... 142 C3
Cambridge House Hotel
　CHTN/BK PR9 .... 200 B2
Camelot Theme Park
　CHLY/EC PR7 .... 206 D7
Canalside Industrial Estate
　MILN OL16 .... 235 L4
Canning Road
　Industrial Estate
　CHTN/BK PR9 .... 200 D5
Cardinal Allen Catholic
　High School
　FTWD FY7 .... 81 K3
Cardinal Newman College
　PRES PR1 .... 9 L5
Carleton Cemetery
　BISP FY2 .... 85 L5
Carleton Green
　Primary School
　PLF/KEOS FY6 .... 85 L5
Carleton St Hildas
　CE Primary School
　PLF/KEOS FY6 .... 85 L6
Carlton Hotel
　BPOOL FY1 .... 104 E4
Carlton Lawn Tennis Club
　STHP PR8 .... 221 J1
Carnforth CC
　CARN LA5 .... 33 H2
Carnforth Christ Church
　CE Primary School
　CARN LA5 .... 33 J2
Carnforth High School
　CARN LA5 .... 33 K2
Carousel Hotel
　BPOOLS FY4 .... 124 D4
Carr Head Primary School
　PLF/KEOS FY6 .... 106 B1
Carr Hill High School
　KIRK/FR/WAR PR4 .... 128 E7
Carrs Industrial Estate
　RAW/HAS BB4 .... 176 D8
Carters Charity
　Primary School
　PLF/KEOS FY6 .... 78 K1
Cartmel College
　LANC LA1 .... 67 G3
Castercliff
　NLSN BB9 .... 123 M2
Casterton County School
　BRFD/BLYE BB10 .... 122 F8
Castle Hill Junior &
　Infant School
　TOD OL14 .... 303 N1
Castleton Swimming Pool
　ROCH OL11 .... 234 F8
Catforth Primary School
　KIRK/FR/WAR PR4 .... 110 C7
The Cathedral
　Catholic Primary School
　LANC LA1 .... 3 J7
Cathedral of Saint Peter
　LANC LA1 .... 3 J6
Caton Primary School
　HGHB LA2 .... 44 D6
Caton St Pauls
　CE Primary School
　HGHB LA2 .... 44 F6
Catteral Hall School
　SETT BD24 .... 265 L6
Cawthorns End
　Primary School
　HGHB LA2 .... 271 R2
Cedar House School
　KKBYL LA6 .... 21 L1
The Cedars Infant School
　BBN BB1 .... 157 J2
Central Lancaster
　High School
　LANC LA1 .... 3 M3
Central Leisure Centre
　MILN OL16 .... 235 K4

Central Pier
　BPOOL FY1 .... 4 B5
Centurion Industrial Estate
　LEYL PR25 .... 168 E8
Chadwick St
　LSTA FY8 .... 145 J7
Chandlers Business Park
　CROS/BRETH PR26 .... 186 B1
Chapel Hill Trading Estate
　GAR/LONG PR3 .... 114 D5
Chapel Lane Business Park
　CHLY/EC PR7 .... 229 J3
Charnley Fold
　Industrial Estate
　BBR PR5 .... 153 H8
Charnock Richard Golf Club
　CHLY/EC PR7 .... 206 E7
Charter Theatre
　PRES PR1 .... 9 J4
Charter Walk Shopping Centre
　BLY BB11 .... 7 G4
Chatburn CE Primary School
　CLI BB7 .... 291 J10
Chaucer Primary School
　FTWD FY7 .... 77 J7
Cherry Fold Community
　Primary School
　BLY BB11 .... 141 M7
Cherry Tree Cricket Club
　BBNW BB2 .... 172 C2
Chesterfield High School
　CSBY/BLUN L23 .... 257 K7
Chichester Business Centre
　MILN OL16 .... 235 K4
Childrens Centre
　ORM L39 .... 241 K8
Chingle Hall
　GAR/LONG PR3 .... 113 G7
Chorley AFC
　CHLY/EC PR7 .... 207 M5
Chorley Business &
　Technology Centre
　CHLY/EC PR7 .... 187 H7
Chorley CC
　CHLY/EC PR7 .... 207 L3
Chorley Cemetery
　CHLY/EC PR7 .... 207 K3
Chorley East Business Centre
　CHLYE PR6 .... 208 C4
Chorley Golf Club
　CHLYE PR6 .... 208 D8
Chorley North Business Park
　CHLYE PR6 .... 188 A8
Chorley North Industrial Park
　CHLYE PR6 .... 208 A1
Chorley Retail Park
　CHLY/EC PR7 .... 207 M4
Chorley & South Ribble
　District General Hospital
　CHLY/EC PR7 .... 187 M8
Chorley West Business Park
　CHLY/EC PR7 .... 207 J3
Christ Church
　CE Primary School
　COL BB8 .... 296 E6
　LANC LA1 .... 3 M5
Christchurch Charnock
　Richard CE Primary School
　CHLY/EC PR7 .... 207 G7
Christ The King Catholic High
　School & Sixth Form College
　STHP PR8 .... 199 L8
Christ The King Catholic
　Maths & Computing College
　PRES PR1 .... 9 L7
Christ the King
　RC Primary School
　BLY BB11 .... 6 C9
　BPOOLE FY3 .... 105 K4
Chromolyte Industrial Estate
　STHP PR8 .... 13 G8
Churchtown Medical Centre
　CHTN/BK PR9 .... 200 D1
Churchtown Primary School
　CHTN/BK PR9 .... 200 E1
City of Preston High School
　FUL/RIB PR2 .... 133 J8
Claremont Hotel
　FUL/RIB PR2 .... 151 L1
Claremont Medical Centre
　MGHL L31 .... 258 E3
Claremont Primary School
　BPOOL FY1 .... 104 F3
Clarence House School
　FMBY L37 .... 237 H5
Clarendon Hotel
　MCMB LA4 .... 41 G7
Claughton Industrial Estate
　GAR/LONG PR3 .... 91 H2
Claylands Caravan Park
　GAR/LONG PR3 .... 284 C1
Clayton Brook
　Primary School
　BBR PR5 .... 169 L6
Clayton Business Park
　ACC BB5 .... 159 J1
Clayton Green
　Business Park
　BBR PR5 .... 169 L7
Clayton Green Sports Centre
　CHLYE PR6 .... 169 K7
Clayton-le-Moors
　Industrial Park
　ACC BB5 .... 159 H2
Clayton le Woods
　CE Primary School
　CHLYE PR6 .... 187 K1
Clayton Street
　Industrial Estate
　NLSN BB9 .... 123 G2
Cleveleys Health Centre
　CLV/TH FY5 .... 85 G1
The Cliffs Hotel
　BISP FY2 .... 104 E2
Clifton Arms Hotel
　LSTA FY8 .... 146 D8
Clifton Primary School
　LSTA FY8 .... 145 M5
Clifton Retail Park
　BPOOLS FY4 .... 126 A3
Clifton Tutorial College
　LSTA FY8 .... 145 H6
Clitheroe Castle
　CLI BB7 .... 99 H4
Clitheroe C&CC Site
　CLI BB7 .... 98 E4
Clitheroe Cemetery
　CLI BB7 .... 99 G1
Clitheroe Cricket Club
　CLI BB7 .... 99 J2
Clitheroe Golf Club
　CLI BB7 .... 99 G8

Clitheroe Health Centre
　CLI BB7 .... 99 H2
Clitheroe Hospital
　CLI BB7 .... 99 K1
Clitheroe Royal
　Grammar School
　CLI BB7 .... 99 J2
Cloughfold CP School
　RAW/HAS BB4 .... 195 M1
Coal Clough CP School
　BLY BB11 .... 6 B6
Coates Lane Primary School
　BWCK/EAR BB18 .... 294 A4
Cobbs Brow
　Community School
　SKEL WN8 .... 243 K8
Cockerham Parochial
　CE Primary School
　HGHB LA2 .... 269 M7
Cockerham Sands
　Country Park
　HGHB LA2 .... 268 G5
Cockersand (Ruined Abbey)
　HGHB LA2 .... 268 E3
Cocker Trading Estate
　BPOOL FY1 .... 104 F4
Colden Primary School
　HBR HX7 .... 301 R6
Collegiate High School
　BPOOLE FY3 .... 105 K2
Colne CC
　COL BB8 .... 296 D6
Colne Cemetery
　COL BB8 .... 296 C6
Colne Golf Club
　COL BB8 .... 296 E4
Colne Health Centre
　COL BB8 .... 296 A6
Colne & Nelson RUFC
　COL BB8 .... 103 M5
Colne Primet High School
　COL BB8 .... 103 L8
Colne Shopping Parade
　COL BB8 .... 296 B6
Common Bank
　Employment Area
　CHLY/EC PR7 .... 207 J4
Common Bank
　Industrial Estate
　CHLY/EC PR7 .... 207 J4
Concourse Shopping Centre
　SKEL WN8 .... 253 L2
Constable Lee CE School
　RAW/HAS BB4 .... 177 K7
Co-operative Museum
　WHIT OL12 .... 235 H3
Cop Lane CE Primary School
　PRES PR1 .... 151 M7
Copper House School
　BBR PR5 .... 158 D2
The Coppice School
　BBR PR5 .... 169 K2
Coppull Community
　Leisure Centre
　CHLY/EC PR7 .... 229 H3
Coppull Parish
　CE Primary School
　CHLY/EC PR7 .... 229 J3
Coppull Primary School
　CHLY/EC PR7 .... 229 G2
Coppull St Johns CE Voluntary
　Aided Primary School
　CHLY/EC PR7 .... 229 G4
Copse View Business Park
　FTWD FY7 .... 81 J1
Coral Island
　BPOOL FY1 .... 4 C3
Corn Exchange
　PRES PR1 .... 9 H4
Cornholme J&I School
　TOD OL14 .... 300 D10
Corpus Christi Catholic
　Primary School
　RNFD/HAY WA11 .... 262 C4
Corpus Christi RC High School
　FUL/RIB PR2 .... 132 B6
Cottage House
　LANC LA1 .... 2 F5
Cottam Primary School
　KIRK/FR/WAR PR4 .... 131 H6
County College
　LANC LA1 .... 67 G3
Coupe Green Primary School
　BBR PR5 .... 154 B7
Cowling Brow
　Industrial Estate
　CHLYE PR6 .... 208 B5
Crawford Village
　Primary School
　SKEL WN8 .... 254 B8
Crawshawbooth CP School
　RAW/HAS BB4 .... 177 K3
Creamery Industrial Estate
　GAR/LONG PR3 .... 284 E10
Cribden House Comm School
　RAW/HAS BB4 .... 195 H2
Crofters Hotel
　GAR/LONG PR3 .... 284 A5
Crookhey Hall Special School
　HGHB LA2 .... 269 P8
Crosby High School
　CSBY/BLUN L23 .... 257 H5
Crossens CC
　CHTN/BK PR9 .... 181 G7
Cross Hall High School Adult
　Education Centre
　ORM L39 .... 241 L6
Crosshill Special School
　BBN BB1 .... 173 M1
Crossley House
　Industrial Estate
　PRES PR1 .... 152 C7
Croston Cemetery
　CROS/BRETH PR26 .... 204 E2
Croston Medical Centre
　CROS/BRETH PR26 .... 184 F8
Croston Sports Club
　CROS/BRETH PR26 .... 204 E1
Crowland Street
　Industrial Estate
　CHTN/BK PR9 .... 200 C5
Crown Stage & Theatre
　CROS/BRETH PR26 .... 167 M8
Crow Orchard
　Primary School
　SKEL WN8 .... 253 J1
Crow Wood Health &
　Leisure Club
　PDHM/BLYW BB12 .... 142 B2
Cuba Industrial Estate
　RAMS BL0 .... 214 F3
Cuerden Church School
　BBR PR5 .... 169 J3

Cuerden Valley Country Park
 LEYL PR25 .... 169 J8
Cutgate Shopping Precinct
 WHIT OL12 .... 234 E2
Dacrelands Clinic
 LANC LA1 .... 3 G1
Daisyfield Business Centre
 BBN BB1 .... 11 K2
Daisyfield Primary School
 BBN BB1 .... 11 K1
Daisyfield Swimming pool
 BBN BB1 .... 11 H1
Daisyhill Industrial Estate
 BBN BB3 .... 158 E2
Dallas Road Primary School
 LANC LA1 .... 2 F6
Dalmeny Hotel
 LSTA FY8 .... 145 H6
Dalton St Michael
 CE Primary School
 SKEL WN8 .... 244 A6
Dalweb Industrial Park
 CHTN/BK PR9 .... 181 M8
Daneshouse Community
 Health Centre
 BRFD/BLYE BB10 .... 142 D3
Darul Uloom Al Arabiya
 Al Islamia
 TOT/BURYW BL8 .... 214 D7
Darwen Cemetery
 DWN BB3 .... 191 L6
Darwen Cricket Club
 DWN BB3 .... 173 H7
Darwen FC
 DWN BB3 .... 173 J6
Darwen Golf Club
 DWN BB3 .... 173 G8
Darwen Leisure Centre and
 Pool
 DWN BB3 .... 191 J2
Darwen Market
 DWN BB3 .... 191 K2
Darwen Moorland
 High School
 DWN BB3 .... 173 L8
Darwen Tennis Club
 DWN BB3 .... 191 H1
Darwen Vale High School
 DWN BB3 .... 173 G6
Dean Wood Golf Club
 SKEL WN8 .... 254 F3
Deepdale County J&I School
 PRES PR1 .... 152 E1
Deepdale Shopping Park
 PRES PR1 .... 132 F8
Deeplish Primary School
 ROCH OL11 .... 235 K6
Delph Side Primary School
 SKEL WN8 .... 253 L3
Dental Health Centre
 FUL/RIB PR2 .... 132 E8
De Vere Herons Reach Hotel
 BPOOLE FY3 .... 105 L7
Devonshire Primary School
 BPOOLE FY3 .... 105 G5
Devonshire Road Hospital
 BPOOLE FY3 .... 105 G5
Dewan Industrial Estate
 RAW/HAS BB4 .... 194 E3
Dewhurst Industrial Estate
 PRES PR1 .... 8 D1
Deyes High School
 MGHL L31 .... 259 G2
Diamond Business Park
 RNFD/HAY WA11 .... 262 E7
Docker Park Working Farm
 KKBYL LA6 .... 28 C3
Docklands Medical Centre
 FUL/RIB PR2 .... 8 B1
Dolphinholme
 CE Primary School
 HGHB LA2 .... 270 G3
Dover Lodge School of
 Equitation
 CHLYE PR7 .... 170 J2
Downham School
 CLI BB7 .... 291 N10
Downholland Haskayne
 CE Primary School
 ORM L39 .... 239 H8
Dukes Playhouse
 LANC LA1 .... 3 H5
Duke Street Cemetery
 STHP PR8 .... 13 J9
Duke Street Primary School
 CHLY/EC PR7 .... 207 M5
Dunkirk Hall Industrial Estate
 CROS/BRETH PR26 .... 185 M3
Durn Street Industrial Estate
 LIT OL15 .... 219 M5
Duxbury Jubilee
 Park Golf Club
 CHLY/EC PR7 .... 208 A8
Duxbury Park Golf Club
 CHLY/EC PR7 .... 208 A7
Dyslexia North West
 LSTA FY8 .... 145 G5
Earby CC
 BWCK/EAR BB18 .... 294 E6
Earby Cemetery
 BWCK/EAR BB18 .... 294 F4
Earby Springfield
 Primary School
 BWCK/EAR BB18 .... 294 F6
East Chorley Business Centre
 CHLYE PR6 .... 208 A3
Eastcroft Park CP School
 NWD/KWIPK L33 .... 260 C6
Eastern Cemetery
 DWN BB3 .... 191 M6
Eastgate Retail Park
 ACC BB5 .... 159 M5
East Gillbrands
 Industrial Estate
 SKEL WN8 .... 253 K4
Eastham Hall Caravan Site
 LSTA FY8 .... 147 G4
East Lancashire Cricket Club
 BBNW BB2 .... 10 A2
East Lancashire
 Institute of FE
 BBNW BB2 .... 10 C4
East Lancashire Railway
 RAMS BL0 .... 214 F6
 RAW/HAS BB4 .... 195 H4
Eaves Hall Country Hotel
 CLI BB7 .... 290 C9
Eccleston Primary School
 CHLY/EC PR7 .... 205 L5
Edenfield CE Primary School
 RAMS BL0 .... 195 G7
Edenfield Cricket Club
 RAMS BL0 .... 195 H8

Edge Hill College of
 Higher Education
 ORM L39 .... 241 K7
Edge Hill University
 (Ormskirk Campus)
 ORM L39 .... 241 K8
Edgeside School
 RAW/HAS BB4 .... 178 B8
Edgworth CC
 EDGW/EG BL7 .... 213 H5
Edisford Primary School
 CLI BB7 .... 98 F4
Egerton CC
 EDGW/EG BL7 .... 212 A8
Egerton Primary School
 EDGW/EG BL7 .... 212 A8
Eldon Primary School
 PRES PR1 .... 152 B1
Ellel St Johns
 CE Primary School
 HGHB LA2 .... 67 G8
Elms Hotel
 MCMB LA4 .... 41 M4
Elms School
 PRES PR1 .... 132 D8
Elswick Trading Park
 KIRK/FR/WAR PR4 .... 108 D2
Emmanuel Christian School
 BPOOLE FY3 .... 105 M3
 WHIT OL12 .... 235 H2
Emmanuel Holcombe
 Primary School
 TOT/BURYW BL8 .... 214 D5
Empire Theatre
 BCUP OL13 .... 197 K1
English Martyrs
 RC Primary School
 PRES PR1 .... 152 B2
Eric Morecambe Statue
 MCMB LA4 .... 41 M5
Ernest Street School
 ACC BB5 .... 159 H5
Euro Trading Estate
 BBN BB1 .... 157 J4
Euxton CE Primary School
 CHLY/EC PR7 .... 206 F1
Euxton Hall Hospital
 CHLY/EC PR7 .... 206 F2
Euxton St Marys RC
 CHLY/EC PR7 .... 186 F8
Evaglades School
 HGHB LA2 .... 38 D4
Fairhaven Golf Club
 LSTA FY8 .... 146 B7
Fairlie CP School
 SKEL WN8 .... 243 L8
Falinge Park High School
 WHIT OL12 .... 235 G2
Farington Business Park
 LEYL PR25 .... 186 D1
Farington Primary School
 LEYL PR25 .... 168 E8
Farington St Pauls
 CE Primary School
 CROS/BRETH PR26 .... 168 C4
Farnborough Road
 J&I School
 STHP PR8 .... 221 J3
Fearns High School
 RAW/HAS BB4 .... 196 D2
Feniscowles
 Primary School
 BBNW BB2 .... 171 M3
Ferney Lee Primary School
 TOD OL14 .... 303 K1
Fernhurst School
 BBNW BB2 .... 172 F4
Festival Market
 MCMB LA4 .... 41 G6
Fieldhouse Cricket Club
 ROCH OL11 .... 234 B5
Fieldhouse Industrial Estate
 WHIT OL12 .... 235 J1
Fishergate Shopping Centre
 PRES PR1 .... 9 G5
Fishwick Hall Golf Club
 PRES PR1 .... 153 J3
Fishwick Primary School
 PRES PR1 .... 153 H3
Flakefleet Primary School
 FTWD FY7 .... 81 H1
Fleetwood CC
 FTWD FY7 .... 81 H3
Fleetwood Cemetery
 FTWD FY7 .... 77 L6
Fleetwood Charles Sear
 Community Primary School
 FTWD FY7 .... 76 F8
Fleetwood Ferry Terminal
 FTWD FY7 .... 77 L7
Fleetwood FC
 FTWD FY7 .... 77 J8
Fleetwood Golf Club
 FTWD FY7 .... 77 G8
Fleetwood Health Centre
 FTWD FY7 .... 77 L7
Fleetwood High
 Sports College
 FTWD FY7 .... 81 G1
Fleetwood Hospital
 FTWD FY7 .... 77 L6
Fleetwood Leisure Centre &
 Swimming Pool
 FTWD FY7 .... 77 K6
Fleetwood Marsh
 Nature Park
 FTWD FY7 .... 81 L1
Fleetwood Museum
 FTWD FY7 .... 77 M6
Fleetwood Pier
 FTWD FY7 .... 77 L5
Fleetwoods Charity
 CE Primary School
 PLF/KEOS FY6 .... 78 E8
Forefield Infant School
 CSBY/BLUN L23 .... 257 K7
Forefield Junior School
 CSBY/BLUN L23 .... 257 J7
Formby AFC
 FMBY L37 .... 237 J8
Formby Business Park
 FMBY L37 .... 237 M8
Formby CC
 FMBY L37 .... 237 J6
Formby Clinic
 FMBY L37 .... 247 J1
Formby Golf Club
 FMBY L37 .... 237 G6
Formby Hall Golf &
 Country Club
 FMBY L37 .... 237 M3
Formby High School
 FMBY L37 .... 237 H7

Formby Junior Sports Club
 FMBY L37 .... 237 K6
Formby Ladies Golf Club
 FMBY L37 .... 237 G6
Formby Lawn Tennis Club
 FMBY L37 .... 237 J6
Formby Point &
 Squirrel Nature Reserve
 FMBY L37 .... 246 D3
Forton Primary School
 GAR/LONG PR3 .... 270 A8
Fort Street Industrial Estate
 BBN BB1 .... 11 J2
The Forward
 Industrial Estate
 LEYL PR25 .... 186 B1
Foulridge Wharf
 COL BB8 .... 296 A1
Four Gates End
 HBR HX7 .... 301 L7
Fox Industrial Estate
 BISP FY2 .... 105 H2
Freckleton CC
 KIRK/FR/WAR PR4 .... 148 E5
Freckleton
 CE Primary School
 KIRK/FR/WAR PR4 .... 148 F4
Freeport Fleetwood
 Outlet Village
 FTWD FY7 .... 77 K8
Frenchwood Primary School
 PRES PR1 .... 9 L6
Freshfield Primary School
 FMBY L37 .... 237 K7
Freshlea Private Clinic
 FMBY L37 .... 247 G2
Friends Meeting House
 LANC LA1 .... 2 F6
Fulwood & Cadley
 Primary School
 FUL/RIB PR2 .... 132 A7
Fulwood Hall Hospital
 FUL/RIB PR2 .... 132 E5
Fulwood High School
 FUL/RIB PR2 .... 132 A5
Fulwood Leisure Centre
 FUL/RIB PR2 .... 132 A6
Funland
 STHP PR8 .... 12 F2
Furness College
 LANC LA1 .... 67 G4
Furthergate Industrial Estate
 BBN BB1 .... 11 L3
Fylde College
 LANC LA1 .... 67 G4
Fylde Cricket Club
 PLF/KEOS FY6 .... 86 B7
Fylde RFC
 LSTA FY8 .... 146 A6
Fylde Road Industrial Estate
 CHTN/BK PR9 .... 180 E7
 PRES PR1 .... 8 D1
Gait Barrows Nature Reserve
 MTHPE LA7 .... 17 K3
Galgate Health Centre
 HGHB LA2 .... 66 F7
Gannow Business Park
 PDHM/BLYW BB12 .... 141 L5
Garden Vale Business Centre
 COL BB8 .... 103 L7
Gargrave CE Primary School
 SKP/WHF BD23 .... 281 J2
Garstang Community
 Primary School
 GAR/LONG PR3 .... 284 A7
Garstang High School
 GAR/LONG PR3 .... 284 C11
Garstang Leisure Centre
 GAR/LONG PR3 .... 284 A8
Garstang St Thomas
 CE Primary School
 GAR/LONG PR3 .... 284 A9
Garstang Swimming Centre
 GAR/LONG PR3 .... 284 B7
Gathurst Golf Club
 WGNNW/ST WN6 .... 245 J6
Gawthorpe Hall
 PDHM/BLYW BB12 .... 141 J2
GEC Business Park
 ACC BB5 .... 159 H2
Ghausia Girls High School
 NLSN BB9 .... 123 G3
Ghyll Golf Club
 BWCK/EAR BB18 .... 294 B2
Giggleswick
 Primary School
 SETT BD24 .... 265 L6
Giggleswick School
 SETT BD24 .... 265 L7
Gillibrand Primary School
 CHLY/EC PR7 .... 207 L5
Gisburn Forest
 Primary School
 SKP/WHF BD23 .... 266 C10
Gisburn Primary School
 CLI BB7 .... 292 E1
Gisburn Road Community
 Primary School
 BWCK/EAR BB18 .... 293 P5
Glades Clinic
 FUL/RIB PR2 .... 153 J1
Glasson Sailing Club
 HGHB LA2 .... 65 K6
Glebe House School
 MILN OL16 .... 235 H5
Glenburn Sports College
 SKEL WN8 .... 253 K3
Glendower Hotel
 LSTA FY8 .... 145 G5
Glenfield Business Park
 BBN BB1 .... 157 L4
Glenfield Park
 Industrial Estate
 BBN BB1 .... 157 L3
 NLSN BB9 .... 123 K2
The Globe Centre
 ACC BB5 .... 159 L6
Goosnargh Oliversons
 CE Primary School
 GAR/LONG PR3 .... 113 G5
Gorrells Industrial Estate
 ROCH OL11 .... 235 H8
Graduate College
 HGHB LA2 .... 66 F5
Grand Cinema
 CLI BB7 .... 99 J2
The Grand Hotel
 LSTA FY8 .... 145 H6
Grand Theatre
 BPOOL FY1 .... 4 C2
Grange Park
 Health Centre
 BPOOLE FY3 .... 105 K3

Grange Primary School
 NTHTN L30 .... 258 B6
Grapevine Fitness &
 Leisure Centre
 BLY BB11 .... 6 C1
Great Arley School
 CLV/TH FY5 .... 81 L8
Great Arley Swimming Pool
 CLV/TH FY5 .... 81 L8
Great Crosby
 RC Primary School
 CSBY/BLUN L23 .... 257 J7
Great Eccleston Copp
 CE Primary School
 GAR/LONG PR3 .... 88 C7
Great Eccleston Health Centre
 GAR/LONG PR3 .... 88 E6
Great Harwood Cricket Club
 GTH/LHO BB6 .... 138 E4
Great Harwood Golf Club
 GTH/LHO BB6 .... 139 J4
Great Harwood
 Primary School
 GTH/LHO BB6 .... 138 E6
Greatwood Primary School
 MCMB LA4 .... 41 M6
The Greaves Hotel
 LANC LA1 .... 54 F5
Greenbank Business Park
 BBN BB1 .... 157 M5
Greenbank High School
 STHP PR8 .... 221 H2
Green Bank Industrial Estate
 BBN BB1 .... 11 M1
Green Haworth
 CE Primary School
 ACC BB5 .... 175 L2
Green Haworth Golf Club
 ACC BB5 .... 175 L2
Greenlands Community
 Primary School
 FUL/RIB PR2 .... 133 H8
Green Park Primary School
 MGHL L31 .... 258 E1
Griffin Park Primary School
 BBNW BB2 .... 156 E8
Grimeford Industrial Estate
 CHLYE PR6 .... 231 G5
Grimsargh St Michaels
 CE Primary School
 FUL/RIB PR2 .... 133 M2
Grimshaw Retail Park
 BBNW BB2 .... 10 F7
Grindleton CE Primary School
 CLI BB7 .... 290 H7
Grizedale College
 LANC LA1 .... 67 G4
Grosvenor Park
 Primary School
 HEY LA3 .... 54 A1
Grove Park Industrial Estate
 CHLY/EC PR7 .... 205 M6
Grundy Art Gallery
 BPOOL FY1 .... 104 D3
Guild Community Healthcare
 FUL/RIB PR2 .... 131 K5
Guild Hall Charter Theatre
 PRES PR1 .... 9 J4
Guild Trading Estate
 PRES PR1 .... 9 M2
Guys Industrial Estate
 BRSC L40 .... 241 L1
Habergham High School
 PDHM/BLYW BB12 .... 141 J4
Haighton Manor
 Country House Hotel
 FUL/RIB PR2 .... 133 K1
Hale Carr Lane Cemetery
 HEY LA3 .... 52 F2
Halfpenny Bridge
 Industrial Estate
 MILN OL16 .... 235 K5
Hall Green Clinic
 SKEL WN8 .... 254 E4
Hall More Caravan Park
 MTHPE LA7 .... 18 B4
Halsall St Cuthberts
 CE Primary School
 ORM L39 .... 239 L2
Hambleton Health Centre
 PLF/KEOS FY6 .... 86 E1
Hambleton Primary School
 PLF/KEOS FY6 .... 87 G1
Hameldon
 Community College
 PDHM/BLYW BB12 .... 141 J4
Hamer County
 Primary School
 MILN OL16 .... 235 L1
Hannah Street School
 ACC BB5 .... 159 L6
Hapton CE Methodist
 Primary School
 BLY BB11 .... 140 F7
Harbour Trading Estate
 FTWD FY7 .... 81 J1
Hardmans Business Centre
 RAW/HAS BB4 .... 195 H2
Hargher Clough Junior School
 BLY BB11 .... 6 A6
Harris Museum & Art Gallery
 PRES PR1 .... 9 J4
Harrison Trading Estate
 PRES PR1 .... 152 F2
Harris Primary School
 FUL/RIB PR2 .... 131 L4
Haslemere Industrial Estate
 LEYL PR25 .... 186 C1
Haslingden Baths
 RAW/HAS BB4 .... 194 E1
Haslingden Cricket Club
 RAW/HAS BB4 .... 194 F3
Haslingden High School
 RAW/HAS BB4 .... 194 E3
Haslingden Primary School
 RAW/HAS BB4 .... 194 E1
Haslingden Sports Centre
 RAW/HAS BB4 .... 194 D2
Hawes Side Clinic
 BPOOLS FY4 .... 125 H4
Hawes Side Primary School
 BPOOLS FY4 .... 125 H4
Hawkins Clinic
 MILN OL16 .... 235 J4
Hawthorne Industrial Park
 BLY BB11 .... 99 K2
Hawthornes Junior School
 RNFD/HAY WA11 .... 157 J3
Hazel Business Park
 RNFD/HAY WA11 .... 262 F7
Hazelhurst Community
 Primary School
 RAMS BL0 .... 214 D7

Headlands Hotel
 BPOOLS FY4 .... 124 D5
Heald Brow (NT)
 CARN LA5 .... 25 G2
Healey Dell Nature Reserve
 WHIT OL12 .... 217 L7
Healey Primary School
 WHIT OL12 .... 218 B8
Healey Wood Infant School
 BLY BB11 .... 6 F7
Healey Wood Road
 Industrial Estate
 BLY BB11 .... 6 F6
Heasandford Industrial Estate
 BRFD/BLYE BB10 .... 143 G3
Heasandford Primary School
 BRFD/BLYE BB10 .... 142 E3
Heathland College
 ACC BB5 .... 160 A6
Helmshore Primary School
 RAW/HAS BB4 .... 194 D4
Helmshore Textile Museum
 RAW/HAS BB4 .... 194 C3
Henrietta Street
 Industrial Estate
 BCUP OL13 .... 197 J1
Hesketh Centre (Hospital)
 CHTN/BK PR9 .... 199 M2
Hesketh Golf Club
 CHTN/BK PR9 .... 200 B1
Hesketh-with-Becconsall
 All Saints CE Primary School
 KIRK/FR/WAR PR4 .... 165 G7
Heskin Football Club
 CHLY/EC PR7 .... 206 A8
Heskin Pembertons
 CE Primary School
 CHLY/EC PR7 .... 228 B1
Hewitt Business Park
 WGNW/BIL/OR WN5 .... 255 H7
Heybrook Primary School
 WHIT OL12 .... 235 K2
Heyhouse Endowed
 CE Junior School
 LSTA FY8 .... 145 J3
Heyhouse Endowed
 CE Primary & Infant School
 LSTA FY8 .... 145 J4
Heysham Business Park
 HEY LA3 .... 64 E1
Heysham Car Ferry Terminal
 HEY LA3 .... 52 B6
Heysham CC
 HEY LA3 .... 52 D4
Heysham Golf Club
 HEY LA3 .... 52 D7
Heysham High School
 HEY LA3 .... 53 G1
Heysham Nature Reserve
 HEY LA3 .... 52 C7
Heysham Nuclear
 Power Station
 HEY LA3 .... 52 B7
Heywood Cemetery
 ROCH OL11 .... 234 C7
Higham CE Primary School
 PDHM/BLYW BB12 .... 121 J5
High Bentham Business Park
 HGHB LA2 .... 39 G5
High Bentham Primary School
 HGHB LA2 .... 39 G5
High Birch Special School
 ROCH OL11 .... 234 E6
Higher Walton
 CE Primary School
 BBR PR5 .... 153 M8
Highfield Cricket Club
 WGNS/IIMK WN3 .... 255 M7
Highfield Hospital
 ROCH OL11 .... 235 G6
Highfield Humanities College
 BPOOLS FY4 .... 125 H5
Highfield Industrial Estate
 CHLY/EC PR7 .... 207 M1
 CLI BB7 .... 99 H3
Highfield Primary School
 CHLYE PR6 .... 208 A3
Highfield Priory School
 FUL/RIB PR2 .... 133 J2
Highfield St Matthews
 CE Primary School
 WGNS/IIMK WN3 .... 255 M7
Highfurlong School
 BPOOLE FY3 .... 105 K1
Hillside Community
 Primary School
 SKEL WN8 .... 254 A3
Hillside Golf Club
 STHP PR8 .... 221 H2
Hillside Health Centre
 SKEL WN8 .... 253 M2
Hillside School
 GAR/LONG PR3 .... 115 G4
Hippings Methodist
 Primary School
 ACC BB5 .... 159 H8
HM Prison
 KIRK/FR/WAR PR4 .... 128 D8
 PRES PR1 .... 9 L3
Hodge Bank Business Park
 NLSN BB9 .... 123 G1
Hodgson High School
 Technical College
 PLF/KEOS FY6 .... 86 D1
Hoghton Tower
 BBR PR5 .... 171 H2
Holcombe Brook Sports
 Club
 RAMS BL0 .... 214 D8
Holgate's Caravan Park
 CARN LA5 .... 16 E7
Holker Business Centre
 COL BB8 .... 103 L7
Holland Business Park
 BRSC L40 .... 242 F7
Holland Moor
 Primary School
 SKEL WN8 .... 254 B4
The Hollins
 Technology College
 ACC BB5 .... 176 A1
Hollygrove Primary School
 BRFD/BLYE BB10 .... 142 F1
Hollywood Park Cinema
 BLY BB11 .... 6 F6
Holme Mills Industrial Estate
 KKBYL LA6 .... 18 F2
Holme Primary School
 KKBYL LA6 .... 19 G1
Holme Slack CP School
 FUL/RIB PR2 .... 132 F8
Holy Cross RC High School
 CHLY/EC PR7 .... 207 M7

Holy Family
Catholic High School
CSBY/BLUN L23 .... 257 K5
Holy Family
Catholic Primary School
CHTN/BK PR9 .... 200 B4
Holy Family
RC Primary School
BPOOL FY1 .... 104 F3
FUL/RIB PR2 .... 131 J7
KIRK/FR/WAR PR4 .... 148 B5
Holy Rosary
RC Junior School
AIN/FAZ L10 .... 259 G8
Holy Rosary
RC Primary School
AIN/FAZ L10 .... 258 F8
Holy Saviour
RC Primary School
NLSN BB9 .... 123 H1
Holy Souls RC Primary School
BBN BB1 .... 157 H2
Holy Spirit RC Primary School
NTHTN L30 .... 258 A8
Holy Trinity
CE Primary School
CHTN/BK PR9 .... 13 J2
LIT OL15 .... 219 M5
Holy Trinity CE School
BLY BB11 .... 6 C5
Holy Trinity
RC Primary School
NLSN BB9 .... 122 F6
Holy Trinity Stacksteads
CE Primary School
BCUP OL13 .... 196 F2
Holy Trinity VC School
DWN BB3 .... 191 K2
Hoohill Industrial Estate
BPOOLE FY3 .... 105 H3
Hoole St Michael
CE Primary School
KIRK/FR/WAR PR4 .... 183 M2
Hopwood Hall College
WHIT OL12 .... 235 H4
Hornby CE Primary School
HGHB LA2 .... 36 B5
Hornby High School
HGHB LA2 .... 36 B5
Horse & Bamboo Theatre
RAW/HAS BB4 .... 196 A3
Horwich Leisure Centre
HOR/BR BL6 .... 231 M8
Horwich Parish
CE Primary School
HOR/BR BL6 .... 231 M7
Hotel Ibis
GAR/LONG PR3 .... 132 B2
Hotel Prospect
MCMB LA4 .... 41 J5
Hotel Sheraton
BISP FY2 .... 104 E1
Houghwood Golf Club
RNFD/HAY WA11 .... 263 L4
Houndshill Shopping Centre
BPOOL FY1 .... 4 C2
Howick CE Primary School
PRES PR1 .... 151 J8
Hud Hey Industrial Estate
RAW/HAS BB4 .... 176 E5
Hudson Primary School
MGHL L31 .... 259 G4
Hugh Business Park
BCUP OL13 .... 196 F3
Hulmes Bridge
Business Centre
ORM L39 .... 239 M1
Huncoat Business Park
ACC BB5 .... 160 A2
Huncoat
Industrial Estate
ACC BB5 .... 159 M3
Hurlston Hall Country
Caravan Park
BRSC L40 .... 240 F1
Hurlston Hall Golf Club
BRSC L40 .... 240 F1
Hutton Grammar School
KIRK/FR/WAR PR4 .... 167 G1
Hyndburn Park Primary
School ACC BB5 .... 159 K5
Hyndburn Sports Centre
ACC BB5 .... 159 J5
ightenhill County School
PDHM/BLYW BB12 .... 141 M4
India Mill Business Centre
DWN BB3 .... 191 K3
Industrial Centre for
the Blind & Disabled
BPOOLS FY4 .... 125 L3
Ingol Community
Primary School
FUL/RIB PR2 .... 131 J7
Ingol Golf Club
FUL/RIB PR2 .... 131 L5
Innes Special School
WHIT OL12 .... 234 F2
Inskip St Peters
CE Primary School
KIRK/FR/WAR PR4 .... 109 L3
Intack Primary School
BBN BB1 .... 158 A5
Islamiyah School
BBN BB1 .... 157 K3
Island Business Centre
GAR/LONG PR3 .... 283 L7
Italian Gardens
BPOOLE FY3 .... 5 L3
Jack Scout (NT)
CARN LA5 .... 24 E3
Jamea Al Kauthar
LANC LA1 .... 54 E6
Jamiatul-Ilm Wal-Huda
UK School
BBN BB1 .... 11 L1
J Nelson War Memorial
Sports Club
NLSN BB9 .... 123 J4
Johnson Fold Community
Primary School
BOL BL1 .... 233 J8
Joint Cemetery
ACC BB5 .... 159 K3
Jubilee Trading Estate
PRES PR1 .... 8 E1
Judge's Lodgings;
Town House &
Gillow Museum
LANC LA1 .... 2 F4
Junction 7 Business Park
ACC BB5 .... 159 H1
Kaymar Industrial Estate
PRES PR1 .... 152 F4

Kelbrook Primary School
BWCK/EAR BB18 .... 294 D10
Kellet Road Industrial Estate
CARN LA5 .... 33 L2
Kellets Trading Estate
PRES PR1 .... 152 B7
Kennington Primary School
FUL/RIB PR2 .... 132 D7
Kensington Industrial Estate
CHTN/BK PR9 .... 13 C5
Kentmere Primary School
WHIT OL12 .... 218 E8
Kenyon Business Centre
NLSN BB9 .... 122 E4
Kestrels Leisure Centre
BLY BB11 .... 162 A5
Kew Medical Centre
STHP PR8 .... 200 B8
Kew Retail Park
STHP PR8 .... 200 D7
Kew Woods Primary School
STHP PR8 .... 200 B8
Kidderow Health Centre
PDHM/BLYW BB12 .... 141 K5
Kincraig Primary School
BISP FY2 .... 85 J5
King Edward & Queen Mary Pre
Preparatory School
LSTA FY8 .... 145 K7
King Georges Hall
BBNW BB2 .... 10 D4
King George V College
STHP PR8 .... 200 B6
Kingsdown High School
WGNW/BIL/OR WN5 .... 255 M4
Kingsfold Christian School
KIRK/FR/WAR PR4 .... 183 H1
Kingsfold Medical Centre
PRES PR1 .... 151 M8
Kingsfold Primary School
PRES PR1 .... 168 A1
Kings Meadow
Primary School
STHP PR8 .... 221 G8
Kingsway West Business Park
MILN OL16 .... 235 L6
Kingswood College at
Scarisbrick School
BRSC L40 .... 223 K5
Kirkby CE Primary School
KKBY L32 .... 260 A8
Kirkham Baths
KIRK/FR/WAR PR4 .... 128 D6
Kirkham Grammar
Junior School
KIRK/FR/WAR PR4 .... 128 C6
Kirkham Grammar
Senior School
KIRK/FR/WAR PR4 .... 128 B6
Kirkham Health Centre
KIRK/FR/WAR PR4 .... 128 D6
Kirkham Museum
KIRK/FR/WAR PR4 .... 128 D6
Kirkham Trading Park
KIRK/FR/WAR PR4 .... 128 E7
Kirkham & Wesham
Primary School
KIRK/FR/WAR PR4 .... 128 C6
Kirkland & Catterall
CE Primary School
GAR/LONG PR3 .... 90 D1
Kneps Farm Holiday Park
PLF/KEOS FY6 .... 77 M6
Knott End Golf Club
PLF/KEOS FY6 .... 77 M6
Knowsley Northern
Primary Support Centre
NWD/KWIPK L33 .... 260 C7
Knowsley Road
Industrial Estate
RAW/HAS BB4 .... 194 E2
Knuzden St Oswalds
CE Voluntary Aided
Primary School
BBN BB1 .... 158 B7
Ladies Walk Industrial Estate
LANC LA1 .... 3 J2
Lakeland Wildlife Oasis
MTHPE LA7 .... 18 C3
Lamberhead Green
Community
Primary School
WGNW/BIL/OR WN5 .... 255 K4
Lamberhead Industrial Estate
WGNW/BIL/OR WN5 .... 255 L6
Lammack Primary School
BBNW BB2 .... 156 F2
Lancashire College of
Agriculture
GAR/LONG PR3 .... 91 G6
KIRK/FR/WAR PR4 .... 151 J8
Lancashire Enterprise
Business Park
CROS/BRETH PR26 .... 168 C6
Lancashire Holistic College
PRES PR1 .... 9 K2
The Lancashire Priory Hospital
KIRK/FR/WAR PR4 .... 130 E2
Lancashire Pupil
Reintegration Service
ACC BB5 .... 159 H7
Lancashire Records Office
PRES PR1 .... 8 E4
Lancaster Castle (HM Prison)
LANC LA1 .... 2 F5
Lancaster CC
LANC LA1 .... 2 C4
Lancaster Cemetery
LANC LA1 .... 55 H3
Lancaster City FC (Giant Axe)
LANC LA1 .... 2 D5
Lancaster City Museum
LANC LA1 .... 3 G5
Lancaster Farms
Remand Centre/
Young Offenders Institution
LANC LA1 .... 55 J2
Lancaster Girls
Grammar School
LANC LA1 .... 2 F7
Lancaster Golf Club
(Ashton Hall)
HGHB LA2 .... 66 B4
Lancaster House Hotel
LANC LA1 .... 66 F5
The Lancaster & Lakeland
Nuffield Hospital
LANC LA1 .... 3 J3
Lancaster Lane Community
Primary School
LEYL PR25 .... 187 G2
Lancaster Leisure Park
LANC LA1 .... 55 H5

Lancaster Maritime Museum
LANC LA1 .... 2 F4
Lancaster & Morecambe
College
HEY LA3 .... 42 A8
Lancaster Postgraduate
Medical Centre
LANC LA1 .... 3 G9
Lancaster Road
Primary School
MCMB LA4 .... 41 L7
Lancaster Royal
Grammar School
LANC LA1 .... 3 J6
Lancaster University
LANC LA1 .... 3 H5
Lancaster University Sports
Centre & Swimming Pool
HGHB LA2 .... 66 C8
Lane Ends Trading Estate
FUL/RIB PR2 .... 151 M1
Laneshawbridge
COL BB8 .... 296 C5
Langcliffe Primary School
SETT BD24 .... 265 P4
Langdale School
BISP FY2 .... 104 F2
Lansil Golf Club
LANC LA1 .... 43 G7
Lansil Industrial Estate
LANC LA1 .... 42 F8
Larkfield Primary School
CHTN/BK PR9 .... 180 D8
Larkholme Primary School
FTWD FY7 .... 81 G3
Lathom High School
SKEL WN8 .... 243 J8
Lathom Park
CE Primary School
BRSC L40 .... 242 D8
Layton Medical Centre
BPOOLE FY3 .... 105 J4
Layton Primary School
BPOOLE FY3 .... 105 J4
Leachfield Industrial Estate
GAR/LONG PR3 .... 284 B6
Lea Community
Primary School
FUL/RIB PR2 .... 151 G2
Lea Endowed CE
Primary School
FUL/RIB PR2 .... 130 F7
Lea St Mary Catholic
Primary School
FUL/RIB PR2 .... 130 C8
Leck CE Primary School
KKBYL LA6 .... 22 F5
Leighton Hall
CARN LA5 .... 25 M2
LEMS Burnley Centre
BLY BB11 .... 6 B6
Lever House Primary School
LEYL PR25 .... 168 F4
Lever Park School
HOR/BR BL6 .... 231 M8
Leyland Golf Club
LEYL PR25 .... 187 G3
Leyland Leisure Centre
LEYL PR25 .... 186 C3
Leyland Leisure Centre
Swimming Pool
LEYL PR25 .... 186 C3
Leyland Methodist
Junior & Infant School
LEYL PR25 .... 186 C2
Leyland St Marys
Catholic Technology College
LEYL PR25 .... 186 B4
Lidun Park Industrial Estate
LSTA FY8 .... 147 H6
Light Industrial Estate
KIRK/FR/WAR PR4 .... 166 C6
Limestone Trail
BRFD/BLYE BB10 .... 300 B5
Linaker Primary School
STHP PR8 .... 13 H4
Lincoln Road Health Centre
STHP PR8 .... 221 K2
Lindum Hotel
LSTA FY8 .... 145 H6
Linkway House School
PDHM/BLYW BB12 .... 6 D3
Lisieux Hall Hospital
CHLYE PR6 .... 187 K3
Littleborough CC
LIT OL15 .... 219 L5
Littleborough Primary School
LIT OL15 .... 219 L4
Little Digmoor
Primary School
SKEL WN8 .... 253 L5
Little Hoole Primary School
KIRK/FR/WAR PR4 .... 166 D6
Little Theatre
CHTN/BK PR7 .... 207 M3
CHTN/BK PR9 .... 13 H3
Lobden Golf Club
WHIT OL12 .... 218 B4
Lomeshaye Business Village
NLSN BB9 .... 122 F3
Lomeshaye Industrial Estate
NLSN BB9 .... 122 D3
Lomeshaye Junior School
NLSN BB9 .... 122 F3
Long Ing Business Park
BWCK/EAR BB18 .... 293 R5
Longridge CE
Primary School
GAR/LONG PR3 .... 114 D4
Longridge Golf Club
(Fell Barn)
GAR/LONG PR3 .... 115 J1
Longridge Health Centre
GAR/LONG PR3 .... 114 E4
Longridge High School
GAR/LONG PR3 .... 114 D5
Longridge Primary School
GAR/LONG PR3 .... 114 C3
Longsands Community
Primary School
FUL/RIB PR2 .... 133 G6
Longshaw Infant School
BBNW BB2 .... 173 H3
Longshaw Junior School
BBNW BB2 .... 173 H2
Longton Business Park
KIRK/FR/WAR PR4 .... 166 B7
Longton County
Primary School
KIRK/FR/WAR PR4 .... 166 D3
Longton Health Centre
KIRK/FR/WAR PR4 .... 166 D2

Lonsdale College
LANC LA1 .... 67 G3
Lordsgate Township
CE Primary School
BRSC L40 .... 225 H7
Lord Street Primary School
COL BB8 .... 103 M6
HOR/BR BL6 .... 231 L7
Lostock Hall Community
High School
BBR PR5 .... 168 F2
Lostock Hall Community
Primary School
BBR PR5 .... 168 E2
Lothersdale Community
Primary School
AIRE BD20 .... 295 P6
Louis Tussauds Waxworks
BPOOL FY1 .... 4 C4
Low Bentham Primary School
HGHB LA2 .... 38 C3
Lower Audley Industrial Estate
BBN BB1 .... 10 F6
Lower Darwen
Primary School
DWN BB3 .... 173 K5
Lowerhouse CC
PDHM/BLYW BB12 .... 141 K6
Lowerhouse County
Junior School
PDHM/BLYW BB12 .... 141 K5
Lowerplace Primary School
MILN OL16 .... 235 L7
The Loyne School
LANC LA1 .... 2 D1
Lune Industrial Estate
LANC LA1 .... 2 B5
Lydiate Primary School
MGHL L31 .... 249 M7
Lyne Riggs Estate
CARN LA5 .... 33 J2
Lytham CE Primary School
LSTA FY8 .... 146 C8
Lytham Community
YMCA Sports Centre
LSTA FY8 .... 146 C8
Lytham Cricket Club
LSTA FY8 .... 146 C8
Lytham Green Drive Golf Club
LSTA FY8 .... 146 E6
Lytham Hall Park
Primary School
LSTA FY8 .... 146 C8
Lytham Hospital
LSTA FY8 .... 147 F8
Lytham Lifeboat Museum
LSTA FY8 .... 146 C8
Lytham Posey Bowl
LSTA FY8 .... 146 E8
Lytham St Annes High
Technology College
LSTA FY8 .... 145 M6
Lytham St Anne's Sports &
Leisure Centre
LSTA FY8 .... 146 A6
Lytham Windmill
LSTA FY8 .... 146 F8
Macdonald
Dunkenhalgh Hotel
ACC BB5 .... 159 G2
Macdonald
Tickled Trout Hotel
BBR PR5 .... 153 L2
Madisons New Leisure Centre
KIRK/FR/WAR PR4 .... 149 M2
Maghull Health Centre
MGHL L31 .... 258 F2
Maghull High School
MGHL L31 .... 258 F4
Maharishi School
BRSC L40 .... 243 K5
Manchester Mill
Industrial Estate
PRES PR1 .... 152 F3
Manor Beach Primary School
CLV/TH FY5 .... 80 F8
Manor Road Primary School
CHLYE PR6 .... 187 L1
Marble Place Shopping Centre
STHP PR8 .... 13 G4
Maricourt Catholic
High School
MGHL L31 .... 259 H3
Marine Business Centre
LSTA FY8 .... 147 H7
Marine Football Club
CSBY/BLUN L23 .... 256 F8
Marine Hall
FTWD FY7 .... 77 K6
Marine Industrial Centre
LSTA FY8 .... 147 H7
Marketgate Shopping Centre
LANC LA1 .... 3 G6
Market Walk Shopping Centre
CHLY/EC PR7 .... 207 M3
Marland Hill Primary School
ROCH OL11 .... 234 F6
Marland Park Golf Club
ROCH OL11 .... 234 D6
Marl Pits Sports Centre
RAW/HAS BB4 .... 177 L8
Marsden Community
Primary School
NLSN BB9 .... 123 G4
Marsden Hall
NLSN BB9 .... 123 L2
Marsden Heights
Community College
NLSN BB9 .... 122 E5
Marsden Park Golf Club
NLSN BB9 .... 123 L3
Marsh House I
industrial Estate
DWN BB3 .... 192 A2
Marsh Mill Museum
CLV/TH FY5 .... 85 K1
Marshside Primary School
CHTN/BK PR9 .... 180 C6
Marshside RSPB Reserve
CHTN/BK PR9 .... 180 A6
Martland Mill
Industrial Estate
WGNW/BIL/OR WN5 .... 255 M1
Marton Medical Centre
BPOOLE FY3 .... 5 K7
Marton Mere Holiday Village
BPOOLE FY3 .... 105 M8
Marton Primary School
BPOOLS FY4 .... 125 J4
Matrix Park Business Area
CHLY/EC PR7 .... 187 G4
Matthew Moss High School
HEYW OL10 .... 234 D7

Mawdesley St Peters
Primary School
BRSC L40 .... 204 F8
Mayfield Primary School
LSTA FY8 .... 145 H3
Mayfield School
CHLY/EC PR7 .... 207 M6
Mayflower Industrial Estate
FMBY L37 .... 247 K2
Meadowcroft Business Park
KIRK/FR/WAR PR4 .... 167 L2
Meadowhead Infant School
BBNW BB2 .... 172 E2
Meadowhead Junior School
BBNW BB2 .... 172 D2
Meanwood Primary School
WHIT OL12 .... 234 F2
Medlar with Wesham
CE Primary School
KIRK/FR/WAR PR4 .... 128 C5
Megabowl
BBR PR5 .... 152 F6
NTHTN L30 .... 258 D8
Melbreak Caravan Park
HEY LA3 .... 64 E2
Melling Primary School
MGHL L31 .... 259 L7
Melling (St Wilfrid)
CE Primary School
KKBYL LA6 .... 29 K8
Mellor St Mary
CE Primary School
BBNW BB2 .... 156 A1
Meols Cop High School
STHP PR8 .... 200 C6
Meols Cop Retail Park
CHTN/BK PR9 .... 200 C7
Mercer Hall Leisure Centre
GTH/LHO BB6 .... 138 F6
Merchant Taylors Junior
School for Girls
CSBY/BLUN L23 .... 257 H8
Merchant Taylors School
CSBY/BLUN L23 .... 257 H8
Merchant Taylors School
for Girls
CSBY/BLUN L23 .... 257 G7
Mere Brow
CE Primary School
KIRK/FR/WAR PR4 .... 202 C1
Merefield Special School
STHP PR8 .... 220 E7
Mereside Primary School
BPOOLS FY4 .... 125 L2
Metropole Hotel
STHP PR8 .... 12 F5
Metropolitan Business Park
BPOOLE FY3 .... 125 L1
Middleforth
CE Primary School
PRES PR1 .... 152 A8
Middleton Business Park
HEY LA3 .... 52 F8
Millbrook Business Centre
RNFD/HAY WA11 .... 262 F8
Millbrook Primary School
KKBY L32 .... 260 A8
WGNNW/ST WN6 .... 245 L5
Millfield Science &
Perf Arts College
CLV/TH FY5 .... 85 M4
Mill House School
CROS/BRETH PR26 .... 168 B8
Mill Lane Industrial Estate
CLI BB7 .... 292 E1
The Millstone Hotel
BBNW BB2 .... 156 A1
Montgomery High School
BISP FY2 .... 85 G6
Moorbrook School
FUL/RIB PR2 .... 132 B8
Moor End Primary School
ACC BB5 .... 158 F6
Moorfield Industrial Estate
ACC BB5 .... 159 L8
Moorfield School
PRES PR1 .... 132 D8
Moorhead High School
ACC BB5 .... 159 K3
Moor Hey School
BBR PR5 .... 168 D2
Moorhouses Brewery
BLY BB11 .... 141 M6
Moorland School
CLI BB7 .... 99 H1
Moorland View
Childrens Home & School
BLY BB11 .... 161 L6
Moor Nook Primary School
FUL/RIB PR2 .... 133 K8
Moor Park High School
PRES PR1 .... 152 D1
Moor Park
Industrial Estate
BISP FY2 .... 85 J7
Moor Park Infant School
BISP FY2 .... 85 H8
Moor Park Primary School
BISP FY2 .... 85 H8
Moor Park Swimming Pool
BISP FY2 .... 85 G7
Moorside Primary School
LANC LA1 .... 55 G7
SKEL WN8 .... 254 B4
Morecambe Bay
Community Primary School
MCMB LA4 .... 41 J6
Morecambe Bay
Nature Reserve
HGHB LA2 .... 42 C1
Morecambe Bay Yacht Club
MCMB LA4 .... 41 J5
Morecambe CC
MCMB LA4 .... 41 H7
Morecambe Cemetery
HEY LA3 .... 41 M8
Morecambe FC
(Christie Park)
MCMB LA4 .... 41 L7
Morecambe Golf Club
MCMB LA4 .... 42 A4
Morecambe & Heysham
Sandylands Community
Primary School
HEY LA3 .... 40 F8
Morecambe High School
MCMB LA4 .... 41 K5
Morecambe Road School
HEY LA3 .... 41 M8
Morecambe Super Bowl
MCMB LA4 .... 41 G6
Mossgate Primary School
HEY LA3 .... 52 E3

Moss Industrial Estate
 MILN OL16 .... 235 L6
Mossock Hall Golf Club
 ORM L39 .... 251 H7
Moss Side Industrial Estate
 CROS/BRETH PR26 .... 167 M8
Moss Side Primary School
 CROS/BRETH PR26 .... 185 L2
Mosswood Caravan Park
 HGHB LA2 .... 269 L11
Mount Carmel
 Preparatory School
 ORM L39 .... 251 G1
Mount Carmel
 RC High School
 ACC BB5 .... 159 K7
Mount Pleasant
 Primary School
 ACC BB5 .... 159 K1
The Mount-St Marys
 Preparatory School
 CSBY/BLUN L23 .... 256 E8
The Museum of Lancashire
 PRES PR1 .... 9 L3
Museum of Yorkshire Dales
 Lead Mining
 BWCK/EAR BB18 .... 294 E4
Myerscough College
 GAR/LONG PR3 .... 91 G7
Myrtle Bank Infant School
 BLY BB11 .... 6 A7
Mytton Fold Hotel
 GTH/LHO BB6 .... 138 B1
Nateby Primary School
 GAR/LONG PR3 .... 283 M9
National College of
 Hypnosis & Psychotherapy
 NLSN BB9 .... 123 G3
National Football Museum
 PRES PR1 .... 152 E1
Natural Therapy Clinic
 BPOOLE FY3 .... 105 J4
Naze Lane Industrial Estate
 KIRK/FR/WAR PR4 .... 148 E6
Nelson AFC
 NLSN BB9 .... 122 E3
Nelson Bowling & CC
 NLSN BB9 .... 122 F2
Nelson Castercliff
 City School
 NLSN BB9 .... 123 K2
Nelson Cemetery
 NLSN BB9 .... 123 K2
Nelson & Colne College
 NLSN BB9 .... 122 F1
Nelson Golf Club
 NLSN BB9 .... 123 J6
Nelson Health Centre
 NLSN BB9 .... 123 H2
Nether Kellet Community
 Primary School
 KKBYL LA6 .... 33 K7
Netherton Moss
 Primary School
 NTHTN L30 .... 258 B8
Network 65 Business Park
 BLY BB11 .... 141 H7
Newburgh CC
 SKEL WN8 .... 243 K2
Newburgh CE Primary School
 SKEL WN8 .... 243 K2
New Cemetery
 PRES PR1 .... 153 H2
Newchurch CE School
 RAW/HAS BB4 .... 196 A4
Newchurch in Pendle St Mary
 CE School
 PDHM/BLYW BB12 .... 101 M8
Newfield School
 BBN BB1 .... 173 L3
Newfield Special School
 CSBY/BLUN L23 .... 257 L6
New Hall Hey Business Park
 RAW/HAS BB4 .... 195 J2
New House Caravan Park
 KKBYL LA6 .... 22 D5
New Line Industrial Estate
 BCUP OL13 .... 197 K3
New Longton All Saints
 CE Primary School
 KIRK/FR/WAR PR4 .... 167 J4
New Mill Industrial Estate
 BBR PR5 .... 169 J4
New Parkside Farm
 Caravan Park
 HGHB LA2 .... 43 M6
Newton Bluecoat
 CE Primary School
 KIRK/FR/WAR PR4 .... 149 K1
The Nook
 COL BB8 .... 296 A9
Norbreck Primary School
 CLV/TH FY5 .... 85 G3
Norden Community
 Primary School
 WHIT OL12 .... 234 C1
Norden Cricket Club
 WHIT OL12 .... 234 B1
Norden High School
 BBN BB1 .... 158 D1
Norley Hall CC
 WGNW/BIL/OR WN5 .... 255 L4
Northbrook Primary School
 LEYL PR25 .... 186 C2
North Cliffe School
 GTH/LHO BB6 .... 138 E5
Northern CC
 CSBY/BLUN L23 .... 257 J5
Northern Primary School
 BCUP OL13 .... 179 J5
Northfold Community
 Primary School
 CLV/TH FY5 .... 81 H7
North Meols Community
 Leisure Centre
 CHTN/BK PR9 .... 181 L6
North Meols Lawn Tennis Club
 CHTN/BK PR9 .... 200 D2
North Mersey Business Centre
 NWD/KWIPK L33 .... 260 F7
North Pier
 BPOOL FY1 .... 4 B1
North Quarry Business Park
 WGNNW/ST WN6 .... 245 G2
North Road Primary School
 CARN LA5 .... 33 J2
North Valley Retail Park
 COL BB8 .... 296 A6
Northway Community
 Primary School
 MGHL L31 .... 250 B8
Norwood Primary School
 CHTN/BK PR9 .... 200 B4

Novotel
 BBR PR5 .... 169 J5
Nye Bevan Swimming Pool
 SKEL WN8 .... 253 L2
Oakfield House School
 KIRK/FR/WAR PR4 .... 129 M7
Oakhill College
 CLI BB7 .... 119 G5
Oaks Hotel
 BRFD/BLYE BB10 .... 122 E7
Ocean Edge Caravan Park
 HEY LA3 .... 64 C1
Ocean Edge Leisure Park
 HEY LA3 .... 52 C5
Odeon Cinema
 BPOOL FY1 4
 NTHTN L30 .... 258 D8
 ROCH OL11 .... 235 H7
Old Barnabys School
 DWN BB3 .... 191 L5
Old Brewery Trading Estate
 PRES PR1 .... 8 D3
Old Hall Caravan Park
 KKBYL LA6 .... 27 K7
Old Hall Farm
 Business Park
 CHTN/BK PR9 .... 200 D6
Old Mill Hotel
 RAMS BL0 .... 214 E4
Old Mil Industrial Estate
 BBR PR5 .... 169 G2
Old Mill Leisure Club
 CHLYE PR6 .... 208 C5
Old Rectory
 CARN LA5 .... 26 A4
Ormskirk Business Park
 ORM L39 .... 241 J5
Ormskirk CE Primary School
 ORM L39 .... 241 J5
Ormskirk College
 ORM L39 .... 241 H6
Ormskirk Cricket Club
 ORM L39 .... 241 J7
Ormskirk & District
 General Hospital
 ORM L39 .... 241 J7
Ormskirk Golf Club
 BRSC L40 .... 242 B4
Ormskirk Rugby Union
 Football Club
 ORM L39 .... 241 H5
Ormskirk School
 ORM L39 .... 241 L6
Orrell Clinic
 WGNW/BIL/OR WN5 .... 255 H4
Orrell Holgate
 Primary School
 WGNW/BIL/OR WN5 .... 255 H6
Orrell Newfold Community
 Primary School
 WGNW/BIL/OR WN5 .... 255 G7
Orrell RUFC
 WGNW/BIL/OR WN5 .... 255 H5
Orrell Water Park
 WGNW/BIL/OR WN5 .... 255 H7
Otters Leisure Pool
 GAR/LONG PR3 .... 132 B1
Oulder Hill Community School
 Language College
 ROCH OL11 .... 234 B2
Our Lady & All Saints
 RC Primary School
 SKEL WN8 .... 243 M1
Our Lady of Compassion
 RC Primary School
 FMBY L37 .... 237 K8
Our Lady of Lourdes
 RC Primary School
 CARN LA5 .... 33 K2
 STHP PR8 .... 221 K2
Our Lady of Perpetual
 Succour RC Primary School
 BBNW BB2 .... 173 H4
Our Lady of the Assumption
 RC Primary School
 BPOOLS FY4 .... 125 J6
Our Lady Queen of Peace
 Catholic High School
 BRSC L40 .... 243 J7
Our Lady & St Anselms
 RC Primary School
 WHIT OL12 .... 218 A1
Our Lady & St Edwards
 RC Primary School
 FUL/RIB PR2 .... 132 A3
Our Lady & St Gerards
 RC Primary School
 BBR PR5 .... 168 D3
Our Lady & St Huberts
 RC Primary School
 GTH/LHO BB6 .... 139 H5
Our Lady & St John
 Catholic Arts College
 BBN BB1 .... 157 M8
Our Ladys Catholic
 High School
 FUL/RIB PR2 .... 131 M7
Our Lady's Catholic School
 LANC LA1 .... 3 G3
Our Lady Star of Sea
 Catholic Primary School
 LSTA FY8 .... 145 J3
Out Rawcliffe
 CE Primary School
 GAR/LONG PR3 .... 88 C1
Overdale Primary School
 KKBY L32 .... 260 C7
Over Wyre Medical Centre
 PLF/KEOS FY6 .... 78 C6
Over Wyre Sports Centre
 PLF/KEOS FY6 .... 78 D6
Oxford Medical Centre
 BPOOL FY1 .... 5 K8
Oxhey Trading Estate
 PRES PR1 .... 152 A1
Padiham Cemetery
 PDHM/BLYW BB12 .... 140 F4
Padiham County
 Primary School
 PDHM/BLYW BB12 .... 141 H3
Padiham Cricket Club
 PDHM/BLYW BB12 .... 140 E2
Padiham Football Club
 PDHM/BLYW BB12 .... 140 E3
Padiham Green
 CE Primary School
 PDHM/BLYW BB12 .... 140 F3
Padiham Leisure Centre
 PDHM/BLYW BB12 .... 140 F3
Padiham Town Hall
 PDHM/BLYW BB12 .... 140 F3
Palace Cinema
 GAR/LONG PR3 .... 114 E4

Palatine Community
 Sports College
 BPOOLS FY4 .... 124 F3
Palatine Leisure Centre
 BPOOLS FY4 .... 124 F3
Paragon Industrial Estate
 LIT OL15 .... 219 J8
Paramount Imperial Hotel
 BPOOL FY1 .... 104 E4
Parbold Douglas
 CE Primary School
 SKEL WN8 .... 227 G8
Park Cemetery
 LSTA FY8 .... 146 B5
Park Crematorium
 LSTA FY8 .... 146 C4
Parker Street
 Industrial Estate
 BBN BB1 .... 151 M1
Park Hall Hotel
 CHLY/EC PR7 .... 206 C8
Park Hall Leisure Centre
 CHLY/EC PR7 .... 206 D7
Park High School
 COL BB8 .... 296 C5
Parklands High School
 CHLY/EC PR7 .... 207 K3
Park Pool
 ORM L39 .... 241 H6
Park Primary School
 COL BB8 .... 296 C6
Park Road Industrial Estate
 BCUP OL13 .... 197 J2
Park School
 BPOOLE FY3 .... 5 J4
Park Wood National
 Nature Reserve
 KKBYL LA6 .... 20 B3
Path Industrial Estate
 BBN BB1 .... 173 L5
Pearlbrook Industrial Estate
 HOR/BR BL6 .... 231 L8
Pear Tree School
 KIRK/FR/WAR PR4 .... 128 D6
Peel Brow Primary School
 RAMS BL0 .... 215 G5
Peel Park Primary School
 ACC BB5 .... 160 H1
Pemberton
 Business Centre
 WGNW/BIL/OR WN5 .... 255 M5
Pendle Business Centre
 NLSN BB9 .... 123 H3
Pendle College
 LANC LA1 .... 67 G5
Pendle Community
 High School
 COL BB8 .... 123 L1
Pendle Community Hospital
 NLSN BB9 .... 123 H2
Pendle Dry Ski Slope
 CLI BB7 .... 120 B1
Pendle Forest Sports Club
 PDHM/BLYW BB12 .... 122 B3
Pendle Heritage Centre
 NLSN BB9 .... 103 H7
Pendle Industrial Estate
 NLSN BB9 .... 123 J4
Pendle Leisure Centre
 COL BB8 .... 103 M7
Pendle Primary School
 CLI BB7 .... 99 J2
Pendle Trading Estate
 CLI BB7 .... 290 H12
Pendle Vale College
 NLSN BB9 .... 123 K1
Pendle View Medical Centre
 NLSN BB9 .... 122 E5
Pendle View Primary School
 NLSN BB9 .... 123 M2
Penwortham Cricket Club
 PRES PR1 .... 152 B7
Penwortham Girls
 High School
 PRES PR1 .... 8 A9
Penwortham Golf Club
 PRES PR1 .... 151 L4
Penwortham Holme
 Recreation Centre
 PRES PR1 .... 8 C7
Penwortham
 Primary School
 PRES PR1 .... 151 K6
Penwortham Sports Club
 PRES PR1 .... 152 B7
Peterhouse School
 CHTN/BK PR9 .... 180 E8
Phoenix Sporting &
 Leisure Centre
 CLV/TH FY5 .... 85 H4
Piers House
 BPOOLS FY4 .... 125 G6
Pike View Medical Centre
 HOR/BR BL6 .... 231 L7
Pilling St Johns CE School
 GAR/LONG PR3 .... 79 M5
Pines Hotel
 CHLYE PR6 .... 169 L8
Pinfold Primary School
 BRSC L40 .... 223 J8
Plantation Mill
 Industrial Estate
 BCUP OL13 .... 197 J2
Platts Lane Industrial Estate
 BRSC L40 .... 242 B1
Playhouse Theatre
 PRES PR1 .... 9 G3
Plaza Shopping Arcade
 MCMB LA4 .... 41 J6
Pleasington Cemetery and
 Crematorium
 BBNW BB2 .... 172 A1
Pleasington Crematorium
 BBNW BB2 .... 156 A8
Pleasington Golf Club
 BBNW BB2 .... 171 M2
Pleasure Island
 LSTA FY8 .... 145 H6
Pleasureland
 STHP PR8 .... 12 C3
Pleckgate High School
 BBN BB1 .... 157 G2
The Point Retail Park
 MILN OL16 .... 235 K4
Pontville School
 ORM L39 .... 241 G8
Pool House Community
 Primary School
 FUL/RIB PR2 .... 131 K5
Porter Brewery
 RAW/HAS BB4 .... 176 E7
Post Graduate Medical Centre
 FUL/RIB PR2 .... 132 C7

Poulton le Fylde Golf Club
 PLF/KEOS FY6 .... 86 A6
Poulton le Sands
 CE Primary School
 MCMB LA4 .... 41 J5
Poulton St Chads
 CE Primary School
 PLF/KEOS FY6 .... 86 A8
Poulton Swimming &
 Fitness Centre
 PLF/KEOS FY6 .... 86 B6
Powderhouse Lane
 Crematorium
 HGHB LA2 .... 42 C7
Preesall Mill Industrial Estate
 PLF/KEOS FY6 .... 82 E1
Premier Business Park
 BBN BB1 .... 157 L3
 CHLY/LHO BB6 .... 139 G5
Premier Inn
 BBR PR5 .... 135 G8
 BBR PR5 .... 169 G4
 BPOOLS FY4 .... 126 B5
 BPOOLS FY4 .... 124 F3
 CHLY/EC PR7 .... 208 B6
 CHLYE PR6 .... 188 B6
 DWN BB3 .... 173 K5
 FUL/RIB PR2 .... 133 J5
 GAR/LONG PR3 .... 91 K7
 KIRK/FR/WAR PR4 .... 128 B1
 KIRK/FR/WAR PR4 .... 150 C3
 LSTA FY8 .... 146 D8
 NTHTN L30 .... 258 E7
 STHP PR8 .... 12 E1
 WCNNW/ST WN6 .... 245 L2
 WGNW/BIL/OR WN5 ...... 255 J4
Presfield Special School
 CHTN/BK PR9 .... 180 D8
Preston Bowl
 BBN BB1 .... 152 A1
Preston CC
 PRES PR1 .... 8 F8
Preston College
 FUL/RIB PR2 .... 132 C6
Preston Crematorium
 FUL/RIB PR2 .... 133 M6
Preston Golf Club
 FUL/RIB PR2 .... 132 E6
Preston Grange
 Primary School
 FUL/RIB PR2 .... 133 J7
Preston Grasshoppers RFC
 KIRK/FR/WAR PR4 .... 131 L3
Preston Markets
 PRES PR1 .... 9 H3
Preston Marriott Hotel
 GAR/LONG PR3 .... 132 A1
Preston Muslim Girls
 Secondary School
 PRES PR1 .... 9 M1
Preston North End FC
 (Deepdale)
 PRES PR1 .... 152 E1
Preston Sports Arena
 FUL/RIB PR2 .... 131 H8
Preston Sports Club
 PRES PR1 .... 8 F7
Primet Business Centre
 COL BB8 .... 103 L7
Primetime Leisure Centre
 BBN BB1 .... 158 D1
Primet Primary School
 COL BB8 .... 103 L8
Primrose Bank Medical Centre
 BBN BB1 .... 11 G2
Primrose Hill Primary School
 CHLY/EC PR7 .... 186 E7
The Priory Pool
 PRES PR1 .... 151 J6
Priory Technology College
 PRES PR1 .... 151 K6
Progress Business Park
 KIRK/FR/WAR PR4 .... 128 D7
Progress School
 BBR PR5 .... 169 L5
Prospect House
 Medical Centre
 WGNW/BIL/OR WN5 ...... 255 K5
Python Industrial Estate
 LIT OL15 .... 219 M5
Quality Hotel
 SKEL WN8 .... 254 C6
Queen Elizabeth School
 KKBYL LA6 .... 21 L1
Queen Elizabeths
 Grammar School
 BBNW BB2 .... 10 B2
Queenscourt Hospice
 STHP PR8 .... 200 C7
Queens Drive Primary School
 FUL/RIB PR2 .... 132 A6
Queens Park Hospital
 BBNW BB2 .... 11 K9
Queens Retail Park
 PRES PR1 .... 9 L3
Queen Street Mill
 BRFD/BLYE BB10 .... 143 J1
Queensway Industrial Estate
 LSTA FY8 .... 145 K1
Queen Victoria Hospital
 MCMB LA4 .... 41 J6
Quernmore CE
 Controlled School
 HGHB LA2 .... 56 A6
Railway Road Industrial Estate
 DWN BB3 .... 191 K2
Rainford CE Primary School
 RNFD/HAY WA11 .... 262 C5
Rainford Health Centre
 RNFD/HAY WA11 .... 262 D5
Rainford High
 Technology College
 RNFD/HAY WA11 .... 262 D3
Rainford Industrial Estate
 RNFD/HAY WA11 .... 262 E7
Ralph Williams Clinic
 WHIT OL12 .... 218 F4
Ramsbottom Cemetery
 RAMS BL0 .... 214 D7
Ramsbottom Cottage Hospital
 RAMS BL0 .... 214 F6
Ramsbottom Health Centre
 RAMS BL0 .... 214 E5
Ramsbottom Swimming Pool
 RAMS BL0 .... 214 F4
Range High School
 FMBY L37 .... 247 G3
Rathmell CE Primary School
 SETT BD24 .... 267 J3
Ravenscroft Primary School
 NWD/KWIPK L33 .... 260 B6
Rawtenstall CC
 RAW/HAS BB4 .... 195 L1

Rawtenstall Cemetery
 RAW/HAS BB4 .... 177 K8
Rawtenstall Water
 Primary School
 RAW/HAS BB4 .... 178 D3
Read Congregational School
 PDHM/BLYW BB12 .... 140 A1
Read Cricket Club
 PDHM/BLYW BB12 .... 140 A2
Read Hall Golf & Country Club
 PDHM/BLYW BB12 .... 139 L1
Read St Johns
 CE Primary School
 PDHM/BLYW BB12 .... 140 A1
Red Bank Farm
 CARN LA5 .... 32 E6
The Redbrick Theatre
 BBNW BB2 .... 173 G2
The Redeemer Primary School
 BBN BB1 .... 173 G4
Redgate Primary School
 FMBY L37 .... 247 K1
Red Lion Shopping Centre
 MGHL L31 .... 259 G2
Red Marsh School
 CLV/TH FY5 .... 81 L8
The Red Rose School
 LSTA FY8 .... 145 G5
Red Scar Industrial Estate
 FUL/RIB PR2 .... 133 L6
Reedley CP School
 BRFD/BLYE BB10 .... 122 F7
Regent Caravan Park
 HEY LA3 .... 53 G1
Renacres Hall Hospital
 ORM L39 .... 222 E6
Revoe Primary
 Community School
 BPOOL FY1 .... 4 F6
Rhyddings Business
 Enterprise
 ACC BB5 .... 159 H7
Ribble Business Park
 BBN BB1 .... 157 L3
Ribble Estuary National
 Nature Reserve
 HTWN L38 .... 256 C1
Ribblesdale Pool
 CLI BB7 .... 98 E3
Ribblesdale
 Technology College
 CLI BB7 .... 99 H4
Ribbleton Avenue
 County Infant School
 PRES PR1 .... 152 F1
Ribbleton Avenue
 Methodist Junior School
 FUL/RIB PR2 .... 153 G1
Ribbleton Hospital
 FUL/RIB PR2 .... 153 J1
Ribbleton Lane Trading Estate
 PRES PR1 .... 9 L2
Ribble Village Health Centre
 FUL/RIB PR2 .... 153 H1
Ribby with Wrea Endowed
 CE Primary School
 KIRK/FR/WAR PR4 .... 127 L7
Ribchester Hospital
 GAR/LONG PR3 .... 115 J5
Ribchester Roman Museum
 GAR/LONG PR3 .... 116 A8
Ribchester St Wilfrid's
 CE Primary School
 GAR/LONG PR3 .... 116 B8
Richard Durnings Endowed
 Primary School
 BRSC L40 .... 227 G5
Richard Thorntons
 CE VA Primary School
 KKBYL LA6 .... 31 G6
Richmond Industrial Estate
 ACC BB5 .... 159 L3
Ridge Primary School
 LANC LA1 .... 3 K3
Ridgeway Park School
 CARN LA5 .... 24 F3
Ridgewood Community
 High School
 PDHM/BLYW BB12 .... 142 C3
Ridgmont Cemetery
 HOR/BR BL6 .... 232 A8
Rimington Caravan Park
 CLI BB7 .... 292 D5
Ringtail Industrial Estate
 BRSC L40 .... 241 L1
Ripley St Thomas
 CE High School
 LANC LA1 .... 3 J7
Ripleys Believe it or Not
 Museum
 BPOOLS FY4 .... 124 D4
Rishton Cricket Club
 BBN BB1 .... 158 D3
Rishton Golf Club
 BBN BB1 .... 158 E3
Rishton Methodist
 Primary School
 BBN BB1 .... 158 E2
Riverside Business Centre
 NLSN BB9 .... 123 H2
Riverside Caravan Park
 HEY LA3 .... 53 L3
 HGHB LA2 .... 38 F5
Riverside Holiday Park
 CHTN/BK PR9 .... 182 A8
Riverside Industrial Estate
 BBN BB1 .... 159 G1
 DWN BB3 .... 173 J4
Riverside Industrial Park
 GAR/LONG PR3 .... 284 A12
Riverside Medical Centre
 BBR PR5 .... 153 G6
Rivington & Blackrod
 High School
 HOR/BR BL6 .... 231 L5
Rivington Castle
 HOR/BR BL6 .... 231 J5
Rivington Country Park
 HOR/BR BL6 .... 231 K3
Rivington Park
 Independent School
 HOR/BR BL6 .... 231 J2
Rivington Primary School
 HOR/BR BL6 .... 231 J2
Roby Mill CE Primary School
 SKEL WN8 .... 244 D7
Rochdale AFC
 (Spotland Stadium)
 ROCH OL11 .... 234 F3
Rochdale Cemetery
 ROCH OL11 .... 234 E4
Rochdale Crematorium
 ROCH OL11 .... 234 E4

Rochdale Cricket, Lacrosse & Squash Club
ROCH OL11 .... 234 F4
Rochdale Curtain Theatre
ROCH OL11 .... 235 H5
Rochdale Golf Club
ROCH OL11 .... 234 D3
Rochdale Healthcare
WHIT OL12 .... 219 G6
Rochdale Industrial Centre
ROCH OL11 .... 235 G5
Rochdale Infirmary
WHIT OL12 .... 235 H2
Rock FM Radio Station
PRES PR1 .... 9 K2
The Roebuck School
FUL/RIB PR2 .... 152 A1
Roefield Leisure Centre
CLI BB7 .... 98 E3
Roe Lee Industrial Estate
BBN BB1 .... 157 H2
Roe Lee Park Primary School
BBN BB1 .... 157 J1
Roman Road Industrial Estate
BBN BB1 .... 173 L4
Roman Road Leisure Centre
BBNW BB2 .... 173 J3
Roman Way Industrial Estate
FUL/RIB PR2 .... 133 M4
Roseacre Primary School
BPOOLS FY4 .... 124 F6
Rose Gardens
BPOOLE FY3 .... 5 K2
Rosegrove Infant School
PDHM/BLYW BB12 .... 141 K5
Rosehill Business Park
CLV/BK PR9 .... 13 M5
Rosehill County Infant School
BLY BB11 .... 6 E9
Rosehill County Junior School
BLY BB11 .... 6 E9
Rosehill House Hotel
BLY BB11 .... 6 D8
Rossall Hospital
FTWD FY7 .... 80 F4
Rossall School
FTWD FY7 .... 81 G5
Rossendale General Hospital
RAW/HAS BB4 .... 194 F2
Rossendale Golf Club
RAW/HAS BB4 .... 194 F4
Rossendale Museum
RAW/HAS BB4 .... 195 H1
Rossendale Road Industrial Estate
BLY BB11 .... 141 L8
Rossendale School
RAMS BL0 .... 215 J4
Rossendale United Football Club
RAW/HAS BB4 .... 196 B2
Roughlee Junior School
NLSN BB9 .... 102 C7
The Royal Birkdale Golf Club
STHP PR8 .... 221 G2
Royal Cross Primary School
FUL/RIB PR2 .... 151 H2
Royal Kings Arms Hotel
LANC LA1 .... 3 G6
Royal Lancaster Infirmary
LANC LA1 .... 3 G8
Royal Lytham & St Annes Golf Club
LSTA FY8 .... 145 K5
Royal Preston Hospital
FUL/RIB PR2 .... 132 C5
Royle Pennine Trading Estate
ROCH OL11 .... 235 G8
Royles Brook Primary School
CLV/TH FY5 .... 85 K1
RSPB Leighton Moss Nature Reserve
CARN LA5 .... 25 J1
Rufford CE School
BRSC L40 .... 203 L7
Rufford Old Hall (NT)
BRSC L40 .... 203 M7
Ruffwood School
NWD/KWIPK L33 .... 260 B8
Runshaw College
CHLY/EC PR7 .... 187 H1
LEYL PR25 .... 186 E5
The Ryan Medical Centre
BBR PR5 .... 169 H2
Rydings Special School
WHIT OL12 .... 218 E7
Ryelands House Health Centre
LANC LA1 .... 3 G2
Ryelands Primary School
LANC LA1 .... 2 D1
Sabden Primary School
CLI BB7 .... 120 C3
Sacred Heart Catholic College
CSBY/BLUN L23 .... 257 H7
Sacred Heart Catholic Primary School
FUL/RIB PR2 .... 8 A1
Sacred Heart Catholic School
CLV/TH FY5 .... 81 L8
Sacred Heart RC Primary School
ACC BB5 .... 159 J5
BBNW BB2 .... 156 E5
CHLYE PR6 .... 208 B4
COL BB8 .... 296 A4
MILN OL16 .... 235 M5
Sadler Street Industrial Estate
ACC BB5 .... 159 H6
St Aidans CE Primary School
BBNW BB2 .... 172 E1
BBR PR5 .... 169 J2
St Aidans CE Technology College
PLF/KEOS FY6 .... 78 E8
St Albans RC Primary School
BBN BB1 .... 11 L1
St Ambrose Barlow Catholic College
NTHTN L30 .... 258 D6
St Andrews Bowling & CC
BRFD/BLYE BB10 .... 142 F7
St Andrews CE Infant School
LEYL PR25 .... 186 C3
St Andrews CE Primary School
ACC BB5 .... 159 J1
FUL/RIB PR2 .... 151 L2
RAMS BL0 .... 214 E6
St Andrews CE Primary School
WHIT OL12 .... 219 H1
St Andrews CE School
BBNW BB2 .... 172 E3

St Andrews Maghull CE Primary School
MGHL L31 .... 259 G2
St Annes Catholic Primary School
LEYL PR25 .... 186 A3
St Annes CE Primary School
RAW/HAS BB4 .... 196 C1
St Anne's Cricket Club
LSTA FY8 .... 145 H2
St Anne's Old Links Golf Club
LSTA FY8 .... 145 G2
St Anne's Pier
LSTA FY8 .... 145 G5
St Annes RC Primary School
BBNW BB2 .... 10 D5
ORM L39 .... 241 G7
St Annes & St Josephs RC Primary School
ACC BB5 .... 160 A6
St Annes Swimming Pool
LSTA FY8 .... 145 G6
St Anthonys RC Primary School
FUL/RIB PR2 .... 131 M7
St Antonys RC Primary School
BBN BB1 .... 157 M8
St Augustines RC High School
CLI BB7 .... 118 D7
St Augustines RC Primary School
PDHM/BLYW BB12 .... 141 L5
St Augustines RC Primary School
PRES PR1 .... 9 K5
St Barnabas CE Primary School
DWN BB3 .... 191 M5
St Barnabas & St Pauls CE Primary School
BBNW BB2 .... 10 B5
St Bartholomews CE Primary School
WHIT OL12 .... 217 M3
St Bartholomews Parish CE Primary School
GTH/LHO BB6 .... 138 F5
St Bedes Catholic High School
LSTA FY8 .... 146 F7
ORM L39 .... 241 G7
St Bedes RC High School
BBNW BB2 .... 172 D3
St Bedes RC Primary School
CHLYE PR6 .... 169 L7
St Benedicts RC Primary School
NTHTN L30 .... 258 C6
St Bernadettes Catholic Primary School
WGNNW/ST WN6 .... 245 K5
St Bernadettes Catholic School
BISP FY2 .... 85 G6
St Bernadettes RC Primary School
LANC LA1 .... 55 G7
St Bernards Catholic Primary School
FUL/RIB PR2 .... 150 F2
St Catherines CE Primary School
HOR/BR BL6 .... 231 L8
St Catherines RC Primary School
LEYL PR25 .... 186 F1
St Cecilias RC High School
GAR/LONG PR3 .... 114 D5
St Chads Catholic Primary School
CHLYE PR6 .... 188 C5
St Charles RC Primary School
BBN BB1 .... 158 D2
St Christophers CE High School
ACC BB5 .... 159 K3
St Clares RC Primary School
FUL/RIB PR2 .... 132 C5
St Cuthberts CE Primary School
DWN BB3 .... 173 H8
St Cuthberts RC Primary School
BPOOLS FY4 .... 124 F3
St Edmunds Catholic Primary School
SKEL WN8 .... 253 J2
St Edwards RC Primary School
DWN BB3 .... 173 H7
St Fillans Medical Centre
PRES PR1 .... 151 L5
St Francis Catholic Primary School
GAR/LONG PR3 .... 113 K1
St Francis CE Primary School
BBNW BB2 .... 172 C2
St Francis of Assisi Catholic Primary School
SKEL WN8 .... 254 A4
St Gabriels CE Primary School
BBN BB1 .... 157 H1
St Georges CE High School
BPOOLS FY4 .... 125 K2
St Georges CE Primary School
CHLY/EC PR7 .... 208 D8
St Georges RC Primary School
MGHL L31 .... 259 G4
St Georges Shopping Centre
PRES PR1 .... 9 H4
St Gregorys Catholic Primary School
CHLY/EC PR7 .... 207 M6
MGHL L31 .... 249 M7
St Gregorys RC Primary School
PRES PR1 .... 132 E8
St Helens CE Primary School
HEY LA3 .... 65 J2
St Ignatius RC Primary School
PRES PR1 .... 9 J1
St Ives Business Park
BBN BB1 .... 158 A7
St James Catholic Primary School
WGNW/BIL/OR WN5 .... 255 G7
St James CE Primary School
BBN BB1 .... 157 H4
CHLYE PR6 .... 208 B4
CLI BB7 .... 99 H4
CROS/BRETH PR26 .... 185 K3
DWN BB3 .... 173 K4
DWN BB3 .... 191 L1
RAW/HAS BB4 .... 176 D3

St James CE Primary School
WHIT OL12 .... 218 F5
St James Clinic
BLY BB11 .... 6 F4
St James RC Primary School
ACC BB5 .... 159 J2
St James Lanehead CE Primary School
BRFD/BLYE BB10 .... 143 G1
St James RC Primary School
SKEL WN8 .... 243 L7
St James the Less RC Primary School
RAW/HAS BB4 .... 177 J8
St John Bosco RC Primary School
MGHL L31 .... 258 E1
St John CE Primary School
BRFD/BLYE BB10 .... 163 L5
St John RC Primary School
ROCH OL11 .... 235 J5
St John Rigby College
WGNW/BIL/OR WN5 .... 255 J1
St Johns Catholic Primary School
BRSC L40 .... 242 B1
St Johns CE/Methodist Primary School
CHLYE PR6 .... 189 H3
St Johns CE Primary School
ACC BB5 .... 159 M4
BPOOL FY1 .... 4 E2
BRSC L40 .... 225 J6
CHTN/BK PR9 .... 200 F6
GTH/LHO BB6 .... 138 F7
NLSN BB9 .... 123 L4
WGNW/BIL/OR WN5 .... 255 L5
St John's Market
BPOOL FY1 .... 4 E1
St John Southworth RC Primary School
NLSN BB9 .... 123 G4
St Johns RC Junior School
BRFD/BLYE BB10 .... 122 F8
St Johns RC Primary School
SKEL WN8 .... 253 M2
St Johns Shopping Centre
PRES PR1 .... 9 J3
St Johns Stonefold CE Primary School
ACC BB5 .... 176 D4
St John Stone Catholic Primary School
STHP PR8 .... 238 A1
St John the Baptist RC Infant School
BRFD/BLYE BB10 .... 142 E2
St John the Baptist RC Primary School
PDHM/BLYW BB12 .... 140 F4
St John Vianney Catholic Primary School
BPOOLE FY3 .... 5 K7
St John with St Augustine CEP School
ACC BB5 .... 159 M4
St John with St Michael Primary School
WHIT OL12 .... 302 B10
St Josephs Catholic Primary School
CHLYE PR6 .... 208 A1
CHLYE PR6 .... 230 E4
CLI BB7 .... 42 E8
PRES PR1 .... 152 F2
WGNW/ST WN6 .... 228 C8
St Josephs Convent School
PDHM/BLYW BB12 .... 141 K3
St Joseph's Primary School
TOD OL14 .... 303 L2
St Josephs RC Primary School
BWCK/EAR BB18 .... 293 Q4
CHLYE PR6 .... 189 K2
CLI BB7 .... 117 J3
DWN BB3 .... 191 K4
KIRK/FR/WAR PR4 .... 128 C4
RAMS BL0 .... 214 E5
TOD OL14 .... 303 K1
St Josephs School
BCUP OL13 .... 197 G2
St Kentigerns RC Primary School
BPOOLE FY3 .... 5 H1
St Laurence CE Primary School
CHLY/EC PR7 .... 207 M2
St Leonards CE Primary School
BBR PR5 .... 152 F7
GTH/LHO BB6 .... 118 B8
PDHM/BLYW BB12 .... 140 F2
St Luke & St Philips CE Primary School
BBNW BB2 .... 10 B8
St Lukes CE Primary School
FMBY L37 .... 247 G2
HEYW OL10 .... 234 A8
St Lukes Halsall CE Primary School
CSBY/BLUN L23 .... 257 G6
St Maria Goretti RC Primary School
FUL/RIB PR2 .... 133 J6
St Marie RC Primary School
NWD/KWIPK L33 .... 260 D8
St Marks RC Primary School
BRSC L40 .... 223 G3
St Martins College
LANC LA1 .... 3 J6
St Mary Magdalenes RC Primary School
PDHM/BLYW BB12 .... 142 A3
St Mary Magdalenes CE Primary School
ACC BB5 .... 159 L4
St Mary Magdalens RC Primary School
PRES PR1 .... 152 B7
St Mary & Michael Catholic Primary School
GAR/LONG PR3 .... 284 A3
St Marys Catholic College
BPOOLE FY3 .... 105 J3
St Marys Catholic Primary School
GAR/LONG PR3 .... 88 G1
GAR/LONG PR3 .... 92 A2
LEYL PR25 .... 186 C2
St Marys CE Primary School
CHLY/EC PR7 .... 205 M5
KKBYL LA6 .... 21 L1
RAW/HAS BB4 .... 177 J8
ROCH OL11 .... 235 K7

St Marys Hall
CLI BB7 .... 97 K8
St Marys Medical Centre
PRES PR1 .... 151 L6
St Marys RC Primary School
ACC BB5 .... 139 J8
ACC BB5 .... 159 J7
BBNW BB2 .... 136 A7
BCUP OL13 .... 197 K1
BRFD/BLYE BB10 .... 143 F2
BRSC L40 .... 223 K4
CHLY/EC PR7 .... 207 K4
CSBY/BLUN L23 .... 257 H3
FTWD FY7 .... 77 K6
GTH/LHO BB6 .... 137 M2
MCMB LA4 .... 41 K5
RAW/HAS BB4 .... 194 F1
St Mary's RC Primary School
CLI BB7 .... 120 C4
LIT OL15 .... 219 K5
St Marys RC Sixth Form College
BBN BB1 .... 157 H4
St Marys & St Andrews Catholic Primary School
GAR/LONG PR3 .... 111 K6
St Marys & St Benedicts RC Primary School
BBR PR5 .... 169 H2
St Marys & St Josephs RC Primary School
BBNW BB2 .... 11 G8
St Matthews CE Primary School
PRES PR1 .... 153 G3
St Matthew's Primary School
BBN BB1 .... 11 H5
St Michaels CE High School
CHLY/EC PR7 .... 207 M1
St Michaels CE Primary School
KIRK/FR/WAR PR4 .... 127 H2
St Michaels Church of England High School
CSBY/BLUN L23 .... 256 F5
St Michaels Primary School
KIRK/FR/WAR PR4 .... 128 E6
St Michael with St John CE Primary School
BBN BB1 .... 10 F2
St Nicholas Arcades
LANC LA1 .... 3 G6
St Nicholas CE Primary School
ACC BB5 .... 159 J4
BPOOLS FY4 .... 125 K7
CSBY/BLUN L23 .... 256 E8
St Nicholas Health Centre
BLY BB11 .... 7 G5
St Oswalds CE Primary School
NTHTN L30 .... 258 C8
St Oswalds RC Primary School
ACC BB5 .... 159 K8
CHLY/EC PR7 .... 228 F3
KIRK/FR/WAR PR4 .... 166 F3
St Patricks RC Primary School
BBR PR5 .... 153 H7
CHTN/BK PR9 .... 200 D1
HEY LA3 .... 52 F3
St Patricks VA RC Primary School
WHIT OL12 .... 235 K2
St Pauls CE Primary School
ACC BB5 .... 159 H7
DWN BB3 .... 230 D3
DWN BB3 .... 192 C2
NLSN BB9 .... 123 G4
St Pauls Medical Centre
BPOOL FY1 .... 104 E4
St Pauls RC Primary School
BBNW BB2 .... 172 A3
St Peter & St Pauls CE Primary School
BBN BB1 .... 158 D2
St Peters Catholic High School
WGNW/BIL/OR WN5 .... 255 J7
St Peters CE Primary School
ACC BB5 .... 175 K1
BLY BB11 .... 7 G3
CHLYE PR6 .... 208 B1
DWN BB3 .... 191 L3
FMBY L37 .... 237 K6
FUL/RIB PR2 .... 132 C4
St Peters CE Primary School Heysham
HEY LA3 .... 52 D4
St Peters CE School Simonstone
PDHM/BLYW BB12 .... 140 B2
St Peters RC Primary School
BBNW BB2 .... 172 E1
LSTA FY8 .... 146 F6
St Peters RC Primary School
RAW/HAS BB4 .... 196 F6
St Peters Smithills Dean CE Primary School
BOL BB11 .... 233 L7
St Peters VC CE Primary School
MILN OL16 .... 235 L6
St Philips CE Primary School
NLSN BB9 .... 123 H3
STHP PR8 .... 13 K6
St Pius X Preparatory School
FUL/RIB PR2 .... 132 B6
St Richards Catholic Primary School
SKEL WN8 .... 252 F2
St Silas CE Primary School
BBNW BB2 .... 156 E6
St Stephens CE Infant School
BBN BB1 .... 157 L4
St Stephens CE Junior School
BBN BB1 .... 157 L4
St Stephens CE Primary School
CHTN/BK PR9 .... 181 K6
St Stephens CE School
BLY BB11 .... 7 K8
St Teresas Catholic Primary School
CLV/TH FY5 .... 85 G1
SKEL WN8 .... 254 E2
St Teresas RC Infant and Nursery School
STHP PR8 .... 199 K7
St Teresas RC Primary School
PRES PR1 .... 151 K2
PRES PR1 .... 153 H3
St Thomas CE Primary School
BBN BB1 .... 11 L4
LSTA FY8 .... 145 J5
MGHL L31 .... 250 A7
St Thomas CE (VA) Primary School
NLSN BB9 .... 103 G7

St Thomas the Martyr CE Primary School
SKEL WN8 .... 254 E4
St Veronicas RC Primary School
RAW/HAS BB4 .... 194 E4
St Vincents RC Primary School
WHIT OL12 .... 234 D2
St Wilfrids CE School
BBNW BB2 .... 10 D6
St Wilfrids CE High School and Technology College
BBNW BB2 .... 10 B7
St Wilfrids CE Primary School
HGHB LA2 .... 43 K4
St Wilfrids RC Primary School
GAR/LONG PR3 .... 114 D3
St William of York RC Primary School
CSBY/BLUN L23 .... 257 L6
St Williams Catholic Primary School
GAR/LONG PR3 .... 282 B2
St Wulstans RC Primary School
GTH/LHO BB6 .... 138 F6
St Wulstans & St Edmunds Catholic Primary School
FTWD FY7 .... 77 H8
Salesbury CE Primary School
BBN BB1 .... 137 G5
Salford Industrial Estate
TOD OL14 .... 303 K2
Salt Ayre Athletics Track
LANC LA1 .... 2 A3
Salt Ayre Sports Centre
LANC LA1 .... 2 B3
Salterforth Primary School
BWCK/EAR BB18 .... 294 A7
Saithill Industrial Estate
CLI BB7 .... 99 K2
Samlesbury Aerodrome
BBR PR5 .... 135 J8
Samlesbury CE Primary School
BBR PR5 .... 154 A2
Samlesbury Hall
BBR PR5 .... 155 H1
Sandbrook Community Primary School
ROCH OL11 .... 235 H8
Sandside Caravan & Camping Park
CARN LA5 .... 32 E6
Sandy Lane Clinic
LEYL PR25 .... 186 D3
Sandy Lane Health Centre
SKEL WN8 .... 253 G2
Sawley Abbey
CLI BB7 .... 291 L6
Sawmill Industrial Estate
BPOOL FY1 .... 105 G5
Saxon Hall Leisure Centre
MILN OL16 .... 235 M3
Scarisbrick Hotel
STHP PR8 .... 12 F3
Science Park
BBN BB1 .... 11 K3
Scorton CE Primary School
GAR/LONG PR3 .... 284 D1
Scotforth Cemetery
LANC LA1 .... 54 E8
Scotforth CE Primary School
LANC LA1 .... 54 E7
Scotshaw Brook Industrial Estate
DWN BB3 .... 173 H4
Scoutbottom Industrial Estate
RAW/HAS BB4 .... 178 C8
Sealife Centre
BPOOL FY1 .... 4 C4
Sedbergh Junior School
HGHB LA2 .... 38 C4
Seedhill Athletics Stadium
NLSN BB9 .... 122 F1
Sefton Lane Industrial Estate
MGHL L31 .... 258 D3
Selby Industrial Estate
KIRK/FR/WAR PR4 .... 128 C5
Settle CE Primary School
SETT BD24 .... 265 N7
Settle College
SETT BD24 .... 265 M6
Settle Golf Club
SETT BD24 .... 265 L5
Settle Leisure Pool
SETT BD24 .... 265 N6
Settle Middle School
SETT BD24 .... 265 N6
Seven Stars Primary School
LEYL PR25 .... 186 A4
Shade Primary School
TOD OL14 .... 303 K4
Shadsworth Industrial Park
BBN BB1 .... 173 L5
Shadsworth Infant School
BBN BB1 .... 158 A7
Shadsworth Junior School
BBN BB1 .... 173 H1
Shadsworth Leisure Centre
BBN BB1 .... 173 H1
Shakespeare Primary School
FTWD FY7 .... 77 H7
Sharneyford County School
BCUP OL13 .... 179 M6
Shawclough Community Primary School
WHIT OL12 .... 218 B8
Shawclough Trading Estate
WHIT OL12 .... 218 A8
Shaw Hall Caravan Park
BRSC L40 .... 223 L7
Shay Lane Industrial Estate
GAR/LONG PR3 .... 114 B6
Sherburn School
PRES PR1 .... 132 D8
Sherwood Primary School
FUL/RIB PR2 .... 132 D4
Shevington Community Primary School
WGNNW/ST WN6 .... 245 J3
Shevington High School
WGNNW/ST WN6 .... 245 L1
Shevington Vale Primary School
WGNNW/ST WN6 .... 245 H3
Shireburn Arms Hotel
CLI BB7 .... 117 J2
Shoreside Primary School
STHP PR8 .... 220 E7
Shorrocks Hill Country Club
FMBY L37 .... 246 D2

Shuttleworth College PDHM/BLYW BB12 ... 141 J4
The Sidings Industrial Estate SETT BD24 ... 265 M7
Silverdale CE Primary School CARN LA5 ... 16 F8
Silverdale Golf Club CARN LA5 ... 17 H8
Simonstone Business Park PDHM/BLYW BB12 ... 140 C3
Simonswood Industrial Park NWD/KWIPK L33 ... 260 E5
Singleton CE Primary School PLF/KEOS FY6 ... 107 H2
Sir John Thursby Community College BRFD/BLYE BB10 ... 143 G2
Skelmersdale & Ormskirk Colleges (Northway Centre) SKEL WN8 ... 253 K2
Skelmersdale & Ormskirk Colleges (Westbank Centre) SKEL WN8 ... 253 K3
Skelmersdale Sports Centre SKEL WN8 ... 253 M4
Skelmersdale United FC SKEL WN8 ... 252 F3
Skerton Cemetery LANC LA1 ... 42 E7
Skerton Community Primary School LANC LA1 ... 3 H2
Skerton High School LANC LA1 ... 3 H2
Skerton St Lukes CE VA Primary School LANC LA1 ... 42 D8
Skipton Road Business Park BWCK/EAR BB18 ... 293 Q4
Ski Rossendale RAW/HAS BB4 ... 177 H8
Slaidburn Health Centre CLI BB7 ... 275 N5
Slaidburn Industrial Estate CHTN/BK PR9 ... 180 D7
Slyne-with-Hest St Lukes CE Primary School HGHB LA2 ... 42 D3
Smallbridge Health Centre WHIT OL12 ... 218 F8
Smallbridge Industrial Park MILN OL16 ... 235 M1
Smallshaw Industrial Estate BLY BB11 ... 141 M6
Smithills Hall Museum BOL BL1 ... 233 L7
Smithills School BOL BL1 ... 233 L8
Smithy Bridge Primary School LIT OL15 ... 219 J8
Southbank Tennis Club STHP PR8 ... 200 B7
Southlands High School CHLY/EC PR7 ... 207 K6
South Pier BPOOLS FY4 ... 124 D3
Southport & Ainsdale Golf Club STHP PR8 ... 220 F1
Southport & Birkdale CC STHP PR8 ... 199 H8
Southport Business Centre CHTN/BK PR9 ... 13 H3
Southport Business Park STHP PR8 ... 199 K8
Southport College of FE CHTN/BK PR9 ... 13 J3
Southport Crematorium STHP PR8 ... 222 E1
Southport FC STHP PR8 ... 200 B6
Southport Flower Show Site STHP PR8 ... 12 D4
Southport & Formby District General Hospital STHP PR8 ... 200 B4
Southport & Formby Hospital CHTN/BK PR9 ... 13 H4
Southport General Infirmary STHP PR8 ... 13 M7
Southport Girls FC STHP PR8 ... 200 C5
Southport Landing Area STHP PR8 ... 199 G5
Southport Model Village STHP PR8 ... 12 E3
Southport Municipal Golf Club CHTN/BK PR9 ... 199 M1
Southport Old Links Golf Club CHTN/BK PR9 ... 200 E2
Southport Pier STHP PR8 ... 199 J2
Southport RFC STHP PR8 ... 221 H2
Southport Sailing Club STHP PR8 ... 199 K2
Southport Swimming Baths STHP PR8 ... 12 D4
South Ribble Industrial Estate PRES PR1 ... 152 F6
South Ribble Museum & Exhibition Centre LEYL PR25 ... 186 D3
South Ribble Tennis Centre BBR PR5 ... 169 G4
South Shore Hospital BPOOLS FY4 ... 124 F6
Sowarth Industrial Estate SETT BD24 ... 265 M7
Sparrow Hawk Hotel BLY BB11 ... 7 H3
Sparth House Hotel ACC BB5 ... 139 J7
Spen Farm Business Park BPOOLS FY4 ... 125 M3
Sphynx Tennis Club STHP PR8 ... 200 B7
The Sporting Edge Track ORM L39 ... 241 K8
Spotland Bridge Industrial Centre ROCH OL11 ... 234 F3
Spotland Primary School WHIT OL12 ... 235 G2
Springfield Industrial Estate PRES PR1 ... 152 B2
Springhill High School MILN OL16 ... 235 M6

Spring Hill Primary School ACC BB5 ... 159 K6
Springvale Business Park DWN BB3 ... 191 L5
Squires Gate Industrial Estate BPOOLS FY4 ... 125 H6
Ss John Fisher & Thomas More High School COL BB8 ... 123 L1
Ss Michael & Johns RC Primary School CLI BB7 ... 99 H3
Ss Michaels & All Angels CE Primary School COL BB8 ... 296 B3
Ss Peter & Paul Catholic School NWD/KWIPK L33 ... 260 C6
Ss Peter & Paul RC Primary School BRSC L40 ... 227 J1
Staining CE Primary School BPOOLS FY3 ... 106 A6
Stalmine Primary School PLF/KEOS FY6 ... 82 F4
Stanah Country Park CLV/TH FY5 ... 86 C1
Stanah Primary School CLV/TH FY5 ... 86 A5
Stancliffe Street Industrial Estate BBNW BB2 ... 10 A9
Standish Community High School WGNNW/ST WN6 ... 245 M1
Stanley County Infant School BPOOLS FY3 ... 125 L1
Stanley High School Specialist Sports College CHTN/BK PR9 ... 180 C7
Stanley Junior School BPOOLS FY3 ... 125 L1
Stanley Park Athletics Arena BPOOLS FY3 ... 5 L4
Stanley Park Boat House BPOOLS FY3 ... 5 L3
Stanley Park Municipal Golf Course BPOOLS FY3 ... 5 K2
Stanley Park Sports Arena BPOOLS FY3 ... 5 K4
Stansfield Hall CE Free Primary School LIT OL15 ... 219 M3
Starkie Industrial Estate FUL/RIB PR2 ... 152 A1
Station Approach Business Estate ROCH OL11 ... 235 J5
Station Road Industrial Estate GTH/LHO BB6 ... 139 H6
Stoneholme Industrial Estate RAW/HAS BB4 ... 177 J4
Stonehouse School LEYL PR25 ... 186 C1
Stoneyholme CP School PDHM/BLYW BB12 ... 142 C3
Stonyhurst College CLI BB7 ... 97 K8
Streatham House School CSBY/BLUN L23 ... 256 F7
Strike Lane Primary School KIRK/FR/WAR PR4 ... 148 E3
Stubbins Primary School RAMS BL0 ... 215 G2
Sudden Health Centre ROCH OL11 ... 234 F7
Sudell Primary School DWN BB3 ... 191 L2
Summerhill Primary School MGHL L31 ... 259 H3
Summersales Industrial Estate WGNS/IIMK WN3 ... 255 L7
Sunnybank Industrial Estate PLF/KEOS FY6 ... 87 G2
Sunnycliff Retail Park HEY LA3 ... 53 L2
Sunnymede School STHP PR8 ... 12 D6
Superbowl Leisure Parcs BPOOL FY1 ... 4 C2
Swallow Lodge AIRE BD20 ... 295 M9
Swimsafe Swimming Pool PDHM/BLYW BB12 ... 141 K6
Sycamore Trading Estate BPOOLS FY4 ... 125 J7
Talbot Road Industrial Centre CROS/BRETH PR26 ... 186 A1
Tardygate Trading Estate BBR PR5 ... 168 D3
Tarleton High School KIRK/FR/WAR PR4 ... 183 K4
Tarleton Holy Trinity CE Primary School KIRK/FR/WAR PR4 ... 183 K6
Tarleton Primary School KIRK/FR/WAR PR4 ... 183 J2
Tatham Fells CE Primary School HGHB LA2 ... 48 D4
Tauheedul Islam Girls High School BBN BB1 ... 10 D2
Taylor Holme Industrial Estate BCUP OL13 ... 196 D3
Taylors Industrial Estate GAR/LONG PR3 ... 282 B2
Thames Primary School BPOOLS FY4 ... 124 E4
Theatre & Floral Hall CHTN/BK PR9 ... 13 G1
Thompson Street Industrial Estate BBNW BB2 ... 10 B6
Thorneyholme RC Primary School CLI BB7 ... 274 C10
Thornton Cleveleys Cricket Club CLV/TH FY5 ... 86 C5
Thornton Cleveleys RUFC CLV/TH FY5 ... 85 K1
Thornton Cleveleys Sports Centre CLV/TH FY5 ... 85 K2
Thornton Crematorium CSBY/BLUN L23 ... 257 M4

Thornton-in-Craven Primary School SKP/WHF BD23 ... 294 E1
Thornton Primary School CLV/TH FY5 ... 81 L8
Thornton Primary School CSBY/BLUN L23 ... 257 L5
Three Point Business Park RAW/HAS BB4 ... 194 C1
Three Worlds Business Centre LSTA FY8 ... 147 G7
Thurnham Glasson CE Primary School HGHB LA2 ... 65 K7
Time Stage School PLF/KEOS FY6 ... 78 E7
Tockholes CE Primary School DWN BB3 ... 172 D8
Todmorden CC TOD OL14 ... 303 K1
Todmorden Community College TOD OL14 ... 303 L2
Todmorden Golf Club TOD OL14 ... 303 M1
Todmorden Health Centre TOD OL14 ... 303 L2
Todmorden High School TOD OL14 ... 301 J12
Toll Bar Business Park BCUP OL13 ... 196 F3
Tonacliffe Primary School WHIT OL12 ... 217 M5
Torrisholme Primary School MCMB LA4 ... 42 A6
Tor View School RAW/HAS BB4 ... 195 G3
Touchstones Arts & Heritage Centre ROCH OL11 ... 235 H4
Tower Hill Health Centre NWD/KWIPK L33 ... 260 C6
Tower World BPOOL FY1 ... 4 C2
Towneley Golf Club BLY BB11 ... 142 E8
Towneley Hall Art Gallery & Museums BLY BB11 ... 162 F1
Towngate Healthcare Clinic LEYL PR25 ... 186 D3
Townsmoor Retail Park BBNW BB2 ... 10 E7
Toy & Teddy Bear Museum LSTA FY8 ... 145 G4
Traceys Industrial Estate LEYL PR25 ... 186 F2
Tram Depot BPOOL FY1 ... 4 D6
Tram Shed BPOOL FY1 ... 4 D7
Trans Britannia Enterprise Estate BLY BB11 ... 141 L8
Trans Pennine Trading Estate ROCH OL11 ... 235 G2
Travelodge BLY BB11 ... 6 B4
Travelodge CHLYE PR6 ... 169 L8
Travelodge DWN BB3 ... 173 J6
Travelodge HGHB LA2 ... 270 D6
Travelodge HOR/BR BL6 ... 231 H7
Travelodge KKBYL LA6 ... 18 F6
Trawden Forest Primary School COL BB8 ... 296 E9
Treales CE Primary School KIRK/FR/WAR PR4 ... 129 H1
Treasure House School of Make Up HOR/BR BL6 ... 231 M7
Trinity Primary School SKEL WN8 ... 253 H2
Trinity & St Michaels CE/Methodist Primary School CROS/BRETH PR26 ... 204 F1
Trumacar Community Primary School HEY LA3 ... 52 D6
Tulketh Community Sports College FUL/RIB PR2 ... 131 L7
Turkey Red Industrial Estate ACC BB5 ... 176 C2
Turton Belmont Primary School EDGW/EG BL7 ... 210 F4
Turton & Edgworth CE/Methodist Primary School EDGW/EG BL7 ... 213 H6
Turton Tower EDGW/EG BL7 ... 212 F8
Twine Valley Country Park & Fishery RAMS BL0 ... 215 K3
Twin Lakes Industrial Park CROS/BRETH PR26 ... 184 D8
UCI Cinema FUL/RIB PR2 ... 8 A3
Unity College BLY BB11 ... 7 L7
Unity Trading Estate BBNW BB2 ... 10 D6
University of Central Lancashire PRES PR1 ... 8 F3
University of Central Lancashire (Burnley Campus) BRFD/BLYE BB10 ... 142 E1
University of Cumbria LANC LA1 ... 3 L9
University of Lancaster LANC LA1 ... 3 G6
Up-Brooks Industrial Estate CLI BB7 ... 99 K2
Up Holland High School WGNW/BIL/OR WN5 ... 254 F7
Upper Lighthouse FTWD FY7 ... 77 M6
Ursuline RC Primary School BLY BB11 ... 256 E8
Vale of Lune RUFC LANC LA1 ... 42 B8
Valewood Primary School CSBY/BLUN L23 ... 257 G6
Valley Shopping Centre RAW/HAS BB4 ... 177 H3
Venture Caravan Park MCMB LA4 ... 41 J8
Vickers Industrial Estate HEY LA3 ... 53 K1
Victoria Business Centre ACC BB5 ... 159 L6

Victoria Business Park FTWD FY7 ... 77 K8
Victoria College LANC LA1 ... 3 G5
Victoria Hospital BPOOLE FY3 ... 105 K6
Victoria Market Hall BPOOLS FY4 ... 124 E2
The Villa Country House Hotel KIRK/FR/WAR PR4 ... 127 K8
Village Medical Centre LIT OL15 ... 219 L6
Virgin Active Swimming Pool BBR PR5 ... 152 F6
Vue Cinema BBR PR5 ... 152 F6
Vue Cinema LANC LA1 ... 3 G5
Waddington & West Bradford CE VA Primary School CLI BB7 ... 290 B10
Wakefield Industrial Estate NTHTN L30 ... 258 D8
Walker Industrial Estate BBN BB1 ... 173 M4
Walkers Industrial Estate HEY LA3 ... 52 E8
Walsden CC TOD OL14 ... 303 L4
Walsden CE (VC) Infant School TOD OL14 ... 303 L6
Walsden Industrial Estate TOD OL14 ... 303 L8
Walsden Junior School TOD OL14 ... 303 K6
Walter Street Community Primary School NLSN BB9 ... 122 E6
Walton le Dale Community Primary School BBR PR5 ... 168 F1
Walton le Dale High School BBR PR5 ... 169 J1
Walton le Dale School Clinic BBR PR5 ... 169 J1
Walverden Primary School NLSN BB9 ... 123 J3
Wardle High School WHIT OL12 ... 219 G6
Warton Aerodrome KIRK/FR/WAR PR4 ... 148 C7
Warwick Hotel BPOOLS FY4 ... 124 C5
Waterfoot Business Centre RAW/HAS BB4 ... 196 C1
Waterfoot County Primary School RAW/HAS BB4 ... 196 C3
Waterfoot Health Centre RAW/HAS BB4 ... 196 C3
Waterfront Marine Business Park LSTA FY8 ... 147 H8
The Watergate Clinic MILN OL16 ... 235 J4
The Waterloo Crown Bowling Green BPOOL FY1 ... 4 F9
Waterloo FC CSBY/BLUN L23 ... 256 E6
Waterloo Medical Centre BPOOL FY1 ... 5 G9
Waterloo Primary School BPOOLS FY4 ... 5 H9
Waterside Industrial Estate COL BB8 ... 296 B7
Waterworks Bridge HGHB LA2 ... 44 E3
Watery Lane Industrial Estate DWN BB3 ... 191 L5
Waverledge Business Park GTH/LHO BB6 ... 138 E7
Waves Leisure Centre BBNW BB2 ... 10 D4
Weavers Triangle Visitor Centre BLY BB11 ... 6 F5
Weeton Primary School KIRK/FR/WAR PR4 ... 107 G5
Welcome Lodge CHLY/EC PR7 ... 206 D8
Wellfield Business & Enterprise College LEYL PR25 ... 186 C2
Wellfield Business Park PRES PR1 ... 8 D3
Wellfield Methodist & Anglican Church School PDHM/BLYW BB12 ... 142 A3
Wennington Hall School HGHB LA2 ... 37 H1
Wensley Business Park BBNW BB2 ... 10 A5
Wensley Fold CE Primary School BBNW BB2 ... 156 E6
Wesham Park Hospital KIRK/FR/WAR PR4 ... 128 C5
Westcliff Primary School BISP FY2 ... 84 F6
West Craven High Technology College BWCK/EAR BB18 ... 293 R6
West Craven Sports Centre & Swimming Pool BWCK/EAR BB18 ... 293 R6
West End Business Park ACC BB5 ... 158 E6
West End Primary School ACC BB5 ... 158 E6
West End Primary School HEY LA3 ... 41 G7
West End Primary School ORM L39 ... 241 H4
Westfield Community Centre WGNW/BIL/OR WN5 ... 255 M5
Westgate County Primary School MCMB LA4 ... 41 J8
West Gillbrands Industrial Estate SKEL WN8 ... 253 H4
Westholme Boys School BBNW BB2 ... 156 D5
Westholme Lower School BBNW BB2 ... 156 D5
Westholme Middle School BBNW BB2 ... 156 D5
Westholme School BBNW BB2 ... 156 B5
West Lancashire Community High School SKEL WN8 ... 253 G1

West Lancashire Golf Club CSBY/BLUN L23 ... 256 D5
West Lancashire Light Railway KIRK/FR/WAR PR4 ... 165 J8
West Lancashire Yacht Club STHP PR8 ... 199 K2
Westmorland School CHLY/EC PR7 ... 207 M6
West Pennine Business Park BCUP OL13 ... 179 H6
West Street Community Primary School COL BB8 ... 296 A7
West Tarn School BPOOL FY1 ... 104 E3
West Tower Country House Hotel ORM L39 ... 250 C3
West View Leisure Centre PRES PR1 ... 152 F1
Westwood Primary School CHLYE PR6 ... 169 L7
Whalley Abbey CLI BB7 ... 118 F6
Whalley Bank Trading Estate BBNW BB2 ... 10 C6
Whalley CE Primary School CLI BB7 ... 118 F6
Whalley Cricket Club CLI BB7 ... 118 E5
Whalley Golf Club CLI BB7 ... 119 J6
Whalley Industrial Park CLI BB7 ... 119 G3
Wheatley Lane Methodist Primary School PDHM/BLYW BB12 ... 122 B3
Wheatsheaf Shopping Centre MILN OL16 ... 235 J3
White Ash School ACC BB5 ... 158 F7
Whitechapel Primary School GAR/LONG PR3 ... 93 G4
White Cross Industrial Estate LANC LA1 ... 3 J7
Whitefield Primary School PRES PR1 ... 151 K8
White House Park School CHLYE PR6 ... 171 H7
Whiteledge Centre SKEL WN8 ... 253 L3
White Lund Trading Estate HEY LA3 ... 41 L8
Whitewalls Industrial Estate COL BB8 ... 103 K8
Whittaker Moss Primary School ROCH OL11 ... 234 A2
Whittingham Hospital GAR/LONG PR3 ... 113 J7
Whittlefield Infant School PDHM/BLYW BB12 ... 6 A2
Whittle le Woods CE Primary School CHLYE PR6 ... 187 L3
Whitworth Community High School WHIT OL12 ... 217 M3
Whitworth Football & Cricket Club WHIT OL12 ... 217 M2
Whitworth Swimming Pool WHIT OL12 ... 218 A1
The Whoop Hall Hotel KKBYL LA6 ... 22 B4
Wildfowl & Wetlands Trust Martin Mere BRSC L40 ... 224 E2
William Thompson Recreation Centre BLY BB11 ... 7 H5
Willowbank Holiday Home & Touring Park STHP PR8 ... 237 L1
Willow Lane Community Primary School LANC LA1 ... 2 C6
The Willows RC Primary School KIRK/FR/WAR PR4 ... 128 C6
Wilpshire Golf Club BBN BB1 ... 137 K5
Wilsons Endowed CE Primary School KKBYL LA6 ... 34 B3
Windmill Animal Farm BRSC L40 ... 202 E7
Windsmoor House School BBNW BB2 ... 172 E1
Wingate Medical Centre NWD/KWIPK L33 ... 260 D8
Winmarleigh CE Primary School GAR/LONG PR3 ... 283 P2
Winstanley College WGNW/BIL/OR WN5 ... 255 H8
Winter Gardens BPOOL FY1 ... 4 D2
Withnell Fold Industrial Estate CHLYE PR6 ... 170 F8
Withnell Fold Primary School CHLYE PR6 ... 188 E1
Witton Country Park BBNW BB2 ... 156 C8
Witton Park Athletics track BBNW BB2 ... 156 D8
Witton Park High School BBNW BB2 ... 156 D7
Woodclose Caravan Park KKBYL LA6 ... 22 B2
Woodhey High School RAMS BL0 ... 214 D8
Woodland Primary School SKEL WN8 ... 253 M1
Woodlands Primary School FMBY L37 ... 237 G8
Woodlands School BPOOLS FY3 ... 5 J4
Woodlea Junior School LEYL PR25 ... 186 C3
Woodnook Primary School ACC BB5 ... 159 M7
Woodplumpton St Annes CE Primary School KIRK/FR/WAR PR4 ... 131 G1
Wood Top CE School BLY BB11 ... 6 A5
Woodvale Airfield FMBY L37 ... 237 J3
Woolworths Sports Club ROCH OL11 ... 234 F8

Worden Arts & Crafts Centre
LEYL PR25 .... 186 C5
Worden Sports College
LEYL PR25 .... 186 A2
Worsthorne CP School
BRFD/BLYE BB10 .... 143 K5

Wray with Botton Endowed
Primary School
HGHB LA2 .... 36 F8
Wrightington
Hospital
WGNNW/ST WN6 .... 245 H2

Wrightington Hotel &
Country Club
WGNNW/ST WN6 .... 228 C8
Wrightington Mossy Lea
Primary School
WGNNW/ST WN6 .... 228 B5

Yealand CE
Primary School
CARN LA5 .... 18 B8
Yorkshire Street
Medical Centre
BLY BB11 .... 7 J4

Zakariya School
PRES PR1 .... 9 H5

Acknowledgements

Schools address data provided by Education Direct.

Petrol station information supplied by Johnsons.

Garden centre information provided by:

Garden Centre Association · Britains best garden centres

Wyevale Garden Centres

The statement on the front cover of this atlas is sourced, selected and quoted
from a reader comment and feedback form received in 2004

Speed camera locations

Speed camera locations provided in association with RoadPilot Ltd

RoadPilot is the developer of one of the largest and most accurate databases of speed camera locations in the UK and Europe. It has provided the speed camera information in this atlas. RoadPilot is the UK's pioneer and market leader in GPS (Global Positioning System) road safety technologies.

microGo (pictured right) is RoadPilot's latest in-car speed camera location system. It improves road safety by alerting you to the location of accident black spots,

fixed and mobile camera sites. RoadPilot's microGo does not jam police lasers and is therefore completely legal.

RoadPilot's database of fixed camera locations has been compiled with the full co-operation of regional police forces and the Safety Camera Partnerships.

For more information on RoadPilot's GPS road safety products, please visit **www.roadpilot.com** or telephone 0870 240 1701

ALARM MODE

GPS Antenna
microGo is directional, it only alerts you to cameras on your side of the road

Visual Countdown
To camera location

Your Speed
The speed you are travelling when approaching camera

Camera Types Located
Gatso, Specs, Truvelo, TSS/DSS, Traffipax, mobile camera sites, accident black spots, congestion charges, tolls

Voice Warnings
Only if you are exceeding the speed limit at the camera

Plug and Go
Easy to move from vehicle to vehicle

64 Colour Options
To match vehicle's illumination

Speed Limit at Camera
Screen turns red as additional visual alert

Single Button Operation
For easy access to speed display, camera warning, rescue me location, trip computer, congestion charge, max speed alarm, date and time

SPEED READING